Web Publishing

Professional Reference Edition

William R. Stanek

sams.net

201 West 103rd Street
Indianapolis, IN 46290

PROFESSIONAL REFERENCE EDITION

International Standard Book Number: 1-57521-198-x

Library of Congress Catalog Card Number: 96-70389

2000 99 98 97 4 3

Interpretation of the printing code: the rightmost double-digit number is the year of the book's printing; the rightmost single-digit, the number of the book's printing. For example, a printing code of 96-1 shows that the first printing of the book occurred in 1996.

Composed in AGaramond and MCPdigital by Macmillan Computer Publishing

Printed in the United States of America

Publisher and President: *Richard K. Swadley*

Publishing Manager: *Mark Taber*

Managing Editor: *Cindy Morrow*

Director of Marketing: *John Pierce*

Assistant Marketing Managers: *Kristina Perry*
Rachel Wolfe

Acquisitions Editor
Beverly M. Eppink

Development Editor
Scott D. Meyers

Software Development Specialist
Bob Correll

Production Editor
Heather Stith

Copy Editors
David Bradford
Kristen Ivanetich
Lisa Lord
Stacey Houston

Indexer
Erika Millen

Technical Editors
Karen Clere
Jeff Shockley

Editorial Coordinator
Bill Whitmer

Technical Edit Coordinator
Lorraine Schaffer

Resource Coordinator
Deborah Frisby

Editorial Assistants
Carol Ackerman
Andi Richter
Rhonda Tinch-Mize

Cover Designer
Tim Amrhein

Book Designer
Gary Adair

Copy Writer
Peter Fuller

Production Team Supervisor
Brad Chinn

Production
Mona Brown
Brad Lenser
Donna Martin
Gene Redding
M. Anne Sipahimalani

Part II Web Publishing with HTML 3.2

Part XI Putting It All Together

// Acknowledgements

After a dozen books or so, and without a full-time day job, you would think writing would not be so extraordinarily taxing. Yet it is not so. Clients and business matters occupy many more hours of my time than is prudent, and the writing still lures me through the wee hours of the night. Sometimes it seems that I work 24 hours a day, 7 days a week, and indeed sometimes I come close. Without the support of my wife and two children, the days would seem eternal. Thank you for your continued support and your extraordinary ability to put up with the clackety-clackety of my keyboard!

I'd also like to thank my mother, who has taken command of my company's electronic publishing operation. Managing four electronic book imprints and answering correspondence is no easy task. Thanks for coming to the rescue to ensure I had time for other projects, such as writing this book. Now if we could only find national distributors that could get our products on the shelves of software and bookstore chains!

As always, the team at Sams.net has been great to work with. I've worked with many of you on previous books and your dedication to excellence is really quite wonderful. Specials thanks to Beverly Eppink and Mark Taber, who recognized the tremendous potential and quality of my message in the original edition of *Web Publishing Unleashed* and believed enough to create the expanded edition you hold in your hands.

Thanks to the many thousands who have read and continue to read my books. As I have stated to the hundreds who have contacted me over the years, I take all comments to heart and relish the contact and input from you, the reader. I will continue to try to answer all correspondence personally. As the dragon sometimes wins, keep in mind that e-mail isn't 100 percent reliable and that many times I am so overwhelmed with work, I don't have time to answer any e-mail, be it business or pleasure, but I do try.

— *William R. Stanek*

Dedication

To my wife, who let me follow my dreams and sincerely believed when others didn't.

— *William R. Stanek*

About the Authors

Lead Author

William R. Stanek (`director@tvp.com`) is a leading industry expert and founder of an Internet start-up company called The Virtual Press (`http://tvp.com/` and mirror site `http://www.tvpress.com/`). As a publisher and writer with over 10 years experience on networks, he brings a solid voice of experience on the Internet and Web publishing to his many projects. He was first introduced to Internet e-mail in 1988 when he worked for the government and has been involved in the commercial Internet community since 1991.

His years of practical experience are backed by a solid education, a Master of Science in Information Systems and a Bachelor of Science in Computer Science. Although his Internet start-up company publishes electronic books under four imprints, the core business revolves around three primary divisions that conduct Internet consulting (`icteam@tvp.com`), Web design (`wdteam@tvp.com`), and multimedia development (`epteam@tvp.com`). The time that isn't spent writing such runaway hits as *Web Publishing Unleashed* is spent consulting with corporate clients and developing hot new Web sites.

William served in the Persian Gulf War as a combat crew member on an Electronic Warfare aircraft. During the war, he flew on numerous combat missions into Iraq and was awarded nine medals for his wartime service, including one of our nation's highest flying honors, the Air Force Distinguished Flying Cross. He has written many books, articles, and essays. His book-length projects include nine fiction titles and eight nonfiction titles. When he's not writing or working, he spends time with his family. His favorite time of the day is when he reads to the youngest.

Contributing Authors

Chris Adams (`adamsc@io-online.com`) is a college student in San Diego and a part-time QA technician at Acucobol, Inc. A confirmed old-school experimenter, he has been, among other things, a programmer, BBS sysop and Fidonet veteran, Webmaster, hardware technician, writer, and network and system administrator.

Mark L. Chambers (`sysop@batboard.org`) has been a PC software freelance writer, BBS sysop, and game programmer for over 10 years. He is the author of *Running a Perfect BBS* and has contributed chapters to *Microsoft Internet Explorer 3 Unleashed, Netscape Unleashed, Introduction to PC Communications,* and *Using PC Tools 8.*

Stephen R. Clark (`srclark@indy.net`) is a consultant who offers business and technical writing, editing, and communications consulting, primarily in the Indianapolis area. He was employed by AT&T for seven years, most recently as a proposal manager for AT&T Solutions, located in Morristown, New Jersey. While at AT&T, Stephen developed executive-level presentations and proposals directed at global clients and gained extensive quality process and project management experience. Prior to AT&T, Stephen was the Managing Editor of Bridge Publishing, Inc., the Director of P.R. and Publications at Bluffton College, and the Senior Editor of *Christian Bookseller Magazine.* He has been writing for more than 20 years, including ghostwriting books. Stephen currently resides in Indianapolis with his wife, Marquetté K. Browning-Clark, and his four-year-old stepdaughter, Melody.

Justin Couch (`justin@vlc.com.au, http://www.vlc.com.au/~justin`) works as Software Engineer for ADI Ltd. He also runs The Virtual Light Company, a small VRML and Java Web publishing company located in Sydney, Australia. Co-author of *Laura Lemay's Web Workshop: 3D Graphics and VRML 2* and a contributing author to *Java Unleashed,* Justin is an active member of both the VRML standards and Java-VRML mailing lists. Currently, he is involved in research on using VRML to create seamless worlds on the Internet and can be found most days in the CyberGate community Point World under the name Mithrandir. When not pushing the limits of technology, he relaxes by playing bassoon and clarinet and going gliding.

Rick Darnell (`darnell@montana.com`), a contributing author to *Java Unleashed, FrontPage Unleashed,* and *Microsoft Internet Explorer 3 Unleashed,* is a Midwest native currently living with his wife and two daughters in Missoula, Montana. He began his career in print at a small weekly newspaper after graduating from Kansas State University with a degree in broadcasting. While working as a freelance journalist and writer, Rick has seen the full gamut of personal computers since starting out with a Radio Shack Model I in the late 1970s. When not in front of his computer, he serves as a volunteer firefighter and member of a regional hazardous materials response team.

Steven J. DeRose (`sjd@ebt.com`) earned his Ph.D. in Computational Linguistics from Brown University in 1989 and served as director of the early FRESS hypertext system there. He has worked as a technical writer and design consultant for the CDWord hypertext system and a variety of other systems in computational linguistics, hypermedia, and related fields. Steven has published a variety of papers on markup systems, hypertext, natural language processing, artificial intelligence, and other topics, plus a book with David Durand entitled *Making Hypermedia Work: A User's Guide to HyTime.* He is now senior system architect at Electronic Book Technologies, whose DynaText product is the leading SGML-based software for delivering large-scale electronic books on CD-ROM, disk, LAN, and the Internet. He is very active in standards development, serving with groups including the ANSI group, the ISO SGML group, the HyTime group, the Text Encoding Initiative, and several Internet and Web-related groups. He lives, works, and ice skates in Rhode Island with his wife, Laurie, and two-year-old son, Todd.

Jon M. Duff (`jmduff@tech.purdue.edu`) is Professor of Technical Graphics in the Department of Technical Graphics at Purdue University's School of Technology in West Lafayette, Indiana. He received his Ph.D. from Ohio State University, where he was a faculty member in Engineering Graphics in the College of Engineering for seven years. Author of a dozen textbooks on a variety of graphics topics and over 40 papers on technical graphics and publishing topics, Dr. Duff worked on electronic authoring technologies as a Battelle Memorial Institute Research Scientist with the Department of the Navy. In addition to his writing, Dr. Duff consults with a number of national clients and was editor of the *Engineering Design Graphics Journal* for six years. At Purdue, he is active in the design and evaluation of curricula and teaches in the technical publications area.

Dennis Hamilton (`cato@iquest.net`) is a freelance writer and president of Software Analytics, Inc., an Indianapolis-based technology analysis firm. He is the author or co-author of five books, including four on cyberspace-related subjects, and has written more than 900 articles in the 22 years he has been covering computers and software. He is formerly vice-president and editor-in-chief for ICP, Inc., a software information publisher, and has designed a variety of Web sites in his spare time.

John Jung (`jjung@netcom.com`) is a professional systems administrator with a worldwide information services company. He graduated from the University of Southern California with a computer science degree. He has been on the Internet for over eight years and spends entirely too much time online. He has worked on almost a dozen books and is the co-author of *Special Edition: Using HTML, Second Edition.*

John J. Kottler (73157.335@compuserve.com, jkottler@aol.com, or jay_kottler@msn.com) has been programming for 14 years and has spent the past 6 years developing applications for the Windows platform. He has been programming multimedia applications for over two years and has spent this past year developing applications for the Web. His knowledge includes C/C++, Visual Basic, Lotus Notes, PowerBuilder, messaging-enabled applications, multimedia and digital video production, and Web page development. John contributed to *Java Unleashed, Presenting ActiveX, Web Publishing Unleashed, Netscape 2 Unleashed,* and *Programming Windows 95 Unleashed,* and co-developed the shareware application Virtual Monitors. A graduate of Rutgers University with a degree in computer science, he enjoys inline skating, cycling, or playing digital music in his spare time.

Greg Kovich (Gmkovich@aol.com) is the Director of Technology for the public school system in Munster, Indiana. Greg has worked in industry as an analyst, programmer, and technician and credits that diverse background for the success he has enjoyed in Munster. Currently, Greg is overseeing the technology portion of a $45 million dollar renovation project in the district, which will eventually bring a WAN, LAN, Internet access, video distribution, and telephones to the classroom. He looks forward to training the staff members so that they will be able to incorporate these tools into the daily instruction of the students.

Dick Oliver (dicko@netletter.com, http://netletter.com/) is the author and co-author of numerous books on computer graphics and the Internet, including *Web Page Wizardry, Creating Your Own Web Graphics, Netscape Unleashed, Internet Explorer Unleashed,* and *Tricks of the Graphics Gurus.* He is also the president of Cedar Software and the publisher of a paper and online newsletter called the *Nonlinear Nonsense Netletter.* Dick lives in Elmore, Vermont, and commutes to work all over the world via the Internet.

Dennis R. Short (drshort@tech.purdue.edu) is a Professor of Technical Graphics in the School of Technology at Purdue University, where he has taught for 13 years. He has published two books, numerous book chapters, and over 50 conference and journal publications. Professor Short was a visiting scholar in Japan in 1991 and has areas of expertise in CAD, networking, and advanced computer graphics systems.

Mark Woodman (woodman@dpc.net) is currently a Multimedia Producer for Ink & Image, Inc., a multimedia and video production firm in Peoria, Illinois. He believes the best joke of the 20th century is that people can get paid to have fun using computers. He has yet to tell his employers this, however.

Tell Us What You Think!

As a reader, you are the most important critic and commentator of our books. We value your opinion and want to know what we're doing right, what we could do better, what areas you'd like to see us publish in, and any other words of wisdom you're willing to pass our way. You can help us make strong books that meet your needs and give you the computer guidance you require.

Do you have access to CompuServe or the World Wide Web? Then check out our CompuServe forum by typing **GO SAMS** at any prompt. If you prefer the World Wide Web, check out our site at `http://www.mcp.com`.

> **NOTE**
>
> If you have a technical question about this book, call the technical support line at (800) 571-5840, ext. 3668.

As the publishing manager of the group that created this book, I welcome your comments. You can fax, e-mail, or write me directly to let me know what you did or didn't like about this book—as well as what we can do to make our books stronger. Here's the information:

FAX: 317/581-4669

E-mail: `newtech_mgr@sams.mcp.com`

Mail: Mark Taber
Sams.net Publishing
201 W. 103rd Street
Indianapolis, IN 46290

Introduction

Web Publishing Unleashed, Professional Reference Edition is the best guide to Web publishing on the market. Not only does this book cover every major Web publishing issue, it unleashes each topic with authoritative coverage from the world's foremost experts in Web publishing. The goal of this book is to help you become one of the thousands of successful Web publishers providing ideas, services, and products to millions of Web users.

Whether your Web publishing plans are large or small, you don't want to wait any longer to get into the action. By the end of 1998, more than 100 million people will have access to the global Internet and to the World Wide Web. What this means is that for a few dollars a month you can reach a potential audience of millions. If you think this is hype, think again. The World Wide Web has caught the eye of the media, businesses, entrepreneurs, and governments. Media coverage of the Internet and related issues grows every day. Thousands of articles related to the Internet are published every month in books, magazines, newspapers, and newsletters. You will find discussions about the Internet and the Web on TV shows, radio, and the news. You will also find addresses to Web pages in all forms of advertising, from magazine ads to television commercials.

As you read this book, you will learn about the things the Web has to offer. I have taken great care to provide invaluable tips and pour my expertise into every page of *Web Publishing Unleashed, Professional Reference Edition.* Today's Web publishers have powerful resources at their fingertips and this book will show you how to use every one of them. Here's a sample of the major topics covered in this book:

- Web site planning and development
- Intranet planning and development
- In-depth coverage of HTML 3.2
- Creating Web publications for the hottest browsers, including Netscape Navigator and Internet Explorer
- Designing documents with hot features such as tables and frames
- Enhancing your pages with style sheets
- Using Web publishing and authoring tools
- Bigger, better, and faster graphics
- Working with audio, video, and animation
- Using Shockwave for Director
- Writing CGI scripts
- Designing interactive documents with forms and image maps

- Using search engines and building indexed databases
- Creating live documents with client push/server pull
- Using SGML
- Exploring virtual reality with VRML 2.0
- 3D modeling
- Java and writing Java applets
- Using VBScript and JavaScript
- Activating your pages with ActiveX and ActiveX controls
- Web server administration
- Managing server security

How This Book Is Organized

This book is designed to be the most comprehensive Web publishing resource available anywhere. Chapter by chapter, you will learn everything you need to know to create, design, and publish dazzling Web publications.

Part I, "A Web Publishing Game Plan," covers everything you need to know to get started as a Web publisher. Chapter 1 provides an overview of Web technologies. Coverage of these technologies is intended to save you time, money, and resources. Chapter 2 answers the questions about why you should publish on the Web, what you can publish on the Web, and who is already publishing on the Web. The final chapter of Part I is designed for anyone who wants to build an intranet. The chapter covers essential issues that will help you develop and plan a successful intranet.

Part II, "Web Publishing with HTML 3.2," explores every facet of the HyperText Markup Language and includes extensive coverage of the hottest and latest issues. Chapter 4 is a power primer for creating Web documents with HTML 3.2. You will find useful tips, expert advice, and a strong emphasis on sound design. Chapter 5 is a comprehensive guide to HTML 3.2, with a focus on its features and enhancements to the HTML standard. Chapter 6 explores one of the hottest elements in Web publishing, tables. Not only do leading browsers, such as Netscape Navigator and Internet Explorer, support tables, but tables are also a part of the new HTML specification. Chapter 7 shows you how to enhance your pages with frames. You will find total coverage of standard frames, floating frames, and borderless frames. The final chapter in Part II examines style sheets. With style sheets, Web publishers finally have sophisticated control over the placement of elements on the page.

After exploring power publishing with HTML, the next section of the book examines tools that make Web publishing easier. In Part III, "Web Publishing Environments and Editors," you get the inside scoop on the best authoring tools on the market. Chapter 9 is designed to help you put together the ultimate Web publishing toolkit. Chapter 10 looks at Internet Assistants for Microsoft Word, Excel, and PowerPoint. Chapter 11 examines publishing with the most robust authoring and Web site management tool available today—Microsoft FrontPage. Other chapters in this section cover Netscape Navigator Gold, Macromedia Backstage, and Adobe PageMill/SiteMill. The final chapter in Part III rounds out the section with a look at other promising Web authoring tools including HotSiteX, HoTMetaL, HotDog, and WebEdit.

Part IV, "Enhancing Web Pages with Graphics," is for everyone that has ever read a Web publishing book and wished that just for once someone would show you how the experts design show-stopping graphics. Six chapters in Part IV examine graphic design for the real world. In Chapter 16, you will learn how to create bigger, better, and faster-loading graphics. Chapter 17 explores fancy type faces, cool page layouts, and insider design tricks. In Web publishing, two graphic formats stand out from the pack: JPEG and GIF. Chapter 18 teaches you everything you'll ever need to know about JPEG and GIF. Creating animation is the subject of Chapter 19. Chapter 20 covers image maps. The section is completed with a look at advanced layout with Adobe Acrobat, Common Ground, and other page layout applications.

Graphics are only one part of multimedia. In Part V, "Extending Your Site with Multimedia," you learn how to create pages with live video, real-time audio, and Macromedia's amazing Shockwave. Creating a multimedia feast for Web surfers is what Chapter 22 is all about. In Chapter 23, you learn how to enhance your pages with soundtracks, real-time audio, and streaming. The next chapter examines video. Not only do you learn how to use video in your Web pages, you also learn how to create video. Finally, the section looks at the hottest multimedia development environment for the Web—Shockwave. Using Macromedia's Shockwave for Director, you can create pages with multimedia sequences that rival the best CD-ROM titles.

Interactivity is the main attraction on the Web, and Part VI, "Adding Interactivity with CGI," provides you with everything you need to know to create truly interactive publications with CGI. Chapter 26 provides a top-notch introduction to CGI scripts that won't leave you confused and wondering how it all works. Chapter 27 tells you in a very straightforward way how to use forms and, more importantly, how to design good forms. Chapter 28 shows you how to use the hypertext facilities of the Web to put the world's most powerful search engines at your fingertips. The chapter also provides in-depth coverage on how to build an indexed database. The final chapter in this section shows you how to create and manage discussion groups on the Web.

Beyond HTML and CGI, a whole world of hot technologies is waiting to be put to use. The hottest of these technologies is ActiveX. ActiveX is a family of technologies for activating the Internet with real-time interaction. In Part VII, "ActiveX and VBScript," you will learn how to use ActiveX, how to write scripts using VBScript, and how to integrate ActiveX and VBScript. As you will discover in Chapters 30 and 31, VBScript provides the development language for activating your pages. But to create truly interactive pages, you need to integrate ActiveX with VBScript. Using ActiveX and integrating ActiveX with VBScript is the subject of Chapters 32 and 33.

Part VIII, "JavaScript and Java," provides a fast track to using JavaScript and Java. Chapter 34 shows you how to use JavaScript in your Web pages. The next chapter follows up by teaching you how to write JavaScripts. But your lesson in object-oriented programming is only beginning. Next, you learn how to write Java applets. Afterward, you see how to integrate JavaScript and Java.

Part IX, "Creating VRML Worlds," is a power tour of virtual reality and Web publishing in 3D. If you've dreamed of creating 3D worlds, Chapters 39 and 40 are for you. Chapter 39 discusses the Virtual Reality Modeling Language (VRML) and how you can use it. Chapter 40 explores the latest VRML specification, called Moving Worlds. Yet VRML 2.0 is only the beginning. Beyond VRML 2.0 are technologies like ActiveVRML and VRMLScript. ActiveVRML is a standard that allows you to activate VR worlds with ActiveX. With VRMLScript, you can create advanced behaviors for objects in your VR worlds. Finally, by putting the VR technologies together with Java, you can create 3D worlds publishers could only dream of until recently.

After a high-speed race through virtual reality, the book explores Web publishing administration. Part X, "Web Publishing Administration," goes well beyond the basics of administering a Web site. In Chapter 42, you will learn tips and techniques for managing large-scale projects. Chapter 43 shows you how to move legacy documents to the Web. Chapter 44 examines SGML—one of the most powerful and versatile markup languages. Chapter 45 covers setting up and administering a Web server. Chapter 46 focuses on optimizing Web sites and intranets. Maintaining the integrity of your server is essential to your success, so Chapter 47 teaches you all about server security.

Practical application of this book's many topics is the subject of Part XI, "Putting It All Together." Every success story has a beginning, and in Web publishing, the first step is creating a Web page. Chapter 48 covers everything you need to know to build a terrific Web page—publishing strategies, page structure, creating the page, adding features, proofing the page, testing the page, and publishing the page. Creating and publishing your first Web page is only a starting point; the next chapter tells you how to build a cool Web site. But Chapter 49 doesn't stop there, it goes on to tell you how to publicize your Web site as well. The next chapter tells you how to build a multimedia presentation that will dazzle the masses.

The final section of the book puts the reference resources you need into your hands. Appendix A, "Sources for Additional Information," tells you where to find more. Appendix B, "HTML Reference," is an invaluable at-a-glance resource for HTML. Appendix C, "Browser Comparison Chart," gives publishers a quick reference to browsers. Appendix D, "Color Table," makes it easier to use a wide range of colors in your Web pages. Appendix E, "MIME Types and File Extensions," provides a quick reference to the MIME standard. These terrific references are followed by many other references you will put to heavy use. Appendix F, "JavaScript Reference," is a resource for anyone wanting to use JavaScript. Appendix G, "ActiveX and VBScript Reference," is a resource for ActiveX and VBScript.

Who Should Read This Book?

This book is perfect for just about anyone. Whether you have been publishing on the Web for years or are just starting, *Web Publishing Unleashed, Professional Reference Edition* is for you.

Beginners: To enter the cutting edge of Web publishing, I recommend that beginners read this book cover to cover. As you read, put the thousands of tips, techniques, and examples to use. Afterward, as you design and publish Web publications, refer to the specific chapters and appendixes that cover the Web publishing aspects you are using.

Casual and Accomplished Users: You may want to jump to specific topics, such as publishing with HTML 3.2 or integrating ActiveX and VBScript. However, keep in mind that this book focuses not only on the how-to, but the why, where, and when of Web publishing as well. Although the three W's are often neglected in other books, *Web Publishing Unleashed, Professional Reference Edition* doesn't forget to combine how-to steps with thorough design tips and expert advice. After you read about hot technologies like HTML 3.2, VBScript, Java, JavaScript, and VRML 2.0, go back and read the other chapters.

Experts: For the experts, this book offers a wealth of knowledge and pooled resources you can't get anywhere else. You will find the thousands of examples contained in this book to be invaluable. Work these examples into 50 chapters and several reference resources, and you've got everything you need to hone your skills to perfection. Put the table of contents and the index to immediate use. Don't worry about wearing out the book by thumbing through the pages in the heat of the moment; this hard-bound edition should definitely last longer than a flimsy soft-cover edition.

I truly hope you find *Web Publishing Unleashed, Professional Reference Edition* to be *the* best Web publishing book available.

Thank you,

William R. Stanek

`(director@tvp.com)`

Part I

A Web Publishing Game Plan

IN THIS PART

CHAPTER 1

Web Publishing: A Technology Overview

by William Robert Stanek

IN THIS CHAPTER

The World Wide Web is rapidly evolving into a medium that rivals television for information content and entertainment value. Millions of people and thousands of businesses around the world are racing to get connected to the global Internet and the World Wide Web because the Web is the most powerful and least expensive medium to publish in. Whether you're an information provider or simply a creative person who wants to publish your own work, no other medium empowers the individual like the Web; it levels the playing field, allowing a one-person operation to compete head-to-head with corporate conglomerates.

To publish successfully on the Web, you don't have to be a genius, a programmer, or a computer guru with insider secrets. What you need are the practical advice, tips, and techniques you will find throughout this book. Many books on Internet and Web publishing discuss theories, but rarely follow a practical approach to Web publishing. Books without practical examples and genuinely useful information can leave you wondering where to start, how to start, and what to do when you do finally manage to start. This chapter, like all the chapters in this book, is filled with useful information designed to unleash the topic of Web publishing and help you become one of the thousands of successful Web publishers offering ideas, services, and products to millions of Web users.

This chapter gives you an overview of the technologies that make Web publishing possible. You can use this information as a launching pad toward success in Web publishing.

Overview of Web Publishing's Past

The World Wide Web is an open-ended information system designed specifically with ease of use and document interchange in mind. In early 1989, Tim Berners-Lee of the European Laboratory for Particle Physics (CERN) proposed the Web as a way for scientists around the world to collaborate, using a global information system based on hypertext.

In the fall of 1990, the first text-only browsers were set up, and CERN scientists could access hypertext files and other information at CERN. However, the structure of hypertext documents and the way they were transferred to remote sites needed to be better defined. Based on proposals by Berners-Lee, the structure of hypertext documents was defined by a new language called the HyperText Markup Language (HTML). HTML was based on a subset of the Standard Generalized Markup Language (SGML), already in wide use. To transfer HTML documents to remote sites, a new protocol was devised called HTTP (hypertext transfer protocol).

HTTP offers a means of moving from document to document and indexing within documents. The power of hypertext is its simplicity and transparency. Users can navigate through a global network of resources at the touch of a button. Hypertext documents are linked together by keywords or specified hot areas—such as graphical icons or even parts of indexed maps—in the document. When a new word or idea is introduced, you can, with the help of hypertext, jump to another document containing complete information on the new topic. Readers see links as highlighted keywords or images displayed graphically and can use these links to access additional documents or resources.

In the fall of 1991, conference-goers around the world started hearing about the promise and ease of hypertext, but sparks still weren't flying. By early 1993, there were only about 50 Web sites worldwide. Then a wonderful thing happened. A browser that allowed users to take advantage of the Web's graphical capabilities was developed at the National Center for Supercomputing Applications (NCSA). NCSA called the browser Mosaic. For a time, it seemed as though the Web and Mosaic were synonymous. Interest in the Web began to grow, from a trickle of interest to a great flood of enthusiasm. Today, the Web is the hottest and fastest growing area of the Internet, and Mosaic is only one of dozens of available browsers.

You've undoubtedly used a browser before, but you might not have thought about what makes a browser work the way it does. The purpose of a browser—also called a *client*—is to request and display information. Clients make requests to servers, then servers process those requests based on a set of rules—called a *protocol*—for communicating on the network. Protocols specify how programs talk to each other and what meaning to give to the data they receive. Many protocols are in use on the Internet, and the Web uses them all; however, the primary protocol is HTTP.

Generally, HTTP processes are transparent to users. To request information from a server, all the user has to do is activate a hypertext reference, and the user's browser takes care of interpreting the hypertext transfer commands and communicating requests. The mechanism on the receiving end, which is processing the requests, is a program called the Hypertext Transfer Protocol Daemon (HTTPD). A *daemon* is a UNIX term for a program that processes requests. If you've used a UNIX system, you have probably unknowingly sent requests to the Line-Printer Daemon (LPD) to print material to a printer by using the commands `lp` or `lpr`. The HTTPD resides on the Web server, which is at the heart of your connection to the Web.

Using the Web's hypertext facilities, you have the freedom to supply information to readers in powerfully innovative ways. The entrepreneurs who fostered the Web's growth started by creating small publications that used few of the Web's graphical and multimedia capabilities. This changed dramatically in a few short years, and today's Web publications use many of the Web's graphical, interactive, and multimedia features. New ways to publish on the Web are constantly being defined, and the features that tomorrow's publications will have may amaze you.

If you've browsed the Web, you've probably seen *image maps*, which are high-power graphical menus. There's no better way to create easy, graphic-based ways for users to browse information at your Web site. Using an image map, you can create a graphic image with multiple hot spots; each hot spot is a specific part of an image that the user can click on to access other documents and objects.

The wonderful thing about images is that you can pack the equivalent of hundreds of words into tiny symbols in your image map. Image maps are so user-friendly that you can pack a lot of information into a relatively small amount of space. Some image maps on the Web lead to dozens of pages, meaning virtually everything on the image is a doorway to something new. You'll learn all about image maps in Chapter 20, "Backgrounds, Image Maps, and Creative Layouts."

The specification for HTML 3.2 is a recent development in HTML publishing; it's a subset of the original HTML 3.0 specification and is based on features and extensions used in Web documents before May 1996. The first draft of the HTML 3.2 specification was released in May 1996.

NOTE

This book features extensive coverage of HTML 3.2. In fact, you will find five chapters loaded with information on HTML 3.2 in Part II, "Web Publishing with HTML 3.2."

However, the Web isn't defined by HTML alone. Many Web publishers are going back to the standard language HTML is based on—SGML. It's an advanced markup language that, although complex, offers better control over documents' layout than HTML does. SGML is also the basis for many page-definition languages used by publishing production systems, such as Adobe Acrobat and Common Ground.

NOTE

SGML is featured in Chapter 44, "Should You Upgrade to SGML?" You will also find a terrific SGML reference on the CD-ROM with this book.

Some Web publishers are looking at the origins of Web publishing, but others are taking giant leaps forward, made possible by innovators like Netscape Communications Corporation, Microsoft Corporation, and Sun Microsystems, Inc. In the fall of 1994, Netscape Communications Corporation released the first browser to support unique extensions to HTML. Netscape Navigator took the Internet community by storm and quickly became the most popular browser on the Net. A developer's site for Netscape products is featured in Figure 1.1.

TIP

The Developer's Edge site (`http://developer.netscape.com`) is the place to find developer's information for Netscape. If you want to stay current with the cutting edge for Netscape products, visit this site often.

The browser that may replace top dog Netscape Navigator is Microsoft's Internet Explorer. Microsoft's Web site is shown in Figure 1.2, and, as you can imagine, the site showcases the browser Internet Explorer; it features extensions that enable Web publishers to add soundtracks and live video segments to their publications. When a reader accesses a publication with a soundtrack or a live video segment, the sound or video plays automatically if the reader's browser supports these extensions. Microsoft has a terrific reference resource for Microsoft Internet products called the Internet Center, pictured in Figure 1.2.

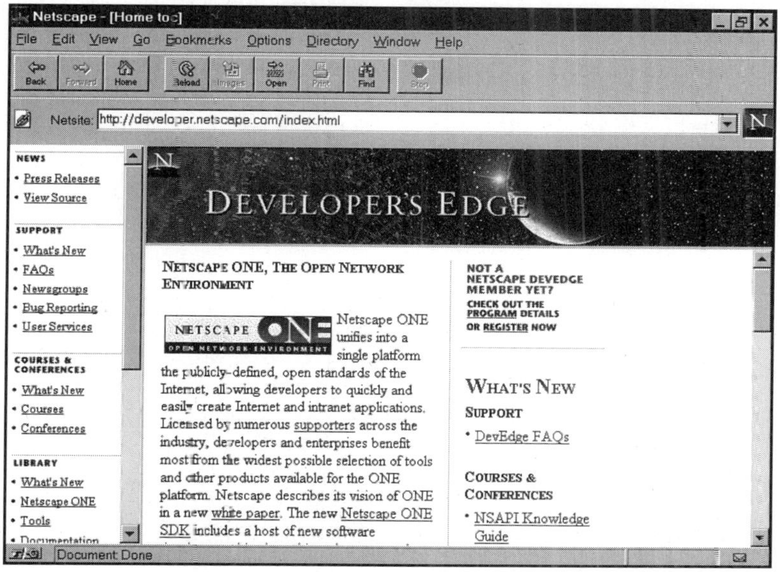

FIGURE 1.1.
The Developer's Edge site from Netscape.

TIP

Those developing Web pages should add the Internet Center (`www.microsoft.com/internet`) to their hot list. It's the place to learn about the latest innovations for Internet Explorer, FrontPage, and many other Internet products from Microsoft.

Sun Microsystems (`www.sun.com`) has been a leading supporter of Web innovation. Recently, Sun Microsystems released the HotJava browser, written entirely in the Java programming language developed by Sun. The Java language is similar to C and C++, but its platform-independence is unique. Using Java, you can add programs called *applets* to your Web publications. Applets are self-running applications that readers can preview and play automatically. Sun has set up several Web servers to handle requests related to Java; the main server is at `http://www.javasoft.com`. Figure 1.3 shows a tribute to Java in the July issue of Sun Microsystem's online magazine.

FIGURE 1.2.
For the latest in Web publishing technology, add the Internet Center to your hot list.

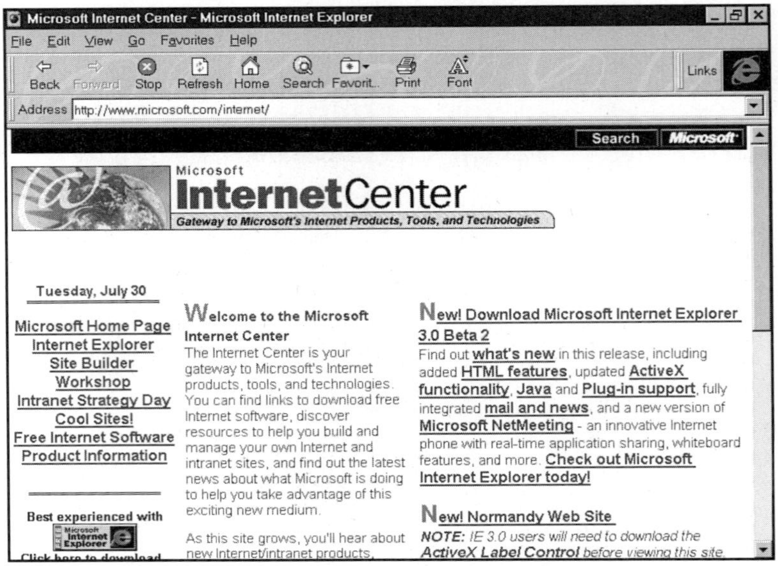

NOTE

The Java programming language is a hot topic in Web publishing. This book has three chapters designed to teach you everything you need to know to use Java in your Web pages; they are Chapter 36, "Including Java Applets in Your Web Pages," Chapter 37, "Writing Java Applets," and Chapter 38, "Integrating JavaScript and Java."

Ever since Java offered a taste of what powerful interactive content is like, Internet users around the world have clamored for more. Web developers and publishers seeking to answer this demand have taken Web publishing to new heights. Breaking new ground often meant thinking in completely new ways. For example, the traditional way to handle interactions between the client browser and the server is for the server to handle all the processing, but server-side processing is very restrictive and resource intensive. Seeking to solve this problem, Web developers looked to client-side handling of interactions, and another doorway was opened for Web publishers.

Through this doorway, you will find client-pull, client-side image maps, and client-side scripting. Client-pull is a wonderfully easy way to create documents that update themselves automatically. With client-side image maps, the user's browser can process the image map coordinates locally and more efficiently. Although client-pull and client-side image maps are terrific, client-side scripting is the innovation with the biggest impact on Web publishing. With client-side scripting, you can add completely interactive programs to your HTML documents.

FIGURE 1.3.
Java is often the main event in Sun's online magazine.

NOTE

You will find in-depth coverage of client-side technology further on in this book. Client-pull is explored in Chapter 19, "Animating Graphical Images," and client-side handling of image maps is explored in Chapter 20.

Hot new scripting languages include the following:

- JavaScript
- VBScript
- VRMLScript

JavaScript is a scripting language based on the Java programming language. This powerful up-and-coming scripting language is being developed by Netscape Communications Corporation. JavaScript can recognize and respond to mouse clicks, form input, and page navigation. This means your pages can "intelligently" react to user input. Using JavaScript is the main subject of Part VIII, "JavaScript and Java."

With VBScript (Visual Basic Script), Microsoft proves once again that it understands the tools developers need. VBScript is a subset of Visual Basic and is used to create highly interactive documents on the Web. As with JavaScript, programs written in VBScript are embedded in the body of your HTML documents. VBScript is covered extensively in Part VII, "ActiveX and VBScript."

Web publishers have been waiting for a scripting language like VRMLScript ever since the VRML standard was introduced. VRMLScript is the perfect marriage of VRML and client-side scripting. With VRMLScript, you can create dynamic interactive content for the Web. You will examine VRMLScript in Chapter 41, "Adding Behaviors with VRMLScript and Java."

Innovations by Netscape, Sun, and Microsoft represent only a small portion of the changes that are revolutionizing the way information is provided to millions of people around the world. These innovations, coupled with the explosive growth and enthusiasm in the Web, make now a more exciting time than ever to be a Web publisher.

As a Web publisher, you can publish information that will be seen by people in dozens of countries around the world, but the best news is that you as an individual can compete solely on the merits of your ideas, products, and services—not the size of your bank account. In Web publishing, you can reach the same audience whether your Web site is based on a $25 basic account from a service provider or a corporate Web server with leased lines costing $1,500 a month. Web users will judge your publications based on their information content and entertainment value.

Internet Standards and Specifications

Several standards in place on the Web allow information to be transferred the way it is; many of them relate to specifications for protocols that predate the Web, such as File Transfer Protocol (FTP) and Gopher. FTP provides a way to access files on remote systems. With FTP, you can log onto an FTP server, search for a file within a directory structure, and download the file. You also can upload files to the FTP server. Searching the file structures on FTP servers is a time-consuming process, especially if you don't know the directory of the file you're looking for. The basic functions of FTP have been extended in different ways. The most popular extension is Archie, which lets you search file archives easily by using keywords.

The Gopher protocol is similar to HTTP, but not as powerful or versatile. You can use it to search and retrieve information which is presented as a series of menus. Menu items are linked to the files containing the actual text. Gopher is most useful as the basis protocol for its more powerful and recent extensions, including Gopher Jewels, Jughead, and Veronica. Gopher Jewels enables you to search catalogs of Gopher resources indexed by category. Jughead lets you search Gopher indexes according to specified information. Veronica enables you to search Gopher menus by keyword.

The major shortcoming of early Internet protocols was the inability to access information through a common interface. Generally, files available through one interface weren't available through another. To get to information on an FTP server, you used FTP; for information on a Gopher server, you used Gopher. For files that weren't available through either FTP or Gopher, you could try to initiate a remote login to a host by using telnet. Sometimes you went from host to host looking for the information you needed.

Even with this simplified scenario, you can probably imagine how time-consuming and frustrating it was to track down information. Consequently, a major design issue for the Web was how to supply a common, easy-to-use interface to get to information on the Internet. To make sure information available through previous protocols is accessible on the Web as well, the Web was built on existing standards and specifications, like those for FTP and Gopher. Using these other protocols in your Web documents is easy—you simply specify the protocol in a reference to a uniform resource locator (URL). URLs give you a uniform way to access and retrieve files. Without one single way to retrieve files, Internet publishers and users would still be pulling their hair out.

Although the specification for URLs is an important specification for finding files on the Web, many other specifications play a major role in defining the Web. Specifications for HTTP define how hypertext documents are transferred, specifications for markup languages define the structure of Web documents, and specifications for multipurpose Internet mail extensions define the type of data being transferred and enable you to transfer any type of data on the Web. Finally, specifications for the Common Gateway Interface (CGI) make it possible for you to create dynamic documents. The following sections briefly explain each of these specifications, with emphasis on how they affect you as a Web publisher.

Transferring Files Using HTTP

HTTP is the primary protocol used to distribute information on the Web. It's a powerful, fast protocol that allows for easy exchange of files and is evolving along with other Web technologies. The original specification for HTTP is HTTP/0.9. HTTP version 0.9 has many shortcomings; for example, HTTP/0.9 doesn't allow for content typing and doesn't have provisions for supplying meta-information in requests and responses.

Content typing enables the computer receiving the data to identify the type of data being transferred. The computer can then use this information to display or process the data. Meta-information is supplemental data, such as environment variables that identify the client's computer. Being able to provide information about the type of data transferred, as well as supplemental information about the data, is important.

To address the shortcomings of HTTP/0.9, the current version of HTTP, HTTP/1.0 allows for headers with a `Content-Type` field and other types of meta-information. The type of data being transferred is defined in the `Content-Type` field. You can also use meta-information to offer additional information about the data, such as its language, encoding, and state information. (See Chapter 4, "Creating Web Documents with HTML," for a preliminary discussion on using meta-information in HTML documents.)

Most Web users and publishers want HTTP to address security; they want to be able to conduct secure transactions. The key issue in security for promoting the widespread use of electronic commerce is the ability to authenticate and encrypt transactions. Currently, there are several proposals for secure versions of HTTP. The two most popular secure protocols are Secure

HTTP (S-HTTP) and Secure Socket Layer (SSL). When one of these specifications is adopted, secure transactions using HTTP will become a reality for mainstream Web users.

HTTP is a powerful protocol because it's fast and light, yet very versatile. To achieve this speed, versatility, and robustness, HTTP is defined as a *connectionless* and *stateless* protocol, which means that generally the client and server don't maintain a connection or state information about the connection.

Connectionless Versus Connection-Oriented Protocols

HTTP is a connectionless protocol. *Connectionless protocols* differ from connection-oriented protocols in the way requests and responses to requests are handled. With a connectionless protocol, clients connect to the server, make a request, get a response, and then disconnect. With a connection-oriented protocol, clients connect to the server, make a request, get a response, and then maintain the connection to handle future requests.

An example of a connection-oriented protocol is FTP. When you connect to an FTP server, the connection remains open after you download a file. The maintenance of this connection requires system resources. A server with too many open connections quickly gets bogged down. Consequently, many FTP servers are configured to allow only 250 open connections at one time, so only 250 users can access the FTP server at once. Additionally, processes that aren't disconnected cleanly can cause problems on the server. The worst of these processes runs out of control, uses system resources, and eventually crashes the server. The best of these processes simply eats up system resources.

In contrast, HTTP is a connectionless protocol. When clients connect to the server, they make a request, get a response, and then disconnect. Because the connection isn't maintained, no system resources are used after the transaction is finished. Consequently, HTTP servers are limited only by active connections and can generally handle thousands of transactions with low system overhead. The drawback to connectionless protocols is that when the same client requests more data, the connection must be reestablished. To Web users, this means a delay whenever they request more information.

Stateless Versus Stateful Protocols

HTTP is a stateless protocol. *Stateless protocols* differ from stateful protocols in the way information about requests is maintained. With a stateless protocol, no information about a transaction is maintained after a transaction has been processed. With a stateful protocol, state information is kept even after a transaction has been processed.

Servers using stateful protocols maintain information about transactions and processes, such as the status of the connection, the processes running, the status of the processes running, and so on. Generally, this state information resides in memory and uses up system resources. When a client breaks a connection with a server running a stateful protocol, the state information has to be cleaned up and is often logged as well.

Stateless protocols are light because servers using them keep no information about completed transactions and processes. When a client breaks a connection with a server running a stateless protocol, no data has to be cleaned up or logged. By not tracking state information, there's less overhead on the server, so it can generally handle transactions swiftly. The drawback for Web publishers is that if you need to maintain state information for your Web documents, you must include it as meta-information in the document header.

Determining the Structure of Web Documents

The way you can structure documents is largely determined by the language you use to lay out the document. Some languages are advanced and offer you extensive control over document layout. Other languages are basic and offer ease of use and "friendliness" instead of advanced features. The following sections take a look at commonly used languages, including

- SGML
- Virtual Reality Modeling Language (VRML)
- HTML
- Page definition

SGML

Most Web documents are structured with a markup language based on SGML. SGML defines a way to share complex documents by using a generalized markup described in terms of standard text. Describing complex structures with plain text ensures the widest distribution to any type of computer and presents the formatting in a human-readable form called *markup*. Because the markup contains standard characters, this also means anyone can create documents in a markup language without needing special software.

SGML is an advanced language with few limitations. In SGML, you have full control over the positioning of text and images, so text and images are displayed by the user's SGML browser in the precise location you designate. Although SGML is a powerful markup language, it isn't widely used on the Web. However, this is changing as more publishers become aware of SGML's versatility.

VRML

Technology on the Web is growing at an explosive pace, and one of the most recent developments is VRML. VRML enables you to render complex models and multidimensional documents by using a standardized markup language.

The implications of virtual reality for Web publishers are far-reaching. Using VRML, you can reduce calculations and data points that would have filled 10 M of disk space to just a few hundred lines of markup code. Not only does this feature drastically reduce the download time for VRML files and save network bandwidth, it also presents complex models in a readable and—gasp—understandable format. VRML isn't widely used on the Web yet, but it's attracting tremendous interest in the Internet community and the world community, as well. Although the current version of VRML is VRML 1.0, the Moving Worlds specification for VRML 2.0 has recently been approved and is gaining widespread support.

NOTE

Exploring the limitless possibilities of VRML is the subject of Part IX, "Creating VRML Worlds." This part of the book contains three chapters that showcase the VRML 2.0 Moving Worlds specification.

HTML

HTML is the most commonly used markup language. HTML's popularity stems mostly from its ease of use and friendliness. With HTML, you can quickly and easily create Web documents, make them available to a wide audience, and control many of the layout aspects for text and images. You can specify the relative size of headings and text, as well as text styles, including bold, underline, and italics. Extensions to HTML enable you to specify font type, but standard HTML specifications don't give you that capability.

Although many advanced layout controls for documents aren't available with HTML, it's still the publishing language of choice on the vast majority of Web sites. Remember, the limitations are a way to drastically reduce the complexity of HTML. Currently, HTML has three specifications: HTML 1.0, HTML 2.0, and HTML 3.2. Each level of specification steadily introduces more versatility and functionality.

In addition to these specifications, several Internet developers have created extensions to HTML. The extensions are nonstandard, but many have been accepted and used by Web publishers. Some extensions, such as Netscape's and Microsoft's, are so popular that they seem to be standard HTML.

Page Definition Languages

Some Web documents are formatted by using page definition languages instead of markup languages. *Page definition languages* often use formats specific to a particular commercial page-layout application, such as Adobe Acrobat or Common Ground. Page-layout applications are popular because they combine fine-tuned control over document layout with user-friendly graphical interfaces. Although the formats these applications use are proprietary, most of the formats are based on the standards set forth by SGML.

Identifying Data Types with MIME

With HTTP, you can transfer full-motion video sequences, stereo soundtracks, high-resolution images, and any other type of media you can think of. The standard that makes this possible is *multipurpose Internet mail extensions* (MIME). HTTP uses MIME to identify the type of object being transferred across the Internet. Object types are identified in a header field that comes before the actual data for the object. In HTTP, this header field is the `Content-Type` header field. By identifying the type of object in a header field, the client receiving the object can handle it appropriately.

For example, if the object is a GIF image, it's identified by the MIME type `image/gif`. When the client receiving the object of type `image/gif` can handle the object type directly, it displays the object. When the client can't handle the object directly, it checks a configuration table to see whether an application is configured to handle an object of this MIME type. If an application is configured for use with the client and is available, the client calls the application, which then handles the object. In this case, the application would display the GIF image.

Not only is MIME typing useful to HTTP, it's useful to other protocols, too. MIME typing was originally developed so that e-mail messages could have several parts, with different types of data in each part. In this way, you can attach any type of file to an e-mail message. The MIME standard is described in detail in Requests for Comments (RFCs) 1521 and 1522. (Many Internet standards and specifications are described in RFCs, which are a collection of documents about the Internet that cover both technical and nontechnical issues.) See Chapter 26, "Writing CGI Scripts," for more information on MIME types and their uses in your Web documents.

TIP

RFCs are great resources to browse. You can find RFCs at the following sites:

`http://ds.internic.net/ds/dspg1intdoc.html`

`http://www.cis.ohio-state.edu:80/hypertext/information/rfc.html`

Accessing and Retrieving Files with URLs

To retrieve a file from a server, a client must know three things: the address of the server, where on the server the file is located, and which protocol to use to access and retrieve the file. This information is specified as a URL. URLs can be used to find and retrieve files on the Internet with any valid protocol.

Although you normally use HTTP to transfer your Web documents, you can include references to other protocols in your documents. For example, you can specify the address to a file available through FTP simply by naming the protocol in a URL. Most URLs you use in your documents look something like this:

```
protocol://server_host:port/path_to_resource
```

The first part of the URL scheme names the protocol the client will use to access and transfer the file. The protocol name is generally followed by a colon and two forward slashes. The second part of the URL indicates the address of the server and ends with a single slash. The server host may be followed by a colon and a port address. The third part of the URL indicates where on the server the resource is located and may include a path structure. In a URL, double slash marks indicate that the protocol uses the format defined by the Common Internet Scheme Syntax (CISS); colons are separators. In this example, a colon separates the protocol from the rest of the URL scheme; the second colon separates the host address from the port number.

NOTE

CISS is a common syntax for URL schemes that involve the direct use of IP-based protocols. IP-based protocols specify a particular host on the Internet with a unique numeric identifier called an *IP address* or with a unique name that can be resolved to the IP address. Non-CISS URL schemes don't name a particular host computer. Therefore, the host is assumed to be the computer providing services for the client.

Here's a URL using HTTP to retrieve a file called `index.html` on the Macmillan Computer Publishing Web server:

```
http://www.mcp.com/index.html
```

URLs, defined in RFC 1738, are powerful because they give you a uniform way to retrieve multiple types of data. Here are the most common protocols you can specify by using URLs:

FTP	File Transfer Protocol
Gopher	Gopher Protocol
HTTP	Hypertext Transfer Protocol
mailto	Electronic mail address
Prospero	Prospero Directory Service
news	Usenet news
NNTP	Usenet news accessed with Network News Transfer Protocol
telnet	Remote login sessions
WAIS	Wide Area Information Servers
file	Files on local host

Using these protocols in your Web documents is explored in Chapter 4.

Creating Dynamic Documents with CGI

The Web's popularity also stems from its interactivity. Web users click on hypertext links to access Web documents, images, and multimedia files, but the URLs in your hypertext links can lead to much more than static resources. URLs can also specify programs that process user input and return information to the user's browser. By specifying programs on the Web server, you can make your Web publications highly interactive and dynamic. You can also create customized documents on demand, based on the user's input and on the type of browser being used.

Programs specified in URLs are called *gateway scripts*; the term comes from the UNIX environment. *Gateways* are programs or devices that supply an interface. Here, the gateway or interface is between your browser and the server. Programs written in UNIX shells are called *scripts* by UNIX programmers because UNIX shells, such as Bourne, Korn, and C-shell, aren't actual programming languages. UNIX shells are easy to use and learn, so most gateway scripts are written in them.

The CGI specification describes how gateway scripts pass information to servers. CGI gives you the basis for creating dynamic documents, which can include interactive forms, graphical menus called image maps, and much more. The power of CGI is that it gives Web publishers a common interface to programs on Web servers. Using this common interface, Web publishers can provide dynamic documents to Web users without regard to the type of system the publisher and user are using.

NOTE

Understanding CGI is important to Web publishing. You will explore CGI in more depth in Part VI, "Adding Interactivity with CGI."

The Evolution of Standards and Specifications

The standards and specifications you read about in the previous section are the result of coordinated efforts by standards organizations and the working groups associated with them. Generally, these organizations approve changes to existing standards and specifications and develop new ones. Three primary standards groups develop standards and specifications for the Internet and networked computing in general:

- ISO: The International Organization for Standardization
- IETF: The Internet Engineering Task Force
- W3C: The World Wide Web Consortium

The International Organization for Standardization

The International Organization for Standardization is one of the most important standards-making bodies in the world. The ISO doesn't usually develop standards specifically for the Internet; rather, it develops standards for networked computing in general. One of the most important developments by the organization is the internationally recognized *seven-layer network model.* The seven-layer model is commonly referred to as the Open Systems Interconnection (OSI) Reference Model.

Most Internet specifications and protocols incorporate standards developed by the ISO. For example, ISO standard 8859 is used by all Web browsers to define the standard character set. ISO 8859-1 defines the standard character set called ISO-Latin-1, which has been added to; the addition is called the ISO-Added-Latin-1 character set. You will refer to these character sets whenever you want to add special characters—such as &, ©, or ®—to your Web documents.

The Internet Engineering Task Force

The Internet Engineering Task Force (IETF) is the primary organization developing Internet standards. All changes to existing Internet standards and proposals for new standards are approved by the IETF, which meets three times a year to set directions for the Internet.

Changes to existing specifications and proposals for new ones are approved by formal committees, called *working groups.* The IETF has dozens of them. Each group typically focuses on a specific topic within a development area.

NOTE

The process for approving and making changes to specifications is standardized. The working groups propose Internet Draft specifications, such as the current specifications for HTML and HTTP. Internet Drafts are valid for six months after they're formalized. If the Internet Draft hasn't been approved in six months, then it expires and is no longer valid. If the Internet Draft is approved, it becomes an RFC.

RFCs are permanently archived and are valid until they're superseded by a later RFC. As their name implies, RFCs are made available to the general Internet community for discussion and suggestions for improvements.

Many RFCs eventually become Internet Standards, but the process isn't a swift one. For example, URLs were introduced by the World Wide Web global information initiative in 1990. They've been in use ever since, but the URL specification didn't become an RFC until December 1994 and was only recently approved as an Internet standard.

Figure 1.4 shows IETF's site on the Web. Here you can find information on current IETF initiatives, which include the latest standards and specifications for the Internet. You can find more information on the Internet Society and membership in the Internet Society at this Web site:

```
http://www.isoc.org/
```

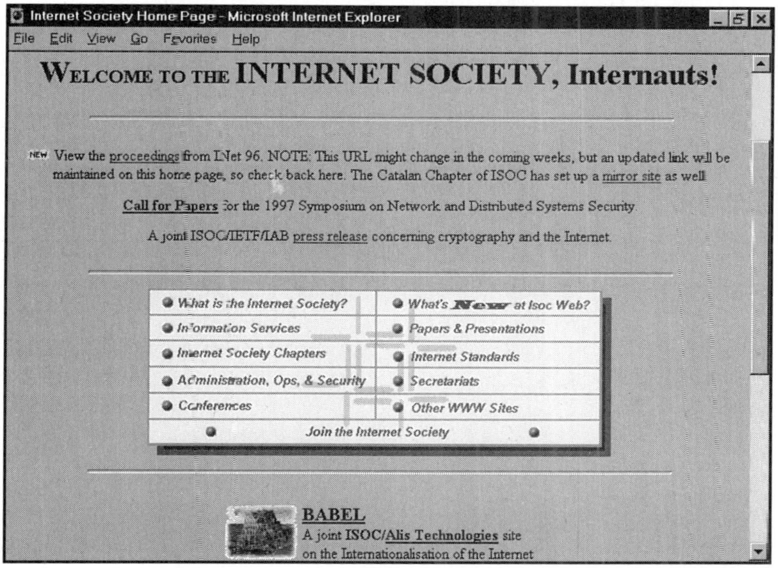

FIGURE 1.4.
The Internet Engineering Task Force Web site.

Membership in the IETF is open to anyone. The directors of the working group areas handle the internal management of the IETF. These directors, along with the chairperson of the IETF, form the Internet Engineering Steering Group (IESG), which handles the operational management of the IETF under the direction of the Internet Society.

The World Wide Web Consortium

The World Wide Web Consortium (W3C) is managed by the Laboratory for Computer Science at the Massachusetts Institute of Technology. The W3C develops common standards for the evolution of the World Wide Web. It is a joint initiative between MIT, CERN, and INRIA. The U.S. W3C center is based at and run by MIT. The European W3C center is at the French National Institute for Research in Computing and Automation (INRIA). CERN and INRIA cooperate to manage the European W3C center.

The W3C was formed in part to help develop common standards for the development of Web technologies. One of the W3C's major goals is to offer a storehouse of information about the Web to Web developers and users. To do that, the W3C has sites where you can find the most current information on Web development. If you visit the page featured in Figure 1.5 and enter your e-mail address in the form at the bottom of the page, you will automatically be notified when the W3C updates the page on HTML.

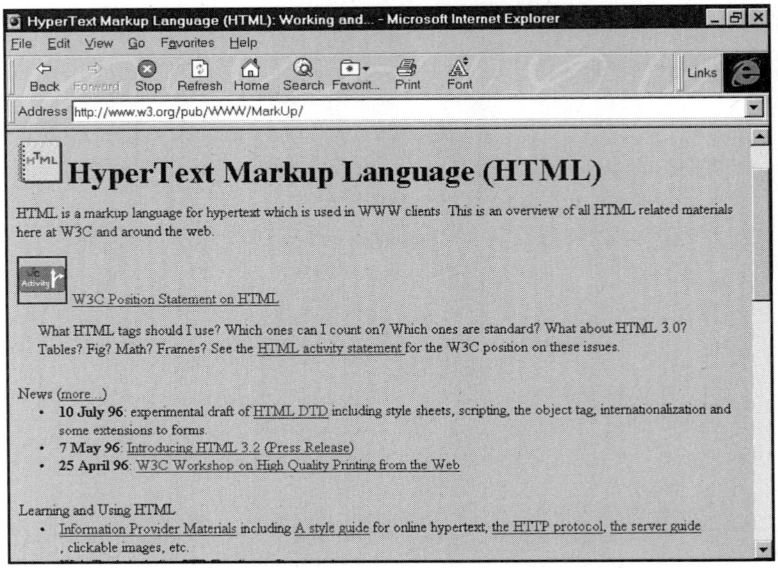

FIGURE 1.5.
The HTML specification documents at the World Wide Web Consortium Web site.

Another goal of the W3C is to supply prototype applications that use new technologies proposed in Internet Drafts. The W3C works with its member organizations to propose specifications and standards to the IETF. Member organizations pay a fee based on their membership status. Full members pay $50,000 and affiliate members pay $5,000 for a one-year membership.

Summary

The Web was built on existing protocols and intended to provide a common interface to other protocols. Because of this design, you can use any valid protocol to transfer files. You primarily use HTTP to access your Web documents, but you can use other protocols, such as Gopher and FTP, to enhance the usefulness of your documents. The face of Web publishing is changing rapidly, and the way you specify the structure of Web documents is changing just as quickly. The most common way to structure Web documents is with HTML, but you can also use SGML, VRML, and page-layout applications to structure Web documents.

The MIME standard is what allows you to provide access to any type of document on the Web. With MIME, you can supply information about documents in the `Content-Type` header field. Browsers use the content type to take appropriate action on the document, such as displaying an image or calling another application. The URL standard, however, is what lets you access and retrieve files on the Web. With URLs, you can locate and retrieve files with the appropriate protocol. The final specification of interest to Web publishers is CGI; by using it, you can create dynamic documents.

To stay current with the latest developments on the Web, you should follow the Internet standards and specifications proposed by Internet standards groups, such as the IETF and the W3C.

CHAPTER 2

Developing and Planning a Web Site

by William Robert Stanek

IN THIS CHAPTER

An entire universe is growing in cyberspace. The Internet connects over 50,000 computer networks and 6 million host computers worldwide. Almost every country in the world and some 50 million people have access to the Internet. Even more incredible, in less than two years, the number of users is expected to double, which means more than 100 million people on the global Internet by the end of 1998. The segment of the Internet driving this tremendous growth is the World Wide Web. Not only can you reach these millions of consumers on the Web, you can do so in ways that are limited only by your imagination.

In 1995 alone, more than 8 million people gained access to the Web. The source of this increase was primarily commercial online services, such as CompuServe, Prodigy, and America Online, which offer their users full access to the Internet. When these figures are added to a conservative growth rate of 10 percent per month for new users of the Web, this means 25 to 50 million people are using the Web as of late 1996.

This chapter gives you the essential background for success in developing and planning your Web site and plenty of information that will help you make important preliminary decisions about your Web site.

NOTE

This chapter explores everything from navigating the Web to examining your access needs, but it's not a step-by-step guide to setting up a Web site. If you're looking for a guide to creating a Web site, see Chapter 49, "Designing and Publishing a Killer Web Site."

Navigating the Web

If you've browsed the Web before, you know that navigating the Web can be as easy as activating a hypertext link—you just move your mouse pointer to the link and click the left mouse button. Text containing a hypertext link is underlined and usually displayed in a different color from other text on the page. By default, most browsers display links that you haven't visited in blue and links that you have visited in purple or light red.

When you move your mouse pointer over a link, most browsers display the URL path to the file or object that will be retrieved if you activate the link. This is useful to identify the type of file the link is referring to.

NOTE

With some browsers, you can select the color of text on the page. The four basic color definitions you can assign to text specify the color of ordinary text, unvisited links, active links, and visited links. In HTML 3.2, you, as the Web publisher, can define the color of text on the page. These color definitions generally override color definitions defined in the user's HTML 3.2-compliant browser.

Following text-based links on Web pages is easy, but following links embedded in graphic objects sometimes isn't. Some images are displayed on the page with a distinctive blue border; this type of clickable image is easy to identify. However, others have no borders at all, primarily because of extensions to HTML that enable Web publishers to suppress the border around images; also, other extensions to HTML enable Web publishers to place borders around images that can't be clicked on. So how do you know when an image is clickable if it has no distinctive border?

One way to tell is to move your mouse pointer over the image. If your browser shows that a URL path is associated with the image, you can click on it. The site featured in Figure 2.1 has a well-designed image map. When you move the mouse pointer over the figure as shown, a reference URL is shown on the browser's status bar. Alternately, some browsers change the pointer to a hand if an image is clickable.

FIGURE 2.1.
An image map used at Planet Direct.

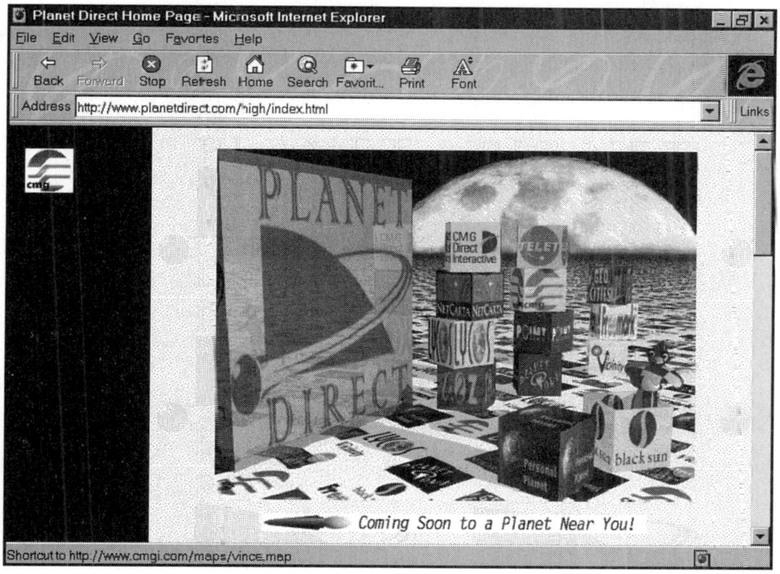

As you point and click your way through the Web, you probably don't stop to think about the URLs you're using to find Web resources. However, as a Web publisher, you should stop and think about them. One of the hottest sites on the Web is the Jose Cuervo Web Site featured in Figure 2.2. I wholeheartedly recommend stopping by and blending up some critter drinks, but first, take a closer look at the page URL.

The page URL `http://www.cuervo.com/main.html` tells a browser to use the hypertext transfer protocol (HTTP) to get a file called `main.html` on the `www.cuervo.com` Web server. However, URLs are much more powerful and complex than this simple example, so the next section examines the structure of URLs and how they are used on the Web.

FIGURE 2.2.
The Jose Cuervo Web site.

Using URLs

URLs give you a uniform way of identifying resources that are available by using Internet protocols (IP). To better understand URLs, you need to know about URL schemes and formats, how URLs are defined, and how to use escape codes in URLs.

URL Schemes and Formats

The standard naming scheme is what makes URLs so versatile. URL schemes name the protocol the client will use to access and transfer the file. Web clients use the name of the protocol to determine the format for the information that follows the protocol name. Here are two general formats:

```
protocol://host name:port/path_to_resource
protocol://user name:password@host name:port/path_to_resource
```

NOTE

If you use a DOS/Windows-based system, you normally type a backslash to change directories and maneuver around the system. Consequently, you might have to remind yourself that the Web follows the UNIX syntax for slashes, and the slashes you type for URLs should be forward slashes.

Defining Host Information in URLs

Host name information used in URLs identifies the address to a host and is broken down into two or more parts separated by periods. The periods separate domain information from the host name. Common domain names for Web servers begin with *www*, such as `www.tvp.com`, which identifies the Web server called *tvp* in the commercial domain. Domains you can specify in your URLs include the following:

COM	Commercial sites
EDU	Education sites
GOV	Nonmilitary government sites
MIL	Military sites
NET	Network sites (developers, Internet Service Providers, and so on)
ORG	Organizational sites

Defining Port Information in URLs

Ports are rather like telephone jacks on the Web server. The server has certain ports allocated for certain things, such as port 80 for incoming requests for hypertext documents. The server listens on a particular port. When it hears something, in essence, it picks up the phone and connects the particular port.

Port information used in URLs identifies the port number to be used for the connection. If you don't specify a port number, a default value is assumed as needed. Generally, you don't have to specify port numbers in your URLs unless the connection will be made to a port other than the default. Default values for ports are defined in the URL specification, as follows:

File Transfer Protocol (FTP)	Port 21
Gopher	Port 70
HTTP	Port 80
Network News Transfer Protocol (NNTP)	Port 119
telnet	Port 23
wide area information server (WAIS)	Port 210

Defining User Name and Password Information in URLs

By specifying the user name and password information in a URL, users can log in to a system automatically. The two protocols that use both user name and password information are FTP and telnet. In a FTP session, the user name and password information are often used to let users log in to FTP servers anonymously. When a connection is made to a FTP server and user name and password information aren't specified, the following default values are assumed: anonymous for user name and the user's e-mail address as the password.

In telnet, there are no default values. If the user name and password aren't supplied, the user is prompted for this information. To avoid this, you could allow users to log in automatically by specifying a user and password in your URL. However, you usually don't want to specify a personal password in a URL, so if you want users to be able to log in automatically using telnet, you should create a guest account with a generic password.

Defining Path Information in URLs

The final part of a URL is the path to the resource. This path generally follows the directory structure from the root or slash directory to the resource specified in the URL. A completely specified path to a resource is called an *absolute path*. You can also specify a path to a resource in relation to the current directory. You will learn more about specifying paths to resources in Chapter 4, "Creating Web Documents with HTML."

Protocol Schemes Defined

Most protocol schemes follow the two general forms of URLs discussed earlier. Protocol schemes conforming to the CISS standard use the double slashes. CISS-compliant protocols are FTP, Gopher, HTTP, NNTP, WAIS, and File. Protocols that don't conform to the CISS standard—such as Mailto and News—omit the double slashes. Table 2.1 shows the URL schemes associated with each protocol.

NOTE

In Chapter 4, you will learn how to refer to alternative protocols in your Web documents.

Table 2.1. URL schemes and formats.

Scheme	*Description/ Protocol*	*URL Format*
FTP	File transfer protocol	`ftp://user name:password@host name:port/path_to_resource`

Scheme	*Description/ Protocol*	*URL Format*
Gopher	Gopher protocol	`gopher://host name:port/path_to_rescurce`
HTTP	Hypertext transfer protocol	`http://host name:port/path_to_resource`
Mailto	Electronic mail address	`mailto:user name@host`
News	Usenet news	`news:newsgroup-name`
		`news:message-number`
NNTP	Usenet news accessed with Network News Transfer Protocol	`nntp://host name/newsgroup-name`
telnet	Remote login sessions	`telnet:/user name:password@host name:port`
WAIS	Wide area information servers	`wais://host name:port/database`
File	Files on local host	`file://host name/path_to_resource`

How URLs Are Defined

URLs consist of characters defined by the ASCII character set, and the URL specification allows for the use of uppercase and lowercase letters. Most Web publishers use only lcwercase letters in their URLs, so most Web documents and object files are named in lowercase letters, too. If you are on a system that has case-sensitive file naming, such as UNIX, then naming your files in lowercase letters helps avoid possible conflicts.

Although URLs consist of characters defined by the ASCII character set, you can't use all ASCII characters in your URLs. You can use the letters *a-z*, the numerals 0-9, and a few special characters, such as the following:

- Asterisks
- Dollar signs
- Exclamation points
- Hyphens
- Parentheses (left and right)
- Periods
- Plus signs
- Single quotation marks
- Underscores

You are limited to these characters because other characters used in URLs have specific meanings, as shown in Table 2.2.

Table 2.2. The meaning of characters used in URLs.

Character	Meaning	Example
:	The colon is a separator.	
	It separates protocol from the rest of the URL scheme.	`http://tvp.com/vpfound.html`
	It separates host name from the port number.	`http://www.tvp.com:80/`
	It separates user name from the password.	`ftp://anonymous:william@tvp.com/ ➥vpinfo.txt`
//	The double slash marks indicate that the protocol uses the format defined by the Common Internet Scheme Syntax.	
	This protocol follows the CISS format.	`ftp://tvp.com/vpinfo.txt`
	This protocol does not follow the CISS format.	`news:newsgroup-name`
/	The slash is a separator used to separate the path from host name and port.	`http://tvp.com/vphp.html`
	The slash is also used to denote the directory path to the resource named in the URL.	`/usr/cgi-bin/useit.pl`
~	The tilde is generally used at the beginning of the path to indicate that the resource is in the specified user's public html directory.	`http://www.aloha.com/~william`
%	The percent sign identifies an escape code, which is used to specify special characters in URLs that otherwise have a special meaning or are not allowed.	`gopher://unm.edu/books english/ ➥Book%20Table%20of%20Contents`

Character	Meaning	Example
@	The at symbol is used to separate user name and/or password information from the host name in the URL.	`mailto:william@tvp.com`
?	The question mark is used in the URL path to specify the beginning of a query string. Query strings are passed to CGI scripts. All the information following the question mark is data the user submitted and is not interpreted as part of the file path.	`/usr/cgi-bin/useit.pl?keyword`
+	The plus sign is used in query strings as a placeholder between words. Instead of using spaces to separate words the user has entered in the query, the browser substitutes the plus sign.	`/usr/cgi-bin/` `➥useit.pl?word1+word2+word3`
=	The equal sign is used in query strings to separate the key assigned by the publisher from the value entered by the user. In the sample URL, user name is the key assigned by the publisher and the value entered by the user is `william`.	`/usr/cgi-bin/useit.pl?user` `➥name=william`
&	The ampersand is used in query strings to separate sets of keys and values.	`/usr/cgi-bin/query.pl?` `➥name=william&question=why+not`

continues

Table 2.2. continued

Character	*Meaning*	*Example*
	In the sample URL, `name` is the first key assigned by the publisher and the value entered by the user is `william`. The second key assigned by the publisher is `question`, and the value entered by the user is `why+not`.	
`^`	The caret symbol is reserved for future use.	
`{}`	The curly braces are reserved for future use.	
`[]`	The brackets are reserved for future use.	

Using Escape Codes in URLs

To make URLs even more versatile, the specification enables you to use escape codes in URLs. *Escape codes* are used to specify special characters in URLs that are either reserved or not otherwise allowed. They are particularly useful for protocols (such as Gopher) that allow resources to be defined with spaces between words. For example, to use the Gopher resource `Book Table of Contents`, you would have to rewrite the resource name using the escape code for spaces. The percent sign identifies an escape code, and the number following the percent sign identifies the character being escaped; therefore, the escape code for a space is a percent sign followed by the number 20. To use the preceding resource name in a URL, you would rewrite it as follows:

```
Book%20Table%20of%20Contents
```

Using the ISO Latin 1 character set, you can determine the values for characters you need to escape. To do this, you convert the decimal value defined in the character set to a hexadecimal value. The decimal value for a space is 32. When you convert this decimal value to hexadecimal, the resulting value is 20. Table 2.3 shows common character values from the ISO Latin 1 character set and the associated escape codes.

Table 2.3. Common character values and their associated escape codes.

Numeric Value	*Character Description*	*Escape Code*
09	Tab	%09
32	Space	%20
35	Number sign (#)	%23
37	Percent sign (%)	%25
38	Ampersand (&)	%26
39	Apostrophe (')	%27
63	Question mark (?)	%3f
64	At symbol (@)	%40
95	Caret symbol (^)	%5f

TIP

When you use escape codes such as %09 for a tab, be sure to include the zero. The computer will interpret the hexadecimal value 09 as a tab.

Who's Publishing on the Web?

The Web is a powerful interface to everything the Internet has to offer. When most people think of the Internet, they think of the dynamic environment that enables them to search through and access complex webs of text, graphics, sound, and video. In short, they equate the Web with the Internet—and that's because the Web has swallowed the Net.

The Web was born at the European Laboratory for Particle Physics (CERN), and it should be no surprise that universities, colleges, and research institutes represent some of the largest segments of Web publishers. Some of the most wonderful Web sites are created by college students and research scientists. These same students and researchers also represent most of the innovators creating new technologies for the Web.

Web sites created by research and educational organizations are plentiful, but their presence has been dwarfed in recent months by commercial sites. Thousands of businesses are already plugged into the Internet and have built some of the hottest sites on the Web, attracting thousands of visitors every day. One of these hot sites is found at Pepsi (`www.pepsi.com`). Pepsi's Psychotropic Sundae page is featured in Figure 2.3.

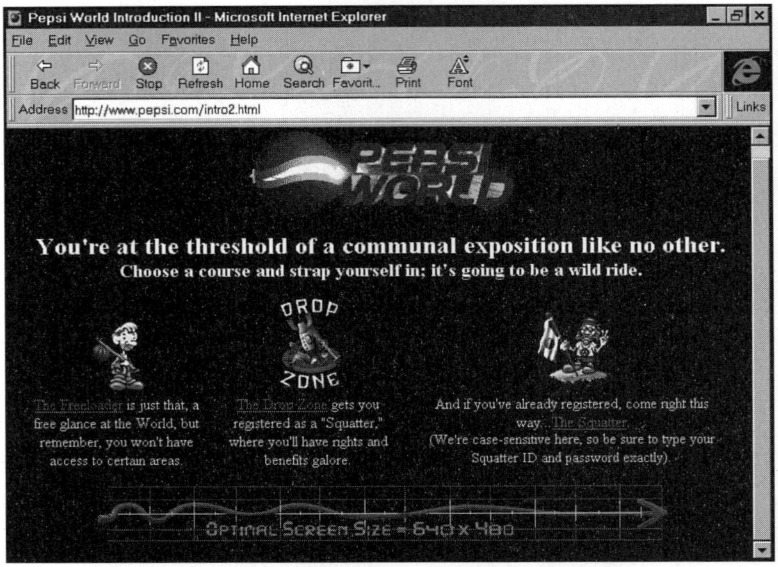

FIGURE 2.3.
Anyone for a Psychotropic Sundae?

Not all the companies running commercial sites are multibillion dollar conglomerates with thousands of employees. Many commercial sites are run by startup companies who represent small groups of entrepreneurs with big dreams, and others are mom-and-pop businesses from down the street and home businesses run from the kitchen table.

An original mom-and-pop kind of business is Ben & Jerry's. Ben & Jerry's is a phenomenal success story because someone there recognized the importance of larger-than-life marketing to customers across the country. Today, Ben & Jerry's continues a tradition of powerful marketing on their Web site, shown in Figure 2.4. At this site, you will find excellent multimedia productions with RealAudio and Shockwave. The URL to this site is `http://www.benjerry.com`.

NOTE

For more information on using the latest audio technologies in your Web pages, see Chapter 23, "Creating Online Audio." To learn more about Macromedia's powerhouse called Shockwave, refer to Chapter 25, "Adding Interactivity with Shockwave for Director."

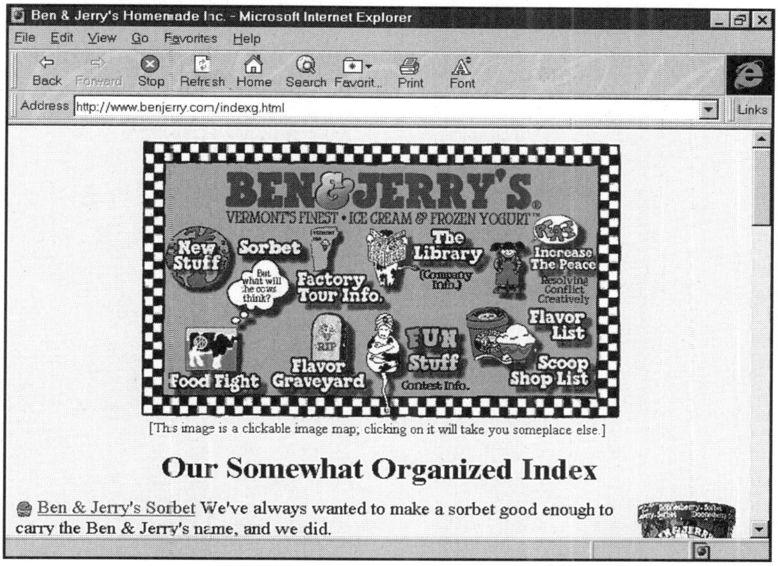

FIGURE 2.4.
Ben and Jerry's site is fully enhanced with RealAudio and Shockwave.

Behind the massive wave of companies and entrepreneurs carving their niche in cyberspace, the governments of the world watch. They know what commerce without national borders, tariffs, and taxes means to global markets and aren't sure how to regulate it—or even whether they *can* regulate it. Many governments are doing much more than watching; they're taking active roles in developing the Internet and fostering its growth with funding. Government agencies are publishing their own Web sites loaded with useful information. U.S. government agencies publishing on the Web include the Environmental Protection Agency, the Central Intelligence Agency, the National Security Agency, the Census Bureau, and a very humorous site from the IRS.

There's a one-stop index to government resources on the Web at the University of Michigan's Document Center. The home page for the list, fittingly called "Government Resources on the Web," is shown in Figure 2.5. This definitive list has links to government sites the world over. If any country's government has a site on the Web, you'll find the links to it in this list. The URL to this site is `http://www.lib.umich.edu/libhome/Documents.center/govwebnew.html`.

Although many Web publishers represent organizations, this isn't always the case—a growing number of Web publishers are individuals who want to share their ideas and interests with the world. They aren't publishing on the Web to make a profit; they're doing it because it's fun to create something people around the world will see, it's challenging to test new publishing techniques, and it's exciting to build something dozens, hundreds, and often thousands of people will talk about.

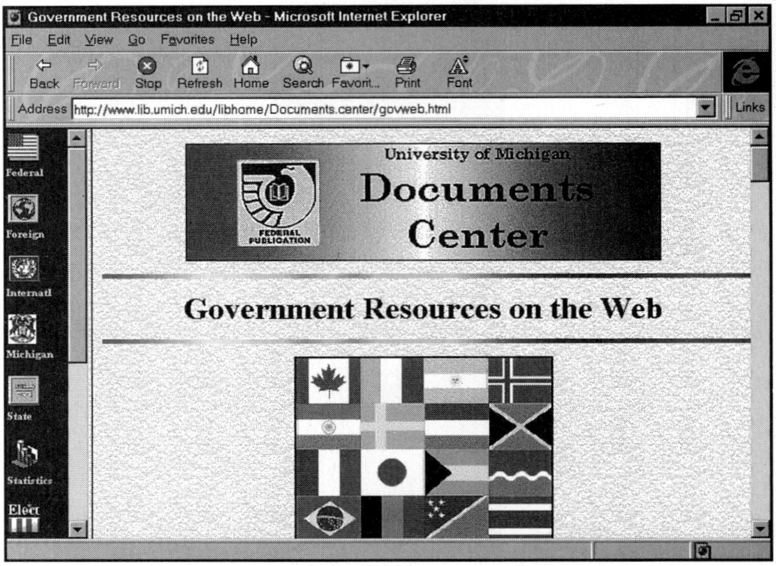

FIGURE 2.5.
Find just about any government resource on the Web at this page.

Conducting Business

On the Web, your business is never closed. Consumers can visit your site 24 hours a day, seven days a week, 365 days a year. They don't have to worry about fighting traffic to get to the mall. They don't have to race to the store after work and hope that it's not closed. They don't have to talk to a sales representative who's having a bad day and doesn't want to answer their questions. They can get information about your products and services at their own pace and when it's most convenient for them, even if it's 3:00 a.m. on Christmas morning.

Businesses are striving to establish a presence on the Web for many different reasons. Some are experimenting and trying to discover the benefits of Web publishing, so they are promoting their company's product and service online. Often, they try to gauge consumer interest areas and figure out the directions the Web site should grow in to best serve customers.

Other businesses focus strictly on profits from Web publishing. They expect to make direct sales to customers and are interested in little else. These businesses are often disappointed when their Web publishing operation doesn't generate thousands of new sales. What these businesses fail to realize is that the benefits of Web publishing aren't always tangible.

Although advertising agencies would undoubtedly argue to the contrary, you can't precisely gauge the sales generated from a $100,000 television commercial. You can estimate the potential sales based on the estimated size of the viewing audience, but you can't directly relate sales to a particular 30-second television commercial. The same is true in Web publishing. If your consumers aren't purchasing your product at your online order center, that doesn't mean they aren't reading about the product online and purchasing the product locally.

Increasing the bottom line because of Web publishing can be a goal, but it shouldn't be the only goal. Internet-savvy businesses have many goals for their Web publishing operations and know the Web is best used for the following:

- Offering enhanced customer service
- Public relations
- Marketing to global audiences
- Direct sales

Enhanced Customer Service

What do you do when the customer has questions and wants answers at 3:00 a.m.? Most customer service departments aren't open 24 hours a day, primarily because of the expense of providing around-the-clock service. The best time to reach customers is at their leisure, and when they have questions about your products or services.

One of the biggest customer complaints is the wait to get service. Nothing frustrates customers more than waiting on the phone or in a line to get service. Some companies solve this problem by hiring additional customer service representatives during peak periods. Other companies simply can't afford the extra expense of hiring more personnel, so the result is long waits for service.

On the Web, there's no wait to get customer support. Customers reach the Web site, follow the links to your customer support area, and find the information they need. Ideally, the customer service area would have search facilities so customers could look for specific information quickly.

The customer support area for Strategic Simulations Incorporated (SSI, `www.ssionline.com`) is shown in Figure 2.6. In this area, SSI customers can download updates and patches for the latest games. Being able to instantly get and download a patch for a game means customers don't have to wait two to four weeks for an update to be sent through the mail.

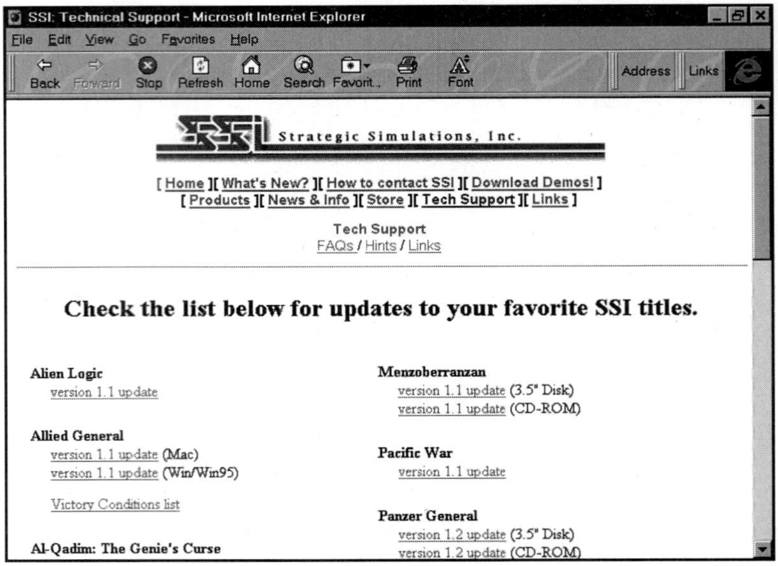

FIGURE 2.6.
Customer service plays a central role at the SSI Web site.

The Web dramatically reduces the cost of publishing product information. Not only can you give customers product information, but you can do so on a scale that would be prohibitively expensive through traditional media. You can turn your one-page ad in a leading magazine into a 20-page exposé on your product for a fraction of the cost of publishing in the magazine. In fact, for the same cost as a one-page ad in a leading magazine, you can probably publish detailed information on your entire product line.

Quick access to information is often critical to the success of your products and services. The Web also reduces the lag time for getting new product information. Instead of having to wait days for product information to arrive in the mail, customers can find new product information at your Web site within seconds after you publish it.

Customers focus on documentation for products, and the manuals delivered with products aren't always detailed enough for them. Poorly written manuals are sometimes the result of a rush to get the product to market or publishing constraints that limit the size of the manual to reduce costs. Many manuals also have typos and inconsistencies, but correcting them is costly and impractical when products have already been shipped to wholesalers, retailers, and customers. You can correct your manual's deficiencies by offering a deluxe version online.

The Web also significantly reduces the costs of distributing upgrades to customers. Not only can you provide information on patches for software products, but you can also make the patches available for downloading online. Giving customers free upgrades to your products is good business, especially since most minor upgrades fix bugs in the original product. The company saves money because disks and documentation don't have to be published and shipped to the customer.

To offer quality customer service and make sure you're meeting the needs of customers, you need feedback from them. Your Web pages can have forms that customers fill out and submit online by e-mail. In this way, you can keep in touch with your customers' needs. Fill-out forms can also be used to get customer opinions on your latest products and services. You can compile these opinion surveys and use the statistics to pinpoint areas for improvement in future product releases.

Public Relations

Building your business's image is important, and one of the best ways to do this is through press coverage. Savvy businesses with Web sites have the online equivalent of neon signs leading the press to special areas set up for their use. For example, the Internet Explorer home page (`www.microsoft.com/ie`) shown in Figure 2.7, has a link to a page specifically directed at the press.

FIGURE 2.7.
The Internet Explorer home page has links to reviews and the latest press releases to improve public relations.

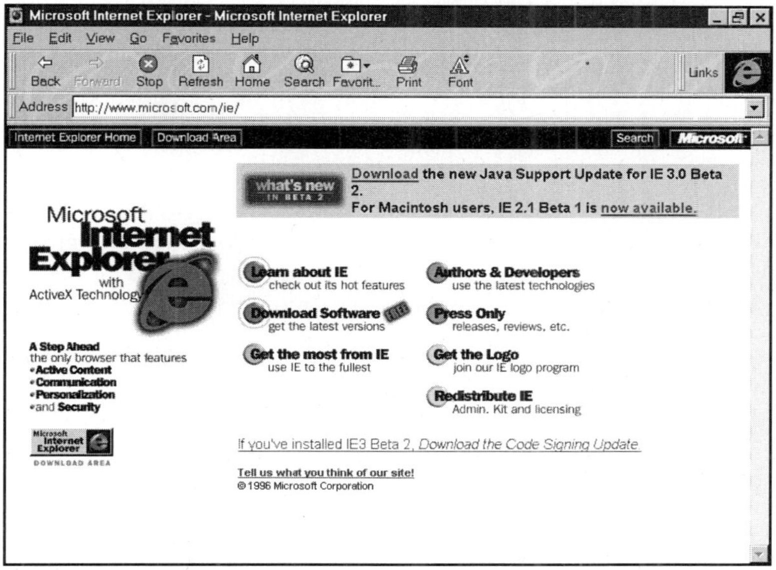

Often these press areas list contacts for key personnel in the company, such as the marketing director, the public relations manager for hardware issues, or the public relations manager for new product releases. On the Web, you can do much more than simply list names; you can include color photos of the company representatives and executive officers. You can also list their phone numbers, fax numbers, and e-mail addresses and even include online forms to submit public relations questions.

Along with contact information, these areas often contain press releases. Press releases on your business's products and services are free advertising. Many Web sites publish current and past press releases as well as information to be freely distributed by the press. Coverage in the press shows interested parties what your company has done in the past and what it's doing now. Press releases aren't just for the press, however. You should also supply press releases in areas frequented by your customers. In this way, customers, too, can see what the company has done in the past and is doing now.

You can also offer demos and screenshots of your products for downloading so that people who are interested in your products can see them firsthand. If they're interested, they can test the demo; if they need screenshots to publish in a book, magazine, or newspaper, they can download and use the material you supply.

Marketing to Global Audiences

Selling your products and services to consumers is done through marketing. The interactive and dynamic nature of the Web makes it a powerful tool for marketing. If you don't market your products, they won't sell. If you don't tell people about your services, no one is going to hire you. Large corporations spend millions of dollars on marketing every year. Traditional direct advertising media include television and radio commercials, display advertising in magazines and newspapers, and mass marketing campaigns done by direct mail.

The problem with direct marketing is that there's no guarantee your product will sell based on the advertisement or that you will actually make sales to the consumers you reach. For example, the typical response rate for direct mailings is 3–4 percent, so if you distribute 10,000 flyers to a targeted mailing list, you generally make 300 to 400 sales.

In recent years, many companies have been turning to marketing media that are more interactive than direct advertising and less expensive than personal sales visits. Companies are using telemarketing to reach potential customers by phone or long, documentary-style commercials called "infomercials" to give customers information about products in a setting that seems interactive.

Although telemarketing and infomercials are more interactive than traditional forms of marketing, they also have drawbacks. Telemarketing is often seen as an invasion of privacy, and even when telemarketers get a person willing to listen, they have only a few minutes to make a sale. Infomercials, like personal sales visits, aren't always practical because they cost hundreds of thousands of dollars to produce and televise. To produce a successful infomercial, you need the right type of product.

The wonderful thing about Web marketing is that it's right for all types of products and offers a level of interaction with customers on a par with personal sales visits. You don't have to spend $100,000 or even $10,000 to reach a global audience. You can publish on the Web for $100 a month or less.

Your Web pages can help you establish connections with new customers and build relationships with your current customers. Web users reach businesses in the world market at the click of a button. One click can take them to a business in London; another click can take them to one in Albuquerque. The image you present through your Web site is often all the potential customer will know about your business, so you can gain a substantial competitive advantage in a global market simply by projecting a strong image.

Web marketing is not a replacement for traditional marketing; it is best used when combined with other types of marketing. However, Web marketing can certainly help companies of any size meet their marketing needs. Consider the comparisons in the following sidebar.

TRADITIONAL ADVERTISING COMPARED TO A COMMERCIAL WEB SITE

Option A: Television commercial
Audience: 1,000,000 television viewers
Cost: $125,000 (development and production: $50,000; broadcast expense: $75,000)
Duration: 30 seconds
Recurring costs for broadcasting same commercial to similar-sized audience: $75,000

Option B: Web site with hundreds of megabytes of data available
Audience: 10,000 hits per day for 365 days (3.65 million hits)
Cost: $120,000
Breakdown of costs:
Purchase high-capacity Web server: $20,000
One-year salary for server administrator: $50,000
Professional site design: $20,000
One-year T1 connection to Internet: $25,000
Installation fees for T1: $5,000
Average duration of exposure to advertising: 3–5 minutes/hit
Recurring annual costs for maintaining Web site: $75,000

Option A: One-page magazine advertisement
Audience: 100,000 readers
Cost: $18,000 (development and design: $8,000; publication expense: $10,000)
Average duration of exposure to advertising: 30–60 seconds
Recurring costs for running same advertisement in other magazines: $10,000

Option B: Web site on ISP's Web server with 10–20 M of available data
Audience: 2,500 hits per day for 365 days (912,500 hits)
Cost: $11,300
Breakdown of costs:
Professional site design: $10,000
One-year account fee: $1200
Phantom domain setup and registration: $100 (includes $50 annual fee for domain registration)
Average duration of exposure to advertising: 3–5 minutes/hit
Recurring annual costs: $1250 minimum, additional $2,000–$5,000 for site maintenance

Option A: Mass marketing campaign through direct mailings
Audience: 10,000 consumers
Cost: $2000
Breakdown of costs:
10,000 sheets paper: $75
10,000 envelopes: $125
10,000 envelope labels: $50
Printer supplies for laser printer: $100
Mail expense (bulk rate): $1400
Targeted mailing list: $250
Average duration of exposure to advertising: 0–60 seconds
Recurring costs for subsequent mailings: $1750–$2000

Option B: Web publication with 23M of data
Audience: 500 hits per day for 365 days (182,500 hits)
Cost: $650
Breakdown of costs:
One-year account fee: $600
Setup: $50
Average duration of exposure to advertising: 3–5 minutes/hit
Recurring annual costs: $600

Electronic Commerce

Making direct sales on the Web is not only a possibility—it's a reality, and the Web's interactive nature is largely responsible for making these sales. Businesses all over the world have online order centers; their customers use fill-out forms to directly submit orders for processing.

Figure 2.8 shows the form used to apply for an account at the Internet Shopping Network (`www.isn.com`). Once you fill out and submit the form, you get an account number you can use when you place orders.

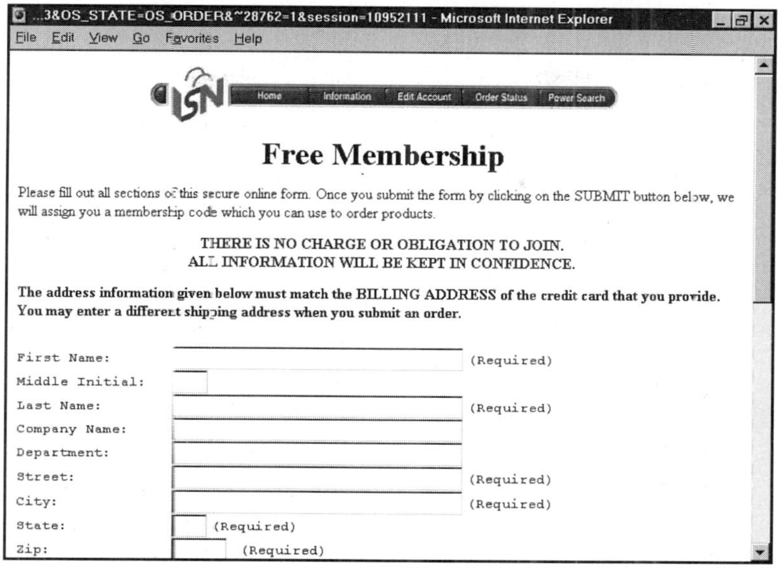

FIGURE 2.8.
Applying for an account at the Internet Shopping Network.

CAUTION

Online ordering has tremendous potential. Dozens of Internet-savvy businesses have increased revenues by 200 to 300 percent through online ordering. However, for every success story, there are several companies who fail miserably. The primary reason companies don't generate sales online is that they don't take the time to learn about the market. Traditional advertising and marketing schemes simply don't work on the Web.

The company I founded, The Virtual Press Inc., offers many services to businesses wanting to establish a presence on the Web. When I wear my Internet consulting hat, the advice I often offer new businesses is this: Don't measure the success of your Web site by the revenues generated from online orders.

The Web is best viewed as an extremely powerful advertising medium and marketing tool. Television commercials don't generate sales that can be specifically correlated to a single commercial, either. You wouldn't pull the plug on your television commercials when 10,000 viewers fail to run out and buy your latest gizmo immediately after the commercial, so why would you pull the plug on your Web site?

Because electronic commerce is in its infancy on the Internet, the mechanism behind direct ordering differs greatly from site to site. A growing number of businesses have set up ways for customers to make secure transfers. In this way, sensitive information, like credit card numbers, is protected by encryption. More businesses will adopt secure transfer methods when true security standards are implemented.

Currently, businesses with online order centers use a variety of methods to secure transfers. Many of them have customers set up an account before ordering online. Customers are assigned an account number that can be used for online ordering at the customer's convenience. Normally, any orders placed with the account number can be shipped only to the address the customer specified when the account was set up.

Some businesses allow customers to place orders online and then ask them to confirm the order by phone or fax. Customers typically get an order reference number they could give to a sales representative or automated voice mail system, along with their credit card number. Because the customer has already provided all the essential information online, the whole confirmation process by phone or fax usually takes less than a minute.

Spreading the Word About Your Ideas

Often the focus of Web publishing is on the business benefits, yet the Web is much more than a place to conduct marketing and advertising. You don't have to publish on the Web for profit. For every business publishing on the Web to increase the bottom line, someone somewhere is publishing on the Web simply to spread the word about his or her ideas.

The Web is an open repository for information. Research institutes, universities, colleges, non-profit organizations, and individuals freely publish information. One of the primary reasons to publish on the Web is to gain recognition for your ideas, research findings, and projects, but you can also do so simply because you want to share information and ideas with others.

Spreading the word about ideas you've published on the Web is easy, and, more important, free. Dozens of Web sites index and catalog information available on the Web. Some of these sites maintain specialized lists of popular, new, and cool documents; others maintain comprehensive lists.

One of the most comprehensive guides to Web resources is found at Lycos (`www.lycos.com`), shown in Figure 2.9. Web users rely on databases like Lycos to find resources on the Web. To add your documents to a list, all you have to do is register them. This generally means filling out a form and submitting it online, which takes only a few minutes. The key information you enter in a fill-out form includes your name, business address, e-mail address, uniform resource locator (URL), and a brief description of your document. You can find a comprehensive list of catalog sites in Chapter 49, "Designing and Publishing a Killer Web Site."

FIGURE 2.9.
Lycos is one of many Web databases.

Features of the Web

The Web is the most dynamic medium you will ever publish in. Using its rich features, you have almost limitless possibilities for publishing your ideas.

Much has changed since the Web's early days. The first Web publications were mostly textual and limited in multimedia features, but today's Web publications are highly graphical and rich in multimedia features. Using the Web's facilities, you can easily incorporate images into your publication.

Interactivity is a key ingredient for making connections with readers. Highly interactive documents invite readers to become participants. When your readers are actively involved, they're no longer simply watching as you unfold ideas in page after page. They are deciding how they want to unfold the story and are choosing their own path through it. The Web isn't the only medium you can use to create interactive publications, but it's the most versatile and least expensive one available.

Creating multimedia documents for use on the Web is easier than you might think. In fact, the Web is the easiest publishing medium for creating multimedia documents. At the Web publisher's fingertips is the world's greatest multimedia library—the Internet and all its archives. Not only does this library have thousands of multimedia clips you can get for free or for a small fee, it's complete with a multimedia developer's toolkit you can also get for free or a small fee. You will explore the possibilities of multimedia in Part V, "Extending Your Site with Multimedia."

If free clips and tools aren't enough to persuade you that Web publishing is your best choice for creating multimedia publications, the wonderful thing about Web technology is that it's advancing at an explosive pace. Even now, you can create publications with animation, soundtracks, and video without needing any special tools at all.

Evaluating Your Access Needs

Before you start publishing on the Web, you must evaluate your access needs so you can determine what type of account will meet your needs as a Web publisher and can get the level of access to the Web that's right for you. If you plan to provide Internet-related services or products specifically for Internet-smart consumers, you should have your own domain. A *domain address* is a unique address only you will have. Web users can use programs, such as Whois, to get information about your domain.

NOTE

Whois is a basic protocol to find information on Internet users and domains. If you have an account with an Internet Service Provider (ISP) with access to a UNIX shell, you can type `whois` at the shell prompt. For example, to find more information on my domain, `tvp.com`, you would type the following at the shell prompt:

```
whois tvp.com
```

Having your own domain is vital to establishing a presence on the Web. Many users make specific judgments about you based on the address URL to your Web pages. Most people believe you must set up a Web server to get your own domain, but this isn't true. Web publishers who want their own domain have several options.

Most people don't need to set up their own Web server. If you plan to go through an ISP to get an account with Web publishing privileges, you don't need to set up your own Web server. You will use your ISP's Web server to publish your Web documents. If you already have an account with an ISP, you may already have all you need to publish on the Web.

Your access options are the following:

- Installing your own Web server
- Using an ISP's Web server with a standard account
- Using a commercial online service's Web server with a standard account
- Getting a phantom domain

Installing Your Own Web Server

Installing your own Web server is the most expensive option for Web publishing, but it offers significant advantages. With a dedicated connection, you can provide 24-hour Web services to users worldwide. You will have complete control over your Web server and can publish whatever you wish. You can configure the server to handle other services as well, such as FTP, Gopher, telnet, and CGI scripts. You will also have your own domain, which will establish a clear presence on the Web for you or your company. Your URL will look something like the following:

```
http://www.your_company.com/
```


Server Software and Platform Options

Web server software is available for almost every platform, including Amiga, Macintosh, Windows, and UNIX systems. A few commercial options, such as the Netscape Commerce Server, are very expensive, but most server software is available free or for a nominal fee. Server software is widely available for downloading from the Internet. You can even get evaluation versions of commercial software that will allow you to try the server software free. Typically, these trial periods are for 90 days; afterward, if you want to continue using the commercial server software, you must pay a fee.

NOTE

Many chapters in this book cover server setup and administration. Installing and managing Web servers is covered in depth in Chapter 45, "Setting Up and Administering a Web Server." Customizing your Web site for speed and performance is covered in Chapter 46, "Optimizing Your Web Site or Intranet." Server security is examined in Chapter 47, "Managing Server Security."

For an individual or small company wanting to set up a Web server, the best server software to use is most likely the software that will run on the computer system you're most familiar with. For a company with an installed computer network, you might want to use one of the computers already available as your Web server. Before you install the Web server, you should carefully consider security options, such as a firewall, to shield your internal network from illegal activities.

If you don't have a computer capable of providing Web services, you will need to buy one at a cost of $3,000 to $25,000 or lease one at a cost of $75 to $500 per month. Before buying or leasing a computer, you must determine what platform the Web server runs on. Again, the best server software for you is usually the software that runs on a platform familiar to you or your support staff. However, before you make any decision, examine carefully how and for what purpose the company plans to use the Web server.

Commercial options are usually the easiest to install, support, and maintain; however, the primary reason for using commercial Web server software is support. If you believe you will need outside software support to keep the server alive, commercial software is the best choice.

Most shareware servers run on UNIX systems. UNIX servers are typically the best maintained and supported, so they're some of the most reliable and secure servers available. If you have a strong need for reliability and security, you should look at UNIX Web server software. However, you might need an experienced team to compile the source code and configure the server parameters.

Internet Connection Options

You will also need to get an Internet connection. Generally, you can do this for a fee from an Internet Service Provider or a commercial online service. The speed of the connection drives the monthly fees. To determine the best connection speed for you, you will need to estimate the volume of traffic for the site. A good way to estimate traffic is to visit a site similar in content and structure to your intended site. Because most popular sites offer some historical information on the site's use, you can use the data to make a better estimate of traffic for your site.

Although the Internet is a global structure, use of your site probably won't be at a steady constant pace throughout the day. For example, a site with 25,000 hits a day may experience peak usage periods within fluctuating time-windows. These peak periods present a problem when assessing your Internet connection needs. For this reason, for a Web site with an anticipated high volume of traffic, such as daily network traffic of more than 25,000 hits per day, you might want to consider using a high-speed T1 connection to the Internet. Leasing a T1 line will cost you $2,500 to $5,000 per month, plus an installation fee of $2,500 to $5,000.

Most Web sites don't need a T1 connection to the Internet. In fact, the average site needs only a 56 Kbps line. A 56 Kbps connection can adequately handle daily network traffic of 2,000 hits per day, and the really good news is that the cost of a 56 Kbps connection to the Internet is only $300 to $500 per month, plus a startup fee of up to $500.

Using an Internet Service Provider's Web Server with a Standard Account

Getting an Internet account with Web publishing privileges is an inexpensive option. Typical costs for such an account are $20 to $50 per month, plus a startup fee of up to $50. The account should include at least 2–3 M of storage space on the service provider's computer. Most ISPs offer unlimited access time to the Internet, meaning whether you log on for 40 or 400 hours a month, you usually pay the same monthly fee. Although your e-mail, standard files, and Web-published files will use this space, 2–3 M is usually enough to maintain a modest-sized site. If you currently have an account with an ISP that allows Serial Line Internet Protocol (SLIP) or Point-to-Point Protocol (PPP) access to the Web, you may already have Web publishing privileges!

Your account with an ISP is available on a dial-up basis. A dial-up connection requires a computer, which might be dedicated to networking, with communications software and a modem. The good news about a dial-up connection is that it uses a regular phone line with speeds ranging from 9.6 Kbps to 28.8 Kbps. Your computer is used to establish a connection over the modem and phone line for a temporary period; at the end of use, the Internet connection is broken. You will use the connection to browse the Web, navigate around the Internet, or check on your site published on the ISP's Web server.

Before you set up an account, check with your ISP for specifics on storage space, additional fees for storage space that shouldn't be more than $2 per megabyte, and possible additional fees if you have a popular site. You should also check on the availability of more services, such as FTP, Gopher, telnet, and CGI scripts, which should be available for use free, if they're available at all.

An account with an ISP is an inexpensive option, but it's also a very basic one. You don't have control over the Web server, so you'll be at the mercy of the ISP for additional services, including CGI scripts. You won't have your own domain, and people will know this immediately because your URL will look something like this:

```
http://www.your_service_provider.com/~you
```

Using a Commercial Online Service's Web Server with a Standard Account

America Online, CompuServe, Genie, and Prodigy all offer or plan to offer Web publishing privileges to their customers. Publishing on the Web through a commercial online service is your least expensive alternative if you use your account wisely. Typical costs for such an account are $10 to $20 per month, plus a small additional fee for maintaining your Web pages on the online service's Web server. Most commercial online services offer only a few hours of connection time free each month. After you use your free connection time, you have to pay additional connection charges. If you currently have an account with a commercial online service, you might already be able to publish on the Web!

Your account with a commercial online service is available on a dial-up basis. You use the connection to browse the Web, navigate around the Internet, or to check on your site published on the online service's Web server. Before you set up an account, check with the commercial online service for specifics on storage space and possible extra fees if you have a popular site.

An account with a commercial online service is the least expensive option, but it's also the most basic option. Many online services are fairly new to Web publishing themselves and don't offer access to essential additional services. This, of course, will change—and probably quickly—but you should ask your online service about additional services, such as FTP, Gopher, and CGI, to find out when they'll be available. You won't have your own domain, which people will know because your URL will look something like this:

```
http://www.commercial_online_service.com/~you
```

TIP

If you're interested in Web publishing with a commercial online service, visit these Web sites to find current rates and publishing options:

America Online	`http://www.aol.com/`
CompuServe	`http://www.compuserve.com/`
Genie	`http://www.genie.com/`
Prodigy	`http://www.prodigy.com/`

Getting a Phantom Domain

Getting a phantom domain is often the best option available for anyone wanting to Web publish. With a phantom domain, you get most of the benefits of having your own Web server, and you get affordability. When you have your own domain, Web users can use programs, such as Whois, to get more information about you.

Typical costs for a phantom domain are only slightly more than a basic account with an ISP and range from $25 to $75. The primary advantage of a phantom domain is that you'll have your own domain, so your URL will look something like this:

```
http://www.your_company.com/
```

This URL is easier to type and remember than a URL containing the tilde. Instead of telling people your URL is `www.yourserviceprovider.com/~yourcompany`, you can tell them your URL is `www.yourcompany.com`. You may be surprised to learn that many users try to find sites based on the company name. For example, when I look for a site associated with a major company, I usually type `http://www.companyname.com` in my browser's URL window. If the URL is valid, then I'm at the company's Web site without having to look up the URL in a Web database that might not have the site's URL.

Some ISPs call this service *Web server hosting.* This generally means that by hosting, the ISP is creating a phantom domain for you on its system. Maintaining a phantom domain is no more taxing on the ISP's server than your standard account and is, in fact, little more than clever linking to make the outside world think you have your own domain. With a phantom domain, you still have no control over the Web server or additional services. However, most ISPs that offer phantom domains include additional services as part of the deal, and these additional services are the only real justification for higher fees.

PHANTOM DOMAINS

Phantom domains are the wave of the future in Web publishing. If you already have an account with an ISP, check to see whether they offer phantom domains. Many ISPs offer phantom domains to their users because it's an easy way to generate extra revenue.

You can get a phantom domain from an ISP, a commercial service provider, or an Internet presence provider. Internet presence providers specialize in setting up Web sites. Most of the sites that presence providers set up are phantom domains. A typical presence provider services hundreds of phantom domains off one or more Web servers. Although this might sound like a lot, the power and capacity of the server and the speed of its connection to the Internet are more important than anything else.

Because Internet presence providers specialize in servicing businesses instead of individual users, business-oriented sites may do better with these providers. Dozens of presence providers are available; for more information, visit this site:

`http://www.isoc.org/~bgreene/nsp1-5c.html`

To find a comprehensive list of Internet service providers, visit The List. This site maintains one of the best ISP listings:

`http://www.thelist.com/`

Or try this site:

`http://www.cybertoday.com/ISPs/ISPinfo.html`

Summary

Navigating the Web is easy if you understand the principles of hypertext linking and URLs. Hypertext references can be text- or graphics-based, but they're all defined by URLs that specify a path to the resources.

The most exciting time to publish on the Web is right now. You have a chance to get in on the ground floor, and for once, it isn't going to cost you a bundle to join. People all around the world are publishing on the Web for fun, profit—and because they can.

The Web is the most versatile medium you will ever publish in. Web publishers have proved time and again that there are no real limits to what can be published on the Web. Not only are they publishing every imaginable type of document ever created, they are doing it successfully and helping to build the most powerful information system in the world: the World Wide Web. So what are you waiting for?

Before you start Web publishing, you should also evaluate your own access needs, even if you already have an Internet account. By doing this, you can determine what type of account will meet your needs as a Web publisher.

CHAPTER 3

Developing and Planning an Intranet

by William Robert Stanek

IN THIS CHAPTER

Although you could design many types of intranets using today's technology, this chapter focuses on using the hypermedia capabilities of the World Wide Web to set up an intranet publishing operation. The Web's power lies in its diversity, and its handling of hypertext objects enables cross-platform solutions. With intranet publishing, you can easily set up a mini-Internet in your company. Your mini-Internet—or *intranet*—can be available to the outside world or just to those in the company.

Taking a Closer Look at Intranets

Millions of people browse the World Wide Web; if you're reading this book, odds are you're one of them. The Web is a networked information system based on hypertext, which allows you to navigate through networked resources at the click of a button.

Beneath the system of hypertext documents and the wonderful graphical interface that makes it all work is a complex network—the Internet. The Internet is a global network of millions of computers. Many different technologies are used on the Internet to find, send, and retrieve information:

- E-mail is used to send electronic mail.
- Gopher, Archie, and Veronica can be used to find information.
- FTP is used to send and retrieve files.
- Telnet is used to log in to remote hosts.
- The Web is used to browse hypertext resources.

Trillions of research dollars went into developing the Internet and the tools that make it work, some of which was paid for with your tax dollars. So wouldn't it be nice to put this technology to work for you and your company? This is where intranets come in.

An *intranet* is a network within an organization that adapts Internet technologies for use in its information infrastructure. The most common Internet technology used in organizations is the Web's hypertext system. For this reason, many developers associate Web publishing on an internal network with intranets.

Ideally, your intranet will use many different Internet technologies, including Internet e-mail, FTP, telnet, and Web services. You might be wondering why you should use all these Internet services. After all, most networks are set up for file transfer with FTP, remote host logins, and e-mail. However, your internal network probably uses commercial software designed for a specific operating system, and this software probably isn't completely user- and administrator-friendly.

Take e-mail, for example. Most networks use an e-mail system. In a large organization, mail gateways and servers are needed to transfer e-mail from one area of the network to another. These gateways and servers are responsible for translating or encapsulating the protocol of the e-mail software so that your messages are readable on the receiving end.

Maintaining this maze of servers and gateways is the responsibility of the network administrator. When the system fails, as it inevitably does from time to time, users may lose mail and the administrator may lose sleep. By using an e-mail system designed for the Internet, you can end the nightmare. Users on any platform, be it UNIX, Mac, or Windows 95, can use the same software to send and receive messages, but best of all, you eliminate the need for e-mail servers.

What Is Intranet Publishing?

Intranet publishing is the practical application of Web publishing to a real-world business problem—publishing on the corporate network. A business reality is that company databases tax resources in both labor costs and real-money terms. Even the best conventional database tools have high learning curves. Another reality is that sometimes you just don't have two to four weeks to train new personnel on using the database, and companywide databases are growing in size and complexity.

Databases aren't the only part of the company that grows as the company grows. The paper trail of documents—brochures, information packets, and policies—also grows with the company. Maintaining an ever-growing paper trail is costly and personnel-intensive. Every time there's a product release, product update, or press release, documents must be distributed to support personnel and other key people in the company. This costs money.

Other problems stem from this paper trail. For example, the customer support department might be misinforming customers based on data that's days or weeks old. To better serve customers, employees need the most current information, and what they really need to stay current is a metaindex of company resources and documents in a format that allows them to easily search for and retrieve information in an instant. However, a companywide metaindex of resources and documents would be astronomically expensive using conventional means. Publishing these documents electronically on an internal network is a nonconventional solution that would drastically reduce costs and save countless hours.

Extending the usefulness of the World Wide Web to corporate networked environments is a cost- and time-effective business solution. The Web's facilities don't have high learning curves—in fact, there isn't much of a learning curve at all if the facilities and tools are a part of the company's infrastructure.

The only thing intranet publishing requires is that you install and configure two things: Web server communications and Web browser communications. Popular server software is examined later in the chapter section "Web Server Software," and popular browsers are examined in Chapter 9, "An HTML Toolkit: Browsers, Converters and Editors."

MANAGING BROWSER LICENSES ON YOUR INTRANET

If you choose a commercial browser, such as Netscape Navigator, you must pay a licensing fee for each copy of the browser used at your site. There are several ways you can find out the number of licenses you need to buy.

You could buy a license for each computer on your network. Although software companies love this model, few network administrators follow it. Under most circumstances, all the computers in a company aren't running the browser.

The trick, then, is to determine what percentage of the users on the network are running the browser at the same time. In a typical network environment, where the intranet documents aren't critical to the corporate mission, probably only 20–25 percent of users will be using the browser at any one time. Therefore, on a 500-node network, you could start with 100 to 120 licenses for the browser of your choice.

To make sure that only the number of browsers you've bought licenses for are running at any one time, you should set up a license server, which tracks the number of licenses in use and denies access to the browser software when needed. When the number of users exceeds the license count, your license server should display a message stating that no licenses are currently available and the user should try again in a few minutes. The license server should also log the number of disallowed accesses with a timestamp; with these server logs, you can periodically re-evaluate your license needs.

Setting up and managing a license server might seem like a hassle, but it can save you and your company thousands of dollars. If the browser software you chose costs $35/license, a 500-node network using 120 licenses will save over $13,000.

With intranet publishing, you can supply a metaindex of documents, access to company databases, and much more. You can directly publish existing documents or convert document formats to the HTML format, which has the advantage of being dynamic. People don't have to rummage through a paper trail or learn the commands to interface with the company database. With HTML, all they have to do is click on links to find a related reference. To perform a database search, they just need to enter a word or two at a prompt. Some of the types of documents you can network-publish include the following:

- Policies
- Standards
- On-the-job training documentation
- Online help manuals
- User manuals
- Department/company memos
- Project descriptions, goals, and contacts

News releases
Trip reports
Employee recognition awards
Company mission, goals, and objectives
Company background and history
Company forms
Company product and sales information
Company telephone directory
Office and key personnel rosters

Why You Don't Have To Be on the Internet

A common misconception about the Web is that you must be on the Internet to set up a Web server. This simply isn't true. The company doesn't have to be connected to the Internet to take advantage of Web tools. The Web server doesn't have to be linked to the Internet, and company personnel don't need to get on the Internet to make intranet publishing a reality within the company.

Several books about the Web and the Internet specifically—and mistakenly—state that a Transmission Control Protocol/Internet Protocol (TCP/IP) connection to the Internet is an absolute requirement for setting up a Web server. It's true that an Internet connection would help in getting Web server software because that software is widely available on the Internet. However, this software, the installation instructions, and manuals can be downloaded from any Internet account and then loaded onto the company network.

A more accurate statement is that if the company wants to use the Internet and take advantage of the World Wide Web, there must be some kind of connection to the Internet. The company doesn't have to be connected to the Internet or any part of the Internet to set up a Web server for use within the company.

The federal government and a growing number of large corporations have private intranets that take advantage of Internet and Web technologies. What these private intranets allow on their networks is their business; therefore, what you provide on your network is your business.

When you set up a Web server, you tell it what domain, or structure, you want it to operate in. You can include or exclude links to the outside world as you see fit. You can even include or exclude divisions within the company. It all depends on how you set up the Web server and the permissions you grant or deny.

Intranet Publishing Versus Paper Publishing

You have probably heard the term *paperless office* before. Don't cringe. Although this eventuality isn't outside the realm of possibility, this isn't a lecture on how Web publishing can help make the office paperless. The truth is that publishing company documents on an intranet won't eliminate the paper trail, but it *can* help dramatically reduce it. It can streamline the update and correction process and distribute large amounts of up-to-date information throughout the organization. The decision to intranet-publish ultimately comes down to simple economics:

- Is intranet publishing affordable?
- Is intranet publishing cost-saving?
- Is intranet publishing cost-effective?

Intranet Publishing Is Affordable

The costs are negligible for incorporating Web publishing into an existing network. Often a network already has a workstation capable of carrying the additional load as the Web server. The Web server doesn't have to be a dedicated machine, especially for small networks or networks with limited personnel using the Web server.

Usually, you won't need a full-time Web server administrator. Existing networks already have, or should have, a system administrator who can handle the additional duties as the Web server administrator. Web servers are easy to administer once they're set up and running.

Although using an existing workstation isn't always possible, the good news is that the Web server doesn't have to be a power machine. Web servers serving thousands of users are running on network-configured computers with Intel Pentium processors.

Intranet Publishing Saves Money

Publishing company documents on an intranet can reduce print costs and other associated costs significantly. Printed documents quickly become outdated. Technical manuals, company policies, and other important documents are expensive to maintain and reprint. With intranet publishing, there aren't any print costs, and maintaining Web documents is easier than maintaining printed documents.

A point-and-click interface environment doesn't have a high learning curve; as a matter of fact, you can even automate the updating of documents. Time savings for easy maintenance and use add up to big money savings over traditional alternatives. The savings also extend to personnel. Your company can realize these savings in personnel in the fewer hours spent building, searching, and maintaining company documents. Ease of use means that finding information is less frustrating for workers, and a less stressful environment is good for the company and its workers.

Ease of use also means that new employees can become productive company assets sooner. Using a Web browser, such as Mosaic, new employees with little training could make retrievals from the company's Oracle database on the first day of the job. To do this, they would access a Web page with a fill-out form or query box like those discussed in Chapter 27, "Form Creation and Design." After typing in the information they wanted to retrieve, users would simply click the submit button; soon afterward, the retrieved information would display on their screens.

Intranet Publishing Is Cost-Effective

Intranet publishing is an efficient way to make sure company information is distributed throughout the organization. Putting a document on the company Web can offer instant access for all personnel, several departments, or an individual department. Web documents are easier to maintain, produce, index, and use—which means cost efficiency.

If cost efficiency is a big consideration for the company (and it should be), consider a company with global offices. These offices are probably already connected through a Wide Area Network (WAN) or have some kind of dial-up access to the Internet. Despite the ease of use of electronic mail, company documents flow back and forth through conventional mail every day because some types of documents aren't suited for posting to e-mail. Posting a 500-page policy manual by e-mail to all company personnel would probably bring the network to a screeching halt. Even if it didn't, the people who should be reading the policy manual wouldn't because of the message's form.

With intranet publishing, the policy manual would be an interactive, indexed document that personnel could easily search for references that affect their departments' operations. More important, the entire manual wouldn't have to be mailed and re-mailed to a dozen global or regional offices.

Determining the Best Organization for Your Intranet

The organization of your intranet is extremely important to its success. Over the years, three organizational models have developed for information systems like your intranet: centralized, decentralized, and a combination of the two.

Learning from the Past

The three organizational models are really driven by the types of computers used at an organization. Following the centralized model, all computer resources are centered in one location and under the management of one organization. When you think of centralized computing, think of mainframes and computer centers.

With the introduction of file-server and client-server computing, most organizations moved away from the centralized model toward a decentralized one. In decentralized computing, computer resources are spread throughout the organization and are under the management of the departments where they're located. When you think of decentralized computing, think of high-power workstations and servers.

After the big move to decentralize computer resources and dismantle massive computer centers, many managers had a rude awakening to the anarchy decentralized computing can cause. Imagine an organization where each department sets the rules and decides the standards—like what hardware and software to purchase and how that hardware and software should be set up. Then imagine the nightmare of trying to support the range of software and hardware installed in an organization the size of AT&T.

Because of the lack of control in decentralized computing, many organizations are moving to the happy middle ground of a mixed computing model. In this mixed model, a centralized IS (information systems) management sets broad policy, such as the direction and purpose of key computing initiatives, and the individual departments are free to work within those guidelines.

Applying the Past to Your Intranet's Future

As you discuss setting up an intranet with management, keep the three computing models in mind. Although your organization may currently use a specific model, you can apply any of the models to the design of your intranet and should encourage management to choose the model that will best serve your organization. Ideally, the final decision will be based on the need for control and who is responsible for the intranet resources.

Following a centralized model, a specific department in the organization is responsible for the intranet. This same department is responsible for the setup, design, and administration of your intranet servers and for creating the needed publications based on user requests.

With a centralized model, there's usually a formal approval process for new publications and services. For example, if the Human Resources department wants an indexed database of employee files, a formal request is required. Once the request is approved, the intranet developers would work with Human Resources to create the database and the associated HTML search forms. The problem with centralized control and formal approval processes is that they put creativity and timeliness in thumbscrews. Can you imagine having to get formal approval to change the dates in an intranet-published memo?

Following a decentralized model, each department within the organization is responsible for its section of the intranet. All departments that want to create intranet services must set up, design, and administer their own intranet servers. Each department is also responsible for creating the publications and services used by the department.

When you use a decentralized model, you cut out the formal approval process for new publications and services, so anyone can create intranet resources. Greater freedom and few controls mean that new services can be set up quickly by anyone who wants to do so; however, these seeming advantages can also lead to abuse of the intranet resources. Who do you blame when someone publishes potentially offensive material or when the usefulness of the intranet deteriorates because so much junk has been created?

By adopting elements of both the centralized and decentralized model to fit the organization's needs, you can balance the need for strict control with the need for creative freedom. For example, you could create an intranet with a centralized Web server that links departmental servers. The IS staff would be responsible for maintaining the central server and updating links to resources throughout the organization, and the individual departments would be responsible for maintaining their own servers. To make sure the intranet is not abused, one person in each department could be responsible for the department's intranet resources.

Intranet Development Tools

After considering the organization style for your intranet, you should examine the tools you'll need to develop the intranet. A tool is anything that supports the task you're working on. The tools for unleashing your intranet's power are based on the existing tools for the Internet itself, which includes protocols, resource tools, and information services.

Implementing TCP/IP Networking

TCP/IP (Transmission Control Protocol/Internet Protocol) is the foundation of the worldwide Internet. To ensure your intranet operates the same as the Web it is based on, you should install TCP/IP on your network. Using TCP/IP, you will be able to access documents using Internet protocols, such as HTTP and FTP.

A *protocol* is a set of rules for programs communicating on the network. It specifies how the programs talk to each other and what meaning to give to the data they receive. Without TCP/IP setting the rules for your network communications, you can't use Internet technologies to their fullest potential.

The good news is that if your organization already has access to the World Wide Web, you may already have the necessary TCP/IP structure in place. Additionally, TCP/IP is built into some operating systems, including Windows 95, Windows NT, and most variants of UNIX.

If you have an operating system without built-in TCP/IP and don't have TCP/IP installed, you'll need to buy TCP/IP software. Fortunately, TCP/IP software is widely available from software vendors. For example, if you want to install TCP/IP on a Macintosh, you can get the software directly from Apple or third-party vendors.

NOTE

If you plan to use a commercial browser, check to see whether the software package includes the necessary TCP/IP software.

Intranet Developer's Resource Tools

Tools are an essential part of any operation. Resource tools give you the means for sending and retrieving information. The three most basic tools of intranetworking are the following:

e-mail: Electronic mail is a great way to communicate. Think of e-mail as a way to send letters to anyone in the company instantly. Many e-mail programs allow delivery of mail to single users or groups of users. Some e-mail programs even offer ways to automate responses. Most browser packages are packaged with e-mail software.

FTP: File transfer protocol supplies the basic means for delivering and retrieving files around the network. The files can be text, sound, or graphics. FTP provides a springboard for many information-based approaches to retrieving information. Many higher level tools that have friendlier interfaces use FTP or a similar protocol to transfer files. Just about every browser currently available supports FTP.

telnet: telnet lets you remotely log in to another system and browse files and directories on that remote system. Telnet is valuable because it's easy to use and basic to the network. When you telnet to another computer, you can issue commands as though you were typing on the other computer's keyboard. On some platforms, like UNIX, telnet is a built-in resource. On other platforms, you need a telnet tool.

The basic resource tools are indispensable when used for the purpose for which they were designed. They are even the basis for many high-level resource tools, but they simply weren't designed for the advanced manipulation of the wealth of information available on the Internet. This is why dozens of information resource tools have been designed to manipulate networked data.

Here's a list of high-level resource tools you might want to use on your intranet:

Archie: A system to automatically gather, index, and serve information on the Internet. Archie is a great tool for searching your intranet's file archives. Once you set up Archie services, users can access Archie resources with their browser.

Gopher: A distributed information service that enables you to move easily through complex webs of network resources. Gopher uses a simple protocol that enables a Gopher client to get information on any accessible Gopher server. Most browsers directly support Gopher.

Listserv: An automated mailing list distribution system. Users can subscribe to listserv lists that you set up on the intranet, which lets them read e-mail posted to the list or post e-mail to the list. Once you set up a listserv server, users can join lists and participate in lists by using standard Internet e-mail software. Most browser packages include e-mail software.

Usenet: A bulletin board system of discussion groups called *newsgroups*. Users can participate in newsgroups posting messages to the group and can read messages posted by other newsgroup members. Once you set up a newsgroup server, users can browse newsgroups and post information by using a newsgroup reader. Most browser packages include a newsgroup reader.

Wide Area Information Servers (WAIS): A distributed information service for searching databases located throughout the network. It offers indexed searching for fast retrieval and an excellent feedback mechanism that enables the results of initial searches to influence later searches. WAIS servers are best accessed with CGI scripts, which allows users to search WAIS databases by using their browsers.

Setting Up Web Services on Your Intranet

An intranet without Web services is like a world without water. The key to the World Wide Web is HTTP, which offers a means of moving from document to document or indexing within documents. Getting to documents published on your intranet involves communication between browsers and servers.

In a browser, such as Netscape Navigator, the HTTP processes are practically transparent to the user. All the user really has to do is activate links to move through your Web presentation. The browser takes care of interpreting the hypertext transfer commands and communicating requests.

TIP

To reduce time spent on training and support, you might want to select a single browser package for use on the intranet. Before selecting a specific browser package, however, you should make sure its developer has versions for all the operating systems in use on your network. If the developer doesn't, you might want to consider another browser.

The mechanism on the receiving end, which is processing the requests, is a program called the Hypertext Transfer Protocol Daemon (HTTPD). A *daemon* is a UNIX term for a program that runs in the background and handles requests. The HTTP daemon resides on your Web server.

Table 3.1 lists some of the most popular server software and the operating systems the servers are available for. To get a better understanding of which servers are the most widely used on the Web, examine the table shown in Figure 3.1; it shows the responses to a recent survey about server use on the Web.

NOTE

The August 1996 NetCraft Web Server Survey is the most comprehensive, current, and honest survey of server use I have found. NetCraft gathered the results of its survey directly from over 342,000 Web servers by polling each server with an HTTP request and compiling the results.

Table 3.1. Popular server software.

	Operating System Available For						
Server Software	*UNIX Solaris*	*SunOS*	*HP/UX*	*IRIX*	*Other*	*Windows NT*	*Windows 95*
Apache	X	X	X	X	X		
CERN	X	X	X	X	X		
Microsoft IIS						X	
NCSA	X	X	X	X	X		
Netscape Communications	X	X	X	X	X	X	
Commerce	X	X	X	X	X	X	
Open Market	X	X	X	X	X		
O'Reilly Website						X	X

The best server software for you is most likely the software that will run on the workstation you plan to use as the network's Web server, but several factors come into play that could change your mind. The four primary factors are

- Expertise of the installation team
- Reliability of the Web server
- Necessity of support
- Security

FIGURE 3.1.
Server software used on the Web.

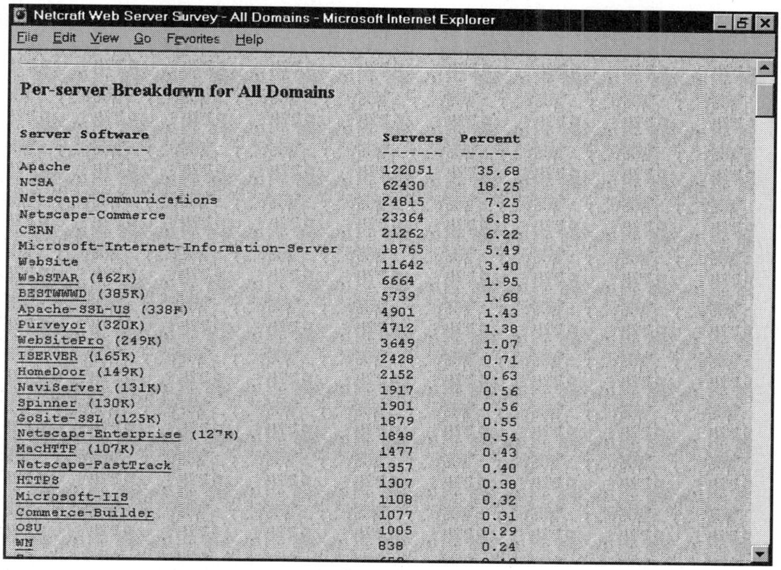

Per-server Breakdown for All Domains

Server Software	Servers	Percent
Apache	122051	35.68
NCSA	62430	18.25
Netscape-Communications	24815	7.25
Netscape-Commerce	23364	6.83
CERN	21262	6.22
Microsoft-Internet-Information-Server	18765	5.49
WebSite	11642	3.40
WebSTAR (462K)	6664	1.95
BESTWWWD (385K)	5739	1.68
Apache-SSL-US (338K)	4901	1.43
Purveyor (320K)	4712	1.38
WebSitePro (249K)	3649	1.07
ISERVER (165K)	2428	0.71
HomeDoor (149K)	2152	0.63
NaviServer (131K)	1917	0.56
Spinner (130K)	1901	0.56
GoSite-SSL (125K)	1879	0.55
Netscape-Enterprise (127K)	1848	0.54
MacHTTP (107K)	1477	0.43
Netscape-FastTrack	1357	0.40
HTTPS	1307	0.38
Microsoft-IIS	1108	0.32
Commerce-Builder	1077	0.31
OSU	1005	0.29
WN	838	0.24

The Expertise of the Installation Team

The installation team's level of expertise will be a major determining factor in your choice of server. To configure for specific types of platforms, and primarily UNIX platforms, some Web server software must be compiled from source code. This is good if you have an experienced team capable of setting parameters within the code to optimize for the intended system. Having the source code also means you can easily trace down and correct bugs and create enhancements to the existing code.

However, having the source code does you no good if you can't optimize and compile it. Therefore, if you don't have an experienced team, or are looking for an easy solution for your intranet publishing operation, you should look at server software that doesn't need to be compiled or optimized.

Reliability of the Web Server

The Web server's reliability is the second major determining factor in choosing a server. Examine carefully how the company plans to use the Web server. The projected nature of its use will help drive your decision. Some server software is continually updated and improved, and some platforms have a variety of support tools. Both are especially true for UNIX platforms, but not necessarily true for other platforms.

UNIX systems are the lifeblood of the Internet, so naturally some of the best server software is for UNIX systems. Because UNIX server software has been around longer, most of the bugs have been worked out, and the software is usually being continually improved. These factors make UNIX the most used operating system for Web servers. (See Figure 3.2.)

FIGURE 3.2.
Web server operating systems.

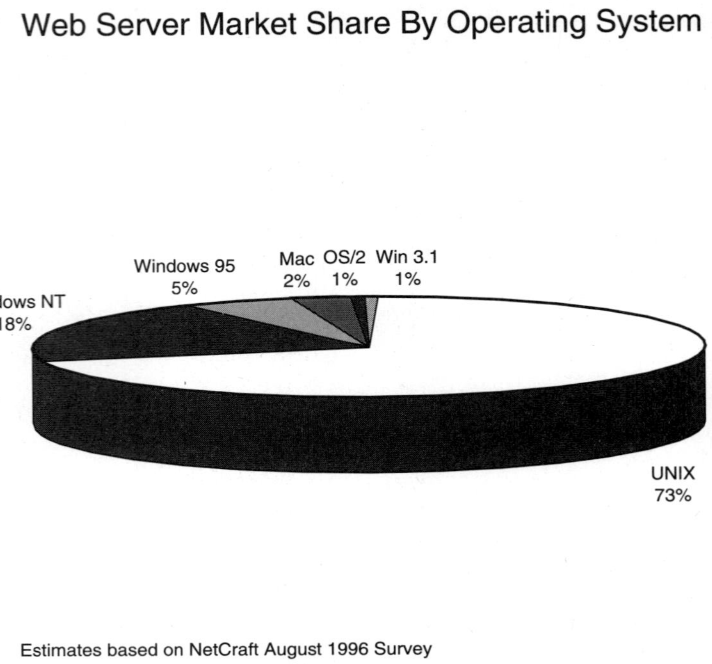

The Necessity of Support

The type of support needed to maintain the Web server is the third major determining factor in choosing your server. The primary reason for opting to use commercial Web server software is software support. If you believe the organization will need software support to keep the operation alive, commercial software is the best choice. Freeware software is generally provided on an as-is basis. The creators ask that if you improve the software or fix bugs, you send them the updates.

NOTE

Because software support may play a major role in your decision to buy Web server software, you should also know about other options, such as hiring a software support firm to give your company technical support. Software support firms are a $100 million-a-year niche of the computer industry and are growing in number. They specialize in offering technical support for a wide range of products and are positioned well to replace many traditional help desk centers. Several of the early software support companies have been tremendously successful because of the strong need in the business community for prompt, reliable, and accurate technical support. As the Internet and the World Wide Web grow, these companies will undoubtedly start to support key Internet and Web software applications.

Security Concerns

Security is the fourth major determining factor in choosing your server. Web server software that lacks adequate security constraints can put the company's network in jeopardy. This factor is critically important when the company plans to connect to the Internet.

Using the security mechanisms built into most server software, you can restrict access to intranet-published information, which allows you to selectively send out information within the company. For example, financial data could be accessible only to personnel in the finance department. You could further restrict access by adding login names and passwords. In this way, corporate financial records would be available only to those who need to use this information.

Web Server Software

This section examines server software. For UNIX platforms, there are dozens of possibilities, but only the most popular server software is described here. Until recently, there was only one good choice for the Windows NT environment, but this has changed. There are now many excellent commercial and freeware choices for Windows NT.

For other platforms, there's generally only one choice in server software. Having only one choice of server software for your Macintosh or Windows 3.1 system doesn't mean the quality of the server software is poor. Quite the contrary—the quality of the software is often quite good.

NOTE

Some servers can proxy serve documents, which means company personnel could get to the Web past an existing firewall, and the outside world could get Web documents on the firewall but shouldn't be able to get *past* the firewall. A *firewall* is a workstation that shields the internal network from the outside network–the Internet. It's the only machine that's directly connected to the Internet. This is a good way to minimize unauthorized access to the company network.

Apache HTTPD

The Apache HTTPD server runs on UNIX platforms and is free. Because Apache is a plug-in replacement for NCSA's Web server Version 1.3 and 1.4, it's very popular. Apache is designed for speed and reliability and fixes security problems found in NCSA HTTPD. Some of Apache's features include the following:

- Access authorization mechanisms
- Content negotiation in which the server can serve clients with documents that offer the best representation of information the client is capable of accepting
- Customized responses to errors and problems

- Directory indexing
- Multihomed servers in which requests made to different IP addresses can be mapped to the same machine
- The capability to include the output of commands or other files in HTML documents
- The capability to process CGI scripts
- Unlimited numbers of Alias and Redirect directives
- User authentication on a database model

You can learn more about Apache HTTPD and get the source code at this address:

`http://www.apache.org/`

CERN HTTPD

CERN HTTPD runs on UNIX platforms and is one of the most popular kinds of server software. It is well-maintained freeware with excellent documentation. One of CERN Web server's best selling points is that it can also be run as a caching proxy server. The server caches recently or frequently retrieved documents to improve response time; its features include the following:

- Access to authorization mechanisms
- Automatic generation of directory tree for browsers
- The capability to process CGI scripts
- Content negotiation in which the server can serve clients with documents that offer the best representation of information the client is capable of accepting
- Directory indexing
- Document name to file name mapping for longer-lived document names

You can learn more about CERN HTTPD and get the source code at this address:

`http://www.w3.org/hypertext/WWW/Daemon/Status.html`

Microsoft Internet Information Server

Microsoft Internet Information Server (IIS) is a powerful option for intranets using Windows NT servers. The main server is an integrated HTTPD, File Transfer Protocol (FTP), and Gopher server with a graphical installation utility that lets you completely install the product in less than 10 minutes. IIS is optimized for performance, speed, and reliability. Currently, you can also get free trial versions of IIS from Microsoft's Web site at `http://www.microsoft.com/`. Some of the features include the following:

- Advanced fault tolerance with disk mirroring, drive duplexing, and RAID 5
- The capability to process CGI scripts
- Graphical server management and performance monitor

- Integration with existing databases using the Internet Database Connector
- Multihomed servers in which requests made to different IP addresses can be mapped to the same machine
- Support for Secure Sockets Layer, which provides strict user and access authentication
- Support for the Internet Server Application Programming Interface (ISAPI)

You can learn more about Microsoft IIS at this URL:

```
http://www.microsoft.com/BackOffice/InfoServ/default.htm
```

NCSA HTTPD

NCSA HTTPD runs on UNIX platforms. NCSA's server was designed to be fast and have a low overhead, which means it's not taxing on the system. This server software is freeware and is rich in features. The current version is 1.5.x; here are some of its features:

- Access to authorization mechanisms
- The capability to include the output of commands or other files in HTML documents
- The capability to process CGI scripts
- Directory indexing
- Multihomed servers in which requests made to different IP addresses can be mapped to the same machine

With NCSA HTTPD, you can make the server more secure by limiting access to server directories. You can learn more about NCSA HTTPD and get the source code at this address:

```
http://hoohoo.ncsa.uiuc.edu/docs/Overview.html
```

Netscape Servers

Netscape offers several commercial server software packages for UNIX and Windows NT platforms. They include the following:

- Netscape Commerce Server—Designed to enable secure commerce on the Internet
- Netscape Communications Server—Designed to handle heavy loads and multimedia

Netscape claims that its server software offers increased performance over the competition and can easily be integrated with commercial or custom applications. The software tends to have higher overhead than other HTTP servers, but it definitely makes up for this by reducing response times and making better use of the communications bandwidth. Netscape servers are also some of the most secure in the world. You can learn more about Netscape servers at this site:

```
http://home.mcom.com/comprod/server_central/index.html
```

Open Market

The Open Market WebServer is a commercial server for UNIX platforms and comes in two versions: standard and secure. The Open Market Secure WebServer offers simultaneous support for both the Secure Hypertext Transfer Protocol (S-HTTP) and the Secure Sockets Layer (SSL). Some of Open Market's features include the following:

- Advanced tools for server administration and performance monitoring
- The capability to process CGI scripts
- Directory indexing
- Enhanced logging of statistics
- Flexible access control with the Tool command language (Tcl)
- A multithreaded design

You can learn more about Open Market servers at this URL:

```
http://www.openmarket.com/segments/servers/
```

O'Reilly Website

O'Reilly Website is an award-winning commercial server that runs on Windows 95 and Windows NT platforms. This server features many advanced utilities for Windows 95/NT environments and is designed for ease of use. Website is an integrated server package that includes an HTML browser, HTML editor, and a comprehensive book; here are some of its features:

- The capability to process CGI scripts
- Directory indexing
- Enhanced logging of statistics
- Graphical server management and performance monitor
- A multithreaded design
- Strict access control

You can learn more about O'Reilly Website at this address:

```
http://website.ora.com/
```

WebStar

WebStar is a server for the Macintosh and, as you might expect, it's one of the easiest Web server software packages to install. This server is great for use on small networks and has one of the lowest fees of any commercial server. The most recent version includes support for CGI scripts. WebStar is based on the commercial version of the original Web server for the Macintosh called MacHTTP.

You can purchase this software from StarNine Technologies Incorporated, and it has a 30-day evaluation period. After the evaluation period, you must register the server or stop using the software. You can find information on WebStar at this address:

```
http://www.starnine.com
```

NOTE

If you have a Macintosh running A/UX, there's a version of CERN's HTTP server that will run on your system. The CERN HTTP server was featured in the section "CERN HTTPD."

WinHTTPD

WinHTTPD is a server for the Windows 3.1 operating system; it installs easily and has low overhead. Just like WebStar, WinHTTPD is a good choice for use on small networks and has a low fee. The server software was ported from NCSA's server. Its features include the following:

- Directory indexing
- Access authorization mechanisms
- The capability to process CGI scripts
- The capability to include the output of commands or other files in HTML documents

You can purchase WinHTTPD from City Net Express, and it has a 30-day evaluation period. After the evaluation period, you must register the server or stop using the software. More information on WinHTTPD can be found on the Web at this site:

```
http://www.city.net/win-httpd/
```

Selecting a Domain Name

After you've selected a platform and server software, you should decide on a domain name for the Web server. During the installation process, you'll have to enter a domain name for the Web server. Common domain names for Web servers begin with www, such as this one:

www.*yourhostname*.com

If the company has decided to connect the server to the Internet, the network must have a unique identifier and domain name. You must register with the Internet Address Naming Authority (IANA), also called the InterNIC. Your company can select any domain name as long as it's unique. The InterNIC charges for domain name registration. If you plan to register a domain, check with the InterNIC for current registration prices.

Each computer connecting to the Internet must have a unique IP address. The requirement may mean changing the IP address on computers you plan to connect to the Internet. Getting IP addresses from the InterNIC is a three-part process:

1. First, get the InterNIC Internet number registration form from

   `ftp://rs.internic.net/templates/internet-number-template.txt`
2. Follow the comprehensive instructions included with the form, using the FTP address to fill out the form.
3. E-mail the completed form to

   `hostmaster@internic.net`

Domain name registration for ROOT, EDU, GOV, COM, NET, and ORG domains is also a three-part process:

1. First, get the InterNIC domain name registration form from

   `ftp://rs.internic.net/templates/domain-template.txt`
2. Follow the comprehensive instructions included with the form to fill out the form.
3. E-mail the completed form to

   `hostmaster@internic.net`

CAUTION

Beware of people trying to sell registration services on the Internet. Ultimately, these individuals must go through the InterNIC to register your domain. These individuals offer easy-to-use fill-out forms for processing your registration and charge fees ranging from $100–$500. As you have seen, the submission process isn't difficult—and certainly not worth $500.

NOTE

The InterNIC is a very busy organization. Not only do they supply detailed explanations with registration forms, they include several sources to find more information with each of their forms. Refer to these sources of additional information before sending inquiries to the InterNIC. If you have a unique situation that's not covered in either the IP or domain registration forms, such as registering as an Internet service provider, you can find a list of registration forms supplied by the InterNIC here:

`http://rs0.internic.net/templates.html`

Mapping Your Intranet in Four Easy Steps

Now that you know intranet basics, you have everything you need to develop a plan that takes you through creating and carrying out your intranet. The best way to start is to break the plan down into a series of steps, which makes developing the intranet more manageable. Here are four steps you should follow:

1. Determining requirements
2. Planning
3. Design
4. Implementation

Step 1: Determining Requirements

In this step, try to figure out what you need to finish the intranet design and setup; start by examining the intranet's purpose, scope, and audience.

Your statement of purpose should identify these factors:

- Why you are building the intranet
- How the intranet will be used in your organization

When you examine the scope for the intranet, think in terms of size and focus. Will the intranet be companywide? What types of documents, files, and software will be permitted on the intranet?

Your audience for the intranet is your customer base. Your customers could include all company employees, employees in specific departments, or employees in a single department.

Here's a preliminary plan for an intranet in a specific department:

Intranet for Sales Department

Purpose:

Give support to the regional sales department. Services include record searches of the customer databases, sales computation, order processing, and inventory checks.

Scope:

25 computers in the sales department. All resources will support and promote regional sales. Limited human resource data will be available to management staff.

Audience:

All personnel assigned to the regional sales department.

After determining the purpose, scope and audience, examine your reasonable expectations for the completed intranet, then translate these needs, goals, and purposes into requirements for the intranet. The basic needs for any intranet are the software development tools that help you build the necessary intranet services. Software tools for carrying out your intranet were examined earlier in the section "Intranet Development Tools."

You should think beyond your software needs and look at your hardware needs, too. Many types of computers are on the market. The IBM PC and PC compatibles have many generations of computer systems based on different chip sets. Some PCs are based on the 80286, 80386, and 80486 chips. Other PCs are based on Intel's Pentium chips. The same is true for Macintoshes—you might choose from a whole line of PowerMacs. There's even a PowerPC, a cross between a Mac and a PC. UNIX systems come in many configurations, from Sun Microsystems' popular SPARC workstations to Silicon Graphics workstations.

Very often, the best platform for your intranet services is the platform you're most familiar with because different computer platforms use different operating systems. If you're unfamiliar with the operating system, you'll have a more extended learning curve as you study both the operating system and the software your intranet runs.

Here's a sample plan for hardware and software requirements:

Hardware

Web server: Existing 486DX/100MHz in system administration area

Gopher server: Add service to Sun SPARC 10 file server in system administration area

Software

Web server: Microsoft IIS for Windows NT

Browser: Internet Explorer 3.0

E-mail: Add-on module for Internet Explorer

Next, you should consider time, budget, and personnel constraints. If you have only six weeks to set up the intranet, you might need to hire other team members to get the intranet finished on time. In this case, hiring a specific number of extra team members would be one of your requirements.

Here's a sample plan for the initial time, budget, and personnel requirements:

Duration

Setup and installation: 30 days

Phase-in and testing: 30 days

Follow-up training and support: 90 days

Budget

$5,000

Personnel

Management and planning: 1
Installation team: 2
Training and support: 2

If you have a $5,000 budget, you will have to scrutinize every aspect of the budget to keep costs down. In this case, you will probably be selective about the development tools you buy and hire outside help only as needed. If the budget constraints are so severe they would affect the intranet's success, you should make sure your superiors are aware of the situation and possibly make a case for getting a larger budget.

Step 2: Planning

After you determine your requirements for the intranet, then start planning it. An essential part of planning is determining how long the project is going to take and the steps needed to carry you through the project. For this reason, the planning step can also be a reality check for constraints or requirements.

For example, say you determine it will take a minimum of three months to finish the intranet and install all the necessary services, yet the deadline for project completion given to you by management is 30 days away. Something would have to give, and you would have to work hard to manage perceptions and expectations of the intranet. You might have to renegotiate the deadline, hire more team members, or eliminate certain time-intensive parts of the intranet.

The more complex your intranet, the more involved your planning will be. The plans for a small intranet could be very basic, such as a list of steps with deadlines for completion written down in a notepad. The plans for a large intranet could be rendered in detail with a project-management tool like Microsoft Project.

Ideally, your deadlines won't be carved in stone. The best planners use windows for project steps, such as five days for planning or two weeks for preliminary design. There could be hundreds of steps, with several steps being performed simultaneously, or a handful of steps, with each step being performed one after the other. Some steps would be dependent on other steps, meaning they couldn't be started until certain other aspects of the intranet were finished. Other steps wouldn't depend on any other steps and could be performed at any time during the intranet's development.

TIP

Part of your planning should include scheduling necessary training on the intranet and promoting the intranet to company employees. If you don't sell the employees—your customers—on the intranet, your intranet won't succeed.

continues

continued

One way to help sell the intranet is to develop focus groups; they get your customers involved with the development process. Continued involvement in the intranet through its development and after its setup ensures an intranet that customers want. This involvement makes sure they have a solid investment in an intranet they will want to promote and support.

Step 3: Design

The design step is one of the most critical steps. During this step, you take your plans to another level of detail by determining how and where the intranet's hardware and software will be set up. For example, will the intranet's main Web server be located in the computer department? How will the software be distributed?

Use this step as a reminder to sit down with your system administrators and network personnel. You should discuss how you plan to install the hardware and software for the intranet. If there are any misgivings about the intranet, it's better to hear about them before you begin installation. If there are great ideas for improving the planned intranet, you definitely want to consider them before installation.

TIP

For a small intranet, you might be inclined to skip this step, but don't. During this step, you may discover something you overlooked in planning.

Part of your design may be to use a specific section of the current network as a "test bed" before you deploy the intranet companywide. To do this, you install the intranet services in a specific department or office. The users in this group are then given access to the intranet for a testing period. Based on the outcome of the testing, you would either continue with the intranet's companywide installation or revise your plans accordingly.

Ideally, your intranet team will work closely with the test group. During installation and when users start using the new services, you should make sure someone is on hand to answer questions and problems that might come up. This individual or group from your intranet team should take notes and make daily progress reports. Based on the input, you could modify your plans as you go through the various phases of the implementation for the test group.

Step 4: Implementation

The implementation step tends to be the longest step in developing your intranet. During this step, you install your intranet services based on the requirements, plans, and designs you created.

NOTE

Don't stop trying to enhance your plans once you have your intranet blueprint. The key to building a better intranet is to improve your ideas.

Using Your Intranet

Managing your new intranet can be frustrating at times, especially when you're first trying to install and configure the server. The important thing to remember is that your intranet can pay off in huge dividends. The time and money savings alone for intranet-publishing company user and technical manuals make intranet publishing worthwhile. Not only could the documentation be maintained so that it's always up-to-date at a lower cost than the original publishing and distribution of the manuals, but employees can search the entire text of manuals in an instant and at the touch of a button.

Although intranet publishing can bring dramatic improvements in the accessibility of information within the company, part of the problem with any project is that people often have unrealistic expectations or mismatched perceptions. The process of setting up your intranet publishing operation is no exception. The best thing you can do is to remember the following:

- Intranet publishing is a learning process.
- Take it one step at a time.
- Set realistic goals.
- Adopt a companywide policy for using and publishing information on the company web.

A Learning Process

This is your first intranet publishing operation, so it should be a learning process. Don't expect all the pieces to fall into place in a day—it simply won't happen. Give yourself and the project a fighting chance, and manage your expectations to help the project become a success. Remember, your expectations might not match those of your superiors.

Before you start to set up the Web server, keep the following in mind:

- Make sure your expectations and those of your supervisors mesh.
- Make sure the communication channels between you and your supervisors are open.
- Discuss expectations at the start and manage them properly.

One Step at a Time

Never let your thoughts about the complexity of the project overwhelm you. Your perceptions about the project play a deciding role in whether you'll ever finish the project, so convince yourself you can do this.

Often, people forget that sometimes you need to take a breather. You can't possibly try to do everything all at once, so set up your intranet publishing operation one step at a time. Begin by planning your course of action, and slowly progress from platform selection to server installation.

Set Realistic Goals

One of the first things you should do is make sure your goals are realistic. They should take into account both the complexities of the project and the possible setbacks. Your goals should be clear and relevant to the problem at hand—setting up the Web server and a networking publishing operation. As you set goals and milestones for each stage of the project, remember to provide flexibility. Never give yourself deadlines you can't meet, and if possible, give yourself a window for project completion.

Adopt a Companywide Policy

When you finish the project, remember to adopt a companywide policy about using and publishing information on the network. The key is to not only adopt a policy, but also to communicate it throughout the organization. Make sure company personnel know the following information:

- Who to contact for technical problems
- Who to contact for setup
- Who to contact for training
- What documents or services are available
- How to access Web documents
- The responsibilities of departments and individuals
- The acceptable uses of the company's intranet publishing operations

Summary

To create an intranet, you need to set up basic networking protocols, like TCP/IP, and services like the WWW. Once you have selected the basic tools you need to create the intranet and considered how you will organize the intranet, you can map the intranet through completion.

Intranet publishing is a cost-effective and time-saving way to publish company documents. To set up a intranet-publishing operation, you need to install and configure a Web server; it could be one of your existing network workstations or a new workstation you buy specifically for the task. Although you must be on the Internet to take advantage of the Web's information resources, you don't have to be on the Internet to take advantage of the features offered by Web servers and browsers.

II

PART

IN THIS PART

Web Publishing with HTML 3.2

CHAPTER 4

Creating Web Documents with HTML

by William Robert Stanek

IN THIS CHAPTER

You can easily create documents with HTML, but it's your design that helps sell your ideas, products, or services to a global audience. You don't have to be a programmer or a computer wizard to design dazzling HTML documents. What you need are a firm understanding of HTML design concepts and the pointers you'll find in this and other chapters in this book. HTML is based on the Standard Generalized Markup Language (SGML). SGML markup code is complex, but HTML markup code is easy to learn and use. It lets you format information so that it's user-friendly, interactive, and visually appealing.

Creating HTML Documents

Formatting HTML documents depends on markup codes called *tags*. Tags define the structure of the document and include an element name enclosed by brackets, such as `<H1>`, which indicates the start of a Level One heading. HTML is not case-sensitive, so `<h1>` and `<H1>` both mean the same thing.

Most tags are used in pairs. A tag called the *begin tag* tells the browser a document element is beginning, and another tag called the *end tag* tells the browser an element is ending. The only difference between the two is that the end tag has a forward slash before the element name. For example, the begin heading tag `<H1>` is paired with the end heading tag `</H1>`. The initial `<H1>` tag tells the browser a Level One heading is starting, and the end tag `</H1>` tells the browser the heading is ending.

TIP

Typically, when you create documents in a word processor or text editor, the documents have text formatting, such as tabs, spacing, paragraph markings, or page breaks. Keep in mind, as you create your first Web page, that ASCII text formatting is normally ignored. When your browser sees any of these text-formatting techniques, no matter how many times you repeat them, it interprets them as a single space. Generally, any of the following are displayed by your browser as a single space:

Single tab/multiple tabs

Single space/multiple spaces

Single paragraph markings/multiple paragraph markings

Single page breaks/multiple page breaks

In HTML, you can also define a special character to display. Special characters are described by an element name preceded by an ampersand and ending with a semicolon, such as `&` for the ampersand symbol. When a browser sees a special character, it interprets the special character and displays the corresponding symbol, if possible. Special characters are discussed in more detail in the section "Using Special Characters."

Defining the Document Structure

Every HTML document should begin with the markup tag <HTML> and end with the markup tag </HTML>. The begin tag <HTML> tells the browser the document is an HTML-formatted document and marks the beginning of the document. The end tag </HTML> marks the end of the document and is always the last item in any HTML document.

Although you might find HTML documents on the Web that don't include the begin and end <HTML> tags, it's poor design style not to use these tags. HTML isn't the only markup language in use on the Web; without identifying your document as HTML, you might confuse the reader's browser.

Every HTML document should also have a header and a body. The header immediately follows the first <HTML> tag and is used to specify key aspects of the document, such as its title. The beginning of the header is specified with the begin header tag <HEAD>, and the end of the header is specified with the end tag </HEAD>.

Following the header is the main section of the document, called the *body*, which contains the text and objects you want to display in the reader's browser. Like the header, the body has the begin tag <BODY> and end tag </BODY>.

NOTE

The examples in this book usually show markup in uppercase letters. This is good form and helps to clearly differentiate between code and text, but uppercase letters aren't necessary, because HTML isn't case-sensitive. Therefore, <BODY>, <body>, <Body>, and <BoDy> all mean the same thing.

Most current HTML browsers can figure out the header and body sections of HTML documents, but it's good design practice to include the HEADER and BODY elements in all your HTML documents. With the three tags discussed in this section, you can create the framework for an HTML document as follows:

```
<HTML>
<HEAD>
. . .
</HEAD>
<BODY>
. . .
</BODY>
</HTML>
```

In this example, the ellipses are used to show where additional information would go in an actual document. Now that you have the framework for an HTML document, take a look at components and concepts for the header and body elements.

HTML Header Design

The header section is primarily used to supply information about the document to the Web server. Everything in the header section is located between the begin and end header tags. Six HTML tags are reserved specifically for the header:

`<TITLE>`	The title of the document
`<BASE>`	Identifies the base URL for the document
`<ISINDEX>`	Provides a way to turn on the browser's textual search mechanism
`<LINK>`	Identifies the document's relationship to other documents
`<META>`	Enables you to identify general or meta-information about the document
`<NEXTID>`	Identifies the next identifier to be generated

NOTE

The `<BASE>`, `<LINK>`, `<META>`, and `<NEXTID>` tags do not display when the document is loaded into the reader's browser; they are used primarily by Web publishers with large sites to manage. These tags are used infrequently, probably because of a lack of understanding about their purpose. They supply information about the document to the Web server and to anyone who reads the HTML source code for the document.

Using Document Titles

The most commonly used header tag is the `<TITLE>` tag. The begin title tag `<TITLE>` identifies the beginning of the document title, and the end title tag `</TITLE>` identifies the ending of the document title. Each document can have only one title. Because a limited number of characters are displayed, your title should be short but descriptive. A general rule to follow for its length is 65 characters or less. Also, the title can have no extra formatting or markup, so it should contain only plain ASCII characters.

NOTE

Think carefully about the title for your document and the information it gives to readers. The title is referred to more than any other component in any document. It appears on a user's bookmark or hot list, which lists a user's favorite online places, for future reference. The title also shows up on the user's history list, a list of places visited during the current session. Most Web browsers prominently display the document title in a special location. Browsers such as NCSA Mosaic display it in a clear window appropriately called "Document Title."

> Browsers like Netscape Navigator display the title at the top of the browser's viewing area. Other browsers, such as Lynx, don't display the title unless the user enters a set of keystrokes telling it to do so.

Because the title might be referred to separately by the user, it should offer insight into the document's contents or topic. A good title for a sports service in Australia could be this:

```
<TITLE>Extreme Sports Australia</TITLE>
```

Depending on the focus of the document, a better title might be one of the following:

```
<TITLE>Extreme Sports in Australia and New Zealand</TITLE>
```

```
<TITLE>Extreme Sport Experiences in Australia and New Zealand</TITLE>
```

The could be added to the framework of a Web document as follows:

```
<HTML>
<HEAD>
<TITLE>Extreme Sport Experiences in Australia and New Zealand</TITLE>
</HEAD>
<BODY>
. . .
</BODY>
</HTML>
```

Using Base Links

Normally, you find files on a local Web server by using a relative file path. When you use a relative path to locate a file, you're locating the file in relation to the current file. Although this is the normal way to use relative paths, you can define a base path for all relative links in your document. Using a base path, you can tell the browser to locate files in relation to a specific path that could actually point to a remote server.

The `<BASE>` tag can appear only within the `<HEAD>` element. The only valid attribute for the `<BASE>` tag is `HREF`.

You could define a base path as follows:

```
<BASE HREF="http://tvp.com/">
```

The base path example tells the browser to add `http://tvp.com/` to all relative links in the document. Defining a base path is most useful when your document is available at two different locations, and you want to relate them to documents at a specific location. For example, you could publish your home page at a free Web mall without changing relative addresses to absolute addresses. Listing 4.1 shows how you would do it.

Listing 4.1. tvphome.htm.

```
<HTML>
<HEAD>
<TITLE>The Virtual Press -- A Hot Spot on the Web</TITLE>
<BASE HREF="http://tvp.com/">
</HEAD>
<BODY>
<P> <A HREF="vpbg.html"><IMG SRC="vpttl11.gif" ALT=""></A></P>
<H2><IMG SRC="bboard.gif" ALIGN="BOTTOM" ALT="* ATTN *">
The Original Virtual Press -- Hot contests for writers &amp; artists,
job information, electronic publishing information and much more!</H2>
<P><STRONG><A HREF="vphp.html">Experience the explosive features we've
created especially for you.</A></STRONG></P>
. . .
</BODY>
</HTML>
```

Whenever a user accesses this sample document, no matter where the document is actually located on the Web, any links the user follows will lead them to pages at the `tvp.com` Web site. The base path also makes sure that other relative paths on the page are valid at the new site, including the path to the images on your page.

Using the base path defined above, the relative references in the document—`vpbg.html`, `vpttl11.gif`, `bboard.gif`, and `vphp.htm`—would be interpreted as the following:

```
http://tvp.com/vpbg.html
http://tvp.com/vpttl11.gif
http://tvp.com/bboard.gif
http://tvp.com/vphp.html
```

Using <ISINDEX>

The `<ISINDEX>` tag is used with interactive searches of your document. To activate an `ISINDEX` query, a user must first access a gateway script that generates an HTML document containing the `<ISINDEX>` tag. When the user enters information requested by the query, a special URL with the path to the original script and the information the user typed in is sent back to the gateway script for processing. The specification that describes how gateways pass information to the server is called Common Gateway Interface (CGI).

CGI enables HTML documents to call external programs called *gateway scripts*. By calling gateway scripts, you can make your Web documents highly interactive and dynamic. CGI provides the basis for creating interactive forms and image maps.

NOTE

Creating forms is discussed in Chapter 27, "Form Creation and Design," and image maps are discussed in Chapter 20, "Backgrounds, Image Maps, and Creative Layouts."

Using <LINK>

Although header links are defined in the HTML 2.0 standard, no HTML 2.0-compliant browsers support this powerful and versatile element. Currently, the <LINK> tag is used primarily with style sheets, which are discussed in detail in Chapter 8, "Using Style Sheets."

Using <META>

When a client application requests an HTML document, a Web server normally passes the document with a response header added at the beginning. This header is separate from the HTML HEAD element and includes information the client needs to interpret the document. At times, you might want to modify the standard header or create your own header for special situations; you might also need to supply information to the client that you couldn't pass by using standard HTML elements. With the <META> tag, you could pass this extra or specialized information in the HEAD element of a document. The server retrieving the document would include this information in the response header for the client's use.

Most markup tags have attributes that describe how the tag is used in the document. The <META> tag has three attributes:

CONTENT

HTTP-EQUIV

NAME

Generally, these three attributes are used with each other. You can specify what information should be included in the response header by using the HTTP-EQUIV attribute. To do this, use a valid HTTP header name and supply a value for it with the CONTENT attribute. If you don't know the valid HTTP header name or don't supply a header name with HTTP-EQUIV, you should use the NAME attribute to identify the value you are referring to with the CONTENT attribute.

In general, you use the <META> tag only when there isn't another HTML tag you could use to supply the information. Header names aren't case-sensitive; therefore, you could use meta-information to specify an expiration date for your document as follows:

```
<META HTTP-EQUIV="expires" CONTENT="Mon, 31 Dec 1998 10:00:00 HST">
```

A Web server would add this meta-information to the document's response header as the following:

```
Expires: Mon, 31 Dec 1998 10:00:00 HST
```

You can also use meta-information to set keywords for the document. Here, the keywords are *publishing, books,* and *magazines*:

```
<META HTTP-EQUIV="keywords" CONTENT="Publishing, Books, Magazines">
```

A Web server would add this meta-information to the document's response header as the following:

```
Keywords: Publishing, Books, Magazines
```

You can use meta-information to specify the amount of time before a client should request a file again. Here, the client will request the file every 30 seconds:

```
<META HTTP-EQUIV="refresh" CONTENT="30">
```

If you use the NAME attribute, the server won't generate a response header. Some information you might want to pass in this way includes an e-mail address for the document's author, the date the document was published, and other information not specifically addressed by other HTML tags. You could specify the document's author as follows:

```
<META NAME="author" CONTENT="william@tvp.com">
```

You could specify the document's publication date as follows:

```
<META NAME="published" CONTENT="Mon, 15 Nov 1995">
```

Your HTML documents can have several <META> tags. The meta-information used as examples in this section could be added to the HEAD element of an HTML document, as shown in Listing 4.2.

Listing 4.2. metasamp.htm.

```
<HTML>
<HEAD>
<TITLE>The Web Book</TITLE>
<META HTTP-EQUIV="expires" CONTENT="Mon, 31 Dec 1998 10:00:00 HST">
<META HTTP-EQUIV="keywords" CONTENT="Publishing, Books, Magazines">
<META HTTP-EQUIV="refresh" CONTENT="30">
<META NAME="author" CONTENT="william@tvp.com">
<META NAME="published" CONTENT="Mon, 15 Nov 1995">
</HEAD>
<BODY>
 . . .
</BODY>
</HTML>
```

Using <NEXTID>

The <NEXTID> tag is used only by HTML editors that generate identifiers for elements. Using <NEXTID>, the editor tracks the next ID value to assign to an element. In this way, the editor uses unique identifiers for elements.

The <NEXTID> tag has only one attribute, N. The value of the N attribute is the next identifier for an element. This identifier should be alphanumeric. You must use the N attribute and specify a value as follows:

```
<NEXTID N="alphanumeric value">
```

In this example, the `ID` value of the next element you create would be `alpha7`:

```
<NEXTID N="alpha7">
```

The `<NEXTID>` tag is used only by HTML editors; browsers don't use the `<NEXTID>` tag in any way.

HTML Body Design

The main section of a Web document is the body. Everything in the body is located between the begin and end body tags. Dozens of HTML tags can be used in the body; these tags are defined throughout this chapter and in other chapters that explore HTML. As you design your document, focus on the structure of the elements you plan to include in the body section.

Well-designed documents look as though they were designed effortlessly. They get their impact from simplicity of design and are organized in a coherent, flowing way. However, designs that seem simple and natural to the reader are often the result of painstaking effort. You can use many techniques to structure the document in powerful, yet uncomplicated, ways.

Sometimes it isn't what you have on the page that helps convey your message, but what you *don't* have on the page. Empty space—also called *white space*—makes material easier to read and helps focus the reader's attention on your ideas. Interestingly enough, it's the separation of material that creates the emphasis and draws the reader's attention. Two key page components that can help you create white space are paragraphs and headings.

Browsers typically display an empty space between paragraphs, so a page with many paragraphs has more white space. You should use short paragraphs, fewer than six lines, as much as possible; try to keep paragraph length under 10 lines. Varying the length of paragraphs is a good technique to keep the reader's attention. If you use the same paragraph length repeatedly, even the most lively material seems monotonous.

Browsers also display an empty space between headings. Using headings, you can divide the document into sections or topics. A document broken into topics looks more manageable and interesting, and headings help the reader identify the main points of the document at a glance. They also help the reader quickly find topics of interest.

Color is another feature you can add to the document. Most browsers display your document on a gray background. HTML 3.2 includes an extension for the `<BODY>` tag that lets you add images and color to the background. Other extensions enable you to specify the color of text and links. If you plan to enhance your documents specifically for users with an HTML 3.2-compliant browser, this can be a good extension to take advantage of. HTML 3.2 is explored in Chapter 5, "Designing with HTML 3.2."

Often the best way to add color to the page is with graphic images. A few pictures placed strategically on the page can dramatically increase its impact. Your pictures don't have to be sophisticated or high-resolution. Simple is usually best. You should place the images so that they focus the reader's attention on the page's key aspects, such as placing a small eye-catching graphic at the beginning of a key paragraph.

NOTE

Adding images to your documents is featured in the section "Adding Images to Your Pages." Because images are so important to Web publications, an entire section of this book is devoted to images and graphic design—Part IV, "Enhancing Web Pages with Graphics."

The key components of a basic HTML document are headings and paragraphs. Most basic documents also use comments, special characters, and text elements like quotes or addresses. The next sections discuss the five basic document components:

Headings

Paragraphs

Comments

Special characters

Additional text elements

Creating Headings

With headings, you can better organize your ideas. The chapters of most nonfiction books use many levels of headings—usually chapter headings, section headings for each major topic, and subheadings for subtopics. Headings are generally in a bold type and larger than normal font size, which usually corresponds to the heading's level. Chapter headings use the largest font size, section headings use a slightly smaller font size, and so on. The boldfaced text at the top of this section is an example of a subtopic heading level.

HTML enables you to create up to six levels of headings, `<H1>` through `<H6>`. Like many other tags, heading tags are used in pairs. For example, the begin Level One heading tag `<H1>` is used with the end Level One heading tag `</H1>`. HTML headings are displayed in bold type. In general, a Level One heading uses the largest font size, and a Level Six heading uses the smallest one. Browsers typically insert a space before and after the heading.

NOTE

As the Web publisher, you have no direct control over font size in HTML; it's determined by configurations set up in the browser displaying the document, and heading sizes are consistent in relation to each other and the main text. Most browsers display visible differences only in heading levels one to four. This means a Level Four heading is often displayed in the same font size as Level Five and Six headings.

You can create headings as follows:

```
<H1> A Level One Heading </H1>
<H2> A Level Two Heading </H2>
<H3> A Level Three Heading </H3>
<H4> A Level Four Heading </H4>
<H5> A Level Five Heading </H5>
<H6> A Level Six Heading </H6>
```

Figure 4.1 shows how the different heading levels are sized in relation to each other. As you can see from the figure, the browser used in the figure—Netscape Navigator 3.0—displays all heading levels in a different font size. However, if you look closely, you can see that the size of Level Four headings and regular text is the same, which means the only difference between the heading and the text is that the heading is in bold type.

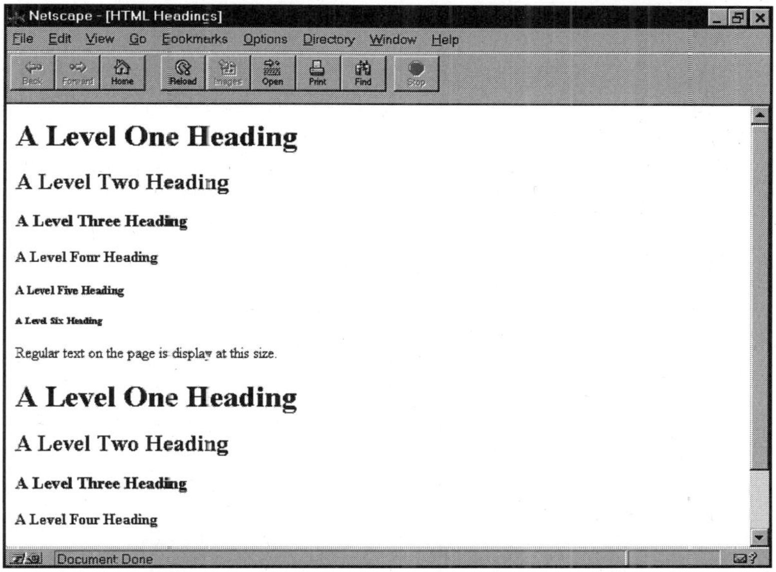

FIGURE 4.1.
Headings are generally sized in relation to each other.

Creating Paragraphs

After years of casual or professional writing, some processes of writing seem automatic. You probably don't think about the need to place a period at the end of a sentence, or why apostrophes are used in contractions. Similarly, when you start a new paragraph, you probably add a blank line, indentation, or both to separate the new paragraph from the previous one, without giving much thought about why. You add the blank line or indentation because it makes sense and because it's what your grammar teacher told you to do. Blank lines and indentations serve to visually separate the paragraphs and break up the document.

In HTML, the way to visually break up the document into paragraphs is to use the paragraph tag `<P>`. When a browser sees the paragraph tag, it ends the current line and inserts a blank space before inserting the text or object following the paragraph tag. If you're using a word processor or text editor to create your Web document, keep in mind that browsers reduce all ASCII text formatting—including multiple spaces, tabs, or blank lines—to a single space.

> **NOTE**
>
> Although an end paragraph tag is defined under the HTML standard, the end paragraph tag `</P>` is currently optional. I use the end paragraph tag in the examples in this chapter whenever I have a paragraph of text. This lets me see at a glance where the text for a paragraph begins and ends.

You can create paragraphs as follows:

```
<P> Insert the paragraph text here. </P>
```

An excerpt from an earlier section of this chapter's text is shown in Figure 4.2. The paragraphs used in this document follow the spacing techniques discussed earlier.

Adding Comments to Your Documents

If you're a programmer or have looked at the printout of a computer program, odds are you have seen comments inserted into the code. *Comments* are used in computer code to make notes or explanations to anyone who might see the code. Even the original programmer finds the comments useful when changes or additions to the code are necessary, especially if they come up months or years after writing the program. Programmers use comments because having to work through a code's logic every time it has to be changed is a waste of time and resources.

Web publishers can use comments similarly to save time and resources when making changes and additions to HTML documents. You can use comments to track the document's update history, to make notes about text, links, or objects in the document, or to pass on information to anyone who might be reading the source code. Comments aren't displayed by the browser with the text and objects on the page and can be viewed only if you view the source code for the document.

FIGURE 4.2.
Well-designed paragraphs vary in length and number of sentences.

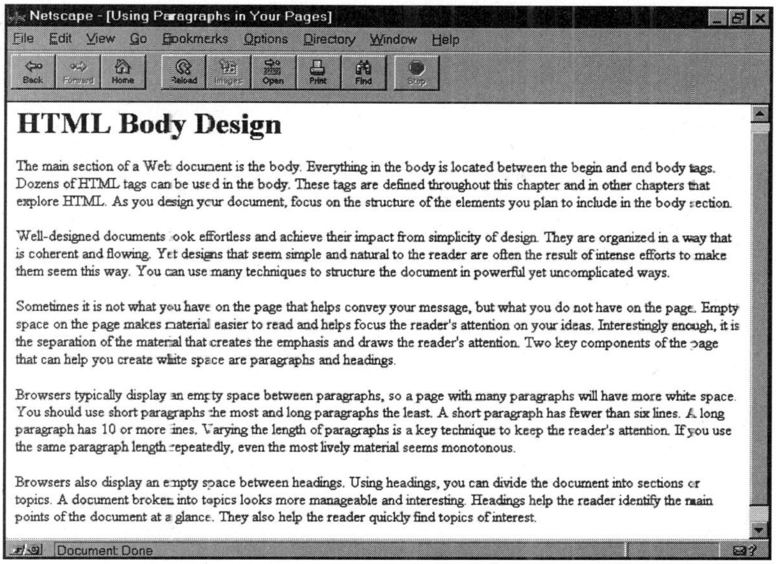

You can add comments to a document using the open comment tag `<!--` and the end comment tag `-->`. Each line of text that you want to be a comment should be individually tagged as a comment. Here are some comments you might make on your document:

```
<!-- Links on this document last checked July 1995 -->
<!-- Don't look at the code too close this document is just for fun -->
<!-- Section Four list needs to be updated -->
```

NOTE

Comment tags are oddballs; the begin and end comment tags have only a single bracket. Consequently, when you add comments, make sure they follow the proper format. Otherwise, your comments could be displayed when you don't want them to be.

Using Special Characters

Special characters are also called *entities*. In HTML, there are two types of entities: character entities and numeric entities. Character entities use actual text characters to define the special character, such as `"` for the double quotation mark symbol. Numeric entities use numbers to define the special character and add a pound symbol before the number, such as `|` for the vertical bar (|) symbol. The numbers used with numeric entities correspond to character positions in the ISO Latin I character set. Lists of the ISO Latin I character set are available on the Web, but Figure 4.3 shows the most commonly used special characters and their values.

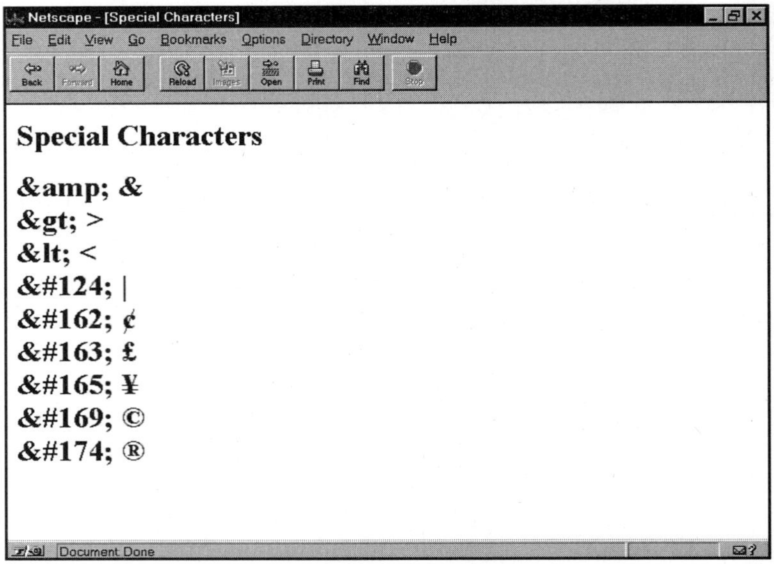

FIGURE 4.3.
Commonly used special characters and their values.

Using special characters in your Web document is easy. Wherever the special character should appear in your document, simply type in the value associated with the character. When a browser sees that special character, it interprets the character and displays the corresponding symbol, if possible. For example, when a browser reads the entity value `|`, it displays the vertical bar symbol.

The typical characters you must use entity values for include any characters used in HTML markup, which is why you must use the `>` entity for the greater than symbol and the `<` entity for the less than symbol when you want them to be displayed with the text in the document. If you use the < or > symbol in text you want displayed, you will confuse the browser and probably get strange results. Watch out for these and other symbols that might confuse your browser. Whenever you find one, check to see whether there's an associated entity value you can use instead of the special character.

The HTML source used to create the document shown in Figure 4.3 is found in Listing 4.3. As you can see from the document, there's a trick to displaying the special character and its value. To display the special character, simply enter the character value, such as `>`. To display an actual value for a special character, convert the initial ampersand to its character value: `&`, then enter the rest of the character value.

Listing 4.3. `specchar.htm`.

```
<HTML>
<HEAD>
<TITLE>Special Characters</TITLE>
</HEAD>
```

```
<BODY>
<H1>Special Characters</H1>
<H1>&amp;amp;          &amp;<BR>
&amp;gt;          &gt;<BR>
&amp;lt;          &lt;<BR>
&amp;#124;        ¦<BR>
&amp;#162;        &#162;<BR>
&amp;#163;        &#163;<BR>
&amp;#165;        &#165;<BR>
&amp;#169;        &169;<BR>
&amp;#174;        &174;
</H1>
</BODY>
</HTML>
```

More Text Elements

In addition to headings, paragraphs, and special characters, many Web documents contain other text elements, such as the following:

- Addresses
- Block quotes
- Preformatted text

Using Addresses

Your contact pages should have an address element that specifies your address or signature information. To add an address element, use the <ADDRESS> tag.

Browsers typically display address text in italics, with a paragraph break before the begin address tag <ADDRESS> and a paragraph break after the end address tag </ADDRESS>. No other special formatting is associated with the <ADDRESS> tag. For example, you can enter an address in multiple lines, as follows:

```
<ADDRESS>
Extreme Sports Hawaii
5300 Kalekaua
Honolulu, HI
</ADDRESS>
```

This address would be displayed in italics, as shown here:

Extreme Sports Hawaii 5300 Kalekaua Honolulu, HI

If you wanted the address to appear on more than one line, you would have to insert the line break tag <BR>, as follows:

```
<ADDRESS>
Extreme Sports Hawaii<BR>
5300 Kalekaua<BR>
Honolulu, HI<BR>
</ADDRESS>
```

Examples of addresses used in a Web page are shown in Figure 4.4.

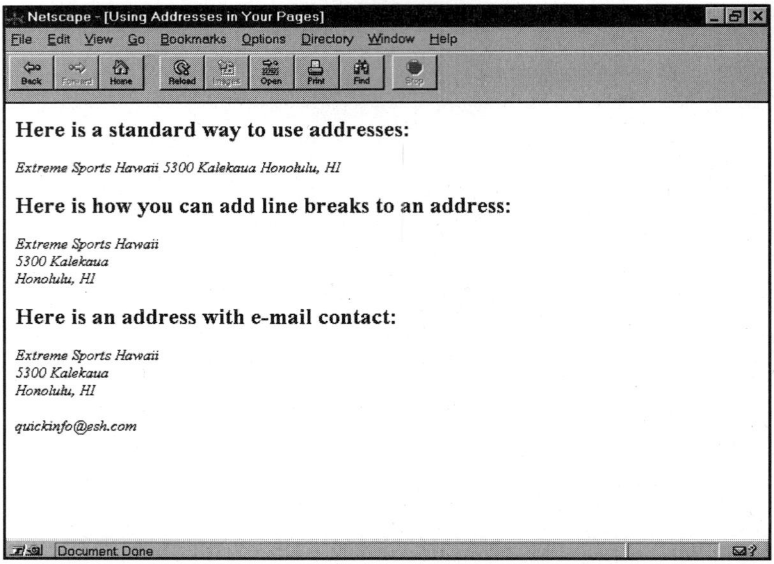

FIGURE 4.4.
Using addresses in your pages.

Using Blockquotes

The `<BLOCKQUOTE>` tag is used to specify a section of the document containing a quotation. Just as browsers display addresses in a unique way, they also display quotations uniquely. Browsers set the quotation off from other text with spacing and indent both the left and right margins. More pages have quotations than you might think, but the element that creates the quotation isn't always used as the developers of HTML intended. The primary reason for this is that you can use quotations to indent any type of text.

As with most HTML tags, you need both a begin `<BLOCKQUOTE>` tag and an end `</BLOCKQUOTE>` tag. Quotations used in a sample document are shown in Figure 4.5. Here's how the final example was added to the page:

```
<BLOCKQUOTE>Sometimes the dragon wins.<BR>
Other times the dragon retires from the field;<BR>
weary from the battle.</BLOCKQUOTE>
```

Using Preformatted Text

Defining a section of text as *preformatted* is very useful and enables you to use standard ASCII text-formatting techniques for text in your documents. In a section of text declared as preformatted, you can use any of your favorite ASCII spacing tricks, including tabs, multiple tabs, multiple spaces, and multiple blank lines.

FIGURE 4.5.
Using quotations in your pages.

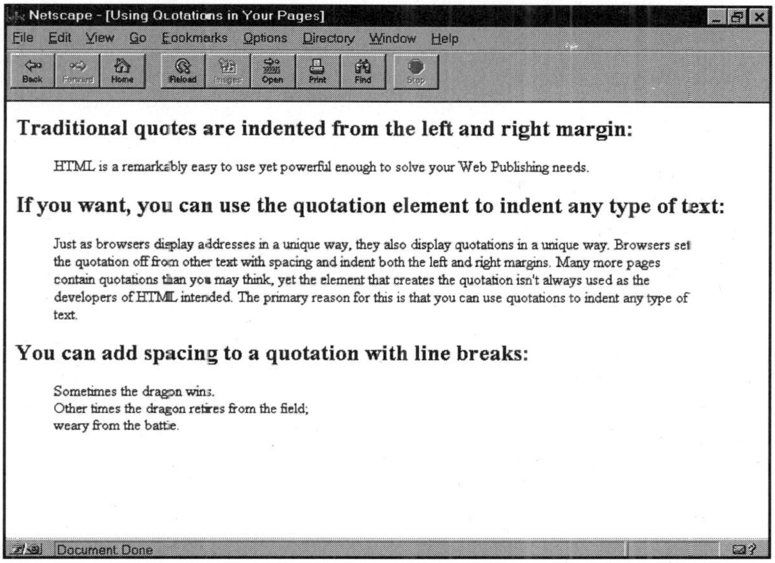

The `<PRE>` tag is used in a pair of tags as follows:

```
<PRE> Preformatted text </PRE>
```

Figure 4.6 shows how you could use preformatted text in your documents. The text in the preformatted page is displayed in a monospaced font called Courier New. Listing 4.4 is the code for the page.

Listing 4.4. `pretext.htm`.

```
<HTML>
<HEAD>
<TITLE>Markup Languages</TITLE>
</HEAD>
<BODY>
<PRE>
Markup Languages

SGML                     HTML                     VRML
-----------              -----------              -----------
Standard generalized     Hypertext                Virtual Reality
markup language          markup language          modeling language
-----------              -----------              -----------
Basis language for       Based on SGML            Based on SGI's Open
most other markup                                 Inventor Format
languages
```

continues

Listing 4.4. continued

```
Language Level
-----------         -----------          -----------
Complex language    Basic language       Advanced language
Powerful/Versatile  Simple/Straight forward  Great for rendering
                                         3-d images and models

Browser Support
-----------         -----------          -----------
Any SGML browser    Any HTML Browser     Any VRML browser
</PRE>
</BODY>
</HTML>
```

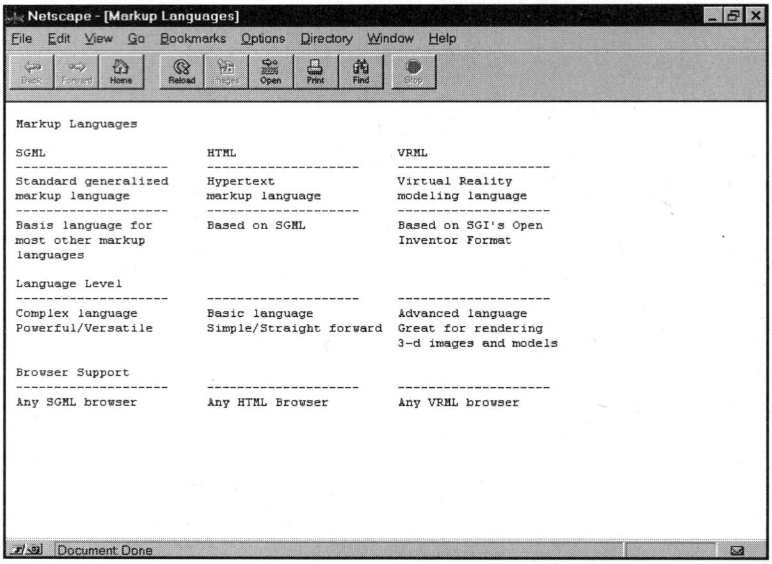

FIGURE 4.6.
Creating a table with preformatted text.

CAUTION

When using the <PRE> tag, keep in mind that monospaced fonts look much wider than proportional fonts. Proportional fonts use the amount of screen space that's proportional to their size, which means that an *i* uses less screen space than a *w*. In a monospaced or nonproportional font, each letter uses the same amount of screen space.

The only attribute for the <PRE> tag in HTML 2.0 is the `WIDTH` attribute. You can use the `WIDTH` attribute with the <PRE> tag to specify the maximum number of characters that should appear on a line. If you don't specify a width, the default is 80 characters. However, since current browsers don't support using the `WIDTH` attribute, there's no real maximum width or default.

Adding Features to Web Documents

Features you should add to your documents are those that increase the document's visual impact and those that make the document interactive. Beyond graphic images, features that add to the visual impact include line breaks to create a column of text and horizontal rules to visually divide the document into sections. To increase the interactive nature of your document, you can create links to other documents on the Web. You can also create internal links in your document to help guide readers to key parts of your publication. You can also add any of several types of lists to your document, which can boost the document's visual impact by clearly organizing material.

Using Line Breaks and Horizontal Rules

The line break tag <BR> enables you to break a line without adding a space between the lines; it's one of the few tags that have only a begin tag. You can use a line break to format text on your document in many creative ways. Sometimes you don't want a space between lines of text, or you want to highlight an example by breaking the line, then starting the example on a new line.

Here's how this could be done:

```
<P>This section will contain:<BR>
An introduction to the document</P>
```

The <BR> tag can also be used to format your text into a column or simple list. Not only does text formatted in a column add to the document's visual impact, but it also gets the reader's attention. The following example shows how you could create a simple list:

```
Our on-line publications include:<BR>
<BR>
Books<BR>
Magazines<BR>
Newspapers<BR>
Newsletters<BR>
```

You can use the <BR> tag inside other tags without affecting the font or style of the previously declared tag. If you insert <BR> into a heading, the text before and after the break is formatted in the style and font of a heading. All the <BR> tag does is start a new line, just as the carriage return on a typewriter does.

Another way to easily add visual impact is to use horizontal rules, shaded lines drawn across the width of the document. The line's shading makes it appear to be engraved into the document. You can add a horizontal rule to the document by using the <HR> tag.

<HR> tags have the advantage of dividing your document visually into sections; however, you should use them sparingly. Too many horizontal rules in the document can spoil the effect. Use the <HR> tag merely to highlight or to help the reader better identify the document's major sections.

Figure 4.7 shows a combination of the <BR> and <HR> tags. The figure shows only the outline of the document, but you can see how horizontal rules could be used to divide the document into four major sections. The complete HTML code for the outline of the document is shown in Listing 4.5.

Listing 4.5. hrbrsamp.htm.

```
<HTML>
<HEAD>
<TITLE>Using Horizontal Rules and Line Breaks</TITLE>
</HEAD>
<BODY>
<P>This section will contain:<BR>
An introduction to the document</P>
<HR>
<P>This section will contain a list of our publications.<BR>
Our on-line publications include:<BR>
<BR>
Books<BR>
Magazines<BR>
Newspapers<BR>
Newsletters<BR>
</P>
<HR>
<P>This section will contain creative works by:<BR>
Writers and poets who want to publish their works on the Web.</P>
<HR>
<P>The final section of the document will contain:<BR>
Contact and copyright information.</P>
</BODY>
</HTML>
```

Adding Visual Variety to Your Documents

A Web document that has just paragraphs and headings would be boring. Since you want to highlight and emphasize key sections of the text, you can use a special set of HTML tags called *character style tags.* These tags highlight your text with techniques such as boldface and italics. Unlike heading and paragraph tags, character style tags do not insert white space, which makes it possible to put them in other tags to highlight a single word or a group of words.

In HTML, there are two subsets of character style tags: physical styles and logical styles.

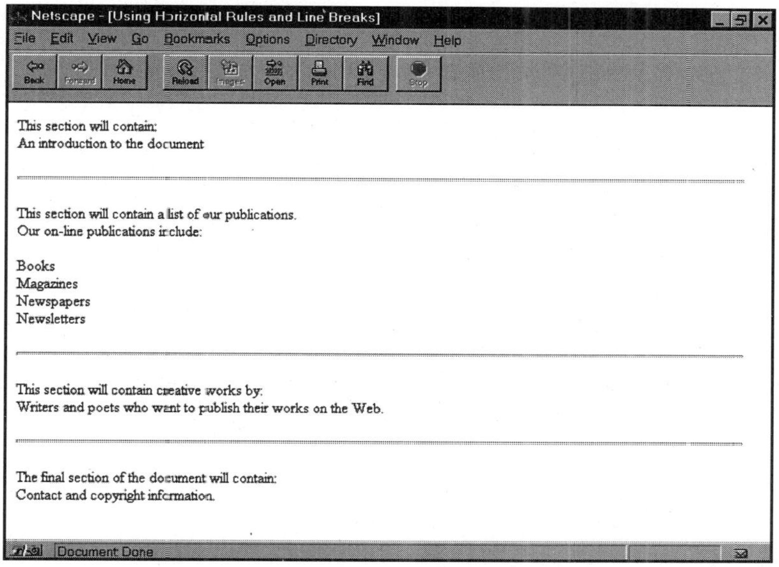

FIGURE 4.7.
You can visually break up the document with horizontal rules and line breaks.

Physical Styles

Physical styles tell the browser the precise format to display. In HTML 2.0, four physical styles correspond to bold, italics, underlined, and monospaced type. Additional physical styles are discussed in Chapter 5, “Designing with HTML 3.2.” Each physical style has a begin tag and an end tag; the four physical style tags are listed here:

<B> Bold type </B>

<I> Italics type </I>

<U> Underline </U>

<TT> Typewriter or monospaced type </TT>

You could use these tags in an HTML document as follows:

```
<P>Physical styles tell the browser the precise format to display.
<B>If you want to display a word or group of words in bold type, you
 use the bold tag just as you see it used in this sentence.</B>
<I>If you want to display a word or group of words in italics type, you
 use the italics tag just as you see it used in this sentence.</I>
<U>If you want to display a word or group of words underlined, you use the
underline tag just as you see it used in this sentence.</U>
<TT>If you want to display a word or group of words in a monospaced or
typewriter type, you use the typewriter tag just as you see it used
in this sentence.</TT></P>
```

You can combine physical style tags with other tags and even with other physical style tags. When combining tags always keep them in parallel order, especially if you are combining style tags. You could, for example, combine the bold and italics styles as follows:

```
<I>When combining tags always keep them in parallel order, especially if
you are combining style tags like <B>bold</B> with another style tag.</I>
```

Figure 4.8 shows how the example combining these styles might look in your browser. A browser accessing documents with physical styles tries to display the text using the strict format you have specified. If it can't, it may substitute another style for the one you're using, or worse, it may ignore the tag and display the text in standard style. Consequently, when you want to make sure text is highlighted, use logical styles. Logical styles are the preferred method of adding highlights to Web documents.

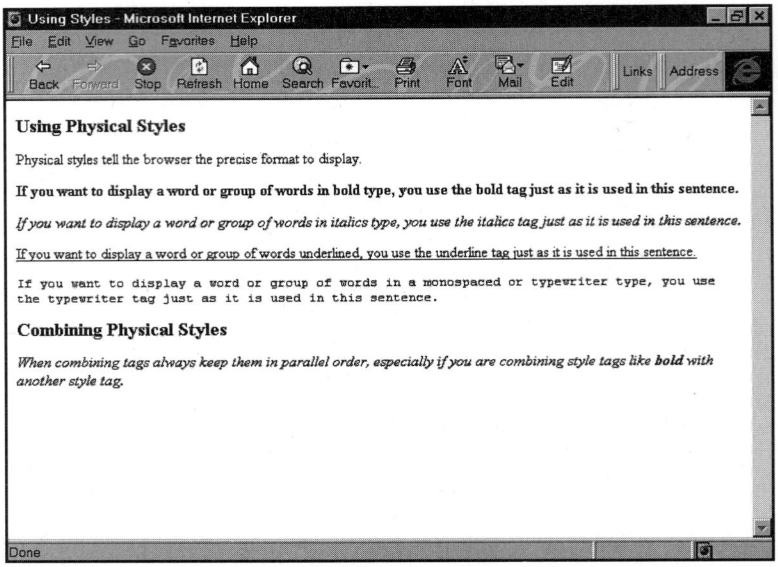

FIGURE 4.8.
Using physical styles.

Logical Styles

Unlike physical style tags, logical style tags don't specify a strict format. They tell your browser how the text should be used and let the browser display the text according to a set of specific configurations. The logical assignment of the style to the browser ensures that your text is highlighted in the document in some way.

HTML 2.0 defines seven logical styles; each has a begin tag and an end tag. Two specific logical styles are used more than any of the others. The begin emphasis tag `<EM>` is used to indicate text that should be emphasized. Browsers usually display emphasized text in italics. The begin strong emphasis tag `<STRONG>` is used to indicate text that should be strongly emphasized. Browsers usually display strongly emphasized text in bold type. You can use these tags in your document as follows:

```
<P>Logical styles tell the browser how the text should be used.
<EM>If you want to emphasize a word or group of words, you
 use the emphasis tag just as you see it used in this sentence.</EM>
<STRONG>If you want to strongly emphasize a word or group of words, you
 use the strong tag just as you see it used in this sentence.</STRONG></P>
```

Figure 4.9 shows how this example might look in your browser.

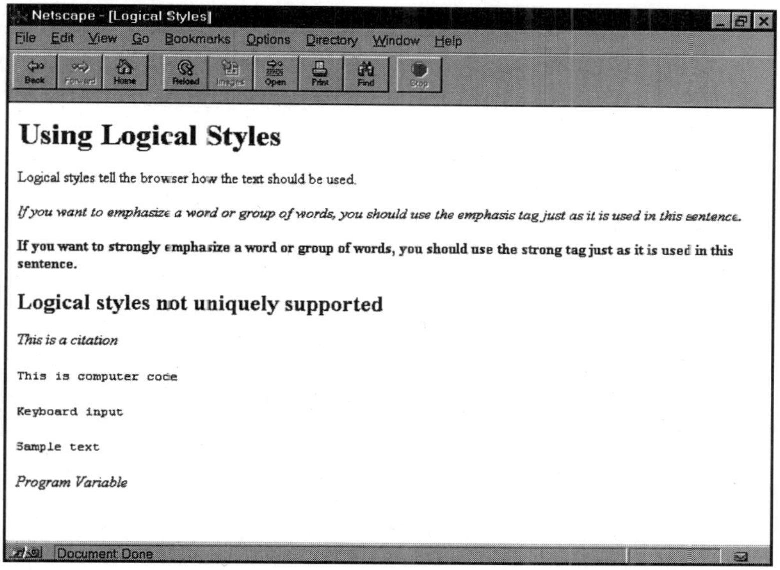

FIGURE 4.9.
Using logical styles.

The other five logical styles aren't uniquely supported by browsers, and because they duplicate styles you can create by other means, they're rarely used. Here are the five styles:

`<CITE>` Indicates the text is a citation. Most browsers display this style in italics. The tag could be used as follows:

`<CITE>Citation</CITE>`

`<CODE>` Indicates text is computer code or a program sample. Most browsers display this style in a monospaced font, such as Courier. The tag could be used as follows:

`<CODE>Computer Code</CODE>`

`<KBD>` Indicates text that a user would type in on the keyboard. Most browsers display this style in a monospaced font, such as Courier. The tag could be used as follows:

`<KBD>Keyboard Input</KBD>`

<SAMP> Indicates a sample of literal characters. Most browsers display this style in a monospaced font, such as Courier. The tag could be used as follows:

```
<SAMP>Sample</SAMP>
```

<VAR> Indicates text is a variable name, such as those used in computer programs. Most browsers display this style in italics. The tag could be used as follows:

```
<VAR>Program Variable</VAR>
```

Using Links

Without links, the Web wouldn't be interactive, so now it's time to put the "hyper" into hypertext. Most Web documents have hypertext links that act as pointers to other resources or files on the Web. Using links, you can connect text, graphic images, and multimedia objects to your documents. The great thing about hypertext linking is that linked text, images, or objects can be located anywhere on the Web. This means you can add images to your document that don't even reside on your Web server. For example, if you have created a resource guide to the latest in cutting-edge Web technologies, you might want to refer to Pepsi's Landing Gear page, shown in Figure 4.10. You could (with Pepsi's permission) use the Landing Gear logo as the link to the Landing Gear page at Pepsi. Here's how you would do it:

```
<P>
<A HREF="http://www.pepsi.com/landinggear/">
<IMG SRC="http://www.pepsi.com/landinggear/images/top2.gif">
</A>
</P>
```

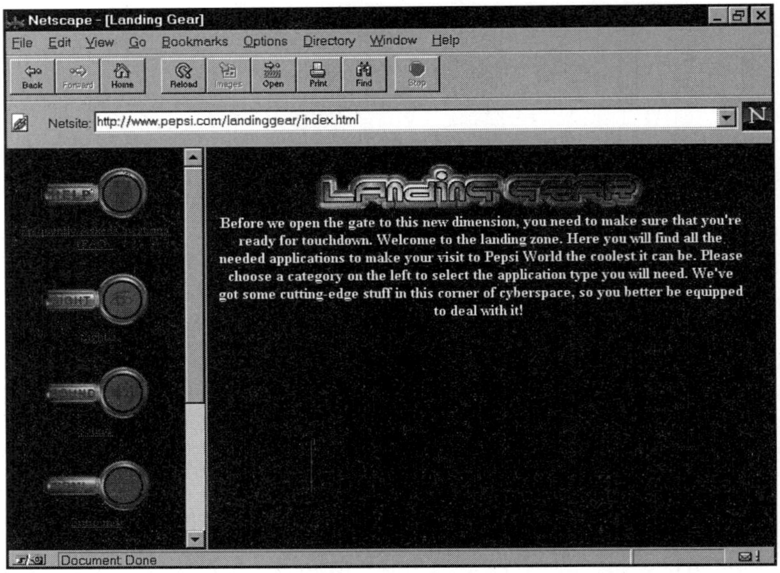

FIGURE 4.10.
Find cutting-edge Web technology at Pepsi's Landing Gear page.

NOTE

The <IMG SRC> tag enables you to display an image along with the text of your document. The <IMG> tag has three basic attributes and no closing element. The only attribute of the <IMG> tag you must use is SRC, which specifies the source, or path, to the image, including the name. Tips and techniques for using the <IMG SRC> tag are explored in the section "Adding Images to Your Pages."

The lines of HTML code in the sample code might look like a tangled mess, but they can be easily untangled. Links tell the browser where to send a request for a particular file. Initially, the browser doesn't care what type of file it's supposed to retrieve; it just tries to retrieve the file. To get to a file, browsers need to know where the resource is. The resource's location is specified as a Uniform Resource Locator, commonly called a URL.

The previous example contained two URLs:

```
http://www.pepsi.com/landinggear/

http://www.pepsi.com/landinggear/images/top2.gif
```

The first URL tells the browser to use the hypertext transfer protocol to access a file on the `www.pepsi.com` Web server. Here, the file is the base document in the `/landinggear` directory. The second URL tells the browser to use the hypertext transfer protocol to access a file called `top2.gif` on the `www.pepsi.com` Web server; the file is a graphic image in the `/images/top2.gif` directory. URLs with complete address information such as these let you link your documents to files on other Web servers.

NOTE

The base document is typically called `index.html` and can be accessed by using the forward slash. Using the slash, you can refer to shorter URLs and supply shorter URLs to those who might want to visit your document. Because the file name for the base document in a directory can vary, depending on the Web server software, here are some of the naming conventions used with popular Web server software:

MacHTTP	`default.html`
WinHTTP	`index.htm`
NCSA HTTPD	`index.html`
CERN HTTPD	`Welcome.html`
	`welcome.html`
	`index.html`

With the anchor tag, you can create a link. The basic format of a hypertext link is this:

```
<A HREF="URL">Text or Object reader sees and can click on</A>
```

The opening `<A>` tag contains the address of the files you're linking. The address isn't visible in a document unless the mouse pointer is over the anchor. The *anchor* is the portion of the link that's visible when a browser displays the document; it's positioned between the begin and end anchor tags. To activate a link, you move your mouse pointer over the anchor and click the left mouse button.

The great thing about the anchor portion of the link is that the anchor can be textual or graphical. If a line of text is the anchor, the reader can click on the text to activate the link. If an image is the anchor, the reader can click on the image to activate the link. You can also create an anchor that uses both text and an image.

Generally, text links are shown in blue letters and images with links have a blue border around them. Using HTML 3.2 enhancements, you can define the color of linked text and eliminate the border around linked images.

Figure 4.11 shows a page with both text and image links. Generally, when you provide both text and image menus like the one shown in the figure, you should interrelate them. Clicking on a text link, such as the one labeled `World Wide Offices`, takes you to a page with information on the worldwide offices of Extreme Sports Hawaii. Clicking on an image link, such as the picture of the globe, takes you to the same page.

NOTE

The page shown in Figure 4.11 illustrates many HTML 3.2 enhancements, such as centering and background images. You will learn all about the elements used to create this page in Chapter 5, "Designing with HTML 3.2."

As you can see, hypertext links to text and objects can be the most powerful features in your document. Adding links to your document can be done in three ways:

- Using relative paths to files in links
- Using direct paths to files in links
- Using links within your documents

Using Relative Paths in Links

You can access local files—files on your local Web server—by using a relative file path. URLs with relative file paths generally don't name a protocol or a Web server in the link. This is because when you use a relative path to locate a file, you're finding the file in relation to the current file. Being able to access a file in relation to the current file implies that you have already accessed a file on a particular Web server.

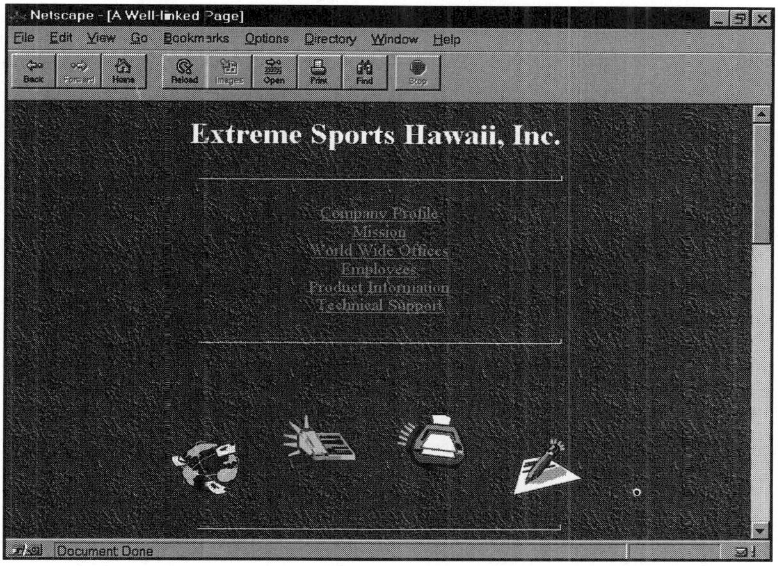

FIGURE 4.11.
A well-linked page that uses both image and text links.

You can use relative file paths in these ways:

- A file in the current directory.

  When you click on this link, your browser expects to find the file `orders.html` in the current directory:

```
<A HREF="orders.html">Orders &amp; Information</A>
```

- A file in a parent directory of the current directory.

  This file is located in the directory above the current directory:

```
<A HREF="../orders.html">Place an order today!</A>
```

  This file is located two directories above the current directory:

```
<A HREF="../../orders.html">Place an order today!</A>
```

- A file in a subdirectory of the current directory.

  This file is in the subdirectory called `info`:

```
<A HREF="info/orders.html">Visit our order center.</A>
```

TIP

Study the links used throughout the chapter as examples of well-designed links. Good links don't say "Click here." A "click here" link disrupts the flow of the text and the user's natural thought processes. The Web's interactive nature is such that you should never have to say "click here." Build hypertext links into the text; by doing so, you'll create documents that flow.

When using links, keep in mind that they're highlighted in the document. Typically, links are shown in underlined blue letters, which makes them stand out from surrounding text.

Here's an example of poorly designed anchor text:

```
<P>To place an order at our on-line order center
<A HREF="info/orders.html">click here</A></P>
```

This is a better way to create the link:

```
<P><A HREF="info/orders.html">Place an order</A> using our on-line
order center.</P>
```

Using Direct Paths in Links

Another way to access files is to specify the complete path to the file you want. Although you must specify the protocol to be used for files directly accessed on a nonlocal Web server, you don't have to do this for files directly accessed on a local Web server. This means there are two ways to access files directly:

1. Specify the full path to the file, including the transfer protocol.

   The following file could reside on a nonlocal server:

   ```
   <P>Find cutting edge Web tools at
   <A HREF="http://www.pepsi.com/landinggear/">
   Pepsi's Web site</A></P>
   ```

2. Specify the full path to the file, excluding the transfer protocol.

   The following file must reside on a local server:

   ```
   <P>Find cutting edge Web tools at
   <A HREF="/landinggear/index.html">
   Pepsi's Web site</A></P>
   ```

TIP

Designing good links is easy once you know the basics of using relative and direct paths. The key is to keep the anchor text for the link short but descriptive. Usually this text should be three to five words describing the link in a way that's clear to the user. Anchor text can be the key words of a sentence, but sometimes you might want the anchor text to include an entire short-but-descriptive sentence. Later sections of this chapter show how you can better organize links by using lists and menus.

Using Links Within Documents

Internal document links can offer powerful navigation methods for your readers and are especially useful in long documents. Using internal document links, you can provide ways to quickly jump to key sections of any document. Creating links within documents is a two-part process. First, you specify a link with a keyword by using the anchor tag the same way you've used other links. The only exception to the rules about links covered earlier is that the keyword for the internal document link is preceded by the pound sign (#), as in this example:

```
<A HREF="#keyword">Text or object to use as the anchor</A>
```

The next step is to label the location in the document you want the reader to jump to. You do this by labeling the `<A NAME>` tag with the keyword you selected earlier in the form:

```
<A NAME="keyword">
```

The keyword used in the link and anchor name must match exactly. When a user activates an internal document link, the section of the document associated with the `<A NAME>` tag is displayed. If the internal document link is in the current document, the browser quickly searches the document for the `<A NAME>` tag with the keyword that matches the keyword in the link. When the browser finds the matching `<A NAME>` tag, it displays the corresponding section of the document. If the internal link is in a different document, the browser loads the document and then searches for the `<A NAME>` tag with the keyword that matches the keyword in the link. The location of the keyword in relation to the link in the document doesn't matter. As long as the keyword is in the body of the document, the browser can find it.

You can specify links in the current document as follows:

1. Create a special link with a keyword, like this:

   ```
   <A HREF="#keyword">Text or object to use as the Anchor</A>
   ```

2. Label the section of the document the user can jump to as follows:

   ```
   <A NAME="keyword">Text or object to jump to</A>
   ```

Using internal document links, you could create an index for your document, such as the one shown in Figure 4.12. If you clicked the Overview link, then your browser would search for the keyword "overview." When your browser found the keyword, the section associated with the keyword would be displayed. In the example, the browser would scroll forward and display the overview section of the document. The ellipses show where actual document content would go. Listing 4.6 contains the code for the sample document.

Listing 4.6. `intrlink.htm`.

```
<HTML>
<HEAD>
<TITLE>Web Publishing</TITLE>
</HEAD>
<BODY>
```

continues

Listing 4.6. continued

```
<H1>The HTML Standard</H1>
<H2><A HREF="#overview">Overview</A></H2>
<H2><A HREF="#html_one">HTML 1.0</A></H2>
<H2><A HREF="#html_two">HTML 2.0</A></H2>
<H2><A HREF="#html_three">HTML 3.2</A></H2>
<HR>
<H2><A NAME="overview">Overview</A></H2>
. . .
<H2><A NAME="html_one">HTML 1.0</A></H2>
. . .
<H2><A NAME="html_two">HTML 2.0</A></H2>
. . .
<H2><A NAME="html_three">HTML 3.2</A></H2>
. . .
</BODY>
</HTML>
```

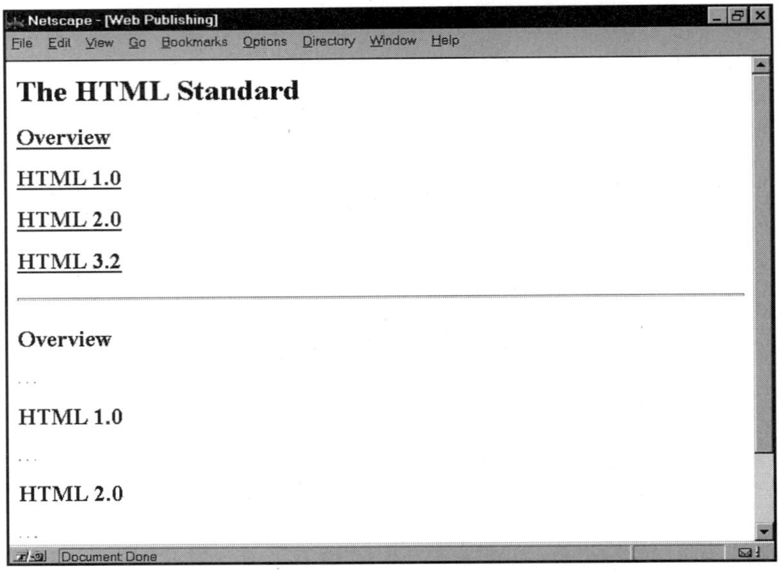

FIGURE 4.12.
After activating a link, your browser would jump to a section associated with the keyword.

NOTE

In the preceding sample code, the <A NAME> tag is placed between a begin and an end heading tag. This ensures that the <A NAME> tag is directly before the text or object the browser should jump to, which is the preferred way to place the <A NAME> tag in your code. If you place the <A NAME> tag before another HTML tag, you might confuse your browser, so always place the <A NAME> tag directly before the text or object the browser should jump to.

You can specify internal links to other documents in many ways. Using relative paths and keywords, you can get to specific locations in documents on the local Web server. With direct paths and keywords, you can reach specific locations in documents located anywhere on the global Web. This is the basic format for internal links to other documents:

```
<A HREF="URL#keyword">Text or object reader can click on</A>
```

Relative paths can be used with internal document links in three ways:

1. An internal link to a file in the current directory can be used.

   When you click on this link, your browser loads the `fiction.html` document from the current directory, searches the document for the keyword "Mystery," and then displays the section of the document corresponding to the keyword:

   ```
   <A HREF="fiction.html#Mystery">Top 100 Mysteries</A>
   ```

   The <A NAME> tag could be defined in the `fiction.html` document as follows:

   ```
   <H1><A NAME="Mystery">The Top 100 Mysteries Available On-line</A></H1>
   ```

2. An internal link to a file in a parent directory of the current directory can be used.

   When you click on this link, your browser loads the `nonfiction.html` document from the parent directory, searches the document for the keyword "Science," and then displays the section of the document corresponding to the keyword:

   ```
   <A HREF="../nonfiction.html#Science">Science &amp; Technology</A>
   ```

   The <A NAME> tag could be used in the `nonfiction.html` document as follows:

   ```
   <H3><A NAME="Science">Resources: Science</A></H3>
   ```

3. An internal link to a file in a subdirectory of the current directory can be used.

   The keyword in this example is "Information":

   ```
   <A HREF="info/orders.html#Information">Ordering Information</A>
   ```

   The <A NAME> tag could be used in the `orders.html` document as follows:

   ```
   <P><A NAME="Information">You can place an order</A> using our on-line
   order form, by sending e-mail to orders@wizard.com, or by sending a check
   or money order to the address below.</P>
   ```

Direct paths can be used with internal links as well; here are the two ways you will use internal links with direct paths:

1. Append the internal link to the full file path that includes the transfer protocol, such as in this example:

   ```
   <A HREF="http://www.tvp.com/viporder.html#Fantasy">
   Virtual Fantasy E-Books</A>
   ```

   The <A NAME> tag could be used in the `viporder.html` document as follows:

   ```
   <H2><A NAME="Fantasy">Virtual Fantasy Imprint</A></H2>
   ```

2. Append the internal link to the full file path that excludes the transfer protocol, as shown here:

```
<A HREF="/home/users/william/index.html#top10">Today's Top 10</A>
```

The `<A NAME>` tag could be specified in the `index.html` document as follows:

```
<P><A NAME="top10">Today's Top 10</A>
begins with an entry from left field . . .</P>
```

CAUTION

Be careful when specifying internal links to someone else's document. Web documents tend to change often, and a keyword that's specified today might not be there tomorrow.

Using Lists

Lists are one of the most useful tools in your writing and publishing toolkit. Lists can clearly organize your ideas and increase your document's visual appeal. You can use lists to grab readers' attention, especially those readers who are simply browsing or Web-surfing your site in their quest to find new and interesting places to visit.

The best lists are designed for a specific purpose. For example, the steps discussed in this chapter for creating a Web document make a great list:

- Develop a strategy.
- Define the document structure.
- Create the document.
- Add features to the document.
- Proof the document.
- Test the document.
- Publish the finished document.

This type of list is called a *bulleted list*, often used to outline goals, objectives, or tasks that have no specific order. Bulleted lists are also called "unordered lists." This list, however, is in a specific order, so a bulleted list isn't the best way to present it.

A better way to present the list of steps for creating a Web document is to number the list:

1. Develop a strategy.
2. Define the document structure.
3. Create the document.
4. Add features to the document.
5. Proof the document.

6. Test the document.
7. Publish the finished document.

This type of list is called a *numbered list*; it's used when tasks must be performed in a specific order. Numbered lists are also called "ordered lists."

Lists are also used in the glossary section many nonfiction books have. A glossary lists keywords and their definitions. You can use glossary lists whenever you want to associate a keyword with a concept or definition. Many glossary lists look something like this:

> **HTML**
>
> HyperText Markup Language
>
> The HyperText Markup Language is a markup language based on the Standard Generalized Markup Language that enables you to format information in visually appealing ways without sacrificing ease of use and the potential for wide distribution.
>
> **SGML**
>
> Standard Generalized Markup Language
>
> The Standard Generalized Markup Language forms the basis for most markup languages and is an advanced language with few limitations.
>
> **VRML**
>
> Virtual Reality Modeling Language
>
> Virtual Reality Modeling Language is an advanced markup language, based on SGI's Open Inventor Format, that enables you to create multidimensional documents.

Although the three fundamental types of lists are strongly supported by the HTML standard, the standard defines two more types of lists designed primarily for programmers. Menu lists can be used to list the contents of program menus, and directory lists can be used to list the contents of directories. Menu lists and directory lists have fallen into disuse and are poorly supported by browsers. If you use a menu or directory list, the chances are high that your browser will display the list following the rules for another list type. Therefore, it's generally not a good idea to use menu or directory lists.

The next sections offer a close look at how the three primary types of lists are used in HTML.

Bulleted Lists

Bulleted lists are used to outline goals, objectives, or tasks with no specific order. The associated HTML tag for this type of list is `<UL>`, which is an abbreviation of "unordered list." Bulleted list tags are used in pairs, and the counterpart of the begin tag `<UL>` is the end tag `</UL>`. Items in the list are preceded by the list item tag `<LI>`. The `<LI>` tag can be used with a begin and end tag, but the end list tag `</LI>` is not required. Listing 4.7 shows how a bulleted list can be added to a sample document.

Listing 4.7. b-list.htm.

```
<HTML>
<HEAD>
<TITLE>Creating Web Documents</TITLE>
</HEAD>
<BODY>
<H1>How to Create Web Documents</H1>
<UL>
<LI> Develop a Strategy
<LI> Define the document structure
<LI> Create the document
<LI> Add features to the document
<LI> Proof the document
<LI> Test the document
<LI> Publish the Finished document
</UL>
</BODY>
</HTML>
```

As the first example in Figure 4.13 shows, bulleted lists are generally single-spaced. When your browser sees the begin list tag <LI>, it does two things:

- Starts a new line
- Inserts a character called a *bullet* before the listed item

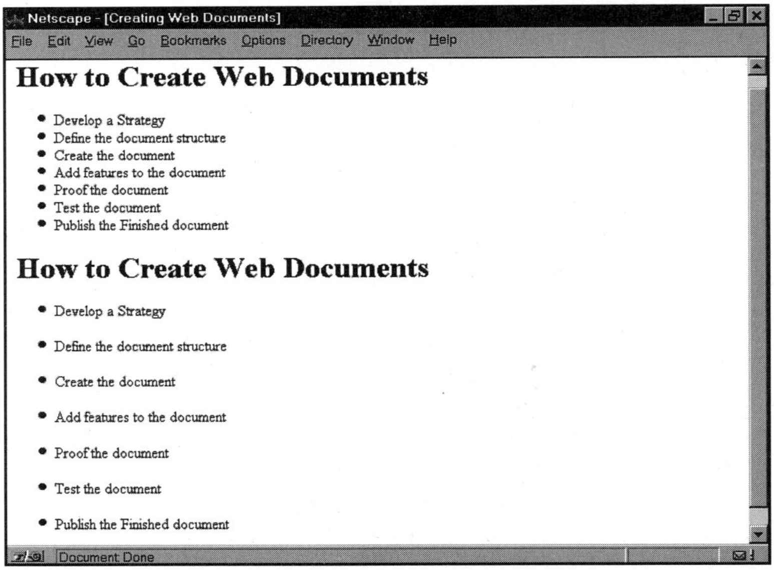

FIGURE 4.13.
Using a bulleted list.

NOTE

Most browsers display the bullet as a large solid dot, but the actual size and shape of the bullet may be different in your browser. Text browsers, such as Lynx, display the bullet as an asterisk. Other browsers use a different symbol for the bullets at each level of nested lists. Also, the Netscape browser uses extensions that let you select the bullet's shape. These Netscape extensions are featured in Chapter 5.

Single-spacing your bulleted list can make it difficult to read. This is especially true when your list has many items, and each list item has two or more lines of text. If readability is a problem with your list, you can introduce a simple spacing technique, such as the one shown in Listing 4.8 that uses the paragraph tag to add white space.

Listing 4.8. `b-list2.htm`.

```
<HTML>
<HEAD>
<TITLE>Creating Web Documents</TITLE>
</HEAD>
<BODY>
<H1>How to Create Web Documents</H1>
<UL>
<LI> Develop a Strategy
<P>
<LI> Define the document structure
<P>
<LI> Create the document
<P>
<LI> Add features to the document
<P>
<LI> Proof the document
<P>
<LI> Test the document
<P>
<LI> Publish the Finished document
</UL>
</BODY>
</HTML>
```


Glossary Lists

Glossary lists are also called *definition lists.* The associated HTML tag for the list is `<DL>`, which is an abbreviation of "definition list." Definition list tags are used in pairs, and the counterpart of the begin tag `<DL>` is the end tag `</DL>`. Each item in a definition list has two elements:

- A keyword, called the *definition title*
- The definition, called the *definition data*

The definition title tag <DT> specifies the glossary term or keyword you're defining. The definition data tag <DD> specifies the definition associated with the glossary term or keyword. You can use more than one definition data tag if the term has multiple definitions. Although a begin and end tag are defined for the <DT> and <DD> tags, only the begin tags are normally used.

TIP

A glossary list is generally for words and their definitions, but that doesn't mean you have to use them just for that purpose. You can use glossary lists whenever you want to associate a keyword, phrase, or sentence with a concept.

Listing 4.9 shows you a sample glossary list.

Listing 4.9. `g-list.htm`.

```
<HTML>
<HEAD>
<TITLE>Web Publishing</TITLE>
</HEAD>
<BODY>
<H1>Markup Languages</H1>
<DL>
<DT>HTML
<DD>Hypertext Markup Language
<DD>The hypertext markup language is a markup language based on the
standard generalized markup language that enables you to format
information in visually appealing ways without sacrificing ease of
use and the potential for wide distribution.
<DT>SGML
<DD>Standard Generalized Markup Language
<DD>The standard generalized markup language forms the basis for most
markup languages and is an advanced language with few limitations.
<DT>VRML
<DD>Virtual Reality Modeling Language
<DD>Virtual Reality Modeling Language is an advanced markup language
based on SGI's Open Inventors Format that allows you to create
multidimensional documents.
</DL>
</BODY>
</HTML>
```

As Figure 4.14 shows, glossary lists are normally formatted with the terms and definitions on separate lines. The terms are aligned with the left margin, the definitions are indented, and generally, just single-spacing is used.

Single spacing is good if you want to squeeze the list into a smaller screen space, but it makes it difficult to distinguish multiple definitions of a term. Introducing a simple spacing technique, such as the one shown in Listing 4.10, can improve the readability of your list. This technique is illustrated in Figure 4.15.

FIGURE 4.14.
Using a glossary list.

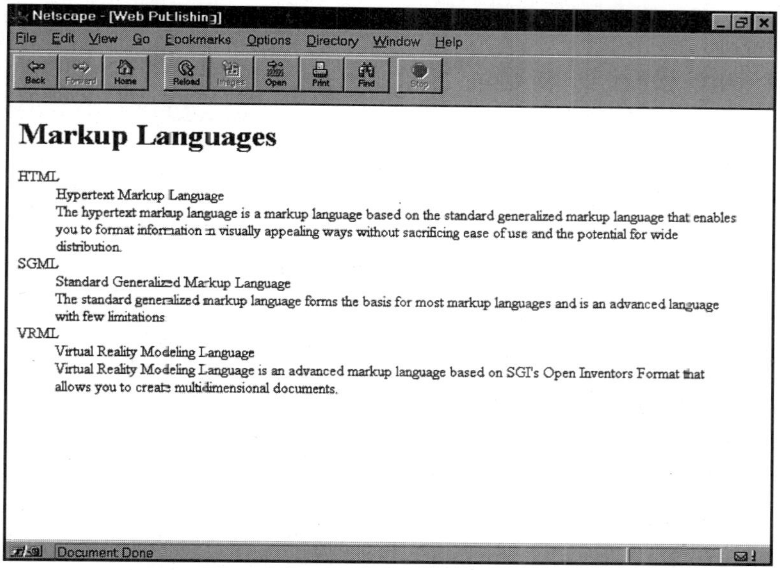

Listing 4.10. `g-list2.htm`.

```
<HTML>
<HEAD>
<TITLE>Web Publishing</TITLE>
</HEAD>
<BODY>
<H1>Markup Languages</H1>
<DL>
<P><DT>HTML</P>
<DD>Hypertext Markup Language
<P><DD>The Hypertext Markup Language is a markup language based on the
Standard Generalized Markup Language that enables you to format
information in visually appealing ways without sacrificing ease of
use and the potential for wide distribution.</P>
<P><DT>SGML</P>
<DD>Standard Generalized Markup Language
<P><DD>The Standard Generalized Markup Language forms the basis for most
markup languages and is an advanced language with few limitations.</P>
<P><DT>VRML</P>
<DD>Virtual Reality Modeling Language
<P><DD>Virtual Reality Modeling Language is an advanced markup language
based on SGI's Open Inventors Format that allows you to create
multidimensional documents.</P>
</DL>
</BODY>
</HTML>
```

FIGURE 4.15.
Adding spacing to a glossary list.

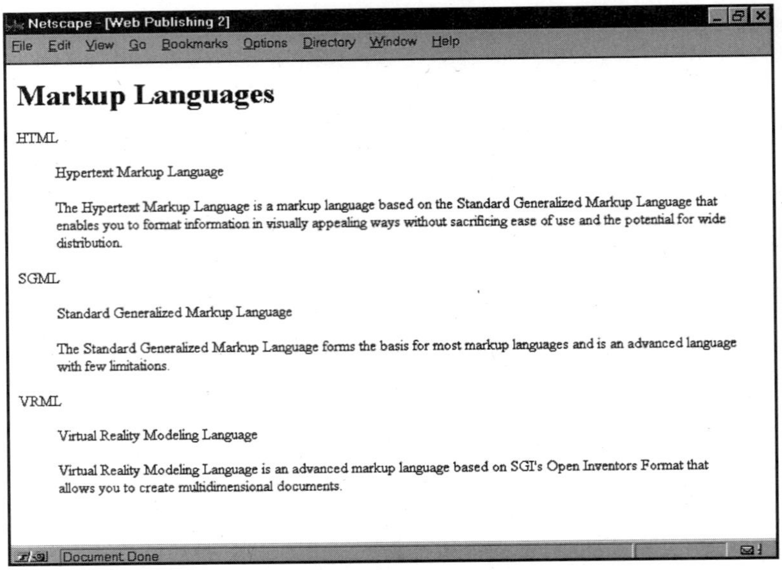

Numbered Lists

Numbered lists are also called ordered lists. The associated HTML tag for the list is `<OL>`, an abbreviation of "ordered list." Ordered list tags are used in pairs, and the counterpart of the begin tag `<OL>` is the end tag `</OL>`. Each item in the ordered list is preceded by the list item tag `<LI>`.

Each item in an ordered list is consecutively numbered or lettered. Letters are used only when you nest lists, and only if the browser you're displaying the list in treats nested ordered lists uniquely. When a browser sees a begin list tag `<LI>`, it does three things:

- Starts a new line
- Indents the text of the list item
- Puts the appropriate number or letter in front of the list item

> **NOTE**
>
> A *nested list* is a list inside another list. In HTML, you nest a list by including the entire structure for a list within your current list. For example, you could put bulleted lists within your numbered list structure.

As you can see from the first example shown in Figure 4.16, numbered lists are single-spaced, just like other types of lists discussed earlier. You should use numbered lists when tasks must be performed in a particular order or when you want to add specificity to the list. When you number and add a label to a list of resources such as those shown in Figure 4.16, you add specificity to the list. Instead of the list being just another list of resources, the list represents *the* 12 reference works you wish were on your bookshelf. Listing 4.11 is the HTML markup for the document.

Listing 4.11. `n-list.htm`.

```
<HTML>
<HEAD>
<TITLE>The Reference Desk</TITLE>
</HEAD>
<BODY>
<P>12 reference works you wish were on your bookshelf</P>
<OL>
<LI>American English Dictionary
<LI>Bartlett's Familiar Quotations
<LI>Computer Dictionary
<LI>Encyclopedia Britannica
<LI>Global Encyclopedia
<LI>Grammar and Style Guide
<LI>Grolier's Encyclopedia
<LI>Handbook of Poetry Terms
<LI>Hypertext Webster
<LI>Roget's Thesaurus
<LI>World Factbook
<LI>Worldwide Telephone Codes
</OL>
</BODY>
</HTML>
```

FIGURE 4.16.
Using a numbered list.

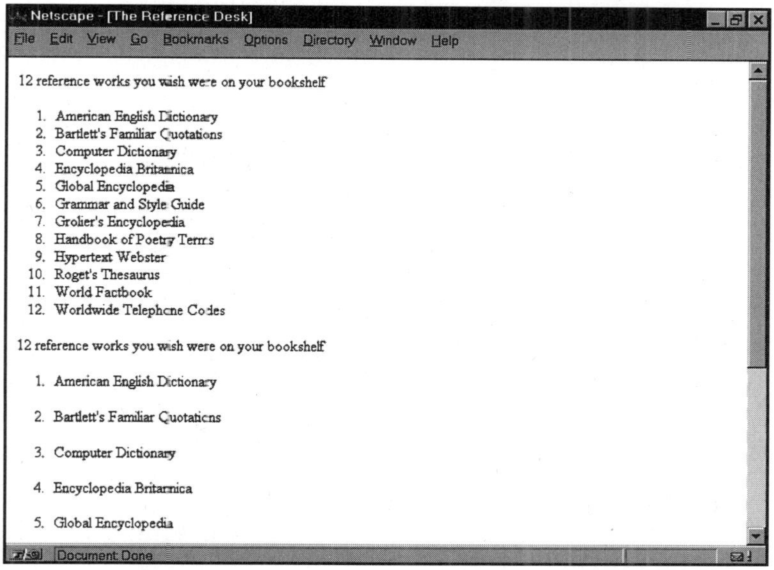

To make the list items more distinct on the page, you could break up the page by using a spacing technique. Although you would generally do this with a short numbered list that you wanted to stand out from the surrounding text, Listing 4.12 shows how this could be done by inserting the paragraph tag into the previous example.

Listing 4.12. nlist2.htm.

```
<HTML>
<HEAD>
<TITLE>The Reference Desk</TITLE>
</HEAD>
<BODY>
<P>12 reference works you wish were on your bookshelf</P>
<OL>
<LI> American English Dictionary
<P>
<LI> Bartlett's Familiar Quotations
<P>
<LI>Computer Dictionary
<P>
<LI>Encyclopedia Britannica
<P>
<LI>Global Encyclopedia
<P>
<LI>Grammar and Style Guide
<P>
<LI>Grolier's Encyclopedia
<P>
<LI>Handbook of Poetry Terms
<P>
<LI>Hypertext Webster
<P>
<LI>Roget's Thesaurus
<P>
<LI>World Factbook
<P>
<LI>Worldwide Telephone Codes
</OL>
</BODY>
</HTML>
```

Adding Images to Your Pages

Images are the key to unleashing the power of your Web publications. Everywhere you look on the Web, you see images. Web publishers use images to enhance their pages and get the reader's attention. You can use thumbnail icons to create highlights and navigation mechanisms. You can use computer-designed images as logos, page titles, illustrations, and maps to the hot features at your site. You can use digitized photos to convey your message more powerfully than text alone does. These photos can help sell your products and services and can even show people what your part of the world looks like.

Adding images to your Web pages is easy and can be done by using either external images or inline images. Readers access external images by activating a hypertext link to the image, such as this one:

```
<P><A HREF="67chevy.gif">67 Chevy</A> fire-engine red.</P>
```

When readers click on the link, the image is downloaded to their computers. If an image viewer is available and configured for use in the reader's browser, the image is displayed; if it isn't, the image is stored on readers' hard disks for later viewing.

Adding external images to your Web publications is as easy as supplying a link to the image, but it does require forethought and a fundamental understanding of image formats and related concepts. Browsers know which image viewer to launch based on the file type extension (`.jpeg`, `.gif`, and so forth) of the external image reference in your document. When a reader uses a link to a GIF image, the browser checks a configuration table to see which application should display the image, which is why your Web files should always be named with the appropriate extension. If the file is in GIF format, name it with a `.gif` extension; if it's in JPEG format, name it with a `.jpeg` or `.jpg` extension.

Unlike external images that aren't displayed directly, inline images can be viewed directly. When a reader with a graphics-capable browser finds your page, the images can be automatically loaded, along with the text on the page. You can add inline images to your publications with the `<IMG>` tag. In HTML 2.0, the `<IMG>` tag has four attributes:

```
SRC
ALT
ALIGN
ISMAP
```

The most important attribute for the `<IMG>` tag is `SRC`, which specifies the path to the image. This path is in the form of a URL that can be a relative path, such as this one:

```
<IMG SRC="67chevy.gif">
```

It can also be a full path, as shown here:

```
<IMG SRC="http://tvp.com/usr/images/gifs/67chevy.gif">
```

The `ALT` attribute for the `<IMG>` tag specifies other text to display in place of the image. Readers with a text-only browser see the alternate text instead of the image. If you don't specify other text to use, readers with a text-only browser see a note that marks the location of the image on the page, such as `[IMAGE]`.

Figure 4.17 shows a cool car—you'll have to take my word for it that it's fire-engine red. The graduated border was done by inserting the image into an HTML table. You'll learn all about HTML tables in Chapter 6, "Effective Use of Tables." Because a page devoted to cars would be pretty useless without any pictures, alternative text and fancy linking is used to allow users in text-only mode to click on the alternative text to see the image in an external image viewer. The HTML to do this is as follows:

```
<A HREF="coolcar.jpg">
<IMG SRC="coolcar.jpg" ALT="Cool Car in Fire-engine Red">
</A>
```

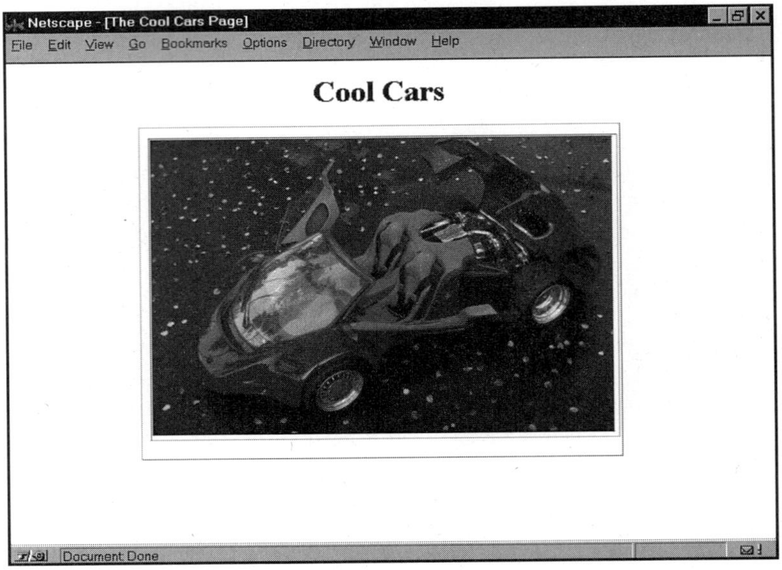

FIGURE 4.17.
Images are powerful additions to any page.

The ALIGN attribute specifies the image's alignment in relation to a line of text. By default, the bottom of the image is aligned with the text, but you can specify this explicitly by using a value of ALIGN=BOTTOM. You can align the top of the image with the text by using a value of ALIGN=TOP, and you can align the middle of the image with the text by using a value of ALIGN=MIDDLE.

The ISMAP attribute specifies that the image is an image map. You can use image maps to create graphical menus with hot areas that the user can click on. (See Chapter 20 for more information.)

Browsers handle inline images in many different ways. Some browsers load all text and associated images before displaying any part of your document. Some browsers display text and graphics as they read in your document. Other browsers load and display the textual portions of the page, leaving placeholders where the images go and then retrieving the images one by one. A few advanced browsers let the reader select options for displaying the components of the page.

Individual browsers handle inline images in many different ways, but all graphics-capable browsers give readers a way to turn off the automatic image-loading feature of the browser. However, this nice feature for readers means more work for Web publishers.

NOTE

This discussion on images is only a preliminary one. Because images are so important to your Web publications, an entire section of this book is devoted to images and graphic design. For more information on using images, see Part IV, "Enhancing Web Pages with Graphics." Part IV has six chapters that explore everything from how to create bigger, better, and faster-loading graphics to how to use animation.

Using Other Protocols in Web Documents

The Web was designed to be an open-ended multimedia system based on hypertext. However, the hypertext transfer protocol isn't the only protocol you can refer to in your Web publications. You can refer to files with any valid protocol. The format of URLs in hypertext references should follow the URL scheme outlined in Chapter 2, "Developing and Planning a Web Site."

The next sections explain how to use these protocols in your Web documents:

- FTP
- Gopher
- mailto
- NNTP and News
- telnet
- WAIS

Using FTP

Thousands of files are available on FTP sites around the world, and your Web documents can have links to files retrieved with FTP. The general form for using a hypertext reference to an FTP file is this:

```
<A HREF="ftp://host/path"> Anchor text </A>
```

If you specify a directory path instead of the full path to a file, the reader's browser lists the directory's contents. The following hypertext reference retrieves a listing of the MS-DOS directory from an FTP server at the University of Florida:

```
<A HREF="ftp://ftp.eng.ufl.edu/pub/msdos">MS-DOS Tools</A>
```

Using Gopher

Gopher information is presented to readers as easy-to-navigate menus. Readers can access Gopher files by using a hypertext reference, such as the following:

```
<A HREF="gopher://host/path"> Anchor text </A>
```

The following hypertext reference retrieves information on the DILS Project from a Gopher server at the University of Toronto:

```
<a href="gopher://gopher.epas.utoronto.ca/11/cch/disciplines/
➥medieval_studies/keefer">DILS Project</A>
```

Using mailto

You could use a special type of link that starts a Create Mail session in the reader's browser:

```
<A HREF="mailto:william@tvp.com">
```

This mailto reference tells the reader's browser to open a Create Mail session that will be sent to `william@tvp.com`. This type of link enhances the page's interactivity and supplies a way to get feedback from readers. Don't forget to anchor the link to the page with text or graphics that readers can click on. Here's one way to do that:

```
<A HREF="mailto:william@tvp.com">Send e-mail to the publisher</A>
```

Using NNTP and News

In your Web documents, you can refer to any of the thousands of newsgroups on the Internet in two main ways: by using the reader's local news server or by using NNTP (network news transfer protocol). Referring to newsgroups on a local news server is easy; you just specify the name of the newsgroup in the form:

```
news:newsgroup.name
```

In this example, you could include a link to the `alt.books.reviews` newsgroup:

```
<A HREF="news:alt.books.reviews"> alt.books.reviews</A>
```

NNTP is used to transfer postings to and from a news server; here's how it's used to link to the `alt.books.reviews` newsgroup:

```
<A HREF="nntp://news.aloha.com/alt.books.reviews"> alt.books.reviews</A>
```

CAUTION

Generally, to get to the news server, the reader must be a known client. Although this protocol could be useful to an exclusive group of known users, most are finding your pages from a remote site and can't use the named news server. Consequently, you should use newsgroups available on the reader's local news server whenever you want to reach the widest possible audience.

Using telnet

With telnet, you can let readers reach an interactive service on a remote host. In the telnet session, readers can input commands at a command prompt as if they were logged on to the remote host. You can refer to telnet in your Web documents in this way:

```
<A HREF="telnet://tvp.com"> Telnet </A>
```

Using WAIS

You can refer to indexed databases on WAIS (wide area information systems) by using a WAIS URL. To use WAIS, the reader's browser must either be configured to invoke a WAIS client that the reader has installed on his or her system or be able to act as a WAIS client. You can refer to WAIS in your Web documents as follows:

```
<A HREF="wais://tvp.com/wwwdata"> Search our World Wide Web database </A>
```

Summary

Web publishing with HTML is easy. Using the techniques discussed in this chapter, you can create simple yet effective Web documents. The two key sections of your HTML documents are the header section and the body section. You can use the header to supply information about the document to the Web server, but the body section is where your document comes to life. Dozens of HTML tags can be used in the body, and they all increase your documents' visual impact.

CHAPTER 5

Designing with HTML 3.2

by William Robert Stanek

IN THIS CHAPTER

The HTML standard is advancing at an explosive pace. Since 1990, when the World Wide Web initiative began, three major specifications for HTML have been defined. The current specification for HTML 3 has taken many twists along the road. First came HTML 3.0, a version of HTML too far ahead of its time; next came HTML 3.2—an attempt to put the future of HTML back on track and also a major success.

HTML 3.2 incorporates and standardizes many extensions of leading browsers such as Netscape Navigator and Internet Explorer. These extensions have long been favorites for cutting-edge Web publishing, and now they're finally moving toward full standardization. This chapter explains how you can use HTML 3.2 in your documents and what design issues you, as a Web publisher, should focus on.

Learning About HTML 3.2

Even before the HTML 2.0 draft was ratified, Web publishers, eager to create better and more powerful documents, started looking to the advanced features offered by HTML version 3. HTML 3 is the next level in HTML publishing.

The original specification for HTML version 3 was called HTML 3.0. HTML 3.0 offered these powerful features:

- Advanced layout control
- Banners
- Client-side handling of hot spots in images
- Customized lists
- Dynamic documents with client-push/server-pull
- Mathematical equations
- Style sheets
- Tables
- Tables within forms

Although HTML 3.0 was widely written about, the specification was never fully carried out in client browsers, mostly because of the complexities in using the advanced features found in HTML 3.0. Instead of fully implementing HTML 3.0, many browsers, including Netscape Navigator, Internet Explorer, and NCSA Mosaic, supported only key enhancements of the HTML 3.0 specification.

As you might expect, the supported enhancements are those high on most Web publishers' wish lists, but not extremely difficult to use. The supported enhancements include the following:

Advanced layout control

Client-side handling of hot spots in images

Customized lists

Dynamic documents with client-push/server-pull

Tables

Tables within forms

This subset of the original HTML 3.0 specification was reworked into a new specification called HTML 3.2. Just as HTML 2.0 is based on the features and extensions used in documents before June 1994, HTML 3.2 is based on features and extensions used in documents before May 1996. HTML 3.2 is designed as a replacement for HTML 2.0 and as such is fully backward-compliant with HTML 2.0 features.

NOTE

The subset of enhancements supported by HTML 3.2 doesn't include all the extensions proposed in HTML 3.0. For example, HTML 3.2 doesn't use the full HTML 3 table model. Instead, HTML 3.2 implements tables as supported by browsers like Netscape and Internet Explorer.

The features HTML 3.0 promised to bring to Web publishing aren't gone with the death of HTML 3.0. Instead, many advanced features are being developed as separate specifications. For example, there's a complete specification for style sheets and one for the HTML 3 table model.

NOTE

You'll explore publishing with style sheets in Chapter 8, "Using Style Sheets." The HTML 3 table model is examined in Chapter 6, "Effective Use of Tables."

A growing number of HTML documents have features defined in the HTML 3.2 specification; you will find thousands of documents featuring tables, client-side image maps, and client-pull/server-push. If you plan to publish HTML documents on the Web, you should definitely consider using HTML 3.2 enhancements.

NOTE

The next version of HTML after HTML 3.2 adds support for embedded multimedia objects, client-side scripting, style sheets, and extensions to fill-out forms. This upcoming version of HTML, code-named Cougar, is currently available as an experimental specification at `http://www.w3.org/`.

Defining Document Backgrounds

Helping you unleash the power of your ideas is what document backgrounds are all about. Most browsers display text on a slate-gray background, but HTML 3.2 lets you add images and color to the background. You can also specify the color of text and links.

Using Background Images

Document backgrounds are a graphic designer's dream come true. To add a background image, all you have to do is specify an image to be used as the document's background with the BACKGROUND attribute of the <BODY> tag. The image is tiled, or repeated, to fill the background area. You can use tiling to create design effects with small images. The best image formats to use for background images are GIF and JPEG, which are fully supported by leading browsers such as Netscape Navigator and Internet Explorer.

Here's an example of a background image inserted in a Web page:

```
<HTML>
<HEAD>
<TITLE>Sample Page</TITLE>
</HEAD>
<BODY BACKGROUND="sample.gif">
 . . .
</BODY>
</HTML>
```

The key to using backgrounds in your pages is to make sure the background doesn't interfere with the page's readability. Figure 5.1 shows how background images can add pizazz to your Web pages without affecting the page's readability. The background image is a grouping of five animals: an eagle, a seal, an ape, a wolf, and a polar bear. Because the image didn't fill the browser's window, it's tiled. Here's how the background image was added to the page:

```
<BODY BACKGROUND="wildlifa.gif">
```

A popular technique to use when adding backgrounds is to create the illusion that the image runs along the margin. (See Figure 5.2.) When the graphic is in the margin, it won't interfere with how easily the page can be read. The trick to the illusion is a spacing technique that makes it seem as though the background image is only in the left margin, when it really extends across the full width of the browser's window.

To tile the background image vertically, make sure the image is at least 800 pixels wide—600×800 is the most popular high-end screen resolution. Next, put dark graphics in the left margin that are 100 to 200 pixels wide and combine them with a light (usually white) graphic 600 to 700 pixels wide that completes the effect. You could also reverse this and put the light graphics in the left margin.

FIGURE 5.1.
Add pizazz to your pages with background images.

FIGURE 5.2.
Vertical tiling, a popular technique for backgrounds.

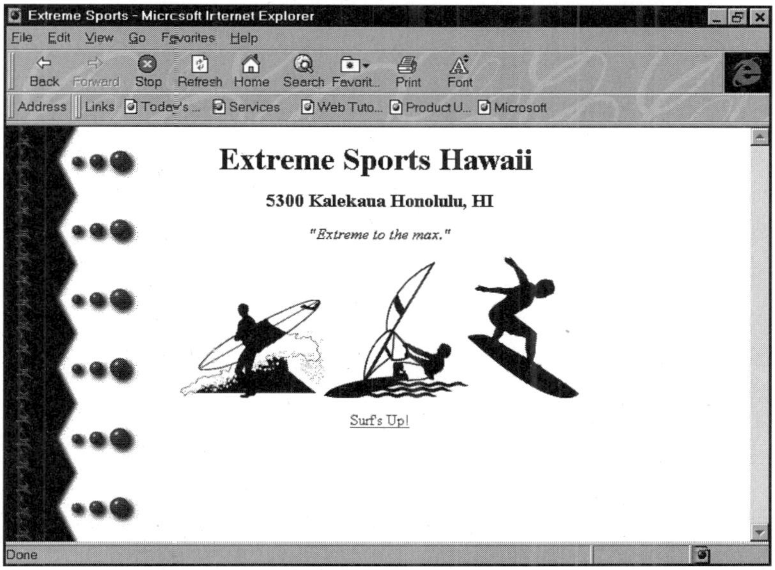

Using Background Colors

Sometimes what your pages need is a splash of color. With the BGCOLOR attribute, you can specify a color for the background. The background color can be expressed as a hexadecimal value or a color name:

```
<BODY BGCOLOR="#00FF00">

<BODY BGCOLOR="BLUE">
```

Basic color combinations using hexadecimal values are shown in Table 5.1. Hexadecimal color values are different from the decimal color values you may be used to seeing. Decimal values allow for 256 colors by using the values 0 to 255, but hexadecimal values allow for 256 colors by using the base 16 numbering system from 00 to FF. For example, the decimal value 0 in hexadecimal is 00, and the decimal value 255 in hexadecimal is FF. By combining values or slightly altering them to create darker or lighter shades, you can create a rainbow of colors.

Table 5.1. Using hexadecimal color values.

Color	*Hexadecimal Values*
Black	00 00 00
Blue	00 00 FF
Brown	99 66 33
Cream	FF FB F0
Cyan	00 FF FF
Dark Blue	00 00 80
Dark Gray	80 80 80
Dark Green	00 80 00
Dark Purple	80 00 80
Dark Red	80 00 00
Dark Yellow	80 80 00
Grass Green	C0 DC C0
Green	00 FF 00
Light Gray	C0 C0 C0
Medium Gray	A0 A0 A4
Purple	FF 00 FF
Red	FF 00 00
Sky Blue	A6 CA F0
White	FF FF FF
Yellow	00 FF FF

The following pages use a background color specified as a hexadecimal value:

```
<HTML>
<HEAD>
<TITLE>Sample Page 2</TITLE>
</HEAD>
<BODY BGCOLOR="#FFFFFF">
 . . .
</BODY>
</HTML>
```

Using a predefined color name is the easiest option; you simply select a color name from a list of accepted ones, shown in Table 5.2.

Table 5.2. The 16 accepted color names for text and backgrounds.

Aqua
Black
Blue
Fuchsia
Gray
Green
Lime
Maroon
Navy
Olive
Purple
Red
Silver
Teal
White
Yellow

This page uses a background color specified as a color name:

```
<HTML>
<HEAD>
<TITLE>Sample Page 2</TITLE>
</HEAD>
<BODY BGCOLOR="WHITE">
 . . .
</BODY>
</HTML>
```

TIP

You can use the BGCOLOR attribute with the BACKGROUND attribute to specify which color to use when the background image can't be displayed. If the background image can't be displayed for some reason, such as the user turning off the browser's auto-load image feature, the background color you specified is displayed. Also, if you don't specify a background color and the image you specified can't be displayed, the browser won't use your color assignments for text and links. This is a fail-safe to make sure you didn't specify text and link colors that would conflict with the standard gray background.

As with background images, the key to using background colors is to make sure the background color doesn't interfere with the page's readability. Figure 5.3 shows what a page showcased earlier in the chapter would look like with white as the background color. As you can see, the impact of the page isn't quite the same. However, a page with a colorful background certainly has more appeal than a plain gray background.

FIGURE 5.3.
Using a background color.

Specifying Default Text and Link Colors

Obviously, black text on a black background is unreadable, so when you use background images or colors, you need to specify the color for text and links to make sure they're readable. The page shown in Figure 5.4 has a black background with white text and red links.

FIGURE 5.4.
Adding color to text and links.

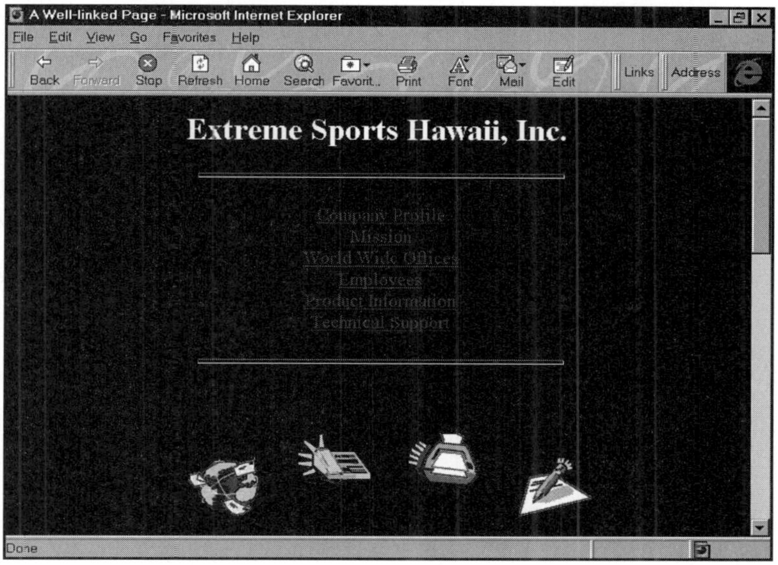

To assign colors to text and links, HTML 3.2 supports four additional attributes for the `<BODY>` tag. You can enter the colors as RGB values:

`TEXT="#rrggbb"`	Specifies the color for normal text
`LINK="#rrggbb"`	Specifies the color for links that are unvisited
`ALINK="#rrggbb"`	Specifies the color for active links
`VLINK="#rrggbb"`	Specifies the color for visited links

You can also specify any of the defined color names instead of a hexadecimal value:

`TEXT="White"`	Specifies the color for normal text as white
`LINK="Yellow"`	Specifies that unvisited links are yellow
`ALINK="Red"`	Specifies that active links are red
`VLINK="Blue"`	Specifies that visited links are blue

Color name values could be used in a sample page as follows:

```
<HTML>
<HEAD>
<TITLE>Sample Page 3</TITLE>
</HEAD>
<BODY BGCOLOR="BLUE" TEXT="WHITE" LINK="YELLOW" ALINK="GRAY" VLINK="SILVER">
 . . .
</BODY>
</HTML>
```

TIP

Using the Internet Explorer 2.0/3.0 extension for background properties, you can create background patterns that don't scroll. Nonscrolling background patterns are called *watermarks*, which are much more effective than the traditional scrolling backgrounds. To create a watermark, you specify a background image and set the `BGPROPERTIES` attribute as follows:

```
<BODY BACKGROUND="dazzle.gif" BGPROPERTIES=FIXED>
```

Layout Extras

HTML 3.2 supports many extensions for document layout. These extras include the following:

- Image extensions
- Center
- Element alignment
- Line break extensions
- Horizontal rule extensions

Image Extensions

HTML 3.2 supports powerful enhancements for images that help you precisely place images in your page. For example, the `LEFT` and `RIGHT` values can be used to align an image and a paragraph of associated text into columns. The `LEFT` value puts the image in the left margin and wraps the text around the right-hand side of the image. Conversely, the `RIGHT` value puts the image in the right margin and wraps the text around the left-hand side of the image.

By aligning text and images into columns with `ALIGN=LEFT` or `ALIGN=RIGHT`, you can lay out documents with styles that merge the image into the text of the document in more effective ways than were previously possible. To get the text to wrap around only the left or right side of the image, place the `<IMG>` tag as the first element in a short paragraph of text, as shown in Listing 5.1. A sample page using image alignment is shown in Figure 5.5.

Listing 5.1. `imageal.htm`.

```
<HTML>
<HEAD>
<TITLE>Aligning Images</TITLE>
</HEAD>
<BODY BGCOLOR="#FFFFFF">
<P><IMG SRC="Scompass.gif" ALIGN="RIGHT">
Text flows around the image on the left.</P>
<P><IMG SRC="Scompass.gif" ALIGN="LEFT">
```

```
Text flows around the image on the right.</P>
<P><IMG SRC="Scompass.gif" ALIGN="RIGHT">
Text flows around the image on the left.</P>
<P><IMG SRC="Scompass.gif" ALIGN="LEFT">
Text flows around the image on the right.</P>
</BODY>
</HTML>
```

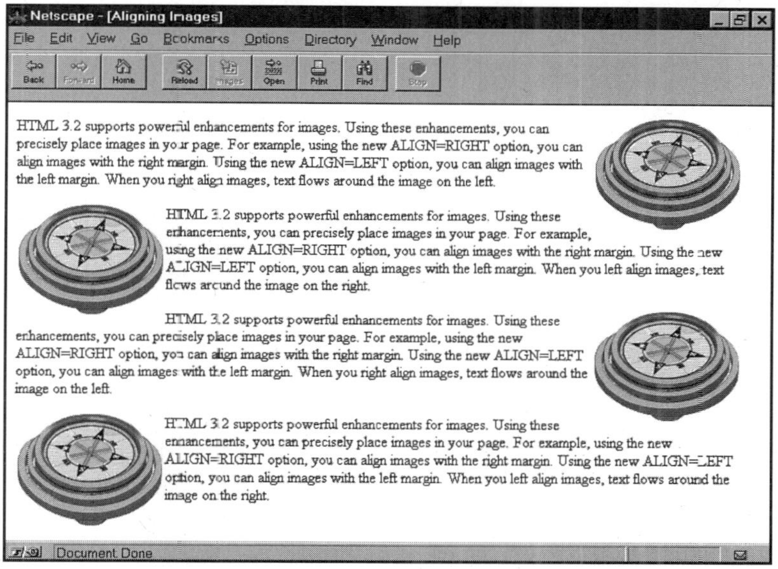

FIGURE 5.5.
Text flows around left- or right-aligned images.

Images and text are aligned with minimal spacing, which sometimes makes the text difficult to read. One way to increase the spacing and make the image more useful is to include the image in a hypertext reference. The image will then have a border around it that clearly separates it from the associated text, and it can also be clicked on.

The `WIDTH` and `HEIGHT` attributes can also be used to create better Web publications. Generally, these attributes are used together to resize an image according to the values you assign. By default, the numeric value you associate with the width and height for an image is a number of pixels.

The original size of the compass shown in Figure 5.5 is 150×119. By defining a new width and height, the image can be shrunk:

```
<IMG SRC="scompass.gif" ALT="" WIDTH=100 HEIGHT=75>
```

You can also enlarge it:

```
<IMG SRC="scompass.gif" ALT="" WIDTH=200 HEIGHT=150>
```

The ability to shrink or enlarge images on the fly is very useful. You can create a menu of consistently sized images without having to create new files containing the resized images. You can then reuse the same images later in the document at their original size or sized to suit your needs, without having to load new image files. This is convenient for you and reduces your document's download time.

NOTE

In addition to the HTML 2.0 and 3.2 alignment values, Netscape and Internet Explorer supports the following unique extensions:

```
ALIGN=TEXTTOP
ALIGN=ABSMIDDLE
ALIGN=ABSBOTTOM
ALIGN=BASELINE
```

The Netscape image alignment values behave exactly as their names imply they should. The value of `TEXTTOP` aligns the top of the image with the top of the tallest element in the line of text associated with the image; the value of `ABSMIDDLE` aligns the center of the image with the center of the line of text associated with it; the value of `ABSBOTTOM` aligns the bottom of the image with the bottom of the line of text associated with the image; and the value of `BASELINE` aligns the base of the image with the baseline of the text associated with the image, which is exactly how the value of `BOTTOM` handles text and image alignment. Internet Explorer doesn't recognize these alignment values.

Keep in mind that other browsers might ignore the unique alignment values and display your images with the default alignment value of `BOTTOM`. Consequently, you should use the Netscape alignment values only on pages that will be displayed by the Netscape browser or when the alignment of the image and text isn't critical.

Other HTML 3.2 innovations for images include these attributes:

```
BORDER
HSPACE
VSPACE
```

The `BORDER` attribute specifies the pixel size of the border to be drawn around an image. Here's how you can add an image with a border five pixels wide surrounding it:

```
<IMG SRC="../graphics/windows.jpeg" BORDER=5>
```

Generally, borders are visible if the image is anchored to the page as a hypertext link and invisible if the image isn't anchored to the page. You can use the `BORDER` attribute to add white space around images that aren't links and to build a picture frame around images that are links. Although both techniques enhance the image's impact, you can also remove the border around linked images by specifying the value of `BORDER=0`.

Figure 5.6 shows a 10-pixel-wide border around an image. Here is the markup for this page:

```
<HTML>
<HEAD>
<TITLE>The Cool Cars Page</TITLE>
</HEAD>
<BODY BGCOLOR="#FFFFFF">
<CENTER>
<H2>Cool Cars</H2>
<IMG SRC="cool.jpg" BORDER="10">
</CENTER>
</BODY>
</HTML>
```

FIGURE 5.6.
Using borders around your images.

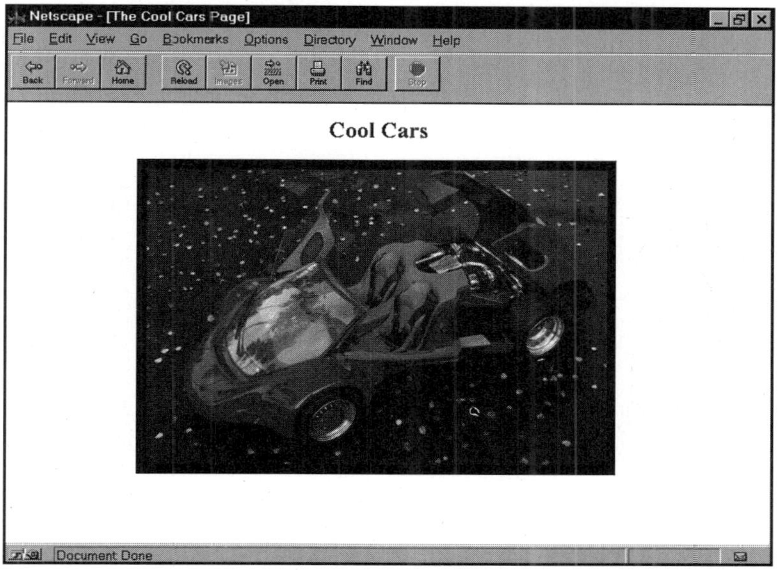

NOTE

The way borders are displayed is browser-dependent. For example, Internet Explorer 3.0 doesn't display borders around images that aren't links, but Netscape Navigator 3.0 does.

The attributes HSPACE and VSPACE are used to increase the amount of white space surrounding the image. HSPACE increases the pixel size of the horizontal margins surrounding the image, and VSPACE increases the pixel size of the vertical margins. These attributes are used to put white space between multiple images or text. You can use these attributes as follows:

```
<IMG SRC="sunset.gif" HSPACE=12 VSPACE=6>
```

NOTE

The discussion on images in this section is only a preliminary one. After reading this section, you should be familiar with the attributes used with images, but not necessarily a design expert. For detailed coverage of images and graphic design, refer to Part IV, "Enhancing Web Pages with Graphics."

Centering Text and Graphics

Centered text and graphics is a Netscape innovation fully supported by HTML 3.2. With the <CENTER> tag, you can center any objects defined between the begin and end <CENTER> tags. The <CENTER> tag is useful for centering sections of your page that include text and objects.

Many of the previous examples in this chapter use the <CENTER> tag. Listing 5.2 shows how the text and images in the Earth!First example are centered.

Listing 5.2. earth.htm.

```
<HTML>
<HEAD>
<TITLE>Wildlife Educational Center</TITLE>
</HEAD>
<BODY BGCOLOR="White">
<CENTER>
<IMG SRC="Gold1e.gif">
<IMG SRC="Gold1a.gif">
<IMG SRC="Gold1r.gif">
<IMG SRC="Gold1t.gif">
<IMG SRC="Gold1h.gif">
<IMG SRC="Gold1_!.gif">
<IMG SRC="Gold1f.gif">
<IMG SRC="Gold1i.gif">
<IMG SRC="Gold1r.gif">
<IMG SRC="Gold1s.gif">
<IMG SRC="Gold1t.gif">
<P ALIGN="CENTER">
<IMG SRC="Earth1.gif"></P>
<CENTER>
<H1><A HREF="enter.htm">Join Us!</A></H1>
</CENTER>
</BODY>
</HTML>
```

Figure 5.7 shows another use of the <CENTER> tag; the markup for this page is given in Listing 5.3.

FIGURE 5.7.
The <CENTER> *tag is great for centering text and graphics.*

Listing 5.3. `coffee.htm`.

```
<HTML>
<HEAD>
<TITLE>Java World Coffee</TITLE>
</HEAD>
<BODY BACKGROUND="BACK/coffee_g.gif" TEXT="#FFFFFF">
<CENTER>
<IMG SRC="IMAGES/coffee_a.gif" ALIGN="bottom" ALT=" [ Java World Coffee ]"><BR>
<I>&quot;The Juice that fuels the World<I>&quot;</I><BR>

<A HREF="products.htm">
<IMG SRC="IMAGES/coffee_e.gif" ALIGN="bottom" ALT="[ Products ]" BORDER="0">
</A>

<A HREF="location.htm">
<IMG SRC="IMAGES/coffee_d.gif" ALIGN="bottom" ALT="[ Locations] " BORDER="0">
</A>

<A HREF="hot.htm">
<IMG SRC="IMAGES/coffee_f.gif" ALIGN="bottom" ALT="[ What's Hot ]" BORDER="0">
</A>

<A HREF="contact.htm">
<IMG SRC="IMAGES/coffee_c.gif" ALIGN="bottom" ALT="[ Contact ]" BORDER="0">
</A>

</CENTER>
</BODY>
</HTML>
```

Element Alignment

With HTML 3.2, you can more precisely align elements on the page. Take a look at element alignments for page divisions, headers, and paragraphs.

Aligning Divisions

Traditional documents are divided into a table of contents, chapters, appendixes, bibliographies, and glossaries. These major sections are usually broken down into subsections corresponding to major topics. In HTML 2.0, there's no way to represent these traditional document sections by using formats specific to the section element. HTML 3.2 corrects this shortcoming with the `<DIV>` tag to specify sections of the document.

Using the `ALIGN` attribute with the `<DIV>` tag, you can specify the alignment for a section of your document. The capability to align an entire section is a feature in high demand by Web publishers.

> **NOTE**
>
> According to the HTML 3.2 specification, the alignment of a division applies only to text associated with block elements, which includes paragraphs and lists but not headings and images. This is supposed to let you align headings and images as needed, without worrying whether you're going to conflict with the alignment of the division. However, most current browsers align all elements in a division, meaning that all block text, headings, and graphics follow the division's alignment.

HTML 3.2 specifies three values for the `ALIGN` attribute. All elements in this division are flush left:

```
<DIV ALIGN=LEFT>
  . . .
</DIV>
```

All elements in this division are flush right:

```
<DIV ALIGN=RIGHT>
  . . .
</DIV>
```

All elements in this division are centered:

```
<DIV ALIGN=CENTER>
  . . .
</DIV>
```

NOTE

The alignment assigned to elements in the division always overrides the alignment set for the division. This means that if the division alignment is flush right and you use the <CENTER> tag to center an image in the division, the image will be centered.

Aligning Headings and Paragraphs

In HTML 3.2, you can align headings and paragraphs, too, with the three alignment values. The default alignment for headings and paragraphs is flush left.

To center a heading, you could use the following:

```
<H1 ALIGN=CENTER> A centered heading </H1>
```

To right-align a paragraph, you could use this:

```
<P ALIGN=RIGHT> This paragraph is aligned with the right margin. </P>
```

NOTE

Because paragraph text can be aligned based on the ALIGN attribute, I recommend you use the begin and end paragraph tags so you have a clear understanding of what text will be aligned and what text won't be aligned.

Figure 5.8 shows a cool HTML 3.2-enhanced page that uses division, heading, and paragraph alignment. The markup for the page is shown in Listing 5.4.

Listing 5.4. htmlfaq.htm.

```
<HTML>
<HEAD>
<TITLE>The HTML Publishing FAQ</TITLE>
</HEAD>
<BODY BACKGROUND="BACK/FAQS.GIF" TEXT="#000000">
<DIV ALIGN=CENTER>

<IMG SRC="IMAGES/FAQTITLE.GIF" BORDER="0">
<H2>The HTML Publishing FAQ</H2>

<IMG SRC="DIVIDERS/LINE2.GIF" BORDER="0" HEIGHT="5" WIDTH="400">

<H3 ALIGN="LEFT">
<IMG BORDER="0" ALIGN="MIDDLE" HSPACE="20" SRC="IMAGES/REDQ.GIF">
<A HREF="#TOPIC1">What is HTML?</A></H3>
```

continues

Listing 5.4. continued

```
<H3 ALIGN="RIGHT">
<A HREF="#TOPIC2">What are the Features of HTML?</A>
<IMG BORDER="0" ALIGN="MIDDLE" HSPACE="20" SRC="IMAGES/YELQ.GIF">
</H3>

<H3 ALIGN="LEFT">
<IMG BORDER="0" ALIGN="MIDDLE" HSPACE="20" SRC="IMAGES/BLUEQ.GIF">
<A HREF="#TOPIC3">What is Netscape?</A>
</H3>
<IMG BORDER="0" HEIGHT="5" WIDTH="400" SRC="DIVIDERS/LINE2.GIF">
</DIV>

<DIV ALIGN=CENTER>
<P>The Full Text of the FAQ</P>
</DIV>
</BODY>
</HTML>
```

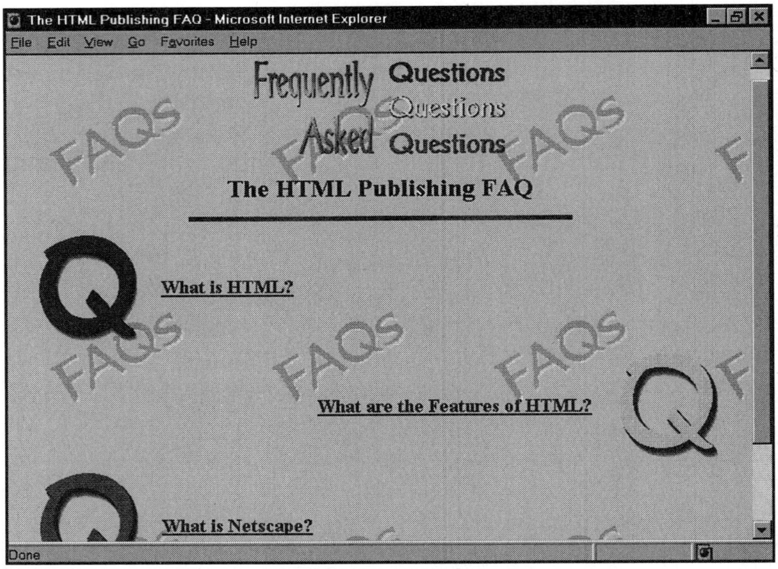

FIGURE 5.8
Aligning elements on the page.

Line Break Extensions

The <BR> tag is useful when you're aligning images and text. Using the <BR> tag and the new CLEAR attribute, you can insert a clean break into the column of text associated with the image. The text before the <BR> tag will be aligned with the image in a column, and the text after the <BR> tag will be inserted after the margin is clear.

HTML 3.2 supports these values for clearing margins:

```
<BR CLEAR=LEFT>
<BR CLEAR=RIGHT>
<BR CLEAR=ALL>
```

An example using line breaks is shown in Figure 5.9. As you can see, if an image is aligned with the left margin, you should use a value of `CLEAR=LEFT` with the `<BR>` tag. This ensures that text following the line break clears the left margin. Similarly, if the image is aligned with the right margin, you should use a value of `CLEAR=RIGHT` with the `<BR>` tag to make sure the text following the line break clears the right margin. To clear both margins, use a value of `CLEAR=ALL`.

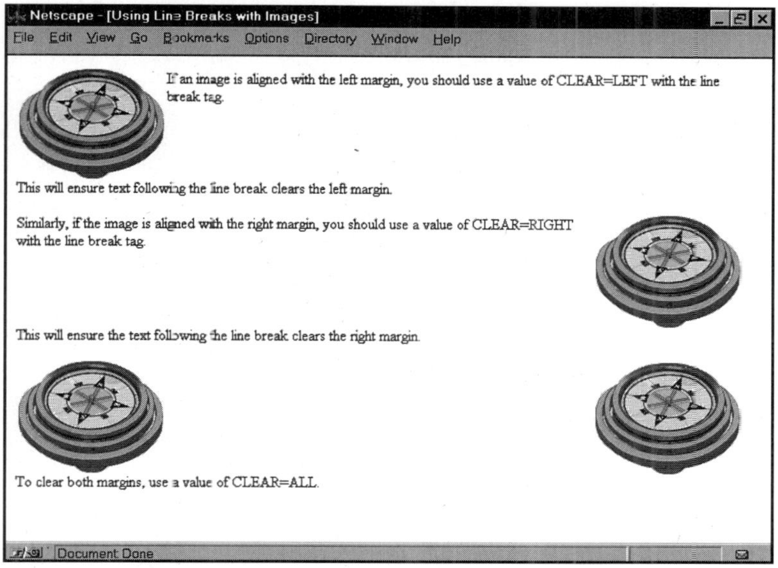

FIGURE 5.9.
Using line breaks with images.

Horizontal Rule Extensions

Horizontal rules become helpful design tools with HTML 3.2. You can use the `SIZE` attribute to make the separation of topics and subtopics on your pages more distinct. The size of a horizontal rule is defined in terms of pixels, as in the following:

```
<HR SIZE=5>
```

A five-pixel size for the horizontal rule isn't very thick. To get a thicker rule, try using a size of 10:

```
<HR SIZE=10>
```

To separate topics and subtopics visually, you could use one size value for main topics and another size value for each level of subtopics. You should experiment with rule sizes in your publications. Five pixels is usually enough to separate main topics, and two pixels is enough for subtopics. Figure 5.10 shows a sample page with horizontal rules of different sizes.

Figure 5.10.
The size of horizontal rules is in pixels.

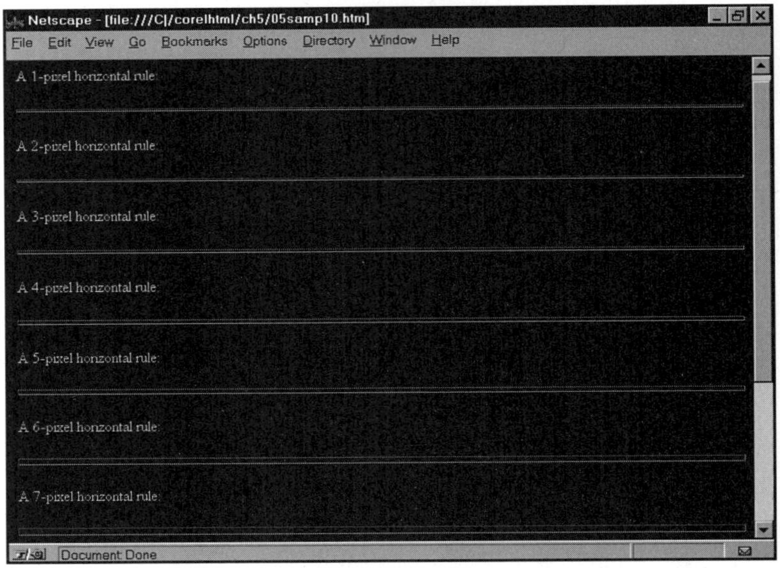

Horizontal rules normally look engraved on the page, but you can define rules without shading by using the `NOSHADE` attribute. You could create a nonshaded rule as follows:

```
<HR SIZE=2 NOSHADE>
```

Other unique attributes for horizontal rules include `ALIGN` and `WIDTH`. These attributes are best used with each other. Using the `ALIGN` attribute, you can align a horizontal rule with the left margin, right margin, or center of the page with the values `ALIGN=LEFT`, `ALIGN=RIGHT`, and `ALIGN=CENTER`, respectively. Using the `WIDTH` attribute, you can define the length of the horizontal rule in pixels or as a percentage of the browser's window width:

```
<HR WIDTH=10>
```

```
<HR WIDTH=5%>
```

More examples of horizontal rules are shown in Figure 5.11. The markup for this page is shown in Listing 5.5.

Listing 5.5. `morehr.htm`.

```
<HTML>
<HEAD>
<TITLE>More Horizontal Rule Examples</TITLE>
</HEAD>
<BODY BGCOLOR="#000000" TEXT="#FFFFFF">
<P>These horizontal rules have no shading:</P>
<HR SIZE="5" NOSHADE>
<HR SIZE="5" NOSHADE>
<P>A horizontal rule 50 pixels in length:</P>
<HR SIZE="5" WIDTH=50>
<P>The length of this horizontal rule is 50 percent of the current window size:</P>
<HR SIZE="5" WIDTH=50%>
<P>By default, horizontal rules are centered, you can change this if you want:</P>
<HR SIZE="5" ALIGN=LEFT WIDTH=50%>
<HR SIZE="5" ALIGN=RIGHT WIDTH=50%>
<HR SIZE="5" ALIGN=LEFT WIDTH=50%>
<HR SIZE="5" ALIGN=RIGHT WIDTH=50%>
</BODY>
</HTML>
```

FIGURE 5.11.
Adjusting the length of horizontal rules in your pages.

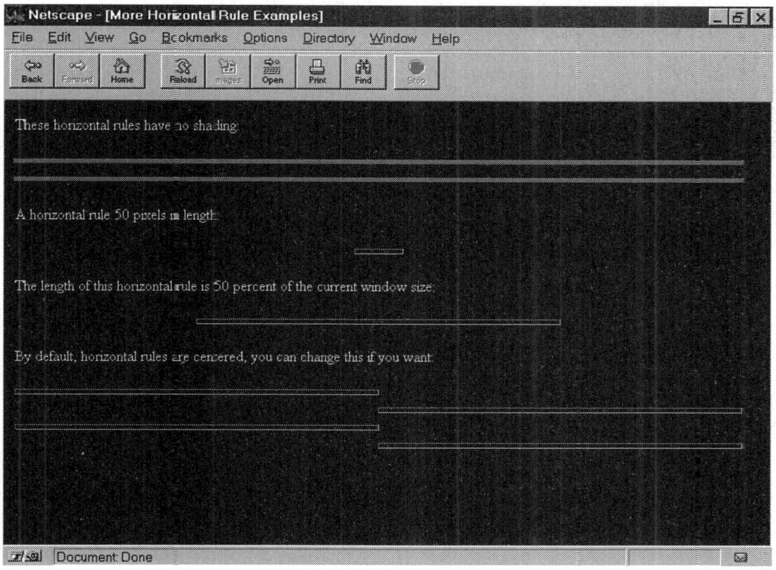

By combining the horizontal rule attributes, you can create powerful effects, such as the one shown in Figure 5.12. The code for the example is shown in Listing 5.6.

Listing 5.6. fancyhr.htm.

```
<HTML>
<HEAD>
<TITLE>Fancy Horizontal Rules</TITLE>
</HEAD>
<BODY BGCOLOR="#FFFFFF">
<HR ALIGN=CENTER SIZE=2 WIDTH=65>
<HR ALIGN=CENTER SIZE=3 WIDTH=75>
<HR ALIGN=CENTER SIZE=4 WIDTH=85>
<HR ALIGN=CENTER SIZE=5 WIDTH=95>
<HR ALIGN=CENTER SIZE=4 WIDTH=105>
<HR ALIGN=CENTER SIZE=3 WIDTH=115>
<HR ALIGN=CENTER SIZE=2 WIDTH=125>
<H1 ALIGN=CENTER>Welcome!</H1>
<HR ALIGN=CENTER SIZE=2 WIDTH=125>
<HR ALIGN=CENTER SIZE=3 WIDTH=115>
<HR ALIGN=CENTER SIZE=4 WIDTH=105>
<HR ALIGN=CENTER SIZE=5 WIDTH=95>
<HR ALIGN=CENTER SIZE=4 WIDTH=85>
<HR ALIGN=CENTER SIZE=3 WIDTH=75>
<HR ALIGN=CENTER SIZE=2 WIDTH=65>
</BODY>
</HTML>
```

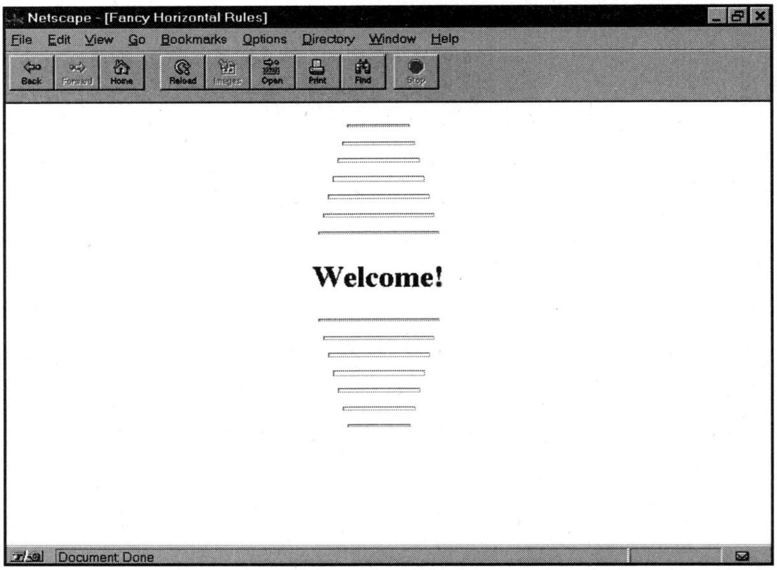

FIGURE 5.12.
Using fancy horizontal rules.

NOTE

Remember, browsers that aren't HTML 3.2-compliant ignore the sizing and alignment values for horizontal rules. These browsers display the multiple horizontal rules in the example as ordinary horizontal rules. Therefore, it's best to use multiple horizontal rules only on pages that will be displayed by HTML 3.2-compliant browsers.

Font Enhancements

HTML 3.2 introduces many useful font enhancements. All these enhancements are defined for use with the `<FONT>` tag, which is used with a begin and end tag. The next sections explore enhancements for the `<FONT>` tag one by one.

Defining Font Size

In the HTML 2.0 specification, there's no way to define a specific font size to use, primarily because the font size is controlled by configurations in the user's browser, and the user is the one who selects the font size she wants to use for viewing Web documents. Using different heading levels, Web publishers had some control over font size in graphical browsers. Generally, a Level One heading could be used to create text 8 to 10 point sizes larger than regular text, a Level Two heading for text 6 to 8 point sizes larger than regular text, and so on. However, this still didn't give Web publishers accurate control over font sizes, especially if the publisher wanted to change font size in the middle of a line of text.

HTML 3.2 corrects this shortcoming by allowing Web publishers to finally define font size. All font sizes are specified as relative values between `1` and `7`. A value of `1` is used for the smallest text, and a value of `7` is used for the largest text. The default value for font size is `3`, which corresponds to the size of standard text.

The following example shows how to set the font size to a specific value:

```
<FONT SIZE=4><P>This line of text is larger than normal</P></FONT>
```

You can also set the font size in relation to the size used with the current text element. To do this, precede the size value by + or – to indicate a relative change in the font size. Here, two relative font sizes are used to adjust the size of the text:

```
<P>Normal text is displayed in font size 3.
<FONT SIZE=-2><P>Text is displayed in font size 1.</P></FONT>
<FONT SIZE=+2><P>Text is displayed in font size 5.</P></FONT>
```

Being able to adjust the font size is very handy. A small font size is useful for disclaimers or copyright notices that you want to display but not take up too much space on the page. A large font size is useful when you want to draw attention to specific keywords or paragraphs of text.

You can adjust the font size to create a large first letter for keywords or the first word in a paragraph, which is called a *drop cap*, a design technique used by many Web publishers. These effects are shown in Figure 5.13. The markup for the example is listed in Listing 5.7.

Listing 5.7. fontex.htm.

```
<HTML>
<HEAD>
<TITLE>Using Font Sizes</TITLE>
</HEAD>
<BODY TEXT="#000000" BGCOLOR="#FFFFFF">
<P>Being able to <FONT SIZE="+3">adjust</FONT> the font size is very handy.</P>
<P></P>
<P><FONT SIZE="2">A small font size is useful for disclaimers or
copyright notices you want to place on the page, but do not want
to eat up page space.</FONT></P>
<P></P>
<P><FONT SIZE="5">A large font size is useful when you want to draw
attention to specific keywords or paragraphs of text.</FONT></P>
<P></P>
<P><FONT SIZE="+7">Y</FONT>ou can adjust the font size to create a large
first letter for keywords or the first word in a paragraph, which is
called a drop cap. </P>
<P><FONT SIZE="+7">D</FONT>rop caps are a design technique used
by many Web publishers.</P>
</BODY>
</HTML>
```

FIGURE 5.13.
Using different font sizes.

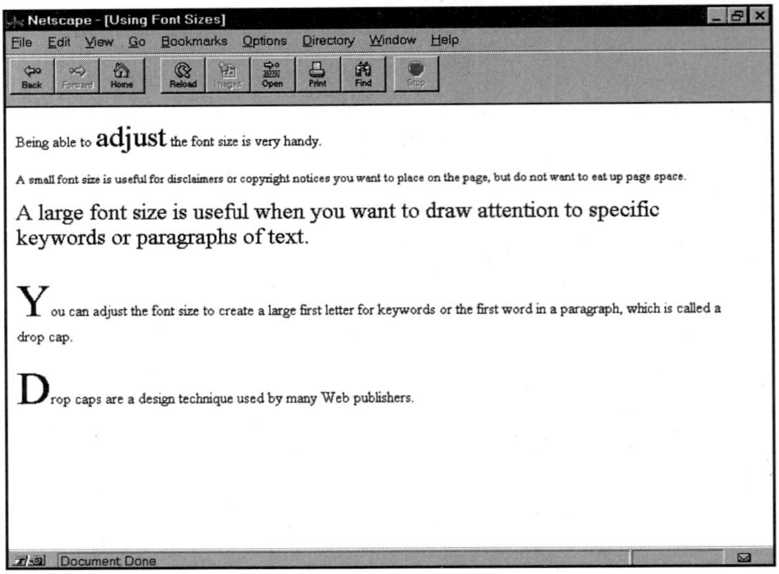

As shown in Figure 5.14, you can also create word art by adjusting the font size within words or sentences. Listing 5.8 contains the markup for the word art example.

Listing 5.8. `relfonts.htm`.

```
<HTML>
<HEAD>
<TITLE>Using Relative Font Sizes</TITLE>
</HEAD>
<BODY BGCOLOR="#000000" TEXT="#FFFFFF">
<HR SIZE=5 NOSHADE WIDTH=50%>
<HR SIZE=5 NOSHADE WIDTH=75%>
<CENTER>
<H1>
<FONT SIZE=-2>T</FONT>
<FONT SIZE=-1>H</FONT>
<FONT SIZE=+0>E</FONT>

<FONT SIZE=+1>H</FONT>
<FONT SIZE=+2>O</FONT>
<FONT SIZE=+3>T</FONT>
<FONT SIZE=+4>T</FONT>
<FONT SIZE=+4>E</FONT>
<FONT SIZE=+3>S</FONT>
<FONT SIZE=+2>T</FONT>

<FONT SIZE=+1>P</FONT>
<FONT SIZE=+0>A</FONT>
<FONT SIZE=-1>G</FONT>
<FONT SIZE=-2>E</FONT>
</H1>
<H1>
<FONT SIZE=+4>H</FONT>
<FONT SIZE=+3>T</FONT>
<FONT SIZE=+2>M</FONT>
<FONT SIZE=+1>L</FONT>

<FONT SIZE=+1>3</FONT>
<FONT SIZE=+2>.</FONT>
<FONT SIZE=+3>2</FONT>
</H1>
<H1>
<FONT SIZE=+1>E</FONT>
<FONT SIZE=+2>N</FONT>
<FONT SIZE=+3>H</FONT>
<FONT SIZE=+4>A</FONT>
<FONT SIZE=+4>N</FONT>
<FONT SIZE=+3>C</FONT>
<FONT SIZE=+2>E</FONT>
<FONT SIZE=+1>D</FONT>
</H1>
</CENTER>
<HR SIZE=5 NOSHADE WIDTH=75%>
<HR SIZE=5 NOSHADE WIDTH=50%>
</BODY>
</HTML>
```

Defining Font Colors

Until recently, the font color used in your documents was either black by default or set by users to a specific color, if their browsers supported a color option. HTML 3.2 has a way for Web publishers to control font color anywhere in the text of the document. Using the `COLOR` attribute for the `<FONT>` tag, you can set the color in one of two ways:

- With a predefined color name, such as this one:

  ```
  <FONT COLOR="RED">
  ```

  See Table 5.2 for a complete list of color names.

- With a hexadecimal value to represent the red, green, and blue content of the color. The basic form of the value is preceded by a number sign:

  ```
  <FONT COLOR=#rrggbb>
  ```

  It's used as follows:

  ```
  <FONT COLOR=#00FF00>
  ```

  See Table 5.1 for a sample of color values.

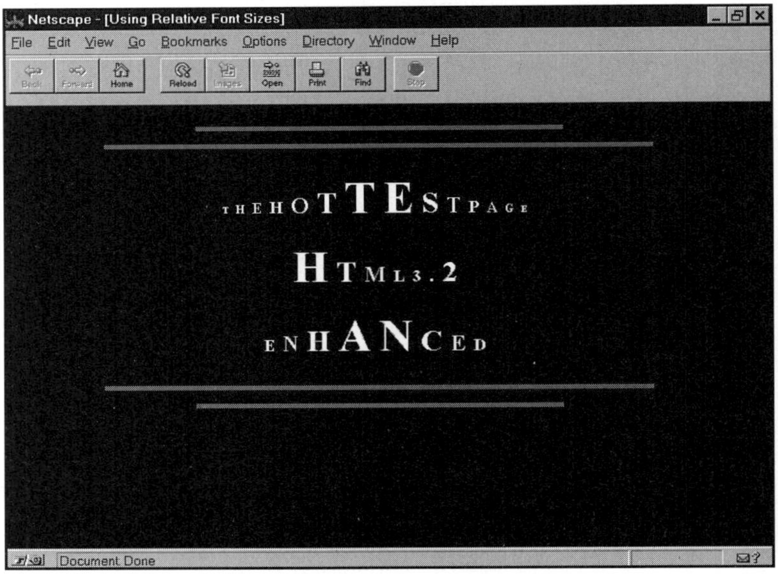

FIGURE 5.14.
Creating word art with relative fonts.

USING COLORFUL FONTS

Although the capability to assign font colors is useful, using color in publications has always caused problems. Some color combinations just don't go together–such as purple, green, and hot pink text all on the same Web page. Don't use color in your publication just because you can–rather, use color as a design technique to enhance your page.

When using colorful text in Web publications, you should follow three general rules:

- Use basic colors for text wherever possible, like black, gray, red, yellow, green, blue, and white.
- Make sure your font colors can be read on the background you've chosen.
- Limit the number of colors you use on any single page, and, if practical, follow the same color scheme throughout your publication. Four colors are usually enough.

Adding Visual Variety to Your Documents in HTML 3.2

With HTML 3.2, you can add more variety to the text part of your page by using strikethrough, big, small, superscript, and subscript text. The associated tags highlight your text, but they don't insert white space into the document. This makes it possible to use character style tags within other tags to highlight a single word or a group of words.

When you're creating a document, often you want some text to be larger than the surrounding text. The only way you could do this in HTML 2.0 was to use a header tag, which isn't how header tags are intended to be used and could cause problems with older browsers, such as Lynx. In HTML 3.2, Web publishers no longer have this problem. Text highlighted with <BIG> is displayed in a larger-than-normal font on the page:

```
<BIG> Large text </BIG>
```

As a Web publisher, sometimes you want sections of small text for copyright notices, disclaimers, or other legal notes in your documents. Text highlighted with <SMALL> is displayed in a smaller-than-normal font on the page:

```
<SMALL> Small text </SMALL>
```

A basic addition to HTML 3.2 is strikethrough text, which is displayed by browsers as text with a line drawn through it. You can define strikethrough text as follows:

```
<S> Strikethrough text </S>
```

Another useful addition to HTML 3.2 is subscripts and superscripts. Subscript text, displayed by browsers in a subscript font, is defined by using the begin and end <SUB> tags; superscript text, displayed by browsers in a superscript font, is defined by using the begin and end <SUP> tags. You can use subscript and superscript as follows:

```
<SUB> Subscript text </SUB>
<SUP> Superscript text </SUP>
```

Figure 5.15 shows an example of the new HTML 3.2 text styles. The markup for the example is given in Listing 5.9.

Listing 5.9. `newstyle.htm`.

```
<HTML>
<HEAD>
<TITLE>Using New HTML 3.2 Text Styles</TITLE>
</HEAD>
<BODY BGCOLOR="#FFFFFF">
<HR SIZE=5 NOSHADE>
<P>Text highlighted with &lt;BIG&gt; is displayed in a larger font
than normal paragraph text on the page:
<P>While this is normal text, <BIG> this is large text.</BIG>
<HR SIZE=5 NOSHADE>
<P>Text highlighted with &lt;SMALL&gt; is displayed in a smaller font
than normal paragraph text on the page:
<P>See the difference between normal text <SMALL> and small text.</SMALL> Yes?
<HR SIZE=5 NOSHADE>
<P><S>Strikethrough text should be displayed by browsers with a line
through it.</S>
<HR SIZE=5 NOSHADE>
<P>Another useful addition to HTML 3.2 are
su<SUB>bscrip</SUB>ts and su<SUP>perscrip</SUP>ts.
Subscript text is displayed by browsers in a <SUB>subscript</SUB> font.
Superscript text is displayed by browsers in a <SUP>superscript</SUP> font.
<HR SIZE=5 NOSHADE>
</BODY>
</HTML>
```

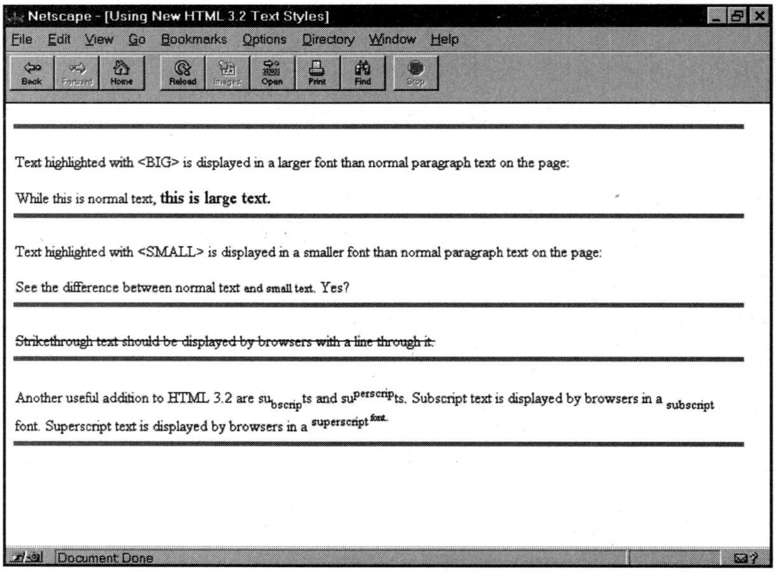

FIGURE 5.15.
New text styles in HTML 3.2.

List Enhancements

HTML 3.2 offers several useful extensions for lists. Using the TYPE attribute, you define the bullet shape to use for unordered lists and the style of lettering or numbering to use for ordered lists.

For unordered lists, you can use these values with the unordered list tag:

`<UL TYPE=CIRCLE>`	Use an open circle for the bullet
`<UL TYPE=SQUARE>`	Use a square for the bullet
`<UL TYPE=DISC>`	Use a solid circle for the bullet, which is the default

An unordered list using these attributes is shown in Figure 5.16. As you can see from the example, each type of bullet—the open circle, square, and solid circle—has a distinct appearance.

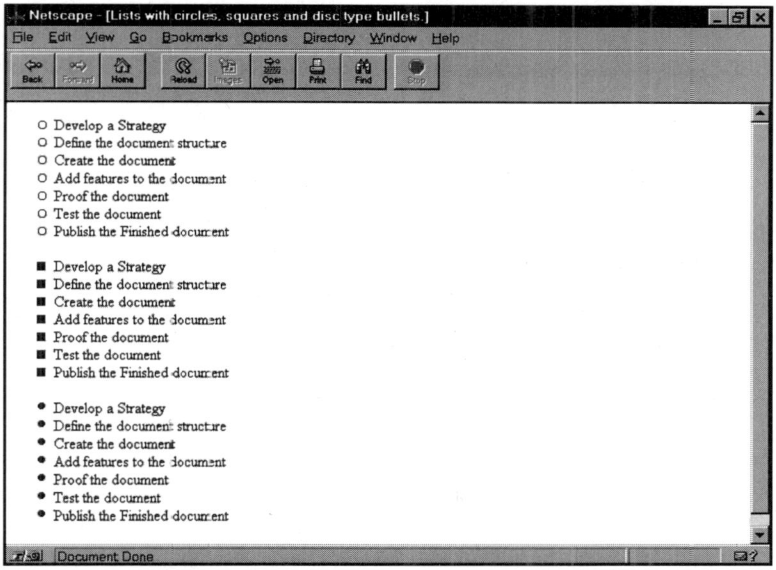

FIGURE 5.16.
Defining bullet shapes for unordered lists in HTML 3.2.

The default values used for ordered lists are numerals. When you nest ordered lists, the numerals change to an appropriate level for outlines. You can override this sequencing with the following attributes:

`<OL TYPE=A>`	Use capital letters for the ordered list elements
`<OL TYPE=a>`	Use lowercase letters for the ordered list elements
`<OL TYPE=I>`	Use Roman numerals for the ordered list elements
`<OL TYPE=i>`	Use lowercase Roman numerals for the ordered list elements
`<OL TYPE=1>`	Use numerals for the ordered list elements, which is the default

Figure 5.17 shows two ordered lists—the first uses Roman numerals and the second capital letters.

You can set items in an ordered list to start at a specific value by using the START attribute. You assign a numeric value to the START attribute even if you're using letters or Roman numerals for your ordered list. This code specifies that the list will start with the capital letter D:

```
<OL TYPE=A START=4>
```

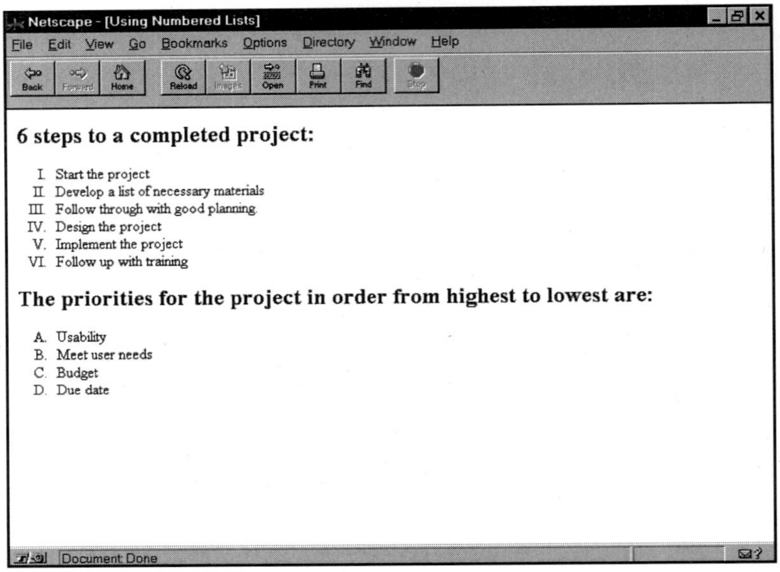

FIGURE 5.17.
Ordered lists in HTML 3.2.

Summary

As you have seen in this chapter, designing with HTML 3.2 is easy. HTML 3.2 features hot enhancements to the HTML specification that you can use to dramatically improve your documents' impact. Image enhancements allow you to create text flow around images, layout extras offer better control over positioning text and objects, font enhancements let you select font color and relative size, and body tag extensions allow you to use background images and colors.

CHAPTER 6

Effective Use of Tables

by William Robert Stanek

IN THIS CHAPTER

No doubt you've seen tables in publications, like those used throughout *Web Publishing Unleashed, Professional Reference Edition*, and you've probably used tables in your own documents as well. Tables are great for organizing and presenting information, so this chapter shows you how to create and effectively use them in your Web pages.

NOTE

Learning the most current information on HTML tables is extremely important. The table model has changed drastically since the original implementation. Consequently, this chapter describes tables as defined in the HTML 3 tables specification (RFC 1942). If you use tables as outlined in this section, your tables will be fully compliant with the HTML 3 tables specification and backward-compatible with HTML 3.2 browsers. Currently, Internet Explorer 3.0 is the only major browser to support most of the elements in the HTML 3 tables specification. The next major upgrades to Netscape Navigator and Internet Explorer should fully support this specification and display your tables precisely as outlined here. However, older browsers can use only attributes defined in their DTDs. Basically, this means your fully HTML 3-compliant tables will look best in a browser fully compliant with the table model.

Table Design

Tables are one of the most sought-after features in the HTML specification. In general, tables have a caption and one or more rows of data organized into columns. The columns of data contain individual cells, each of which is either a header or a data set. Although a table can have several levels of headings, all headings serve to identify the data sets in the table's body. Some tables also have footers, used to make annotations within the table. Therefore, tables have three basic parts: header, body, and footer.

After breaking tables into their component parts, developers of the table model looked at how the data in a table should be displayed by browsers—a major concern. Web publishers have no direct control over the size of the window used to display a table, which means table data defined in absolute terms, such as pixels or characters, could easily get obscured or clipped. To avoid this, developers made it possible to define column width in relative terms as well as absolute terms.

Defining a table in relative terms enables you to specify a size that's a percentage of the current window size. The browser displaying the table will size it accordingly, using the currently defined font. The default size for a table is the current window size, so if you don't specify a width for your table, the `WIDTH` attribute is set to 100 percent. However, tables created with the default sizing use only as much space as they need.

Another item developers of the table model considered is network speed versus table size. Under the original implementation, the entire table had to be downloaded before any part of it could be displayed. On a slow network or with a large table, the wait could be rather long—sometimes longer than a Web user is willing to wait. To alleviate this problem, the current table model allows for incremental downloading of tables if you specify the number of columns and their widths in the beginning table tag <TABLE>.

The table model is dynamic in other ways as well; you can do the following:

- Add images to your table by defining the image in a cell of your current table
- Add lists to your table by defining the list in a cell of your current table
- Build forms within your table by defining the form in a cell of your current table
- Create tables within your table by defining the new table in a cell of your current table

This chapter explores both traditional and creative uses for tables. Traditionally, tables are used to organize data sets such as those shown in Figure 6.1. The table shown in that figure is very useful, but tables can be powerful additions to your pages if you can think beyond the bounds of tradition. For example, the Discovery Web site shown in Figure 6.2 uses tables to add creative flair to its home page.

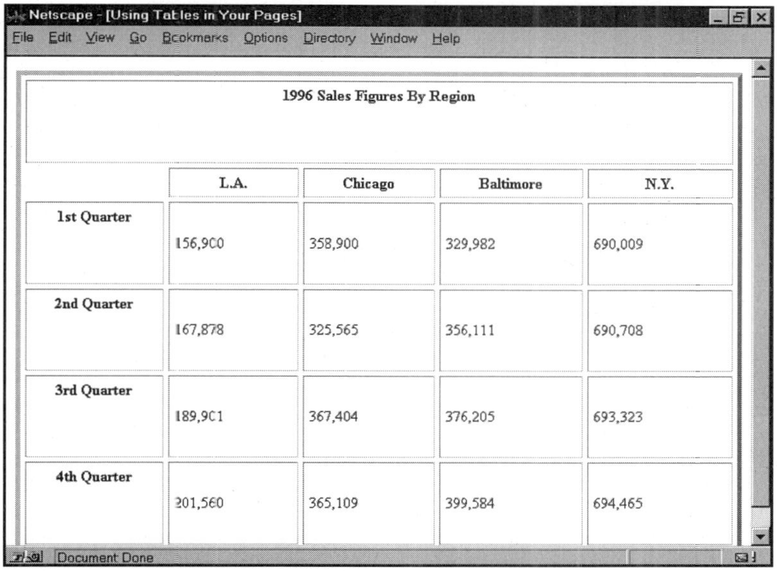

1996 Sales Figures By Region				
	L.A.	Chicago	Baltimore	N.Y.
1st Quarter	156,900	358,900	329,982	690,009
2nd Quarter	167,878	325,565	356,111	690,708
3rd Quarter	189,901	367,404	376,205	693,323
4th Quarter	201,560	365,109	399,584	694,465

FIGURE 6.1.
A traditional use of tables.

FIGURE 6.2.
Adding creative flair to your page with tables.

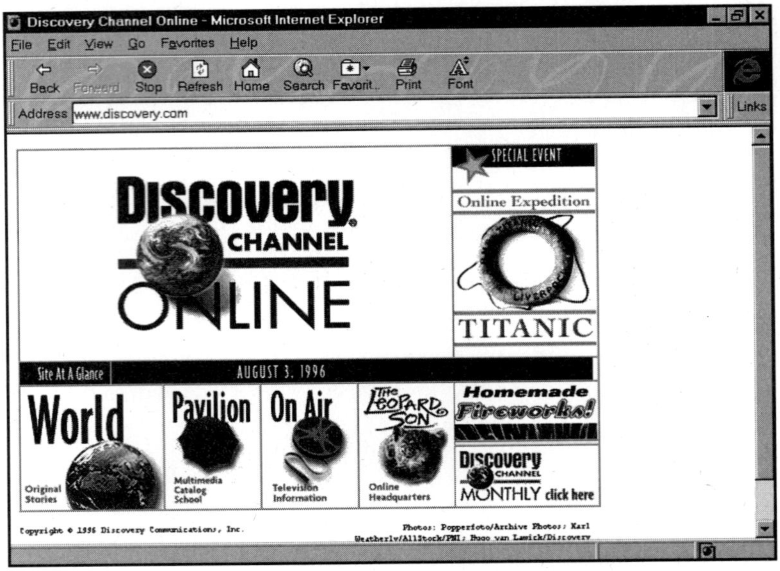

Building the Framework of Your Table

To build the framework for your table, you need to define its sections, including the header, body, and footer. Just as some of these parts are optional in traditional tables, they are also optional in HTML tables. The only mandatory part of a table is the table body. Each table you create can have one header section, one or more body sections, and one footer section. The most basic components of any table are the columns and rows that make up the table.

You specify the basic components of a table as follows:

```
<TABLE>
<THEAD>
Header Information
<TBODY>
Data Set 1
<TBODY>
Data Set 2
<TBODY>
 . . .
<TBODY>
Data Set N
<TFOOT>
Footer Information
</TABLE>
```

Many attributes are used to define what tables look like on the page and whether the table should be incrementally loaded. The following attributes are common to most table elements:

`CLASS` Specifies a subclass for a tag. `CLASS` is normally used to display a tag in a different style, based on a class type you've specified in a style sheet.

DIR	Specifies the direction for text layout. English text is read from left to right, but some Asian languages are read from right to left. Using DIR with the LANG attribute, you can specify the text layout as left to right by setting a value of DIR=LTR or as right to left by setting a value of DIR=RTL.
ID	Labels an element with a keyword. If you activate a hypertext reference containing a keyword that matches the element's ID, the browser jumps to the section of the document containing the ID.
LANG	Specifies the language to be used for the element. You can use this attribute with the optional DIR attribute if the language is read from right to left instead of left to right.
UNITS	Specifies the type of unit for all numeric values in the associated tag. The implied default is UNITS=PIXELS. You can also specify en units with UNITS=EN.

The <TABLE> Tag

The table model has advanced significantly since it was first drafted. In many ways, the current model is more flexible and more powerful, mostly because of the control you have over the way tables are used in your documents. Using the many attributes of the <TABLE> tag, you can define precisely where and how tables are displayed on the page. To specify a table, you use the begin and end <TABLE> tags.

Valid attributes for the begin table tag <TABLE> include the following:

CLASS

DIR

ID

LANG

UNITS

BORDER

CELLPADDING

CELLSPACING

COLS

FLOAT

FRAME

RULES

WIDTH

The ID, CLASS, DIR, LANG, and UNITS attributes are used as described earlier; the other attributes have unique uses when applied to the <TABLE> tag.

BORDER and FRAME

Creating the border for a table is generally a two-part process. You use the BORDER attribute to specify the width for framing around the table and the FRAME attribute to specify the style of the frame around the table.

You specify the type of framing for a table with these values:

FRAME=VOID	No frame around the table, the default.
FRAME=ABOVE	Put a frame only on the top of the table.
FRAME=BELOW	Put a frame only on the bottom of the table.
FRAME=HSIDES	Put a frame on the top and bottom of the table.
FRAME=VSIDES	Put a frame on the left and right sides of the table.
FRAME=LHS	Put a frame only on the left side of the table.
FRAME=RHS	Put a frame only on the right side of the table.
FRAME=BOX	Put a frame on all four sides of the table.
FRAME=BORDER	Put a frame on all four sides of the table, which is the same as the value BOX.

Although the values FRAME=BORDER and FRAME=BOX mean the same thing, they are used for different purposes. For backwards compatibility, if you insert the attribute BORDER into the <TABLE> tag without a value, such as <TABLE BORDER>, a browser with the table specification assumes you want the table to have a border on all four sides. The browser makes a substitution using the value FRAME=BORDER and interprets <TABLE BORDER> as <TABLE FRAME=BORDER BORDER=implied>.

Similarly, if you specify <TABLE BORDER=0>, as you can under the HTML 3.2 table model, a browser compliant with the table model assumes you want the table to be displayed without a border. The browser interprets <TABLE BORDER=0> as <TABLE FRAME=VOID BORDER=0>. You can use the value FRAME=VOID as a design technique to remove extra white space around the table.

Figure 6.3 shows an example of tables with and without borders. By default, tables do not have a border or frame, which you can see in the first table example. The second table shown in the figure has a 15-pixel border. To set a border for a table, you must specify a width in pixels for the BORDER attribute, such as BORDER=15. Listing 6.1 shows the markup for the sample page.

Listing 6.1. Table borders.

```
<html>
<head>
<title>Frames for Your Tables</title>
</head>

<body bgcolor="#FFFFFF">
<div align=center>
<h2 align=left>A table without a border or frame:</h2>
<table>
<caption align=top>Cool WWW Technologies</caption>
```

```
<tr>
<td align=center width=50%>HTML</td>
<td align=center width=50%>SGML</td></tr>
<tr>
<td align=center width=50%>VRML</td>
<TD align=center width=50%>Java</td></tr>
<tr>
<td align=center>ActiveX</td>
<td align=center>VBScript/JavaScript</td></tr>
</table>
<h2 align=left>A table with a 15-pixel border</h2>
<table border=15>
<caption align=top>Cool WWW Technologies</caption>
<tr>
<td align=center width=50%>HTML</td>
<TD align=center width=50%>SGML</td></tr>
<tr>
<td align=center width=50%>VRML</td>
<td align=center width=50%>Java</td></tr>
<tr>
<td align=center>ActiveX</td>
<td align=center>VBScript/JavaScript</td></tr>
</table>
</div>
</body>
</html>
```

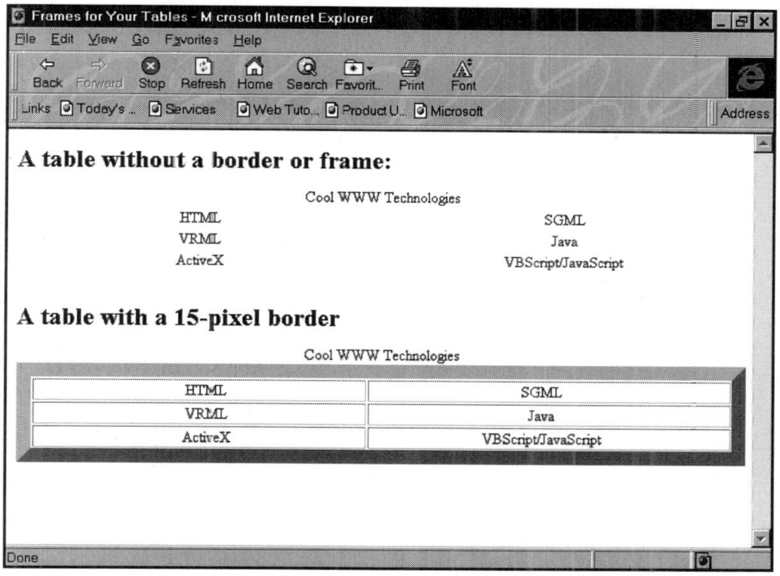

FIGURE 6.3.
Tables with and without borders.

Once you set a border for your table, you can define how you want the table to be framed. Figure 6.4 shows the use of framing in tables. The first example uses the default framing, and the second example shows a table with no frame around the border. Listing 6.2 shows the markup for the sample page.

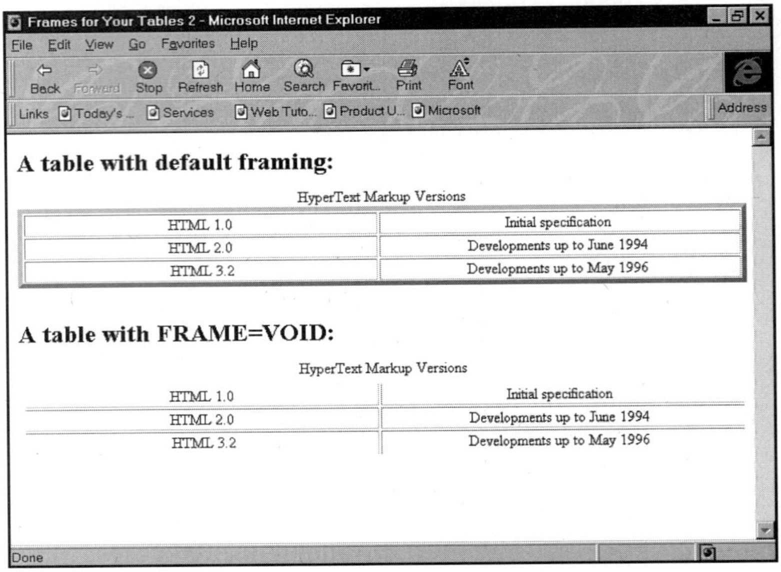

FIGURE 6.4.
Tables that illustrate framing techniques.

Listing 6.2. Table frames.

```
<html>
<head>
<title>Frames for Your Tables 2</title>
</head>

<body bgcolor="#FFFFFF">
<div align=center>
<h2 align=left>A table with default framing:</h2>
<table border=5>
<caption align=top>HyperText Markup Versions</caption>
<tr>
<td align=center width=50%>HTML 1.0 </td>
<td align=center width=50%>Initial specification</td></tr>
<tr>
<td align=center width=50%>HTML 2.0 </td>
<td align=center width=50%>Developments up to June 1994</td></tr>
<tr>
<td align=center>HTML 3.2</td>
<td align=center>Developments up to May 1996</td></tr>
</table>
<h2 align=left>A table with FRAME=VOID:</h2>
<table border=5 frame=void>
<caption align=top>HyperText Markup Versions</caption>
<tr>
<td align=center width=50%>HTML 1.0 </td>
<td align=center width=50%>Initial specification</td></tr>
<tr>
<td align=center width=50%>HTML 2.0 </td>
<td align=center width=50%>Developments up to June 1994</td></tr>
<tr>
```

```
<td align=center>HTML 3.2</td>
<td align=center>Developments up to May 1996</td></tr>
</table>
</div>
</body>

</html>
```


CELLPADDING and CELLSPACING

For table readability, CELLPADDING and CELLSPACING are the most important attributes you define for the table. CELLPADDING is used to specify the spacing within data cells, and CELLSPACING is used to specify the spacing between data cells. You specify padding and spacing in the current unit, normally pixels.

In Figure 6.5, there is a stark contrast between the two tables. The table without padding or spacing has thin framing with very little space between the cells; it's perfect for cramming a lot of data into a small space. The second table uses the same framing but adds cell padding, which makes the data sets stand out better and improves readability. The markup for the table padding example is in Listing 6.3.

Listing 6.3. Cell padding and spacing.

```
<html>
<head>
<title>Using Cell Padding In Your Tables</title>
</head>
<body bgcolor="#FFFFFF">
<h2>A table without cell padding or spacing:</h2>
<table border=5 cellpadding=0 cellspacing=0 width=100%>
<tr>
<th colspan=5 width=100%>1996 Sales Figures By Region</th></tr>
<tr>
<th valign=bottom width=20%></th>
<th valign=bottom width=20%>L.A.</th>
<th valign=bottom width=20%>Chicago</th>
<th valign=bottom width=20%>Baltimore</th>
<th valign=bottom width=20%>N.Y.</th></tr>
<tr>
<th width=20%>1st Quarter</th>
<td width=20%>156,900</td>
<td width=20%>358,900</td>
<td width=20%>329,982</td>
<td width=20%>690,009</td></tr>
<tr>
<th width=20%>2nd Quarter</th>
<td width=20%>167,878</td>
<td width=20%>325,565</td>
<td width=20%>356,111</td>
<td width=20%>690,708</td></tr>
<tr>
```

continues

Listing 6.3. continued

```
<th width=20%>3rd Quarter</th>
<td width=20%>189,901</td>
<td width=20%>367,404</td>
<td width=20%>376,205</td>
<td width=20%>693,323</td></tr>
<tr>
<th>4th Quarter</th>
<td>201,560</td>
<td>365,109</td>
<td>399,584</td>
<td>694,465</td></tr>
</table>
<h2>A table with cell padding of 10 pixels:</h2>
<table border=5 cellpadding=10 cellspacing=0 width=100%>
<tr>
<th colspan=5 width=100%>1996 Sales Figures By Region</th></tr>
<tr>
<th valign=bottom width=20%></th>
<th valign=bottom width=20%>L.A.</th>
<th valign=bottom width=20%>Chicago</th>
<th valign=bottom width=20%>Baltimore</th>
<th valign=bottom width=20%>N.Y.</th></tr>
<tr>
<th width=20%>1st Quarter</th>
<td width=20%>156,900</td>
<td width=20%>358,900</td>
<td width=20%>329,982</td>
<td width=20%>690,009</td></tr>
<tr>
<th width=20%>2nd Quarter</th>
<td width=20%>167,878</td>
<td width=20%>325,565</td>
<td width=20%>356,111</td>
<td width=20%>690,708</td></tr>
<tr>
<th width=20%>3rd Quarter</th>
<td width=20%>189,901</td>
<td width=20%>367,404</td>
<td width=20%>376,205</td>
<td width=20%>693,323</td></tr>
<tr>
<th>4th Quarter</th>
<td>201,560</td>
<td>365,109</td>
<td>399,584</td>
<td>694,465</td></tr>
</table>
</body>

</html>
```

When you create a table with spacing between the cells and no cell padding, you create the unique look shown in Figure 6.6. In the table with cell spacing, each cell is distinct. Listing 6.4 shows the markup for the table spacing example.

Listing 6.4. Cell spacing.

```
<html>
<head>
<title>Using Cell Spacing In Your Tables</title>
</head>
<body bgcolor="#FFFFFF">
<h2>A table without cell padding or spacing:</h2>
<table border=5 cellpadding=0 cellspacing=0 width=100%>
<tr>
<th colspan=5 width=100%>1996 Sales Figures By Region</th></tr>
<tr>
<th valign=bottom width=20%></th>
<th valign=bottom width=20%>L.A.</th>
<th valign=bottom width=20%>Chicago</th>
<th valign=bottom width=20%>Baltimore</th>
<th valign=bottom width=20%>N.Y.</th></tr>
<tr>
<th width=20%>1st Quarter</th>
<td width=20%>156,900</td>
<td width=20%>358,900</td>
<td width=20%>329,982</td>
<td width=20%>690,009</td></tr>
<tr>
<th width=20%>2nd Quarter</th>
<td width=20%>167,878</td>
<td width=20%>325,565</td>
<td width=20%>356,111</td>
<td width=20%>690,708</td></tr>
<tr>
<th width=20%>3rd Quarter</th>
<td width=20%>189,901</td>
<td width=20%>367,404</td>
<td width=20%>376,205</td>
<td width=20%>693,323</td></tr>
<tr>
<th>4th Quarter</th>
<td>201,560</td>
<td>365,109</td>
<td>399,584</td>
<td>694,465</td></tr>
</table>
<h2>A table with cell spacing of 10 pixels:</h2>
<table border=5 cellpadding=0 cellspacing=10 width=100%>
<tr>
<th colspan=5 width=100%>1996 Sales Figures By Region</th></tr>
<tr>
<th valign=bottom width=20%></th>
<th valign=bottom width=20%>L.A.</th>
<th valign=bottom width=20%>Chicago</th>
<th valign=bottom width=20%>Baltimore</th>
<th valign=bottom width=20%>N.Y.</th></tr>
<tr>
<th width=20%>1st Quarter</th>
<td width=20%>156,900</td>
<td width=20%>358,900</td>
<td width=20%>329,982</td>
<td width=20%>690,009</td></tr>
```

continues

Listing 6.4. Cell spacing.

```
<tr>
<th width=20%>2nd Quarter</th>
<td width=20%>167,878</td>
<td width=20%>325,565</td>
<td width=20%>356,111</td>
<td width=20%>690,708</td></tr>
<tr>
<th width=20%>3rd Quarter</th>
<td width=20%>189,901</td>
<td width=20%>367,404</td>
<td width=20%>376,205</td>
<td width=20%>693,323</td></tr>
<tr>
<th>4th Quarter</th>
<td>201,560</td>
<td>365,109</td>
<td>399,584</td>
<td>694,465</td></tr>
</table>
</body>

</html>
```

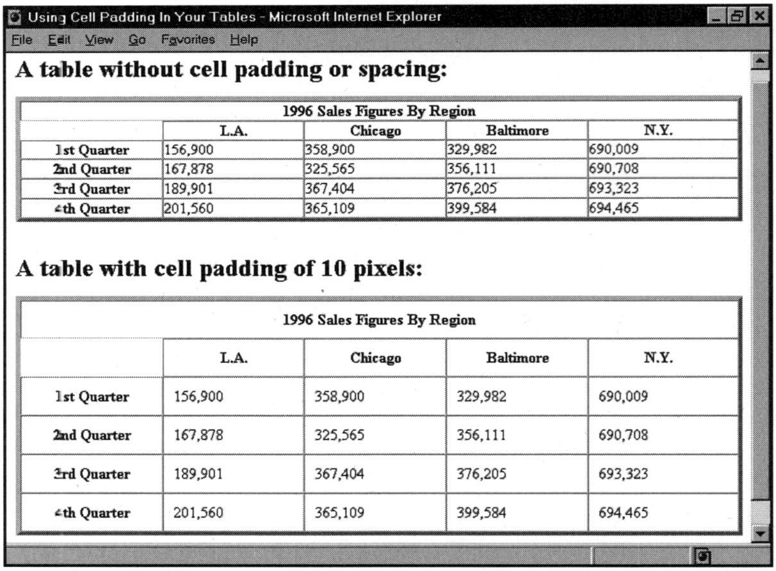

FIGURE 6.5.
Tables with and without cell padding.

FIGURE 6.6.
Tables with and without cell spacing.

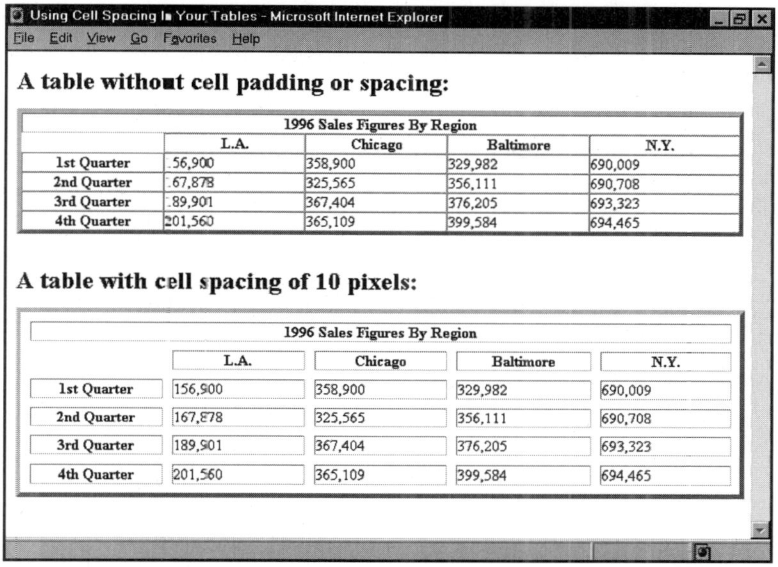

1996 Sales Figures By Region				
	L.A.	Chicago	Baltimore	N.Y.
1st Quarter	56,900	358,900	329,982	690,009
2nd Quarter	67,878	325,565	356,111	690,708
3rd Quarter	89,901	367,404	376,205	693,323
4th Quarter	201,560	365,109	399,584	694,465

1996 Sales Figures By Region				
	L.A.	Chicago	Baltimore	N.Y.
1st Quarter	156,900	358,900	329,982	690,009
2nd Quarter	167,878	325,565	356,111	690,708
3rd Quarter	189,901	367,404	376,205	693,323
4th Quarter	201,560	365,109	399,584	694,465

The final example in this section combines cell spacing and cell padding. As you can see, a table with lots of spacing and padding is very readable, yet also fills a lot of screen space. Ideally, tables you use in your pages will have the right balance of padding and spacing.

FIGURE 6.7.
A table with both cell spacing and padding.

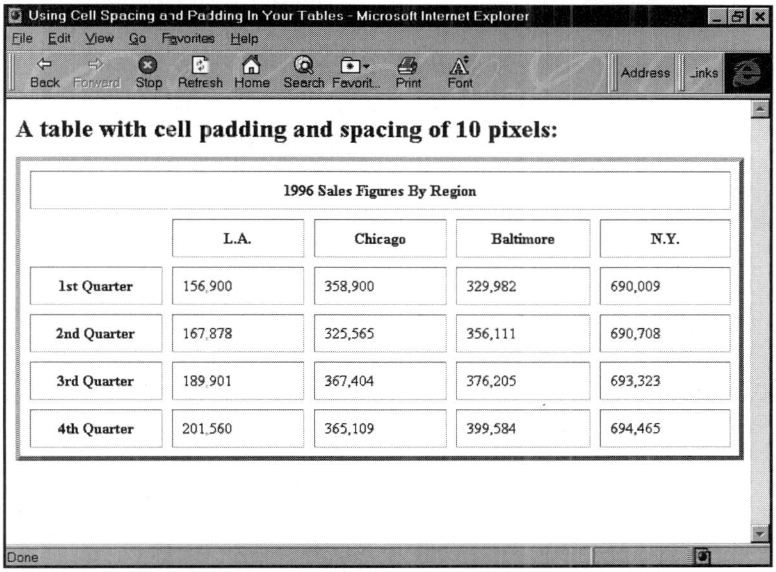

1996 Sales Figures By Region				
	L.A.	Chicago	Baltimore	N.Y.
1st Quarter	156,900	358,900	329,982	690,009
2nd Quarter	167,878	325,565	356,111	690,708
3rd Quarter	189,901	367,404	376,205	693,323
4th Quarter	201,560	365,109	399,584	694,465

COLS

The `COLS` attribute specifies the number of columns in a table and is used by your browser to display the table incrementally as it's received. If you don't specify the number of columns, the browser reads all the table data before displaying any portion of the table.

You can specify a table with four columns as follows:

```
<TABLE COLS=4>
```

NOTE

Even if you don't specify a `COLS` attribute for your table, the table will display just fine. However, the browser won't be able to display the table incrementally.

FLOAT

Text in your documents can flow around tables. By default, tables are aligned with the left margin, and text flows around the table's right side. You can also align tables with the right margin, which causes text to flow around the table's left side. You set the alignment of your table by using the `FLOAT` attribute. Values associated with the `FLOAT` attribute identify where the table floats on the page.

The developers of the table model chose the word *float* so as not to conflict with the `ALIGN` attribute used for other purposes in the table model. These are the two values for the `FLOAT` attribute:

```
<TABLE FLOAT=LEFT>
<TABLE FLOAT=RIGHT>
```

NOTE

Neither Internet Explorer 3.0 or Netscape Navigator 3.0 supports floating tables. Look for floating table support in future versions of this software.

RULES

The `RULES` attribute is used to specify the type of horizontal and vertical lines to display within a table. By default, tables have no horizontal or vertical ruling lines separating columns and rows, and it's only when you specify a border or frame for your table that `RULES` comes into play.

Rules visually separate the parts of the table. You can increase the table's impact by including some type of rules. The default `rules` value separates all columns and rows with horizontal and verticle rules.

These are the values for the `RULES` attribute:

`RULES=NONE`	No horizontal or vertical rules separating rows and columns.
`RULES=GROUPS`	Separate the header, body, and footer elements with a horizontal rule.
`RULES=ROWS`	Separate all rows in the table with horizontal rules; some browsers may add a thicker line to the header, body, and footer elements.
`RULES=COLS`	Separate all columns in the table with vertical rules and add horizontal rules between header, body, and footer elements.
`RULES=ALL`	Separate all elements in the table with horizontal and vertical rules. Some browsers may add a thicker line to the header, body, and footer elements.

Combining cell padding and spacing with various rule settings can create many different looks for your tables. Figure 6.8 shows two sample tables. The first table uses cell spacing and padding but has no rules; the second table uses rules for rows. The markup for the example is in Listing 6.5.

Listing 6.5. Table rules.

```
<HTML>
<HEAD>
<TITLE>Using Rules in Tables</TITLE>
</HEAD>
<BODY BGCOLOR="#FFFFFF" LINK="#000000" TEXT="#000000">
<H2>A table with RULES=NONE</H2>

<CENTER>
<TABLE BORDER=5 RULES=NONE CELLPADDING=5 CELLSPACING=5>
<TR>
<TD><IMG HEIGHT="50" WIDTH="100"   SRC="BULLETS/BUTT10A.GIF">
<TD><IMG HEIGHT="50" WIDTH="100"   SRC="BULLETS/BUTT10B.GIF">
<TD><IMG HEIGHT="50" WIDTH="100"   SRC="BULLETS/BUTT10C.GIF">
</TR>
<TR>
<TD><IMG HEIGHT="50" WIDTH="100"   SRC="BULLETS/BUTT10D.GIF">
<TD><IMG HEIGHT="50" WIDTH="100"   SRC="BULLETS/BUTT10E.GIF">
<TD><IMG HEIGHT="50" WIDTH="100"   SRC="BULLETS/BUTT10F.GIF"></TR>
<TR><TD><IMG HEIGHT="50" WIDTH="100"   SRC="BULLETS/BUTT10G.GIF">
<TD><IMG HEIGHT="50" WIDTH="100"   SRC="BULLETS/BUTT10H.GIF">
<TD><IMG HEIGHT="50" WIDTH="100"   SRC="BULLETS/BUTT10I.GIF"
</TR>
</TABLE>
</CENTER>
```

continues

Listing 6.5. continued

```
<H2>A table with RULES=ROWS</H2>
<CENTER>
<TABLE BORDER=5 RULES=ROWS CELLPADDING=5 CELLSPACING=5>
<TR>
<TD><IMG HEIGHT="50" WIDTH="100"   SRC="BULLETS/BUTT10A.GIF">
<TD><IMG HEIGHT="50" WIDTH="100"   SRC="BULLETS/BUTT10B.GIF">
<TD><IMG HEIGHT="50" WIDTH="100"   SRC="BULLETS/BUTT10C.GIF">
</TR>
<TR>
<TD><IMG HEIGHT="50" WIDTH="100"   SRC="BULLETS/BUTT10D.GIF">
<TD><IMG HEIGHT="50" WIDTH="100"   SRC="BULLETS/BUTT10E.GIF">
<TD><IMG HEIGHT="50" WIDTH="100"   SRC="BULLETS/BUTT10F.GIF">
</TR>
<TR>
<TD><IMG HEIGHT="50" WIDTH="100"   SRC="BULLETS/BUTT10G.GIF">
<TD><IMG HEIGHT="50" WIDTH="100"   SRC="BULLETS/BUTT10H.GIF">
<TD><IMG HEIGHT="50" WIDTH="100"   SRC="BULLETS/BUTT10I.GIF">
</TR>
</TABLE>
</CENTER>

</BODY>
</HTML>
```

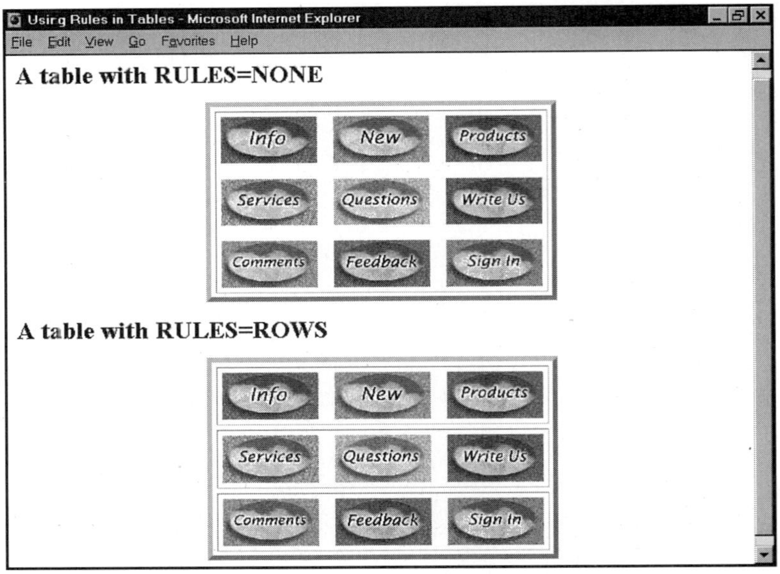

FIGURE 6.8.
Using rules in your tables.

Figure 6.9 shows more examples of using rules in tables. The first table shown in the figure uses the default rule setting, and the second example uses rule for columns. Listing 6.6 is the markup for this example.

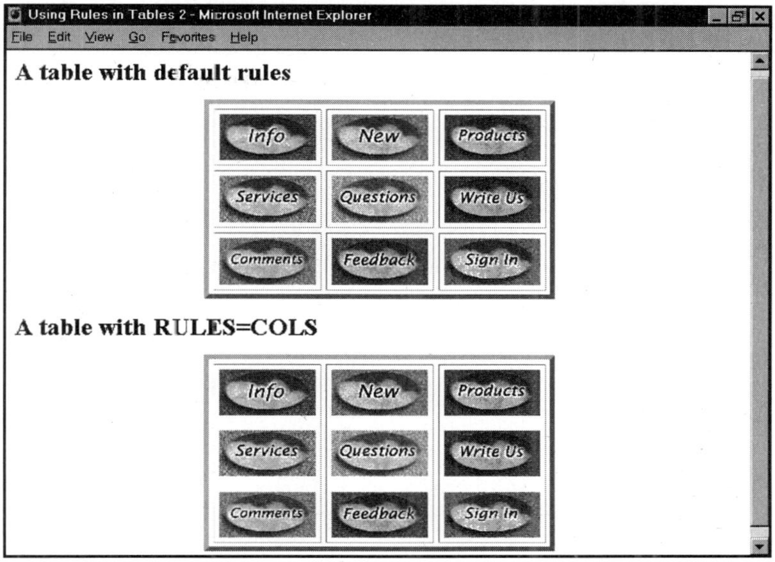

FIGURE 6.9.
More examples of rules in tables.

Listing 6.6. More table rules.

```
<HTML>
<HEAD>
<TITLE>Using Rules in Tables 2</TITLE>
</HEAD>
<BODY BGCOLOR="#FFFFFF" LINK="#000000" TEXT="#000000">
<H2>A table with default rules</H2>
<CENTER>

<TABLE BORDER=5 CELLPADDING=5 CELLSPACING=5>
<TR>
<TD><IMG HEIGHT="50" WIDTH="100"   SRC="BULLETS/BUTT10A.GIF">
<TD><IMG HEIGHT="50" WIDTH="100"   SRC="BULLETS/BUTT10B.GIF">
<TD><IMG HEIGHT="50" WIDTH="100"   SRC="BULLETS/BUTT10C.GIF">
</TR>
<TR>
<TD><IMG HEIGHT="50" WIDTH="100"   SRC="BULLETS/BUTT10D.GIF">
<TD><IMG HEIGHT="50" WIDTH="100"   SRC="BULLETS/BUTT10E.GIF">
<TD><IMG HEIGHT="50" WIDTH="100"   SRC="BULLETS/BUTT10F.GIF">
</TR>
<TR>
<TD><IMG HEIGHT="50" WIDTH="100"   SRC="BULLETS/BUTT10G.GIF">
<TD><IMG HEIGHT="50" WIDTH="100"   SRC="BULLETS/BUTT10H.GIF">
<TD><IMG HEIGHT="50" WIDTH="100"   SRC="BULLETS/BUTT10I.GIF">
</TR>
</TABLE>
</CENTER>

<H2>A table with RULES=COLS</H2>
<CENTER>
<TABLE BORDER=5 RULES=COLS CELLPADDING=5 CELLSPACING=5>
```

continues

Listing 6.6. continued

```
<TR>
<TD><IMG HEIGHT="50" WIDTH="100"    SRC="BULLETS/BUTT10A.GIF">
<TD><IMG HEIGHT="50" WIDTH="100"    SRC="BULLETS/BUTT10B.GIF">
<TD><IMG HEIGHT="50" WIDTH="100"    SRC="BULLETS/BUTT10C.GIF">
</TR>
<TR>
<TD><IMG HEIGHT="50" WIDTH="100"    SRC="BULLETS/BUTT10D.GIF">
<TD><IMG HEIGHT="50" WIDTH="100"    SRC="BULLETS/BUTT10E.GIF">
<TD><IMG HEIGHT="50" WIDTH="100"    SRC="BULLETS/BUTT10F.GIF">
</TR>
<TR>
<TD><IMG HEIGHT="50" WIDTH="100"    SRC="BULLETS/BUTT10G.GIF">
<TD><IMG HEIGHT="50" WIDTH="100"    SRC="BULLETS/BUTT10H.GIF">
<TD><IMG HEIGHT="50" WIDTH="100"    SRC="BULLETS/BUTT10I.GIF">
</TR>
</TABLE>
</CENTER>

</BODY>
</HTML>
```

WIDTH

The `WIDTH` attribute is used to specify a table's relative or absolute width. The default `WIDTH` is the current window size. This means if the table exceeds the current window size, it's resized to fit the current window. Figure 6.10 shows a table that would normally exceed the window size, but because the default width is used, the table is resized to fit the window. The second example in the figure shows the same table with a fixed width of 400 pixels.

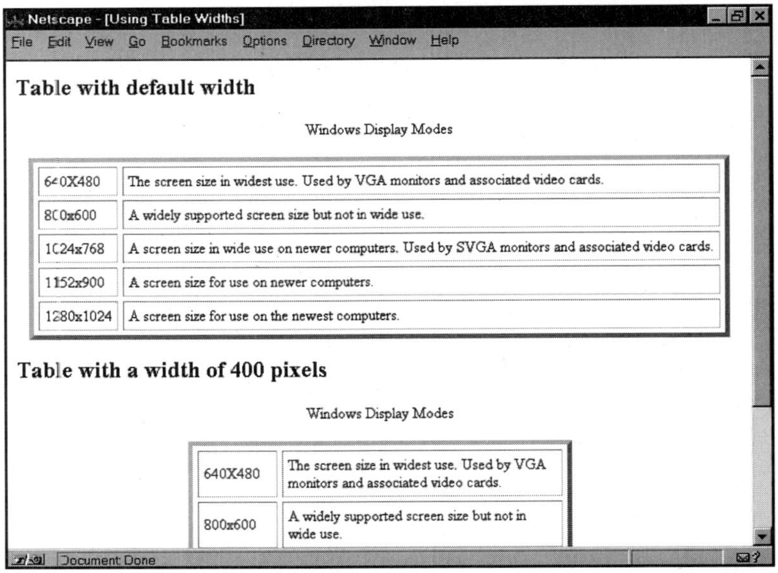

FIGURE 6.10.
Sizing your tables.

The HTML code for the table example is in Listing 6.7.

Listing 6.7. Table widths.

```
<html>
<head>
<title>Using Table Widths</title>
</head>
<body bgcolor="#FFFFFF">
<div align=center>
<h2 align=left>Table with default width</h2>

<table border=5 cellpadding=5 cellspacing=5>
<caption align=top>Windows Display Modes</caption>
<tr>
<td>640X480</td>
<td>The screen size in widest use. Used by VGA monitors and associated video
cards.</td>
</tr>
<tr>
<td>800x600</td>
<td>A widely supported screen size but not in wide use.</td>
</tr>
<tr>
<td>1024x768</td>
<td>A screen size in wide use on newer computers. Used by SVGA monitors and
associated video cards.</td>
</tr>
<tr>
<td>1152x900</td>
<td>A screen size for use on newer computers.</td>
</tr>
<tr>
<td>1280x1024</td>
<td>A screen size for use on the newest computers.</td>
</tr>
</table>

<h2 align=left>Table with a width of 400 pixels</h2>
<table border=5 cellpadding=5 cellspacing=5 width=400>
<caption align=top>Windows Display Modes</caption>
<tr>
<td>640X480</td>
<td>The screen size in widest use. Used by VGA monitors and associated video
cards.</td>
</tr>
<tr>
<td>800x600</td>
<td>A widely supported screen size but not in wide use.</td>
</tr>
<tr>
<td>1024x768</td>
<td>A screen size in wide use on newer computers. Used by SVGA monitors and
associated video cards.</td>
</tr>
<tr>
```

continues

Listing 6.7. continued

```
<td>1152x900</td>
<td>A screen size for use on newer computers.</td>
</tr>
<tr>
<td>1280x1024</td>
<td>A screen size for use on the newest computers.</td>
</tr>
</table>

</div>
</body>
</html>
```

DETERMINING THE BEST WIDTH FOR YOUR TABLE

When you design your table, keep in mind that screen sizes vary. Not all readers will view your page using the screen size you are working in. Macintoshes display 72 pixels per inch, and the number of pixels that can be viewed on the screen depends on the screen's size. Monitor sizes vary from as small as 9" diagonal on older Macs to typical sizes of 13" and 14" diagonal—all the way up to 25" or more.

The Windows system for determining the number of pixels on the screen is different from the Macintosh system. On Windows systems, these are the common screen sizes:

640×480	The screen size in widest use. Used by VGA monitors and associated video cards.
800×600	A widely supported screen size but not used as commonly.
1024×768	A screen size in wide use on newer computers. Used by SVGA monitors and associated video cards.
1152×900	A screen size for use on newer computers.
1280×1024	A screen size for use on the newest computers.

Often, you can use relative widths for your tables, which leaves the sizing of the table in the hands of the readers' browsers. Still, sometimes you need to use an absolute size for your table. For example, if your table contains graphic images, like those used in Figure 1.2, you should use an absolute table size to get a specific result. If you decide to use an absolute size for your table, test your page on other screen or display sizes. Usually, you design your table for the smallest common screen size, such as the popular 640×480 display mode for Windows systems.

You can specify the table width in units or as a percentage of the current window size. Any numeric value is interpreted in the current unit, normally pixels, unless you follow the value by a percent sign to define a relative width. Figure 6.11 shows two tables that use relative sizing.

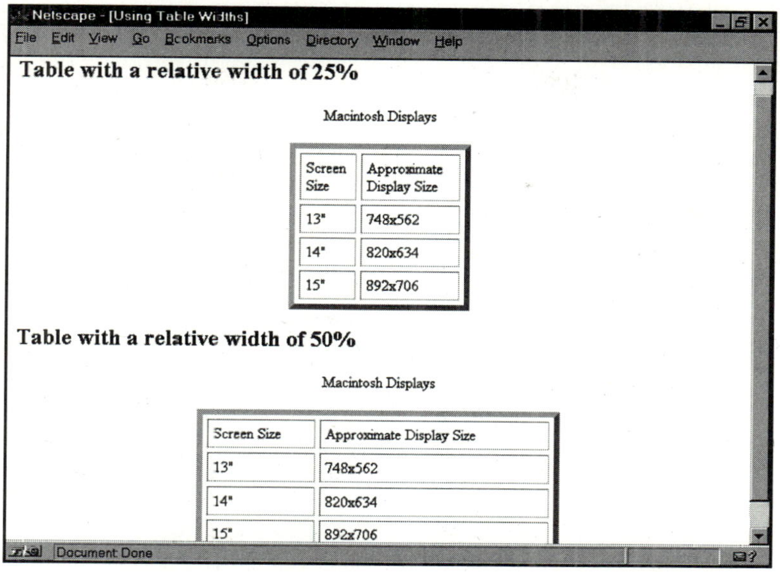

FIGURE 6.11.
More examples of rules in tables.

Listing 6.8 shows the markup for the example.

Listing 6.8. Relative table widths.

```
<HTML>
<HEAD>
<TITLE> Using Table Widths</TITLE>
</HEAD>
<Body BGCOLOR="#FFFFFF">
<DIV ALIGN=CENTER>
<H2 ALIGN=LEFT>Table with a relative width of 25%</H2>
<TABLE BORDER=6 CELLPADDING=5 CELLSPACING=5 WIDTH=25%
. . .
</TABLE>
<H2 ALIGN=LEFT>Table with a relative width of 50%</H2>
<TABLE BORDER=6 CELLPADDING=5 CELLSPACING=5 WIDTH=50%>
 . . .
</TABLE>
</DIV>
</BODY>
</HTML>
```

Adding a Table Caption

After you specify what you want the table's basic components to look like, you might want to add a caption to the table. Captions supply an explanation or description of the data sets in a table. To define a caption, use the begin and end `<CAPTION>` tags as follows:

```
<CAPTION>HTML Design Processes</CAPTION>
```

The table specification gives you some control over the placement of table captions with the `ALIGN` attribute. Used with captions, the `ALIGN` attribute has four values:

`ALIGN=TOP`	Place the caption above the table.
`ALIGN=BOTTOM`	Place the caption below the table.
`ALIGN=LEFT`	Place the caption on the left side of the table.
`ALIGN=RIGHT`	Place the caption on the right side of the table.

The exact positioning of right- or left-aligned captions is determined by the browser displaying the caption. According to the specification, browsers should try to display the caption so it fits the table's width and height. When Internet Explorer 3.0 displays left- or right-aligned captions, the caption is displayed with the specified alignment above the table, as you can see in Figure 6.12.

FIGURE 6.12.
Aligning captions in your tables.

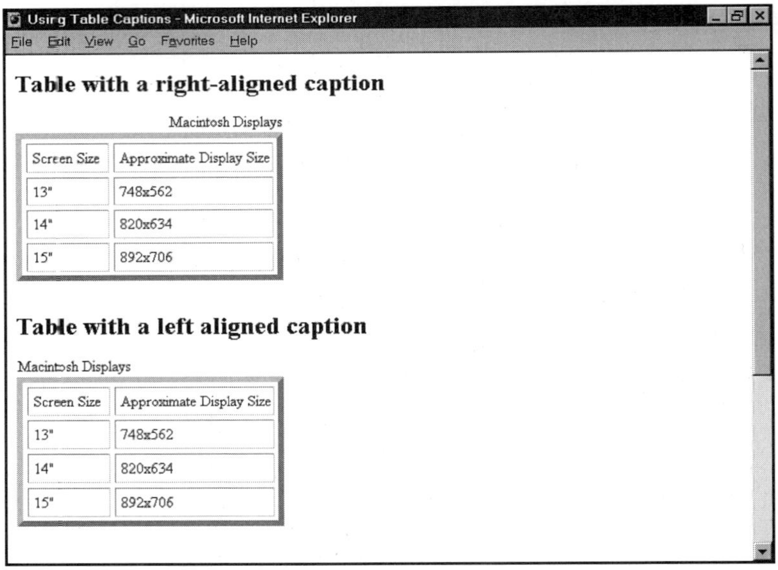

Generally, the caption tags are placed just after the begin `<TABLE>` tag as shown in Listing 6.9.

Listing 6.9. Table captions.

```
<html>
<head>
<title>Using Table Captions</title>
</head>
<body bgcolor="#FFFFFF">
<h2>Table with a right-aligned caption</h2>
```

```
<table border=6 cellpadding=5 cellspacing=5>
<caption align=right>Macintosh Displays</caption>
<tr><td>Screen Size</td><td>Approximate Display Size</td></tr>
<tr><td>13&quot;</td><td>748x562</td></tr>
<tr><td>14&quot;</td><td>820x634</td></tr>
<tr><td>15&quot;</td><td>892x706</td></tr>
</table>

<h2>Table with a left aligned caption</h2>
<table border=6 cellpadding=5 cellspacing=5>
<caption align=left>Macintosh Displays</caption>
<tr><td>Screen Size</td><td>Approximate Display Size</td></tr>
<tr><td>13&quot;</td><td>748x562</td></tr>
<tr><td>14&quot;</td><td>820x634</td></tr>
<tr><td>15&quot;</td><td>892x706</td></tr>
</table>

<h2>Generally, table captions are not in bold,
but you can add highlighting if you want to:</h2>
<table border=6 cellpadding=5 cellspacing=5>
<caption align=top><B>Macintosh Displays</B></caption>
<tr><td>Screen Size</td><td>Approximate Display Size</td></tr>
<tr><td>13&quot;</td><td>748x562</td></tr>
<tr><td>14&quot;</td><td>820x634</td></tr>
<tr><td>15&quot;</td><td>892x706</td></tr>
</table>

</body>
</html>
```

When adding a table caption, keep in mind that the best captions are short and descriptive. One way to make the caption more readable is to use bold type. You can add bold type to a caption placed on the right side of a table as follows:

```
<CAPTION ALIGN=RIGHT><B>HTML Design Processes</B></CAPTION>
```

Other attributes you can use with the begin caption tag `<CAPTION>` include `ID`, `LANG`, `CLASS`, and `DIR`.

Defining Columns for Your Table

Before you define the rows and individual cells that make up a table, you might want to specify general rules for all the columns in the table. You do this by using the optional `<COL>` tag.

Generally, if you want to assign an alignment rule to any column in your table, you should assign rules to all the columns in your table. This helps you avoid problems that could happen when you make changes to the table. Therefore, if your table has three columns, your table would have three `<COL>` tags. The first `<COL>` tag would apply to the first column of data cells; the second `<COL>` tag to the second column of data cells; and the third `<COL>` tag to the third and final column of data cells.

Besides the common attributes defined earlier, you can use these attributes with the `<COL>` tag:

```
ALIGN
CHAR
CHAROFF
VALIGN
WIDTH
SPAN
```

TIP

Don't confuse the `<COL>` tag with the `<COLS>` tag. The `<COLS>` tag is used to specify the number of columns in your table and is used only by browsers during the table's download. The `<COL>` tag is used to specify the alignment and positioning of text and objects in individual columns.

Horizontal Alignment of Cells in a Column

You can specify the horizontal alignment of data within a cell by using the `ALIGN` attribute. For the `<COL>` tag, you can use these alignment values:

```
ALIGN=LEFT
ALIGN=RIGHT
ALIGN=CENTER
ALIGN=JUSTIFY
ALIGN=CHAR
```

The default alignment for headings in a table is `ALIGN=CENTER`, and the default alignment for data sets is `ALIGN=LEFT`. Aligning data in column cells based on a character—done by using the value `ALIGN=CHAR`—is often useful, especially for numeric values that have decimal points. For a column aligned on a character, you must specify what character to align with by using the `CHAR` attribute. The key to using characters for alignment in cells is to use a unique character. To align a column of cells based on a decimal point, you could use the following:

```
<COL ALIGN=CHAR CHAR=.>
```

With the `CHAROFF` attribute, you can specify an offset for the character you're using for alignment. The *offset* is a positional value expressed as a percentage of the cell width. The default offset of 50 centers the unique character within the cell, so an offset of 0 aligns your unique character with the left cell wall, and an offset of 100 aligns it with the right cell wall. You should use the CHAR and CHAROFF attributes only with the ALIGN attribute. Here's an offset to partially right-align the data points, using a percent sign as the unique character:

```
<COL ALIGN=CHAR CHAR=% OFFSET=75>
```

Figure 6.13 shows an example of using horizontal alignment for columns in a table. Listing 6.10 shows the markup for this example.

Listing 6.10. Horizontal column alignment.

```
<html>
<head>
<title>Alignment of Cells in a Column</title>
</head>
<body bgcolor="#000000" text="#FFFFFF">
<h2>Aligning columns of cells</h2>
<center>
<table border=10 cellpadding=10 cellspacing=10 width=100%>
<col align=left>
<col align=center>
<col align=right>

<tr>
<td >A left-aligned Column</td>
<td>A centered Column</td>
<td >A right-aligned Column</td>
</tr>

<tr>
<td >A left-aligned Column</td>
<td>A centered Column</td>
<td >A right-aligned Column</td>
</tr>

<tr>
<td >A left-aligned Column</td>
<td>A centered Column</td>
<td >A right-aligned Column</td>
</tr>

<tr>
<td >A left-aligned Column</td>
<td>A centered Column</td>
<td >A right-aligned Column</td>
</tr>

<tr>
<td >A left-aligned Column</td>
<td>A centered Column</td>
<td >A right-aligned Column</td>
</tr>

</table>

</center>
</body>
</html>
```

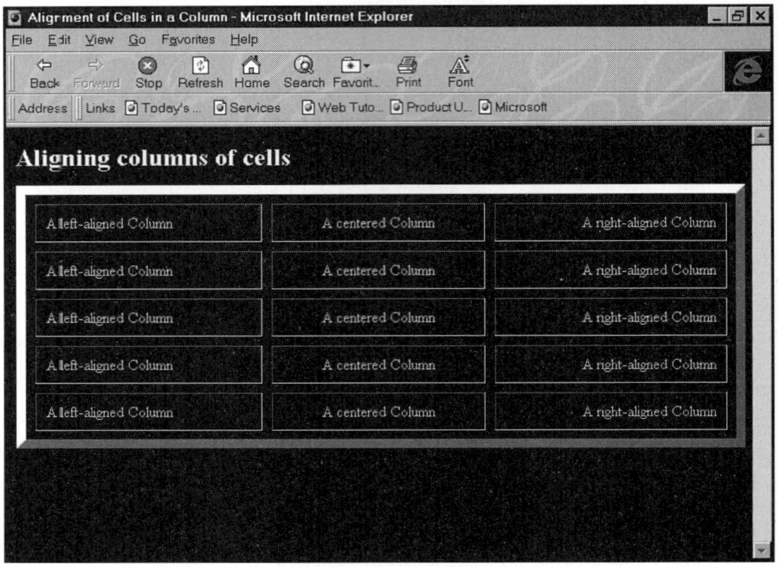

FIGURE 6.13.
Horizontal alignment for columns.

Vertical Alignment of Cells in a Column

You can specify the vertical alignment of data within a cell by using the `VALIGN` attribute. For the `<COL>` tag, you can use these alignment values:

```
VALIGN=TOP
VALIGN=MIDDLE
VALIGN=BOTTOM
VALIGN=BASELINE
```

The default alignment for headings and data used in tables is `VALIGN=MIDDLE`. To vertically align the first line of text in all the cells in the same row, you can use the `VALIGN=BASELINE`. Although the baseline alignment is useful, keep in mind that subsequent lines of text after the first line may not be aligned along a common baseline. Here's how you can align the cells of a column with the bottom of the cell:

```
<COL VALIGN=BOTTOM>
```

An example of using vertical alignment for columns in a table is shown in Figure 6.14. Listing 6.11 the markup for this example.

Listing 6.11. Vertical column alignment.

```
<html>
<head>
<title>Vertical Alignment of Cells </title>
</head>
```

```
<body bgcolor="#000000" text="#FFFFFF">
<H2>Vertical alignment of cells</H2>
<center>
<table border=5 cellpadding=2 cellspacing=2 width=100%>
<col valign=top>
<col valign=middle>
<col valign=bottom>

<tr>
<td >A top-aligned cell</td>
<td>A middle-aligned cell</td>
<td >A bottom-aligned cell</td>
</tr>

<tr>
<td >A top-aligned cell</td>
<td>A middle-aligned cell</td>
<td >A bottom-aligned cell</td>
</tr>

<tr>
<td >A top-aligned cell</td>
<td>A middle-aligned cell</td>
<td >A bottom-aligned cell</td>
</tr>

<tr>
<td >A top-aligned cell</td>
<td>A middle-aligned cell</td>
<td >A bottom-aligned cell</td>
</tr>

<tr>
<td >A top-aligned cell</td>
<td>A middle-aligned cell</td>
<td >A bottom-aligned cell</td>
</tr>

</table>

</center>
</body>
</html>
```

Applying Attributes to Multiple Columns

Usually, the attributes assigned to a particular `<COL>` tag apply to one column in a table, so a four-column table could have up to four `<COL>` tags to define the attributes for cells associated with each column. Using the `SPAN` attribute, you can apply assignments in a `COL` element to two or more columns.

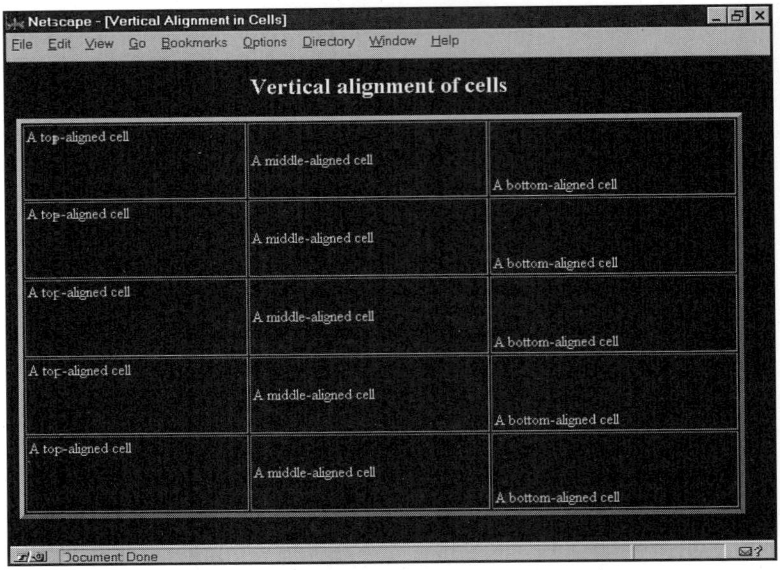

FIGURE 6.14.
Vertical alignment for columns.

The next example has a partial definition for a table of five columns. Data within the cells of the table's first column is justified and aligned with the top of the cell. Data in the next four columns is defined by the single `COL` element with the `SPAN` attribute and is aligned based on the position of the colon character. Here is the sample code:

```
<TABLE BORDER=5 FLOAT=RIGHT CELLPADDING=5 FRAME=BOX RULES=BASIC COLS=5>
<CAPTION ALIGN=LEFT>HTML Design Processes</CAPTION>
<COL ALIGN=JUSTIFY VALIGN=TOP>
<COL ALIGN=CHAR CHAR=: CHAROFF=25 SPAN=4>
 . . .
</TABLE>
```

Defining a Width for a Column of Cells

Usually, column width is determined by the number of characters in the first heading or data set in the column. You can override this function by specifying a relative or absolute width for the column with the `WIDTH` attribute of the `<COL>` tag. For compatibility with table representation in other table models and particularly in the SGML CALS model, column width doesn't follow the same rules for widths used elsewhere in HTML. You specify absolute widths in the current unit by specifying a value. However, you don't specify the relative column width with the percent sign; instead, you add an asterisk as the value's suffix, as in this example:

```
<COL WIDTH=0.25*>
```

The asterisk character used with widths may seem confusing, but it reminds you that the behavior of relative widths for columns is different from other relative widths. The value `0.25` isn't a percentage of the cell size, and the total of your column widths don't need to add up to 100. Rather, the value `0.25` is a weighted factor, compared to the allocated widths for other columns. If you assigned 2.0 units of width to all columns in the table, the column with the value `0.25` would have a width approximately 12.25 percent of the table's total width.

Using relative widths this way is better than using percentages. It saves you the trouble of trying to make sure all your column widths add up to 100 percent of the table width and lets you manipulate an individual column size as needed. This method also enables you to remove or add columns without recomputing percentages for width.

Defining the Main Sections of Your Table

The main sections of any table are the head, body, and foot elements. You define these elements with the following tags:

```
<THEAD> Table Header </THEAD>
<TBODY> Table Body </TBODY>
<TFOOT> Table Footer </TFOOT>
```

The only mandatory part of a table is the body element. Although all tables must include one or more body elements, a table can have only one header section and one footer section. The table model defines a begin and end tag for the head, body, and foot elements. However, the end tags for these elements can generally be omitted. If the table has only body elements, the begin and end body tags can also be omitted, so the minimum table definition could look like this:

```
<TABLE>
 . . .
</TABLE>
```

You would place row, column, and cell assignments where the ellipses are. At a minimum, each defined element must contain one row of data. Keep in mind that if you use a head or foot element, you will need to use the appropriate start tags to separate the table's body component. Ideally, browsers use the head, body, and footer elements to display tables smartly. If the table extends beyond the current window, the browser may let the reader scroll through the data sets of the body section while the header and footer sections remain onscreen, or browsers may simply display the header and footer sections with the current page of the table. When the user advances to the next page, the browser would display a header and footer, as appropriate.

The `<THEAD>`, `<TBODY>`, and `<TFOOT>` tags can be used with the following common attributes:

```
CLASS
DIR
ID
LANG
UNITS
```

You can also use these alignment attributes:

```
ALIGN
CHAR
CHAROFF
VALIGN
```

The alignment attributes for header, body, and footer sections are used as described in the previous section. By making assignments in the header, body, or footer, you can override the defaults and column assignments you made with the <COL> tag.

The following example shows how the header, body, and footer sections could be added to a table. Note that the header section for the table has vertical and horizontal alignments that override the assignments made with the <COL> tag. Likewise, the footer for the table has vertical and horizontal alignments that override the assignments made with the <COL> tag. If you use a header or footer in your tables, you probably want unique alignment for the data in associated cells. Here's the example:

```
<TABLE BORDER=5 FLOAT=RIGHT CELLPADDING=5 FRAME=BOX RULES=BASIC COLS=5>
<CAPTION ALIGN=LEFT>HTML Design Processes</CAPTION>
<COL ALIGN=JUSTIFY VALIGN=TOP>
<COL ALIGN=CHAR CHAR=: CHAROFF=25 SPAN=4>
<THEAD ALIGN=CENTER VALIGN=MIDDLE>
 . . .
<TBODY>
 . . .
<TBODY>
 . . .
<TBODY>
 . . .
<TFOOT ALIGN=LEFT VALIGN=BOTTOM>
</TABLE>
```

Adding Rows to Your Table

All tables must have one or more rows of data cells. Rows are defined within the header, body, or footer section of a table. Using the <TR> tag, you can define rows for each section your table has. Therefore, a table with one header, two body, and one footer sections would have at least four rows. Generally, only the begin <TR> tag is used in tables, but you can use the optional end </TR> tag if you want to.

Table row tags can be used with the following common attributes:

```
CLASS
DIR
ID
LANG
UNITS
```

You can also use these alignment attributes:

```
ALIGN
CHAR
CHAROFF
VALIGN
```

The alignment attributes for table rows are used as described previously. By making assignments in a table row, you can override the defaults, the column assignments you made with the <COL> tag, and the section assignment you made with the <THEAD>, <TBODY>, or <TFOOT> tag. All table rows consist of one or more data cells. No matter what the cells' placement is, they can be defined as header cells or data cells.

The following is an example of row assignments in a table:

```
<TABLE BORDER=5>
<CAPTION ALIGN=LEFT>Adding Rows to Your Table</CAPTION>
<THEAD ALIGN=CENTER VALIGN=MIDDLE>
<TR> . . .
<TBODY>
<TR> . . .
<TR> . . .
<TR> . . .
<TBODY>
<TR> . . .
<TR> . . .
<TR> . . .
<TBODY>
<TR> . . .
<TFOOT ALIGN=LEFT>
<TR> . . .
</TABLE>
```

Creating Table Cells for Data and Headers

The assignments you make at the cell level are for the individual data sets or headings. *Data cells* contain the numbers, facts, and statements to display in the table.

Using the <TD> tag, you can define data cells. As with the <TR> tag, the end </TD> tag is optional. The default vertical alignment for data cells in tables is VALIGN=MIDDLE, and the default horizontal alignment is ALIGN=LEFT.

Heading cells contain headings for sections, columns, and rows. Using the <TH> tag, you can define heading cells. The end </TH> tag is optional. Text in a heading cell is usually displayed in bold. The default horizontal alignment for heading cells in a table is ALIGN=CENTER, and the default vertical alignment is VALIGN=MIDDLE.

To define cells within a row, you simply insert the cell data into the table after a row assignment, as shown in the following example:

```
<TABLE BORDER=5 FLOAT=RIGHT CELLPADDING=5 FRAME=BOX RULES=BASIC COLS=5>
<CAPTION ALIGN=LEFT>HTML Design Processes</CAPTION>
<THEAD ALIGN=CENTER VALIGN=MIDDLE>
<TR><TH>Header Cell 1<TH>Header Cell 2<TH>Header Cell 3
<TH>Header Cell 4<TH>Header Cell 5
<TBODY>
<TR><TD>Body Row 1 Cell 1<TD>Body Row 1 Cell 2<TD>Body Row 1 Cell 3
<TD>Body Row 1 Cell 4<TD>Body Row 1 Cell 5
<TR><TD>Body Row 2 Cell 1<TD>Body Row 2 Cell 2<TD>Body Row 2 Cell 3
<TD>Body Row 2 Cell 4<TD>Body Row 2 Cell 5
</TABLE>
```

The definitions for table cells are very dynamic. Table cells use most of the previously defined attributes, including these:

- ALIGN
- CHAR
- CHAROFF
- CLASS
- DIR
- ID
- LANG
- UNITS
- VALIGN

By making assignments in a table cell, you override the defaults, the column assignments you made with the <COL> tag, the section assignment you made with the <THEAD>, <TBODY>, or <TFOOT> tag, and the row assignment you made with the <TR> tag. Figure 6.15 shows how individual cells can be vertically aligned. Lisitng 6.12 shows the markup for this example.

Listing 6.12. Vertical alignment of cells.

```
<html>
<head>
<title>Vertical Alignment of Individual Cells</title>
</head>
<body bgcolor="#FFFFFF" TEXT="#000000">
<div align=center>

<table border=10 cellpadding=5 cellspacing=5 width=100%>
<tr>
<td valign=tcp >A top-aligned cell<p> </p>
</td>
<td >A middle-aligned cell</td>
<td valign=bottom >A bottom-aligned cell</td>
</tr>

<tr>
<td valign=top >A top-aligned cell<p> </p></td>
```

```
<td >A middle-aligned cell</td>
<td valign=bottom >A bottom-aligned cell</td>
</tr>

<tr>
<td valign=top >A top-aligned cell<p> </p></td>
<td >A middle-aligned cell</td>
<td valign=bottom >A bottom-aligned cell</td>
</tr>

<tr>
<td valign=top >A top-aligned cell<p> </p>
</td>
<td >A middle-aligned cell</td>
<td valign=bottom >A bottom-aligned cell</td>
</tr>

<tr>
<td valign=top >A top-aligned cell<p> </p>
</td>
<td >A middle-aligned cell</td>
<td valign=bottom >A bottom-aligned cell</td>
</tr>
</table>

</div>
</body>

</html>
```

NOTE

To increase the amount of space table cells occupy, you can insert a paragraph with a non-breaking space, as shown in the previous listing. The code for this is `<P> </P>`.

Using the following additional attributes, you can define cells that span multiple columns and rows, disable automatic wrapping of text, and more:

AXIS

AXES

BGCOLOR

COLSPAN

ROWSPAN

NOWRAP

FIGURE 6.15.
Aligning individual cells in a column.

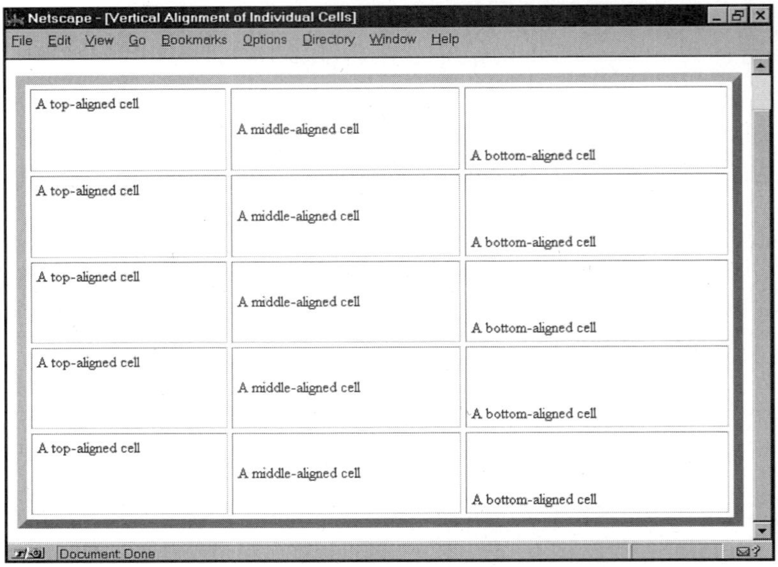

Using the AXIS and AXES Attributes

The `AXIS` and `AXES` attributes are used to label cells. Using the `AXIS` attribute, you can label one cell with a keyword; with the `AXES` attribute, you can label row and header attributes for the cell. The keyword for the row label is separated from the header label by a comma. Values you assign to the `AXIS` and `AXES` attributes aren't displayed with the text of your table. Most tables you create don't need these attributes; however, you can use cell labels to represent field names from a database or to help convert table data to other formats.

For example, you could label a cell with these attributes:

```
<TD AXIS="keyword" AXES="row header keyword, column header keyword">
```

Using Backgrounds in Table Cells

Internet Explorer enables you to add color to header and data cells with the `BGCOLOR` attribute. You can add color to a cell with a color name or hexadecimal value, such as

```
<TH BGCOLOR=WHITE>
```

or

```
<TD BGCOLOR=#FF00FF>
```

The key to using color in your tables is to use it sparingly. You should test the text's readability when used with a color. If the text is unreadable, use the `<FONT>` tag to change the color of the cell's text:

```
<TR><TD BGCOLOR=BLUE><FONT COLOR=WHITE>12.5%<TD BGCOLOR=BLUE>
<FONT COLOR=WHITE>15.8%<TD BGCOLOR=BLUE><FONT COLOR=YELLOW>28.3%
```


Using the BACKGROUND attribute, you can also add images to the table backgrounds in Internet Explorer. If you want to use the image as a background for an entire table, place the BACKGROUND attribute in the <TABLE> tag definition, but if you want to use the image as a background for an individual cell, place the BACKGROUND attribute in the <TD> or <TH> tag definition.

Figure 6.16 shows how background images can be used in tables. When you combine unique page colors or backgrounds with a table that has backgrounds, be sure to check the table for readability. The table shown in the figure worked great against a white background. When the background color of the page is changed to black, the color of text on the page needs to be changed to ensure readability of the text. The obvious choice is to change the text color to white. White text on a black background is easy to read. However, white text creates a readability problem in the table on the sample page because of the light background image used in the table. To correct the readability problem, table text was changed to black to be seen on the white background of the table. To see how this was handled, examine Listing 6.13.

Listing 6.13. Table backgrounds.

```
<head>
<title>Using Backgrounds in Tables</title>
</head>
<body bgcolor="#000000" TEXT="#FFFFFF">
<h2>A table with a background image:</h2>
<center>
<table border=5 cellpadding=5 cellspacing=10 width=75%
background="wildlifa.gif" bgcolor="#FFFFFF">
<caption align=top>
<FONT COLOR="BLACK">
<B>The Wildlife Preservation Society</B></FONT>
</caption>
<tr>
<th><FONT COLOR="BLACK">Quarter</FONT></th>
<th valign=top width=33%><FONT COLOR="BLACK">Wolf Status</FONT>
<p> </p></th>
<th valign=top width=33%><FONT COLOR="BLACK">Bear Status</FONT></th>
<th valign=top width=34%><FONT COLOR="BLACK">Eagle Status</FONT></th>
</tr>
<tr>
<th><FONT COLOR="BLACK">1st</FONT></th>
<td width=33%><FONT COLOR="BLACK">1800</FONT></td>
<td width=33%><FONT COLOR="BLACK">500</FONT></td>
<td width=34%><FONT COLOR="BLACK">300</FONT></td>
</tr>
<tr>
<th><FONT COLOR="BLACK">2nd</FONT></th>
<td width=33%><FONT COLOR="BLACK">1200</FONT></td>
<td width=33%><FONT COLOR="BLACK">450</FONT></td>
<td width=34%><FONT COLOR="BLACK">275</FONT></td>
</tr>
<tr>
```

continues

Listing 6.13. continued

```
<th><FONT COLOR="BLACK">3rd</FONT></th>
<td><FONT COLOR="BLACK">900</FONT></td>
<td><FONT COLOR="BLACK">425</FONT></td>
<td><FONT COLOR="BLACK">250</FONT></td>
</tr>
<tr>
<th><FONT COLOR="BLACK">4th</FONT></th>
<td><FONT COLOR="BLACK">875</FONT></td>
<td><FONT COLOR="BLACK">415</FONT></td>
<td><FONT COLOR="BLACK">235</FONT></td>
</tr>
</table>
</center>
<p>If you use background images in your table, be sure to check
the readability of the data. You may have to change the font
color within the table as you see here.</p>
</body>
</html>
```

NOTE

The table in the previous example also uses the `WIDTH` attribute with header cells. This attribute is not part of the current table specification, but is supported by Netscape Navigator and Internet Explorer for both <TH> and <TD>.

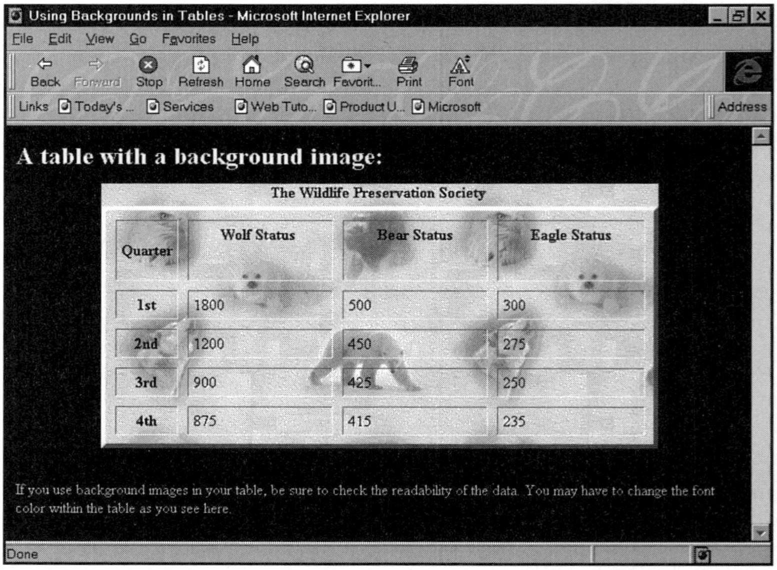

FIGURE 6.16.
Using background images in your tables.

Creating Cells That Span Rows and Columns

The table specification gives you advanced control over the placement of cells in your tables. Using the COLSPAN attribute, you can create cells that span two or more columns; with the ROWSPAN attribute, you can create cells that span two or more rows. By combining the COLSPAN and ROWSPAN attributes, you can create cells that span multiple columns and rows.

You can use the COLSPAN and ROWSPAN attributes with header and data cells. In a header, you can use COLSPAN to create major headings for sections of a table. If you use COLSPAN to span several column headers and define subheadings, you will need to use ROWSPAN in columns with only one level of heading to make sure headings and cells line up appropriately.

Figure 6.17 shows an example of using COLSPAN and ROWSPAN in a multicolumn table with subheadings. Listing 6.14 shows the markup for this example.

Listing 6.14. Spanning columns and rows.

```
<HTML>
<HEAD>
<TITLE>Using Spanning columns and rows</TITLE>
</HEAD>
<BODY BGCOLOR="#000000" TEXT="#FFFFFF">
<DIV ALIGN=CENTER>
<H2 ALIGN=LEFT>Creating columns and rows that fill more than one cell</H2>
<P> </P>
<TABLE BORDER=5>
<CAPTION ALIGN=LEFT>Developing HTML Publications</CAPTION>
<TR><TH ROWSPAN=2>Project Creation<TH COLSPAN=2>Project Design
<TH ROWSPAN=2>Project Publication
<TR><TH>Preliminary Design<TH>Phase II Design
</TABLE>
<P> </P>
<H2 ALIGN=LEFT>Adding a cool effect with top and bottom framing:</H2>
<P> </P>
<TABLE BORDER=5 FRAME=VOID>
<CAPTION ALIGN=LEFT>Developing HTML Publications</CAPTION>
<TR><TH ROWSPAN=2>Project Creation<TH COLSPAN=2>Project Design
<TH ROWSPAN=2>Project Publication
<TR><TH>Preliminary Design<TH>Phase II Design
</TABLE>
</DIV>
</BODY>
</HTML>
```

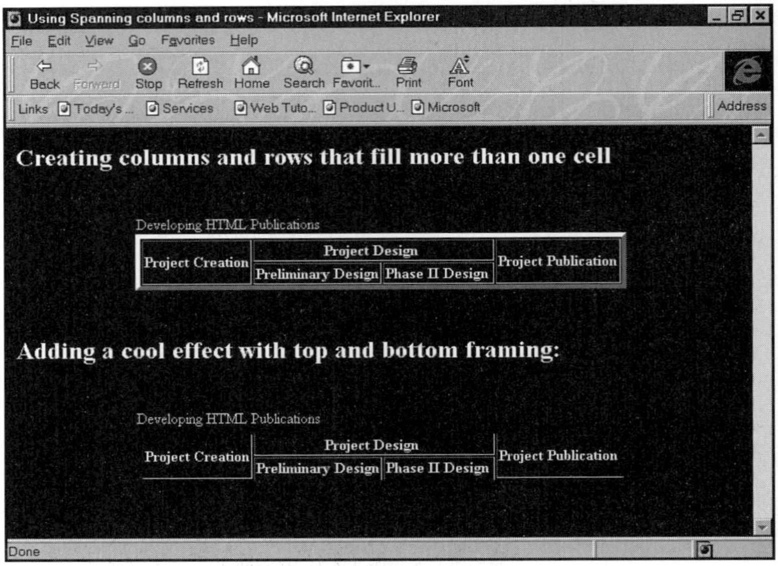

FIGURE 6.17.
Creating columns and rows that span multiple cells.

Using NOWRAP

The `NOWRAP` attribute for header and data cells is used to disable the automatic wrapping of text. Lines of text that don't wrap can alter your table's appearance by creating excessively wide cells. Therefore, you should use the `NOWRAP` attribute cautiously, if at all. If you do use `NOWRAP`, view your table with a small screen size, such as 640×480 for Windows systems or 13-inch for Macintosh systems. Here's how you can add `NOWRAP` to a data cell:

```
<TR><TH>Precise Calculation<TH>Variance
<TR><TD NOWRAP>12.872653872<TD NOWRAP>0.00000001
```

Summary

Tables can be a powerful addition to your documents. Study the key concepts of column and row headers, alignments for columns and rows, and column and row spanning. Use the examples in this chapter as guidelines for creating well-designed tables. The design concepts that went into making the tables are simple, but when combined, these concepts can be used to create more powerful tables. For example, cell padding and spacing can be used to increase the white space in the table and to make sure the data doesn't touch the cell walls.

CHAPTER 7

Creating and Enhancing Web Pages with Frames

by William Robert Stanek

IN THIS CHAPTER

Frames are an idea slightly ahead of their time—they enable you to create documents with multiple windows and, in doing so, open the door for an entirely new way to publish on the Web. Each frame is a mini-page in your Web publication. You can add scrollbars to a frame, let users manipulate the size of the frame, and add frames for permanent headers, footers, and menu bars. Hypertext references in frames can have pointers to any window defined on the page or can be used to launch an entirely new full-sized window. You can even create frames within frames.

Frame-Enhancing Your Documents

With frames, you can create documents with multiple windows. Netscape Navigator and Internet Explorer are currently the only browsers to support frames, but this will change quickly. There are plans to incorporate frames into the HTML 3.2 specification, and several other browsers plan to support frames in their next major release.

The best thing about frames is that they finally give Web publishers a way to easily create unique pages for users with Netscape Navigator and Internet Explorer. The two primary tags you use to create frames are `<FRAMESET>` and `<NOFRAME>`. Using the `<FRAMESET>` tag, you specify a section of a document that will be used by frame-capable browsers; with the `<NOFRAME>` tag, you specify a section of a document that will be used by browsers that cannot use frames.

Within the begin and end `<FRAMESET>` tag, you can only nest `FRAME` tags, which are used to identify the source of your document's frames. Although sources can be any type of document, they're typically HTML pages. The frame-enhanced page in Figure 7.1 uses three window frames. The contents of each mini-window come from a separately defined HTML document merged into a common window by using frames. As you can see, some of the frames have horizontal and vertical scrollbars that readers can use to read the additional material in the document.

In Figure 7.1, the left-hand frame was created from a document with a title image. The title image is fully animated using client-pull/server-push and can be clicked on. The right-hand frame is the primary frame; as shown here, it contains the contents of a home page created specifically for Netscape and Internet Explorer-enhanced browsers. The bottom frame contains a text-based menu. When a menu item is clicked on, the contents of the associated document are normally loaded into the main frame.

You don't have to frame-enhance all the pages at your Web site. A key concept in designing publications for frames is to define frames only on the main page readers use to access the publication. This can be your home page or any top-level page at your site. Using a top-level page reduces the amount of work you must do to frame-enhance your site and lets you use frames as they were meant to be used.

Improvements have been made to frames since they were originally implemented. Internet Explorer 3.0 made the best improvement—users can now view frame-enhanced pages without borders. (See Figure 7.2.) These so-called *borderless* frames are the key to making frame-enhanced pages more user-friendly and may help propel frames into the spotlight where they belong.

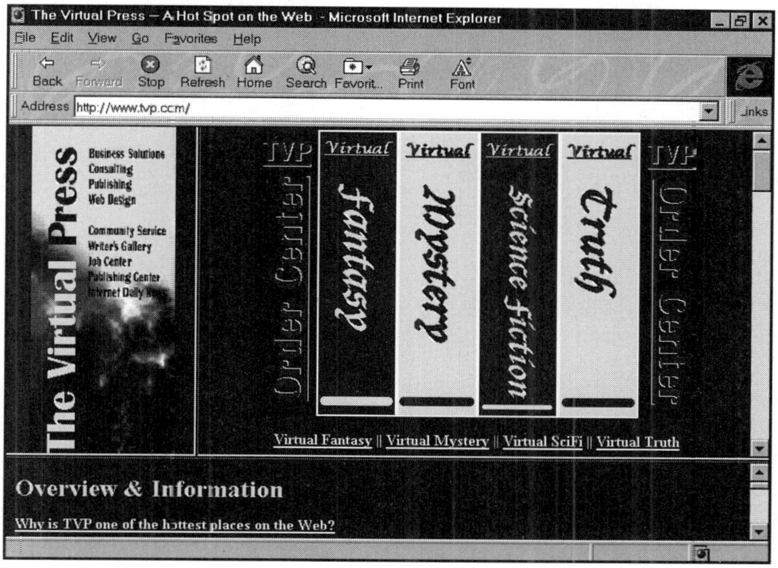

FIGURE 7.1.
The frame-enhanced Virtual Press home page.

The page shown in Figure 7.2 has four frames. The six spheres in the upper-left corner supply a link to the workshop's home page. The frame below it on the left contains a title logo, and the frame to the right of the spheres has an image map menu to key areas of the workshop. The large main frame holds the main contents for the page.

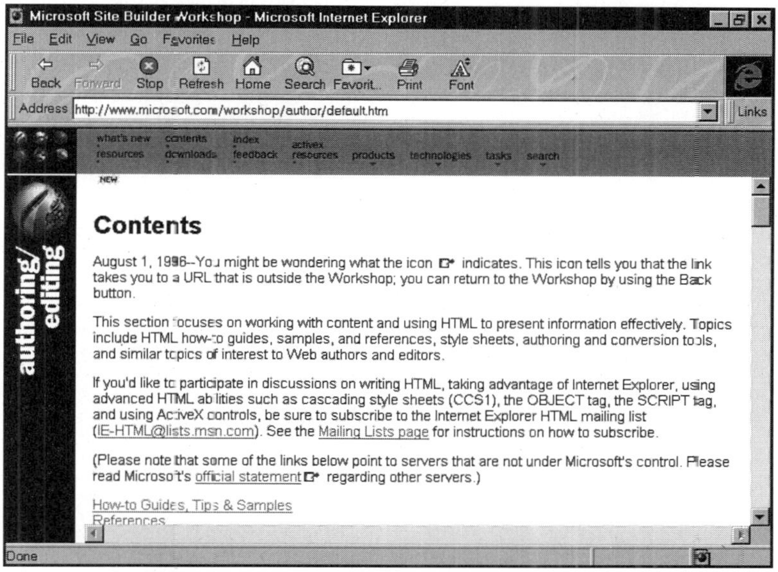

FIGURE 7.2.
The Microsoft Internet workshop with borderless frames.

Dividing a Browser Window into Frames

At first glance, the way you divide a browser window into frames can seem confusing. This is because window frames are organized much like a table is, with each window divided into one or more rows and columns. You count the rows for a window as the number of horizontal frame partitions and the columns for a window as the number of vertical frame partitions.

Using the ROWS attribute, you can define the number and size of the rows to display in your browser window. The vertical size of a row is expressed as an absolute or relative value with multiple row assignments separated by a comma. The number of rows is equal to the number of items in the comma-separated list.

With the COLS attribute, you can define the columns to display in your browser window. The size of a column is expressed as an absolute or relative value. When you have multiple columns, separate the column assignments with a comma. The number of columns is equal to the number of items in the comma-separated list.

Column and row size can be defined in three ways:

1. As an absolute value in pixels
2. As a relative value in percentage of window width
3. As a relative value following the CALS table model syntax

Assigning an absolute value in pixels may seem the easiest way to create a column or row of frames, but it's never a good idea to define all the rows or columns in terms of pixels. The size of the browser window can vary quite a bit, depending on the display mode and sizing being used. To avoid filling the window with empty space, the browser will probably override the values you've assigned to make sure the entire window is filled. This can distort your row and column assignments. Consequently, you should use fixed pixel values with relative values. The following <FRAMESET> tag defines three rows of frames with fixed pixel sizes:

```
<FRAMESET ROWS="100,300,240">
  . . .
</FRAMESET>
```

Relative values can be expressed as a percentage or on a proportionate scale of the total window size. To use percentages, assign a value between 1 and 100 and follow it with a percent sign. If the total of all percentages assigned is greater than 100, the values are scaled down to 100. If the total of all percentages assigned is less than 100, the relative sizes are scaled up to 100—in this way, the relative-sized frames are given the extra space. The following <FRAMESET> tag defines two columns of frames with relative sizes:

```
<FRAMESET COLS="10%,90%">
  . . .
</FRAMESET>
```

For relative scaling, use an asterisk with or without a value. An asterisk with no associated value is interpreted as a request to give all remaining space in the row or column to the frame you're creating. An asterisk with a value in front of it is used to scale how much relative space to assign to a frame. A frame with the value `"3*"` would get three times as much relative space as other frames that have been assigned a relative value. The following `<FRAMESET>` tag defines two relatively scaled rows and two fixed-sized rows:

```
<FRAMESET ROWS="3*,*,100,150">
 . . .
</FRAMESET>
```

The way columns and rows of frames are displayed depends on how you make row and column assignments. Each column assignment you make after your row assignments divides successive rows of frames into columns. Conversely, each row assignment you make after your column assignments divides successive columns of frames into rows.

In the example that follows, three rows are defined. The first row is divided by two columns of equal size. The other two rows extend across the entire width of the screen. Figure 7.3 shows how the following sample code is displayed:

```
<HTML>
<HEAD>
<TITLE>New Frameset</TITLE>
</HEAD>
<FRAMESET ROWS="34%,33%,33%">
    <FRAMESET COLS="50%,50%">
        <FRAME SRC=FIRST.HTM>
        <FRAME SRC=SECOND.HTM>
    </FRAMESET>
    <FRAME SRC=THIRD.HTM>
    <FRAME SRC=FOURTH.HTM>
</FRAMESET>
</HTML>
```

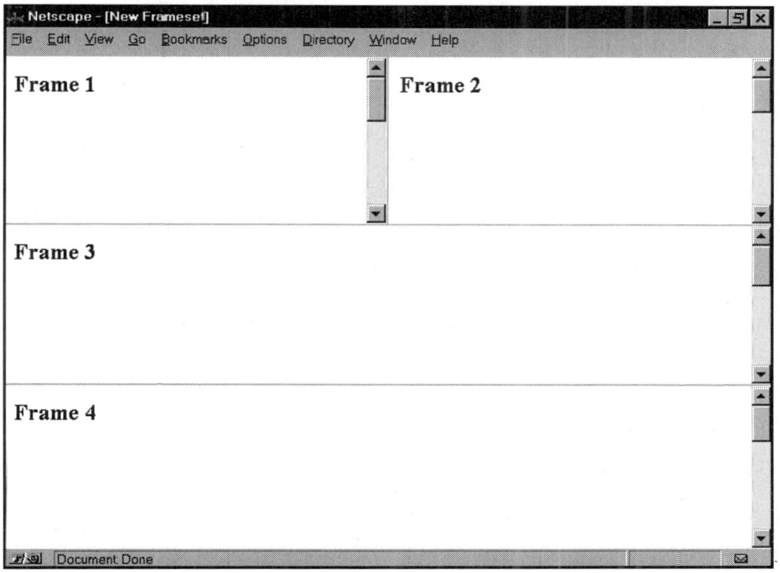

FIGURE 7.3.
Creating frames is easiest when using percentages.

By reversing the order of the column and row assignments, you create an entirely different window. The next example has two columns of equal size. The first column is divided by three rows, and the second column extends down the full length of the window. Figure 7.4 shows a sample frame-enhanced page; the sample code is available in Listing 7.1.

Listing 7.1. Creating framesets.

```
<HTML>
<HEAD>
<TITLE>Frameset 2</TITLE>
</HEAD>
<FRAMESET COLS="50%,50%">
    <FRAMESET ROWS="34%,33%,33%">
        <FRAME SRC=FIRST.HTM>
        <FRAME SRC=SECOND.HTM>
        <FRAME SRC=THIRD.HTM>
    </FRAMESET>
    <FRAME SRC=FOURTH.HTM>
</FRAMESET>
</HTML>
```

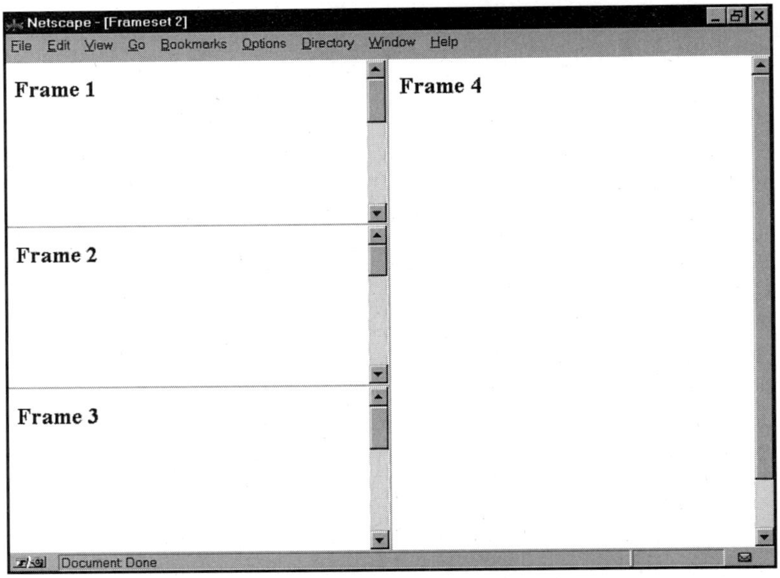

FIGURE 7.4.
A new window created by reversing column and row frames.

Defining the NOFRAME Area

With the `<NOFRAME>` tag, you can define an area of the document that's displayed by browsers that can't use frames. The `<NOFRAME>` tag is used in a pair with the begin tag `<NOFRAME>` specifying the start of the area for browsers that aren't frame-capable and the end tag `</NOFRAME>` specifying the end of this area. All frame-enhanced pages should have a fully defined `NOFRAME` area, which could simply contain your original page before you frame-enhanced it. Listing 7.2 shows a sample document with a NOFRAME area.

Listing 7.2. Defining a NOFRAME area.

```
<HTML>
<HEAD>
<TITLE>Your Home Page [Frame Enhanced]</TITLE>
</HEAD>
<FRAMESET COLS=25%,75%>
    <FRAMESET ROWS="20%,80%">
        <FRAME SRC="title.html">
        <FRAME SRC="menu.html">
</FRAMESET>
<FRAME SRC="main.html">
</FRAMESET>
<NOFRAME>
<HEAD>
<TITLE>Your Home Page [Non-Frame Enhanced]</TITLE>
</HEAD>
<BODY>
  . . .
</BODY>
</HTML>
```


As you can see from the preceding example, documents with frame assignments aren't organized like other documents. In general, they don't need a header or body section. However, you can add a header section to the top of the document to specify the title for the frame-enhanced page. You can also add a header and body section to the NOFRAME area of the document. The header and body sections in the NOFRAME area are used by browsers that can't use frames; therefore, the second title will be used by browsers that aren't frame-capable.

Creating Individual Frames

The only tag you can use within the begin and end <FRAMESET> tag is the <FRAME> tag, used to specify the source for the frame and to assign the frame's key characteristics. The source document or object for the frame is specified with the optional SRC attribute. If you don't use the SRC attribute, the frame is displayed as a blank space in the window. Because only advanced browsers, like Netscape Navigator and Internet Explorer, support frames, the source you specify is usually a document with advanced features.

In the following example, the window is divided into two columns. Although the first column is divided into three rows, the second column extends the full length of the windows. The first source assignment fills the first frame in column one, which is in the upper-left corner. The second source assignment fills the frame in the middle of column one, and the third source assignment fills the frame in the bottom column one. The final source assignment fills the large area for column two. Here is the code for the example:

```
<FRAMESET COLS="25%,75%">
    <FRAMESET ROWS="25%,25%,50%">
        <FRAME SRC="titlepage.htm">
        <FRAME SRC="subtitlepage.htm">
        <FRAME SRC="menu.htm">
    </FRAMESET>
<FRAME SRC="homepage.htm">
</FRAMESET>
```

The way you nest tags within <FRAMESET> tags is extremely important. The first <FRAMESET> tag should enclose all further assignments for frame sets and frames. In the previous example, all elements of the first column were defined first, and then elements of the second column were defined. You should define elements for rows and columns in the same way.

Other optional attributes for the <FRAME> tag include the following:

MARGINHEIGHT

MARGINWIDTH

NORESIZE

SCROLLING

NAME

Adding Frame Borders with Margins

The MARGINHEIGHT attribute controls the top and bottom margin size for the frame. Browsers that don't support borderless frames set a minimum margin size of one. For these browsers, if you assign a margin size of less than one, the browser displays the frame with a margin to make sure frame edges don't touch. If you do not assign a margin size, the browser uses a default margin size, which can vary. Consequently, you might want to assign a margin size for the frame's top and bottom margins.

The MARGINWIDTH attribute controls the left and right margin size for the frame. For browsers that don't support borderless frames, the minimum margin size is also one. You can assign MARGINHEIGHT and MARGINWIDTH as follows:

```
<FRAME SRC="titlepage.htm" MARGINHEIGHT=2 and MARGINWIDTH=2>
```

Figure 7.5 shows a frame-enhanced page that uses wide margins. The markup for the frame source page is available in Listing 7.3.

Listing 7.3. Using margins in frames.

```
<HTML>
<HEAD>
<TITLE>Frameset Using Margins</TITLE>
</HEAD>
<FRAMESET ROWS="15%,85%">
    <FRAME SRC="BANNER.HTM" MARGINWIDTH="10"
    MARGINHEIGHT="10">
```

```
    <FRAMESET COLS="50%,50%">
        <FRAME SRC="CONTEN.HTM" MARGINWIDTH="10"
        MARGINHEIGHT="10">
        <FRAME SRC="MAIN.HTM" MARGINWIDTH="10"
        MARGINHEIGHT="10">
    </FRAMESET>
    <NOFRAMES>
    <BODY>
    <P> </P>
    <P>This web page uses frames, but your browser doesn't
    support them.</P>
    </BODY>
    </NOFRAMES>
</FRAMESET>
</HTML>
```


If you examine the frame assignments in the previous listing, you will find references to three separate HTML documents. The first frame reference identifies a document called BANNER.HTM. Listing 7.4 shows the markup for the BANNER.HTM page.

Listing 7.4. The BANNER.HTM page.

```
<HTML>
<HEAD>
<TITLE>Banner Frame</TITLE>
</HEAD>
<BODY BGCOLOR="#000000" TEXT="#FFFFFF">
<H3>Banner Frame</H3>
<P>This frame should contain the main navigation links.</P>
</BODY>
</HTML>
```

The second frame assignment references a document called CONTEN.HTM. The markup for the CONTEN.HTM page is shown in Listing 7.5.

Listing 7.5. The CONTEN.HTM page.

```
<HTML>
<HEAD>
<TITLE>Table Of Contents</TITLE>
</HEAD>
<BODY BGCOLOR="FFFFFF">
<H3>Table Of Contents Frame</H3>
<P>This frame should contain links to the main pages.</P>
</BODY>
</HTML>
```

The final document referenced by the frame set is called MAIN.HTM. The markup for this page is shown in Listing 7.6.

Listing 7.6. The MAIN.HTM page.

```
<HTML>
<HEAD>
<TITLE>Main Frame</TITLE>
</HEAD>
<BODY BGCOLOR="#FFFFFF">
<H3>Main Frame</H3>
<P>This frame holds the contents of the main page.</P>
</BODY>
</HTML>
```

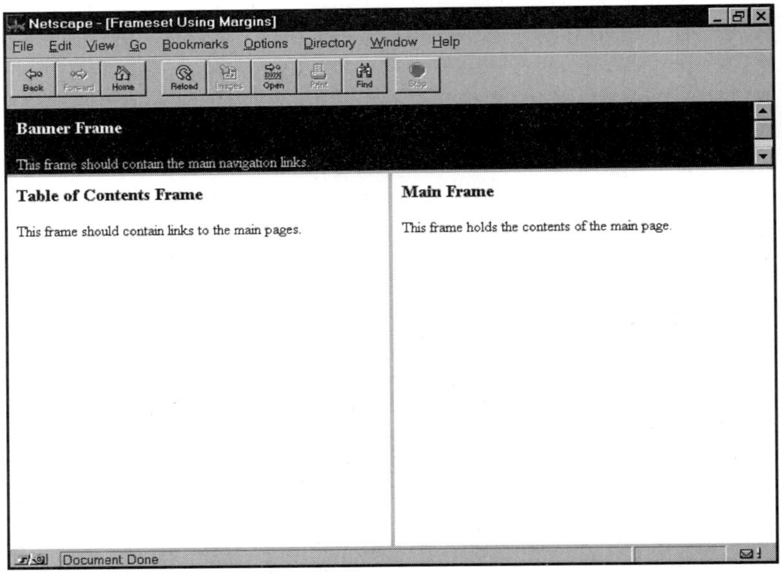

FIGURE 7.5.
Using margins in your frame-enhanced pages.

User Adjustment of Frames

Users can adjust frames in two key ways: by using scrollbars and by resizing the frame. In general, users want to be able to manipulate your frames, especially if they're using a screen size other than the one you created the publication for. However, you can turn these features on or off by using the `SCROLLING` and `NORESIZE` attributes.

By default, the browser decides whether a window should have scrollbars. If the entire document is visible in the frame, the browser automatically displays the frame without scrollbars, but if it isn't, the browser automatically displays the frame with scrollbars. The browser displays both horizontal and vertical scrollbars, regardless of whether both are needed. The `SCROLLING` attribute has three values:

```
<FRAME SCROLLING=AUTO>

<FRAME SCROLLING=YES>

<FRAME SCROLLING=NO>
```

You can override the default AUTO value for the SCROLLING attribute by setting SCROLLING=YES or SCROLLING=NO. The value SCROLLING=YES ensures that scrollbars are always visible, and the value SCROLLING=NO makes sure scrollbars are never visible.

By default, the size of all frames can be adjusted by the user. Users adjust frames by moving the cursor over a frame edge, holding down the left mouse button when the resizing icon appears, and dragging the frame edge to a new position. You can turn the resizing feature off with the NORESIZE attribute. Keep in mind that even a single frame that cannot be resized affects whether other frames in the window can be adjusted.

Targeting and Naming Frames

The NAME attribute plays a key role in how your frames interact with other frames and windows. By default, hypertext references in a frame are targeted to the frame, so when you activate a link within a frame, the new document is normally loaded into the same frame. By naming a frame, you can target it from other frames on the page. To name a frame, use a keyword that begins with an alphanumeric character, as in this example:

```
<FRAME SRC="homepage.html" NAME="MAIN">
```

By default, all frames are unnamed, but once you've assigned a name to a frame, the frame can be targeted by other frames. Usually, these frames are on the same page. For example, your page could have a main section named MAIN and a menu section targeted at the main frame. In this way, when a user clicked on a hypertext reference in the menu, the corresponding document would be loaded into the main frame.

To target a frame, use Netscape's TARGET attribute for the anchor tag <A>. The value assigned to the TARGET attribute should be the name of the frame you want to target. If you wanted to target the frame called MAIN in the window described earlier, here is how you would do it:

```
<A HREF="subpage.html" TARGET="MAIN">
```

You can assign a base target for all links in a document with the <BASE> tag. In this way, you don't have to insert target information for all links in a document. Keep in mind that a target defined in a link overrides the base target defined. Therefore, if you want to target most of the links to a single frame and some links to other frames, you can easily do this. Here's how you can assign the base target to the frame called MAIN:

```
<BASE TARGET="MAIN">
```

An interesting way to use the base target is to target a name you haven't used elsewhere. If the target name is not a frame in the currently defined window, the browser opens a new window in addition to the current window. If the current window has two unnamed frames and one frame named CENTRAL1, this base target would open a new window:

```
<BASE TARGET="WINDOW2">
```

The NAME and TARGET attributes can also be used to establish the current document's relationship to other documents. Currently, four relationships are defined:

_blank	Load this link into a new, unnamed window.
_self	Load this link over yourself.
_parent	Load this link over yourself and reset the window.
_top	Load this link at the top level.

Although all these relationships are useful, the most useful relationship is _parent. By using the _parent relationship, you force the browser to reset the window entirely and avoid loading a frame document within the current frame. You should use this relationship whenever you have a link that leads to a page containing frame assignments. For example, if lower-level documents refer to your home page, you can use the following assignment to avoid getting a frame within a frame:

```
<A HREF="yourhomepage.html" TARGET="_parent">
```

An example of frames with links targeted as other frames is shown in Figure 7.6. The code for the frame source page is available in Listing 7.7.

Listing 7.7. Using targeted links.

```
<HTML>
<HEAD>
<TITLE>Targeting Frames</TITLE>
</HEAD>
<FRAMESET ROWS="20%,80%">
    <FRAME SRC="FRBANNER.HTM" NAME="BANNER" MARGINWIDTH="5"
    MARGINHEIGHT="5">
    <FRAMESET COLS="20%,80%">
        <FRAME SRC="FRCONTEN.HTM" NAME="CONTENTS" MARGINWIDTH="5"
        MARGINHEIGHT="5">
        <FRAME SRC="FRMAIN.HTM" NAME="MAIN" MARGINWIDTH="5"
        MARGINHEIGHT="5">
    </FRAMESET>
    <NOFRAMES>
    <BODY>
    <P> </P>
    <P>This web page uses frames, but your browser doesn't
    support them.</P>
    </BODY>
    </NOFRAMES>
</FRAMESET>
</HTML>
```

As you can see in the previous listing, the frame set references three HTML documents: FRBANNER.HTM, FRCONTEN.HTM, and FRMAIN.HTM. The markup for the FRBANNER.HTM document is shown in Listing 7.8.

Listing 7.8. The FRBANNER.HTM document.

```
<HTML>
<HEAD>
<TITLE>Banner Frame</TITLE>
<BASE TARGET="CONTENTS">
</HEAD>
<BODY BGCOLOR="#888888" TEXT="#FFFFFF">
<H3>Banner Frame</H3>
<P>This frame should contain the main navigation links.
The links in this frame target
the table of contents frame.</P>
</BODY>
</HTML>
```


The contents of the FRCONTEN.HTM document are listed in Listing 7.9.

Listing 7.9. The FRCONTEN.HTM document.

```
<HTML>
<HEAD>
<TITLE>Table Of Contents</TITLE>
<BASE TARGET="MAIN">
</HEAD>
<BODY BGCOLOR="000000" TEXT="FFFFFF">
<H3>Table Of Contents Frame</H3>
<P>This frame should contain links to the main pages.
Links in this frame target
the main frame.</P>
</BODY>
</HTML>
```

The FRMAIN.HTM document is shown in Listing 7.10.

Listing 7.10. The FRMAIN.HTM document.

```
<HTML>
<HEAD>
<TITLE>Main Frame</TITLE>
</HEAD>
<BODY BGCOLOR="#FFFFFF">
<H3>Main Frame</H3>
<P>This frame holds the contents of the main page.
Links in this page do not
target any other frame.</P>
</BODY>
</HTML>
```

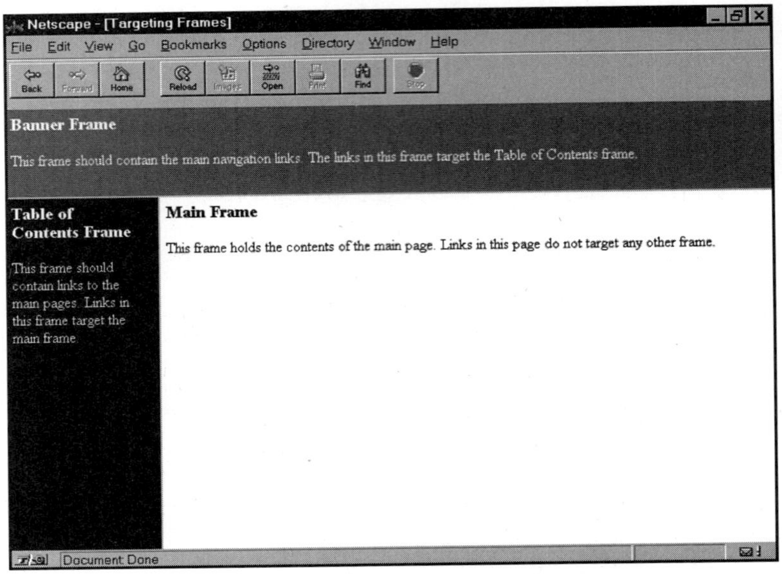

FIGURE 7.6.
Targeting your frames.

Creating Borderless Frames

Internet Explorer 3.0 supports enhancements that let users view frames without borders. If you're frame-enhancing your pages specifically for Internet Explorer 3.0, you might want to use optional `FRAMEBORDER` and `FRAMESPACING` attributes for the `<FRAMESET>` tag. Set the `FRAMEBORDER` and `FRAMESPACING` field values to zero for all frames in your document, which is a trick you can use to get borderless frames. Keep in mind that borders and scrollbars are automatically added if the content of the frame is larger than the area dedicated to the frame, so keep document content to a minimum if you want to get borderless frames.

Figure 7.7 shows a page with borderless frames. The markup for the frame source page is shown in Listing 7.11.

Listing 7.11. Using borderless frames.

```
<HTML>
<HEAD>
<TITLE>Borderless Frames</TITLE>
</HEAD>
<FRAMESET ROWS="20%,80%" FRAMEBORDER="0"
    FRAMESPACING="0">
    <FRAME SRC="BANNER.HTM">
    <FRAMESET COLS="50%,50%" FRAMEBORDER="0"
        FRAMESPACING="0">
        <FRAME SRC="CONTEN.HTM">
        <FRAME SRC="MAIN.HTM">
    </FRAMESET>
    <NOFRAMES>
```

```
    <BODY>
    <P> </P>
    <P>This web page uses frames, but your browser doesn't
    support them.</P>
    </BODY>
    </NOFRAMES>
</FRAMESET>
</HTML>
```

FIGURE 7.7.
A page with borderless frames.

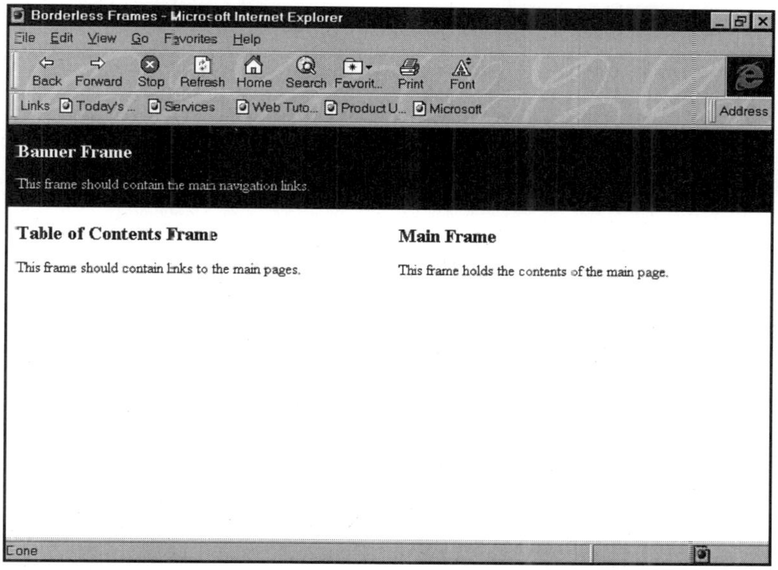

Creating Stylish Frames

Frames offer endless possibilities for your pages. This section highlights the most common styles for frame-enhanced pages. You will find the complete HTML markup for these pages on the CD-ROM accompanying this book. Use the source code as a template to help you frame-enhance your own pages.

Main Document with Footnotes

Figure 7.8 shows a document with a Main frame and a scrolling Footnote frame. The Main frame targets the Footnote frame and should hold the main information for the document. When users click a link in the Main frame, the corresponding footnotes are displayed in the Footnote frame. Listing 7.12 contains the source code for this example.

Listing 7.12. Using footnotes.

```
<html>
<head>
<title>Frame With Footnotes</title>
</head>
<frameset rows="78%,22%">
    <frame src="frmain.htm" name="main" marginwidth="1"
    marginheight="1">
    <frame src="frfootno.htm" name="footnotes" marginwidth="1"
    marginheight="1">
    <noframes>
    <body>
    <p>This web page uses frames, but your browser doesn't
    support them.</p>
    </body>
    </noframes>
</frameset>
</html>
```

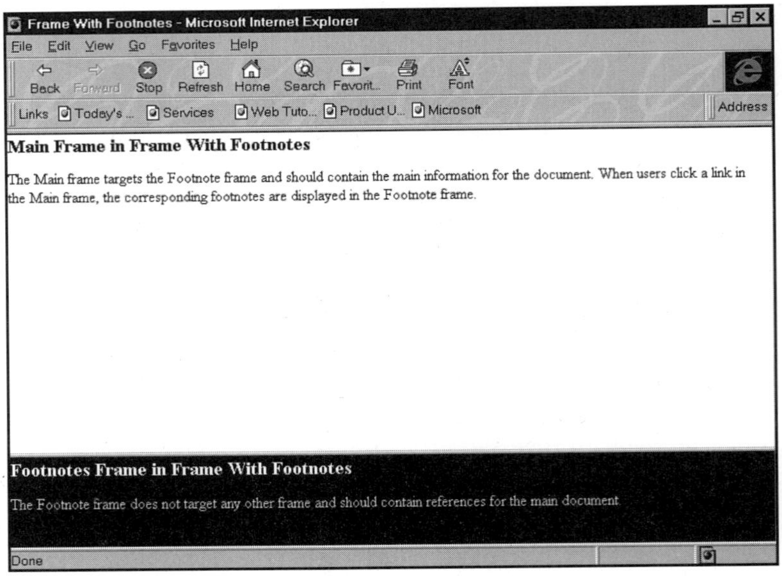

FIGURE 7.8.
Creating a document with footnotes.

Navigation Bars with a Table of Contents

Figure 7.9 shows a document with navigation bars at the top and bottom, a Table of Contents frame, and a Main frame. Navigation bars are usually image map banners. Both navigation bars target the Table of Contents frame and should contain the main navigation links. When users click a link in either navigation bar, their browser will load the referenced document into the Table of Contents frame. The frame source page for this example is shown in Listing 7.13.

Listing 7.13. Using navigation bars.

```
<html>
<head>
<title>Frameset with Navigation bars</title>
</head>
<frameset rows="13%,73%,14%">
    <frame src="frtop.htm" name="top" noresize>
    <frameset cols="25%,75%">
        <frame src="frconten.htm" name="contents">
        <frame src="frmain01.htm" name="main">
    </frameset>
    <frame src="frbottom.htm" name="bottom" noresize>
    <noframes>
    <body>
    <p>This web page uses frames, but your browser doesn't
    support them.</p>
    </body>
    </noframes>
</frameset>
</html>
```


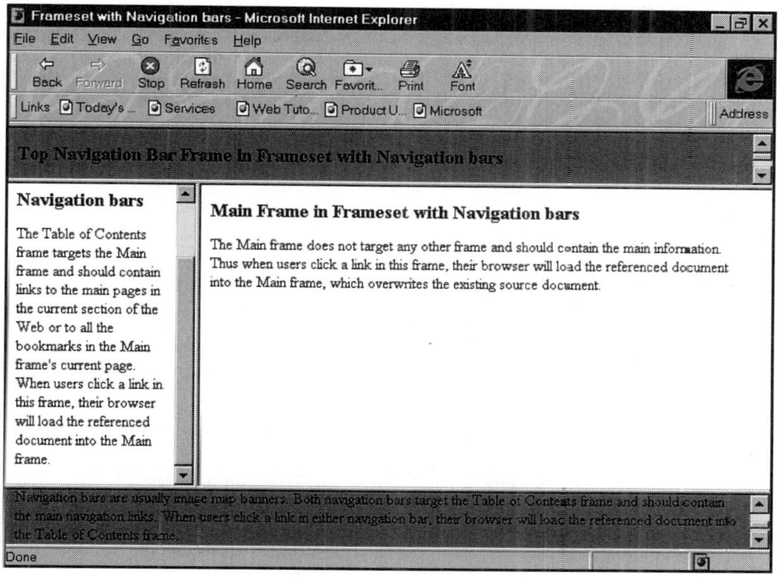

FIGURE 7.9.
Creating a document with navigation bars.

A Top-Down, Three-Level Hierarchy

Figure 7.10 shows a document with a top-down hierarchy split into three frames. The top frame targets the middle frame and should contain the main sections of your Web site. When users click a link in the top frame, their browser will load the referenced document into the middle frame. Listing 7.14 contains the source code for the frame-enhanced page shown in the figure.

Listing 7.14. A three-level hierarchy.

```
<html>
<head>
<title>A Top-Down Hierarchy</title>
</head>
<frameset rows="15%,29%,56%">
    <frame src="frtop01.htm" name="top" marginwidth="1"
    marginheight="1">
    <frame src="frmiddle.htm" name="middle" marginwidth="1"
    marginheight="1">
    <frame src="frbott01.htm" name="bottom" marginwidth="1"
    marginheight="1">
    <noframes>
    <body>
    <p>This web page uses frames, but your browser doesn't
    support them.</p>
    </body>
    </noframes>
</frameset>
</html>
```

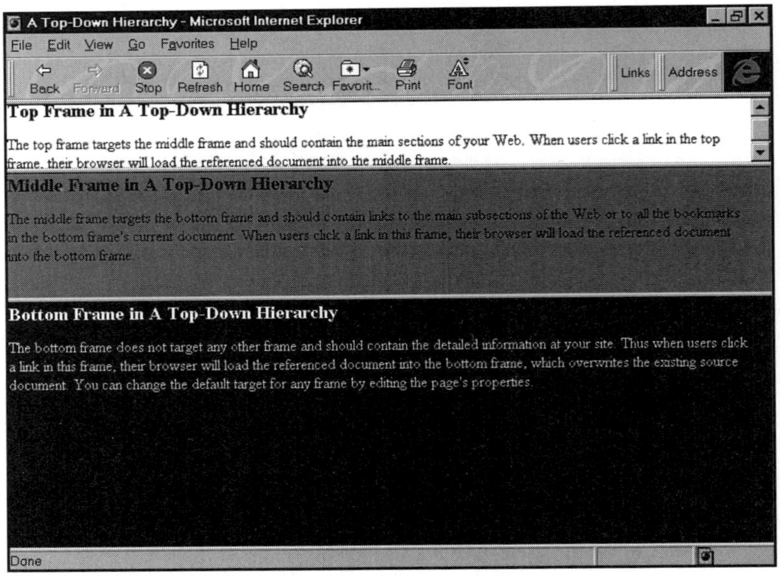

FIGURE 7.10.
Creating a document with a top-down hierarchy.

A Nested Three-Level Hierarchy

Figure 7.11 shows a document with a nested hierarchy split into three frames. The left frame targets the right top frame and should contain the main sections of your Web site. When users click a link in the top frame, their browser will load the referenced document into the right top frame. The source code for the figure is shown in Listing 7.15.

Listing 7.15. Using a nested hierarchy.

```
<html>
<head>
<title>Nested Three-level Hierarchy</title>
</head>
<frameset cols="23%,77%">
    <frame src="frleft.htm" name="left" marginwidth="1"
    marginheight="1">
    <frameset rows="18%,82%">
        <frame src="frrtop.htm" name="rtop" marginwidth="1"
        marginheight="1">
        <frame src="frrbotto.htm" name="rbottom" marginwidth="1"
        marginheight="1">
    </frameset>
    <noframes>
    <body>
    <p>This web page uses frames, but your browser doesn't
    support them.</p>
    </body>
    </noframes>
</frameset>
</html>
```


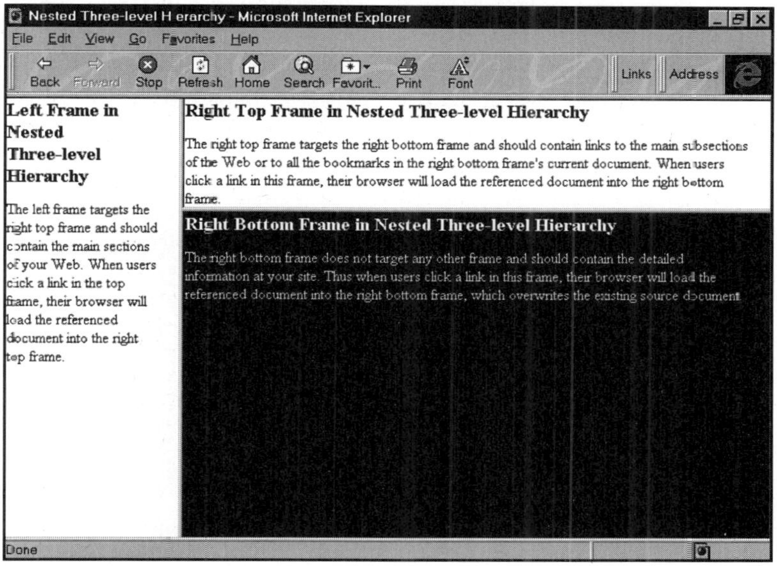

FIGURE 7.11.
Creating a document with a nested hierarchy.

A Simple Table of Contents

Figure 7.12 shows a document with a Table of Contents frame and a Main frame. The Table of Contents frame targets the Main frame and should contain links to the main pages in the current section of the Web or to all the bookmarks in the Main frame's current page. When users click a link in this frame, their browser will load the referenced document into the Main frame.

The source code for the frame-enhanced page with a table of contents is shown in Listing 7.16.

Listing 7.16. Using a table of contents.

```
<html>
<head>
<title>Frameset with Table of Contents</title>
</head>
<frameset cols="18%,82%">
    <frame src="frcont01.htm" name="contents" marginwidth="1"
    marginheight="1">
    <frame src="frmain02.htm" name="main" marginwidth="1"
    marginheight="1">
    <noframes>
    <body>
    <p>This web page uses frames, but your browser doesn't
    support them.</p>
    </body>
    </noframes>
</frameset>
</html>
```

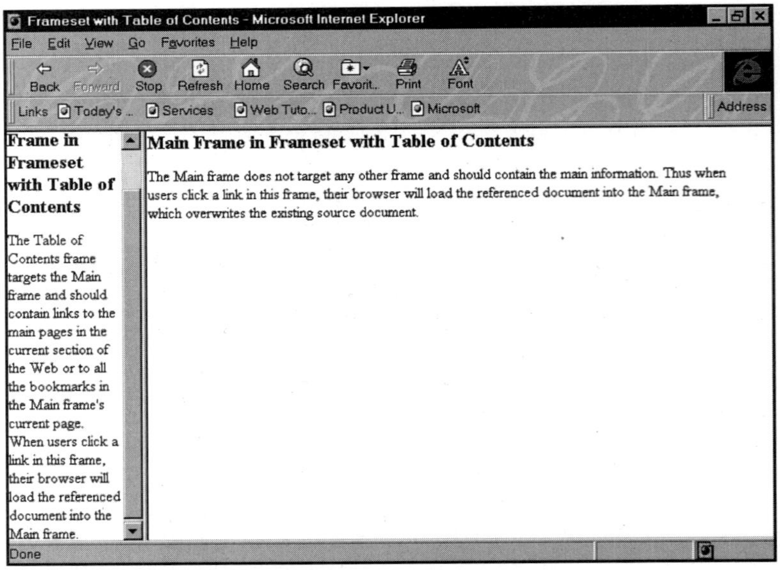

FIGURE 7.12.
Creating a document with a table of contents.

Summary

You can frame-enhance a single page or your entire Web site. Frames are more than mini-windows within the larger browser window—they are the gateway to an entirely new way to publish on the Web. If you've ever wanted to add powerful features to your Web publications, frames offer definite starting points.

CHAPTER 8

Using Style Sheets

by William Robert Stanek

IN THIS CHAPTER

Style sheets offer total control over every aspect of your Web page, and the Cascading Style Sheets Level 1 specification lives up to that promise. With style sheets, you can set specific font sizes, types, and colors anywhere in your Web page. You can add and change background colors to highlight sections of text. You can control margins and spacing around text and graphical elements. You can even control the placement of design elements and the style of borders to display around images.

What Are Style Sheets and How Are They Used?

Style sheets are a dream come true for Web publishers who wanted their Web pages to use the same advanced design and layout techniques offered by popular desktop publishing software. With style sheets, you can specify design and layout parameters for every element in your Web page. If you want all Level 1 headings to be in 45-point Times Roman, you simply add a single specification to your page to take care of all Level 1 headings. If you also want all headings displayed in brown and paragraph text in blue, you can add this specification, too.

Adding a style sheet to your page is easier than you might think. Compare the page shown in Figure 8.1 to the page shown in Figure 8.2. Both pages have the same contents, but the first page uses a style sheet that gives the page a unique look. The second example is a plain old run-of-the-mill HTML page without a style sheet. The difference between these pages is striking, especially if you view them in color with your browser.

NOTE

To view pages that use style sheets, you need a style sheet-capable browser. The primary browser that supports style sheets is Internet Explorer 3.0/4.0. If you have problems viewing the style sheet examples in your browser, check that your version of Internet Explorer is current.

The style sheet used in Figure 8.1 sets the following design parameters:

- All Level 1 headings are in 45-point Times Roman and displayed in brown.
- All paragraphs are in 12-point Times Roman and displayed in blue.
- The first line of all paragraphs is indented one inch.
- The right margin for paragraphs is set to one inch.
- All block quotations are in 10-point Helvetica and displayed in black.
- Highlighting with a yellow background is added to all block quotations.

Listing 8.1 shows the complete markup for the sample page.

Listing 8.1. Using style sheets.

```
<HTML>
<HEAD>
<TITLE>Designing Powerful Pages With Style Sheets</TITLE>
<STYLE>
H1  {font: 45pt Times; color: brown}
P  {font: 12pt Times; color: blue; text-indent: 1in; margin-right: 1in}
BLOCKQUOTE  {font: 10pt Helvetica; color: black; background: yellow}
</STYLE>
</HEAD>
<BODY BGCOLOR=#FFFFFF>
<H1 ALIGN=CENTER>Designing Great Pages</H1>
<P> </P>
<P ALIGN=RIGHT>Pages with high visual impact will leave a lasting impression
 on readers. High visual impact does not necessarily correlate to high
 resolution graphics. Some of the most visually stunning pages contain
 no graphics at all. They achieve their impact from simplicity of design.
 They use screen space, color, fonts and headings to their advantage.</P>
<P ALIGN=RIGHT>The best writing looks effortless. Words seem to flow straight
 from the writer's pen. The same is true about the best designed pages.
 Well-designed pages look effortless. They are organized in a way that is
 coherent and flowing.</P>
<P ALIGN=LEFT>
<BLOCKQUOTE>The secret to making words seem to flow effortlessly
 is simple. Good work is the result of hard work-careful editing, revision
 and proofreading. Creating a single polished page may take hours.
 Well-designed pages are also the result of hard work. Designs that seem simple
 and natural to the reader are often the result of intense efforts to make
 them seem this way.-
<FONT SIZE=-3>William R. Stanek</FONT>
</BLOCKQUOTE>
</P>
</HTML>
```

8 USING STYLE SHEETS

NOTE

For now, don't worry about the syntax used to set style sheet parameters. You will find detailed instructions later in the chapter.

If you examine Listing 8.1, you can see that nine design parameters are set with the following five lines of markup code:

```
<STYLE>
H1  {font: 45pt Times; color: brown}
P  {font: 12pt Times; color: blue; text-indent: 1in; margin-right: 1in}
BLOCKQUOTE  {font: 10pt Helvetica; color: black; background: yellow}
</STYLE>
```

Defining a style sheet within the page header is just one way you can add style to your Web pages. If you define your style parameters in a separate document, you can import this *style sheet* into any page at your Web site. This allows you to apply a single style sheet to multiple pages, which adds a consistent look and feel to your Web pages.

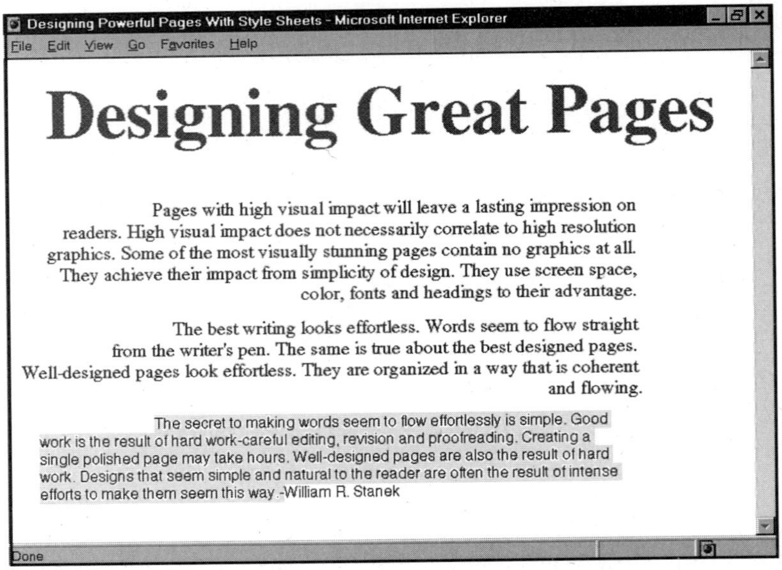

FIGURE 8.1.
Adding style to your pages.

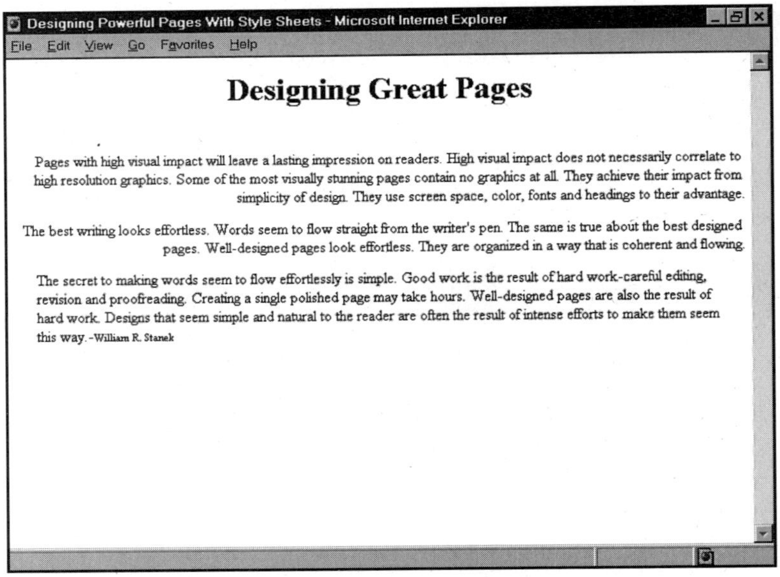

FIGURE 8.2.
A page without a style sheet.

Using the same parameters in the earlier listing, you could create a document called `Style1` with the following contents:

```
H1  {font: 45pt Times; color: brown}
P  {font: 12pt Times; color: blue; text-indent: 1in; margin-right: 1in}
BLOCKQUOTE  {font: 10pt Helvetica; color: black; background: yellow}
```

After saving the style sheet as standard ASCII text, you could then import the style sheet into your Web page, as shown in Listing 8.2.

Listing 8.2. Using imported style sheets.

```
<HTML>
<HEAD>
<TITLE>Designing Powerful Pages With Style Sheets</TITLE>
<STYLE>
@import url(http://www.tvp.com/Style1);
@import url(http://www.tvp.com/Style2);
@import url(http://www.tvp.com/Style3);
</STYLE>
</HEAD>
<BODY BGCOLOR=#FFFFFF>
 . . .
</HTML>
```

TIP

The style sheet specification allows you to import style sheets from multiple sources. If a conflict occurs, such as one style sheet sets the color of paragraph text to blue and another style sheet sets the color to brown, the specification sets up clear rules to handle it–more on this later in the section titled "Cascading Style Sheets."

Another way to refer to external style sheets is with the `<LINK>` tag and its relationship attribute `REL`; this method is shown in Listing 8.3.

Listing 8.3. Referring to an external style sheet.

```
<HTML>
<HEAD>
<TITLE>Designing Powerful Pages With Style Sheets</TITLE>
<LINK REL=STYLESHEET HREF="Style1" >
</HEAD>
<BODY BGCOLOR=#FFFFFF>
 . . .
</HTML>
```

Sometimes, you want to add only a few style parameters to your page. No problem—the style sheet specification lets you add style elements wherever and whenever you want to in your pages by using inline style notation; an example of this is shown in Listing 8.4.

Listing 8.4. Using inline style references.

```
<HTML>
<HEAD>
<TITLE>Designing Powerful Pages With Style Sheets</TITLE>
</HEAD>
<BODY BGCOLOR=#FFFFFF>
<H1 ALIGN=CENTER STYLE="font: 45pt Times; color: brown">
Designing Great Pages</H1>
<P> </P>
<P ALIGN=RIGHT STYLE="font: 12pt Times; color: blue;
➥text-indent: 1in; margin-right: 1in">
Pages with high visual impact will leave a lasting impression
 on readers. High visual impact does not necessarily correlate to high
 resolution graphics. Some of the most visually stunning pages contain
 no graphics at all. They achieve their impact from simplicity of design.
 They use screen space, color, fonts and headings to their advantage.
<P ALIGN=RIGHT STYLE="font: 12pt Times; color: blue;
➥text-indent: 1in; margin-right: 1in">
The best writing looks effortless. Words seem to flow straight
 from the writer's pen. The same is true about the best designed pages.
 Well-designed pages look effortless. They are organized in a way that is
 coherent and flowing.</P>
<P ALIGN=LEFT STYLE="font: 12pt Times; color: blue;
➥text-indent: 1in; margin-right: 1in">
<BLOCKQUOTE STYLE="font: 10pt Helvetica; color: black; background: yellow">
The secret to making words seem to flow effortlessly
 is simple. Good work is the result of hard work-careful editing, revision
 and proofreading. Creating a single polished page may take hours.
 Well-designed pages are also the result of hard work. Designs that seem simple
 and natural to the reader are often the result of intense efforts to make
 them seem this way.-
<FONT SIZE=-3>William R. Stanek</FONT></BLOCKQUOTE>
</P>
</HTML>
```

When you place inline style notations throughout your page, you lose the greatest benefit of style sheets—the ability to separate the presentation from the content. Still, there are many times when defining inline style parameters makes sense, especially if you want to override a default style set in the page header.

Examining the <STYLE> Tag

Using the <STYLE> tag, you can add style sheet parameters to the header of your Web pages. The only attribute for the <STYLE> tag is the TYPE attribute that assigns a style sheet language. If you don't set the TYPE attribute to a specific value, this default for the Cascading Style Sheet specification is generally assumed to be the following:

```
<STYLE TYPE="text/css">
```

If you assign a different style notation, it must be a recognized style notation in the browser's document type definition, such as `dssl-lite`.

NOTE

DSSL is the Document Style Semantics and Specification Language. This very complex style notation isn't well-suited for use on the World Wide Web, which is why a subset of DSSL called DSSL Lite was defined. You may hear more about DSSL or DSSL Lite as the style sheet specification evolves.

Style assignments you make between the begin and end `STYLE` tags override the browser's defaults and are based only on a known style sheet referred to in the `TYPE` attribute or the widely accepted default of `text/css`. This is the key difference between a style sheet defined with the `<STYLE>` tag and one assigned using the `<LINK>` tag. A style sheet specified in the `<STYLE>` tag is a reference to a standard style sheet known to the browser, and any style changes are assigned between the open and close `STYLE` tags. A style sheet specified in a link can be a reference to a style sheet anywhere on the Internet and isn't included as part of the document.

You could add the `<STYLE>` tag to your document as follows:

```
<HTML>
<HEAD>
<TITLE>The Web Book</TITLE>
<STYLE NOTATION=dsssl-lite"> . . . </STYLE>
</HEAD>
<BODY>
 . . .
</BODY>
</HTML>
```

NOTE

Style sheets are fairly new to Web publishing but are powerful enough to warrant close attention. Currently, the only major browsers to support style sheets are Internet Explorer 3.0 and Netscape Navigator 4.0. As more browsers support style sheets, you will see dramatic changes in the way information is published on the Web. One way to keep pace with changes in Web publishing associated with style sheets is to add the following address to your browser's hot list:

`http://www.w3.org/hypertext/WWW/Style/`

Style Sheet Basics

Before getting into the really fun stuff, take a look at some style sheet basics, such as:

- Grouping styles
- Learning about cascading style sheets

- Using class types
- Spanning document sections

Grouping Styles

Every textual or graphical element in your Web page can have a unique look. According to what you've learned so far for style sheets, you would apply one style parameter to each element. For example, to set the color of all headings to brown, you might use the following:

```
<STYLE>
H1  {color: brown}
H2  {color: brown}
H3  {color: brown}
H4  {color: brown}
H5  {color: brown}
H6  {color: brown}
</STYLE>
```

Having to define each style element separately would mean using very large style sheets and increasing the download time of your page. However, you can combine similar definitions by grouping them in a comma-separated list, such as in this example:

```
<STYLE>
H1, H2, H3, H4, H5, H6  {color: brown}
P, BLOCKQUOTE  {color: blue}
</STYLE>
```

Cascading Style Sheets

Being able to import multiple style sheets into the same page comes in handy more times than you might expect, especially if you rely on external style sheet definitions. The cascading effect of the style sheet specification is a tremendous advantage for resolving style conflicts that might happen. When style sheets cascade, they follow a specific precedence order for style definitions, which is based on three key factors, listed in lowest to highest precedence order:

- The weight of the definition
- The origin of the definition
- The specificity of the definition

When resolving a style conflict and determining which style to display when, the first factor a client examines is the weight of the definition. By default, all definitions have a weight of `normal`. You can change the weight of a definition by declaring it as `important`:

```
<STYLE>
H1, H2, H3, H4, H5, H6  {color: brown ! important}
P, BLOCKQUOTE  {color: blue ! important}
</STYLE>
```

The second factor examined is the origin of the definition. The current specification allows both Web publishers and Web users to create style sheets. The publishers' definitions have higher precedence than users' definitions.

The final factor examined is the specificity of the definition. A definition that applies to a general element on the page, such as a page division, has a lower precedence than a specific element, such as a listed item in an unordered list. Similarly, a definition imported from an external style sheets has a lower precedence than a definition defined inline.

Don't try to memorize the precedence order. Knowing that a precedence order exists is usually enough for most Web publishers and can explain why a section of the page doesn't display exactly the way you want it to. If you understand that there is a precedence order, you can fix a troublesome element simply by giving an inline style definition to the page element you want to correct.

Class Types

Using class types, you can create sets of style rules, and then apply them to elements in your pages by referring to the class type. Defining a class type is easy—all you have to do is append a class label to your style definition. You separate the style definition and the class label with a period, as in the following example:

```
<STYLE>
H1.styleA  {font: 45pt Times; color: brown}
H1.styleB  {font: 30pt Arial; color: blue}
</STYLE>
```

To apply the style definition in your page, you must refer to the class type; examine Listing 8.5 to see how you do this.

Listing 8.5. Using class types.

```
<HTML>
<HEAD>
<TITLE>Using Classes in Style Sheets</TITLE>
<STYLE>
H1.styleA  {font: 45pt Times; color: brown}
H1.styleB  {font: 30pt Arial; color: blue}
</STYLE>
</HEAD>
<BODY>
<H1 CLASS="styleA"> This heading is in styleA</H1>
<P> . . . </P>
<H1 CLASS="styleB"> This heading is in styleB</H1>
<P> . . . </P>
</HTML>
```

Spanning Document Sections

The <SPAN> tag is a useful markup tag introduced by style sheets. Using this tag, you can apply style definitions to entire sections of your page. Here's how you specify the style for the spanned section in the document header:

```
SPAN { font: Arial; color: white}
```

Then, in the body of the document you simply insert the begin and end <SPAN> tag wherever you want to apply your style definition:

```
<SPAN>
<H1> A heading using the SPAN style definitions.</H1>
<P> A paragraph using the SPAN style definitions.</P>
<P> A paragraph using the SPAN style definitions.</P>
</SPAN>
```

You can specify style definitions for spanned sections directly in the text, as well:

```
<SPAN STYLE="font: Arial; color: white">
<H1> A heading using the SPAN style definitions.</H1>
<P> A paragraph using the SPAN style definitions.</P>
<P> A paragraph using the SPAN style definitions.</P>
</SPAN>
```

Decorating Your Text with Fancy Styles

The font you use defines the way text looks. When publications were typeset for a printing press, the number of fonts publishers used were limited. Each new font in the publication cost the publisher money. Some companies that specialized in creating fonts charged thousands of dollars for a single font; because of this, even in the early days of computing, fonts were still expensive.

Thankfully, this isn't true today. The power of type was unleashed in the early days of the desktop publishing revolution. Now, you can buy fonts for pennies, and there are thousands to choose from.

Using Font Styles

Beyond the uppercase and lowercase characters that make up fonts, fonts have many different characteristics. You can use normal type, bold type, italic type, and bold italic type. These different font types add emphasis and convey meanings. For example, italics can convey a sense of nostalgia, and bold type seems to be shouting at you.

Style sheets give you precise control over font characteristics with three properties: `font-weight`, `font-style`, and `text-transform`. Using the `font-weight` property, you control the boldness of text on the page, which makes text lighter or darker. Using the `font-style` property, you control the style of the font as normal, italic, or small caps. Using the `text-transform` property, you specify whether text is in uppercase, lowercase, or title case.

The `font-weight` for normal text is `medium`. You can adjust the boldness of the text with these relative values:

`lighter`: Displays text one step lighter than other text in the same element.

```
font-weight: lighter
```

`bolder`: Displays text one step darker than other text in the same element.

```
font-weight: bolder
```

Or you can use these absolute values:

```
font-weight: extra-light
font-weight: light
font-weight: demi-light
font-weight: medium
font-weight: demi-bold
font-weight: bold
font-weight: extra-bold
```

The default `font-style` of text on the page is `normal`, but you can change the style of the font as follows:

```
font-style: normal
font-style: italic
font-style: small-caps
```

To change text case, you can use the `text-transform` property with these values:

capitalize: Displays the first character of each word in uppercase.

```
text-transform: capitalize
```

uppercase: Displays all characters in uppercase.

```
text-transform: uppercase
```

lowercase: Displays all characters in lowercase.

```
text-transform: lowercase
```

none: Displays all characters in default style and eliminates an inherited style.

```
text-transform: none
```

NOTE

As more browsers support style sheets, you can use font styles to create a unique look for your pages. Unfortunately, current browsers, including Internet Explorer 3.0, support only a minimal set of font styles. You'll have to wait for browsers to catch up with the standard to take full advantage of font styles.

Examine Listing 8.6 to see how you can add font styles to your pages.

Listing 8.6. Using font styles.

```
<HTML>
<HEAD>
<TITLE>Using Font Styles</TITLE>
</HEAD>

<BODY>
<P>The font-weight for normal text is medium. You can adjust the
 boldness of the text with these relative values:</P>

<DL>
<DT>lighter
<DD STYLE="font-weight: lighter">Displays text in one step lighter
 than other text in the same element.</DD>
<DD STYLE="font-weight: lighter">font-weight: lighter</DD>
<DT>bolder
<DD STYLE="font-weight: bolder">Displays text in one step darker than
 other text in the same element.</DD>
<DD STYLE="font-weight: bolder">font-weight: bolder</DD>
</DL>

<UL>
<LI STYLE="font-weight: extra-light">font-weight: extra-light</LI>
<LI STYLE="font-weight: light">font-weight: light</LI>
<LI STYLE="font-weight: demi-light">font-weight: demi-light</LI>
<LI STYLE="font-weight: medium">font-weight: medium</LI>
<LI STYLE="font-weight: demi-bold">font-weight: demi-bold</LI>
<LI STYLE="font-weight: bold">font-weight: bold</LI>
<LI STYLE="font-weight: extra-bold">font-weight: extra-bold</LI>
</UL>

<P>The default font-style of text on the page is normal. You can change
 the style of the font to normal, italic or small-caps as follows:</P>

<UL>
<LI STYLE="font-style: normal">font-style: normal</LI>
<LI STYLE="font-style: italic">font-style: italic</LI>
<LI STYLE="font-style: small-caps">font-style: small-caps</LI>
</UL>

<P>To change the case of text, you can use the text-transform property
 with these values:</P>

<DL>
<DT>capitalize
<DD STYLE="text-transform: capitalize"> Display the first character
 of each word in uppercase.</DD>
<DD STYLE="text-transform: capitalize">text-transform: capitalize</DD>
<DT>uppercase
<DD STYLE="text-transform: uppercase">Display the all characters in
 uppercase.</DD>
<DD STYLE="text-transform: uppercase">text-transform: uppercase</DD>
<DT>lowercase
<DD STYLE="text-transform: lowercase">Display the all characters
 in lowercase.</DD>
```

```
<DD STYLE="text-transform: lowercase">text-transform: lowercase</DD>
<DT>none
<DD STYLE="text-transform: none">Displays all characters in default
 style and eliminates an inherited style.</DD>
<DD STYLE="text-transform: none">text-transform: none</DD>
</DL>

</BODY>
</HTML>
```

Using Font Sizes

Fonts come in many sizes. The larger the type size, the larger the type. Font size is specified in units called *points*. A point is a printing unit that equals approximately 1/72 inch. However, the true size of the point really depends on how the font was designed. Words in 10-point type using one font may not be the same as words in 10-point type in another font. This ambiguity in font sizes is something computers and desktop publishing have brought to the art of printing.

The most common point size for material designed to be read on a computer is 12-point. This is a good size for the main textual portions of the publication. Other common sizes range from 9 to 12 for the main text; here are two rules of thumb for font size:

Don't make the type size so small the reader has to squint to read.

Don't make type size so large that readers feel they have to sit across the room from the screen.

To set font size in your style sheets, you can use the `font-size` property. The two-letter abbreviation for a font point is `pt` and is used as follows:

```
font-size: 12pt

font-size: 40pt
```

Figure 8.3 shows a page that uses font size. To see how font sizes were changed within the document, examine Listing 8.7.

Listing 8.7. Using font sizes.

```
<HTML>
<HEAD>
<TITLE>Using Font Sizes</TITLE>
</HEAD>
<BODY BGCOLOR="#FFFFFF">
<P Style="font-size: 12pt">Fonts come in many sizes. The larger the type size,
 the larger the type. The most common point size for material designed to
 be read on a computer is 12-point. This is a good size for the main textual
 portions of the publication. Other common sizes range from 9 to 12 for the
 main text.</P>
```

continues

Listing 8.7. continued

```
<P Style="font-size: 12pt">Two rules of thumb for font size are:</P>
<UL>
<LI Style="font-size: 6pt">Do not make the type size so small the reader
 has to squint to read.</LI>
<LI Style="font-size: 40pt">Do not make type size so large that the readers
 feel they have to sit across the room from the screen either.</LI>
</UL>
</BODY>
</HTML>
```

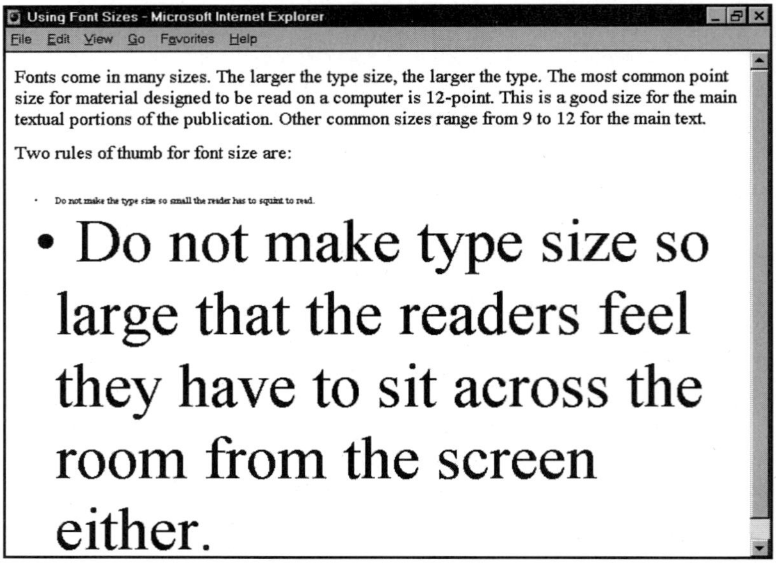

FIGURE 8.3.
Changing font size with style sheets.

Using Font Faces

Fonts come in thousands of styles named by their designers. Many font styles in use today are hundreds of years old. Fonts like Baskerville have been around since 1766. Some types considered modern first appeared over 200 years ago, but others like Castellar, Contemporary Brush, and BriemScript have been around for only a few decades.

The name of a font sometimes conveys a message about the style of the font, but not always. Fonts like Ransom, Futura, Century Gothic, and NuptialScript carry distinct messages about the style, and fonts like New Century Schoolbook, Contemporary Brush, Courier New, and Times New Roman all seem to be saying they are modern styles. However, thousands of other font faces simply have a name that may or may not convey a meaning to you.

TIP

The font you choose for the main text doesn't have to be the font you use for headings. Some fonts were meant to be used in headings, some were designed to be decorative, and others were designed to be used in normal text. The key to selecting a good font style is to use one that's easy to read in a variety of conditions and works well for the purpose you have in mind.

A key concept in using fonts in your publications is to limit the number of font styles you use on any one page. For the sake of consistency, you should also limit the number of fonts you use throughout the publication. A good rule of thumb is to use no more than three different font styles on any page and, if possible and practical, use the same fonts throughout the publication.

To specify the font face, use the `font-family` property. Font families are specified by a precise name, such as New Century Schoolbook, or in terms of a general font style, such as serif. If the font type isn't available on the user's system, the default font set in the user's browser is used to display your text. When you specify a font face, you must use the full name, as follows:

```
font-family: Helvetica
```

If the font name is more than one word, enclose the font name in quotations:

```
font-family: "New Century Schoolbook"
```

To increase this property's usefulness, you can specify more than one font face. The browser will try to use each font face in turn until it finds one that can be used to display your text. If none of the specified font faces is available, the default font is used. You can specify multiple font types, as shown in this example:

```
font-family: "Arial Narrow", "Lucida Handwriting", "Times New Roman"
```

CREATING TEXT APPEAL

The fonts you use define the way text looks in your documents. Fonts have many different characteristics and are classified in three key ways: by family; proportionally, as *monospace* or *proportional*; and stylistically, as *serif* or *sans serif*.

Normal, bold, and italic type form a basic font family, which is simply a group of related fonts. Some font families include variations like normal type, bold type, italic type, and bold italic type. These different font types add emphasis and convey meanings. Italics can convey a sense of nostalgia. Bold type seems to be shouting at you.

continues

continued

Most typewriters use monospace type, in which each alphabetic or numeric character takes equal space—a monospaced *l* takes the same amount of space as a monospaced *w*. Monospace type is easy to read and great for tired eyes. Another kind of type is proportional type, in which each alphabetic or numeric character takes up a different amount of space. For example, a *w* takes up more room than an *l*. Most fonts today use proportional type, which adds visual variety to your text.

Serifs are the stylistic flourishes, like cross strokes or curves, added to the end of strokes in a character. *Sans* is a French word that means "without," so sans serif fonts don't have stylistic flourishes. For a classical or traditional look, you should use serif fonts; they are the primary fonts used in books, magazines, and newspapers because they're easier to read. Sans serif fonts have a more contemporary look and are often used for book or magazine titles, captions, and headings. You might want to use a sans serif font for headings and a serif font for normal text.

Unfortunately, font faces aren't universal across platforms. If you want to make sure your text has a certain style, you should use a general font style. Here are some types of general font styles with examples of a font that can be used by the user's system:

`serif`: A generic font family with stylish flourishes, such as Times Roman.

```
font-family: serif
```

`sans-serif`: A generic font family without stylish flourishes, such as Helvetica.

```
font-family: sans-serif
```

`cursive`: A font that looks handwritten, such as Lucida Handwriting.

```
font-family: cursive
```

`fantasy`: A modern font family, such as Western.

```
font-family: fantasy
```

`monospace`: A non-proportional font family, such as Courier.

```
font-family: monospace
```

Examine Listing 8.8 to see how font families can be used in your pages. As you can see, the example uses class types and spanning to apply styles to sections of the page. Figure 8.4 shows this example in a browser.

Listing 8.8. Using font families.

```
<HTML>
<HEAD>
<TITLE>Using Font Families</TITLE>
<STYLE>
.serif { font-size: 14pt; font-family:serif }
.sans { font-size: 14pt; font-family: sans-serif }
```

```
.cursive { font-size: 14pt; font-family: cursive }
.fantasy { font-size: 14pt; font-family: fantasy }
.monospace { font-size: 14pt; font-family: monospace }
</STYLE>
</HEAD>
<BODY BGCOLOR="#FFFFFF">
<DL>
<SPAN CLASS=serif>
<DD>serif</DD>
<DT>A generic font family with stylish flourishes, such as Times Roman.</DT>
<DT>font-family: serif</DT>
</SPAN>
<BR>
<BR>
<SPAN CLASS=sans>
<DD>sans-serif</DD>
<DT>A generic font family without stylish flourishes, such as Helvetica.</DT>
</SPAN>
<BR>
<BR>
<SPAN CLASS=cursive>
<DD>cursive</DD>
<DT>A font that looks hand written, such as Lucida Handwriting.</DT>
</SPAN>
<BR>
<BR>
<SPAN CLASS=fantasy>
<DD>fantasy</DD>
<DT>A modern font family, such as Western.</DT>
</SPAN>
<BR>
<BR>
<SPAN CLASS=monospace>
<DD>monospace</DD>
<DT>A non-proportional font family, such as Courier.</DT>
</SPAN>
</DL>
</BODY>
</HTML>
```


Adjusting Space Between Text Elements

With style sheets, you can clearly separate text elements, such as paragraphs and headings, by adjusting the space between them. The property you use to adjust element spacing is the `line-height` property, which is set in units of measurement or as a percentage in relation to the original spacing.

NOTE

Keep in mind that normal line spacing is a factor of font-size and element type. For instance, a Level 1 heading has more line spacing after it than a paragraph does, and paragraphs with 14-point text have more line spacing than paragraphs with 10-point text do.

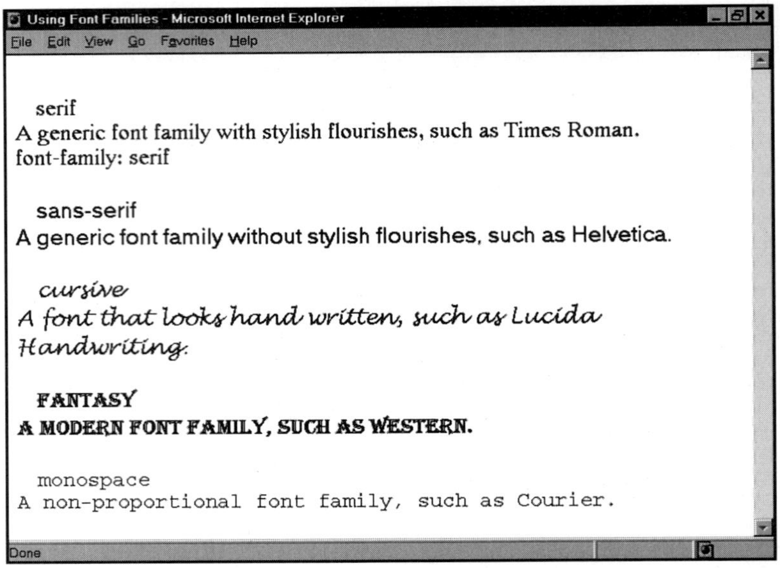

FIGURE 8.4.
Using font families in your pages.

Here's how you set the element spacing that uses font points:

```
line-height: 14pt
```

To set the element in relation to the original spacing, specify a percentage by which you'll increase or decrease the spacing. You can double the element spacing by using this example:

```
line-height: 200%
```

Grouping Font Properties

Entering each font property into your style sheet separately is tedious; however, you can combine any and all font-related properties.

When you combine font-related properties, the following style definition

```
H1 { font-weight: bold;
    font-size: 12pt;
    line-height: 14pt;
    font-family: courier;
    font-style: small-caps}
```

can be changed to

```
H1 { font: bold 12pt/14pt courier small-caps}
```

NOTE

The order of the property values isn't important. You can group the property values any way you like.

Figure 8.5 shows an example that combines many of the font properties discussed in this section. The style definitions and outline of the page are available in Listing 8.9.

Listing 8.9. Combining font properties.

```
<HTML>
<HEAD>
<TITLE>Creating Text Appeal</TITLE>
<STYLE>
H1 { font-weight: bold;
       font-size: 35pt;
       font-family: Harrington;}
P { font: bold 12pt/14pt "Lucida Handwriting"}
</STYLE>
</HEAD>
<BODY BGCOLOR=#FFFFFF>
<H1 ALIGN=CENTER>Creating Text Appeal</H1>
  . . .
</BODY>
</HTML>
```


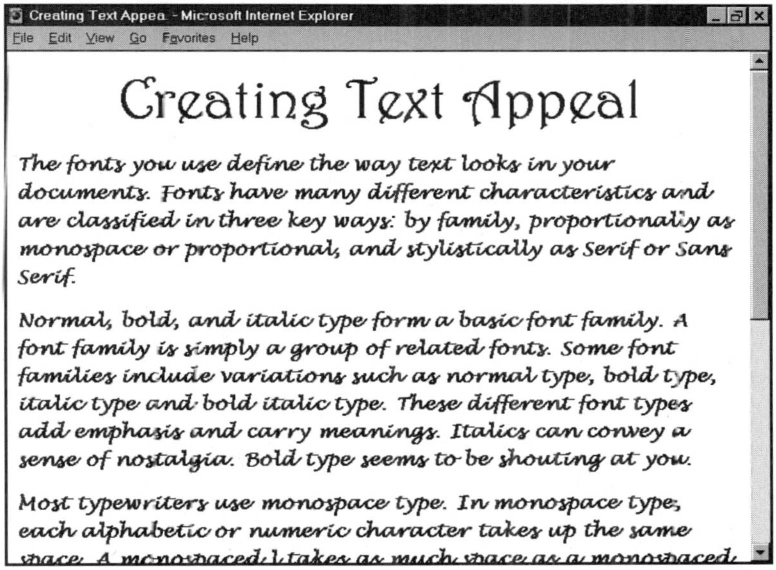

FIGURE 8.5.
Creating text appeal.

NOTE

Keep in mind that in order to use a specific font, the font must exist on your computer. If you do not have the Lucida Handwriting font, your browser will not display the font as intended. Sometimes you can correct this shortcoming by using a generic font family, such as cursive. This way, the browser will select any available font that follows the cursive style.

Showing Your True Colors with Styles

You can easily add splashes of vivid color to your pages with style sheets. Color can be added to text, backgrounds, and images used in your pages.

Using Colorful Backgrounds and Text

The two properties you use to add color to your pages are the `color` property and the `background` property. The `color` property is used to set text color, and the `background` property sets the background color the text is displayed against.

TIP

With the wide range of colors available, there are bound to be problems. This is especially true when you use color combinations with text and backgrounds. For example, light-colored text against a white background is almost always a poor combination.

In the following example, black text is displayed against a yellow background:

```
<P STYLE="color: black; background: yellow">
Black text against a yellow background</P>
```

Both properties can be expressed as a color name or a hexadecimal value:

```
color: black
color: #000000
```

However, using a predefined color name is the easiest option; simply select a color name from the list of 16 widely known color names. The currently defined color names are in the following list:

Aqua	Navy
Black	Olive
Blue	Purple
Fuchsia	Red
Gray	Silver
Green	Teal
Lime	White
Maroon	Yellow

A sample page using the `color` and `background` properties is shown in Figure 8.6, and the markup for the page is shown in Listing 8.10.

Listing 8.10. Combining colors.

```
<HTML>
<HEAD>
<TITLE>Combining Colors</TITLE>
<STYLE>
H1  {font: 25pt Arial; color: white; background: blue}
P  {font: 12pt/12pt Times;
    color: blue;
    text-indent: .5in;
    margin-left: .5in;
    margin-right: 1in}
UL LI {font: 10pt Times;
    color: black;
    background: yellow;
    margin-left: 1.5in;
    margin-right: 1.5in}
</STYLE>
</HEAD>
<BODY BGCOLOR=#000000>
<H1 ALIGN=CENTER>Using Color <BR> in Your Pages</H1>
<P>The use of color in publications has always caused problems.
 In the early days of desktop publishing, people were discovering
 color printers. Documents were printed in red, yellow, blue,
 purple and combinations of any other colors you can think of.
 This was not done because it was a sound design technique,
 rather because the desktop publisher could.</P>
<P>With the wide range of colors available, there are bound to be problems.
 This is especially true when you use color combinations with text and
 backgrounds. For example, lightly colored text against a white background
 is almost always a poor combination.</P>
<P>The best rules to follow when using colorful text or backgrounds are</P>
<UL>
```

continues

8 USING STYLE SHEETS

Listing 8.10. continued

```
<LI>Use basic colors for text, like black, gray, red, yellow,
 green, blue, and white.
<LI>Use basic colors for backgrounds but contrast them with the
 text colors. For example, if you use a dark blue background,
 try using white, bright yellow, or black text.
<LI>Do not use too many different color combinations with text
 and backgrounds on the same page.
</UL>
</HTML>
```

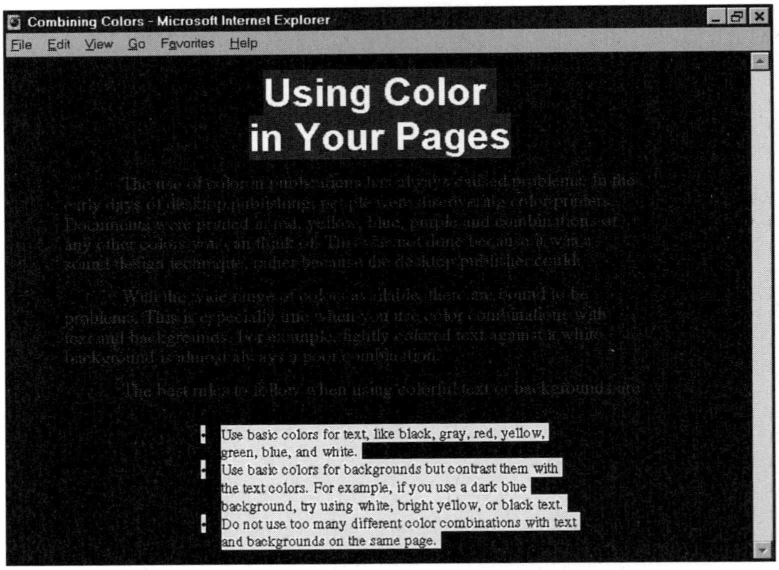

FIGURE 8.6.
Using color in text and backgrounds.

Using Images in Backgrounds

In addition to using colors with backgrounds, you can also specify an image to display in the background. Although in theory you can add a background image to any text element, current browsers allow you to add the image only to the body of the page. Here's how to add a background image:

```
BODY  { background: url(Globe1.gif)}
```

NOTE

The URL parameter for the background property can be a relative URL or an absolute URL.

By default, the background image is tiled to fill the window and is overlaid on top of any specified color. This allows you to combine a background color and a floating object. To avoid a conflict, assign the background image in the style sheet and the background color in the <BODY> tag, as follows:

```
<HTML>
<HEAD>
<TITLE>Combining Colors</TITLE>
<STYLE>
BODY  { background: url(Globe1.gif)}
</STYLE>
</HEAD>
<BODY BGCOLOR=#000000>
  . . .
</HTML>
```

As you might expect, the style sheet specification allows you to precisely define how and where the background image is displayed. To control the image's tiling, the specification introduces the `repeat` attribute, which has four valid settings:

`repeat`: repeat the image both horizontally and vertically in the background.

```
BODY  { background: url(cool.gif) repeat}
```

`repeat-x`: repeat the image along the x axis (horizontally) in the background.

```
BODY  { background: url(cool.gif) repeat-x}
```

`repeat-y`: repeat the image along the y axis (vertically) in the background.

```
BODY  { background: url(cool.gif) repeat-y}
```

`no-repeat`: do not repeat the image in the background; display it on the window only one time.

```
BODY  { background: url(cool.gif) no-repeat}
```

With the `scroll` attribute, you can make the image scroll in the background, which is the current default setting for background images. To make the image fixed on the page, simply use the `fixed` keyword:

```
BODY  { background: url(Globe1.gif) fixed}
```

The most powerful feature offered for background images is precise positioning with a grid coordinate system or keywords. The coordinate system style sheet's use may be slightly different from what you're used to. The upper-left corner of the current element is at coordinate `0% 0%`, which is the default position. As you move outward to the right in a straight line, the x coordinates grow larger. As you move downward in a straight line, the y coordinates grow larger.

To start tiling the background image in the middle of the page, you could use the following style sheet definition:

```
BODY  { background: url(Globe1.gif) 0% 50%}
```

Or you could use this definition:

```
BODY  { background: url(Globe1.gif) left middle}
```

The keywords `left` and `middle` correspond to preset locations in the grid system. There are six valid settings:

`left:` Start at the x position 0 percent, which is the left-hand side of the element's window.

`center:` Start at the x position 50 percent, which is in the middle of the element's window.

`right:` Start at the x position 100 percent, which is the right-hand side of the element's window.

`top:` Start at the y position 0 percent, which is the top of the element's window.

`middle:` Start at the y position 50 percent, which is the middle of the element's window.

`bottom:` Start at the y position 100 percent, which is the bottom of the element's window.

Figure 8.7 combines some of the properties for background images. The image is tiled along the y axis by using the value `repeat-y` and placed precisely on the page with a y axis value of 25 percent. To make sure the paragraph text isn't displayed on top of the image, the left margin is indented. Listing 8.11 shows the style definitions for the example.

Listing 8.11. Placing background images on the page.

```
<HTML>
<HEAD>
<TITLE>Placing Background Images on the Page</TITLE>
<STYLE>
H1 {font: 25pt Arial; background: blue}
P { font: 12pt/8pt Times;
    color: blue;
    text-indent: .5in;
    margin-left: 1.5in;
    margin-right: 1in }
BODY { background: url(Globe.gif) repeat-y 0% 25%}
</STYLE>
</HEAD>
<BODY BGCOLOR="#FFFFFF">
 . . .
</BODY>
</HTML>
```

FIGURE 8.7.
Precisely placing background images on the page.

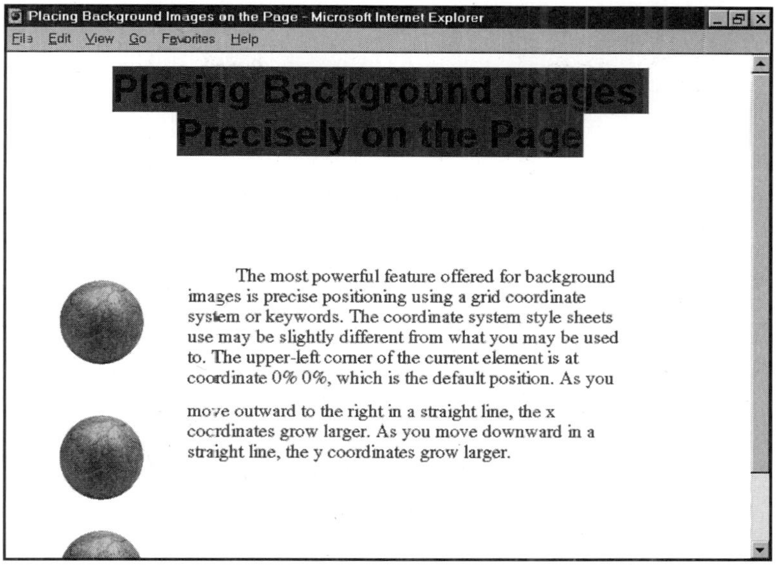

Cool Spacing Techniques with Style Sheets

In many of the previous examples, spacing techniques added flair to the page. This section shows how you can use the same spacing techniques in your pages to control the size of margins, line spacing, word and letter spacing, and more.

Getting the Most Out of Margins

Sometimes it isn't what you have on the screen that helps convey your message—it's what you don't have on the screen. Empty space on the screen makes the material easier to read by drawing the reader's attention to the screen area that has material in it. The separation of the material creates emphasis and draws the reader's attention.

Using space effectively isn't a new idea. In traditional publications, graphics designers carefully balance the amount of empty space on the page to emphasize material by using wide margins whenever possible. Open your favorite textbook and you'll probably notice that the top margin is smaller than the bottom margin. Next, compare the margins on two opposing pages. On the left-hand page, the left margin is wide and the right margin near the binding is narrow, but on the right-hand page, the left margin near the binding is narrow and the right margin is wide. Print publications are usually designed this way to make them more visually appealing.

These are some of the ways you can use screen space to enhance your Web pages:

Don't center the text window on the screen.

Use a wide left margin and a narrow right margin.

Indent the first line of every paragraph.

You can vary these techniques to fit the needs of your publication. If you want to off-center text to the left, do so, or use a wide right margin and a narrow left margin.

A page that's entirely graphical can also benefit from using spacing techniques. If text is secondary to an image on the page, the centerpiece of the page should be the image, so you would design the page to enhance the image's value. The key is to use space in a way that enhances the design and draws attention to what you want to emphasize.

These and many more spacing techniques can be achieved with style sheets. To adjust the width of the margins, use these properties:

`margin-left`: Sets the size of the element's left margin.

```
P  { margin-left: .5in}
```

`margin-right`: Sets the size of the element's right margin.

```
P  { margin-right: 1.5in}
```

`margin-top`: Sets the size of the element's top margin.

```
P  { margin-top: .5in}
```

`margin-bottom`: Sets the size of the element's bottom margin.

```
P  { margin-bottom: .5in}
```

`margin`: Sets the size of all margins around the element.

```
P  { margin-all: 1in}
```

You can specify the size of the margin in a specific unit of measurement by using a two-letter abbreviation, such as `in` for inches. Here are other units of measurement you can use:

`px`: screen pixels

```
P { margin-left: 50px margin-right 25px }
```

`cm`: centimeters

```
P { margin-left: 1cm margin-right 1cm }
```

`mm`: millimeters

```
P { margin-left: 50mm margin-right 25mm }
```

`en`: en units

```
P { margin-left: 3en margin-right 3en }
```

NOTE

An *en* is a unit used by typesetters that's equal to half the point size of the associated text. If the reader is displaying your page in a 12-point font size, an en unit for the page would be roughly six points in size. Remember that one point is roughly equal to 1/72 of an inch, but that can vary depending on the actual font used. This means six points would equal approximately 1/12 of an inch. Therefore, for every whole digit increment in en units, the tab position for this reader moves 1/12 of an inch. Sound like rocket science? Well, maybe it is. However, the developers of HTML 3 and the style sheets specification needed a generic unit that could be sized in relation to the current font, and the en unit filled this need quite well.

You can create powerful spacing effects by changing the margins within the body of your page. One way to do this is to alternate margin widths, like the example you see in Figure 8.8. Listing 8.12 shows the HTML for the example.

Listing 8.12. Using margins.

```
<HTML>
<HEAD>
<TITLE>Cool Spacing Techniques With Margins</TITLE>
<STYLE>
BODY { background: white;}
H1 {font: 25pt Helvetica;
        background: yellow;}
P.first { font: 10pt Arial;
    color: blue;
    margin-left: .25in;
    margin-right: 2.5in;}
P.second { font: 10pt Arial;
    color: blue;
    margin-left: 2.5in;
    margin-right: .25in;}
</STYLE>
</HEAD>
<BODY>
<H1 ALIGN=CENTER>Using Spacing Techniques</H1>
<P CLASS=first>Sometimes it is not what you have on the screen that helps
 convey your message; rather it is what you do not have on the screen. Empty
 space on the screen makes the material easier to read by drawing the
 reader's attention to the area of the screen that has material on it.
 It is the separation of the material that creates emphasis and draws
 the reader's attention.</P>
<P CLASS=second>Using space effectively is not a new idea. In traditional
 publications, graphic designers carefully balance the amount of empty space
 on the page to emphasize material. They do this by using wide margins
 whenever possible. Open your favorite textbook and you will probably
 find that the top margin is smaller than the bottom margin. Next, compare
 the margins on two opposing pages. You may find that on the left-hand
 page the left margin is wide and the right margin near the binding is
 narrow. On the right-hand page, the left margin near the binding is narrow,
 and the right margin is wide. Print publications are usually designed this
 way to make them more visually appealing.</P>
<P CLASS=first>A page that is entirely graphical can also benefit from spacing
 techniques. If text is secondary to an image on the page, the centerpiece
 of the page should be the image, so you would design the page to enhance
```

continues

Listing 8.12. continued

```
 the value of the image. The key is to use space in a way that enhances the
 design and draws attention to what you want to emphasize.</P>
</BODY>
</HTML>
```

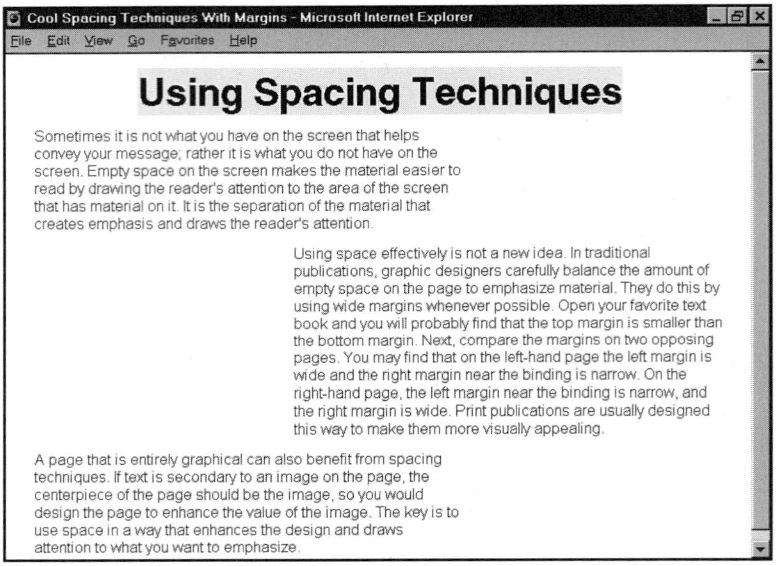

FIGURE 8.8.
Cool spacing techniques with margins.

HOW GRAPHICS DESIGNERS USE GRIDS

By adjusting margins for text and graphical elements, you can create grids. The *grid system* is a way of designing pages that can help you create a uniform, symmetrical look to the published page. Graphics designers have used the grid system for many years to design pages. Using the grid system, you break the page into columns. Text, graphics, and other objects on the page are lined up within the columns.

A simple page could be broken into three grid columns, and complex pages could be divided into 10 or more grid columns. The number of imaginary grid columns depends on the type and number of objects you're placing on the page.

For example, a newsletter could be divided into three grid columns. Header and title information could go across the whole top of the page, meaning this text would be in all three grids. Pictures could be aligned in the first or leftmost grid, one under the other down the page, and text could be placed in columns two and three.

The grid system is used primarily in print publications, but it also makes sense to use the grid system in electronic publications. Your publication shouldn't look like a mess on the reader's computer screen; it should be pleasing to look at. Using the grid system will help you add symmetry to your pages.

Just as you can group style sheet elements, you can group related element properties. When you group elements related to margins, you simply specify them after the generic `margin` property in the following order: top margin, right margin, bottom margin, and left margin. What this means is that the following style definition

```
P { margin-top: .5in;
margin-right: 1.0in;
margin-bottom: .75in;
margin-left: 1.0in }
```

is equivalent to

```
P { margin: .5in 1.0in .75in 1.0in }
```

NOTE

If you use the `margin` property and set only one value, the margin value applies to all margins. If you use the `margin` property and specify only two values, the margin values are applied to opposing sides.

Using Borders to Add Spacing

Borders offer another way to add spacing to elements on your page. Like the `margin` property, there's a set of related properties for borders: `border-top`, `border-right`, `border-bottom`, `border-left`, and `border`. You can set the width of the border as a relative or absolute value:

```
border: thin
border: medium
border: thick
border: .25in
```

You can add color to the border simply by specifying a color name or value:

```
border: medium red
border: .25in #FF00FF
```

To add a unique style to the border, you can use any of the following:

`none`: Do not draw a border

`border: none`

`dotted`: Draw the border as a dotted line.

`border: dotted medium red`

`dashed`: Draw the border as a dashed line.

`border: dashed thin blue`

`solid`: Draw the border as a solid line.

```
border: solid thick green
```

`double`: Draw the border as a double line.

```
border: double thin white
```

`groove`: Draw the border as a 3D line.

```
border: groove medium red
```

`ridge`: Draw the border as a raised 3D line.

```
border: ridge .5in blue
```

`inset`: Draw the border as an inset 3D line.

```
border: insert medium red
```

`outset`: Draw the border as an outset 3D line.

```
border: outset 25px white
```

When you use a 3D border, you can specify an image to display in the border space that will be repeated throughout the border. Here's how you could create a fancy border with an image:

```
IMG { border: groove .5in url(coolrule.gif) }
```

To increase the spacing between borders and content, use the `padding` property. Like other spacing properties, there's a set of related properties for padding. Still, the best way to set padding is with the general property. Here's how you can set a border and padding for the `IMG` element:

```
IMG { border: solid .5in white; padding: .25in }
```

Another way to give your pages a unique look is to adjust the spacing between words and letters. You can do this to give a monospace look to a proportional font face or to create long banner-like headings. To adjust the spacing between words, use the `word-spacing` property; between letters, use the `letter-spacing` property.

Playing with the Text

Style sheets create entirely new ways to enhance your pages. Some of the best style sheet properties are those that let you play with the text on the page. You can indent the first line of each block-level element by using the `text-indent` property, which adds visual appeal to your text.

Figure 8.9 shows how you can use indented text and shading to create a powerful effect in your Web page. The markup for the example is available in Listing 8.13.

Listing 8.13. Using indentation and shading.

```
<HTML>
<HEAD>
<TITLE>Using Text Indentation and Shading</TITLE>
```

```
<STYLE>
H1 {font: 35pt Times;
        color: blue}
P.orig { font: 14pt Arial;
    color: brown;
    text-indent: 1.5in;
    margin-left: .25in;
    margin-right: 1.25in}
P.note { font: 15pt "Lucida Handwriting";
    background: Silver;
    color: blue;
    margin-left: 2.5in;
    margin-right: .1in}
</STYLE>
</HEAD>
<BODY BGCOLOR="white">
<H1 ALIGN=CENTER>Creating Powerful Pages <BR> with Style Sheets</H1>
<P CLASS=orig>
Style sheets create entirely new ways to enhance your pages.
 Some of the best style sheet properties are those that let you
 play with the text on the page. You can indent the first line
 of each block level element using the text-indent property, which
 adds a style to your text never before seen in Web publications.
</P>
<P CLASS=note>
Note:<BR>
You can add notes, tips, warnings and cautions to your pages
 by creating a shaded box with the style sheet.
</P>
</BODY>
</HTML>
```


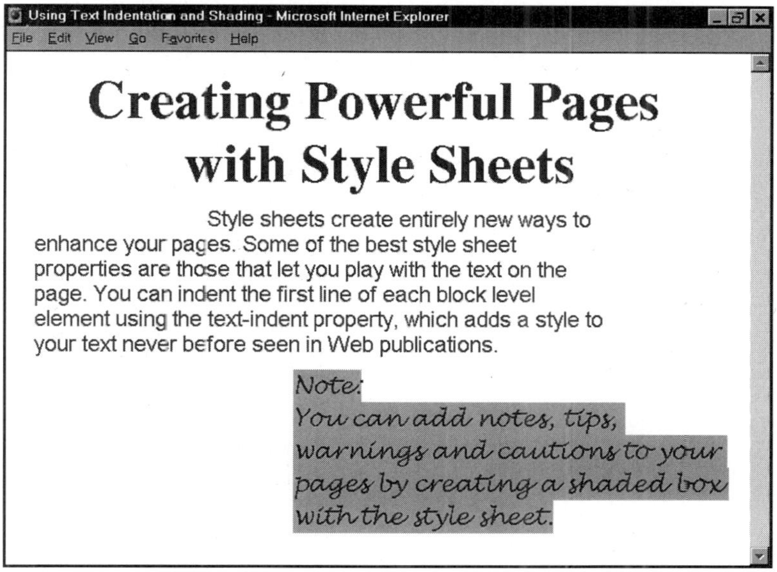

FIGURE 8.9.
Using indentation and shading.

Another way to play with the text on the page is with pseudo elements like `first-line` and `first-letter`. The `first-line` element allows you to define unique characteristics for the first line of any block-level element. With this element, you can apply any style sheet definition for fonts, colors, and even backgrounds. When you use this element, enter it as a separate definition, as in this example:

```
P:first-line {font: 16pt Times; color: blue}
```

Another cool element is the `first-character` element. Like the `first-line` element, you can apply any style sheet definition to the `first-character` element. When you use this element, enter it as a separate definition:

```
P:first-character {font: 30pt Arial; color: black}
```

If you want to add drop caps to your Web pages, you don't need to look any further. (See Figure 8.10.) The `first-character` element makes creating stylish drop caps a snap, especially if you combine it with the `float` property. When you float the first character, text can flow around the contour of the letter or along a straight-line box around the letter.

Here are some ways you can float the first character in a text element:

```
P:first-character {float: left contour}

P:first-character {float: left box}

P:first-character {float: right contour}

P:first-character {float: right box}
```

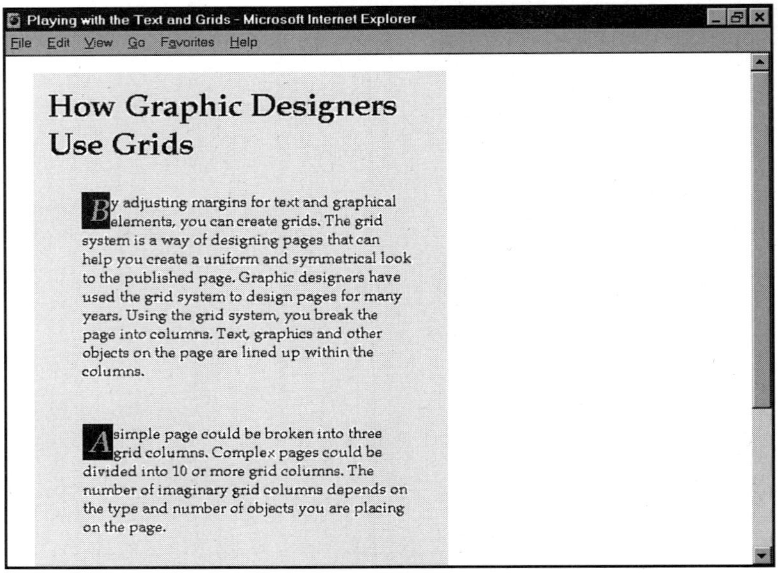

FIGURE 8.10.
Creating drop caps with style sheets.

Summary

Style sheets allow you to customize your Web pages and control every aspect of the layout and design of your page. With style sheets, decorating your text with fancy styles has never been easier. Finally, you can use any font face, type, size, or color you want. You can easily add color to text, backgrounds, and images used in your pages. You can even boost the impact of your pages with spacing techniques adopted from desktop publishers.

III

PART

IN THIS PART

Web Publishing Environments and Editors

CHAPTER 9

An HTML Toolkit: Browsers, Converters, and Editors

by William Robert Stanek

IN THIS CHAPTER

No matter what computer platform you use, this chapter introduces the ingredients to make the ultimate HTML publishing toolkit for your system. In this chapter, you will get the inside scoop on:

- Web browsers
- HTML converters
- HTML editors

Web Browsers

Following the wild success of the World Wide Web, the number of organizations developing browsers grew explosively. Currently, more than 60 organizations have entered the browser development race and are vying for Netscape's coveted position as the leader in browser development. Browsers are available for use on almost any computer operating system, including Amiga, DOS, Macintosh, NeXT, RISC, Windows, Windows 95, Windows NT, and UNIX.

Browsers: Your Windows to the Web

A *browser* is a software application that enables you to access the World Wide Web. You can think of a browser as your window to the Web. Change your browser and you get a whole new view of the Web. When you use Lynx, your window to the Web has only text. Text-only browsers are the original browsers for the Web. Although it may be hard to believe, several text-only browsers are still being developed.

When you use NCSA Mosaic, your window to the Web has text and graphics. Browsers that enable you to view Web documents containing text and graphics are the second generation of browsers. These browsers are largely responsible for the phenomenal success of the Web.

When you use Netscape Navigator, your window has text, graphics, and live animation. Browsers that enable you to view Web documents containing text, graphics, and inline multimedia are the third generation of browsers. These browsers are driving the Web's transition to an extremely visual medium that rivals the television for information content and entertainment value.

Although the Web is increasingly commercial, you can still find freeware and shareware browsers. One reason to keep abreast of browser developments is that somewhere in the myriad of options is the gem that may one day replace Netscape Navigator as top dog. If you have heard about the Netscape Navigator, you may not think this is possible, but keep in mind that until Netscape Navigator came along a browser called Mosaic was king.

Examining Netscape Navigator

NAVIGATOR AT A GLANCE

Tool Type:	Advanced Web browser
Developer:	Netscape Communications, Inc.
Version:	3.0/4.0
Availability:	Windows 3.1, Windows 95/NT, Macintosh, and UNIX

Netscape Navigator is the most widely used Web browser. Versions of Netscape Navigator are available for Macintosh, Windows, and UNIX systems. Driven by Netscape's rise as a commercial corporation worth billions of dollars, all Netscape's products are shifting to a commercial model. However, you can still download evaluation versions of the Netscape Navigator.

Since Netscape Navigator's initial release, it has gone through three major revisions. The final edition of Netscape Navigator, version 3.0, was released in the summer of 1996. The next edition of Netscape Navigator is already in development and promises to revolutionize the way you and I surf the Web. One of the major enhancements is the incorporation of Macromedia Shockwave into the browser.

Netscape has many unique extensions. These extensions, like the HTML specification itself, are changing. Many Web users confuse Netscape extensions and HTML 3.2 enhancements. Although Netscape did create extensions to HTML that are incorporated into HTML 3.2, Netscape adopted key features, like tables, from early drafts of the HTML 3 standard.

Netscape implemented the following unique extensions with the release of Netscape Navigator 1.0:

- Layout extras, like center and blink
- Horizontal rule extensions for width, length, and shading
- Control over relative font sizes
- Control over font color
- Use of images or colors to form a background for a document

Although these extensions were once unique to Netscape Navigator version 1.0, other companies are adopting these extensions for use in their browsers as well. The development team at Netscape didn't stop with the original extensions. Netscape introduced the following extensions with the release of Netscape Navigator 2.0:

- Additional control over font sizes
- Support for multiple windows, called frames, in a document
- Netscape scripting language for client-side scripts

The capability to embed multimedia objects and use an add-on module for the browser called a plug-in

The latest version of Netscape Navigator to be officially released is 3.0. New extensions introduced by this version of the Navigator include support for the following:

Internet Explorer's font face extension

Multicolumn text layout

Spacers that provide total control over the vertical and horizontal white space on a page

Enhancements for frames

The frame enhancements allow you to specify a color for frame borders and to remove frame borders. Although Navigator 3.0 does not introduce as many new extensions as previous versions, it is bundled with many client applications, including CoolTalk (an Internet phone software package), and features broader support for new Internet technologies, such as JavaScript and Java.

Netscape extensions offer terrific solutions for your advanced Web publishing needs. Keep in mind that if you use Netscape extensions, only browsers capable of handling Netscape extensions will display your document as you intended. Because approximately 50 percent of Web users have at least a Netscape version 1.0-capable browser, using Netscape extensions in your publications is something you should seriously consider.

Netscape Navigator is available for most operating systems, including Windows, Windows 95/NT, Macintosh, and UNIX. To learn more about Netscape Navigator, visit the following Web site:

`http://home.netscape.com/`

Examining Microsoft Internet Explorer

INTERNET EXPLORER AT A GLANCE

Tool Type:	Advanced Web browser
Developer:	Microsoft
Version:	3.0/4.0
Availability:	Windows 95/NT, Macintosh

The most exciting browser to be released recently is Microsoft's Internet Explorer. Already Internet Explorer has gone through three versions, and every version has introduced hot new features to the Web. Internet Explorer is the premier browser that directly supports internal multimedia. With direct support for internal multimedia, users are freed from the hassles of installing and configuring helper applications to view the multimedia, and Web publishers have greater freedom to include multimedia in their publications.

Internet Explorer supports Netscape 1.0 and 2.0 extensions to HTML. Internet Explorer also supports the SSL secure transfer protocol and will support the new, more secure, transfer protocol called STT. Like Netscape Navigator, the Internet Explorer supports unique extensions. Extensions unique to Internet Explorer 2.0/3.0 include:

Scrolling marquees

Dynamic sources to create inline motion video

Documents with soundtracks

Internet Explorer extensions are powerful multimedia solutions for your advanced Web publishing needs. However, only browsers capable of handling Internet Explorer extensions can use these features. Currently, Internet Explorer extensions support video in Microsoft AVI format and sound in WAV, AU, and MIDI formats. If you plan to incorporate sound and video into your Web publications, you should seriously consider using Internet Explorer extensions in addition to hypertext references to the multimedia files.

Internet Explorer version 3.0 was released in the summer of 1996. When Internet Explorer 3.0 was introduced, it featured the most complete support for the HTML table model standard first proposed in HTML 3.0 and was the only browser to support the cascading style sheets standard.

Internet Explorer version 3.0 features complete support for HTML 3.2 and has the broadest support for the latest Internet technologies and standards. It supports TrueType fonts, ActiveX, VBScript, Java, VRML, and Active VRML, and features enhancements for frames.

TIP

With Internet Explorer 3.0, you can view documents with borderless frames and floating frames. Refer back to Chapter 7, "Creating and Enhancing Web Pages with Frames," for more information. For more cool frame enhancements, look for a new version of Internet Explorer in early 1997.

Internet Explorer is available for Macintosh, Windows 95, and Windows NT. International versions of Internet Explorer are available for over a dozen languages. Internet Explorer 3.0 is included on the CD-ROM that accompanies this book. For more information about Internet Explorer, visit Microsoft's Internet Explorer page at this URL:

```
http://www.microsoft.com/ie/
```

HTML Converters

Although the task of creating HTML code is fairly complex, some helper applications called *converters* try to automate the task. HTML converters convert your favorite document formats into HTML-formatted documents and vice versa.

Using Converters

With a converter, you can transform a Word 7.0 document into an HTML document at the touch of a button. Converters are especially useful when you are converting simple documents; they are less useful when you are converting documents with complex layouts.

You can find HTML converters for every major word processor and document design application, including BibTeX, DECwrite, FrameMaker, Interleaf, LaTeX, MS Word, PageMaker, PowerPoint, QuarkXPress, Scribe, and WordPerfect. HTML converters are available to convert specific formats, such as ASCII, RTF, MIF, PostScript, and UNIX man pages. There are even converters to convert source code from popular programming languages to HTML. You can convert your favorite programs to HTML if they are in C, C++, FORTRAN, Lisp, or Pascal.

The definitive site on the Web to learn more about HTML converters and download dozens of converters is the W3C. Their section on HTML converters is the best you will find on the Web. Visit this page at the W3C:

```
http://www.w3.org/hypertext/WWW/Tools/Filters.html
```

Some HTML converters are template utilities that enable you to add the functionality of an HTML editor to your favorite word processor. This enables you to use the familiar features of your word processor to add HTML formatting to your documents. The best known template utility on the market is Internet Assistant from Microsoft.

Introducing Internet Assistant

INTERNET ASSISTANT AT A GLANCE

Tool Type:	Converter/template utility
Developer:	Microsoft
Version:	Used with Microsoft Office and Office 97
Availability:	Windows 95/NT and Macintosh

Using Internet Assistant, you can create HTML documents using the familiar interface of Microsoft Office products. You can also easily convert existing documents to HTML. Versions of Internet Assistant are available for Microsoft Word, Excel, PowerPoint, and Schedule+. Internet Assistant is also directly integrated into all Microsoft Office 97 applications. You will learn all about Internet Assistant in Chapter 10, "Publishing with Microsoft Internet Assistants."

HTML Editors

HTML editors enable you to easily create documents in HTML format. The job of the editor is to help you place HTML tags in your document. Early HTML editors were simple tools that allowed you to insert tags into your pages, but current HTML editors have developed into advanced turnkey solutions for Web publishing. Often these advanced editors are called authoring systems. Authoring systems have features akin to your favorite word processor and are complete with pulldown menus, macros, quick keys, and automation wizards.

This section introduces the most powerful and popular authoring systems available today including: Microsoft FrontPage, Netscape Navigator Gold, Macromedia Backstage, and Adobe PageMill/SiteMill. To give you a thorough understanding of these tools, each tool is featured in separate chapters that follow this chapter.

Introducing Microsoft FrontPage

FRONTPAGE AT A GLANCE	
Tool Type:	Authoring and Web site management system
Developer:	Microsoft
Version:	1.1/Office 97
Availability:	Windows 95/NT (Soon Macintosh)

Microsoft FrontPage is an all-in-one solution for creating and managing Web sites. This solution includes two powerful tools for creating advanced HTML documents using a what-you-see-is-what-you-get (WYSIWYG) authoring environment: the FrontPage Explorer and the FrontPage Editor.

The FrontPage Explorer, as shown in Figure 9.1, presents your Web site in a manner similar to the Windows 95 Explorer and simplifies Web site creation and maintenance, particularly for complex sites. With the FrontPage Editor, as shown in Figure 9.2, you can create your Web pages in a fully WYSIWYG environment.

FrontPage provides everything you need to design, publish, and manage your Internet or intranet Web site. Some of the most advanced features you will find are Page Wizards, WebBots, and backlink updating.

Page Wizards help you generate content for your Web page. If you want to create Netscape frame-enhanced documents, follow the frame wizard's step-by-step advice. If you want to create tables using the advanced layout features of HTML 3.2, use the table wizard, and you will be able to create an advanced table in minutes.

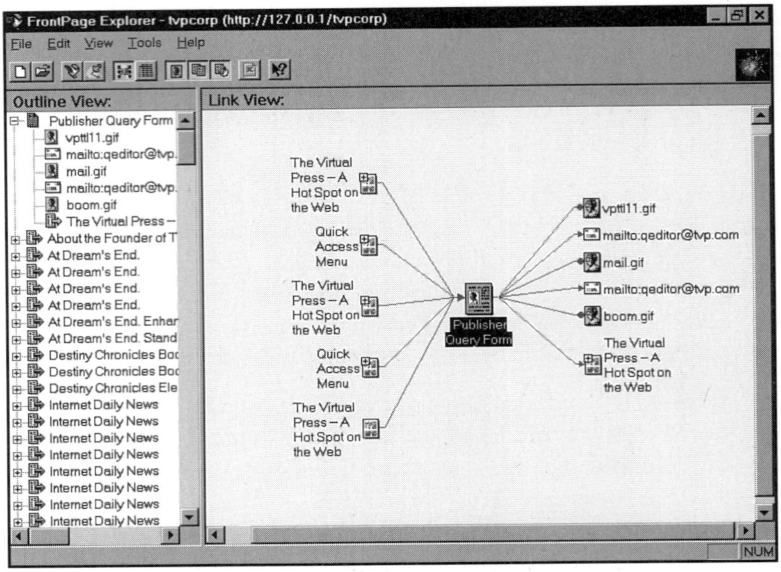

FIGURE 9.1.
The FrontPage Explorer is a hot graphical display tool.

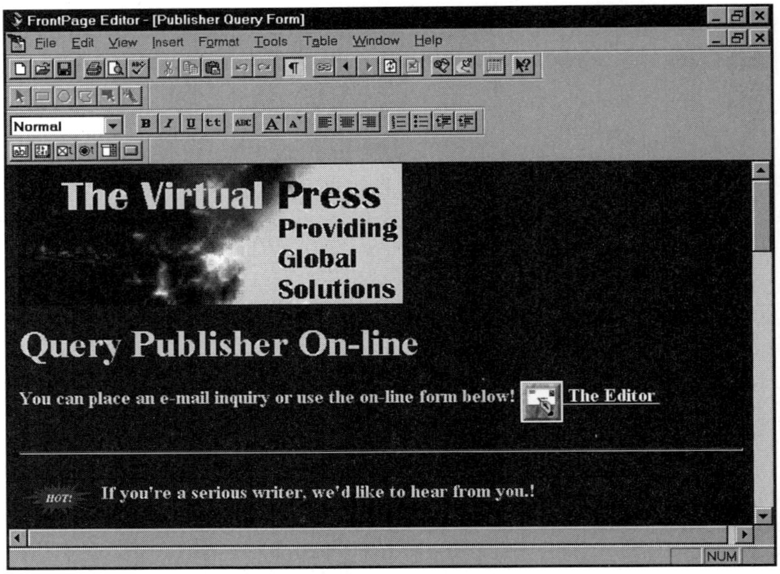

FIGURE 9.2.
The FrontPage Editor is WYSIWYG authoring at its best!

With FrontPage WebBots, you can add advanced capabilities to your Web site, including interactive forms, navigation bars, search engines, and discussion forums. WebBots offer drop-in interactive functionality, which greatly streamlines the development process and eliminates the need to write your own scripts or add complicated HTML commands. No programming is involved at all.

Using a feature called backlink, you can tell FrontPage to verify every link in your entire Web site. FrontPage examines onsite and offsite links in the background while you go on to other tasks. When it finishes, you will see a complete report of all invalid and questionable links. Using a single interface, you can then update these links automatically for specific pages or for all pages in your Web site. This capability means an end to chasing down broken links.

FrontPage includes a Web server called the Personal Web Server that fully supports the Hypertext Transfer Protocol (HTTP) and the Common Gateway Interface (CGI) standards. FrontPage also includes a server administration tool that manages security and access to your server.

Introducing Navigator Gold

NAVIGATOR GOLD AT A GLANCE

Tool Type:	HTML editor/authoring system
Developer:	Netscape Communications, Inc.
Version:	3.0/4.0
Availability:	Windows 3.1, Windows 95/NT, Macintosh, and UNIX

Navigator Gold is a WYSIWYG HTML authoring system that has a marketplace advantage because it is directly integrated into the Netscape Navigator browser. In fact, the only visible difference between the browser used with the Navigator Personal Edition and the Navigator Gold Edition is the addition of the Edit icon you see in Figure 9.3. When you click on this icon, you start an authoring session in the Navigator Gold Editor.

If you compare the Navigator Gold Editor shown in Figure 9.4 and the FrontPage Editor shown earlier in Figure 9.2, you will see they are very different editors indeed. The FrontPage Editor interface looks and feels like a familiar Microsoft Office application. The Navigator Gold interface is appealing once you get used to it.

Unlike Microsoft FrontPage, Navigator Gold is not a complete authoring and Web management solution. The focus in Navigator Gold is on authoring and publishing Web pages. With this focus in mind, Navigator Gold has many features that make content creation easy and fast. In addition to dozens of ready-made page templates, you will find a Page Wizard that helps you create pages. Other cool features include the following:

- Automatic color scheme mapping, which allows you to select predefined color schemes for text, links, and page backgrounds
- One-button publishing of the page you are creating
- Drag-and-drop link creation and updating

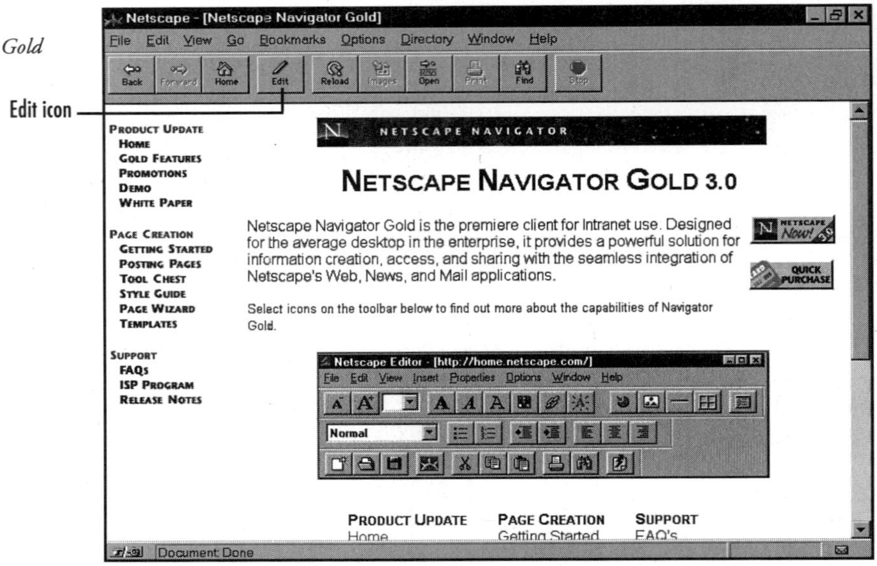

FIGURE 9.3.
The Navigator Gold browser.

Because Navigator Gold is integrated into the existing Netscape Navigator framework, it is available on most operating systems, including Windows 3.1, Windows 95/NT, Macintosh, and UNIX. Similarly, version numbers of Navigator Gold coincide with the Navigator Personal Edition versions.

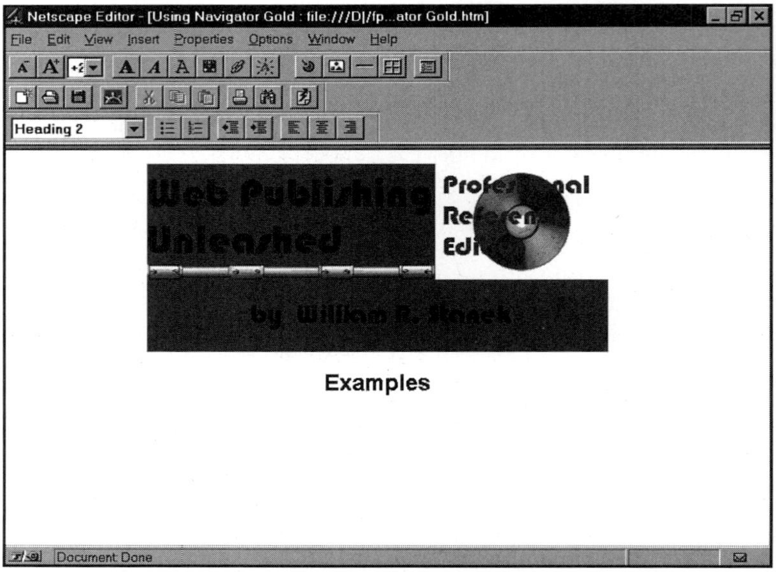

FIGURE 9.4.
The Navigator Gold Editor.

Introducing Macromedia Backstage Designer and Studio

BACKSTAGE DESIGNER AT A GLANCE

Tool Type:	HTML editor/authoring system
Developer:	Macromedia
Version:	1.0/1.1
Availability:	Windows 3.1, Windows 95/NT, and Power Macintosh

BACKSTAGE STUDIO AT A GLANCE

Tool Type:	Authoring and Web site management system
Developer:	Macromedia
Version:	1.0/1.1
Availability:	Windows 95/NT and Power Macintosh

Macromedia professes that Backstage is a Web development environment and indeed has all the ingredients for a very complete Web authoring and management system. As you see in Figure 9.5, Backstage is actually a family of related products.

The most basic offering in the lineup is the Backstage Designer. Using the Backstage Designer, you can create advanced HTML pages in a WYSIWYG environment. Backstage Designer is similar to the editor found in FrontPage and Navigator Gold. Because Backstage Designer is a product of Macromedia, the professional edition called Backstage Designer Pro has something other HTML editors don't—the ability to add Macromedia PowerApplets.

PowerApplets use Macromedia Shockwave and Java to add motion and interactivity to your pages. Versions of the Backstage Designer and Designer Pro are available for Windows 3.1, Windows 95/NT, and Power Macintosh.

A more advanced solution from Macromedia is the Backstage Desktop Studio. The Desktop Studio integrates the Backstage Designer with Web server management and database connectivity tools. Backstage Designer also includes a powerful object toolkit that allows you to instantly create pages with search engines, form management, discussion groups, and Web-based front ends to databases. Beyond the Desktop Studio is the Enterprise Studio with its full support for linking to RDBMS databases such as Oracle and Informix. Versions of the Desktop Studio and Enterprise Studio are available for Windows 95/NT and Power Macintosh.

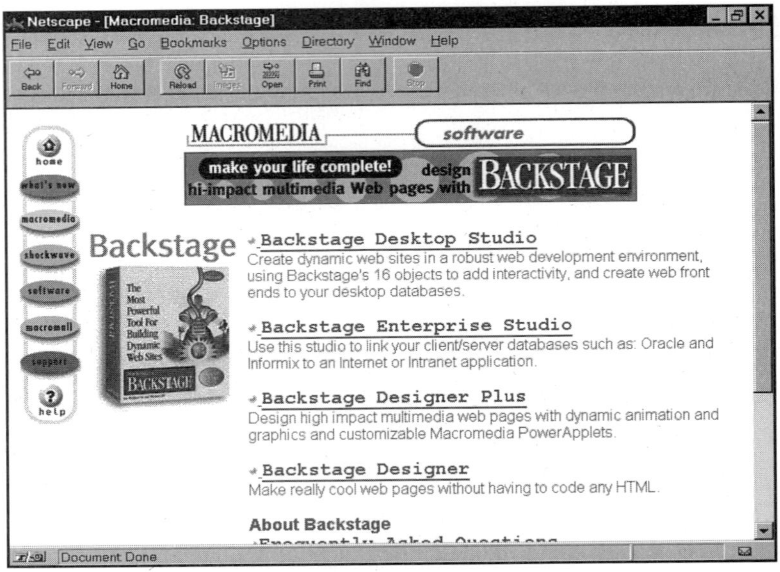

FIGURE 9.5.
Macromedia Backstage.

Introducing Adobe PageMill and SiteMill

PAGEMILL AT A GLANCE

Tool Type: HTML editor/authoring system
Developer: Adobe Systems, Inc.
Version: 2.0
Availability: Macintosh (Soon Windows 95/NT)

SITEMILL AT A GLANCE

Tool Type: Authoring and Web site management system
Developer: Adobe Systems, Inc.
Version: 1.0/2.0
Availability: Macintosh (Soon Windows 95/NT)

PageMill and SiteMill are two terrific Web publishing solutions from Adobe. PageMill (see Figure 9.6) is a WYSIWYG HTML editor, much like FrontPage Editor, Navigator Gold Editor, and Macromedia Designer. SiteMill is a complete management system for Web sites, much like Backstage Studio. Although versions of PageMill and SiteMill will soon be available for Windows 95/NT, Macintosh users will be happy to know that Adobe developed these applications first and foremost for the Macintosh and the Power Macintosh.

As you would expect, PageMill and SiteMill feature advanced support for other Adobe products such as Adobe Postscript and the Adobe Portable Document Format, which differentiates PageMill and SiteMill from the other applications examined in this chapter. Additionally, because Adobe has a lot of experience in the document conversion arena, PageMill and SiteMill have built-in document conversion utilities that allow you to instantly add documents in multiple formats to a Web page. Some of the formats supported are Microsoft Word, Corel WordPerfect, Excel, and dBase.

FIGURE 9.6.
Using PageMill.

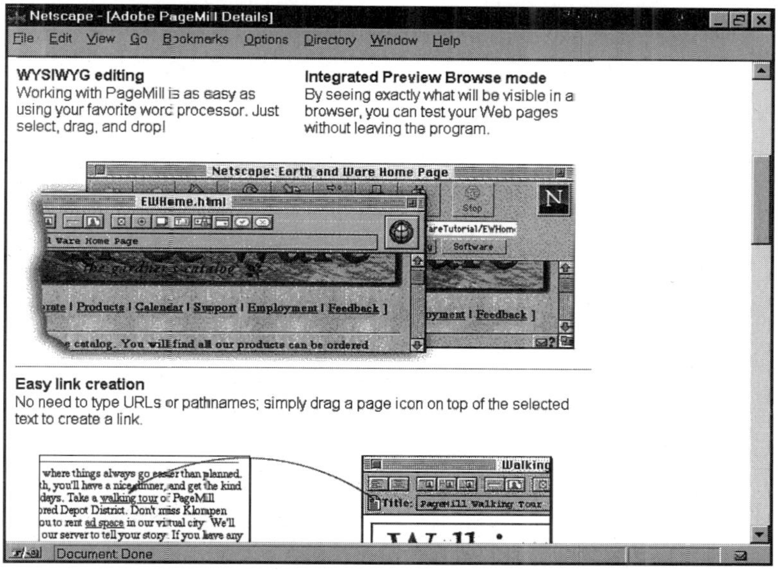

Summary

Web publishers can use many different types of tools to make their endeavors in cyberspace a little easier. Web browsers provide your window to the Web. Two of the hottest browsers around are Netscape Navigator and Internet Explorer. HTML converters help you convert document formats. Some converters, such as Internet Assistant, allow you to create HTML pages using the familiar interface of your favorite word processor, spreadsheet application, or database system.

Creating advanced pages featuring the latest interactive and multimedia features is a snap with HTML editors and authoring systems. Navigator Gold, Backstage Designer, and PageMill all offer basic authoring solutions. Beyond these basic solutions are complete authoring and management systems such as FrontPage, Backstage Desktop Studio, and SiteMill. Using these advanced solutions, you can create pages and manage your Web site.

CHAPTER 10

Publishing with Microsoft Internet Assistants

by Sean F. Leinen and Stephen R. Clark

IN THIS CHAPTER

With all the various specialized (and sometimes cryptic) tools for creating Web pages that exist on the Internet, have you ever said to yourself, "Gee, it'd be really nice if I could just use my everyday office productivity tools, such as my word processor, to create smart-looking Web pages with a minimum of hassle"? If so, then this chapter is for you!

This chapter introduces you to five free add-on programs that plug right into the Microsoft Office and Office 95 family of productivity tools, extending those productivity tools as quick, easy-to-use, and powerful Web authoring platforms. Although the focus in this chapter is on the Internet Assistants for the Office 95 family of productivity tools, most are available for Windows 3.x and function similarly. The Office 95 family of productivity tools includes Word 7.0, Excel 7.0, PowerPoint 7.0, and Access 7.0. You'll learn how to create a Web site using the most powerful of the Internet Assistants, Word Internet Assistant, and then augment that site with specialized documents created using the Internet Assistants for the other members of the Office 95 family.

NOTE

It is anticipated that the Office 97 products will include all or most of the Web-related functionality currently available only through the various Internet Assistants. In other words, the capability to create Web pages in Word, Excel, and so on will be integrated into the applications.

Microsoft Word Internet Assistant

The Microsoft Word Internet Assistant is a free add-on program for users of Microsoft Word version 6.0 or higher that enables users to create documents in Word or convert existing Word documents for publishing on the World Wide Web. It also enables users to browse the Web from within Word, without having to use an external Web browser program; a special built-in Web browsing component is never more than a mouse click away.

With Word Internet Assistant, you can publish basic or very sophisticated Web pages quickly and easily. With the wide availability of Microsoft Office in corporate environments, minimal training and no additional software investment are needed to enable employees to share information on internal intranets. Entrepreneurs and small businesses can also create and maintain professional Web pages on their own without having to purchase Web creation services.

Hardware and Software Requirements

If you're already a Microsoft Word user and have had a little exposure to the Internet, chances are that you already have what you need to use Word Internet Assistant. The following are the most basic requirements to run Microsoft Word Internet Assistant for Office 95:

- A minimum of a 386 PC with at least 8 M of RAM, but it is recommended that you have at least a 486 with 16 M of RAM
- Microsoft Word for Windows 6.0, 6.0a, 6.0c, or higher
- Windows 95 or Windows NT version 3.51 or later
- 2 M of hard disk space
- Microsoft mouse or compatible pointing device
- 14.4 Kbps modem or faster
- An existing Internet connection

The last two items are not required if you want to use Word Internet Assistant for creating and reading hypertext documents over an existing local area network (for example, for corporate intranet Web pages). However, in order to use Word Internet Assistant to browse and create pages for the World Wide Web, you'll need either a direct Internet connection through your institution or business or a SLIP/PPP account obtained with a private Internet access provider.

If you already have the basic hardware and software requirements to run Microsoft Word, you probably don't need to upgrade your hardware. Word Internet Assistant is not a big program and adds very little to Word's existing hardware requirements; 2 M of free hard disk space is all that's required for the entire program.

WORD PRANK MACRO SCANNER

If you plan on working with Word documents to create Web pages, you should install a Microsoft scanner/cleaner for the much-publicized Word *prank macros* (`WinWord.Concept`, `WinWord.Nuclear`, and so on). Prank macros, as the name implies, are rogue scripts created in WordBasic (the scripting language built into every copy of Microsoft Word) whose function is to carry out whatever mischievous deed their miscreant authors intend. These prank macros attach themselves to Word documents and can easily infect another machine when a user uses Word to open an infected document. The prank macros can not only cause Word to behave strangely (`WinWord.Concept`, for example, blocks navigation through the directory tree in the `File | Save As` dialog box, and makes it impossible to save the current document as anything other than a template), but they can cause file and directory corruption and deletion, in the case of the more malicious prank macros. The latest revision of the Microsoft scanner/cleaner, at the time of this writing, is ScanProt Version 1.0. Check Microsoft's WWW home page for updates:

```
http://www.microsoft.com./msoffice/msword/freestuff/mvtool/mvtool2.htm
```

After you download this file, place it in an empty directory and execute it to unarchive it. Two files are unarchived: `SCANPROT.DOT` and `README.DOC`. Follow the instructions in the `README.DOC` file to install the program into your copy of Microsoft Word. The installation program scans your copy of Microsoft Word for any existing prank macro infection, scans

continues

continued

your hard disk for documents that carry any prank macros, and installs macros to protect your copy of Microsoft Word from future infection. This process takes only a couple of minutes.

Downloading and Installing Microsoft Word Internet Assistant

Microsoft Word Internet Assistant is easy to install. While it is installing, it will add the appropriate menus and toolbars to Microsoft Word to enable you to begin writing HTML documents (and export existing Word documents into HTML) immediately. A copy of Microsoft Word Internet Assistant Version 2.03z is available on the included CD-ROM. Internet Assistant 2.03z is required if you are using Microsoft Word for Windows 95 and have installed Microsoft Internet Explorer 3.0. For all other versions of Word, download Internet Assistant 2.0z.

After you have located the appropriate file, follow this procedure for installation:

1. Place `wdia203z.exe` in any empty directory. Consider placing it in its own directory (something like `C:\DELIVERY\WORDIA30`) in case you need to uninstall or reinstall Microsoft Word Internet Assistant in the future.
2. Close all active Windows/Windows 95/Windows NT applications that you are running, including Microsoft Word, before you install Word Internet Assistant. The reason for this step is that the Word Internet Assistant installation program might have to update some shared files (like dynamically linked libraries) that other running applications might be using.
3. Execute the `wdia203z.exe` file to start the unarchive and installation process.
4. One of the first questions the installation program will ask is if you want to install Internet Assistant for Microsoft Word. Because this is exactly what you want to do, click `Yes`.
5. You'll then see the installation program extracting files, followed by a Welcome dialog box informing you about the licensing agreement for Microsoft Word Internet Assistant. You'll have two buttons here: `Continue` and `Exit Setup`. Click `Continue`; however, keep in mind that any time during this procedure that you see the `Exit Setup` button, you can click it to end the installation process.
6. A dialog box appears and states that it's searching for installed components; it's followed by another dialog box with the actual licensing agreement. Read through this licensing agreement, and if you agree with its terms, click `Accept`.
7. You should now see the Internet Assistant for Microsoft Word Setup dialog box with two buttons: a large button that says `Complete` and a small button that says `Change Folder`. Just to the left of the `Change Folder` button, you'll see the default installation

directory, which is usually `C:\Program Files\Internet Assistant`. If you want to change that directory, click `Change Folder` and change the default installation folder. When you're satisfied with the folder settings, click the large `Complete` button.

8. The installation program begins installing the Microsoft Word Internet Assistant files. When it is finished, the installation program presents a final dialog box stating that installation of the Internet Assistant for Microsoft Word was completed successfully. This dialog box has two buttons: `Launch Word` and `Exit Setup`. Click `Exit Setup` for now, and click `OK` in the ensuing dialog box.

Reinstalling, Uninstalling, and Getting Updates for Word IA

If you ever need to reinstall the Microsoft Word Internet Assistant for any reason, just repeat the preceding procedure. After the dialog box that states that it's searching for installed components appears, you'll see the Internet Assistant for Microsoft Word Setup dialog box with two new buttons: `Reinstall` and `Remove All`. Click `Reinstall` if you want to reinstall Microsoft Word Internet Assistant, or click `Remove All` if you want to completely remove it.

You can obtain updates for Microsoft Word Internet Assistant from Microsoft's Web site or FTP site. Point your Web browser at the following URL:

```
http://www.microsoft.com./msword/internet/ia/
```

Your First Home Page with Word Internet Assistant

Now that you have installed Microsoft Word Internet Assistant (IA), you are ready to use it to compose a home page from scratch. The hardest, and most important, step in this process is deciding what to put on your home page. Remember the old real estate joke, "What are the three most important items in real estate? Location, location, and location." An analogous joke works here: "What are the three most important items in Web authoring? Content, content, and content." The content of your page is what attracts people and will keep them coming back.

After you decide upon content, the next most difficult task is figuring out how to present it—how your page will look and feel. The Web site should be laid out logically so that the visitor can easily see what your Web site is about. Draw a map of your proposed site to ensure the flow of your links and pages makes sense. The first page should be more or less a table of contents of your site, telling the user what can be found at the site and providing links that the user can click to easily navigate around.

The example presented in this chapter guides you through the task of creating a Web presence for an imaginary bookstore called Book Binders, a medium-sized bookstore with a good inventory of books in stock that holds weekly book signings by various authors. You'll use the various Microsoft Internet Assistants to create a home page (the first page a visitor to the site sees) for Book Binders. This home page will include links to other pages (which the user can just click to view) and will provide links to some of Book Binders' documents and brochures that have been turned into Web pages. The next section takes a look at some of the issues you need to consider when you design the Web site.

Creating and Setting Up the Web Directory

An excellent way to set up your Web site logically is to create a directory structure in order to organize and contain all the documents and images that you plan to publish on Web Site. The idea here is that after you've created all the pages, images, and links to connect them all together, "packaging up" the whole directory structure for publishing on a Web server is a simple matter. Start by creating this directory structure:

1. Create a main directory called `c:\Website`. The home page will reside in this directory with the file name `default.htm`. This file is considered the starting point for anyone visiting your site. For organizational purposes, this file should be the only one in this directory.
2. Within `c:\Website`, make two subdirectories called `c:\Website\images` and `c:\Website\pages`. As their names imply, the `c:\Website\pages` directory is for all the documents to which you want to create links, and `c:\Website\images` is for all the images. Figure 10.1 shows how this directory structure should look.
3. After you complete the construction of all the pages using Microsoft Word Internet Assistant, it's an easy matter to copy the whole `c:\Website` directory tree to the Web server for posting on the Web.

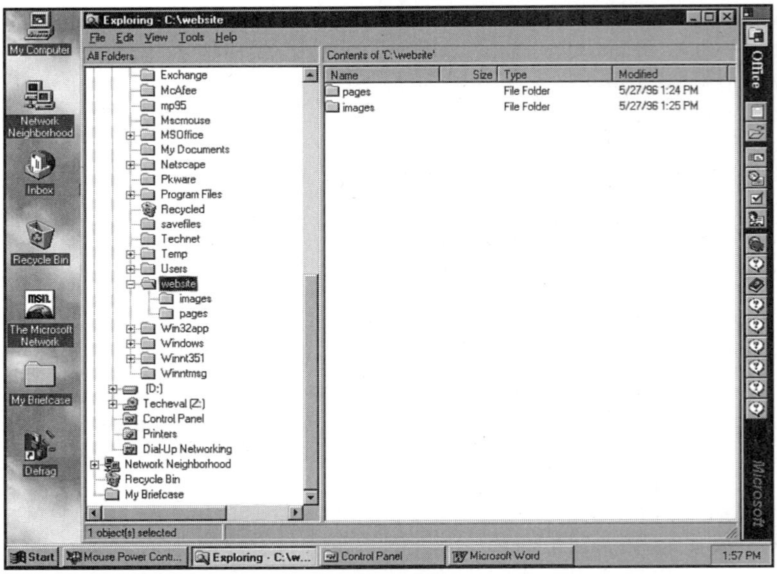

FIGURE 10.1.
Starting your Web site with a simple directory structure greatly eases the Web creation process.

Creating the Home Document

In this section, you're going to see just how easy it is to create Web pages with Microsoft Word IA. Start up Microsoft Word, select `File | New`, select `HTML.DOT` from the `General` tab, and click `OK` (see Figure 10.2). This template came from the Word Internet Assistant installation program, which added it to the list of templates your copy of Word already had. This template adds a few new options (discussed as they come up in the example) to your toolbar when you select it and hides those Word toolbar options that are not applicable to HTML documents.

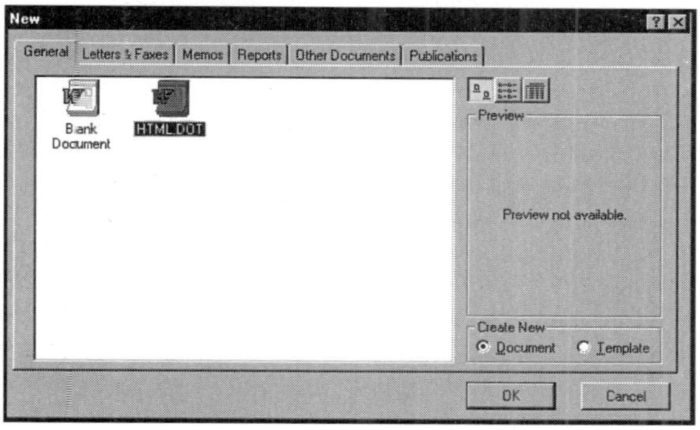

FIGURE 10.2.
Beginning an HTML document is as easy as choosing the `HTML.DOT` *template from the* `General` *tab.*

Now you're at the beginning of a new document, ready to begin typing your Web page. Notice that the Formatting toolbar (the second toolbar down from the menu bar) no longer sports the Font and Size drop-down selection lists. These toolbar options are not applicable to Web authoring because the visiting person's browser program (the client Web browsing software) determines what font and size to use. As a Web author, you're concerned only with the structure of the document, which makes your job easier. You're probably wondering, "OK, but *how* does the client Web browsing program know to display some text larger than the rest, and know when to bold, italicize, and so on?" This information is part of the structure of the HTML document; an HTML document is divided into different parts by *tags*.

Figure 10.3 shows some of the tags that are available from the Styles drop-down list in the Formatting toolbar. This figure shows the six standard heading levels for HTML documents; H1 displays the largest text available, and H6 displays the smallest text available. Again, keep in mind that size is relative—the client Web browsing program determines precisely what font and size to use for displaying the various heading levels.

The first step is to add a title to the top of the home page. (The title is usually the name of the company or institution.) From the Style drop-down list in the Formatting toolbar, choose the largest heading, Heading 1 or H1, click the Center Text icon (indicated in Figure 10.3), and type in the title **Book Binders**. While you're at it, add a subtitle to let people know what Book Binders is all about. Choose Heading 2 (H2), click the Center Text icon, and type in the subtitle **A Bookstore For The Masses**.

FIGURE 10.3.
The Styles drop-down list on the Formatting toolbar shows the six standard heading levels for HTML documents.

Before you get any farther, name the document `default.htm` by saving it to disk in the `c:\Website` directory you created. In the Save As dialog box, make sure the `Save as type:` drop-down list at the bottom displays `HTML Document (*.htm)`, and then type `default.htm` in the `File name:` field (see Figure 10.4). After you've saved the document for the first time as the proper type and with the name of `default.htm`, you can use `File | Save`, and Word will save the document properly from here on out.

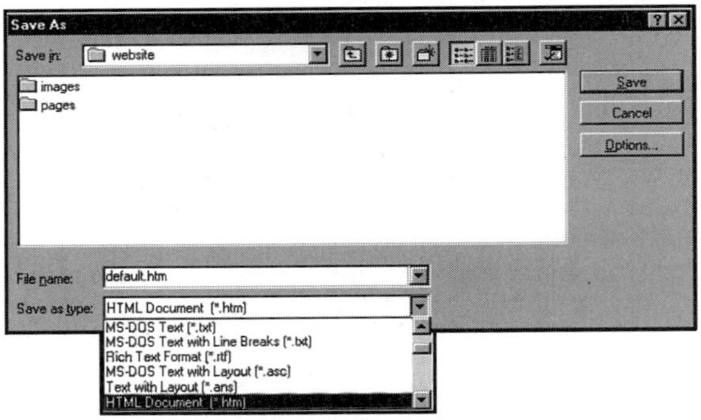

FIGURE 10.4.
Always be sure to select `HTML Document (*.htm)` *in the* `Save as type:` *field when you save the document for the first time.*

CAUTION

Do not be tempted to merely type in the file name with an `.htm` extension, thinking that Word Internet Assistant will automatically save the document as the correct type. If you initially save the document and do not change the `Save as type:` field to `HTML Document (*.htm)`, Word will save the document as a normal Word document by default. The next time you work on the document, it will still look like a valid HTML document because the same toolbars, editing screen, and HTML template will display as they did before, but the document will not function as an HTML document.

It's time to add some descriptive information to the page. Keep this information short and sweet because the home page is basically just a table of contents for the whole Web site. Select the `Normal,P` paragraph style from the Style drop-down menu in the Formatting toolbar, and type in the company description shown in Figure 10.5. This new home page is starting to take shape! Of course, just as you can with any good word processor, you can copy and paste text from any document into your HTML document and then edit that text's properties to fit HTML standards.

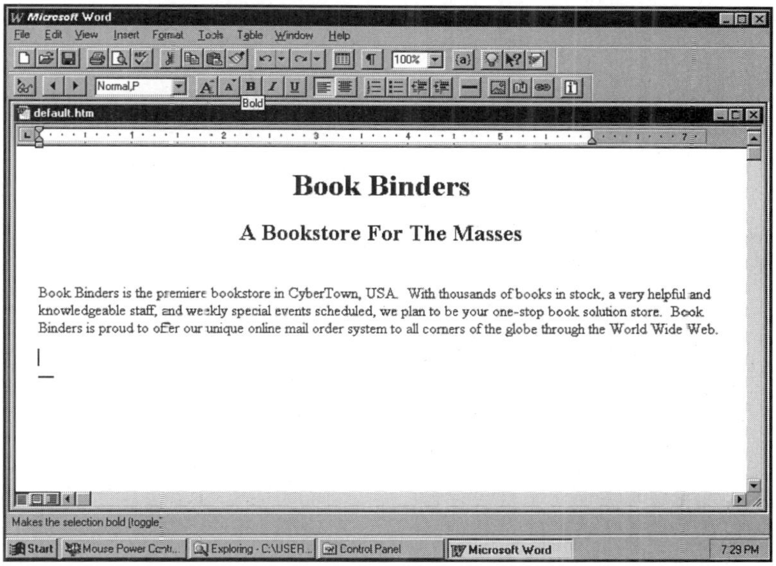

FIGURE 10.5.
With a selection of two different HTML headings, text centering, and a normal paragraph style, the home page is taking shape.

NOTE

You can type paragraphs one right after the other using the default paragraph style (Normal,P). When you press the Enter key at the end of each paragraph, a new paragraph is started automatically.

Creating Lists

So far, the home page looks more like a normal document than a table of contents. One way to spruce it up a bit is to provide a list. There are two types of lists in HTML: numbered lists and bulleted lists. You can easily insert them into the document by using Word IA's Numbered List and Bulleted List icons (see Figure 10.6). The numbered list tends to denote a certain order or sequence to the items, so a bulleted list is more appropriate for this example. Visitors to the Book Binders home page might not be interested in the order of the items that they see on the page, and more than likely want to go straight to the information they need.

A bulleted list would work well just below the short introductory paragraph. From the `Style` drop-down list in the Formatting toolbar, select `List Bullet,UL` (or click the Bulleted List icon). Type in the bulleted list items you see in Figure 10.6. (Word Internet Assistant automatically provides the bullets for you in a bulleted list when you press Enter; it also automatically provides the numbers for numbered lists.)

NOTE

The `UL` next to `List Bullet` in the Style drop-down list stands for Unordered List—the standard HTML tag for specifying a bulleted list. Likewise, the `OL` next to `List Number` means Ordered List—the standard HTML tag for specifying a numbered list.

TIP

Besides being able to create a bulleted or numbered list by selecting one or the other from the `Style` drop-down list *before* typing the text, you can also highlight existing paragraph text and make a bulleted or numbered list out of it by selecting the `List Bullet` or `List Number` style as appropriate. After you highlight the text and select the list type from the `Style` drop-down menu, just position the flashing cursor in this text and press the Enter key where you want each new bullet (or number) to appear.

Making Rules, Rules, and More Rules

If you've surfed the Net before, you've probably noticed the heavy use of something called rules, or horizontal bars, in Web pages. The reasons for their frequent use are simple: they make a page look sharper and they add a kind of delineation or page separation in long documents. Many variations of rules exist; some of the fancier ones include solid bars of color, bars of rainbow hues, and those yellow-and-black diagonally striped bars that you recognize from construction sites. This example uses a basic rule as a separator.

FIGURE 10.6.
Word Internet Assistant automatically provides the bullets for a bulleted list when you select `List Bullet,UL` *from the* `Style` *drop-down list.*

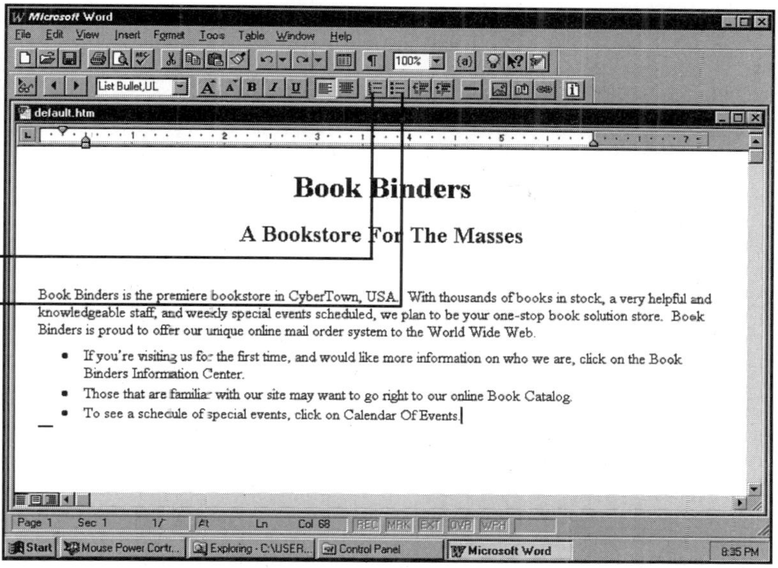

The first thing to ask yourself when you are deciding where to put rules in your HTML document is where you want the appearance of separation in your document. In the Book Binders home page, a rule between the subtitle and the body text seems natural. To place one there, position your flashing cursor at the end of the subtitle and press Enter. To create the horizontal rule, select `Horizontal Rule,HR` from the `Style` drop-down list, or click the Horizontal Rule button (fifth button from the far right side of the Formatting toolbar). A horizontal rule appears right on the new line that occurred when you pressed Enter.

Another good place for a horizontal rule would be right after the bulleted list, because you're going to be inserting some more material there. Position the flashing cursor at the end of the last item in the bulleted list. Press Enter to drop the cursor to the next line, press the Backspace key twice to get out of bulleted list mode, and then click the Horizontal Rule button on the toolbar.

Creating Hyperlinks to Other Documents

So far, the home page you are creating doesn't seem all that special. However, you're about to get into the meat of what HTML is about: hyperlinks. The key to hyperlinks are things called *anchors*, or highlighted text (usually blue in color). When a user clicks an anchor, it jumps the user to the destination to which it's linked. The Book Binders home page has three items in its bulleted list that inform the user what to click to navigate around the Web site, and you need to create those hyperlinks. First, however, you must create the linked documents, because part of the hyperlink process is selecting the file to which a particular anchor jumps.

Select File | Save to save the latest changes to your default.htm home page, but do not close default.htm. Begin a new HTML document as you did before, selecting File | New and selecting HTML.DOT from the General tab. For the purposes of brevity (and quick illustration), select Heading 1,H1 from the Style drop-down list, and type in **Book Binders Information Center**. Save this document as an HTML document, with the name c:\Website\pages\infocntr.htm.

Switch your Word view back to default.htm. To create a hyperlink between the words Book Binders Information Center in the first item of the bulleted list and the document c:\Website\pages\infocntr.htm, follow these steps:

1. If you haven't recently saved default.htm, do so now. Valid hyperlinks between documents cannot be achieved if the file hasn't been saved or has been edited since the last save.
2. Highlight the text you want to be your anchor for the hyperlink. If you haven't typed in your anchor text, just position your cursor where you want it to appear—a subsequent step takes care of the text itself.
3. Click the Hyperlink icon (second button from the far right of the Formatting toolbar). The Hyperlink dialog box, shown in Figure 10.7, appears.
4. In the Text to Display entry field, enter the text you want to become your anchor (in the case where no text was highlighted initially), or edit the text that you highlighted.
5. Using the Browse button, navigate down the c:\Website\pages directory and select the infocntr.htm file. Click Open in the Select File to Link dialog box.

NOTE

Hyperlinks can contain two types of file paths: relative and absolute. A *relative* path is relative to the current HTML document's location on the Web server. For example, say that the currently displayed HTML document is default.htm, and there exists a pages subdirectory in which default.htm is located; a hyperlink using a relative path to the infocntr.htm document in the pages subdirectory would use the path pages/infocntr.htm (notice the lack of a leading slash).

An *absolute* path includes a full path to the document to which it's anchored, regardless of where in the server's directory tree the currently displayed HTML document is located. These absolute paths usually have a leading slash (for example, /pages/infocntr.htm). It is highly recommended that you use relative paths in your hyperlinks wherever possible, because when you copy your Web site's directory structure to the Web server, the links will remain accurate no matter where in the Web server's directory tree your home page's directory structure is located.

To see how absolute paths are created, click the `Link Path` button on the Hyperlink dialog box to see the Use fixed file location option. Enabling this option will cause all hyperlinks from that point out to use absolute paths. The Book Binders example used in this chapter uses relative paths for all hyperlinks, so make sure that Use fixed file location is not enabled. You should leave this option disabled unless you have specific reasons to use absolute paths.

FIGURE 10.7.
Ready to create a hyperlink from the words Book Binders Information Center to the document `c:\Website\pages\infocntr.htm`.

Hyperlink icon

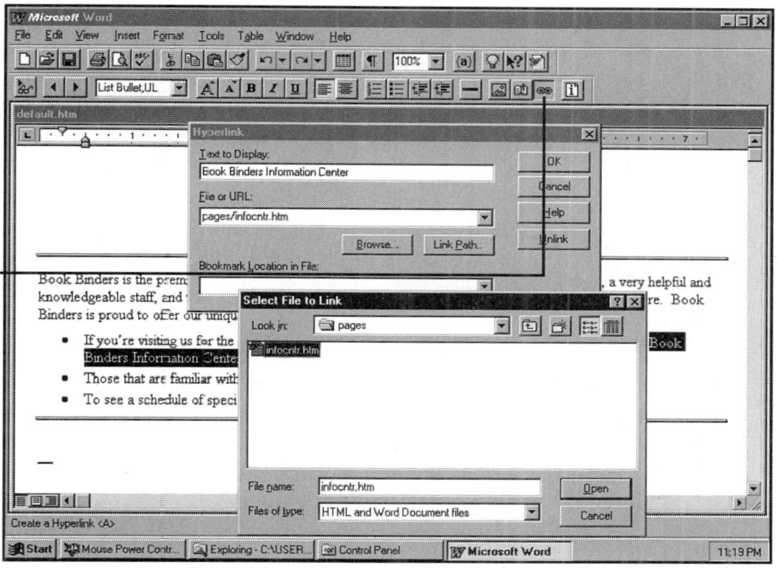

6. Click `OK` in the Hyperlink dialog box; the hyperlink, shown in Figure 10.8, should be created in bright blue.

Inside Microsoft Word, hyperlinks work just as they do on a Web site, with an exception; a single mouse click on the anchor merely highlights it (for use in editing the properties of that anchor), whereas a double mouse click navigates you to the document to which it's linked. This is most likely the opposite of what you're used to with a standard Web browser; single-clicks in a Web browser navigate, and double-clicks highlight. The reason Microsoft Word with Internet Assistant works this way is because you're *editing* a document; because the phrase `Book Binders Information Center` is now considered a single object in the document (an anchor in this case), it's standard fare in authoring tools to use a single mouse click to select that object for editing purposes. Try this out. Single-clicking `Book Binders Information Center` should highlight the whole phrase, giving you the opportunity to edit the link properties with the Hyperlink icon on the Formatting toolbar; a double-click should navigate you to the `c:\Website\pages\infocntr.htm` file you created earlier.

FIGURE 10.8.
The resulting hyperlink.

hyperlink

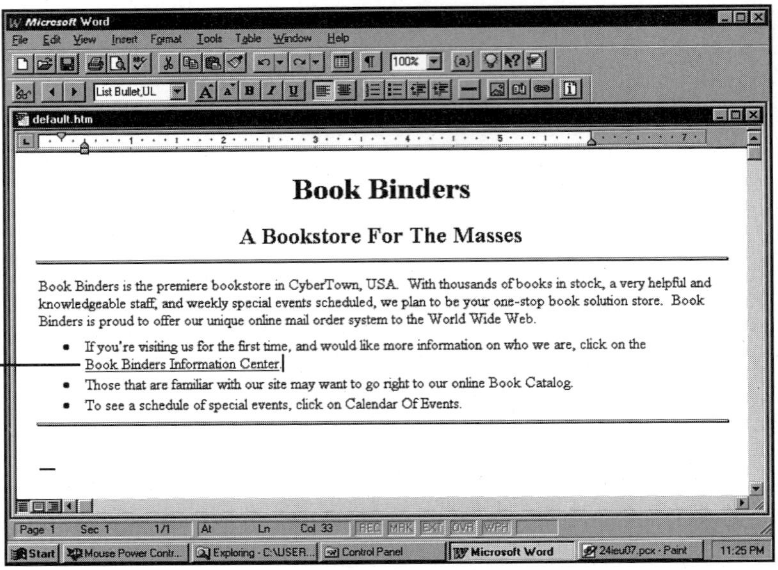

NOTE

Word Internet Assistant's Web Browse view enables you to test-drive your page thus far. In Browse view, mouse clicks work the way you'd expect them to in a browser program: single-clicks navigate you to the document that the anchor is linked to, and double-clicks highlight the anchor. To try this out, notice the very first icon over on the far left of the Formatting toolbar (the one that looks like a pair of eyeglasses). That's the Switch to Web Browse View icon, and as its name implies, it switches from Edit mode to Browse mode. With the `default.htm` file as the active document, click the Switch to Web Browse View icon and watch what happens. Now, instead of the I-beam mouse cursor you see in Edit mode, there's a normal arrow cursor like you'd see in a Web browser program. Single-click `Book Binders Information Center` in your Web page, and notice how it immediately navigates you to the linked document behind it—no double-clicking necessary.

Word Internet Assistant even enables you to create hyperlinks to documents that do not exist yet. In the second item of your bulleted list, highlight the two words `Book Catalog` at the end of the sentence. Click the Hyperlink icon on the Formatting toolbar, and use the Browse button to navigate to the `c:\Website\pages` directory. In the `File Name` field of the Select File to Link dialog box, type in **bkcatlog.htm** (you'll create this file later) and click `OK`. Click `OK` in the Hyperlink dialog box to complete the link. Notice that you have created an anchor out of `Book Catalog`, which, when double-clicked, displays the error dialog box shown in Figure 10.9. You'll fix this error later when you use Excel Internet Assistant to create the `bkcatlog.htm` file. For now, just dismiss this error dialog box by clicking `OK`.

FIGURE 10.9.
With Word Internet Assistant, you can create hyperlinks to documents that you haven't yet created.

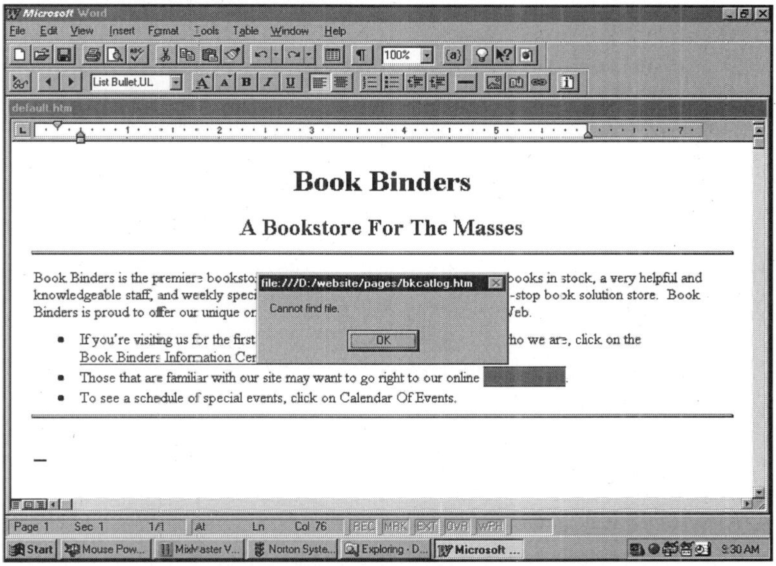

Hyperlinks are not limited to just documents resident on your local machine; you can create hyperlinks to other Web sites, or even to specific documents located several layers deep on other Web sites. Word Internet Assistant makes this easy; all you have to know is the URL (Uniform Resource Locator) path name to that Web site or remote document.

Try this feature by adding a new item to your bulleted list that will jump the user to the Library Of Congress search engine. Position your cursor at the end of the third bullet item and press Enter to create a fourth bullet. Type the text you see in Figure 10.10 and create an anchor out of the words `Library Of Congress search engine`. Instead of using the Browse button to look for a local document, type in the following for the `File or URL` field of the Hyperlink dialog box: **http://lcWeb.loc.gov./harvest/**.

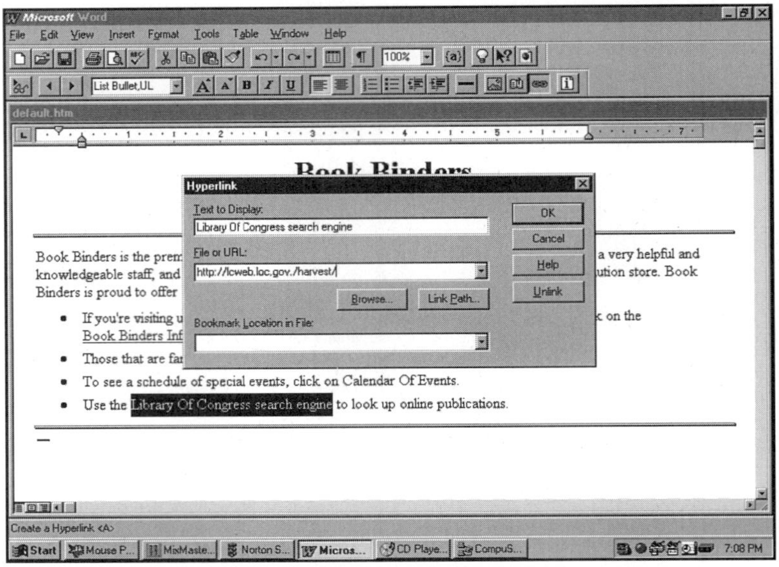

FIGURE 10.10.
Creating a link to a document that's not local to your machine, but on a remote machine out on the Web.

Click OK in the Hyperlink dialog box. If you're anxious to see what this anchor is going to do, start up your Internet connection (if it's via a dial-up modem connection), click the Switch to Web Browse View icon (the little eyeglasses), and single-click the Library Of Congress search engine anchor. Word IA attempts to contact the remote site, as shown in Figure 10.11. After contacting the site, Word IA downloads the appropriate HTML documents to display the Library Of Congress search engine (see Figure 10.12). You can use this search engine to search for online publications such as public domain newsletters, reports, and so on.

NOTE

Notice that you're still in Word, which opens up a new window to display this site. This window works just like any Web browser; this is not a static Word document at all. You can click the hyperlinks presented, fill in the text entry fields, and click any buttons presented from the remote site. If you didn't know you were in Word, you'd probably swear you were using a Web browser. You know what? You are! In the beginning of this chapter, I mention "a Web browsing component that is never more than a mouse click away." That Web browsing component is InternetWorks, a product developed by a company called BookLink Technologies, Inc. and owned by America Online. Just before InternetWorks was sold to America Online, Microsoft licensed enough of its code to create the Web browsing component of Word Internet Assistant.

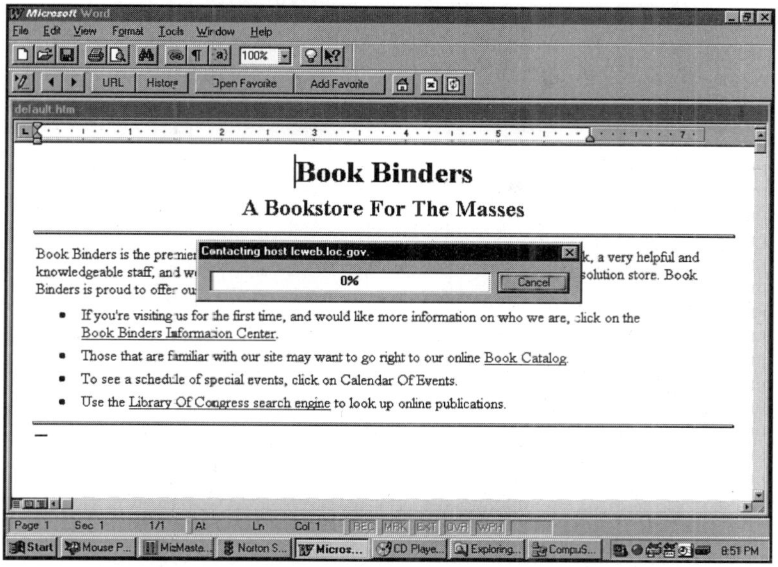

FIGURE 10.11.
A click on the link to the Library Of Congress causes Word to attempt to contact the site.

Titling and Signing Your Home Document

To form good Web authoring habits from the beginning (as well as to be kind to potential Web site visitors), you should title and sign your Web page. Titling a page is not the same as putting title text at the top of the page; instead, it's giving your page the name by which it is known on the Web. Web indexing/search engines use this information to find your site. This information is not always visible on the page itself; if it displays anywhere, it'll more than likely show up on the Web browser program's title bar. The title information is some of the hidden code that Word Internet Assistant inserts at the top of your HTML document.

Word Internet Assistant provides two ways to title a Web page: you can click on the Title icon on the toolbar (the last icon on the far right of the Formatting toolbar—it looks like a sheet of paper with a lowercase *i* in it), or you can select `File | HTML Document Info`. Either way, the HTML Document Head Information dialog box appears. Click the Title button on the Formatting toolbar, and type in **Book Binders Bookstore**, as shown in Figure 10.13. This title is descriptive enough that Web search/indexing engines will be able to help a person looking for book resources to find this page. Click `OK`.

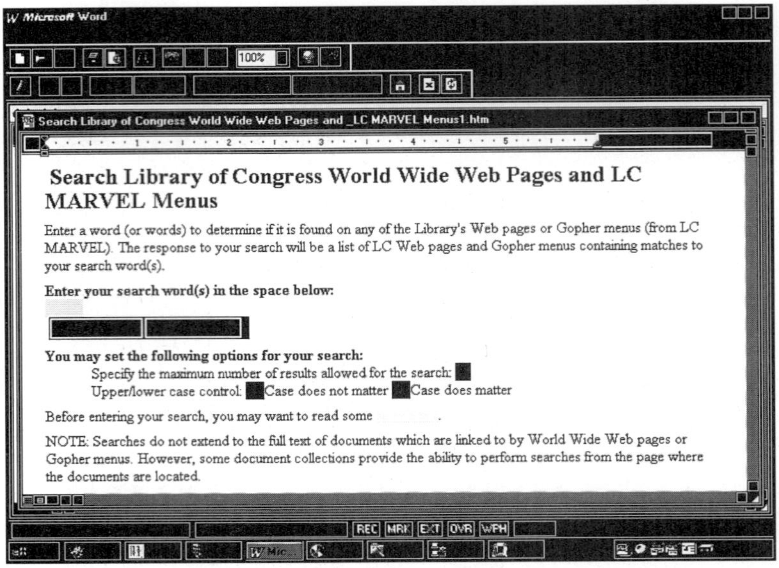

FIGURE 10.12.
The Library of Congress search engine is now displayed in Word IA's Browse view, which looks and feels just like a standard Web browser.

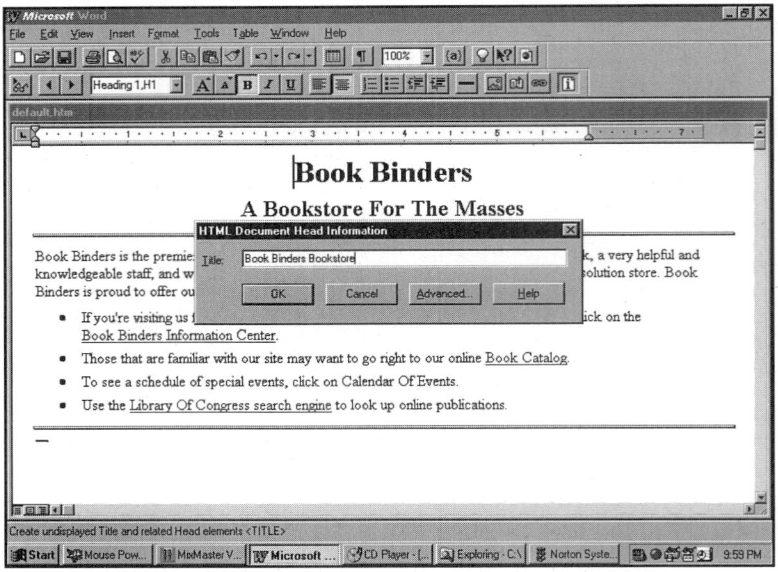

FIGURE 10.13.
Titling the home page.

Signing a Web page means placing information on it (usually at the bottom) that enables visitors to contact the people behind the Web site and putting a date on the page. You can sign a page neatly by using the Address style on the Formatting toolbar. The Address style is the Web convention of displaying the address information in a special way. Browsers such as Internet

Explorer, Netscape, and Mosaic might show this information in italicized text; other browsers might show the address information indented or right-justified. Either way, the address information will be set off in a way that makes it clearly different from the rest of the document.

From the Formatting toolbar, select `Address` from the `Style` drop-down menu, and then enter information something like that shown in Figure 10.14. Also notice that the e-mail path is anchored so that visitors can merely click the e-mail path to send you e-mail. To set up this procedure, highlight the e-mail path, click the Hyperlink button on the Formatting toolbar, and in the `File or URL` field of the Hyperlink dialog box, type in the e-mail path again, only this time prefaced with `mailto:`. This special HTML tag tells the local browser software to spawn the local e-mail program with the specified e-mail path as the recipient; all the viewer has to do is type the e-mail message body. Although the Web browsing component of Word Internet Assistant doesn't recognize this tag, most stand-alone Web browsers do, and I've included it here because most of the Web pages you see out on the Internet are set up much the same way.

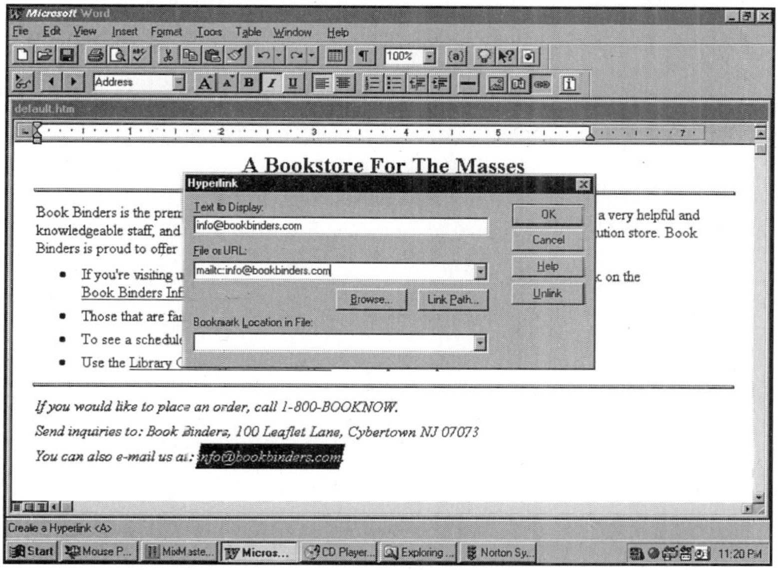

FIGURE 10.14.
Creating a special link to the e-mail path that enables the viewer to merely click it to send e-mail.

Viewing Source Code

You're probably wondering all along what all this Internet Assistant GUI stuff has been doing behind the scenes. With the `default.htm` file as the active window, select `View | HTML Source`. Believe it or not, you wrote all that HTML code! As shown in Figure 10.15, there should be a two-button toolbar kind of floating around the top of this HTML Source window; the left button returns you to Edit mode, and the right button formats and color codes the HTML. Click the left button to return to Edit mode.

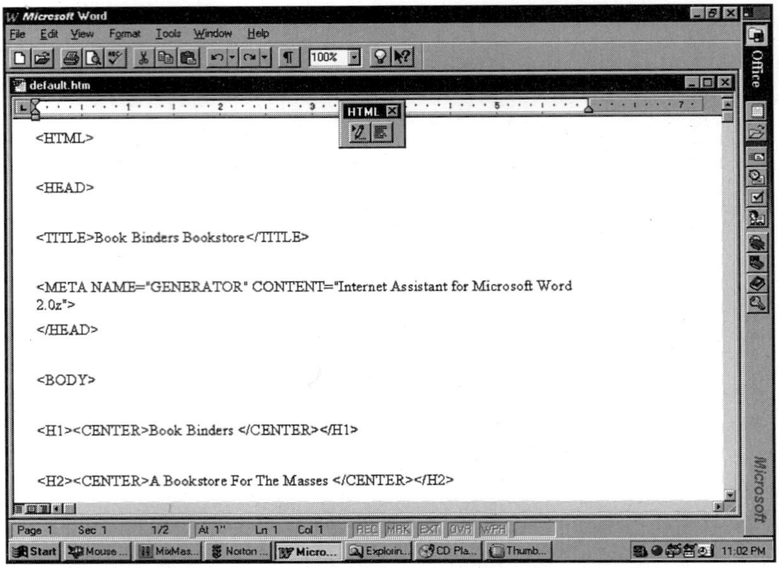

FIGURE 10.15.
This is what Word Internet Assistant has been doing behind the scenes while you were working in the GUI.

Using Graphics

One of the main attractions to the Web is its capability to incorporate pictures into documents, as evidenced by the abundance of Web pages with pictures and graphics. Word Internet Assistant makes the process of incorporating pictures and graphics into the HTML document easy; just place your I-beam cursor where you want the picture to appear, and click the Picture icon on the Formatting toolbar (the fourth button from the far right). In the dialog box that appears, specify the path name of the picture (there's a `Browse` button that'll help you do this) and click `OK`.

One thing that Word Internet Assistant does not have in its arsenal, however, is an image editing capability. You'll need a separate graphics package to do that, preferably one that can work with both GIF (Graphics Interchange Format) and JPEG (Joint Photography Exchange Group) images. Sorry, the built-in Windows 95/Windows NT PaintBrush just won't do. You can create and edit GIF and JPEG files in the PowerPoint Internet Assistant, which is covered later in this chapter.

Microsoft includes an excellent online tutorial for using Word Internet Assistant. The tutorial directs you to other Web sites where you can learn more about and download software for creating graphics, doing image mapping, and more. It also points you to sites that were created using Word IA. The tutorial is located at the following URL:

```
http://www.microsoft.com/msword/internet/ia/step.htm
```

Microsoft Excel Internet Assistant

Microsoft Excel Internet Assistant is an add-in wizard that enables users to create and distribute Microsoft Excel documents online for viewing with any popular browser. It helps Excel users convert their spreadsheet data to HTML format, either as a separate document or as part of an existing document.

Hardware and Software Requirements

The hardware and software requirements for Excel Internet Assistant are basically the same as for the Internet Assistants for the other members of the Office 95 family; in the case of the Excel application itself, you need version 7.0 or higher.

One highly recommended software item is a minor patch to Excel to correct three known bugs. This free patch corrects the following known problems: the 15-digit number bug, the Link to same cell on different sheets bug, and the Transposing ranges bug. To get a copy of the patch, as well as a more in-depth description of the three known bugs, point your Web browser to the following URL:

```
http://www.microsoft.com./kb/softlib/mslfiles/XL15LINK.EXE
```

After you download the file, place the `XL15LINK.EXE` file in a separate empty directory and execute it to unarchive it. Follow the instructions in the resulting `README.TXT` file for further installation information.

Installing Excel Internet Assistant

After you've applied the patch to your copy of Excel, you're ready to install the Excel Internet Assistant. You can find the Excel Internet Assistant on the CD-ROM, but you can get updates by pointing your Web browser at the following URL:

```
http://www.microsoft.com/msexcel/internet/ia/
```

Installing Excel Internet Assistant is a little bit different than installing Word Internet Assistant; instead of running an executable file to start the installation process as you would with Word Internet Assistant, you merely drop the file `HTML.XLA` into the `LIBRARY` subdirectory of your Excel product directory. Just follow this easy procedure to install and enable the Excel Internet Assistant:

1. Close Microsoft Excel if it's already running.
2. Copy the `HTML.XLA` file to the Microsoft Excel Library directory (for example, `C:\MSOFFICE\EXCEL\LIBRARY`).
3. Start Microsoft Excel.

4. Select `Tools | Add-Ins`. The Add-Ins dialog box appears.
5. Check the `Internet Assistant Wizard` checkbox (see Figure 10.16) by clicking it.
6. Click `OK`.

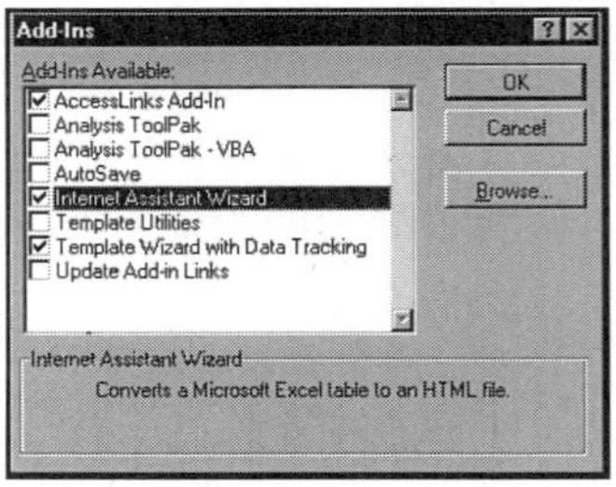

FIGURE 10.16.
To use the Excel Internet Assistant, just enable the Internet Assistant Wizard on the Add-Ins dialog box.

Using Excel Internet Assistant

Excel Internet Assistant is one of the very best tools to use if you have to create tables for Web pages. If you have a spreadsheet with a certain look and feel, you can maintain this look and feel as you export it to an HTML table. If your spreadsheet includes various colors, different fonts, text formatting, and so on, Excel IA can create a Web page table from this spreadsheet with all these things. Use the following basic procedure to create a Web page table from any spreadsheet:

1. Start Excel.
2. Choose `Tools | Internet Assistant Wizard`.
3. Highlight the cells containing the data you want to convert to an HTML table. Click `Next`.
4. Select whether you want to create an independent HTML file or insert the table in an existing HTML document. Click `Next`.
5. If you chose to insert the table into an existing HTML document, make sure that the string, `<!—##Table##—>` exists at the exact location in the HTML document in which you want this table to appear. Down at the bottom of the Internet Assistant Wizard - Step 3 dialog box, type in (or use the `Browse` button to navigate to) the path to the existing HTML file where you want the table to be inserted. Click `Next`.

   If you instead chose to create an independent HTML document, enter into the Internet Assistant Wizard - Step 3 dialog box the header and footer information that you want to appear on the new HTML document. You can also choose to have horizontal lines inserted before and/or after the table by clicking the appropriate checkboxes. Click `Next`.
6. Select whether to convert just the cell data that you highlighted or to retain rich color, font, and text formatting used by the original spreadsheet. Click `Next`.

7. Enter the path name for the file that you want to save.
8. Click `Finish` to generate an HTML document with spreadsheet data.

To illustrate this process, the next paragraphs explain how to create a simple Excel spreadsheet that shows an excerpt from an online book catalog and import that into the Web page as a table. Start Excel and type in a small spreadsheet like the one shown in Figure 10.17. Don't be afraid to spiff up the looks of this simple spreadsheet; use bold text for the column headers, add some color text in certain places, and so on.

FIGURE 10.17.
Creating a simple spreadsheet and preparing to export it with Excel IA.

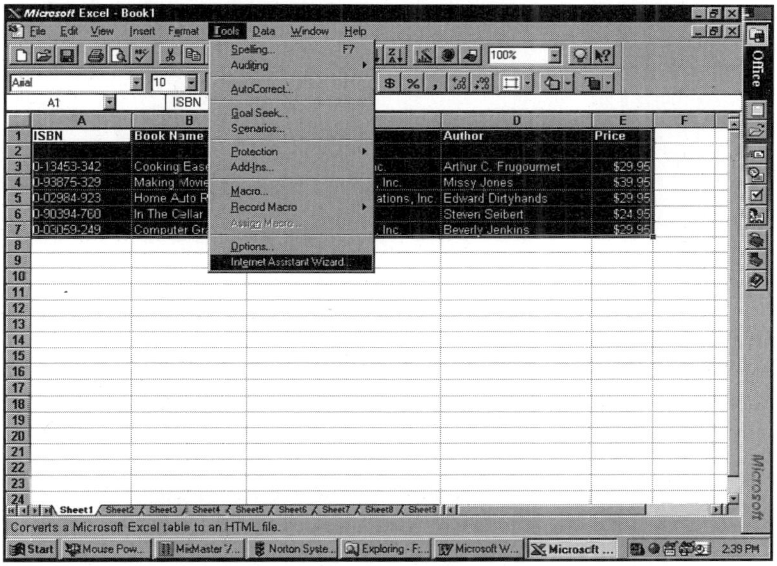

Next, highlight the whole block of rows/columns where you typed text (including any column headers). An easy way to do this is to position your mouse at the top left cell where you typed something, press and hold your primary mouse button, and drag diagonally until you end up at the bottom right cell. Release the primary mouse button. Select `Tools | Internet Assistant Wizard`. The first dialog box asks what cells you want to convert to an HTML table; by default, the location range of the cells you highlighted already appears there. Click `Next`.

The second dialog box asks where you want the resulting table to appear, either in a new HTML document (which you'll get to select a file name for in a subsequent step) or in an existing HTML document. Have Excel IA create a new document; you can use this as an opportunity to fix the link you made from the anchor Book Catalog (in the second item of the bulleted list) to a previously nonexistent document `c:\Website\pages\bkcatlog.htm`. Use the `Browse` button to navigate to it, and click `Next`.

The third dialog box asks for more specific information that would be relative to a stand-alone HTML document—things like Title, Heading, Footer information, and so on. Fill these fields in, using Figure 10.18 as your guide, and click `Finish`. Remember, the Title information is the information that appears in the title bar of the visiting person's Web browser, whereas the Header information appears as part of the HTML document at the very top. If you've done this successfully, clicking the Book Catalog anchor in `default.htm` (while in Web Browse mode) should navigate you to the nicely formatted table shown in Figure 10.19.

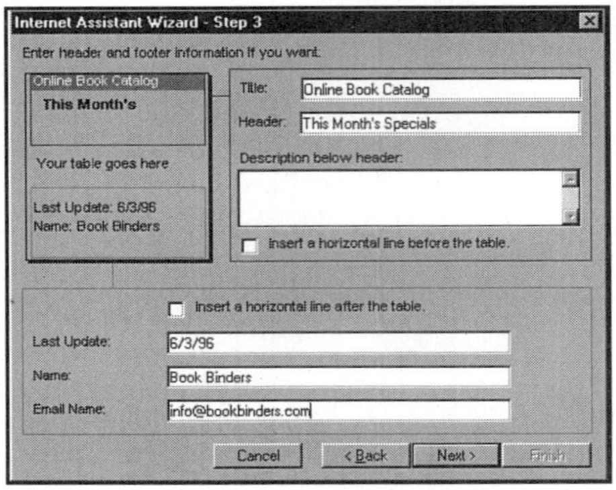

FIGURE 10.18.
Filling in the information for a stand-alone HTML document.

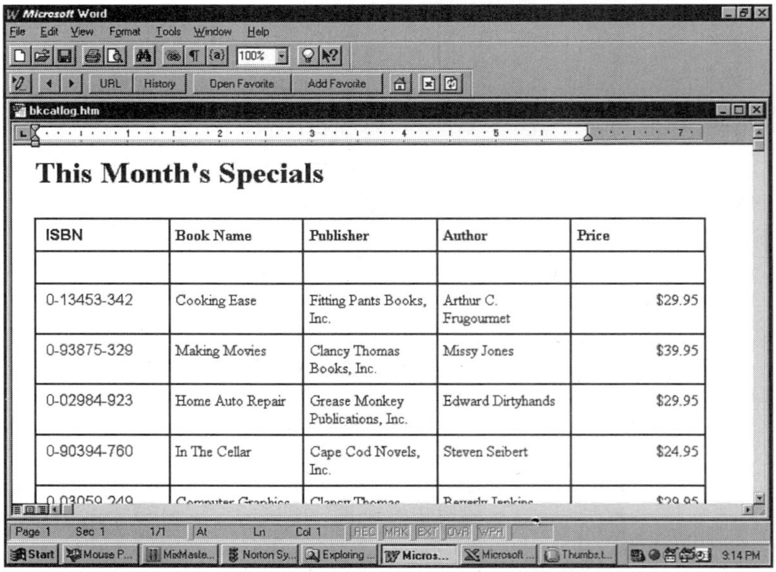

FIGURE 10.19.
Congratulations! A very nicely formatted HTML table from a simple Excel spreadsheet.

NOTE

If you do not see a cleanly formatted table while in Word Internet Assistant, but rather one with what seems to be HTML comments between the Header and the table (which might be blue in color), you are still in Edit mode. Click the little eyeglasses icon on the far left of the Formatting toolbar to switch to the Web Browse mode, and you should see the document properly.

Microsoft PowerPoint Internet Assistant

The Microsoft PowerPoint Internet Assistant enables users of PowerPoint for Windows 95 to create professional-looking Web pages merely by creating a PowerPoint presentation and then saving it as HTML. Because most Web sites consist of multiple pages that are linked together using hyperlinks, PowerPoint lends itself well as a Web authoring tool. A typical workflow would be to create the PowerPoint presentation first, and then convert it to HTML.

Hardware and Software Requirements

The minimum version of PowerPoint needed is version 7.0. The hardware and other software requirements are pretty much the same as the other Internet Assistants, so this section focuses on a free patch you might need, depending on your version of PowerPoint. Check your version of PowerPoint 95 by selecting `Help | About Microsoft PowerPoint`. The second line down from the top should report the version number. If you have version 7.0a, you need the patch. If your version number is merely 7.0 (without the *a*), you do not need the patch.

PowerPoint version 7.0a has a bug in it that causes it to exhibit a screen redraw problem in certain views after several minutes of use. This bug exists only in the *a* release of PowerPoint 95. It makes PowerPoint drain system resources, causing screen redraws to distort and system performance to degrade upon continued use. When the bug manifests itself, you might receive system alerts notifying you of low system resources. If you do receive these alerts, immediately save your work and exit PowerPoint. Your files will be OK, right up to, and including, the last changes you made to them. If, on the other hand, you do not save and exit PowerPoint as soon as you notice the symptoms, you are susceptible to losing any recent changes to the open PowerPoint files. After you exit PowerPoint, system resources (and the responsiveness of other running applications) will return to normal. The problem occurs only under Windows 95, although it can occur under Windows NT 3.51 with heavy PowerPoint use.

To get the patch for this bug, point your Web browser to the following URL:

`http://www.microsoft.com./kb/softlib/mslfiles/PPREDRAW.EXE`

Place this file in an empty directory, and execute it to unarchive it. Next, follow the instructions in the resulting `README.TXT` file to apply the patch.

Downloading and Installing Microsoft PowerPoint IA

PowerPoint Internet Assistant is included on the CD-ROM, but updates can be had by pointing your Web browser to

`http://www.microsoft.com./mspowerpoint/internet/ia/`

Place the `PPTIA.EXE` file in its own empty directory, and execute it to unarchive it. This step should result in four new files: `IA4PPT95.EXE`, `IA4PPT95.HTM`, `IA4PPT95.DOC`, and `README.TXT`. The `IA4PPT95.EXE` file is the setup program, and `README.TXT` is nothing more than a packing list file (something like a `MANIFEST.TXT`). The real documentation is in the `IA4PPT95.DOC` and `IA4PPT95.HTM` files. These files are essentially the same document but in different formats: Word and HTML, respectively. Use whichever of the two formats is more convenient for you. When you double-click either file in Explorer, it should spawn the appropriate application to read it: Word, in the case of `IA4PPT95.DOC`, or your Web browser, in the case of `IA4PPT95.HTM`.

To install PowerPoint Internet Assistant, first check to see whether PowerPoint is already running; if it is, close it. Next, double-click the `IA4PPT95.EXE` file in Explorer. From here, you can pretty much follow the instructions on the screen. User intervention is required only twice, and in both cases, a click of the `OK` button continues the installation. After the installation completes, start PowerPoint. You should notice a new item added to the `File` menu: `Export as HTML` (see Figure 10.20).

NOTE

If you use a network installation of PowerPoint (that is, you run PowerPoint from a network-mounted drive on a server), running the preceding installation procedure will not work. You'll need to contact your site system administrator to have him or her install PowerPoint Internet Assistant into that server's PowerPoint installation.

Using PowerPoint Internet Assistant

In both the `IA4PPT95.DOC` and `IA4PPT95.HTM` files, there is a basic procedure that you can use to create HTML documents from a PowerPoint presentation. It's located in the section Step by Step with the Internet Assistant for PowerPoint. Rather than repeating those steps, this section focuses on using the PowerPoint Internet Assistant to create an information center for the Book

Binders company Web page. Remember the short `infocntr.htm` file you created with Word Internet Assistant to illustrate Word IA's ease of creating hyperlinks to other local documents (the one where you only typed in **Book Binders Information Center** at the top of the document)? This section shows you how to flesh out that file with a PowerPoint presentation.

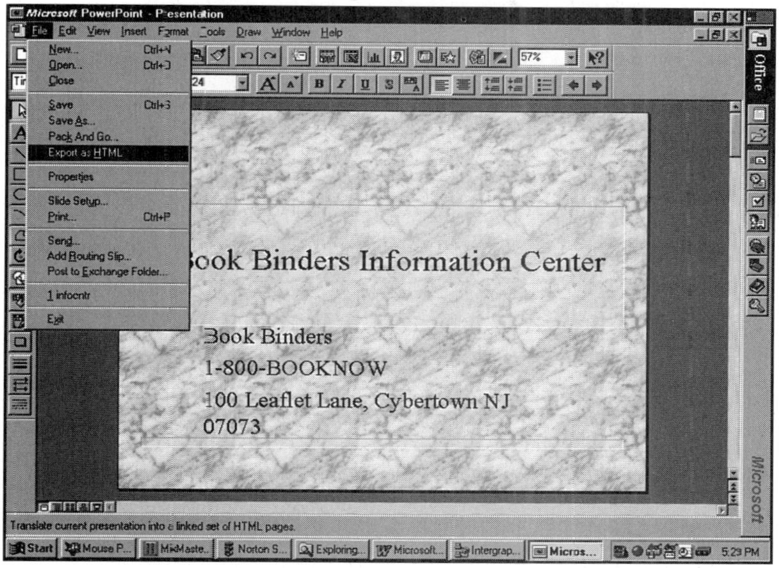

FIGURE 10.20.
Installation of PowerPoint Internet Assistant adds a new `Export as HTML` *option to the* `File` *menu of PowerPoint.*

Start PowerPoint and create a very short PowerPoint presentation on Book Binders. Feel free to use PowerPoint's AutoContent Wizard or one of your own templates. In Figure 10.20, I used AutoContent Wizard, answering it with the following options:

First dialog box

- "What is your name?" Book Binders
- "What are you going to talk about?" Book Binders Information Center
- "Other information you'd like to display?" 1-800-BOOKNOW
  100 Leaflet Lane, Cybertown NJ 07073

Second dialog box

- Select `Selling a product, service or idea`, and then click the `Next` button.

Third dialog box

- Select `Professional` for the visual style of the presentation and `Haven't decided` for the length of the presentation.
- Click the `Next` button.

Fourth dialog box

- Select `On screen presentation` for the type of output, and select `No` for printing handouts.
- Click the `Next` button.

Fifth (and final) dialog box

- Click `Finish` at the last dialog box.

You should now have an eight-slide presentation with boilerplate text that you can replace with any text you want. To save time (and because this is only a sample Web site anyway), go right to exporting this eight-slide presentation as is to HTML. Select `File | Export as HTML` as shown in Figure 10.20. You should then see the HTML Export Options dialog box, which enables you to choose the output style, output format (GIF or JPEG), JPEG image quality and file size, and the folder where the resulting HTML files will go.

CAUTION

When PowerPoint Internet Assistant exports a presentation as HTML, it creates not only HTML files, but GIF/JPEG images as well. PowerPoint Internet Assistant exports both the HTML files and the GIF/JPEG images to one directory—the directory you specify in the `Folder for HTML Export` in the HTML Export Options dialog box. You should export every PowerPoint presentation you plan to use in your Web site to its own subdirectory of your Web site tree; otherwise, you will end up with an incredible mess of HTML files and GIF/JPEG images in what you might have thought was an HTML-only directory.

In Figure 10.21, notice that the sample PowerPoint presentation is being exported to `c:\Website\pages\infocntr`. Even though this directory doesn't exist yet, PowerPoint Internet Assistant will create it. The reason we're not just exporting to the `c:\Website\pages` directory is not only to avoid a mixture (a mess) of GIF/JPEG images and HTML files in this directory, but to have all the HTML and images for the presentation located in one place, their own subdirectory, in case they ever need to be removed, edited, or replaced.

To make a change, it's a simple matter to remove the files in the Web presentation's subdirectory, make the necessary changes to the parent PowerPoint presentation, and then re-export the parent PowerPoint presentation as HTML to that subdirectory. If the Web presentation were exported to, say, `c:\Website\pages`, you'd have a mess to clean up in there, for you'd have to remove all the Web presentation-related files without disturbing the other HTML files already there.

After you have typed in the path `c:\Website\pages\infocntr` for the folder to export to (or you can use the `Browse` button as shown in Figure 10.21), click `OK`, and immediately slide your mouse all the way to the bottom of the screen, out of the PowerPoint window. The export process will begin.

FIGURE 10.21.
Selecting the directory to which to export the presentation.

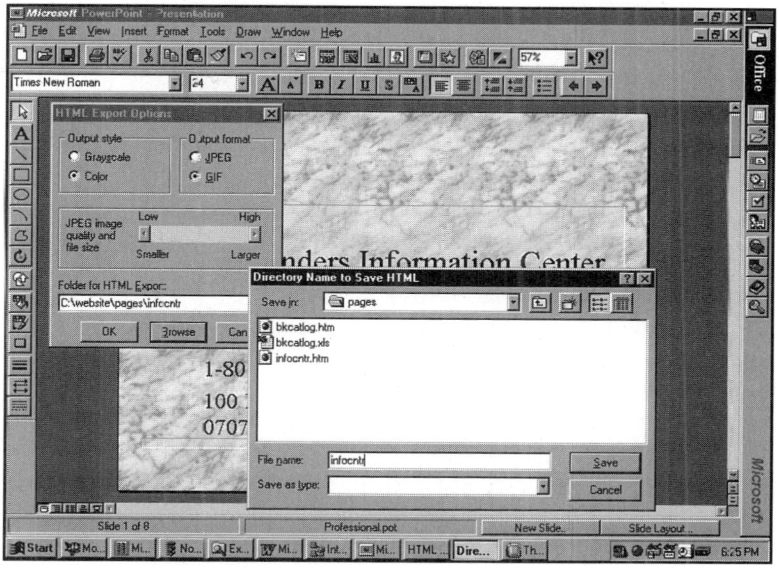

CAUTION

During the export process, you will see various dialog boxes and windows appearing and disappearing on your screen (as in Figure 10.22). The Scroll Lock indicator on your keyboard may also flash on and off. Do not move your mouse anywhere near the PowerPoint window during this time, or you might get stray graphics in the resulting Web presentation.

After the export is completed, you'll see a Status dialog box informing you that the export completed successfully. You can move your mouse now. Click `OK` in this dialog box, save your PowerPoint presentation to a safe place (you might want to consider the `c:\Website\pages` directory itself for later edits/updates), and exit PowerPoint.

What happened here is that all the PowerPoint slides themselves were exported to graphics files of the type you chose on the HTML Export Options dialog (`sldXXX.gif` or `sldXXX.jpg`). Along with those graphics files, the following were created:

- `p2hgraph.gif` (or `p2hgraph.jpg`), a little presentation icon
- `p2hnext.gif` (or `p2hnext.jpg`), a right-pointing arrow icon that looks a lot like the Play button on electronic equipment
- `p2hprev.gif` (or `p2hprev.jpg`), a left-pointing arrow icon that looks a lot like the Reverse button on electronic equipment

- `p2htext.gif` (or `p2htext.jpg`), an icon that implies ASCII text
- `p2hup.gif` (or `p2hup.jpg`), a doubled left-pointing arrow icon that looks a lot like the Rewind button on electronic equipment
- `sldXXX.htm`, an HTML file that displays its associated slide graphics file with the button icons described above to navigate forward, backward, and so on through the presentation
- `tsldXXX.htm`, which is an HTML text-only version of each slide for those people using text-only Web browsers like Lynx

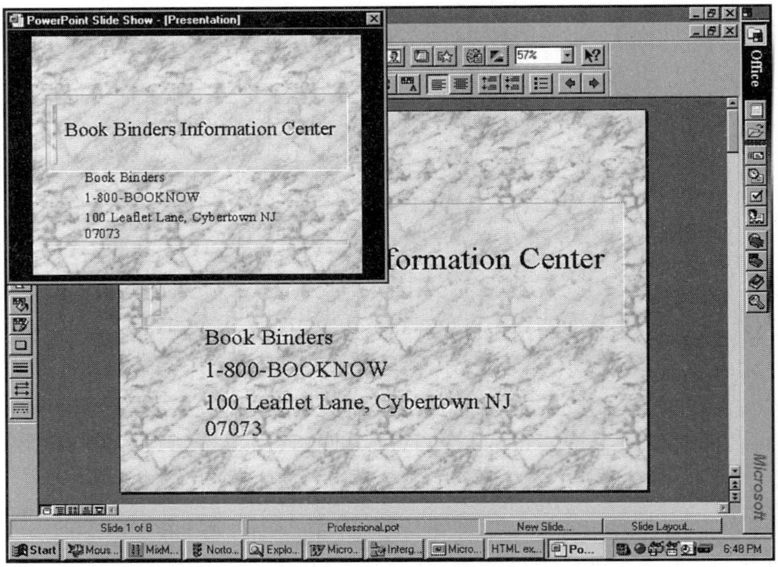

FIGURE 10.22.
Various splash dialog boxes and windows appear and disappear during the HTML export process. Don't move that mouse!

Both the images and the HTML text files went to the `c:\Website\pages\infocntr` directory, which itself was created by the export process. The HTML files are set up so that one links to the next, just like a PowerPoint presentation, but with a twist: an `index.htm` file was also created that acts as a master menu of them all. It is this `index.htm` file that you want to link to the `Book Binders Information Center` anchor on the main page. To view the `index.htm` file, just double-click it in Explorer, and you should see something like what's shown in Figure 10.23.

Notice a cool feature of the PowerPoint Internet Assistant: it names each anchor on the `index.htm` according to the text found at the top of each slide; that is, the title text at the top of each slide is now an anchor on the `index.htm`—just click it to go to that document. Imagine the possibilities; if you had to create a bunch of small Web documents with a master menu from which the user could pick, you could simply create a PowerPoint presentation with descriptive document titles at the top of each slide (each slide being a stand-alone document). Export that presentation as HTML, and voilà! An entire technical data center, or card catalog, or recipe list, or—you get the idea.

FIGURE 10.23.
The resulting `index.htm` *file from the PowerPoint HTML export. Notice that the PowerPoint product registration information made its way into this file.*

You might notice that the product registration information you entered when initially installing PowerPoint made its way into this file and appears at the top. If that's the case in your `index.htm` file, it's easily fixed. Just open that file inside of Word (with Word IA installed, of course), edit out the registration information, and save it as an HTML file.

To create a link from the `Book Binders Information Center` anchor to this `index.htm` file, start Word and open up the `c:\Website\default.htm` file. Single-click the `Book Binders Information Center` anchor to highlight it, and click the Hyperlink icon on the Formatting toolbar (the icon that looks like three links of chain). Using the `Browse` button on the Hyperlink dialog box, navigate down to the `c:\Website\pages\infocntr` directory and select the `index.htm` file (see Figure 10.24). Click `Open` in the Select File To Link dialog box, and then click `OK` in the Hyperlink dialog box. This procedure orphans the original file `c:\Website\pages\infocntr.htm` that you used as a placeholder for the Book Binders Information Center anchor, so you can now just delete the `infocntr.htm` file altogether.

TIP

The first section of this chapter mentions that Word IA lacks a native graphics editor capable of dealing with GIF/JPEG files. Remember how I hinted that PowerPoint Internet Assistant can? Just use PowerPoint to create a one-slide presentation, export it as HTML to a temporary directory (say, `c:\temp`), and grab the `sld001.gif` or `sld001.jpg` file (as appropriate) that the export process creates.

continues

continued

You might be interested in the little button images that the export process creates as well; these are useful to place at the bottom of your pages so the users can navigate back and forth. Without their `.gif`/`.jpg` file extensions, these little button images are called `p2hnext` (an arrow pointing to the right), `p2hprev` (an arrow pointing to the left), and `p2hup` (a double arrow pointing to the left). You might also want to take a peek at the other p2h files to see whether you can use them. The remainder of the files from the one-slide presentation export process can be deleted.

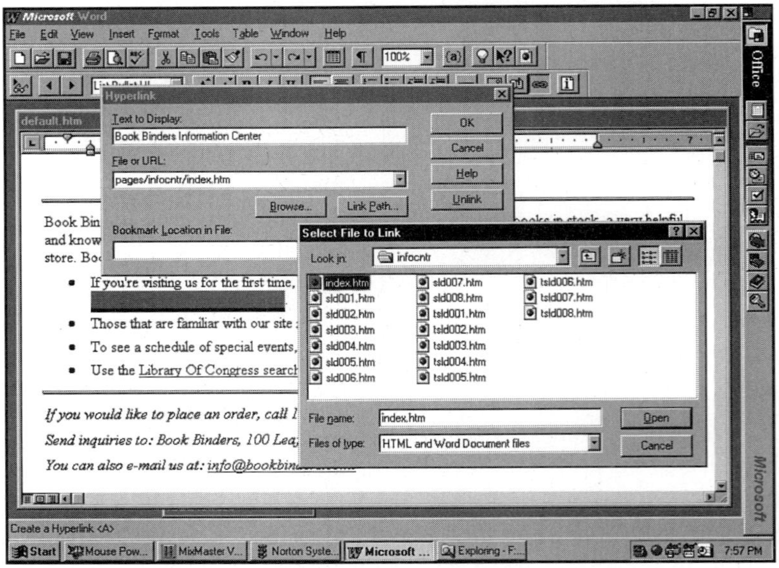

FIGURE 10.24.
Editing the link behind the anchor `Book Binders Information Center` *to point to the* `index.htm` *of the exported Web presentation.*

Now to create a logo for the Book Binders home page. In PowerPoint, pick a template/slide style that you like, and type the introductory company text and subtitle on it. Delete any extraneous empty slides that might also be in that presentation set—you want only one slide. (This saves on the time required for the export and avoids creating extra files for slides you don't need.) Export that single-slide presentation to a temporary directory. Copy the `sld001.gif` (or `sld001.jpg`) file to your `c:\Website\images` directory as `logo.gif` (or `logo.jpg`). Next, open the `default.htm` file in Word and insert the picture where you want it to appear by using the Picture icon on the Formatting toolbar (see Figure 10.25). You might want to use this logo to replace the name and subtitle, so after inserting the picture, just delete the text for the name and subtitle (see Figure 10.26).

TIP

Notice the use of the Alternative Text field on the Picture dialog box to display text for text-only Web browsers.

Picture icon

FIGURE 10.25.
Using Word Internet Assistant's insert picture feature to add the company logo created from PowerPoint Internet Assistant.

FIGURE 10.26.
The resulting home page with the PowerPoint Internet Assistant-created company logo. Because the picture says it all as far as the name and subtitle of the home page go, we deleted the text for the name and subtitle.

Summary

This chapter covered a lot of ground. You've learned how to use the Word, Excel, and PowerPoint Internet Assistants as integrated tools to create a sample Web site. The majority of the sample site was created with Word Internet Assistant for general layout and look and feel; you then filled in the site using the other Internet Assistants. If you've used relative path names for all the hyperlinks in your HTML documents, copying the entire `c:\Website` directory structure to the Web server for publishing is now easy. With relative paths, you can transfer Web site directory structures without having to worry about "breaking" the hyperlinks.

Note that from within the Word Internet Assistant you can use the icons on the toolbar to insert things like spreadsheets and presentations. Another tool you have in your arsenal is to use normal Windows drag-and-drop functionality to insert these objects into your HTML document, and Word IA will then take care of the translation to HTML. One of the more detailed things you didn't learn but you might want to use is Word IA's capability to create fill-in forms. This feature is accessible within Word IA by selecting `Insert | Form Field`.

The two other Internet Assistants are the Schedule+ Internet Assistant and the Access Internet Assistant. The Access Internet Assistant works only with the Windows 95 version of Access and requires database knowledge of tables, queries, form datasheets, and reports, all of which are beyond the scope of this chapter. The Schedule+ Internet Assistant also is available only for the Windows 95 version and was in a beta version at the time of this writing. Although individual users may not find many uses for these two tools, those using intranets may find them invaluable. For example, project team members could post their calendars for viewing by others by using the Schedule+ Internet Assistant. You can obtain Schedule+ Internet Assistant at the following URL:

```
http://www.microsoft.com./msscheduleplus/internet/ia/
```

To get Access Internet Assistant, go to this URL:

```
http://www.microsoft.com./msaccess/internet/ia/
```

You should now have a good idea of how to use the various Internet Assistants for Office products to create logically laid out and aesthetically pleasing Web pages.

CHAPTER 11

Microsoft FrontPage

by Dennis R. Short

IN THIS CHAPTER

FrontPage Version 1.1, by Microsoft, is a suite of three sets of tools that help you to develop and administer local and remote Web sites. The three components of FrontPage are the FrontPage Client, the Personal Web Server, and a set of utilities. FrontPage Client consists of FrontPage Explorer, FrontPage Editor, FrontPage Wizards, and the To Do List. The Personal Web Server is a 32-bit PC-based Web server running under Windows 95 or Windows NT that supports the HTTP (Hypertext Transfer Protocol) and CGI (Common Gateway Interface) standards. The final component of FrontPage is a set of utilities; FrontPage TCP/IP verifies the TCP/IP configuration of a PC hosting a Personal Web Server, and FrontPage Server Administrator handles server administration tasks.

NOTE

All of the components described in this chapter are installed in a typical installation. To install any component or subset of a component, select custom installation.

Although FrontPage is marketed as a package that enables non-programmers to develop professional-quality Web sites, FrontPage is useful as a productivity and development tool for professionals as well. You can make the most of FrontPage by using it with the family of Internet Assistants available for Microsoft Office applications. You also can extend FrontPage's functionality by using the FrontPage Software Developer's Kit (SDK) to develop templates, wizards, and custom CGI scripts.

FrontPage Client

FrontPage Client is the set of productivity tools that are part of FrontPage. These tools include FrontPage Explorer for Web site administration, FrontPage Editor for creating and modifying Web pages, the To Do List for managing the tasks involved in Web creation and maintenance, and FrontPage Wizards for the development of Webs, Web pages, and pages utilizing forms or frames.

Front Page Explorer

FrontPage Explorer is a tool used to view and administer a Web site. Information on the Web site is presented in both hierarchical and graphical forms. The visual interface provided by FrontPage Explorer is extremely useful in helping the developer understand how the Web components are associated and linked. Icons indicate the type of Web element and whether a problem, such as a broken link, exists. The application is closely integrated with FrontPage Editor and helps you to create links and relocate files between directories while dynamically modifying all links for pages effected. You can quickly create Web sites by using the wizards and templates that FrontPage Explorer provides.

Web Display

With FrontPage Explorer, you can display link, outline, and summary views of a Web site (see Figure 11.1). All files, documents, and links are displayed in the Web view. The usual configuration, selected in the View menu, is a side-by-side display of the outline view and the link view. Double-clicking an icon opens that HTML component in FrontPage Editor. You can direct FrontPage to recalculate all Web links and to refresh the display lists by using the `Tools | Recalculate Links` command.

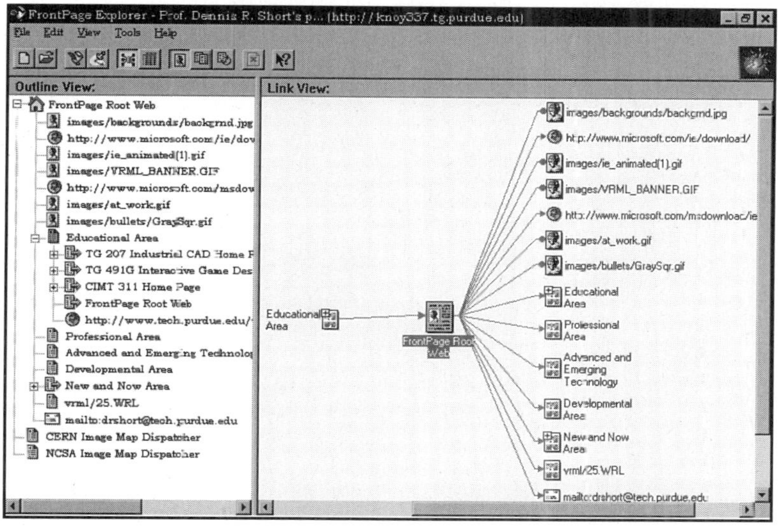

FIGURE 11.1.
FrontPage Explorer window.

> **CAUTION**
>
> If you manipulate the Web file area outside of the FrontPage Explorer environment while Explorer is open, you must select `View | Refresh` from the menu bar to display the Web hierarchy correctly.
>
> The recalculation of Web links for a large Web site can take a long time. Not only are all internal links verified but all external links are tested also. Depending on network traffic, this recalculation can be quite time-consuming.

Web Creation and Manipulation

You can create new Webs or add elements to the current Web by using available wizards and templates. The Corporate Presence Wizard (see Figure 11.2 and Figure 11.3) and the Discussion Web Wizard are included in FrontPage. FrontPage also includes five templates: Normal

Web, Empty Web, Customer Support Web, Personal Web, and Project Web. You can develop other Web wizards and templates using the FrontPage Software Developer's Kit. These wizards are selected when a new Web is created. Each wizard takes the user through a series of questions that establish the Web content.

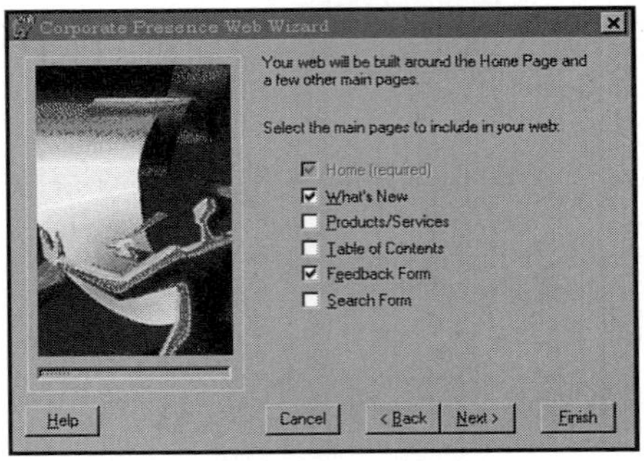

FIGURE 11.2.
This dialog box from the Corporate Presence Web Wizard allows the users to specify the main components of the Web.

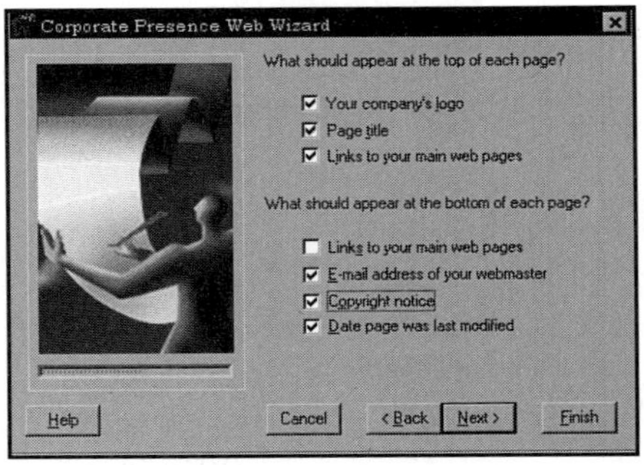

FIGURE 11.3.
Users can specify Web page elements that will appear on all pages in this dialog box from the Corporate Presence Web Wizard.

You can establish links by dragging a file from FrontPage Explorer on top of text (the link description) in FrontPage Editor. By using the `File | Copy Web` command, you can copy existing Webs and all their components to or from another Web server with server extensions installed (see Figure 11.4). Although some CGI programming may not transfer (WebBot generated code will transfer), you can move Webs between platforms without having to make many corrections. Individual files and Web components can be imported from or exported to other servers by using the `File | Import` and `File | Export` commands. To use these commands, you must have read/write access for the target system. Common problems encountered when importing or exporting Webs include incompatible file naming conventions or extensions such as mixed-case file names or three- versus four-character extensions (for example, `.htm` and `.jpg` versus `.html` and `.jpeg`), fragmented directory structures, and references to local applications not found on the target system.

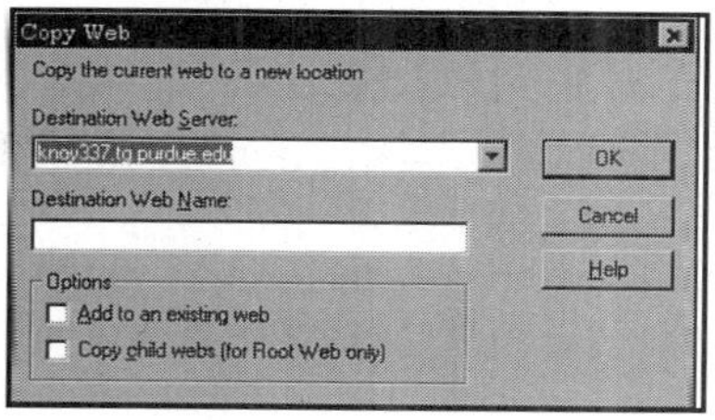

FIGURE 11.4.
The Copy Web dialog box.

Verification and Testing

FrontPage automatically updates all files and directories for a published Web if any changes have occurred. For example, Explorer can automatically fix related links when a document is renamed or moved. FrontPage Explorer also can verify and flag all broken internal and external links (see Figure 11.5).

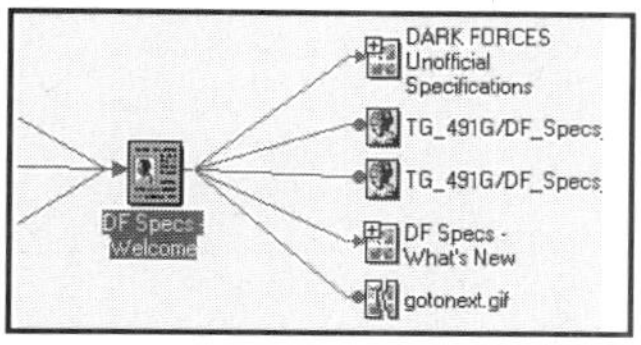

FIGURE 11.5.
An example of a broken link icon in the Link View of FrontPage Explorer.

The verify link function tests all internal and external links. Figure 11.6 shows the results of this procedure. The summary view allows failed links to be edited or to be added to the To Do List.

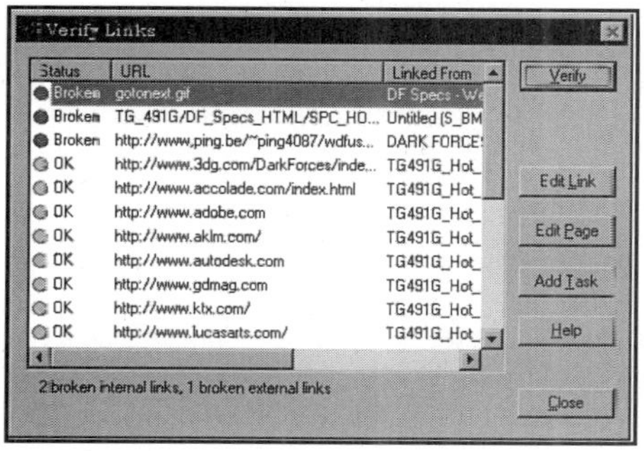

FIGURE 11.6.
The Verify Links dialog box showing broken links to an internal GIF image and an external HTTP site.

Configuration Options

FrontPage Explorer launches the correct Microsoft application for any file created using a Microsoft application. The extension and application is then added to the configure editors list. You must add non-Microsoft extensions to the list manually in order for the specified editor to recognize them.

You can configure the editors that FrontPage uses. You can map file extensions to the application that you would like to use for editing or viewing that file type by selecting `Tools | Configure Editors` and adding, modifying, or removing a file extension and the related application. Applications referenced in the Configure Editors dialog box (see Figure 11.7) must include the full path for the required executable.

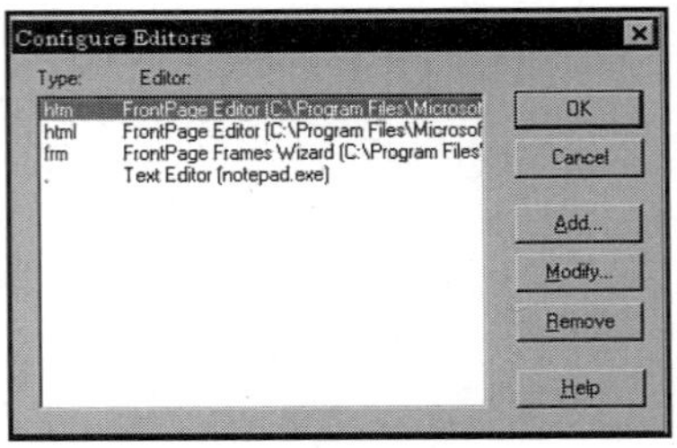

FIGURE 11.7.
The Configure Editors dialog box showing the default FrontPage Explore file types and editor associations.

FrontPage Editor

FrontPage Editor is a WYSIWYG editor used to create and develop Web pages. The Editor does not require a knowledge of HTML and presents the user with an interface very similar to Microsoft Word with Microsoft Internet Assistant for Word. Using wizards or templates, you can create Web pages with features that normally would require special programming, including forms and frames. You can create specialized HTML coding such as scheduled images, timestamps, which indicate the last date of page modification, and includes through WebBots. Server-side includes references to fragments of HTML code that can be embedded in Web pages. By updating this fragment of HTML code, commonly used elements, such as copyright notices or Webmaster e-mail addresses, can be updated on all pages in a uniform manner.

FrontPage Editor enables you to control and implement most HTML-related functions through icon and menu selection. Standard word-processing functions including font style, font size, font attributes, paragraph style, and paragraph alignment are directly translated into HTML code. However, FrontPage Editor does not directly support tabs and tabbing for the layout of text.

CAUTION

Text imported into or pasted into the FrontPage Editor will display tabs present in the text. However, when the page is viewed from a external browser, the tabs are not part of the page formatting, and unpredictable results may occur.

FrontPage has other limitations as well. Although you can view HTML code within FrontPage Editor, you cannot directly manipulate it. Instead, you must use another editor, such as Microsoft Word with Internet Assistant for Word. The example of the FrontPage Editor window shown in Figure 11.8 illustrates some of the limitations of the internal Web browser. In this example, the Editor is unable to display the scrolling marquee and font specification for a page developed with Internet Assistant for Microsoft Word.

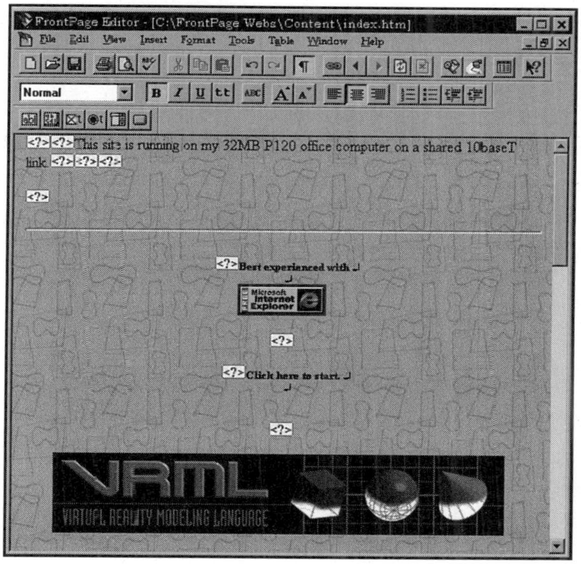

FIGURE 11.8.
The FrontPage Editor window.

Creating and Editing Pages

To create a page in FrontPage Editor, you either open a normal template, use one of several special templates, or invoke a wizard. You can open existing pages from any source, including an existing URL, and you can save the page directly to that URL if you have the correct permissions set. You can save images and other components of the page locally from the remote URL. By double-clicking the Page icon, you can open pages directly from FrontPage Explorer.

You can edit pages by using drag-and-drop, directly manipulating an object (such as text), or by editing the object or page properties. Double-clicking a component, such as an image, brings up the properties window for that component. You can then modify these properties as required. In Figure 11.9, an existing JPEG image of a diesel engine is being changed into an interlaced GIF image to improve page display performance.

FIGURE 11.9.
An Image Properties dialog box.

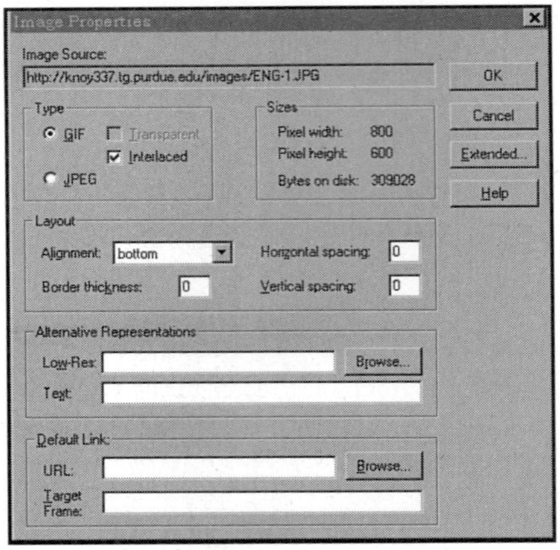

A number of frequently used Web page formats and constructs are automated by FrontPage Editor. These formats and constructs are accessed through the `Insert` menu for each category, such as `Headings` or `Form Field`. Figures 11.10 and 11.11 show two form field constructs for a drop-down menu and an image insert. Available formats and constructs accessed through the `Insert` menu include the following:

- Bulleted headings
- Numbered headings
- Directory headings
- Menu headings
- One-line text box
- Scrolling text box
- Checkbox
- Radio button
- Drop-down menu
- Pushbutton

FIGURE 11.10.
The Drop-Down Menu Properties dialog box.

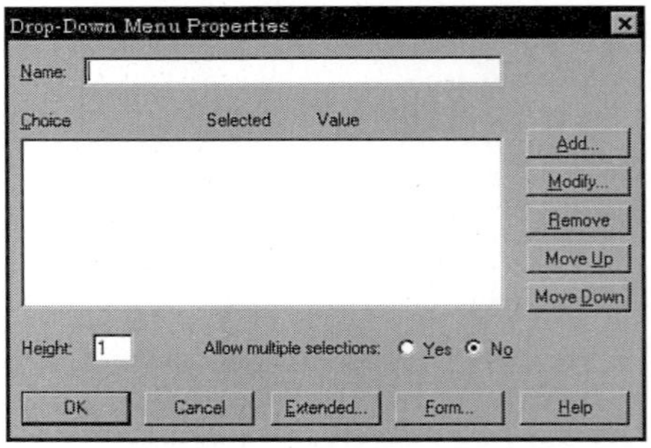

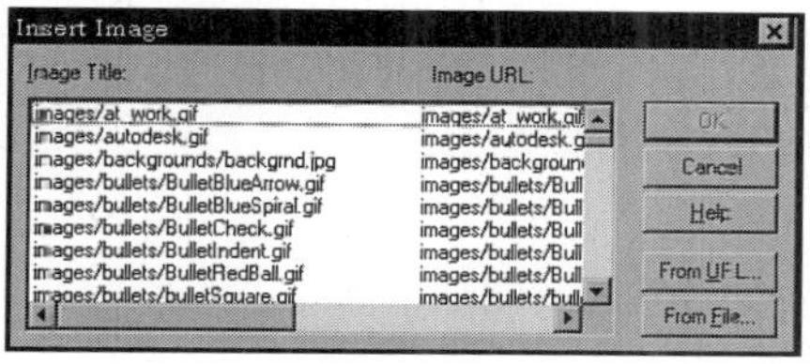

FIGURE 11.11.
The Insert Image dialog box.

FrontPage Editor Templates

FrontPage Editor includes several Web page templates for commonly created pages (see Figure 11.12). These templates are oriented toward commercial or professional sites with `Normal Page` being the system default. Templates are available when a new Web page is created. The templates consist of a series of dialog boxes that guide the user in the creation of the page through a series of selections. The following templates are included in FrontPage Editor for the creation of new Web pages:

Normal page	Lecture abstract
Bibliography	Meeting agenda
Confirmation form	Office directory
Directory of press releases	Press release
Employee directory	Product description
Employment opportunities	Product or event registration
Feedback form	Search page
Frequently asked questions	Software data sheet
Glossary of terms	Survey form
Guest book	Table of contents
Hot list	User registration
HyperDocument page	What's new

FrontPage Editor Wizards

FrontPage Editor includes three wizards: Form Page Wizard, Frame Wizard, and Personal Home Page Wizard. The two most useful are the Form and Frame wizards. The Form Page Wizard prompts you for each type of question the form is to include and allows you to edit the text and the attributes for each question (see Figures 11.13 and 11.14). The Frame Wizard presents a number of common frame arrangements for Web pages and enables you to select the frame arrangement and name the frame elements before creating the Web page (see Figure 11.15). You also can use custom frame sizes and configurations rather than the predefined frames.

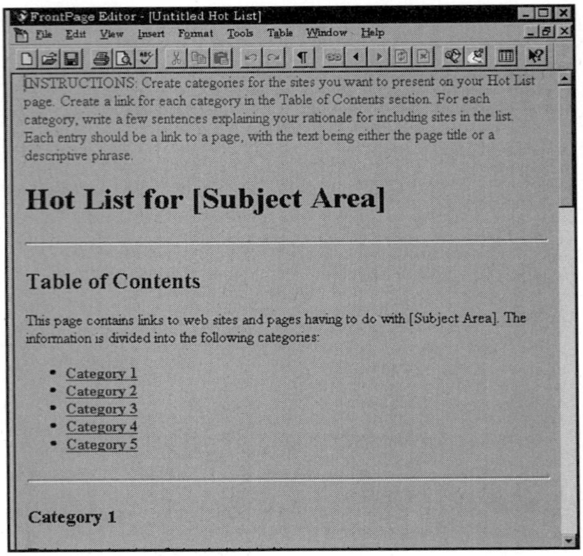

FIGURE 11.12.
An unedited Web page created with the Hot List template in FrontPage Editor.

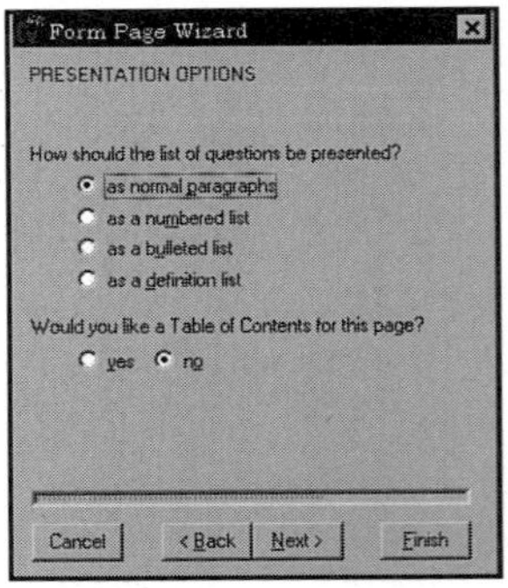

FIGURE 11.13.
A dialog box from the Form Page Wizard setting up the general characteristics of the new Web page.

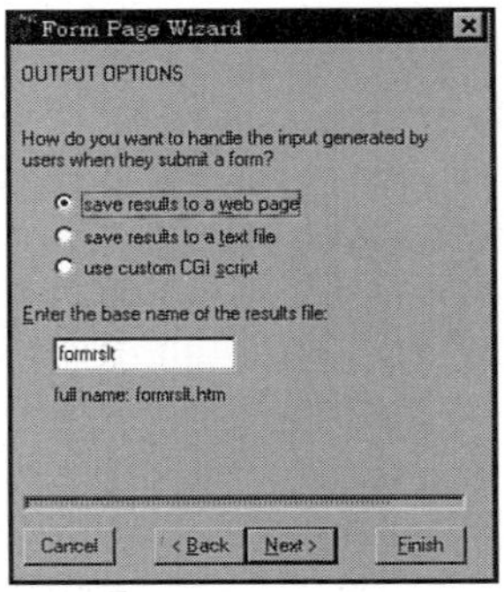

FIGURE 11.14.
A dialog box from the Form Page Wizard defining the output options.

FIGURE 11.15.
Selecting the frame style from the Frames Wizard - Pick Template Layout dialog box.

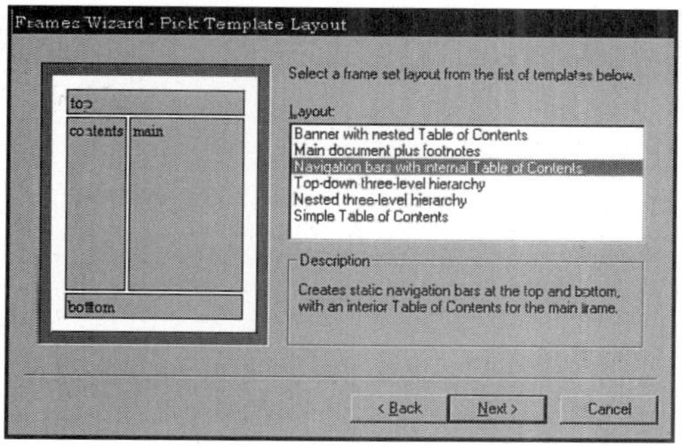

The Personal Home Page Wizard presents a list of common personal home page elements from which you can choose (see Figure 11.16). A Web page template including the selected elements is then created for you, providing a basis for further Web page development. The Personal Home Page is based on a single page rather than a series of linked pages.

FIGURE 11.16.
The contents dialog box of the Personal Home Page Wizard.

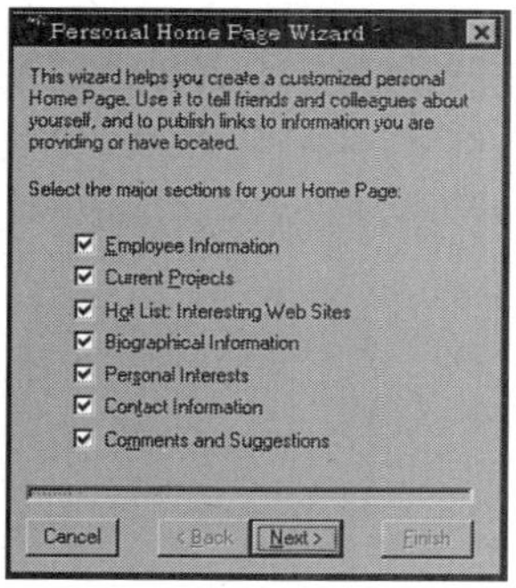

Working with Images

FrontPage Editor can import images in a number of formats, including BMP, EPS, GIF, JPEG, MAC, MSP, PCD, PCX, TIFF, WPG, and WMF. All images inserted into a page or table in FrontPage Editor are converted into either GIF or JPEG (quality 75 by default) formats. An image, after it's inserted by using either the `Insert | Image` or the `Insert | Form Field | Image` commands, can be converted between JPEG and GIF by editing the image properties (refer to Figure 11.11). The `HTML IMAGE` code that is created when you insert an image includes the image size in order to increase the speed at which the page can be viewed by a compliant browser.

CAUTION

Because image size information is included in the HTML code, you must open and save a Web page in FrontPage Editor if you have changed the size of an image on that page by using an external image editor. This action allows the Editor to update the size information in the `IMAGE` code. Failure to update the image size can affect the appearance of the page.

You can edit images within FrontPage Editor. For example, you can make a selected color in a GIF transparent by using the Make Transparent tool from the image toolbar and selecting the color that will be transparent.

You also can use FrontPage Editor to create clickable images by using the image toolbar edit commands for circular, rectangular, and irregular polygons to insert hotspots on an image. After you create a hotspot, FrontPage automatically prompts you for the URL link information. To create client-side image maps, access the image properties by clicking the image with the right mouse button and adjust the Web settings by selecting the `Generate Client-Side Image Maps` option. Both client-side and server-side image maps can be supported at one time. You can control more advanced image manipulation, including interlaced GIFs, alternate images or text, and extend attributes, by editing the image properties.

WebBots

WebBot components can be described as smart page objects and are inserted using the `Insert | Bot` command. WebBots allow the Web page developer to include capabilities that would normally require CGI programming. For example, WebBots can help you create discussion groups with full-text search capabilities, schedule images and other Web components to be included on Web pages, perform registration and confirmation functions, allow HTML markup, and use include functions to simplify site administration. There are two types of WebBots: static and dynamic. Static WebBots are components that do not change when a user fetches a Web page. Dynamic WebBots change each time a user fetches a Web page. The WebBots available in FrontPage Editor Version 1.1 are all static WebBots.

When you insert a WebBot into a Web page, you are prompted for the configuration required by that particular WebBot. For example, after inserting the Include WebBot, you would be prompted for the needed URL. If you inserted the Timestamp WebBot, you would be prompted for the date format and to indicate whether the time is to be for the last edit or the last automatic update of the Web page. Figure 11.17 shows the dialog box for the Scheduled Image WebBot used to insert images in a Web page for defined time periods.

One of the more useful WebBots is the Annotation WebBot. This WebBot enables you to include information on a Web page that is only viewable within FrontPage Editor and is not seen by the user when the page is displayed by a Web browser. This WebBot enables you to add production comments directly to the page and permits the developer to simply reference the annotation in the To Do List.

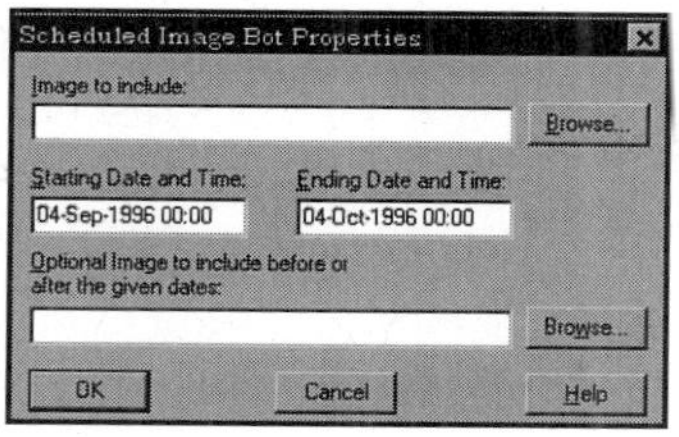

FIGURE 11.17.
The Scheduled Image Bot Properties dialog box.

To Do List

FrontPage Client includes an integrated To Do List that is accessible from both the FrontPage Explorer and the FrontPage Editor. The To Do List allows the developer to maintain a list of tasks that need to be accomplished for a Web site. The list indicates the task, who is responsible for the task in a multiple-author environment, the priority of the task, the affected page, and a description of the task that needs to be performed (see Figure 11.18).

The To Do List also can maintain and display a history of assigned and accomplished tasks. The usefulness of the To Do List is extended if an Annotation WebBot is used on the page to describe the work needing to be done or the problem that must be corrected.

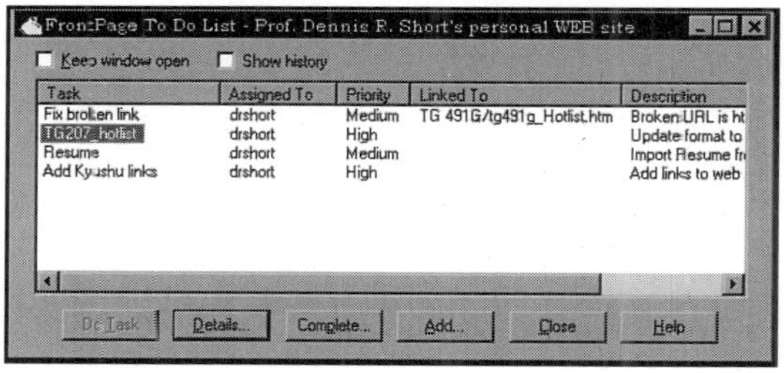

FIGURE 11.18.
A To Do List from a Web site under development.

FrontPage Personal Server and Components

The FrontPage Personal Web Server is a 32-bit Web server that can run under either Windows 95 or Windows NT. The server supports both the Hypertext Transfer Protocol (HTTP) and the Common Gateway Interface (CGI) standards. The principal use for the FrontPage Personal Web Server is to allow Web developers to run a Web server on their local machines for the development and testing of a Web site. Another use for the Personal Web Server is to operate a small Web site for a collaborative workgroup or an isolated intranet.

Installation and Configuration

System requirements for the FrontPage Personal Web Server include an Intel Pentium-based system (a 486 processor is **not** adequate), a minimum of 16 M of memory for the Personal Web Server, 15 M minimum of disk space (more will be required), and the Windows 95 or Windows NT operating system.

The installation process is straightforward. If you are installing all of the FrontPage components, two main directories are created by default. The applications programs are installed in the `Programs Files` directory in a directory called `Microsoft FrontPage`. The tutorial files, templates, wizards, clip art, and other files are located in various subdirectories.

The FrontPage Personal Web Server creates a new directory at the root level of the selected drive called `FrontPage Webs`. This directory contains two main components: the `Server` directory and the `Content` directory. The `Content` directory holds the files and directories that make up the Web page. The installation process also prompts you for a name and password for page administration. You cannot recover this information if the name and password are lost. You must use the `Custom Install` option to reinstall the Personal Web Server in this case.

Limitations

The main limitations to the FrontPage Personal Web Server are the lack of secure transaction options (some encryption is supported) and the limited number of users the server can effectively serve on Windows 95 and smaller Windows NT servers. Personal Web Server was not designed as a production server.

CAUTION

When you name files and directories for a Web under FrontPage Personal Web Server in a Windows 95 or Windows NT environment, don't use spaces, special characters, or long file names that would normally be legal under these two operating systems. If you do, browsers running under different operating systems, such as Windows 3.1, will not be able to access the page because the file names will either be truncated or appear to be invalid. A `File not found` error will be returned to the browser.

FrontPage Server Extensions

Server extensions allow FrontPage Explorer to work directly with a variety of different WWW servers running under several different operating systems. FrontPage includes server extensions for FrontPage Personal Web Sever, O'Reilly Website 1.1, Netscape Communications Server v11.2, and Netscape Commerce Server on Windows NT. FrontPage server extensions can be configured to support single and multiple daemons and can support multihoming.

CAUTION

The FrontPage server extension for Netscape Commerce Web Server does not support SSL (Secure Sockets Layer). You must disable SSL while using FrontPage Explorer or Editor to manage the site. SSL may be turned on again when site management tasks are completed.

Additional server extensions are available for popular WWW servers for the following operating systems: Solaris 2.4, SunOS 4.13, IRIX 5.3, HP/UX 9.03, and BSD/OS 2.1. The current listing of available FrontPage server extensions is on the Microsoft Web site at `http://www.microsoft.com/FrontPage/softlib/fs_fp_extensions.htm`; you can download these server extensions from the site as well. Note that server extensions for the popular IBM operating systems, including the RS/6000 platforms, are not currently available. For unsupported systems, you will need to use the FrontPage Publishing Wizard. This Wizard does not provide functionality equivalent to using FrontPage with server extensions.

FrontPage server extensions could weaken a Web site's security if they are not properly configured. Most of the known security cases involve running a Web as root and thereby allowing the possibility of forged root access. If you are using FrontPage server extensions, download the Known Security Issues Web page for FrontPage from Microsoft's Web site.

FrontPage Utility Programs

Two utility programs are included in FrontPage to aid in the performance of systems administration tasks: Front Page TCP/IP test and FrontPage Server Administrator. Additional utility programs and aids may be downloaded from Microsoft's Web site at `http://www.microsoft.com/FrontPage/softlib`.

FrontPage TCP/IP Test

FrontPage TCP/IP Test (`TcpTest.exe`) verifies the installation of either 16-bit or 32-bit Winsock DLL's and returns information on the system's Internet connectivity, including host name, IP address, and local host IP address (see Figure 11.19). Run this utility before installing FrontPage Personal Web Server by double-clicking the software icon located in the `bin` subdirectory of the `Microsoft FrontPage` folder.

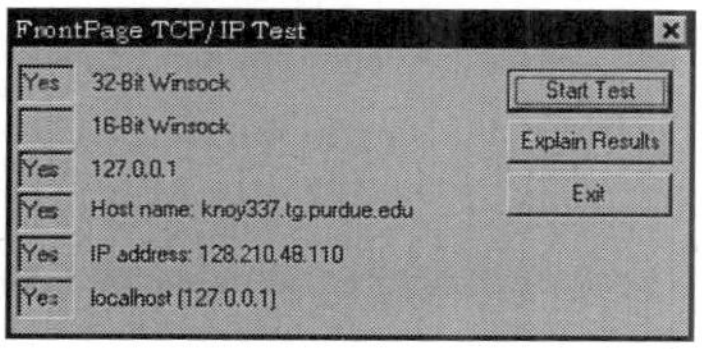

FIGURE 11.19.
An example of the TCP/IP Test dialog box after testing a site.

FrontPage Server Administrator

FrontPage Sever Administrator is available as a Windows (`fpservwin.exe`) program or as a command-line (`fpsrvadm.exe`) application located in the `bin` subdirectory of the `Microsoft FrontPage` folder. Although you can handle most of the administration of a Web site from FrontPage Explorer, tasks that must be performed or run from the server's local host machine require FrontPage Server Administrator. This application enables you to change the administrator password and other parameters on the host machine and change permissions for FrontPage Editor and FrontPage Explorer so that they can function with a particular server (see Figure 11.20). FrontPage Server Administrator works only with systems running the appropriate FrontPage server extension.

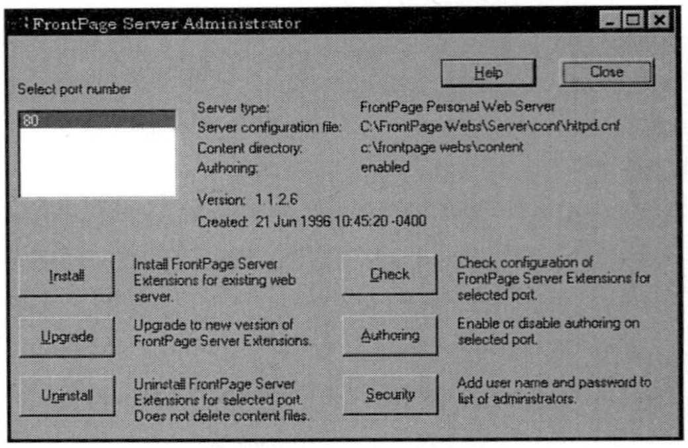

FIGURE 11.20.
The starting dialog box for FrontPage Server Administrator.

FrontPage Publishing Wizard

An additional utility that you can download from Microsoft's Web site is FrontPage Publishing Wizard (`fpposit.exe`). This application helps you to perform many of the same Web administration functions as FrontPage Server Administrator does, but it's for systems that do not have FrontPage server extensions available. The application is particularly useful for moving a Web site onto or out of the FrontPage Client environment. The starting dialog box for FrontPage Publishing Wizard that controls the FTP access to the remote Web is shown in Figure 11.21.

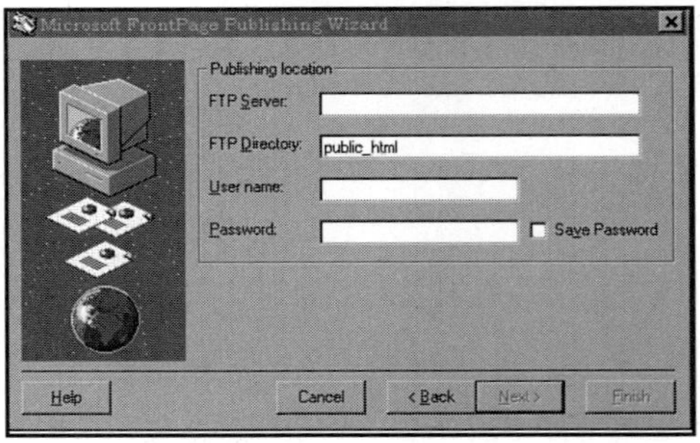

FIGURE 11.21.
The beginning dialog box for FrontPage Publishing Wizard.

FrontPage Software Developer's Kit

Microsoft FrontPage Software Developer's Kit (SDK) is used to extend the functionality of FrontPage by allowing developers to create templates and wizards for Web pages or Webs and helping them to develop CGI-based programs or scripts. The development of templates does not require programming knowledge, but the development of wizards or OLE Automation for the external control of FrontPage components requires that you know either Microsoft Visual C++ or Visual Basic. A Visual Basic program called Web Template Maker is included in the SDK to help automate the process of creating Web templates. The SDK includes a number of coding examples as well.

You can use the Developer's Kit to develop prototype Web components and to distribute these components to developers or to end users. Examples of applications you could create with this kit include the development wizards for employee information Web pages or wizards for product catalog page development, including graphics and CGI scripts. You can download the FrontPage Software Developer's Kit from Microsoft's Web site at `http://www.microsoft.com/FrontPage/softlib/fs_fp_sdk.htm`.

Summary

Microsoft FrontPage is an integrated set of tools for the creation and maintenance of Web sites and Web pages. Using FrontPage in combination with Microsoft's Internet Assistant family provides for a powerful Web development and administration environment supported by a single vendor. The automation of tasks through wizards and WebBots greatly simplifies many repetitive Web creation functions. Through the use of the FrontPage SDK, a competent programmer can automate a variety of templates and wizards that would allow less skilled personnel to assist in the development of robust, professional, and consistent Web pages for larger organizations.

CHAPTER 12

Netscape Navigator Gold

by Dick Oliver

IN THIS CHAPTER

The Gold edition of Netscape Navigator is not only a Web browser, but also a Web publishing tool. In this chapter, you will learn about the Web publishing capabilities built into Netscape Gold.

Why Go for the Gold?

As discussed in previous chapters, the HTML code used to define the appearance and contents of a Web page is basically a set of commands stored in a text file. The problem for many people who are new to Web publishing is that the almost cryptic appearance of HTML code can be very disconcerting.

For example, to create the simple Web page shown in Figure 12.1, the following HTML code was used:

```
<HTML>
<HEAD><TITLE>Hi-Ku</TITLE></HEAD>
<BODY BACKGROUND="dotty.gif" TEXT="#880000" LINK="#880000" VLINK="#FFFFFF">
<DIV ALIGN="center">
<TABLE BORDER=0><TR><TD VALIGN="top">
<IMG SRC="hiku.gif" ALT="modern moments; hi-tech haiku">
</TD><TD>
<FONT SIZE=+1><I><DIV ALIGN="center">
<PRE>



</PRE>
pick up and you know<BR>
from the pause before the voice<BR>
telemarketer<P>
CDs never change<BR>
but every time I play one<BR>
it's not quite the same<P>
traffic jam? no prob<BR>
I've got a cel modem and<BR>
lots of batt life left<P>
RuPaul and Limbaugh<BR>
are now in the same time slot<BR>
this seems important<P>
</I></FONT></DIV>
</TD><TD VALIGN="bottom">
<A HREF="dicko.htm"><IMG SRC="dicko.gif" ALT="dicko" BORDER=0></A>
</TD></TR></TABLE></DIV>
</BODY>
</HTML>
```

To anyone from the Windows or Macintosh world, this need for hard coding Web pages is often hard to understand. In a world where programming languages such as Delphi, Visual Basic, and even Visual FoxPro use graphical environments for application development, and word processors provide on-screen approximations of their final output as a matter of course, the World Wide Web has in many ways been slow to adopt this obvious technology.

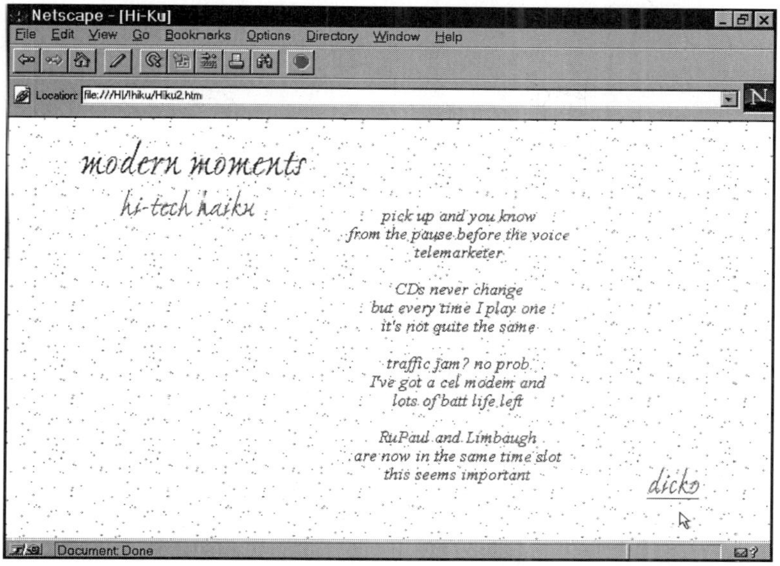

FIGURE 12.1.
The HTML code used to describe even the simplest Web page can often be confusing.

Of course, some notable exceptions include the powerful Live Markup Pro system and other commercial products such as PageMill, but on the whole, most people—even those using HTML editors—spend most of their time dealing with raw HTML code.

Netscape Gold as a Visual Editor

In creating Netscape Gold, its developers aim to move the focus of Web publishing from the mechanics of writing HTML code to the more creative aspects of Web design by reducing and eventually removing the need for hard coding Web pages.

In the place of HTML coding, Netscape Gold offers a visual editing environment that closely approximates that of a Web page and at the same time adopts many of the concepts used by word processors and document publishing tools (see Figure 12.2).

This is not to say that Netscape Gold does away with HTML altogether. At its heart, Netscape Gold still generates true HTML code, but during the editing phase, this code is hidden from the user by the graphical interface.

In addition, in its current incarnation, Netscape Gold is limited in some ways by the fact that it does not directly support all the functionality possible when hard coding HTML source code. For this reason, when creating complex Web pages, you will still need to understand the principles behind the HTML language and its various constructs.

As a result, much of the content of this book still deals with the mechanics of writing HTML code, and it would appear that Netscape Gold users will need this information for some time to come.

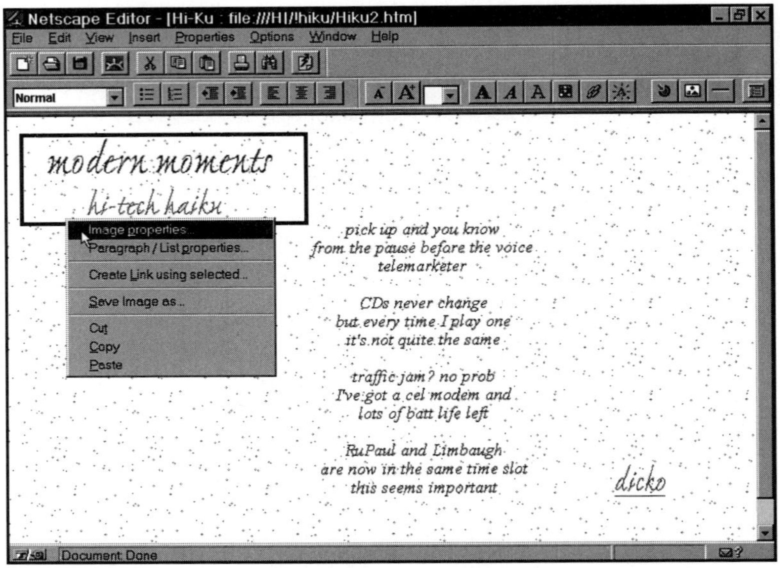

FIGURE 12.2.
Netscape Gold provides a Web publishing environment that looks and feels like a Web page.

Visual Editing and Hard Coding

As things currently stand, there are some limits to what you can achieve using a program like Netscape Gold. Basically, some of the more powerful HTML features such as forms and frames cannot—yet—be visually added to your Web pages. That is, you cannot insert them into your Web page by selecting an option from a menu or by clicking on a toolbar. (Note that Microsoft FrontPage does support some visual editing of some of these advanced features.)

As you will learn later, there is nothing stopping you from adding all your basic Web page functionality using Netscape Gold and then hard coding only those items that specifically require such steps. This is, in fact, one of the most powerful features of Netscape Gold. It does not limit your Web publishing requirements to only those features it supports internally. Instead, you are free to extend the Web pages it creates in any way you see fit.

The following sections will guide you through the steps involved in creating Web pages from scratch. In the section "Using Templates and the Page Wizard," later in this chapter, you will discover some of the tools Netscape has created to reduce the amount of work you need to do when getting started.

Creating a New Web Page

To get started using the Netscape Gold editing environment, you can follow a number of different paths. For the time being, the quickest way to create a blank Web page is to open the `File` menu on the Web browser window and select `New Document | Blank`, as shown in Figure 12.3. Netscape will display an editing window like the one shown in Figure 12.4.

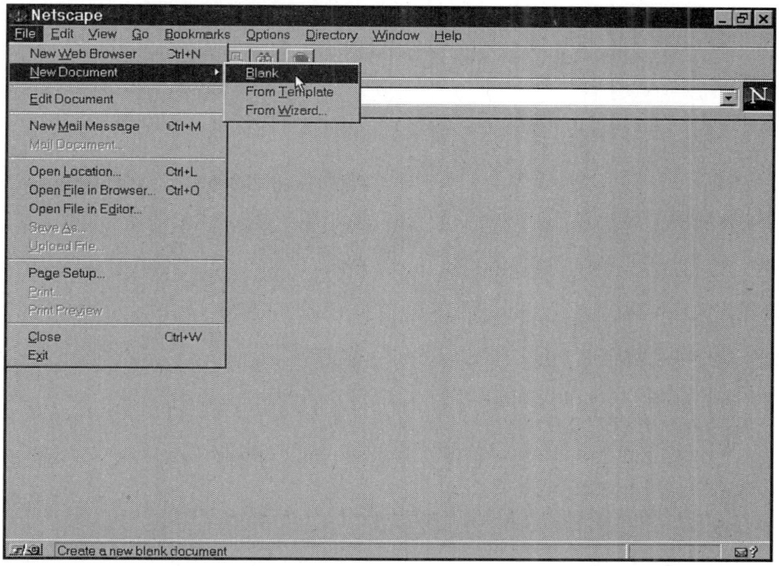

FIGURE 12.3.
Access the editing environment by creating a blank Web page.

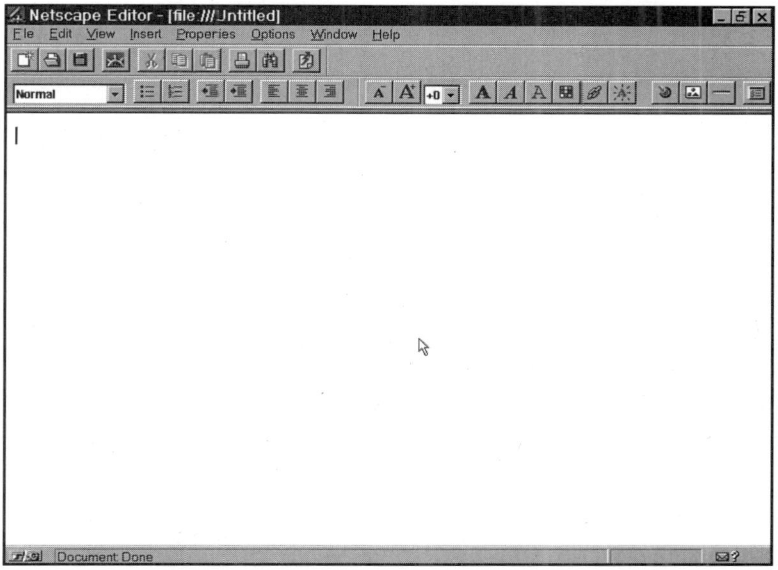

FIGURE 12.4.
The Netscape Editor window.

With the editing window open, you are just about ready to create your first Web page. Before you get started, however, you need to do one more thing. Unlike most word processors and document editors (which will let you create the contents of a new document before saving it to disk), before you can do any serious Web publishing with Netscape Gold, you need to name the page you are creating and save a copy to your hard drive.

To do this, select the `Save` option from the `File` menu. You'll see a dialog box similar to the one shown in Figure 12.5. Select the folder on your hard drive where you want to store your Web pages and give the file a name that ends with `.htm`. For now, use something like `goldpage.htm`.

FIGURE 12.5.
You should give each new Web page a name and save it to disk.

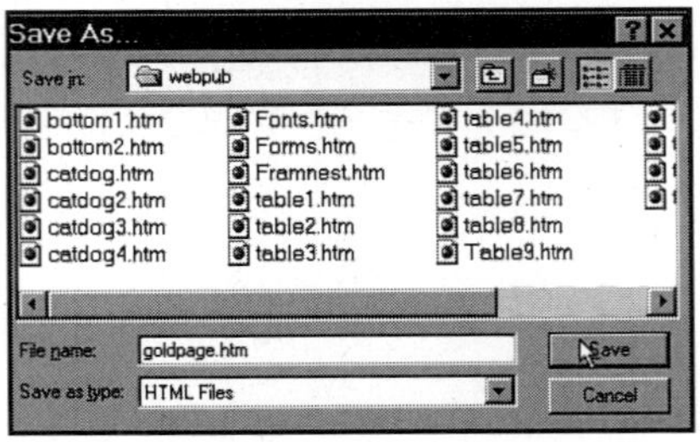

Document Editing

As in a normal Web browser, the most important area of the Netscape Gold editing window is the document area. Unlike the Web browser, this editing window will let you enter new text, edit existing text, add images, insert hyperlinks, and control the appearance of the Web page in general.

If you have ever used a word processor or any other form of editor, the basics of the editing window will be relatively straightforward. Wherever the insertion point cursor—the blinking vertical bar—is currently located is where you are currently working.

Whatever you type on the Web page will appear at the insertion point. Pressing the Delete button on the keyboard will delete text and elements, as will pressing the backspace key. In addition, you can use the up, down, right, and left cursor keys to move the insertion cursor around the Web page, or alternatively, you can move it by clicking with your mouse cursor.

The two most important menus for editing Web pages are the Insert menu and the Properties menu. The Insert menu contains a list of the different types of elements that you can add to a Web page. When you select any of the entries on this menu, Netscape Gold will automatically add the element to your Web page—and you don't need to know about the HTML codes for it.

To control the positioning of the elements available on the Insert menu, place your cursor at the point in the document where you want the element to be inserted and click with the mouse. A vertical positioning bar like that found in many word processors will indicate the current edit point.

The Properties menu enables you to control the appearance and actions of the various elements that you can place on a Web page, in much the same way that you can alter the appearance of text in a word processor. Most of the functions on the Properties menu are controlled by the type of text or element that is currently selected in the editing window. To select an element or block of elements and text, click where you want to start highlighting and then drag your mouse down to highlight all the required information.

The Toolbars

Although the menus across the top of the Editor window give you access to the Web publishing features provided by Netscape Gold, for the most part, you will find that accessing the various functions via the toolbars is a far more efficient way of working.

Below the menu, you will find three separate toolbars that give you access to specific sets of functions.

- The File/Edit toolbar—This toolbar basically duplicates the features provided by the File menu along with the basic editing tools from the Edit menu.
- The Character Format toolbar—Many of the buttons on the Character Format toolbar duplicate the formatting options on the Insert and Properties menus. More specifically, each of these options deals with settings that you can apply to an individual character or element.
- The Paragraph Format toolbar—Navigator Gold includes a number of paragraph formatting tools and predefined paragraph styles that you can assign to blocks of text and objects on your Web pages. The Paragraph Format toolbar lets you easily assign paragraph formatting to the text you currently have selected.

Starting from Scratch

With your new Web page ready to go, the first thing you need to do is edit the document properties. Select the Document item from the Properties menu.

The Document properties dialog box contains three tabbed windows. The first, shown in Figure 12.6, contains General properties for your Web page. As a rule, you should always complete the `Title` and `Author` fields at the very least. The remaining fields are optional and can be left blank for now. The `Description`, `Keywords`, and `Classification` fields have no physical effect on the appearance of your Web page and are only of real relevance to certain Web servers and search engines.

The second tabbed window—Appearance—is where you define the default color for your Web page. You can set the color for individual elements such as the background, text, and links, or alternatively, you can select one of the predefined color schemes such as Black on Yellow, as shown in Figure 12.7. There is also a provision for defining a background image to be tiled behind the Web page.

The final tabbed window of the Document Properties window—Advanced—is used predominantly for special HTTP-EQUIV instructions, and as such, it is beyond the scope of this section of the book.

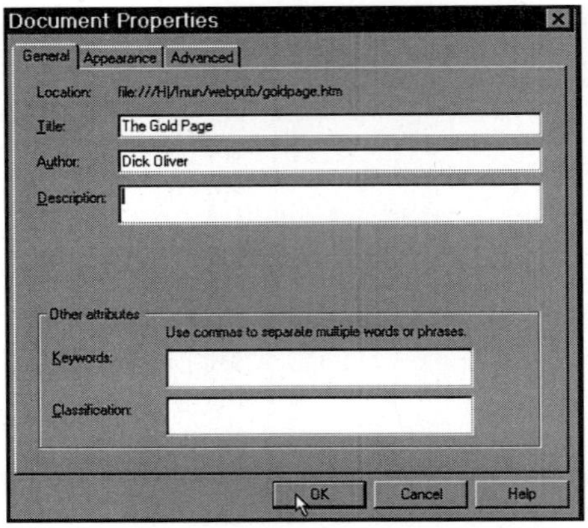

FIGURE 12.6.
Make sure you define at least the `Title` *and* `Author` *properties for every Web page you create.*

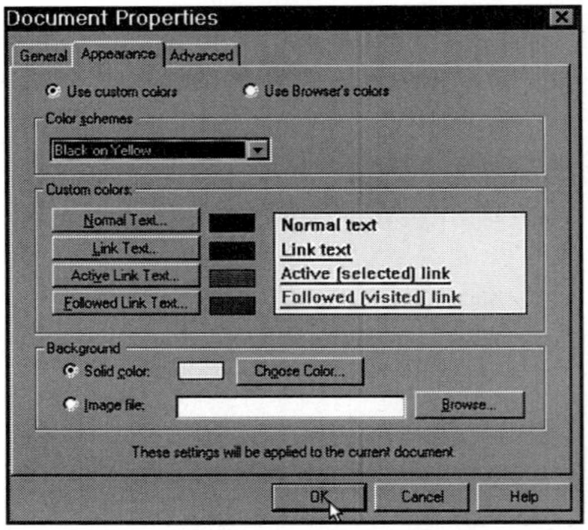

FIGURE 12.7.
The Document Appearance dialog lets you define the overall visual appearance of your Web page.

After you have finished making your changes to Document properties, click on the `OK` button to save the settings.

The next step is to add some text and formatting to the page. To begin, type a heading for the page as in the following:

`The Quest for Gold`

Press the Enter key and then type

`For ages, humankind has navigated the unknown in search of gold. This site will help you find gold on the wild electronic frontier.`

On lines below this one, enter the names of some of your favorite financial (or maybe Olympic sports?) Web sites. Three or four will do for now, but you can add more later if you like.

Finally, enter one last line that says:

`Page created by Dick Oliver - May 20, 1996.`

Remember, of course, to insert your own name and the current date. At this stage, if you've been following along, you should have a Web page that looks something like the one shown in Figure 12.8, and if you click on the View in Browser button or select `Browse document` from the `File` menu, your Web page will be displayed as a document in the browser window.

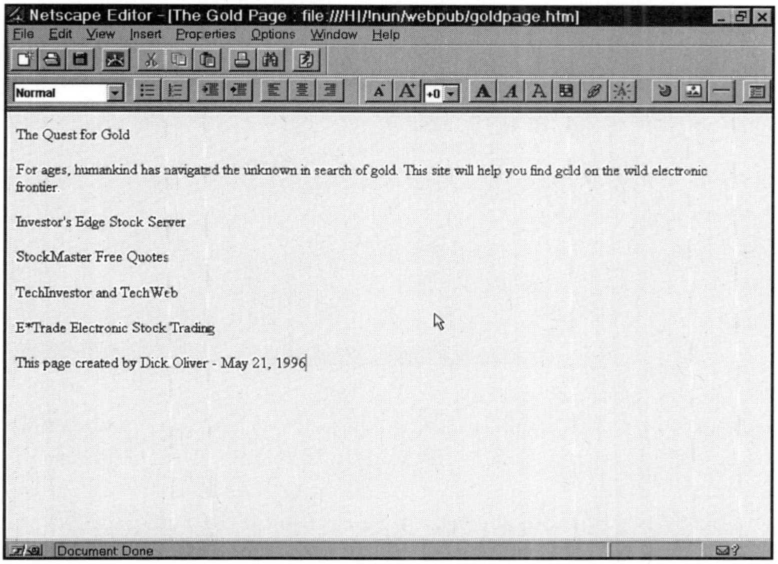

FIGURE 12.8.
The beginnings of a simple Web page.

Spicing Things Up

Although you have created a Web page, at this stage it looks a little bit bland. Take a look at what it will take to turn `goldpage.htm` into something a little more impressive.

To begin, highlight the text in the first line—`The Quest for Gold`. Because it is the main title for our page, either select the `Heading 1` submenu item from the `Paragraph` item of the `Properties` menu, or alternatively, simply select Heading 1 from the Paragraph Style list box on the Paragraph Format toolbar.

When you select Heading 1, the font size of the selected text should become very large. To add even more emphasis to the heading, with the text still selected, click on the Center button, which is also located on the Paragraph Format toolbar.

With these changes made, the first line of text on your Web page should look like that shown in Figure 12.9.

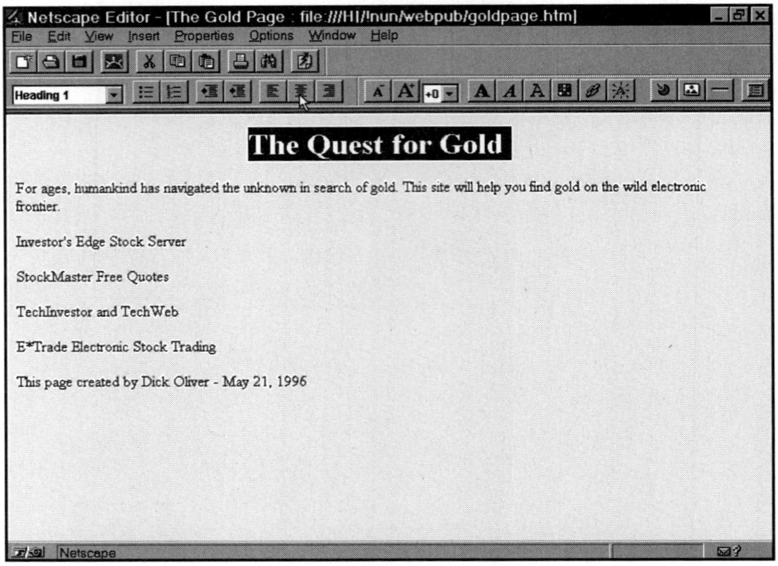

FIGURE 12.9.
A few clicks of the mouse added a Heading 1 style and centering.

The next step in this exercise is to turn your list of sites into a bulleted list. Highlight the list of site names you entered earlier. Click on the first letter of the first line and then drag your mouse down until all the lines are highlighted. With all the lines selected, all you need to do to create a bulleted list is click on the Bullet List button on the Paragraph Format toolbar.

Because there isn't very much text on this page, you might also decide to increase the size of the text by selecting all of it and clicking on the A+ button on the Character Format toolbar.

To finish the page, change the style for the last line to the paragraph style Address and add a horizontal rule before it by clicking on the Horizontal Rule button on the Character Format toolbar. The result is a list like the one shown in Figure 12.10.

Adding Links to the Page

You now have a good-looking Web page to show your friends, but at the moment, it is not very functional. To make the page functional, what you need to do is add some hyperlinks to the page.

Highlight the text of the first name—in this case, Investor's Edge Stock Server—and click on the Make Link button located on the Character Format toolbar. Alternatively, you can also select the `Link` item from the `Insert` menu.

Regardless of which option you choose, you'll see a dialog box like the one shown in Figure 12.11 on screen. In the top section of the window, the text you selected is shown under the title Linked Text, and below it is a field where you can enter the address of the Web page you want to link to.

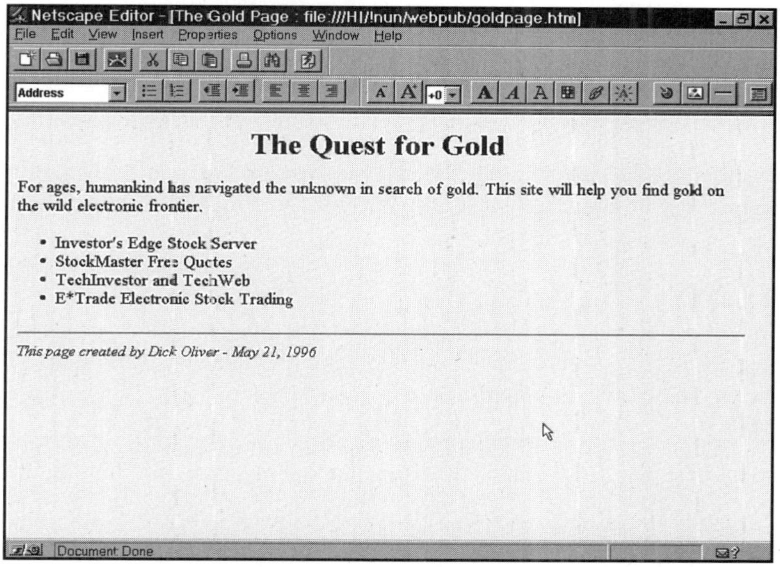

FIGURE 12.10.
Your first Web page all spiced up.

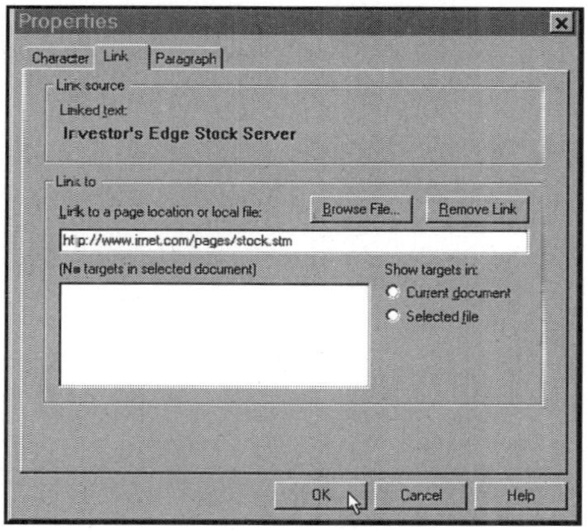

FIGURE 12.11.
The Link dialog box.

After entering the URL address of the site in the `Link to` field, click on the `OK` button to complete the creation of your hyperlink. You then need to work down through your list of sites, highlighting the appropriate text, clicking on the Make Link button, and entering the appropriate URL address.

> **NOTE**
>
> In addition to defining links to other Web sites, you can also use the Link dialog to point to other links stored on your local computer. To create such links, use the `Browse File` button on the Link dialog to select the file you want to link to.

Once you have finished adding a hyperlink to each of your listed sites, it's time to add a special link that will help people get in touch with you via e-mail. On the last line of your Web page, highlight your name and click on the Make Link button. Then, in the `Link` field, enter a special URL that takes the following form:

```
mailto:your@email.address
```

So that people can e-mail me, I entered `mailto:dicko@netletter.com` in the `Link to` field, but you will need to replace my e-mail address with your own. Once you have done this, click on the `OK` button to complete the link.

If you have been following along with the past few steps, you should now have a fully functional Web page that looks something like the one shown in Figure 12.12.

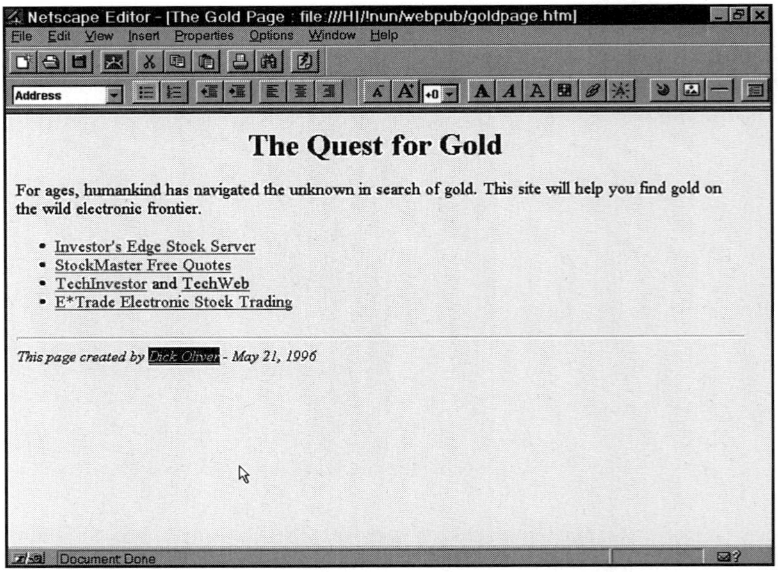

FIGURE 12.12.
Now that the links have been added, this Web page is almost complete.

Adding Images to a Web Page

To complete the Web page in Figure 12.12, you might like to add some graphics. Move the cursor so that it is positioned before the first word in the title and click on the Insert Image button on the Character Format toolbar, or alternatively, select the `Image` item from the `Insert` menu. You'll see a dialog box like the one shown in Figure 12.13.

FIGURE 12.13.
The Image dialog box.

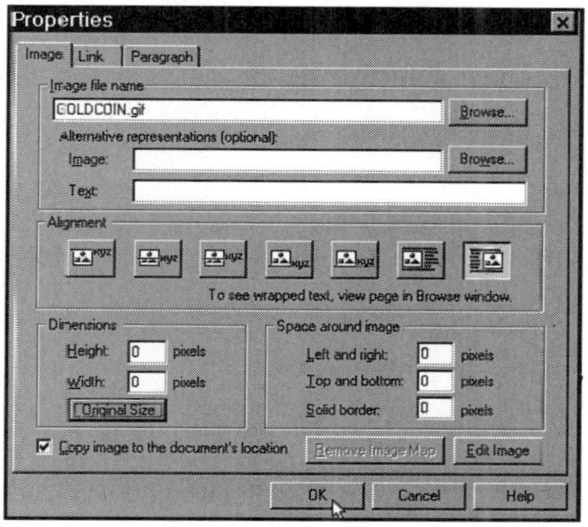

The Image Properties dialog box consists of three tabbed windows. The first, Image, deals with the appearance of the image itself. The Link tab lets you turn an image into an hyperlink, and the Paragraph tab controls the paragraph formatting associated with the image.

For now, confine your interest to the Image tab. In this example, the file name for the image to be displayed is `goldcoin.gif`, and it is located in the same directory as the HTML file. Enter the name of the image you want to use in the `Image file name` field.

NOTE

The image file name can also be a URL or a file in a different directory. To help you locate an image, use the `Browse` button included next to the `Image file name` field.

Below the `Image file name` field are two `Alternative representation` fields. As a rule, you do not need to include an alternative image here, but you should always include some alternative text for those people who prefer not to display images on the Web browser. For this exercise, enter **Gold Coin** into the text field.

Directly below the `Image file name` area is a row of buttons that let you control the alignment of your image. These buttons from left to right are Top, Absolute Center, Center, Baseline, Bottom, Wrap Left, and Wrap Right.

For this exercise, you want to choose the last button on the right, which is Wrap Right. Finally, to add a bit of spacing around the image, enter a value of 4 into the Left and Right spacing box. If you want this image to be a clickable hyperlink, click on the Link tab and fill in the location where the hyperlink should lead.

If you now click on the `OK` button, a copy of the image will be displayed at the front of the document, as shown in Figure 12.14. Note that Figure 12.14 also shows a background image, which I specified by returning to the Properties/Document dialog box discussed earlier.

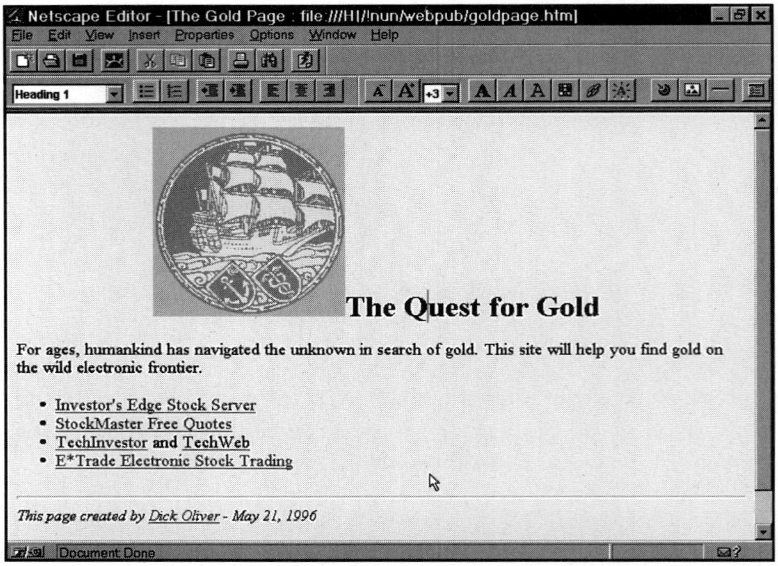

FIGURE 12.14.
The Navigator Gold editing window previews graphics and backgrounds but does not preview text-wrapping alignment.

Note that the gold coin image in Figure 12.14 is not aligned to the right, as requested, because the Navigator Gold editing window does not preview any text-wrapping alignment. In order to see the text wrap correctly, you'll need to click on the View in Browser button on the File/Edit toolbar. A browser window will appear, as in Figure 12.15.

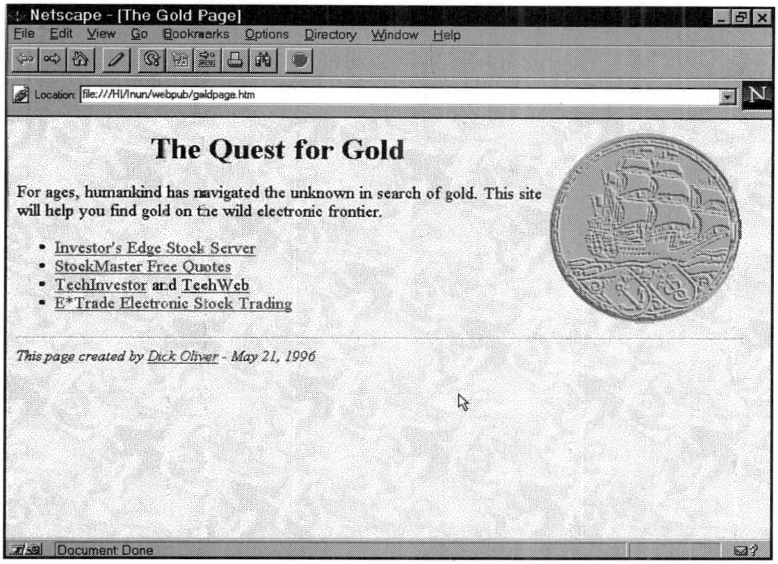

FIGURE 12.15.
To see text wrapping, view the page in the browser window.

Using Templates and the Page Wizard

To help you get up to speed quickly using Netscape Gold, Netscape Communications created a collection of Web pages on its host site that lets you build impressive-looking Web pages by starting with a basic template and then adding your own information and images as required.

Web Templates

To access the templates provided by Netscape, open the `File` menu and choose the `From Template` submenu item below the New Document entry. Doing so will request a copy of the current templates index from the Netscape Web site. (See Figure 12.16.) The Templates page includes a detailed list of instructions describing how to use the templates with Netscape Gold, along with a list of the currently available files.

To use any of the listed templates with Netscape Gold, simply click on the corresponding hyperlink and wait for the template page to display on your browser. Then, if you like the look of the chosen template, click on the Edit button located in the browser toolbar or select `Edit Document` from the `File` menu.

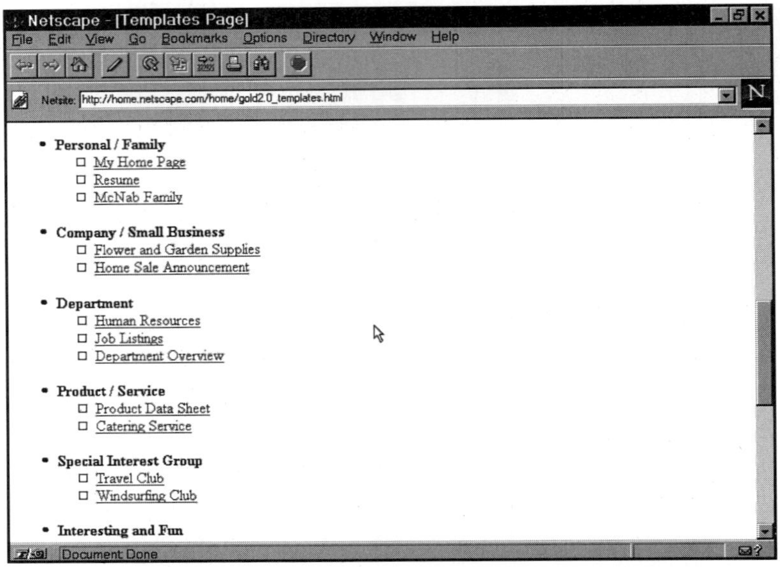

FIGURE 12.16.
The Netscape Web page Templates page.

You'll see a dialog box like the one shown in Figure 12.17, informing you that you need to save the template file to your local hard drive before you can edit it. As a rule, simply click on the `Save` button to proceed with the download.

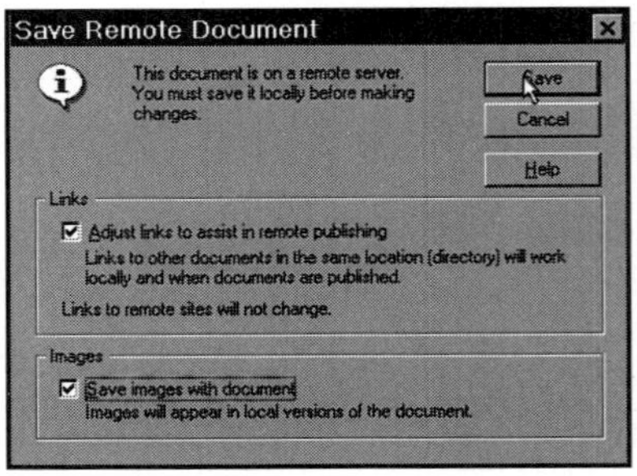

FIGURE 12.17.
You must save templates to your local hard drive before you can edit them.

CAUTION

At this stage, you might encounter a warning regarding the use of copyrighted material. All of the templates provided by Netscape are freely available for your use; however, if you attempt to edit files from other Web sites, copyright restrictions could apply.

Finally, to complete the download process, you'll see a file requester dialog box. Use this dialog box to indicate where to store the template file and also define what to call it. Then, when you click on the `Save` button, a copy of the template and any image associated with it is saved to your local hard drive. Once this process is complete, you can then edit the template and adjust it to your own purposes using the Editor window. (See Figure 12.18.)

FIGURE 12.18.
Once the template is stored locally, you can edit it to suit your needs.

The Page Wizard

If none of the predefined templates is suitable to your needs, then you might like to try the Page Wizard shown in Figure 12.19. To try the Page Wizard for yourself, open the `File` menu and choose the `From Wizard` submenu item below the New Document entry. Doing so will start the Page Wizard system.

The Page Wizard guides you step-by-step through the process of creating a basic Web page, and when the page is complete, you simply download it to your local hard drive, as was the case for templates; select the Edit button from the Navigator Gold browser and save the file to your hard drive.

NOTE

As was the case with using templates, you need to be connected to the Internet to use the Page Wizard.

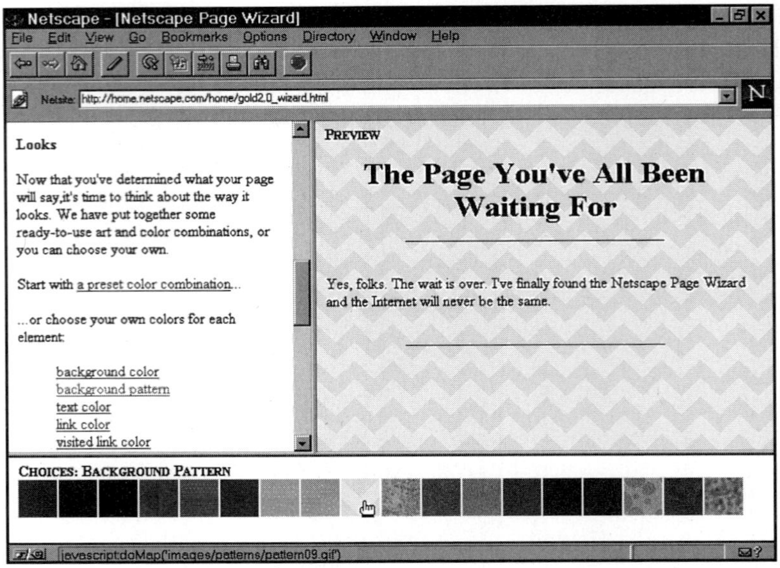

FIGURE 12.19.
The Netscape Page Wizard.

One-Click Publishing

All the Web pages you've created in this chapter were saved to your local hard drive, and as a result, they could be viewed only by you. Naturally, however, as you begin to build Web pages, your main aim will be to publish your Web page creations on the Internet for everyone to view.

To do this, you need to take a number of steps, the most significant of which is gaining access to a Web server to house your Web pages. Your Internet service provider (ISP) can provide you with specific information about hosting pages on its Web server.

The Publish Button

Assuming now that you have managed to obtain access to a Web server, the next issue you need to deal with is how you get all the files and images you have stored on your local hard drive onto the Web server that is going to publish your files.

This is where the Publish button on the Netscape Gold editor window comes into its own. Traditionally, the process of installing files onto your Web server has been a manual, time-consuming task, but with Netscape's one-click publishing system, the entire process can be completely automated.

To demonstrate how the system works, return to the `goldpage.htm` file created earlier in the chapter and work through the steps involved in publishing that file on my Web site at `http://netletter.com/`.

First, load the file you want to publish into the Editor window and then click on the Publish button on the File/Edit toolbar. You'll see a dialog box like the one shown in Figure 12.20.

FIGURE 12.20.
The Publish Files dialog box.

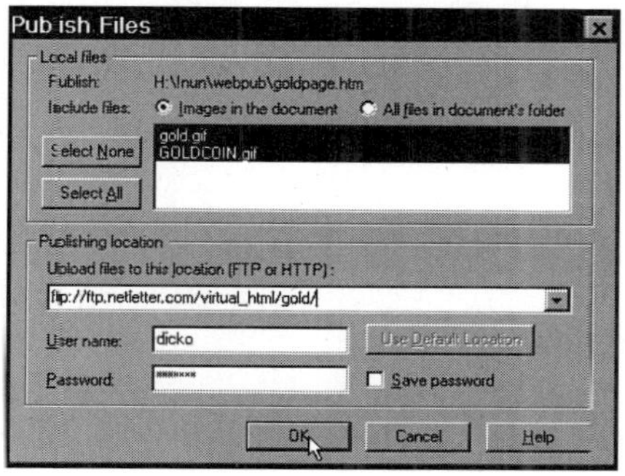

The top section of the dialog box lets you control what files are to be published. In this case, there are two files, the HTML page itself and the gold coin image. In addition, it is possible to publish the entire contents of a directory or just a small group of files by selecting the appropriate radio button and files.

The bottom section of the Publish Files dialog box is where you indicate the location of the Web server that is to publish your Web pages. You can define either an FTP or HTTP URL here depending on the capabilities of your Web server, and in most cases, you will also need to supply a user name and password.

Once you've entered all the appropriate information, all you need to do to publish your files is click on OK. Netscape Gold will then take over and look after the task of installing the selected Web pages and images onto your Web server.

The Web Page Starter Site

To help people learn more about the process of Web publishing, Netscape Communications created a special area on its Web site called the Web Page Starter Site. (See Figure 12.21.) To access the Web Page Starter Site, open the `Help` menu and select the `Web Page Starter` option.

This site contains a wealth of information about the intricacies of Web publishing and covers a wide variety of topics including instructions on finding a Web server, copyright and legal issues, Web style guides, links to popular Web publishing information sites, and a special area devoted to Netscape Navigator Gold users called the Netscape Gold Rush Tool Chest.

In the Tool Chest, you will find links to the templates mentioned previously, a collection of clip art and graphics, more style guides, and various hints and tips on how to create Web pages with Netscape Gold.

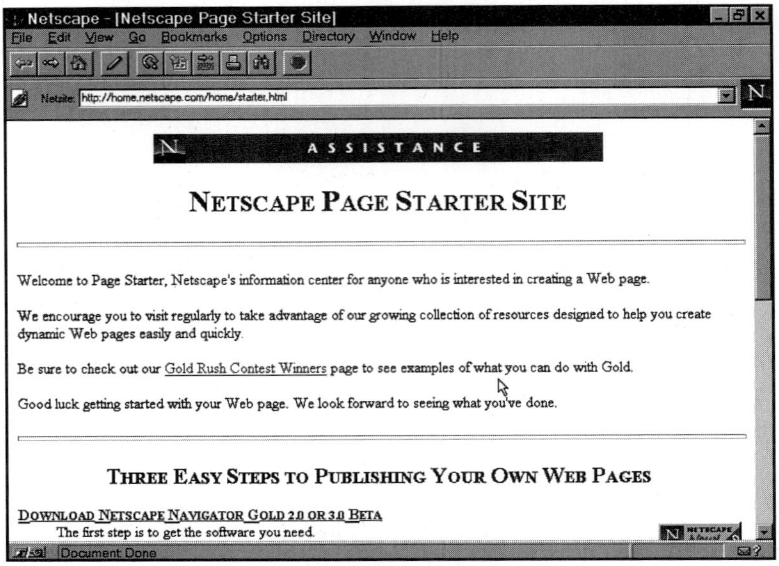

FIGURE 12.21.
The Web Page Starter Site.

Interactive Table Design

Unfortunately, the current version of Netscape Navigator Gold—24.0b2—does not directly support the use of frames and other advanced extensions to HTML. However, you can use the HTML tag option to hard code these features into your Web pages. See Chapter 7, "Creating and Enhancing Web Pages with Frames," for details on these more advanced HTML tags.

The good news is that Navigator Gold does support interactive table editing. To see how this feature works, use a table to change the layout of the graphics and text on the Quest for Gold page.

First, create a new table by selecting `Insert | Table`. The dialog box in Figure 12.22 appears, allowing you to specify the size and attributes of the table. Eventually, you'll give this table a border size of zero to make the borders invisible, but it is much easier to work with tables when the borders are showing, so leave the border size at 1 for now. Enter 1 row and 3 columns, and then click `OK`.

The new table appears as small, empty cells. To move elements of the page into the cells, select the material you want to place in a cell and then select `Edit | Cut`. Then, place the cursor inside the cell and select `Edit | Paste`. Figure 12.23 shows a three-cell, single-row table with all the text and graphics from the page moved into it.

On the Insert and Properties menus, you'll find menu items for creating, deleting, and controlling the attributes of each row and cell in a table. Figure 12.24, for example, shows the Cell crosstab of the Properties/Table dialog box, which lets you change the alignment, size, and background color of an individual cell. You can also make cells span more than one row or column in the table.

FIGURE 12.22.
The Insert Table dialog lets you create complex tables without writing any HTML code.

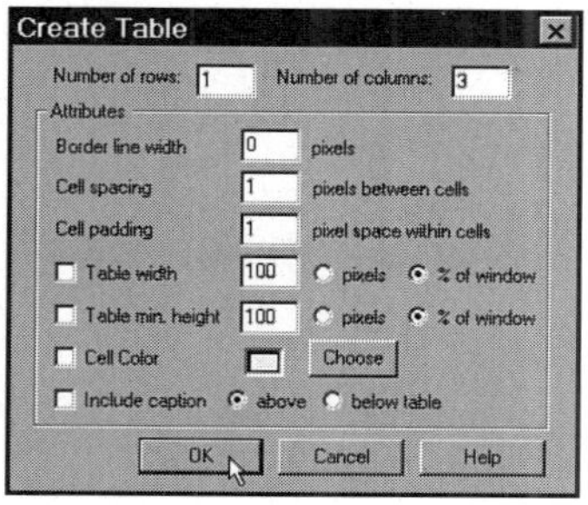

FIGURE 12.23.
You can use tables as a powerful page layout feature.

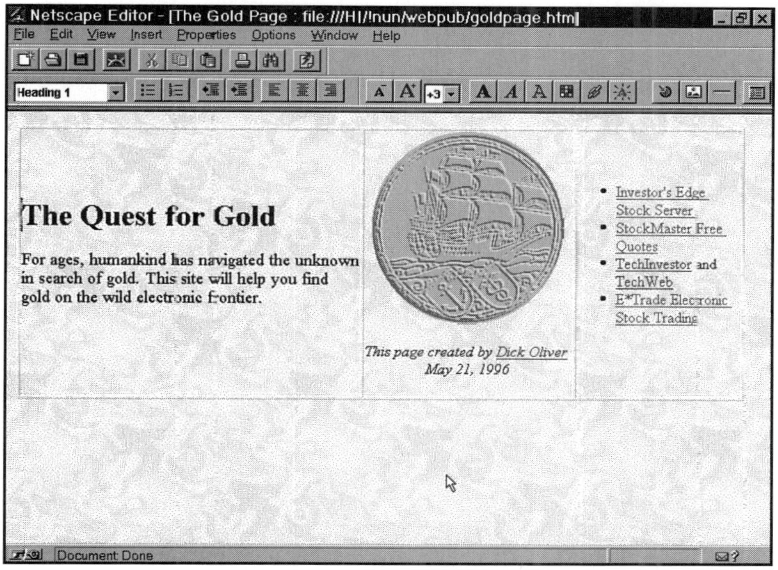

FIGURE 12.24.
You can change an individual cell in a table with Properties/ Cell.

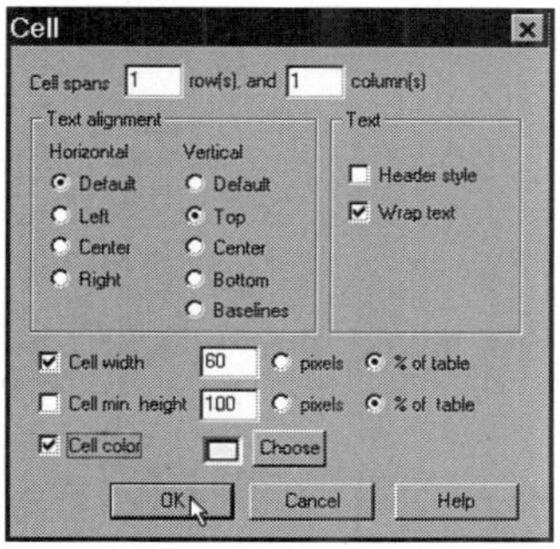

To create the layout in Figure 12.25, I added a row with `Insert|Row` and then used `Properties|Cell` to make the two rightmost cells span both rows. Finally, I forced the empty cell on the bottom-left corner to have a fixed height of 40 percent of the overall table height. (This control is also within the Properties/Cell dialog box.) Finally, I hid the borders of the entire table by selecting `Properties|Table` and setting the border width to 0. With a little practice, you'll be making creative Web pages with Netscape Gold that would be very confusing to code by hand with `TABLE`, `TR`, `TD`, and `TH` tags.

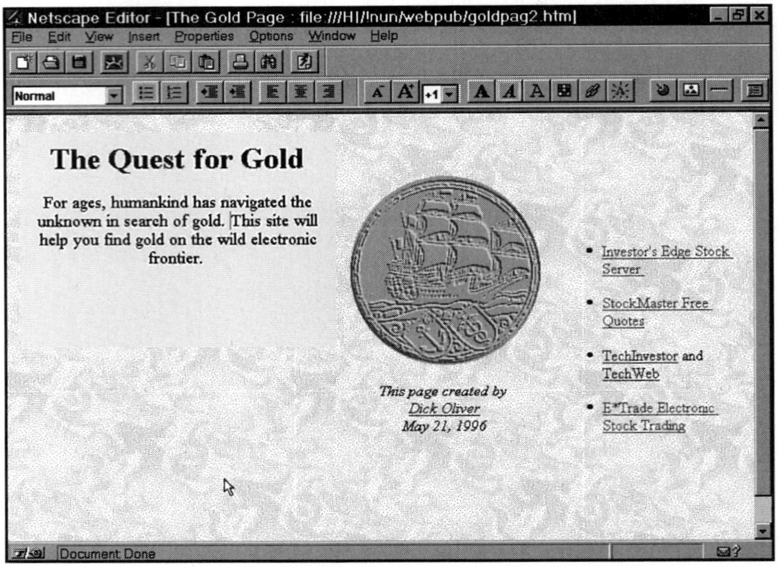

FIGURE 12.25.
By tweaking the properties of each cell, you can add a great deal of variety to your Web pages.

Summary

This chapter introduced you to interactive Web page creation and editing with Netscape Navigator Gold 3. When you combine the speed and interactive layout capabilities of Navigator Gold with the handcrafted HTML tricks you learned in previous chapters, your productivity and enjoyment will soar.

CHAPTER 13

Creating Web Sites with Macromedia's Backstage Desktop Studio

by Dennis Hamilton

IN THIS CHAPTER

Macromedia's Backstage Desktop Studio is one of a new generation of tools that combine dynamic Web page authoring facilities with Web site management features. The key word in all of that is dynamic. That means adding, with relative simplicity, multimedia and database connectivity into pages whose information needs to change as often as the person viewing it changes. In their ultimate form, dynamic pages are pages tailored specifically to the person who calls them up.

At the time of this writing, the majority of pages being created for the World Wide Web—and there are more than seven million of them—are static monuments to passivity. No motion, no interactivity, no applications, no database access, no viewer customization. For a lot of sites, these are lost opportunities.

The most successful, useful, and visited sites are dynamic in one way or another. They involve the viewer. They enable viewers to correspond with web page creators. They provide gateways to specific information. They help them solve problems. And they do it in interesting and creative ways. With 3,000 new pages being added to the Web every day, the question becomes one of new objectives: If dynamic sites are the future, how do you build and manage them today?

Macromedia, known for such multimedia tools as Shockwave and Director, purchased the original developer of the Backstage line—iband, based in Campbell, California—last March. It has moved with the Backstage line into the total Web site management end of things, from creating through administering, and now has assembled a variety of tools flying the Backstage colors (see Figure 13.1).

These tools range from a WYSIWYG authoring environment called Backstage Designer on the low end to a comprehensive Web site creation and management system with client/server facilities called Backstage Enterprise Studio on the high end. The former is for anyone, Web professional or otherwise, who wants to create fast, interesting Web pages; the latter is for high-end pros looking for optimum multimedia pages, client/server Web applications, and maximum database connectivity, including mainframes.

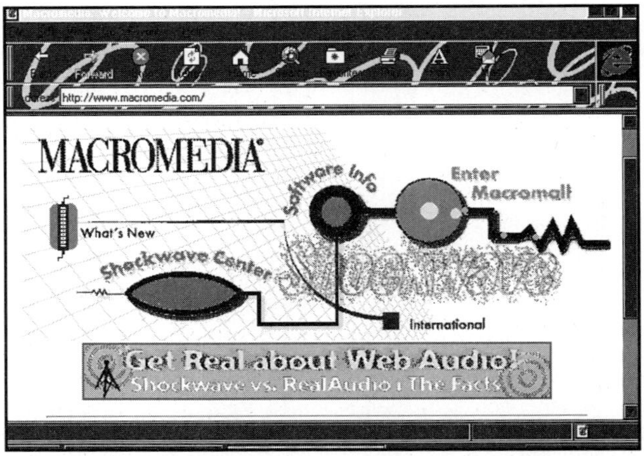

FIGURE 13.1.
Macromedia's home page— `www.macromedia.com`*—offers a prime look at a Backstage-developed dynamic page.*

Backstage Desktop Studio, which lies between the two, contains all of the facilities found in Enterprise Studio except for the extensive client/server application development and connectivity tools. It does have facilities for connecting to popular desktop databases such as Microsoft Access, FoxPro, and Paradox.

Who Backstage Desktop Studio Is for

Backstage Desktop Studio is an extremely function-rich suite of tools. That often has meant it is too advanced for personal Web-page developers or Webmasters at smaller sites who have limited technical knowledge. But in fact Backstage Desktop Studio, thanks to the tools in its suite, is as good as the people using it and can even make the site better. If you're creating your first Web site, you can do some interesting things quickly; if you're a high-level Webmaster, you can apply your own custom techniques and ideas to bring truly unique pages to life.

Backstage Desktop Studio's preinstalled links to popular desktop databases acknowledge a trend in Web publishing: you don't need a mainframe client/server environment to have a useful, functioning Web server with database applications.

The software was developed with Web dynamism in mind. That means being able to create or change pages quickly and easily, as information needs demand. It means being able to link into desktop databases quickly and easily. It means having an "intelligent" site that is able to customize itself to the person viewing it. It means the fast, simple insertion of compelling visual images.

While all of that functionality isn't needed on every Web page or even every Web site, the process of making it available helped make Desktop Studio useful for almost any level of expertise. The point-and-click features, the ability to drag-and-drop heretofore complex functionality onto a page, and the WYSIWYG HTML editor all turned the software into a tool for the masses, even if it wasn't necessarily intended that way originally.

The ability to add customized HTML by using the source edit mode enables high-tech professionals to add even more functionality to their pages. Another development aid—this one is not included with the Desktop Studio suite but is available from Macromedia for use with it—is the Xtras Developer's Kit (XDK), which higher-level developers can use to create their own custom objects.

The creative end of the Web page development process is helped by the management end of it. Backstage Manager, the Web site project management and administration system that is included with Desktop Studio, enables developers of any level to keep track of their work easily. As Web sites grow and their pages multiply, the complexity and coherence of the whole gets tough to control. Because Backstage Manager is a visual tool, control is simpler to see and maintain, as are logical extensions to what should be developed next to make a better site.

Backstage Desktop Studio is only for developers who really need strong page-creation tools along with accessibility to desktop databases. If you do not need to interact with desktop databases (and don't intend to in the near future), you should probably consider Backstage Designer Plus, which is the page-creation element of Desktop Studio. You can bring all of the same design tools, including the Objects Library, to bear on your Web site. You just won't have the database tools. But Backstage Designer Plus is considerably less expensive when purchased alone.

Conversely, if you need the highest-end tools available—for example, to connect client/server applications from your Web site to a remote mainframe database—the Backstage Enterprise Studio is the option you would consider. But at close to $3,000, this option is only for the most advanced Web sites and developers.

For most people, Backstage Desktop Studio is the happy medium. It brings a strong suite of easy-to-use design tools, site management features, and connectivity options. Both new developers (it helps to be at least technically intuitive) and tenured high-tech Web wizards can use it, and that makes it one of the more interesting tools to come along this year.

Point-and-Click Simplicity

Backstage Desktop Studio puts its emphasis on creating highly functional dynamic Web pages with point-and-click simplicity. Anyone who has labored through coding with HyperText Markup Language (HTML), the pre-eminent page language of the Internet, knows how tedious it is. Desktop Studio brings a WYSIWYG HTML editor that enables designers to build multimedia pages without coding any HTML.

Backstage Desktop Studio has a strong variety of point-and-click features to render HTML, so you don't need to code every tag; skilled HTML developers also can use the source edit mode to create even more customized page designs. An HTML validation facility reviews all of the HTML tags so the developer doesn't have to do so.

But HTML alone has limitations, no matter how patient and creative the developer. Backstage Desktop Studio takes the point-and-click functionality beyond HTML into multimedia and desktop database connectivity. Using Backstage Objects, a library of which is included with the software, page developers can create and integrate robust database front ends, discussion groups, forms to e-mail, and much more in a simple drag-and-drop environment. And they can manage all of these things, including remote servers, from a central Backstage Desktop Studio site.

To do this, Macromedia has tied together several discrete tools to create the Backstage Desktop Studio suite. A discussion of the basic components of Backstage Desktop Studio follows.

Backstage Designer Plus

Backstage Designer Plus is the primary design tool for building Web pages in any of the Backstage environments. Using simple point-and-click, drag-and-drop, WYSIWYG tools,

Backstage Designer Plus was created to make dynamic, multimedia page creation easy for just about anyone (see Figure 13.2). It is available from Macromedia as a separate Web page authoring product but is included as part of the Backstage Desktop Studio suite. It's also the tool used to build interactive Web-based applications using Backstage Objects. Backstage Designer provides a visual Web page editor that enables developers to insert Backstage Objects as they build the pages. It provides standard word processing features and supplements them with a range of HTML-specific functions. They include text and hyperlink formatting, an HTML source edit mode, a form-building toolbar, and menu selections and toolbar buttons for a wide range of standard HTML tags.

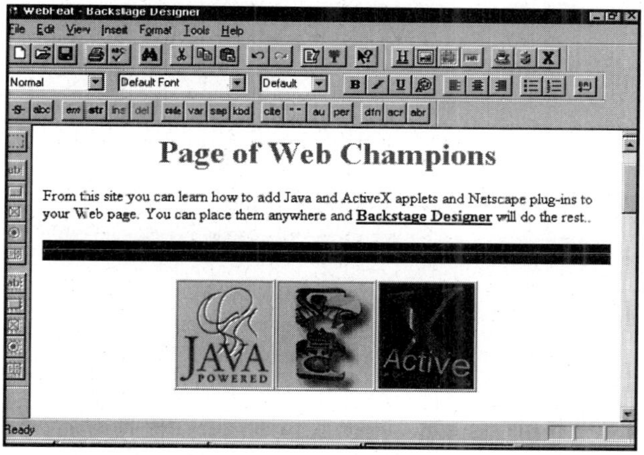

FIGURE 13.2.
Backstage Designer Plus, the page design tool of Desktop Studio, enables you to turn a page of text into a fully-coded, full-color, multimedia Web page with just a few point-and-click commands.

Backstage Manager

A key component of Backstage Desktop Studio, Backstage Manager is a project management system that helps Web site developers create and administer their sites. It is used in tandem with Backstage Designer Plus. It provides a project-level view of all of the pages that make up a site, enabling developers to visualize and manage the site in its entirety (see Figure 13.3). It is also the source of Backstage Objects that provide the functionality to Backstage-developed pages.

Backstage Manager organizes Web sites into four major categories:

- Web pages
- Discussion groups
- Database queries
- User profiles

Using remote file transfer protocol (FTP) servers, Backstage Manager also enables Webmasters and developers to administer remote sites. The local site is where developers usually keep the applications they are developing. When an application is ready to be deployed, Backstage Manager automatically posts all components of the Web application to a remote site.

If you travel on business, Backstage Manager enables you to download an entire site, work on it wherever you might be, and then upload changes and additions when you dock with your Web server or dial in to your local area network.

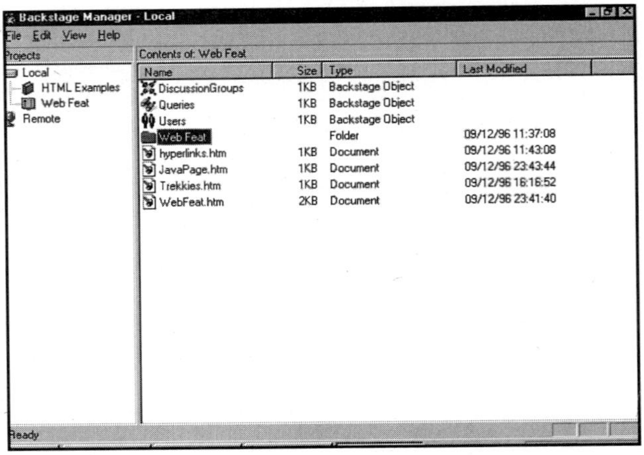

FIGURE 13.3.
Backstage Manager provides an overview of all of the pages of a Web site, local and remote, to help developers and Webmasters manage the entire site.

Backstage Objects

The library of Backstage Objects contains most of the advanced functionality of Backstage Desktop Studio (see Figure 13.4). They are used to develop Web-based applications. The 16 scalable, built-in objects provide connectivity to desktop databases, forms, threaded discussion groups, automated e-mail, user log-in and authentication, page hit count, browser ID, and more, all without scripting or programming.

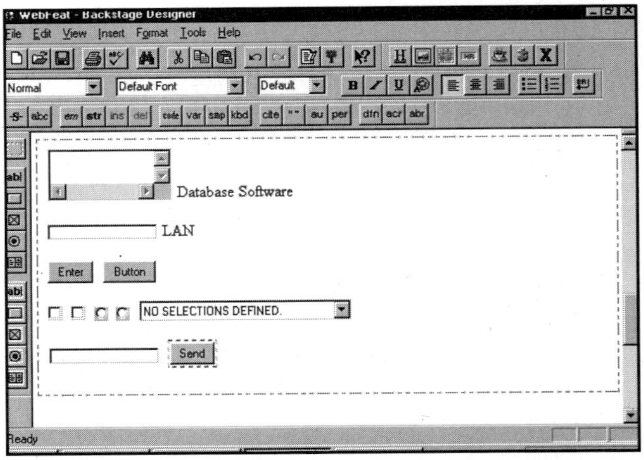

FIGURE 13.4.
Instead of programming functionality into Web pages, developers can drag and drop functional objects into place from Backstage's Objects Library.

Most of the objects can be inserted into a Web page right from the Insert menu on the toolbar, and then configured quickly by double-clicking on the object to display its Properties dialog boxes.

Backstage Object Server

The Backstage Object Server for Desktop Studio works with most Web servers and all Web browsers. It serves up the functions of the Backstage Objects that have been inserted into the Web pages—dynamic features such as e-mail, discussion groups, and so forth. It uses ODBC compliance to be instantly compatible with most popular desktop databases. It can also tailor page visits to the page visitor. The authentication object identifies the visitors to your site and then tailors your site to their profiles. Dynamic HTML page generation creates pages that are customized at run time, each time a visitor accesses a page.

These components constitute the core of Backstage Desktop Studio, but other tools extend its dynamic page creation functionality even further. Included in the suite of tools are what Macromedia calls PowerApplets, six fully customizable applets using Director and Java. You can use them to instantly add multimedia features to any Backstage-developed Web page (see Figure 13.5). Included are Animator, SlideShow, Icons, Banners, Bullets, and Charts.

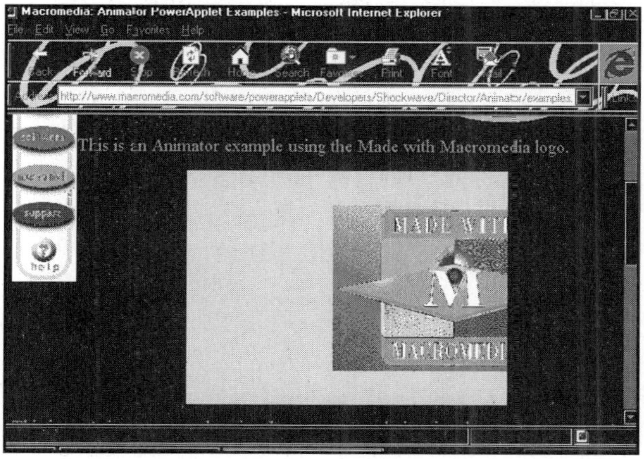

FIGURE 13.5.
Backstage's PowerApplets combine two strong Web technologies—Java and Director—to create six ready-to-use multimedia applets that turn visually static pages into dynamic ones.

Desktop Studio also includes Macromedia xRes SE, a powerful image editor for creating Web graphics, a collection of Web-page templates, and a library of clip art. In practical terms, these tools mean a developer could get a functioning Web site up and running in just a few hours.

What Equipment and Software You Need

Like most full-featured Web-page development environments, Backstage Desktop Studio takes up quite a bit of disk and RAM space, though it is by no means the worst. Developers can actually do all of the design work with fairly old equipment; the Backstage Server and Backstage Object Library require a boost in power and memory to work well.

The four components are installed in twos. The Backstage Designer Plus and Backstage Manager components, which run on a client computer, require

- Minimum of 486/33; a Pentium is recommended
- Windows 3.1, Windows 95, or Windows NT

  A minimum of 8 M of RAM is recommended for Windows 3.1.

  A minimum of 16 M of RAM is recommended for Windows 95.

  A minimum of 24 M of RAM is recommended for Windows NT.
- 7 M of free disk space

The Backstage Server and Backstage Object Library, which are intended to run on your Web server, require 24 M of RAM for Windows NT or 16 M RAM for Windows 95.

NOTE

Although the Backstage Server and Objects Library are meant to run on your Web server, they can also be installed on the client computer. The latter requires you to have the same recommended disk and RAM storage on the client as you would on the server.

You will also need the following:

- You need an HTTP-compliant Web server (that supports virtual paths) that also runs on Windows 95 or Windows NT.
- You also need an HTTP-compliant Web browser (for example, Mosaic, Netscape Navigator, or Microsoft's Internet Explorer).
- For database connectivity, you need 32-bit ODBC drivers installed on Windows 95 or Windows NT for the particular database program you want to use. Backstage provides ODBC compatibility for the database products such as Oracle, Access, Sybase SQL Server, Informix, CA-Ingres, FoxPro, Paradox, and dBase.
- For remote access, a File Transfer Protocol (FTP) server must be installed on your Web server computer.

Creating a Backstage Site

The first thing to do in creating a Backstage site, and then individual Backstage pages, is to start Backstage Manager. This is the control point for the site. All pages from the home page on are originally created and named in Backstage Manager. Backstage Designer Plus is then used to do the actual creative work on the Web pages. Unlike a lot of project management systems, Backstage Manager does not require that you configure it extensively. It simply provides a control point for and access path to all of the pages in your site.

To creating a new site project with Backstage Manager is a simple three-step process:

1. Start Backstage Manager by double-clicking the icon.
2. Select the Local icon in the Projects pane (see Figure 13.6).
3. Select `File` | `New` | `Project`.

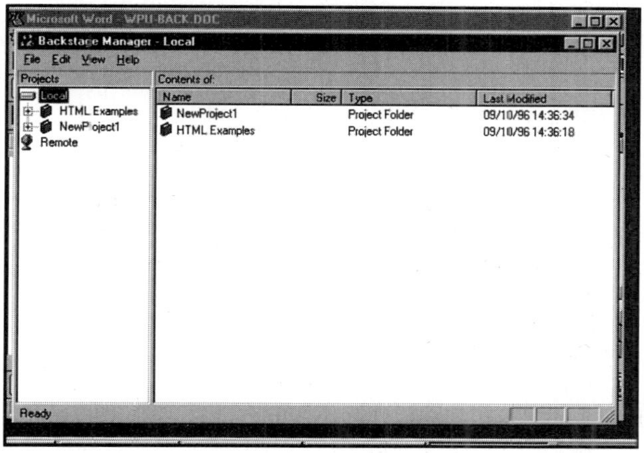

FIGURE 13.6.
Projects and pages are created and named in Backstage Manager, which then works in tandem with Backstage Designer Plus while you develop the pages.

This creates a new project icon under the Local icon. The default name of the project is `NewProject`, which you will see has been selected. Just enter the name of the new project and you're off and running into Backstage Designer Plus to begin creating.

Creating the Backstage Home Page

The home page is just what its name implies. It is the point of entry for anyone who wishes to access your Web site, the most important page you will create. The best way to think of a home page is like a magazine cover or a table of contents. It is from here that viewers will find a link to the specific information they're seeking when they visit.

Backstage Manager is used to create the home (and other) pages for the Web. The pages then are kept in the project folders and any one can be accessed just by double-clicking on the project (Web site) name. This will open Backstage Designer Plus (see Figure 13.7), where you can begin the process of actually developing the creative content of the home page.

FIGURE 13.7.
Once you create the Web site project and home page in Backstage Manager, it automatically opens this screen in Backstage Designer Plus to begin the page development process.

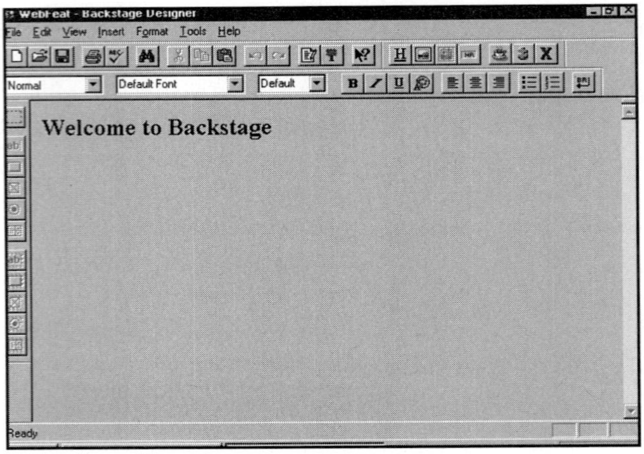

Designing in WYSIWYG

WYSIWYG is the acronym for "what you see is what you get." In the online world, that has two special meanings: what you see when you design the page and what you see when you view the page in a browser. The first point is that WYSIWYG development enables designers to create a Web page much as they would a page of text (with design elements added), and then have it show up in their browser exactly as they designed it. Before the automatic HTML creation that Backstage and others have brought to Web page development, designers would code the HTML tags onto text, and then switch to a browser to check their work (often finding several elements not as they had intended). Then it was back and forth, back and forth, until the bugs were out.

Backstage's WYSIWYG, an extremely important feature of the software, enables Web page designers to create the text naturally, in a browser-like screen, without worrying about HTML.

Without WYSIWYG, for example, you would write a Web page this way:

```
<HTML>
<HEAD>
<TITLE>WebFeat Home Page</TITLE>
</HEAD>
<BODY>
<CENTER>
<H1><FONT COLOR="Maroon">WebFeat</FONT></H1>
<H1>
<FONT COLOR="Teal">Java Page of Web Champions</FONT></H1>
</CENTER>
<P ALIGN="LEFT">From this site, you can learn how to add fast, easy Java to your
➥Web page.
You can place your applet anywhere and Backstage Designer will do the rest. </P>
<P ALIGN="LEFT"> </P>
```

With WYSIWYG in Backstage Designer Plus, you would write this to do the same thing:

```
WebFeat
Java Page of Web Champions
From this site, you can learn how to add fast, easy Java to your Web page.
You can place your applet anywhere and Backstage Designer will do the rest.
```

The second aspect of WYSIWYG is how different browsers present the Web pages you create. Is what you see in one browser what you see in another? Not always. Developers have suffered through five years (the World Wide Web was started in 1991 with the NCSA Mosaic browser) of finding their pages sometimes looking fine in one browser and awful in another. There were line breaks in text where there shouldn't be. Some design elements weren't accommodated. Some pages were barely recognizable as coming from the same source.

Macromedia has eliminated some of the problems. Web pages created in Backstage are largely browser-independent (though they clearly get the best servicing from Netscape Navigator 2.0 or 3.0 and Microsoft Internet Explorer 3.0, which together constitute at least 85 percent of the browser market; they also support the widest range of plug-ins and applets that can bring a Web page to life and that are Backstage Desktop Studio's strength). The HTML 2.0 tags that are the standard output for Backstage Designer Plus are usable on virtually any Web server (and you can still add, while in source mode, the latest HTML tags developed to create even more advanced pages).

There is a little work to be done here, however. Although first-hand examinations show that most browsers display Backstage-developed pages similarly, one of its own Web site pages still broke the headlined word "Plus"—as in Backstage Designer Plus—in half while being viewed in Netscape Navigator 2.0, dropping the "us" to a second line. The same problem wasn't evident in Internet Explorer. It was the only anomaly among all the pages at the site. A minor point, but interesting.

Using the WYSIWYG facility is fairly simple, especially if you are familiar with any Microsoft Office products. Once you set the Properties for a page—a quick procedure from the File menu—you can start creating the text using the WYSIWYG editor. This is one of the real joys of Backstage, especially for developers who can remember encoding every HTML tag manually.

Via point-and-click facilities, you can do the following:

- Center text
- Align left
- Align right
- Add color
- Add boldface
- Add italics
- Create numbered lists
- Create bulleted lists

In addition, the Backstage Designer toolbars enable you to insert design features such as horizontal rules, plug-ins for browsers such as Netscape, Java applets, images, and objects. Placing these features into your WYSIWYG-created page automatically adjusts the HTML coding to accommodate them.

In Figure 13.8, the WYSIWYG page looks pretty much as if it had been created with a typewriter. You enter text right on a screen that looks very much like one you might see (and far too often do see) on the World Wide Web. This default look gives you a better sense of what you would have as a starting point if you just sent basically unformatted text out as your home page.

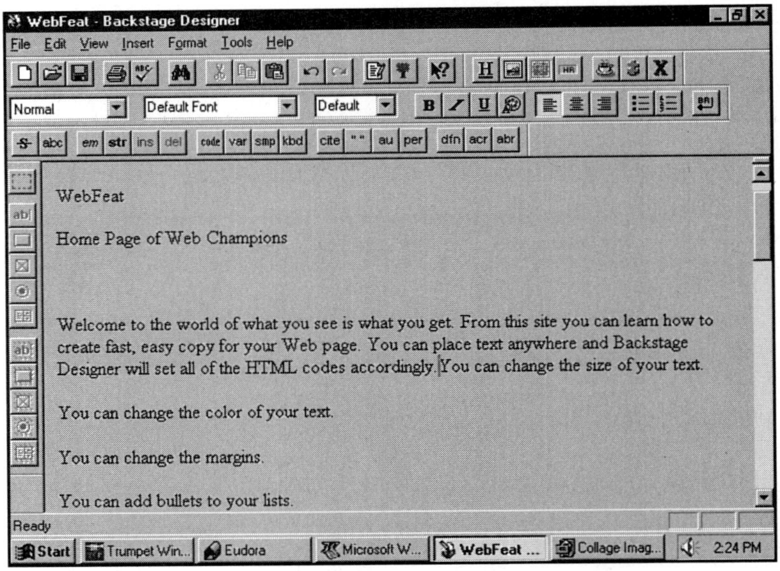

FIGURE 13.8.
You can enter text for your home page, or open a file of text that you want to display. This is what it looks like before you do some quick WYSIWYG formatting.

From this starting point, you can work quickly to add the touches that will separate your Web pages from the millions that compete with it (see Figure 13.9). Adjust the sizes of your headlines and subheads, add color to the words you want to draw attention to, and add links to the "hot words" you'll use to jump to other pages.

If you want to view or modify the HTML coding that has been created while you developed the page, you can display it by a simple click on the toolbar (see Figure 13.10).

Adding Hypertext Links

In the final analysis, the thing that makes the Web navigable is the hypertext link. Without these links, you would need to find and enter uniform resource locators (URLs)—the name for Web addresses—every time you wanted to advance to another destination page. With the links, you need only click on a word or image to make the jump.

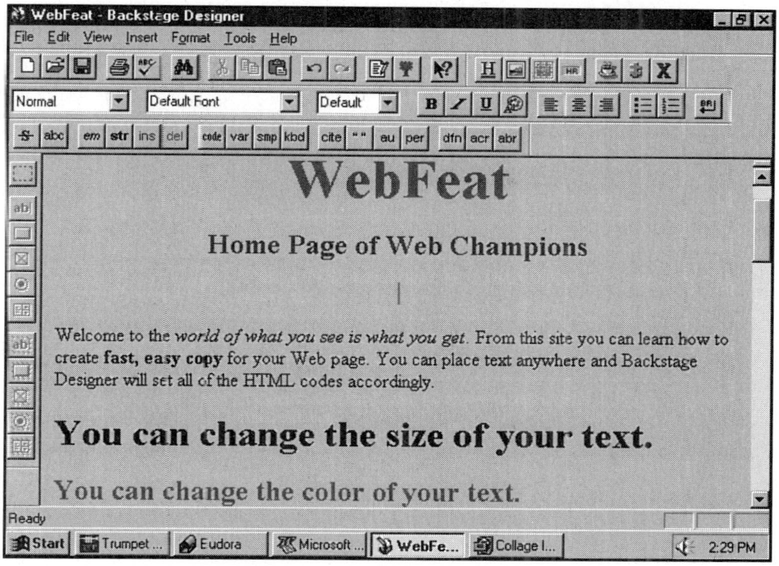

FIGURE 13.9.
The changes to the text took about 60 seconds and required not a single line of manual HTML coding.

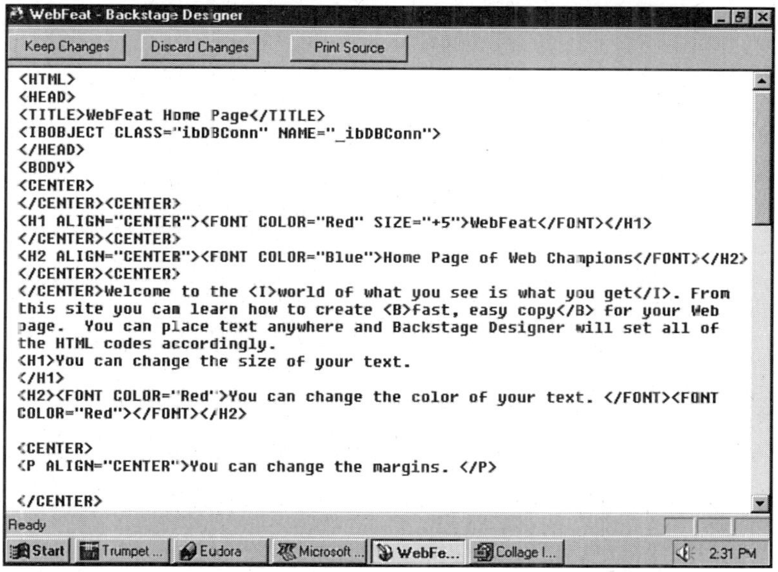

FIGURE 13.10.
All of the HTML code seen here, which once had to be tediously coded tag by tag, is generated automatically by Designer Plus. If you want to add more HTML functionality by adding new code, just enter it from this screen.

The process of adding hypertext links used to be a tedious affair, but Backstage has greatly simplified it. Adding hypertext links in Backstage requires only highlighting the text that you want to link, and then entering the URL in the Hyperlink properties dialog box. In the field designated `URL:`, type the address or click the `Browse` button next to the field to navigate to the file you want users to go to when they select the hyperlink.

It is no more complicated to create links to one Backstage Object that you will work with in Desktop Studio (e-mail, forms, discussion groups, and so forth). You do it by linking to the Backstage page containing the object. In the Hyperlink properties dialog box, click the radio button for Hyperlink to Backstage Page instead of that for Standard Hyperlink. Then in the URL field, enter what is called a relative URL—that is, one that is not fully specified. For example, a specified URL might be: `http://www.ibm.com/software/client_server.htm`. A relative URL might look more like this: `client_server.htm`. Fully specified URLs don't work here.

After you've entered the relative URL, determine the Backstage link option (see Figure 13.11). When you click the `Hyperlink to Backstage Page` radio button, it will enable the controls just beneath it in the dialog box. You can choose `Start New Session`, which means you will be using a new object; `Preserve Existing Session`, which just extends the use of the object you have been using; or `Custom`, which enables you to configure a custom session link.

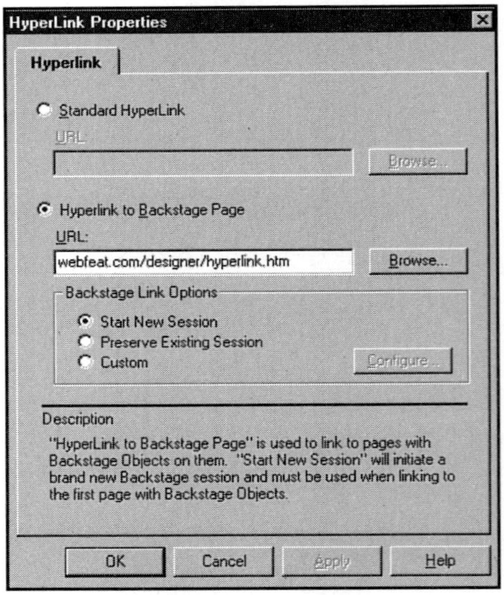

FIGURE 13.11.
In the past, using a hyperlink to link to objects required HTML coding and perhaps even some programming, depending on the object. Backstage has reduced the creation of hyperlinks to a 10-second proposition, just as long as you know the URL.

The distinguishing feature for Backstage in all of this is that most of the linking is done via point-and-click configuring. The default hyperlink color is the standard blue, but you can choose any color you like from the Backstage palette. Anytime you need to recheck or change a URL, you can do it right from the Hyperlink properties dialog box instead of sifting through the HTML source. Just highlight the URL, and then click the Hyperlink button on the toolbar. No more needle-in-a-haystack searches, which are especially difficult when you have a lot of URLs listed together in HTML source.

Using Backstage's Objects Library

Backstage Desktop Studio comes with a library of Backstage Objects that, along with the WYSIWYG facilities, are what really speed up the Web page development process. All of the Backstage Objects are point-and-click elements. Inserting them is a matter of placing your cursor where you want the object on the page, and then double-clicking the object to display a dialog box in which you configure it.

The following list describes the objects in the Objects Library in Backstage Desktop Studio. The references to a "Backstage Web page" distinguish it from a standard Web page, which does not have any objects in it. The preprogrammed Backstage Objects include the following:

Authentication. Defines attributes of a user profile to allow or restrict access.

Backstage Button. Specifies attributes associated with a button placed on a Backstage Web page.

Backstage Checkbox. Specifies attributes associated with a checkbox placed on a Backstage Web page.

Backstage Menu/List. Specifies attributes associated with a list or menu placed on a Backstage Web page.

Backstage Radio Group. Specifies attributes associated with a radio button group placed on a Backstage Web page.

Backstage Table. Specifies attributes associated with a table and associated columns placed on a Backstage Web page.

Backstage Text. Specifies attributes associated with a Backstage text object placed on a Web page.

Backstage Text Field. Specifies attributes associated with a Backstage text field object placed on a Backstage Web page.

Browser Information. Defines browser attributes that can be placed on Web pages.

Conditional Include. Defines conditions and files to include in a Web page display based on whether the condition is TRUE or FALSE.

Database Connection. Specifies logon, database connection, and query attributes.

Date & Time. Specifies format of date and time stamp, which can be included on a Web page.

Debug Dump. Displays HTTP parameters from the last page.

Discussion Group. Specifies attributes associated with discussion groups, topics, and topic messages.

Field Link. Specifies attributes associated with a Backstage field link specified on a Backstage Web page.

Next Data-Page. Specifies processing for a Next Data-Page object placed on a Backstage Web page (when displaying multiple pages of data retrieved from a database).

Pagehit Counter. No attributes. Corresponds to the `Pagehit` object that indicates the number of times users have accessed a specific Web page.

Previous Data-Page. Specifies processing for a Previous Data-Page object placed on a Backstage Web page (when displaying multiple pages of data retrieved from a database).

Session Link. Specifies attributes associated with a Web page session link and associated database connection and processing of page-to-page links.

Although it isn't possible in this chapter to go into detail about each Backstage Object (some are self-explanatory), I'll discuss some of their more important uses.

Creating Forms with Backstage

Backstage Desktop Studio makes it a relatively simple job to create both standard and Backstage (those with objects in them) forms for your Web site. It uses a library of point-and-click form elements. You can place any of them simply by putting the cursor at the point in the form you wish the element to appear, and then adding that element. You can add the following elements:

- Text fields
- Buttons
- Checkboxes
- Radio buttons
- List menus
- Drop-down menus

These elements make forms creation pretty much a mouse-based affair. You can access all of these form elements from a toolbar along the left side of the Backstage Designer Plus screen. You can also reach them from the Insert menu.

Forms enable Web site developers to collect information from people. Backstage provides two types of forms: standard and Backstage. With the standard forms, you can use the library of form elements to create your standard form via pointing and clicking (see Figure 13.12). The Backstage forms differ in that they contain Backstage objects. The forms creation process is similar regardless of which type of form you are creating.

FIGURE 13.12.
Forms contain a variety of common elements, all of which are available from the Insert menu on the Backstage Designer toolbar.

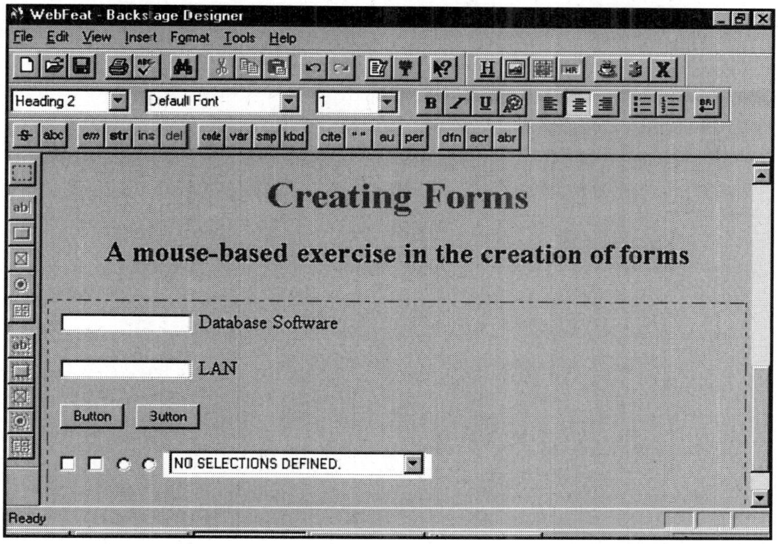

After you have placed the standard form elements into your form, you can change the properties of each one by placing the cursor on the form element and double-clicking. This displays the Properties dialog box for whichever element you clicked on (text field, radio button, and so on). You customize your form's content in these Properties dialog boxes(Figure 13.13). Your options include the following:

- Choosing single lines or multiple lines for text fields
- Designating a password field
- Determining character width
- Naming the buttons
- Assigning values to checkboxes and radio buttons
- Determining the initial state of a button (selected or unselected)
- Adding contents to scrolling lists

This part of the forms creation process departs only slightly from point-and-click construction. The Properties dialog boxes demand a small amount of naming and value defining, but you can do this extremely quickly if you know the parameters before starting.

You could create an "average" form—defined here as one with 10 form elements—and define its values in 5 to 15 minutes (only something such as a lengthy scrolling list could slow the process at all).

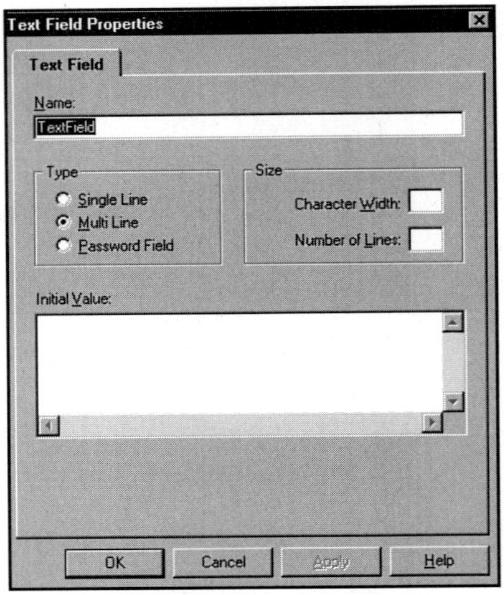

FIGURE 13.13.
The Text Field Properties box illustrates how much latitude a developer has in customizing a form element.

Inserting a Form Object

Backstage's Objects are often the primary reason that a form might exist, but adding them is somewhat more complex than setting up a standard form. Even so, much of the configuration manages to stick with Backstage's commitment to a point-and-click world. The form elements for Backstage Objects appear the same on the screen, but in fact are quite different underneath. You must select these form elements from the Backstage Form Field (not the Standard Form Field, as previously described). Figure 13.14 illustrates how many additional specifications potentially need to be set to create a Backstage Object form.

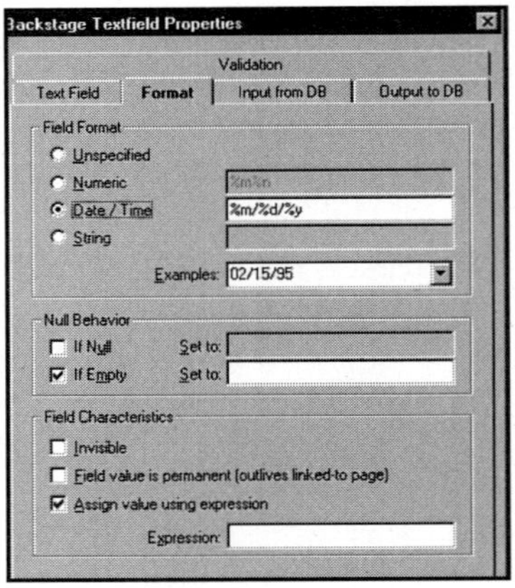

FIGURE 13.14.
Each of the Properties tabs for the form elements needs to be configured for the database the form will interact with. In this figure, by double-clicking on the form element itself you can configure the Textfield properties in the dialog box.

Backstage Desktop Studio has a great deal of built-in interconnectivity with several popular desktop databases such as FoxPro, Paradox, and Access, thanks to its ODBC standards compliance. This means that while the delivering information to and from these databases via forms isn't exactly simple, it doesn't require a database guru either.

Creating Discussion Groups with Backstage

Backstage Desktop Studio is delivered with a Discussion Group Object, with which you can create discussion groups. Discussion groups are like newsgroups you would find on the Internet. They contain one or more groups devoted to specific subjects. Viewers can select a subject, read postings from other people, and post messages themselves. The responses can be threaded, meaning they are linked to an original posting. The difference is that discussion groups are essentially confined to subjects your particular Web site deals with, instead of the more generic newsgroup approach.

Discussion groups can be used for gathering information from clients, posting research and getting comments on it, and debating the merits of new products, even as a form of online help (with messages from people with product problems and replies from people with solutions). They can have juries or moderators to keep the postings relevant.

Creating an actual discussion group page in Backstage is a simple four-step process (although this procedure only places the object onto your Web page; there still is some configuring to do):

1. Place your cursor on your Web page at the point you want the discussion group page to appear.
2. Choose the `Insert | Backstage Object` command from the menu bar.
3. From the Insert Backstage Object dialog box that appears, choose `Community Objects` (as shown in Figure 13.15).
4. Choose `Discussion Group`, and then click `Insert`. The Discussion Group Object is then inserted into your Web page.

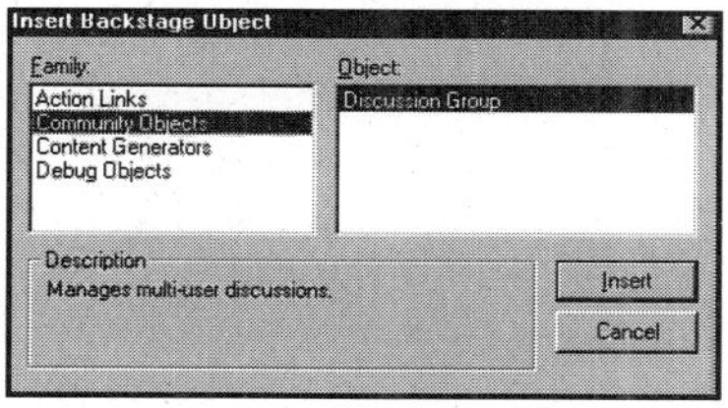

FIGURE 13.15.
Adding the Discussion Group Object from Backstage's Object Library is a four-step process during which your index finger never leaves the mouse.

After you insert the Discussion Group Object into the page, you need to set its properties. This is done from two dialog boxes that you access from Backstage Manager, which always works in conjunction with Backstage Designer Plus in creating pages. You will be asked for information such as the name of the discussion group, a URL (optional) to return a visitor to when they exit the discussion group, the name of the administrator and the administrator's e-mail, and what access privileges you wish to assign. Then you just need to set your topic headings (to establish precisely what you want discussed, lest it become an open forum), and the site is ready (see Figure 13.16). The entire process consumes only a few minutes.

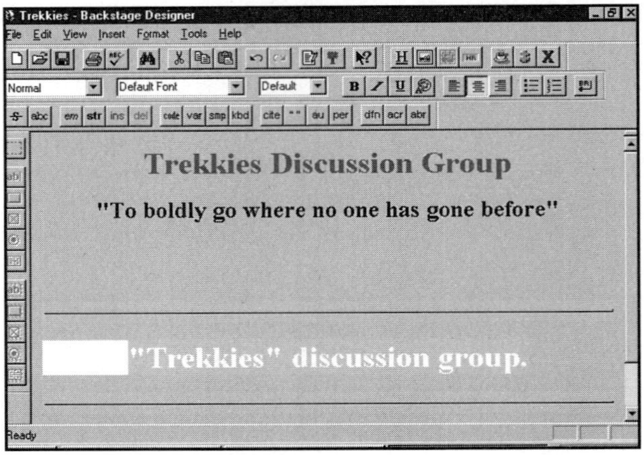

FIGURE 13.16.
The inserted Discussion Group Object shows up on your screen as shown here, with the group name between two bold lines.

Adding Plug-ins, Java Applets, and ActiveX

Backstage Desktop Studio was developed with page dynamism in mind, so dynamic elements such as Java applets, plug-ins for Netscape Navigator and Microsoft Internet Explorer, and ActiveX applets all have been accommodated in the point-and-click scheme.

Java and ActiveX applets, along with plug-ins such as VRealm (a Virtual Reality Modeling Language—VRML—viewing tool) and Shockwave (Macromedia's tool for video/sound/animation support), are placed into pages using the Insert menu. Put your cursor where you want the applet or plug-in to go and then choose the `Insert` menu and select `Java applet/ActiveX/Netscape Plug-in`. Backstage Designer Plus then places an icon on the page at the location you designated (see Figure 13.17).

When an applet icon has been inserted into the page, you need to double-click the icon to display the Java Applet Properties dialog box (see Figure 13.18). Just select the applet you want to place, set the dimensions and attributes, and click OK.

All of these elements are installed in essentially the same way, which is using the place cursor/insert icon/double-click icon/set properties sequence. Versions of Backstage Desktop Studio, at this writing, include several applets called PowerApplets (but no plug-ins); many more applets and plug-ins, along with Microsoft's ActiveX applets, are increasingly plentiful and often available as freeware or shareware on the Web. (To check out the range of plug-ins that have been developed for Netscape Navigator, go to `http://home.netscape.com` on the Web; to see what is actually being done with some of the plug-ins, Macromedia—`http://www.macromedia.com`—has a gallery of best sites showing how Shockwave and other plug-ins have been creatively added to sites.)

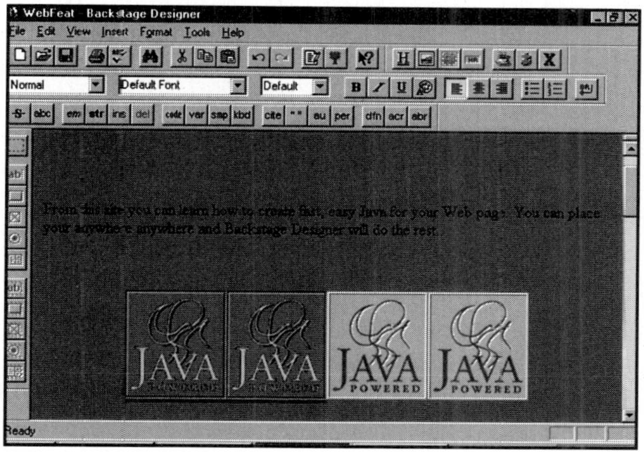

FIGURE 13.17.
To insert a Java applet, just place your cursor in the position on the page you want the applet to appear, and then click `Insert` *and select* `Java Applet`*. An icon like those here will be displayed.*

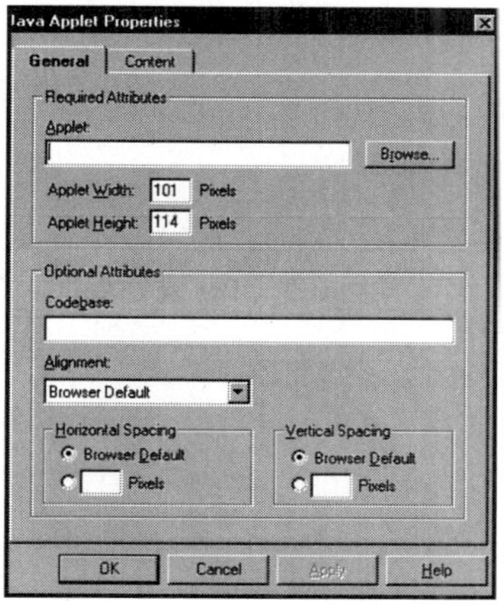

FIGURE 13.18.
You can configure the Java Applet Properties in a few seconds as long as you know the location of the applet you wish to insert.

Using PowerApplets to Jazz up Pages

PowerApplets are about instant dynamism. They are a collection of Shockwave for Director and Java applets that will help you rapidly create multimedia Web pages. Macromedia's goal here, as in the WYSIWYG HTML editor and the point-and-click objects, was to make it easy for you to achieve compelling visual impact without complex programming.

PowerApplets are installed through Backstage Designer Plus and are easy to customize so that your page design can be uniquely tailored to your specific needs. The AppletAce is a new utility that makes configuring the PowerApplets a fairly simple, visual task. Together, AppletAce and the PowerApplets enable you to add memorable effects to your Web pages quickly. Although more PowerApplets are said to be coming, the current portfolio includes the following features.

Animator

You can animate your company's logo, or anything else, right on your Web page. Animator enables you to animate an image or image sequence across a display area by using a simple set of animation paths and options. A single screen interface enables you to determine the motion path, timing, and duration of the animation.

Banners

The Banners PowerApplet will make your text message stand out with animation of its own. It will display text in several animated styles against a background image or solid color. Using Banners, you will be able to select animation styles, font and color combinations, and special text effects that will stand out when visitors view your site. Additionally, the displayed text will also serve as a link to other locations, either on your site or elsewhere on the Web. You can configure Banners in dozens of ways to best suit your application.

Bullets

The non-static bullets in the Bullets PowerApplet add a distinct design flair. You can add color-cycling to bullets and horizontal bars for a unique online look (see Figure 13.19). With this applet, you can simply insert bullets and horizontal bars to spice up the look of a page. There are several options with Bullets. There are five from which to choose, and each has five styles that can be applied to it.

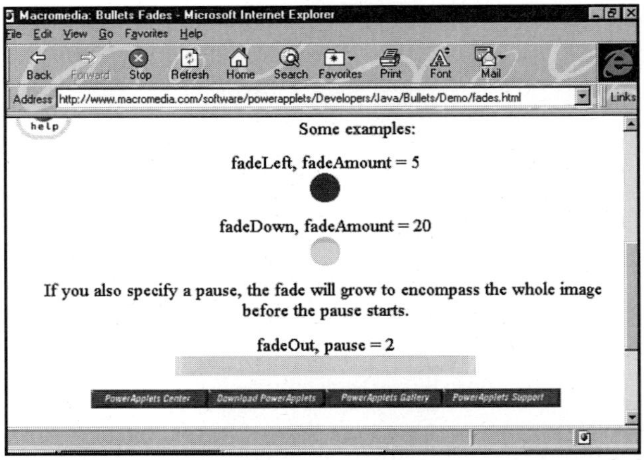

FIGURE 13.19.
These bullets, called Fades, display a continuous rolling change of colors that can draw attention to special items on your Web page.

Charts

You can add bar charts to your Web page to communicate complex numeric data simply. The Chart applet reads a simply formatted data file and plots up to six data series together in a bar chart (see Figure 13.20). Read data from a local file or one located anywhere on the Web and plot its contents. Select from vertical bars, stacked vertical bars, horizontal bars, or stacked horizontal bars.

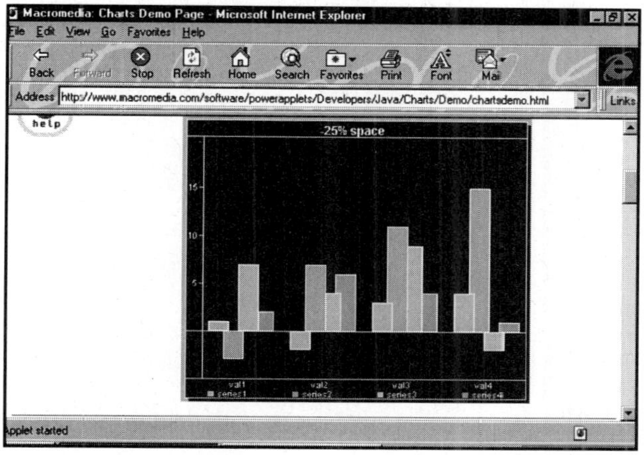

FIGURE 13.20.
Like conventional bar chart applications such as PowerPoint, the Charts PowerApplet converts data from a file into a Web-ready image.

Imagemap

Image maps are increasingly popular as more graphics and multimedia are added to Web pages. Instead of clicking on hyperlinked text, you can click on a relevant image to jump to a site (see Figure 13.21). You can use the Imagemap applet to highlight hot regions with any color, invert the colors, or replace the region with a new image. You can assign separate effects to each region—one effect when the mouse enters a region and one when it is clicked. You can also add ToolTips of any color to a region, displaying different explanations for each area.

Icons

Icons is a collection of animation objects. This collection helps you to add professionally designed, graphically coordinated buttons and icons to your Web pages (see Figure 13.22). To the icons, you can assign links to other pages on your Web site or anywhere on the World Wide Web.

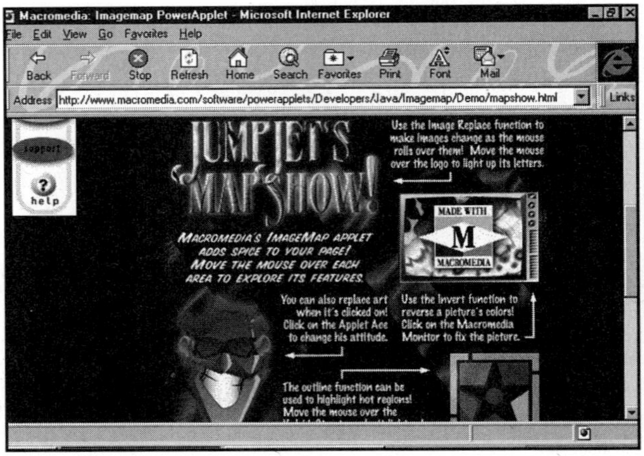

FIGURE 13.21.
You can combine image maps such as this one with Backstage Desktop Studio's image mapping facilities to create compelling visual links in your Web site.

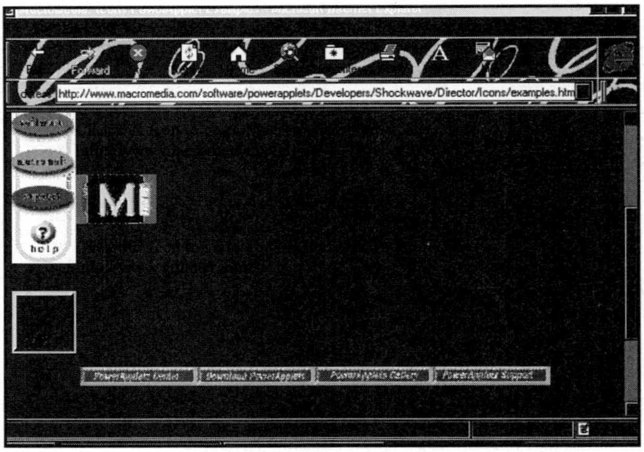

FIGURE 13.22.
Animated icons such as a spinning cube spelling out H-O-M-E can direct people to your home page and are placed with simple point-and-click procedures.

Using xRes SE for Dynamic Images in Backstage

Macromedia's xRes SE is a tool primarily for graphic designers developing images for Backstage Web pages, which is to say it doesn't include features that are designed for use in printing (such as those found in its standard xRes). It enables designers to edit high-resolution files fast with a complete suite of retouching, natural texture painting, and compositing tools (see Figure 13.23). Another point-and-click-driven component of Backstage Desktop Studio, the software provides print designers and multimedia artists with a solid creative tool in the Web page development arena. It provides built-in support for Web- and Internet-friendly formats such as GIF89, Progressive JPEG, and PNG.

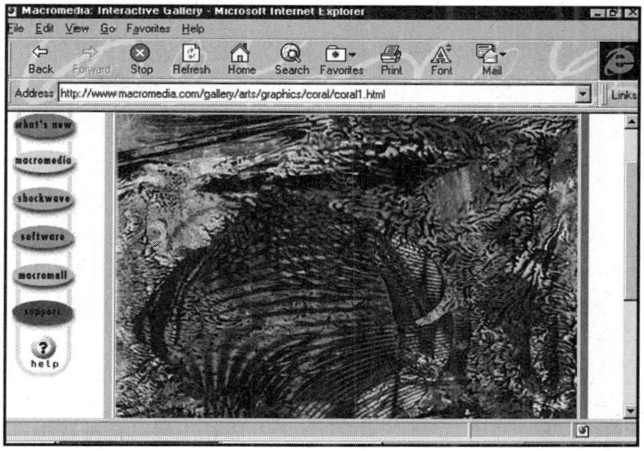

FIGURE 13.23.
You can use xRes SE to create even complex and subtle images such as this coral reef. Then you can let it stand alone or map it with hotlinks.

One of xRes SE's strengths is time management, which can be a sensitive area when dealing with sometimes slow images on the Web. xRes SE uses delayed processing to bypass big-image RAM bottlenecks. Selective processing enables designers to see their edits of even high-resolution bitmaps onscreen in near real time.

If you use Adobe Photoshop, you'll find xRes SE more than a little familiar. It uses similar imaging metaphors and conventions, including floating objects, selections, filters, and alpha channel transparency. Macromedia xRes SE also features a direct mode for processing low-resolution pixel data in real time with a suite of features, such as support for plug-ins, RGB, CMYK, index color, and multi-object editing. Layering multiple image elements is relatively simple with xRes SE objects, which include their own undo and channel information.

xRes SE provides developers with considerable flexibility in developing Web page images. Multiple undos (a terrific facility) let graphic designers test images without committing to them. Text objects enable multimedia artists to place and move text at any time. And a complete suite of customizable artistic brushes and textures enables them to create complex images. With the power to create and edit high-resolution files quickly without extra RAM or hardware, xRes SE is a useful tool for any Web page graphic designer.

Summary

Backstage Desktop Studio is an ambitious suite of tools that attempts to assemble almost anything a Web page developer or Webmaster requires for end-to-end site management. The advantage that Macromedia brings to the effort is its undeniable excellence in multimedia Web authoring. By combining that experience in imagery with the simplicity of a point-and-click, drag-and-drop, WYSIWYG strategy for the implementation tools, Macromedia has come up with a winner. The product's shortcomings really lie in its documentation, which at this stage isn't very visual (which is unusual for a highly visual product such as this) and is missing some explanation of the latest components to be included in the suite (such as the PowerApplets and the xRes SE facilities). But this examination of the software was done with a beta product and with beta documentation. By the time the product is introduced—about the time this book is published—the problems will likely be fixed.

Although you can't download a test version of Backstage Desktop Studio, Macromedia does have a free version of Backstage Designer Plus, the principal Web page design tool, that you can download. It would be worthwhile to check it out at `http://www.macromedia.com`.

CHAPTER 14

Adobe PageMill and SiteMill

by Gregory M. Kovich

IN THIS CHAPTER

For too long, Web pages have been created by professionals well-versed in UNIX with tools resembling simple text editors, but no longer! Adobe Systems now offers two programs for both the beginning HTML author and the experienced Web site manager. PageMill and SiteMill feature a WYSIWYG interface, which makes operating them easy to figure out, as well as incorporating typical Macintosh ease of use. PageMill is an excellent choice for creating Web pages; it allows even a novice to create a Web page complete with forms, graphics, and formatting. SiteMill is the perfect choice for both managing and editing Web pages on the server; it catalogs a Web site, checks each link, and displays all errors. Currently, both programs support HTML version 2.0, as well as certain Netscape plug-ins. Minimum system requirements for both PageMill and SiteMill are as follows: Macintosh OS 7.1 or greater, Drag Manager (if Macintosh OS version is less than 7.5), 8 M RAM, and 10 M of hard disk space.

NOTE

If you're using version 1.0 of either PageMill or SiteMill, check Adobe's Web site at `http://www.adobe.com/supportservice/custsupport/LIBRARY/pmlmac.htm` and `http://www.adobe.com/supportservice/custsupport/LIBRARY/smlmac.htm` for the free updates to 1.0.2.

Because both PageMill and SiteMill share the same feature sets, techniques and tools learned on one program can be used on the other. Each of these tools offers an easy system for creating Web pages or managing a Web site.

PageMill 1.0.2

PageMill can be operated in two separate modes: Browse and Edit. The Browse mode is the default mode when you're opening a saved page; it shows a view of the page as though it were being served over the Internet to your browser. The Edit mode is for creating and editing your page. You can toggle between the two modes by simply clicking the Browse/Edit icon at the screen's upper right. The Browse mode icon looks like a globe, and the Edit mode icon looks like a quill and scroll. The remainder of this section explains the feature sets available in the Edit mode; they include a menu, a button bar, and a floating palette called the Attributes Inspector. Figure 14.1 shows the edit screen containing the feature sets.

PageMill lets you easily create Web pages that have forms, backgrounds, internal links, external links, images, image maps, and detailed text formatting. Thanks to the program's WYSIWYG interface, you can accomplish all of this without any knowledge of HTML.

FIGURE 14.1.
PageMill Edit page.

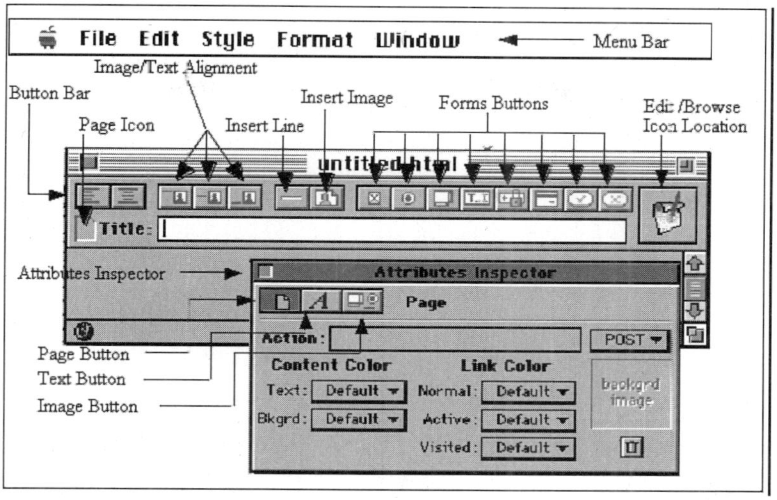

Adding Text to Your Page

Adding text to the page is as simple as typing with a word processor. Just click on the area of the page where you want to add text and start typing! Text wraps at the end of a line, so carriage returns are necessary only for creating paragraphs or extra spacing. In addition, PageMill supports normal cut-and-paste, as well as Macintosh OS drag-and-drop. Macintosh OS *drag-and-drop* allows you to select text in another application and drag it to the page you're currently editing. If the dragged or copied text is RTF-formatted, the attributes and styles are preserved; otherwise, you have to reformat the text.

NOTE

RTF (Rich Text Format) is a formatting option common in many word processors. Saving a file in RTF allows for cross-platform and cross-application compatibility without losing formatting.

NOTE

PageMill 1.0.2 uses the <BR> tag to end a paragraph instead of the <P> tag. Some browsers have trouble with line spacing when the <BR> tag is used (the spacing is simply ignored). It's best to view your page in Netscape or your favorite browser to figure out the page's formatting. This feature will be a choice with PageMill 2.0.

The Attributes Inspector

When you're through typing the text, formatting it is much like formatting text in a word processor. Select the text to be formatted by double- or quadruple-clicking (a single word or the entire paragraph) and choose the format option you want from the available feature set options. The button bar allows simple alignment changes, and the Attributes Inspector, shown in Figure 14.2, lets you format the selected text in many different ways.

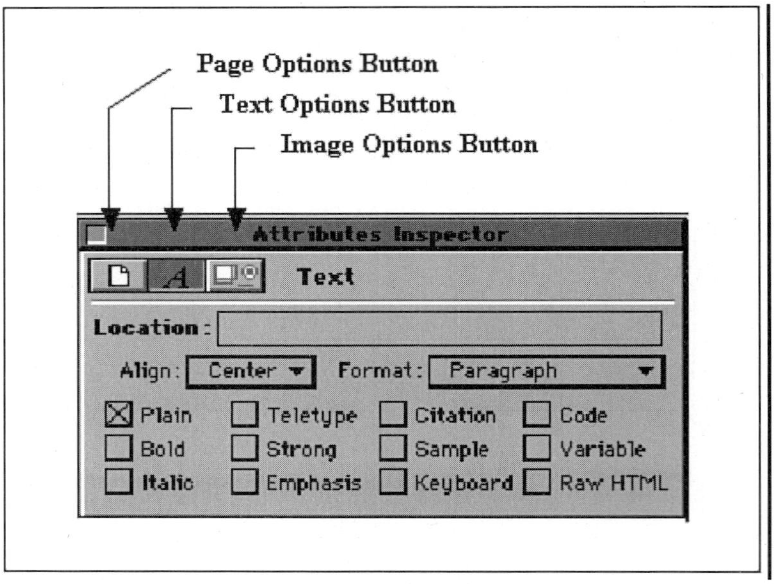

FIGURE 14.2.
The Attributes Inspector.

The Attributes Inspector has three formatting modes: Page, Text, and Image. (See Figure 14.2.) Each of these modes gives you specialized formatting.

In the Page mode, you can select what colors to use for plain text, active links, visited links, normal links, and page background. You can also create a page background by inserting an image into the "backgrd image" well (see the "Including Images" section for more detail) and associate any CGI actions for forms located on the page (covered in more depth in the "Forms" section).

In the Text mode, selected text and paragraphs can be formatted with the following options:

- **Alignment.** You can choose either Left or Center.
- **Physical Styles.** You can choose from Bold, Italic, Teletype, and Plain.
- **Logical Styles.** You can choose from the following:

  Strong

  Emphasis

Citation
Sample
Keyboard
Code
Variable
Raw HTML

- **Paragraph Formats**. You can choose from the following:
  Paragraph
  Address
  Preformatted
  Bullet List
  Definition List
  Directory List
  Menu List
  Numbered List
  Term List
  Small Heading
  Smaller Heading
  Smallest Heading
  Large Heading
  Larger Heading
  Largest Heading

With this variety of options, PageMill enables you to use nearly all the major features of HTML code by simply selecting the text and applying the format. Savvy HTML users can even apply the `Raw HTML` formatting to selected text, which will identify it as specific HTML tags and code.

CAUTION

When you're using `Raw HTML`, PageMill doesn't error check the text. Be careful when using this format option, because the results might not be what you intended.

In the Image mode, you can choose whether an image is a map, button, or picture and manually resize the selected image. Other features of this mode let you create a border around the image and display a descriptive name for browsers whose graphics capability is either turned off or nonexistent.

Format and Styles Menu

If the Attributes Inspector is not to your liking for formatting text, the Format and Style menus contain all the formatting options found in the Inspector. Just as you do when using the Attributes Inspector, select the text and go to the Format or Style menu to choose the option best suited to your needs. A rule of thumb is that logical and physical styles are found in the Style menu, and paragraph formats are found in the Format menu.

PageMill supports the six levels of headings described in HTML 2.0. These levels are available in both the Attributes Inspector and Format menu. Each heading level gives you incremental size and bolding changes for the selected text. Figure 14.3 illustrates the differences between these heading formats.

Figure 14.3.
Format of the six heading levels.

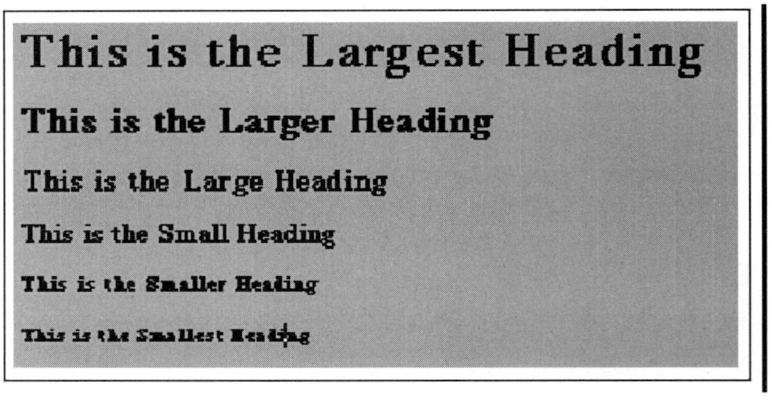

List formats are especially valuable for displaying information to your anticipated audience. The ability to display bullet points, automatically number lines, and easily separate terms from their definitions are several reasons for choosing from the list formats. Once again, PageMill allows format changes simply by typing the text and then selecting the format, either through the Attributes Inspector or the Format menu. Figure 14.4 displays several of the list formats.

Including text from another application is easy and quick. With Macintosh OS drag-and-drop support, found in System 7.1 and above, you can place a selected portion of text from another application inside an edit document. To accomplish this, have both windows open (the PageMill document and source text document), select the text from the source text document, and drag it to the PageMill document. Position the mouse where you want the text to be and release the mouse button. If the text is formatted in RTF, it will keep all the formatting shown in the source document. Otherwise, the text will have to be formatted by using one of the previously described methods.

FIGURE 14.4.
Different list formats.

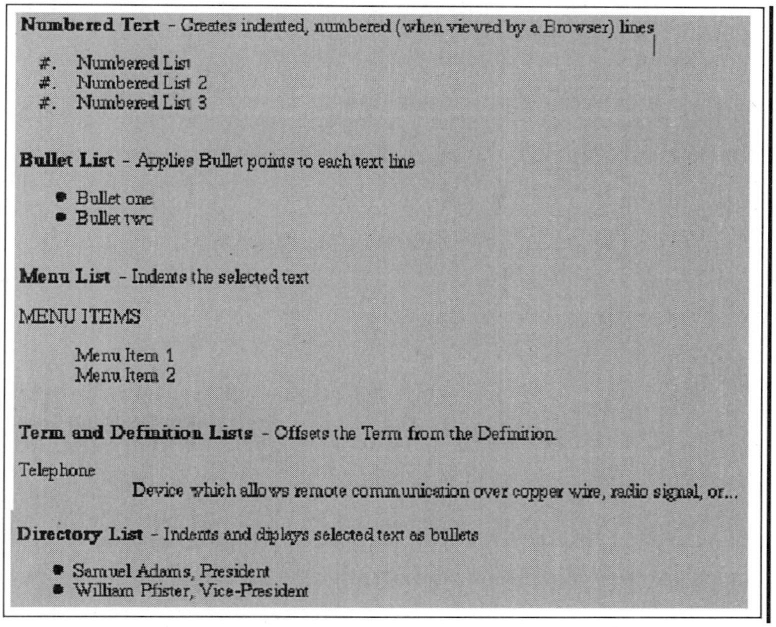

NOTE

The installation of PageMill and SiteMill includes the addition of the Drag Manager. This isn't necessary for System 7.5 and above machines; nevertheless, it's installed anyway.

Including Images

One of the best features of browsing the Web is the rich images and graphics embedded in the pages at your favorite Web sites. Many tools have been created to help the budding Web author change a normal or boring text page into a multimedia extravaganza. PageMill 1.0.2 doesn't have a plethora of built-in tools to help with image animation or multimedia sensations; however, it does allow simple drag-and-drop inputting of images into any page. PageMill also contains a graphics editor that makes it easy to modify and enhance the image.

Popular Web browsers such as Netscape, Mosaic, and Internet Explorer display both GIF and JPEG images. PageMill 1.0.2 automatically changes a PICT image into a GIF image copy just by including it in the page, so including screen captures, scanned images, TV, or CD QuickTime frames into a page is as easy as saving the image and directing PageMill to the saved location.

You can include an image by clicking the Insert Image button on the button bar (shown in Figure 14.1). Once the image is included on the page, you can change its characteristics with the Image Editor, invoked by simply double-clicking on the image. The Image Editor has several tools that give you the ability to have the image display in an interlaced "venetian blind" format (resolved in the browser in stages), make certain portions transparent, shuffle one image on top of another, and permit the image's name to be displayed for text-only browsers. You can also easily create image maps in the editor window by simply drawing rectangles, ovals, polygons, or other shapes inside the image, then linking that shape to either a URL or an anchor located in another part of the current page. Figure 14.5 shows the Image Editor in the process of creating an image map.

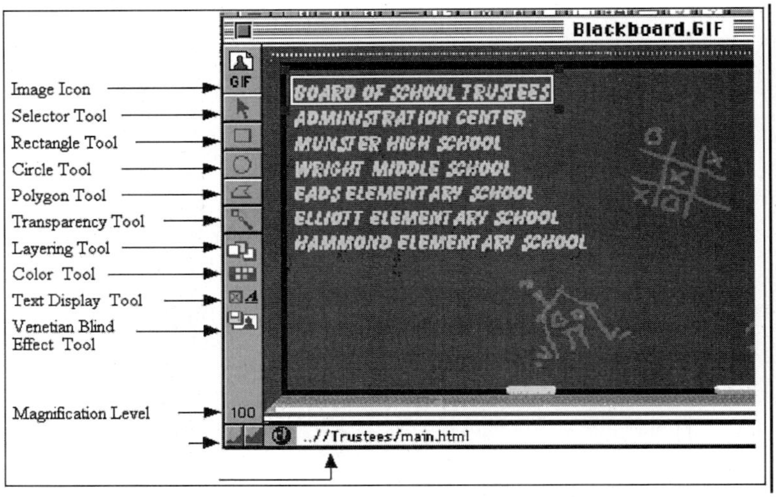

FIGURE 14.5.
Image Editor window.

Images can also be used as a background to spruce up otherwise dull-looking pages. In PageMill, it's as easy as selecting the image and dragging it to the Attributes Inspector "backgrd image" well (shown in Figure 14.1). You can perform all these enhancements with either a button click or with drag-and-drop.

Creating Links

A *link* is a section of text or image that, when clicked, sends the browser to another location. The linked location could be on the same page, the same server, or an entirely different continent! PageMill enables you to do both types of linking: the same page or pages on the same server (internal links) and another page on a different server (external links).

You can create another type of internal link by sending the browser to an anchor. Creating anchors is easy and quick. Scroll to a heading or other area on the page where you want to establish an anchor, drag the Page icon to that area, and release the mouse. When the mouse is released, you'll see an image of an anchor that's associated with that portion of the page. To create a link between the anchor and some text, select the text, scroll down to the anchor, click and drag the anchor to the selected text, and release the mouse. You can also establish links to anchors on other pages by using the same procedure.

Internal Links

An *internal link* directs the browser to a location on either the same page or another page on the same server. In PageMill, you can create anchors in a page, and then create a link to the anchor elsewhere in the document. This technique is best used in a table of contents or index-type page that has many lines of text and offers links to certain sections, giving the viewer the option of jumping directly to information of interest rather than reading everything in between (or worse, scrolling through and missing it).

To create a link to another page, select the text that sends the viewer to that page and enter the URL (uniform resource locator) in the Link Location Bar (see Figure 14.6 for its position) or in the Attributes Inspector. An easier method is to open the target page in PageMill and drag its Page icon to the text you want to link with.

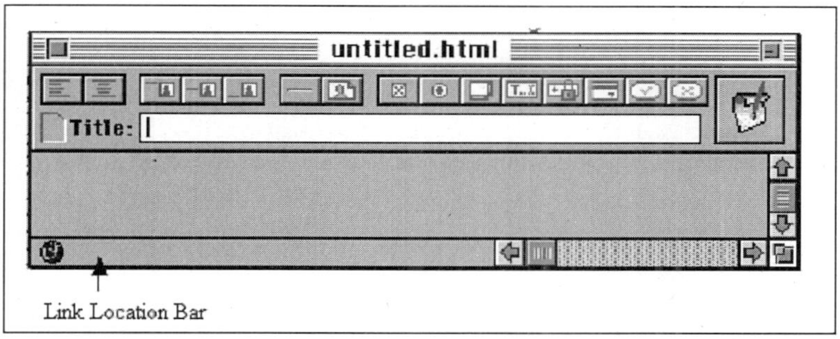

FIGURE 14.6.
The Link Location bar.

External Links

External links send the browser to another server. This type of link is difficult to manage because you have no control over the name or content of pages on other servers. To create an external link in PageMill, follow the same technique described in the internal link section, except that you must type the URL that the browser goes to.

PageMill accommodates different URL types; however, make sure the browser can accept the protocol or action you present. URLs on the Web invariably begin with `http://`; however, other resources on the Internet have URL types that perform different functions. Table 14.1 lists several common URL types recognized by PageMill.

Table 14.1. Common Internet URL types.

`file://`	Opens a file on the server
`ftp://`	Connects to a server by using FTP (File Transport Protocol)
`gopher://`	Connects to a Gopher server
`http://`	Connects to a WWW server
`mailto:`	Sends an e-mail
`news:`	Connects to a newsgroup

NOTE

It's important to type the URL correctly. A broken link is both frustrating and hard to discover without a live test.

Forms

Forms are very versatile, because they let a Webmaster or owner of a Web site know who's interested in the site or products and topics presented on the site's Web pages. Forms are a nifty way to gather information from visitors to your Web page or to share information with them. Another use is for commerce—actually selling merchandise at your Web site. The visitor uses a form to send in the necessary information to complete a transaction. This information is then sent to the Web server, processed by a CGI, and stored for retrieval during normal business hours.

PageMill makes it easy to create several different types of forms. A common form on a Web site is one used for logging the visitor's name and e-mail address. (See Figure 14.7.)

The PageMill users' guide has a tutorial that includes a form-editing section demonstrating how easily PageMill permits changes and additions to a form. The form in Figure 14.7 was created by simply typing the labels for each field, then clicking the appropriate forms-related button in the button bar. Refer to Figure 14.8 for a display of the button bar and the associated forms buttons.

Figure 14.8 shows a variety of common form features, such as the checkbox, radio button, and pop-up menu; they're as simple to include as clicking a button. One drawback is that only one form per page is allowed, or more accurately, one Submit button per page. However, an easy workaround solution for this limitation is to link the submit button for one form to another page and another form.

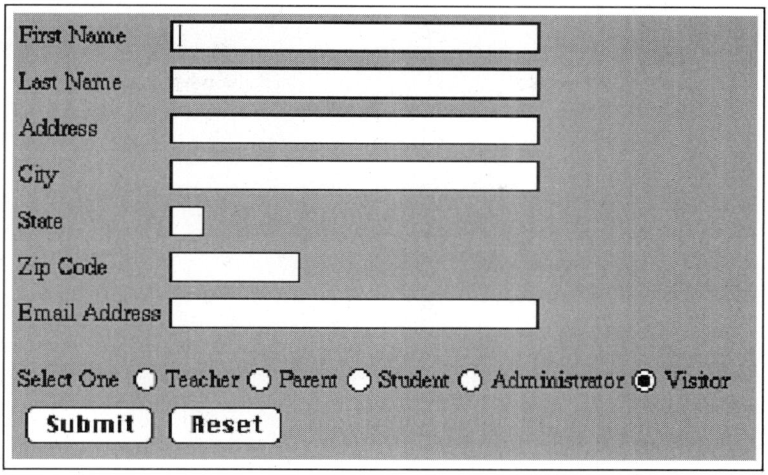

FIGURE 14.7.
Common Web site form.

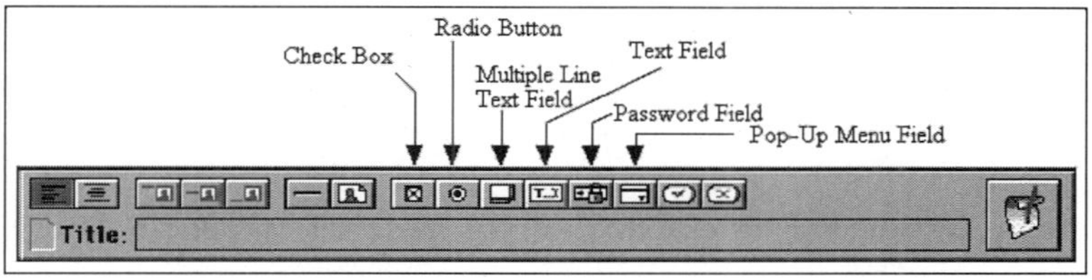

FIGURE 14.8.
The button bar and forms field buttons.

NOTE

PageMill allows only one submit button per page, so whatever form is on that page is sent to the server to be handled by a CGI.

Although forms are versatile and helpful to a Web site owner, it can require some work to get them operating correctly. For your form to work with the database program on a Web server, you must open the Attributes Inspector, select a field, and give it a name indicating what the field represents in the database. This process must be repeated until all the fields on the form have been associated with a field in the database. The submit button sends the contents of the form to the server, based on the CGI script associated with the form's page. To associate a CGI script with a page, enter the CGI's path and name in the `Action` field of the Attributes Inspector. When you're designing a form, contact your Webmaster or database administrator for the correct procedure to follow for your database or CGI.

NOTE

Check with the CGI script author about the value of the Action Option (GET or POST). Don't try to create a form and associate it with a CGI on your own; it's better to involve as many people as you can.

PageMill 2.0

As easy as PageMill 1.0.2 is to use, some limitations for the serious technical author are addressed in version 2.0. Adobe Systems has been quick to respond with a new and improved edition of this application and has been beta-testing PageMill 2.0 throughout the summer. The commercial version is scheduled to be released in November 1996. This version, for both the Macintosh and DOS/Windows platform, will be a welcome tool for many. Version 2.0 will follow the current HTML 3.0 standards and include the capability to do the following tasks that aren't available in version 1.0.2: frames, tables, direct import of Excel files, support for multimedia plug-ins, enhanced text formatting options (color, font, size of individual characters), animated GIF images, text "wrap-around" images, ability to play sounds, spell checking, direct source code editing, <BR> and <P> support, document statistics (estimated time for document viewing), direct source code editing, placeholder support, and Java applets! You can see from this list that version 2.0 will answer many of the technical questions and drawbacks that had prompted users of more robust (but more difficult to use) HTML editors to criticize version 1.0.2.

SiteMill

When calculating the cost of creating a Web presence, invariably the cost for maintaining the site is either forgotten or unknown. Tasks such as evaluating the links, updating images, uploading, and storing pages all seem practically impossible to keep straight, especially at large sites with dozens of pages. SiteMill was created for the beleaguered Webmaster; not only does it have the same functions as its sister application, PageMill (all authoring tools are available), but it also offers tools to keep your Web site operating in tiptop shape. This program can be used on the server (if it's a Macintosh) or on the authoring station.

As you've probably discovered, the best Web sites update their content regularly. If this constant renewal didn't take place, then there wouldn't be any repeat visitors. Unfortunately, when a page's content is changed, links from other pages to the changed page might become broken. Discovering these broken links manually would take hours, and several more hours would be required to fix them. This is where SiteMill saves the day—it gives you a Site menu for loading the root folder (directory) into the program and directing the management software to analyze your site. After the analysis is finished, three windows are displayed: the Site window, the

Error window, and the Extended URL window. Navigating between these windows lets you see what's wrong with your site, and more important, fix it fast!

In the Error window (show in Figure 14.9), errors are displayed as icons with question marks. The icons are different for images, pages, maps, and other files, so it's easy to understand the error's severity. Double-clicking on the question mark produces a dialog box that prompts you for the location of the missing file, image, page, or whatever error SiteMill discovered. Next to the file icon and name is a symbol resembling two arrowheads pointing at each other. Clicking this symbol reveals all the pages affected by this error. Finally, there's a description of the full path where SiteMill thought the file or link should be. Armed with this information, the savvy Webmaster could make short work of even the most complicated site! One last practical tool is the ability to do a "find-and-change" on URLs. This tool comes in handy when a popular external reference has been changed. Simply choose `Site ¦ Replace Links`, and all references to the incorrect URL are changed to the correct one.

FIGURE 14.9.
The Error window.

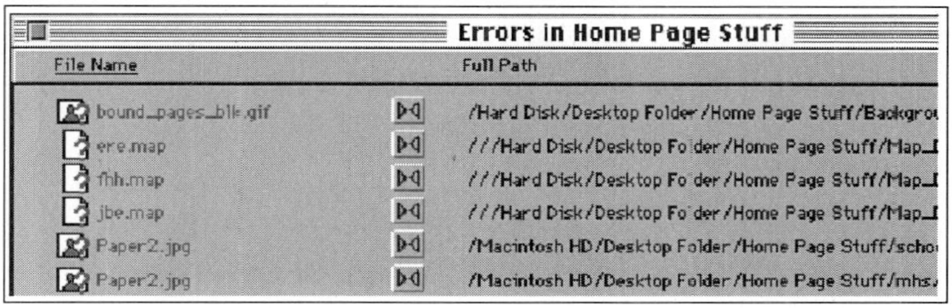

Unlike the Error window, which displays all the internal links, pages, images, and files causing problems, the External URL window (shown in Figure 14.10) displays all external link references. SiteMill doesn't verify whether an external link is broken. However, if you get complaints that the link to a popular site no longer works properly, all you have to do is find the correct link (or an adequate substitute) and use the Replace Links menu option in the Site menu.

FIGURE 14.10.
The External URL window.

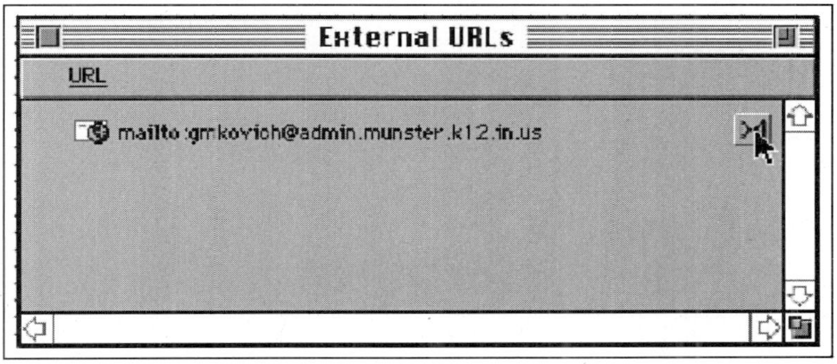

Finally, the Site window (shown in Figure 14.11) allows you to view your entire Web site, errors and all. This window can be configured to view by name, date modified, or kind, which is surprisingly helpful when several people have access and authorization to upload files to the Web server. In the Site window, you can rename files, move them to different folders, examine all incoming and outgoing links for each file, create new folders, and display each page's anchors. When moving files in the Site window, any link referring to that file is automatically updated. This feature is available only in the Site window; moving or renaming files in the Finder will cause broken links.

FIGURE 14.11.
The Site window.

The Site window's title is always the name of the root folder that contains all your Web site's information—in this case, it's `Home Page Stuff`. A file with an × to its right is an unreferenced file. In this case, there are three unreferenced files that could be deleted or moved to another folder. Each folder's contents are accessible by simply clicking the triangle to the left of the folder icon. Pages that display a triangle to the left of the icon will reveal all the anchors on that page when the triangle is clicked.

In addition to these features, each page can also display every incoming and outgoing link. The icon with two arrowheads pointing toward each other represents incoming files, and the icon with two arrowheads pointing away from each other displays all the outgoing links in that page. This feature is helpful when you're looking for a summary of the links and images a certain page contains.

With the incredible power of cataloging a Web site for errors and links, coupled with the point-and-click ease of updating errors, SiteMill is an important tool for the serious Webmaster.

Summary

Adobe Systems has given the beginning Web author and the experienced Web site manager two powerful tools: PageMill and SiteMill. With the WYSIWYG interface and the support of Macintosh drag-and-drop, it's easy to create and manage your pages. Adobe will continue to enhance and hone these two new Web products to be current with the everchanging Internet standards. PageMill and SiteMill should be in the repertoire of any serious Web author or site manager.

CHAPTER 15

Other Web Publishing Tools

by William Stanek

IN THIS CHAPTER

Beyond the mainstream high-end publishing solutions covered in previous chapters, there is a wide array of other Web publishing tools. Many of these tools offer value-pricing, which makes them extremely attractive if you are looking for a budget alternative.

Until now, the focus in this section of the book has been on WYSIWYG publishing tools. While high-end WYSIWYG tools are great, HTML editors come in two general categories: those that follow a WYSIWYG approach to Web publishing and those that generate raw HTML markup. Unlike their WYSIWYG counterparts that shield users from the markup, content generators insert markup directly into your pages in a viewable format.

Being able to see the markup directly has its advantages and disadvantages. You don't have to wonder about the structure of your pages. You don't have to wonder whether you inserted extra tag pairs or inconsistent tag pairs. You do have to take extra steps to view the page in its final form. With many non-WYSIWYG tools, however, you can configure a browser for viewing your pages. You can then preview a page in your browser of choice at the touch of a button.

This chapter examines six alternative publishing solutions:

WebEdit and WebEdit Pro

HotDog and HotDog Pro

HoTMetaL and HoTMetaL Pro

NOTE

Trial versions of WebEdit, HotDog, and HoTMetaL are included on the CD-ROM accompanying this book. If you want to test-drive the professional version, visit the developers' Web sites to obtain a limited demo version. Limited demos of WebEdit Pro and HotDog Pro are currently available.

Introducing WebEdit and WebEdit Pro

Nesbitt Software Corporation (`www.nesbitt.com`) offers two versions of its popular authoring tool called WebEdit. The basic edition, the WebEdit Standard version, retails for $39.95 and is available for Windows 3.1 and Windows 95. The more advanced edition, the WebEdit Professional version (called Web Edit Pro), retails for $109.95 and is available for Windows 3.1 and Windows 95.

For the price, the WebEdit Standard edition is a better value than the WebEdit Professional edition. Both editions of WebEdit fully support HTML 3.0, Netscape 2.0 extensions to HTML, and Internet Explorer 2.0 extensions to HTML. Both editions of WebEdit include a configurable toolbar, shortcut keys, and a spell checker. Where the editions differ is in the automation routines for creating advanced HTML elements such as forms and frames. The professional edition has many wizards to guide you through the creation process and the basic edition has only a few.

NOTE

The current version of WebEdit is 2.0. The developers of WebEdit 2.0 wanted their editor to be on the cutting edge and chose to fully support HTML 3.0. Unfortunately, as you know from reading this book, the HTML standard changed dramatically in early 1996 and HTML 3.0 is now a defunct standard replaced by HTML 3.2.

Still, the Cougar specification, which I'll call HTML 3.4, does reintroduce many aspects of the original HTML 3.0 specification. This means that in the coming months, you may be able to put to use some of the advanced tags you will find in this editor.

Using WebEdit

As you can see in Figure 15.1, WebEdit has an extensive toolbar. Using this toolbar, you can perform most of the routine functions without having to access a menu or memorize shortcut key combinations.

With WebEdit, you can have multiple documents open at one time. Although WebEdit doesn't use a Window or Document menu with which you may be familiar to access open documents, it does provide access to the documents using quick tabs. In Figure 15.1, three open documents are in the editor. You can access these documents from the toolbar by clicking the appropriately labeled tab.

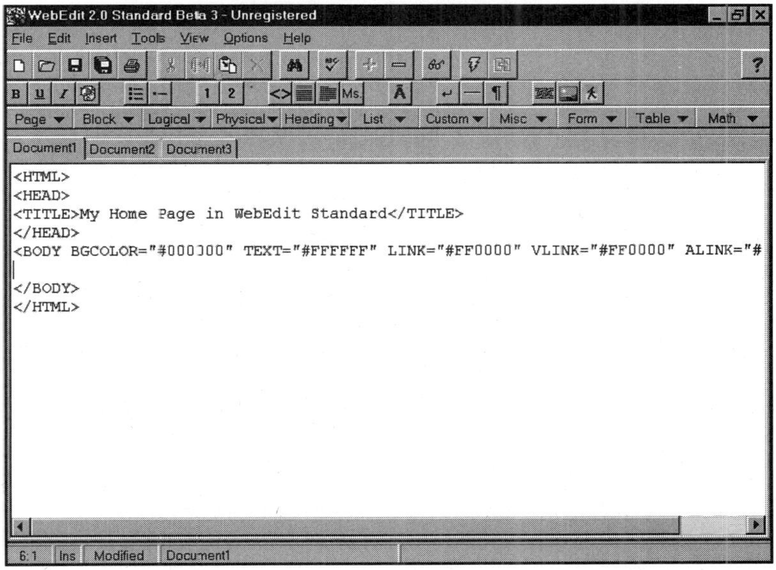

FIGURE 15.1.
Examining WebEdit Standard and its toolbar.

Generally, WebEdit inserts markup as a complete HTML element with a begin and end tag. One key way to insert tags into a page is through the Tools menu. This menu is divided into submenus that are organized by element type.

If you examine the Tools menu, you will see options with which you can add every type of HTML element imaginable. With the SSI menu, you can add tags for server side includes. From the Object menu, you can add tags for embedded multimedia objects. From the Java menu, you can add `<APPLET>` and `<PARAM>` tags. If an element you are adding to the page has special attributes, WebEdit displays a user-friendly dialog box that shows you all acceptable attributes and enables you to assign values to those attributes.

TIP

Right-clicking the mouse displays an extremely useful shortcut menu. Use this menu to save time.

As you see in Figure 15.2, you can add the HTML element to a page by selecting `HTML` from the `Page Structure Tags` submenu. WebEdit then inserts the following tag pair into your page:

```
<HTML> </HTML>
```

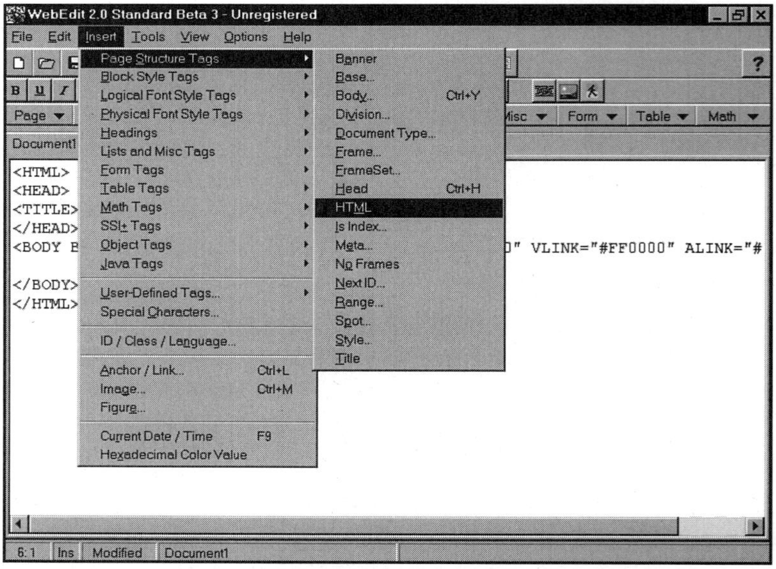

FIGURE 15.2.
Inserting an HTML element.

WebEdit's toolbar saves you keystrokes by placing the most commonly used option menus directly on the toolbar. Thus, another way to add page structure tags to your page is to click the `Page` menu from the toolbar and select an option. Figure 15.3 shows these menus in action. By selecting the `Physical` menu from the toolbar, you can add physical character elements, such as bold and blink, to your pages.

FIGURE 15.3.
Inserting the `<FONT>` *tag using the Physical menu.*

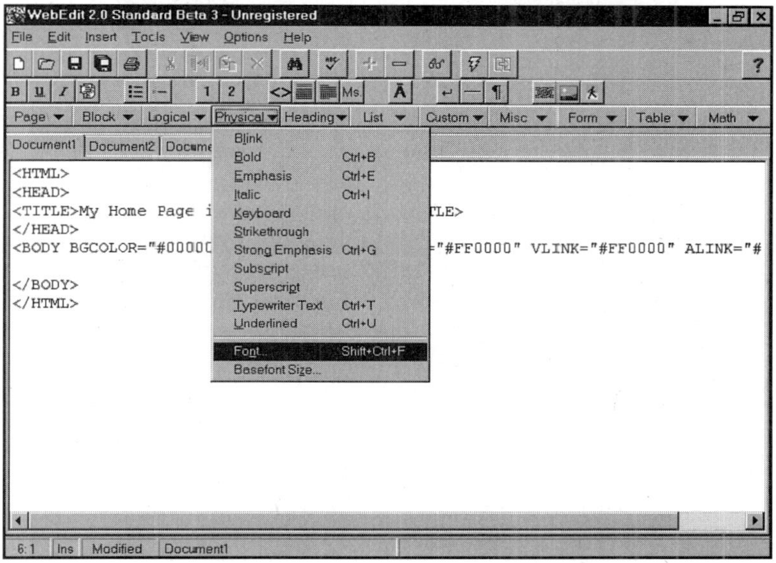

Following the example, you could add a `<FONT>` tag to your page by selecting the `Font` option of the `Physical` menu. When you do this, WebEdit displays the dialog box shown in Figure 15.4. You can use this dialog box to select the size, color, and typeface of the font you want to use.

FIGURE 15.4.
WebEdit's Font dialog box.

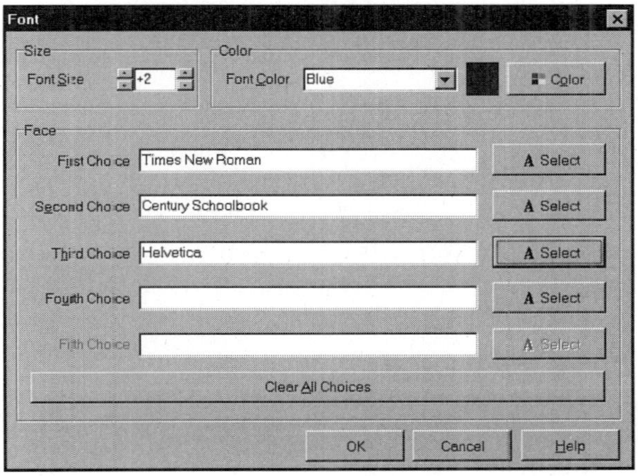

Using WebEdit Pro

The WebEdit Professional edition features an interface that is almost identical to the standard edition. You will find the same friendly toolbar and menus. The professional edition differs from the standard edition in features—the standard edition has a table builder and a home page wizard but that's about it for helper tools.

The professional edition adds to this list of helper tools considerably. You will find a tag checker, Frame Wizard, form builder, Multimedia Wizard, and much more. Most of these helper tools are accessible from the Tools menu shown in Figure 15.5.

FIGURE 15.5.
Examining WebEdit Pro and the Tools menu.

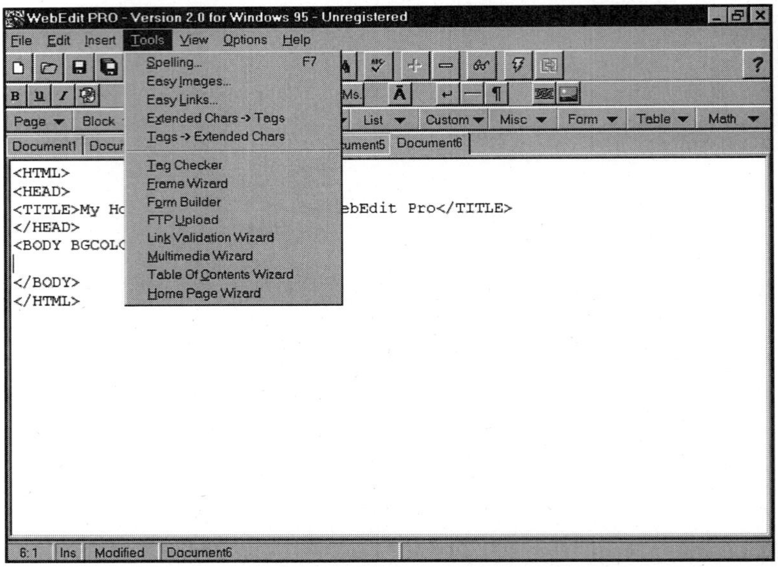

Using the Frame Wizard shown in Figure 15.6, you can frame-enhance your pages using an intuitive graphical interface. Step by step, the Frame Wizard guides you through the frame creation process.

Using the wizard page shown in Figure 15.6, you can divide a page into frames simply by selecting either a horizontal or vertical divider and left-clicking to place the divider on the page. You can adjust the size of any frame by moving the pointer over the divide then clicking and holding the left-mouse button as you drag the divider to a new location on the page.

TIP

If you make a mistake, you can clear the page and start anew by clicking the `Clear` button.

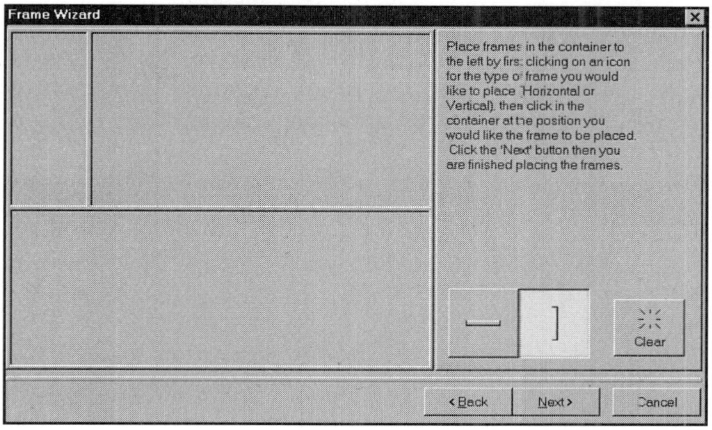

FIGURE 15.6.
Creating frames with the Frame Wizard.

With the Home Page Wizard shown in Figure 15.7, WebEdit guides you through the home page creation process. The first step is to select a heading and subtitle for the page and define the layout style. Next, define the background style and text colors for the page. Then add a logo to the page. Afterward, the wizard helps you finish the page with text, links, and contact information.

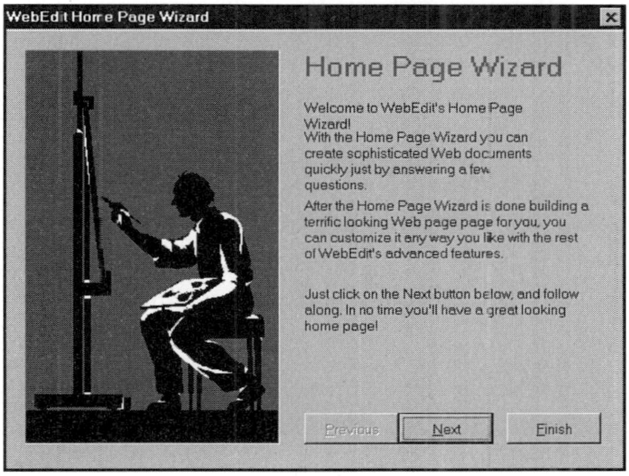

FIGURE 15.7.
Creating a home page with the Home Page Wizard.

Introducing HotDog and HotDog Pro

While Sausage Software's HTML editor, called HotDog, is very comparable to WebEdit, you will find that HotDog is loaded with extras. Like WebEdit, HotDog is available in two versions: The standard edition, called simply HotDog, retails for $39.95 and the professional edition, HotDog Pro, retails for $99.95.

Currently this editor is only available for Windows 3.1 and Windows 95. Although Sausage Software's Web Site (`www.sausage.com`) has long displayed a message stating that HotDog will soon be available for Macintosh and UNIX, it will probably be well into 1997 before the editor is available on other operating systems—if at all.

NOTE

The version of HotDog and HotDog Pro featured in this section is 2.5.3. This version features many improvements over previous versions.

Using HotDog

As with WebEdit, the standard edition is a better value than the professional edition. HotDog fully supports HTML 3.0, Netscape 2.0 extensions to HTML, and Internet Explorer 2.0 extensions to HTML. When you have multiple documents open in the editor, you can switch between them quickly using tabs at the bottom of the editor window.

HotDog features one of the friendliest interfaces you'll find in value-priced HTML editors (see Figure 15.8). As with WebEdit, with HotDog you can select a browser in which to view your pages. Unlike WebEdit, with HotDog you can preview your pages without having to save the page before you preview it. HotDog does this by automatically parsing the file before passing the file to your browser. Other features include an advanced correction system that automatically replaces text and file paths when you publish your pages.

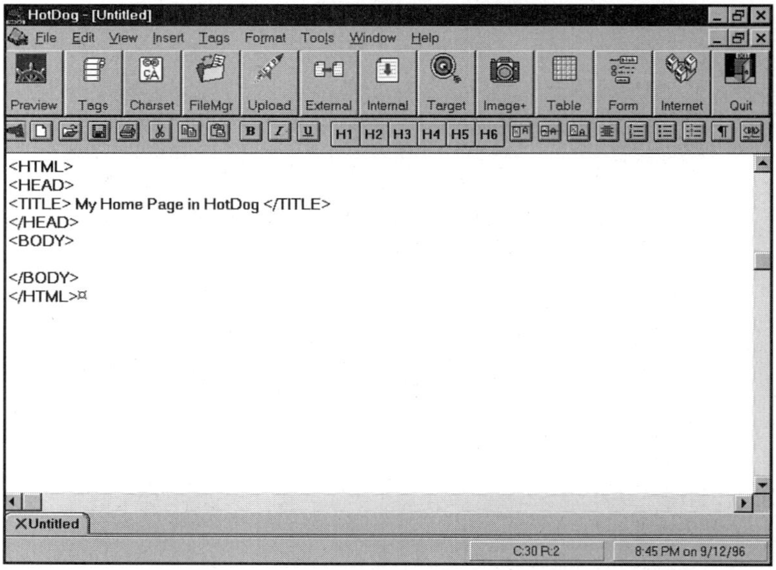

FIGURE 15.8.
HotDog has a very friendly interface.

HotDog is designed for beginners and experts alike. You'll know this immediately when you start HotDog and see the dialog box shown in Figure 15.9. Using this dialog box, beginners can access the help file tutorials to learn about HTML, use HotDog to create Web pages, and also cover HotDog's features.

FIGURE 15.9.
Accessing help files from the HotDog startup dialog box.

In addition to being able to insert many common tags into a page directly from the toolbar, HotDog has a terrific dialog box for adding tags (see Figure 15.10). Once the Tags dialog box is displayed, you can add a tag by finding it in the option list and double-clicking. HotDog has a similar dialog box that lets you add character entities, such as `&` for the ampersand symbol. Another way to add tags is via the popup menus accessible by selecting options on the Tag menu.

TIP

A problem beginners may encounter with the Tags dialog box is that tags and their attributes are displayed. After adding an HTML element, such as the begin and end tags for the BODY element, you must then select attributes for the tag individually. Therefore, to create a BODY element with a background image, you would select the <BODY> tag, then select the BACKGROUND attribute.

Creating forms with HotDog is easy—just click the Forms icon on the toolbar and HotDog displays a form builder. As you can see from Figure 15.11, the form builder provides a friendly interface for selecting the type of element you want to add to a form.

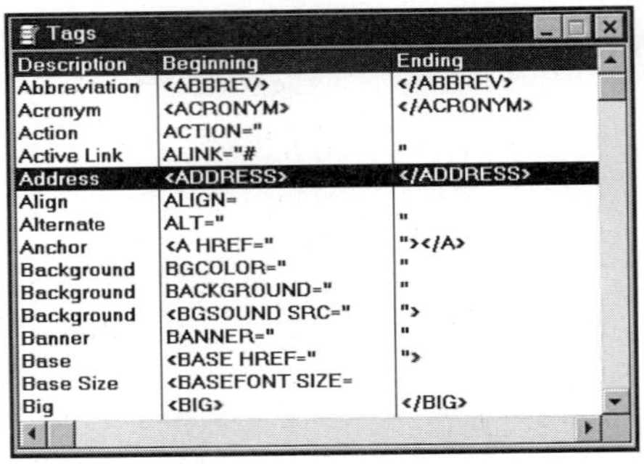

FIGURE 15.10.
Using the Tags dialog box to insert tags and attributes.

Simply click the appropriately labeled button, such as `Text Area`, and you can define the attributes for a `<TEXTAREA>` form element. To insert the form element after you define it, click the `Insert` button. By repeating these steps, you can add as many form elements as you want.

> **TIP**
>
> When you first open the Define Form Elements dialog box, click the `Insert` button immediately to define the submission method, action, and encoding type for the form.

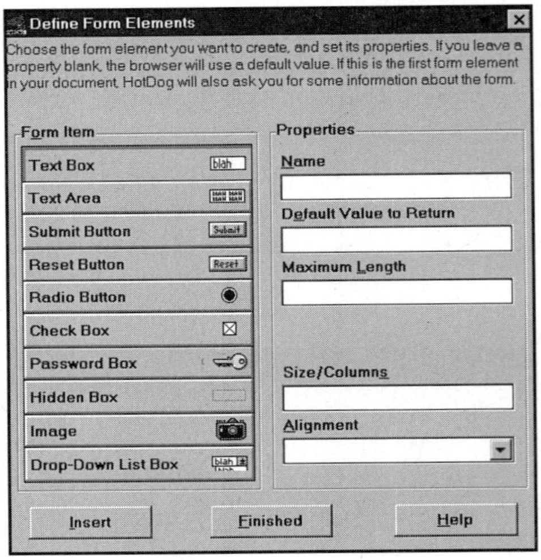

FIGURE 15.11.
Building a form using the Define Form Elements dialog box.

HotDog features many other friendly tools for managing links, building tables, and creating frames. Figure 15.12 shows the Create Table dialog box. Not only can you create a table with this dialog box, you can also use it to display the table with the columns and rows you've defined then enter text directly into the cells of your table. When you are finished defining the table, click the `OK` button to insert the table into your page.

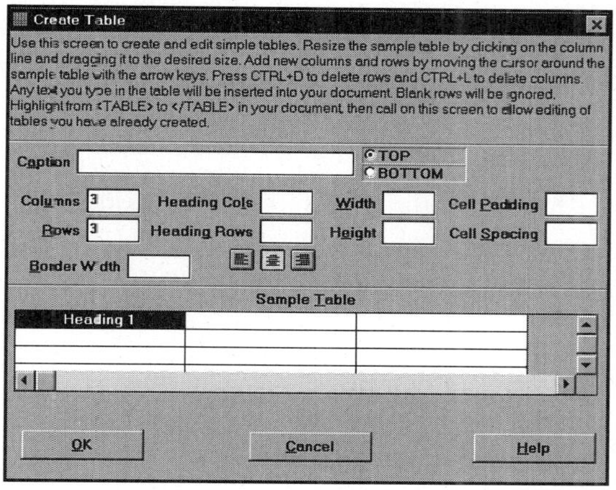

FIGURE 15.12.
Creating a table in HotDog.

Using HotDog Pro

HotDog Pro features the same friendly interface as the standard HotDog editor, yet it has many advanced features that make it a terrific editor of choice. Unlike WebEdit, only the professional version of HotDog includes a spell checker. HotDog Pro further separates itself from the standard edition with multilevel undo and the ability to handle files of unlimited size. HotDog is limited to an arbitrary file length of 32 K, however, which is disappointing because these are useful features that should be included in both editions of HotDog.

With HotDog Pro, not only can you customize the toolbar, you can select the icons and labels for toolbar buttons as well. To do this, select `Tools | Customize Button Bar`. This displays the dialog box shown in Figure 15.13. Next, click the button you want to redefine. You can now reset the label, icon, and function of the button.

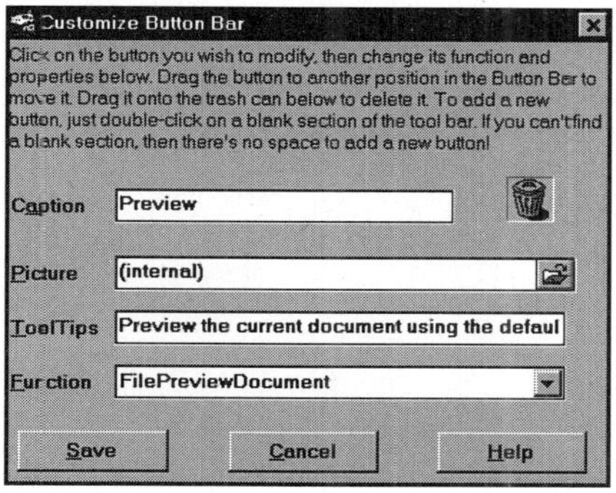

FIGURE 15.13.
Customizing the HotDog Pro toolbar.

Another nice feature of HotDog Pro is the ability to define your own tags or tag sets that can be accessed via the menus. Using this customizing feature, you can add new tags to any of the tag-related menus and redefine any existing tab-related options. Keep in mind that tag-related menus are accessed as pop-up menus by selecting options on the Tag menu.

To define tags, select `Tag Information` from the `Edit` menu. This displays the dialog box shown in Figure 15.14. Next, select the menu to which you want to add or redefine options. You can now create or update a tag definition.

If you are creating a new tag, do the following:

1. Insert the name for the option in the `Item` field.
2. Define the begin tag, such as `<BLOCKQUOTE>`, in the `Beginning Markup` field.
3. Define the end tag, such as `</BLOCKQUOTE>`, in the `Ending Markup` field.
4. Click the `Add New Tag` button.
5. Save the changes by clicking the `Save` button.

If you are updating an existing tag, do the following:

1. Select the option that corresponds to the tag, such as HTML, in the `Item` field.
2. Update the option name related to the tag using the `Item` field.
3. Update the begin tag definition using the `Beginning Markup` field.
4. Update the end tag definition using the `Ending Markup` field.
5. Click the `Edit Tag` button.
6. Save the changes by clicking the `Save` button.

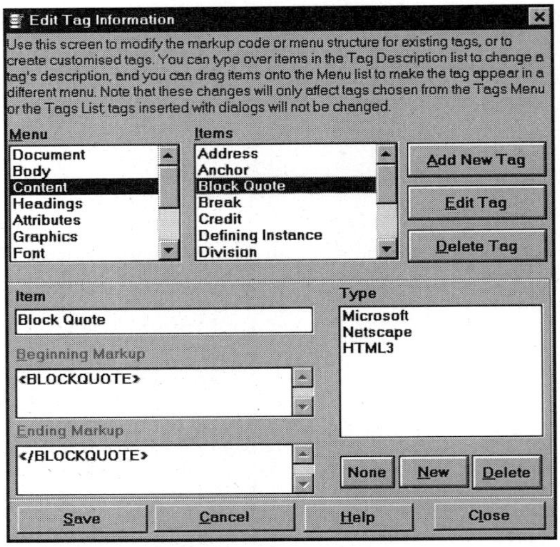

FIGURE 15.14.
Defining new tags for use with HotDog Pro.

With HotDog Pro, you can group pages into projects, which allows quick access to groups of pages for editing and publishing. HotDog Pro even has a Project Manager to help you through the projection creation and management process—to access it, select `Project Manager` under the `File` menu. Once you create a project using the `Project Manager`, you can open any of your projects using the `Open Project` option of the `File` menu.

TIP

If you are using projects in HotDog Pro, be sure to use the `Save Project` or `Save All` options of the `File` menu versus the `Save` option. This lets you save all the files in your project at one time and ensures that the updates you've made are saved.

The Project Manager has three setup pages that are accessed using tabs at the top of the Project Manager dialog box:

Details

Files

Links

Using the Details page shown in Figure 15.15, you can select a name for the project and define the directory in which to store the project. If you plan to use HotDog Pro's quick publishing feature, you can configure the editor to access your Web server of choice.

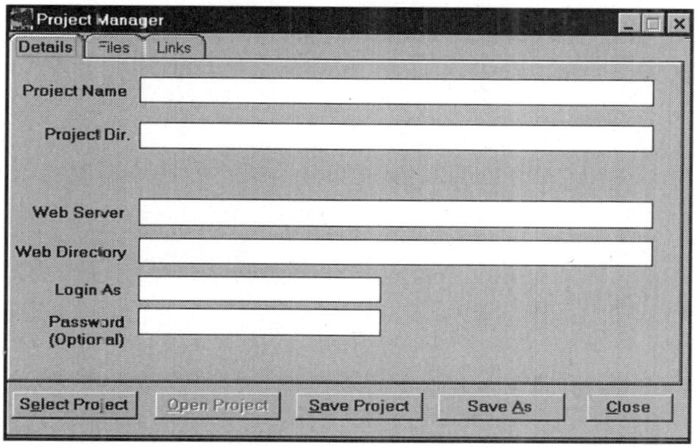

FIGURE 15.15.
Setting project details in the Project Manager.

Using the Files page of the Project Manager, you can add and delete pages (see Figure 15.16). A handy feature is the ability to add all open documents to the current project using the button labeled `Add Opened Docs`.

Using the Links page of the Project Manager, you can check the accuracy of links used in the pages of your project (see Figure 15.17). You can do this on a page-by-page basis, or you can check all the links in all your pages.

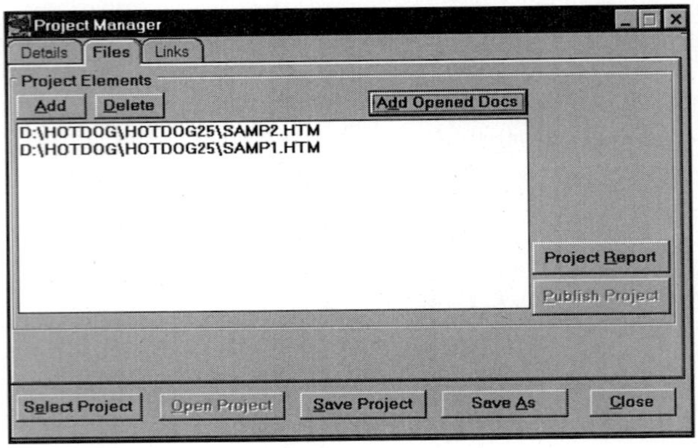

FIGURE 15.16.
Adding files to a project in the Project Manager.

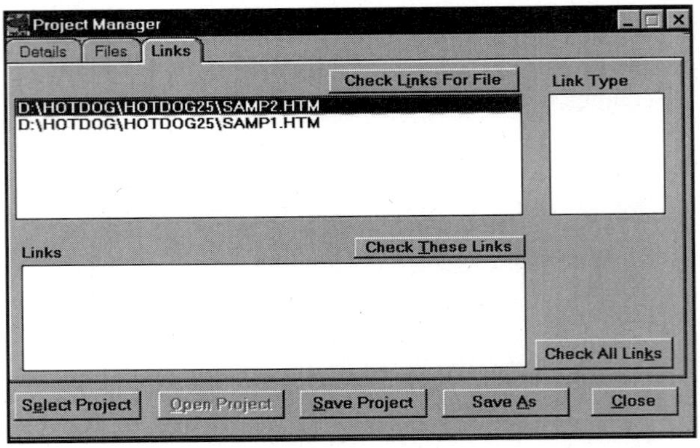

FIGURE 15.17.
Checking links in your project.

Introducing HoTMetaL and HoTMetaL Pro

HoTMetaL is an editor from SoftQuad Incorporated (`www.sq.com`). Like the other editors examined in this chapter, there are two editions of HoTMetaL. Value hunters will want to test drive HotMetaL immediately—it is free! What is even better is that SoftQuad has made a serious commitment to continue to develop and improve this freeware editor. HotMetaL Pro, on the other hand, carries a $159 price tag and supports features that put it in the same league as Microsoft FrontPage and Macromedia Backstage.

Still, SoftQuad has the market experience to back its offerings with solid support and continual upgrades. Before you make a decision on the editor you need, you should give HoTMetaL and HoTMetaL Pro a serious look. Versions of this editor are available for Windows, Macintosh, Power Macintosh, and UNIX.

Using HoTMetaL

As you see in Figure 15.18, HoTMetaL is a unique editor because it enters elements using a WYSIWYG approach, yet it inserts tag markers like the content generators examined earlier. This approach to authoring Web pages works well for beginners and advanced publishers alike. After using both WYSIWYG editors and content generators, you will appreciate the skillful combination that gives you the best of both worlds.

NOTE

The version of HoTMetaL featured in this section is version 2.0. The improvements over version 1.0 are vast, so if you used HoTMetaL 1.0 in the past, be sure to check out HoTMetaL 2.0.

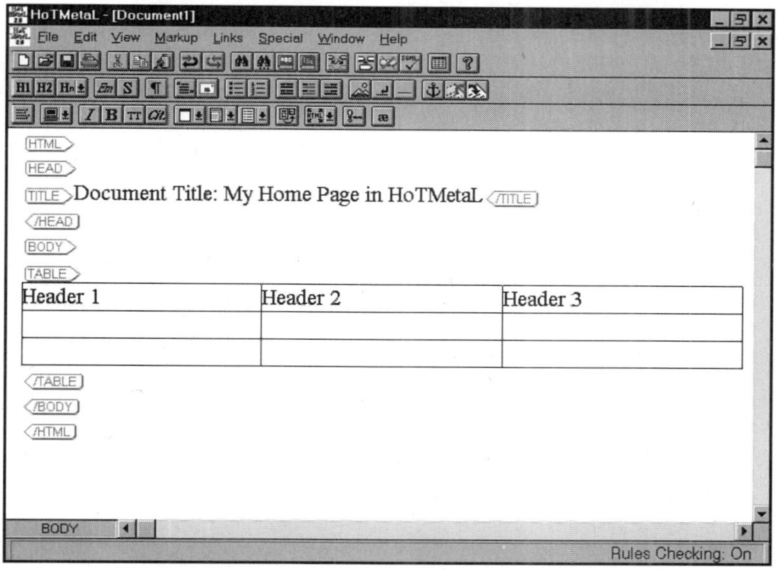

FIGURE 15.18.
HoTMetaL has a unique interface that integrates a WYSIWYG approach with the tag markers used by content generators.

Because HoTMetaL has been through numerous revisions, you will find that it runs fast, handles updates smoothly, and is relatively free of bugs. The same cannot be said about many other HTML editors entering today's market. HoTMetaL is also fully compliant with HTML 3.0 and Netscape 2.0 extensions to HTML.

As you see in Figure 15.19, HoTMetaL lets you hide tags to give your document a complete WYSIWYG feel. To do this, select `Hide Tags` from the `View` menu. Later if you want to view the tags, select `Show Tags` from the `View` menu. Using a similar feature, HoTMetaL lets you hide or display invisible elements like comments. You can also hide or display inline images.

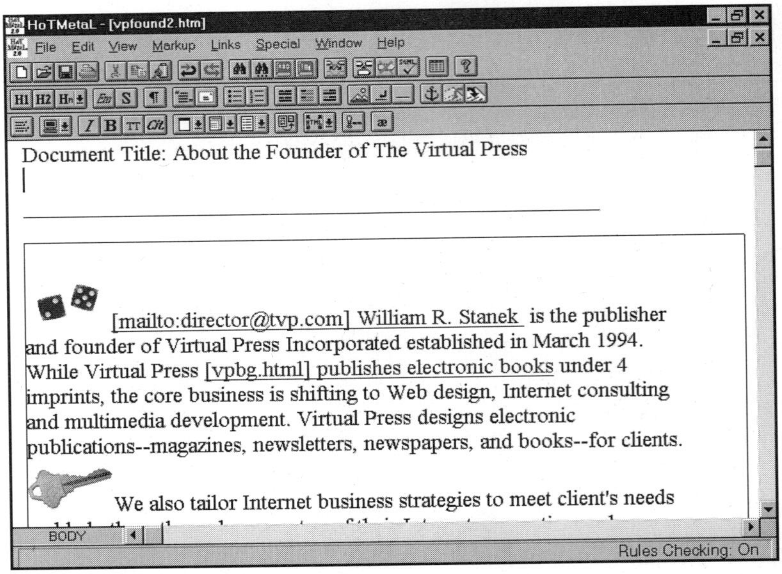

FIGURE 15.19.
With HoTMetaL, you can hide the markup tags.

Although HoTMetaL features an extensive toolbar for adding markup to your pages, the easiest way to add markup is to select `Insert Element` from the `Markup` menu. Using the dialog box shown in Figure 15.20, you can select from a list of elements to add to the page. When you find the right element, double-click its listing, and HoTMetaL will insert the appropriate tag markers and, if necessary, display a dialog with which you can define attributes for the element.

TIP

Often when you are adding a new element, HoTMetaL will display a dialog box that lets you define only the required attributes. You can later define extended attributes for the element. To do this, after you insert the element and close the associated dialog box, move the cursor between the begin and end tag markers for the element, then press `F6`. You should now see a dialog box that lets you set all attributes associated with the element.

The Insert Element dialog box is context-sensitive when rules checking is on. What this means is that the dialog box only displays elements that can be inserted at the current cursor position.

Using the rule checking feature in HoTMetaL, you cannot insert markup where it does not belong. For example, if you move the cursor between the begin and end markers for an `IMG` element, the `Insert Element` option on the `Markup` menu is grayed out because there are no tags you can insert into an `IMG` element. If you move the cursor between the begin and end markers for a `HEAD` element, the Insert Element dialog box displays only elements you can use in page headers, such as the `TITLE` element.

TIP

You can turn rules checking on or off by pressing `Ctrl+K` or by selecting `Turn Rules Checking On/Off` from the `Special` menu.

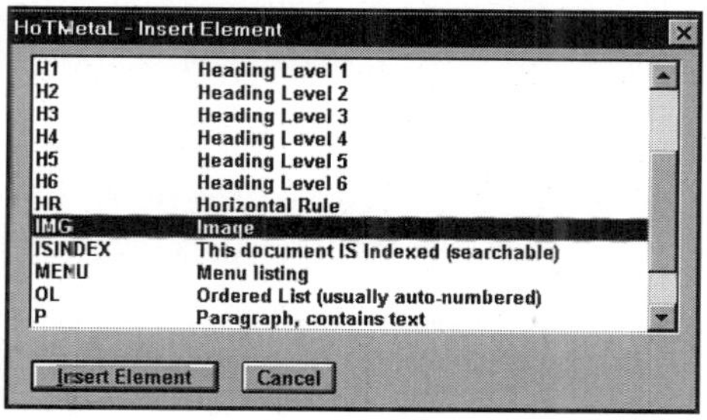

FIGURE 15.20.
Adding tags with the Insert Element dialog box.

Using HoTMetaL Pro

HoTMetaL Pro 3 is an advanced authoring system that supports the most current HTML specification and extensions. You will find that HoTMetaL Pro supports everything you want to use, including HTML 3.2, Java, ActiveX, objects, scripts and even Shockwave.

Like its counterpart HoTMetaL, HoTMetaL Pro follows an integrated WYSIWYG and tag marker approach. If you like the look and feel of HoTMetaL and are looking for advanced help with your page creation efforts, HoTMetaL Pro is for you.

A feature you'll want to check out is the multiple browser preview with which you can preview your page in any browser at the touch of a button. This feature is great if you want to test your page in several browsers. Other features include automatic conversion of other document formats to HTML. All you have to do is open a MS Word, WordPerfect, or AmiPro document in HoTMetaL Pro, and it is instantly converted to HTML.

The best feature of HoTMetaL Pro is the template system. Unlike the basic templates included with most of the other editors discussed in this chapter, HoTMetaL Pro's templates are as advanced as they come. You will find hundreds of templates with which you instantly can create pages, ready-made tables, frames, Java applets, scripts, and Shockwave animation.

You can access templates whenever you create a new page. To do this, select `New` from the `File` menu, and then select a template group. As you see in Figure 15.21, HoTMetaL Pro provides three general template groups: Company, Personal, and Intranet.

Another terrific feature of HoTMetaL Pro is the Frames Editor, which is one of the most advanced you'll find anywhere. As you see in Figure 15.22, creating a frame-enhanced page is done completely with an easy-to-use graphical interface. As you define frames, you can also define the document sources for the frames by dragging and dropping Web pages into your frames.

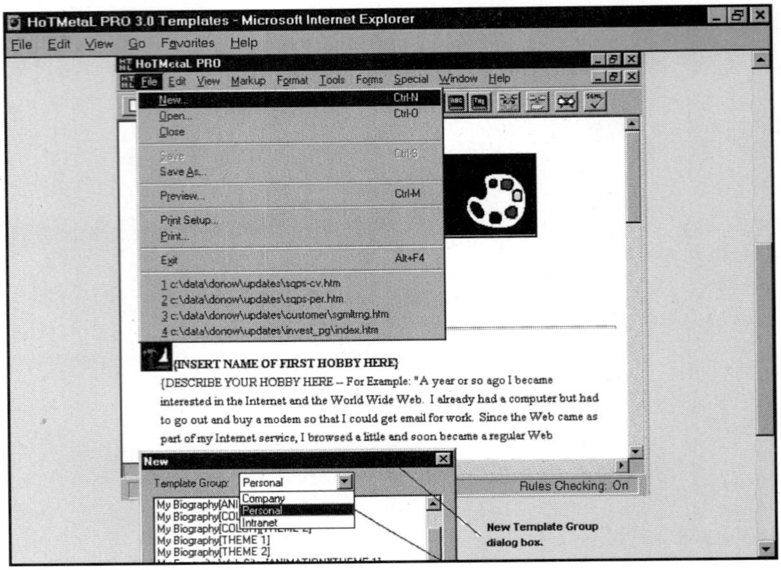

FIGURE 15.21.
Creating pages the easy way—with templates.

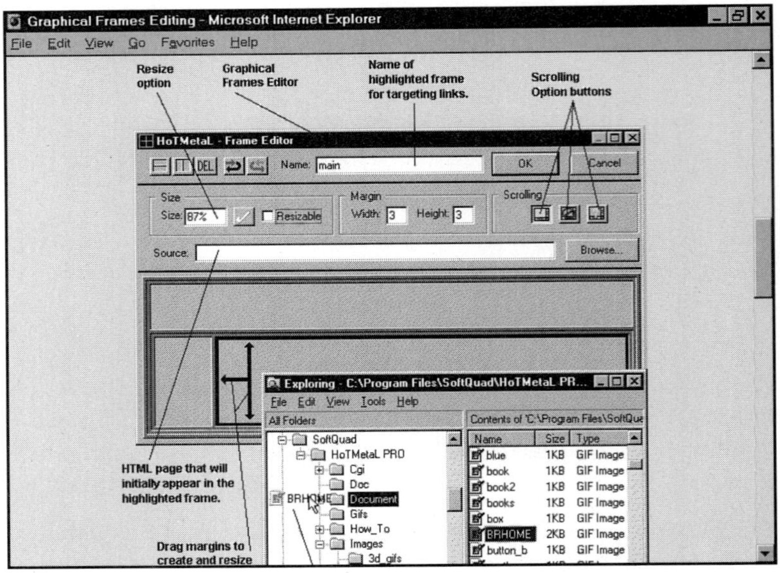

FIGURE 15.22.
HoTMetaL Pro's Frames Editor is terrific for creating frames without hassles.

HoTMetaL Pro comes with a built-in graphics editor called MetalWorks. Whenever you want to manipulate an image, all you need to do is right-click on the image to display a pop-up menu with which you can define image attributes, create transparent images, and build image maps. HoTMetaL Pro supports both server-side and client-side image maps.

As shown in Figure 15.23, building an image map from an existing image is handled through a dialog box called MetalWorks Map. Using this dialog box, you can create very precise image maps by enlarging or shrinking the image to suit your needs. Before you can define hot spots on the map, you must select a shape for the hot spot. Hot spots are circular, rectangular, or polygonal.

FIGURE 15.23.
Creating an image map with the built-in MetalWorks graphics editor.

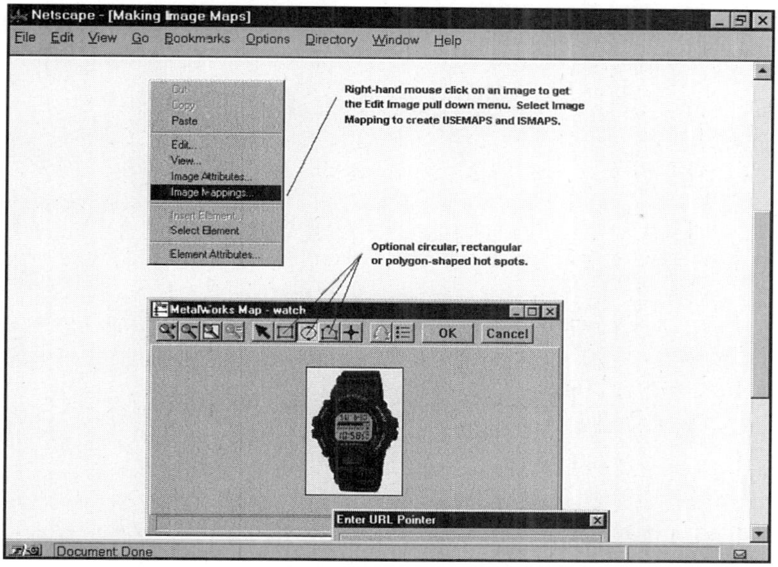

Summary

Many different types of HTML editors are available today. Beyond the high-end WYSIWYG tools is a whole range of editors. One of these editors may just fit your needs. Most developers produce a basic and an advanced version of their editor. Sometimes the basic version of an editor is the better value, especially if you don't need the fancy automation tools built into the advanced version.

Part IV

IN THIS PART

Enhancing Web Pages with Graphics

CHAPTER 16

Bigger, Faster, Better Graphics

by Dick Oliver

IN THIS CHAPTER

You don't have to be an artist to put high-impact graphics and creative type on your Web site. You don't need to spend hundreds or thousands of dollars on software, either. In this chapter, I show you the latest techniques to make the static elements on your pages look great and display quickly. I assume you are already familiar with HTML, though I do explain the syntax for implementing several advanced HTML tricks.

Don't Forget the Basics

The best place to begin gathering inspiration and raw materials for your new improved Web pages is the World Wide Web itself. When you see a fun or impressive graphic site, imagine what it would look like without the graphics, and think about how its creators made the images and coded any fancy text formatting.

Figure 16.1, the Entertainment Radio Network Web site, is the kind of site many Web wizards-to-be lust after: lots of highly polished graphics, an animated masthead that pieces itself together, and a professional announcer's voice that automatically welcomes you to the site if you have a sound card.

Figure 16.2, the Modern Ferrets home page, is pretty nifty, too—but far less polished and more than a little hokey. At least, that might be what you think when you see these two pages next to one another in a book. But the experience when you log on to these sites with a typical 28.8 Kbps modem is another story; 60 seconds after you log on to the Modern Ferrets home page, you will have read intriguing descriptions of the magazine, seen several photos of cute ferrets, and probably moved on to enjoy an illustrated ferret fairy tale or tips on keeping your furry friend well-groomed. But after 60 loooooong seconds at the "impressive" site, you will still be drumming your fingers waiting for the oh-so-prettily-rendered word *Talk* to slowly pour onto the screen and wondering what the name of the site might be as you watch all those puzzle tiles at the top of the screen move around.

The professional Web development team members who got paid big bucks for designing the Entertainment Radio Network site in Figure 16.1 knew that part of their job was to target people who would have the bandwidth to handle long audio downloads. A snazzy but slow site was the perfect choice for them.

The two young self-publishers who put together the Modern Ferrets home page in Figure 16.2 knew they didn't have to spend big money or long hours to build their home page. They also knew that most of their readers were probably low-budget modem users, so the speed of the site was important. The result may not be cutting-edge multimedia, but it does illustrate some important points that apply to all good graphic sites:

- The graphics convey the theme and mood of the topic effectively but are simple enough for a not-too-artsy person to create in an afternoon.
- The image looks big, but it is designed to compress efficiently and load quickly, even over a slow modem connection.

- Elements of the page could be reused on other pages (perhaps even your own, if you ask permission).

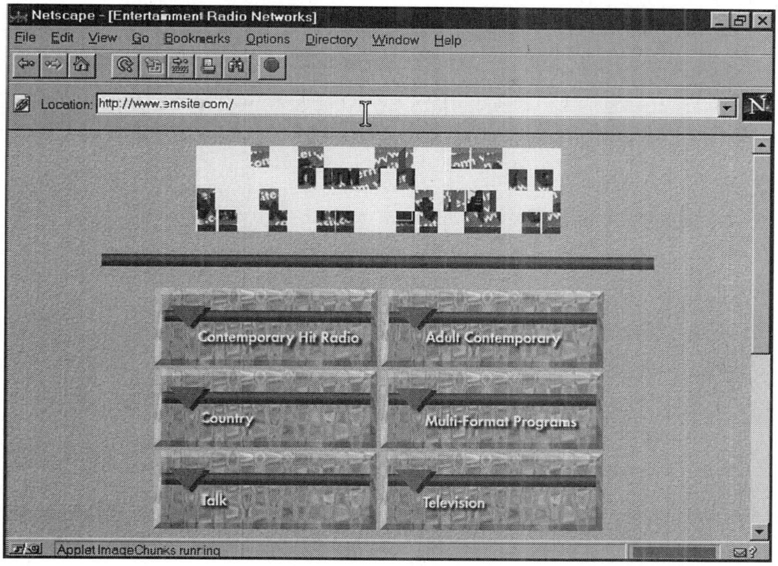

FIGURE 16.1.
This site was designed for high-bandwidth users; it's pretty, but deathly slow to display.

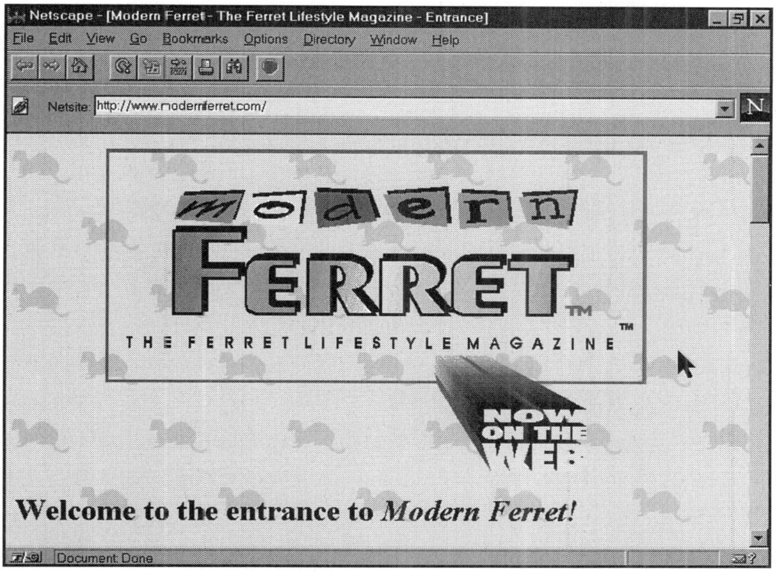

FIGURE 16.2.
Though not as polished as the site in Figure 16.1, this page displays much more quickly and conveys its message just as effectively.

As you explore the far reaches of contemporary Web publishing, keep in mind the principles that make the Modern Ferrets site serve its purpose well: simplicity, speed, and reusability. These principles become even more important as you invest more time and energy into creating a modern Web site.

To create effective Web sites, you need to know the needs of your intended audience and carefully balance coolness with quickness. In this chapter, I show you how to get the flavor of a high-end site without using large amounts of bandwidth and development time.

Finding Graphics on the Internet

One of the best ways to save time in creating graphics files is to avoid creating them altogether. With the entire World Wide Web at your fingertips, you have access to thousands of images and animations. Any graphic you see on any site is instantly reusable, as soon as the copyright holder grants (or sells) you the right to copy it. Because almost all Web pages include the e-mail address of their creators, asking permission to download and adopt a piece of artwork is usually quick and easy.

The familiar Web search engines and directories such as Yahoo! (`http://www.yahoo.com/`), Lycos (`http://lycos.cs.cmu.edu`), and InfoSeek (`http://www.infoseek.com/`) can become a gold mine of graphics images by leading you to sites related to your own theme. They can also help you discover the oodles of sites specifically dedicated to providing free and cheap access to reusable media collections.

A Lycos search for "background textures" turns up, among many other sites, Gini Schmitz's Texture and Background Wonderland, located at `http://netletter.com/cameo/hotlist/hotlist.htm` and pictured in Figure 16.3. This hotlist is one of my favorites, with links to consistently high-quality sites for finding great background tiles and graphic accents for Web pages. (Gini Schmitz is also the artist who created many of the graphics on the CD-ROM that comes with this book. These graphics are discussed later in this chapter.)

On the CD-ROM that comes with this book, you'll find live links to many other graphics and multimedia hotlists and hot sites. Links to all the major search engines are on there, too; just in case you don't already have them all on your own bookmark list.

Grabbing the Graphics You Find

Grabbing a graphic from a Web page is as simple as clicking it with the right mouse button and then picking `Save this image as` in Netscape Navigator or `Save Picture as` in Microsoft Internet Explorer (refer to Figure 16.3).

FIGURE 16.3.
Gini Schmitz's Textures and Backgrounds Wonderland is one of the best places to find lively graphics for your own Web pages.

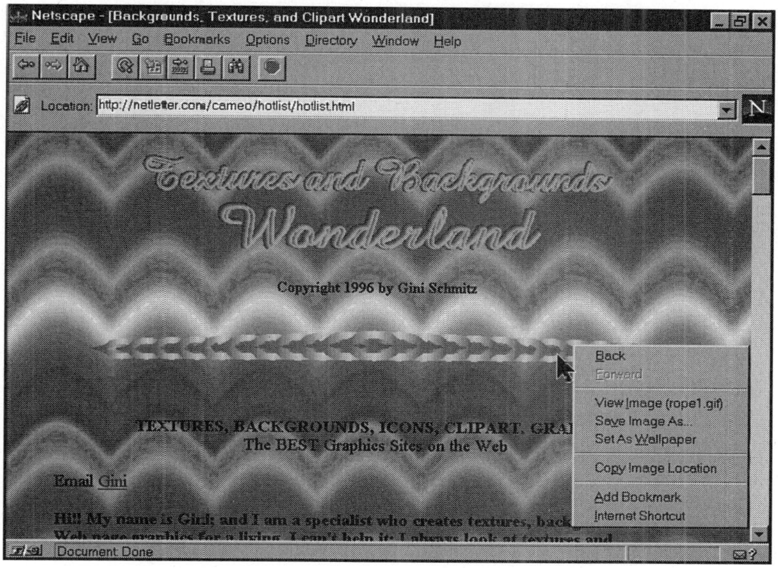

With Microsoft Internet Explorer, extracting a background image from a page is just as easy. Right-click the image and pick `Save Background As`. The procedure for grabbing a background image isn't quite so obvious in Netscape Navigator and most other Web browsers:

1. View the source code (select `View | Document Source` in Netscape; see Figure 16.4).
2. Select the file name in the `BACKGROUND=` attribute in the `<BODY>` tag and copy it to the Clipboard. (In Windows, hold down the Control key and press the Insert key.)
3. Close the source window.
4. Paste the file name by clicking in the `Location` box and pressing Shift+Insert, and then press Enter to go to that address.
5. The background file should appear, as shown in Figure 16.5. You can now use the `Save this image as` command from the menu bar or the right-click graphic menu to save the file.

FIGURE 16.4.
To find out the address of a background graphic in Netscape Navigator, view the source code for the HTML file.

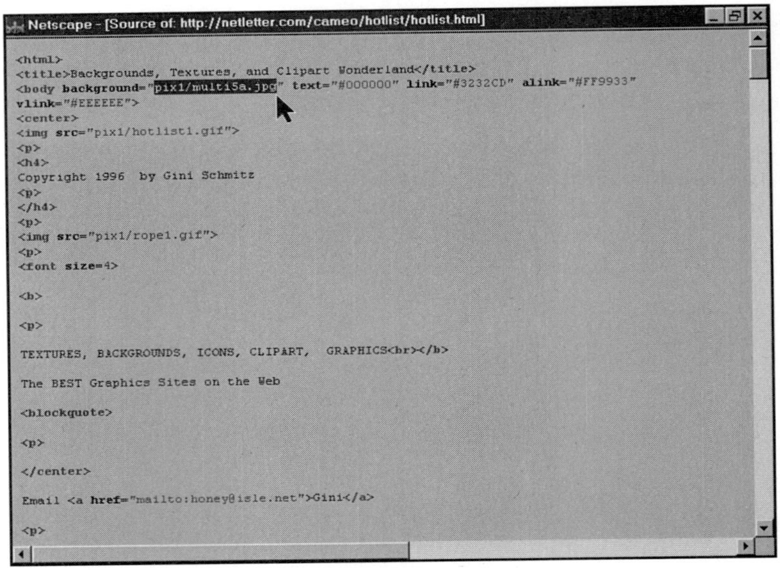

FIGURE 16.5.
When you load the background tile by itself, you can save it as you would any other image.

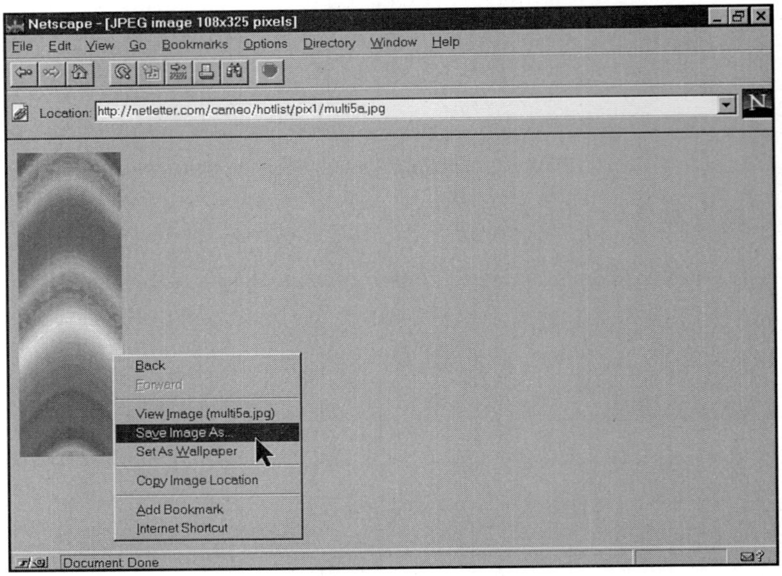

Archie and Veronica Go to the Pictures

If you're looking for something so specific that you can guess part of the file name or title, you can use the Internet indexing systems called Archie and Veronica to find graphics files that may not be accessible through the World Wide Web.

Even some experienced Webmasters have never used Archie and Veronica, so I'll explain the basics of using them to find graphics. I'll also let you in on the secret codes that enable you to limit your search to only graphics files.

NOTE

In the old days, you had to have special programs to access Archie and Veronica, but nowadays you can access them easily through the same browser program you use for the World Wide Web. Some advanced users still prefer the old-style search programs, but I'll explain how to do it without them.

Archie

Archie is a comprehensive, freely accessible, and automatically searchable index of every file accessible through public File Transfer Protocol (FTP). The bad news is that Archie only knows the names of the files and the names of the disk directories they're stored in. The files don't have any text description attached, so a picture of five elephants juggling on bicycles might be called `ejob5.jpg`. You could search Archie for the text *elephant*, *juggle*, and *bicycle* all day and not find the picture.

The good news is that people are generally nice, and they often give files descriptive names. There very well might be a picture file named `elephants-juggling.gif` stored right next to `ejob5.jpg`. The even better news is that many images have such specific content that you can easily guess what somebody would name the image file. If you were looking for an image of *The Three Stooges* TV show, an Archie search for the word *stooges* would be a pretty good bet. Archie also indexes directory names, so you may discover a whole directory full of files related to your search topic.

To search Archie, start by pointing your browser to the list of all Archie servers at

`http://pubweb.nexor.co.uk/public/Archie/servers.html`

Choose the Archie server nearest you or one located in a time zone where it is night and few local people will be using it.

To run a search, click the `What would you like to search for?` box and type the letters you want to search for. For the search type, you'll almost always want `Case Insensitive Substring Match` unless you know the exact name of the file you're looking for. Click the `Submit` button, and in a few seconds (sometimes longer at busy times), you will have a list of clickable links to every publicly archived file in the world containing the letters you searched for in its name.

Veronica

The image files that Archie finds are almost always hiding in a long list of other types of files with similar names. Of course, you can tell Archie to look for images containing the letters GIF or JPG if you want to increase the chances of hitting a graphics file. But wouldn't it be nice if you could just say, "Just find me image files, nothing else"? And while you're making out a wish list, it would also be handy if the files had short descriptions attached to them so you could search the descriptions for keywords, too.

Veronica is another master searchable index of public files. Like Archie, all Veronica needs from you is a few letters or words to search for, and away she goes to fetch every file she can find that matches your query. Most of the files Archie has access to are also accessible through Veronica.

Often, however, Veronica has access to longer descriptions of the files than Archie does. And more importantly, Veronica knows what type of file she's looking at and tells you by displaying the appropriate icon on the search result menu. Veronica searches often turn up thousands of matching files, only 200 or so of which are shown unless you request to see more. Even with handy icons to guide you, weeding through 200 files or more for the desired images is no fun.

TIP

You may notice that the search list Veronica comes up with is titled `Gopher menu`. The file system that Veronica indexes is called *Gopher* or sometimes *GopherSpace*. Gopher itself has been largely superseded by the World Wide Web, so you probably won't have much reason to access Gopher menus directly unless you're doing a Veronica search.

To save time, you can tell Veronica to find just graphics files and ignore everything else by entering `-tIg` (that's hyphen, small t, capital I, small g) as one of the words to search for. This code will command Veronica to show you only graphics.

The following example of a Veronica search should give you an idea of how the process works. First, pick a Veronica server from the list at

`http://www.scs.unr.edu/Veronica.html`

The Veronica search form (see Figure 16.6) is pretty basic. Just type the keywords and hit the Enter key. Along with the words to search for (which can be entered in any order), you can also give special commands to Veronica. For more information on the command language, choose the `How to Compose Veronica Queries` link from the Veronica server list page. As mentioned previously, if you enter `-tIg` as if it were one of your search words, Veronica will return only graphics images and ignore all other file types. You may also include menus and Web pages with the command `-tIgh1` (a hyphen followed by the letters *tIgh* and the number *1*) instead of just `-tIg`.

Figure 16.6 shows a Veronica query for images whose names or descriptions include the letters *wizard.* Veronica responds by building the Gopher menu shown in Figure 16.7, which leads to several images along the lines of Figure 16.8.

FIGURE 16.6.
Veronica offers an express lane down the yellow brick road.

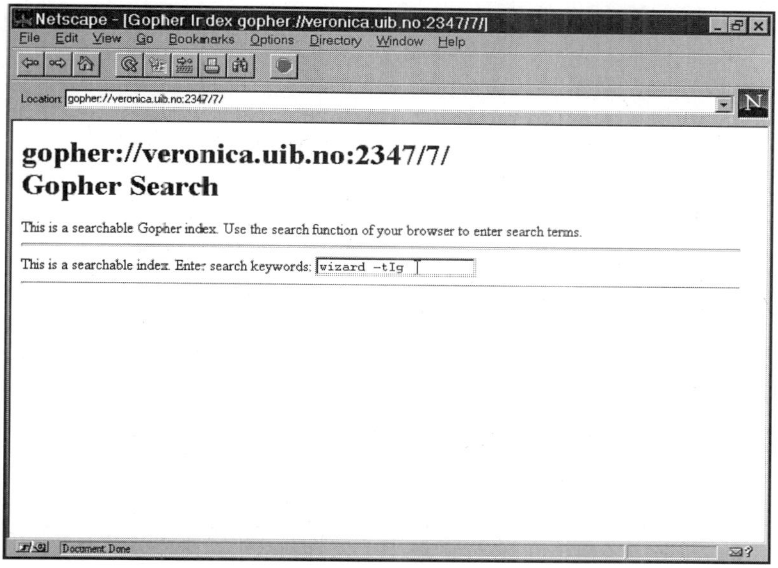

FIGURE 16.7.
In a flash of shimmering light, 24 wizards appear. Clicking each menu item will display or download the associated image.

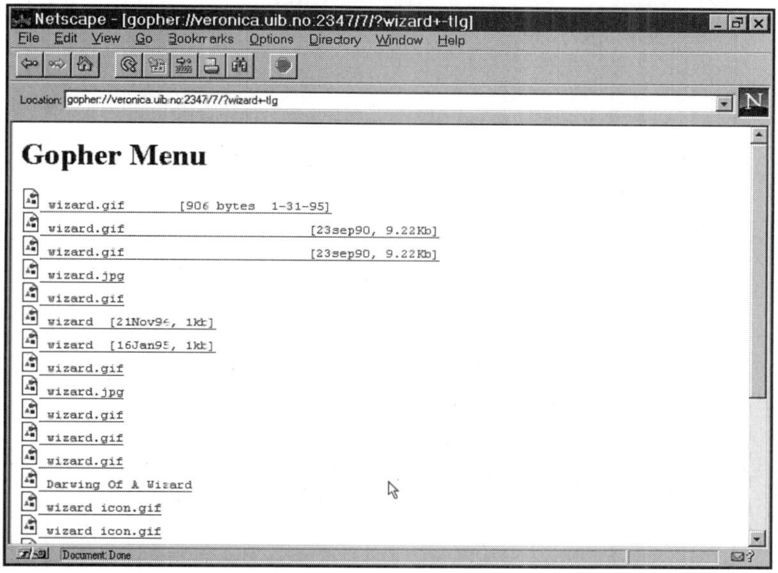

FIGURE 16.8.
This image could be handy if, for example, you want to illustrate the wizardry of searching the Internet for graphics.

How to Make 90 Percent of the Web Page Graphics You'll Ever Need

In this section, I explain some tricks that savvy Webmasters like you can use to maximize the impact and speed of the graphics on your pages. These techniques are illustrated with Paint Shop Pro, a shareware Windows graphics editor that comes on the CD-ROM with this book. If you haven't already installed Paint Shop Pro, you might want to do it before reading the rest of this chapter so you can play with the techniques as you go along.

NOTE

The Paint Shop Pro software on the CD-ROM is a fully functional shareware evaluation copy. If you agree with me that it's essential for working with Web page images, please be prompt about sending the $69 registration fee to the program's creators at JASC Software. (The address is in the online help in the software.) I'm confident that you're not going to find any other graphics software even close to the power and usability of Paint Shop Pro for anywhere near $69. (I have all the leading super-expensive commercial graphics programs from Photoshop on down, and Paint Shop Pro is the best by far for day-to-day work with Web graphics.)

There are so many ways to produce images with Paint Shop Pro, I can't even begin to explain them all. In this chapter and the next, I do offer a quick overview of some not-so-obvious techniques that are particularly well-suited for Web page graphics, but they barely scratch the surface of what you can do. You'll have to explore the rest on your own.

Make sure you check out the `Defornation` browser and `Filter` browser on the `Image` menu. These browsers give you access to a wide range of cool effects such as embossing, warping, and smearing, which are demonstrated by some of the images in this chapter. You should also make good use of the text tool, which can use any TrueType or Postscript font on your system to make fancy graphic headings for your Web pages.

Transparency

By setting a color in your GIF image to be transparent, you can make nonrectangular graphics look good over any background color or background image tile. To make a color in a GIF file transparent, follow these steps in Paint Shop Pro:

1. Choose the eyedropper tool.
2. Right-click the color you want to make transparent.
3. Select `File | Save As`.
4. Choose the `GIF file format` and `Version 89a-Noninterlaced` subformat (interlaced transparent GIFs are possible, but often don't display correctly).
5. Click the `Options` button.
6. Choose `Set the transparency value to the background color` as shown in Figure 16.9 and click `OK`.
7. Enter a name for the file, and then click `OK` to save it.

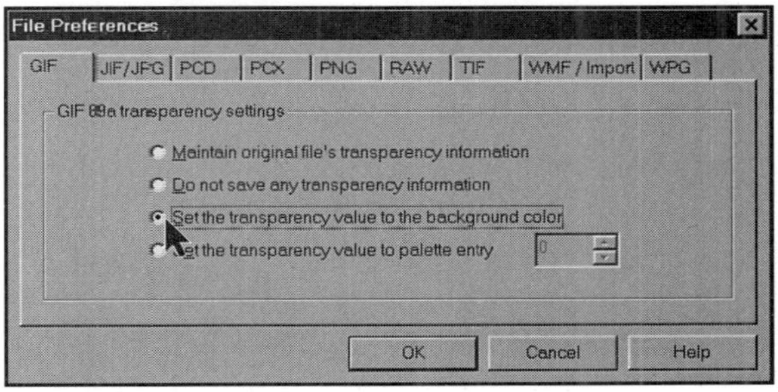

FIGURE 16.9.
Paint Shop Pro's File Preferences dialog box lets you choose which palette color will become transparent.

TIP

For a masked preview of which part of the image will be transparent, select `Colors | Edit Palette` and change the transparent palette color to some outrageous fluorescent green or another highly visible hue. Or you may want to set it to the dominant color of the background you plan to place the image over to get an idea of how the image will look on the page.

Backgrounds and Text Colors

Background tiling started as another unofficial extension to HTML, but it has quickly gained near-universal support. This powerful feature enables you to specify an image file to be used as a wallpaper tile behind all text and images in a document. It is implemented as an attribute in the `<BODY>` tag like in the following:

```
<BODY BACKGROUND="blues.gif"> (document text goes here) </BODY>
```

As Figure 16.10 shows, background tiling can be combined with transparent images to add flair to your pages. Be warned, however, that some browsers don't always handle backgrounds and transparent images correctly. Background tiling also can significantly increase the time it takes for a page to download and display if you're not careful to keep your background image files reasonably small.

FIGURE 16.10.
A good background can add color and interest to transparent graphics.

A faster way to wield some control over the background in Netscape is to use the body color extensions. These extensions enable you to specify a color for the background, text, and hotlinks. No extra images must be loaded or processed, so images still download and display at maximum speed.

You can specify colors by name or number. You can specify the basic colors by using the English words *blue*, *green*, *purple*, and so forth. To make the background blue, the text white, and the links yellow, for example, you would use the following:

```
<BODY BGCOLOR="blue" TEXT="white" LINK="yellow">
```

You can also specify a color for links that have already been visited with `ALINK=` and a color for links to blink when they're activated with `VLINK=`.

TIP

If you set `VLINK` and `BGCOLOR` to the same color on a home page or hotlist, every link the visitor has already been to seems to disappear!

You can mix your own custom colors in the format *#rrggbb*, where *rr*, *gg*, and *bb* are a two-digit hexadecimal values for the red, green, and blue components of the color. If you're not familiar with hexadecimal numbers, don't sweat it: just remember that `FF` is the maximum, `00` is the minimum, and `88` is in the middle. To make the background white, the text black, and the links blue, you would say

```
<BODY BGCOLOR="#FFFFFF" TEXT="#000000" LINK="#0000FF">
```

Use custom colors with caution, however, because they can make many computers display distracting dithered patterns behind text. You should generally stick to the basic named colors that almost every computer will show without any dithering: black, white, red, green, blue, yellow, magenta, and cyan. Aqua, fuchsia, lime, maroon, navy, olive, gray, silver, and teal are also valid color names, but they are not as reliable as the pure colors.

NOTE

You can change the text colors at any point during the document with the `FONT COLOR=` attribute. For example, to make the word *CAUTION* appear red, you could say

```
<FONT COLOR="red">CAUTION:</FONT> this page is HOT!
```

You'll find out much more about the `<FONT>` tag in Chapter 18, "Creative Uses of Text, Fonts, and Type."

Matters of Size

Two forces are always at odds when you post graphics and multimedia on the Net. Your eyes and ears want everything to be as detailed and accurate as possible, but your clock and wallet want files to be as small as possible. Intricate, colorful graphics mean big file sizes, which can take a long time to transfer even over a fast connection. Add smooth animation and high-quality sound, and file sizes get truly astronomical. As a result, quality usually has to take a back seat to file size, especially now that most people on the Net are using inexpensive modems and not high-speed university trunk lines.

So how do you find the right balance? And how do you maximize the quality of your presentation while minimizing file size? To make these choices, you need to understand what your options are and how color depth and resolution work together to create a subjective sense of quality. The next few paragraphs contain a concise summary of what you need to know about color and resolution. Quality and size issues for sound, animation, and interactive media are also discussed.

Graphics Resolution

The vertical and horizontal resolutions are the height and width of the image, measured in pixels (the individual dots that make up a digital image). Color depth is the number of bits of information used to describe each pixel. Each bit can have two values, so two bits can have four unique values (2×2), four bits can have 16 unique values (2×2×2×2), and so on. For most images you put on the Net, a color lookup table or palette is included in the image file to specify which color corresponds to each value.

If you use enough bits per pixel, however, you can describe the color in terms of its red, green, and blue color components, and you don't need a color lookup table. Most often, these true color images use 24 bits per pixel, which provide more colors than the human eye can distinguish. Some graphics cards use only 15, 16, or 18 bits to display true color images, but the graphics files themselves usually include all 24 bits of color information even if you can't see them all on your graphics card.

All these factors together determine the overall size of the image file. Table 16.1 shows all the common color depths, resolutions, and the resulting theoretical size of the image, including the color lookup table. Before you dive into the long list of numbers in Table 16.1, take a look at Figures 16.11 through 16.16. Figures 16.11 through 16.13 show an image at one size, but with increasing color depth (here the images are of course approximated in gray—the differences would be even more pronounced in full color). Figures 16.14 through 16.16 show a black-and-white image at increasing horizontal and vertical resolution.

FIGURE 16.11.
An image using two colors.

FIGURE 16.12.
The same image using 16 colors.

FIGURE 16.13.
The same image using 256 colors.

FIGURE 16.14.
A two-color image at a resolution of 160×120 pixels.

FIGURE 16.15.
A two-color image at a resolution of 320×240 pixels.

FIGURE 16.16.
A two-color image at a resolution of 640×480 pixels.

Table 16.1. How color depth and resolution affect the theoretical (uncompressed) file size (1 K=1,024 bytes=8,192 bits).

	Bits Per Pixel(Number of Colors)				
Resolution	*1(2)*	*4(16)*	*8(256)*	*15(32,768)*	*24(16,777,216)*
160×120 pixels	3 K	10 K	20 K	35 K	58 K
320×200 pixels	8 K	31 K	64 K	117 K	188 K
640×480 pixels	37 K	150 K	300 K	563 K	900 K
800×600 pixels	59 K	234 K	469 K	879 K	1,406 K
1024×768 pixels	96 K	384 K	769 K	1,440 K	2,304 K

To estimate how long it will typically take for your images to download, you can assume that a standard 28.8 Kbps modem with a good connection to a Net site can pull about two kilobytes (that is, 2 K) per second on average.

Remember, though, that many people are still accessing the Net through 14.4 Kbps or slower modems. As a general rule, any Web page that includes more than 50 K worth of graphics should only be accessed from another, less graphics-intensive page. Links to the graphics-intensive page should warn the readers so they can turn off their Web browsers' automatic graphics downloading if they are using a slow dial-up modem connection.

Reducing Color Depth

As Table 16.1 suggests, one of the most effective ways to reduce the download time for an image is to reduce the number of colors. In Paint Shop Pro, you can do this by selecting `Colors | Reduce Color Depth`. (Most other graphics programs have a similar option.) The software will automatically find the best palette of 16 or 256 colors for approximating the full range of colors in the image.

When you reduce the number of colors in an image, you will see a dialog box with several choices (see Figure 16.17). For Web page images, you will almost always want to choose an `Optimized` or `Weighted` palette and `Nearest Color` instead of `Error Diffusion` or any form of dithering.

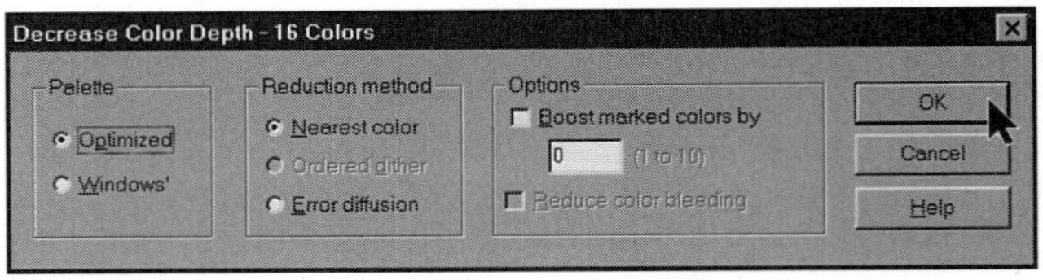

FIGURE 16.17.
Reducing the color depth of an image can dramatically reduce file sizes without changing the appearance of the image too much.

> **TIP**
>
> *Dithering* (called *error diffusion* in Paint Shop Pro) means using random dots or patterns to intermix palette colors. This process can make images look better in some cases, but you should usually avoid it for Web page graphics. It substantially increases the information complexity of an image, and that almost always results in much larger file sizes and slower downloads. So, listen to your Great Uncle Oliver and "don't dither!"

Achieving Maximum Compression

Most images will actually take much less space on your hard drive than Table 16.1 indicates because they are stored in a compressed format. How much an image can be compressed depends on the image. A truly random sea of static image wouldn't compress at all, and a solid color image would compress to well under a kilobyte no matter what its resolution. Generally the GIF images most often found on the Net achieve somewhere around 4:1 compression (meaning that a file would typically take up a quarter as much space as is listed in Table 16.1).

JPEG compression, however, can squeeze images even smaller. They'll usually start showing noticeable degradation at compression ratios greater than 4:1, but true color photographic images will sometimes tolerate JPEG compression as tight as 10:1 without too much uglification. You can control the JPEG compression ratio in many graphics programs, including Paint Shop Pro. Figure 16.18 shows the JPEG Save As Options dialog box. You can control the compression ratio for saving JPEG files by adjusting the compression level setting between 1 percent (low quality, small file size) and 99 percent (high quality, large file size).

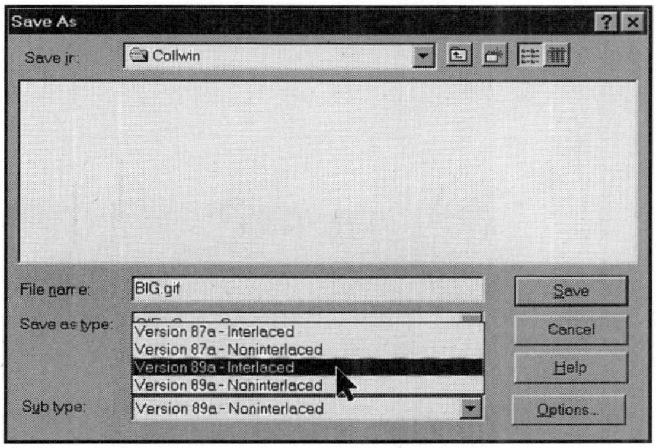

FIGURE 16.18.
Paint Shop Pro allows you to trade reduced file size for image quality when saving JPEG images.

Figures 16.19 through 16.22 compare the results of saving a graphics file at various JPEG compression quality settings (keep in mind that the differences are more obvious in color), and Table 16.2 indicates how these settings affect the file size. If you were surfing the Net, would you rather wait nearly half a minute to see this image in its full glory, or watch it pop onto your screen at 75 percent quality in less than six seconds? That's the kind of difference that makes JPEG a hard format to beat for storing true color graphics on the Net. Unfortunately, images that are larger than this 320×200 example usually don't compress quite as efficiently.

Table 16.2. Relative file sizes of the image in Figures 16.19 through 16.22, and approximate transfer time over a 25.8 Kbps modem connection.

Color Depth	*Actual File Format*	*Approximate File Size*	*Approximate Compression Ratio*	*Transfer Time*
24 bit	Uncompressed TGA	190.5 K	1:1	95 seconds
8 bit	Compressed GIF	51.4 K	4:1	26 seconds
24 bit	"Near perfect" JPEG	54.3 K	4:1	27 seconds
24 bit	95 percent JPEG (see Figure 16.19)	32.5 K	6:1	16 seconds

continues

Table 16.2. continued

Color Depth	*Actual File Format*	*Approximate File Size*	*Approximate Compression Ratio*	*Transfer Time*
24 bit	75 percent JPEG (see Figure 16.20)	11.3 K	17:1	6 seconds
24 bit	50 percent JPEG (see Figure 16.21)	7.3 K	26:1	4 seconds
24 bit	25 percent JPEG (see Figure 16.22)	4.6 K	40:1	2 seconds

FIGURE 16.19.
A scanned photo saved as a JPEG file at 95 percent compression quality.

FIGURE 16.20.
A scanned photo saved as a JPEG file at 75 percent compression quality.

FIGURE 16.21.
A scanned photo saved as a JPEG file at 50 percent compression quality.

FIGURE 16.22.
A scanned photo saved as a JPEG file at 25 percent compression quality.

Progressive Display and Interlacing

After you've compressed your files as tightly as possible, what more can you do to make them download and display faster? A lot! There are three ways to make a rough draft of an image appear well before the entire image is finished downloading. This can have a dramatic psychological effect, making the images seem to come up almost instantly even though they may take quite a while to completely finish downloading.

Interlaced GIFs

The most popular way to get an illusion of speed is to use a special kind of GIF file called an *interlaced GIF.* In a noninterlaced image file, the top line of pixels is stored first, and then the next line down is stored, and then the next line after that, and so on. In an interlaced file, only every other line is saved and then the missing lines are filled in at the end of the file. Most Web browsers will display interlaced GIFs as they are being read, so a rough draft of the image appears quickly. The details are filled in as the download finishes.

Most graphics programs that can handle GIF files enable you to choose whether to save them interlaced or noninterlaced. In Paint Shop Pro, for example, you can choose the `Version 89a—Interlaced File` sub-format on the Save As dialog box just before you save a GIF file (see Figure 16.23).

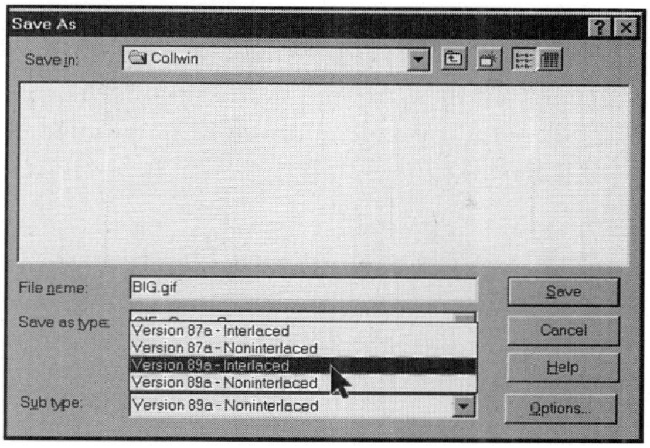

FIGURE 16.23.
Paint Shop Pro lets you save interlaced GIF images, which appear to display faster when loading.

Progressive JPEGs

The JPEG format has its own corollary to interlaced GIF, called *progressive JPEG*. The mathematics are a bit more complex than interlacing, but the effect is essentially the same: a blurry version of the picture appears first and is replaced by a more precise rendition as the image finishes downloading.

Unfortunately, at this writing, the progressive JPEG standard is quite new and is only supported by the latest versions of Netscape Navigator and Microsoft Internet Explorer. As older browsers become less commonplace, progressive JPEGs will undoubtedly become quite popular.

NOTE

Browsers that don't support progressive JPEG will *not* display the file as if it were just a regular JPEG; they will display nothing at all or a message saying the file isn't recognizable. So don't put progressive JPEGs on your pages unless you're sure that all your intended audience will be using a browser that supports them! (Interlaced GIFs, on the other hand, will appear correctly even in older browsers that don't support two-stage display.)

HTML Extensions for Speedy Display

The third way for graphics to appear faster than they really are is to use the `LOWSRC`, `WIDTH`, and `HEIGHT` attributes, which are HTML extensions to the `<IMG>` tag. These attributes are currently only supported by Netscape Navigator, but other browsers will just ignore these tags. So you can use them safely even if some visitors to your site may not be using Netscape.

The LOWSRC attribute specifies an image to be loaded and displayed before the image specified in the SRC attribute. The idea is to load a quick two-color GIF or lossy JPEG image first, and then immediately replace it with a more colorful or detailed version of the same image. Basically, LOWSRC enables you to simulate the effect of an interlaced GIF or progressive JPEG by using two separate images.

The two images don't have to look similar. By using two completely different images, you can create a clever little two-frame animation or overlay effect. Keep in mind, however, that the LOWSRC image is not displayed at all if Netscape can find the SRC image in its memory or disk cache from a recent download. So if viewers return to your page more than once in a session, they usually won't see your nifty LOWSRC animation effect.

The WIDTH and HEIGHT attributes specify the size (in pixels) to make an image. Normally, these attributes are the actual width and height of the image and are used by Netscape to lay out the page quickly and display any text that follows an image without having to load the image first. But they can also be used to resize an image to fit a larger (or smaller) space. For example, if big.gif was a 200×200 pixel image, you could make a 100×100 pixel version called small.gif and use the following HTML command on your Web page:

```
<IMG SRC="big.gif" LOWSRC="small.gif" WIDTH=200 HEIGHT=200>
```

The smaller version would load first, and Netscape would automatically enlarge it to 200×200 pixels. Then the full-size version would overlay it as soon as it loaded.

Doing It All at Once

By using transparency, interlaced GIFs, and LOWSRC all at once, you can make the image display in several separate stages, with each stage appearing more detailed. Even the slowest modem users get something to look at quickly and an interesting progression of layers to keep them entertained while the final image loads.

Figures 16.24 through 16.28 show the four stages that appear when you load the sample document designed earlier in this chapter. (To see this for yourself, open the /examples/look/bfb.htm file on the CD-ROM with Netscape Navigator.) Figure 16.28 is the final appearance of this page.

TIP

If you're going to the trouble of making graphics appear fast to slow modem users, don't forget that many people will not see the graphics on your Web pages at all. Even those using graphics-capable browsers often surf with graphics downloading turned off to reduce download times over a slow modem connection.

HTML gives you a way to send a special message to readers who don't see your graphics. Each image can be given an ALT= attribute that will display the text you specify whenever the image itself can't be shown. Here's an example:

```
<IMG SRC="triangle.gif" ALT="WARNING:"> This page is radioactive on some
monitors.
```

If the image file `triangle.gif` couldn't be displayed, most browsers would display the word `WARNING:` instead.

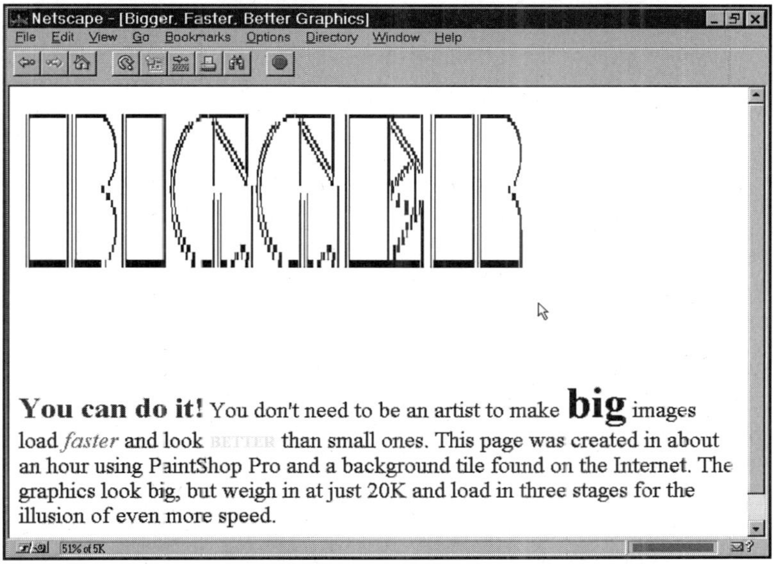

FIGURE 16.24.
The first thing you see is a blocky image. This is the first pass of the interlaced `LOWSRC` *image loading.*

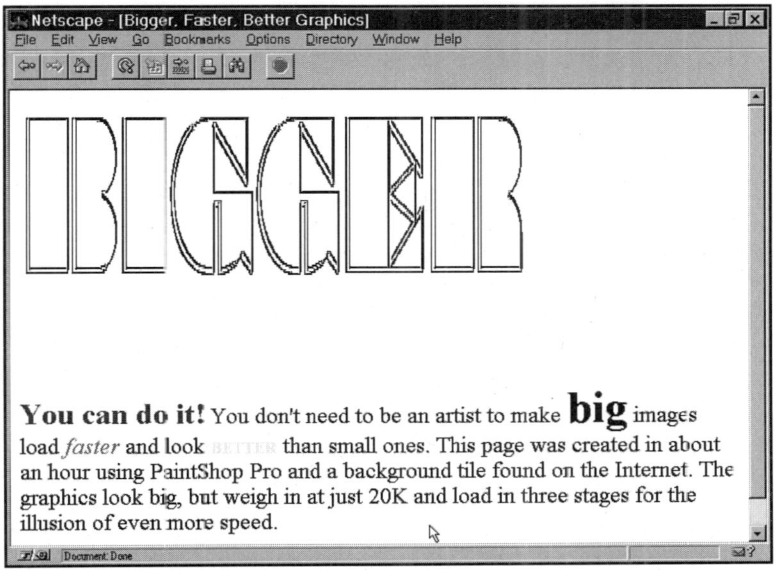

FIGURE 16.25.
Next, the more detailed second pass loads.

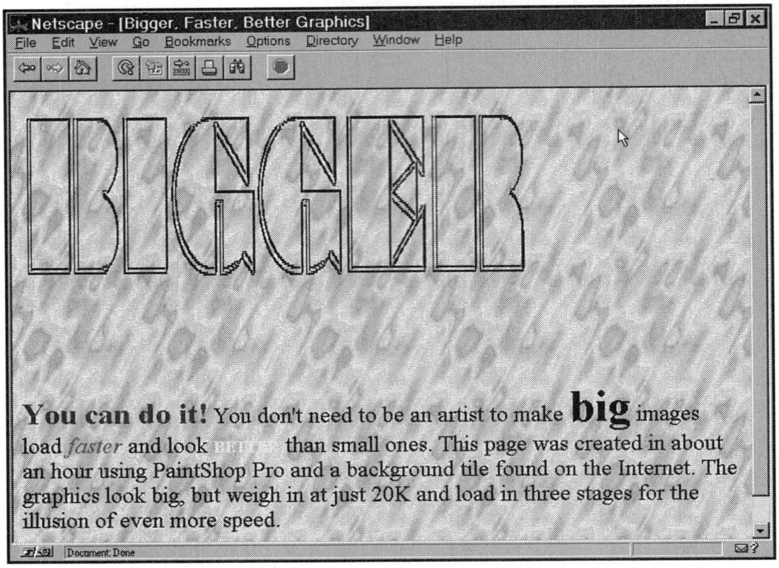

FIGURE 16.26.
As soon as Netscape finishes loading the background tile image, it is displayed under whatever is on the screen at that moment.

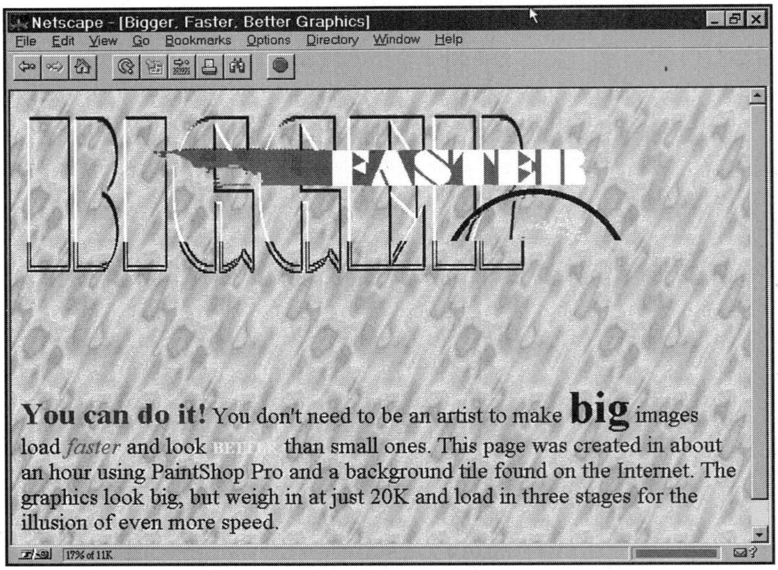

FIGURE 16.27.
Finally, the LOWSRC *image is gradually replaced by the* SRC *image as it downloads.*

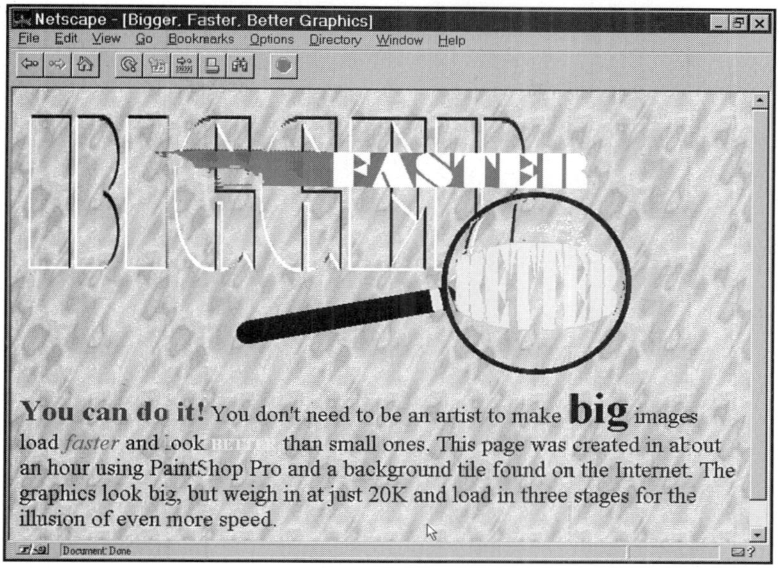

FIGURE 16.28.
The page shown in Figures 16.24 through 16.27 as it looks when it's completely finished loading.

Summary

This LOWSRC business can be a cheap and easy way to do super-simple animation without the need for you or your viewing audience to mess with extra plug-ins, helper applications, or Java applets. Chapter 19, "Animating Graphical Images," shows you some much better—and almost as cheap—ways to get animation without the fuss.

Meanwhile, Chapter 17, "Working with JPEG and GIF Images," explains in detail how to create and enhance Web graphics with Paint Shop Pro. Chapter 18, "Creative Uses of Text, Fonts, and Type," explores some sneaky ways to get creative with the words on your Web pages.

CHAPTER 17

Working with JPEG and GIF Images

by Dick Oliver

IN THIS CHAPTER

Whether you are painting your Web page graphics "by hand," modifying existing artwork, or scanning your favorite photos, graphics software like Paint Shop Pro can do some of the hardest work for you.

This chapter shows you how to find, scan, or capture existing graphics and introduces a host of automatic tools to create, modify, and enhance images at the push of a button. Then it explains how to use certain effects to create snazzy buttons, 3D titles, and backgrounds as quick as you can click.

Most of the examples in this chapter will use Paint Shop Pro, a shareware graphics program included on the CD-ROM with this book and introduced in Chapter 16, "Bigger, Faster, Better Graphics." Most other commercial graphics programs include similar commands to the ones demonstrated in Paint Shop Pro.

Capturing Screen Shots

You probably use your computer for other things besides building Web pages. You may even use it to build old-fashioned paper pages with a word processor or page layout program. Or perhaps you've created or bought some other programs that display interesting graphics or type. In any of these situations, and many others, transferring part of an image you see on your computer screen to a Web page can be useful.

Figure 17.1 shows a carefully laid-out page that I created in Adobe PageMaker for a paper publication. Suppose I wanted to post this page on the Internet. How would I do it? Even though PageMaker has a built-in Web page export feature, I would lose all the fancy typography and borders at the top of the page if I used it. PageMaker doesn't have a command that enables me to export this entire title as a graphic that I could load into Paint Shop Pro.

The solution to my dilemma is to capture an image of the title from my computer screen while the PageMaker program is running. There are two easy ways to do this:

- Use Windows' built-in screen capture capabilities by pressing the Print Screen key to capture the entire screen or Alt+Print Screen to capture the active window. Then select `Edit | Paste | Into New Image` Paint Shop Pro to paste the image from the Clipboard.
- Use Paint Shop Pro's `Capture` menu to grab the image directly. This method is usually faster and gives you a number of options (see Figure 17.2) that Windows' built-in screen capture doesn't provide.

In this case, I opened both PageMaker and Paint Shop Pro at the same time and hid all page layout guidelines in PageMaker. Then I selected `Capture | Setup` in Paint Shop Pro, made sure that `Capture/Area` was selected, and clicked the `Capture Now` button. Paint Shop Pro automatically minimized its own window so PageMaker's window became visible.

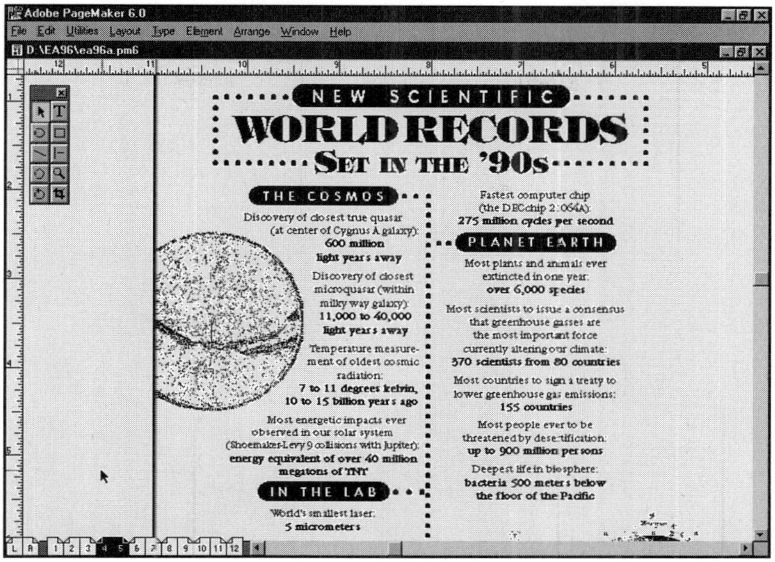

FIGURE 17.1.
You can't export the title and layout of this page to a Web page without losing formatting.

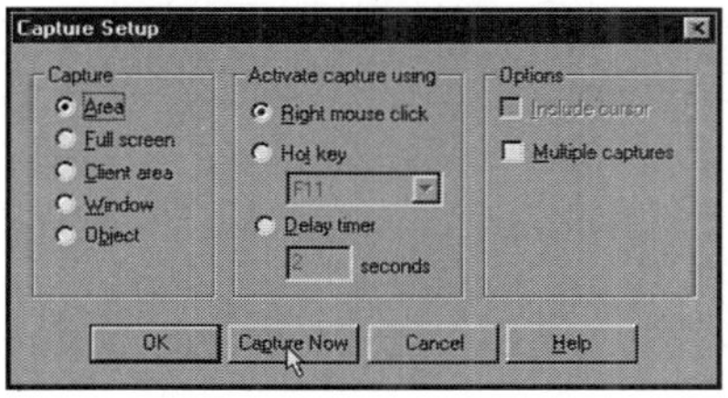

FIGURE 17.2.
Paint Shop Pro offers a number of time-saving options for screen captures that the Print Screen key doesn't provide.

I clicked with the right mouse button inside the PageMaker window, and the mouse cursor turned to a crosshair. This crosshair indicates that Paint Shop Pro is ready for an area to be specified. One left-button click to the top left of the title and one click to the lower right corner of the title is all it takes for the image to be cropped and captured directly into Paint Shop Pro. (If I had selected `Full Screen`, `Client Area`, `Window`, `rom` or `Object` instead of `Area` in the `Capture Setup` dialog box, only one right mouse click would have been needed to capture the image.)

Once the title graphic has been captured, you can use any of Paint Shop Pro's tools and commands to modify the image. Generally, I recommend saving one copy of the image as captured (see top image in Figure 17.3) and using `Edit | Copy` followed by `Edit | Paste | As new image` to create a working copy before you make any modifications (see bottom image in Figure 17.3). That way, if you don't like your changes, you won't have to set up the screen capture again to get the original file back.

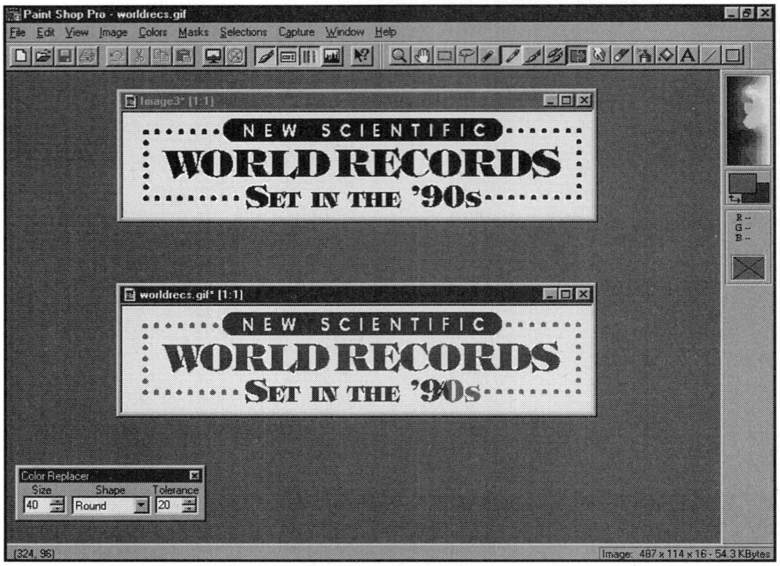

FIGURE 17.3.
A screen capture brought this title into Paint Shop Pro from PageMaker at just the right resolution for a Web page.

> **TIP**
>
> If you have other graphics software, such as CorelDRAW!, Adobe Illustrator, or a 3D rendering program, it is probably capable of exporting some file format that Paint Shop Pro can open. (To browse the extensive list of file formats which Paint Shop Pro can handle, select `File | Save As` and pull down the `Save As Type` list.)
>
> However, the graphics files that your applications save may be at a resolution that is better for paper printing or video production than Web pages, and there can often be a significant difference between the colors you see on the screen and the colors you'll see when you open the resulting graphics file.
>
> You may often find it faster and more reliable to simply capture images straight from the screen while a graphics application is running. That way you know the image will appear on your Web page exactly as you see it when you do the capture. This method is also an easy way to capture still images from video clips as you play them back on your screen.

Modifying Graphics for Your Pages

Imagine for a moment that you want to put that "Scientific World Records" page on the Web. You've captured the fancy title shown in Figure 17.3. You've selected a suitable background graphic, and you've got all the graphics files that were used to print the paper version of the page. So you toss all those graphics together with a little HTML and you should be all set, right?

Wrong. The requirements for Web graphics are radically different than the requirements for printed graphics. In fact, almost all the rules are reversed:

- For paper, you want giant, high-resolution graphics files. For the Web, you want small graphics that load fast and look good on a relatively low-resolution computer screen.
- Printing color ain't cheap, and preparing color graphics for printing is a complex and often agonizing endeavor. On the Web, color is easy to work with and is almost free.
- Once a document is on paper, it doesn't change until the next print run. Web documents often need to be updated quickly.
- On paper, dark colors bleed into the light colors, and it's a struggle to make bright colors shine. On a computer screen, lighter colors leap out and overwhelm nearby dark areas.

The bottom line is that graphics created for print publications seldom work unmodified for Internet publication. Because most clip art and stock photography was originally designed for print publications, you need to be aware of these differences even if you've never printed a paper page in your life.

Resizing Graphics

Figure 17.4 shows two fairly typical images from a clip art collection, which were used to illustrate the paper version of the article on scientific world's records. Notice that the files are very large; the lower right corner of the Paint Shop Pro window indicates that the image of the Earth is 1,656 by 1,131 pixels. Also notice that the one-third-sized rendition shown doesn't look very interesting because much detail is lost.

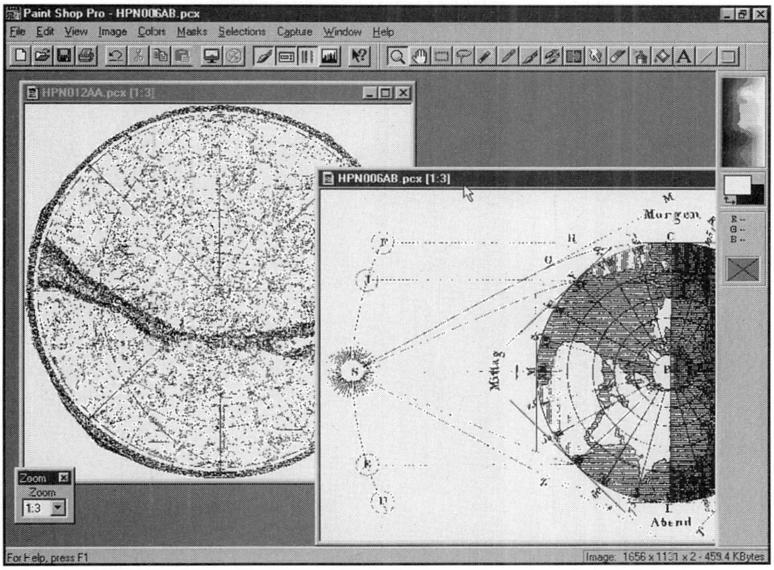

FIGURE 17.4.
These clip art images would print well on paper, but are too big and too intricate for Web pages.

To make these images smaller while losing as little detail as possible, I converted them to grayscale by choosing `Colors | Increase Color Depth | 256 Colors` and then selecting `Image | Resample`. The `Resample` command uses sophisticated image processsing math to maintain the best quality when shrinking an image. If I had used `Image | Resize` instead, the results would have been dramatically less detailed.

TIP

To squeeze the absolute best out of images when you reduce their size, always try to resample to exactly one-half, one-quarter, or one-eighth the original size if possible. The mathematical reasons why this works better are beyond what I could explain in this little tip, but trust me, it works.

For example, a 1200×800 pixel image will usually look better when resampled down to exactly 300×200 pixels than it would if you resampled it to 312×208 pixels, even though the 312×208 image is slightly bigger. If the requirements of your page don't allow a division in size by exactly two, four, or eight, stick to other simple division factors like three, five, or six.

Another technique for bringing out detail in graphics that will be viewed mostly on a computer screen is to make sure that any thin lines are in a lighter color than the background around them (the opposite of what you'd do on paper). In this case, simply negating the image colors works well to portray stars and a planet in space. Figure 17.5 shows the final images reduced, recolored, and ready for the Web.

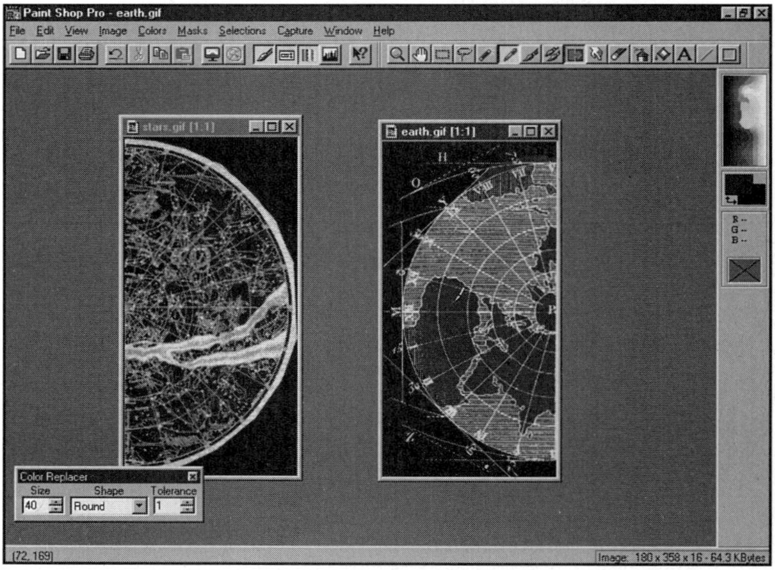

FIGURE 17.5.
White-on-black shows details better on computer screens than black-on-white.

Once the overall size of the images is reduced, you may still need to crop them and reduce the number of colors to get the file size down. The images in Figure 17.5 were reduced to 16 colors with the `Colors | Increase Color Depth` command after some color adjustments with the `Colors | Adjust | Gamma Correct` and `Colors | Adjust | Brightness | Contrast` commands.

All these techniques together reduced the star map image file from 180 K to 23 K in size and the Earth image from 90 K to 18 K. These images are still a bit large for Web pages, but they couldn't be reduced much more without losing so much detail that they'd be difficult to recognize. Because of the relatively large file sizes, I chose to save them as interlaced GIFs, which will display a blurred version of the file long before it is completely done downloading. Because these graphics aren't essential in understanding the text content of the page, visitors won't need to wait for the images to finish downloading before they start reading the page.

Customizing and Correcting Images

Such cosmic graphics deserve a suitably celestial background. A starry background tile I found through the Textures and Backgrounds Wonderland site mentioned in Chapter 16 (`http://netletter.com/cameo/hotlist/hotlist.htm`) does the trick nicely. However, like many backgrounds available on the Web, this background is intentionally provided at a larger size than is appropriate for most Web pages. (Gini Schmitz, the background guru who created it, knows that it's easier to reduce the size of an image than to increase it.)

As with the grayscale graphics discussed earlier, `Image | Resample` is also the command of choice for reducing the size of full-color graphics. In Figure 17.6, the image is resampled to exactly half its original size in each dimension (from 250×250 pixels to 125×125 pixels).

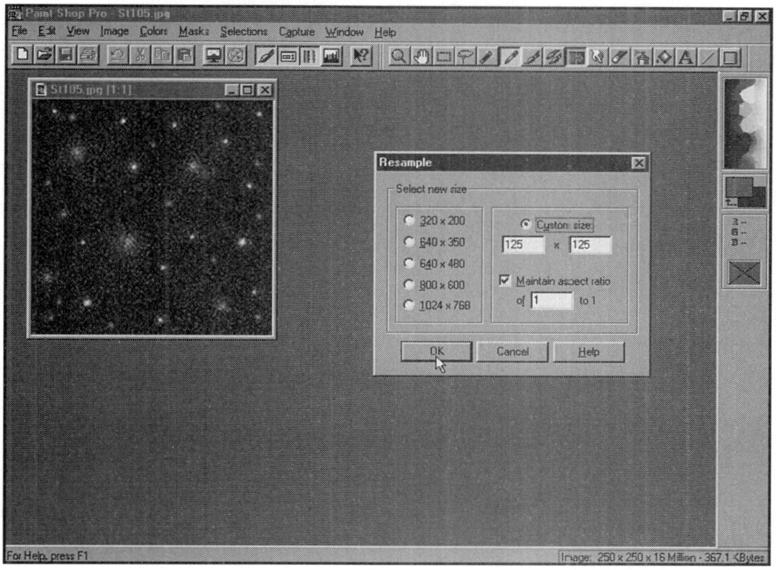

FIGURE 17.6.
The Resample command almost always works better than Resize when reducing the size of a full-color or grayscale image.

Most images also have too much contrast and too wide a color range for use as Web page backgrounds. As with size adjustment, it's always easier to decrease contrast and get rid of too much color than the other way around. The most useful command for adjusting background colors is `Colors | Adjust | Gamma Correct`. This command changes the bright/dark balance in an image without losing any color information. This command is usually better than the `Brightness/Contrast` adjustment because `Brightness/Contrast` often washes out the brightest whites or blacks out dark colors. A gamma correction factor between 0 and 1 darkens an image, and a factor between 1 and 4 lightens an image.

A correction of 0.81 is applied in Figure 17.7. I came up with 0.81 just by twiddling the setting up and down until it looked as though white text would show up clearly over the background, but the stars were still easily visible.

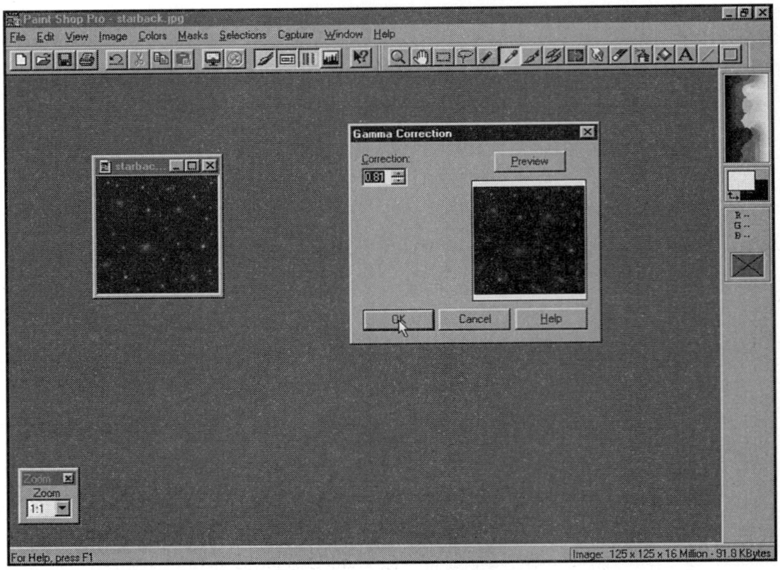

FIGURE 17.7.
Gamma correction is the best way to fade background images without losing detail.

Finishing Touches

You've seen three of the four key steps involved in adapting almost any image for use on a Web page:

1. Find or capture a promising image.
2. Adjust the colors to match the other elements of the page.
3. Resize the image and reduce the color depth.
4. Touch up any colors or details that don't quite work.

Step 4 on the list is often the most time-consuming step. The other steps become almost automatic after you've created a few pages. But the more you explore Paint Shop Pro's powerful capabilities, the more tempted you'll be to spend half an hour with `Colors | Edit Palette` to get that title color just right or playing around with `Image | Special Effects | Drop Shadow` for the precise 3D look you're after.

But take my advice, discipline yourself to spend only a few minutes perfecting the graphics on each page. I indulged in a couple of worthwhile improvements to the completed page pictured in Figures 17.8 and 17.9. The gradient fill of *World Records* and filling in the words *New Scientific* with white were well worth the minimal effort these procedures involved. Likewise, using the color replacer tool to fill the continents of the Earth with a nontransparent shade of black definitely made the graphic more easily recognizable.

But will my picky adjustments and re-adjustments of the palette of colors in the title really make any difference to the people who visit this site? Probably not. And that glow effect experiment I tried when you weren't looking was a nice idea, but it increased the file size of the title image from 4 K to 23 K. (Oops! Never mind.) So do as I say, not as I do; stop having so much fun playing around with your pages and focus on productivity and serious stuff like that. And, hey, I don't want to see anybody fooling around with that `Image | Deformation Browser` command any more, got it? Good.

FIGURE 17.8.
The completed masterpiece is less detailed but far more colorful than the original two-color printed version.

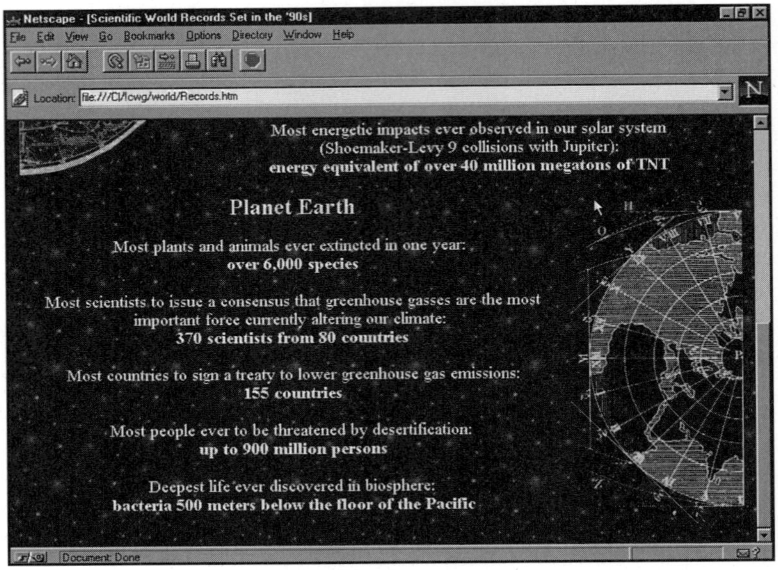

FIGURE 17.9.
As a final touch, I had to touch up the Earth so you couldn't see the stars through the continents.

Scanning and Enhancing Photos

To incorporate photographic images into your Web pages, you need some kind of scanner to transform the colors of the photo into bits that the computer can handle. You can buy a decent handheld color scanner for as little as $200, which should prove quite sufficient for most images at the relatively low resolutions appropriate for the Net.

Of course, to properly prepare photographic images for online display, you need some photo retouching software—like our familiar friend, Paint Shop Pro. It can handle almost any image correction and enhancement task you need for the Net, and Paint Shop Pro even includes the standard TWAIN interface for scanners so you can scan without leaving the program. To scan an image, select `File | Acquire` and the scanning controls for your particular scanner will appear (see Figure 17.10).

NOTE

The dialog box that you see when you select `File | Acquire` will probably look different than the one shown in Figure 17.10. The exact interface will depend on which scanner you have and the software drivers that you installed when you connected the scanner to your computer. (Figure 17.10 shows the interface for my Logitech Color ScanMan.)

If you get an error message or nothing happens when you select `File | Acquire`, then you either don't have a scanner or your scanner is not compatible with the TWAIN standard. If that's the case, you will need to use the software that came with your scanner to scan and save images. You can then open them in Paint Shop Pro.

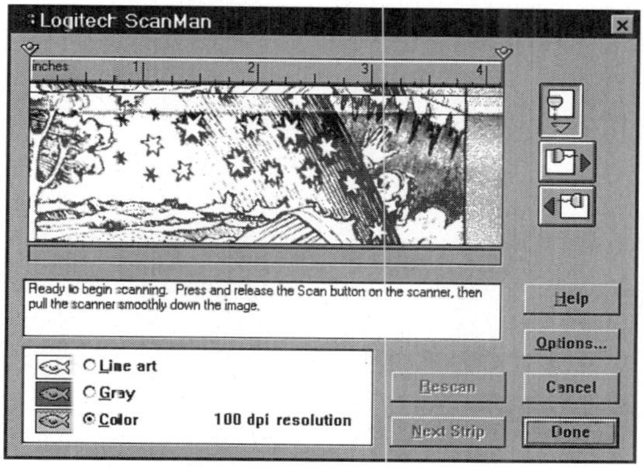

FIGURE 17.10.
Pressing the `Acquire Image` *button brings up the dialog box for your specific TWAIN-compatible scanner driver without leaving Paint Shop Pro.*

If you plan to scan images often, you should add the `Acquire Image` button to your toolbar. To do so, select `File | Preferences | Customize Toolbar`, highlight the `Acquire Image` icon as shown in Figure 17.11, and click the `Add` button. While you're at it, you might like to add the `Brightness/Contrast`, `Adjust RGB`, and `Gamma Correction` buttons to your toolbar as well. These functions are frequently used to enchance scanned images.

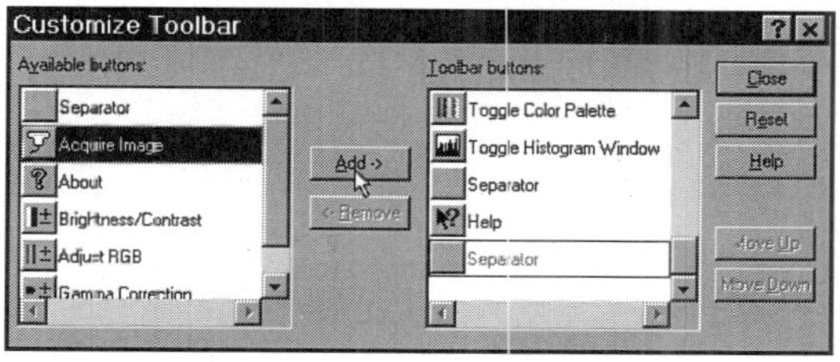

FIGURE 17.11.
If you scan photos often, add the `Acquire Image` *icon to the Paint Shop Pro toolbar.*

Paint Shop Pro's `Colors | Gamma Correct` and `Brightness/Contrast` commands, which are used to correct the overall tone of images, were demonstrated earlier in this chapter under "Customizing and Correcting Images." Several other useful color correction tools are available on the Paint Shop Pro `Colors` menu (and in most other photo editing programs).

Isolating Subjects from the Background

You will often want to isolate the main subject of an image from its original background before you place it on your Web page. (Isolating a subject from its background becomes especially useful when you use transparent images, as discussed in Chapter 16.) Figure 17.12 is an image of a flat-coated retriever that I retrieved from the `alt.binaries.pictures.animals` newsgroup. If I wanted to publish a flat-coated retriever home page on the Web, I'd probably want to remove the distracting background from this image.

FIGURE 17.12.
A bad picture of a good dog.

The hard way to free this dog would be to outline him with the lasso hand-selection tool. Given the irregular boundaries of a flat-coated retriever, that task would be impossible with a mouse and tiresome with a drawing tablet. An easier way would be to use the magic wand tool to automatically select a similarly colored area. In this image, the dog contrasts fairly well with the background, so this approach has promise. By double-clicking the magic wand, I can even adjust the tolerance to best capture the range of colors that distinguishes the dog from the background. Selecting a region this way generally takes some trial-and-error to find the best tolerance, but this method can save a lot of work in high-contrast images. Figure 17.13 shows the Magic Wand control box and tool ready to make a selection.

After highlighting the dog (and some unwanted but similarly colored background details) with the magic wand, I can then select `Edit | Copy` and `Edit | Paste | As New Image` to produce a cutout picture. By carefully tweaking the tolerance and using the other painting tools to smooth the edges, I could get a better outline than this. Figure 17.14 shows the start of this approach, but I didn't bother finishing because it was a lot of picky work and I could see that, for this particular image, there was a better way.

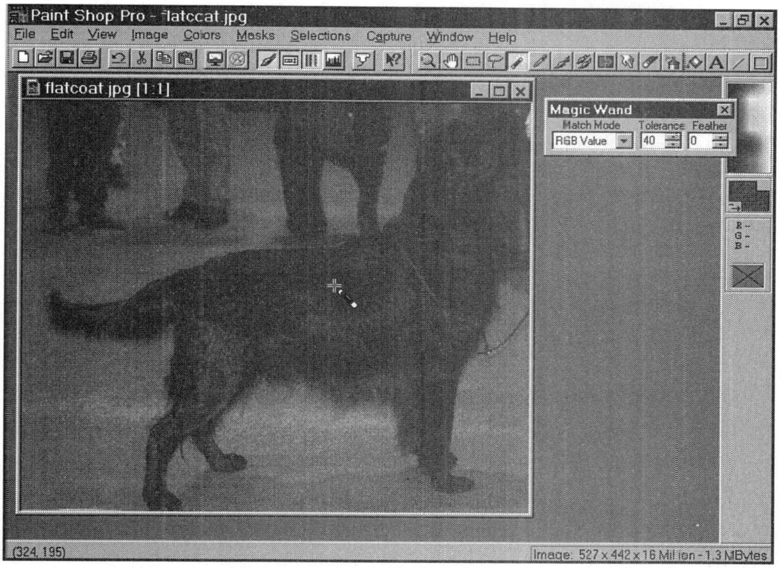

FIGURE 17.13.
The magic wand tool automatically selects a region based on color similarity.

FIGURE 17.14.
Careful tuning of the magic wand tolerance and meticulous hand editing (shown here in progress) can liberate even the most complex object from any background.

The better way in this case was to use the brightness and contrast controls to fade most of the background out to pure white. Figure 17.15 shows the result, which has much cleaner edges than any magic wand selection could achieve on a low-resolution image.

FIGURE 17.15.
Using brightness and contrast controls to wash out a light background sometimes works wonders that no magic wand can match.

NOTE

All the tools mentioned in the following paragraph are on the Select toolbar in Paint Shop Pro. Similar tools are also found in almost every major image-processing or photo-editing program. For more details on how these tools work, consult the online help for Paint Shop Pro or your favorite comparable software.

To remove the rest of the background, I first eliminated the people's legs and shadows with the rectangular selection tool, the lasso selection tool, and the `Edit | Clear` menu command. Then I went in by hand with the paintbrush and push brush tools to clear away the stuff around the dog's head. Finally, I touched up a bit with the softening tool to eliminate any jagged edges. I chose to leave the small shadows under his feet, but I did use the image clone tool to get rid of that pesky leash. In Figure 17.16, the retriever is finally free.

FIGURE 17.16.
A bit of touching up with the painting tools and he's a free dog.

Image Filters

A good photographer or publishing professional can do very impressive color correction in a traditional darkroom. Other forms of digital image enhancement, however, are difficult or impossible to do without a computer. Image filters based on a mathematical technique called convolution may seem especially magical in their ability to bring out detail, sharpen or soften edges, and automatically produce complex-looking special effects like embossing. But you don't have to understand the math or the magic to use filters. In fact, PaintShop Pro's `Image | Filter Browser` control (see Figure 17.17) makes it easy to choose and apply a filter.

TIP

Note that the edge and emboss filters give better results on images that aren't scanned with a hand scanner, as the `flatcoat.jpg` file appears to have been. The extra noisy edges are by-products of the scanning process.

You can often avoid or reduce this problem by reducing the contrast in the image before embossing it. Selecting `Colors | Posterize` can also help tidy up messy images before you use an edge-oriented filter on them.

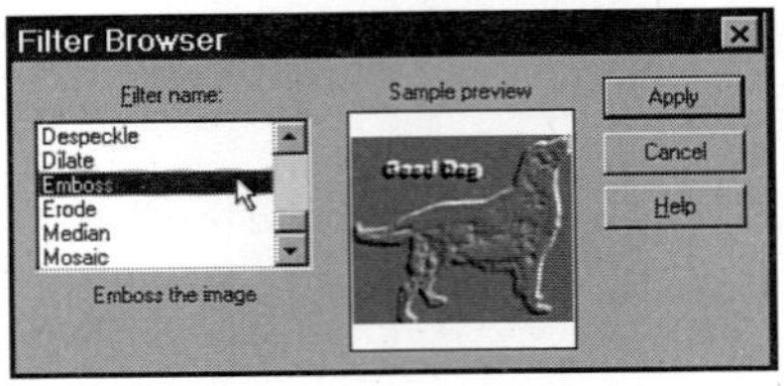

FIGURE 17.17.
Use the filter browser to preview any of PaintShop Pro's image filters.

You should be able to tell from the Filter Browser which filter might do your image some good. When it doubt, try it! You can always select `Edit` | `Undo` afterward if you need to.

Deforming Images

Retouching images can be a lot of work. It can also be a lot of fun, especially when you use image deformation tools. As with filters, Paint Shop Pro gives you an interactive preview browser for deformations (see Figure 17.18). When you pick a deformation in the browser and click the `Apply` button, you get a dialog box that enables you to adjust the effect settings for that particular deformation and preview the results on the entire image before committing to it (see Figure 17.19).

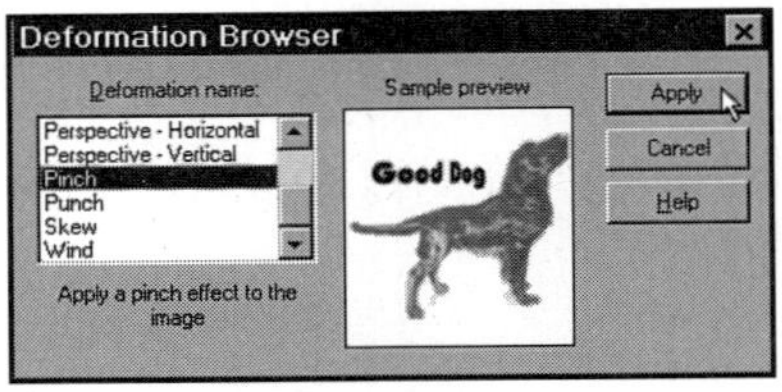

FIGURE 17.18.
The Deformation Browser is your own computer-controlled funhouse mirror.

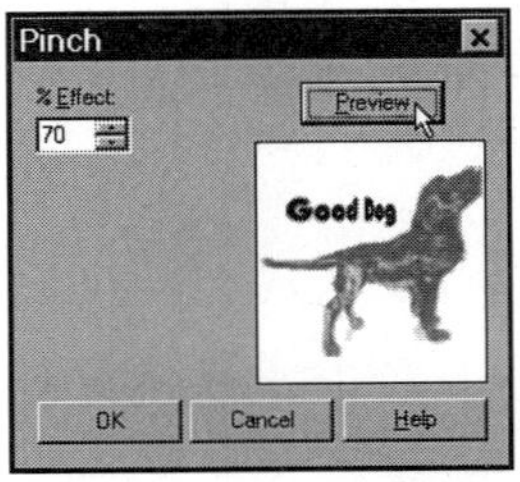

FIGURE 17.19.
Before you deform an image, you can adjust the amount of effect to apply.

Combining and Layering Images

You can create dramatic and useful graphics effects by combining two images with image arithmetic. To combine images in a variety of ways, use the `Image` | `Arithmetic` menu choice in Paint Shop Pro. For example, you can add two images together, making one appear superimposed over the other with partial transparency, as shown in Figures 17.20 and 17.21.

Here's a quick tour of the Image Arithmetic dialog box shown in Figure 17.20:

- Choose the images you want to combine from the `source image #1` and `source image #2` lists. For best results, make sure the two images are the same size.
- Select a function such as `Add` or `Multiply`.
- For color images, you can choose to work with the red, green, and/or blue color channels only. Normally, however, you would select `All channels`.
- Enter a `Divisor` suitable for the operation you have in mind. For most operations, you should start with a divisor of 1. The two exceptions to this rule of thumb are the Multiply function, which will usually give you a completely white image unless you use a divisor of at least 100, and the Add function, which generally works best with a divisor of 2. Higher divisors generally make the resulting image darker, and lower divisors make it brighter.
- Enter a `Bias` between -255 and 255 to change the overall brightness of the entire image. Generally, you should use 0 unless you find that an image is coming out too light or dark, in which case the bias setting provides an easy way to correct the problem.
- You will almost always want `Clip color values` selected. If it isn't selected, super-bright whites turn to black or gray, and super-dark blacks turn to white or gray. This result can create interesting effects, but it is difficult to predict and control.

When you click on `OK`, Paint Shop Pro goes through each pixel in the first image and adds (or multiplies, subtracts, and so on) its value to the corresponding pixel color value in the second image. The result is divided by the `Divisor` you entered, and then the `bias` is added. In Figure 17.20, I selected `Add` and entered a `Divisor` of two. The pixel color values of the two source images were added together and then divided by two, effectively averaging the two images together as shown in Figure 17.21.

Image addition is relatively easy to describe, but the other operations offer creative possibilities that words could never begin to convey. If you want to combine two images for a layered or faded look, your best bet for finding the right effect is good old-fashioned trial and error.

Note that the Subtract function isn't symmetrical, meaning that subtracting image #1 from image #2 would give a significantly different result that subtracting image #2 from image #1. All the other Image Arithmetic functions are symmetrical, however.

TIP

Simple gradations created with the paint bucket tool (like the rightmost image in Figure 17.21) are especially useful for creating special effects with the Image Arithmetic dialog box. You can select radial, sunburst, or linear fill in the paint bucket style palette, and then use the Image Arithmetic dialog box to fade out a corresponding pattern in another image.

FIGURE 17.20.
The Image Arithmetic dialog box allows you to combine two images mathematically.

FIGURE 17.21.
The settings shown in Figure 17.20 create a third image by adding together the source images and dividing by two to take the average.

Special Effects

Paint Shop Pro's `Image | Special Effects` menu is a treasure chest of time-saving gems to make your Web pages richer. You won't find most of these tricks in many other graphics programs.

> **NOTE**
>
> One of the most magical and practical items on the Image | Special Effects menu is Create Seamless Pattern. Because this is specifically for making background tiles, it's covered in Chapter 20, "Backgrounds, Image Maps, and Creative Layouts" instead of this chapter. All the other items on the Special Effects menu are discussed in this section.

Drop Shadows and Highlights

One of the most popular effects used by every graphics pro is the drop shadow, which is a subtle darkening of the area directly behind a graphic or some text to make it look like it's floating above the page. Unlike many automatic computer effects, shadowing is in no danger of becoming an overused visual cliche. Shadows are just too prevalent in the physical world. In fact, *not* knowing how to use shadows effectively is more likely to make your pages look mundane than overusing them is.

Fortunately, Paint Shop Pro makes drop shadows incredibly easy to create. You can add a shadow behind any selected text or region with the `Image | Special Effects | Add Drop Shadow` command. The dialog box that appears (see Figure 17.22) lets you pick the color of the shadow and gives you several other controls as well. You can set the `Opacity` of the shadow to any number from 1 (almost completely transparent) to 255 (solid with none of the existing image showing through). The `Blur` setting controls how many pixels across the fuzzy edge of the shadow will be. A `Blur` setting of 1 makes the edges crisp with no fuzziness, and the maximum setting of 36 will make a hazy shadow or a glowing effect if you use a bright color. In Figure 17.22, I chose a medium-bright shadow color around the light text, which gives both a shadow and a glow effect to the letters.

To control how far your object leaps out of the page, use the slider controls in the bottom part of the `Drop Shadow` dialog box. These controls set the vertical and horizontal offset of the shadow from the selection in pixels. Larger values make the selection look further from the page, and negative values put the shadow on the upper left instead of the lower right of the object. For a glow effect, set both offsets close to zero and use a high blur setting, or select the `Add Drop Shadow` command twice and put one shadow below and the other above, as I did in Figure 17.22.

> **NOTE**
>
> To select the Add Drop Shadow command, you must have an open full-color or grayscale image and an active selection (with moving dotted lines around it). These requirements are also necessary in order to use most other Special Effects commands; Paint Shop Pro can't add an effect if you haven't selected anything to add the effect to!

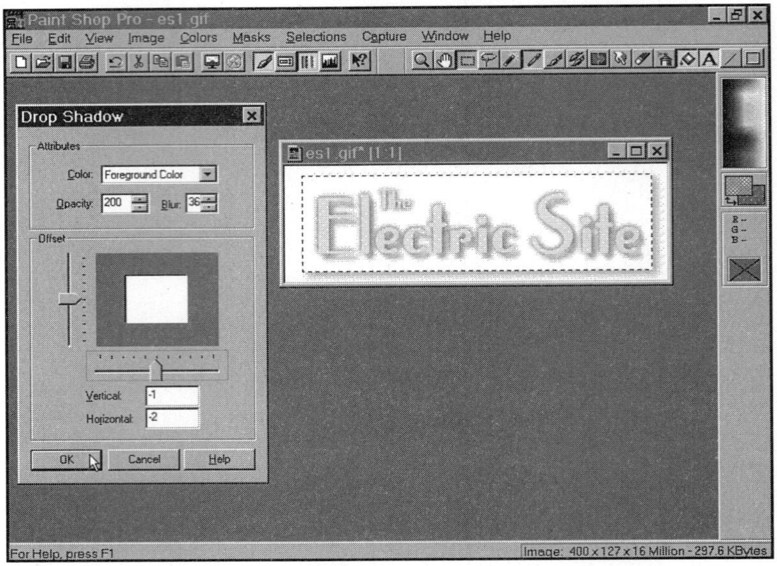

FIGURE 17.22.
You can use the `Add Drop Shadow` *command to create glow effects and fuzzy outlines as well as shadows.*

Creating 3D Buttons

When you have an impressive title with a drop shadow behind it, you'll naturally want to create some 3D buttons for the links between your Web pages. Once again, Paint Shop Pro makes this effect a snap to create. Select a rectagular area with the selection tool, and choose the `Image | Special Effects | Buttonize` command. Choose the exact button effect you want from the `Buttonize` dialog box shown in Figure 17.23.

The height of the button is set with `Edge Size` as a percent of the total button width. You can also choose between a button with transparent edges (such as the push me button in Figure 17.23) or solid edges (such as the ok? button in Figure 17.23). In either case, the button will be shaded with a combination of the current foreground color, the existing image, and a shade of gray to create the 3D look.

Figure 17.23 also uses two of the three remaining options on the Paint Shop Pro `Special Effects` submenu. `Chisel` outlines the current selection for a chiseled effect, and `Hot Wax Coating` tints and chisels at the same time. The final option, `Cut Out`, creates a beveled effect at the edges of the selection so it appears to be dropped slightly into the page. This is the same idea as the 3D-look borders of most inset controls in Windows 95 programs.

FIGURE 17.23.
The ok? button has solid edges, while the other two have transparent edges. `Chisel` *and* `Hot Wax Coating` *highlight the button labels.*

The last item on Paint Shop Pro's `Special Effects` list is a bit different than the rest. `Hot Wax Coating` doesn't sound like something you'd do with your computer, let alone a graphics program. Nonetheless, it is a very useful tool for Web pages because it combines a number of common tasks into a single one-click operation. The math behind `Hot Wax Coating` is tricky, and the effect is too; basically, this tool tints the current selection with the foreground color while also enhancing the edges, improving the contrast, and darkening the highlights in a way that would be difficult to achieve without applying a number of other tools one after the other. This tool is an excellent choice for any part of a page or image where you want a button or illustration to look like it is layered over something else. The Just don't button in Figure 17.23 shows an example of this effect.

Though this chapter has covered just about every special effect tool that Paint Shop Pro offers, I would be remiss in my duties if I didn't remind you that Paint Shop Pro also supports standard graphics plug-in filters created by third-party developers. These plug-ins, from serious graphics gurus such as the makers of Kai's Power Tools and Adobe Photoshop, can give you even more creative power to make your Web pages fly.

Summary

In this chapter, you've seen how to capture, scan, enhance, and add special effects to the graphics on your Web pages. Chapter 18, "Creative Use of Text, Fonts, and Type," helps you add the same pizazz to the text on your Web pages.

CHAPTER 18

Creative Uses of Text, Fonts, and Type

by Dick Oliver

IN THIS CHAPTER

Every time you sit down to design a Web page today, you're faced with an agonizing decision: Do you use lots of big graphics for maximum impact, or do you stick to plain old text that will convey information quickly and clearly? In this chapter, I show you how to get the best of both worlds by pushing Web page text to its creative limits.

I also take you step-by-step through creating graphical titles and buttons, which you can substitute for "real" text to give your pages a stylistic flair.

Some of the fancier stuff covered in this chapter currently shows up only in Netscape Navigator 3.0 and Microsoft Internet Explorer 3.0. However, because everything is in HTML, the same pages will still look great in most other popular browsers.

Dare to Be Different

Face it, after a few hours of surfing, most of the pages on the Web all start to look the same—the logo, the heading, the too-wide single column of text with cute little iconic images to the left every once in a while. Then there are those all-one-big-graphic pages that take forever to download and contain only six words for you to read before you click yet another all-one-big-graphic page that takes forever to download.... It's enough to put you to sleep, even after that fifth cup of coffee.

But just when you're nodding off, you come across a page like the one in Figure 18.1 (which you can view online at `http://www.iterated.com/`). Most of the text is real text, so it pops up fast. But then those snappy little title graphics appear one by one, each in just the right place next to the text it refers to, and the whole thing is laid out in a distinctive, attractive way that just oozes "cool" without reeking of some artist's overripe ego.

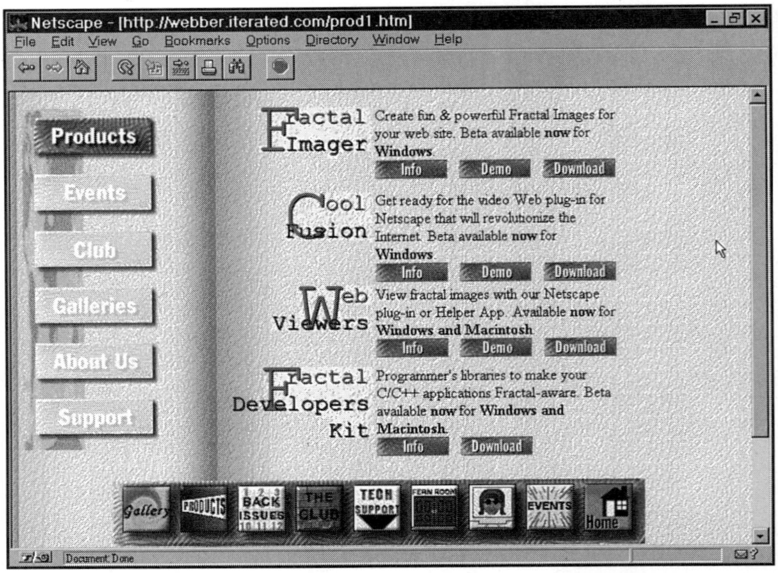

FIGURE 18.1.
This site features a unique, distinctive layout and look without giant, bandwidth-hogging graphics files.

Now, you might prefer a different aesthetic than what this page displays, but the tricks its designer used to make it stand out can be adapted to make your pages unique in a totally different direction. The key elements to notice, in any case, are the following:

- Most graphics that substitute for text are small, so they load and display first. The larger graphics are less essential for reading the page, so it's okay that they appear more slowly.
- Some of the graphics are used more than once (the Info and Demo buttons, for instance). This technique speeds display because they need to be loaded only once.
- The background image is quite small (just a thin horizontal strip, tiled down the page), but it creates a large and visually striking design element on the page.
- Multicolumn text and a unique layout make this page (and the others at this site) stand out from the crowd of "me-too" pages on the Internet.
- Almost all the actual text content of the page is "real text," not graphics, so visitors can use their browser's `Find` command to search it for keywords. More important, Internet search indexes can index this page according to its text content so potential visitors can find it easily.

In this chapter, you'll learn how to make highly expressive pages that meet all these criteria and more.

Font Manipulation and Text Formatting

You'll notice the `FONT` tag used often in the examples throughout this chapter. Using this tag to set the size and color of text is pretty much a no-brainer: The `SIZE` attribute can take any value from `1` (tiny) to `7` (fairly big), and the `COLOR` attribute can take the standard English color names (black, white, red, green, blue, yellow, magenta, cyan, aqua, fuchsia, gray, lime, maroon, navy, olive, silver, and teal). The actual size and exact color of the fonts depend on the user's screen resolution and preference settings, but you can be assured that `SIZE=6` will be a lot bigger than `SIZE=2`, and that `COLOR="red"` will certainly show its fire. Both Netscape Navigator and Microsoft Explorer now support `FONT SIZE` and `COLOR`, and most other browsers will soon support this tag, too.

Another font trick you should know about is the `<TT>` tag, which changes from the user's normal, proportionally spaced font to a monospaced "typewriter type" font. Theoretically, each user can choose any font he or she wants when configuring the browser, and the "monospaced" font may not even be monospaced for some crazy users. But most people just stick with the standard fonts their browser comes set up with, so you should design and test your pages with those default fonts, too. (The standard proportional font is usually Times New Roman, and the standard monospaced font is almost always Courier or Courier New.)

Putting a New Face On Your Page

With the new 3.0 versions of both Navigator and Internet Explorer, Netscape and Microsoft have added another powerful form of font control: the `FONT FACE` attribute. It allows you to specify the actual typeface that should be used to display text—and has been the source of much rejoicing among Webmasters who are *awfully* sick of Times and Courier!

The site in Figure 18.2 uses these font controls (and another new feature, borderless frames) to present a warmly welcoming homestyle site.

FIGURE 18.2.
If you have Lucida Handwriting or Brush Script installed on your computer, the text of this page appears in a handwritten style (`/maple/syrup.htm`).

The code to set the font used in Figure 18.2 (in the file `examples/maple/main.htm` on the CD-ROM) is this:

```
<FONT FACE="Lucida Handwriting, Brush Script, Brush Script MT" SIZE=5
COLOR="#800000">
```

If the browser can find a font named Lucida Handwriting on a user's system, that font is used. Otherwise, it checks for a font named Brush Script or Brush Script MT and uses whichever of those it can find. If the user doesn't have any of those fonts installed, the default font is used (this is usually Times New Roman).

TIP

Note that both TrueType and Postscript fonts installed on the user's system can be used in Web pages. TrueType fonts are more common, but it's always a good idea to include the name of a similar Postscript font (if you know one), because some people don't use TrueType at all.

In this example, Brush Script is the customary name for the Postscript version of the font, but Brush Script MT is the most common name of the TrueType version of the same font. I included both names just to be on the safe side.

Browsers other than Navigator 3.0 and Microsoft Explorer 3.0 will ignore the `FONT FACE` attribute and display the default fonts they always use. Figure 18.3 shows the same page as in Figure 18.2, displayed with Netscape Navigator 2.0.

FIGURE 18.3.
Netscape Navigator 2.0 doesn't recognize the `FONT FACE` *attribute, so it displays the page in plain old Times New Roman.*

Currently, only fonts that each user happens to have on his or her system will show up, and you have no control over which fonts are installed. Furthermore, the exact spelling of the font names is important, and many common fonts go by several slightly different names. Extensions to HTML will soon support a new, highly compact font format that can be automatically downloaded along with your pages to solve these problems. But for now, you just have to stick to the most common fonts and make sure your pages still look acceptable in Times New Roman.

Figure 18.4 shows the most common TrueType fonts, many of which are also available in Postscript format. Microsoft offers a number of these fonts available for free download from this site:

`http://www.microsoft.com/truetype/`

Microsoft has also included these fonts (and variations on them) in Windows and other popular software packages.

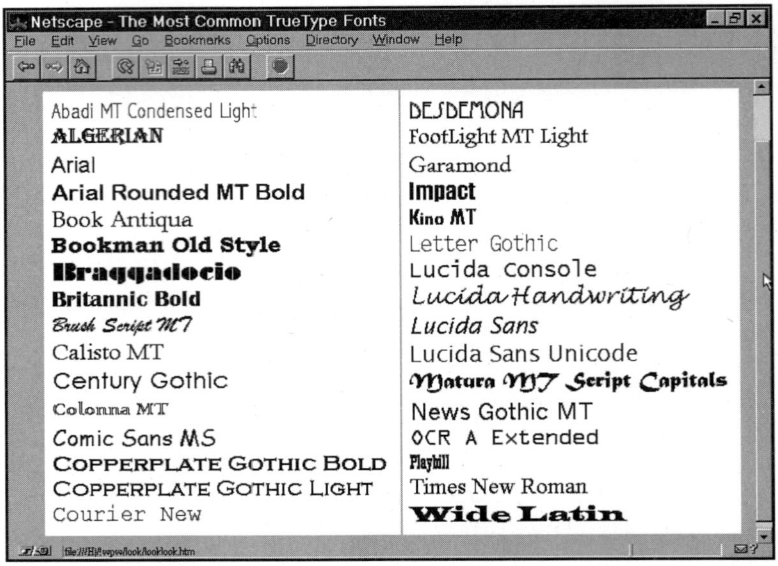

FIGURE 18.4.
The most popular TrueType fonts are good bets for your Web pages. Arial is especially reliable since most computers now come with it installed (`/bfb/fonts.htm`*).*

If you want to use a font on your Web page that isn't on this list, don't be afraid to do so! The user will never see an error message if the font can't be found—the worst thing that could happen is that the user won't see your special font, but will still see the text in the next best font that can be found. If one of the fonts in Figure 18.4 has a similar feel to the one you want, include it as a "second choice," as I did with Brush Script in the preceding example.

Style Sheet Font Controls

As you saw in Chapter 8, "Using Style Sheets," style sheets are without a doubt the Next Big Thing in the fast-paced world of the Web. The concept is simple: You create a single "style sheet" document that specifies the fonts, colors, backgrounds, and other characteristics that establish a unique "look." Then you link every page that should have that "look" to the style sheet, instead of specifying all those style elements over and over again in each document separately. When you decide to change your official corporate typeface or color scheme, you can modify all your Web pages at once just by changing one or two style sheets.

If style sheets accomplished this and nothing else, they'd save millions of dollars worth of Webmasters' time and become an integral part of most Web-publishing projects, but they aim to do this and much more. The proposed HTML style sheet standard enables Web authors to set many formatting characteristics that were never possible to modify before with any amount of effort. These include exacting typeface controls, letter and line spacing, margins and page borders, and expanded support for non-European languages and characters. They also let you specify sizes and other measurements in familiar units, such as inches, millimeters, and picas.

In short, style sheets bring the sophistication level of paper-oriented publishing to the Web. And they do so—you'll pardon the expression—"with style."

A Basic Style Sheet

Despite their intimidating power, style sheets can be very simple to create. Take a look at the documents shown in Figures 18.5 and 18.6. They share several properties that could be put into a common style sheet:

- They use the Lucida Handwriting font in both body text and headings.
- They use the paper.JPG image as a background tile.
- They use reddish-brown (color #800000) text throughout.

(Note that Figure 18.5 is the same document as Figure 18.2, displayed by Microsoft Explorer instead of Netscape Navigator.)

FIGURE 18.5.
This page shares several characteristics in common with the page in Figure 18.6.

Here's how an HTML style sheet that specified these properties would look:

```
BODY {font: 12pt Lucida Handwriting;
      color: #800000;
      background: url(paper.JPG) #E0E080}
H1 {font: 18pt Lucida Handwriting}
H2 {font: 14pt Lucida Handwriting}
```

18 CREATIVE USES OF TEXT, FONTS, AND TYPE

FIGURE 18.6.
Style sheets let you specify the common elements of several pages in a separate document.

The first thing you'll undoubtedly notice about this style sheet is that it doesn't look anything like normal HTML. Style-sheet specifications are really a separate language in and of themselves.

Of course, there are some familiar HTML tags in there. As you might guess, `BODY`, `H1`, and `H2` in the style sheet refer to the corresponding tags in the HTML documents to which the style sheet will be applied. The specifications for what all text within that tag should look like are in curly braces after each tag name.

In this case, all `BODY` text that isn't within some other tag should be rendering at a size of 12 points, in the Lucida Handwriting font, if possible, and with the color `#800000`. The `BODY` background should be the image found at the relative URL `paper.JPG`—or if no image of that name can be found, the background color should be set to `#E0E080`. Any text within `H1` or `H2` tags should be rendered in Lucida Handwriting at a size of 18 points and 14 points, respectively.

NOTE

The "point sizes" used in the HTML `<FONT>` tag are *not* the same as the point sizes specified in style sheets. `<FONT SIZE=3>` corresponds to approximately 12-point text, `<FONT SIZE=1>` is about 6-point text, and `<FONT SIZE=7>` (the maximum size for the `FONT` tag) is about 24-point text. You can specify font sizes as large as you like with style sheets, although most display devices and printers won't correctly handle fonts over 200 points.

All that remains is to link this style sheet to the HTML documents. You do this by including a <LINK> tag in the <HEAD> section of each document:

```
<HEAD>
    <TITLE>A Very Stylish Page Indeed</TITLE>
    <LINK REL=STYLESHEET TYPE="text/css" HREF="mystyle.css">
</HEAD>
```

This assumes the style sheet was saved under the name `mystyle.css` in the same directory folder as the document containing the preceding HTML. Internet Explorer then gives the body and heading text the properties specified in the style sheet, without the need for any FONT tags or BODY BACKGROUND attribute in the document itself.

Specifying Inline Styles

In some situations, you might want to specify styles that will be used in only one Web page. You can then enclose a style sheet between <STYLE> and </STYLE> tags and include it in the beginning of an HTML document, between the </HEAD> and <BODY> tags. No <LINK> tag is needed, and you can't refer to that style sheet from any other page (unless you copy it into the beginning of that document, too).

If you want to specify a style for only a small part of a page, you can go one step further and put a STYLE attribute within a <P>, <DIV>, or <SPAN> tag. (<SPAN> and </SPAN> are "dummy" tags that do nothing in and of themselves, except specify a range of text to apply any STYLE attributes you add.)

Here's how a sample STYLE attribute might look:

```
<P STYLE="color: green">This text is green, but
<SPAN STYLE="color: red"> this text is red.</SPAN>
Back to green again, but...</P>
<P>...now the green is over, and we're back to the default color for this page.
```

Although this example's effect could be achieved as easily with the <FONT COLOR> tag, many style specifications have no corresponding HTML tag. Generally, you should avoid inline styles except when there's no way to do what you're after in HTML and you feel that using an external style sheet would be too cumbersome.

TIP

Even when you use a separate style sheet document, you can specify any unique style changes you want for a particular document inline. The most local style specification overrides any conflicting styles previously specified. This principle is central to the style sheet concept and is why they're officially called *Cascading Style Specifications* (CSS).

Now We're *Really* Stylin'

The style sheet standard is actively under development, and the implementation of style sheets in MS Internet Explorer 3.0 is by no means complete. The style specifications currently supported by Internet Explorer are explained in the following list, but be sure to check Microsoft's Web site (`http://www.microsoft.com/`) for any late-breaking enhancements and changes in the standard.

- `font:` lets you set many font properties at once. You can specify a list of font names separated by commas; if the first isn't available, the next is tried, and so on. You can also include the words `bold` and/or `italic` and a font size. Each of these font properties can be specified separately with `font-family:`, `font-size:`, `font-weight: bold`, and `font-style: italic`, if you prefer.
- `text-decoration:` is useful for turning link underlining off—simply set text decoration to `none`. The values of `underline`, `italic`, and `line-through` are also supported.
- `line-height:` is also known in the publishing world as leading. This sets the height of each line of text, usually in points.
- `background:` places a color or image behind text, either with a color or a `url(`*`address`*`)`, in which *`address`* points to a background image tile. Note that this can be assigned not only to the `<BODY>` tag, but also to any tag or span of text to "highlight" an area on a page.

The ability to specify these few style properties for many documents at once—or any portion of a document—is already revolutionary. Expect the next versions of Internet Explorer and Netscape Navigator (and of other Web browsers) to take style sheets even further toward the ideal of online publishing with all the flexibility of traditional publishing tools.

Type That Isn't Type (and Other Illusions)

In situations where you want to make sure all viewers see a special font, you can substitute graphics images for a few key words in the text of your pages. Figures 18.7 and 18.8 show two very simple but visually powerful examples of real text mixed with graphics images of text in a fancy font. These two-color graphics are quite large, but they compress tightly and load quickly because they're so simple.

Note that the image in Figure 18.8 doesn't use transparency, but appears to because the graphic's background color matches the page's background color. (See Chapter 16, "Bigger, Faster, Better Graphics," for details on how to set the text and background colors and which colors can be relied on to match a graphic on most computers.)

The page in Figure 18.9 is a little trickier. Here, the text appears to "bleed" off the top of the page because it's actually a background tile. You can use background graphics for nonrepeating elements, as long as you make the image wider than about 1000 pixels and taller than 750 pixels, and put little enough text on the page so that it usually fits on a single screen without scrolling. (Very few people surf the Internet at screen resolutions greater than 1024×768.)

FIGURE 18.7.
Powerful visual effects don't have to be complex.

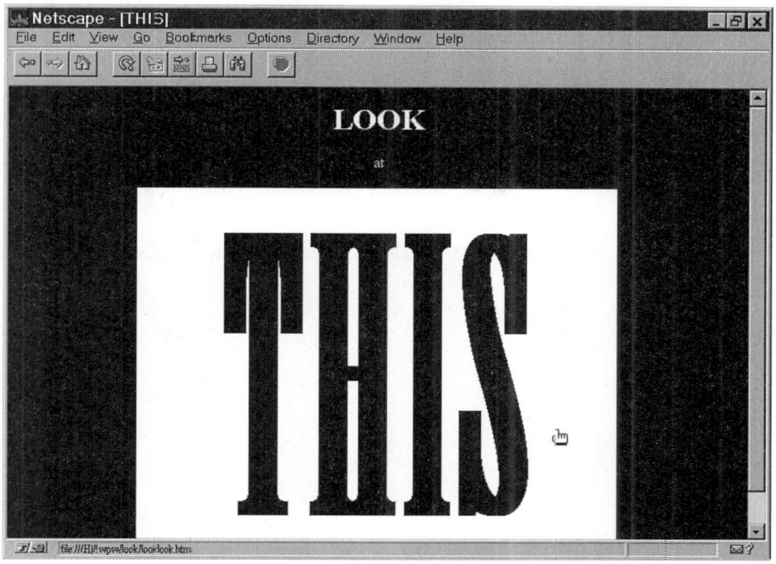

FIGURE 18.8.
Nontransparent images can look transparent if you match the page's background color.

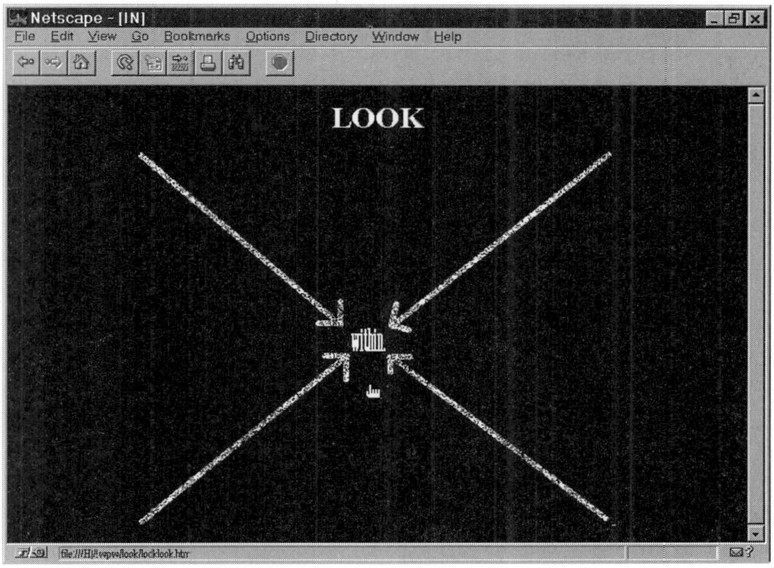

FIGURE 18.9.
You can make graphics bleed right up to the edge of the viewing window by using them as backgrounds.

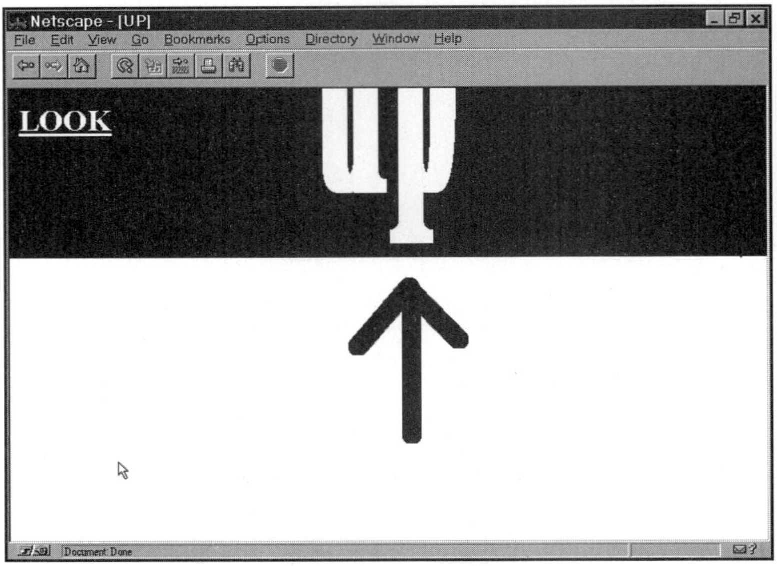

TIP

You might think that a 1000×750-pixel image would be too big to be practical as a background, but the black-and-white background graphic in Figure 18.9 is actually only 4 K and loads in less than two seconds over a 28.8 Kbps modem. Because GIF and JPEG files are compressed efficiently, the size of the image always depends more on its visual complexity than on the actual resolution.

In fact, blank space of *any size* takes up almost no space in the graphics file when compressed, so you could even use a 1000×3000-pixel image with 2500 pixels worth of blank space at the bottom for your text to scroll over and still keep the file size under 5 K.

The moral of the story: When you want to grab visitors' attention fast, don't be afraid to think *big* as long as you also think *simple*.

Figure 18.10 illustrates yet another background-as-graphic-as-text stunt. Visitors to this page can scroll down through several copies of the background image, even though no text or foreground images appear on most of the page.

There are three ways to get this effect. The most common is to include a long, totally transparent GIF image as a "spacer" to fill the empty region on the page where you want just the background to show. Another, which is even faster and more efficient, is to set the text color to match the background color and insert some "invisible" text down the page. The HTML code for Figure 18.10 appears in Listing 18.1. The third technique for getting the same result is to insert several blank lines between `<PRE>` and `</PRE>` tags, which specify preformatted text, including line breaks.

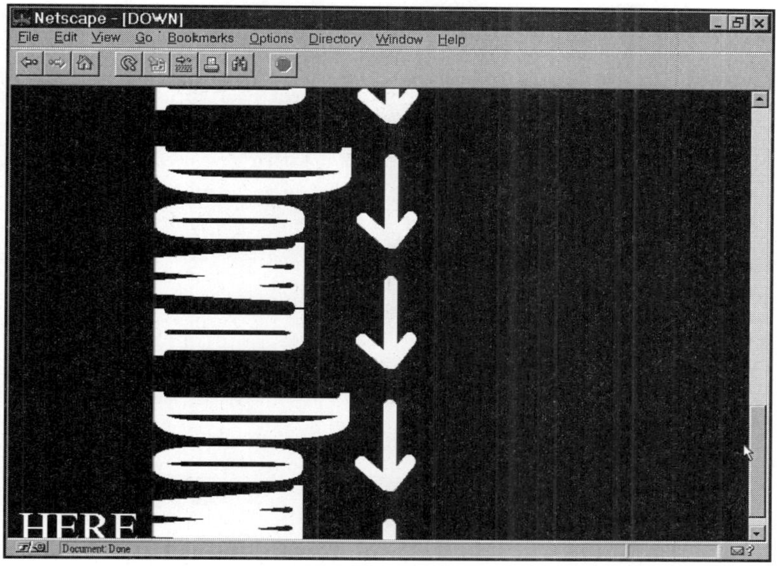

FIGURE 18.10.
With invisible text, the user can scroll down several times without seeing anything but the repeating background.

Listing 18.1. Inserting invisible text.

```
<HTML>
<HEAD><TITLE>DOWN</TITLE></HEAD>
<BODY BACKGROUND="down.gif" BGCOLOR="black"
  TEXT="black" VLINK="white" ALINK="white" LINK="white">
<H1><A HREF="looklook.htm">LOOK</A>
i<P>
n<P>
v<P>
i<P>
s<P>
i<P>
b<P>
l<P>
e<P>
-<P>
t<P>
e<P>
x<P>
t<P>
!<P>
<A HREF="looklook.htm">HERE.</A></H1>
</BODY>
</HTML>
```

Notice that no `FONT COLOR` commands need to be used because all the letters I wanted to be visible are within links, and the link color is set to white in the `<BODY>` tag.

Far-Out Layouts

The simplified demonstration pages in Figures 18.7 through 18.10 are just a warm-up to get you thinking about ways to do things differently while staying within the "letter of the law" of HTML. The page in Figure 18.11 takes creative text layout a bit further, to demonstrate the kind of creative freedom you have to put expressive and stylistic text on your Web pages.

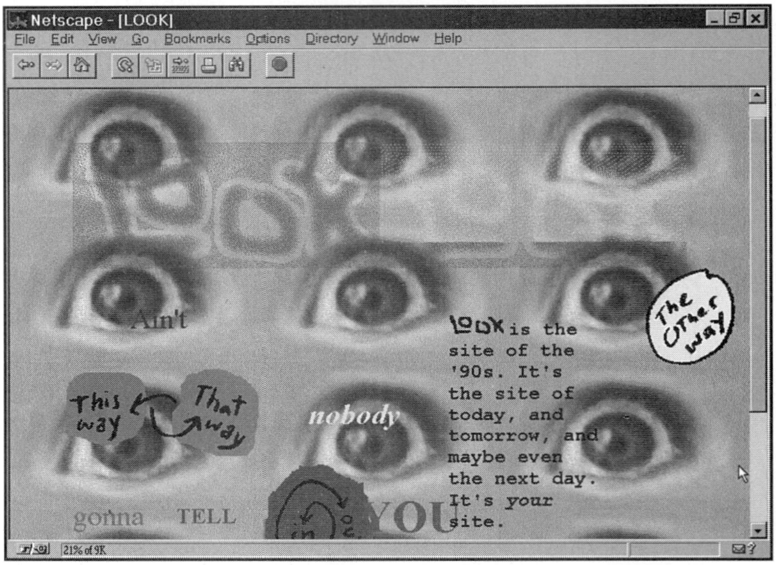

FIGURE 18.11.
Graphical text and creative layout can give your pages plenty of personality.

NOTE

The pages featured in the following section obviously involve some tricks that don't directly relate to type layout. For details on how to make seamless backgrounds, image maps, and multicolumn tables, refer to Chapter 20, "Backgrounds, Image Maps, and Creative Layouts."

Graphical Titles and Buttons

The most common situations where you should substitute graphics images for text are when you're using stylistic buttons and titles. Of course, you can always make links and headings with ordinary text, but using graphics gives you much more flexibility. It also ensures that every visitor to your page sees the same font and color scheme for the key design elements.

The rest of this chapter gives you detailed instructions and examples for creating graphical buttons and bars in Paint Shop Pro, the shareware graphics program most recommended for this type of work. Paint Shop Pro is introduced in Chapter 16, and many of the effects used in this chapter are discussed in Chapter 17, "Working with JPEG and GIF Images."

Creating Buttons in Paint Shop Pro

A frightening number of people, when they notice that Paint Shop Pro has a Buttonize command on the Special Effects menu, start using it to create every button on their Web pages. And why not? It's quick, it's easy, and you can't argue with the fact that it makes something that looks an awful lot like a button.

This might, in fact, be a satisfactory approach if you're short on time and creativity—and if you don't mind your Web pages looking exactly like every other amateur Web page in the universe. However, chances are you're looking for something more than a quickie "me-too" page. Fortunately, it's almost as quick and easy to create truly unique buttons that communicate what *your* site is all about.

In this section, I outline a general formula you can follow to create an unlimited variety of professional-quality buttons without hiring (or becoming) a professional graphics artist. To illustrate the principles in action, I explain exactly how to create each of the four buttons shown in Figure 18.12, step by step.

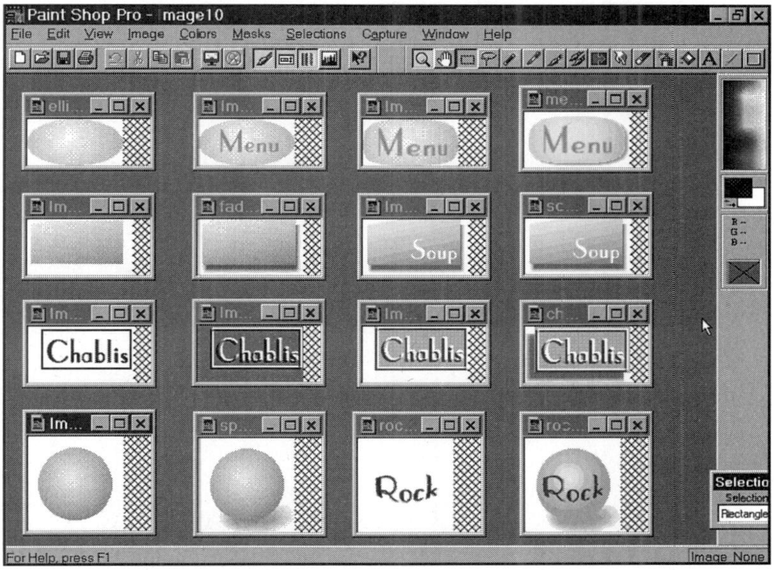

FIGURE 18.12.
Paint Shop Pro's special effects can help you produce a wide variety of button styles.

The first—and most important—step in designing a button takes place in your imagination. What colors, shapes, and textures best express the mood and message of your Web site? In the examples for this chapter, I use the same color scheme (electric blue and white) and text font (Parisian) throughout every example, to highlight the other differences between them. Naturally, you want to select a font (or, at most, two) and a color scheme that reflect the style you're after.

1. **Select a shape**

   The first thing you'll need to decide is a shape for your buttons. Iconic links (buttons that don't look like buttons) are discussed later in this chapter. For now, though, stick to easily recognized button shapes, such as rectangles and ellipses. Each of the buttons in Figure 18.12 started as a selection made with the rectangle, ellipse, or circle selection tool.

2. **Fill in or shade it**

   To make your shape stand out from the background, you need to fill it with some color. For a 3D-look with round buttons, use the fill bucket tool with Sunburst Gradient, as I did with the ellipse and sphere buttons in Figure 18.12.

   A Linear Gradient usually looks better with rectangular buttons—on the Soup button in Figure 18.12, I clicked on Options in the fill bucket style palette to set the direction of the gradient to 350 degrees. Another option is to distinguish the outline of the button with a drawing tool, as I did with the Chablis button in Figure 18.12.

3. **Add a shadow**

   The `Image | Special Effects | Add Drop Shadow` command can give almost any button more visual impact and "pushability." I used it to add a shadow to all the buttons in Figure 18.12, with the exception of the sphere. That shadow I added by hand with the brush tool for the specific three-dimensional effect I was after.

   Generally, you should add a shadow before you label the button, and then save the blank button as a full-color TIF or JPG file. That way, you can use the same basic button many times simply by adding different labels. The exception to this rule is when you're going to distort or filter the entire button, including the text label. Then you'll need to wait and put the shadow on after you're done so the button's color and shape don't change in unrealistic ways. The Menu button and Chablis button in Figure 18.12 are examples of waiting to add a last-minute shadow.

4. **Label it**

   Use the text tool to choose a font and put an appropriate label on your button. While the text is selected, you could use the fill bucket to shade it with a gradient fill that contrasts with the button. To make the text transparent, fill it with the background color and make sure you save the file as a transparent GIF when you finish the rest of the following steps.

5. **Add a cool special effect**

   Any of the filters, distortions, and effects discussed in Chapter 17 are available to make your button stand out and look "smart." The buttons in Figure 18.12 show off just three of the infinite possibilities: I used `Image | Distortions | Punch` to warp the Menu button. For the Chablis button, I applied the `Image | Special Filters | Emboss` filter, and then used `Colors | Adjust | Brightness` and `Colors | Colorize` to make it light blue. After applying `Image | Distortions | Circle` twice to the word *Rock*, I used `Image | Arithmetic | Darkest` to overlay it on the sphere.

   Of course, sometimes the best special effect is *no* special effect. I didn't do any fancy image processing at all to the Soup button, for example.

6. **Reduce the color depth**

   Fancy buttons don't do much good if nobody can see them for 25 seconds after your Web page starts loading. A key move for keeping button graphics files small is to reduce the number of colors. Almost any good button should reduce nicely to 16 colors; select `Colors | Reduce Color Depth | 16 Colors` and choose `Palette | Optimized` with `Reduction Method | Nearest Color`.

   If you look closely, you'll notice some color "banding" in 16-color buttons that use gradient fills, but this slight aesthetic compromise is well worth the faster speed at which the buttons come through your viewers' modems.

7. **Save as a transparent GIF**

   Rectangular buttons with no shadow don't need to be transparent, but any button with a shape should be. That way, you can change the background on your Web pages any time you like without having to change the buttons.

   To save a transparent GIF, select the eyedropper tool and click with the right mouse button on the region you want to be transparent. Then select `File | Save As` and choose `GIF89A Noninterlaced`. Click the `Options` button and choose `Set the transparency value to the background color`.

NOTE

Occasionally, a rectangular button with lots of gradually changing colors will save more efficiently and look better as a JPEG file. Be warned, though, that the JPEG compression algorithm can blur text if you're not careful with the amount of compression.

8. **Touch up anything that looks amiss**

   Often, you'll find the odd pixel or color shade that needs a bit of adjustment with the brush tool or `Colors|Edit Palette` command to look "just so."

   Another common problem with 16-color buttons is that parts of the button with colors similar to the background may become transparent when you meant for them to be opaque. For example, the word *Soup* in Figure 18.12 turned transparent when I reduced the image to 16 colors. To fix this problem, I selected a foreground color that looks almost as white as the background and used the color replacer tool to paint over the word *Soup*.

By following these eight basic steps and adding your own choice of effects, you can create beautiful buttons that convey the unique flavor of your own Web pages.

Matching Titles and Bars

A Webmaster does not live by buttons alone. You'll almost certainly want some other matching graphics for your pages. Since the title is probably the first thing that people will look at on your page, you might want to make it a fancy graphic instead of (or in addition to) a text heading. In fact, aside from graphical buttons, fancy titles are probably the most common use of graphics on the Web.

Almost as common are graphical bars, rules, or page dividers. If your page has a lot of text, a thematic bar or rule is a great way to offer a visual break to readers. Whether your pages are text intensive or not, bars can add flair and help remind people where they're at on the page.

Figures 18.13 through 18.16 are pages from a fictitious Web site I created for this chapter. For each of the four button styles you saw in Figure 18.12, I used similar shapes and effects to make matching titles and bars.

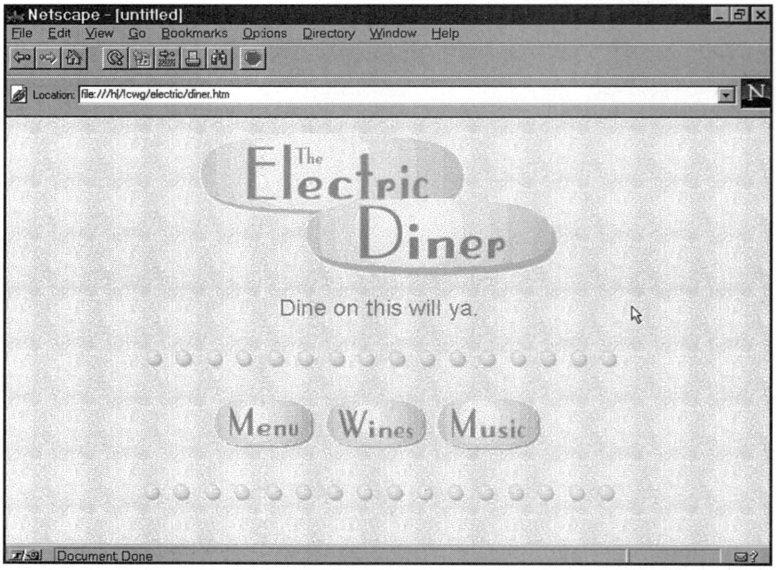

FIGURE 18.13.
Rules don't have to follow the rules—and who says titles have to be just text?

Figure 18.13 demonstrates how a little creativity can go a long way toward giving a page its own identity. By applying the same button effects to larger words, I made a title that follows the same theme. Cutting and pasting one word over the other and using a slightly deeper shadow enhances the three-dimensional effect. Similarly, cutting and pasting a line of shaded and shadowed dots fits the page's theme better than simply drawing a horizontal line.

FIGURE 18.14.
The Cut Out effect can make something drop into the page, but drop shadows make elements stand out above the page.

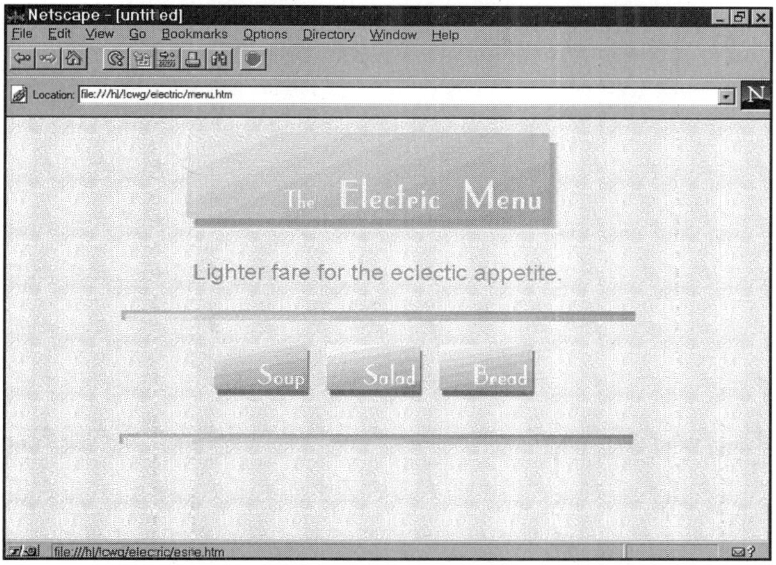

The title in Figure 18.14 was a no-brainer once the buttons were designed. It uses precisely the same fill and shadow settings—which Paint Shop Pro remembers until you change them, even if you close down the program and start it up again. The only change was that I saved the title as a 256-color image instead of a 16-color image. The color banding in the large region of gradient fill would have been too pronounced with only 16 colors. For a little visual variety, I used the `Image | Special Effects | Cut Out` command to drop the rules into the page, instead of the Drop Shadow command to elevate them above the page. The resulting Web page took only minutes to make, but looks sharp and loads fast.

Of course, titles don't have to look exactly the same as buttons to give a page visual consistency. In Figure 18.15, I used the same Emboss and Colorize filters on the title that I did on the buttons, but instead of adding a frame and drop shadow, I simply made the background color transparent. This is a popular (and very easy) trick, which makes the title seem to have been embossed onto the page. The horizontal rules above and below the title are actually separate graphics, which could be used anywhere on the page for dividers.

FIGURE 18.15.
Embossing gives titles and rules that oh-so-chic stamped-paper look.

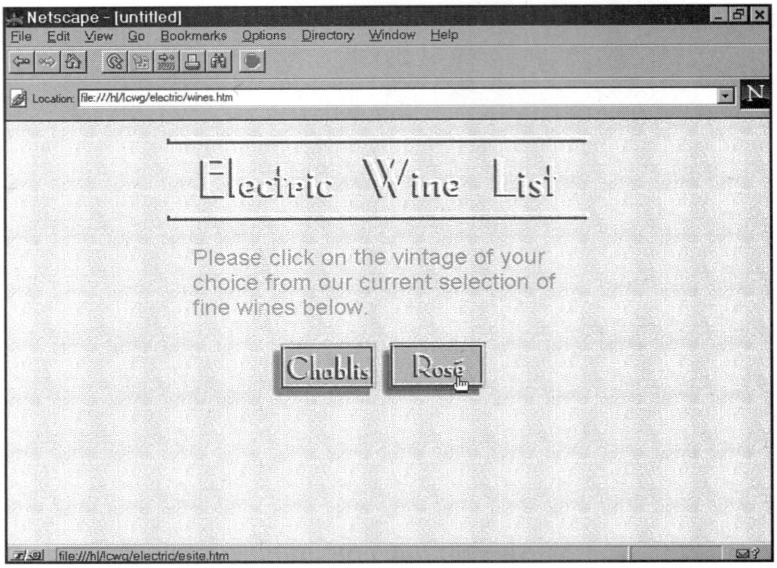

TIP

Notice that the text in Figure 18.15 stays neatly near the center of the page and lines up nicely with the title. Doing this is simple; just put the text in a one-cell table with the width you want. In this case, the HTML was this:

```
<TABLE WIDTH=440><TR><TD>
Please click on the vintage of your choice from our current selection
of fine wines below.
</TD></TR></TABLE>
```

You'll find more details on making tables in Chapter 20.

If you choose to use multiple effects in a graphic, it can be tedious and trying to exactly repeat all the steps you took when you go to make another matching image. To make the title in Figure 18.16, for example, I played around a bit with Hot Wax Coating, Negative Image, and other color replacements and adjustments. When I finally got a result I liked, I would have been hard put to remember just what I'd done to arrive at it.

How, then, did I make the matching horizontal bar? Easy. I just cut out the letter *l* from the word *Electric* and pasted copies of it together to form a long vertical bar. Then I rotated it and added a drop shadow in the same direction as I had for the title. I often copy the letter *l* or *I* from text quite often to make a horizontal rule. Dots from an *i* can make nice dotted bars, too.

FIGURE 18.16.
As long as you're careful not to get toooo wild, multiple effects can give your pages a singular personality.

Summary

This chapter has explored four ways to add flair to your pages while making your work as a Web author more efficient. Font controls and style sheets let you customize the mood of your text; special effects and creative layouts let you do the same with your graphics and overall page appearance.

I hope this chapter has inspired you to be more creative than you thought you could be with the words on your Web pages. Chapter 19, "Animating Graphical Images," tells you how to make your Web pages dynamic with moving images and icons.

CHAPTER 19

Animating Graphical Images

by Dick Oliver

IN THIS CHAPTER

There are several ways to add some movement to a Web page. You could hire a programmer or spend a few months learning the Java language. You could use a pre-built applet or OLE component to play some sort of video or interactive media file. Or you could ask all the visitors to your Web site to go get a helper application or plug-in program to play your favorite media file format. All of these can be excellent solutions in many situations, but every one of them involves an investment of time and resources, even before you start to produce the animation itself.

Wouldn't it be nice if you could just "snap together" three or four GIF images to make a simple animated graphic, without having to deal with any extra software components or media viewers at all? And wouldn't it be great if people using older Web browsers automatically saw at least the first frame of your animation, without your having to do any extra coding or producing additional graphics files? And while we're wishing, how about an animation format that can save a cool animated icon in a 20 K or smaller file?

Believe it or not, these utopian dreams have already become a reality. In fact, multiframe animation was built into the GIF file format way back in 1989. The compression is very efficient, and it's almost shamefully easy to make GIF animations. Every user of Netscape Navigator and Microsoft Internet Explorer (which means the vast majority of Internet surfers) can see animated GIFs without any additional software or add-ons. You can include these animations in a Web page exactly as if they were "ordinary" GIFs, with the `<IMG>` tag. Most browsers will support GIF animation in their next releases, but in the meantime, those who use browsers other than Navigator or Explorer will always see just the first (or in some cases, the last) image in the animation.

Ease of creation and use makes GIF animations a great choice for simple animated icons and any Web page graphics that could use a little motion to spice them up. In this chapter, you'll learn how to create GIF animations and how to optimize them for the fastest possible display.

You'll also learn some even sneakier tricks to create movement and interactivity on your Web pages with ordinary HTML. These include dynamic documents that automatically load another document after a specified time period as well as an example of how to use embedded frames to create images that respond to user interaction.

Building a GIF Animation

The first step in creating a GIF animation is to create a series of images to be displayed one after the other. You can use any graphics software you like to make the images. You don't even need to use software that supports GIF to make the images; Alchemy Mindworks' GIF Construction Set, a nifty little utility designed especially for assembling multi-image GIFs, can import BMP, JPEG, PCX, TIFF, and almost any other graphics file format you throw at it.

TIP

The fastest way to create a simple GIF animation with GIF Construction Set is to select `File | Animation Wizard`. This will start an "interview" that leads you through all the steps discussed below.

You can also automatically create scrolling text and a number of transition effects with the `Edit | Banner` and `Edit | Transition` commands. These commands provide an easy way to add some quick animation effects to still images.

In this chapter, however, I show you how to create animations "by hand," without using the Wizard or automatic effects. This will give you a head start when you want to use the advanced animation tricks discussed toward the end of the chapter.

The following numbered steps show you how to make a simple GIF animation. This animation will flip back and forth between two artistic renderings of the word "LOOK" that I created in Paint Shop Pro.

1. Before you assemble an animation with GIF Construction Set, you may want to open the images you'd like to include from another graphics program so you can refer to them as you put the animation together. Figure 19.1 shows the two images for this example opened in Paint Shop Pro, with the GIF Construction Set program in the foreground.

TIP

You'll find it easier to build and modify animations if you give the images for each animation similar names. You might name the images for a dog animation `dog1.gif`, `dog2.gif`, `dog3.gif`, and so on.

2. To start a new animation, start GIF Construction Set and select `File | New`. At the top of the white area, "`HEADER GIF 89a Screen (640×480)`" should appear. This is the first "block" in the GIF file, to which you will be adding additional image blocks and control blocks that will be listed below it.
3. Click the `Edit` button and the dialog box in Figure 19.1 appears. Enter the screen width and depth (height) of the largest image you want to use in the animation and click `OK`. (Not sure how big your images are? Paint Shop Pro displays the width and depth of the current image at the lower left corner of the screen.)

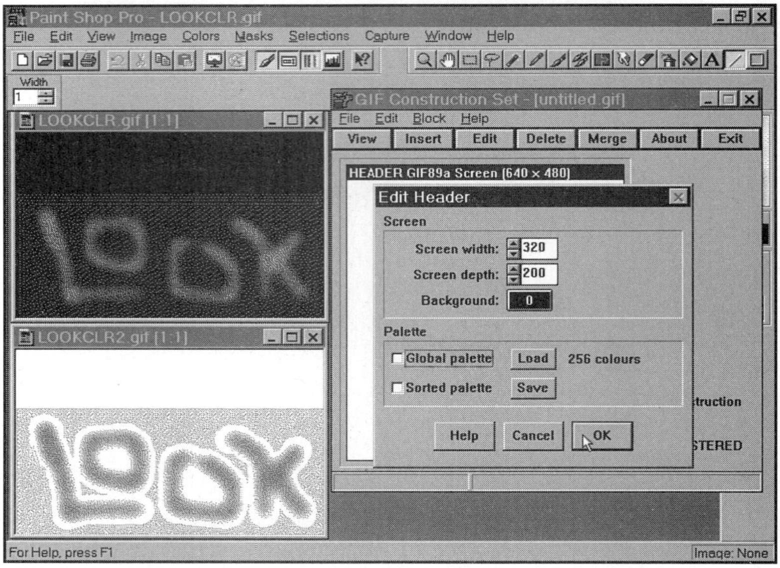

FIGURE 19.1.
GIF Construction Set runs in a fairly small window, so you can see other applications—such as Paint Shop Pro—at the same time. Here, the Edit Header dialog box displays information.

4. If you want the animation to loop continuously when you view it in Netscape Navigator, click the `Insert` button and then click `Loop` to insert a special control block telling it to immediately restart the animation every time it finishes. If you want to create an animation that plays only once and then stops (leaving the last image on display), skip this step.
5. Click `Insert` then `Image` and choose the first image in the animation, as shown in Figure 19.2. This is also the image that will be displayed by browsers that don't support GIF animation.
6. A dialog box will appear saying `The palette of the image you have imported does not match the global palette for this file`. Later in this chapter I'll explain in detail the other options included in this dialog box, but for now, choose `Use a local palette for this image` and click `OK`.

FIGURE 19.2.
Even in Windows 95, GIF Construction Set uses a Windows 3.x style file selection box. (Tsk, tsk. But then again, who really cares?)

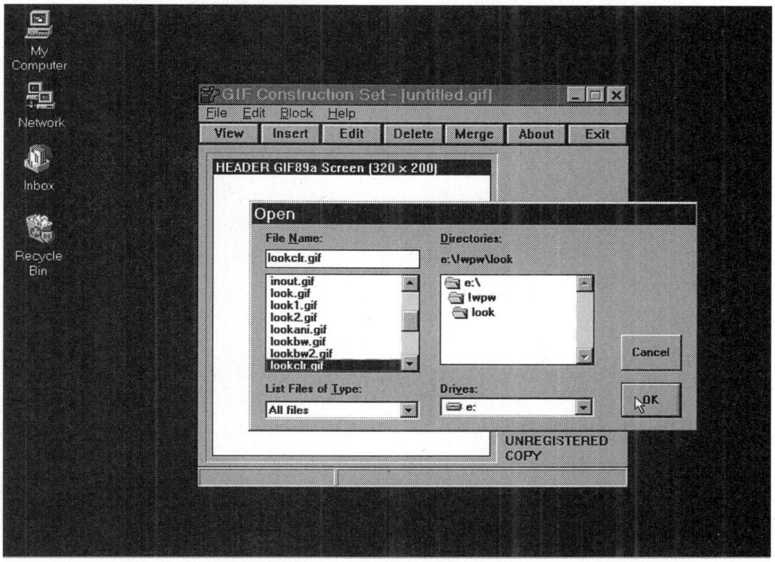

7. If you want the image you just inserted to be transparent, press the up arrow once or click on `LOOP`, then click `Insert`, then `Control`. This inserts a control block in front of the image.

   Then click `Edit` to get the Edit Control Block dialog box shown in Figure 19.3. Check Transparent colour and then click the little eyedropper icon button. The image is displayed and the cursor turns to an eyedropper. Click the tip of the eyedropper on the color you want to appear transparent when the image is displayed.

   Before you click `OK`, be sure to select `Background` under the `Remove by:` selection list. (The other options are explained later in this chapter.)

FIGURE 19.3.
With control blocks, you can make images transparent or insert a time delay between images.

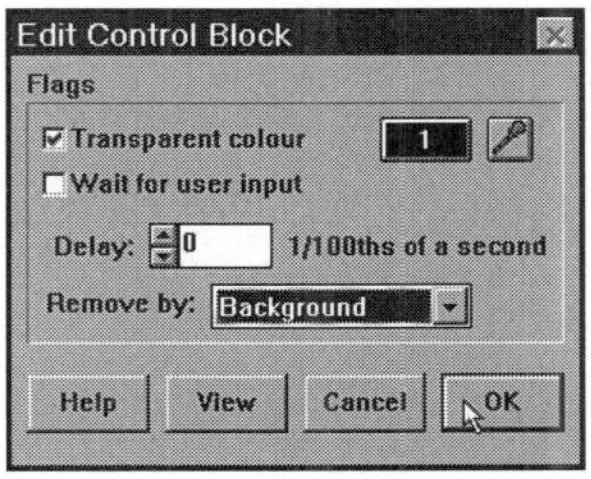

8. Repeat steps 5 through 7 for every image in the animation. Remember that the control block for an image has to appear just above the image block in the list, but you need to insert the image first and then go back to edit the control block to add transparency.

   A little confusing? Don't worry, you'll be an old pro at it by the end of this chapter. In the meantime, if you make a mistake, you can highlight any block and click `Delete` to get rid of it.

9. When all the images and control blocks are inserted in the right order, select `File` | `Save As` to save the animation (see Figure 19.4). Be sure to give it a name ending in `.gif`!

10. Using your favorite Web page editor, make an HTML document with an `IMG` tag referring to the `.gif` file you just saved as the `SRC` (an example tag might be <IMG SRC="lookani.gif">). Load the document in Netscape Navigator version 2.0 or higher to see the results.

    You can also preview the animation within GIF Construction Set by clicking View at any time during the construction process.

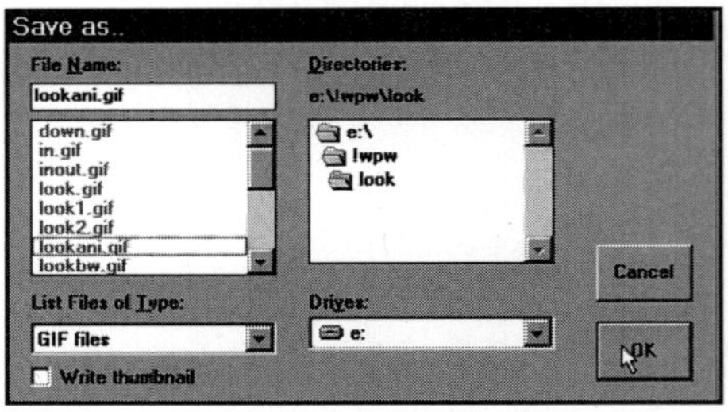

FIGURE 19.4.
Save your file with the `.gif` *extension.*

I obviously can't illustrate the animated effect of flipping back and forth between two images with a printed figure in a book. But you can load the `look.htm` document on the CD-ROM if you'd like to see the action.

GIF Animation Tips and Tricks

Figure 19.5 shows a page I created for the CD-ROM to accompany my book *Web Page Wizardry* from Sams.net Publishing. *Web Page Wizardry* is an excellent choice if you want to learn about more advanced animation and multimedia techniques after you finish this book.

The page in Figures 19.5 through 19.7 is also on the CD-ROM included with this book, as `/examples/wpw/wpw/wpw.htm`. If you view the page with Netscape Navigator version 2.0 or higher or with Microsoft Internet Explorer 3.0, you'll notice that all the icons are animated: a vision appears in the crystal ball, the scepter flashes, the cauldron bubbles, the mirror revolves, the book pages turn. These icons are actually five separate multi-image GIFs, and the HTML code for this snazzy action-filled page looks just like an ordinary static Web page (see Listing 19.1).

Listing 19.1. The Web Page Wizardry Page (`wpw.htm`)

```
<HTML>
<HEAD><TITLE>Web Page Wizardry</TITLE></HEAD>
<BODY BACKGROUND="bubsmoke.jpg" BGCOLOR="black">
<CENTER>
<IMG SRC="wpwtitle.gif" LOWSRC="hat.gif"><P>

<A HREF="visions.htm"><IMG SRC="visions.gif" BORDER=0></A>
<A HREF="programs.htm"><IMG SRC="programs.gif" BORDER=0></A>
 <IMG SRC="spacer.gif"><IMG SRC="spacer.gif">
<A HREF="brews.htm"><IMG SRC="brews.gif" BORDER=0></A>
 <IMG SRC="spacer.gif"><IMG SRC="spacer.gif">
<A HREF="worlds.htm"><IMG SRC="worlds.gif" ALIGN="absmiddle" BORDER=0></A>
<A HREF="pages.htm"><IMG SRC="pages.gif" BORDER=0></A><BR>

<A HREF="visions.htm"><IMG SRC="vistext.gif" BORDER=0></A>
<A HREF="programs.htm"><IMG SRC="prgtext.gif" BORDER=0></A>
<A HREF="brews.htm"><IMG SRC="brwtext.gif" BORDER=0></A>
<A HREF="worlds.htm"><IMG SRC="wrltext.gif" BORDER=0></A>
<A HREF="pages.htm"><IMG SRC="pagtext.gif" BORDER=0></A>
</CENTER>
</BODY>
</HTML>
```

NOTE

If this were a page on the Internet instead of a CD-ROM, I would have included ALT attributes so that users of very old browsers or very slow modems would see some text without having to wait for the graphics to download. For example, `<IMG SRC="wpwtitle.gif" ALT="Web Page Wizardry">`.

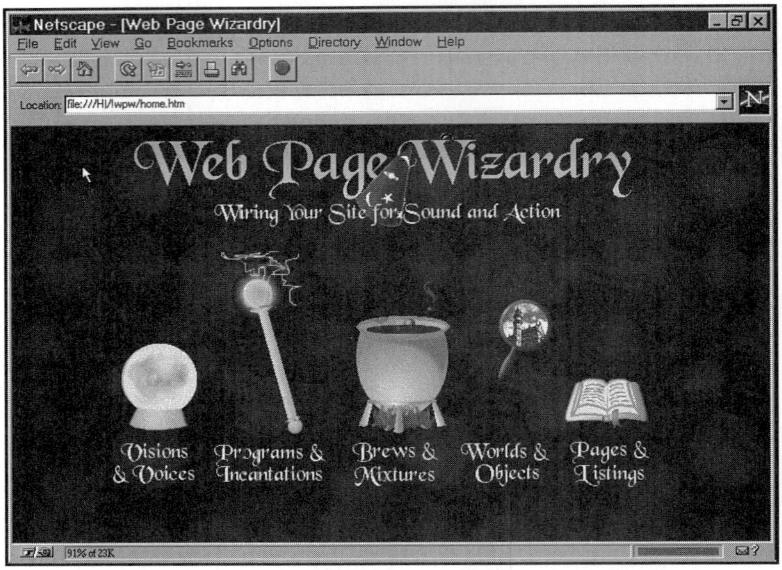

FIGURE 19.5.
At first glance, and to non-Netscape users, this looks like a page full of regular GIF images.

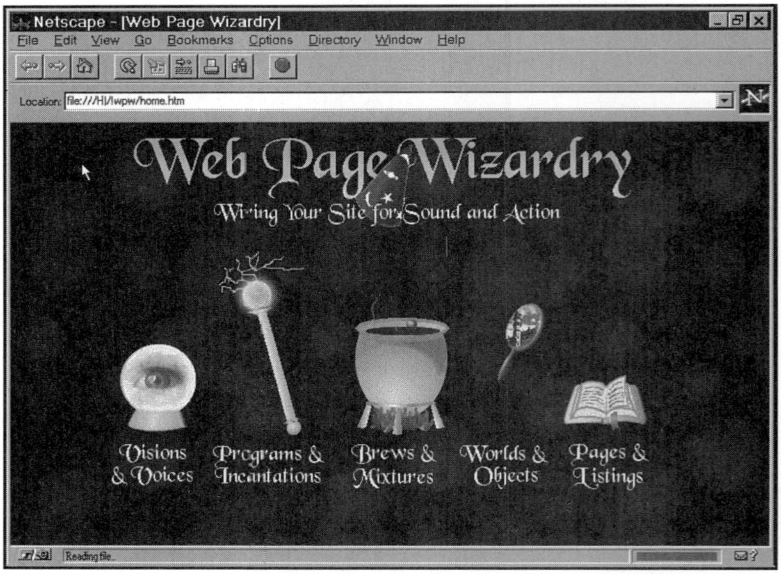

FIGURE 19.6.
Users of Netscape, however, will quickly notice that all the GIFs are actually multi-image animation.

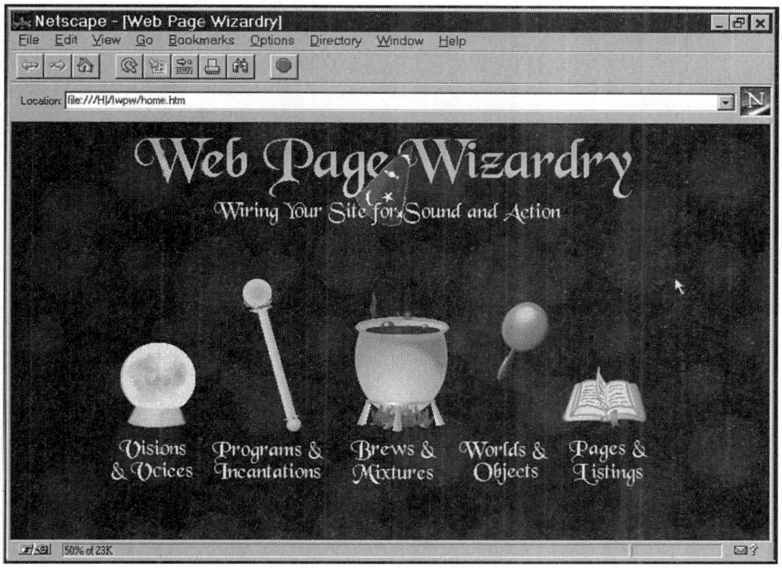

FIGURE 19.7.
Netscape gracefully handles the logistics of displaying five separate GIF animations all at once.

A Hand-Crafted Animation

I could have created all this animation in Paint Shop Pro or another shareware graphics program, but I decided to bring in the heavy artillery and create it in Adobe Photoshop instead. Not only does Photoshop offer more advanced drawing and coloring tools, but more importantly, with it you can keep various parts of an image in separate layers that you can modify independently. This feature (which is also found in a number of other commercial graphics editors) makes drawing simple animation a breeze.

For example, let me explain how I created the spell book that flips its own pages. To start, I just sketched the first image from scratch and then drew five views of the turning page on separate layers, as shown in Figure 19.8.

NOTE

To make "layered" animations like this in Paint Shop Pro, start by drawing the basic image (in this case, the book), and using `Edit | Copy` and `Edit | Paste | As New Image` to create multiple copies of it. Then add the details for each image (in this case, the turning page) separately.

FIGURE. 19.8.
Photoshop makes it easy to build animation because you can just draw the changes from frame to frame and use transparency to show or hide it at will.

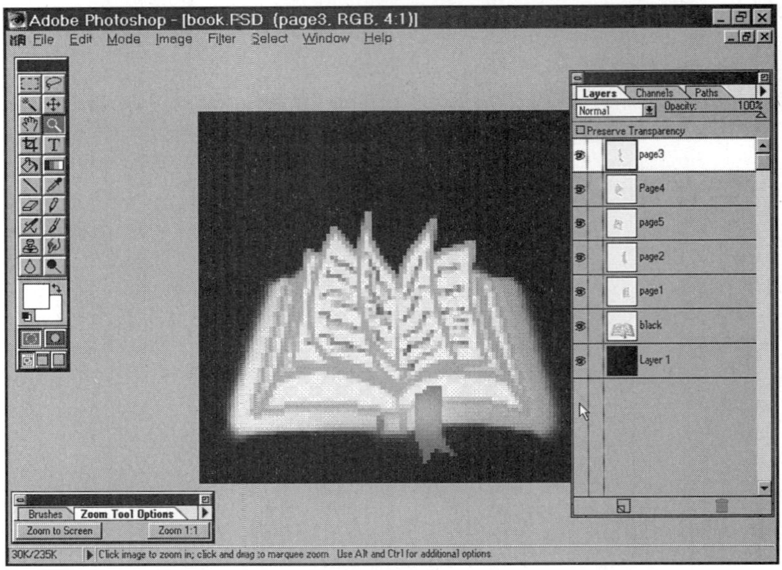

After I drew all the pages, I turned on each layer one at a time (keeping the book and background layers always on) and used Photoshop's `File` | `Save a Copy` command to save each view as a separate true-color BMP file.

TIP

If you're wondering how I did the rotating mirror within Photoshop, know that I didn't. I used a 3D modeling program to build a 3D model of the mirror and a keyframe animation of it rotating. Then I brought the images from that animation into Photoshop to add the magic window through which you can see the castle. You can find out more about creating 3D models and putting "virtual reality" scenes on your Web pages in the *Web Page Wizardry* book.

Handling Palettes

When I created the spell book, I knew that GIF Construction Set is able to import BMP files and dither them down to 256 colors. I also knew that I could get the best results by giving GIF Construction Set one file that was already dithered to 256 colors, however, so that GIF could use that file's colors as the global palette to which all other files in the animation could be matched. Therefore, I used Photoshop's `Mode | Index Color` command to change the first image in the sequence (the book with flat pages) to 256 colors and saved that in the GIF format. In Paint Shop Pro, you could achieve the same thing with the `Colors | Decrease Color Depth` command.

Next, I fired up GIF Construction Set and assembled the images the same way I assembled the images in the step-by-step example earlier in this chapter. The only difference between the present example and the previous example is how I handled the global palette and the dithering of the imported BMP files. For the first image in the spell book GIF, I inserted the 256-color GIF file and chose `Use this image as the global palette`, as shown in Figure 19.9. For all other images, I inserted the true-color BMP files and chose `Dither this image to the global palette`, as in Figure 19.10.

TIP

In this case, the subtle gradations of color in these images look a lot better when dithered, so I was willing to put up with the slightly larger file sizes that dithering creates.

For most situations, however, you should use Paint Shop Pro's nearest color algorithm to change all images to 256 colors before bringing them into GIF Construction Set, and then choose `Remap this image to the global palette` when importing them, rather than `Dither this image to the global palette`. They might not look quite as pretty, but they'll often come out a lot smaller and faster.

On the other hand, when you need the absolute best possible quality and don't care so much about size or speed, you have the option of using a separate optimized palette of colors for each image. To do this, choose `Use a local palette for this image` when you insert each image.

FIGURE 19.9.
For at least one image in your animation (usually the first one), you should select `Use this image as the global palette` *after you insert the image.*

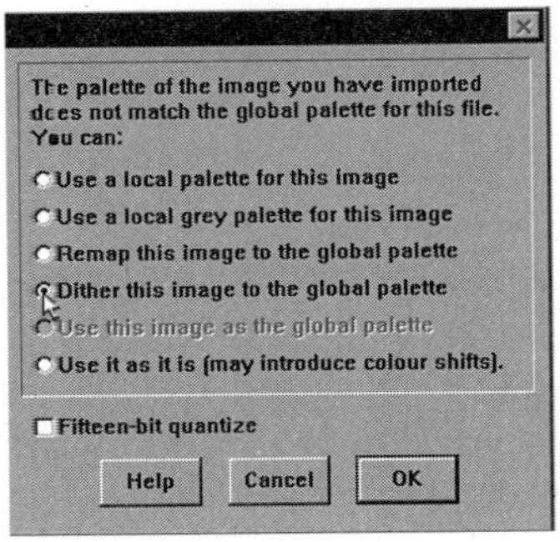

FIGURE 19.10.
Once you have a global palette from one image, you can reduce file size and improve display speed by remapping or dithering all other images to that palette.

Tips on Transparency

As demonstrated in the earlier `LOOK` example, you can make the background transparent by inserting a control block in front of each image and choosing `Transparent colour` and `Remove by: Background` when you edit the control block (see Figure 19.11). You can use the eyedropper tool (mentioned previously in this chapter) to pick the transparent color or you can click the number next to the eyedropper to pick the color directly from the global or local palette (see Figure 19.12).

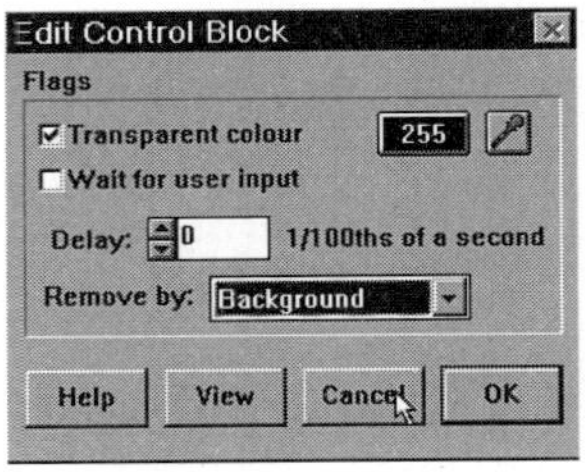

FIGURE 19.11.
If you want the animation to have a transparent color, insert and edit a control block before each image.

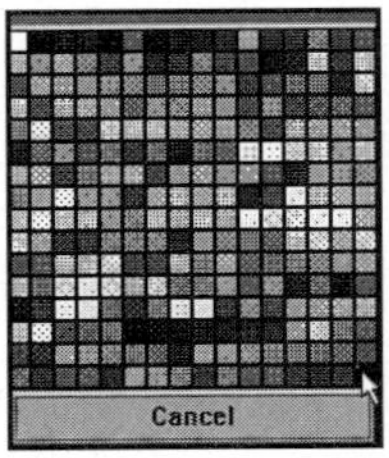

FIGURE 19.12.
To pull up this color-picking palette, click the number next to the eyedropper tool (255 in Figure 19.11).

To make sure you pick the right color you want to be transparent, you can click on the `View` button to preview the animation. Note that the background color used during the preview can be set by selecting `File | Setup` and picking a color from the `Edit view mode background` drop-down list box (Figure 19.13). You may want to choose a contrasting color (in this example, white or gray) to check the transparency value, and then choose a color similar to your Web page background (in this example, black) to see what the animation will look like on the page.

TIP

Notice that the Setup dialog box also includes some controls to fine-tune the dithering of true-color images. You'll probably never need these, but if you're not happy with the results of a dithered image, this is where you go to fuss and fiddle with it.

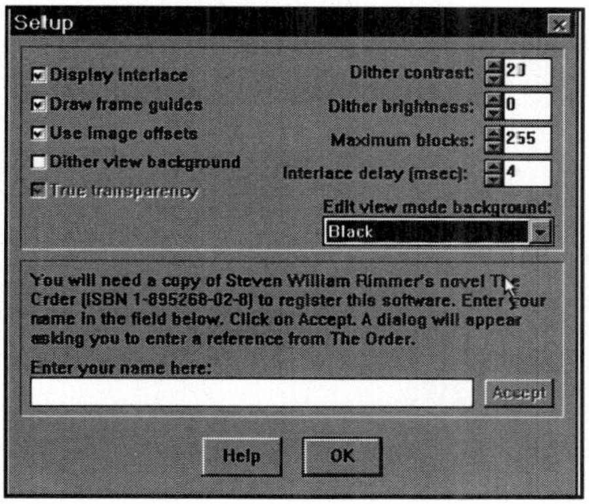

FIGURE 19.13.
In this dialog box, you can choose a preview background color and fine-tune some other picky stuff.

Doing the Loop

In the first example in this chapter, I mentioned that you can make an animation continuously loop by clicking `Insert` then `Loop` in GIF Construction Set. You need to know one more thing to create a successful looped animation, however, and it isn't at all obvious. Because of the way that Netscape Navigator processes and displays multi-image GIF files, you will often find that the first frame of a looping animation is skipped or only half displayed, making a noticeable jerk or some other subtle-but-annoying effect.

The way to avoid this is to always repeat the first image at the end of the animation. This way, the "jerk" becomes invisible because it occurs between two identical images. For example, Figure 19.14 shows the complete `pages.gif` animation. This animation actually contains only six separate images—the seventh image is a repeat of the first.

Repeating the first image does increase the size of the GIF file, so you may be willing to tolerate a little jerkiness to keep the size down. Also, in an animation such as the LOOK logo example, you never notice or care about the jerk anyway. It's a good idea to try the animation without the first image repeat to see whether you're happy with the results. If you are, the only reason to consider repeating the first image is that a few older browsers will display only the last image in the animation. (Most older browsers will display only the first image, however.)

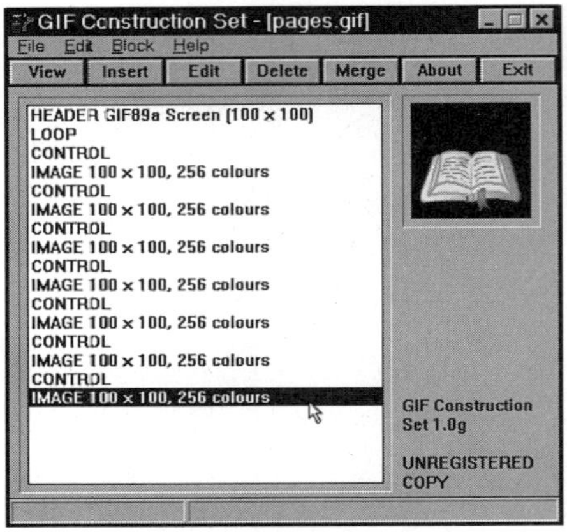

FIGURE 19.14.
For smooth animation, it often helps to make the first and last images identical.

TIP

One more tip on looping: If you highlight the LOOP block and click the `Edit` button, you can set a number of iterations for the animation to repeat before stopping. This doesn't work in Netscape Navigator 2.0, but it does work in Navigator 3.0 and Microsoft Explorer 3.0.

Optimizing GIF Animation for Speed and Size

You can improve the speed and reduce the size of GIF animation in two ways. One way is to save only the part of the image that changes from one frame to the next and insert this smaller GIF file instead of replacing the whole image. The other way is to make transparent any part of the image that doesn't change. This can also dramatically reduce the size of the file because a solid region of transparency will compress much more efficiently than the same region filled with complex image data.

The most impressive application of these techniques is an animation in which a small moving character or object is superimposed over a complex backdrop. You can save the backdrop only once as the first image and then insert only the images of the small changing region for subsequent images. This can easily reduce the size of the animation file by a factor of 10 or more. I'll use a less dramatic example, though, where we'll actually only shave about 6 K off a 26 K animation file. You can, of course, apply the same technique to a larger file.

Cropping the Crystal

Like the spell book, the crystal ball animation was created as a number of separate image layers in Photoshop (see Figure 19.15). Instead of saving each frame in the animation as a layer, in this case I used the opacity slider to vary the transparency effects between layers as I swirled the "fog" layer around with the smudge brush. You could achieve the exact same effect in Paint Shop Pro by using the smudge brush on multiple copies of the original image.

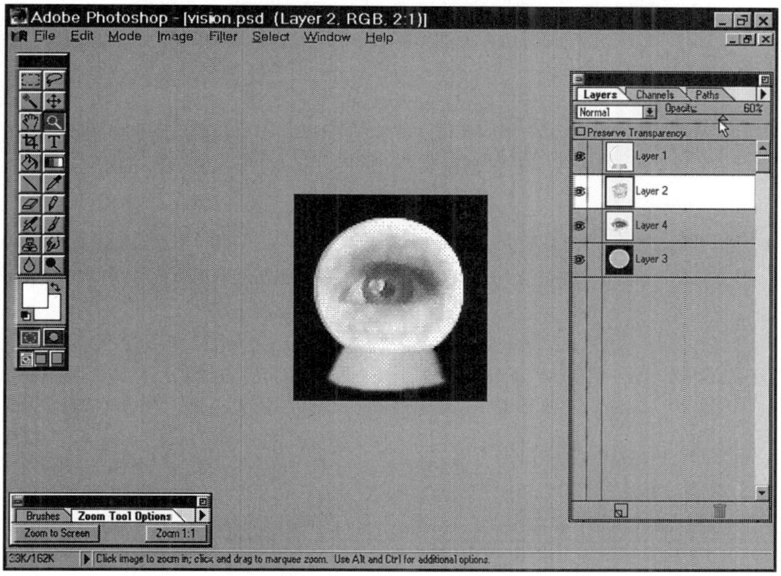

FIGURE 19.15.
The crystal ball animation was created by varying the opacity of the layers in a Photoshop image.

Only the first image of the series was saved in its entirety, however. I cropped off the bottom part (including the gold stand) of all the other images. Figure 19.16 shows the five images used to build the animation. Note that these include a cropped copy of the first image to put at the end of the animation.

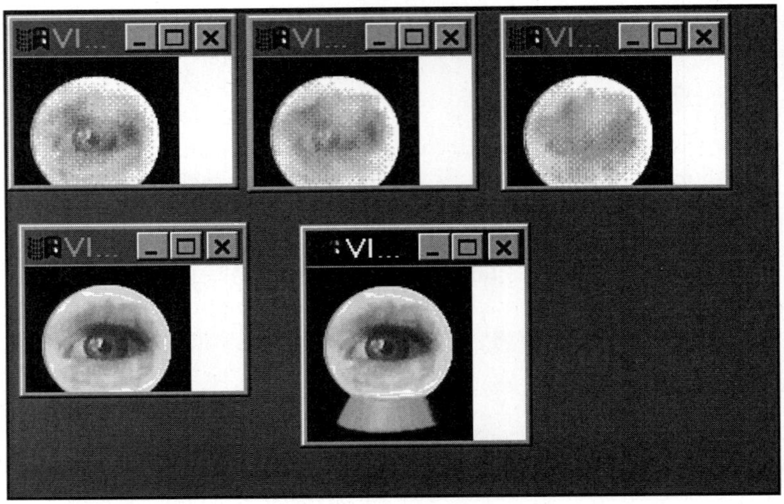

FIGURE 19.16.
To make the file sizes smaller, I stored only the part of the animation that changes from frame to frame.

When I assembled these images in GIF Construction Set, I set each Edit Control Block to `Remove by: Previous Image` instead of `Remove by: Background` (Figure 19.17). This keeps the previous image visible under any transparent areas—or areas not covered by the current image if the current image is smaller than any of those previous. This way, the gold stand from the first image remains unchanged when the smaller cropped frames are displayed.

You may also notice in Figure 19.17 that I specified a delay of 20/100 (or 1/5) of a second between animation frames. This slows the animation down enough so that the foggy haze seems to drift in and out, rather than snap back and forth like someone changing TV channels.

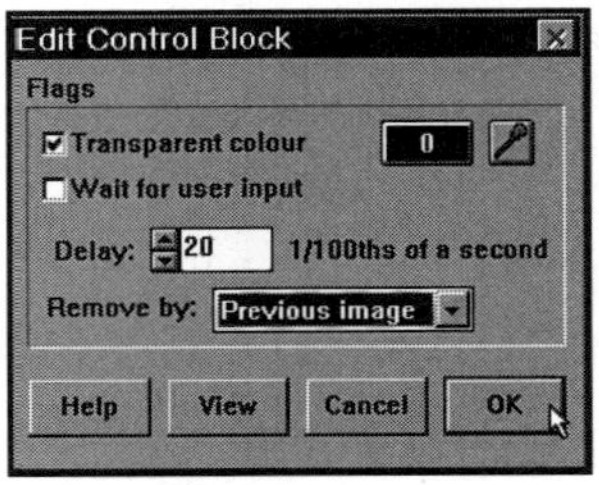

FIGURE 19.17.
By setting each Edit Control Block to `Remove by: Previous Image`, *you can leave parts of a previously displayed frame visible.*

TIP

You can control where a smaller image appears over a larger one by highlighting the image block and clicking `Edit` (see Figure 19.18). In this example, both the Image left (horizontal offset) and Image top (vertical offset) values are `0`, meaning that the top left corner of the image should be placed exactly over the top left corner of the entire animation. If you have a small object to place in the middle of a large backdrop, however, you can adjust these offsets to place the object just where you want it.

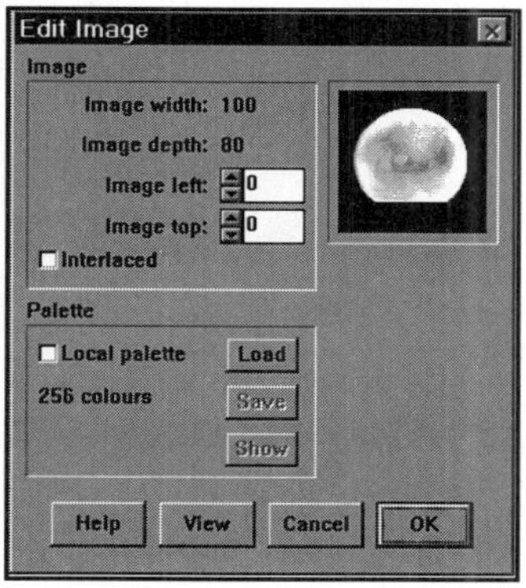

FIGURE 19.18.
You can use the `Image left` *and* `Image top` *settings to place a smaller image in the middle of a larger one. (Here, no offset is needed so they are both set to* `0`*.)*

Emptying the Pot

The largest animation on the *Web Page Wizardry* home page is the bubbling cauldron. Because the big fat pot had to be dithered for the shading to look good, the animation weighs in at more than 40 K—about twice as large as the other multi-image GIFs on the page.

There's a sneaky way to cut that file size almost in half. In Figure 19.19, I placed a blue rectangle over the unchanging (and biggest) part of each image, except for the first one. Then, when I pulled these images into GIF Construction Set, I set blue to be transparent and chose `Remove by: Previous Image` in the Edit Control Box, as I did for the crystal ball images.

Unfortunately, this sneaky stunt only works when you don't need to use the transparency for the background of a Web page to show around the edges of an image. (If I used the same black color to block out the pot as I used for the background around the top and bottom, parts of the steam, bubbles, and fire would not get erased properly between frames.)

If I were posting this page on the Internet, I would probably choose to use a solid black background on the page so I could use the optimized `Remove by: Previous Image` version of this animation (26 K) instead of the fully transparent `Remove by: Background` version (40 K). But, because this is for CD-ROM, I splurged and went with the fancy background and the 40 K image. Even with this move of reckless abandon, all the animation on the page still only adds up to 120 K, which is smaller than the static graphics on many Web pages these days.

FIGURE 19.19.
By blocking out the unchanging part of a large image, you can save a lot of space in the GIF file.

Chapter 16, "Bigger, Faster, Better Graphics," reveals a number of other ways to reduce the size and increase the speed of your GIF graphics.

Dynamic Documents

Dynamic documents are pages that automatically change without any action from the user. Dynamic documents are not new to Internet Explorer 3.0 (they were first introduced in version 2.0), but they represent yet another very striking development in HTML content presentation.

There are two basic approaches to producing a dynamic document: server push and client pull. As these terms suggest, server-push documents are sent automatically by the server without being "asked for." A client-pull document, on the other hand, is a page that instructs the browser (client) program to automatically initiate a request for another page.

TIP

Dynamic documents work beautifully within frame documents. You can have one frame automatically refreshing itself while the other frames display ordinary static pages. (See Chapter 7, "Creating and Enhancing Web Pages with Frames," for an introduction to frames.) Oh, and whatever you do, don't put a server-push animation into your background image. On second thought....

Server-Push

Server-push is different from standard HTTP information transfers. Normally, when you use Internet Explorer (or any other Web browser) to request a document from a site on the World Wide Web, your computer makes a request of another computer, the other computer processes your request and sends back the information you requested (if it is available), and that is the end of the communication.

With server-push, however, Internet Explorer establishes a connection to an HTTP server and keeps that connection open, enabling content to be "streamed" out of the server until the parameters of the HTTP request have been satisfied. Server-push programming usually involves some kind of Perl or C programming knowledge.

Before you embark on any substantial work, though, be sure to check with your Internet access provider to find out whether their server is capable of handling server-push programs or whether you could expect to be billed extra for the service. Server-push scripts are known to bring the most robust servers down.

Unlike many other Internet Explorer extensions, Internet Explorer's implementation of server-push has not been very widely adopted by other browsers, and for the most part, server-push programs can be viewed only by Internet Explorer. The multimedia dimensions that server-push offers are expected to be superseded by more advanced animation and multimedia interfaces such as Java.

For a fun demonstration of server-push, point your Internet Explorer browser to `http://anansi.panix.com/~sorabji/smile.smile.smile.html`.

Client-Pull

Client-pull is different from server-push in that the main "work" involved is performed by the Web browser. The `<META>` tag is used to automatically request another page after a specified time period. The syntax of the `<META>` tag looks somewhat bizarre at first.

```
<META HTTP-EQUIV="Refresh" CONTENT="2; URL=http://someplace.com/page2.html">
```

What this tag does is send a message pretending to be from the server saying `Refresh: 2; URL=http://someplace.com/page2.html`. When Internet Explorer sees this message, it waits two seconds, and then loads the URL given. In this case, a document named `page2.html` is loaded from `someplace.com`, but the URL could be any other document anywhere else on the Internet (or a file on the local hard drive). It could also be any type of viewable file, such as a sound or multimedia file for which a plug-in or helper application has been configured.

The net effect is simple: Internet Explorer retrieves one document and then pauses for a couple of seconds before loading a second document. This can be very striking when used as an attention-getting device, but it can also be useful if you want to be reasonably certain that visitors to your page will see a set of pages in a certain sequence.

Depending on what you wish to accomplish, server-push can be more efficient and reliable than client-pull because client-pull involves multiple HTTP requests and because the speed of HTTP requests can vary considerably.

For a working example of client-pull animation, open the `catdog2.htm` file on the CD-ROM that accompanies this book. The HTML for this animation is listed here and illustrated in Figure 19.20.

```
<HTML>
<HEAD>
<META HTTP-EQUIV="Refresh" CONTENT="2; URL=catdog3.htm">
<TITLE>Meow</TITLE></HEAD>
<BODY>
<IMG SRC="catdog2.gif"><A HREF="catdog4.htm">Click here to stop.</A>
</BODY>
</HTML>
```

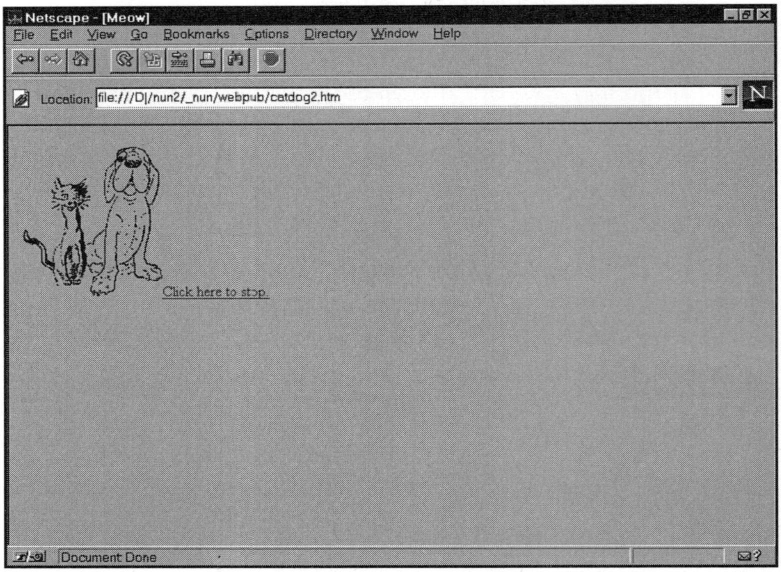

FIGURE 19.20.
This page (`catdog2.htm`) automatically turns into Figure 19.21 after two seconds.

After two seconds, the page automatically replaces itself with the `catdog3.htm` file, listed here and shown in Figure 19.21.

```
<HTML>
<HEAD>
<META HTTP-EQUIV="Refresh" CONTENT="2; URL=catdog2.htm">
<TITLE>Meow</TITLE></HEAD>
<BODY>
<IMG SRC="catdog.gif"><A HREF="catdog4.htm">Click here to stop.</A>
</BODY>
</HTML>
```

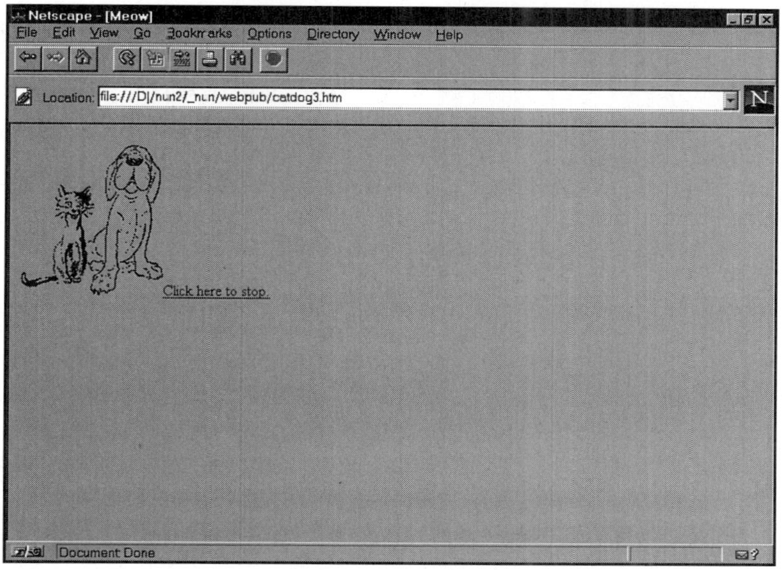

FIGURE 19.21.
This page (`catdog3.htm`) automatically turns back into Figure 19.20 after two seconds.

When the user clicks the `Click here to stop.` link, a similar page without any client-pull animation tags is loaded. This page, called `catdog4.htm`, is listed following:

```
<HTML>
<HEAD>
<TITLE>Meow</TITLE></HEAD>
<BODY>
<IMG SRC="catdog.gif"><A HREF="catdog2.htm">Click here to start.</A><P>
<A HREF="catdog.htm">Click here to go back.</A></BODY>
</HTML>
```

Interactive Floating Frames

One very interesting use of client-pull animation is to put a client-pull page inside a floating frame. Chapter 7, "Creating and Enhancing Web Pages with Frames," explains all the nitty-gritty of floating frames, but I'll review the essentials here and show how they can be used to change or animate graphics on a Web page in response to someone clicking on a link.

With floating frames, you can embed one Web page into another. The `<FRAME>` tag works just like the `<IMG>` tag except that the `SRC` can be an HTML document. For example, you could place the Microsoft home page in a 400×400-pixel area on one of your own Web pages, as in the following code:

```
<FRAME SRC="http://www.microsoft.com/" WIDTH=400 HEIGHT=400>
```

This area would have its own little scrollbar, and any links that the user clicks within the frame will display their corresponding documents within the frame without changing the main page at all. You can even use the standard `IMG ALIGN` attribute to center the frame or wrap text around it.

The real fun begins when you give a frame a name with the `<FRAME NAME>` attribute. You can then make any link on the page change the contents of that frame using only the `<A TARGET>` attribute. For example, the page in Figure 19.22 includes the following tag in the upper-left cell of the table:

```
<FRAME SRC="tabula.gif" NAME="picture">
```

This displays the `tabula.gif` image in that cell when the page loads. Each of the product names is a link that displays an image of the corresponding table in the frame named `"picture"`, as in the following:

```
<A HREF="table1.gif" TARGET="picture"><H2>Tabula Suprema</H2></A>
```

When the user clicks one of these links, the picture immediately appears in the frame without any reloading of the main page (see Figure 19.23).

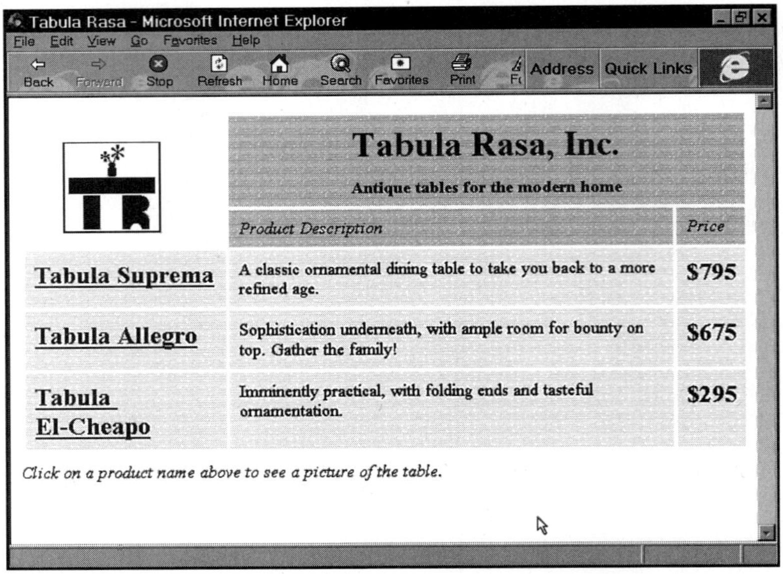

FIGURE 19.22.
The top-left cell in this table contains a named frame that initially contains the logo image.

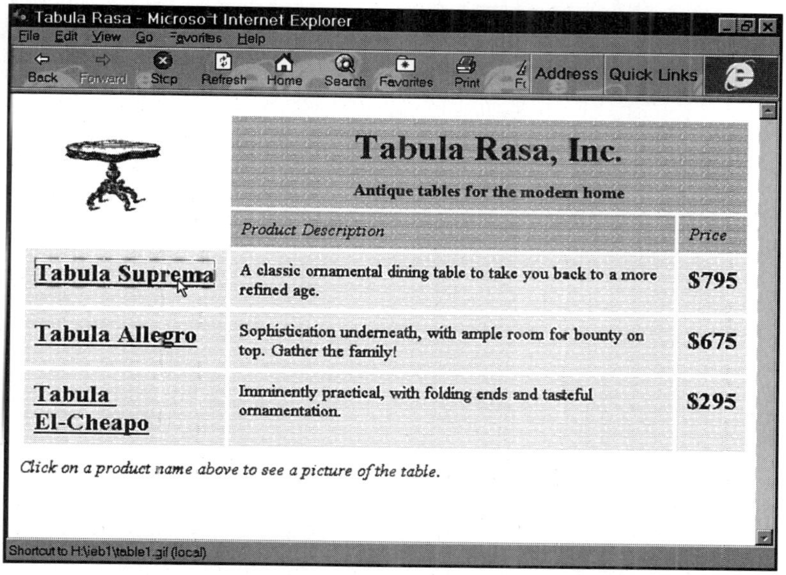

FIGURE 19.23.
When a user clicks one of the product names, a picture of the corresponding product immediately replaces the logo image.

NOTE

For details on how to make colorful tables like the one in Figures 19.22 and 19.23, refer to Chapter 6, "Effective Use of Tables."

When used in conjunction with GIF animations and/or client-pull animation, floating frames turn your Web pages into an interactive, action-filled experience. To accomplish this sort of interactivity before the invention of floating frames, you would have had to use complex programming or scripting languages. Now you can do it as easily as placing any other image on the page!

Summary

This chapter has shown you how to spice up your Web graphics with animation and interactivity. Chapter 20, "Backgrounds, Image Maps, and Creative Layouts," brings all the ingredients of a full-flavored graphical Web site together and serves up some creative examples for you to enjoy.

CHAPTER 20

Backgrounds, Image Maps, and Creative Layouts

by Dick Oliver

IN THIS CHAPTER

This chapter demonstrates how creative use of backgrounds, image maps, and layouts can ensure that Web surfers don't need to reach for the coffee while exploring your site. It helps you pull together all the tools and techniques covered in this book to create a cohesive and attractive Web site.

Making Seamless Background Tiles

If eye-catching is what you're after, what better way to start than by catching an eye? Figure 20.1 is my two-year-old daughter's left eye, scanned with a cheap hand-scanner from a snapshot and color-corrected a bit in Paint Shop Pro. (See Chapter 17, "Working with JPEG and GIF Images," for help with doing that.)

FIGURE 20.1.
The edges of this scanned photo don't fit together very well when tiled as a background.

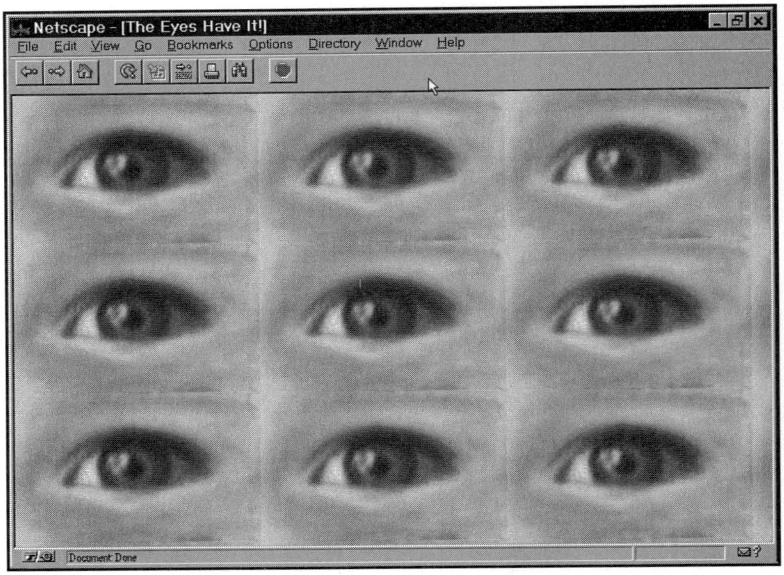

Seamless Backgrounds by Hand

The eye is pretty effective as an attention-getting background—but wouldn't it be slick if the tiles all fit together seamlessly? Since you might not know how to turn this image into a seamless background tile, I'll explain it step-by-step. You can follow these steps to turn almost any interesting pattern or image into a repeating tile.

NOTE

The following 11 steps do essentially the same thing as Paint Shop Pro's one-click `Image | Special Effects | Create Seamless Pattern` command. After I show you how to do it "the hard way," I'll show you the easy way. I'll also explain why this particular image (and many others) comes out much better if you *don't* use the Create Seamless Pattern command.

The following instructions are specifically for Paint Shop Pro, but you can do the same thing in any good graphics-editing program.

1. Open the graphics file you want to start with, and resize or crop it to suit the layout you have in mind. In this case, I chose a size that would tile nicely in a 640×480, 800×600, or 1024×768 window without the eye being cut in half on the right edge. (The image is 255×161 pixels.)
2. Select `Image | Enlarge Canvas` and double both the vertical and horizontal size of the canvas to leave room for arranging four copies of the image next to one another.
3. Using the rectangle selection tool, select the original image (in this case, the rectangle from 0,0 to 254,160). Paint Shop Pro displays the current location of the cursor at the bottom of the screen to help you get exactly the region you want.
4. Using the move selection tool (the one with two people in dotted boxes on the toolbar), move a copy of the selection down, as shown in Figure 20.2.

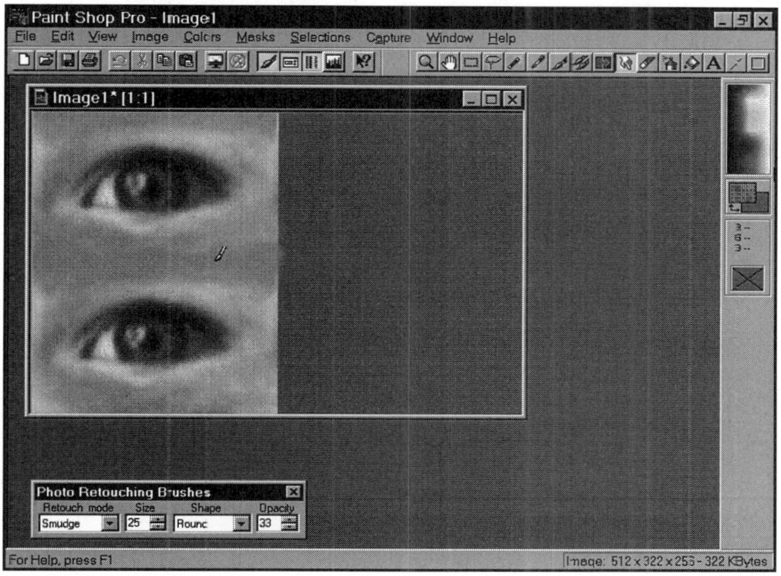

FIGURE 20.2.
To make a seamless tile, start by copying the image and smoothing the top and bottom edges together.

5. Using the smudge brush and/or the copy brush, smooth the edge between the two copies of the image.
6. Select the top part of the bottom image (here, the rectangle from 162,0 to about 350,255), and move it up to replace the top part of the top image. Now the top image will tile seamlessly in the vertical direction.
7. Repeat steps 3 through 6 for the horizontal direction: Move a copy of the top image to the right, smooth the edge between them, and copy the leftmost half back onto the original image. (See Figure 20.3.)

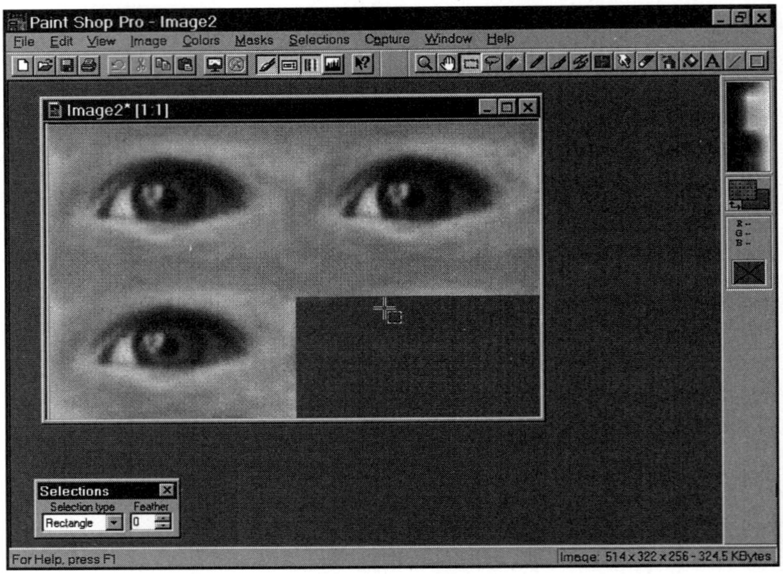

FIGURE 20.3.
Smooth the left and right edges together, being careful not to change the corners too much.

8. There may still be some abrupt color changes at the image's corners. To check for and correct these, copy the upper-left image down into the empty region at the lower right. Use the smudge or copy brushes to smooth the corner at the center of the four images, then copy that corner carefully back up into the upper left.
9. Copy the upper-left image into the clipboard, paste it into a new image file, and save it in the JPEG or GIF format.

10. Create a quick test document like this:

```
<HTML><BODY BACKGROUND="myimage.jpg"></BODY></HTML>
```

    Then open it in your Web browser, as shown in Figure 20.4.

    Note that most JPEG files show barely visible seams between tiles—even if you followed these steps perfectly—because the exact color information is distorted slightly during compression. Most people won't even notice this subtle effect once the tile is on your page, but if it bothers you, use a GIF image for tiling instead.

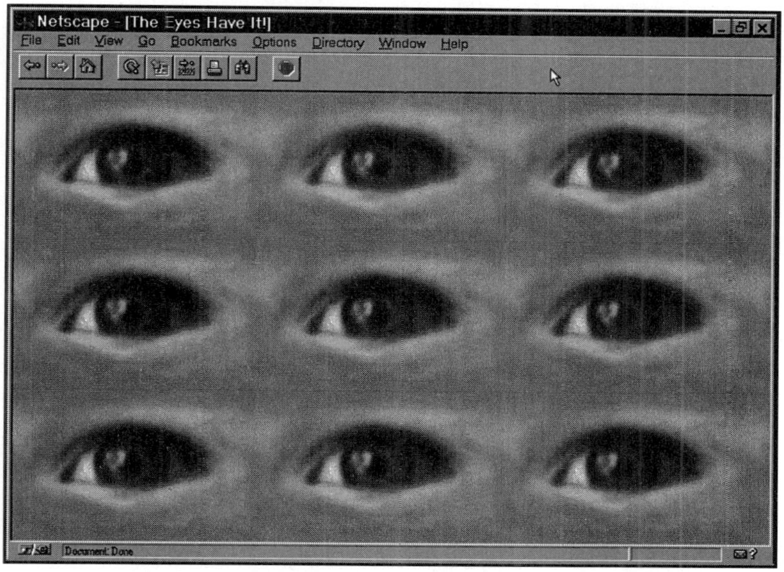

FIGURE 20.4.
JPEG images usually have barely visible "cracks" between tiles due to the lossy compression algorithm.

11. Once you see the tile in your browser, you might see a few spots that need touching up in Paint Shop Pro before you pronounce your work a success.

You can use essentially the same process of copying and shuffling pieces of an image to draw your own seamless tiles from scratch or add artwork to existing tiles. Figure 20.5 is a simple example, created by painting a colored stripe onto the image and its copies, then tweaking it as described here. Figure 20.6 shows the result in Netscape.

Dramatic accents like this can make the subtle seams between JPEG tiles less noticeable, too.

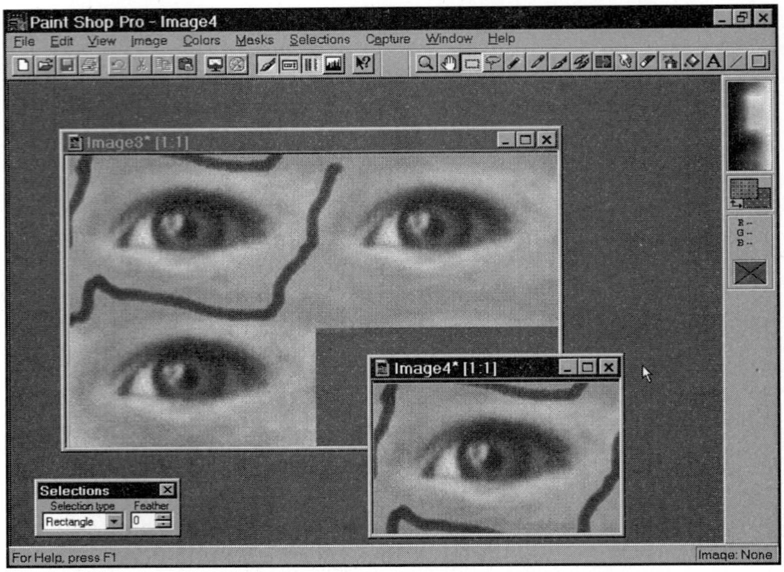

FIGURE 20.5.
When you get the hang of tiling, you can add any number of artistic effects to your backgrounds.

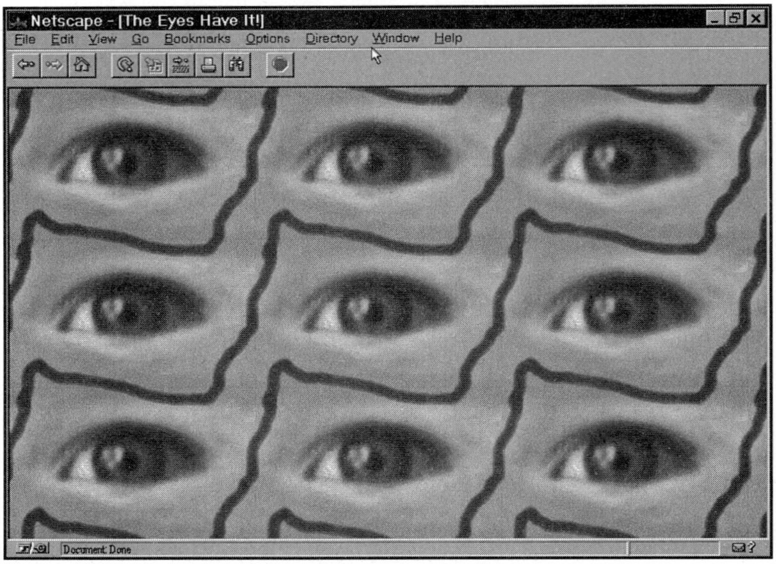

FIGURE 20.6.
The modified tile in Figure 20.5, as seen in Netscape Navigator.

Seamless Backgrounds Automatically

If you made it through all the preceding steps for creating a background tile by hand, you're probably eager for the "easier way" I promised to explain. Paint Shop Pro actually has a special command for creating seamless background tiles; you can simply select a rectangular region of any full-color image and `Image | Special Effects | Create Seamless Pattern` does all the hard work for you.

The left image in Figure 20.7 is a modified photo of a taro plant, and the two smaller images to its right are tiles taken from the same rectangular region of the taro leaf. They may look the same in Figure 20.7, but Figures 20.8 and 20.9 reveal the difference. One was simply cropped out of the larger image (Figure 20.8) and doesn't make a very good background tile, but the other was done with the `Create Seamless Pattern` command (Figure 20.9) and tiles much more smoothly. With some color adjustment, it would make a lovely background for a Web page.

> **TIP**
>
> Watch for ugly "banding" that can show up in the background if the tile pattern is too distinctive (such as the same light patch repeating over and over so that it paints a light stripe down the side of the page). Unless the background is theme-related, subtlety should be the key.

FIGURE 20.7.
The upper-right image was cut out of the larger image on the left. The lower-right image was created with Paint Shop Pro's Create Seamless Pattern command.

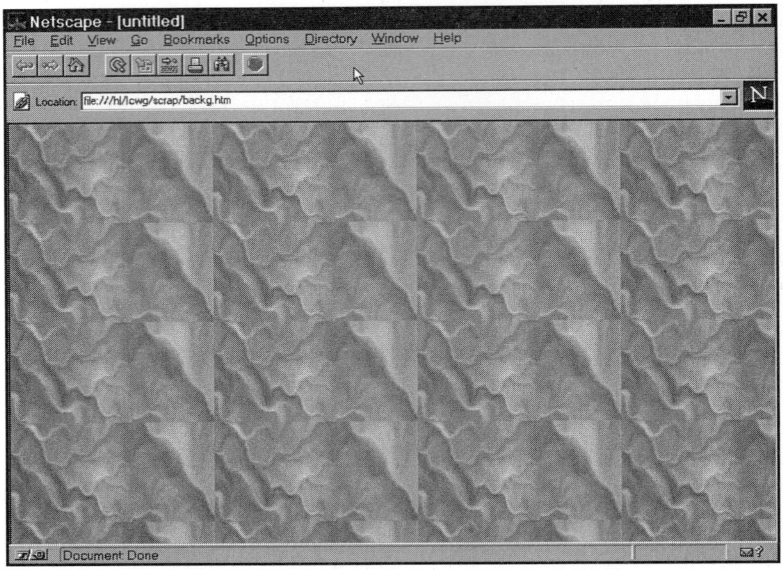

FIGURE 20.8.
The upper-right image from Figure 20.7 doesn't make a very effective background tile because the edges are too abrupt.

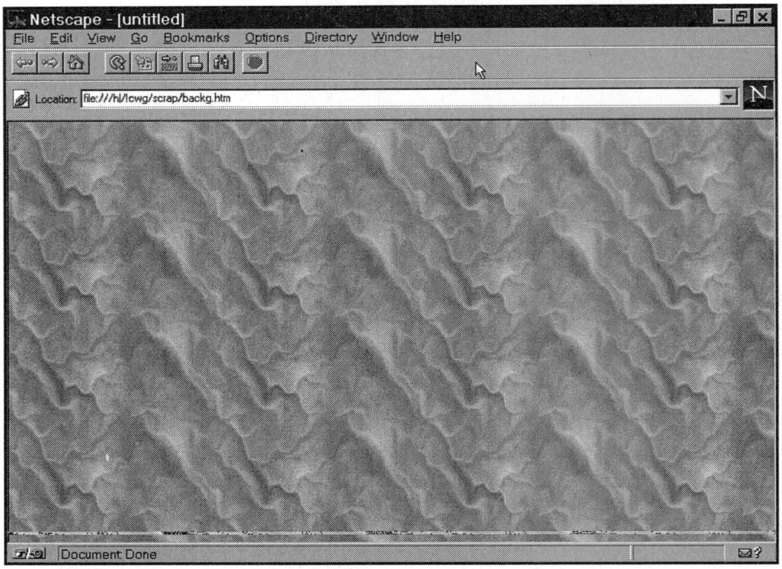

FIGURE 20.9.
The lower-right image from Figure 20.7 makes a better tile because its edges match up more smoothly.

Unfortunately, the range of background images that Create Seamless Pattern works well with is fairly limited. For it to work at all, you must have an image at least twice as large as the background tile you want to create, and the area to make into a tile must be far enough from the edges of the original image so that Paint Shop Pro can use the area around the selection to do its magic.

For the background tile to actually look good, the requirements of your original image are much more stringent. It must be a photo or full-color artwork with gradual changes in color and fairly low contrast. A scanned image of gravel or grass would work well, for example. The image of the eye presented earlier in this chapter, however, would get a bit mangled when the surrounding face was "faded" into it by the `Create Seamless Pattern` command. When the background you have in mind has a high-contrast, recognizable image or pattern, you almost always have more success with the labor-intensive manual techniques discussed previously.

Hand-drawn Backgrounds

Figures 20.10 and 20.11 show two seamless backgrounds that the `Create Seamless Pattern` command wouldn't have been any help in creating. However, these were still quite easy to construct with Paint Shop Pro's other tools.

To make the chain-link fence in Figure 20.10, I used the line and fill tools to make two crossed bars, then touched up the elbow with the paintbrush tool. I then cut and pasted four copies of the link around the original and carefully cropped the image so that all four corners fell exactly on the center of the elbow. All this took a few minutes and some concentrated squinting at the screen, but a bachelor's in fine arts certainly wasn't required (good thing, too—I majored in engineering).

FIGURE 20.10.
You don't have to be van Gogh to draw an interesting and effective background tile.

Despite the artsy theme of Figure 20.11, it took almost no artistic skill to draw the canvas background (and not much more skill to draw the other elements on the page, for that matter). I simply picked an ivory color and painted a square with Paint Shop Pro's Paper Texture setting on the brush tool stylebar set to Canvas. And voila! Canvas!

You can quickly make any of the other paper textures listed in the brush tool stylebar the same way. You can also make some attractive papers with the `Image | Special Filters | Add Noise` command, especially when combined with the Blur or Erode filters and `Colorize` command. Play around with the powerful tools Paint Shop Pro offers, and you'll be surprised how easy it is to get some delightful results.

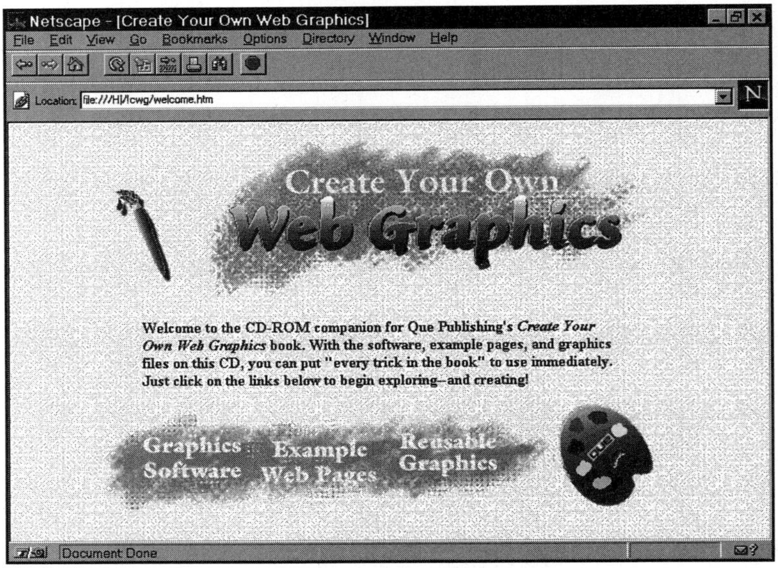

FIGURE 20.11.
Paint Shop Pro offers several canvas paper textures built into the brush tool, so making a classy page like this is amazingly easy.

NOTE

As you might have guessed, the pages shown in Figures 20.10 and 20.11 are from the CD-ROMs accompanying two of my recent books, *Netscape 3 Unleashed* from Sams.net Publishing and *Creating Your Own Web Graphics* from Que Publishing. Both of these books are (in my humble opinion) excellent resources for anyone who wants more in-depth coverage of Netscape Navigator and/or Web page graphics than this book provides.

Translucent Images

When you're using not-so-subtle background tiles, it would be rather counterproductive to cover them up with a big foreground image. Of course, it would be even more counterproductive not to have big foreground images announcing the content of your eye-popping site. An interesting compromise that has many applications is to create translucent foreground images and allow the background to show through to varying degrees. You can get this uncommon effect quite neatly by dithering a color or grayscale image down to two colors, as shown in Figure 20.12.

FIGURE 20.12.
Ordered dither gives a regular pattern, but error diffusion adds a degree of randomness.

Paint Shop Pro (like most other graphics programs) gives you several dithering options. *Ordered dither* places pixels in a regular pattern, and three types of *error diffusion* offer subtle differences in how they randomly place pixels. Try them all, and you'll see the difference much more clearly than I could ever explain.

Figure 20.13 shows the two variations on the image in Figure 20.12, each dithered with the Floyd-Steinberg error diffusion method down to two colors and saved as transparent GIFs. The difference between the left and right images is that the left one was lighter shades of gray before being dithered, so the pattern is more sparse and allows more of the background to show through.

If the figure was in color, you'd also see that, after I dithered each image down to two colors, I increased the color depth up to 16 colors and edited the palette entry of the black color to be light blue (in the left image) or red (in the right image). The net effect is a colored, translucent image that clearly shows both the LOOK logo and the background beneath it. You could also use the color replacement tool in Paint Shop Pro's Paint palette to make multicolored translucent images easily.

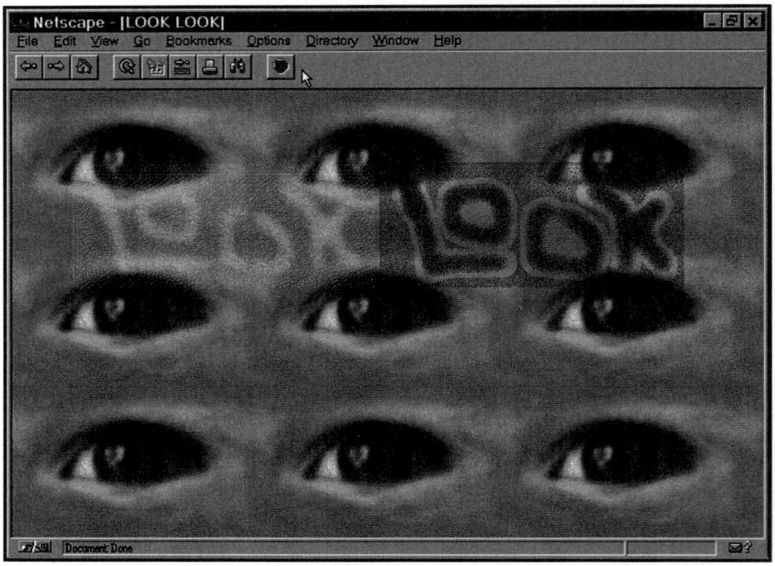

FIGURE 20.13.
Translucent, colored images show up clearly but also let the background show through.

As mentioned in Chapter 16, "Bigger, Faster, Better Graphics," the complexity of error diffusion dithering can significantly increase file sizes. However, reducing the color depth tends to *decrease* file sizes, so all in all, translucent images don't usually get too big. The examples in Figure 20.13 are only about 5 K each, even though they're quite large (320×200 pixels).

Do-It-Yourself Image Mapping

If you've ever put a page up on the Web, you know how to make an image link to another document, but if you haven't, it looks like this:

```
<A HREF="whatever.htm"><IMG SRC="myimage.gif"></A>.)
```

You can also subdivide an image into regions and link to different documents, depending on which region the user clicks. This is called an *image map*, and any image can be made into an image map.

Netscape Navigator and Microsoft Explorer both allow you to choose between two different methods for creating image maps: *server-side image maps* and *client-side image maps.* Nowadays, all your image maps should be client-side because you can easily make them automatically work the old server-side way for users of older browser programs. I'll explain both kinds in the following sections, but first a tip that will help you with either of them…

TIP

To make any type of image map, you need to figure out the numeric pixel coordinates of the regions you want to become "hot spots" in an image. An easy way to do this is to open the image with Paint Shop Pro and watch the coordinates at the bottom of the screen as you use the rectangle selection tool to select a rectangular region of the image. (See Figure 20.14.) When the mouse button is down, the coordinates at the bottom of the screen show both the upper-left and lower-right corners of the rectangle, instead of just a single X,Y position, as shown here.

There are also some fancy freeware programs that let you highlight a rectangle with your mouse and automatically spew out image map coordinates into a file, but I personally find them much more cumbersome to use.

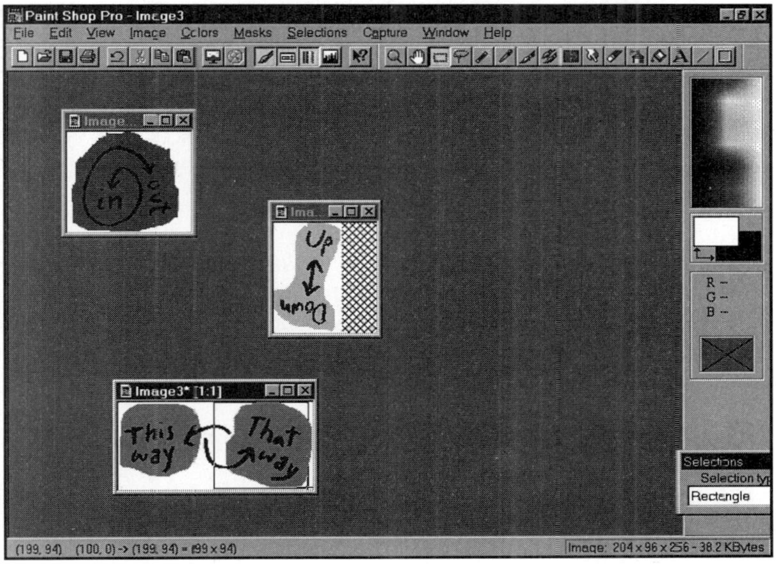

FIGURE 20.14.
Paint Shop Pro can easily tell you the coordinates for image map regions without mucking around with special image-mapping utilities.

Server-Side Image Maps

The old-fashioned way to do an image map is to let the server computer where the Web page resides do all the work. When the user clicks an image that has been mapped this way, the browser program just sends the X,Y coordinates of the mouse pointer's location to a special script on the server. Usually, this script is called `image map` and is located in the `cgi-bin` directory on the server; the HTML to create the image map is just a normal anchor link:

```
<A HREF="/cgi-bin/imagemap/thisthat"><IMG SRC="thisthat.gif"></A>
```

Simple—but when you install a Web page including such a link, you need to tell the image map script which parts of the image should be associated with which link addresses. This is normally done in a *map file*. Each line in the map file is simply the word *rect* followed by a URL address and two sets of X,Y coordinates representing the upper-left and lower-right corners of a region of the image. The first line in a map file begins with the word *default*, followed by the URL address that should be used if the user happens to click outside any rectangular region defined by a `rect` line. A map file named `thisthat.map` might look like this:

```
default /top/this.htm
rect /top/this.htm 0,0,102,99
rect /top/that.htm 103,0,205,99
```

The final step in setting up a server-side image map is telling the image map script which map file to use for which image by adding a line to a system file named `imagemap.conf`. This file will already exist and includes entries for every image map defined on the server. You simply add a line with the name used in the `HREF` attribute of the `<A>` tag, a colon, and then the actual location and name of the associated map file. For example, the previous reference is `HREF="/cgi-bin/imagemap/thisthat"`, and the preceding map file is named `thisthat.map`. If this map file was in a directory named `/mapfiles`, then the line in `imagemap.conf` would look like this:

```
thisthat : /mapfiles/thisthat.map
```

All this isn't nearly as difficult as it might sound if you've never set up an image map before, but it can be a hassle—especially if your pages reside on somebody else's server, and you don't have the rights to modify system files like `imagemap.conf` yourself. What's worse, server-side image maps don't work at all on Web pages located on your hard drive, a CD-ROM, or most local networks.

There are also some variations in the exact syntax for image map implementation, depending on the software installed on your server. If you move your pages to a different server, the image maps may not work anymore. Yuck. Fortunately, there's now an easier and more reliable way to set up image maps.

Client-Side Image Maps

The latest versions of all the major browsers support client-side image maps, where associating links with specific regions in an image is handled by the browser itself instead of a server script.

This means you can include image maps in your HTML files without imposing an additional burden on your Internet Service Provider's server, and you can be more certain they will be processed correctly and dependably. The HTML to create a client-side image map looks like Listing 20.1.

Listing 20.1. HTML for a client-side image map.

```
<MAP NAME="thisthat">
<AREA SHAPE="RECT" COORDS="0,0,102,99" HREF="this.htm">
<AREA SHAPE="RECT" COORDS="103,0,205,99" HREF="that.htm">
</MAP>

<-- any amount of HTML could go here -->

<IMG SRC="thisthat.gif" USEMAP="#thisthat">
```

TIP

Remember that links don't necessarily have to lead to HTML documents. You could make an image map link to sound files, video clips, or any other media that you know the user has a plug-in or helper application to handle.

You'll find several sample client-side image maps in the `look.htm` document on the *Web Publishing Unleashed* CD-ROM. In that document (and the preceding example), the `<MAP>` and `<AREA>` tags were located in the same file as the `<IMG>` tag. It's also possible to put the map definition in a separate file by including that file's name in the `USEMAP` attribute, like this:

```
<IMG SRC="/thisthat.gif" USEMAP="maps.htm#thisthat">
```

Combined Client/Server Image Maps

You can also supply client-side image maps that automatically switch to server-side image maps if the user's browser doesn't support client-side maps. With a single line of code, you can allow an image map to be interpreted either by the end user's software or by the server by including the `ISMAP` attribute in the `<IMG>` tag, and then including both a `USEMAP=` attribute and `cgi-bin/imagemap` reference:

```
<A HREF="/cgi-bin/imagemap/thisthat">
<IMG SRC="thisthat.gif" USEMAP="#thisthat" ISMAP>
</A>
```

Here, as with any unrecognized tag, browsers that don't support client-side image maps simply ignore the `<USEMAP>` and `<ISMAP>` tags and treat the preceding code like an old-fashioned server-side image map.

TIP

You might want to include an HREF anchor link with client-side image maps, even if you don't implement server-side image maps at all. For example, the following would bring up the document nomaps.htm when clicked from a browser that didn't support client-side image maps:

```
<A HREF="nomaps.htm"><IMG SRC="thisthat.gif" USEMAP="#thisthat"></A>
```

The nomaps.htm document might include a text list of choices equivalent to the various regions in the image or simply an error message telling users that their browser doesn't support client-side image maps.

Using Tables to Lay Out Graphics

Tables are your most powerful tool for creative Web page layouts. The boring, conventional way to use tables is for tabular arrangements of text and numbers. However, the real fun begins when you make your table borders invisible and use them as guides for arranging graphics and columns of text any which way you please.

TIP

Tables were once visible only to users of Netscape Navigator, but now that the current version of Microsoft Internet Explorer (and the next version of every other major browser) supports tables, you can use tables without fearing they will turn into a mish-mash of text before the eyes of non-Netscapers.

Laying It Out on the Table

In Figure 20.15, I've arranged some scanned handwriting with type of different sizes and colors into a table. I left the borders visible so I could make sure everything was placed the way I wanted; however, before putting this on a Web page, I would use the `TABLE BORDER=0` command to make the lines invisible. Listing 20.2 shows the HTML to make the table in Figure 20.15.

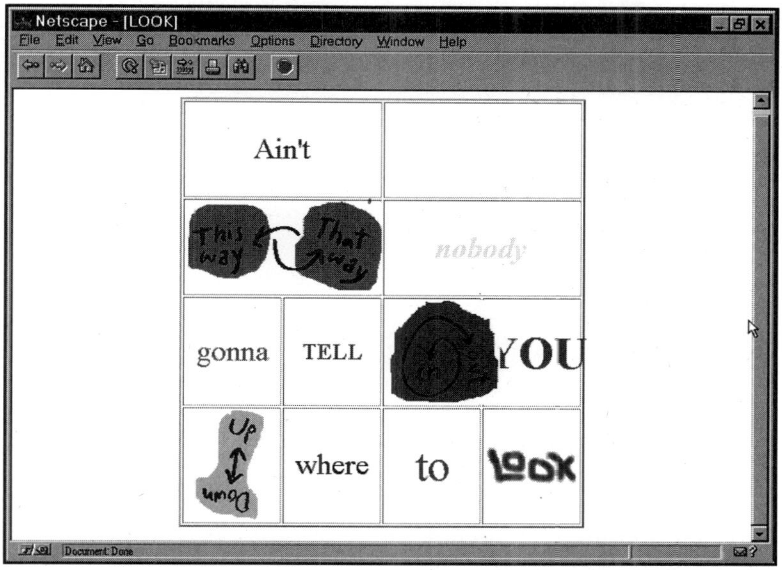

FIGURE 20.15.
Tables can include text, graphics, or a combination of both.

Listing 20.2. Making a table for text and graphics.

```
<TABLE BORDER=2>
<TR VALIGN="middle" COLSPAN=2>
  <TD ALIGN="center" WIDTH=200 COLSPAN=2>
     <FONT SIZE=6 COLOR="blue">Ain't</FONT></TD>
  <TD ALIGN="center" WIDTH=200 COLSPAN=2>
     <IMG SRC="space100.gif"></TD>
</TR>
<TR VALIGN="middle">
  <TD ALIGN="left" WIDTH=200 COLSPAN=2>
     <IMG SRC="thisthat.gif" USEMAP="#thisthat" BORDER=0></TD>
  <TD ALIGN="center" WIDTH=200 COLSPAN=2>
     <FONT SIZE=6 COLOR="yellow"><I><B>nobody</B></I></FONT></TD>
</TR>
<TR VALIGN="middle">
  <TD ALIGN="center" WIDTH=100>
     <FONT SIZE=6 COLOR="fuchsia">gonna</FONT></TD>
  <TD ALIGN="center" WIDTH=100>
     <FONT SIZE=5 COLOR="green"><B>TELL</B></FONT></TD>
  <TD ALIGN="center" WIDTH=100>
     <IMG SRC="inout.gif" USEMAP="#inout" BORDER=0></TD>
  <TD ALIGN="center" WIDTH=100>
     <FONT SIZE=7 COLOR="teal"><B>YOU</B></FONT></TD>
</TR>
<TR VALIGN="middle">
  <TD ALIGN="center" WIDTH=100>
     <IMG SRC="updown.gif" USEMAP="#updown" BORDER=0></TD>
  <TD ALIGN="center" WIDTH=100>
```

continues

Listing 20.2. continued

```
      <FONT SIZE=6 COLOR="purple">where</FONT></TD>
   <TD ALIGN="center" WIDTH=100>
      <FONT SIZE=7 COLOR="gray">to</FONT></TD>
   <TD ALIGN="center" WIDTH=100>
      <IMG SRC="look2.gif"></TD>
</TR>
</TABLE>
```

In case you're not familiar with the HTML syntax for tables, here's a quick run-down of how all the code works. The `<TABLE>` and `</TABLE>` tags always start and end a table, and the `BORDER` attribute sets the border width.

A `<TR>` and `</TR>` tag enclose each row in a table and accept the `VALIGN` attribute, which controls whether the contents of the row are vertically aligned to the center, top, or bottom. You could also use `HEIGHT` to set an exact height for the row in pixels, but in this example, I just let the browser automatically figure out the right height based on the tallest item in the row.

Each cell in the table starts with `<TD>` and ends with `</TD>`. The `ALIGN` attribute sets the horizontal alignment within the cell to either center, left, or right. I used `WIDTH` to set the cell widths to exactly 200 or 100 pixels, and `COLSPAN` to indicate that each cell in the top two rows should span two columns.

That's all there is to it! I did use a few sneaky tricks: a totally transparent 100×100-pixel image called space100.gif to fill an empty cell and an image too big to fit in its cell (more on that shortly).

Nested Tables

Now suppose you wanted to add a column of text to the page, placed to the right of the table in Figure 20.15. No current extension to HTML allows you to wrap text to the right (or left) of a table—but that doesn't mean there isn't a way to do it! You can create another table, like the one shown in Figure 20.16 and insert the table in Figure 20.15 into a cell in that new table.

Figure 20.16.
To wrap text to the right or left of a table, create another table and insert the first one inside it.

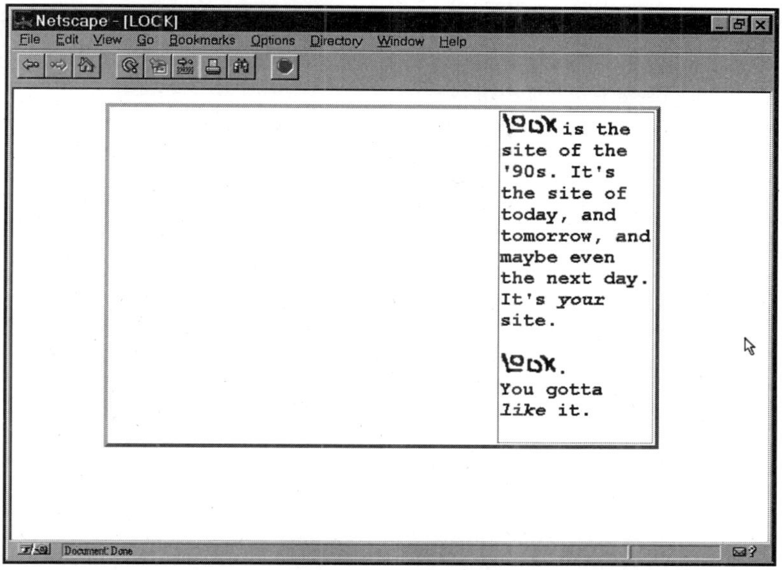

The code to create a nested table with the arrangement shown in Figure 20.17 would look like Listing 20.3.

Listing 20.3. Creating nested tables.

```
<TABLE BORDER=4>
<TR VALIGN="middle">
<TD WIDTH=400>
(the table in Figure 20.15 goes here)

</TD>
<TD WIDTH=160>
<IMG SRC="look1.gif" ALIGN="bottom">
<FONT SIZE=5><TT><B>is the site of the '90s.
It's the site of today, and tomorrow, and maybe even the next day.
It's <I>your</I> site.<P>
<IMG SRC="look1.gif">.<BR> You gotta<BR> <I>like</I> it.</B></TT><P>
</TD>
</TR>
</TABLE>
```

Figure 20.17 shows the two tables from Figures 20.15 and 20.16 put together. It also demonstrates a useful "bug" that you can use on purpose to create a sort of "grunge" layout effect. By putting a table in a space that's just a little too small to hold it, you can make text or images from one cell overlap into another. (Although both the table and the space to put it in are 400 pixels wide, the borders make it just a tad too big to fit.) Unfortunately (or fortunately, depending on whether you did it on purpose or by accident), this trick fools only Netscape Navigator. Microsoft Internet Explorer will automatically resize all cells to fit properly, as shown in Figure 20.18.

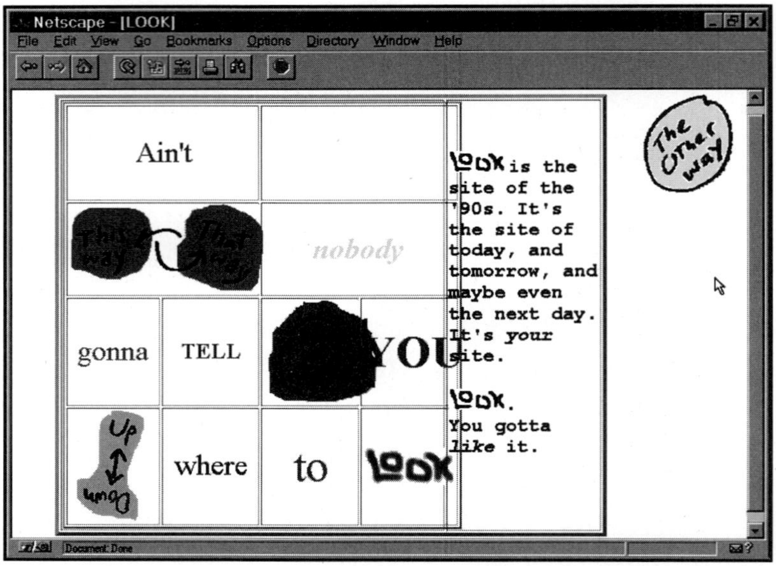

FIGURE 20.17.
Putting a table where it won't quite fit within another table can create an overlapping postmodern effect in Netscape Navigator.

As an added touch, notice that I inserted yet another graphic to the right of the nested table in Figures 20.17 and 20.18 by placing the following tag *before* the table code:

```
<IMG SRC="other.gif" ALIGN="right" BORDER=0>
```

The image appears on the far righthand margin and all graphics, text, or tables that follow are automatically placed to the left of it.

The finished LOOK page, complete with borderless table layouts, is shown in Figure 20.19. However, if you look at this page on the CD-ROM (it's `examples/look/look.htm`), you'll see more than a figure in a book could show! The logo at the top of the page is animated in flashing colors, and each of the handwritten images is a clickable image map.

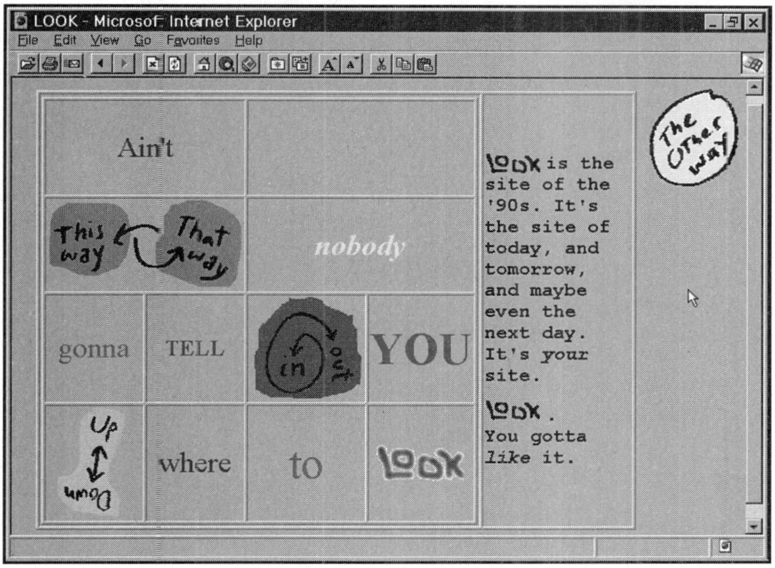

FIGURE 20.18.
Microsoft Internet Explorer is a little more fussy than Netscape Navigator and adjusts the size of all cells to hold any oversized content.

NOTE

Chapter 19, "Animating Graphical Images," reveals how the animated GIF images were produced. Creating and using clickable image maps was explained earlier in this chapter in the section "Do-It-Yourself Image Maps."

TIP

Note that Microsoft Internet Explorer 3.0 and Netscape Navigator 3.0 now allow you to specify a separate background for each cell in a table by placing the `BGCOLOR=` or `BACKGROUND=` attributes in a `<TR>` or `<TD>` tag, just as you would use these attributes in the `<BODY>` tag. Refer to Chapter 6, "Effective Use of Tables," for more details and examples.

Microsoft Internet Explorer 3.0 and Netscape Navigator 2.0 (or later) support frames, which are similar to tables except that each frame contains a separate HTML page and can be updated independently of the others. Refer to Chapter 7, "Creating and Enhancing Web Pages with Frames," for more information.

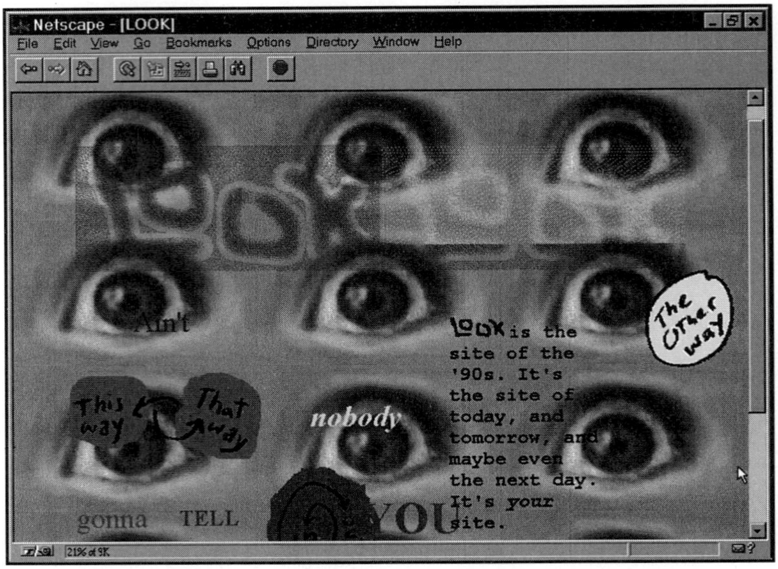

FIGURE 20.19.
When the borders of the tables are hidden and a wild background is added, the result is an unquestionably unique look!

Tips and Tricks for Creative Design

This chapter—and the previous four chapters—have given you a wide range of techniques for creating Web page graphics and examples of Web pages specifically created as examples. Your task is to adapt those techniques to make your pages unique in a totally different direction. To help you take that leap, here are a few final pointers for designing and laying out your pages:

- Maintain a consistent color scheme and visual flavor throughout your site. Resist the temptation to use *all* of Paint Shop Pro's fantastic tools at once, and stick to a few "signature" effects that express your pages' themes.
- Keep any graphics that substitute for text small so that they load and display first. Try to make sure that any larger graphics aren't essential for reading the page, keeping in mind that they'll display more slowly.
- When possible, use the same graphics repeatedly on a page and throughout your site. This technique speeds display because they need to be loaded only once.
- It's fine for background images to be bold and eye-catching, but not if it means your text is difficult to read. Either make sure your text falls over quiet regions of the background or stick to subdued colors and designs for your background tiles.
- Make almost all the actual text content of your pages "real text," not graphics, so visitors can use their browsers' `find` command to search it for keywords. And, more important, Internet search indexes will index your pages according to their text content so potential visitors can find them easily.

- Even if you want a much more businesslike look than the wild examples in this chapter, multicolumn text and a unique layout can make pages stand out from the crowd of "me-too" pages on the Internet.

Summary

Seamless backgrounds give your pages that extra professional touch. Image maps allow you creative freedom in helping users navigate through your site. When these and other creative design techniques are combined, your pages become both more attractive and more intuitive for visitors to explore.

In this chapter and the previous four chapters, you've seen how to design, create, and arrange highly expressive graphics. Part V, "Extending Your Site with Multimedia," takes you beyond graphics into the world of sound, video, and interactive media.

CHAPTER 21

Publishing Other File Formats

by Jon M. Duff

IN THIS CHAPTER

Every computer file has a format. Unfortunately, most data formats were designed long before the Internet and the World Wide Web were even a glimmer in someone's eye. Because of this, publishing on the Web presents a completely different set of problems than does traditional publishing. You want to be able to take a file in file format Z and include it in your Web page or view it. The problem was that first-generation Web browsers only accepted files in formats A, B, and C (HTML, GIF, and JPEG). Data formats recognized by a browser without additional resources, such as plug-ins, are called supported formats. If you must supplement your browser with additional resources to display, play, or hear a file, the file is in an unsupported format. As new generation browsers evolve, more of the commonly encountered text, graphic, and multimedia formats are supported without additional resources.

NOTE

Many Web file format issues revolve around audio, video, animation, and multimedia applications. When you think about it, almost every entertainment medium is less effective when delivered via the Web. On the other hand, information published on the Web can be more flexible, more available, and often more usable than in its original form. Keep this fact in mind when choosing data in unsupported formats.

Publishing on the Web is a powerful way to distribute and gather information. Yet in almost all instances, it is unnecessary, even unwise, to distribute information in its native file format because of the following points:

- A native application file has an overhead of program-specific information that's not needed for display on the Web. The native file is also more platform- and operating system-dependent than is necessary.
- The more obscure the application and its file format, the less the chance that someone will have the correct resources to be able to use the data.
- You want clients to benefit from the information, not be able to easily use the file for their own purposes. At least make them pound the text, capture the graphic, record the sound, or re-enter the data themselves.
- You want your pages to download quickly and naturally, without the burden of loading a helper application or prompting clients to download additional resources themselves.

In the following chapters, you will learn the ins and outs of making the most of varied resources on the Web. Consider this chapter to be a starting point for using exciting video, audio, multimedia, technical graphic, page layout, database, and spreadsheet information on your Web pages.

As browsers become more capable, taking on more of the characteristics of an operating environment, many of these issues will take care of themselves. Browsers will be able to provide text, vector and raster graphics, video, animation, and sound without additional resources. They will accept additional application formats with greater ease. But until that time, you'll have to juggle file formats if you work on the Web. This process entails one of three basic operations:

- Translating files into formats that browsers naturally accept
- Using features in application programs to change files into standard HTML format
- Including plug-ins for formats that don't lend themselves to either of the first two operations

In this chapter, you do the following:

- Understand how Web browsers handle various file formats
- Learn how embedded plug-ins extend the functionality of your Web site
- Know when to use a helper application to view an unsupported data type
- Understand which popular programs easily create Web-savy files
- Learn how to translate raster and vector files into Web-compatible formats
- Learn how to integrate video, animation, and sound elements into Web pages
- Know how to use the latest virtual reality resources

Web File Formats Explained

A collection of data, when it is committed to a storage medium, is organized in a standard way. This standard is referred to as its *file format*. File formats are recognized by standard *file extensions*, which take the form of a period followed by 1-3 characters. For Web work, always use lowercase file extensions. The formats that programs use to store data are called *native file formats.*

Table 21.1 lists file format extensions commomly encountered on the Web. Raster formats contain only information about bitmaps. Vector formats contain graphic information as calls to mathematical routines. Text formats contain alphanumeric information and formatting instructions. Meta formats contain raster, vector, and textual information. Formats using encoded data change the data structure for easier transmission. Compression is a type of encoding that decreases memory requirements by removing redundant or unnecessary information.

NOTE

Macintosh and Windows 95 operating systems don't require file extensions because they use a creator type that's saved with the file. However, HTML does require file extensions to correctly locate and display files. Always use consistently correct file extensions even though they are not an operating system requirement.

Table 21.1 File Extensions and their descriptions

Extension	*Type*	*Description*
`.a3m`	Multimedia	Authorware Macintosh
`.a3w`	Multimedia	Authorware Windows
`.aif`	Audio	Audio Interchange
`.avi`	Video	Audio Video Interface
`.bmp`	Raster	Windows bitmap
`.cgm`	Meta	Computer graphics metafile
`.dcr`	Multimedia	Macromedia Director
`.doc`	Text	Microsoft Word
`.dwg`	Vector	AutoCAD drawing
`.dxf`	Vector	AutoCAD intermediate
`.eps`	Meta	Encapsulated PostScript
`.flc`	Animation	AutoDesk animation
`.gif`	Raster	Graphics interchange
`.gz`	Compression	GZIP compression format
`.hqx`	Encoding	Mac byte-stream encoded
`.html`	Text	Hypertext markup language
`.jpg`	Raster	Hoint Photographic Experts Group
`.mid`	Audio	Musical instrument digital
`.mov`	Video	QuickTime movie
`.mpg`	Video	Motion Picture Experts Group
`.pcx`	Raster	Windows Paintbrush
`.pdf`	portable	Portable document format
`.pic`	Meta	Macintosh picture
`.png`	Raster	Portable network graphic
`.ppt`	Slides	PowerPoint presentation
`.ps`	PostScript	ASCII PostScript file
`.rgb`	Raster	Silicon Graphics 24-bit color
`.sea`	Compression	Self-extracting archive
`.sun`	Raster	Sun 24-bit color
`.tga`	Raster	Truevision Targa 24-bit

Extension	Type	Description
.tif	Raster	Tagged image file format
.txt	text	Raw, unformatted text
.viv	Video	Compressed live video
.wav	Audio	Windows audio-visual
.wmf	Meta	Windows Meta file
.wrl	Text	Virtual reality modeling
.zip	Compression	PKZIP compression
.zoo	Compression	ZOO compression

The organization of native data is determined by programmers who create the application. It will differ from other file formats due to the unique needs of the application. For example, Word and WordPerfect files don't share the same format because the needs of each program are different. Inside the file, a textual passage may be the same, but the way that the text is recorded differs. Additionally, each program adds application-specific, operating system-specific, and platform-specific information (such as formats, links, or special characters).

Stripping this specific information from a native file creates an intermediate file format. Files in intermediate format are transportable between programs and platforms. However, stripping out the program-specific information may make certain features of the data unavailable.

You can reduce the amount of storage space required for given file by using a data compression format. In compression, redundant data (such as repeating characters in a text document, repeating numerals in a spreadsheet, or repeating pixels in a graphic) are replaced with identifiers or tokens that take up less space (fewer bits). Compressed files download faster but must be decompressed to be viewed or worked on and generally require more time to load. You must also have access to the correct codecs (compression-decompression). Uncompressed files load faster, but they require more storage space.

NOTE

Many applications have proprietary compression algorithms. This feature usually shows up as a "Save Smaller" option and is tailored for and usually only recognized by the application. Avoid using proprietary program-based compression for files you want to publish on the Web.

You may be tempted to load a Web site with as many indications of your prowess as possible. Although doing so may be technologically interesting (and tons of fun), it may do nothing for the readability and effectiveness of the site. Follow these Golden Rules of Web File Formats:

1. Use supported file formats first. Rely on your creativity and content knowledge, not on tricks.
2. Publish textual, numerical, graphical, visual, or auditory data only if it enhances the effectiveness of the site.
3. Translate unsupported files into supported file formats first.
4. Always choose a file format with the lowest practicable data transmission requirements that still satisfies design and communication requirements.
5. Never force a client to do anything other than browse. Provide links to video, animation, sound, and multimedia.
6. Embed resources for unsupported file formats in the Web site if translation into a supported format isn't feasible or possible.
7. Point to URLs for file format resources that are unsupported and for which you haven't embedded the resource in your site.

Supported Web Formats

Text is read by the browser in plain ASCII text format (`.txt`). All the special instructions of a word processor are not needed because HTML structures and formats the text as it is read and displayed. Is this a limitation? Hardly. HTML is a structural formatting language, not a page description language like PostScript. A structural formatting language emphasizes content and structure, which are more important than appearance for the communication of information.

Graphics are supported in 8-bit, 256 color CompuServe Graphic Interchange Format (`.gif`) or in the more capable 24-bit Joint Photographic Experts Group (`.jpg`) format. Because there is no standard object imaging display language across PC, Mac, and UNIX platforms, graphics are supported only in raster format. Is this a limitation? Again, hardly. The vast majority of potential display monitors are limited to 8-bit (256) colors, 640x480 pixel screen dimensions, and 72-80 dpi (.25-.28 mm) resolution. Choose file formats appropriate for your audience.

Sound, video, and animation were not part of the original Web vision because, until recently, browsing computers were not configured to make use of multimedia resources. Is this a limitation in delivering Web-based publications? If these multimedia features are indespensible for the effectiveness of your Web publication, it could be.

MIME Data Types

In order for files of different types and formats to be correctly encoded and decoded, the Multipurpose Internet Mail Extensions (MIME) standard is used. Each file is tagged so that servers can send the files and browsers can interpret them. The relationship between the MIME decoder and external programs (helper applications, plug-ins) is established in your browser. Figure 21.1 shows the Netscape browser's provision for establishing MIME types for expected file types and helper applications.

FIGURE 21.1.
Establishing MIME types in Netscape's browser.

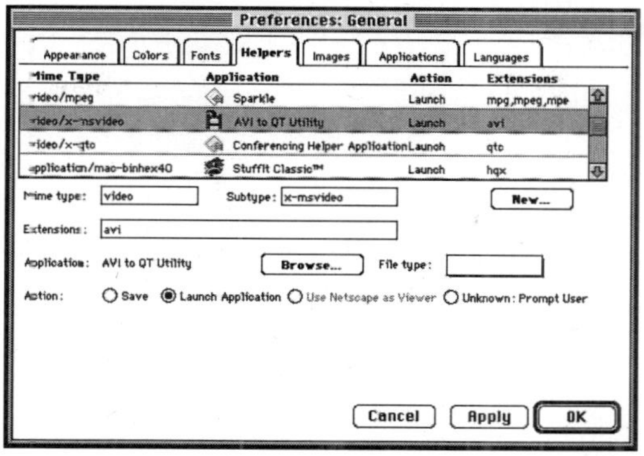

MIME is divided into various content types. Each content type is subdivided into data types. Table 21.2 shows this organization and Table 21.3 lists common MIME types encountered on the Web.

Table 21.2. Organization of common MIME content and data types.

MIME	*Data*	*Description*
Text	Plain	ASCII text with no formatting
	Enriched	Word-processed text text formatted
Audio	Basic	Single-channel, 8-bit sound
Image	GIF	8-bit color raster image
	JPEG	24-bit color raster image
	TIFF	24-bit color raster image
Video	MPEG	Video and audio
	QuickTime	Video and audio
Application	Octet-stream	Binary data
	PostScript	PostScript data
	Mac-binhex	Mac-encoded data and resource

Table 21.3. Common file formats and their corresponding MIME types.

File	*MIME Type*	*Subtype*
`.a3m`	Application	x-authorware
`.a3w`	Multimedia	x-authorware

continues

Table 21.3. continued

File	MIME Type	Subtype
`.aif`	Audio	x-aif
`.avi`	Video	x-avi
`.bmp`	Image	x-MS-bmp
`.cgm`	Image	x-cals
`.dcr`	Application	x-director
`.doc`	Application	x-doc
`.dxf`	Image	x-dxf
`.eps`	Image	epsf
`.flc`	Video	x-flc
`.mid`	Audio	x-midi
`.mov`	Video	QuickTime
`.mpg`	Video	MPEG
`.pcx`	Image	x-pcx
`.pdf`	Image	x-pdf
`.pic`	Image	x-pic
`.ppt`	Application	x-ppt
`.tif`	Image	TIFF
`.wav`	Audio	x-wave
`.wrl`	x-world	x-vrml

Display Options for Unsupported File Formats

You've determined that you want to use an unsupported file format on your Web page. What are your options? First, you can use the `<EMBED>` tag to include the plug-in for that format in the HTML page specification. This is called an *embedded plug-in* and displays the file actively on the page just like a supported file type (see Figure 21.2). It presents the most seamless and natural solution.

The second option is to anchor the file using the `<A HREF=>` tag. When the appropriate plug-in is in the browser's plug-in directory and matches the file's MIME and file extension types, a separate full-page browser window is opened and the file is displayed. This is shown in Figure 21.3. This option is appropriate when the information is best viewed separately, removed from the page.

FIGURE 21.2
An embedded video running on a Web page.

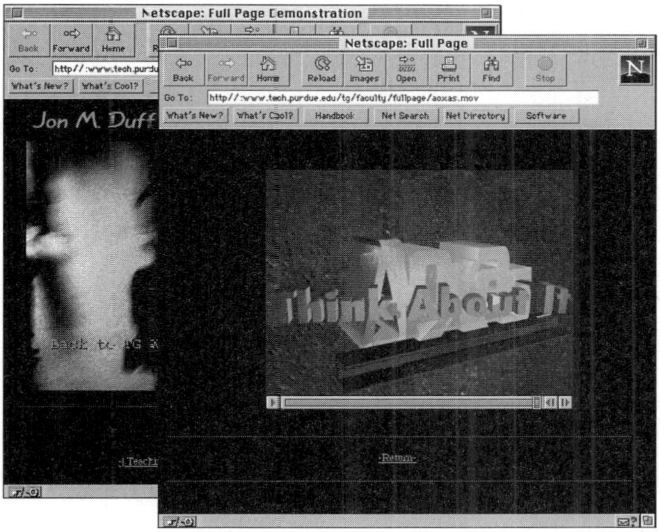

FIGURE 21.3.
A full-page display of an unsupported graphic file type.

Browser Helper Apps and Plug-Ins

A *helper application* is a program residing on the user's hard disk that extends the functionality of a browser. When associated with a file type by its extension, this program is called a *helper app*. You can see why it's so important to use a consistent file extension scheme. For example, assume you want to view animations in AutoDesk's `.flc` format. You can set up your browser to do one of the following:

- When your browser encounters an `.flc` animation file, a helper application such as AA Player starts and plays the animation in the browser.
- When your browser encounters an `.flc` animation file, a helper application such as AA Player launches and displays the animation outside the browser in a separate window. This allows you to suspend the animation and continue viewing the Web pages, returning to the animation as needed.
- When your browser encounters an `.flc` animation file, it opens the `.flc` file in a full-fledged application such as Animator Studio so that the animation can be edited and archived.

The strong point of using a helper app is that you can have much greater control over interacting with the file than if you simply play or view the file in the browser. The downside of using a helper app is that the operation of your browser is interrupted, which changes the natural flow of information.

A plug-in also extends functionality by adding the capability to display files in formats not naturally understood (supported) by your browser. When the browser is launched, it looks into its plug-ins directory and builds a list of the MIME and file types supported by the plug-ins located there. These plug-ins aren't loaded at this time; they are loaded only when an `<EMBED>` or an `<A HREF>` tag calls for a file type in the list.

Most people find as many plug-ins as they can and put them in their plug-ins directory. That way, whenever the browser encounters a nonsupported file type, it will look for a plug-in that will display it. For plug-ins to work, the server and your browser must match file and MIME types. Many plug-ins can be downloaded directly from the URLs listed in the next section. Remember, plug-ins have no permanent overhead. Each utility is loaded when needed and flushed from memory when you leave the Web page that needed it.

By having the largest collection of plug-ins, you have access to the coolest sites and their content on the Web. However, plug-ins are browser-dependent, and as you change browsers or upgrade from one version of a browser to another, you may also have to update your plug-ins. Refer to the previous discussion of MIME types for additional information on configuring plug-ins. Plan ahead for demanding temporary plug-in memory requirements by allocating as much memory to your browser as you can.

Resources for Publishing Unsupported File Formats

Companies want you to include their files in your Web pages and generally distribute plug-ins to help you. The easier it is to get their product's files published, the greater their potential market share. However, plug-ins are platform- and browser-specific. Not everyone has bought into Netscape's plug-in specification. Remember your potential market when you plan on using file formats that require additional resources.

Plug-ins are generally compressed to make download times as short as possible. Configure your browser to recognize typical compression formats. For Windows computers, files will usually be in `.zip` format. Configure PKUNZIP to extract these files. Find PKUNZIP at `http://www.pkware.com`. After you unzip a plug-in, place it in the browser's plug-in directory and restart your browser.

For Macintosh computers, files will be in `binhex` format and stuffed as a self-extracting archive in `.sea` format. Use Stuffit Expander to extract these files. Find Stuffit Expander at `http://www.aladdinsys.com`. After you unstuff a plug-in, place it in the browser's plug-in folder and restart your browser.

On the UNIX side, files are often encountered in GZIP's `.gz` format. More than one file can be compressed into a single GZIP archive. As part of a UNIX pipeline, files can be sent to the GZIP codec for compression or decompression and passed along for storage or to another program. In addition to GZIP, UNIX users will run across ZOO files in `.zoo` format. This technique uses LZW lossless compression to reduce the size of files within a ZOO archive and packs the data after archiving to remove previous versions of the data.

Most plug-ins are available freely for noncommercial purposes such as browsing, public service, or self-promotion. If you want to include a plug-in in a commercial site, a small licensing fee is usually charged. If you plan on making money, the software companies should make some money too.

Almost every new release of software touts itself as "Web-enabled." This feature is usually an option to save or export the data as an HTML file. Explore this option first and you may not need to locate additional resources. However, be prepared to do some fine-tuning because the HTML code probably won't do exactly what you want.

The following information is organized alphabetically by file type. The list is by no means exhaustive, but it represents a good cross-section of technical, corporate, and graphical file types one encounters in Web publications.

.a3w, .a3m

Format:	Macromedia Authorware
Plug-in name:	Shockwave for Authorware
URL:	`http://www.macromedia.com/shockwave/`
Platforms:	Mac, Power Mac, Windows 3.1, Windows 95, Windows NT

This plug-in plays Authorware applications that have been processed with Afterburner.

.ai

Format: Adobe Illustrator illustration

Export files in this format as `.eps` graphics. Use the FIGleaf Inline or Adobe Acrobat plug-ins to publish these files in `.eps` format (see `.eps` listing for more information).

.aif

Format: Audio Interchange file
Plug-in name: KM's Multimedia Plug
URL: `http://www.wco.com/~mcmurtri`
Platforms: Mac, Power Mac

This plug-in plays sampled sounds and musical instruments used on Macintosh and SGI platforms.

.asn

Format: Gold Disk Astound presentation
Plug-in name: Astound Web Player
URL: `http://astoundinc.com/awp/awplinked.html`
Platforms: Power Mac, Windows 3.1, Windows 95

This plug-in plays back Astound slide presentations from within your Web pages.

.avi

Format: Microsoft Audio Video Interface
Plug-in name: ClearFusion
URL: `http://webber.iterated.com/coolfusn`
Platforms: Windows 95, Windows NT

This plug-in plays `.avi` movies with user control. These files can be very large, requiring significant download times for dial-up connections. For compressed `.avi` movies, see `.viv` format.

.bmp

Format: Windows bitmap
Plug-in name: FIGleaf Inline
URL: `http://www.ct.ebt.com/figinline/`

Platforms: Power Mac coming, Windows 95, Windows NT, and UNIX (SunOS, Solaris, IRIX) available in beta form

This plug-in streams .bmp raster graphics into your browser.

.cgm

Format: Computer graphics metafile

Plug-in name: FIGleaf Inline

URL: http://www.ct.ebt.com/figinline/

Platforms: Power Mac coming, Windows 95, Windows NT

This plug-in streams .cgm graphics into your browser. Because .cgm is a vector format, a pop-up menu gives the viewer zooming options.

.dcr

Format: Macromedia Director movie

Plug-in name: Shockwave for Director

URL: http://www.macromedia.com/shockwave/

Platforms: Mac, Power Mac, Windows 3.1, Windows 95, Windows NT

This plug-in plays Director movies that have been processed with Afterburner.

.doc

Format: Microsoft Windows text document

Save files in this format as HTML documents or use Sausage's Hot Dog editor (available at http://www.sausage.com) to convert them to HTML.

.dwg

Format: AutoDesk drawing

Plug-in name: AutoCAD DXF Viewer

URL: http://www.softsource.com/softsource/plugins/plugins.html

Platforms: Windows 95, Windows NT

AutoCAD drawings in .dwg format carry considerable application-specific file information and can be several megabytes in file size. Convert these drawings to .dxf format and remove geometry and notes not required for Web browsing. For viewing on Macintosh platforms, save the file in EPS format using the EPSOUT option and use the FIGleaf Inline plug-in.

.dxf

Format: Drawing interchange
Plug-in name: AutoCAD DXF Viewer
URL: `http://www.softsource.com/softsource/plugins/plugins.html`
Platforms: Windows 95, Windows NT

This format is AutoCAD's intermediate vector file format. Its universal acceptance enables files from other CAD programs to be displayed on the Web.

.eps

Format: Encapsulated PostScript
Plug-in name: FIGleaf Inline
URL: `http://www.ct.ebt.com/figinline/`
Platforms: Power Mac, Windows 95, Windows NT, and UNIX (SunOS, Solaris, IRIX) available in beta form for download

This plug-in streams `.eps` graphics into your browser. This plug-in provides access to the huge amounts of PostScript art available as clip art as well as the output from PostScript illustration programs such as Freehand, Illustrator, and CorelDRAW!. See also `.pdf` format.

.fh5

Format: Macromedia Freehand Illustration
Plug-in name: Shockwave for Freehand
URL: `http://www.macromedia.com/shockwave/`
Platforms: Mac, Power Mac, Windows 3.1, Windows 95, Windows NT

This plug-in displays Freehand vector illustrations without turning them into fixed-resolution bitmaps. As vector files, the graphics are of considerably smaller file size.

.flc

Format: AutoDesk animation

Convert files in this format to `.avi` format in Animator Studio or to `.mov` format in Graphic Converter and use the appropriate plug-in. Or use Astound's Web Player. Find this plug-in at `http://www.astoundinc.com/awp/awplinked.html`.

.gif

Format: Graphics interchange
Plug-in name: FIGleaf Inline

URL:	`http://www.ct.ebt.com/figinline/`
Platforms:	Power Mac coming, Windows 95, Windows NT, and UNIX (SunOS, Solaris, IRIX) available in beta form for download

This plug-in streams `.gif` graphics into your browser. This plug-in gives you greater control over color palette assignments, border characteristics, and whether the graphic appears on the page, in a new window overlaying the current window, or in a new window substituting for the existing window.

`.jpg`

Format:	Joint Photographic Experts Group
Plug-in name:	FIGleaf Inline
URL:	`http://www.ct.ebt.com/figinline/`
Platforms:	Power Mac, Windows 3.1, Windows 95, Windows NT, and UNIX (SunOS, Solaris, IRIX) available in beta form for download

This plug-in streams `.jpg` graphics into your browser. This plug-in gives you greater control over color palette assignments, border characteristics, and whether the graphic appears on the page, in a new window overlaying the current window, or in a new window substituting for the existing window.

`.mid`

Format:	Musical instrument digital interface
Plug-in name:	KM's Multimedia Plug
URL:	`http://www.wco.com/~mcmurtri`
Platforms:	Mac, Power Mac

This plug-in plays MIDI music files with user control.

`.mpg`

Format:	Motion Picture Experts Group
Plug-in name:	KM's Multimedia Plug
URL:	`http://www.wco.com/~mcmurtri`
Platforms:	Mac, Power Mac

Multimedia Plug plays `.mpg` video and animation files with user control.

Format:	Motion Picture Experts Group
Plug-in name:	InterVU MPEG Player

URL:	`http://www.intervu.com/player/player.html`
Platforms:	Windows 95, Windows NT

InterVU lets you know how much of the file has been downloaded.

.mov

Format:	QuickTime movie
Plug-in name:	Apple QuickTime Plug-in
URL:	`http://www.quicktime.apple.com`
Platforms:	Mac, Power Mac
Format:	QuickTime movie
Plug-in name:	Apple QuickTime Plug-in for Windows
URL:	`http://www.quicktime.apple.com/sw/sw.html`
Platforms:	Windows 3.1, Windows 95

This plug-in plays back inline QuickTime movies and movies with MIDI soundtracks. A great technique for low-overhead background music is to make a blank movie with MIDI sound.

.pcx

Format:	Windows Paintbrush
Plug-in name:	Quick View Plus
URL:	`http://www.inso.com/frames/product/product.htm`
Platforms:	Windows 3.1, Windows 95, Windows NT

On the Macintosh side, convert files in this format to `.jpg` format in Photoshop, Hyjaak Pro, or DeBabelizer and include them with the `<IMG SRC=>` tag in an HTML document.

.pdf

Format:	Adobe Portable Document Format
Plug-in name:	Adobe Acrobat Reader 3.0
URL:	`http://www.adobe.com/acrobat/`
Platforms:	Mac, Power Mac, Windows 95, Windows NT

Adobe's Portable Document Format creates a scalable, resolution-independent, searchable, and hyperlinkable text file out of any compliant PostScript file. Any word processor, page layout, graphics, database, or spreadsheet program that can print PostScript to a disk file is a candidate for using the `.pdf` format.

Additionally, existing documents can be scanned into `.pdf` format—a technique that makes existing publications and documents Web-ready. Of course, to do all this, you need Adobe's Acrobat Reader plug-in.

.pic

Format:	Macintosh picture
Plug-in name:	KM's Multimedia Plug
URL:	`http://www.wco.com/~mcmurtri`
Platforms:	Mac, Power Mac

This plug-in displays `.pic` object and raster data.

.pm6

Format:	Adobe PageMaker Page Layout

When you have files in this format, use PageMaker HTML Addition in release 6 to convert them to an HTML document. PageMaker 6.5 also provides a facility to directly write `.pdf` files.

.png

Format:	Portable network graphics
Plug-in name:	FIGleaf Inline
URL:	`http://www.ct.ebt.com/figinline/`
Platforms:	Power Mac coming, Windows 95, Windows NT and UNIX (SunOS, Solaris, IRIX) available in beta form for download

This plug-in streams `.png` graphics into your browser. This plug-in gives you greater control over color palette assignments, border characteristics, and whether the graphic appears on the page, in a new window overlaying the current window, or in a new window substituting for the existing window.

.ppt

Format:	Microsoft PowerPoint presentation
Plug-in name:	PointPlus Viewer
URL:	`http://www.net-scene.com/down2.htm`
Platforms:	Windows 95, Windows NT

PowerPoint presentations must be converted to NetScene's `.slc` format for viewing. PowerPoint 5 includes a `Save as HTML` option that makes the need for a plug-in less critical.

.qxp

Format:	Quark Express page layout

Use Quark HTML Xtension found in version 3.5 to convert files in this format into an HTML document.

.rgb

Format:	Silicon Graphics RGB
Plug-in name:	FIGleaf Inline
URL:	`http://www.ct.ebt.com/figinline/`
Platforms:	Power Mac coming, Windows 3.1, Windows 95, Windows NT, and UNIX (SunOS, Solaris, IRIX) available in beta form for download

This plug-in streams `.rgb` graphics into your browser. This plug-in gives you greater control over color palette assignments, border characteristics, and whether the graphic appears on the page, in a new window overlaying the current window, or in a new window substituting for the existing window.

.rtf

Format:	Rich text

Use Microsoft Word to read the `.rtf` file, and then save the file as an HTML document.

.sun

Format:	Sun raster
Plug-in name:	FIGleaf Inline
URL:	`http://www.ct.ebt.com/figinline/`
Platforms:	Power Mac coming, Windows 95, Windows NT, and UNIX (SunOS, Solaris, IRIX) available in beta form for download

This plug-in streams `.sun` graphics into your browser. This plug-in gives you greater control over color palette assignments, border characteristics, and whether the graphic appears on the page, in a new window overlaying the current window, or in a new window substituting for the existing window.

.tga

Format:	Targa raster graphic

Convert files in this format to `.jpg` format in Photoshop, Hyjaak Pro, or DeBabelizer and include them with the `<IMG SRC=>` tag in an HTML document.

.tif

Format:	Tagged image file
Plug-in name:	FIGleaf Inline
URL:	`http://www.ct.ebt.com/figinline/`

Platforms: Power Mac coming, Windows 95, Windows NT, and UNIX (SunOS, Solaris, IRIX) available in beta form for download

This plug-in streams `.tif` graphics into your browser. This plug-in gives you greater control over color palette assignments, border characteristics, and whether the graphic appears on the page, in a new window overlaying the current window, or in a new window substituting for the existing window.

.txt

Format: ASCII text

You can include files in this format directly in HTML files with proper formatting and structuring tags. Use products such as Hot Dog or BBEdit to add tags.

.viv

Format: Compressed live video

Plug-in name: Vivoactive

URL: `http://www.vivo.com/vivoactive/index.html`

Platforms: Windows 95

This plug-in displays the first frame of a VivoActive compressed live video while the rest of the file continues to load. Download both the Player and the Producer so you can create compact `.viv` files from `.avi` videos.

.wav

Format: Windows Audio Video Exchange

Plug-in name: KM's Multimedia Plug

URL: `http://www.wco.com/~mcmurtri`

Platforms: Mac, Power Mac

This plug-in plays `.wav` audio files with user control.

.wmf

Format: Windows metafile

Plug-in name: FIGleaf Inline

URL: `http://www.ct.ebt.com/figinline/`

Platforms: Power Mac coming, Windows 95, Windows NT, and UNIX (SunOS, Solaris, IRIX) available in beta form for download

This plug-in streams `.wmf` graphics into your browser. This plug-in gives you greater control over color palette assignments, border characteristics, and whether the graphic appears on the page, in a new window overlaying the current window, or in a new window substituting for the existing window. A zoom pop-up menu allows you to magnify areas of the display.

.wp

Format:	Corel WordPerfect text document

Print files in this format to disk as PostScript and view in your browser in `.pdf` format using Adobe Acrobat Reader plug-in, or place them into a page layout program and use Xtension (Quark) or Addition (PageMaker) to create an HTML file.

.wrl

Format:	Virtual Reality Modeling Language (VRML)
Plug-in name:	Netscape Live3D
URL:	`http://home.netscape.com/comprod/products/navigator/live3d/`
Platforms:	Power Mac, Windows 3.1, Windows 95, Windows NT

This plug-in allows the viewer to navigate around VRML worlds using navigation bars and controls.

.xls

Format:	Microsoft Excel spreadsheet
Product name:	Hot Dog
URL:	`http://www.sausage.com`
Platforms:	Windows 95, Windows NT

Use Sausage Software's Hot Dog HTML editor to turn Excel worksheets into HTML tables. Save Excel 5.0 for Windows 95 worksheets directly as HTML documents.

File Formats Q&A

Q I'm planning a Web site but I have no idea what browsers will be used to access it. What should I do about publishing unsupported file formats?

A This is a matter of design philosophy. First, design your site for the lowest level graphic browser. (The time for text-only browsers has passed. It's time to upgrade!) Don't substitute bells and whistles for sound design, layout, and graphics. Second, include unsupported file types only if they are critical to the success of your site. A general-purpose informational site's needs for unsupported file formats is much less than one targeted to a specific group who may have specific needs to see, hear, or use information.

Q Do I have more flexibility in designing an intranet?

A Absolutely. An intranet should specify a browser and default plug-in package. Plus, it's much more common for members within a company to need information in native application file formats.

Q A friend of mine gave me several plug-ins but they don't work. What did I do wrong?

A Well, where should I start? Are the plug-ins for the same platform? Are they for compatible operating systems on the same platform (Mac 68XXX vs. PPC; Windows 3.11 vs. 95 vs. NT)? If so, are they for the same or compatible browser? Did you put the plug-ins in the correct directory or folder?

Q I want to design my own plug-in. Where do I start?

A Such an ambitious goal! You'll need to know as much as possible about how the data within the file format is structured. You normally get this information from the software vendor or by dissecting a test file. You may have to enter into a developer's agreement with the vendor to have access to this information. You'll also need the Netscape Plug-in Software Development Kit available at `http://www.netscape.com/comprod/development_partners/plugin_api/index.html`.

Q My company has extensive libraries of TIFF images that I want to make available on the Web. What's the best way to do this?

A First, understand that the TIFF format is a print media format. It works best when sending continuous tone images to imagesetters for screens and halftones. There is no advantage to publishing TIFF images on the Web, unless you want clients to eventually use the TIFF files for their own printing. A better solution is to selectively convert the TIFF images to JPEG format and include them as a supported graphic file type.

Summary

Great Web sites make use of data in many forms: text, graphics, sound, and multimedia. In this chapter, you developed an understanding of how Web browsers handle data in different file formats. Hopefully, you also developed an understanding of the appropriateness of including certain types of data. You now know the importance of correctly establishing MIME data types so that Web servers and browsers can sucessfully transfer and read information stored in many formats. Armed with this knowledge, you are now able to choose between displaying files inline or opening a separate browser window. Finally, you have been presented a series of strategies for including a multitude of file types in Web publications.

The Web landscape is constantly changing. The resources cited in this chapter simply represent a snapshot of what is currently available. Be prepared to do additional browsing to locate the latest and greatest Web resources. Now that you have a better understanding of file formats and how to get them into your Web page, learn how to include animation, sound, and interactivity by reading the chapters in Part V, "Extending Your Site with Multimedia."

IN THIS PART

V

Part

Extending Your Site with Multimedia

CHAPTER 22

Adding Multimedia to Your Web Site

by Dick Oliver

IN THIS CHAPTER

For better or worse, multimedia has come to the Web—and in a big way. In the last year, dozens of new formats for the compression or streaming transmission of audio and video data have been released publicly or incorporated into widely distributed software products. Meanwhile, the HTML specification has evolved so quickly that two variant forms—each with its own strong and weak suits regarding multimedia content—have advanced well beyond the canonical version overseen by the Internet Engineering Task Force and the World Wide Web Consortium. The trend seems to be picking up speed, as developer after developer rushes to lay claim to that most elusive of all digital media titles: "The Industry Standard."

The new wave of World Wide Web applications is providing multimedia developers and content creators with more bells, whistles, gongs, and interactive-design options than ever possible before. The question is no longer "Can I add multimedia to my Web site?" but rather "Which tools are best for the specific type of multimedia experience I'm envisioning?" There are also many to choose from. This chapter provides you with a solid understanding of how to make your way through this minefield of choices and add multimedia content to your Web pages.

Content First

Obviously, before you can place *anything* on your Web page, you first have to obtain it—or create it from scratch. Creating multimedia of any kind is a challenging and complicated task—one that is made no easier by the fact that the very tools used in its creation are constantly changing. If you're planning to create your own content from scratch you might want to consider skipping ahead to Chapter 23, "Creating Online Audio," Chapter 24, "Working with Video," or Chapter 25, "Adding Interactivity with Shockwave for Director." There you will find detailed information regarding the creation and formatting of your content. You can return to this point when you're ready to begin looking at how to place your new creations into your Web pages.

For those of us who are artistically challenged, a number of alternative ways to obtain useful multimedia assets are available. Aside from the obvious ("hire an artist"), here are a few suggestions:

- *Stock media.* The Web itself is chock-full of useful content in all media types, and stock-media clearinghouses of all shapes and sizes now exist online. At these places, you can find all the sounds, music, textures, video, and 3D models you need—just name it. Of course, prices can vary greatly from one clearinghouse to the next, so be sure to shop around. See the hotlist on the CD-ROM for links to some of the best stock-media sources on the Web.
- *Free for all.* Don't feel like spending any money? Much of the material on the Internet is deliberately "anti-copyrighted" or has reverted to public domain.

NOTE

It's still a good idea to double-check with the accredited author or current owner of the content; you don't want to get sued for copyright infringement. In addition, various offices of the U.S. government have spent a good deal of time and money generating content that, by law, belongs to all Americans (any NASA footage found online, for instance); these assets are free for you to use. Consult your favorite search engine or the hotlist on the CD-ROM.

- *Bartering for art: a win-win situation.* Want to show video on your site? Go find some videographers. Hang out in camera stores, leave a flyer on the school bulletin board, or (easiest of all) check out the online forums and Usenet newsgroups that cater to the interests of videographers. As clearly as possible, describe your site and what you want to do with it and offer to trade Web-page coding or other services for permission to use art. Chances are you'll find a few up-and-coming artists who'd be more than happy to let thousands of people peruse their work online.

NOTE

If you plan to make money off your site in any way—and maybe even if you don't—it is advisable to seek the services of an attorney who is familiar with copyright law and to spell out the terms of ownership in a formal agreement.

For the examples in this chapter, we created a Web page allowing hungry Web surfers a chance to preview the daily menu for a (fictitious) seafood restaurant. A picture of a lobster was morphed with PhotoMorph 2 software to create a short video (see Figure 22.1). We then recorded and mixed a voice-over with GoldWave (see Figure 22.2), with some music by a friend (Dana Robinson) in the background. Finally, the sound and video were combined, clipped, and compressed with Video Action ED (see Figure 22.3), a low-cost, commercial video-editing program.

All these tools—and many similar ones—are inexpensively available in software stores and on the Internet (except Windows Sound Recorder, which is included with Microsoft Windows). The quality of the end result (which you can see in `examples/downeast/downeast.htm` on the CD-ROM) isn't great, but it's about as good as anything on the Web that you can reasonably play back over a 28.8 Kbps or slower modem. The point is that you don't need to own a multimillion-dollar production studio to create multimedia that looks and sounds as good as you can expect within the bandwidth restrictions of today's Web.

For more details on producing and optimizing multimedia content with free and inexpensive tools, refer to Chapters 23 and 24.

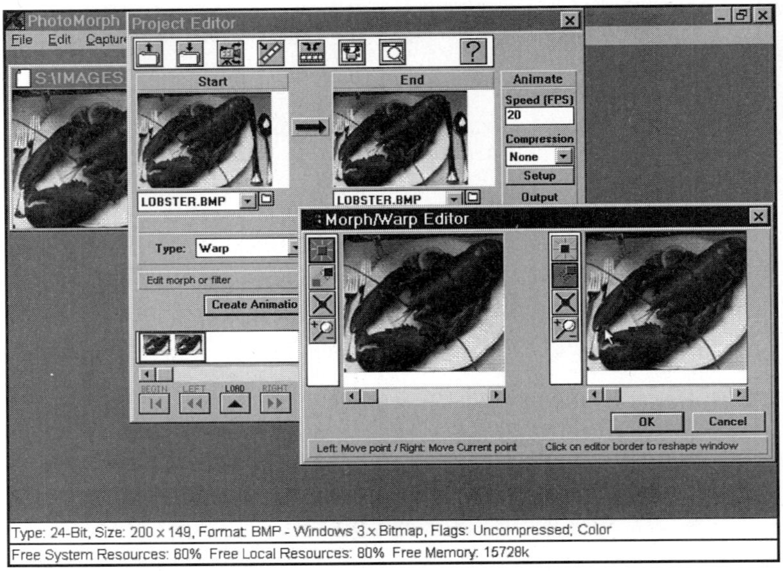

FIGURE 22.1.
PhotoMorph 2 is an inexpensive graphics program that makes it easy to create interesting videos from still images.

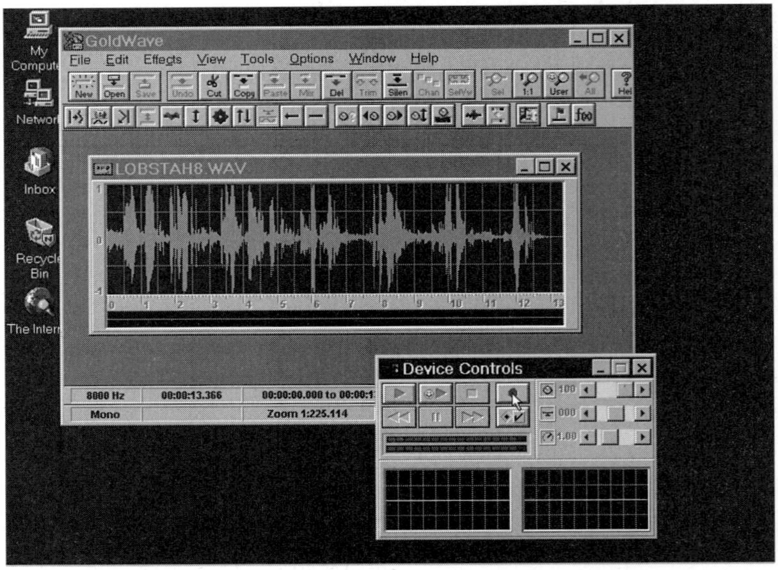

FIGURE 22.2.
Any sound card and microphone, combined with the GoldWave shareware on the CD-ROM, can be used to record Internet-quality audio.

FIGURE 22.3.
Now that low-cost video-editing programs such as Video Action ED are widely available, you have no excuse not to hop aboard the multimedia bandwagon.

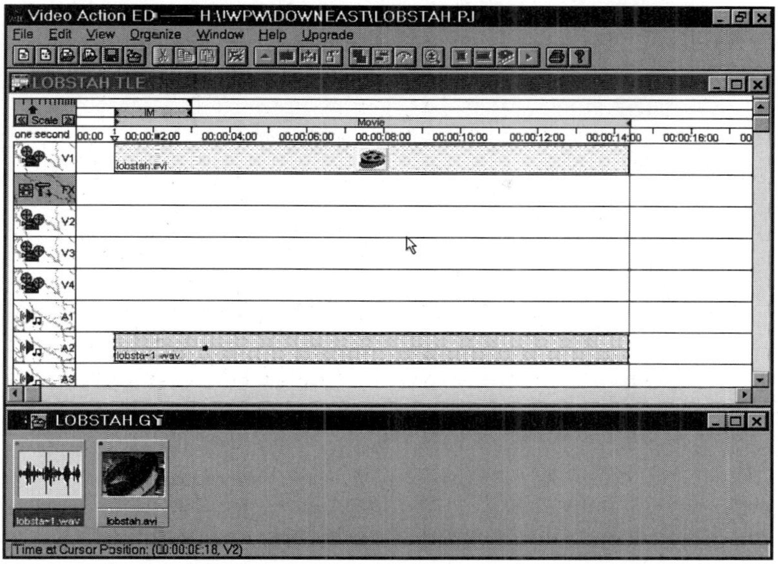

Streaming Over the Web

In the past, browsers have been limited to prerecorded and canned sequences, retrieved as full files. Video and audio files took minutes and sometimes hours to retrieve, thus severely limiting the inclusion of video and audio. The goal that everyone is moving toward is the creation of video that will be small enough to "stream" over the Web. This means you will not have to completely download the clip before you can start to watch it. Streaming video or audio will play in real time while the data is being received.

The real-time transfer of video data streams introduces new problems of maintaining adequate playback quality in the face of network congestion and client load. Nevertheless, a large number of companies are making streaming video a reality (with varying levels of success).

MPEG-1 is emerging as the video file-format standard because it produces video files that are typically one-quarter the size of other video formats. Unfortunately, MPEG-1 is not currently supported by QuickTime, so at present most of the streaming video technologies are limited to PC users.

A number of packages are cross-platform at present, but they require special server software that is out of the price range of most individual users. By the time you read this, however, Apple should have released a beta version of QuickTime 2.5, and a number of other companies are also planning products to serve and receive streaming MPEG over normal modem lines. For late-breaking news on this promising development, keep your eye (and ear) on the multimedia news-sites hotlist on the CD-ROM included with this book.

Meanwhile, streaming playback is now widely supported for Windows AVI and WAV files through Microsoft Internet Explorer and Netscape Navigator plug-ins. The examples in this chapter use these media types to demonstrate both streaming and the old-fashioned, download-and-play methods of delivering audiovisual media.

Laying It Inline

When it comes to placing audio, video, and animation (as well as any other sort of data you might want to send to a browser) in your Web pages, these media are not that different at all. In fact, as far as standard HTML is concerned, the only difference between one kind of file and another is the corresponding *media type*, which is indicated by the file extension (the three or four letters following the dot at the end of the filename). Given this significant piece of information (and, of course, the data in the file itself), the browser will marshal its helpers or plug-ins to handle everything as seamlessly as possible.

The tag you use to place a file into your Web page determines how (and if) it responds when browsed. There are a couple of things you'll have to consider when doing this—namely, which browsers you intend on serving best, and whether or not you're going to stick to the authorized, "official" HTML spec (which is specifically designed to minimize incompatibilities and display errors among all known browsers).

The following discussion demonstrates how to embed video and sound into your Web pages so that users of all major browsers can enjoy the multimedia experience.

The Public `<IMG>`

You are by now familiar with the function of the `<IMG>` tag, which is used to incorporate inline graphics (which are displayed directly "in" the page, as opposed to within the window of an external viewer). As of this writing, the `<IMG>` tag as implemented by Netscape Navigator 3.0 recognizes only GIF or JPG formats, but Microsoft Internet Explorer 3.0 enables you to include BMP images and—more significantly—AVI videos and three-dimensional VRML worlds.

Figure 22.4 shows an AVI video clip embedded in a Web page in Microsoft Internet Explorer 3.0.

The HTML code to include the video can be as simple as:

```
<IMG DYNSRC="lobstah.avi" WIDTH=160 HEIGHT=120>
```

The `DYNSRC` stands for *dynamic source* and tells Explorer that this is a motion video file instead of just a still `SRC` image.

If you include both `SRC` and `DYNSRC` attributes in an `<IMG>` tag, older browsers that don't support `DYNSRC` will simply display the `SRC` image instead. This is a very painless way to ensure backward compatibility!

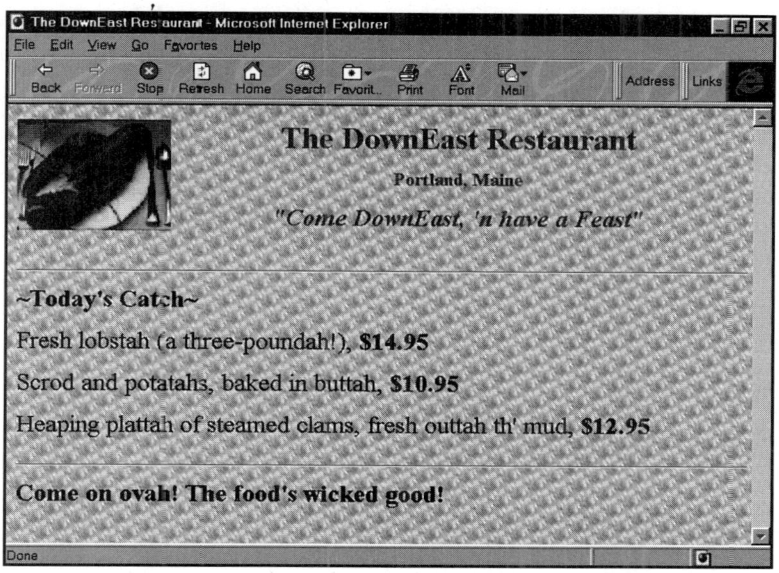

FIGURE 22.4.
Open `examples/downeast/downeast.htm` *on the CD-ROM, to see a short video of the lobster image.*

Two more new attributes can be used along with `DYNSRC` in an `<IMG>` tag, too. `CONTROLS` causes a set of controls to be displayed beneath the video clip. `LOOP=INFINITE` makes the video automatically repeat forever, whereas `LOOP=`*n* plays the video *n* times and then stops (for example, `LOOP=3` would play three times). Naturally, you can also use any of the standard `<IMG>` attributes, such as `ALIGN`, `BORDER`, and so on.

NOTE

As of version 3.0, Netscape Navigator does not support the `DYNSRC` attribute. You'll see how to handle embedded video for Netscape later in this chapter.

Link-and-Load

You can achieve a click-and-download effect by simply placing the file name in an anchor tag with an `HREF`, as shown in this line:

```
<A HREF="/WINDOWS/MEDIA/CANYON.MID">Click Here to Download</A>
```

This way, of course, the associated helper program is triggered as soon as the file has finished downloading, and executes the file (in the example above, for instance, the MIDI helper would fire up and play `CANYON`). If no helper program has been specified under General Preferences (in Netscape) or the Windows Associations (in Explorer), your browser will ask if you wish to save the file.

To make the lobster video in the DownEast Restaurant sample page available to users who don't have Internet Explorer 3.0, you could enclose the IMG tag with an ordinary A HREF link, and perhaps include the words "Click me!" or something similar in the SRC image; for example,

```
<A HREF="lobstah.avi">
<IMG DYNSRC="lobstah2.avi" SRC="lobstah.jpg" WIDTH=160 HEIGHT=120>
</A>
```

Figure 22.5 shows the result of an Internet Explorer 2.0 user clicking on the lobstah.jpg image; a separate AVI window appears and plays back the video. This is exactly the same page as seen with Explorer 3.0 in Figure 22.4 (examples/downeast/downeast.htm). Users of other browsers would see whatever AVI viewer their software was configured to use as a helper app, or they would be given the chance to save the AVI file to disk if no viewer was available.

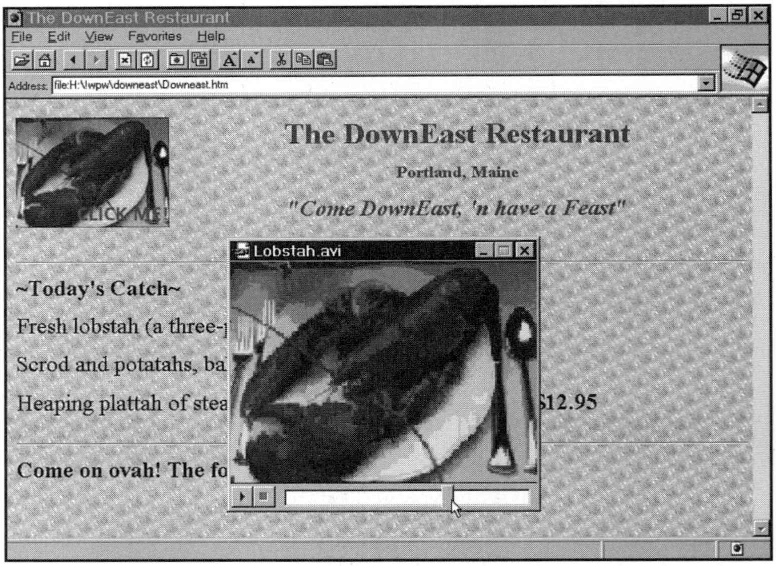

FIGURE 22.5.
Users of older browsers (such as Explorer 2.0, shown here) see a still image, which they can click to download and display the AVI animation.

> **NOTE**
>
> Note that DYNSRC begins playing video clips as soon as they begin downloading, but users whose browsers don't support DYNSRC have to wait until the video is completely done downloading before they begin to see it.

Microsoft Background Sounds

Video files embedded with `IMG DYNSRC` can include soundtracks, but Microsoft Internet Explorer also lets you specify a background sound for a page like this:

```
<BGSOUND SRC="lobstah.wav">
```

The background sound may not synchronize exactly with video content on the page, but in situations where that's okay `BGSOUND` can offer several advantages. Not only does the background sound usually start playing sooner than video, but you can include more than one video on the page *and* use `BGSOUND` to provide a master soundtrack for all of them.

A particularly effective way to reduce the file sizes on your page is to use a short video with the `LOOP` attribute to repeat it several times (or continually), while a longer background sound plays. This was used in the `downeast.htm` example on the CD-ROM to reduce the total multimedia file size for the page from over 500 K (`lobstah.avi`) to less than 200 K (`lobstah8.wav` and `lobstah2.avi`), while keeping the same voice over and a similar video effect.

To save even more space, you can specify a MIDI music file as the `BGSOUND SRC`. Because MIDI files are usually at least ten times as compact as a WAV file of the same time duration, you can use MIDI to effectively serve quite lengthy soundtracks—even to 14.4 Kbps modem users.

Netscape Plug-Ins

Netscape Navigator versions 2.0 and 3.0 can be extended to handle inline data of any type. This makes for a seamless presentation, compared to the original method of making the target app a helper for nonnative media types; the nonnative data is output right into the displayed page, rather than being sent to any external applications or opening more windows.

In order for the seamless presentation to occur, however, the user must have a *plug-in* that recognizes the incoming data type and knows what to do with it. A plug-in is like a helper that is fused into Navigator itself. Rather than executing anything external or launching files from the desktop, it adds a new set of display capabilities directly into the Netscape browser.

The Plug-Ins Development Kit, available for free from Netscape, enables developers to create new plug-ins for their own products and data types. For more information, see Netscape's Web site at

`http://www.netscape.com/comprod/development_partners/plugin_api/index.html`

In addition to the audio, video, and virtual reality plug-ins that are included with Netscape Navigator 3.0, third-party plug-ins are available for almost all common media types. Many of the most promising plug-ins make use of special encoding techniques that enable streaming of massive data files (such as high-fidelity audio or video data); this makes for more immediate output and shorter download time, without degrading the quality of the user's experience.

Where to Find Plug-Ins

Netscape maintains a Web page that lists all registered plug-ins and plug-in developers. To check out the current assortment, simply fire up your trusty browser and head out to the Netscape home site:

`http://home.netscape.com/`

If you're serious about staying up-to-date as far as your plug-in collection is concerned, you'll probably want to stop by fairly regularly because new plug-ins are frequently added to the list.

Media Types and Plug-Ins

As mentioned earlier, every media file embedded within an HTML page possesses a media type, which tells the browser how the file should be handled upon receipt (that is, which plug-in or helper app the data should be passed to). Media types are automatically associated with the appropriate files (based upon file extensions or the existence of a self-descriptive header within the body of the file itself). The transmission process is fairly transparent while it happens—assuming proper installation, the flow of multiple media formats can be quite seamless.

Unfortunately, the programs used to process these files—plug-ins especially—are still relatively new (even by the youthful standards of the World Wide Web). In realistic terms, this means that many users will have to expend some effort to obtain and install the necessary plug-ins or helper programs before they'll be able to view your media files.

Basically, we're talking about asking your online visitors to undergo the equivalent of a software upgrade. Even though most plug-ins are easy to install and available as freeware (for the time being, at least), this is still something that many people may be reluctant to do. Fortunately, you can do a number of simple things to help make this entire process as painless as possible for your Web guests. Keep these details in mind:

- Different systems handle media types differently. The tone and timbre of any note played will differ depending on the hardware involved (both the audio card and the physical speaker). Likewise, the color and quality of video and graphic elements can vary between computers and browsers.
- Unassociated files may or may not be visible. Depending on which browser you use, which tag you happen to run across, and what the contents of that tag are, a file that has no helper program (in Netscape's General Options) or association (in Windows systems) may or may not be represented in the rendered page. By definition, the file cannot be literally displayed, so if it is represented at all it will be by an icon. If an icon is displayed, the user will often be able to download a copy of the file by performing a `Save File As`.
- All required software should be made available. There are few things more frustrating than successfully finding your way to what sounds like a great Web site, only to find that you now need to go chasing plug-ins and helpers all over cyberspace before you'll

be able to experience it. It's not very difficult—and it's certainly conscientious—to make the required software available right there on your home page, or to give visitors a link to the home page of the software's developer or publisher.

- You might need a FAQ or newbie page. The purpose of this page is simply to welcome newcomers to your site and to explain what's going on. As long as the link to the FAQ or newbie page is prominently located near the top of your home page, it will generally function as intended, steering newcomers aside just long enough to give them a clue. This approach is somewhat of a compromise between structure and style, enabling you to make any initiatory information available without intruding into the structure of the home page.
- Give credit where credit is due. This may seem like something of a side point, but it's worth mentioning. If you do make use of someone else's technology on your page, it's only fair (and often legally required) that you credit your source for it.

How <EMBED> Works and What You Can Do with It

Just when you think you've mastered the last HTML element you'll ever need to know, along comes another set of expansions to the specification. You might as well get used to it—HTML's rapid evolution shows no sign of stopping any time soon. Besides, they wouldn't add a new tag if it weren't a good and necessary thing, right? (Don't answer that question without donning your asbestos longjohns; this is the sort of stuff religious wars are based on….)

Whereas Microsoft opted to add the `DYNSRC` attribute to the old, familiar `<IMG>` tag, Netscape chose instead to introduce an entirely new tag called `<EMBED>`. The `<EMBED>` tag enables you to place *any* type of file directly into your Web page, but only for people who have a plug-in or helper app installed and configured to accept the media type you embed. For example, the following line of HTML

```
<EMBED SRC="lobstah.avi">
```

would embed a video clip named `lobstah.avi` at the current position on the page, as long as visitors to the page have an AVI-compatible plug-in or helper app. (You'll find out shortly what happens if the user *doesn't* have an AVI viewer.)

Notice that, like the `<IMG>` tag, `<EMBED>` possesses an `SRC` attribute, which indicates the URL of the embedded document or application. Also like `<IMG>`, the `<EMBED>` tag can take `ALIGN`, `WIDTH`, and `HEIGHT` attributes.

The `<EMBED>` tag also enables you to set any number of optional parameters in order to pass startup values to the program being called. For instance, the page in Figure 22.6 includes the following:

```
<EMBED SRC="lobstah.avi" WIDTH=160 HEIGHT=120
ALIGN="left" AUTOPLAY="on" ONCURSOR="play">
```

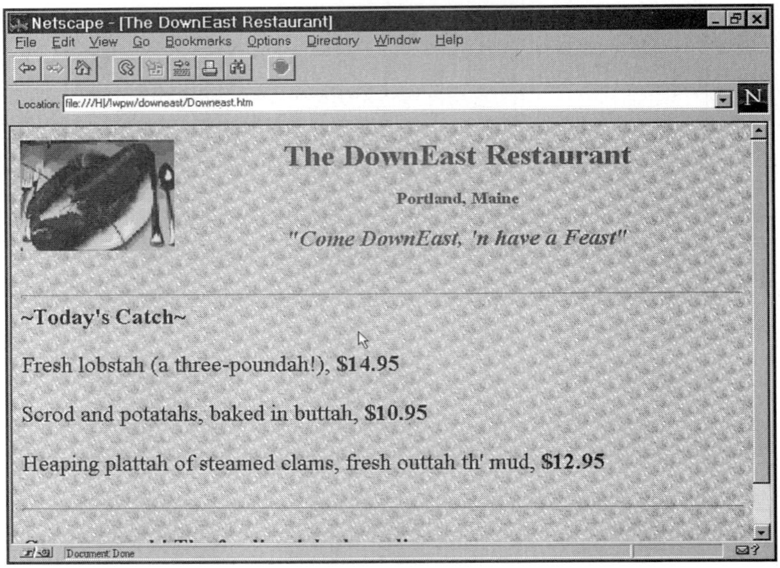

FIGURE 22.6.
With the appropriate Navigator plug-in installed, AVI files appear on the Web page just as if the plug-in functionality were built into Netscape Navigator.

NOTE

Netscape Navigator 2.0 did not include a plug-in to view AVI files, so users had to install a third-party plug-in, such as CoolFusion, before they could view video clips. But the Navigator version 3.0 comes preconfigured with a plug-in for AVI files, so most new users of Netscape will be able to see embedded videos without installing any additional software.

The `SRC`, `WIDTH`, `HEIGHT`, and `ALIGN` attributes are interpreted by the browser just as they would be for a still image. However, the actual display of the video is handled by whichever plug-in or helper app each user may have installed.

The `AUTOPLAY` and `ONCURSOR` parameters are not standard attributes of the `<EMBED>` tag, so the browser simply hands it over to the user's plug-in program to interpret. If a user happens to have the CoolFusion AVI viewer plug-in installed, CoolFusion will interpret the `ONCURSOR="play"` command to mean that whenever the user passes the mouse cursor over the video, it should restart. It is important to know that this parameter is meaningful only to CoolFusion, and that most other plug-ins have their own particular parameters that they can understand. If a user has a different AVI plug-in, or no plug-in at all for handling AVI files, then this parameter will do nothing at all. The LiveVideo plug-in included with Netscape Navigator 3.0, for example, will ignore the `ONCURSOR` parameter but will interpret the `AUTOPLAY="on"` parameter as an instruction to immediately play the video when it loads. Refer to the Web pages of each plug-in developer for information on the commands that its plug-in will accept as attributes in the `<EMBED>` tag.

TIP

If you want to support two or more popular plug-ins for the same media type that understand different parameters, you can put parameters for each of them in the same <EMBED> tag. Any parameters that aren't meaningful to the particular plug-in a user has installed will simply be ignored.

What Can Go Wrong?

`<EMBED>` works great when all the visitors to your site have the appropriate plug-in installed. But what will people who don't have the right plug-in see? That depends, unfortunately, on circumstances beyond your control as a Web-page publisher.

One thing you can be certain of is this: Users of Microsoft Internet Explorer 2.0 (and most other older browsers) will ignore the `<EMBED>` tag completely. However, users of Netscape Navigator 2.0 may see an unsightly puzzle-piece icon and a message saying `Plugin Not Loaded`, as shown in Figure 22.7. If they click on the `Get the Plugin` button, they will be taken to a page on Netscape Corporation's Web site explaining how to get and install plug-ins and helper apps (see Figure 22.8).

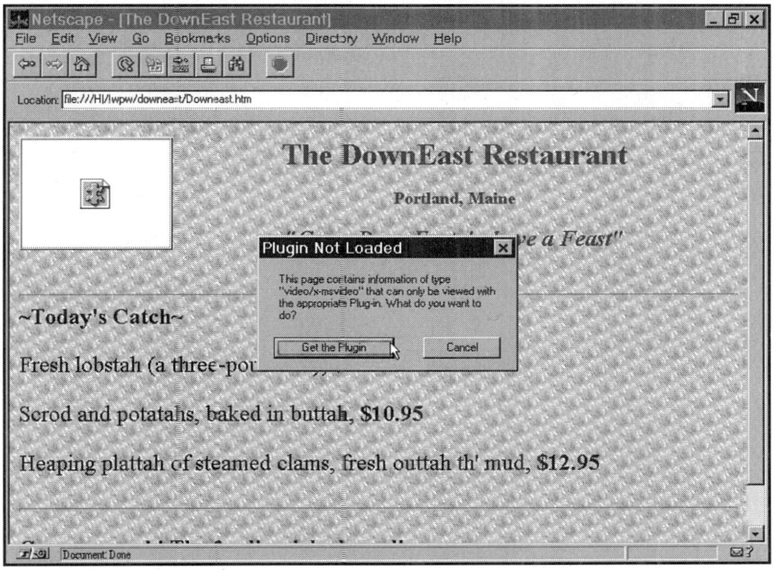

FIGURE 22.7.
When no plug-in or helper app can be found to handle an `<EMBED>` *tag, Netscape Navigator displays this message.*

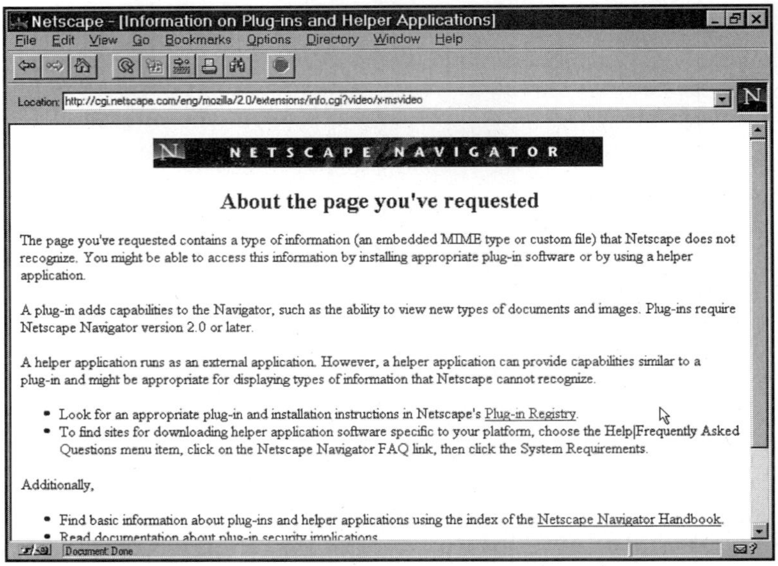

FIGURE 22.8.
Clicking `Get the Plugin` *in Figure 22.7 takes you to this page on Netscape's site.*

Experienced Web surfers will probably find it fairly easy to navigate from the links on Netscape's "About the page you've requested" page to the site where the plug-in they need can be downloaded. But many novice users are likely to throw up their hands in confusion, and blame the problem on something they "shouldn't have done." Those people may or may not ever make it back to your Web page. To avoid this confusion, you should provide your own links to any plug-ins that visitors to your site will need, along with an explanation of how to download and install them. This preferably should be done on a home page that will be seen *before* any pages where `<EMBED>` tags are used.

Helper Apps to the Rescue

To thicken the plot, Microsoft Internet Explorer 3.0 interprets the `<EMBED>` tag differently from previous versions of Explorer. Although Internet Explorer does not support Netscape plug-ins, it does support embedded helper applications. This means that when Explorer encounters an `<EMBED>` tag, it looks for the Windows 95 program that is registered to display the media type specified in the SRC attribute and embeds that application in the Web page. Figure 22.9 shows this for the AVI video and the `<EMBED>` tag in the page from Figure 22.6. Netscape Navigator 3.0 also supports embedded helper applications (see Figure 22.10), but only when it can't find a suitable Netscape plug-in.

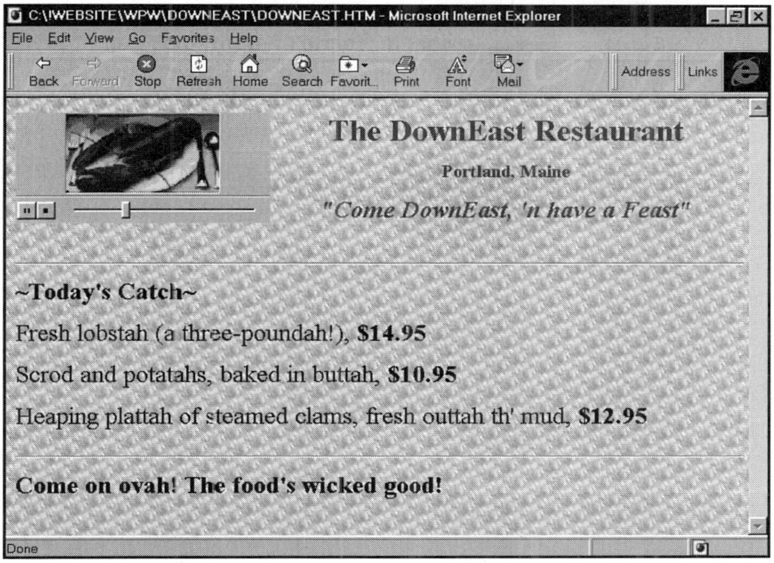

FIGURE 22.9.
Internet Explorer 3.0 interprets the <EMBED> *tag as an instruction to embed a helper application.*

NOTE

Embedded helper apps work only in Windows 95 and Windows NT. They will not function for Macintosh or UNIX users. Also, you should not confuse this use of Windows Object Linking and Embedding (OLE) with the OLE plug-in controls discussed later in this chapter. Though they do rely on the same underlying software technology, embedded helper apps do not require any sort of Netscape plug-in to function.

Note that the helper app will restrict its display to the area you specified with the `WIDTH` and `HEIGHT` attributes, which may result in squashed or warped output if controls are included that a plug-in wouldn't display (see Figure 22.11). You can avoid this by leaving out the `WIDTH` and `HEIGHT` attributes, but then any text or images further down the page will not be displayed until the entire media file is done downloading—which might be a long time if you've embedded a big video file!

You may be wondering how Internet Explorer and Netscape Navigator know which helper app to invoke to go with each embedded media type. If you guessed that they refer to the helper app list that a user can access by selecting `Options ¦ General Preferences ¦ Helpers`, you're wrong! Those helper configurations are used only for media linked with an `<A HREF>` tag and are ignored for the `<EMBED>` tag. Instead, the Windows file-type associations registry is used to find the appropriate application to handle the embedded media type.

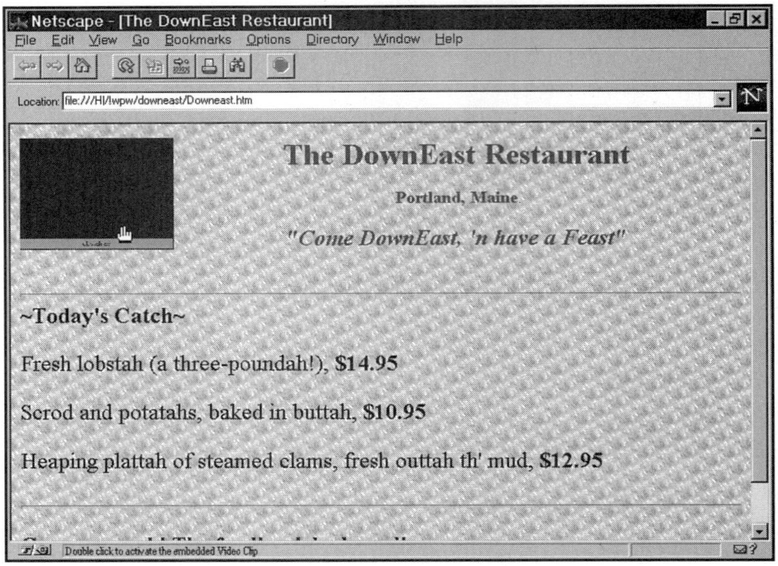

FIGURE 22.10.
Here, the MPLAYER.EXE *program that comes with Windows 95 is displaying the first frame of a video as an embedded object.*

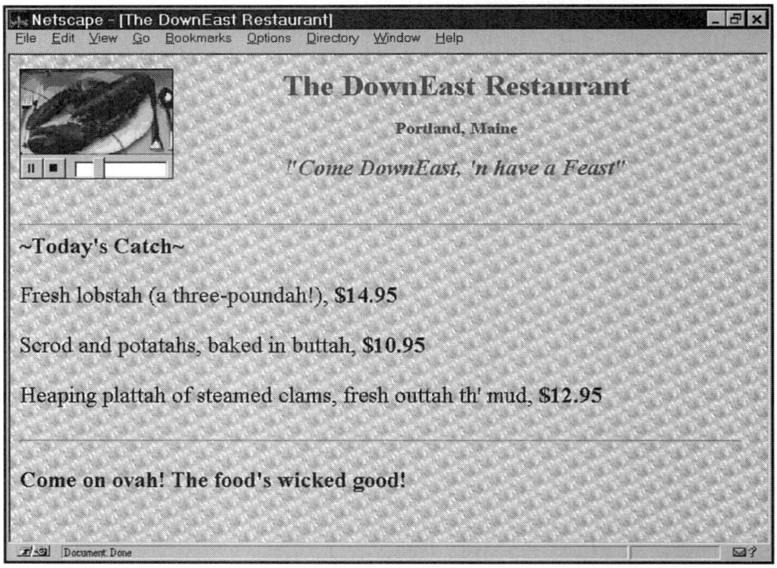

FIGURE 22.11.
Double-clicking on the frame in Figure 22.10 plays the video, still embedded in the Web page.

Figure 22.12 shows how to edit the Windows 95 associations to control which embedded helper app will get which file types, and the following list steps you through the process in more detail.

1. Start Windows Explorer (or Windows Internet Explorer), and select `View | Options`.
2. Click on the `File Types` tab, and choose the file type you want to configure from the scrolling list.
3. Click the `Edit` button, and choose the MIME Content Type and Default Extension for this file type. (Note that the Confirm open after download setting here applies only to Microsoft Internet Explorer and has no effect on Netscape Navigator 2.0.)
4. To change which program is invoked for this file type, choose one of the Actions and click the `Edit` button. You can then specify the Application used to perform action, including any parameters you want to have passed to that application.

Be aware that any changes you make here will affect all OLE embedding in any Windows program—not just Netscape Navigator. For example, if you change the application program associated with AVI video files, any AVI video embedded in Microsoft Word documents is displayed with the new application from then on.

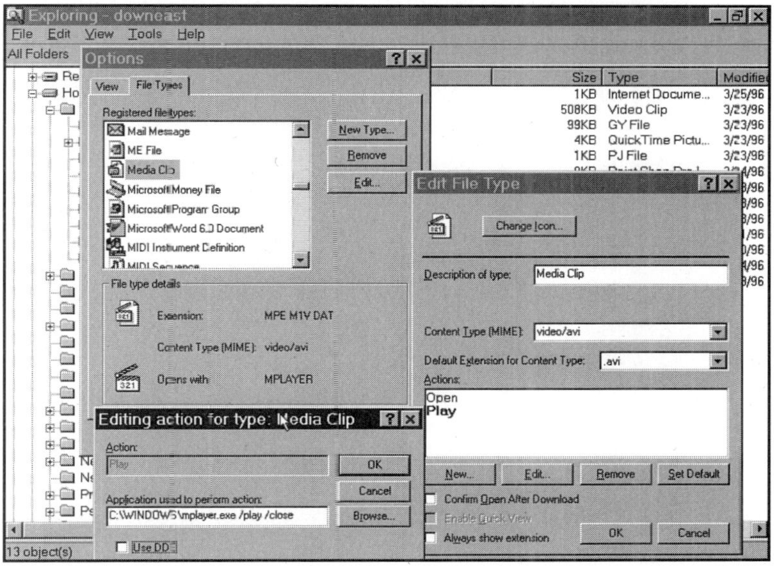

FIGURE 22.12.
As with all OLE applications, Netscape Navigator and Internet Explorer use the Windows file type registry to associate media types with applications to display them.

Though multimedia files are an obvious use of embedding, you can actually embed any media type for which a plug-in or OLE application is configured. In Figure 22.13, for instance, a TIF image has been embedded into a Web page and Netscape invoked Paint Shop Pro to display it. (The separate Paint Shop Pro editing window was opened only when the embedded image was double-clicked.)

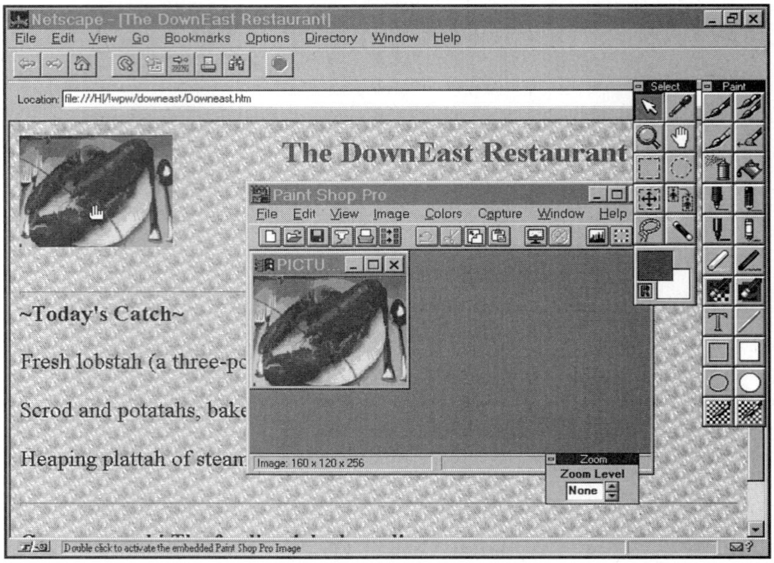

FIGURE 22.13.
When a user double-clicks on an embedded TIF file, the OLE application associated with that file type is opened.

The HTML code to embed this TIF was just the same as for any other media type: `<EMBED SRC="lobstah.tif">`

Unfortunately, you as a Web page author have no control over or knowledge of which file types and applications that people who visit your pages will have configured on their computers, or even how many visitors will be using a Microsoft Windows operating system. So the exotic uses of `<EMBED>` are probably best left to corporate intranets or other situations in which the page publisher has some control over the intended audience's computer setup.

Supporting Older Browsers

Because Netscape and Microsoft knew that their browsers would be the first (and perhaps only) to support the `<EMBED>` tag, they provided an easy way to provide alternate content for other browsers. Immediately following an `<EMBED>` tag, you can specify any amount of HTML code for other browsers, surrounded by `<NOEMBED>` (and `</NOEMBED>`) tags. For example, the `examples/downeast/downeast.htm` document shown in the figures throughout this chapter contains the following code:

```
<EMBED SRC="lobstah.avi" WIDTH=160 HEIGHT=120 ALIGN="left" AUTOPLAY="on">
<NOEMBED>
 <BGSOUND SRC="lobstah8.wav">
    <A HREF="lobstah.avi">
    <IMG SRC="lobstah.jpg" DYNSRC="lobstah2.avi" LOOP=INFINITE
      WIDTH=160 HEIGHT=120 ALIGN="left" BORDER=0>
  </A>
</NOEMBED>
```

Here's how this code will work in various browsers:

- Netscape Navigator 2.0 sees only the `<EMBED>` tag and ignores everything between `<NOEMBED>` and `</NOEMBED>`. If the LiveVideo plug-in is installed, it interprets the `AUTOPLAY="on"` command as discussed earlier. Otherwise, whatever plug-in or helper app that Netscape can find to display AVI files is used.
- Microsoft Internet Explorer 3.0 tries to embed a helper app associated with the AVI media type. If no such helper app is registered with Windows, it ignores the `<EMBED>` tag and sees the `<BGSOUND>` and `<IMG>` tags. In that case, it plays the `lobstah8.wav` sound file in the background while it loops the `lobstah2.avi` video specified in the `<DYNSRC>` tag. Note that this is a different video clip than Netscape will play—it contains no sound, and is a shorter clip designed to loop over and over again as the sound plays in the background.
- Most other browsers see only the `IMG SRC` attribute and display the `lobstah.jpg` still image. I added the words "CLICK ME!" to this image so that users with an AVI helper app can click on the image to play the `lobstah.avi` video clip specified in the `A HREF` attribute.
- Netscape Navigator version 1.2 is a problem case because it recognizes the `<EMBED>` tag but not the `<NOEMBED>` tag. It displays *both* the image specified in `IMG SRC` *and* an embedded OLE display or—more often—a broken image icon resulting from a failed attempt to display the `<EMBED>` tag. This can result in a Security Hazard message, or in the more innocuous but less hopeful message in Figure 22.14. Although these messages may be bothersome, the essential information on the page is still displayed successfully, and clicking on the "CLICK ME!" image will still launch an AVI helper app if one is available.

Forcing a Download with <EMBED>

The preceding sections detail the principle uses of the `<EMBED>` tag—namely, to display inline versions of the specified file or to enable the user to launch the associated helper program in order to view/play the file. However, `<EMBED>` has a tricky side as well: The tag can be used to push just about any common type of file to the user's machine by causing the client to perform what you might call a *forced download.*

The syntax for this function is exactly the same as the typical `<EMBED>` tag, including an `SRC` attribute that refers to the URL of the file you want to send, as shown in this line:

```
<EMBED SRC="filename.zip">
```

There are two major conditionals on the use of `<EMBED>` for this purpose. First, it does not work with EXE files (obviously, this would be a major security risk). Second, it will work only as described here if the user has a helper application associated with the media type (file extension) in question. If no helper (or plug-in) exists on the user's machine, all the user receives is an inline picture of the default "dead" icon, indicating that Netscape doesn't know what to do with the file. When working with the more common file types, this stipulation should pose no problem at all; but if the file is of some rare type, it is necessary to make the associated helper app available before the forced download will work.

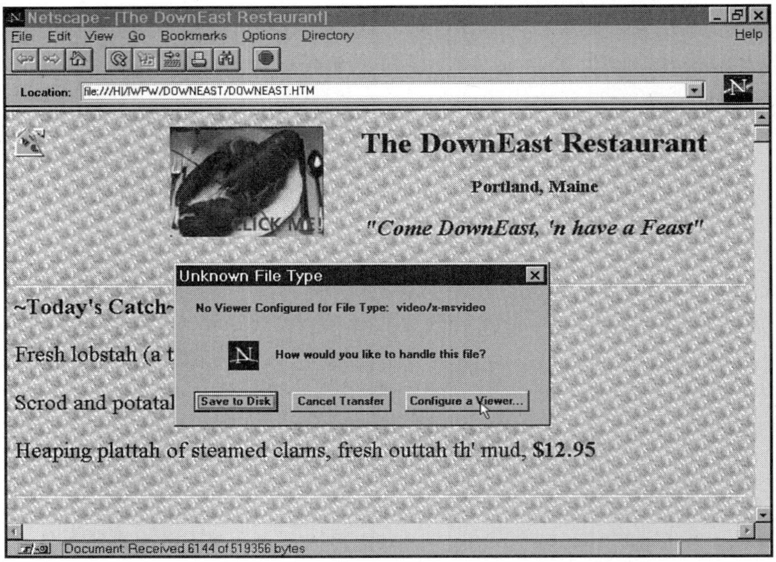

FIGURE 22.14.
Users of of Netscape Navigator version 1.2 may see some odd icons or messages when they look at pages intended for newer browsers, but they'll also see the rest of your page just fine.

This function is useful if you want to send a file automatically on page load (that is, as soon as a Netscape browser displays your page), or if you need to get a file to people who are unfamiliar with FTP and uncomfortable with computers in general. *The user doesn't even have to click on an icon to receive the file*, which will be sent automatically to whatever folder is specified in his or her Temporary Directory settings under `General Preferences | Apps`.

Another thing that makes this feature so useful is that the source file (on the server) does *not* have to exist within a publicly accessible directory (as would be the case with a typical FTP); embedding the file's URL into your page effectively bypasses this necessity.

Needless to say, this function should be used rarely and responsibly.

Where Things Stand

The `<EMBED>` tag has come under fire for a number of reasons, both technical and political. As of this writing, the W3C seems highly unlikely to accept the `<EMBED>` tag; in fact, they've even drafted a sort of counter-proposal that specifies a new tag called `<OBJECT>` (both Netscape and Microsoft were involved in the creation of this second proposal, though it was Microsoft's idea to call the tag `<OBJECT>` instead of the originally proposed `<INSERT>`). The `<OBJECT>` tag will do everything Netscape wants the <EMBED> tag to do, plus a lot more. You'll find out the details of how to use the <OBJECT> tag with Microsoft Internet Explorer and Macromedia's Shockwave player in Chapter 25.

None of this has stopped Netscape from using <EMBED> as originally proposed. Indeed, the <EMBED> tag is an integral element of Netscape's current plug-in system, which has already won much support from users and vendors alike. Obviously, the goal for Netscape is to make sure that use of the <EMBED> tag becomes so common that the WC3 has no alternative but to accept it as an official part of HTML. Netscape has moved quickly and openly toward this goal, and thanks to the dozens of third-party vendors who've already invested time and money in the creation of plug-ins for embedded media, Netscape may stand a chance of getting what it wants.

Microsoft, meanwhile, has decided to stick with the original unfortunately named <IMG> tag, and has proposed a number of additional attributes that would enable it to be used for embedding sound and AVI files, as explained earlier in this chapter.

Keep your eye on the W3C pages at `http://www.w3.org/pub/WWW/` for more on this topic—the <EMBED> wars are far from over.

Summary

In this chapter, you've seen how to embed video and sound into a Web page. But remember that the <EMBED> tag can be used to include a vast array of media types besides just Windows AVI and WAV files. Some of these media types are alternative audio and video formats that aim to achieve greater compression, quality, or compatibility than the Windows standard formats. Others, such as Shockwave and QuickTime VR, add a variety of interactive features that old-fashioned audiovisual media types lack.

In Chapter 23, "Creating Online Audio," and Chapter 24, "Working with Video," you'll get some tips and instructions for producing your own clips for use on the Web. Chapter 25, "Adding Interactivity with Shockwave for Director," introduces true interactive multimedia for the Web, with the ever-popular Macromedia Director software.

CHAPTER 23

Creating Online Audio

by Dick Oliver and John J. Kottler

IN THIS CHAPTER

Sounds have the power to completely alter the perceived message of the visuals they accompany. If you need to create your own source audio, there are a number of things you should keep in mind. Working with audio can be a tricky task, one made even more confounding by the limitations imposed on content on the Web in order for it to be viewed or heard reasonably over slow connections. The following quick introduction to digital audio should help you better understand how to add sound to your Web pages.

Working with Digital Audio

Just as with moving pictures, the quality and convincing nature of a digital audio file is largely dependent on its speed. More precisely, this depends on the distance in time between one *sample*, or frame, and the next. In digital audio, this distance is known as the *sampling rate* and is generally expressed in KiloHertz (KHz). A digital audio device that records or plays back 11,000 samples per second (a fairly poor rate, but adequate for low-end professional audio) is said to operate at 11 KHz. If the sampling rate during recording or conversion is too low, the whole thing will sound terrible.

If sampling rate can be likened to the frames of a movie, *sample resolution* might represent the number of colors available for use on the screen. Whereas the sampling rate indicates how often a sample is taken, the sample resolution determines the degree of *detail* with which each sample is recorded—that is, the number of bits dedicated to each sample.

Take, for instance, the ruler that you use to make measurements. Typically you will find inches on the ruler as well as halves, quarters, eighths, and sixteenths of an inch. If you measured the length of a pencil using inches only, you wouldn't get a very accurate measurement. However, if you measured that same pencil using sixteenths of an inch, you would get a much more accurate measurement. It is the same with sampling resolution; the finer the measurements you make (using higher rates), the more accurate the sound recording will be.

QUICK LESSON ON DIGITAL AUDIO

A sound wave is much like a water wave; it contains highs and lows, crests and troughs. A sound wave can be recorded by measuring its highs and lows (amplitude) over time. In order to capture sound digitally, an infinite amount of time must be broken into a definite number of points (this is referred to as the *sampling frequency* or *rate*). The amplitude of the sound wave at each point in time may then be measured and stored as a digital code. There are additional compression techniques, in which the differences between actual points on a sound wave and data points predicted mathematically by the compression algorithm are stored. By storing only these differences and not every data point, audio information can be stored using less space.

Sample size is also referred to as *bit depth*. The bit depth of an audio file indicates the number of bits that are grouped together in order to represent the "shape" of each sample. The more bits you use to record something, the more detail and subtlety are caught by your recording. The sample sizes of digital audio files are almost always either 8-bit (as in most multimedia files) or 16-bit (as in CD audio).

Sampling rate and sample size determine both the subjective quality of the sound and the size of the sound file. For Internet audio, you will almost always want to use the lowest sample rate (8 KHz) and sample size (8 bits) available. A CD-quality, 44 KHz sample may sound terrific, but just five seconds of speech at this quality takes up over 350 K. If you were using a 14.4 Kbps modem, this little track would take over five minutes to download!

TIP

Here's a general rule of thumb to help you quickly make a ballpark estimate of how big an 8-bit sound sample is. Each second of most music or sound effects produces a file size (in kilobytes) approximately equal to the sample rate (in KiloHertz). For example, a one-second sound sampled at 8 KHz is about 8 K. Ten seconds at 16 KHz is about 160 K.

Double those estimated file sizes for speech or complex, chaotic sounds. And, of course, double them again if you use 16-bit samples instead of 8-bit. This is a general rule for monophonic sound. If you plan on using stereo sound, the size of the file is double what it would be for mono. Digital-stereo recordings require that both the left and right audio channels be stored.

Audio File Formats

In the early days of multimedia computers, most machines (such as Apple, IBM, Tandy, and IBM clones) possessed their own, native audio file formats. Moving audio from one platform to another—especially without loss of sound quality—was a difficult procedure. Soon enough, audio card manufacturers began to develop audio file formats of their own, each with its own specific strengths and weaknesses. As you might expect, this confused the issue even further.

However, in the intervening years, the audio side of multimedia development has stabilized considerably, and a number of cross-platform solutions have found their way into popular acceptance. Today, those with digital audio enjoy a somewhat more stable and standardized set of file formats and protocols than their counterparts in video. It's also fairly easy to locate software utilities that enable you to record, edit, or convert audio files from one format to another. Sometimes, however, this process noticeably degrades the quality of the sound.

The most common file formats for digital audio on the Web are `.aiff`, `.au`, `.mid`, `.snd`, and `.wav`. Table 23.1 provides an overview of the strong and weak points of all these common audio formats.

Table 23.1. The five most common audio formats on the Internet.

Audio Interchange File Format (.aif, .aiff)*—The audio file format of choice in the Mac world*	
Media type:	audio/x-aiff
Native platform:	Apple, SGI
Sample size:	Typically 16-bit (variable from 1-bit to 32-bit)
Sampling rate:	16 KHz
File size per minute:	960 K
Sound quality:	Very good; close to FM radio
Sun Audio (.au)*— The native UNIX audio file format*	
Media type:	audio/basic
Native platform:	NeXT, Sun
Sample size:	8-bit
Sampling rate:	8 KHz
File size per minute:	480 K
Sound quality:	Fairly good; television/telephone quality
Musical Instrument Digital Interface (.mid, .midi)*—Protocol for exchanging music notation electronically (known as MIDI)*	
Media type:	audio/midi, audio/x-midi
Native platform:	N/A
Sample size:	N/A
Sampling rate:	N/A
File size per minute:	50 K
Sound quality:	Unpredictable; depends on listener's sound card
Macintosh Sound Files (.snd)*—Nearly identical to .au files in performance features*	
Media type:	audio/basic
Native platform:	Mac, NeXT, Tandy
Sample size:	8-bit
Sampling rate:	8-KHz
File size per minute:	480K
Sound quality:	Fairly good; television/telephone quality

Waveform Audio (.wav)*—Microsoft Windows native audio format*	
Media type:	audio/x-wav
Native platform:	PC
Sample size:	8-bit or 16-bit
Sampling rate:	8 to 22 KHz
File size per minute:	480 to 1024 K
Sound quality:	Good to excellent; AM radio to CD quality

WHAT IS MIDI?

MIDI (Musical Instrument Digital Interface) files are not waveform files and therefore operate differently from any of the other file types listed in Table 23.1. Created and maintained by the International MIDI Manufacturers Association—a coalition of musical instrument manufacturers and electronics firms—MIDI is a protocol that allows information to be exchanged between synthesizers, tone boxes, computers, and other compatible devices. MIDI files don't contain any sounds at all, in the sense that a digital sample such as an `.aiff` or `.wav` file can be said to contain a sound.

Instead, a MIDI file consists of a stream of numbers, each of which corresponds to a specific audio event or attribute, such as voice, pitch, volume, sustain, decay, bend, and so on. Like the screen layout of an HTML document that may be viewed through various browsers, the audible result of a MIDI file's execution is *informed*—but not *dictated*—by its content. For example, some sound cards use extremely high-quality digital samples of a real piano, while others synthesize a "piano" sound that resembles a baby duck as much as a baby grand.

Furthermore, some MIDI devices may have a tuba or trombone sound loaded into the channel usually used for piano, so your New Age keyboard improvisation may sound like a brass band tuning up before a parade. Though MIDI sound cards are getting better every year and do generally follow the standard instrument mappings, it can still be difficult to predict exactly how a MIDI file will sound when played on someone else's machine.

Recording and Mixing Internet Audio

Now that you have some familiarity with how digital audio is stored, let's look at how to create some new audio files of your own. To create and edit audio content, you must use an appropriate tool. GoldWave is a program included on the CD-ROM with this book. This software enables you to record, edit, convert, and play digital audio on your Windows 3.*x* or Windows 95 computer. Figure 23.1 shows GoldWave in action.

FIGURE 23.1.
GoldWave is an audio-editing program you can use to record, play, convert, and apply numerous special effects to sound files.

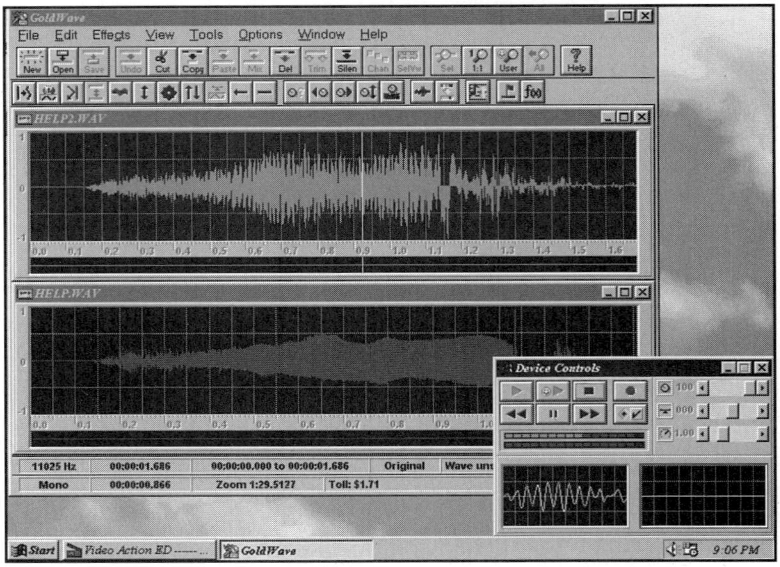

After you start GoldWave, you will notice that the program produces two windows. The first window is the Editor window, where graphical representations of sound waves are drawn. In the lower-right corner of your screen, a second Device Controls window presents you with some familiar buttons for controlling the playback or recording process. To begin recording, you must first create a new audio file using the `File | New` menu option. Choosing this option presents you with a dialog box, prompting you to choose the qualities of the sound you are creating.

TIP

When creating Internet sound files, remember that the smaller a file is, the better. Unfortunately, as stated earlier, this requires a compromise with the quality of the sound. To minimize file size, consider creating your new sound files as 8-bit, 11 KHz, monophonic (not stereo) files. This will add more noise to your sounds, but will significantly decrease the amount of storage space required for the sound file.

After you have created the new sound file, a new window is created in GoldWave's editor window. To record into this window, simply click on the red record button in the Device Controls window. The record button then changes into a purple stop button, and a vertical beam slowly progresses across the length of the new window you created. This beam is the position bar, which indicates how far along in the sound file you have recorded. When you click on the stop button, or when the position bar reaches the end of the file, the recording process stops. Whatever audio you have recorded is then converted to a graphical representation and displays in the Editor window.

TIP

Remember to check the audio settings and connections for your sound card prior to recording. You should make certain that the source you are recording is connected appropriately to the sound card. If you are using a microphone, make sure it is connected to the MIC input. If you are recording from a device such as an external CD player or stereo, make certain that these devices are connected to the LINE input.

Most sound hardware in computers is accompanied by software for controlling the sound card. Usually, this software includes mixer software for controlling the input and output levels of the sound card. Before recording, make sure that these settings are correct so that the correct input device is captured.

You can play, pause, rewind, and forward the contents of the sound file in the Editor window at any time by clicking on the appropriate buttons in the Device Controls window. You will use the play button often to audition the sound that you are creating.

Trimming the Fat

Typically, after you have captured the sound file, you need to alter it in some fashion. Most likely, you will need to trim the sound file that you have just recorded. Unless you are extremely coordinated, you often must start the recording process on the computer before actually capturing the audio input. This is necessary to avoid missing the introduction of the audio clip you are attempting to record. However, depending on the length of the pause between clicking on the record button in GoldWave and beginning the audio clip, you may have a considerable amount of silence at the beginning of your audio file. Silence before or after an audio clip in a file is both annoying and wastes valuable space. Therefore, you should immediately trim the audio file you have captured.

In GoldWave, you may specify a region of the audio file by using the mouse. As you pass the mouse cursor over an audio file in GoldWave, the cursor changes into an icon of two arrows pointing toward a vertical bar between them. Place this icon at the front of the sound file, where the squiggly line that represents the sound first appears, and click the left mouse button.

You can then move the mouse cursor to where all of the squiggly lines stop in your audio file and click the *right* mouse button. After doing so, a range is defined that includes only the sound itself, not the silence before or after the sound. The selected range is indicated by a blue highlight in the window for the sound you are editing.

After you have selected just the sound from a sound file, choose the `Edit | Trim` command. GoldWave discards all information that is not within the region you defined.

TIP

You may wish to save your sound files periodically, using different file names for each version you create. As you experiment with multiple effects and edit the sound wave, you may wish to undo your changes. Although GoldWave supports the Undo command, it will undo only your most recent change. If you apply three different effects and wish to undo them all, the only choice you have is to start over or load a previous copy of the sound file.

Adding Audio Effects

Ranges that you define in GoldWave are important for other features than simply trimming the sound file. You can think of the highlighted section of the sound file as selecting several words in a word processing program. Any action you perform applies only to the selected region. Therefore, you can copy a section of the entire sound and paste it somewhere else later in the sound file, just as you can with text in a word processor. You may also apply a variety of special effects to the selected region of a sound.

Pump Up the Volume

No matter how hard you try, certain sounds that you record are going to be too quiet. You can tell this because the graphical representation of the sound does not occupy the entire height of the window in which it is drawn. To maximize the amplitude of the sound wave to fill the height of the window (or *normalize* the sound wave), open the `Effects | Volume` menu. Also included in this menu are volume commands for fading in, fading out, changing the overall volume of the sound, and creating custom volume controls over time.

Mix Well

Another common function of sound-editing software such as GoldWave is the `Mix` command. This command enables you to take two entirely different sound files and mix them into one sound file. The result is a single sound file that plays both of the original sounds, at the same time. For instance, let's assume you would like to mix two sound files included with Windows: `chimes.wav` and `chord.wav`. To mix these two files together, first open the two files in GoldWave. Then select the `chord.wav` window, set the range for the sound file to include the entire sound file, and choose the `Edit | Copy` command from the menu. With the chord sound in the Clipboard buffer, choose the other window (`chimes.wav`) and then `Edit | Mix` from the menu. A dialog box appears, asking which volume to use when mixing the files together. A value of **`100`** indicates that both sounds will be the same volume when played together. Values higher than `100` instruct GoldWave to mix the sound file that is currently in the Clipboard so that it is louder than the original file. Likewise, lower values indicate that the content in the Clipboard should be quieter than the original sound file. The `Mix` command uses the contents of the Clipboard to mix with a sound file. After you have performed the mix, the Clipboard data will remain in the Clipboard for you to paste when desired, although it is not necessary to use the `Paste` command with the mix effect.

Echo, Flange, and Doppler Effects

GoldWave supports numerous effects that cannot be covered in depth in this section of the book. However, the "Skiing" video example we create later in this book mixes the sound of a person yelling "Help!" into the video. Two digital audio files are included on the CD-ROM with this book: `help.wav` and `help2.wav`. The first is a simple recording of someone screaming "Help!" The second file is the same audio recording of the word "Help," but after some special effects have been applied. After playing each file, you should be able to quickly distinguish the difference.

The second audio file (`help2.wav`) applies the echo, flange, and Doppler effects to the original sound. The echo effect, as its name implies, adds an artificial echo to the sound. The flange effect, which can make your voice sound like a mechanical robot, was then applied to make the voice file sound more like two people. The Doppler effect was used to simulate the fall-off in the voice, as if the skier were moving away down the hill. Figure 23.2 shows the Doppler effect with a curve that slowly falls down. This curve is then applied to the entire region selected in the sound file.

NOTE

The *Doppler effect* is an effect that can be heard in everyday life. Take, for instance, a train that blares its horn as it passes you. The train's horn uses only one pitch. But as the train approaches, you may notice that the pitch of the horn seems to rise. After it passes by, the pitch falls off. You can also hear this effect when an emergency vehicle with a siren passes by or someone drives by with a loud stereo.

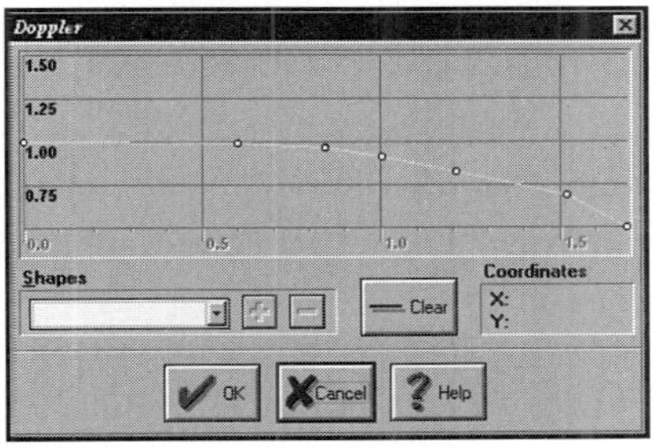

FIGURE 23.2.
You can create your own curves for the Doppler effect in GoldWave. In this example, the pitch of the sound drops quickly toward the end of the sound.

Compressing and Saving Audio Files

After you have perfected the sound, you need to save it. As with almost anything else on the Internet, saving the sound is not quite as simple as it first appears. First, you must determine which file format is best for storing the audio file. If you plan on using this file with the greatest number of computers from around the world on the Internet, you may consider using the Sun/NeXT (`.au`) format or Mac/SGI (`.aif`) format. Netscape provides an audio player that can easily play sound files of either type on any computer platform. In any case, when you have decided on the format that best matches your needs, you must save your work using the `File` | `Save` option in GoldWave. A dialog box then appears, prompting you to specify the path and file name for the sound, as well as to determine what file format to use (see Figure 23.3).

NOTE

The WAV (`.wav`) file format contains many additional file attributes that may not be found in the other audio file formats. One important attribute is MSADPCM. Using this attribute will effectively halve the size of the overall sound file. ADPCM (Adaptive Differential Pulse Code Modulation) is a compression technique that can save a considerable amount of space (and therefore time transferring the file across the Internet). As sound players that support the .wav format become available on non-Windows computers, you may decide to use this format for storing your audio content. The GoldWave audio editor included on the CD-ROM enables you to save your files using any of these compression techniques.

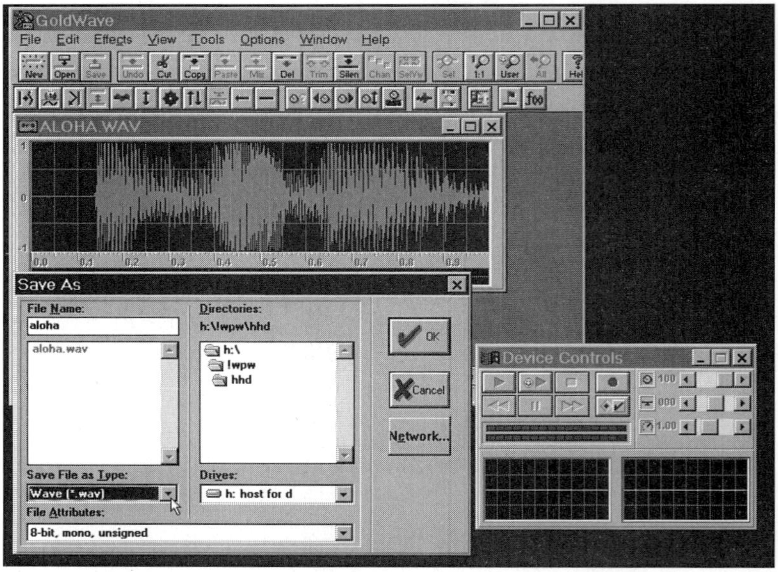

FIGURE 23.3.
GoldWave enables you to save (and convert between) a wide variety of sound file formats and to choose attributes such as bit depth and compression type.

Audio Conversion

No matter what platform or operating system you use, sooner or later you'll come across an audio file that you'd love to have a copy of—except for one little problem: it's encoded in a file format you're unfamiliar with, or one for which you have no player. When this happens, you will need to use a conversion utility to translate the file into a format that your player software can understand.

In essence, all conversion utilities do exactly the same thing: They effectively perform a `Save As...` or `Export` command on the designated source file, creating a replica of the original data "as heard through the ears" of the target format. Because the various file formats all have different features and performance statistics, it helps to play around with them for a while, tweaking and comparing them until you get a feel for each format's particular strengths and weaknesses. Your trusty conversion utilities are your best tools for this sort of experimentation. You can convert between most common formats within GoldWave (and most other sound-editing programs) simply by opening the file you have and saving it in the format you want.

When you select a file format for output (that is, the target format), what you're really doing is telling the converter which algorithms and ranges or boundaries you want it to use in the upcoming translation process. The conversion utility then reads the file from end to end—applying a predetermined set of algorithms to the data in the file, multiplying, dividing, averaging, truncating, and rounding to the nearest equivalent—and finally saves the output of these calculations in the style of the target format.

NOTE

Conversion utilities can vary greatly in the amount of control they give to their users, as well as in the quality of their output. Generally speaking, they will produce translations that approach–but do not quite equal–the quality of the original. Of course, depending on the formats involved, the conversion software used, and the contents of the original (source) file, the differences between the two versions may sometimes turn out to be more drastic than you had expected. And in any case, the result file rarely (if ever) comes out sounding *better* than the original–unless you have some sort of rare and wondrous talent!

For this reason, it is a good idea to view or play a converted file *immediately after performing the conversion*. If the result file is unsatisfactory, be sure to delete it right away; this will protect you from the possibility of confusing the two files later on.

Audio Helper Apps and Plug-Ins

Helper apps are programs that are external to the browser, but that are called into action when the browser receives files of their designated media type. They are alternately known as *players* or *viewers*.

Plug-ins differ from helper apps in that they insert their associated media files *inline*—that is, directly within the body of the rendered HTML document. Unlike audio helper apps, audio plug-ins can generally be set up to begin playing immediately upon page load—the user doesn't even have to click on anything. The following is a sample of audio helper applications and plug-ins that are available:

- GSM Audio Players/Converters
  `http://www.cs.tu-berlin.de/~jutta/toast.html`
- Netscape Audio Player
  `http://home.mcom.com/newsref/ref/winaudio.html`
- RealAudio Client
  `http://www.realaudio.com`
- ToolVox for the Web
  `http://www.voxware.com`
- TSPlayer, WHAM, PLANY, and other audio helper apps
  `ftp://ftp.winsite.com/pub/pc/win3/sounds/`

Many of the newer helper apps and plug-ins utilize a technology known as *streaming.* They receive and use audio data so that they can begin playing the file before the entire download is completed. In the past, in order to hear an audio file, you first were required to download the audio file in its entirety from the Internet. Depending on the size of the audio file, this could take some time. Streaming audio (and video) enables the helper application or plug-in to download the beginning of the file. This portion is then interpreted by the plug-in or helper application, and the audio (or video) starts playing the little data that is available. As that content is playing, additional information is downloaded from the Internet in the background. This gives the appearance of much quicker connectivity to information-rich content, such as video and audio. Streaming technology is made possible by efficient data compression and the power of today's multithreading and multitasking operating systems.

One nice feature of streaming audio and video is that it requires no special action from the user. The user simply clicks on a link to play the audio clip, and the appropriate helper application or plug-in is invoked automatically (assuming that the program is available on the user's computer). In most cases, the only way in which streaming audio is differentiated from standard audio files is by conscious efforts made by Web-page developers to place text or graphics indicating that streaming audio is available on a page.

It is important to recognize that not all streaming technologies are created equal. All are bound to have strong points and weak points (and in these early days of Web-based multimedia, there are still more weak points than the average TV viewer or radio listener would care to put up with). Each does a better job at compressing certain types of sound, depending on the volume, pitch, and tone of the sound, and the algorithm used to represent that sound digitally.

NOTE

TSPlayer is unique among audio helper apps in the previous listing. It does not play any audio files on its own. Rather, it passes audio data (in .wav format) through itself to the actual audio helper app (which may be any application that can play .wav files). This produces an effect similar to streaming, in that the audio file begins playing before the download is completed.

Summary

This chapter explained the basics of creating your own digital audio. Chapter 24, "Working with Video," initiates you into the art of motion-video production for the Internet.

CHAPTER 24

Working with Video

by Dick Oliver

IN THIS CHAPTER

So you think you want to create some video for the Internet. The first question to ask yourself is "Do I really need video, or can I create a similar effect using GIF animation, client pull, or a multimedia authoring program like Macromedia Director?" All of these approaches are usually much faster and easier, both for you and the people who will visit your Web site.

Likewise, ask yourself, "Which would be more effective for the amount of space required: a few seconds of video, or a slickly produced audio piece replete with sound effects and music?"

When you are sure that video is the best or easiest thing to use for the task at hand, the question becomes "How much and what kind of video will best suit the requirements of my intended Internet site?" For example, imagine you are designing an online demonstration of the inner workings of the pistons of an engine. In this case, you could set the video to loop using Movie Player, which would allow you to run your presentation indefinitely in the space of about 100 K or less. Likewise, perhaps your movie will be almost as effective, or more effective, in 1-bit or 4-bit rather than 16-bit. Often, you can cut your frame rate and playback size and still create the effect you are seeking. Remember, people have to download your clip, and in most cases users will happily trade some quality to have the clip quicker.

Moreover, most people will simply not be able to enjoy high-quality video—even if they don't mind the download—because they do not have enough video RAM to display at color depths greater than 256 colors, or a processor capable of pushing large, high-quality video images.

All this is not to suggest that you should avoid video, especially if you want it or need it. Nor is it to suggest that the average user cannot enjoy beautiful video created by you and transmitted over the Internet. The real issue here is to determine how to create the best effect for the least bandwidth.

For example, a stark black-and-white image is not only far easier to download, but in many cases it is far more compelling than any color version of the same thing—in much the same way that a black-and-white movie is often more enjoyable than a colorized version of the same motion picture. Would Charlie Chaplin or Orson Welles be as powerful in color? Imagine further the riveting photographic images of Ansel Adams or Richard Avedon—they simply would not have the same dramatic impact if they were in color.

Before deciding how to create the desired video, one should look at the tools that are at hand and what effect is desired. Ideally, what you create will be a match between the tools and the concept. In many cases, you will have to be clever in fashioning your concept to match the tools you have available to you in order to create the most powerful effect.

Creating the Original Content

Unless you plan to reuse digital video from another source, the first thing you'll need to do is to get a camera. You can easily rent video cameras in most cities, but if you want to invest further and purchase a video camera for creating your own video movies, we suggest selecting a good Hi-Band 8 video camera with a plug-in for an external microphone.

Although Hi-Band 8 is not quite broadcast quality, it is substantially better than Regular 8 or VHS. When you digitize the video, the difference in picture quality between Hi-Band 8 (about a thousand dollars) and professional equipment (about 10 thousand dollars) will be nonexistent.

When choosing a Hi-Band 8 camera or other video camera, camera sensitivity is one of the most important factors to consider. The camera sensitivity is measured in *lux*, which means the light level at which the camera is able to pick up images. Most Hi-Band 8 cameras can shoot down to about 2 or 3 lux. The lower the lux, the darker the environment you can successfully videotape and thus the less will be your need for cumbersome lighting equipment.

TIP

The cheapest method of all may be to use the Connectix camera. These little color cameras cost only $199 (including all hardware and software you need to get started) and are available for both Mac and Windows. The camera can be used for video teleconferencing (software and instruction for teleconferencing available at `http://www.wpine.com/ins.html`) as well as capturing live video—but, of course, this is not a real-time capture, so do not be disappointed.

The Connectix camera captures sound video in full color and works well in low light situations. The only drawback of the camera is that it needs to be connected to a computer, but if you want to go mobile, you can connect the camera to a notebook computer (either Mac or PC) and shoot your own version of *Citizen Kane* on location.

The software included with the Connectix camera doesn't enable editing, but it does provide a variety of effects and frames for video playback. For $199 this little camera is hard to beat. More information on the Connectix camera is available at the `http://www.connectix.com/` Web site.

As any video producer knows all too well, there are many, many factors that go into a successful video shoot—more than we have room to cover in this book. But for the two- to ten-second clips that are currently viable for most Web uses, the lighting and choice of subject matter will matter more than anything else. The subject matter is, of course, up to you, but we can offer a few tips on lighting that can make a dramatic difference in the quality of your video.

TIP

One quick note to those who wish to digitize home movies or 16 mm films for playback on the Internet using a projector and a video camera. You will need a five-blade projector. A five-blade projector has the same shutter speed as a standard video camera. If you do not have a five-blade projector (you probably don't—most are four-blade) and try to digitize

continues

continued

anyway, your videotaped image will appear to strobe and the video will be unusable. If you are not sure, you can try it and see, or open your shutter gate and make a small mark on one of the blades (located behind the lens) and count the number by turning the mechanism manually.

Five-blade projectors are available for rent at most A/V rental houses, or they can be purchased for about two hundred dollars through an industry magazine called *The Big Reel*. You can also have your home videos transferred to videotape at many photo labs, such as Fox Photo.

Lighting a Video Shoot

Good lighting and careful planning are essential for a successful video shoot, no matter how good your equipment is and no matter how low a lux your camera can handle. There are numerous books on video lighting and production at any public library or camera store. You can also check out the Videomaker's Glossary of Terms at `http://www.videomaker.com/edit/other/glossa~1.htm`.

All of these resources will emphasize the same basic *lighting triangle*, which consists of three lights arranged in a triangle around your subject. The three lights are as follows:

- The *key light* is the brightest light, and it represents the main light source on a subject (for example, the "table lamp," if you are photographing someone in a room at night).
- The *fill light* should be more diffused and half as bright as the key light, and placed opposite to the key light. The fill light is used to eliminate unwanted shadows on your subject.
- The *back light* is placed behind the subject to illuminate the top and back of the subject. The back light should also be about half as bright as the key light. Its purpose is to define your subject and separate the subject from the background.

Digitizing Video

After you have successfully lit and captured a scene using a video camera, you must digitize it into the computer. This process varies, depending on the hardware and software you use on your computer. For instance, if you are using an Apple Macintosh computer with Audio/Video capabilities, you may simply connect your video source to the computer and begin recording the content digitally. If, however, you are using a PC, you first must purchase a video-capture card. These cards range from a few hundred dollars to several thousand dollars, depending on the level of quality you are striving to obtain. Obviously, the most expensive cards are intended for video professionals who are creating digital studios with their computers. However, the price of typical capture cards has dropped below five hundred dollars.

TIP

When shopping for a video-capture card, make sure that it is capable of digitizing motion video. There are numerous devices on the market today that accept a video signal from a source such as a video camera, but merely take a single unmoving "snapshot" photo from a moment of video. This photo can be useful for making still images to put on a Web page, but won't allow you to put moving video onto a Web page.

Most capture equipment includes software for capturing video input. Adobe Premier, Microsoft VidCap, and Video Action Pro (registered version) all offer the capability of recording digital video. Most programs enable you to specify the format of the video file that will be captured. You may choose settings such as the following:

- The rate at which video is recorded in frames per second (fps)
- The quality of the audio to be recorded with the video
- The dimensions of the video window in pixels
- The compression algorithm to apply to the video

Although you will ultimately wish to create a video that is highly compressed so that it requires very little space, capture your original footage using the highest settings possible. Then, when you are editing the footage with other material, you can be sure that the final, compressed video will be as clear as possible. If you use a high amount of compression when initially recording, those compressed files will be further compressed when they are edited and used to produce another final file. Be aware however, that minimizing compression during the recording process will generate mammoth files.

Figure 24.1 demonstrates a video capture in progress, including the numerous option windows that VidCap provides. You may capture video using any number of settings. To conserve space and transmission times, Internet videos should be relatively small in dimension with low-quality audio and high video compression.

To begin recording video content digitally, simply start the recording software. In the case of Figure 24.1, `Capture Video Sequence` was chosen from the `Capture` menu. When all settings have been verified, clicking on the `OK` button starts the recording process. Logically, pressing the Esc key on your keyboard halts the recording process.

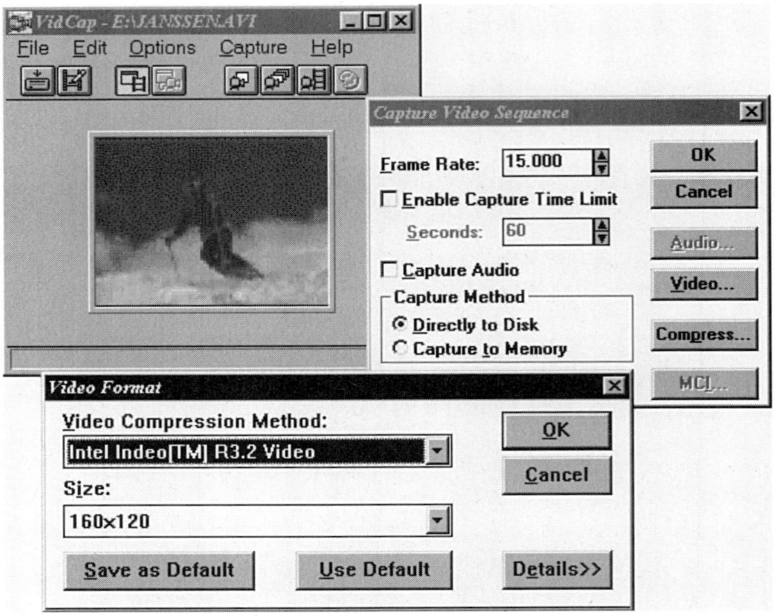

FIGURE 24.1.
A VidCap video capture in progress.

> **TIP**
>
> Because it takes a moment to actually start the process, start recording first and then begin the actual video signal output. Although you may record either video noise or blank input, you can be sure that you will not miss the introduction of the video clip. You may always use video-editing software to remove those blank sections of your video file.

> **NOTE**
>
> If you do use VidCap to capture your video files, it is important to remember to set the capture file each time you wish to record. This may be accomplished through the `Set Capture File` option in the `File` menu or by clicking on the left-most toolbar button. Setting the capture file allocates space for recording the digital video. However, if you forget to reset the capture file, you may inadvertently overwrite your previous work.

Editing Video

After you capture your video, you will need to edit it. There are many different editing packages available—too many to examine in depth in this book. If you already have a video capture board, it was probably bundled with an editing package. Most video-editing packages are fairly similar, unless you are using a very low-end package or desire elaborate effects. For those wishing to explore creating more elaborate videos, you may consider using more advanced software such as Adobe Premier.

If you are a Mac user with only the Connectix camera, or with only a video-capture board and no software for editing, try QuickEditor—a low-cost shareware movie editor. It is Mac and PowerMac native and offers features including 2D and 3D plug-in transitions and effects and stereo soundtrack editing. QuickEditor is available at `ftp://sumex-aim.stanford.edu/info-mac/_Graphic_%26_Sound_Tool/_Movie/`.

The Video-Action Screen

As an example of the steps involved in digital-video editing, this section shows you how to create a simple video production using Video Action ED for Windows-based machines.

NOTE

Video Action ED was chosen to demonstrate video editing because it is the only full-featured video-editing program available for under $30. This makes it a good choice for Internet work, where a $595 program like Adobe Premier is definitely overkill. You can get Video Action ED, along with a complete 3D graphics and animation package on the *Videology 3D* CD-ROM from Andover Advanced Technologies, Inc. (`http://www.andatech.com/`), or free with the Sams.net Publishing book *Web Page Wizardry*.

Andover Advanced Technology also offers a more advanced video-editing and special-effects program called VideoCraft, priced at $99. See their Web site at `http://www.andatech.com/` for details.

Regardless of which video-editing software you choose, the basic steps in the following discussion of video editing will be essentially the same.

When you first start Video Action, you will be greeted with two windows: a timeline in the top half of the Video Action window and a gallery in the lower half. A *timeline* or *storyboard* is common to almost all video editing software; it enables you to position elements such as video, audio, or pictures at some exact moment in time. When the final movie is played, the items placed in the timeline will be played in the order in which they appear from left to right.

The gallery is a collection window that displays all of the multimedia content currently in use for the final video production. Figure 24.2 displays a Video Action screen, in which the order of videos and transitions may be found in the timeline window at the top. The original video, a static bitmapped file, and an additional audio file may be found in the gallery window at the bottom of the screen.

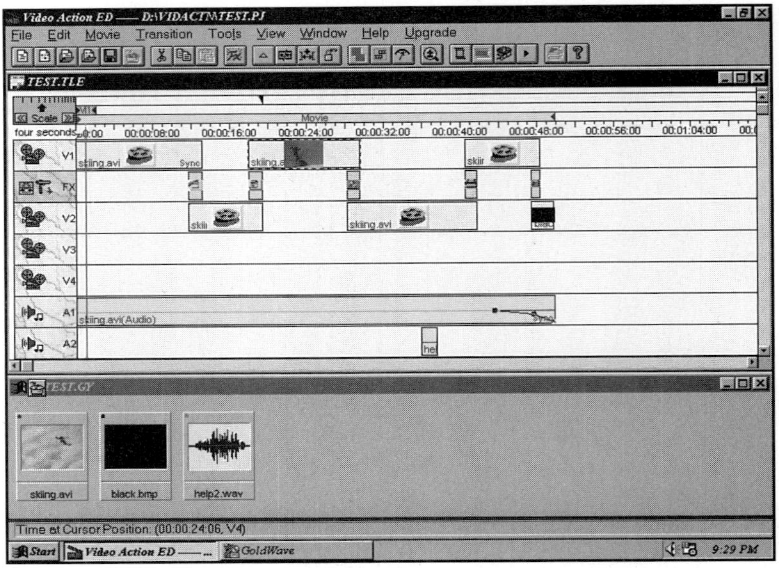

FIGURE 24.2.
As with Video Action ED, most video-editing programs use a graphical timeline to organize the sequence of video and audio clips.

Collecting Content

Before you can place any multimedia elements on the timeline, you must first import them into the gallery window. To do this, you can simply click on the small button in the top-left corner of the gallery window (this button appears as a pot with four colored balls and an arrow pointing into the pot). You may also select the `Collect` command from the `Organize` menu when the gallery window is active.

No matter how you do it, a dialog box will prompt you to select content to import. Simply select the bitmaps, videos, or audio files you wish to import and click on the `OK` button. The items you have selected will then appear in the gallery window at the bottom of the Video Action window. A small thumbnail drawing of the original item will be displayed as well.

Editing a Timeline

After you have imported the content necessary for your video production, you may begin dragging the items from the gallery onto the timeline. You may drag graphical material on any of the four video tracks or audio material on any of the four audio tracks. After you have dropped a video or graphic item on the timeline, it will be represented by a yellow rectangle with a thumbnail of the content. The length of the yellow regions on the timeline are directly proportional to the length of the actual clip.

Similarly, you may drag audio resources from the gallery onto the timeline. These files will appear as light blue regions in the audio tracks of the timeline. You may place either type of resource anywhere on the timeline. If audio and video clips overlap in the timeline, they will be played together. Any blank space in the timeline indicates silence in the video, represented by muted audio tracks and simply a black screen in the video tracks.

Let's assume you had three video clips that you wanted to play immediately after each other. Let's also assume that you have a single audio file that is long enough to span the length of the three video clips. To create a final video, you simply drag the three video clips onto one track in the timeline, ensuring that the beginning of each subsequent clip lines up with the end of the preceding clip. The audio file is then dragged onto its own audio track, such that the beginning of the audio file lines up with the beginning of the first video clip.

Trimming Clips

As mentioned earlier, it is possible that you may record signal noise or "blank" frames before or after the actual content you intended to record. The starting and ending positions of each video clip identified on the timeline may be adjusted. To adjust these settings, double-click on a clip in the timeline. A window similar to the one shown in Figure 24.3 is displayed.

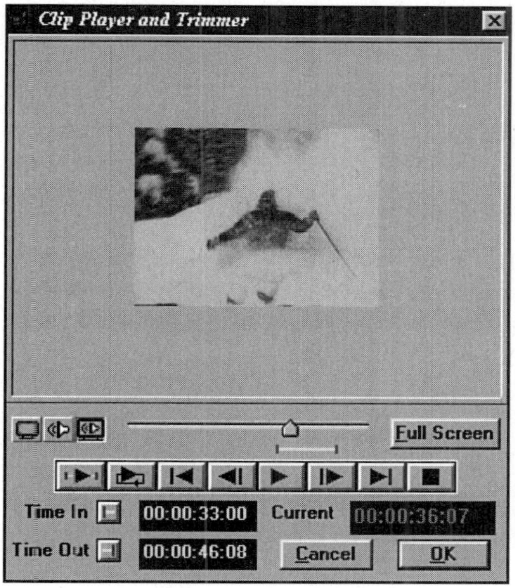

FIGURE 24.3.
You may specify the starting and ending positions of each clip in Video Action's timeline window.

A preview of the clip being modified is available in the center of this window. Beneath this preview is a scrollbar that enables you to seek a specific frame in the video. Just beneath this scrollbar is a range marked by a yellow line with two red end points. This range identifies how much of the clip is being used in the timeline window.

If you find that you need to trim the beginning of the video clip, simply drag the scrollbar to the new starting position for the video clip and click on the "Time In" button. The range that identifies the video clip will be adjusted appropriately. These "Time In" and "Time Out" buttons simply enable you to specify where you want a video clip to begin playing and where you want it to stop.

Transitions

There is nothing wrong with placing video clips right up against each other on the timeline. The clips will be played in the final movie production, but will there will be no transitions between them; when one clip is finished, the second will immediately appear. Although this is not unacceptable, there may be occasions when you prefer to create a smoother transition. For example, if you had one clip that was dark and another that was bright, playing those clips back-to-back would create a flash between the dark and light clips. Depending on the effect you are trying to create, you may prefer one clip to transition gradually into another via a dissolve effect.

Let's create a dissolve transition in Video Action, using the three back-to-back clips discussed earlier. Between the first and second video tracks in Video Action, there is an additional transition track. This transition track specifies which transitions are to occur between the first and second video tracks when the final movie is rendered. To create a transition in this track, simply drag one clip to the second video track so that the beginning of that clip starts before the clip on the first track finishes. The transition effect, indicated by a green region in the timeline, will be created automatically between the time in which the second track's video clip starts and the first track's video clip ends. The timeline window in Figure 24.2 includes five separate transitions for the movie being created.

When you have defined the transition region, you may then specify which transition you wish to use between the video clips on the first and second video tracks. To change transition effects, click once on the transition you wish to alter in the transition track. Then click on the `Transition` menu to display a Transition Group window. This window enables you to select from 20 different transition types including: wipes, dissolves, zooms, and even page-turns. Double-clicking on the appropriate animated icon replaces the selected transition with the new effect and displays a Transition Viewer window, as shown in Figure 24.4. This transition window enables you to modify specific properties regarding the transition or preview how the effect will appear in your movie.

If you wish to create a second transition, you will need to place the starting position of the third video clip just before the end of the second video clip. This time however, you must place the third clip back on the first track. Because the transition track is applied between only the first and second tracks, all video clips that are to be included in a transition must exist on either side of the transition track.

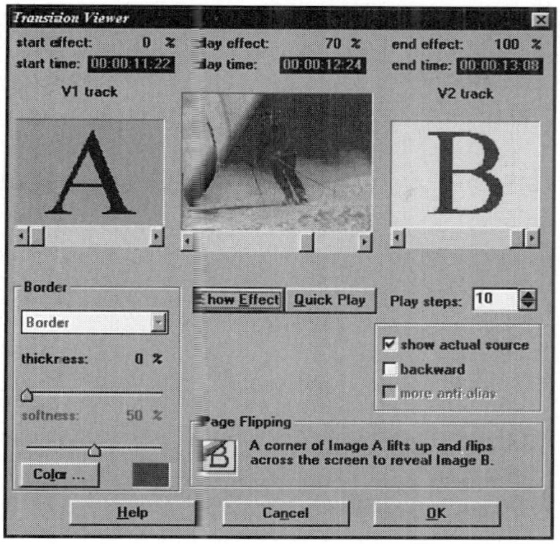

FIGURE 24.4.

The Transition Viewer window in Video Action ED enables you to modify the details of a transition and preview the results.

Video FX

Video Action—like all other major video-editing programs—enables you to incorporate special effects into your own digital movies. Some special effects are absolutely legitimate and necessary. For instance, if you digitized a video clip and the lighting was not suitable, you could adjust the brightness or contrast of the clip and save the modified version in your final movie. Yet there are also several cool effects such as Old Movie, Kaleidoscope, Star Highlight, or Title Generator that can make your movies stand out.

To add a special effect to a video clip, first select the video clip in the timeline window. Then choose the `Video Effects & Titler` option from the `Tools` menu or click on the FX button on the toolbar. A window similar to that shown in Figure 24.5 is displayed, enabling you to select special effects and tweak the results of each effect.

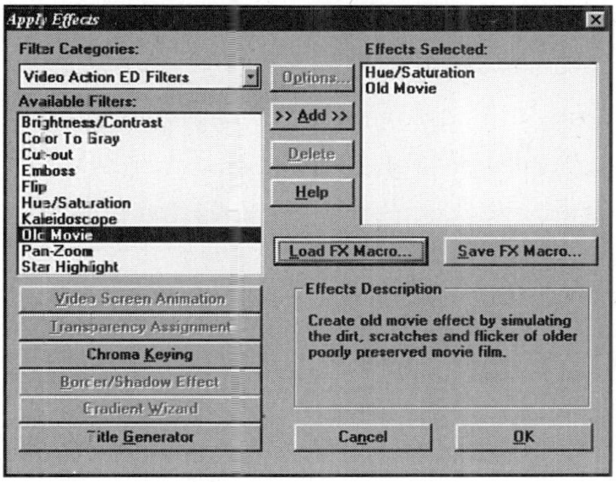

FIGURE 24.5.

Video Action supports numerous special effects that can make your movies more compelling.

Let the Movie Roll

When you have finished designing the timeline for your digital movie and are satisfied with the layout, you may create the final movie. To create the movie in Video Action, you must first specify the settings for the final production. Settings for the final movie may be altered by selecting `Movie Settings` from the `Movie` menu while the timeline window is selected. Figure 24.6 is an example of some of the settings that may be modified for video files being created.

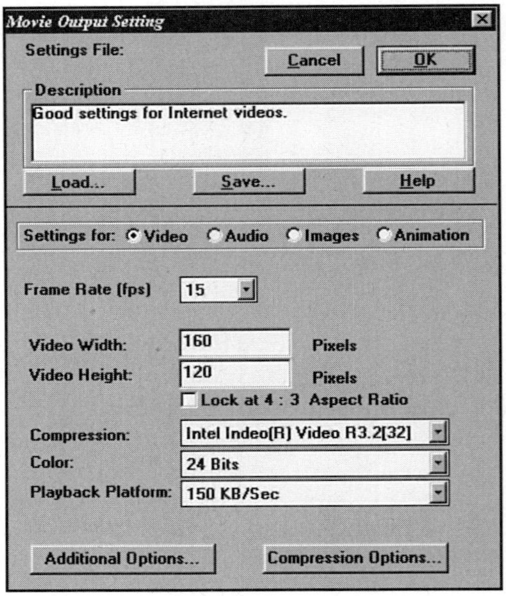

FIGURE 24.6.
You may specify a number of settings for the final video file that you create with Video Action ED.

When creating Internet videos, remember to keep the size of the final video file relatively small. Smaller files require less time to transmit over the Internet and are therefore more effective for the person viewing them. You can adjust the settings in the Movie Settings window to achieve optimal compression by doing the following:

- Minimizing the dimensions of the final video window
- Limiting the number of frames per second (fps) of the video
- Choosing a video compressor and reducing its quality as a compromise to the final size of the video
- Limiting audio to 8-bit, 11 KHz

After you have established the appropriate settings for an Internet video, you must select the region of the timeline you wish to export as the final movie. A yellow bar with red triangles at each end of the bar and the word *Movie* on it should be present near the top of the timeline window. Simply stretch the ends of this rectangle to enclose the multimedia elements in the tracks below. In other words, ensure that the beginning of the Movie meter is at the same position as the beginning of the very first video clip. Similarly, make certain that the end of the meter is at the same ending position as the last video clip.

To create the final digital movie, select `Make Movie/AVI File Output` from the `Movie` menu. When a dialog window appears prompting for the name of the final movie file, type in an appropriate name and click on the `OK` button. All of the content in the timeline window will then be assembled appropriately and written to a final `.avi` file.

Squeezing It through the Pipe: Codecs

How your video picture looks and how long it takes to stream across the Net will be largely determined by which video *codec* you choose when compressing your video clip. Codecs (short for compressor-decompressor) compress the enormous amount of video information needed to display a video movie on your computer. When the user plays your video, the codec decompresses the video on the fly while the movie plays back.

NOTE

A quick lesson on digital video: Most digital video must be compressed in order to be stored with a reasonable amount of space. Then when the stored video is played, the data must be decompressed in order to be displayed. For example, a 320 × 240 pixel video clip with 24-bit color depth and a frame rate of 15 fps would take up just under 3.5 M of space for just one second of video without compression!

Several companies, such as Intel, Cinepak, and Microsoft, have designed digital-video compression technologies—each with varying quality and amount of storage space saved. These compression/decompression techniques are accomplished using software, but there several hardware-based codecs as well. MPEG (Motion Pictures Expert Group) is an example of a hardware-based compression/decompression scheme.

Codecs can be *lossy*, meaning various areas of the picture are simplified, or *lossless*, meaning all areas of the video are kept intact. Lossy codecs have lower overall quality but offer much greater compression than lossless codecs.

There are numerous different types of codecs available, both hardware- and software-based. Although hardware-based codecs offer far greater compression, they also require the user to have similar hardware for playback; software-based codecs require only similar software (which is usually free). Consequently, because the Web is worldwide and very diverse, we will cover only software-based compression solutions.

MPEG-1 and MPEG-2

MPEG (software-based version) is the most commonly used type of compression on the Internet—first, because freeware MPEG converters are commonly available on the Web, and second, because MPEG offers the best compression ratio of any commonly used codec.

However, MPEG does have the disadvantage of being lossy and not allowing 8-bit compression. Although 16-, 24-, or even 32-bit video is great, most computer users cannot display it properly. Consequently, the quality of MPEG is substantially degraded for many users. Another disadvantage of MPEG is that most of the freeware converters on the Web do not offer a facility for playing back audio along with the video image, although MPEG-1 can support audio and video tracks. MPEG-2 is designed for commercial-broadcast applications and is not currently applicable to Web-based applications.

Cinepak

Cinepak is the most commonly used video codec for CD-ROM production. Cinepak, although lossy, offers very good compression and enables you to embed an 8-bit palette within a 16-bit or 32-bit movie. Embedding an 8-bit palette within your movie significantly improves the visual quality of your video when played back on a computer unable to display at higher color depths.

The biggest drawback of Cinepak is the significantly longer time it takes to compress the video. Typically, Cinepak takes between 30 seconds to 2 minutes per frame to compress a piece of video footage. Thirty seconds of video, captured at 10 frames per second, could take as long as 10 hours to compress.

Indeo R.32

Indeo R.32 (which stands for "release 32") is similar to Cinepak and is rapidly replacing it for CD-ROM production. Although lossy, Indeo offers good compression and enables you to embed an 8-bit palette within a 16-bit or 32-bit movie. Embedding an 8-bit palette within your movie significantly improves the visual quality of your video when it is played back on a computer unable to display at higher color depths. Indeo's 8-bit playback quality is substantially higher than that of Cinepak, and Indeo R.32 also compresses substantially faster than Cinepak.

In comparison to Cinepak, Indeo R.32 does have a few disadvantages. Cinepak offers slightly smoother playback at high frame rates and slightly better compression. Indeo R.32 is available at `http://www.intel.com/pc-supp/multimed/indeo/`.

Indeo Video Interactive

Indeo Video Interactive is perhaps one of the most exciting new codecs available. According to Intel, Indeo Video Interactive offers new features, including:

- Transparency Support, which enables video or graphics to be overlaid on top of another video or background graphic. The graphics can then be controlled in real-time via a joystick, keystroke, or mouse.
- Local Window Decode, which gives programmers the ability to create an independent video playback "window" within a larger video playback display or graphics scene, thus enabling fast branching and panning.
- Random Keyframe Access, which enables placement of keyframes (used to "refresh" image quality within a video stream) at any arbitrary interval. This makes it possible to quickly or dynamically adjust video-quality level and frame rate during playback. This feature can offer big savings in file size and improved playback quality.
- Saturation/Contrast/Brightness controls, which can be adjusted on the fly (as a video file is being played).
- Password protection, which enables programmers to assign passwords to keyframes to protect video clips from alteration or from being played back with applications that cannot provide the correct password.
- Exceptional video quality on Pentium-based systems, with full-screen, near VHS quality comparable to software MPEG-1 players at 2X CD-ROM data rates. Indeo Video Interactive's scalable-quality feature also enables quality to scale between several different "quality levels" or "bands," depending upon the capability of the PC's CPU to minimize frame-dropping.

As was the case with Indeo Video release 3.2, Intel continues to license Indeo Video Interactive to software developers for free and on a royalty-free basis. Indeo Video Interactive is available for both Mac and Windows platforms, and offers better compression than earlier versions of Indeo. It is available at `http://www.intel.com/pc-supp/multimed/indeo/`.

Animation Compression

Animation compression (lossy) offers decent compression and fairly good playback speed with the added advantage of color depth settings ranging from 1-bit to 32-bit color or black and white. If the material is appropriate, a 1-bit or 4-bit video clip can produce stunning results and substantial file-size savings using the animation compressor. For example, Expressionist motion pictures such as *Nosferatu* or the *Cabinet of Dr. Caligari* would translate nicely using a 4-bit black and white compression. Likewise, animations such as a typical Charlie Brown special would drop down to 4-bit color fairly successfully (see the section on DeBabelizing video later in this chapter). Many animated logos could drop down to 4-bit color with this process, as well.

JPEG

JPEG (lossy) compression, although offering incredible compression ratios, decompresses so slowly that this method is rendered almost useless for anything other than a slide-show style presentation. Like MPEG, it does have the disadvantage of being 32-bit based and is often extremely lossy.

Graphics Compression

Graphics compression is lossless and offers the major advantage of giving the user the option of creating a custom palette for 8-bit video. When displayed in 256 colors (if you DeBabelize your video), the picture quality is perhaps the best of any codec. However, graphics compression and decompression rates are so poor that it is hard to achieve an adequate frame rate.

General Codec Options and Settings

With all of the preceding codecs, you will be given a choice of frame rate. With many of them, you will also be given a choice of quality. (It is best to capture at the color depth and frame rate you plan to use for your final output.)

Action Sequence Settings

The quality and frame rate settings you choose will probably depend upon the content of your clip. For action sequences, you will probably want to choose a higher frame rate and lower quality. Otherwise, in an action sequence, the jerkiness caused by a low frame rate would be more noticeable, whereas the image improvements from the high-quality setting would not even be noticed (so trade these two options, as first stated, for best effect).

Nonaction Sequence Settings

For nonaction sequences, choose the exact opposite quality and frame rate settings than for action sequences. A lower frame rate, but with a higher quality setting, is appropriate—jerkiness will be less noticeable, whereas artifacting will be far more noticeable.

DeBabelizing Your Video

The best way to ensure a high-quality video for the majority of users is to do what most multimedia folks call DeBabelizing, after the popular Macintosh video processing program named DeBabelizer. This program enables you to process video and graphic files in a number of ways as well as import and export using a multitude of file formats.

In this section, you will see how it is important to create a common color palette to be used throughout your digital video. For instance, by optimizing your video to be used with the default colors of the system palette, you can use your video files neatly with other graphics. If you do not perform such a process, machines with lower color resolutions such as 256 colors may constantly remap colors in the system when playing video content. This may cause adverse color effects in other programs in the rest of the system.

NOTE

Windows 95 has made significant improvements in this area, attempting to resolve color resolution problems and color mappings automatically. However, if you wish to control the color output of your video files on a Windows-based machine, you may use Video Action ED. In the Movie Settings window you may specify which compressor to use when creating a final video. If you instead choose `No Compression` for the compression option, the color depth option then enables you to choose from several palettes (including custom palettes) when rendering the final movie. Similar settings can be specified in Adobe Premier and other video-editing software.

The DeBabelizing process *polls* the frames, looking at each of them to count and notate the colors contained in each. Then it compares all of the colors used in the movie and picks the best 256 colors to represent the millions of colors contained in that exact movie. This Super Palette can be embedded in movies made for QuickTime 2.1 or higher. (QuickTime 2.1 is available free of charge for both Mac and Windows from Apple Computer at `http://www.astro.nwu.edu/lentz/mac/qt/`).

When the movie is played back in 8-bit, QuickTime calls up the palette and resets the monitor temporarily to that color palette, which eliminates much of the graininess of 8-bit playback while not affecting the playback quality of the movie at higher color depths, such as 32-bit. It is possible to do this using both Indeo and Cinepak, but Indeo does a far superior job.

TIP

Although the `Graphics` compression setting does a better job of rendering an 8-bit palette than either Indeo or Cinepak, it requires that you remap your movie to the 8-bit palette, resulting in an overall poorer quality at higher color depths, a significantly poorer quality of encode and decode, larger file sizes, and poorer playback.

The best solution possible when size is the determining factor? If the movie is a color movie, use Cinepak with a DeBabelized 8-bit movie. This has only recently become a possibility. (Note: You will need QuickTime 2.1.)

By reducing the color depth of your movie to 256 colors, you will be able to reduce your compressed movie size by about two-thirds (as compared to a 24-bit version of the same movie). Follow these steps:

1. Capture your movie at the highest color depth possible and at the window size you want your final movie to be.
2. In DeBabelizer, select `File` and pull down until `Batch` is highlighted. Under `Batch`, select `Super Palette`, as shown in Figure 24.7.

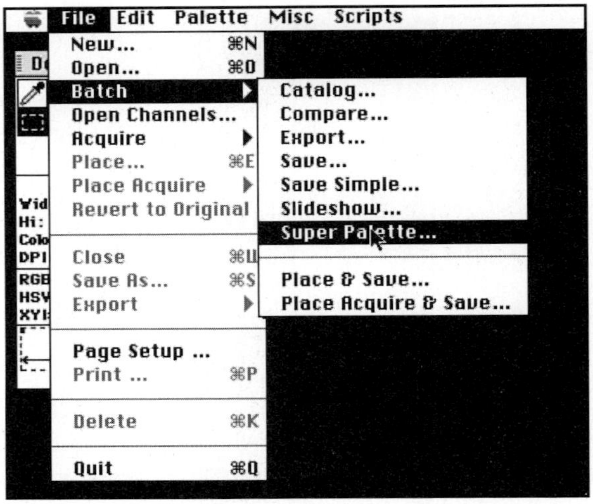

FIGURE 24.7.
The first step in optimizing your video color palette in DeBabelizer is to create a Super Palette.

3. A dialog box appears. Select the movie you wish to work on by highlighting it and clicking the `Append` button, located in the middle of the dialog box. (See Figure 24.8.)

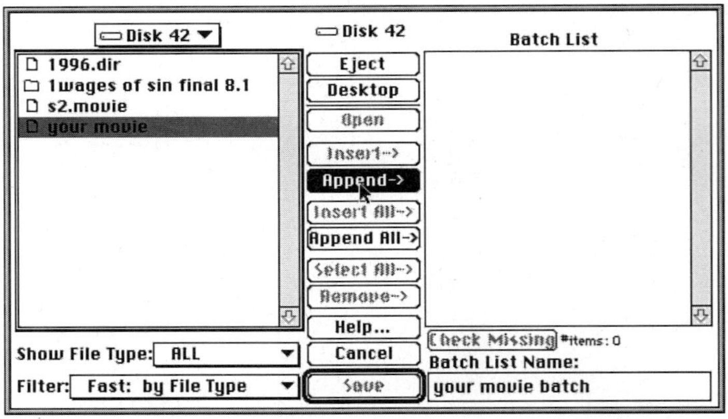

FIGURE 24.8.
You must select the movie you wish to DeBabelize.

4. Give the project a new name by typing the new name in the `Batch List Name` text box, located in the lower-right corner. Click `Save`. This will launch the Batch SuperPalette dialog box. (See Figure 24.9).
5. In the upper-right section of the menu, set the `Display` feature to `Display off`. Below that, set `Number of colors in Super Palette` to `256`.
6. Click the `DO IT` button located in the lower-right corner of the menu.
7. A Preview box opens and displays the first frame of the QuickTime movie you wish to poll. Click the `OK` button and the process will begin, as shown in Figure 24.10. At 10 frames per second, a one-minute clip will take several hours to complete.

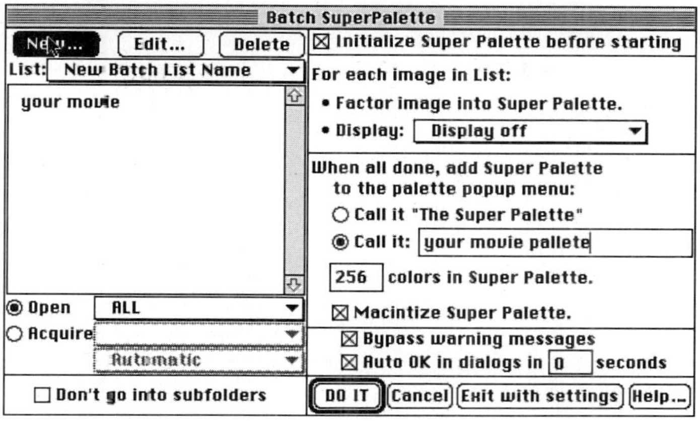

FIGURE 24.9.
DeBabelizer features numerous options for controlling your video's color palette.

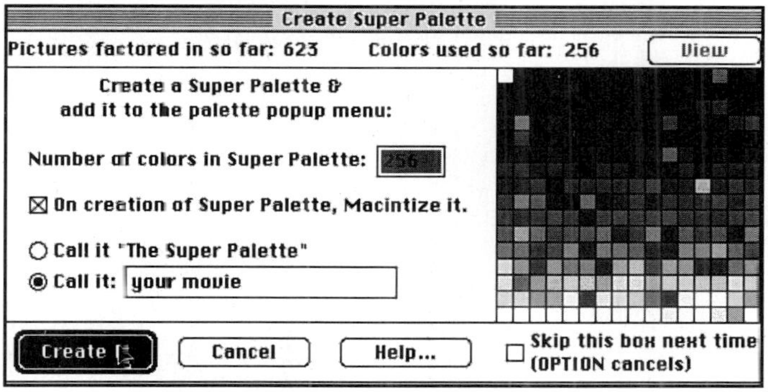

FIGURE 24.10.
After DeBabelizer has analyzed the entire movie, the optimal palette is displayed.

8. When DeBabelizer has completely finished polling each of the frames, a new dialog box appears containing the optimal palette for the movie. The Create Super Palette dialog box appears. When it is finished, give the palette an appropriate name by typing it in next to the `Call It` button near the bottom of the dialog box. Click the `Create It` button.
9. Select `File | Batch Save`. Save the file to a separate folder using the `Auto Naming` option, select `Quicktime Movie` under the file type, and choose `256` under `Colors`. Click on the `DO IT` button. An Auto Namer dialog box appears, as shown in Figure 24.11. Choose `Cinepak` from the `Extension` menu. Click `OK`.
10. The Auto Remap dialog box appears. Choose the palette you just created under the `Remap to palette` pulldown menu and select the `Dither when remapping` check box. (See Figure 24.12.) Click `OK`. The Compression Settings dialog box (Figure 24.13) opens automatically.

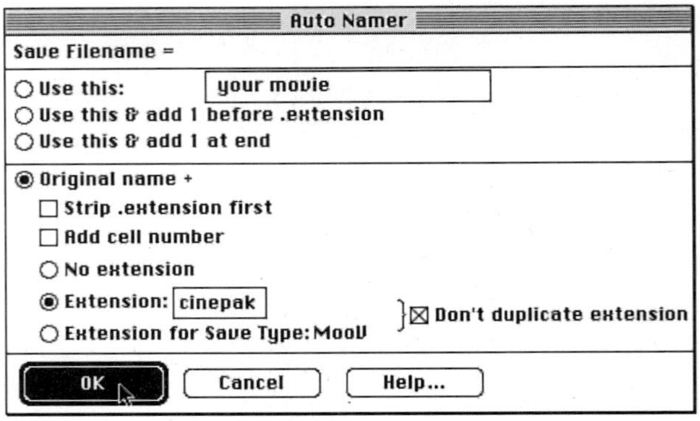

FIGURE 24.11.
After you have determined the optimal color palette, you must resave the movie.

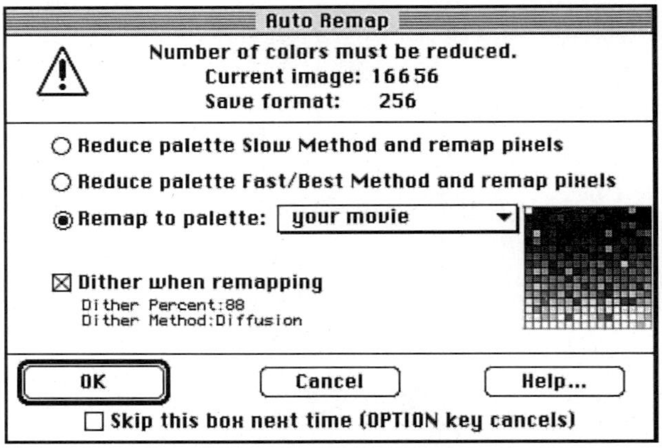

FIGURE 24.12.
When resaving the movie, you will need to specify which color palette to use—in this case, the optimal palette that DeBabelizer found earlier.

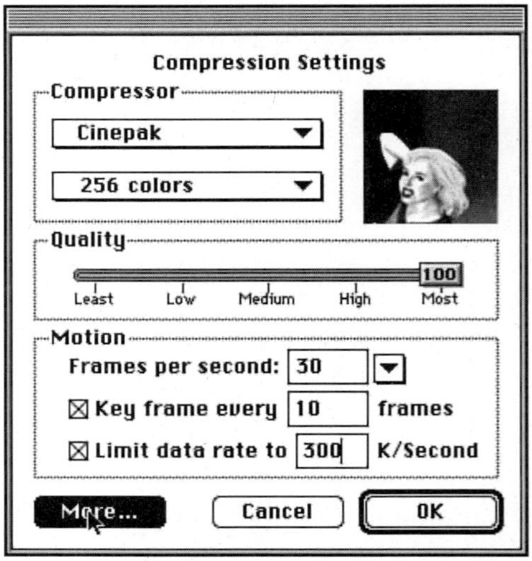

FIGURE 24.13.
Because the new movie is in Cinepak format, you can adjust the final compression settings for the movie.

11. Choose `Cinepak` as your compressor. Adjust the `Quality` slider bar. Choose your frame; it's best to choose the same frame rate as the rate at which you originally digitized your movie. Set your key frame. If you have quite a bit of action, you will probably want to set a low number as your key frame rate; try a number that is approximately one third of your frame rate. Be advised, however, that the lower the number you choose, the bigger your movie will be. If your movie doesn't contain a great deal of movement, you can choose a much higher number as your key frame rate. Leave `Limit data rate to` set to the default.
12. Click the `More` button, located in the lower-left corner. Another dialog box appears, as shown in Figure 24.14. `Set Frames Per Second in previous dialog box from` should be set to `Latest setting`. `For Time Scale, use:` should be set to `600`. All other check boxes should be activated. Finally, and most importantly, make sure that the `Save Palette From Menu` pulldown list indicates the palette you created previously. Click `OK` to close the dialog box and then click it again to close the Compression Settings dialog box. Now you are all set!

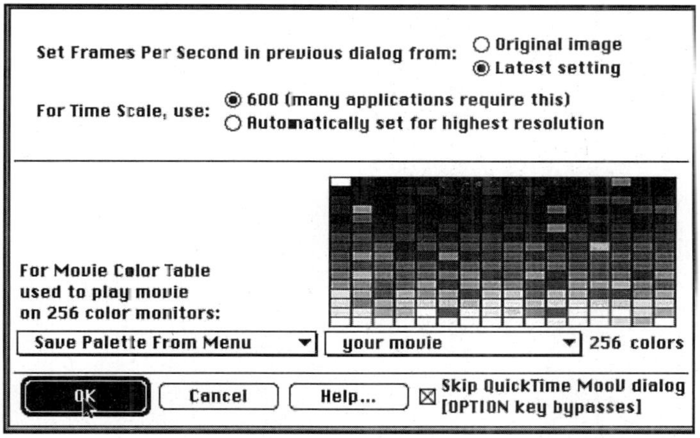

FIGURE 24.14.
Some advanced options may be set for the Cinepak code.

DeBabelizer now generates an 8-bit Cinepak movie. The time it takes will depend upon the size of your movie, but it will take approximately twice as long as it took to poll the color information and create the Super Palette.

Summary

This chapter has given you a quick crash course in creating digital audio and video suitable for the kind of uses you saw in Chapter 22, "Adding Multimedia to Your Web Site." In Chapter 25, "Adding Interactivity with Shockwave for Director," you'll learn how to take visitors to your site beyond passive listening and viewing, into the new world of interactive media.

CHAPTER 25

Adding Interactivity with Shockwave for Director

by Mark "Woody" Woodman

IN THIS CHAPTER

Few plug-ins for Netscape Navigator and Navigator-compatible browsers have created as much of a stir as Macromedia's Shockwave for Director. Arguably the industry standard for creating interactive multimedia, Director is the software used to create thousands of popular CD-ROM titles like *Passage to Vietnam*, *MYST*, and *Total Distortion*. The Shockwave plug-in enables you to view Director files (called *movies*) right inside an HTML page without an external viewer. The release version of the Shockwave for Director plug-in was introduced in the spring of 1996 and was immediately one of the most popular plug-ins available.

NOTE

Macromedia has released several other plug-ins with the name Shockwave for viewing files made with various applications like Freehand and Authorware. Unless otherwise stated, any mention of Shockwave in this chapter implies Shockwave for Director 5.0.

Netscape Navigator uses plug-ins to extend functionality with third-party software; Microsoft Internet Explorer uses what it calls ActiveX controls. Plug-ins and ActiveX controls are, for the most part, identical in purpose and function, so for the purposes of this chapter, I will use the generic term plug-in to accommodate either browser.

With this chapter and a little work, you can embed Director-made applications right in your Web pages, regardless of whether you use Macromedia Director. To make the most of what Shockwave can do for you, however, you should learn Director. If you are already a Director user, you will find step-by-step instructions for making your own Shockwave movies that use the new Lingo commands built into the Shockwave plug-in.

Placing a Shockwave File in Your HTML Page

Using Shockwave movies in your Web pages requires a simple one-time server configuration. Once that has been done, you use HTML tags within your Web pages to signal the browser to load the Shockwave plug-in. If you haven't already done so, download and install the plug-in from Macromedia's site at `http://www.macromedia.com` (see Figure 25.1). You also can find the software by following the links from Netscape's plug-in directory at `http://home.netscape.com`.

Configuring Your Server

The Shockwave for Director plug-in (or control) loads when it detects an embedded file with one of the Shockwave file extensions. A `.dcr` file is a Director movie that has been compressed and protected with the Afterburner Xtra and is the most common Shockwave for Director format on the Internet. (An Xtra is a plug-in for Director 5.x that adds functionality to your movie. Afterburner is discussed later in this chapter.) A `.dxr` movie is one that has not been compressed with Afterburner, but has been protected from within Director itself. A file with the `.dir` extension is an uncompressed and unprotected Director movie. Unless you plan on sharing your code and cast members with other Director users, do not put `.dir` files on the Internet.

You must configure your server to handle these file types and serve them properly to a Web browser. If you don't have root access to your Web server, have no fear; the process is simple and takes about five minutes. Chances are pretty good your server's administrator will be only too happy to configure things for a bag of corn chips. If he holds out, you may need to resort to throwing in a couple of Twinkies. Use this tactic sparingly, however; you may need it for Part VI when you want to start playing with CGI scripts.

The server must be configured to handle the following MIME types:

```
application/x-director dir
application/x-director dcr
application/x-director dxr
application/x-director fgd
```

TIP

If you or your sysop is unsure of how to configure your server to handle the MIME types described previously, Macromedia provides excellent online technical support. You should be able to find the information you need at `http://www.macromedia.com/shockwave`. Macromedia is always thorough in documenting its products, so don't hesitate to look around for plenty of good technical information.

FIGURE 25.1.
The Shockwave starting point at Macromedia.

Writing the HTML to Use Shockwave Files

Placing a Shockwave movie into your Web page requires you to use the `<EMBED>` or `<OBJECT>` tags. The `<EMBED>` tag is the Netscape-compatible command for invoking a plug-in, and the `<OBJECT>` tag is for use primarily in the Microsoft Internet Explorer 3.x browser. `<EMBED>` is recognized by any browser that uses the Netscape-compatible plug-in architecture. Among such browsers are Navigator 2.x, Navigator 3.x, Attachmate Emissary, WebSurfer by Netmanage, and Microsoft's Internet Explorer 2.0 beta 3 for the Macintosh. At the time of this writing, `<OBJECT>` tags can only be used with the Microsoft Internet Explorer 3.x browser for Windows or Macintosh.

TIP

A Shockwave file can only be loaded once per HTML page. If you need to have the same file appear in several places on the same page, you must duplicate the file and give it a different name. For example, if you want to load the file `myshock.dcr` three times, you will need to copy and rename it twice so you have the files `myshock.dcr`, `myshock2.dcr`, and `myshock3.dcr` to use on the same page. Be careful not to load too many Shockwave files on the same page, however, because each one uses a 50-70 K chunk of available RAM. Macromedia suggests you limit yourself to three Shockwave movies per HTML page.

Using the <EMBED> and <NOEMBED> Tags

Netscape plug-ins are loaded when the browser detects the `<EMBED>` tag in your HTML. If the plug-in hasn't been installed, the browser displays a missing plug-in icon (see Figure 25.2) and alerts the user that the plug-in is required. To accommodate browsers that do not use Netscape plug-ins, such as the America Online Web browser, you can display alternate content between the tags `<NOEMBED>` and `</NOEMBED>`.

NOTE

Netscape Navigator normally checks `<EMBED>` to see whether the user has the necessary plug-in to view the file. If not, the browser alerts the user that the plug-in is needed and takes them to an URL to find it. Navigator 1.1 is the exception to this and will only display a missing plug-in icon where the `<EMBED>` is placed. (See Figure 25.2.) Unfortunately, it won't display the content in `<NOEMBED>` either. Because there is not a readily available solution to this problem, most Web sites with Shockwave make a note that the user needs Netscape 2.0 or later to view the site.

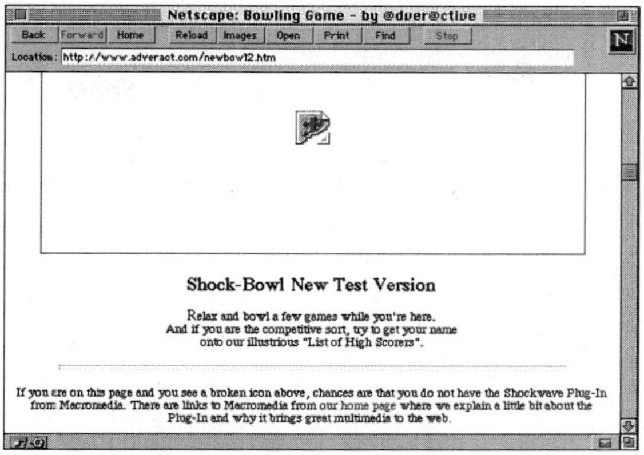

FIGURE 25.2.
Without the Shockwave plug-in installed, Netscape displays a missing plug-in icon where the Shockwave movie should be.

The basic structure for an `<EMBED>` tag is as follows:

```
<EMBED SRC=filename WIDTH=width HEIGHT=height VSPACE=vspace
HSPACE=hspace ALIGN=align BGCOLOR=color PALETTE=ground>
```

You can use these basic parameters with any Shockwave file:

The `SRC` parameter should be a file name with one of the appropriate extensions mentioned in "Configuring Your Server." To specify the location of the file, use the standard format of *`path/filename`*. You can use the file's relative path, such as `"intro/welcome.dcr"`, or use an absolute path, such as `"http://my.domain.net/intro/welcome.dcr"`, if you prefer. In some situations, people have had trouble using relative paths; if this happens to you, make the paths absolute instead. Either way, don't forget the quotes around the file name parameter, or evil things will happen to your Web page. (Okay, evil may be a stretch, but chances are good that your Shockwave movie won't load.)

The `WIDTH` and `HEIGHT` parameters tell the browser how much space (measured in pixels) to reserve for the Shockwave file while it is loading. If you use numbers that are smaller than the dimensions of the file, the browser will crop off the excess accordingly.

`VSPACE` and `HSPACE` tell the browser how much of an empty margin (again measured in pixels) to place around the file. `VSPACE` means vertical space and controls the empty margin above and below the file. `HSPACE` means horizontal space and controls the empty margin to either side of the Shockwave movie.

Use `ALIGN` to place the file either in the left, the center, or the right of the window. If you're sharp and got plenty of sleep last night, you may have already guessed that you can use `ALIGN=left`, `ALIGN=center`, or `ALIGN=right` to do this.

`BGCOLOR` is a parameter that lets you specify the color you want to be displayed behind the Shockwave movie. This parameter works just like it would for the `<BODY>` tag of your Web page. You can get more information about how to specify a certain color in the Chapter 5 section titled "Using Background Colors."

The `PALETTE` option is a tricky one and should be used with care. The default setting is `PALETTE=background`, but if the Shockwave file has its own custom palette, and you want to force the whole page to be displayed with that palette, use `PALETTE=foreground`.

CAUTION

Be careful when using `PALETTE=foreground`. On machines that can only display 256 colors, forcing the screen to change palettes may produce a "palette flash" and alter the colors of anything else on the screen. This tends to be uglier than a Mac versus PC flame war in a chat room and nearly as annoying.

In addition to these basic parameters, Macromedia has custom parameters that allow you to pass information, such as a user name or a string of text, to the Shockwave movie. These options are covered in "Passing Information from HTML to Shockwave" later in this chapter.

A complete `<NOEMBED>` tag has the following structure:

```
<NOEMBED>
     Alternate content
</NOEMBED>
```

Using `<NOEMBED>` is straightforward. Any HTML you put between `<NOEMBED>` and `</NOEMBED>` is displayed to browsers that do not use Netscape-compatible plug-ins. Many Webmasters provide an image map that mirrors the Shockwave file, and some even provide a link to a non-shocked version of the Web site.

The final HTML in your page for these tags might look like the following:

```
<EMBED SRC="shockstuff/intro/welcome.dcr" WIDTH=300 HEIGHT=235
VSPACE=5 HSPACE=5 ALIGN=left BGCOLOR=#FFFFFF PALETTE=background>

<NOEMBED>
     <IMG SRC="images/getnn.gif"><BR>
     Sorry, you need a browser that uses Netscape plug-ins to view
     this site. To download a trial version of Netscape,
     <A HREF="home.netscape.com">Go here.</A>
</NOEMBED>
```

Using the <OBJECT> and <NOOBJECT> tags

Microsoft's Internet Explorer 3.0 uses a software architecture called ActiveX that allows developers to write plug-ins (called *controls*) for it. Any file using such a control is inserted into HTML pages with the `<OBJECT>` tag, which is similar in purpose to Netscape's `<EMBED>` tag. In fact, `<EMBED>` works just fine with Internet Explorer. If you need to write your HTML specifically for Explorer with `<OBJECT>`, however, here are the elements you need:

```
<OBJECT CLASSID=classid CODEBASE=codebase WIDTH=width HEIGHT=height NAME=name
ID=idname>
     <PARAM NAME="SRC" VALUE=filename>
     <PARAM NAME="PALETTE" VALUE=ground>
     <PARAM NAME="BGCOLOR" VALUE=color>
</OBJECT>
<NOOBJECT>
     Alternate content
</NOOBJECT>
```

You may have noticed that `<NOOBJECT>` seems to mirror the function of `<NOEMBED>`. Any browser that cannot use the `<OBJECT>` tag will display whatever you put in the `<NOOBJECT>` tag instead. If you did in fact notice this, consider yourself part of the coding elite that will one day rule the world. Either way, here's an example of how `<OBJECT>` and `<NOOBJECT>` may look in your source code:

```
<OBJECT CLASSID="clsid:166B1BCA-3F9C-11CF-8075-444553540000"
CODEBASE="http://active.macromedia.com/director/cabs/sw.cab#version=5,0,1,61"
WIDTH=300 HEIGHT=235
NAME="Shockwave" ID="swwelcome">
     <PARAM NAME="SRC" VALUE="shockstuff/intro/welcome.dcr">
     <PARAM NAME="PALETTE" VALUE="background">
     <PARAM NAME="BGCOLOR" VALUE="white">
</OBJECT>
<NOOBJECT>
     <IMG SRC="images/getmsie.gif"><BR>
     Sorry, you need MSIE 3.0 to view Shockwave files in this site.
     <A HREF="www.microsoft.com'>Get it here.</A>
</NOOBJECT>
```

Let's break this code down and take a look at the pieces:

The `CLASSID` parameter is a mind-numbingly long string of code to tell the browser that you are using a certain plug-in. Be sure this string is exactly as you see it in the preceding example, or Explorer will not be able to load the Shockwave for Director control.

`CODEBASE` is where you specify the URL where the latest version of the plug-in is. If the user doesn't already have the Shockwave control, Explorer will prompt her and ask whether she wishes to download it. Again, use the exact URL you see in the preceding example for this to work properly.

`WIDTH` and `HEIGHT` function just as they do in the `<EMBED>` tag and specify the dimensions of the stage in the Shockwave file. Note that you must enclose the numbers in quotation marks when using `<OBJECT>`. If you use numbers that are smaller than the stage, the excess will be cropped off in your page.

If you use a `FORM` in your page, use the `NAME` parameter to tell Explorer how to identify this object. You must use `NAME="Shockwave"` for this to work.

The `ID` parameter is where you can give the Shockwave file a unique name or document identifier. This name lets you and the browser refer to the Shockwave file by `ID` for hypertext linking and communication between objects. This value can be any string you like.

Internet Explorer has other parameters as well:

<PARAM NAME=*paramname* VALUE=*value*>. The only one that you must use with Shockwave is the SRC parameter, which should have the path and file name of your Shockwave file in the value. The preceding example illustrates this parameter.

The BGCOLOR parameter is where you can indicate the color to be displayed behind the Shockwave movie. The section "Using Background Colors" in Chapter 5 gives you more information on this parameter.

The PALETTE parameter can have VALUE="foreground" or VALUE="background". It tells the browser whether to use the palette of colors specific to the Shockwave file, or the colors native to the browser, respectively. See the caution about the PALETTE parameter with the <EMBED> tag above for additional information.

As with the <EMBED> tag for Netscape, there are other parameters you can add to pass information directly into the Shockwave movie with <OBJECT>. Some of these are discussed in "Passing Information from HTML to Shockwave" later in this chapter. For more information on using the <OBJECT> tag with Shockwave, look for technical support documentation at Macromedia's site at http://www.macromedia.com/shockwave.

Putting It All Together

By now you may be asking yourself, "What if I want to try to load Microsoft's ActiveX control first, and then fall back to load a Netscape plug-in if the user's browser doesn't recognize <OBJECT>?" Good question; give yourself 15 seconds to feel smugly superior. The following code uses the previous examples with slight modifications to cover the bases in one fell swoop:

```
<OBJECT CLASSID="clsid:166B1BCA-3F9C-11CF-8075-444553540000" CODEBASE="http://
active.macromedia.com/director/cabs/sw.cab#version=5,0,1,61" WIDTH=300 HEIGHT=235
NAME="Shockwave" ID="swwelcome">
     <PARAM NAME="SRC" VALUE="shockstuff/intro/welcome.dcr">
     <PARAM NAME="PALETTE" VALUE="background">
     <PARAM NAME="BGCOLOR" VALUE="white">
</OBJECT>
<NOOBJECT>
     <EMBED SRC="shockstuff/intro/welcome.dcr" WIDTH=300 HEIGHT=235
     VSPACE=5 HSPACE=5 ALIGN=left BGCOLOR=#FFFFFF PALETTE=background>
     <NOEMBED>
        <IMG SRC="images/getaclue.gif"><BR>
        Sorry, you need a browser that uses Netscape plug-ins or
        Microsoft ActiveX controls. You can
        <A HREF="home.netscape.com">Get Netscape</A> or
        <A HREF="www.microsoft.com">Get Internet Explorer</A>.
     </NOEMBED>
</NOOBJECT>
```

The browser will try to use Microsoft's <OBJECT> tag first, and then try Netscape's <EMBED> tag. If the browser can't use plug-ins compatible with either method, you will see the contents of <NOEMBED>. This last part is particularly handy if the user who pulls up your page has something like an older AOL browser.

One final note: When Shockwave first came out, it was necessary with some older versions of Netscape to use JavaScript work-arounds to get it to behave properly. You may run into online documentation that suggests you take this route, but this should no longer be necessary with the latest versions of Netscape- and Explorer-compatible browsers. However, the mantra of the Internet is "whatever works." If you run into problems using standard `<EMBED>` or `<OBJECT>` specifications, the work-arounds might be exactly what you need. One source of excellent information is the ShockeR Listserv, maintained at `http://www.ShockeR.com/ShockeR`. The e-mail listserv is for Shockwave developers to exchange ideas and tips with each other about using the latest developments in Shockwave. You'll even find a few of the Macromedia tech-heads who invented Shockwave lurking about and answering technical questions. Chances are that if something cool is being done with Shockwave, the ShockeR subscribers know about it.

Creating Shockwave Files in Macromedia Director

This section assumes you are comfortable working with Macromedia Director and have at least a basic knowledge of using Lingo. (If you're not used to seeing the splash screen in Figure 25.3, this next section may be a challenge for you.) The methods you use to create Shockwave movies will be nearly identical to those you use to create anything else in Director. However, there are a few disabled features, a few new Lingo commands, and bandwidth issues to be taken into account. With a little patience and a little experimenting, you'll be churning out your own Shockwave movies with abandon.

FIGURE 25.3.
The birthplace of Shockwave—the splash screen for Macromedia Director 5.x.

Planning Your Shockwave Movie

Your capacity for presenting a professional, polished Shockwave-enhanced site directly correlates to how much planning you do ahead of time. As tempting as it can be to "shoot from the hip" and see what happens, you will do yourself a significant favor by making some key decisions about the uses of Shockwave in your site ahead of time.

To illustrate my point with a non-Shocked example, think of the most graphically appealing Web site you've browsed lately. Chances are the graphics and artwork fit a specific theme, integrated closely with the content, and didn't overshadow that content. Graphics should be more than just eye candy; they should be tools to evoke a theme, idea, or consistent frame of reference. Your Shockwave movies can and should perform the same function. The difference is that Shockwave provides you with a vastly superior set of tools. Now you can have something that not only looks good, but also sounds good and responds to user input. Making the best use of this potential involves two basic stages of planning: deciding what role Shockwave will take in your Web site and determining what parameters to set to keep your file sizes small.

Deciding How "Shocking" Your Site Will Be

Any plans you make about using Shockwave in your Web site should probably center around the question, "Who is my audience?" Out of this question are numerous other questions for you to consider before building a site that uses Shockwave. This section contains a few of these questions to prime the pump.

Shockwave is only available for Navigator- or Explorer-compatible browsers; does your audience use such a browser? If so, do they have the Shockwave plug-in or control? If not, will they know how to get it? Will you provide information to help them do this?

You can create an entire Web site with one HTML page and a series of Shockwave movies, but if your audience doesn't have access to Shockwave, will you provide them with alternative content? Will that alternative content be on different HTML pages, or will it exist on the same page as the Shockwave movies?

What function will Shockwave play in your Web site? Is it appropriate to use it for navigation (toolbars, icons, and so on)? Is it appropriate to deliver the main content of the page? Will you be able to navigate from one Shockwave movie to another from within the movie, from HTML links, or from a separate "toolbar" movie? You can use Shockwave as a form of entertainment that attracts the user's attention but doesn't have the real meat of your information. Is this a better or worse use of Shockwave? If you are paying somebody to write Shockwave movies for you, will you have to pay them to update the content? How often?

After you have weighed all of these options, there is one more question to ask: "Is Shockwave the best way to get the job done?" For the average Web site, the answer may be, "Probably not." But if you need the extra punch of interactivity and multimedia in your site, Shockwave for Director is one of the best ways to go.

Keeping File Sizes Small

Your Shockwave movie can be anything from a CD-ROM-sized application to a simple looped animation. The former may not be the best approach; most users don't like waiting for a 650 M download. Until the curse of limited bandwidth lifts from the Internet, you have the task of keeping your Shockwave movies at a reasonable size for your users. Shockwave does not currently stream its information to your browser. The entire movie file must load before you can see it. (Shockwave Audio is a different story, however. See the section "Using Streamed Shockwave Audio" for more information.)

If you have the freedom to design your Shockwave movies for an intranet platform where users will have unlimited bandwidth, you can smugly skip this section altogether. The other 99.9 percent of you may glean a helpful hint or two in avoiding insufferably long download times. If your users are accessing your Web site over the Internet, you can safely expect that they will load files at about 1000-1500 bytes per second. So if your Shockwave movie is 200 K, your users may have to wait over three minutes to view it. Granted, that's a poor-case scenario. (The worst-case scenario happens when the user is getting about 65 bytes per second of data transfer. This typically happens in one of two situations: just after you finished bragging about your bandwidth to a potential client or when you use AOL during any of its 22 "peak hours" in the day.)

Many professionals using Shockwave have adopted an unofficial standard of keeping their movie files under 200 K. This seems to be a reasonable amount of time for the user to wait without doing something drastic to their keyboard in frustration. The following sections have some tips on keeping your file sizes friendly to the user.

Limit Your Bitmap Cast Members

Limiting your bitmap cast members is by far the best way to keep your movie size down. Bitmap cast members are the real bandits in bloating a movie's file size, so try to reuse the same bitmap cast members as much as possible. For instance, instead of making five bitmap buttons with different labels, make one bitmap button and use it five times. Text cast members don't take up nearly the same memory that bitmap members do, so you could label each of your generic button sprites with a different text cast member placed over it.

Another way to keep your movie file size smaller is by keeping your overall dimensions smaller. You may be used to producing applications for full-screen delivery; coming up with something visually stimulating to fill a 640×480 or 800×600 screen can be quite a challenge. With Shockwave, chances are good you will never need to cover that much screen area. Your movie will be playing in the browser window, remember, and you don't want users to have to scroll back in forth in their browsers to see the whole thing. The stage size itself has little bearing on the file size. What you put *inside* that stage determines the file size. If you can accomplish your purpose with a smaller stage size, you'll be doing yourself and your users a favor.

Another way to keep your bitmap cast members manageable is to reduce their color palette. This palette determines the colors that can be displayed in the image, but it is not limited to the colors actually used in the image. So even if the image uses only several of the available colors, the entire palette is still built-in. Therefore, if you can reduce the palette without compromising the quality of the image, you'll save memory.

The buttons named Press in Figure 25.4 serve as a good example of how much of a difference it makes to lower the color resolution of your bitmap cast members. The top button at 16 bits (thousands of colors) is roughly twice as large as the identical button reduced to 8 bits (256 colors). Generally speaking, you can cut a bitmap's file size in half by taking it down one level in palette resolution. Black-and-white, or 1-bit images, are the smallest of all, if you can use them without compromising the artistic considerations of your movie. If you can make use of 1-bit or 2-bit images in any involved animation sequences, the memory savings you make could be enormous. Experiment with ink effects on these images to give you variety without additional cast members.

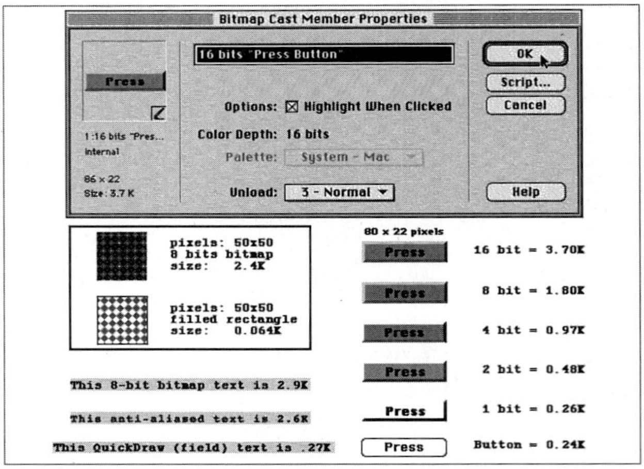

FIGURE 25.4.
Examples of memory sizes among different cast members.

To set the color resolution on a bitmap cast member in Director 5.0, select the item in the cast window and choose `Modify | Transform bitmap`. Or if you have the cast member open in the Paint window, the resolution appears below the tool palette on the left side. Double-click the resolution to display the Transform bitmap window. Director doesn't let you undo resolution changes, so you may want to experiment with expendable copies of your cast member first.

Use QuickDraw Shapes with Patterns

The floating Tool Palette window lets you put QuickDraw text and shapes into your movie with very little cost in added bytes. Creating something visually stimulating with only QuickDraw shapes may feel prohibitive, but you can use them for borders, backgrounds, separators, buttons, and the like. Again, try experimenting with ink effects to add variety to these sprites without adding cast members.

NOTE

QuickDraw shapes are the plain boxes, ovals, and lines you can create from the Tool Palette. They take up very little memory because Director stores only their boundary coordinates, not a bitmap of the entire shape.

Another way to make the most of QuickDraw shapes is by using the tile patterns Director offers. They enable you to have textured backgrounds and shapes in your movie without large bitmaps. Figure 25.5 shows two 50×50 boxes. The top one is a bitmap, considerably larger in file space than its QuickDraw filled rectangle counterpart below. If you don't like the patterns built into Director, you can import your own. Follow these steps:

1. Create a seamless tile in a graphics program like Adobe Photoshop or Macromedia xRes. The dimensions should be any combination of 16, 32, 64, or 128 pixels (for example, 16×16, 32×64, 128×32) Save it as a PICT and import it into your movie as a cast member.
2. Select `Window | Tool Palette`. In the Tool Palette, double-click the pattern bar beneath the foreground/background selections. (It's the bar just above the line-width options.) The Tile Settings window appears (see Figure 25.5).
3. Highlight the built-in pattern you want to override. For the `Source` option, choose the `Cast Member` radio button. Use the arrow buttons to go through the cast members until you find your imported pattern.
4. At the bottom left of the window, select the dimensions of your pattern from the `Width` and `Height` menus.
5. The left half of this window shows your pattern and a selection box of what Director will try to tile. The right half of the window shows what the tiling will look like. If you need to, adjust the selection box on the left side until your pattern tiles properly on the right side.
6. Click the `OK` button when you are finished. Now you can select your custom pattern to fill any QuickDraw shape in your movie.

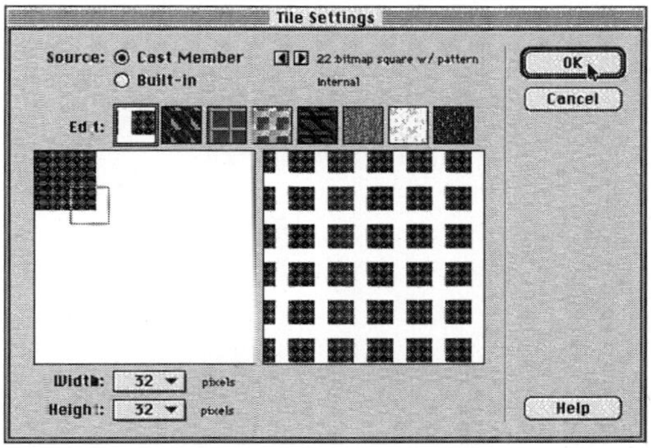

FIGURE 25.5.
The Tile Settings window.

Display Text in Field Cast Members

Director 5 allows you to use anti-aliased text, but be warned that this kind of text takes up considerably more file space than plain text in a field cast member. (Anti-aliasing makes the letters appear smoother by filling in jagged edges with transition colors.) When Director applies anti-aliasing to a block of text, the text is changed to a bitmap. The text in field cast members, however, is stored as plain ASCII information and not as a bitmap. Figure 25.5 shows three boxes of text in the lower left of the stage. The top box was created in the paint window, the second with the text tool (with anti-aliasing on), and the third in a field cast member. If you have a lot of text to put into your Shockwave movie, pick the size savings that the field cast members give you. You won't get the eye-pleasing results of anti-aliasing, but sometimes form has to give way to function.

Use `getNetText uri` for Dynamic Content

The Shockwave lingo command `getNetText` is an often-overlooked command that enables you to use the same movie over and over again while changing any text content. You will learn how to use this command in "Learning the New Lingo," but this space-saving feature bears mentioning here. If you have a Shockwave movie that has text that must be updated on a regular basis, consider designing your movie to act as a player or kiosk for that text. `getNetText` lets you import a text file from anywhere on the Internet directly into your Shockwave movie while it is running.

For example, imagine a certain college wants to have a Shockwave kiosk on its home page that displays the latest athletic scores and scheduled events. The departments responsible for keeping the information current need only update the text, and the Shockwave kiosk movie will display the latest information each time it is loaded. See Figure 25.6 for an example of what this might look like.

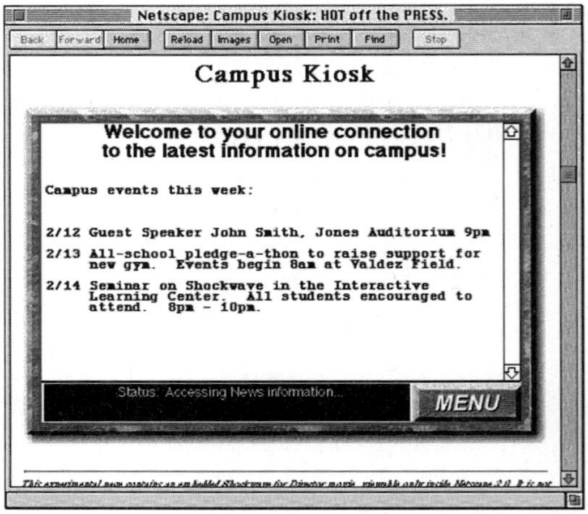

FIGURE 25.6.
One use of `getNetText` *is to create a kiosk that draws on regularly updated text files.*

Use Sound Cast Members Frugally

Using sound in your Shockwave movies always adds a nice touch to normally mute Web pages. Sound cast members quickly bloat the size of your movie, however, so you have to weigh the desire for a feature-length soundtrack with a reasonable download time.

When possible, use the smallest sound files possible. If you need a music soundtrack, try to use short clips that can be seamlessly looped for an extended period of time. You can also experiment with different sampling rates to reduce the file size, but down-sampling a sound too much makes it unusable. A common sound format is to record at an 8-bit, 22 MHz resolution. With the proper recording equipment, this format is usually satisfactory for narration and sound effects. Avoid using sounds recorded at an 8-bit, 11 MHz resolution if at all possible.

You also have the option of using external audio files that can load and play independently of your Shockwave movie. They have the `.swa` extension and can be compressed with Xtras provided by Macromedia. See the section "Using Streamed Audio with Shockwave" for more information.

Learning the New Lingo

The real power of Director is found in Lingo, the internal programming language that gives your control over virtually everything in the movie. Although you don't need to be a certified propeller-head (also known as a programmer) to use Director well, the more Lingo you know, the better.

There are new considerations you have to take into account when designing Director movies for Shockwave. Some of the features you may be used to are disabled for security or practical reasons. Furthermore, the Shockwave plug-in uses Lingo commands to give you added functionality and access to network-related functions.

Disabled Lingo Commands

Several commands normally available to you in Director have been disabled in Shockwave to protect users from security breaches on their computers. These commands perform system-related functions or give directory and file information on the host computer. At the time of this writing, Macromedia listed the following commands and features as disabled in Shockwave:

```
closeDA, closeResFile, closeXLib, close window

custom menus

fileIO

fileName of cast, fileName of castLib, fileName of window

getNthFileNameInFolder

importFileInto
```

`keyUp (Netscape 2.x only)`

`mci command`

`moviePath`

`open, openDA, openResFile, open window, openXLib, openCastlib`

OrthoPlay functions

`pathName`

`printFrom, pasteFromClipboard`

`quit`

`restart`

`saveMovie`

`searchCurrentFolder, searchPaths`

`serialIO`

`shutdown`

XObjects, XCMDs, XFCNs

From the preceding list, you may have gathered that several powerful features of Director are not available to you. One of these, regrettably, is the "Movie in a Window" method of having multiple movies open at the same time and passing information between them. Macromedia has indicated that it is working on this problem, but for the moment, there is no easy way to have Shockwave movies pass information to each other. (You can have one movie load and play another movie when it is finished, however. Keep reading for details.)

Despite the list of verboten commands, Shockwave does allow the movie to access Xtras and linked media. The item must be in the Shockwave Plug-in Support folder, however, so the user must download the Xtra or media and place it in the folder before your movie will be able to use it. It's a hassle, but it's also an understandable security restriction. You don't want somebody's malicious movie traipsing about your hard drive while supposedly looking for a missing Xtra.

For an updated list of disabled commands, refer to Macromedia's Shockwave Developer's Guide online at `http://www.macromedia.com/shockwave`.

Shockwave Lingo Commands

There are all sorts of new things you can do in Shockwave that you can't do in a normal Director movie. In this section, you'll learn what they are and how they work so that you can build your own Net-aware Shockwave movies.

NOTE

The Internet is unreliable. (Propeller-heads call this *asynchronous*, but don't let that fool you.) When you want something done on a network, you have to ask for it and keep checking to make sure you are going to get it. This process holds true for using the new Lingo commands with Shockwave. Suppose you want to load an external text file into a variable. Your movie has to tell the server to go get the content of the file, monitor whether the request is being filled, and then put the text into a variable when it is finally retrieved. Don't assume that asking is enough; always monitor asynchronous functions.

getNetText uri

The `getNetText` command searches for a text file at *`uri`* and imports the text directly into your Shockwave movie while it is playing. *`Uri`* stands for universal resource indicator and is a standard HTTP file location (URL). The following is an example of how this command might be used:

```
on startMovie
      getNetText "http://www.blahblah.com/welcome.txt"
      go to "Intro"
   end startMovie
```

This is a wonderful command to use if you want your movie to act like a kiosk to display constantly updated information. Instead of updating your Shockwave movie with time-sensitive information on a regular basis, have the movie retrieve the text with `getNetText` instead. This way, you only have to update the text file and not the Shockwave movie.

If you are proficient in CGI or Perl-esque programming, there are all sorts of nifty things you can do with importing text files that are generated on-the-fly. You could show a Shockwave movie that shows the latest usage statistics on a certain Web site, the highest bid on a `FORM`-fed auction, or the current weather forecast. The following are some related commands:

```
getLatestNetID, netAbort(), netDone(), netTextResult()
```

getLatestNetID()

Because more than one asynchronous task can be executed at once, you need to be able to refer to each task by a unique ID. Right after you have started an asynchronous task, such as `GetNetText`, you can use `getLatestNetID()` to get the unique network ID number for it.

The following example shows how you can use this command:

```
on startMovie

  -- Declare a global variable to store a network task ID.
  global textTaskID
```

```
  -- Get the text located in an external file.
  getNetText "http://www.blahblah.com/welcome.txt"

  -- Put the task ID of the recent command into the variable.
  set textTaskID=getLatestNetID()

  -- Take the user to wherever the movie begins.
  go to "Intro"

end startMovie
```

When you are using asynchronous commands with Shockwave, your movie is instructing the user's browser to perform that command. A limited number of commands can be performed at once, and most browsers default to four sockets or connections. Use `getLatestNetID()` to keep track of the different tasks in progress and assign them their own variables. If a command can't be carried out on the first try, your movie may need to `netAbort()` and try again. The following are some related commands:

`netAbort(), netDone()`

getPref(prefName)

The `getPref` command is used to retrieve user preference data that you have defined with `setPref`. The `prefName` parameter is the name of your preference file, located in the `Prefs` folder of the `Plug-In Support` folder. If no such file exists, the result of this command will be `void`. The following is an example of how this command is used:

```
on startMovie

  -- Define a global variable to store the user's preferences.
  global userPref

  -- Get the preferences from the file previously created.
  set userPref = getPref("shockfun.prf")

  -- If there are no existing preferences, take the user to
  -- A first-time visitor's area. Otherwise, take the user to
  -- the area where repeat visitors begin.
  if voidP(userPref) then
    go to "Firstvisit"
  else
    go to "Repeatvisit"
  end if

end startMovie
```

The preference file contains information the program has established about the user for future reference. The capability to retrieve this information is especially helpful in situations where you want to customize what the user sees. You may have first-time visitors fill out their favorite interests, for example, and record them with `setPref` to a preference file. Later, when they return to your site, you could utilize `getPref` to automatically show them the things they might be the most interested in. Preference files may also be useful in establishing statistics on how many visitors return to your site on a regular basis.

gotoNetMovie uri

The `gotoNetMovie` command loads the movie file specified in `uri`, halts the current movie, and begins playing the new one in the same position on the HTML page. Macromedia has indicated that, for the time being, the movie called must be in a standard HTTP file location. (Not, for instance, on an FTP server.) You can even have the movie begin at a certain internal marker by using a target-style modifier, such as `"http://path/filename.dcr#target"`.

```
on exitFrame

  -- Tell the user another movie is about to play.
  put "Returning to main menu...." into field "StatusWindow"

  -- Load and play the next movie.
  gotoNetMovie "main.dcr#menu"

  -- Go to a frame that waits for the next movie to load.
  go to "Hold"

end exitFrame
```

Something to keep in mind when using this command is that you can only have one active `gotoNetMovie` in progress at the same time. If you issue `gotoNetMovie` with another one already in progress, the second command will override the first. Because the called movie will begin playing as soon as it is loaded without warning, you might want to use `preLoadNetThing` as a helpful way of loading the movie into the user's cache without immediately launching it. When your first movie is finished with whatever it needs to do, it can then use `gotoNetMovie` without an abrupt transition. The following are some commands related to this command:

`getLatestNetID, preLoadNetThing`

gotoNetPage uri, target

You can use `gotoNetMovie` to play a sequence of movies on one HTML page, but if you need the browser to switch to a different HTML page, `gotoNetPage` is the command to use. The `uri` parameter can be any HTTP file location, and if your Web site uses frames, you can specify a frame with the optional `target` parameter. The site in Figure 25.7 uses this function.

The following is an example of how this command might be used:

```
on mouseUp

  -- This button, labelled Home, is on a Shockwave menu bar at
  -- the bottom of the HTML page.

  -- Play a sound that resembles a mouse button being released.
puppetSound "mouseUp.wav"
  updateStage

  -- Load a new HTML page in the current browser window.
  gotoNetPage "http://myserver.myschool.edu/index.html#top"

end mouseUp
```

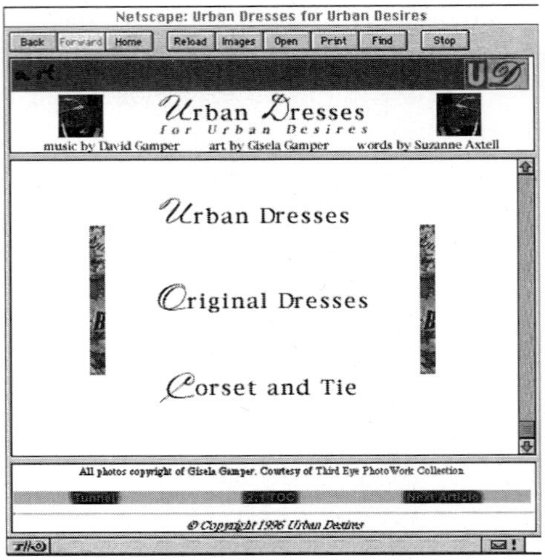

FIGURE 25.7.
A site that uses Shockwave navigation inside browser frames.

If the specified `target` frame doesn't exist, the user's browser loads the `uri` in a new window with `target` as its name. This feature can be handy if the `uri` is a link to a page not in your Web site. The user can explore the link in a new window, but yours will still be in the background when he is ready to return. This setup is often a much nicer alternative to hitting the Back button a dozen times.

Don't forget to monitor the progress of this command to see whether it is being accomplished. If the page located at `uri` doesn't exist or is not accessible, you need to provide a way for your Shockwave movie to deal with this situation. Use `getLatestNetID()` and `netDone()` to monitor the `gotoNetPage` operation. You might even want to use `preLoadNetThing` to load the page ahead of time.

TIP

You can use `gotoNetPage` to bring up an e-mail window for the user. The HTML method of doing this is as follows:

```
<A HREF="mailto:username@server.org">Email me.</A>
```

To accomplish the same thing in Shockwave, use the following line of code in Lingo:

```
gotoNetPage("mailto:username@server.org")
```

The result is that an e-mail composition window pops up in front of your HTML window, and the `To` line contains the value of `username@server.org`.

netAbort()

Without a specified task ID, the `netAbort()` command cancels the last asynchronous command executed. It aborts a specific asynchronous command by referring to it by task ID. (For information on how to identify a command's ID, refer to the information on `getLatestNetID`.) The following is an example of how this command might be used:

```
on exitFrame

  -- In a previous frame, the timer was started and a network
  -- command was given. The task ID was placed in the global
  -- variable 'netTask'.
  global netTask

  -- If the task is completed successfully, leave this frame loop.
if netError(netTask)="OK" then
    go to "Success"
    exit

    -- The task isn't completed, so if the 10-second limit is reached,
    -- abort the task, alert the user, and leave the frame loop.
else
    if the timer>600 then
      netAbort(netTask)
      alert "Operation timed out or failed. Please try again."
      go to "Menu"
      exit
    end if
  end if

  -- Repeat this frame. The user won't exit from this frame until
  -- either the task is completed or the time limit is reached.
  go to the frame

end exitFrame
```

You should always program "outs" for yourself in any given situation. When you execute a network (asynchronous) command, be sure to account for the possibility that it doesn't work. Typically, the way you would do this is by putting the program into a loop until one of three things happens: the command is successfully completed, an error is returned, or a time limit you set is exceeded.

CAUTION

When you are checking on the status of an asynchronous command in progress, it is tempting to use a `repeat while` loop to make your movie concentrate on that one thing. Don't! Repeat loops are very CPU-intensive and can slow down the user's machine to a crawl. Use frame loops whenever possible; they allow the movie to check on any other

continues

continued

events that need attention. (See the code sample for `netAbort()` as an example.) A "go to the frame" loop also frees up the user's browser to perform other functions. If you must use a `repeat while` loop, always provide a way for time to run out or the user to cancel the loop. It's a good idea, in fact, to incorporate similar safety measures into any kind of loop your movie may perform.

The following commands are related to this command:

`getLatestNetID, netError, netDone()`

netDone()

The `netDone()` command returns the status of the last network command given. If you specify a task ID number within the parentheses, it returns the status of that particular task. The result of this command is either `TRUE` or `FALSE`. The command only returns `FALSE` if a task is in progress; it returns `TRUE` if there is no task being executed, if a task has finished, or if a task has been aborted.

The following is an example of how this command might be used:

```
on exitFrame

  -- In a previous frame, the movie has issued a getNetText
  -- command to retrieve a weather report text file. The task ID
  -- is in the global variable called "getTheWeather".
global getTheWeather

  -- If the task is done, put the result into "theReport".
if netDone(getTheWeather)=TRUE then
    set theReport = getTextResult(getTheWeather)

    -- If the result of the task is empty, something went
    -- wrong, and the text file wasn't retrieved.
    if theReport = "" then
      alert "I didn't get the weather report. Try again."
      go to "Menu"
      exit

    else

      -- Display the weather report text in a field and exit.
      put theReport into field "Weather Report"
      go to "Menu"
      exit
    end if
  end if

end exitFrame
```

Be sure to account for the fact that when `netDone() = TRUE`, it means that the task is no longer in progress. It does not imply that the command was successful, however, so be sure to check the result of the command and make sure you got what you needed.

The following commands are related to this command:

`getLatestNetID, getNetText, getTextResult, gotoNetMovie, gotoNetPage, netAbort, netError, preLoadNetThing`

netError()

Use `netError()` to monitor a network task in progress for a specific error. The command returns the status on the most recent network command given unless a specific task ID is provided by `getLatestNetID`. The result of `netError` is one of four strings: `"OK"` if the task was successfully completed, `"NONE"` if there is no task in progress, an error string if something went wrong, and an empty string (`""`) if the task is still in progress.

The following is an example of how this command might be used:

```
on mouseUp

  -- This is the handler for a button labeled 'Check Status".
-- The task ID for a network command initiated in an
  -- earlier frame is stored in the global variable "myTask".
  global myTask

  -- If the result is "OK", the command worked.
if netError(myTask)="OK" then
    go to "Success"
    exit
  else

    -- If the result is "", the command is still in progress.
if netError(myTask)="" then
      put "Still waiting." into field "Report"
      exit
    else

      -- If the result is "NONE", the command was never given.
if netError(myTask)="NONE" then
        put "Nothing to check on.' into field "Report"
        exit
      else

        -- The result isn't one of the other three options, so
        -- the remaining option is that an error occurred.
        put "ERROR: " & netError(myTask) into field "Report"
        exit
      end if
    end if
  end if

end mouseUp
```

This command can be useful if `netDone()` isn't giving you the feedback you need when a command is issued. There is one case, however, where using `netError()` will give you trouble. If you have given a command with a `uri` that doesn't exist, `netError()` will return an empty string indefinitely. So be sure to code a way for the movie to abort after a certain amount of time or at the user's discretion.

The following commands are related to the `netError()` command:

```
getLatestNetID, netAbort, netDone()
```

netLastModDate(uri)

Use the `netLastModDate` command to return the date that the specified HTTP item was last modified. The `uri` parameter must be a valid HTTP file name. The result of this command will be a string. The following is an example of how this command might be used:

```
on enterFrame

  -- Check the last-modified date on a file that changes often.
set myFile = "news/pressrelease/press.txt"
  set myFileModDate = getNetModDate(myFile)

  -- Put the result into a display field on the stage.
  put "Last press release: " & myFileModDate into field "Status"

end enterFrame
```

Programs called *spiders* roam and catalog a Web site for the user on command, and Shockwave spiders can be a great alternative for people who don't have access to CGI scripting. The command `netLastModDate` in particular is helpful for any Shockwave movie that is keeping track of a large number of files at the same time, be they HTML pages or graphics. You might find it helpful to build a spider that only monitors your own Web site and alerts you to pages that haven't been updated in, say, three months. Or if you have more than one person maintaining your site, you could keep track of which pages have been most recently updated in order to monitor quality control.

The following command is related to the `netLastModDate` command:

```
netMIME()
```

netMIME(uri)

The `netMIME` command returns the MIME type of the HTTP item specified in `uri`. The result is contained in a string. The following is an example of how this command might be used:

```
on enterFrame

  -- Establish a list of files to check the MIMe types on.
  set fileList=[news.txt","home.dcr","logo.jpg"]

  -- Set a variable to hold the output.
  set report=""
```

```
  -- Repeat this process with each file in fileList.
  repeat with eachFile in fileList

    -- Output the name and MIME type of each file into 'report'.
    put eachFile & " is: " & netMIME(eachFile) after report
  end repeat

  -- Put the contents of 'report' into a field on the stage.
  put report into field "File Types"

end enterFrame
```

Like `netLastModDate`, this command is provided to allow you to glean information about HTTP files on a network. A file's MIME type describes what kind of application it is associated with and is usually indicated by the file's three-letter extension. This command will become increasingly useful as Xtras for Shockwave are developed to import new file types.

netStatus msg

If you are using Netscape Navigator, the `netStatus` command puts a string into the status message at the bottom of the window. Macromedia indicates that this command does not work with Microsoft Internet Explorer 3.0 and, at the time of this writing, has offered no information as to when or if it will.

The following is an example of how this command might be used:

```
on startMovie

  -- Put a message in the status window of the browser.
  netStatus("Welcome to our Shocked Web site!')

end startMovie
```

This isn't one of the more awe-inspiring commands that Shockwave provides, but it has its usefulness. There are probably thousands of different JavaScripts on the Net to accomplish the same thing within HTML, so why not have it in Shockwave? Hopefully, the technical folks at Macromedia will make this command work with Internet Explorer in the near future.

The following command is related to the `netStatus` command:

```
netAbort()
```

netTextResult()

Use the `netTextResult()`command after issuing a `getNetText` command on a text file. Providing that the `getNetText` command was successful, the `netTextResult()` command will return a string of the text contained in the file. Figure 25.8 shows a site that uses this command for an online quiz.

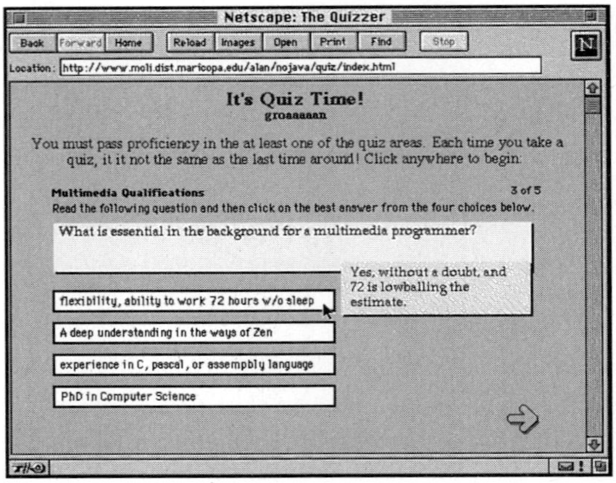

FIGURE 25.8.
A light-hearted online quiz using `getNetText` *and* `netTextResult()` *by Alan Levine.*

The following is another example of how this command might be used:

```
on exitFrame

  -- For this example, getNetText("usernames.txt") has
  -- already been given, and the movie has used netDone() to
  -- confirm that it worked.

  -- Put the text from the file into a field on the stage.
 put netTextResult() into field "Imported Text"

end exitFrame
```

This command must be used in conjunction with the `getNetText` command. You will need to use either `netAbort` or `netError` to monitor the progress of `getNetText` until it is completed. (See the notes on these commands for more information.) After you have stored the result of `netTextResult` in a variable or field, you will probably need to format it to fit the aesthetics of your Shockwave movie. Keep in mind that text created in Windows and text created on a Macintosh use different ASCII characters for a line feed (carriage return). Consult your Director manuals for more information on ASCII tables for each platform.

For more information, check the descriptions of these related commands:

`getNetText, netDone, netError`

preLoadNetThing uri

The `preLoadNetThing` command is one of the hidden gold mines in working with Shockwave. The `uri` parameter can be any HTTP file, and the result is that the specified file will begin to load into the browser's cache. Use `netDone` or `netError` to monitor the progress of this command. The following is an example of how this command might be used:

```
-- This script is in a frame script at the beginning of the
-- Shockwave movie. The idle script executes as soon as the movie
```

```
-- isn't executing another handler. We only want the preLoad
-- commands to be called the first time, however, so we'll use a
-- global variable called NextMovieIsLoading to prevent repeats.

on idle

  -- 'NextMovieIsLoading' is set to FALSE before the first time
  -- that this handler executes. The global 'preLoadTask' will
  -- hold the task ID of the preLoadNetThing command.
  global NextMovieIsLoading , preloadTask

  if NextMovieIsLoading = FALSE then

    -- Preload the Shockwave movie that will come after this one.
preLoadNetThing "part2.dcr"

    -- Store the command's task ID in a global for later use.
    put getLatestNetID() into preloadTask

    -- Make sure this script won't run again
    set NextMovieIsLoading = TRUE

  end if

end idle
```

Keep in mind that this command only preloads *one* file into the browser's cache. If the `url` you specify is a HTML page, it will preload the HTML, but it won't preload any of the graphics or embedded files in that page. To load the individual elements into the cache, you have to refer to them specifically. Many browsers only allow four asynchronous commands to be in progress at once, so you may have to write a script to deal with what is often called the *four-socket barrier.*

These commands are related to the `preLoadNetThing` command:

`getLatestNetId, netAbort, netDone, netError`

setPref prefName, prefValue

If you need to record the user's preferences concerning certain aspects of your Shockwave movies, use the `setPref` command. The `prefName` parameter is the name of a file that will be created in the `Prefs` folder of the `Plug-In Support` folder. If the folder does not already exist, it will be created the first time `setPref` is used. The `prefValue` parameter is a text string that contains any information you want to be stored.

Macromedia recommends that you keep the file name to eight characters long with an optional three character extension, but the naming convention you use is up to you. Make the file name fairly unique to avoid the possibility that somebody else's Shockwave movie has created a preference file with the same name; avoid names like *shockwave, shockdata, shockinfo,* and anything else you might think of off the top of your head. The last thing you want is somebody else's Shockwave movie overwriting your preference data.

The following is an example of how the `setPref` command might be used:

```
on enterFrame

  -- The user has filled out several items of information
  -- which have been stored in global variables.
  global userName, userAge, userGender

  -- Prepare a string of the preferences delimited by spaces.
  set userPrefs = userName & " " & userAge & " " & userGender

  -- Create a user preference file called "1732prefs".
setPref "1732prefs",userPrefs

end enterFrame
```

The term for a preference file created by a Net-accessed application is *cookie*. This file contains information the program has established about the user for future reference. You may have first-time visitors fill out their favorite interests, for example, and record them with `setPref` to a cookie.

NOTE

Be advised that many users are wary of letting Web sites glean to much information about them. Commercial programs are being developed to prevent cookie files from being maintained on the user's computer, so it is considered polite to inform the user that you plan to create a preference file.

Passing Information from HTML to Shockwave

Sometimes you will want to specify variable information in your HTML page rather than inside of the Shockwave movie. You could, of course, put the information into a text file and use `getNetText` to retrieve it. For small strings of text, however, there is an easier way.

Your Shockwave movie can detect custom parameters and their values specified in the `<EMBED>` or `<OBJECT>` tag of the `<HTML>` tag. If you are coding for the Netscape broswer with `<EMBED>`, these parameters can be named anything you like. If you are coding to accommodate both Netscape and Microsoft browsers, limit yourself to the preset parameter names recognized by Internet Explorer in the `<OBJECT>` tag. They are as follows:

```
swAudio
swBackColor
swBanner
swColor
swForeColor
swFrame
```

```
swList
swName
swPassword
swPreLoadTime
swSound
swText
swUrl
sw1, sw2, sw3, sw4, sw5, sw6, sw7, sw8, sw9
```

Macromedia recommends you use values with these parameters that are logical to the person writing the HTML page. Assigning the parameter `swForeColor` a value of "Lord of the Flies", for example, might be a tad confusing. However, these parameters are just variable holders and do not automatically change the behavior of anything in your Shockwave movie. If you use up `sw1` through `sw9` and need more custom parameters, you can commandeer any of the other parameter names for whatever values you like.

Using Custom Parameters with <EMBED>

The format for specifying custom parameters in the `<EMBED>` tag is simply `paramName=paramValue`. For example:

```
<EMBED SRC="myshock.dcr" WIDTH=100 HEIGHT=100 swForeColor="212" swBackColor="14"
swText="Additional parameters are cool.">
```

In addition to the preset parameter names, you can create any parameter name you like. If you know how to generate HTML pages on the fly with a CGI script, custom parameters becomes a very powerful method of sending information to your Shockwave movies. If the user answered a quiz inside a `FORM`, you could generate an HTML page with custom Shockwave parameters that contain the answers. It might look something like the following:

```
<EMBED SRC="scoretest.dcr" WIDTH=500 HEIGHT=400 userName="Mark Woodman"
userEmail="woodman@inkimage.com"
 answer1="A" answer2="B" answer3="C" answer4="B" favoriteBook="Web Publishing
Unleashed">
```

Using Custom Parameters with <OBJECT>

To specify custom parameters for Shockwave in the `<OBJECT>` tag, use the following format:

```
<PARAM NAME=paramName VALUE=paramValue>
```

The following code is an example of using custom parameters with `<OBJECT>`:

```
<OBJECT CLASSID="clsid:166B1BCA-3F9C-11CF-8075-444553540000"
 CODEBASE="http://active.macromedia.com/director/cabs/sw.cab#version=5,0,1,61"
 WIDTH=100 HEIGHT=100 NAME="Shockwave" ID="myshock">
     <PARAM NAME="SRC" VALUE="myshock.dcr">
     <PARAM NAME="swForeColor" VALUE="212">
```

```
    <PARAM NAME="swBackColor" VALUE="14">
    <PARAM NAME="swText" VALUE="Additional parameters are cool.">
</OBJECT>
```

Unlike `<EMBED>`, you cannot create your own parameter names. (See the list of available parameter names under "Passing Information from HTML to Shockwave.") You do have 22 parameters at your disposal, however, and you can give them whatever custom parameter values you need to get the job done.

Detecting Custom Parameters in Lingo

Now that you can provide custom parameter values through HTML for Shockwave, you need to know how to bring those values into your movie. There are three Shockwave Lingo commands that you can use to detect and import custom parameter values: `externalParamCount()`, `externalParamName()`, and `externalParamValue()`.

The command `externalParamCount()` returns an integer that is equal to the number of parameters detected in the `<EMBED>` or `<OBJECT>` tag. The `SRC`, `WIDTH`, and `HEIGHT` parameters are included in this number.

The command `externalParamName(n)` returns the name (in a string) of the `n`th parameter detected. If an `nth` external parameter is not detected, the result is `void`.

The command `externalParamValue(n)` returns the value of the parameter specified in `n`. You can use the parameter name in a string for `n`, or use an integer to indicate the `n`th parameter detected. If an `n`th external parameter does not exist, the result is `void`.

A Sample Use of Custom Parameters

This example is a simple Shockwave movie that displays the custom external parameters specified in the HTML page. The cast of the Shockwave movie consists of a Movie Script and a field named `Status` placed on the stage. The content of the Movie Script is as follows:

```
on startMovie

  -- Look for external parameters specified in HTML.
  put externalParamCount() into exPC

  -- Display how many parameters are detected.
  put "Parameters detected: " & exPC & RETURN into field "Status"

  -- Display each parameter name and its value.
  repeat with eachParam = 1 to exPC
    set eachPName=externalParamName(eachParam)
    set eachPValue=externalParamValue(eachParam)
    put eachPName & " = " & eachPValue & RETURN after field "Status"
  end repeat

end startMovie
```

You might think it is necessary to include an `if...then` statement in the preceding script to make sure that the number of parameters detected is greater than zero. However, because the

SRC parameter is always detected, you are guaranteed that `externalParamCount()` will return a value of at least 1.

For this example, the HTML of the embedded Shockwave movie is as follows:

```
<EMBED SRC="params.dcr" WIDTH=496 HEIGHT=200 sw1="hello" swText="This is my text."
swName="Joe Bob"  myCustomParameter="123 abc doh ray me">
```

When the Shockwave movie runs, the output to the stage would look something like the following:

```
Parameters detected: 7
SRC = params.dcr
WIDTH = 496
HEIGHT = 200
sw1 = hello
swText = This is my text.
swName = Joe Bob
myCustomParameter = 123 abc doh ray me
```

Using Shockwave Lingo Offline

The new Lingo commands you have learned are actually executed by the Shockwave plug-in and are not built into Director. Thus, when you are testing your movies in Director before putting them online, you need to trick Director into allowing the Shockwave Lingo commands to parse.

The best way to accomplish this task is to create an external cast with dummy Shockwave handlers that will disable the `Script Error: handler not defined` alerts. (The commands themselves will not function beyond whatever output you have them fake.) When you are finished testing your movie and are ready to try it in your browser, unlink the external cast. In the simplest use, have each dummy handler do nothing but allow your scripts to compile without `handler not defined` errors. If you need to have the handlers return sample values, however, you must add some custom scripting.

Whoever first thought of this idea deserves our thanks. This practice has become so common among Shockwave developers today that it is hard to imagine making Shockwave movies without it. Listing 25.1 is a sample movie script that you can use to start your own dummy handlers. Some of them do nothing more make a note in the message window; others are examples of how to fake the output of a Shockwave handler for offline testing. The script in Listing 25.1 is only one way to accomplish this, and considerably more sophiticated scripts are often made available by Director users on the Internet (see Figure 25.9). See "Online Resources for Shockwave Developers" for some ideas of where to look.

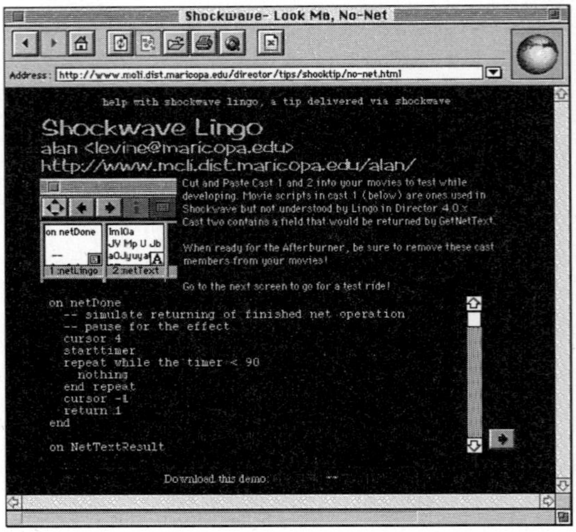

FIGURE 25.9.
One of several public-domain Shockwave movies that can help you do offline testing.

Creating an External Cast

To create a set of dummy Shockwave handlers for yourself, follow these steps:

1. Select `Modify | Movie | Casts`.
2. In the window that appears, click the `New` button.
3. In the window that appears, set the `Name` field to **SWdummy.cst** or something that you will remember.
4. Select the `External` radio button next to the `Storage` option. Leave the `Use in current movie` check box unchecked.
5. Click the `OK` button.
6. Create a Movie Script cast member and place the script found in Listing 25.1 into it.
7. Save the external cast file.

Listing 25.1. `SWdummy.cst`.

```
-- The following handlers should be placed in a Movie Script in an
-- external cast member. They will disable the "Handler not defined"
-- error in Director while you are making a Shockwave movie. Most of
-- these handlers only output a result to the message window for your
-- convenience. You can modify them to fit the conditions of your own
-- movies as needed.

on getNetText uri
  put "Shockwave: getNetText " & uri
end

on getLatestNetID
  put "Shockwave: getLatestNetID"
```

```
    -- Your script will expect a returned value from this handler.
    -- You should modify this script to return a sample value
    -- of what your script is looking for. This example assigns a random integer
    -- to your taskID.
return random(10000)
end

on getPref prefName
  put "Shockwave: getPref " & prefName
  -- Your script will expect a returned value from this handler.

  -- You should add to this script so that it will return a string
  -- in the same format your preference file will be in.
end

on gotoNetMovie uri
  put "Shockwave: gotoNetMovie " & uri
  alert "The next movie to play would be: " & uri
end

on gotoNetPage uri, target
  if the paramCount = 1 then
    put "Shockwave: gotoNetPage " & uri
    alert "The next page to load would be: " & uri
  else
    if the paramCount = 2 then
      put "Shockwave: gotoNetPage " & uri & "#" & target
      alert "The next page to load would be: " & uri & "#" & target
    end if
  end if
end

on netAbort taskID
  if the paramCount = 0 then
    put "Shockwave: netAbort()"
  else
    put "Shockwave: netAbort " & taskID
  end if
end

on netDone taskID
  if the paramCount = 0 then
    put "Shockwave: netDone()"
  else
    put "Shockwave: netDone " & taskID
  end if
end

on netError taskID
  if the paramCount = 0 then
    put "Shockwave: netError()"
  else
    put "Shockwave: netError " & taskID
  end if
end

on netLastModDate uri
  put "Shockwave: netLastModDate " & uri
```


continues

Listing 25.1. continued

```
  -- Your script will expect a returned value from this handler.
  -- You should modify this script to return a sample value
  -- of what your script is looking for.
  return the date
end

on netMIME uri
  put "Shockwave: netMIME " & uri
  -- Your script will expect a returned value from this handler.
  -- You should modify this script to return a sample value
  -- of what your script is looking for.
  return "application/x-director"
end

on netStatus msg
  put "Shockwave: netStatus -> " & msg
end

on netTextResult taskID
  if the paramCount = 0 then
    put "Shockwave: netTextResult()"
    return "This is sample text."
  else
    put "Shockwave: netTextResult " & taskID
    set mySample="This is sample text from taskID " & taskID
    return mySample
  end if
end

on preLoadNetThing uri
  put "Shockwave: preLoadNetThing " & uri
end

on setPref prefName, prefValue
  put "Shockwave: setPref " & prefName & " = " & prefValue
end

on externalParamCount
  put "Shockwave: externalParamCount()"
  -- Your script will expect a returned value from this handler.
  -- You should modify this script to return a sample value
  -- of what your script is looking for.
end

on externalParamName param
  put "Shockwave: externalParamName " & param
  -- Your script will expect a returned value from this handler.
  -- You should modify this script to return a sample value
  -- of what your script is looking for.
end

on externalParamValue param
  put "Shockwave: externalParamValue " & param
  -- Your script will expect a returned value from this handler.
  -- You should modify this script to return a sample value
  -- of what your script is looking for.
end
```

Linking an External Cast

To link an external cast, follow these steps:

1. Select `Modify | Movie | Casts`.
2. In the window that appears, click the `Link` button. (See Figure 25.10.) In the dialog box that appears, locate the external cast you saved and click the `Open` button.

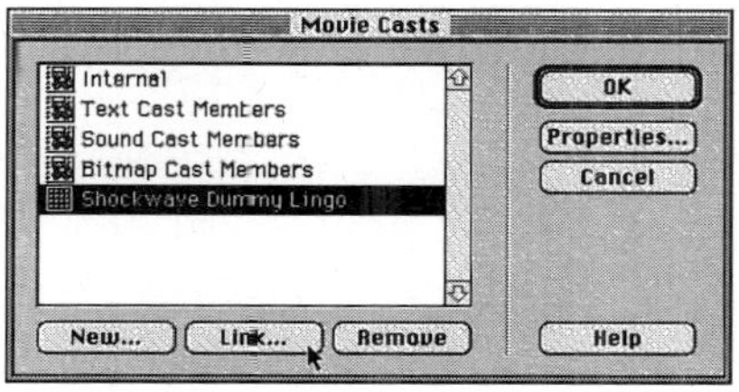

FIGURE 25.10.
The Movie Casts window.

Now your movie will be able to use all the Shockwave dummy handlers that are in your external cast. You can't use an external cast with an online movie, though, so remember to unlink it when you are done testing offline.

Unlinking an External Cast

To unlink an external cast, follow these steps:

1. Select `Modify | Movie | Casts`.
2. In the window that appears, highlight the external cast and click the `Remove` button.

Compressing Your Shockwave Movies with Afterburner

Macromedia has made a compression Xtra for Director called Afterburner freely available to Shockwave developers. It will take any loaded Director `.dir` file and "burn" a compressed version of the file for use online. The resulting "burned" file has the extension of `.dcr` and can only be accessed within a browser equipped with the Shockwave plug-in or control. A movie compressed with Afterburner cannot be examined for contents or Lingo scripting and is often compressed from 60 to 40 percent of the original file size.

You can, of course, leave your raw Director movie (`.dir`) in its unprotected format for testing purposes, but anyone with Director will be able to open your file. You can also use a protected movie (`.dxr`), but as with a `.DIR` file, a significant amount of file space is wasted.

The process of burning an Afterburner file is simple:

1. If you don't already have it, download Afterburner from Macromedia and go through the installation process. The Afterburner Xtra is added to the others in your `Director Xtras` folder.
2. Open the movie you intend to burn into Director.

3. Select Xtras | Afterburner.
4. Name and save the Shockwave (.dcr) file.

Watch the little progress bar march along, and you will have instant Shockwave! (See Figure 25.11.) There is typically a list of concerns and workarounds that Director issues with each release of the Afterburner Xtra. Consult the Read Me files that come with the Afterburner Xtra for this information.

FIGURE 25.11.
Afterburner at work compressing a .dir file.

Using Streamed Audio with Shockwave

One of the newer features of Shockwave is the capability to play streaming audio files. This powerful feature allows the user to hear an audio file as it is downloading rather than having to wait for the download to be completed. Audio can be compressed in a variety of ways to best suit the intended audience. In a best-case scenario for users with T1 access, you can deliver CD-quality audio in real time.

At the time of this writing, Shockwave audio was quite new to the Web scene and still had some glitches to be worked out by Macromedia, especially with cross-platform creation of streamed audio files. Committing anything to print here would have been premature, so I encourage you to visit Macromedia's site at http://www.macromedia.com for current developers' information on using Shockwave audio.

Online Resources for Shockwave Developers

There are many Web sites that make good starting places for getting help and hints on doing your own Shockwave projects. Macromedia's Shockwave site is the jumping-off point for just about everything you will do with Shockwave. Go here for the latest downloads, technical releases, and the famous Shocked Site of the Day gallery. (See Figure 25.12.) The URL is as follows:

```
http://www.macromedia.com/shockwave/
```

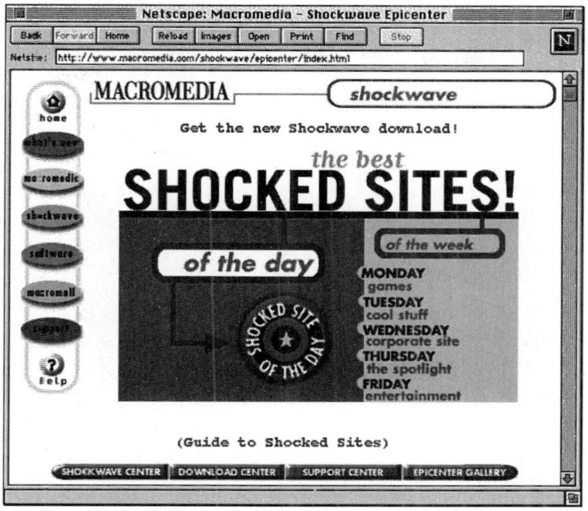

FIGURE 25.12.
Macromedia's listing of some hot new Shockwave sites.

Perhaps the best Shockwave-related e-mail listserv in circulation, the ShockeR listserv is frequented by some of the best minds in the industry. You will find the brains behind the latest developments in Shockwave technology lurking here, as well as a few Macromedia employees who have the inside scoop on how things work. The URL is as follows:

`http://www.ShockeR.com/ShockeR/`

Director Web is an all-around good resource for Director users, and the resources and information are not limited to Shockwave. It is also the starting point for getting yourself on the Direct-L listserv, arguably *the* e-mail group for Director users. The URL is as follows:

`http://www.mcli.dist.maricopa.edu/director/`

Summary

Developing your own Shockwave movies for the Web is an exciting and rewarding way to use your Macromedia Director skills. As with anything related to the Internet, however, there is no way a single chapter or book can hold everything you need to know about Shockwave. Use this chapter as a reference to the Shockwave basics, and make a habit of checking Macromedia's Web site for updates and new features to Shockwave. For added support, join a user group or listserv that discusses Shockwave and Director issues. Don't hesitate to experiment with everything you've read here, and above all, have fun!

Part VI

IN THIS PART

Adding Interactivity with CGI

CHAPTER 26

Writing CGI Scripts

by William Robert Stanek

IN THIS CHAPTER

Using CGI scripts, you can create powerful, personalized, and professional Web publications that readers can interact with. CGI scripts are external programs that act as gateways between the Web server and other applications. You can use CGI scripts to process input from readers and thus open a two-way communication channel with your readers. Reader input can be data from fill-out forms, keywords for a database query, or values that describe the reader's browser and connection.

Your CGI scripts can use this input to add entries to an index, to search databases, to create customized documents on the fly, and much more. Yet the most wonderful thing about CGI scripts is that they hide their complexities from users. If you've used a fill-out form or an image map on the Web, you've probably used a gateway script without even knowing it. With CGI scripts, everything seems to happen automatically. You enter data and click a mouse button, and a moment later, a result is displayed. Learning what happens between the click of the mouse button and the display of the result is what this chapter is all about. This chapter explains what you need to know about CGI scripts: what they are, how to use them, and why to use them.

What Are CGI Scripts?

CGI scripts are external programs that run on the Web server. You can use CGI scripts to create highly interactive Web publications. The standard that defines how external programs are used on Web servers and how they interact with other applications is the common gateway interface. The three keywords that comprise the name of the standard—common, gateway, and interface—describe how the standard works:

Common. By specifying a common way for scripts to be accessed, CGI enables anyone, regardless of platform, to pass information to a CGI script.

Gateway. By defining the link (gateway) between the script, the server, and other applications, CGI makes it possible for external programs to accept generalized input and pass information to other applications.

Interface. By describing the way external programs can be accessed by users (the interface), CGI reduces the complex process of interfacing with external programs to a few basic procedures.

The developers of CGI worked these key concepts into the CGI standard to create a powerful and extendable advanced feature for Web publishers that shields readers of your publications from its complexities. Readers need only click an area of an image map or submit their fill-out forms after completing them. Everything after the click of the mouse button seems to happen automatically, and the readers don't have to worry about the how or why. Web publishers, however, must understand how CGI scripts work, especially if they want to take advantage of the ways CGI can be used to create powerful Web publications.

Although readers see only the results of their submissions or queries, behind the scenes many things are happening. The process consists of the following steps:

1. The reader's browser passes the input to the Web server.
2. The server, in turn, passes the input to a CGI script.
3. The CGI script processes the input, passes it off to another application if necessary, and sends the output to the Web server.
4. The Web server passes the output back to the reader's browser. The output from a CGI script can be anything from the results of a database search to a completely new document generated as a result of the reader's input.

On UNIX systems, CGI scripts are located in a directory called `cgi-bin` in the `usr` file system, and CGI utilities are located in a directory called `cgi-src` in the `usr` file system. On other systems, your Web server documentation explains where CGI scripts and utilities should be placed.

Choosing a Programming Language for Your CGI Scripts

CGI scripts are also called *gateway scripts*. The term *script* comes from the UNIX environment, in which shell scripts abound, but gateway scripts don't have to be in the format of a UNIX script. You can write gateway scripts in almost any computer language that produces an executable file. The most common languages for scripts are the following:

Bourne Shell

C Shell

C/C++

Perl

Python

Tcl

Visual Basic

When you use the traditional scripting languages, your scripts are located on the server and are executed when a user submits a fill-out form. Scripts located on a server are called server-side scripts. In contrast, some scripts, called client-side scripts, are embedded in HTML documents and are executed by your browser. JavaScript and VBScript are two up-and-coming client-side scripting languages.

The best programming language to write your script in is one that works with your Web server and meets your needs. Preferably, the language should already be available on the Web server, and you should be proficient in it (or at least have some knowledge of the language). Keep in mind that most user input is in the form of text that must be manipulated in some way, which makes support for text strings and their manipulation critical.

The easiest way to determine whether a language is available on a Web server is to ask the Webmaster or system administrator responsible for the server. Because most Web servers operate on UNIX systems, you may also be able to use the `which` or `whereis` UNIX commands to check on the availability of a particular language. To use commands on UNIX systems, type `which` or `whereis` at the shell prompt and follow the command with a keyword on which you want to search, such as the name of the programming language you want to use. For example, to see whether your UNIX server supports Perl, type either one of the following lines:

```
which perl

whereis perl
```

As Perl, C/C++, and UNIX shell are the most popular languages for scripts, the following sections look briefly at these languages, with emphasis on why and when to use them. Each section contains a checklist for features and systems supported that contains the following categories:

Operating system support lists the operating systems on which the language can be used.

Programming level specifies the level of difficulty involved in using and learning the language.

Complexity of processing indicates the complexity of the tasks you can process with the language.

Text-handling capabilities are the capability of the language to manipulate text and strings.

The sections on common scripting languages are followed by discussions of the newest scripting languages: JavaScript and VBScript. Both JavaScript and VBScript are hot topics on the Net right now. If you want to be on the cutting edge of Internet technologies, keep both eyes on these languages.

Using UNIX Shell

Operating system support: UNIX

Programming level: Basic

Complexity of processing: Basic

Text-handling capabilities: Moderately advanced

The UNIX operating system is in wide use in business, education, and research sectors. There are almost as many variations of the UNIX operating system as there are platforms that use it. Even platforms produced by the same manufacturer use different variants of the UNIX operating system. For example, DEC has variants of UNIX for the Dec-Alpha, Decstation, and Dec OSF platforms.

What these operating systems have in common is the core environment on which they are based. Most UNIX operating systems are based on Berkeley UNIX (BSD), AT&T System V, or a combination of BSD and System V. Both BSD and System V support three shell scripting languages:

Bourne shell

C shell

Korn shell

TIP

You can quickly identify the shell scripting language that is being used by examining the first line of a script. Bourne shell scripts generally have this first line:

```
#!/bin/sh
```

C shell scripts generally have a blank first line or the following:

```
#!/bin/csh
```

Korn shell scripts generally have this first line:

```
#!/bin/ksh
```

All UNIX shells are interpreted languages, which means the scripts you create do not have to be compiled. Bourne shell is the most basic shell. C shell is an advanced shell with many features of the C programming language. Because Bourne shell uses a completely different syntax than C shell, scripts written in Bourne are not compatible with scripts written in C. If you create a script in Bourne shell and later want to use C shell to interpret the script, you must rewrite the script for C shell.

Many programmers often want to merge the simplicity of Bourne shell with the advanced features of C shell, and this is where Korn shell comes in handy. Korn shell has the same functionality as the Bourne shell and incorporates many features of the C shell. Any shells you've written in Bourne shell can be interpreted directly by the Korn interpreter. This capability prevents you from having to rewrite a Bourne shell script when you later find you want to use a feature supported by Korn. Although the Korn shell is gaining popularity, Bourne and C shell are the two most widely used UNIX shells.

You can change your current shell any time from the shell prompt by typing one of the following:

`/bin/sh` to change to Bourne shell

`/bin/csh` to change to C shell

`/bin/ksh` to change to Korn shell

Usually, you will see differences between the various shells immediately. For example, the default command prompt for Bourne shell is the dollar sign, and the default command prompt for C shell is usually your host name and user ID followed by a colon. Beyond this difference, C shell supports a history function, aliasing of commands, and many other controls that the Bourne shell does not. However, these differences are generally not important to the CGI programmer. Your primary concern should be the features that the shell directly supports and how scripts behave when executed in it.

Bourne shell is the smallest of the shells and the most efficient. Consequently, a Bourne shell script generally executes faster and uses fewer system resources. When you want more advanced features, such as arrays, use Korn shell. Korn shell has more overhead than Bourne shell and requires slightly more system resources. When you want to make advanced function calls or assignments, use C shell. Because C shell is larger than Bourne and Korn shell, scripts written in C shell generally have higher overhead and use more system resources.

Although UNIX shells have good built-in facilities for handing text, such as `sed`, `awk`, and `grep`, they are not as powerful or extendable as traditional programming languages. Consider using shell scripts when you want to perform simple tasks and moderately advanced text or file manipulation.

Using C/C++

Operating system support: UNIX, DOS, Windows, Mac, and others

Programming level: Advanced

Complexity of processing: Advanced

Text-handling capabilities: Difficult to use

When you want your scripts to perform complex tasks, you call in the big guns. Two of the most advanced languages used in CGI scripts are C and C++. C is the most popular programming language in use today. C++ is the object-oriented successor to C. Both C and C++ are advanced programming languages that require you to compile your scripts before you can use them. The major advantages of C and C++ is that they enjoy widespread use and versions are available for virtually every operating system you can think of.

Use C (rather than C++) when your scripts must execute swiftly and use minimal system resources. Compiled C programs are very small—tiny compared to programs with similar functionality programmed in other languages. Small programs use minimal system resources and execute quickly. However, C is a very complex language with difficult-to-use facilities for manipulating text. Therefore, if you are not proficient in C, be wary of using C to perform advanced text string processing.

Use C++ when certain functions of your scripts will be reused and when long-term development costs are a major concern. C++ is an object-oriented language that enables you to use libraries of functions. These functions form the core of your CGI scripts and can be reused in other CGI scripts. For example, you can use one function to sort the user's input, another function to search a database using the input, and another function to display the output as an HTML document. Keep in mind that C++ is an object-oriented language that is very different from other languages. If you have not used an object-oriented language before, are not familiar with C, and plan to use C++ for your CGI scripts, be prepared for a steep learning curve.

Using Perl

Operating system support: UNIX, DOS, Windows, Mac, and others

Programming level: Advanced

Complexity of processing: Advanced

Text-handling capabilities: Easy to use

If you want to be on the inside track of CGI programming, learn and use the Practical Extraction and Report Language (Perl). Perl combines elements of C with UNIX shell features like `awk`, `sed`, and `grep` to create a powerful language for processing text strings and generating reports. Because most of the processing done by CGI scripts involves text manipulation, Perl is rapidly becoming the most widely used language for CGI scripts. As with C and C++, a major advantage of Perl is its widespread use. Versions of Perl are available for virtually every operating system you can think of. You can use Perl to do the following tasks:

- Easily manipulate files, text, and processes
- Extract text strings and manipulate them in complex ways
- Quickly and easily search files, databases, and indexes
- Print advanced reports based on extracted data

Perl, like Bourne and C shell, is an interpreted language. However, Perl does not have the limitations of most interpreted languages. You can use Perl to manipulate extremely large amounts of data, and you can quickly scan files using sophisticated pattern-matching techniques. Perl strings are not limited in size. The entire contents of a file can be used as a single string. Perl's syntax is similar to C's. Many basic Perl constructs, like `if`, `for`, and `while` statements, are used just as you use them in C.

TIP

Like a UNIX shell script, a Perl script will usually specify the path to the source routines in the first line. Therefore, the first line of a Perl script should specify the path to where Perl is installed on the system. This path is usually one of the following:

```
#!/usr/local/perl

#!/usr/local/bin/perl
```

Perl is surprisingly easy to learn and use, especially if you know the basics of C or UNIX shell. Perl scripts are usually faster than UNIX shell scripts and are slightly slower than compiled C/C++ scripts. You should use Perl whenever you have large amounts of text to manipulate.

Using JavaScript

JavaScript is a client-side scripting language based on the Java programming language developed by Sun Microsystems. This powerful up-and-coming scripting language is being developed by Netscape Communications Corporation, and, as you may have guessed, Netscape Navigator 2.0/3.0 fully supports JavaScript.

Netscape Navigator 2.0/3.0 interprets JavaScript programs embedded directly in an HTML page, and, just like Java applets, these programs are fully interactive. JavaScript can recognize and respond to mouse clicks, form input, and page navigation. This capability means your pages can "intelligently" react to user input. The JavaScript language resembles the Java programming language—with a few important exceptions, as you can see from the comparisons in the following lists:

JavaScript is the following:

- An interpreted language
- Object-based, without classes and inheritance
- Embedded in HTML
- Loosely typed with undeclared variable data types
- Checked at run time
- Secure because you cannot write to hard disk

Java is the following:

- Compiled to bytecode before execution on client
- Object-oriented, with classes and inheritance
- Referenced from HTML, with separate source code
- Strongly typed with declared variable data
- Checked at compile time and at run time
- Secure because you cannot write to hard disk

JavaScript is designed to complement the Java language and has some terrific features for Web publishers. For example, by creating a JavaScript program that passes parameters to a Java applet, you could use the JavaScript program as an easy-to-use front-end for your Java applets. Because a Web publisher is not required to know about classes to use JavaScript and to pass parameters to a Java applet, JavaScript provides a simple solution for publishers who want to use the features of the Java language but don't want to learn how to program in Java. The JavaScript scripting language is featured in the chapters in Part VIII, "JavaScript and Java."

Using VBScript

With VBScript, Microsoft proves once again that it understands the tools developers need. Visual Basic Script is a subset of Visual Basic and is used to create highly interactive documents on the Web. Similar to JavaScript, programs written in VBScript are embedded in the body of your HTML documents.

Visual Basic Script also enables dynamic use of OLE scripting management with ActiveX Controls. The Object Linking and Embedding of scripts enables Web publishers to dynamically embed VBScript run-time environments. Basically, this capability enables you to use VBScripts as plug-in modules. You can, for example, embed a VBScript program in your Web document that calls other VBScript programs to use as plug-ins. The exact plug-in calls could be dynamically selected based on user input. The VBScript scripting language is featured in the chapters of Part VII, "ActiveX and VBScript."

Why Use CGI Scripts?

At this point, you may be worried about having to program. You may also be wondering why you would want to use gateway scripts at all. These are valid concerns. Learning a programming language isn't easy, but as you will see later, you may never have to program at all. Dozens of ready-to-use CGI scripts are freely available on the Web. Often you can use these existing programs to meet your needs.

The primary reason to use CGI scripts is to automate what would otherwise be a manual and probably time-consuming process. Using CGI scripts benefits both you and your reader. The reader gets simplicity, automated responses to input, easy ways to make submissions, and fast ways to conduct searches. Gateway scripts enable you to automatically process orders, queries, and much more. CGI programs are commonly used to do the following tasks:

- Process input, typically search strings, and output a document containing the results of the search
- Validate user identification and password information and grant readers access to restricted areas of the Web site
- Process input from image maps and direct the reader to associated documents
- Add the reader's feedback or survey responses to a database or index
- Track visitors to Web pages and post continually updated numbers to the Web page as it is accessed
- Generate documents based on the type of browser the reader is using
- Perform post-submission processing and possibly output results for the reader

How CGI Scripts Work

Gateway scripts are used to process input submitted by readers of your Web publications. The input usually consists of environment variables that the Web server passes to the gateway script. Environment variables describe the information being passed, such as the version of CGI used on the server, the type of data, the size of the data, and other important information. Gateway scripts can also receive command-line arguments and standard input. To execute a CGI script, the script must exist on the server you are referencing. You must also have a server that is both capable of executing gateway scripts and configured to handle the type of script you plan to use.

Readers pass information to a CGI script by activating a link containing a reference to the script. The gateway script processes the input and formats the results as output that the Web server can use. The Web server takes the results and passes them back to the reader's browser. The browser displays the output for the reader.

The output from a gateway script begins with a header containing a directive to the server. Currently, the three valid server directives are Content-type, Location, and Status. The header can consist of a directive in the format of an HTTP header followed by a blank line. The blank line separates the header from the data you are passing back to the browser. Output containing Location and Status directives usually consists of a single line because the directive contained on the Location or Status line is all that the server needs, and when there is no subsequent data, you do not need to insert a blank line. The server interprets the output, sets environment variables, and passes the output to the client.

Any transaction between a client and server has many parts. These parts can be broken down into nine steps as follows:

1. The client passes input to a server.
2. The server sets environment variables pertaining to input.
3. The server passes input as variables to the named CGI script.
4. The server passes command line input or a standard input stream to the CGI script if one is present.
5. The script processes the input.
6. The script returns output to the server. This output always contains a qualified header and contains a body if additional data is present.
7. The server sets environment variables pertaining to output.
8. The server passes output to the client.
9. The client processes input from the server.

Input to CGI Scripts

When a user activates a link to a gateway script, input is sent to the server. The server formats this data into environment variables and checks to see whether additional data was submitted via the standard input stream.

Environment Variables

Input to CGI scripts is usually in the form of environment variables. The environment variables passed to gateway scripts are associated with the browser requesting information from the server, the server processing the request, and the data passed in the request. Environment variables are case-sensitive and are normally used as described in this section. Although some environment variables are system-specific, many environment variables are standard. The standard variables are shown in Table 26.1.

As later examples show, environment variables are set automatically whenever reader input is passed to a server. The primary reason to learn about these variables is to better understand how input is passed to CGI scripts, but you should also learn about these variables so you know how to take advantage of them when necessary.

Table 26.1. Standard environment variables.

Variable	*Purpose*
`AUTH_TYPE`	Specifies the authentication method and is used to validate a user's access.
`CONTENT_LENGTH`	Used to provide a way of tracking the length of the data string as a numeric value.
`CONTENT_TYPE`	Indicates the MIME type of data.
`GATEWAY_INTERFACE`	Indicates which version of the CGI standard the server is using.
`HTTP_ACCEPT`	Indicates the MIME content types the browser will accept, as passed to the gateway script via the server.
`HTTP_USER_AGENT`	Indicates the type of browser used to send the request, as passed to the gateway script via the server.
`PATH_INFO`	Identifies the extra information included in the URL after the identification of the CGI script.
`PATH_TRANSLATED`	Set by the server based on the `PATH_INFO` variable. The server translates the `PATH_INFO` variable into this variable.
`QUERY_STRING`	Set to the query string (if the URL contains a query string).

continues

Table 26.1. continued

Variable	*Purpose*
REMOTE_ADDR	Identifies the Internet Protocol address of the remote computer making the request.
REMOTE_HOST	Identifies the name of the machine making the request.
REMOTE_IDENT	Identifies the machine making the request.
REMOTE_USER	Identifies the user name as authenticated by the user.
REQUEST_METHOD	Indicates the method by which the request was made.
SCRIPT_NAME	Identifies the virtual path to the script being executed.
SERVER_NAME	Identifies the server by its host name, alias, or IP address.
SERVER_PORT	Identifies the port number the server received the request on.
SERVER_PROTOCOL	Indicates the protocol of the request sent to the server.
SERVER_SOFTWARE	Identifies the Web server software.

AUTH_TYPE

The AUTH_TYPE variable provides access control to protected areas of the Web server and can be used only on servers that support user authentication. If an area of the Web site has no access control, the AUTH_TYPE variable has no value associated with it. If an area of the Web site has access control, the AUTH_TYPE variable is set to a specific value that identifies the authentication scheme being used. Otherwise, the variable has no value associated with it. A simple challenge-response authorization mechanism is implemented under current versions of HTTP.

Using this mechanism, the server can challenge a client's request and the client can respond. To do this, the server sets a value for the AUTH_TYPE variable and the client supplies a matching value. The next step is to authenticate the user. Using the basic authentication scheme, the user's browser must supply authentication information that uniquely identifies the user. This information includes a user ID and password.

Under the current implementation of HTTP, HTTP 1.0, the basic authentication scheme is the most commonly used authentication method. To specify this method, set the AUTH_TYPE variable as follows:

```
AUTH_TYPE = Basic
```

CONTENT_LENGTH

The CONTENT_LENGTH variable provides a way of tracking the length of the data string. This variable tells the client and server how much data to read on the standard input stream. The value of the variable corresponds to the number of characters in the data passed with the request. If no data is being passed, the variable has no value.

As long as the characters are represented as octets, the value of the CONTENT_LENGTH variable will be the precise number of characters passed as standard input or standard output. Thus, if 25 characters are passed and they are represented as octets, the CONTENT_LENGTH variable will have the following value:

```
CONTENT_LENGTH = 25
```

NOTE

An octet is a set of eight bits. Thus, when characters are represented as octets, they are passed in eight-bit groupings.

CONTENT_TYPE

The CONTENT_TYPE variable indicates the data's MIME type. MIME typing is a feature of HTTP 1.0 and is not available on servers using HTTP 0.9. This variable is set only when attached data is passed using the standard input or output stream. The value assigned to the variable identifies the MIME type and subtype as follows:

```
CONTENT_TYPE = type/subtype
```

MIME types are broken down into basic type categories. Each data type category has a primary subtype associated with it. Table 26.2 shows the basic MIME types and their descriptions.

Table 26.2. Basic MIME types.

Type	*Description*
application	Binary data that can be executed or used with another application
audio	A sound file that requires an output device to preview
image	A picture that requires an output device to preview
message	An encapsulated mail message
multipart	Data consisting of multiple parts and possibly many data types
text	Textual data that can be represented in any character set or formatting language
video	A video file that requires an output device to preview
x-world	Experimental data type for world files

MIME subtypes are defined in three categories: primary, additionally defined, and extended. The primary subtype is the primary type of data adopted for use as a MIME content type.

Additionally defined data types are additional subtypes that have been officially adopted as MIME content types. Extended data types are experimental subtypes that have not been officially adopted as MIME content types. You can easily identify extended subtypes because they begin with the letter *x* followed by a hyphen. Table 26.3 lists common MIME types and their descriptions.

Table 26.3. Common MIME types.

Type/Subtype	*Description*
`application/mac-binhex40`	Macintosh binary-formatted data
`application/msword`	Microsoft Word document
`application/octet-stream`	Binary data that can be executed or used with another application
`application/pdf`	ACROBAT PDF document
`application/postscript`	Postscript-formatted data
`application/rtf`	Rich Text Format (RTF) document
`application/x-compress`	Data that has been compressed using UNIX `compress`
`application/x-dvi`	Device-independent file
`application/x-gzip`	Data that has been compressed using UNIX `gzip`
`application/x-latex`	LATEX document
`application/x-tar`	Data that has been archived using UNIX `tar`
`application/x-zip-compressed`	Data that has been compressed using PKZip or WinZip
`audio/basic`	Audio in a nondescript format
`audio/x-aiff`	Audio in Apple AIFF format
`audio/x-wav`	Audio in Microsoft WAV format
`image/gif`	Image in GIF format
`image/jpeg`	Image in JPEG format
`image/tiff`	Image in TIFF format
`image/x-portable-bitmap`	Portable bitmap
`image/x-portable-graymap`	Portable graymap
`image/x-portable-pixmap`	Portable pixmap
`image/x-xbitmap`	X-bitmap
`image/x-xpixmap`	X-pixmap
`message/external-body`	Message with external data source
`message/partial`	Fragmented or partial message

Type/Subtype	*Description*
`message/rfc822`	RFC 822-compliant message
`multipart/alternative`	Data with alternative formats
`multipart/digest`	Multipart message digest
`multipart/mixed`	Multipart message with data in multiple formats
`multipart/parallel`	Multipart data with parts that should be viewed simultaneously
`text/html`	HTML-formatted text
`text/plain`	Plain text with no HTML formatting included
`video/mpeg`	Video in the MPEG format
`video/quicktime`	Video in the Apple QuickTime format
`video/x-msvideo`	Video in the Microsoft AVI format
`x-world/x-vrml`	VRML world file

Some MIME content types can be used with additional parameters. These content types include `text/plain`, `text/html`, and all multipart message data. The `charset` parameter, which is optional, is used with the `text/plain` type to identify the character set used for the data. If a `charset` is not specified, the default value `charset=us-ascii` is assumed. Other values for `charset` include any character set approved by the International Standards Organization. These character sets are defined by ISO-8859-1 to ISO-8859-9 and are specified as follows:

```
CONTENT_TYPE = text/plain; charset=iso-8859-1
```

The `version` parameter, which also is optional, is used with the `text/html` type to identify the version of HTML used. If this parameter is set, the browser reading the data interprets the data if the browser supports the version of HTML specified. The following document conforms to the HTML 3.2 specification:

```
CONTENT_TYPE = text/html; version=3.2
```

The `boundary` parameter, which is required, is used with multipart data to identify the boundary string that separates message parts. The `boundary` value is set to a string of 1 to 70 characters. Although the string cannot end in a space, it can contain any valid letter or number and can include spaces and a limited set of special characters. `Boundary` parameters are unique strings that are defined as follows:

```
CONTENT_TYPE = multipart/mixed; boundary=boundary_string
```

GATEWAY_INTERFACE

The GATEWAY_INTERFACE variable indicates which version of the CGI specification the server is using. The value assigned to the variable identifies the name and version of the specification used as follows:

```
GATEWAY_INTERFACE = name/version
```

The current version of the CGI specification is 1.1. A server conforming to this version would set the GATEWAY_INTERFACE variable as follows:

```
GATEWAY_INTERFACE = CGI/1.1
```

HTTP_ACCEPT

The HTTP_ACCEPT variable defines the types of data the client will accept. The acceptable values are expressed as a type/subtype pair. Each type/subtype pair is separated by commas, as in

```
type/subtype, type/subtype
```

Most clients accept dozens of MIME types. The following lines identify all the MIME content types accepted by this particular client:

```
HTTP_ACCEPT = application/msword, application/octet-stream,
application/postscript, application/rtf, application/x-zip-compressed,
audio/basic, audio/x-aiff, audio/x-wav, image/gif, image/jpeg, image/tiff,
image/x-portable-bitmap, message/external-body, message/partial,
message/rfc822, multipart/alternative,
multipart/digest, multipart/mixed, multipart/parallel, text/html,
text/plain, video/mpeg, video/quicktime, video/x-msvideo
```

HTTP_USER_AGENT

The HTTP_USER_AGENT variable identifies the type of browser used to send the request. The acceptable values are expressed as *software type/version* or *library/version*. The following HTTP_USER_AGENT variable identifies Netscape Navigator Version 2.0:

```
HTTP_USER_AGENT = Mozilla/2.0
```

As you can see, Netscape uses the alias Mozilla to identify itself. The primary types of clients that set this variable are browsers, Web spiders, and robots. Although this variable is useful for identifying the type of client used to access a script, keep in mind that not all clients set this variable.

Here's a list of software type values used by popular browsers:

```
Arena
Enhanced NCSA Mosaic
Lynx
MacWeb
```

```
Mozilla
NCSA Mosaic
NetCruiser
WebExplorer
WinMosaic
```

These values are used by Web spiders:

```
Lycos
MOMSpider
WebCrawler
```

PATH_INFO

The PATH_INFO variable specifies extra path information and can be used to send additional information to a gateway script. The extra path information follows the URL to the gateway script referenced. Generally, this information is a virtual or relative path to a resource that the server must interpret. If the URL to the CGI script is specified in your document as

```
/usr/cgi-bin/formparse.pl/home.html
```

then the PATH_INFO variable would be set as follows:

```
PATH_INFO = /home.html
```

PATH_TRANSLATED

Servers translate the PATH_INFO variable into the PATH_TRANSLATED variable by inserting the default Web document's directory path in front of the extra path information. For example, if the PATH_INFO variable were set to home.html and the default directory were /usr/documents/pubs, the PATH_TRANSLATED variable would be set as follows:

```
PATH_TRANSLATED = /usr/documents/pubs/home.html
```

QUERY_STRING

The QUERY_STRING variable specifies an URL-encoded search string. You set this variable when you use the GET method to submit a fill-out form or when you use an ISINDEX query to search a document. The query string is separated from the URL by a question mark. The user submits all the information following the question mark separating the URL from the query string. The following is an example:

```
/usr/cgi-bin/formparse.pl?string
```

When the query string is URL-encoded, the browser encodes key parts of the string. The plus sign is a placeholder between words and acts as a substitute for spaces:

```
/usr/cgi-bin/formparse.pl?word1+word2+word3
```

Equal signs separate keys assigned by the publisher from values entered by the user. In the following example, `response` is the key assigned by the publisher, and `never` is the value entered by the user:

```
/usr/cgi-bin/formparse.pl?response=never
```

Ampersand symbols separate sets of keys and values. In the following example, `response` is the first key assigned by the publisher, and `sometimes` is the value entered by the user. The second key assigned by the publisher is `reason`, and the value entered by the user is `I am not really sure`:

```
/usr/cgi-bin/formparse.pl?response=sometimes&reason=I+am+not+really+sure
```

Finally, the percent sign is used to identify escape characters. Following the percent sign is an escape code for a special character expressed as a hexadecimal value. Here is how the previous query string could be rewritten using the escape code for an apostrophe:

```
/usr/cgi-bin/formparse.pl?response=sometimes&reason=I%27m+not+really+sure
```

REMOTE_ADDR

The `REMOTE_ADDR` variable is set to the Internet Protocol (IP) address of the remote computer making the request. The IP address is a numeric identifier for a networked computer. The following is an example of the `REMOTE_ADDR` variable:

```
REMOTE_ADDR = 205.1.20.11
```

REMOTE_HOST

The `REMOTE_HOST` variable specifies the name of the host computer making a request. This variable is set only if the server can figure out this information using a reverse lookup procedure. If this variable is set, the full domain and host name are used as follows:

```
REMOTE_HOST = www.tvp.com
```

REMOTE_IDENT

The `REMOTE_IDENT` variable identifies the remote user making a request. The variable is set only if the server and the remote machine making the request support the identification protocol. Further, information on the remote user is not always available, so you should not rely on it even when it *is* available. If the variable is set, the associated value is a fully expressed name that contains the domain information as well:

```
REMOTE_IDENT = william.www.tvp.com
```

REMOTE_USER

The REMOTE_USER variable is the user name as authenticated by the user, and as such is the only variable you should rely upon to identify a user. As with other types of user authentication, this variable is set only if the server supports user authentication and if the gateway script is protected. If the variable is set, the associated value is the user's identification as sent by the client to the server:

```
REMOTE_USER = william
```

REQUEST_METHOD

The REQUEST_METHOD variable specifies the method by which the request was made. For HTTP 1.0, the methods could be any of the following:

```
GET
HEAD
POST
PUT
DELETE
LINK
UNLINK
```

The GET, HEAD, and POST methods are the most commonly used request methods. Both GET and POST are used to submit forms. The HEAD method could be specified as follows:

```
REQUEST_METHOD = HEAD
```

SCRIPT_NAME

The SCRIPT_NAME variable specifies the virtual path to the script being executed. This information is useful if the script generates an HTML document that references the script. If the URL specified in your HTML document is

```
http://tvp.com/cgi-bin/formparse.pl
```

the SCRIPT_NAME variable is set as follows:

```
SCRIPT_NAME = /cgi-bin/formparse.pl
```

SERVER_NAME

The SERVER_NAME variable identifies the server by its host name, alias, or IP address. This variable is always set and could be specified as follows:

```
SERVER_NAME = tvp.com
```

SERVER_PORT

The `SERVER_PORT` variable specifies the port number on which the server received the request. This information can be interpreted from the URL to the script if necessary. However, most servers use the default port of 80 for HTTP requests. If the URL specified in your HTML document is

```
http://www.ncsa.edu:8080/cgi-bin/formparse.pl
```

the `SERVER_PORT` variable is set as follows:

```
SERVER_PORT = 8080
```

SERVER_PROTOCOL

The `SERVER_PROTOCOL` variable identifies the protocol used to send the request. The value assigned to the variable identifies the name and version of the protocol used. The format is *name/version*, such as `HTTP/1.0`. The variable is set as follows:

```
SERVER_PROTOCOL = HTTP/1.0
```

SERVER_SOFTWARE

The `SERVER_SOFTWARE` variable identifies the name and version of the server software. The format for values assigned to the variable is *name/version*, such as `CERN/2.17`. The variable is set as follows:

```
SERVER_SOFTWARE = CERN/2.17
```

CGI Standard Input

Most input sent to a Web server is used to set environment variables, yet not all input fits neatly into an environment variable. When a user submits data to be processed by a gateway script, this data is received as an URL-encoded search string or through the standard input stream. The server knows how to process this data because of the method (either `POST` or `GET` in HTTP 1.0) used to submit the data.

Sending data as standard input is the most direct way to send data. The server tells the gateway script how many eight-bit sets of data to read from standard input. The script opens the standard input stream and reads the specified amount of data. Although long URL-encoded search strings may get truncated, data sent on the standard input stream will not. Consequently, the standard input stream is the preferred way to pass data.

Clarifying CGI Input

You can identify a submission method when you create your fill-out forms. Under HTTP 1.0, two submission methods for forms exist. The HTTP `GET` method uses URL-encoded search strings. When a server receives an URL-encoded search string, the server assigns the value of the search string to the `QUERY_STRING` variable.

The HTTP `POST` method uses the standard input streams. When a server receives data by the standard input stream, the server assigns the value associated with the length of the input stream to the `CONTENT_LENGTH` variable.

Supose you have a Web document containing a form with three key fields: `NAME`, `ADDRESS`, and `PHONE_NUMBER`. Assume the URL to the script is `http://www.tvp.com/cgi-bin/survey.pl`, and the user responds as follows:

```
Sandy Brown
12 Sunny Lane WhoVille, USA
987-654-3210
```

Identical information submitted using the `GET` and `POST` methods is treated differently by the server. When the `GET` method is used, the server sets the following environment variables, and then passes the input to the `survey.pl` script:

```
PATH=/bin:/usr/bin:/usr/etc:/usr/ucb
SERVER_SOFTWARE = CERN/3.0
SERVER_NAME = www.tvp.com
GATEWAY_INTERFACE = CGI/1.1
SERVER_PROTOCOL = HTTP/1.0
SERVER_PORT=80
REQUEST_METHOD = GET
HTTP_ACCEPT = text/plain, text/html, application/rtf, application/postscript,
audio/basic, audio/x-aiff, image/gif, image/jpeg, image/tiff, video/mpeg
PATH_INFO =
PATH_TRANSLATED =
SCRIPT_NAME = /cgi-bin/survey.pl
QUERY_STRING = NAME=Sandy+Brown&ADDRESS=12+Sunny+Lane+WhoVille,+USA
&PHONE_NUMBER=987-654-3210
REMOTE_HOST =
REMOTE_ADDR =
REMOTE_USER =
AUTH_TYPE =
CONTENT_TYPE =
CONTENT_LENGTH =
```

When the `POST` method is used, the server sets the following environment variables, and then passes the input to the `survey.pl` script:

```
PATH=/bin:/usr/bin:/usr/etc:/usr/ucb
SERVER_SOFTWARE = CERN/3.0
SERVER_NAME = www.tvp.com
GATEWAY_INTERFACE = CGI/1.1
SERVER_PROTOCOL = HTTP/1.0
SERVER_PORT=80
REQUEST_METHOD = POST
HTTP_ACCEPT = text/plain, text/html, application/rtf, application/postscript,
audio/basic, audio/x-aiff, image/gif, image/jpeg, image/tiff, video/mpeg
PATH_INFO =
PATH_TRANSLATED =
SCRIPT_NAME = /cgi-bin/survey.pl
QUERY_STRING =
```

```
REMOTE_HOST =
REMOTE_ADDR =
REMOTE_USER =
AUTH_TYPE =
CONTENT_TYPE = application/x-www-form-urlencoded
CONTENT_LENGTH = 81
```

The following POST-submitted data is passed to the gateway script through the standard input stream:

```
NAME=Sandy+Brown&ADDRESS=12+Sunny+Lane+WhoVille,+USA&PHONE_NUMBER=987-654-3210
```

Output from CGI Scripts

After the script finishes processing the input, the script should return output to the server. The server will then return the output to the client. Generally, this output is in the form of an HTTP response that includes a header followed by a blank line and a body. Although the CGI header output is strictly formatted, the body of the output is formatted in the manner you specify in the header. For example, the body can contain an HTML document for the client to display.

CGI Headers

CGI headers contain directives to the server. Currently, these three server directives are valid:

- Content-Type
- Location
- Status

A single header can contain one or all of the server directives. Your CGI script outputs these directives to the server. Although the header is followed by a blank line that separates the header from the body, the output does not have to contain a body.

Content Types Used in CGI Headers

The Content-Type field in a CGI header identifies the MIME type of the data you are sending back to the client. Usually the data output from a script is a fully formatted document, such as an HTML document. You could specify this output in the header as follows:

```
Content-Type: text/html
```

Locations Used in CGI Headers

The output of your script doesn't have to be a document created within the script. You can reference any document on the Web using the Location field. The Location field references a file by its URL. Servers process location references either directly or indirectly depending on the location of the file. If the server can find the file locally, it passes the file to the client. Otherwise, the server redirects the URL to the client and the client has to retrieve the file. You can specify a location in a script as follows:

```
Location: http://www.tvpress.com/
```

NOTE

Some older browsers don't support automatic redirection. Consequently, you may want to consider adding an HTML-formatted message body to the output. This message body will only be displayed if a browser cannot use the location URL.

Status Used in CGI Headers

The `Status` field passes a status line to the server for forwarding to the client. Status codes are expressed as a three-digit code followed by a string that generally explains what has occurred. The first digit of a status code shows the general status as follows:

`1XX` Not yet allocated

`2XX` Success

`3XX` Redirection

`4XX` Client error

`5XX` Server error

Although many status codes are used by servers, the status codes you pass to a client via your CGI script are usually client error codes. Suppose the script could not find a file and you have specified that in such cases, instead of returning nothing, the script should output an error code. Here is a list of the client error codes you may want to use:

Status: 401 Unauthorized Authentication has failed. User is not allowed to access the file and should try again.

Status: 403 Forbidden. The request is not acceptable. User is not permitted to access file.

Status: 404 Not found. The specified resource could not be found.

Status: 405 Method not allowed. The submission method used is not allowed.

Clarifying CGI Output

Creating the output from a CGI script is easier than it may seem. All you have to do is format the output into a header and body using your favorite programming language. This section contains two examples. The first example is in the Perl programming language. The second example is in the UNIX Bourne shell.

If you wanted the script to output a simple HTML document using Perl, here is how you could do it:

```
#!/usr/bin/perl
#Create header with extra line space
print "Content-Type: text/html\n\n";
#Add body in HTML format
print <<"MAIN";
<HTML><HEAD><TITLE>Output from Script</TITLE></HEAD>
<BODY>
<H1>Top 10 Reasons for Using CGI</H1>
<P>10. Customer feedback.</P>
<P>9. Obtaining questionnaire and survey responses.</P>
<P>8. Tracking visitor count.</P>
<P>7. Automating searches.</P>
<P>6. Creating easy database interfaces.</P>
<P>5. Building gateways to other protocols.</P>
<P>4. HTML 2.0 image maps.</P>
<P>3. User authentication.</P>
<P>2. Online order processing.</P>
<P>1. Generating documents on the fly.</P>
</BODY>
MAIN
```

If you wanted the script to output a simple HTML document in Bourne shell, here's how you could do it:

```
#!/bin/sh
#Create header with extra line space
echo "Content-Type: text/html"
#Add body in HTML format
cat << MAIN
<HTML><HEAD><TITLE>Output from Script</TITLE></HEAD>
<BODY>
<H1>Top 10 Reasons for Using CGI</H1>
<P>10. Customer feedback.</P>
<P>9. Obtaining questionnaire and survey responses.</P>
<P>8. Tracking visitor count.</P>
<P>7. Automating searches.</P>
<P>6. Creating easy database interfaces.</P>
<P>5. Building gateways to other protocols.</P>
<P>4. HTML 2.0 Image maps.</P>
<P>3. User authentication.</P>
<P>2. Online order processing.</P>
<P>1. Generating documents on the fly.</P>
</BODY>
MAIN
```

The server processing the output sets environment variables, creates an HTTP header, and then sends the data on to the client. Here is how the HTTP header might look coming from a CERN Web server:

```
HTTP/1.0 302 Found
MIME-Version: 1.0
Server: CERN/3.0
Date: Monday, 4-Mar-96 23:59:59 HST
Content-Type: text/html
Content-Length: 485
```

```
<HTML><HEAD><TITLE>Output from Script</TITLE></HEAD>
<BODY>
<H1>Top 10 Reasons for Using CGI</H1>
<P>10. Customer feedback.</P>
<P>9. Obtaining questionnaire and survey responses.</P>
<P>8. Tracking visitor count.</P>
<P>7. Automating searches.</P>
<P>6. Creating easy database interfaces.</P>
<P>5. Building gateways to other protocols.</P>
<P>4. HTML 2.0 image maps.</P>
<P>3. User authentication.</P>
<P>2. Online order processing.</P>
<P>1. Generating documents on the fly.</P>
</BODY>
```

How to Use Server-Push

Server-push technology allows you to make dynamic updates to your documents. Server-push and gateway scripts make perfect combinations. The output of your gateway scripts generally has a defined HTTP header. Using this header, you can create a document that will reload itself or call another document.

Server-push is designed to complement client-pull and behaves similarly. Client-pull is used to refresh or retrieve an entire document with header directives in the document specifying time intervals; server-push is generally used to dynamically update a component of a document, such as an image, with server-side scripts setting the time intervals.

Using client-pull, the client must contact the server, wait for a reply, establish a connection, retrieve the data, close the connection, and repeat the entire process when requesting new data. Using server-push, the client contacts the server, waits for a reply, establishes a connection, retrieves the data, and then retrieves any new data it requests without repeating the process. Besides giving the server total control over when and how often data is sent, server-pull enables users to easily interrupt data updates using the Stop feature of their browsers.

To create a document that updates itself using server-push, you can use the Content-Type directive. The `Content-Type` field in a header identifies the MIME type of data you are sending back to the client. Use the following MIME content type with client-pull:

```
multipart/x-mixed-replace
```

Although most HTTP responses consist of only a single message or document, the multipart message type enables a single response to contain multiple messages or documents. The multipart message type encapsulates other message types within the document you are sending to the client.

When you use the MIME type `multipart/mixed`, you must also specify the boundary string that separates the messages. This string should be unique and not used elsewhere in the text of the message. After the boundary string, you specify the MIME type of the individual message in a header. The header should be followed by a blank line if the message has a body section as well.

The following sample response header for a multipart message contains three messages that are separated by a unique boundary string:

```
Content-type: multipart/mixed;boundary=--YourUniqueBoundaryString

--YourUniqueBoundaryString
Content-type: text/plain

Text for the first message.
--YourUniqueBoundaryString
Content-type: text/plain

Text for the second message.
--YourUniqueBoundaryString
Content-type: text/plain

Text for the third message.
--YourUniqueBoundaryString
```

CAUTION

Some servers have problems processing the multipart message type if you put any spaces after the `multipart/mixed` assignment. For this reason, do not insert spaces after the semicolon or around the equal sign when you assign the mandatory boundary string.

To use server-push, you use Netscape's experimental `multipart/x-mixed-replace` message type. This message type tells the client to replace the current data with the new data. The client finishes loading the current document before loading and displaying the new document. Transforming the `multipart/mixed message` type into a `multipart/x-mixed replace` message is easy. You simply change the type assignment in the first line as follows:

```
Content-type: multipart/x-mixed-replace;boundary=--YourUniqueBoundaryString

--YourUniqueBoundaryString
Content-type: text/plain

Text for the first message.
--YourUniqueBoundaryString
Content-type: text/plain

Text for the second message.
--YourUniqueBoundaryString
Content-type: text/plain

Text for the third message.
--YourUniqueBoundaryString
```

Ideally, you would send the client a multipart message as the output from a gateway script. Because the multipart message can contain as many sections as you want, you can use a `for` loop or a `do-while` loop to keep the script running indefinitely. By building hypertext links into the output documents, you can enable the reader to interact with your publication. The links could even call other gateway scripts that use server-pull animation.

This simple script uses server-pull to display the current time once each second:

```
#!/bin/sh
# Build multipart message using the x-mixed-replace format
# Ensure header is separated from body with space
cat << MAIN
Content-type: multipart/x-mixed-replace;boundary=--YourUniqueBoundaryString

--YourUniqueBoundaryString
MAIN
# Set while to true to loop continuously
while true
do
#Create Document
cat << TIME
Content-type: text/html
<HTML>
<HEAD>
<TITLE>Current Time in Hawaii</TITLE>
</HEAD>
<BODY BGCOLOR="#0000ff" text="#ffff00" link="#fffbf0" vlink="#808000"
➥alink="#ff0000">
<BIG>
date
</BIG>
</BODY>
</HTML>

--YourUniqueBoundaryString
TIME
#wait 1 second before repeating the loop
sleep 1
done
```

CAUTION

Although this Bourne shell script works, you should not use UNIX shell scripts with server push if the connection is going to be open indefinitely. The primary reason for this is that shell scripts will not stop running when the user severs the connection, and if the script is running on your server, it is using system resources. For this reason, if the server-push will open a connection of indefinite duration, use a language that handles interrupts well, such as C or Perl.

A neat trick you can do with server-push is to have the server update an inline image in the current document. Creating an inline animation is as easy as adding an inline image with an URL to a gateway script that uses server-push. Although the current document will not get updated, the image will. The following document contains an inline image that is updated:

```
<HTML>
<HEAD>
<TITLE>Server Push</TITLE>
</HEAD>
```

```
<BODY>
<CENTER>
<IMG WIDTH=64 HEIGHT=64 SRC="http://tvp.com/cgi-bin/doit.cgi">
</CENTER>
<P>Only the image in this document will get updated.
<P>The rest of the document will not be updated.
</BODY>
</HTML>
```

Creating a gateway script that uses server-push is also easy. All you have to do is create a script that builds a document in multipart message format. The following script in the C programming language called `doit.c` was created by Rob McCool. The script enables you to animate a series of images. The number of stages for the animation is determined by the variable `LASTCHAR`.

With the `LASTCHAR` variable, you set the last character of the file name for your images, which are uniquely named and end in an alphabetic letter from lowercase *a* to the value for `LASTCHAR`. To use this script with images in GIF format, all you have to do is modify the `LASTCHAR` variable as necessary and compile the script using your favorite compiler. Listing 26.1 shows the `doit.c` script.

Listing 26.1. Modified doit.c script.

```
/*
 * doit.c: Quick hack to play a sequence of GIF files.
 *
 * This is a modified version of Rob McCool's original script.
 *
 * This code is released into the public domain.  Do whatever
 * you want with it.
 *
 */
 /* the following lines set up the libraries and variables
  * The most important variables are: HEADER and LASTCHAR
  * With the HEADER variable, you set the HTTP response header.
  * With the LASTCHAR variable, you set the last character of the
  * file name for your images. As this animation has 10 stages,
  * the image names will end in a to j.
  */
#include <sys/types.h>
#include <sys/mman.h>
#include <unistd.h>
#include <fcntl.h>
#include <sys/stat.h>
#include <stdio.h>
#define LASTCHAR 'j'
#define HEADER \
"Content-type: multipart/x-mixed-replace;boundary=YourUniqueBoundaryString\n" \
#define RANDOMSTRING "\n--YourUniqueBoundaryString\n"
#define ENDSTRING "\n--YourUniqueBoundaryString--\n"
#define CTSTRING "Content-type: image/gif\n\n"
int main(int argc, char *argv[])
{
    struct stat fi;
    char fn[32];
    caddr_t fp;
```

```
    unsigned char x;
  int fd;
    if(write(STDOUT_FILENO, HEADER, strlen(HEADER)) == -1)
        exit(0);
    if(write(STDOUT_FILENO, RANDOMSTRING, strlen(RANDOMSTRING)) == -1)
        exit(0);
    x = 'a';
    while(1) {
        sleep(1);
        if(write(STDOUT_FILENO, CTSTRING, strlen(CTSTRING)) == -1)
            exit(0);
    /* The next line defines the name of the images to use for creating
     * the inline animation. Here, the images are located in the images
     * subdirectory of the current directory which should be cgi-bin.
     * The image files must be named as follows:
     * images/Aa.gif
     * images/Ab.gif
     * images/Ac.gif
     * images/Ad.gif
     * images/Ae.gif
     * images/Af.gif
     * images/Ag.gif
     * images/Ah.gif
     * images/Ai.gif
     * images/Aj.gif
     */
        sprintf(fn, "images/A%c.gif', (char) x);
        if( (fd = open(fn, O_RDONLY)) == -1)
            continue;
        fstat(fd, &fi);
        fp = mmap(NULL, fi.st_size, PROT_READ, MAP_PRIVATE, fd, 0);
        if(fp == (caddr_t) -1)
            exit(0);
        if(write(STDOUT_FILENO, (void *) fp, fi.st_size) == -1)
            exit(0);
        munmap(fp, fi.st_size);
        close(fd);
        if(write(STDOUT_FILENO, RANDOMSTRING, strlen(RANDOMSTRING)) == -1)
            exit(0);
        if(x == LASTCHAR)
            exit(0);
        else ++x;
```

Summary

The common gateway interface opens the door for adding advanced features to your Web publications. This workhorse running quietly in the background lets you use fill-out forms, database queries, and index searches and create documents on the fly. You use CGI whenever you want to open a two-way communication channel with the reader.

Although CGI enhancement is a click of the mouse button away for most readers, CGI enhancement means extra work for Web publishers. Still, the payoff associated with CGI makes the extra effort truly worthwhile.

CHAPTER 27

Form Creation and Design

by William Robert Stanek

IN THIS CHAPTER

In previous chapters, you learned how to create wonderful Web publications that include multimedia and sizzling HTML 3.2 features. Yet now that you've created the beginnings of a wonderful publication, how do you get the feedback, comments, and praise from visitors that will make all your hard work worthwhile? The answer is easy: add a fill-out form to an appropriate place in your Web publication and invite the reader to participate.

Since HTML 2.0 introduced forms, Web publishing has never been the same. Forms are the primary way to add interactivity and two-way communication to your Web publications. They provide friendly interfaces for inputting data, searching databases, and accessing indexes. To submit a fill-out form as input to a CGI script, the user only has to click on the Submit button. Your forms can contain pulldown menus, pushbuttons, text, and graphics.

What Forms Are and Why You Want To Use Them

In your daily life, you see forms all the time:

- Forms you fill out at the doctor's office
- Credit card bills that require you to fill in the dollar amount in tiny boxes
- Surveys and questionnaires you receive in the mail
- Magazine compatibility polls that you fill out at the checkout counter

Although you may not think of these items as forms, all of them require you to fill in information or make selections from groups of numbered or lettered items. When you submit a printed form, someone on the receiving end has to handle the information. In an increasingly computerized world, this usually means entering the information into a database or spreadsheet. Major companies hire dozens of people for the specific task of entering the information on thousands of forms that flood the company every day into the company database. This huge expense is a tremendous burden on the company.

Imagine a virtual office where thousands of forms are entered into the company database every day without a single worker. The forms are processed efficiently, almost instantly, and the customer can get feedback within seconds of submitting a form. The cost for what otherwise would be a mammoth undertaking is a few hours—the time it takes you to design a fill-out form and build a CGI script to process the information.

Using forms, you open a two-way communication channel between you and visitors to your Web publications. Visitors can send comments directly to you. You can create CGI scripts to process the input automatically. In this way, readers can get immediate results. You can e-mail the input to your e-mail address. This way, you can respond to readers' questions and comments easily and personally. You can also set up a script to process the input, give results to the reader, and send yourself e-mail.

While the scripting part of the process runs in the background, the reader sees the fill-out form. Readers can interact with forms by entering information in spaces provided, by making selections from pulldown menus, by activating pushbuttons, and by submitting the data for instant processing. Figure 27.1 shows a simple form with areas for text entry. Even this simple form is a powerful tool for inviting reader participation.

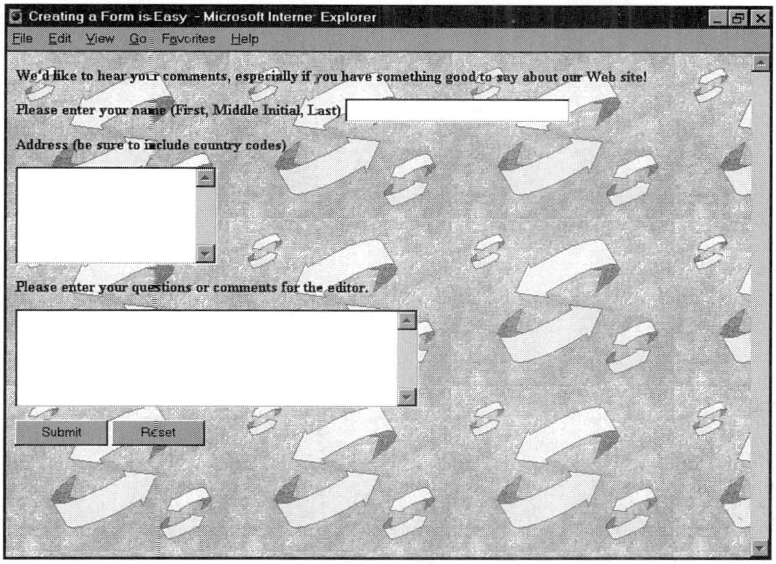

FIGURE 27.1.
Even simple forms are useful for inviting reader participation.

Form Design

Although creating a form is easy, designing a good form can be a little difficult. Some publishers use generic all-purpose forms that fail because the form wasn't designed with a specific purpose in mind. The key to designing forms is to use them for a specific purpose. When you want to get feedback from readers, you create a form for reader feedback. When you want to take orders online, you create a form for submitting online orders.

Designing forms that are useful to readers and to you as the publisher should be your primary goal. A form that is useful to readers will be used. A form that is useful to you as the publisher makes your job easier. When designing forms, keep the following guidelines in mind.

A form that is useful to the reader is

- Friendly
- Well-organized
- Sized correctly

A form that is useful to you as the publisher does the following:

- Uses uniquely named and easily identifiable keywords for fields
- Allows for brevity of processing and quick indexing whenever possible
- Provides subtle guidance to the reader on the amount of input you are looking for

The <FORM> Tag

All elements of your forms are enclosed by the beginning tag `<FORM>` and ending tag `</FORM>`. Within these tags, you can include almost any valid HTML tag, such as paragraph and heading tags. Although multiple forms can be on a single Web page, you cannot create subforms within a form. The reason for this restriction is that the form must be submitted to be processed in a specific manner. The way forms are submitted is based on the following things:

- The method used to submit the form
- The action to be performed when the form is submitted
- The optional type of encoding to be performed on the form

The METHOD Attribute

The `METHOD` attribute specifies the method for submitting the form. Currently, this attribute has two acceptable values:

```
METHOD=GET
```

```
METHOD=POST
```

As discussed briefly in the previous chapter, the preferred submission method is `POST`. When you use `POST`, the data is sent as a separate input stream through the server to your gateway script. This method enables the server to pass the information directly to the gateway script without assigning variables or arguments. The value of the `CONTENT_LENGTH` environment variable tells the CGI script how much data to read from the standard input stream. With this method, there is no limit on the amount of data that can be passed to the server.

The default submission method is `GET`. Data submitted using `GET` is appended to the script URL. The script URL and the data are passed to the server as a single URL-encoded input. The server receiving the input assigns the data being passed to two variables. The script URL is assigned to the environment variable `SCRIPT_NAME`. The data is assigned to the environment variable `QUERY_STRING`.

Assigning the data to variables on a UNIX system means passing the data through the UNIX shell. The number of characters you can send to UNIX shell in a single input is severely limited. Some servers restrict the length of this type of input to 255 characters. This restriction means only a limited amount of data can be appended to a URL before truncation occurs. When truncation occurs, you lose data. Consequently, you should use `GET` only when the length of data input is small.

The ACTION Attribute

The `ACTION` attribute specifies the action to be performed when a form is submitted. A form without an `ACTION` attribute will not be processed, so your forms must always include this attribute. You can define an action for your forms as the URL to a gateway script to be executed or as an action.

By specifying the URL to a gateway script, you can direct input to the script for processing. The URL provides a relative or an absolute path to the script. Scripts defined with relative URLs are on your local server. Scripts defined with absolute URLs can be on a remote or local server. Most CGI scripts are located in the `cgi-bin` directory. You could access a script in a `cgi-bin` directory as follows:

```
ACTION="http://tvp.com/cgi-bin/your_script"
```

An `ACTION` could be inserted in the `<FORM>` tag as follows:

```
<FORM METHOD="POST" ACTION="http://tvp.com/cgi-bin/datasort.pl">
 . . .
</FORM>
```

You can also use the `ACTION` attribute to specify an action to be performed. The only action currently supported is `mailto`, which mails the contents of a form to the address you specify. Most current browser and server software support the `mailto` value. You can use the `mailto` value as follows:

```
<FORM METHOD="POST" ACTION="mailto:publisher@tvp.com">
 . . .
</FORM>
```

A form created using the preceding example would be sent to `publisher@tvp.com`. The `mailto` value provides you with a simple solution for using forms that does not need to be directed to a CGI script to be processed. This is great news for Web publishers who don't have access to CGI. Because the contents of the form are mailed directly to an intended recipient, the data can be processed offline as necessary.

The ENCTYPE Attribute

The `ENCTYPE` attribute specifies the MIME content type for encoding the form data. The client encodes the data before passing it to the server. Data from fill-out forms is not encoded to prevent the data from being read. Data from fill-out forms is encoded to ensure input fields can be easily matched to key values. By default, the data is `x-www-form-encoded`. This encoding is also called URL encoding and was discussed in the previous chapter. If you do not specify an encoding type, the default value is used automatically.

Although, in theory, you can use any valid MIME type, such as `text/plain`, most forms on the Web use the default encoding to prevent problems you would experience when trying to manipulate data that has not been encoded in some way. You can use the `ENCTYPE` attribute in your forms as follows:

```
<FORM METHOD="POST" ACTION="cgi-bin/query.pl" ENCTYPE="x-www-form-encoded">
 . . .
</FORM>
```

Adding Content to the Form

The elements designed specifically for use within forms are what make fill-out forms useful and interactive. When adding content to your forms, keep in mind the simple rules outlined earlier in this chapter. One way of following these rules is to always provide descriptions along with form fields. As with print forms, the descriptions for fields should be brief. Short field descriptions make the form easier to read.

Here is a wordy field description:

> You should enter your full name in the adjacent text window using your first name, middle initial, and last name as appropriate.

Here is a better field description:

> *Please enter your name (First, Middle Initial, Last):*

Input fields should be correctly sized to ensure they are usable. A good field size ensures all key information entered by the user is visible in the input area. For a telephone number, you could define an input field 12 characters in length to enable customers to enter their phone numbers and area codes. If a reader puts parentheses around the area code, the length of the input field should be stretched to 14 characters. If the reader lives in another country, the length of the input field should be stretched to at least 16 characters.

The form itself should be correctly sized and well-organized to ensure readers will take the time to fill it out. A good form balances the number of fields against the length of the fields. This guideline means that a form that requires lengthy input from readers should have few fields and a form that requires the reader to make many selections but requires limited input could have many fields.

Three key elements are used to add content to forms:

`INPUT`	Used to define input fields.
`SELECT`	Used to create selection menus.
`TEXTAREA`	Used to define a multiple-line text input window.

Adding Input Fields

Using the `INPUT` element, you can add check boxes, radio buttons, images, text windows, and other elements to your forms. You define an `INPUT` element by labeling it with a `TYPE` and a `NAME`. The input `TYPE` determines how the input field looks on the screen. `NAME` labels the field with a keyword you can use in your CGI scripts.

The basic format of the `INPUT` element is as follows:

```
<INPUT TYPE="type of field" NAME="input field name">
```

Input fields and associated data are sent to a CGI script as keyword and value pairs. The method used to submit the form determines the way the data is submitted to the CGI script. Let's look at two examples of the data flow from a form to a script. Both forms have three input fields, and the user submits the forms with the following values:

```
answer1 = Monday night football

answer2 = Chicago Bears

answer3 = Super bowl bound
```

The first example uses the `GET` method:

```
<FORM METHOD="GET" ACTION="cgi-bin/query.pl">
<INPUT TYPE="text" NAME="answer1">
<INPUT TYPE="text" NAME="answer2">
<INPUT TYPE="text" NAME="answer3">
</FORM>
```

When the `GET` method is used, the server sets the following environment variables, and then passes the input to the `query.pl` script:

```
PATH=/bin:/usr/bin:/usr/etc:/usr/ucb
SERVER_SOFTWARE = NCSA/1.3
SERVER_NAME = www.tvpress.com
GATEWAY_INTERFACE = CGI/1.1
SERVER_PROTOCOL = HTTP/1.0
SERVER_PORT= 80
REQUEST_METHOD = GET
HTTP_ACCEPT = application/octet-stream, application/postscript,
application/rtf, application/x-compress, application/x-dvi,
application/x-gzip, application/x-zip-compressed, audio/basic, audio/x-aiff,
audio/x-wav, image/gif, image/jpeg, image/tiff, image/x-portable-bitmap,
message/external-body, message/partial, message/rfc822, multipart/alternative,
multipart/digest, multipart/mixed, multipart/parallel, text/html, text/plain,
video/mpeg, video/quicktime, video/x-msvideo
PATH_INFO =
PATH_TRANSLATED =
SCRIPT_NAME = /cgi-bin/query.pl
QUERY_STRING = answer1=Monday+night+football&answer2=Chicago+Bears&
answer3=Super+bowl+bound
REMOTE_HOST =
REMOTE_ADDR =
REMOTE_USER =
AUTH_TYPE =
CONTENT_TYPE =
CONTENT_LENGTH =
```

The second example uses the `POST` method:

```
<FORM METHOD="POST" ACTION="cgi-bin/query.pl">
<INPUT TYPE="text" NAME="answer1">
<INPUT TYPE="text" NAME="answer2">
<INPUT TYPE="text" NAME="answer3">
</FORM>
```

When the `POST` method is used, the server sets the following environment variables, and then passes the input to the `query.pl` script:

```
PATH=/bin:/usr/bin:/usr/etc:/usr/ucb
SERVER_SOFTWARE = NCSA/1.3
SERVER_NAME = www.tvpress.com
GATEWAY_INTERFACE = CGI/1.1
SERVER_PROTOCOL = HTTP/1.0
SERVER_PORT= 80
REQUEST_METHOD = POST
HTTP_ACCEPT = application/octet-stream, application/postscript,
application/rtf, application/x-compress, application/x-dvi,
application/x-gzip, application/x-zip-compressed, audio/basic, audio/x-aiff,
audio/x-wav, image/gif, image/jpeg, image/tiff, image/x-portable-bitmap,
message/external-body, message/partial, message/rfc822, multipart/alternative,
multipart/digest, multipart/mixed, multipart/parallel, text/html, text/plain,
video/mpeg, video/quicktime, video/x-msvideo
PATH_INFO =
PATH_TRANSLATED =
SCRIPT_NAME = /cgi-bin/query.pl
QUERY_STRING =
REMOTE_HOST =
REMOTE_ADDR =
REMOTE_USER =
AUTH_TYPE =
CONTENT_TYPE = application/x-www-form-urlencoded
CONTENT_LENGTH = 75
```

The following data is passed to the `query.pl` script using the standard input stream:

```
answer1=Monday+night+football&answer2=Chicago+Bears&answer3=Super+bowl+bound
```

TYPE has eight possible values. Although forms will let you try to associate just about any attribute with any input type, certain attributes should be used with certain types. Knowing this will save you a lot of time when you create forms. The next sections describe the useful attributes for each of the following input types:

Input Type	*Description*
TEXT	A one-line text field of a width defined in the form
CHECKBOX	One or more boxes that a user can select
HIDDEN	A field that is not displayed to the user but is sent to your script
IMAGE	An image that can be clicked on to submit the form
PASSWORD	A text field where all data entered is seen as the * character
RADIO	One or more radio buttons that a user can turn on or off
RESET	A button that clears the form when clicked
SUBMIT	A button that submits the form when clicked

Using TEXT Fields

The TEXT type enables you to define a basic input field for text. TEXT fields are displayed on a single line. You can use these four attributes with TEXT fields:

`MAXLENGTH`	The maximum allowable length of the field. Beware, if this attribute is not set, there is no limit.
`NAME`	The keyword associated with the input field.
`SIZE`	The width of the input field, expressed as the number of characters for the text area.
`VALUE`	An initial value for the field that will be displayed in the text area. The user can add to this information and, if necessary, delete the information to enter new information.

The following is an example of the code for a `TEXT` input field:

```
<INPUT TYPE="TEXT" NAME="answer1" SIZE="60">
```

In the example, the `SIZE` attribute defines the visible area for the `TEXT` field on the screen to be 60 characters wide. Because the example does not specify the maximum length of the field, the text will scroll, enabling the user to enter more than 60 characters. To limit the input to a specific value, use the `MAXLENGTH` attribute, as in the following example:

```
<INPUT TYPE="TEXT" NAME="answer1" SIZE="60" MAXLENGTH="60">
```

Figure 27.2 shows a form that uses text fields. As you can see from the figure, this form is used to get contact information from a customer. The markup for this page is in Listing 27.1.

FIGURE 27.2.
Using text elements in a form.

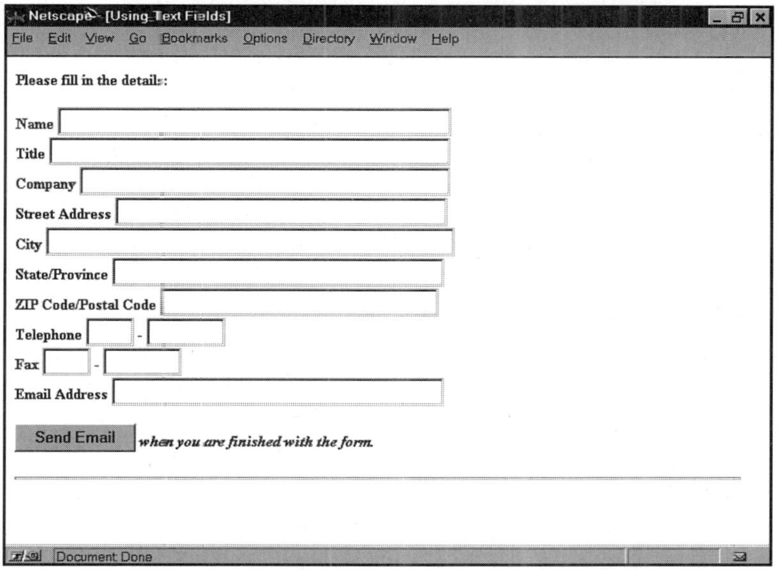

Listing 27.1. Using text fields.

```
<HTML>
<HEAD>
<TITLE>Using Text Fields</TITLE>
</HEAD>
<BODY BGCOLOR="#FFFFFF">
<B>Please fill in the details:</B>
<FORM METHOD="POST" ACTION="cgi-bin/contact.pl">
<P>
<B>
Name
<INPUT TYPE="TEXT" NAME="nameField" SIZE="49">
<BR>
Title
<INPUT TYPE="TEXT" NAME="titleField" SIZE="50">
<BR>
Company
<INPUT TYPE="TEXT" NAME="companyField" SIZE="46">
<BR>
Street Address
<INPUT TYPE="TEXT" NAME="streetField" SIZE="41">
<BR>
City
<INPUT TYPE="TEXT" NAME="cityField" SIZE="51">
<BR>
State/Province
<INPUT TYPE="TEXT" NAME="stateField" SIZE="41">
<BR>
ZIP Code/Postal Code
<INPUT TYPE="TEXT" NAME="zipField" SIZE="34">
<BR>
Telephone
<INPUT TYPE="TEXT" NAME="telepreField" SIZE="4">
-
<INPUT TYPE="TEXT" NAME="teleField" SIZE="8">
<BR>
Fax
<INPUT TYPE="TEXT" NAME="faxpreField" SIZE="4">
-
<INPUT TYPE="TEXT" NAME="faxField" SIZE="8">
<BR>
Email Address
<INPUT TYPE="TEXT" NAME="emailField" SIZE="41">
</B>
</P>
<P ALIGN="LEFT">
<INPUT TYPE="SUBMIT" NAME="Button" VALUE="Send Email">
<I><B>when you are finished.</B></I>
</P>
<HR>
</FORM>
</BODY>
</HTML>
```

Figure 27.3 shows another form for submitting contact information using text fields. The form uses formatting techniques to make it more visually appealing. To see how this was done, refer to Listing 27.2.

FIGURE 27.3.
Formatting techniques can add to the visual appeal of your form.

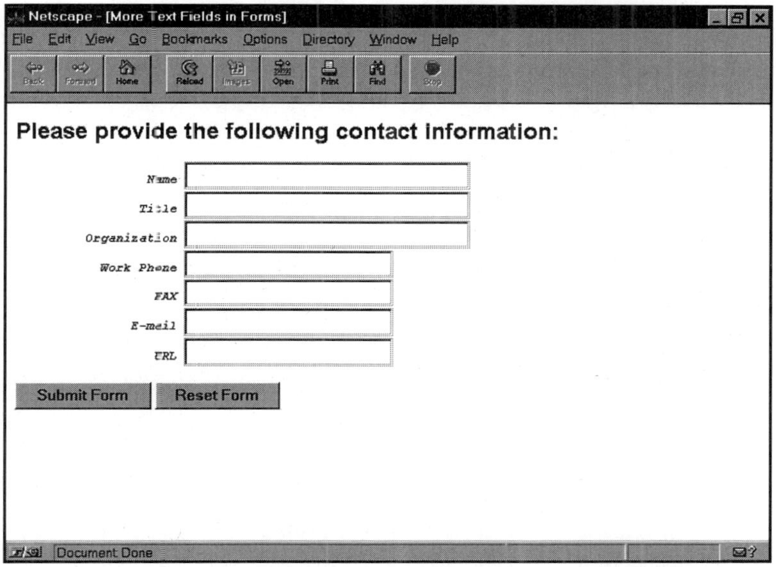

Listing 27.2. More text fields.

```
<HTML>
<HEAD>
<TITLE>More Text Fields in Forms</TITLE>
</HEAD>
<BODY BGCOLOR="#FFFFFF">
<H2><B>Please provide the following contact information:</B></H2>
<FORM METHOD="POST" ACTION="mailto:user@tvp.com">
<P></P>
<BLOCKQUOTE>
<PRE><EM>            Name </EM>
<INPUT TYPE="text" SIZE="35" MAXLENGTH="50" NAME="Contact_FullName">
<EM>           Title </EM>
<INPUT TYPE="text" SIZE="35" MAXLENGTH="50" NAME="Contact_Title">
<EM>    Organization </EM>
<INPUT TYPE="text" SIZE="35" MAXLENGTH="50" NAME="Contact_Organization">
<EM>      Work Phone </EM>
<INPUT TYPE="text" SIZE="25" MAXLENGTH="25" NAME="Contact_WorkPhone">
<EM>             FAX </EM>
<INPUT TYPE="text" SIZE="25" MAXLENGTH="25" NAME="Contact_FAX">
<EM>          E-mail </EM>
<INPUT TYPE="text" SIZE="25" MAXLENGTH="50" NAME="Contact_Email">
<EM>             URL </EM>
<INPUT TYPE="text" SIZE="25" MAXLENGTH="25" NAME="Contact_URL">
</PRE>
```

continues

Listing 27.2. continued

```
</BLOCKQUOTE>
<P></P>
<P>
<INPUT TYPE="submit" VALUE="Submit Form">

<INPUT TYPE="reset" VALUE="Reset Form">
</P>
</FORM>
</BODY>
</HTML>
```

Using Check Boxes and Radio Buttons

The `CHECKBOX` input field creates boxes that a user can select. The `RADIO` input field creates circular buttons that a user can select. Some browsers display selected check boxes and radio buttons using an x for a check box and a round bullet for a radio button. Other browsers display check boxes and radio buttons as graphical pushbuttons with 3D flair. These input fields have four attributes:

`CHECKED`	The check box or radio button is automatically selected when viewed. The best use of this attribute is for default options that can be deselected if necessary.
`DISABLED`	The user cannot manipulate the check box or radio button. You will probably want to use this attribute only for testing your forms.
`NAME`	The keyword associated with the input field.
`VALUE`	The value to assign if the user activates the check box or radio button.

Although the primary difference between a check box and a radio button may seem to be their shape, a fundamental difference exists in the way they behave. Check boxes allow users to make multiple selections. Radio buttons, on the other hand, allow users to make only one selection.

When creating check boxes and radio buttons, carefully consider how you will use them. Use radio buttons with a single associated keyword value when the user should make only one selection, such as a choice of A, B, or C. Use check boxes with multiple associated keyword values when the user can make multiple selections, such as a choice of all or any of A through E. Figure 27.4 depicts how check boxes and radio buttons can be used in a form. Listing 27.3 shows the code for the form.

Listing 27.3. Sample form using check boxes and radio buttons.

```
<HTML>
<HEAD>
<TITLE>Using Check Boxes & Radio Buttons</TITLE>
</HEAD>
<BODY BGCOLOR="#FFFFFF">
<STRONG>
```

```
<FORM METHOD="POST" ACTION="/cgi-bin/survey.pl">
<H1>Optimism Survey</H1>
<P>1. Do you consider yourself to be an optimist or a pessimist?
<P><INPUT  TYPE="checkbox" NAME="optimist"  VALUE="yes" >Optimist</P>
<P><INPUT  TYPE="checkbox" NAME="optimist"  VALUE="no" >Pessimist</P>
<P>2. Is a rainy Sunday?
<P><INPUT  TYPE="checkbox" NAME="rainyday"  VALUE="A" >Soothing
<INPUT  TYPE="checkbox" NAME="rainyday"  VALUE="B" >Restful
<P><INPUT  TYPE="checkbox" NAME="rainyday"  VALUE="C" >Dreary
<INPUT  TYPE="checkbox" NAME="rainyday"  VALUE="D" >Dreadful
<P>3. Is a partially filled glass of water
<P><INPUT  TYPE="radio" NAME="glass"  VALUE="A" >Half Empty
<INPUT  TYPE="radio" NAME="glass"  VALUE="B" >Half Full
<P>4. What do you think about Monday Mornings?
<P><INPUT  TYPE="radio" NAME="mondays"  VALUE="A" >First day of a great week
<INPUT  TYPE="radio" NAME="mondays"  VALUE="B" >First day back to work
<P><INPUT  TYPE="radio" NAME="mondays"  VALUE="C" >Four days to go till Friday
<INPUT  TYPE="radio" NAME="mondays"  VALUE="D" >Five days till freedom
</FORM>
</BODY>
</HTML>
```


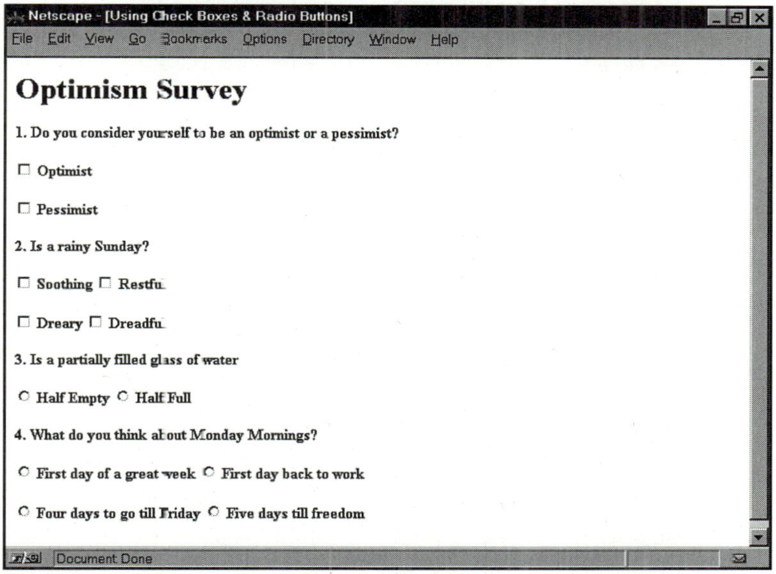

FIGURE 27.4.
A survey using check boxes.

Hidden Fields in Forms

The `HIDDEN` input field is not displayed and is only useful to provide essential input to your script. Hidden elements have two attributes:

`NAME`	The keyword associated with the input field
`VALUE`	The value of the field

Use `HIDDEN` fields when you want the same script to serve more than one purpose. The Web publisher using this `HIDDEN` input field has several publications that may be subscribed to:

```
<INPUT  TYPE="hidden" NAME="subscription"  VALUE="magazine-NewsDay">
```

The publisher uses the `HIDDEN` field to track the publication the customer is subscribing to by setting a unique value for the subscription input field in the form. As all subscriptions require the same information from customers, the publisher uses a single CGI script to process subscriptions from multiple sources. Listing 27.4 is the outline of a Perl script that could be used to process the subscription information.

Listing 27.4. Partial Perl script for processing subscriptions.

```
#!/usr/bin/perl
#Check the method used to submit the form
$METHOD = $ENV{'REQUEST_METHOD'};
#Tell script where to look for POST-submitted input
if  ( $METHOD eq 'POST' )
{
read(stdin, $SINPUT, $ENV{'CONTENT_LENGTH'});
}
else
#Tell script where to look for POST-submitted input
if  ( $METHOD eq 'GET' )
{
$SINPUT = $ENV{'QUERY_STRING'};
}
else
#Tell script to exit if neither POST or GET are used
{
exit( 1 );
}
#Process URL-encoded input into keywords and value pairs
foreach $SINPUT (split(/&/))
{
$SARRAY[$i] =~ s/\+/ /g;
($input_name, $value) = split(/=/,$SARRAY[$i],2);
$input_name =~ s/%(..)/pack("c",hex($1))/ge;
$value =~ s/%(..)/pack("c",hex($1))/ge;
$SARRAY{$input_name} = $value;
}
#Set the output file for the subscription information
if ($SARRAY{'subscription'} eq 'magazine-NewsDay')
{
$DATAOUTFILE = "news.db"
}
else
if ($SARRAY{'subscription'} eq 'magazine-WebTimes')
{
$DATAOUTFILE = "webtimes.db"
}
else
{
$DATAOUTFILE = "running.db"
}
#The rest of the script would process the customer's subscription information,
#such as name, address, and payment method.
```

Using PASSWORD Fields

To allow users to enter password information without revealing the password to onlockers, you can use the PASSWORD input field. All text entered in a PASSWORD field is seen as asterisks. The asterisks are used only to mask the characters and do not affect how the text is passed to your gateway script. If you combine this element with a TEXT input field for the user's login ID, you can pass this information to a script that would validate the user's access to protected areas of your Web site.

This element has four attributes:

MAXLENGTH	The maximum allowable length of the field. Beware, if this attribute is not set, there is no limit.
NAME	The keyword associated with the input field.
SIZE	The width of the input field, expressed as the number of characters for the text area.
VALUE	An initial value for the field that will be displayed in the text area. The user can add to this information and, if necessary, delete the information to enter new information.

The following is a sample PASSWORD element:

```
<INPUT  TYPE="password" NAME="net_password" SIZE=12 MAXLENGTH=12 >
```

Figure 27.5 shows a great use of password fields in a Web page. The HTML used to create this page is shown in Listing 27.5.

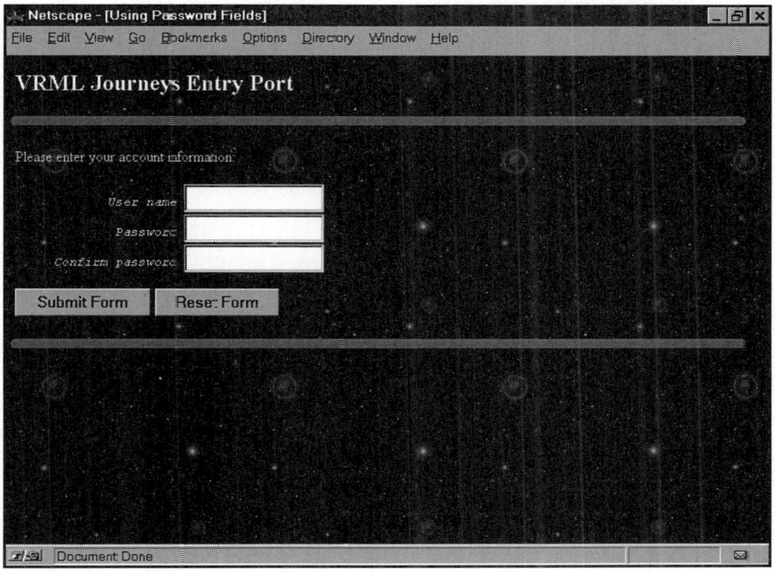

FIGURE 27.5.
Using password fields in your forms.

Listing 27.5. Entering account information.

```
<HTML>
<HEAD>
<TITLE>Using Password Fields</TITLE>
</HEAD>
<BODY BGCOLOR="#000000" BACKGROUND="Space.gif" TEXT="#FFFFFF">
<H2>VRML Journeys Entry Port</H2>
<HR SIZE="10" NOSHADE>
<FORM METHOD="POST" ACTION"enter.pl">
<P>Please enter your account information:</P>
<BLOCKQUOTE>
<PRE><EM>       User name </EM>
<INPUT TYPE="text" SIZE="16" MAXLENGTH="16" NAME="Account_Username">
<EM>        Password </EM>
<INPUT TYPE="password" SIZE="16" MAXLENGTH="16" NAME="Account_Password">
<EM>Confirm password </EM>
<INPUT TYPE="password" SIZE="16" MAXLENGTH="16" NAME="Account_PasswordConfirm">
</PRE>
</BLOCKQUOTE>
<P>
<INPUT TYPE="submit" VALUE="Submit Form">

<INPUT TYPE="reset" VALUE="Reset Form">
</P>
</FORM>
<HR SIZE="10" NOSHADE>
<P> </P>
</BODY>
</HTML>
```

Using RESET and SUBMIT

Two extremely useful input types are RESET and SUBMIT. Usually these features for forms are displayed as graphical pushbuttons. A reset button clears the form when selected. A submit button submits the form when selected. By default, the reset buttons are labeled with the value of RESET, and submit buttons are labeled with the value SUBMIT. You change the label for these buttons using the VALUE attribute, as shown in the following examples:

```
<INPUT TYPE="reset" VALUE="Clear Form">
<INPUT TYPE="submit" NAME="button1" VALUE="Submit Form">
```

Another useful attribute for the submit button is the NAME attribute. Using the NAME attribute, you can track which SUBMIT button a user pressed. This provides another way of tracking the precise form used to submit input. Using this feature of the NAME attribute, you can create a quick menu for your site.

The form in Figure 27.6 uses a CGI script to process the input and direct the user to a new page. When a user clicks on a button, the input is passed to the named script for processing. Listing 27.6 shows the markup for the example.

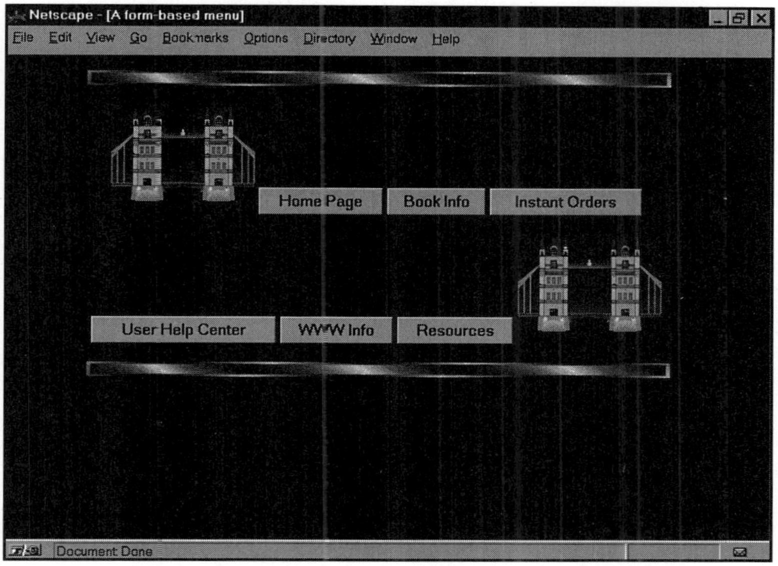

FIGURE 27.6.
A quick menu using a form.

Listing 27.6. Creating a form-based menu.

```
<HTML>
<HEAD>
<TITLE>A form-based menu</TITLE>
</HEAD>
<BODY BGCOLOR="#000000" TEXT="#FFFFFF">
<P ALIGN="CENTER"><IMG SRC="blackdiv.jpg"></P>
<DIV ALIGN=CENTER>
<FORM METHOD="GET" ACTION="../cgi-bin/quick-menu">
<IMG SRC="tower.gif">
<INPUT TYPE="SUBMIT" NAME="BUTTON1" VALUE="Home Page">

<INPUT TYPE="SUBMIT" NAME="BUTTON4" VALUE="Book Info">
<INPUT TYPE="SUBMIT" NAME="BUTTON5" VALUE="Instant Orders">
<P>
<INPUT TYPE="SUBMIT" NAME="BUTTON6" VALUE="User Help Center">
<INPUT TYPE="SUBMIT" NAME="BUTTON7" VALUE="WWW Info">
<INPUT TYPE="SUBMIT" NAME="BUTTON8" VALUE="Resources">
<INPUT TYPE="HIDDEN" NAME="MENU" VALUE="MENU1">
<IMG SRC="tower.gif">
</FORM>
</DIV>
<P ALIGN="CENTER"><IMG SRC="blackdiv.jpg"></P>
</BODY>
</HTML>
```

The form in Figure 27.7 uses multiple forms to create a menu. An `ACTION` attribute is defined for each form. When a user clicks on a button, the browser carries out the assigned action. Because the actions can all be processed by the client, no CGI script is involved. The code for the example is available in Listing 27.7.

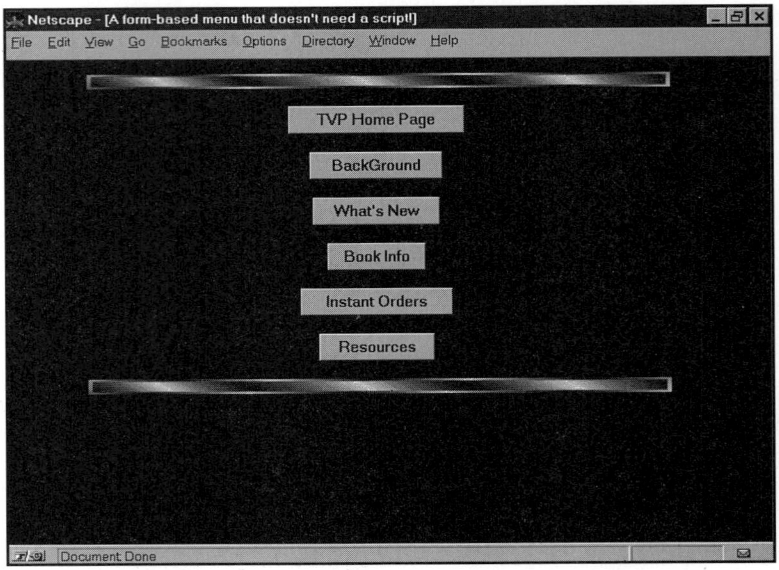

FIGURE 27.7.
A quick menu using multiple forms processed by client.

Listing 27.7. A form-based menu without a script.

```
<HTML>
<HEAD>
<TITLE>A form-based menu that doesn't need a script!</TITLE>
</HEAD>
<BODY BGCOLOR="#000000" TEXT="#FFFFFF">
<P ALIGN="CENTER"><IMG SRC="blackdiv.jpg"></P>
<DIV ALIGN=CENTER>
<FORM METHOD="GET"  ACTION="vphp.html">
<INPUT  TYPE="SUBMIT"  NAME="BUTTON1"  VALUE="TVP Home Page">
</Form>
<FORM METHOD="GET"  ACTION="vpbg.html">
<INPUT  TYPE="SUBMIT"  NAME="BUTTON2"  VALUE="BackGround">
</Form>
<FORM METHOD="GET"  ACTION="new.html">
<INPUT  TYPE="SUBMIT"  NAME="BUTTON3"  VALUE="What's New">
</Form>
<FORM METHOD="GET"  ACTION="books.html">
<INPUT  TYPE="SUBMIT"  NAME="BUTTON4"  VALUE="Book Info">
</Form>
<FORM METHOD="GET"  ACTION="orders.html">
<INPUT  TYPE="SUBMIT"  NAME="BUTTON5"  VALUE="Instant Orders">
</Form>
<FORM METHOD="GET"  ACTION="resources.html">
<INPUT  TYPE="SUBMIT"  NAME="BUTTON8"  VALUE="Resources">
</Form>
</DIV>
<P ALIGN="CENTER"><IMG SRC="blackdiv.jpg"></P>
</BODY>
</HTML>
```

An alternative to the default style of the submission button is to define a fancy button the user can click to submit the form. You do this with the `IMAGE` input field. Image elements have three attributes:

`ALIGN`	Used to align the image with text in the same line. Valid values are `TOP`, `MIDDLE`, and `BOTTOM`.
`NAME`	The keyword associated with the input field.
`SRC`	The image to be displayed.

The following is a sample image element:

```
<FORM METHOD="POST" ACTION="/cgi-bin/clickit.pl">
<INPUT  TYPE="image" NAME="pubform"  SRC="fancybutton.gif" ALIGN="MIDDLE">
</FORM>
```


NOTE

You do not need a `SUBMIT` type in the `INPUT` field containing the `IMAGE` type declaration. The `IMAGE` type is used in place of the `SUBMIT` type; if you click the image, the form will be automatically submitted.

Adding Selection Menus

Beyond input fields for forms, you can also use selection fields. The `SELECT` element is used to create two types of selection menus for your forms. An onscreen menu has selections that are completely visible. A pulldown menu has selection elements that are hidden until the reader activates the menu.

The `SELECT` element has a beginning and an ending tag associated with it. You use the `NAME` attribute to specify a keyword for the selection menu. Using the `SIZE` attribute, you can specify the number of selection elements to display on the screen, as in the following examples:

```
<SELECT SIZE=1 NAME="Menu1"> . . . </SELECT>
<SELECT SIZE=7 NAME="Menu2"> . . . </SELECT>
```

By default, the user can only select one option from the menu. The first selection menu in the preceding example has a one-line window with a pulldown menu. The second selection menu is an onscreen menu with seven displayed items and a scrollbar for accessing additional elements.

To allow the user to make multiple selections, use the `MULTIPLE` attribute. Most browsers allow you to make multiple selections by holding down the Control key on the keyboard and clicking with the left mouse button when the pointer is over the additional item you want to select. The following is an example of this attribute in use:

```
<SELECT SIZE=7 NAME="books" MULTIPLE> . . . </SELECT>
```

You define selections for the menu using the `OPTION` element. This element has two basic formats:

```
<OPTION>Item 1
<OPTION SELECTED>Item 2
```

The first menu item can be selected by a user. The second menu item is selected by default. Users can unselect the default option by clicking it.

Figure 27.8 shows several types of selection menus. The first example shows a pulldown menu as it first appears on screen. The second example shows an onscreen menu. This menu accepts multiple selections. Note that onscreen menus occupy more space than pulldown menus. Consider using onscreen menus when the user can make multiple selections and using pulldown menus when the user can make only one selection. Listing 27.8 contains the HTML for the form.

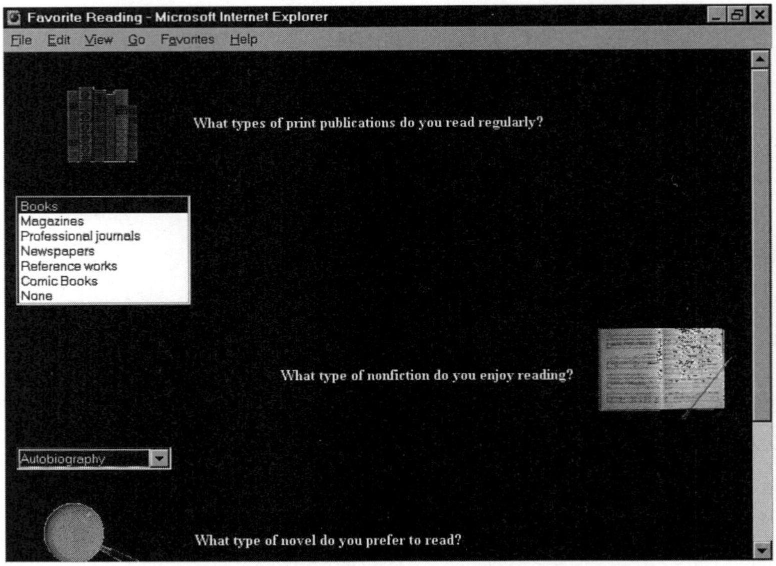

FIGURE 27.8.
Using selection menus.

Listing 27.8. Creating a selection menu in a form.

```
<HTML>
<HEAD>
<TITLE>Favorite Reading</TITLE>
</HEAD>
<BODY BGCOLOR="#000000" TEXT="#FFFFFF">
<FORM METHOD="POST" ACTION="/cgi-bin/books.pl">

<P ALIGN=LEFT><IMG SRC="Books.gif" ALIGN="ABSMIDDLE">
<B>What types of print publications do you read regularly?</B></P>
<SELECT NAME="publications" SIZE="7" MULTIPLE>
<OPTION>Books
</OPTION>
```

```
<OPTION>Magazines
</OPTION>
<OPTION>Professional journals
</OPTION>
<OPTION>Newspapers
</OPTION>
<OPTION>Reference works
</OPTION>
<OPTION>Comic Books
</OPTION>
<OPTION>None
</OPTION>
</SELECT>

<P ALIGN=RIGHT><B>What type of nonfiction do you enjoy reading?</B>
<IMG SRC="Openbook.gif" ALIGN="ABSMIDDLE"></P>
<SELECT SIZE="1" NAME="NonFiction">
<OPTION>Autobiography
</OPTION>
<OPTION>Biography
</OPTION>
<OPTION>Computers/Internet
</OPTION>
<OPTION>Cooking
</OPTION>
<OPTION>Health/Medicine
</OPTION>
<OPTION>How-To
</OPTION>
<OPTION>Money/Finance
</OPTION>
<OPTION>New age
</OPTION>
<OPTION>Parenting
</OPTION>
<OPTION>Reference
</OPTION>
<OPTION>Self-Help
</OPTION>
<OPTION>Sports
</OPTION>
<OPTION>Travel
</OPTION>
</SELECT>
</P>

<P><IMG SRC="Magnify.gif" ALIGN=ABSMIDDLE>
<B>What type of novel do you prefer to read?</B></P>
<SELECT NAME="Fiction" SIZE="3">
<OPTION>Adventure
</OPTION>
<OPTION>Fantasy
</OPTION>
<OPTION>Horror
</OPTION>
<OPTION>Humor
</OPTION>
<OPTION>Mystery
```


continues

Listing 27.8. continued

```
</OPTION>
<OPTION>Romance
</OPTION>
<OPTION>Science fiction
</OPTION>
<OPTION>Suspense
</OPTION>
<OPTION>Western
</OPTION>
</SELECT>

<P><BR CLEAR="ALL"></P>
<P>
<INPUT TYPE="reset" VALUE="Clear Form">
<INPUT TYPE="submit" NAME="button1" VALUE="Submit Form">
</P>
</FORM>
</BODY>
</HTML>
```

Selection elements and associated data are sent to a CGI script as keyword and value pairs. As with other elements, the method used to submit the form determines the way the data is submitted to the CGI script. To see exactly how this works with selection menus and options, follow the data flow from the user's browser to the CGI script in the example. The user selected the following options from the preceding form:

```
publications = Books, Magazines, Newspapers

nonfiction = Computers/Internet

fiction = Adventure
```

The form uses the `POST` method to submit data to the `books.pl` script. The client passes the data to the server. The server sets the following environment variables before passing the data to the script:

```
PATH=/bin:/usr/bin:/usr/etc:/usr/ucb
SERVER_SOFTWARE = CERN/3.0
SERVER_NAME = www.tvp.com
GATEWAY_INTERFACE = CGI/1.1
SERVER_PROTOCOL = HTTP/1.0
SERVER_PORT= 80
REQUEST_METHOD = POST
HTTP_ACCEPT = application/octet-stream, application/postscript,
application/rtf, application/x-compress, application/x-dvi,
application/x-gzip, application/x-zip-compressed, audio/basic, audio/x-aiff,
audio/x-wav, image/gif, image/jpeg, image/tiff, image/x-portable-bitmap,
message/external-body, message/partial, message/rfc822, multipart/alternative,
multipart/digest, multipart/mixed, multipart/parallel, text/html, text/plain,
video/mpeg, video/quicktime, video/x-msvideo
PATH_INFO =
PATH_TRANSLATED =
SCRIPT_NAME = /cgi-bin/books.pl
```

```
QUERY_STRING =
REMOTE_HOST =
REMOTE_ADDR =
REMOTE_USER =
AUTH_TYPE =
CONTENT_TYPE = application/x-www-form-urlencoded
CONTENT_LENGTH = 88
```

The following data is passed to the `books.pl` script using the standard input stream:

```
publications=Books,Magazines,Newspapers&nonfiction=Computers/Internet&
fiction=Adventure
```


Adding Text Windows

The final element you can use with your forms is the TEXTAREA element. This element has more functionality than the text field used with the INPUT element because it enables you define text windows of any size to display onscreen. Text windows can be used to input large amounts of data. Although the size of the window is defined in rows and columns, you have no real control over how much data the user can enter into the window because text windows have vertical and horizontal scrollbars that enable the user to scroll left to right as well as up and down.

Text windows are defined with a pair of tags. Any text between the beginning and ending TEXTAREA tags is used as the initial input to the text window. Default text provided for a text window is displayed exactly as entered. Although the user can erase any default input if necessary, initial input should be used primarily to save the user time. TEXTAREA has three attributes:

NAME	The keyword associated with the input field.
ROWS	The height of the text window in number of lines.
COLS	The width of the text window in number of characters.

To define a text window 8 rows tall and 60 characters wide, you would use the following:

```
<TEXTAREA NAME="Publisher_Query" ROWS=8 COLS=60></TEXTAREA>
```

This sample form contains two text areas:

```
<FORM METHOD="POST" ACTION="/cgi-bin/job.pl">
<P>Describe your current job.</P>
<TEXTAREA NAME="JobDescription" ROWS=10 COLS=60></TEXTAREA>
<P>What would your dream job be like?</P>
<TEXTAREA NAME="DreamJob" ROWS=10 COLS=60></TEXTAREA>
<INPUT TYPE="reset">
<INPUT TYPE="submit" VALUE="Submit Form">
</FORM>
```

Figure 27.9 shows a sample form using a text window. The source for the form page is shown in Listing 27.9.

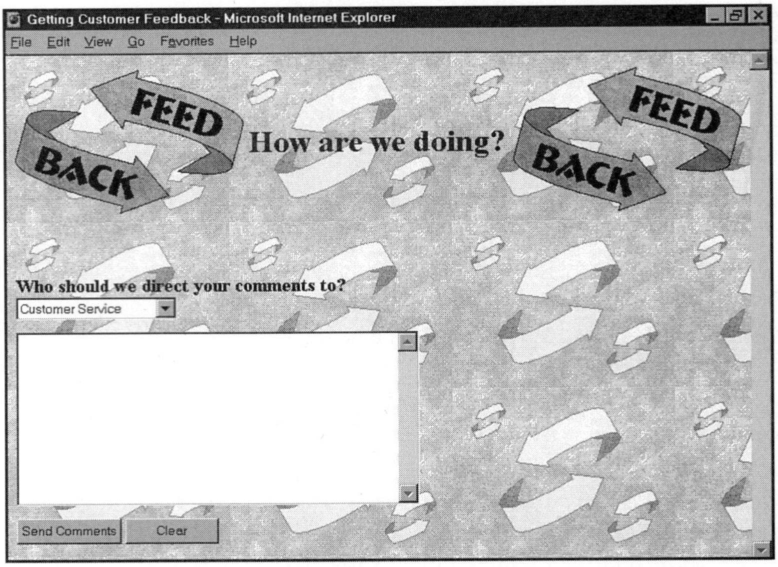

FIGURE 27.9.
Using text windows.

Listing 27.9. Text windows in forms.

```
<HTML>
<HEAD>
<TITLE>Getting Customer Feedback</TITLE>
</HEAD>
<BODY BACKGROUND="BACKGROUND.GIF" VLINK="#00F0FF" LINK="#000000" TEXT="#000000">
<H1>
<IMG ALIGN="ABSMIDDLE" HSAPCE="100" SRC="FEEDBACK.GIF">
<FONT COLOR="Navy">How are we doing?</FONT>
<IMG ALIGN="ABSMIDDLE" HSAPCE="100" SRC="FEEDBACK.GIF">
</H1>
<BR CLEAR=ALL>
<FORM METHOD="POST" ACTION="comment.pl">
<P><FONT COLOR="Black" SIZE="4"><B>Who should we direct your comments to?</B>
</FONT>
<BR>
<SELECT NAME="select">
<OPTION VALUE="cservice" SELECTED>Customer Service</OPTION>
<OPTION VALUE="techsupport">Technical Support</OPTION>
<OPTION VALUE="pr">Public Relations</OPTION>
<OPTION VALUE="general">General Information</OPTION>
</SELECT>
</P>
<P><TEXTAREA COLS="60" NAME="TextField" ROWS="10"></TEXTAREA></P>
<INPUT TYPE="SUBMIT" NAME="Button" VALUE="Send Comments">
<INPUT TYPE="RESET" NAME="Button" VALUE="Clear">
</FORM>
</BODY>
</HTML>
```

Creating a Form Results Page

After submitting a form, users usually want to see a page that verifies the input has been accepted, such as the one shown in Figure 27.10. The creation of the results page is normally handled by the CGI script processing the user's input.

The results page can contain the input the user entered and prompt the user to confirm the input, or it can be a page that simply thanks users for their input. Listing 27.10 shows a scripting routine written in Perl that displays a results page.

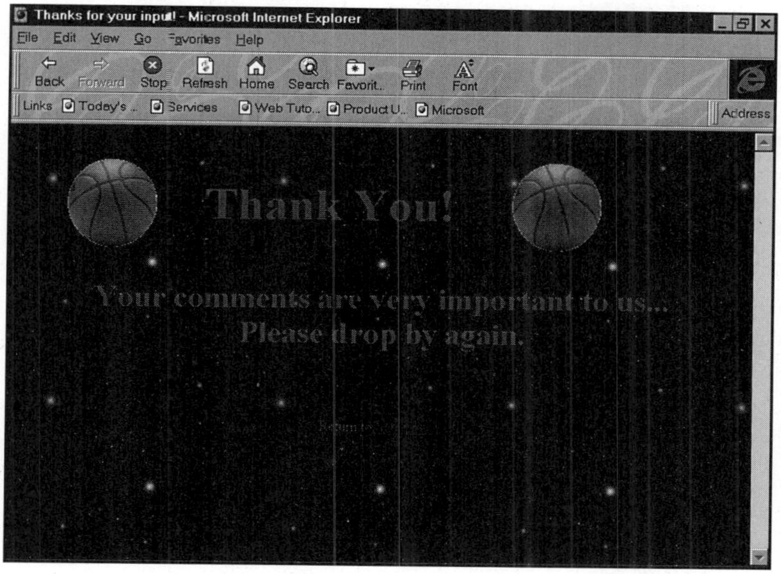

FIGURE 27.10.
An input verification page.

Listing 27.10. A Perl scripting routine that displays a results page.

```
#!/usr/bin/perl
#Display results routine
print "Content-Type: text/html\n\n";
#Add body in HTML format
print <<"MAIN";
<HTML>
<HEAD>
<TITLE>Thanks for your input!</TITLE>
</HEAD>
<BODY BACKGROUND="Space1.jpg" TEXT="#FF0000">
<H1>
<IMG SRC="Baskbal1.gif" ALIGN="ABSMIDDLE" HSPACE="5" VSPACE="5">
<FONT SIZE="+7">Thank You!</FONT>
<IMG SRC="Baskbal1.gif" ALIGN="ABSMIDDLE" HSPACE="5" VSPACE="5">
</H1>
<DIV ALIGN=CENTER>
```

continues

Listing 27.10. continued

```
<H1>Your comments are very important to us...<BR>Please drop by again.</H1>
<BR>
<BR>
<BR>
<BR>
<P>Return to <A HREF="../">home page.</A></P>
</DIV>
</BODY>
</HTML>
MAIN
```

Summary

Forms add interactivity and provide friendly interfaces for inputting data, searching databases, and accessing indexes. Your forms can contain many types of input fields. Some input fields are graphical in nature, like radio buttons and check boxes. Other input fields are textual in nature, like text areas and password fields. Designing forms that are useful to readers and to you as the publisher should be your primary goal.

CHAPTER 28

Search Engines and Indexed Databases

by William Robert Stanek

IN THIS CHAPTER

The hypertext facilities of the World Wide Web put the world's most powerful search engines at your fingertips. Search engines are the gateways to the vast storehouses and databases available on the Web. Thousands of Web search engines are used every day, and if you've browsed the Web, you know online searches are easy to perform. You simply enter keywords, press Enter, and the search engine takes over.

A *search engine* is an application specifically designed and optimized for searching databases. Search engines can race through megabytes of information in nanoseconds. They achieve this terrific speed and efficiency thanks to an application called an *indexer.* An indexer is an application specifically designed and optimized for indexing files. Using the index built by the indexer, the search engine can jump almost immediately to sections of the database containing the information you are looking for. Thus, creating an indexed database of documents at your Web site requires two applications: a search engine and an indexer. The search engine and indexer are normally a part of a larger application, such as a Wide Area Information Server (WAIS).

The trick to creating Web documents that provide access to a search engine is knowing how to integrate the capabilities of the search engine using the existing structure of hypertext and CGI. This chapter unlocks the mysteries of search engines and indexed databases.

What Are Indexers and How Are They Used?

The index for *Web Publishing Unleashed* is an invaluable resource for quickly finding information in this book. Using the index, you can quickly find the topic or subtopic you want to learn more about. You do this by following an alphabetical listing of keywords selected by the human indexer who combed the manuscript in search of the gems you would be interested in.

The indexer used the text of the entire book to create an alphabetical list of keywords and related concepts. The alphabetical listing is broken down into categories and subcategories. The first categories are broad and divided based on the letters *A* to *Z.* Next, the broad categories are subdivided based on keywords. The keyword categories are sometimes further divided based on related concepts. For quick reference, a page number is associated with keywords and their related concepts. You've probably noticed that articles, such as *a, an,* and *the,* and prepositions, such as *in, with,* and *to,* are never listed in the index. The indexer has a list of hundreds of common words such as these that should be excluded from the index because they occur too often to be helpful.

A computer-coded indexer builds an index in much the same way. The indexer application uses a list of common words to figure out which words to exclude from the index, searches through the list of documents you specified, and finally, builds an index containing the relevant associations between the remaining words within all the specified documents. As most indexers build a full-text index based on your documents, the index is often larger than the original files. For example, if your Web site has 15 M of data in 125 documents, the indexer would create an index slightly larger than 15 M.

Most indexers enable you to add to or subtract from the list of common words. Often you can do this by editing an appropriate file or by creating a *stop word* file. A stop word file contains an alphabetized list of words that the indexer should ignore. Most indexers have a predefined stop word file, but you can override it to use your list of stop words instead.

Another type of word list indexers use is the *synonym list.* Synonym lists make it easier for readers to find what they need on your Web site without knowing the exact word to use in the search. Each line of a synonym file contains words that can be used interchangeably. A search for any word in the list will be matched to other words in the same line. Instead of getting no results from the search, the reader will get a list of results that match related words.

Suppose a reader wants to learn how forms are processed on the server but doesn't know the right keyword to use to get a related response. This line from a synonym file could be used to help the reader find what she is looking for:

```
cgi cgi-bin script gateway interface programming
```

Before you create a synonym list, think carefully about the words you want to use in the list. The indexer program uses synonym lists to create an index. Whenever you change the synonym list, you will have to reindex your Web site.

What Are Search Engines and How Are They Used?

Hundreds of search engines are used in commercial and proprietary applications. Usually search engines are part of a larger application, such as a database management system. When Web publishers looked for indexing and searching solutions, they looked at the search engines available and found that most of them were not well-suited for use on the World Wide Web. The main reason they were ill-suited for use on the World Wide Web was because they weren't designed to be used on distributed networks.

One solution Web publishers did find was the *Wide Area Information Server* (*WAIS).* WAIS is a database retrieval system that searches indexed databases. The databases can contain any type of file, including text, sound, graphics, and even video. The WAIS interface is easy to use; you can perform a search on any topic simply by entering a keyword and pressing Enter. When you press the Enter key, the WAIS search engine takes over. You can find both commercial and freeware versions of WAIS.

WAIS was developed as a joint project whose founders include Apple Computers, Dow Jones, Thinking Machines, and the Peat Marwick group. In the early days of WAIS, Thinking Machines maintained a free version of WAIS suitably titled freeWAIS. This version of WAIS enjoys the widest usage. freeWAIS is now maintained by the Clearinghouse for Networked Information Discovery and Retrieval. CNIDR started handling freeWAIS when the founders of WAIS turned to commercial ventures such as WAIS, Inc. Because freeWAIS is so popular and easy-to-use, it is heavily featured in this chapter. Beyond freeWAIS, there are many commercial, shareware, and freeware options. This chapter examines many of those options, including wwwwais.c, SFGATE, SWISH, Excite for Web servers, and Livelink search.

The largest database on the Web, the Lycos Catalog of the Internet, enables you to perform searches for information on over 90 percent of Internet sites using a powerful indexer called a Web crawler. The Web crawler uses URLs at Web sites to find new information, and thus can index every page at a Web site and even find new Web sites. Lycos combines the Web crawler with a powerful search engine. Using the search engine, Web users can find the information they are looking for in a matter of seconds.

NOTE

A Web crawler is a generalized term for an indexer that searches and catalogs sites using the links in hypertext documents. By using the links, the indexer crawls through a document and all its related documents one link at a time.

The Lycos search engine is characteristic of the dozens of search engines you will find on the Web that use WAIS or are modeled after WAIS. You can enter a query at Lycos using the simple one-box form shown in Figure 28.1. By default, the Lycos search engine finds all documents matching any keyword you type in the query box. Because the exclusion list for Lycos contains

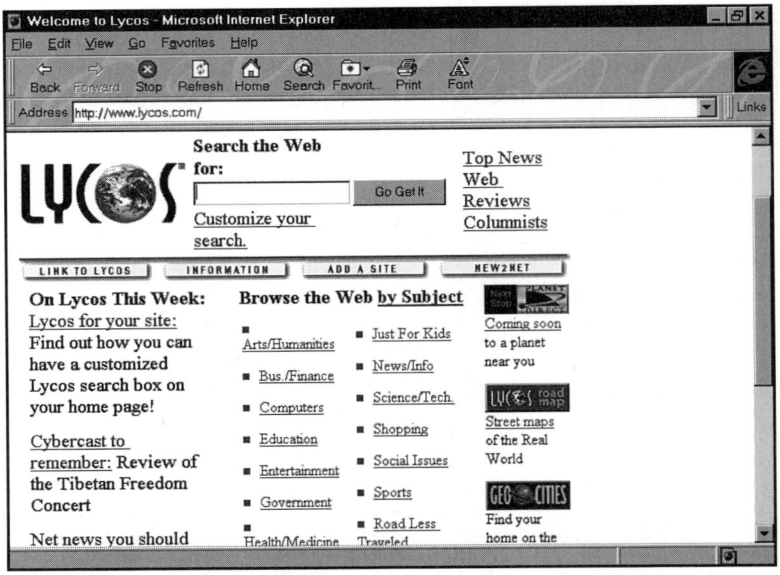

FIGURE 28.1.
Lycos search engine.

articles, prepositions, and other nonuseful words for searching, you can enter a query as a complete sentence, as demonstrated in the following examples:

```
What is WAIS?
Where is WAIS?
How do I use WAIS?
```

You can enter as many keywords as you want on the query line. Because the search is not case-sensitive, the keywords do not have to be capitalized. If you type in two keywords that are not on the exclusion list, the search engine assumes you want to search on both words. For example, if you entered the following:

```
WAIS Web
```

The search engine would search its index for all documents containing either *WAIS* or *Web*. Although you could specify the "or" explicitly in a search, such as WAIS OR Web, you generally do not have to; the OR is assumed whenever you do not specify otherwise. To search the index only for documents containing both *WAIS* and *Web*, you could use the following:

```
WAIS AND Web
```

The AND tells the search engine you are only interested in documents containing the words *WAIS* and *Web*. You can combine the basic functions of logical OR and logical AND in many ways. Often, you will be searching for material on a specific subject; you can use multiple keywords related to the subject to help you get better results on your searches. Suppose you are looking for publishers on the Web; you might try the following keywords:

```
book
fiction
magazine
nonfiction
publisher
publishing
```

Often your main topic will reveal dozens or hundreds of relevant sites. As Figure 28.2 shows, a single search on the keyword *WAIS* at Lycos returned over 26,000 matches. The Lycos search engine returns a summary of each document matching the search. The summary is in the form of an abstract for small documents and a combined outline and abstract for long documents. However, most search engines return a two-line summary of the related document that includes the size, type, and title of the document.

Documents matching your search are weighted with what should be the most relevant documents displayed first and what should be the least relevant documents displayed last. These scores are usually on a 0.0-1.0 scale or a zero to 1,000 scale. The most relevant documents (the documents with the greatest number of search words that are closest together) have a high score, with the highest score being 1.0 or 1,000. The criteria used to figure out relevancy are the number of words that match the search string and the proximity of the words to each other in the document.

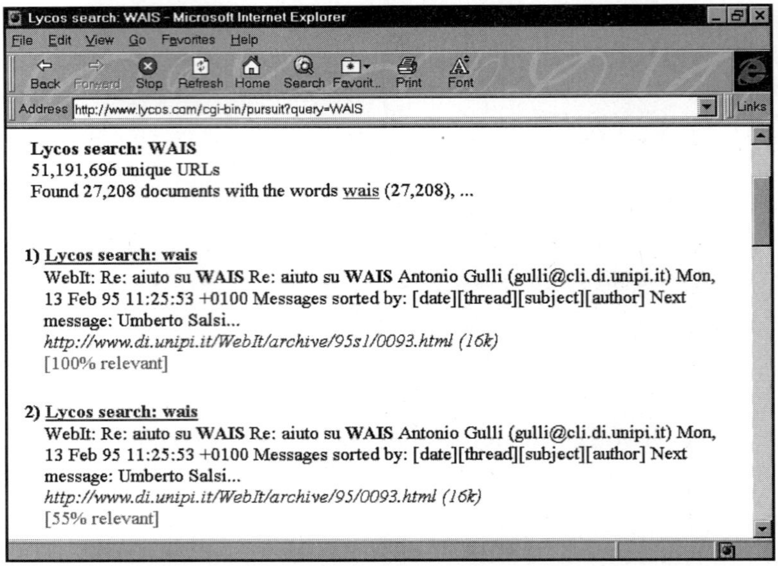

FIGURE 28.2.
Results of a Lycos search.

The overall scores based on these two criteria are used to present the matching documents in order from most relevant to least relevant. Although this method of ranking by relevance is used widely, it can be misleading. For this reason, other descriptive features, like a title and summary, are provided with the search results.

Accessing a WAIS Database

Originally, you could only access a WAIS database using a WAIS client. WAIS clients have built-in functions and are used much like other clients. Yet few people want to download a new type of client onto their system and learn how to use it, especially when the client can be used only for the specific purpose of searching a database. If you've ever used a WAIS client, you know they aren't the friendliest clients on the block. This is why Web users prefer to use their browsers, which provide a simple interface to just about every resource on the Internet.

Currently, most Web users access WAIS databases using a simple fill-out form, such as the one shown in Figure 28.1. When a user enters data into the form, the data is passed to the server and directed to a gateway script designed for search and retrieval. The script does five things:

1. Processes the input
2. Passes the input to the search engine
3. Receives the results from the search engine
4. Processes the results
5. Passes the output to the client

The gateway script creates the interface between the client browser and WAIS. Creating a gateway script to interface with WAIS is not an extremely complex process. Although you could create such a script using fewer than 100 lines of Perl code, dozens of ready-made WAIS gateways are already available. Some of these WAIS gateways are simple and involve efficient Perl scripts packed into a few kilobytes of file space. Other WAIS gateways are part of all-in-one software packages that contain an indexer and search engines as part of a WAIS server and a gateway script to create the Web-to-WAIS interface. The sections that follow discuss five freeware options for WAIS gateways.

Basic WAIS Gateways

Three ready-made solutions for processing the information from WAIS searches are

`wais.pl`

`son-of-wais.pl`

`kidsofwais.pl`

`wais.pl`

The very first WAIS gateway, a Perl script called `wais.pl`, is a quick-and-dirty solution for accessing WAIS. The `wais.pl` script was created by Tony Sanders and is included with the NCSA Web server software. You can obtain `wais.pl` from NCSA's FTP server at

`ftp://ftp.ncsa.uiuc.edu/Web/httpd/Unix/ncsa_httpd/cgi/wais.tar.Z`

`son-of-wais.pl`

Although `wais.pl` is used widely on the Web, it is slowly being replaced by its offspring: `son-of-wais.pl` and `kidofwais.pl`. The `son-of-wais.pl` script is the second evolution of `wais.pl`. This Perl script created by Eric Morgan beats its generic parent hands down because it is more advanced than the original and more robust. You can obtain `son-of-wais.pl` from NCSU at

`http://dewey.lib.ncsu.edu/staff/morgan/son-of-wais.html.`

`kidofwais.pl`

The third evolution of WAIS.PL is a script called `kidofwais.pl`. This script, created by Michael Grady, is a somewhat advanced WAIS gateway programmed entirely in Perl. The features of `kidsofwais.pl` include debugging, multiple formatting options, table titles, and more. You can obtain `kidsofwais.pl` from UIUC at

`http://www.cso.uiuc.edu/grady.html.`

The results of a search on the word *computer* using the `kidofwais.pl` script is shown in Figure 28.3. Many Web publishers prefer the clean output of `kidofwais.pl`. As you can see, matches are generally displayed on a single line of a bulleted list. Each item on the list is displayed in ranked relevance order with the scores omitted. The title, size, and type of matching documents form the basis of each list item.

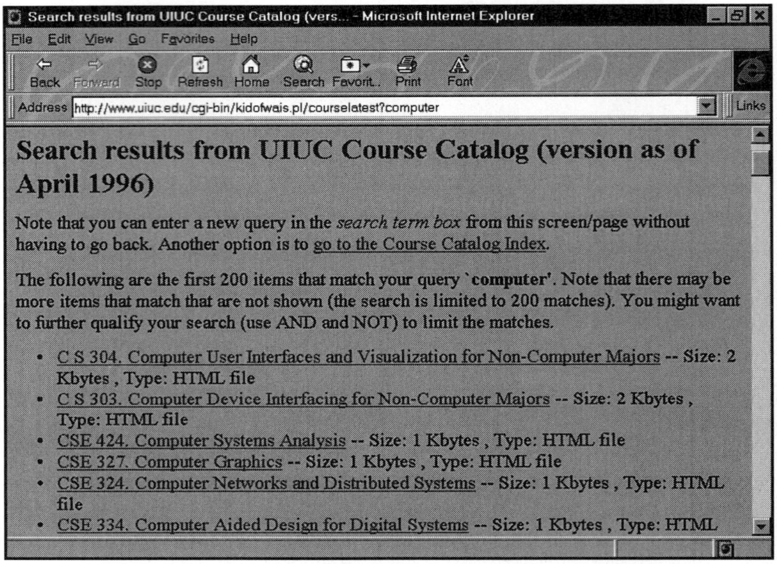

FIGURE 28.3.
Search results using the `kidofwais.pl` *script.*

Advanced WAIS Gateways

Two advanced and powerful solutions for your WAIS needs are

```
SFgate
wwwwais.c
```

SFgate

Created by Miao-Jane Lin and Ulrich Pfeifer, `SFgate` is one of the most advanced freeware WAIS gateways. Unlike other gateways discussed so far, `SFgate` uses a group of shell scripts to create a smooth and feature-rich interface to your WAIS server. This WAIS gateway is several orders of magnitude larger than other WAIS gateways and uses more than 500 K of disk space. In the days of 2 G hard drives, 500 K of disk space is negligible, but when you compare this amount to the `kidofwais.pl` script that is only 24 K in size, you can easily see that `SFgate` is certainly a more involved gateway. Fortunately, the `SFgate` distribution includes an installation routine and good documentation.

`SFgate` provides you with advanced control over the search options. Not only can you search on a keyword, but you can also tell `SFgate` the specific areas of the indexed database to search. You can search by document type, title, author, date, and contents. You can also tell `SFgate` precisely how to format the search results. Increased flexibility in the search parameters and output style produces more meaningful results. You can learn more about `SFgate` and download the latest version at

```
http://ls6-www.informatik.uni-dortmund.de/SFgate/SFgate.html
```

`wwwwais.c`

The `wwwwais.c` gateway is proof positive that you can pack a lot of power into a small C script. Created by Kevin Hughes of Enterprise Integration Technologies and packed into 54 K of C code, `wwwwais.c` is arguably the most powerful freeware WAIS gateway. EIT uses the `wwwwais.c` gateway to search the databases at its Web site. Figure 28.4 shows the results from a `wwwwais.c` search using EIT's `wwwwais.c` gateway.

The output from `wwwwais.c` is similar to other WAIS gateways discussed previously. Matches are generally displayed in a numbered list. Each item on the list is displayed in ranked relevance order. The title, size, type, and ranked score of the matching documents form the basis of each list item. You can download the latest version of this WAIS gateway at

```
http://www.eit.com/software/wwwwais/
```


FIGURE 28.4.
Using `wwwwais.c`.

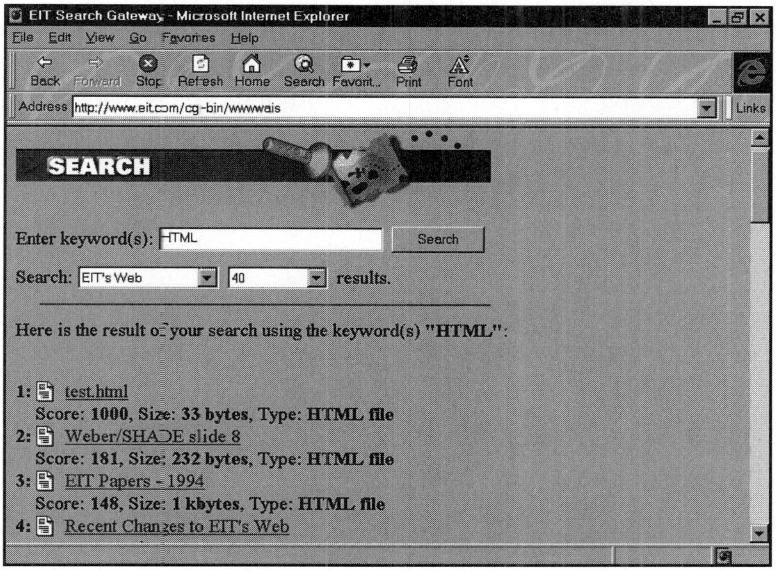

How WAIS Gateways Work

The best way to see how a WAIS gateway works is to examine the code for a script. Ideally, the script should be slightly advanced, yet not too advanced so that its inner workings cannot be easily studied. The son-of-wais script fits this description well. Listing 28.1 shows the code for `son-of-wais.pl` for you to study.

If you go through the code line by line, you will see that the first part of the script begins with an overview of changes Eric Morgan made to `wais.pl`. This section also contains contact information. Because such documentation makes it easier to use and maintain a script, good programmers always add it to a script.

After the overview, the code assigns configuration variables. Because these variables will be unique to your Web server, you will need to update them accordingly. Follow the inline documentation to update the paths to where your data is stored on the server, and be sure to update the contact and title information. One variable that you should pay particular attention to is the one that sets the location of the search engine to be used to perform the search. In the script, the variable is `$waisq`. Using `waisq` and `waissearch` to perform access WAIS databases is discussed later in this chapter.

The next section creates the output to `waisq`. The brevity of this section of the code surprises most beginning Web programmers. Yet keep in mind that `waisq` is the script performing the search against your WAIS database.

The final section of the script creates the output. Although the code for the search fills only a handful of lines, massaging the output and creating the textual portion of the output fills dozens of lines. You can modify the output message to suit your needs. However, the output page should contain the general information provided in the script, which ensures the reader knows how to use the index if they've had problems. If you follow the script, you can see that brief summaries for documents matching the search are displayed according to their relevance. Ranked relevance is described by scores associated with the documents.

Listing 28.1. The `son-of-wais.pl` script.

```
#!/usr/bin/perl
#
# wais.pl -- WAIS search interface
#
# $Id$
#
# Tony Sanders <sanders@bsdi.com>, Nov 1993
#
# Example configuration (in local.conf):
#     map topdir wais.pl &do_wais($top, $path, $query, "database", "title")
#
# Modified to present the user "human-readable" titles, better instructions as
# well as the ability to do repeated searches after receiving results.
#
# by Eric Lease Morgan, NCSU Libraries, April 1994
# eric_morgan@ncsu.edu
# http://www.lib.ncsu.edu/staff/morgan/morgan.html
# To read more about this script try:
# http://www.lib.ncsu.edu/staff/morgan/son-of-wais.html
#
# where is your waiq binary?
$waisq = "/usr/users/temp/wais/freeWAIS-0.202/bin/waisq";
```

```
# where are your source files?
$waisd = "/usr/users/temp/gopher/data/.wais";

# what database do you want to search?
$src = "ncsu-libraries-www";

# what is the opening title you want to present to users?
$openingTitle = "Search the NCSU Libraries Webbed Information System";

# after searching, what to you want the title to be?
$closingTitle = "Search results of the NCSU Libraries Information System";

# specify the path to add
# this is the same path your subtracted when you waisindexed
$toAdd = "/usr/users/temp/www/httpd/data/";

# specify the leader to subtract
# again, this is the same string you added when you waisindexed
$toSubtract = "http://www.lib.ncsu.edu/";

# who maintains this service?
$maintainer = "<A HREF=http://www.lib.ncsu.edu/staff/morgan/morgan.html>
Eric Lease Morgan</A> (eric_morgan@ncsu.edu)";

# and when was it last modified?
$modified = "April 15, 1994";

# you shouldn't have to edit anything below this line,
except if you want to change the help text

sub extractTitle {
  # get the string
  $theFile = $headline;

  # parse out the file name
  $theFile =~ s/^.*$toSubtract//i;

  # Concatenate the "toAdd" variable with the file name
  $theFile = $toAdd.$theFile;

  # open the file
  open( DATA, $theFile) || die "Can't open $theFile\n";

  # read the file and extract the title
  $linenum = 1;
  $foundtitle = 0;
  $humanTitle = "(No title found in document!) Call $maintainer.";
  while ( $line = <DATA>) {
    last if ($linenum > 5);
    $linenum++;
    if ($line =~ s/^.*<title>//i ) {
      chop( $line);
      $line =~ s!</title>.*$!!i;
      $humanTitle = $line;
      $humanTitle =~ s/^\s*//;
      $humanTitle =~ s/\s*$//;
      $foundtitle = 1;
      last;
```

continues

Listing 28.1. continued

```
    }
  }

  # close the file
  close (DATA);

  # return the final results
  return $humanTitle;
  }

sub send_index {
    print "Content-type: text/html\n\n";

    print "<HEAD>\n<TITLE>$openingTitle</TITLE>\n<ISINDEX></HEAD>\n";
    print "<BODY>\n<H2>", $openingTitle, "</H2>\n";

    print "<p>";
    print "This is an index of the information on this server. ";
    print "To use this function, simply enter a query.<P>";
    print "Since this is a WAIS index, you can enter complex queries.
    For example:<P>";
    print "<DT><b>Right-hand truncation</b> (stemming) queries";
    print "<DD>The query 'astro*' will find documents containing the words";
    print " 'astronomy' as well as 'astrophysics'.<P>";
    print "<DT>Boolean '<b>And</b>' queries";
    print "<DD>The query 'red and blue' will find the <B>intersection</b> of
    all";
    print " the documents containing the words 'red', and 'blue'.";
    print "The use of 'and' limits your retrieval.<p>";
    print "<DT>Boolean '<b>Or</b>' queries";
    print "<DD>The query 'red or blue' will find the <B>union</b> of all the";
    print " documents containing the words 'red' and 'blue'.";
    print "The use of 'or' increases your retrieval.<p>";
    print "<DT>Boolean '<b>Not</b>' queries";
    print "<DD>The query 'red not green' will find the all the documents
    containing";
    print " the word 'red', and <b>excluding</b> the documents containing the
    word 'green'.";
    print "The use of 'not' limits your retrieval.<p>";
    print "<DT><b>Nested</b> Boolean queries";
    print "<DD>The query '(red and green) or blue not pink' will find the
    union of all";
    print " the documents containing the words 'red', and 'green'. It will
    then add (union)";
    print " all documents containing the word 'blue'. Finally, it will exclude all
    documents";
    print " containing the word 'pink'";
    print "<HR>";
    print "This page is maintained by $maintainer, and it was last modified on
    $modified.<p>";
}

sub do_wais {
#    local($top, $path, $query, $src, $title) = @_;

    do { &'send_index; return; } unless defined @ARGV;
    local(@query) = @ARGV;
```

```
    local($pquery) = join(" ", @query);

    print "Content-type: text/html\n\n";

    open(WAISQ, "-|") || exec ($waisq, "-c", $waisd,
                               "-f", "-", "-S", "$src.src", "-g", @query);

    print "<HEAD>\n<TITLE>$closingTitle</TITLE>\n<ISINDEX></HEAD>\n";
    print "<BODY>\n<H2>", $closingTitle, "</H2>\n";

    print "Index \`$src\' contains the following\n";
    print "items relevant to \`$pquery\':<P>\r";
    print "<DL>\n";

    local($hits, $score, $headline, $lines, $bytes, $type, $date);
    while (<WAISQ>) {
        /:score\s+(\d+)/ && ($score = $1);
        /:number-of-lines\s+(\d+)/ && ($lines = $1);
        /:number-of-bytes\s+(\d+)/ && ($bytes = $1);
        /:type "(.*)"/ && ($type = S1);
        /:headline "(.*)"/ && ($headline = $1);         # XXX
        /:date "(\d+)"/ && ($date = $1, $hits++, &docdone);
    }
    close(WAISQ);
    print "</DL>\n";
    print "<HR>";
    print "This page is maintained by $maintainer.<P>";

    if ($hits == 0) {
        print "Nothing found.\n";
    }
    print "</BODY>\n";
}

sub docdone {
    if ($headline =~ /Search produced no result/) {
        print "<HR>";
        print $headline, "<P>\n<PRE>";
# the following was &'safeopen
        open(WAISCAT, "$waisd/$src.cat") || die "$src.cat: $!";
        while (<WAISCAT>) {
            s#(Catalog for database:)\s+.*#$1 <A HREF="/$top/$src.src">
            ➥$src.src</A>#;
            s#Headline:\s+(.*)#Headline: <A HREF="$1">$1</A>#;
            print;
        }
        close(WAISCAT);
        print "\n</PRE>\n";
    } else {
        $title = &extractTitle ($headline);
        print "<DT><A HREF=\"$headline\">$humanTitle</A>\n";
        print "<DD>Score: $score, Lines: $lines, Bytes: $bytes\n";
    }
    $score = $headline = $lines = $bytes = $type = $date = '';
}

eval '&do_wais';
```

How to Create an HTML Document for a WAIS Gateway

Creating an HTML document for your WAIS gateway is easy. All you have to do is create a document with a fill-out form that sends the proper values to your WAIS gateway of choice. Depending on the WAIS gateway you choose, this form can be a simple one-line form for entering keywords or a complex multiple-line form that has space for entering keywords as well as search and retrieval options. Listing 28.2 is the HTML code for a document using a simple form for use with `wwwwais.c`.

Listing 28.2. Simple form for use with `wwwwais.c`.

```
<HTML>
<HEAD>
<TITLE>Using WWWWAIS.C</TITLE>
</HEAD>
<BODY>
<CENTER>
<FORM METHOD=GET ACTION="/cgi-bin/wwwwais">
<P><B>Search for:</B>
<INPUT TYPE=TEXT NAME="keywords" SIZE=40>
</FORM>
</CENTER>
</BODY>
</HTML>
```

Because the previous form has only one input field, the submit and reset buttons are not necessary. When the user presses return, the form is automatically submitted to `wwwwais.c`. The `wwwwais.c` script passes the value of the *`keywords`* variable to the WAIS search engine you have installed on your system.

Forms designed for use with the `SFgate` script can be as simple or complex as you make them because SFgate gives you advanced control over how searches are performed and the way results are formatted. Figure 28.5 shows the search section of an advanced form designed to be used with `SFgate`. Figure 28.6 shows how users could be allowed to alter your default search and debug parameters. Listing 28.3 is the HTML code for the document shown in Figure 28.5 and Figure 28.6.

Listing 28.3. Advanced form with use with SF`gate`.

```
<HTML>
<HEAD>
<TITLE>Using SFgate</TITLE>
</HEAD>
<BODY>
<H1>Accessing a WAIS database with SFgate</H1>
<FORM METHOD=GET ACTION="/usr/cgi-bin/SFgate">
<INPUT NAME="database" TYPE="hidden" VALUE="www.tvpress.com/site.db">
<H2>Search by:</H2>
```

```
<DL>
<DT>Title
<DD><INPUT TYPE=TEXT NAME="ti">
<DT>Author name
<DD><INPUT TYPE=TEXT NAME="au">
<DT>Text
<DD><INPUT TYPE=TEXT NAME="text" SIZE=60>
<DT>Publication year
<DD><SELECT NAME="py_p">
<OPTION> &gt;
<OPTION> =
<OPTION> &lt;
</SELECT>
<INPUT TYPE=TEXT NAME="py" SIZE=4 VALUE="1995">
</DL>
<INPUT TYPE="submit">
<INPUT TYPE="reset">
<H1>Change default search and debug parameters</H1>
<H2>Enter search and retrieval options:</H2>
<P>Fetch documents using direct WAIS URL?</P>
<SELECT NAME="directwais">
<OPTION> off
<OPTION> on
</SELECT>
<P>Use redirection capabilities?</P>
<SELECT NAME="redirect">
<OPTION> off
<OPTION> on
</SELECT>
<P>Language for return results?</P>
<SELECT NAME="language">
<OPTION>english
<OPTION>french
<OPTION>german
</SELECT>
<P>How do you want the results to be listed?</P>
<INPUT TYPE="radio" NAME="listenv" CHECKED VALUE="DL">descriptive list
<INPUT TYPE="radio" NAME="listenv" VALUE="PRE">preformatted list
<P>What type of title headings do you want to see in the list?</P>
<INPUT TYPE="radio" NAME="verbose" CHECKED VALUE="1">verbose headings
<INPUT TYPE="radio" NAME="verbose" VALUE="0">short headings
<P>What is the maximum number of hits you want the search to return?</P>
<INPUT NAME="maxhits" TYPE=TEXT VALUE="40" SIZE=3>
<H2>Enter debug options:</H2>
<P>Dump environment to an HTML document instead of processing the query?</P>
<SELECT NAME="dmpenv">
<OPTION> no
<OPTION> yes
</SELECT>
<P>Show Debug information?</P>
<SELECT NAME="debug">
<OPTION> off
<OPTION> on
</SELECT>
</FORM>
</BODY>
</HTML>
```

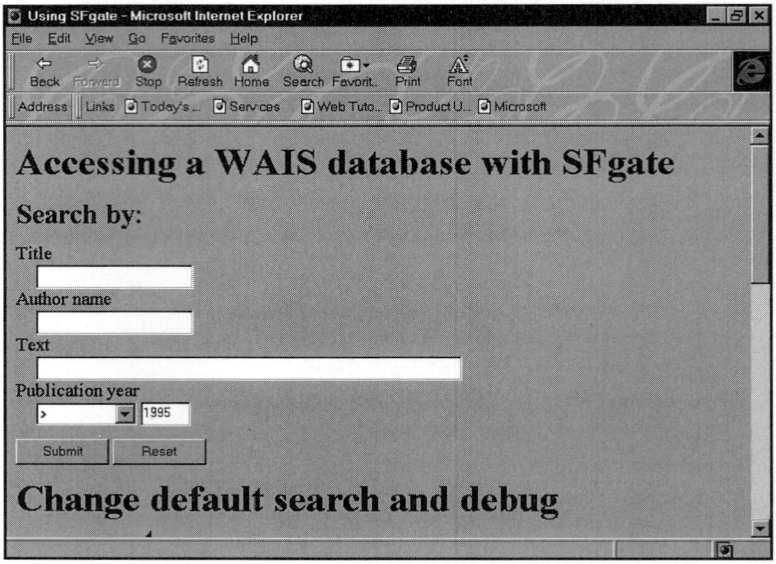

FIGURE 28.5.
Advanced form for use with `SFgate`.

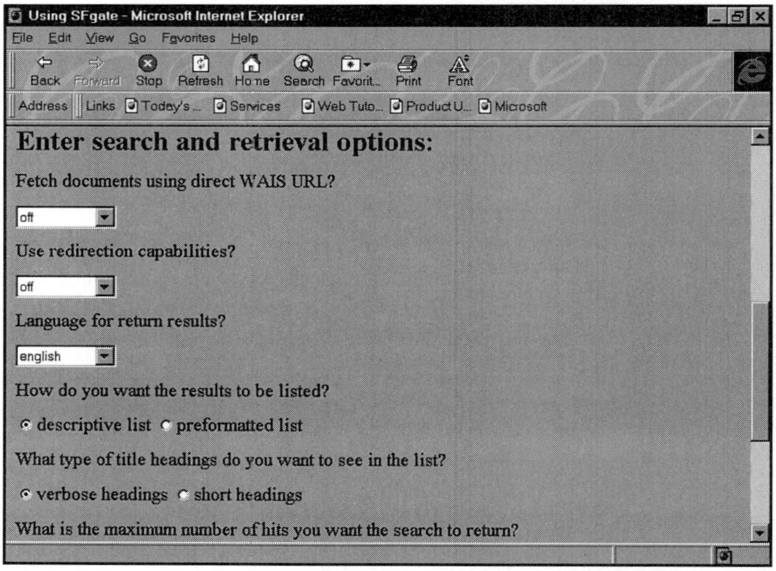

FIGURE 28.6.
Setting additional search and debug parameters.

The form used with the `SFgate` script has many fields. You can assign the `NAME` field to key values that have special meaning to `SFgate`. The primary search and retrieval parameters are `ti`, `au`, `text`, and `py`. The title parameter `ti` enables keyword searches of titles. The author parameter `au` enables keyword searches of the authors of documents indexed in the database. The text parameter `text` enables keyword searches of the full text of documents indexed in the database. The publication year parameter `py` is used to search based on the date the indexed documents were published.

The `database` variable defines the name of the WAIS database you want to search. In this example, this variable is assigned to a hidden input field; in this way, you could use `SFgate` to search different databases at your Web site. You could even let the user search different databases at your Web site using the same form by changing the input field for the database from a hidden field to one the user can manipulate.

Most of the additional search variables are set to default values automatically and do not have to be specified. Specifying parameters for these variables enables you to provide additional controls to users. The debug parameters are used for testing and troubleshooting problems and are not normally included in your final search form.

Installing a WAIS Gateway

Installing a WAIS gateway may not be as easy as you think. This section looks at installing basic and advanced WAIS gateways.

Configuring Basic WAIS Gateways

Installing one of the basic WAIS gateways (`wais.pl`, `son-of-wais.pl`, and `kidsofwais.pl`) is easy. You simply obtain the script, move it to an appropriate directory, such as `cgi-bin`, and modify the configuration parameters in the beginning of the script. The easiest gateway to configure is `wais.pl`. Configuring `wais.pl` involves modifying four lines of code at the beginning of the script:

1. Set the path to the search engine, which is normally `waisq` if you've installed the freeWAIS server:

   ```
   $waisq = "/usr/local/bin/wais/waisq";
   ```

2. Specify the location of the directory containing your WAIS databases:

   ```
   $waisd = "/usr/local/wais.db/";
   ```

3. Specify the indexed database for the search:

   ```
   $src = "sitedb.src"
   ```

4. Specify the title for the HTML document used to display the results:

   ```
   $title = "Search Results"
   ```

If all WAIS gateways were as easy to configure as `wais.pl`, Web publishers would have no problems creating an interface to WAIS. Although configuring `son-of-wais.pl` and `kidofwais.pl` is slightly more difficult, the scripts have good step-by-step documentation that explains the process.

Configuring Advanced WAIS Gateways

Advanced WAIS gateways present more problems to Web publishers because more options and variables are involved. This section looks at configuring an advanced WAIS gateway called `wwwwais.c`. To install EIT's `wwwwais.c`, you have to make a minor modification to the source code, compile the source code, move the compiled script to an appropriate directory, and update the configuration file.

Preparing the `wwwwais.c` Script

Because the `wwwwais.c` gateway uses a separate configuration file, you can install the configuration file wherever you would like. For this reason, you must specify the path to the configuration file in the source code. This minor modification is easy to make; simply edit the source code using your favorite editor. To ensure that the configuration file will be easy to find if you need to update it later, you may want to place the file in the same directory as the configuration file for your Web server, such as

```
/usr/local/httpd/conf/wwwwais.conf
```

NOTE

Because you specify the full path to the configuration file in the source code, you can name the file anything you want. In the preceding example, the configuration file is called `wwwwais.conf`.

After you modify the source code, compile it using your favorite C compiler, such as `gcc`. The `wwwwais.c` script should compile without errors. After the program is compiled, move it to an appropriate directory on your Web server. Usually this directory is your server's `cgi-bin` directory. After moving the script, make sure the script is executable. You may want to use `chmod 711`, which allows you to read, write, and execute the program, but only allows others to execute it.

Updating the `wwwwais.c` Configuration File

The `wwwwais.c` configuration file enables you to set many useful parameters for searching indexed databases and displaying the results. The configuration file contains parameters that can be passed to `wwwwais.c`. Variables are specified by variable name and associated value. The space between the variable name and value is necessary. Listing 28.4 is an example of a `wwwwais.c` configuration file.

Listing 28.4. Sample wwwwais.c configuration file.

```
# WWWWAIS configuration file

# If PageTitle is a string, it will be a title only.
# If PageTitle specifies an HTML file, this file will be prepended to
# wwwwais results.
PageTitle "waistitle.html"

# The self-referencing URL for wwwwais.
SelfURL "http://www.tvpress.com/cgi-bin/wwwwais"

# The maximum number of results to return.
MaxHits 40

# How results are sorted. This can be "score", "lines", "bytes",
# "title", or "type".
SortType score

# AddrMask is used to specify the IP addresses of sites authorized access
# to your database
# Only addresses specified here will be allowed to use the gateway.
# These rules apply:
# 1) You can use asterisks in specifying the string, at either
#    ends of the string:
#    "192.100.*", "*100*", "*2.100.2"
# 2) You can make lists of masks:
#    "*192.58.2,*.2", "*.100,*171.128*", ".58.2,*100"
# 3) A mask without asterisks will match EXACTLY:
#    "192.100.58.2"
# 4) Define as "all" to allow all sites.
AddrMask all

# The full path to your waisq program.
WaisqBin /usr/local/bin/waisq
# The full path to your waissearch program.
WaissearchBin /usr/local/bin/waissearch
# The full path to your SWISH program.
SwishBin /usr/local/bin/swish

# WAIS source file descriptions
# These represent the path to the indexed databases
# For SWISH sources:
#    SwishSource full_path_to_source/source.swish "description"
SwishSource /usr/local/httpd/wais/index/index.swish "Search our Web"
SourceRules replace "/usr/local/www/" "http://www.tvpress.com/"
# For waisq sources:
#    WaisSource full_path_to_source/source.src "description"
WaisSource /usr/local/httpd/wais/index/index.src "Search our Web"
SourceRules replace "/usr/local/www/" "http://www.tvpress.com/"
WaisSource /usr/local/httpd/wais/index/index.src "Search our Web"
SourceRules replace "/usr/local/www/" "/"
SourceRules prepend "http://www.tvpress.com/cgi-bin/print_hit_bold.pl"
SourceRules append "?$KEYWORDS#first_hit"
# For waissearch sources:
#    WaisSource host.name port source "description"
WaisSource quake.think.com 210 directory-of-servers "WAIS directory of servers"
```

continues

Listing 28.4. continued

```
# Do you want to use icons?
UseIcons yes

# Where are your icons are kept?
IconUrl http://www.tvpress.com/software/wwwwais/icons

# Determining file type based on suffix.
# Suffix matching is not case sensitive is entered in the form:
#    TypeDef .suffix "description" file://url.to.icon.for.this.type/ MIME-type
# You can use $ICONURL in the icon URL to substitute the root icon directory.
# You can define new document types and their associated icons here.
TypeDef .html "HTML file" $ICONURL/text.xbm text/html
TypeDef .txt "text file" $ICONURL/text.xbm text/plain
TypeDef .ps "PostScript file" $ICONURL/image.xbm application/postscript
TypeDef .gif "GIF image" $ICONURL/image.xbm image/gif
TypeDef .src "WAIS index" $ICONURL/index.xbm text/plain
TypeDef .?? "unknown" $ICONURL/unknown.xbm text/plain
```

When you update the configuration file for use on your system, look closely at every line of the file containing a parameter assignment. Because you will need to change almost every parameter assignment, be wary of any assignments that you do *not* change. The most important updates to the configuration file involve specifying the proper paths to essential files on the system. Here's how you should assign these essential values:

`SelfURL` The URL path to `wwwwais.c`.

`WaisqBin` The full path to your `waisq` program.

`WaissearchBin` The full path to your `waissearch` program.

`SwishBin` The full path to your `SWISH` program. `SWISH` is similar to `wwwwais.c` and is discussed later in the chapter.

`SwishSource` The location of local databases indexed with `SWISH` and a brief description. If there are multiple `SwishSource` lines, the user is prompted to specify the database to search.

`WaisSource` The local WAIS database name and location. Local WAIS databases are accessed with `waisq`, and remote WAIS databases will be accessed with `waissearch`. For local WAIS databases, you must specify the location of the database and a brief description. All local database names should include the `.src` extension. For remote WAIS databases, you must specify a host name, port, database name, and description. All remote database names should *not* include the `.src` extension.

`SourceRules` The action to take on the results. Valid actions are:

- `append` Add information after the results
- `prepend` Add information before the results

`replace`	Replace the local path with a URL path so Web users can access the documents
`TypeDef`	The MIME type definition. This parameter allows the script to match file name extensions to MIME types. Any MIME types not configured are assigned to the type `unknown`.

Passing Additional Parameters to wwwwais.c

You can pass additional parameters to `wwwwais.c` as input from a fill-out form or with environment variables set in a script that calls `wwwwais.c`. Any additional parameters you reference override parameters set in your configuration file. The simple form used earlier to pass keywords to `wwwwais.c` can be easily updated to accommodate these additional parameters. The variables you can set include the following:

`host` — The name of the remote host machine to search with `waissearch`. The host information should include the domain, as this example does:

```
host=tvp.com
```

`iconurl` — The URL path to icons. The `iconurl` should include the transfer protocol, as in the following example:

```
iconurl=http://tvp.com/icons/
```

`isindex` — The index to search on.

`keywords` — The keywords to search on.

`maxhits` — The maximum number of matches to return after a search.

`port` — The port number to contact the remote host machine on.

`searchprog` — The search engine to use. This variable can be set to one of the following:

`searchprog=swish`	A local search using `SWISH`
`searchprog=waisq`	A local search using `waisq`
`searchprog=waissearch`	A remote search using `waissearch`

`selection` — The indexed database to use as specified by the description set in the configuration file.

`sorttype` — The sorting method for the results. This variable can bet set to the following:

`sorttype=bytes`	Sort by the byte size of the documents
`sorttype=lines`	Sort by the number of lines
`sorttype=score`	Sort by score
`sorttype=title`	Sort by document title
`sorttype=type`	Sort by document type

`source`	The indexed database to search.
`sourcedir`	The directory of the indexed database.
`useicons`	Whether icons based on file type are used. This variable can be set to one of the following: `useicons=no` Do not use icons `useicons=yes` Use icons
`version`	Verification of the version number of your WAIS applications. The default value `false` can be set to `true` as follows: `version=true`

You can use either the `GET` or `POST` method to submit data from an HTML form to `wwwwais.c`. You can set variables yourself using hidden fields or allow the users to set these variables using input fields. The `wwwwais.c` script supports the `PATH_INFO` variable as well, so you can add additional parameters to the end of the URL path to `wwwwais.c` in URL-encoded format. Listing 28.5 shows how you could create a form with additional parameters already added to the URL path:

Listing 28.5. `wwwwais.c` form with additional parameters.

```
<HTML>
<HEAD>
<TITLE>Search our Web site</TITLE>
</HEAD>
<BODY>
<FORM METHOD=GET
ACTION="/cgi-bin/wwwwais/useicons=yes&maxhits=50&sorttype=score">
<P><B>Search for:</B>
<INPUT TYPE=TEXT NAME="keywords" SIZE=40>
</FORM>
</BODY>
</HTML>
```

To set parameters in a script that calls `wwwwais.c`, you use environment variables. You can change any of the variables discussed earlier into an environment variable that `wwwwais.c` will recognize by putting `wwww` before the variable name. All variable names should be in uppercase. Listing 28.6 is a simple `csh` script to show how you could set variables and call `wwwwais.c`.

Listing 28.6. `csh` script to set variables for `wwwwais.c`.

```
!/bin/csh
#Shell script for setting environment variables for wwwwais
setenv WWWW_USEICONS = yes
setenv WWWW_MAXHITS = 50
setenv WWWW_SORTTYPE = type
#Call wwwwais
/usr/local/cgi-bin/wwwwais
exit
```

Building an Indexed Database

So far this chapter has discussed the basics of indexers, search engines, WAIS, and WAIS gateways. Now that you have read the section on accessing a WAIS database, you should understand how WAIS gateways work and how to create an HTML document for a WAIS gateway. The next step is to install a search and retrieval application that includes an indexer and a search engine.

As I mentioned earlier in this chapter, one of the most widely used Wide Area Information Servers is `freeWAIS`. The `freeWAIS` server is actually a series of scripts for building and searching an indexed database. An alternative to `freeWAIS` is `SWISH`. Developed by the team at EIT Corporation, the Simple Web Indexing System for Humans offers ease of installation and ease of use.

Installing and Configuring freeWAIS

Many versions of `freeWAIS` are in use on the Internet. The two main variants you may be interested in are the standard `freeWAIS` package and the `freeWAIS-sf` package. Standard `freeWAIS` is the most widely used WAIS system. The `freeWAIS-sf` package is optimized for use with `SFgate`.

You can find information on the current version of `freeWAIS` and obtain the source code at these locations:

```
http://www.eit.com/software/

http://cnidr.org/

ftp://ftp.cnidr.org/pub/NIDR.tools/freewais/
```

You can find information on the current version of `freeWAIS-sf` and obtain the source code at these locations:

```
http://ls6-www.informatik.uni-dortmund.de/SFgate/SFgate.html

ftp://mirror-site/mirror-dir/SFgate/

ftp://mirror-site/mirror-dir/freeWAIS-sf-1.2/freeWAIS-sf/
```

After you download the source code to your computer from one of the listed locations and uncompress the source code as necessary, you can begin installing and configuring `freeWAIS`. Both variants of `freeWAIS` include essentially the same applications:

```
waisserver
waisq
waissearch
waisindex
```

Using waisserver

The waisserver program is the primary server program. You need to run waisserver only if you want to be able to search locally available databases. Before you start waisserver, you will need to know three things:

- You need to know the port on which you want the waisserver to allow connections. This port is normally 210. You invoke waisserver with the -p option to set the port number.
- You need to know the directory where your source databases are located. The waisserver program will allow any database in the specified directory to be searched. You invoke waisserver with the -d option to set the directory path to your indexed WAIS databases.
- You need to know how you want errors to be treated. Although tracking errors is not mandatory, it is a sound administrative practice. Invoke waisserver with the -e option to specify a log file for tracking errors.

To start waisserver, change directories to where waisserver is installed. In the following example, waisserver answers requests on port 210, source databases are in the /usr/local/httpd/wais/sources, and errors are logged in /usr/local/httpd/logs/wais.log. To start waisserver using these options, you would type the following all on one line:

```
./waisserver -p 210 -d /usr/local/httpd/wais/sources -e
➥/usr/local/httpd/logs/wais.log &
```

NOTE

The ampersand symbol puts waisserver in the background. If you do not put the server process in the background, the server will stop running when you exit your login. Additionally, to ensure waisserver is started if the host computer is rebooted, update the appropriate configuration files. For example, you could add the following to the rc.local file on most UNIX systems to make sure that waisserver is started automatically:

```
#Added to start the waisserver process
#waisserver is used to enable searching of the local WAIS databases
/usr/local/httpd/wais/waisserver -p 210 -d /usr/local/httpd/wais/sources -e
➥/usr/local/httpd/logs/wais.log &
```

Using waisq and waissearch

The waisq and waissearch programs search WAIS databases for the information you're looking for. The waisq search engine looks in databases on the local host, and waissearch looks in databases on remote machines. The waissearch program does things remotely by contacting WAIS servers on different machines, each of which has its own database. In order for waissearch to work properly, you must tell it a host name and a port to which to connect. Additionally, the remote host must have a WAIS server of its own running on the port you specify. Your WAIS gateway calls waisq or waissearch for you, so you generally do not access these search engines directly.

Using waisindex

The waisindex program creates indexed WAIS databases. When you create an index, you can index all or any portion of the files on the host computer. Generally, files are indexed into a database according to their directory. When you index files, you can specify the following information:

- Invoke waisindex with the -d option to set the directory path to the files you want to index.
- Invoke waisindex with the -r option to specify that you want subdirectories to be indexed.
- Specify the name of the database that is created as a result of running waisindex, including the file path. Indexed WAIS databases end with the .src extension, but are named *without* the .src extension.
- Specify whether you want waisindex to index the full contents of the document or just the file name. The default is to index the full contents of the documents. For files indexed with the nocontents flag, only the file names are indexed.

You can specify these additional parameters if you wish:

- Invoke waisindex with the -e option to specify a log file for tracking errors.
- To specify the level of detail for logging what waisindex is doing on your system, invoke waisindex with the -l option to specify logging verbosity. The higher the number, the more verbose and detailed the logging will be.
- Invoke waisindex with the -m option to specify the amount of memory and resources to use for indexing. The higher the number, the more system resources will be used.

To run waisindex, either change to the directory where waisindex is installed or specify the full path to the program. In the following example, waisindex is located in the /usr/local/httpd/wais directory, the verbosity of the output is set to 1 for minimal logging, errors are logged in /usr/local/httpd/logs/waisindex.log, the directory to index is /users/webdocs, the path to the database is /usr/local/httpd/wais/sources, and the name of the database is webdocuments. To run waisindex using these options, you would type the following all on one line:

```
/usr/local/httpd/wais/waisindex -l 1 -d /users/webdocs -e /usr/local/httpd/logs/
➥wais.log -r /usr/local/httpd/wais/sources/webdocuments
```

Although you could run waisindex by hand whenever you needed to reindex your site, the best way to handle indexing is to set up a cron job to handle the task. In UNIX environments, cron jobs are run automatically at times you specify. Most systems have multiple cron tables. Jobs in a cron table are run by the owner of the cron tab, which is normally located in the `/usr/spool/cron/crontabs` directory.

You will usually want to update your indexes daily, especially on a host that changes frequently. The best time to run `waisindex` is when system usage is low. Often, this is in the early morning hours. To add a statement to the root cron table to update your index daily at 1 a.m., you could insert the following lines:

```
# Root Cron
# Entry added to build waisindex
00 01 * * * /usr/local/httpd/wais/waisindex -l 1 -d /users/webdocs -e
➥/usr/local/httpd/logs/wais.log -r /usr/local/httpd/wais/sources/webdocuments
```

The previous example assumes you want to index only a single directory and its subdirectories, but you can add more statements to the cron tab to build additional indexed databases. This solution for indexing your site works best on simple document structures. If your host has a complex document structure, you can build the index using links or build the index using a script.

Building a WAIS Index Using Links

You can add links from your document directories to a base directory that you will index using the `-r` option to recursively index subdirectories. To do this, you could create a base directory, such as `/users/webdocs`, add subdirectories to this directory, and link your document directories to the subdirectories. Here's how you would do this on most UNIX systems that enable symbolic links:

```
$ mkdir /users/webdocs
$ cd /users/webdocs
$ mkdir HTML
$ mkdir TEXT
$ mkdir PDF
$ mkdir GIF
$ ln -s /users/webdocs/HTML /usr/local/httpd/docs/html
$ ln -s /users/webdocs/TEXT /home/users/local/text
$ ln -s /users/webdocs/PDF /usr/bin/adobe/acrobat/docs
$ ln -s /users/webdocs/GIF /usr/local/images/samples/gif
```

Now if you ran the command defined earlier, you would index all the appropriate directories you have linked to the `/users/webdocs` directory. Keep in mind that the actual database would be located in the `/usr/local/httpd/wais/sources` directory and would have the name `webdocuments.src`. The `waisindex` program adds the `.src` extension to the database name to indicate that the file is a source file.

Building a WAIS Index Using a Script

For the most complex document structures, you should use a shell script. A script also enables you to easily specify the types of files you want to be indexed and the types of files you want to ignore.

The csh script in Listing 28.7 was written by Kevin Hughes of EIT and can be used to index documents at your site with waisindex. Documents you don't want to index the contents of, such as GIF images, are specified with the nocontents flag. This flag tells waisindex to index only the file name and not the contents.

Listing 28.7. csh script for indexing documents using waisindex.

```
#! /bin/csh

set rootdir = /usr/local/www
#       This is the root directory of the Web tree you want to index.

set index = /usr/local/httpd/wais/sources/index
#       This is the name your WAIS indexes will be built under.
#       Index files will be called index.* in the /usr/local/httpd/wais/sources
#       directory, in this example.

set indexprog = /usr/local/httpd/wais/waisindex
#       The full pathname to your waisindex program.

set nonomatch
cd $rootdir
set num = 0
foreach pathname ('du $rootdir ¦ cut -f2 ¦ tail -r')

        echo "The current pathname is: $pathname"
        if ($num == 0) then
                set exportflag = "-export"
        else
                set exportflag = "-a"
        endif
        $indexprog -l 0 -nopairs -nocat -d $index $exportflag $pathname/*.html
        $indexprog -l 0 -nopairs -nocat -d $index -a $pathname/*.txt
        $indexprog -l 0 -nopairs -nocat -d $index -a $pathname/*.c
        $indexprog -nocontents -l 0 -nopairs -nocat -d $index -a $pathname/*.ps
        $indexprog -nocontents -l 0 -nopairs -nocat -d $index -a $pathname/*.gif
        $indexprog -nocontents -l 0 -nopairs -nocat -d $index -a $pathname/*.au
        $indexprog -nocontents -l 0 -nopairs -nocat -d $index -a $pathname/*.hqx
        $indexprog -nocontents -l 0 -nopairs -nocat -d $index -a $pathname/*.xbm
        $indexprog -nocontents -l 0 -nopairs -nocat -d $index -a $pathname/*.mpg
        $indexprog -nocontents -l 0 -nopairs -nocat -d $index -a $pathname/*.pict
        $indexprog -nocontents -l 0 -nopairs -nocat -d $index -a $pathname/*.tiff
        @ num++
end
echo "$num directories were indexed."
```

The script shown in Listing 28.8 for indexing directories based on file type was created by Michael Grady from the University of Illinois Computing & Communications Services Office. This Perl script is based on the csh script in Listing 28.7. Although both scripts are terrific and get the job done right, the Perl script offers more control over the indexing.

Listing 28.8. Perl script for indexing documents using waisindex.

```
#!/usr/local/bin/perl
# Michael Grady,  Univ. of Illinois Computing & Communications Services Office
# Perl script to index the contents of a www tree. This is derived from a csh
# script that Kevin Hughes of EIT constructed for indexing files.

$rootdir = "/var/info/www/docs";
#       This is the root directory of the Web tree you want to index
$index = "/var/info/www/wais-sources/ccso-main-www";
#       This is the name and location of the index to be created
$indexprog = "/var/info/gopher/src/fw02sf/bin/waisindex";
#       The full pathname of the waisindex program
$url = "http://www.uiuc.edu";
#       The main URL for your Web. No slash at the end!

$numdir = $num = 0;

# Generate a list of directory names, then for each directory, generate an
# array of all the filenames in that directory except for . and .. . Sort this
# list so that if there is an .htaccess file in that directory, it comes near
# the front of the list. We assume that if you've bothered to put special
# access controls into a directory, then maybe you don't want these files
# indexed in a general index. You of course can remove this restriction if you
# want. Then we separate all the files in the directory into two lists: one
# list is those file types for which it is appropriate to index the contents of
# the files, and the second list are those whose file types are such we don't
# want to index the contents, just the filename (gif, for instance). Then
# if there are any files in either of these lists, we call waisindex to index
# them. The first time we index, we do not include the -a flag, so that the
# index replaces the current one. Every subsequent call to waisindex includes
# the -a flag so that we then add to the new index we are building. We include
# the -nopairs option on all waisindex calls, because this saves a lot of
# unused info from being put into the index.

# If this is run by cron, redirect print statements to file (or /dev/null).
# Probably want to add a "-l 0" option to the waisindex call also.
#open (LOGIT, ">>/tmp/waisindex.run");
#select LOGIT;

# Put in the appropriate path on your system to each of the commands
# "du", "cut" and "tail", in case you want to run this from a cronjob and
# these commands are not in the default path. Note that "du" will not follow
# symbolic links out of this "tree".
open (PATHNAMES,"/usr/bin/du $rootdir ¦ /usr/bin/cut -f2 ¦/usr/bin/tail -r ¦");
DO_PATH: while ( $pathname = <PATHNAMES>) {
        chop $pathname;

        # The following are "path patterns" that we don't want to
        # follow (subdirectories whose files we do not want to index).
        # Add or subtract from this list as appropriate. These may
        # be directories you don't want to index at all, or directories
        # for which you want to build their own separate index.
        next DO_PATH if $pathname =~ /uiucnet/i;
        #next DO_PATH if $pathname =~ /demopict/i;
        next DO_PATH if $pathname =~ /images/i;
        next DO_PATH if $pathname =~ /testdir/i;
```

```
        print "Current pathname is: $pathname\n";
        $numdir++;
        @contents = @nocontents = ();
        opendir(CURRENT_DIR, "$pathname")
                        || die "Can't open directory $pathname: $!\n";
        @allfiles = sort (grep(!/^\.\.?$/, readdir(CURRENT_DIR)));
        closedir(CURRENT_DIR);

        DO_FILE: foreach $file (@allfiles) {
                        # skip directories that contain a .htaccess file
                        # note this is NOT smart enough to be recursive (if a
                        # directory below this does not itself contain an
                        # .htaccess file, it WILL be indexed).
                next DO_PATH if $file eq '.htaccess';
                        # filetypes for which we want to index contents
                $file =~ /\.html$/i &&
                   do { push(@contents, "$pathname/$file"); next DO_FILE;};
                $file =~ /\.te?xt$/i &&
                   do { push(@contents, "$pathname/$file"); next DO_FILE;};
                $file =~ /\.pdf$/i &&
                   do { push(@contents, "$pathname/$file"); next DO_FILE;};
                #$file =~ /\.ps$/i &&
                   #do { push(@contents, "$pathname/$file"); next DO_FILE;};

                        # filetypes for which we DON'T want to index contents
                $file =~ /\.gif$/i &&
                   do { push(@nocontents, "$pathname/$file"); next DO_FILE;};
                #$file =~ /\.au$/i &&
                   #do { push(@nocontents, "$pathname/$file"); next DO_FILE;};
                #$file =~ /\.mpg$/i &&
                   #do { push(@nocontents, "$pathname/$file"); next DO_FILE;};
                #$file =~ /\.hqx$/i &&
                   #do { push(@nocontents, "$pathname/$file"); next DO_FILE;};
        # Comment out the above lines to your liking, depending on what
        # filetypes you are actually interested in indexing.
#       For instance, if the ".mpg" line is commented out, then
#       MPEG files will *not* be indexed into the database (and thus
#       won't be searchable by others).
        } # end DO_FILE loop

        if ($#contents >= 0) {          # Index if any files in list.
                @waisflags = ("-a", "-nopairs");
                @waisflags = ("-nopairs") if $num == 0;
                $num ++;
                system($indexprog, "-d", $index, @waisflags, "-t", "URL",
                                $rootdir, $url, @contents);
        }
        if ($#nocontents >= 0) {        # Index if any files in list.
                @waisflags = ("-a", "-nopairs");
                @waisflags = ("-nopairs") if $num == 0;
                $num ++;
                system($indexprog, '-d", $index, @waisflags, "-t", "URL",
                                $rootdir, $url, "-nocontents", @nocontents);
                # note that "-nocontents" flag must follow any -T or -t option
        }
} # end DO_PATH loop

close(PATHNAMES);
```

continues

Listing 28.8. continued

```
print "Waisindex called $num times.\n";
print "Tried indexing $numdir directories.\n";
# end of script
```

Testing the WAIS Database

After you have installed `freeWAIS`, started `waisserver`, and built an index, you will want to test your new WAIS system. You can do this using `waisq`. If the database was indexed with the following command,

```
00 01 * * * /usr/local/httpd/wais/waisindex -l 1 -d /users/webdocs -e
➥/usr/local/httpd/logs/wais.log -r /usr/local/httpd/wais/sources/webdocuments
```

you could invoke `waisq` as follows to test the database:

```
/usr/local/httpd/wais/waisq -m 40 -c /usr/local/httpd/wais/sources -f -
➥-S webdocuments -g Stanek
```

This command tells `waisq` to return a maximum of 40 matches and to search the `webdocuments` source file located in the `/usr/local/httpd/wais/sources` directory for the keyword `Stanek`. If all goes well and some documents contain the keyword, the server should respond with output similar to the following:

```
Searching webdocuments.src . . . Initializing connection . . . Found 28 items.
```

After this message, the server should produce output containing the search word used and the results of the query. Keep in mind that this output is normally interpreted by your WAIS gateway. The WAIS gateway processes this output, creates a document containing the results, and sends the document to the client originating the search.

Installing and Configuring SWISH

`SWISH`, the Simple Web Indexing System for Humans, is an easy-to-use alternative to `freeWAIS`. `SWISH` is good choice if you want to experiment with indexing and search engines. Besides being easy to install, `SWISH` creates very small indexes compared to a WAIS index. Using the environment variables `PLIMIT` and `FLIMIT`, you can squeeze what otherwise would be a large index into about one-tenth of the file space. As a smaller file is quicker to search, `SWISH` can display results faster than many other search engines. However, there is a trade-off between file size and search results. A smaller file contains less data, and the smaller the file size, the less accurate the results of the search.

`SWISH` has a couple of limitations. Because it can search only local `SWISH` databases, you must use another indexing system if you need to access remote hosts. Additionally, `SWISH` works best with small to medium-size databases, so if you have a large site with hundreds of megabytes of files to index, you may want to use `freeWAIS` instead of `SWISH`.

You can find information on the current version of `SWISH` and obtain the source code from EIT corporation at

`http://www.eit.com/software/`

After you download the source code to your computer from the EIT Web site and uncompress the source code as necessary, you can begin installing and configuring `SWISH`. The first step is to change directories to the `SWISH` source directory and update the `config.h` file. If you've just uncompressed `SWISH`, you should be able to change directories to `swish/src` or simply `src`.

In the `config.h` file, you need to set parameters for your specific system. This file is also where you update the `PLIMIT` and `FLIMIT` variables that control the size of your index files. After you set those parameters by following the inline documentation, you can compile `SWISH`. `SWISH` compiles fine with any C compiler, even plain old `gcc`.

Setting Up the SWISH Configuration File

The next step is to edit the `SWISH` configuration file. This file is usually located in the `src` directory and is used to configure environment variables for search and retrieval results. After you've updated the configuration file, you can name it anything you want, such as `swish.conf`. Listing 28.9 is a sample configuration file for `SWISH`.

Listing 28.9. Sample SWISH configuration file.

```
# SWISH configuration file

IndexDir /usr/webdocs
# This is a space-separated list of files and directories you want to index.

IndexFile /usr/local/httpd/swish/sources/index.swish
# This is the name your SWISH-indexed database.

IndexAdmin "William Stanek publisher@tvp.com"
IndexDescription "Index of key documents at the Web site"
IndexName "Index of TVP Web site"
IndexPointer "http://tvp.com/cgi-bin/wwwwais/"
# Additional information that can be used to describe the index,
# the WAIS gateway used, and the administrator

FollowSymLinks yes
# If you want to follow symbolic links, put yes. Otherwise, put no.

IndexOnly .html .txt .c .ps .gif .au .hqx .xbm .mpg .pict .tiff
# Only files with these suffixes will be indexed.

IndexVerbose yes
# Put this to show indexing information as SWISH is working.

NoContents .ps .gif .au .hqx .xbm .mpg .pict .tiff
# Files with these suffixes won't have their contents indexed,
# only their file names.
```

continues

Listing 28.9. continued

```
IgnoreLimit 75 200
# To ignore words that occur too frequently, you will want to
# set this parameter. The numbers say ignore words that occur
# in this percentage of the documents and occur in at least this
# many files. Here, ignore words that occur in 75% of the files
# and occur in over 200 files. If this variable is not set, SWISH
# uses a default setting.

IgnoreWords SwishDefault
# This variable allows you to set your own stop words.
# To do this, you replace the word SwishDefault with a space-
# separated list of stop words. You can use multiple assignments
# if necessary.
```

The most important variables in the configuration file are `IndexDir` and `IndexFile`. The `IndexDir` variable enables you to specify the files and directories to index. If you enter multiple directories and file names, separate them with spaces. You can make more than one `IndexDir` assignment, if necessary. The `IndexFile` variable tells `SWISH` where to store the index. Because `SWISH` does not add the `.src` extension to the file name, you can name the file anything you want. However, you may want to use an extension of `.swish` so you know the file is a `SWISH`-indexed database.

Compiling and Running SWISH

After you update the configuration file, you can move the compiled `SWISH` program, `swish`, and the configuration file to an appropriate directory, such as:

```
/usr/local/httpd/swish/
```

To run `SWISH` and index the files and directories specified in the configuration file, change directories to where `SWISH` is located and type the following:

```
./swish -c /usr/local/httpd/swish/swish.conf
```

Based on the settings in the previously defined configuration file, when `SWISH` finishes indexing your site, the indexed database will be located here:

```
/usr/local/httpd/swish/sources/index.swish
```

Because `SWISH` lets you specify the full path to the configuration file, you can have different configuration files for different databases. To use `SWISH` with a gateway, you must ensure that the script has been modified to work with `SWISH` or is `SWISH`-friendly. To modify a gateway so that it is `SWISH`-friendly, you may only have to change the path for its search engine from its current setting to the full path to the `SWISH` executable file. An example of a `SWISH`-friendly gateway is `wwwwais.c`. The `wwwwais.c` program enables you to set the path to `SWISH` executable files and sources.

These are the settings that make the program SWISH-friendly:

```
# The full path to your SWISH program.
SwishBin /usr/local/bin/swish

# WAIS source file descriptions
# These represent the path to the indexed databases
# for SWISH sources:
#    SwishSource full_path_to_source/source.swish "description"
SwishSource /usr/local/httpd/wais/index/index.swish "Search our Web"
SourceRules replace "/usr/local/www/" "http://www.tvpress.com/"
```

Other Search Engines

Dozens of commercial, freeware, and shareware search engines are available. If you are looking for a commercial-grade search engine that is free, you may have to look no further than Excite for Web Servers (see Figure 28.7).

Excite for Web Servers is a next-generation search engine that accepts natural language input, which means users can enter search information in whole sentences and don't have to use keywords. Another great feature of EWS is the capability to browse the index, which allows users to search through the database using a directory tree structure. EWS is available for most UNIX operating systems and Windows NT. You can test drive EWS at Excite before you download and install it:

```
http://www.excite.com/navigate/home.html
```

The developers at Excite claim you can download, install, and have EWS running on your system in 30 minutes. Although this claim is definitely true, there is a downside to EWS. EWS requires a minimum of 32 M RAM, and EWS searches are system resource-intensive. Therefore, before you install EWS, carefully consider how your server will handle the additional load.

If you are looking for the best search engine available and cost is not a major consideration, you may be looking for Livelink Search from Open Text, Inc (see Figure 28.8). Most search engines only allow you to search HTML and ASCII formatted documents, but Livelink Search allows you to search just about any type of text-based document, including HTML, SGML, Acrobat PDF, Microsoft Word, WordPerfect, and most other word-processing and spreadsheet formats. Not only will Livelink Search allow you to index non-HTML documents, it also converts non-HTML documents on the fly to HTML for viewing in Web browsers.

Livelink Search is a complete Web publishing solution and includes the Netscape Enterprise Web server. You can test drive Livelink Search at Open Text:

```
http://www.opentext.com/livelink/ll_search.html
```

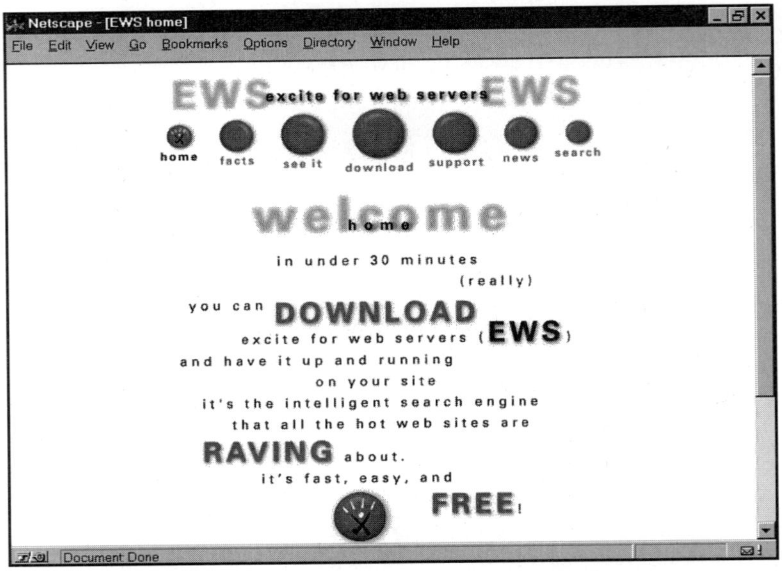

FIGURE 28.7.
Excite for Web Servers: a next-generation search engine.

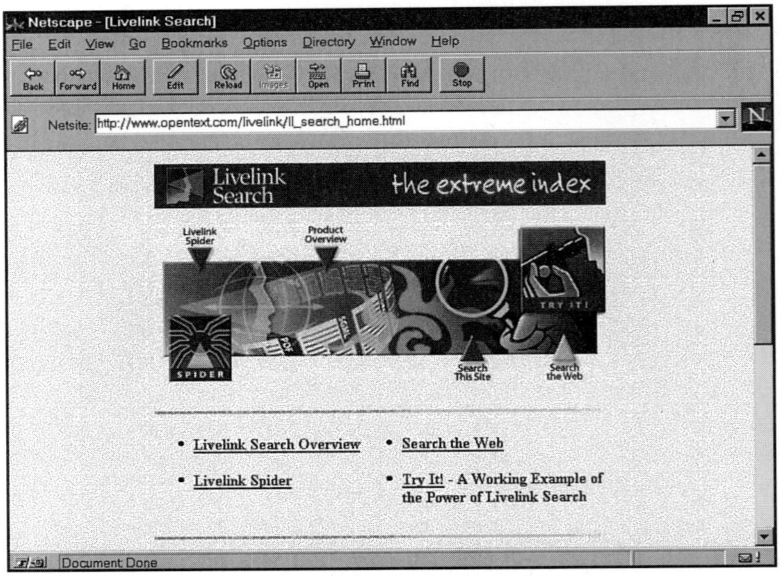

FIGURE 28.8.
Livelink Search allows searching and indexing of non-HTML documents in dozens of popular formats.

Summary

Building an indexed database and creating Web documents that access the database via a gateway requires a lot of effort on the part of the Web publisher. Yet if you take the process one step at a time, you can join the thousands of Web publishers who have indexed their Web sites and thus provide to Web users the ability to search the site quickly and efficiently. Enabling the interface from a fill-out form in your Web document to an indexed database involves these steps:

1. Obtain the appropriate software. If you use `freeWAIS`, the package includes `waisserver`, `waisq`, `waissearch`, and `waisindex`. These programs will handle searching and indexing. You will also need to select a gateway, such as `wwwwais.c`.
2. Install and configure the software.
3. Build your indexed databases.
4. Create a fill-out form to submit data to the gateway.
5. Test the search capabilities of the index.

CHAPTER 29

Creating and Managing Discussion Groups on the Web

by John Jung

IN THIS CHAPTER

People, and companies, often create Web pages that target a single topic. Web pages aimed at fans of a particular star, or show, are widely accessible on the Web. Companies create Web pages to promote themselves and possibly help their customers. Often it is useful for the visitors of these sites to be able to talk together. This chapter explains how you, as a Web publisher, can make such discussions possible.

Why Use Discussion Groups?

Probably the first question that most readers have is, "Why do I want to use a Web-based discussion group?" The answer is quite simple: To allow many people to talk to each other about a common topic. Web browsing is one of the fastest growing activities on the Net. Traditional activities, such as FTP, e-mail, and Usenet, are still being accessed, but they are not growing as fast as the Web. Consequently, there is a need for Web-based discussion groups. Two main groups of Web authors can make use of a discussion group: the fans of a celebrity, or show, and organizations, such as companies.

Fan-based Discussion Groups

Although many people enjoying gawking at celebrities or chatting about television shows, some people are more enthusiastic than others. It's these people who would most likely create a Web page just for their favorite celebrity or show. Many such Web pages are very straightforward, offering any information the Web author has about the subject. Extremely popular celebrities or television shows may have large numbers of such fans who want to talk about their fondness for a particular subject.

Although Usenet newsgroups can be created for the purpose of discussing such subjects, not everybody has access to such groups. The reason these groups don't have that much exposure on Usenet is because of their transient nature. Once a show is cancelled or a star loses his or her appeal, such newsgroups typically fade away. Many Usenet administrators won't carry such newsgroups precisely for these reasons.

A good alternative to this type of Usenet newsgroup is a Web-based discussion group. In such a board, fans can find, or give, information on the celebrity or show. Whether it's the latest gossip or a report on some related news article, such information can be incorporated into the Web page itself. This result brings a certain sense of pride to the participants of a Web-based discussion group. The only problem with a Web-based discussion group is that it doesn't get the exposure that other discussion forums do. A Usenet newsgroup can reach millions of readers; a Web discussion group can only reach whoever accesses the page. However, a Usenet newsgroup won't necessarily be carried by all sites at all times. A Web-based discussion group is carried by the Web author for as long as he wants. If he's particularly enthusiastic about his Web page, it can stay up forever.

Corporate-based Discussion Groups

Every corporation wants to know what its customers are thinking. After all, if it knows what the people want, it can try to provide it for them. A Web discussion group can be a good way to get this information. Corporate-based discussion groups tend to focus on the corporation where the Web site is located. Chances are, if the Web site is for Ed's CompuHut, the discussion group will focus on the store. Customers can post their opinions about a particular product or salesman, questions about using software, or compliments. Similarly, the employees at the corporation can help customers with problems, respond to complaints, and provide late-breaking news about the company. This type of discussion group provides one of the most open channels of communication for a company. It allows them to be insulted and praised on their own systems.

What's Wrong with Usenet Groups?

Usenet is a collection of newsgroups, each of which contains news articles. These general groups are broken up into more specific groups where the content is defined and regulated by its participants. There are a number of problems with using a Usenet-style newsgroup for Web pages. First and foremost is that you need special user privileges to create and maintain each group. For fan-based Web pages, this approach is generally unworkable.

Another problem with the Usenet model is that the specific newsgroup is accessible by a limited number of computers. When an article is posted to a newsgroup, it's handed off to other computers that are capable of recognizing that newsgroup. The problem with narrowly-focused newsgroups, such as for a company, is that most computers outside the company won't carry it. It's not that the noncompany computers necessarily have a problem with the content; it's just that there's little or no demand for those groups. Consequently, creating a Usenet-style discussion group for a Web page is a tremendous amount of work. Aside from the privileges problem, there is the problem of convincing many systems administrators to carry a single Usenet-style group.

Because of these two problems, it is extremely difficult to use Usenet-style newsgroups for a Web-based discussion group. The best method of allowing people to talk about a particular topic is to use a Web-based discussion group. Other options, such as mailing lists or restricted newsgroups, are basically derivatives of a Web-based discussion group.

Discussion Group Issues

Before creating a discussion group, you have to decide who should, and shouldn't, be able to post to the board. This choice isn't as obvious as it may seem; certain conditions must be weighed. On the one hand, you can have unrestricted access, which means anybody can post to it. This is similar to most Usenet newsgroups, where anybody can subscribe to a group, and post to it. With restricted access, only authorized people can post information. This approach is much like private chat areas, where only invited people can participate. Related to deciding who can post is the decision as to whether the discussion group should be moderated. Moderated discussion groups are sort of a middle ground between completely open access and completely restricted access.

Unrestricted Access

One of the best aspects of Usenet is its complete openness. Because anybody can post anything he or she wants, all opinions are heard equally. Consequently, if a point is argued or defended well, the author will probably command respect. This atmosphere makes it possible for minority opinions to be exposed to everybody at large. In this respect, unrestricted access is great for allowing everyone a complete perspective on any given topic. Another benefit of an open-ended discussion group is the many different viewpoints from other participants. If you have a problem with something and you live far from civilization, an unrestricted discussion group can bring you a great deal of help. You don't necessarily need to drive many miles just to get an opinion; you can simply post your query to the board. Whoever reads the board may respond with some useful answers.

The obvious downside of an open-ended discussion group, such as Usenet, is the easy abuse of it. People can easily post topics that are unrelated to your board. Anybody who's read Usenet for very long knows how annoying chain letters and advertisements can be. Although they are less likely to appear, these types of messages are also possible on Web-based discussion groups. Another downside of a discussion group such as Usenet is that everybody can post. Without someone to regulate what's posted, there is little accountability. Anybody can write to your board and disrupt the ongoing discussions. Unrestricted access is a double-edged sword; on the one hand, you let in many viewpoints. On the other hand, you have to deal with possible abuse from the throngs of potential posters.

Restricted Access

Restricted access to a discussion group usually takes the form of a password-protected Web page. Only people with accounts that can bypass the Web page can post to the board. This type of discussion group is best suited for service-oriented companies. Customers of the company, as well as employees, can be given accounts in the protected Web page. As a result, both the vendor and customer can privately discuss issues in peace. Additionally, because the Web page is password-protected, the customer's competition won't be able to read proprietary information.

On the whole, restricted discussion groups tend to be more focused. Depending on the criteria for restricting access to a discussion group, the content can be very helpful. The downside of a restricted discussion group is a lack of more diverse information. Because the discussion group participants have been filtered already, there are fewer voices to be heard. This means that most mainstream opinions are heard, but few extremes are. If you post a query to a restricted discussion group, you may or may not get an answer. If you send that same message to an unrestricted board, you'll almost always get a reply—right or wrong.

Suppose you posed an obscure trivia question about a television show to a restricted discussion group for that show. If nobody with access knows the answer, you won't get any help. However, if you post that question to an unrestricted discussion group, your chances will improve. Another down side to a restricted discussion group is the problem of stagnation. After a while, all the old-timers tend to dominate the topics. Because the discussion has fewer participants, there tend to be fewer new topics. Most of the old-timers have already expressed their opinions to each other, and few want to explain themselves again. Open discussion groups tend to have a constantly changing mix of new participants.

Moderated Board

The middle ground between unrestricted access and completely restricted access is a moderated board. A moderated discussion group is one where anybody can participate in the discussion group. However, when someone posts something, it's not posted directly to the discussion group. Rather the post is sent to a moderator. This person is the only one authorized to post anything to the discussion group. Although this person doesn't write the posts, he or she is the filter for the content of the board.

The primary advantage of having a moderated board is that you have the best of both worlds. You have access to a wide diversity of facts and opinions. At the same time, undesirables are kept from polluting your discussion group. Topics of discussions are relevant, and the participants won't (publicly) insult each other. Best of all, there are no disruptions from unrelated posts.

The big drawback of a moderated discussion group is that you need a moderator. Individuals who run discussion groups don't want to have to sift through and determine what is, and isn't, an acceptable post. For these individual discussion groups, a moderated discussion group isn't an available option. Large organizations, however, might find this approach worthwhile. It allows them to keep their discussion group focused on whatever they like. If the organization is a company, only posts concerning the company's products are likely to be approved. Praise for a competitor's product will also be rejected, for obvious reasons.

Components of a Web-based Discussion Group

The majority of Web-based discussion groups have three basic components. The first is a table of contents, which shows some information about the messages themselves. The second component is some sort of mechanism that assigns each message its own unique file name. The individual messages are the final component. Generally, the individual messages are stored in their own directory to isolate them from other Web pages. The following sections describe the components and how they interact with each other.

Table of Contents

Every Web-based discussion group has to have some place where the messages are referenced. The messages themselves are not stored in this place, only their URLs are. The table of contents for a Web board is often a Web page itself. Usually the subject, author, and corresponding URL of each article are displayed on separate lines. When someone wants to read a message on a Web-based discussion group, he'll point his browser to the table of contents. If a particular subject interests him, he simply has to click on the appropriate link.

Maintaining Unique File Names

In all likelihood, you don't want to keep all messages for a particular board in one file. After all, if there is a lot of posting, the file will grow exceptionally large. Additionally, if the single file were corrupted in some manner, you would lose all topics of discussion. Consequently, you should keep each post in its own file. Another component in Web-based discussion groups is some mechanism for creating unique file names.

The most direct approach in implementing this capability is to assign each message a number. This number can be saved in a plain text file for easy retrieval. When someone posts a message to the discussion group, you simply have to fetch the current message number. Next, save the newly posted message to a unique file name by using the message number. You can then update the file that holds the message number. On DOS-based machines, this naming scheme limits you to a maximum of 99,999,999 messages. If your operating system supports long file names, you can have significantly more messages.

Another approach to this problem is to dynamically assign each file name. To make it unique, you can use current date and time as part of the file name. Although this method makes the file names for each message a little complicated, it is a viable solution. This approach wouldn't require any extra file to hold the unique file name. However, the downside of this approach is that it's possible to have a conflict, which can result in a corrupt message. Also, it is, theoretically, possible for several people to try and save different messages at the exact same time. Certainly, the probability of this scenario happening is very remote, but it does exist.

The Messages Themselves

The final component in a Web-based discussion group is the messages themselves. Because you want to keep each message independent of all others, you will need to keep each individual message. These messages are often stored in their own directory, so as to not clutter up a directory full of Web pages. Most of the time, each message is wrapped in some HTML code. The HTML code typically allows the user to go to the next, or previous, message. The capability to post a new message, or a reply to the current one, is also part of the HTML code.

How to Create a Discussion Group

Now that you know what all the parts of a discussion group are, it's time to put them all together. The table of contents is instrumental in making use of the other components. That is, the table of contents usually has links to a `cgi-bin` script. That script looks at the second component, the last uniquely assigned message number. Finally, the `cgi-bin` script creates the final component, the message itself, by saving the posted message. Although each component of a discussion group is important, you don't need to write `cgi-bin` scripts for each of them. It's possible to create a good `cgi-bin` script that can handle all the components.

Structuring the Table of Contents

Before creating a discussion group, you have to create a table of contents. Although having a table of contents of nothing might seem a little strange, it is necessary. The table of contents should be an HTML file, so that all the contents can formatted as links to the messages. When new messages are posted, this Web page has to be modified. At the very least, the information for the new post has to be added. The table of contents page should also allow users to post to the discussion group. You can provide this feature most easily by having a separate page to take the user's input.

The Posting Page

The page that the table of contents page can point to is the posting page. This Web page has fill-out forms asking for the user's name, e-mail address, subject, and message body. Obviously, you'll also need to point to a `cgi-bin` script to handle the input. The only real purpose of this page is to not clutter up the other pages of the discussion group. Although you could embed this Web page with other discussion group-related pages, you generally don't want to. The contents of the posting page are rather extensive and usually take up a lot of space. This space could be better spent in storing information for more messages or showing more of the body of the message.

The `cgi-bin` Script

When the user is happy with what he's entered into the posting page, he clicks a button. This button should point to a `cgi-bin` script file that will process the input. It should check to make sure that none of the fields in the forms was empty. If anything was left out, the script should send an error message to the user. Although it'd be nice for the script to be able to check for valid inputs, such as a valid e-mail address, it's not realistically possible. From the Web, it's very difficult to accurately verify information entered by the user through form fields.

After the post has passed through the very simple checking process, the file has to be created. The `cgi-bin` script file should first read the message number file, and open it for writing. Next, the parsed message has to be printed out to the newly opened file. The form values should be formatted and sent to the file in a reasonable fashion. For example, create some sort of message header that holds the user name, e-mail address, and subject line. The body can be separated from the header by using an HTML horizontal rule. The purpose of nicely formatting the message is to make it easier for users to read.

Finally, the `cgi-bin` script has to update the table of contents file to provide access to the new message. You can use a text parsing program called by the `cgi-bin` script to handle this task. One approach would be to have an HTML comment in the table of contents. When a post is being added to the table of contents, the comment line is looked for. The location of this comment line is returned from the parsing program to the `cgi-bin` script. Once it's found, the important information for the new article is put in, and the rest of the table of contents is appended. Using the HTML comment, you can also put new messages at the end of the table of contents.

Another approach would be to hard code the number of lines that lead up to the beginning of the table of contents. Suppose that your table of contents Web page uses 10 lines to create the general appearance of the discussion topics. After the new message has been saved, you read it in, and ignore the first 10 lines. Next, you add in the information for the new message, and then append the existing information to the end.

Advanced Discussion Group Issues

With the basic components laid down, you can create a very simple and basic Web-based discussion group. This discussion group lacks a number of useful items that non-Web discussion groups have, however. An obvious feature that's lacking is the capability to reply to the current message. Another feature that is missing is the capability to manage the messages themselves. You can also add intelligent parsing to the Web-based discussion group. The following sections explain the general approaches to implementing each of these features.

Replies

A feature that's very obviously missing from the current outline of a discussion group is the ability to reply to a message. With the current approach, there is no easy method of allowing replies. The best way to enable replies is to embed posting abilities within each message. At the bottom of each article, you could have fill-out forms with the original message. When readers want to reply to the message, they edit the fill-out forms, and then click a button. Make the fill-out form field variable names the same as those on the posting page.

With this approach, one `cgi-bin` script could handle both new postings and replies. When someone wants to reply to an article, the form field values are already entered, and the writer just has to modify them. Though this approach will clutter up the individual messages, it does provide an easy reply mechanism.

Article Maintenance

Another useful capability that's lacking in the currently outlined Web-based discussion group is any type of article maintenance. Theoretically, if a discussion group were never cleaned out, you could read all the articles ever posted. With many messaging systems, however, each forum has a certain amount of space allocated to it. When someone tries to create a new message, and can't, an old message is deleted to make room. Although adequate in most cases, this system suffers when a discussion area stagnates. In such a situation, the discussion group could contain articles that are many months old simply because no new articles have been posted to get rid of the old ones.

Another approach to managing disk space and discussion groups is the Usenet approach. In this approach, each site mandates a maximum amount of time that any article can be kept on the system. This limit allows for an automatic expiring mechanism that is uniform and consistent. Although this limit means there are no truly old articles, it also means that some discussion groups might not have any articles at all. On Usenet, it's not unusual to see stagnant newsgroups with absolutely no content.

The current example of a discussion group has no article management facility. You can add this type of functionality by creating a separate discussion group Web page. Make the page password-protected so that only you, the board maintainer, can access it. This private Web page should also have a separate `cgi-bin` file to do all the dirty work. The private Web page need not be elaborate, after all, it's intended only for one person. However, it should be functional and easy to use, for your sake. It should have form fields that give you a number of useful options, such as listing articles by an author, by a date, or by subject. It should also have links and form fields for deleting articles.

The private `cgi-bin` script is perhaps much more important than the Web page itself. This script should be capable of doing a great deal of text processing for the discussion group Web page. The purpose of most of the `cgi-bin` script will be to give you, the board maintainer, meaningful information. It should return items such as message subject, author, URL, and message number. The rest of the script file will focus on the information. The file should be capable of deleting files entirely or deleting individual lines from a file. When you want to delete an article, the `cgi-bin` file should already know which article you want deleted. Next, it should go out and remove the article's file. Finally, it should update all messages that replied to that article. Obviously, this process involves a great deal of talking and passing of information between the private Web page and `cgi-bin` script. As a result, some Web-based discussion groups put the two, the `cgi-bin` script and the private Web page, together.

Intelligent Parsing

Even though you've probably already implemented a simple routine to check the form fields of a new article, you can do much more. Although you can't reasonably check for a valid user name or e-mail address, you can enhance each post. You can run a simple text parser through the form field values of a post and check for certain strings of characters. For example, you could parse URLs and put HTML code around them to enable readers to directly access a referenced URL.

Similarly, you could modify your parser to look for certain words. Suppose that your Web-based discussion group is about your company's products. You might want to parse the form field values and look for your competitor's names. Although you might not necessarily reject the article, it does give you the ability to filter it out, if necessary. Or suppose there's a discussion group that's geared towards children. You might want to have a text parser to filter out any profanity, so as to not offend anyone. Depending on the level of parsing that you want to implement, the parsing routine could come before, during, or after the post is to be saved in a file.

How to Manage Discussion Groups

Any Web-based discussion group is at the mercy of the person whose account it's residing in. If it's a fan-oriented board and only one person is running it, she'll have absolute say over what should, and shouldn't, be on the board. Similarly, corporate-backed discussion groups are likely to be filled mostly with praise for the company. However, you should know about some aspects of maintaining a discussion group and its topics.

Be Willing to Accept Contrary Opinions

Even though you're the person responsible for the discussion group, you should be willing to keep an open mind. For example, if you feel that an actor was bad in a show's performance, don't delete contrary viewpoints. Be willing to let posts that you personally disagree with get posted, and stay posted, on the board. A healthy debate is good for any conversation, Web-based or not. Try to remember the focus of the discussion group, and don't let your own feelings get in the way. That's not to say that you should let all conflicting viewpoints in, just be willing to accept them. It's no use to set up a discussion group about a TV show if everybody who participates complains about it. Rather, try to strike a balance between pro and con positions.

Corporate discussion groups are different. Although you might be willing to let competitors' products get mentioned, your supervisor might not want you to. She might tell you to filter out any messages that portray the competition in a good light. Customer complaints usually provide the balance to company praise in corporate discussion groups. Chances are pretty good that no matter what company you're with, it will want to hear complaints. Your company can't improve its product if it doesn't know what the customer wants. As a result, even if the complaints are fierce, they probably won't be filtered out.

Try to Be Polite

Another important aspect to remember in being the maintainer of a discussion group is to be polite. Even though you (usually) wield supreme power over your board, you shouldn't flex your muscle. If an article's content was inflammatory and unreasonable, don't respond in kind. Politely reason with the person and try to persuade him to resubmit his opinions in a more suitable manner. Don't be too quick to say, "Well, I run things around here, and I say you're wrong, so you're *wrong*!"

Your discussion group will become more popular if people know it's okay for them to express themselves openly and freely. Let the users complain about your system, your discussion group, even about you. That's what an open discussion is all about. Even though you are in complete control of a discussion group, you should be careful when exercising your position. Supreme executive power derives from a mandate from the users. It helps to keep the participants happy, even when you might not be.

Summary

For people who want to encourage discussion about a particular topic, a Web-based discussion group is a good idea. It gives people interested in the same topic a place to go to talk about whatever they want. However, implementing such a board can be difficult, depending on what functionality you want to offer. A discussion group where people simply write new messages and have no reply capability is easy to implement. A discussion group that more closely resembles other discussion forums, such as Usenet, requires more work. Such a board requires more text parsing and `cgi-bin` scripting, but the payoffs can make the extra work worthwhile.

Also, creating a discussion forum isn't simply putting Web pages and `cgi-bin` scripts together. It's also a fair amount of responsibility. You should be patient and understanding and be willing to listen to complaints. Depending on the purpose of your discussion group, you might not be able to, but you should at least try. The main goal of any discussion group is to allow people a chance to talk about whatever the board was created to talk about. If it's about a TV show, let the users talk about the TV show. If it's about a product, let the users talk about the product. Don't, however, get so engaged in a discussion that you let your personal feelings get in the way. If people disagree with you on something, don't condemn or censor them; let them have their say.

VII
Part

IN THIS PART

ActiveX and VBScript

CHAPTER 30

Introducing Visual Basic Script (VBScript)

by William Robert Stanek

IN THIS CHAPTER

Microsoft's Visual Basic Script (VBScript) offers the functions of a programming language and the simplicity of a technology streamlined for the Web. With VBScript, you can bring your Web pages to life with real-time interaction; there's no more waiting for a server to respond to button clicks and mouse movements. A click of a button gets an instant reaction, and the movement of the mouse over an object brings the object to life.

When you enhance your Web pages with VBScript, you insert scripts directly into your pages. Because VBScript is a subset of Microsoft's Visual Basic, your scripts resemble programs written in Visual Basic. If you aren't a programmer, don't worry. The wonderful thing about VBScript is that it's a very simple programming language to learn and to use. Many Web publishers who aren't programmers use VBScript to enhance their Web pages.

Learning VBScript

If there was ever a programming language that should have been adopted for use on the Web, it's Visual Basic. Microsoft's Visual Basic is founded on the simplest programming language ever designed, called Basic. Extending the simplicity of Basic to a more structured and modern object-oriented programming approach made Visual Basic a smashing success story. A language that understands objects—like buttons, toolbars, and menus—and is easy to use is a dream come true for programmers.

When the developers at Microsoft redesigned Visual Basic for the Web, they knew they had to get rid of the massive overhead associated with Visual Basic programs. This meant streamlining every aspect of Visual Basic and keeping only the essentials of the language. The developers also knew that security was a key concern for Web programming languages. A Web programming language that opened the end user's system to attack and compromise wouldn't succeed.

To protect the end user's computer, VBScript eliminates the cause of most security problems. For example, VBScript doesn't allow scripts to modify files on the end user's computer in any way. By preventing the reading and writing of files and directories on the end user's computer, VBScript closes the door on most security problems.

NOTE

Although VBScript couples the best aspects of Visual Basic with a strict security model, it can be used with other Internet technologies, like ActiveX. You will learn all about integrating ActiveX and VBScript in Chapter 33, "Integrating ActiveX and VBScript."

Like most basic programming languages, VBScript is an interpreted language, which is both good news and bad news. The good news is that you don't need to compile your scripts as you would with a program written in C or C++. Your scripts are directly interpreted, line by line, when they're executed in the user's browser. The bad news is that before anyone can run your scripts, he or she needs a VBScript interpreter, which is part of the standard Internet Explorer browser package. It's installed automatically when you install Internet Explorer.

Although Microsoft's Internet Explorer 3.0 and later versions include a VBScript interpreter, most other browsers don't. However, there's an add-on module for Netscape Navigator 3.0/4.0 that supports VBScript. Netscape Navigator users will need to install this add-on module before they can fully use your VBScript-enhanced pages.

Putting VBScript to Work for You

The possible uses for VBScript in your Web pages are endless. You can use scripts to create forms that change in response to users' questions; these customized forms could tailor orders, surveys, and customer support to the customer's needs. The results from VBScript-enhanced forms can be processed locally by the user's browser or can be passed on to a server script for further processing.

VBScript can be used to add interactive menus and buttons to the page. When the user makes a menu selection, portions of the page can change in response to the selection. At the click of a button, a dialog box can open to answer the user's question, offer helpful hints, or prompt the user when errors occur. (See Figure 30.1.)

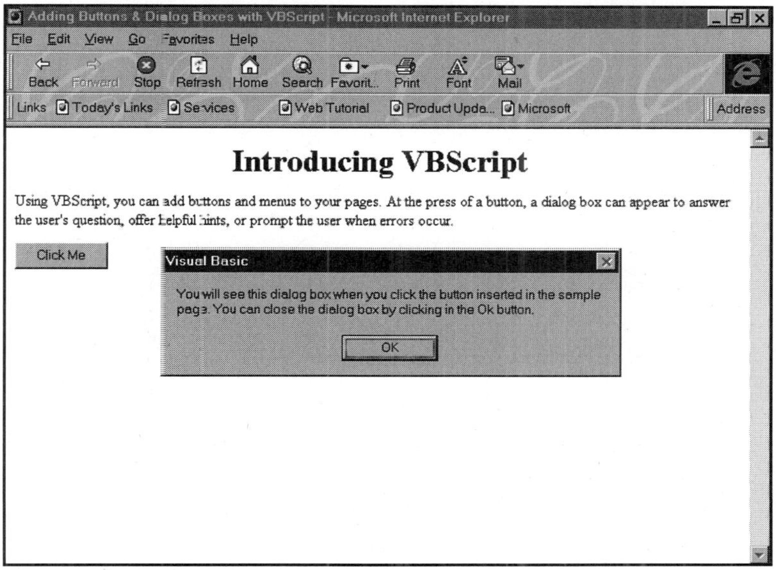

FIGURE 30.1.
Using VBScript to display dialog boxes.

To add these graphical objects to your pages, use the basic controls offered by HTML forms. For example, the button shown in the sample page was added with the following line of code:

```
<INPUT TYPE=BUTTON NAME=cmdButton VALUE="Click Me">
```

You should recognize the `<INPUT>` tag from Chapter 27, "Form Creation and Design." As discussed in that chapter, the `TYPE` attribute is used to set which type of form element to add to the page. Here, the form element is a button—named `cmdButton`—displayed with the label `Click Me`.

By combining the form elements you learned about in Chapter 27, you can easily create interactive Web pages complete with buttons, text fields, text areas, radio buttons, and checkboxes. Later in the chapter, you will learn more about adding controlled objects to your VBScript-enhanced pages.

Displaying the dialog box associated with the button was done with the following code:

```
Sub cmdButton_OnClick

     Msgbox "You will see this dialog box when you click the button inserted
in the sample page. You can close the dialog box by clicking in the OK button."

End Sub
```

By examining this code, you can see how VBScript works. The name of the button is `cmdButton`; it has an event related to it called `OnClick`. When the button is clicked, the subroutine `cmdButton_OnClick` is automatically executed. VBScript features many ways of automatically handling user events, such as button clicks, mouse movement, and detecting when the pointer is over an object. The `Msgbox` statement tells the user's browser to display a dialog box with the contents you define between the quotation marks.

Listing 30.1 shows the complete markup for the page shown in Figure 30.1. As you examine Listing 30.1, don't worry about the syntax used to add scripts to your pages; you'll find detailed instructions later in this chapter.

Listing 30.1. Using buttons.

```
<HTML>
<HEAD>
<TITLE>Adding Buttons &amp; Dialog Boxes with VBScript</TITLE>
</HEAD>

<BODY BGCOLOR="#FFFFFF">
<CENTER>
<H1>Introducing VBScript</H1>
</CENTER>

<P ALIGN="LEFT">Using VBScript, you can add buttons and menus to your pages.
 At the press of a button, a dialog box can appear to answer the user's
 question, offer helpful hints, or prompt the user when errors occur.</P>

<INPUT TYPE=BUTTON NAME=cmdButton VALUE="Click Me">

<SCRIPT LANGUAGE="VBScript">
<!--

' This procedure is executed whenever the button labeled cmbButton is clicked
Sub cmdButton_OnClick
```

```
    Msgbox "You will see this dialog box when you click the button inserted
➥in the sample page. You can close the dialog box by clicking in the Ok button."

End Sub

-->
</SCRIPT>

</BODY>
</HTML>
```

VBScript is great for crunching numbers, too. You can create a script to perform calculations, such as computing your annual salary based on wages and investment income or determining the time it will take to travel from one city to another.

With CGI, the user would have to fill out a form, submit the form to a server, and then wait for the server to respond. When the server finished the calculations, the results would then be sent back to the client, which would display the results. As you know from earlier discussions on CGI, the results are usually displayed on a separate results page. With VBScript, all this back-and-forth processing is eliminated. The user can fill out a form and see the results instantly—and on the same page!

The sample page shown in Figure 30.2 uses VBScript to compute the sales tax on an order. The user simply enters the appropriate values and clicks a button that causes a script to compute and display the results.

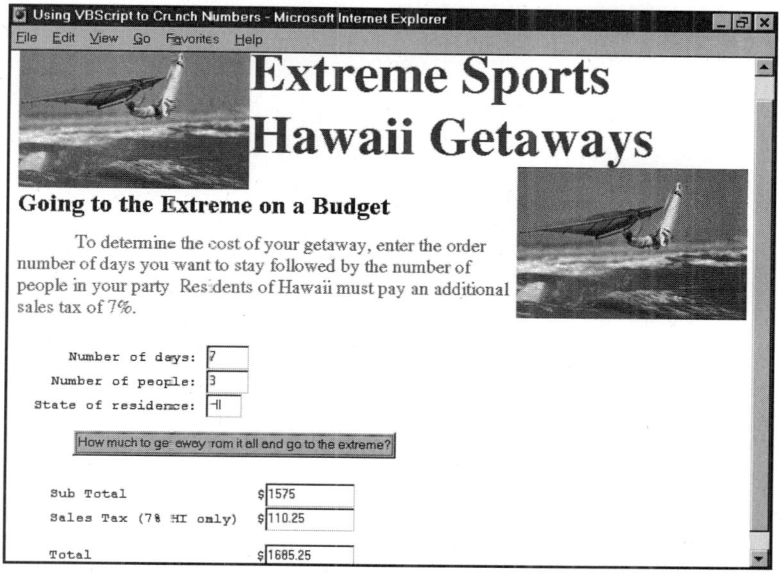

FIGURE 30.2.
Using VBScript to compute sales tax.

Although the script used to perform the calculation shown in Listing 30.2 is longer than the previous script example, the script has a fairly basic structure. Simply put, the script accepts three values and displays the results after computations are made.

Listing 30.2. Calculating costs and sales tax.

```
<HTML>
<HEAD>
<TITLE>Using VBScript to Crunch Numbers</TITLE>
<STYLE>
H1  {font: 35pt Times; color: blue}
P  {font: 12pt Times; color: red; text-indent: .5in; margin-right: 1in}
</STYLE>
</HEAD>

<BODY BGCOLOR="#FFFFFF">

<H1>
<IMG SRC="power.jpg" ALIGN=LEFT>
Extreme Sports Hawaii Getaways
<IMG SRC="power.jpg" ALIGN=RIGHT>
</H1>

<BR CLEAR=LEFT><H2>Going to the Extreme on a Budget</H2>

<P>To determine the cost of your getaway, enter the order number of days
you want to stay followed by the number of people in your party.
Residents of Hawaii must pay an additional sales tax of 7%.</P>

<PRE>
      Number of days: <INPUT NAME="tripDays" SIZE=3>
    Number of people: <INPUT NAME="tripSize" SIZE=3>
  State of residence: <INPUT NAME="resState" SIZE=2>
</PRE>

<P><B><INPUT TYPE=BUTTON VALUE="How much to get away from it
➥all and go to the extreme?" NAME="cmdCost"></B></P>

<PRE>
    Sub Total                $<INPUT NAME="tripCost" SIZE=10>
    Sales Tax (7% HI only)   $<INPUT NAME="tripTax" SIZE=10>

    Total                    $<INPUT NAME="tripTotal" SIZE=10>
</PRE>

<SCRIPT LANGUAGE="VBScript">
<!-- Option Explicit

   Sub cmdCost_OnClick()

Dim State
Dim tripLength
Dim tripParty
Dim Cost
Dim Tax
Dim Total
```

```
tripLength = tripDays.Value
tripParty = tripSize.Value
State = resState.Value

If tripLength = 0 Then
    MsgBox "Please enter the length of your getaway."
    Exit Sub
End If
If tripParty = 0 Then
    MsgBox "Please enter the number of people in your party."
    Exit Sub
End If

Cost = 75.00 * tripLength * tripParty

If State = "HI" Then
     Tax = Cost * 0.07
Else
     Tax = 0
End If

Total = Cost + Tax

tripCost.Value = Cost
tripTax.Value = Tax
tripTotal.Value = Total

   End Sub

-->
</SCRIPT>

</BODY>
</HTML>
```

Getting Ready to Use VBScript

As a VBScript developer, you have an expanded role in Web publishing and may need to modify options in your browser for this new role. Most browsers consider VBScript to be a form of active content. You'll learn about active content and ActiveX in Chapter 31, "Exploring ActiveX and ActiveX Controls." Because running active content can present security concerns, the ability to run scripts is sometimes disabled.

If you're using Internet Explorer 3.0, you can check the security options by choosing Options from the View menu and clicking the Security tab. Figure 30.3 shows the options for the Security tab. Generally, you should select all the available options so you can see active content in any form, whether it's VBScript, JavaScript, Java, or ActiveX.

You should also check your browser's current safety level setting; to do this, click the button shown in Figure 30.3 labeled Safety Level. By default, Internet Explorer is set to the highest safety level, so scripts with errors or safety problems won't be executed. As a VBScript developer, you should probably set the safety level to Medium, as shown in Figure 30.4, which allows you to execute and view potentially unsafe content.

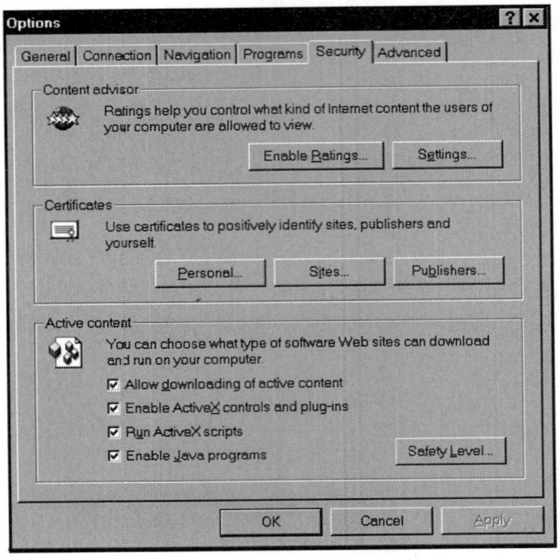

FIGURE 30.3.
Setting security options in Internet Explorer 3.0.

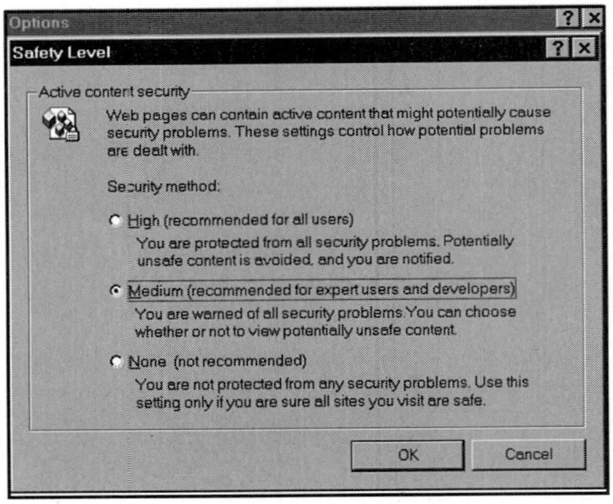

FIGURE 30.4.
Choosing a safety level for active content in Internet Explorer 3.0.

Adding Scripts to Your Page

Adding scripts to your Web pages is easy. All you have to do is place the begin tag `<SCRIPT>` where the script starts and the end tag `</SCRIPT>` where it ends. The `<SCRIPT>` tag has one attribute called `LANGUAGE`, which identifies the scripting language you're using. Since you're creating scripts in VBScript, use the value `LANGUAGE="VBScript"` to tell this to your browser.

Here's an example of how to add a script to your page:

```
<HTML>
<HEAD>
<TITLE>Example</TITLE>
</HEAD>
<BODY>

<SCRIPT LANGUAGE="VBScript">

Insert your script here!

</SCRIPT>

</BODY>
</HTML>
```

Although the most popular browsers available today support scripts, browsers that don't support scripts display your script's code with the contents of your Web page. To avoid this problem, follow the begin script tag with a begin comment tag, and precede the end script tag with an end comment tag. Here's how you can hide the script from non-compatible browsers:

```
<HTML>
<HEAD>
<TITLE>A Better Example</TITLE>
</HEAD>
<BODY>

<SCRIPT LANGUAGE="VBScript">
<!--

Your script is safely hidden here!
Non-compatible browsers will not display
the script with the contents of the page.

-->
</SCRIPT>

</BODY>
</HTML>
```

Scripts in pages may be executed as the page loads. If the script refers to objects that aren't downloaded to the browser, there could be problems. To avoid possible conflicts, make your scripts the last element in the page. To do this, insert the script into the page just before the end body tag `</BODY>`, and place all other markup before the script element, as shown here:

```
<HTML>
<HEAD>
<TITLE>Placing Scripts in Your Pages</TITLE>
</HEAD>
<BODY>

Insert Markup and Main Contents Here!

<SCRIPT LANGUAGE="VBScript">
<!--
Insert Your Script Here!
-->
</SCRIPT>
```

```
</BODY>
</HTML>
```

VBScript Basics

The syntax and structure of programs written in VBScript are like a familiar shoe for anyone who has programmed before. This is true regardless of which programming language you might have used.

Variables

Creating variables in VBScript is easy—all you need to do is give the variable a name. If you assign a name to a variable, you can later refer to the variable by name in your code. There are two ways to declare variables: explicitly or implicitly.

When you declare an explicit variable, you tell VBScript with the keyword `Dim` that you're creating a variable, then follow the `Dim` keyword with the variable name. If you wanted to explicitly declare a variable called `eValue`, you could use the following:

```
<SCRIPT LANGUAGE="VBScript">
<!--

Dim eValue

eValue = eValue + 1

-->
</SCRIPT>
```

When you implicitly declare a variable, you use the variable without first declaring it, so you don't need to use the `Dim` keyword. VBScript creates the variable for you as necessary. If you wanted to use a variable called `iValue` implicitly, you could use the following:

```
<SCRIPT LANGUAGE="VBScript">
<!--

iValue = 150

-->
</SCRIPT>
```

By default, VBScript allows you to mix implicit and explicit variables in your code. The problem with this is that any variable name is assumed to be valid. For example, if you used a variable called `iValue` and later assigned a value to a variable called `iVale`, VBScript would create instances of both variables, even if `iVale` is a typo for `iValue`. To avoid this, you can set the `Explicit` option.

Using the `Explicit` option forces you to declare all variables explicitly with the `Dim` keyword and makes sure your variables are valid. This option should immediately follow the begin comment tag, as follows:

```
<SCRIPT LANGUAGE="VBScript">
<!-- Option Explicit

Your script here.

-->
</SCRIPT>
```

As most programmers know, normally when you use variables in a program, you must state the type of variable. If the variable is used with integers, you declare the variable as an integer; if the variable is used with strings, you declare the variable as a string. However, typing variables appropriately can lead to problems in code and also creates a complex structure that increases the overhead required for programs.

To avoid problems and streamline VBScript, VBScript automatically allocates a variable type to any variable you use in your programs. Variable types used by VBScript include: Boolean, Byte, Integer, Long, Single, Double, Date, String, Object, Error, Empty, and Null.

Generally, if you use whole numbers, such as 5 or 8, with a variable, VBScript creates the variable as an integer. Variables with values that use decimal points, such as 3.5 or 5.82, are usually assigned as double-precision floating-point values—Doubles. Variables entered with a mixture of alphabetical and numeric characters, such as H2O or 4-H, are created as Strings.

Because VBScript can automatically convert between some variable types, most variable conflicts are eliminated. However, if you try to add a String variable to a numeric variable type, you will get an error, so if a variable has alphanumeric characters, don't try to perform numeric calculations with it.

NOTE

Before performing calculations, you can make sure variables are numeric by using the `IsNumeric` function. This function returns a value of `true` if the variable is numeric and `false` if it isn't. This sample code checks for a numeric variable:

```
If IsNumeric(Value1) = True Then
    Value2 = Value1 + 5
```

These related functions check other variable types: `IsDate`, `IsEmpty`, `IsNull`, `IsNumeric`, and `IsObject`.

Arrays

Arrays allow you to group related sets of data together. When you create an array, you must specify its number of dimensions. VBScript allows you to create arrays with up to 60 dimensions. A one-dimensional array is like a column of tabular data; a two-dimensional array is like a spreadsheet with rows and columns; and a three-dimensional array is like a 3D grid that takes time and space into account.

You could create a one-dimensional array from a single column of tabular data. If there were 20 data points in the column, you could declare the array as follows:

```
Dim myArray(19)
```

NOTE

Arrays always begin at 0 and end at the number of data points in the array minus 1. Therefore, an array with 20 data points is initialized as `Array_Name(19)`.

You could create a multi-dimensional array from the cells of a spreadsheet. If the spreadsheet has three columns, each with five rows of data points, you could declare the array as follows:

```
Dim myArray(2,4)
```

If you want to get the value of a specific cell in the spreadsheet, you could use the following:

```
myValue = Array_Name(columns -1, rows -1)
```

In this statement, `columns` is the column position of the cell, and `rows` is the row position of the cell, so if you want to know the value of the cell in column 1, row 4, you could use the following:

```
myValue = myArray(0,3)
```

Although these sample arrays have fixed sizes, you can also size arrays dynamically. This allows you to use input from users to drive the size of the array. Here's how to declare a dynamic array:

```
Dim dynamicArray()
```

Later you can tell VBScript the size of the array by using the `ReDim` function in one of these two ways:

```
ReDim dynamicArray(iCount - 1)

ReDim dynamicArray(columnCount - 1, rowCount - 1)
```

NOTE

Once you create an array at a specific dimension, you can't change the dimension. This means that if you create a two-dimensional array, you can't change it later to a three-dimensional array.

To determine the size of an array at any time, you can use the `UBound` function, which returns the array's upper boundary. The following sample returns the upper boundary of the array in a message box:

```
Dim myArray(99)
Dim x
For x = 0 to UBound(myArray)
     myArray(x) = "Initial"
Next
Msgbox "The upper boundary of the array is" & UBound(myArray)
```

Arithmetic Operators

You perform calculations in VBScript in much the same way as you write out calculations long-hand. The only difference is that you usually assign the result to a variable.

To add numbers, use the + operator, as shown in these two examples:

```
Result = 1 + 5
```

```
Result = ValueA + ValueB
```

To subtract numbers, use the - operator, as these two examples show:

```
Result = 5 - 1
```

```
Result = ValueB - ValueA
```

To multiply numbers, use the * operator; here are two examples of how to do that:

```
Result = 2 * 4
```

```
Result = ValueA * ValueB
```

To divide numbers, use the / or \ operator, as shown in the following examples:

```
Result = 2 / 4
```

```
Result = ValueA / ValueB
```

In division, you often have a remainder. Since you might want to perform calculations based on the remainder, you need a way to determine it. In VBScript, you do this by using the `Mod` function. For the following expression, the value of the result is set to `1`:

```
Result = 7 Mod 2
```

To multiply by an exponent, use the ^ operator. This example is the same as `3 * 3 * 3 * 3`:

```
Result = 3 ^ 4
```

You can also use this example, which is the same as `ValueC * ValueC`:

```
Result = ValueC ^ 2
```

You can negate a value by using the - operator, as shown in these two examples:

```
Result = -2 * 3
```

```
Result = -ValueA * ValueB
```

When you mix operators, VBScript performs calculations using the same precedence order your math teacher taught you. For example, multiplication and division in equations are carried out before subtraction and addition, as shown in these examples:

3 + 2 * 6 = 15

2 / 2 + 3 = 4

The complete precedence order of operators is shown in Table 30.1. According to the table, exponents have the highest precedence order and are always calculated first.

Table 30.1. The precedence order of arithmetic operations.

Order	*Operation*
1	Exponents (^)
2	Negation (-)
3	Multiplication (*) and Division (/)
4	Remainders (Mod)
5	Addition (+) and Subtraction (-)

Comparison Operators

When you perform comparisons, you check for certain conditions, such as “Is A equal to B?” To perform comparisons in VBScript, you use a set of comparison operators that aren’t much different from the comparison operators used in math every day. The only difference is that in your scripts, you typically use a control flow, such as conditional looping, with your comparison. For example, if A is equal to B, then you will perform a specific task; if A is not equal to B, then you will perform a different task.

To see whether a variable is equal to another variable or to a specific value, use the equal sign. Here’s an example that checks for equality:

```
if myValue = 0 Then
   Msgbox "The variable is set to zero."
if myValue = Input Then
   Msgbox "The values are equal."
```

To see whether variables aren’t equal, use the inequality operator, as shown in this example:

```
if myValue <>0 Then
   Msgbox "The variable is NOT set to zero."
if myValue <>Input Then
   Msgbox "The values are NOT equal."
```

To check whether one variable is less than or greater than another variable, use the less than and greater than operators. You can check for values greater than or less than a variable as follows:

```
if myValue < 0 Then
   Msgbox "The value is less than zero."
if myValue > 0 Then
   Msgbox "The value is greater than zero."
```

Another type of comparison you can perform is to see whether a variable is less than or equal to a value. Likewise, you can see whether a variable is greater than or equal to a value. Here is an example of this type of comparison:

```
if myValue <= Input Then
   Msgbox "myValue is less than or equal to Input."
if myValue >= 0 Then
   Msgbox "The value is greater than or equal to zero."
```

NOTE

There is no set precedence order for comparison operators. Comparisons are always performed from left to right.

When you compare objects, such as buttons, you use a special comparison operator called `Is`. By using the `Is` operator, you can see whether two objects are equivalent. The operator returns a result that is true if the objects are equivalent, or false if they aren't. This example shows how you can check whether the object reference `cmd_Button` refers to the object `Button`:

```
Result = cmd_Button Is Button
If Result = True Then
    Msgbox "The objects are equivalent."
Else
        Msgbox "The objects are NOT equivalent."
```

You can also perform the comparison directly in the control flow statement:

```
If cmd_Button Is Button Then
    Msgbox "The objects are equivalent."
Else
        Msgbox "The objects are NOT equivalent."
```

Strings

Strings are sets of alphabetical and numeric characters. In VBScript, there are many ways to use strings. Because VBScript automatically types variables for you, you don't need to declare a variable as a string. You can declare a variable this way:

```
Dim aString
```

Then later you can define a string value for the variable:

```
aString = "This is a String."
```

Often, you want to add strings together. For example, if a user enters his or her full name as three separate variables representing the first, middle, and last name, you might want to add these strings together. Although you may see scripts that use the + operator to concatenate strings, the normal operator for string concatenation is the & operator. With the & operator, you can add strings together as follows:

```
fullName = firstName & " " & Middle & " " & lastName
```

Sometimes you also want to display the value of a string in a message box. To do this, use the & operator, as shown in the following sample code:

```
bString = "Cool"
Msgbox "The value of the string is: " & bString
```

This code displays a dialog box with the following message:

```
The value of the string is: Cool
```

Comments

Just as you can add comments to HTML markup, you can add comments to your VBScript code. To add comments, use the single quotation mark. All text after the single quotation mark and on the same line is interpreted as a comment. Here are some examples of using comments in your code:

```
'This variable holds the first name of the customer
Dim firstName
'This variable holds the middle name of the customer
Dim Middle
'This variable holds the last name of the customer
Dim lastName
```

Control Flow with Conditionals

In much the same way as traffic lights control the flow of traffic on the street, conditional instructions control the flow of instructions in your code.

If...then

If you want to execute a set of instructions only when a certain condition is met, you can use an `If...then` condition. You can control the execution of instructions based on a true condition, as follows:

```
if condition = True Then
  A = B
End If
```

An `If...then` condition can also be used in this way:

```
if condition Then
  A = B
End If
```

You can control the execution of instructions based on a false condition, as follows:

```
if condition = False Then
  A <> B
End If
```

You can also use this form:

```
if Not condition  Then
  A <> B
End If
```

You can extend the `If…then` condition with the `Else` and `ElseIf` statements. The `Else` statement offers an alternative when a condition you specified isn't met. Here's the structure of an `if…then…else` condition:

```
if homeRun = True Then
    Msgbox "The condition has been met."
Else
    Msgbox "The condition has not been met."
End If
```

To add more conditions, you can use the `ElseIf` statement. In this way, each condition you add to the code is checked for validity. Here's an example that uses the `ElseIf` statement:

```
if firstValue < 0 Then
  Msgbox "The value is less than zero."
ElseIf firstValue = 0 Then
  Msgbox "The value is equal to zero."
ElseIf firstValue = 1 Then
  Msgbox "The value is equal to one."
ElseIf firstValue = 2 Then
  Msgbox "The value is equal to two."
ElseIf firstValue = 3 Then
  Msgbox "The value is equal to three."
ElseIf firstValue = 4 Then
  Msgbox "The value is equal to four."
Else
  Msgbox "The value is greater than 4."
End If
```

Select Case

Checking for multiple conditions with the `ElseIf` structure can be tedious. When you want to check more than three conditions, you should probably use the `Select Case` statement. In the `Select Case` structure, the last example in the previous section can be transformed into code that's clearer and easier to understand:

```
Select Case firstValue
   Case < 0
     Msgbox "The value is less than zero."
   Case 0
     Msgbox "The value is equal to zero."
   Case 1
     Msgbox "The value is equal to one."
   Case 2
     Msgbox "The value is equal to two."
```

```
   Case 3
     Msgbox "The value is equal to three."
   Case 4
     Msgbox "The value is equal to four."
   Case Else
     Msgbox "The value is greater than 4."
End Select
```

If you compare the `ElseIf` example and the `Select Case` example, you can see that the `Select Case` example requires less code and has a simpler structure. You can apply this same structure any time you want to check for multiple conditions. Here's another example of `Select Case`:

```
Select Case Abbrev
   Case "HTML"
     Message "The HyperText Markup Language."
   Case "SGML"
     Message "The Standard Generalized Markup Language."
   Case "VRML"
     Message "The Virtual Reality Modeling Language."
   Case Else
     Message "You have entered an abbreviation not known to the system."
End Select
```

Control Flow with Looping

Sometimes you want to repeatedly execute a section of code. In VBScript, there are three ways you can do this:

- Execute a code segment for a specific count by using `For...Next` looping
- Execute a code segment while a condition is met by using `Do While` looping
- Execute a code segment until a condition is met by using `Do Until` looping

For...Next

To execute a code segment for a specific count, use `For...Next` looping. The structure of `For...Next` is as follows:

```
For Counter = Start to Finish
   insert code to repeat
Next
```

Using `For...Next` looping in your code is easy. The following example uses this structure to initialize an array of 20 elements:

```
For x = 0 to 19
   aStruct(x) = "Unknown"
Next
```

After the `For...Next` loop is executed, all 20 elements in the array are initialized to the value `Unknown`. To make the `For...Next` loop more versatile, you can step through the counter at specific intervals. To do this, follow the `Step` keyword with a positive or negative value. The following example sets the array positions 0, 2, 4, 6, and 8 to `Even`:

```
For x = 0 to 8 Step 2
   aStruct(x) = "Even"
Next
```

This loop sets the array positions 3, 6, and 9 to `Multiple`.

```
For x = 3 to 9 Step 3
   aStruct(x) = "Multiple"
Next
```

When you use a negative step value, you should reverse the normal order of the counter. Therefore, instead of going from the lowest value to the highest value, you go from highest to lowest:

```
For x = 8 to 0 Step -2
   aStruct(x) = "Even"
Next

For x = 9 to 3 Step -3
   aStruct(x) = "Multiple"
Next
```

Do While

To execute a code segment while a condition is met, use `Do While` looping. The structure of this loop is as follows:

```
Do While condition
   insert code to repeat
Loop
```

As long as the condition is met, the loop is executed. To break out of the loop, you must change the condition at some point within the loop. Here's an example of a `Do While` loop that changes the status of the condition:

```
Do While homeRun = True

   If basesLoaded Then
      Message "Great time to hit a home run."
   ElseIf Balls = 3 And Strikes = 2 Then
      Message "Go for it!"
   Else
      homeRun = False
   EndIf

Loop
```

By placing your condition at the top of the loop, you make sure the loop is executed only if the condition is met. Sometimes you want to execute the loop at least once before you check the condition; to do this, you can place the check for the condition at the bottom of the loop, as shown in this example:

```
Do

   If basesLoaded Then
      Message "Great time to hit a home run."
```

```
   ElseIf Balls = 3 And Strikes = 2 Then
      Message "Go for it!"
   Else
      homeRun = False
   EndIf

Loop While homeRun = True
```

Do Until

If you want to execute a loop *until* a condition is met instead of *while* a condition is met, use `Do Until` looping, as shown in this example:

```
Do Until condition
    Insert code to repeat
Loop
```

To make sure the loop is executed at least once, you can use the following structure:

```
Do
    Insert code to repeat
Loop Until condition
```

Here's another example of a `Do Until` loop:

```
Do

   If basesLoaded Then
      Message "Great time to hit a home run."
   ElseIf Balls = 3 And Strikes = 2 Then
      Message "Go for it!"
   Else
      homeRun = False
   EndIf

Loop Until homeRun = True
```

> **NOTE**
>
> If you compare the `Do While` loops in the previous section to the `Do Until` loops in this section, you can see that the logic for both types of loops is similar. The key difference is in how the logic is applied. In a `Do While` loop, you execute code *while* a condition is met; in a `Do Until` loop, you execute code *until* a condition is met.

Going Beyond the Basics with VBScript

As you've seen in the previous section, programming with VBScript is fairly straightforward. To go beyond the basics, take a look at how to group sections of code into procedures.

Basic Procedure Classes

Procedures you create in VBScript are groups of statements that perform a particular task. After creating a procedure, you can call it from different locations in your code. When the procedure finishes executing, control returns to the code that called the procedure and your script continues executing from there.

The two basic classes of procedures are these:

- Functions—procedures that return a value to the caller
- Subroutines—procedures that don't return a value to the caller

Functions

Functions—procedures that return a value to the statement that called them—are very useful in your scripts. When you create a function, you can define parameters required to execute the function. Parameters are optional variables that you can use to pass values to the function.

Here is the basic structure of a function:

```
Function functionName(argument1, argument2, ..., argumentN)
   Insert function code here.
End Function
```

You can use functions in your code as follows:

```
Function getName
   Dim goodName
   Do While goodName = ""
      goodName = InputBox "Enter your full name:"
   Loop
   getName = goodName
End Function
```

In the example, `getName` is the name of the function. Because the function accepts no parameters, none are defined after the function name. A temporary variable called `goodName` is created to make the code easier to follow and debug. The temporary variable is used to store the user's input. Once the user enters a valid name, the `Do While` loop is exited. The value the user entered is assigned to the function, allowing the value to be returned to the calling statement.

CAUTION

Variables used within functions or subroutines are temporary variables. These variables exist only within the scope of your function or subroutine, so local variables are another name for variables used within procedures.

You can call a function in one of these two ways:

```
Call getName()
```

```
fullName = getName()
```

Another way to call a function is within a statement:

```
Msgbox "The name you entered is: " getName()
```

When there are no parameters to pass to the function, the parentheses are optional:

```
fullName = getName
```

To better understand how parameters are used, try creating a function that converts a time entry to seconds. This function, called `countDays`, accepts four parameters: `nYears`, `nDays`, `nHours`, and `nMinutes`. Because these parameters are passed directly to the function, you don't need to create temporary variables in the function. The code for the function `countSeconds` is as follows:

```
Function countSeconds(nYears, nDays, nHours, nMinutes)
   Dim tempSeconds
   tempSeconds = ((365 * nYears + nDays) * 24 + nHours) * 3600 + 60 * nMinutes
   countSeconds = tempSecounds
End Function
```

When you call this function, the parameters are mandatory and must be entered in the order defined. Here's a statement that calls the `countSeconds` function:

```
numSeconds = countSeconds(1,69,24,5)
```

NOTE

You can break out of a function and return to the caller at any time by using the `Exit Function` statement. This statement is useful when a predetermined condition has been met and you want to return to the calling statement without finishing the function's execution.

Subroutines

You can also use subroutines in your scripts. A *subroutine* is a procedure that can be called anywhere in the code but doesn't return a value to the caller. You can pass parameters to a subroutine just as you do to a function.

The structure of a subroutine is almost identical to the structure of a function:

```
Sub subroutineName(argument1, argument2, ..., argumentN)
   Insert subroutine code here.
End Sub
```

You can use subroutines in your code as follows:

```
Sub displayError(errorMessage)
   MsgBox "Error: " & errorMessage
End Sub
```

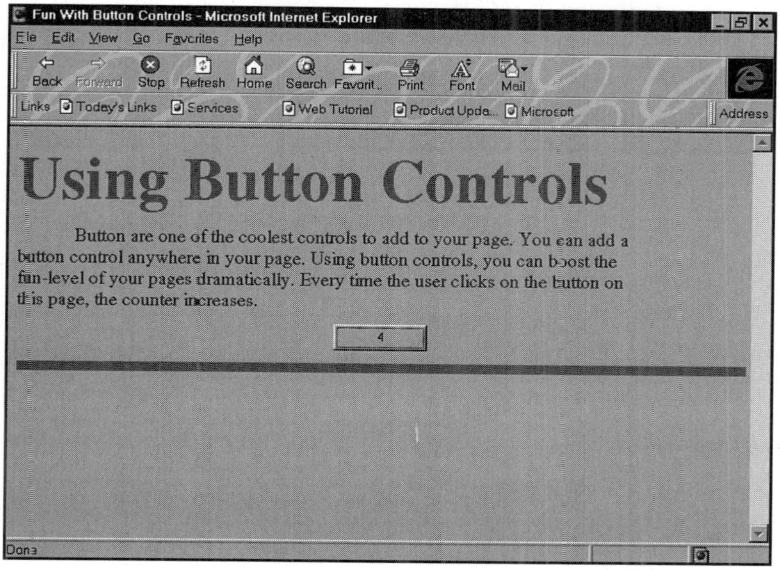

FIGURE 30.5.
An example of a button control.

Listing 30.3. A script with a method call.

```
<HTML>
<HEAD>
<TITLE>Fun With Button Controls</TITLE>
<STYLE>
H2  {font: 40pt Times; color: red}
P  {font: 12pt Times; color: blue; text-indent: .5in; margin-right: 1in}
</STYLE>
</HEAD>

<BODY>
<H2>Using Button Controls</H2>
<P>Button are one of the coolest controls to add to your page. You can add
 a button control anywhere in your page. Using button controls, you can
 boost the fun-level of your pages dramatically. Every time the user clicks
 on the button on this page, the counter increases.</P>
<CENTER>
<INPUT TYPE=BUTTON VALUE="Click Me" NAME="funButton">
</CENTER>

<HR SIZE=10 NOSHADE>

<SCRIPT LANGUAGE="VBScript">
<!--  Option Explicit

Dim Counter

Sub funButton_OnClick()
     Counter = Counter + 1
     funButton.Value = Counter
End Sub
```

continues

Listing 30.3. continued

```
-->
</SCRIPT>
</BODY>
</HTML>
```

Fun with Message Boxes

Message boxes are used to display information to users. VBScript offers many ways to add pizazz to message boxes. To display a message box, simply add this statement:

```
Msgbox "The message you want to display."
```

NOTE

Alert boxes are a special type of message box and can be used to display error messages, cautions, and warnings. To display an alert box, use the `Alert` function as follows:

```
Alert "The error, caution, or warning to display."
```

You can customize message boxes with titles, icons, and several button styles. To add these elements to your message boxes, you must use the following syntax:

```
Msgbox "The message to display", buttonType + iconType, _
        "Title for message box", helpFile, helpFileContext
```

Buttons for Message Boxes

The OK button is the default button for all message boxes, but there's a whole host of useful buttons, including Yes, No, Cancel, Retry, Ignore, and Abort. To add your own buttons to a message box, you must do two things:

- Declare the parameter with a specified value
- Pass the parameter to the function call

Here's how you would add Yes and No buttons to a message box:

```
dim vbYesNoCancel : vbYesNoCancel = 3
Msgbox "The message to display.", vbYesNoCancel
```

`vbYesNoCancel` are the button types you want to add, and `3` is the parameter value.

A message box with the Yes, No, and Cancel buttons is shown in Figure 30.6. The markup and source code for the page is shown in Listing 30.4.

Listing 30.4. Adding buttons to message boxes.

```
<HTML>
<HEAD>
<TITLE>Adding Buttons to Your Message Boxes</TITLE>
<STYLE>
H2  {font: 40pt Times; color: blue}
P  {font: 12pt Times; color: gray; text-indent: .5in; margin-right: 1in}
</STYLE>
</HEAD>

<BODY BGCOLOR="#FFFFFF">
<H2>Using Unique Buttons</H2>
<P>The OK button is the default button for all message boxes. To specify
 buttons, you must pass the second parameter to the function call. When
 you add buttons, you normally add them in specific combinations, such
 as a Yes button with a No button.</P>
<CENTER>
<INPUT TYPE=BUTTON VALUE="Display Message Box" NAME="displayButton">
</CENTER>

<HR SIZE=10>

<SCRIPT LANGUAGE="VBScript">
<!--

dim vbYesNoCancel : vbYesNoCancel = 3

Sub displayButton_OnClick
     Msgbox "Do you want to try again?", vbYesNoCancel
End Sub

-->
</SCRIPT>
</BODY>
</HTML>
```

When you add buttons, you normally add them in specific combinations, such as a Yes button with a No button. The available button combinations and their associated values are summarized in Table 30.3.

Table 30.3. Buttons for message boxes.

Parameter Name	*Purpose*	*Value*
`vbOk`	Shows the OK button	0
`vbOkCancel`	Shows OK and Cancel buttons	1
`vbAbortRetryIgnore`	Shows Abort, Retry, and Ignore buttons	2
`vbYesNoCancel`	Shows Yes, No, and Cancel buttons	3
`vbYesNo`	Shows Yes and No buttons	4
`vbRetryCancel`	Shows Retry and Cancel buttons	5

FIGURE 30.6.
Making your message boxes more useful with buttons.

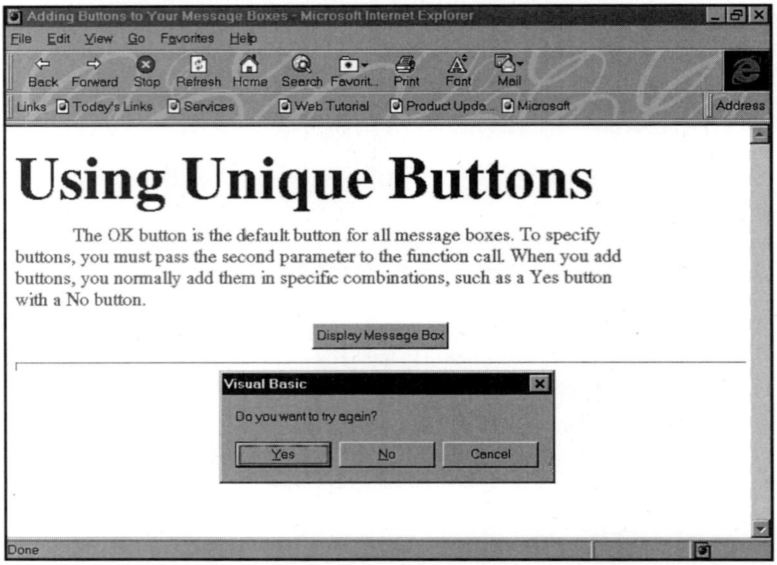

Icons for Message Boxes

Adding a unique icon to a message box is easy. Just remember that buttons and icons are part of the same parameter, which is why you use the plus sign to separate the button types from the icon type. To add icons to a message box, you must do two things:

- Declare the parameter with a specified value
- Pass the parameter to the function call

Here's an example of a message box with an icon:

```
Dim vbRetryCancel: vbRetryCancel=5
Dim vbInformation: vbInformation=64
Msgbox "The message to display.", vbRetryCancel + vbInformation
```

A message box with an information icon is shown in Figure 30.7, and the source for the page is shown in Listing 30.5.

Listing 30.5. Adding icons to message boxes.

```
<HTML>
<HEAD>
<TITLE>Adding Icons to Your Message Boxes</TITLE>
<STYLE>
H2  {font: 40pt Times; color: blue}
P  {font: 12pt Times; color: gray; text-indent: .5in; margin-right: 1in}
</STYLE>
</HEAD>

<BODY BGCOLOR="#FFFFFF">
```

```
<H2>Using Icons</H2>
<P>Adding a unique icon to a message box is easy. Just remember that buttons
 and icons are part of the same parameter, which is why you use the plus sign
 to separate the button types from the icon type.</P>
<CENTER>
<INPUT TYPE=BUTTON VALUE="Display Message Box" NAME="displayButton">
</CENTER>

<HR SIZE=10>

<SCRIPT LANGUAGE="VBScript">
<!--

Dim vbRetryCancel: vbRetryCancel=5
Dim vbInformation: vbInformation=64

Sub displayButton_OnClick
     Msgbox "This option allows you to compute averages. If you want to see" & _
    "the calculator compute averages, click on the Retry button.", _
     vbRetryCancel + vbInformation
End Sub

-->
</SCRIPT>
</BODY>
</HTML>
```

FIGURE 30.7.
Adding icons to message boxes.

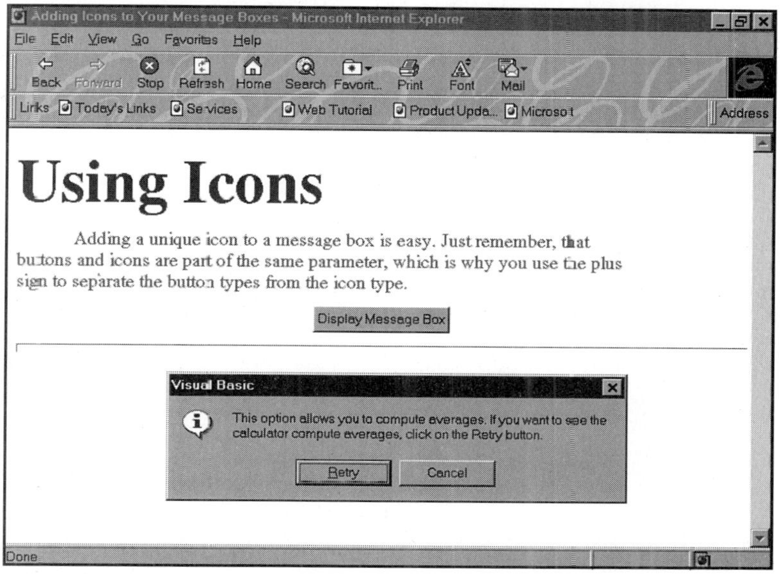

The complete list of icons you can add to your message boxes is shown in Table 30.4.

Table 30.4. Icons for message boxes.

Parameter Name	*Value*	*Purpose*
`vbCritical`	16	Shows an icon with an ×, used for critical errors
`vbQuestion`	32	Shows an icon with a question mark, used for questions
`vbExclamation`	48	Shows an icon with an exclamation point, used for minor errors, cautions, and warnings
`VbInformation`	64	Shows an icon with an *I*, used for informational messages

Titles for Message Boxes

You can easily add descriptive titles to your message boxes. (See Figure 30.8.) All you need to do is to specify the title in the third parameter passed to the `Msgbox` function call. Here's an example of a message box with a descriptive title:

```
Msgbox "You have made an error. Do you want to try again?", _
       vbAbortRetryIgnore + vbExclamation, "Error in Entry: Improper Format"
```

Listing 30.6 shows the contents of the sample page.

Listing 30.6. Using message box titles.

```
<HTML>
<HEAD>
<TITLE>Titles for Your Message Boxes</TITLE>
<STYLE>
H2  {font: 40pt Times; color: blue}
P  {font: 12pt Times; color: gray; text-indent: .5in; margin-right: 1in}
</STYLE>
</HEAD>

<BODY BGCOLOR="#FFFFFF">
<H2>Adding Titles</H2>
<P>You can easily add descriptive titles to your message boxes.
 All you need to do is to specify the title in the third parameter
 passed to the Msgbox function call. </P>
<CENTER>
<INPUT TYPE=BUTTON VALUE="Display Dialog" NAME="displayButton">
</CENTER>

<HR SIZE=10 NOSHADE>

<SCRIPT LANGUAGE="VBScript">
<!--

Dim vbAbortRetryIgnore: vbAbortRetryIgnore=2
Dim vbExclamation: vbExclamation=48
```

```
Sub displayButton_OnClick
Msgbox "You have made an error. Do you want to try again?", _
       vbAbortRetryIgnore + vbExclamation, "Error in Entry: Improper Format"
End Sub

-->
</SCRIPT>
</BODY>
</HTML>
```

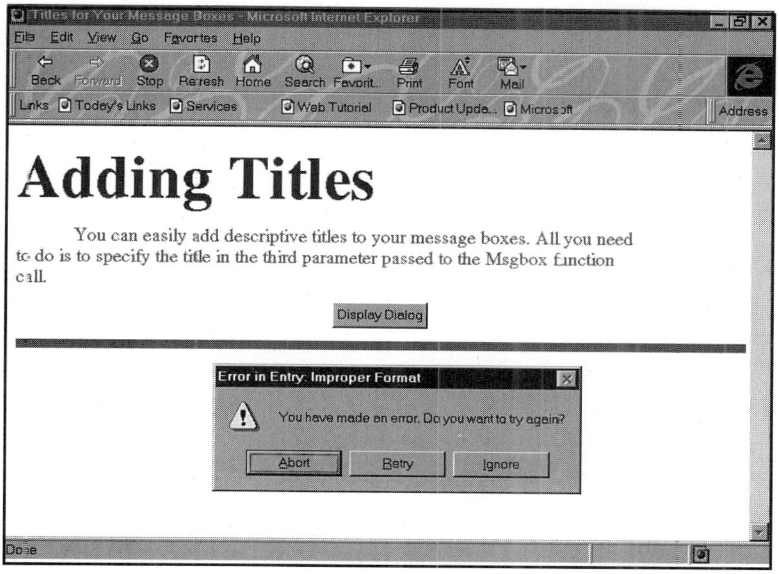

FIGURE 30.8.
Adding titles to your message boxes.

Using Help Files with Message Boxes

When you use the help parameters, the message box is displayed with a Help button that calls the designated help file when it's clicked. Using the help file context parameter, you can identify a specific topic in the help file to be displayed. Once you designate a help file, the Help button is automatically added to the message box. Users can open the help file by clicking the Help button or pressing the F1 key.

Evaluating Button Clicks in Message Boxes

When you give the user several options, such as Yes/No or Abort/Retry/Ignore, you need to know what button the user selected. Because message boxes return a status code, you can easily evaluate button clicks. All you need to do is assign the message box call to a variable, then evaluate the variable.

Because you're using a procedure call to make the evaluation, the syntax for the message box changes slightly, as shown here:

```
evaluateButtonClick = Msgbox ("The message to display", buttonType + iconType, _
      "Title for message box", helpFile, helpFileContext)
```

Anytime this line of code is inserted in a script, a message box is displayed; when the user clicks a button, the returned status code is stored in the variable:

```
tryAgain = Msgbox ("Do you want to try again?", vbYesNoCancel)
```

Once you assign a variable to store the returned status code, you can use an `If…then` or `Select Case` structure to perform actions in response to the button click. Table 30.5 lists message box buttons and the status codes returned when they're clicked.

Table 30.5. Status codes for message box buttons.

Button	*Parameter Name*	*Status Code*
OK	`vbOk`	1
Cancel	`vbCancel`	2
Abort	`vbAbort`	3
Retry	`vbRetry`	4
Ignore	`vbIgnore`	5
Yes	`vbYes`	6
No	`vbNo`	7

A script that evaluates button clicks in message boxes and then directs the result to a text control is shown in Figure 30.9. To see how this was done, examine the source for this page in Listing 30.7. Although the example uses an `If…then` loop to evaluate the button click, you could just as easily use a `Select Case` structure.

NOTE

Text controls are just one of many HTML controls you can add to VBScript-enhanced Web pages. You will learn about these controls in Chapter 32, "Using VBScript to Enhance Your Web Pages."

Listing 30.7. Determining button clicks.

```
<HTML>
<HEAD>
<TITLE>Evaluating Button Clicks In Message Boxes</TITLE>
<STYLE>
H2  {font: 40pt Times; color: blue}
P  {font: 12pt Times; color: gray; text-indent: .5in; margin-right: 1in}
</STYLE>
</HEAD>

<BODY BGCOLOR="#FFFFFF">
<H2>Button Clicks In Message Boxes</H2>
<P>When you present the user with multiple options, such as Yes/No or
 Abort/Retry/Ignore, you need to know what button the user selected.
 Because message boxes return a status code, you can easily evaluate
 button clicks. All you need to do is assign the message box call to
 a variable and then evaluate the variable.</P>

<FORM NAME="coolForm">
<P><INPUT TYPE=BUTTON VALUE="Display Dialog" NAME="displayButton"></P>
<P>Button Evaluation: <INPUT TYPE=TEXT NAME="textControl" SIZE=50 MAXLENGTH=50></P>
</FORM>
<HR SIZE=10 NOSHADE>

<SCRIPT LANGUAGE="VBScript">
<!--

Dim vbYesNoCancel: vbYesNoCancel=3
Dim vbExclamation: vbExclamation=48
Dim vbYes: vbYes=6
Dim vbNo: vbNo=7
Dim vbCancel: vbCancel=2
Dim form
Set form = document.coolForm

Sub displayButton_OnClick
tryAgain = Msgbox ("Do you want to try again?", vbYesNoCancel)

If tryAgain = vbYes Then
     form.textControl.Value = "You clicked on the Yes button."
ElseIf tryAgain = vbNo Then
     form.textControl.Value = "You clicked on the No button."
Else
     form.textControl.Value = "You clicked on the Cancel button."
End If

End Sub

-->
</SCRIPT>
</BODY>
</HTML>
```

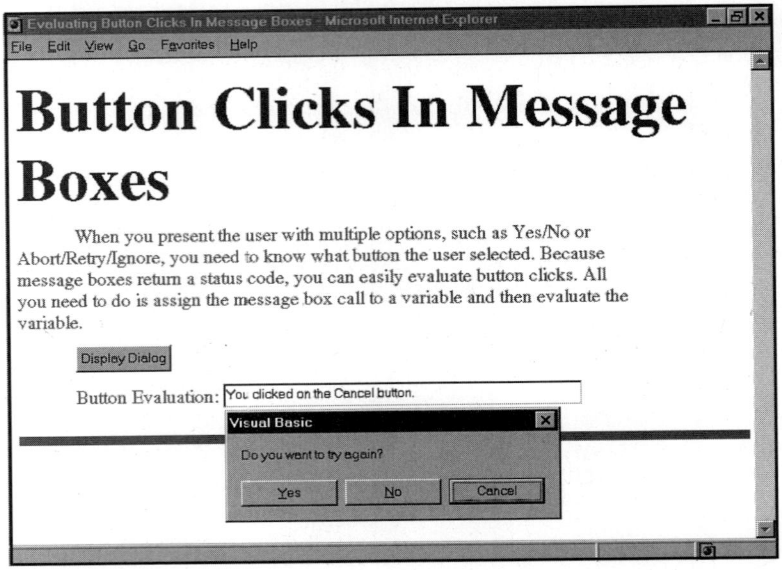

FIGURE 30.9.
Evaluating button clicks in message boxes.

Summary

VBScript is a powerful tool for enhancing your Web pages. Because it's so easy to use, learning VBScript basics, such as how to perform calculations or how to concatenate strings, is a snap. These basic concepts are the building blocks to more advanced subjects such as controlling the flow through your scripts and creating procedures.

Once you understand procedures, you're ready to add interactivity to your pages. One way to do this is with message boxes. There are many uses for message boxes in your scripts, especially if you create "intelligent" message boxes that react to button clicks.

CHAPTER 31

Exploring ActiveX and ActiveX Controls

by William Robert Stanek

IN THIS CHAPTER

Creating documents that come to life before your eyes is what Microsoft's ActiveX is all about. ActiveX-enabled pages can feature powerful yet easy-to-use interfaces that merge virtual reality, 360-degree control over video, real-time audio, and even games into Web pages. Recently, ActiveX technology has come to the forefront as a hot Internet innovation; it's even stealing the spotlight from Java.

This chapter explores ActiveX, the control components that make it work, and how to activate your Web pages with ActiveX.

What Is ActiveX?

At the heart of ActiveX is a concept for merging technologies by using an enhanced object linking and embedding (OLE) interface. OLE is certainly not a new technology, but applying OLE to the Internet is a groundbreaking innovation—this is what ActiveX is all about. ActiveX *is* OLE for the Internet.

ActiveX in Action

With ActiveX, your Web pages can include live multimedia effects. You don't just add a video to the page that plays when the page is loaded; you add a video to the page that the user can control in a panoramic 360 degrees. To experience total control over video, check out Surround Video from Black Diamond. (See Figure 31.1.) If seeing 360-degree control over video with ActiveX technology doesn't make you an immediate ActiveX convert, it will certainly change your view about how to activate the World Wide Web. You can find Surround Video on the Web at this site:

```
http://www.bdiamond.com/surround/surround.htm
```

Live documents you can create with ActiveX aren't restricted to HTML. Beyond 360-degree video, entire worlds are waiting to be created and explored. You can experience the wonders of the marriage of ActiveX and VRML technologies with the TerraForm VRML browser from Brilliance Labs, Inc. (See Figure 31.2.) This browser uses ActiveX to link to a Direct 3D component module that serves up VR images many times faster than normal VR browsers. The TerraForm VRML browser and great demos are at this site:

```
http://www.brlabs.com
```

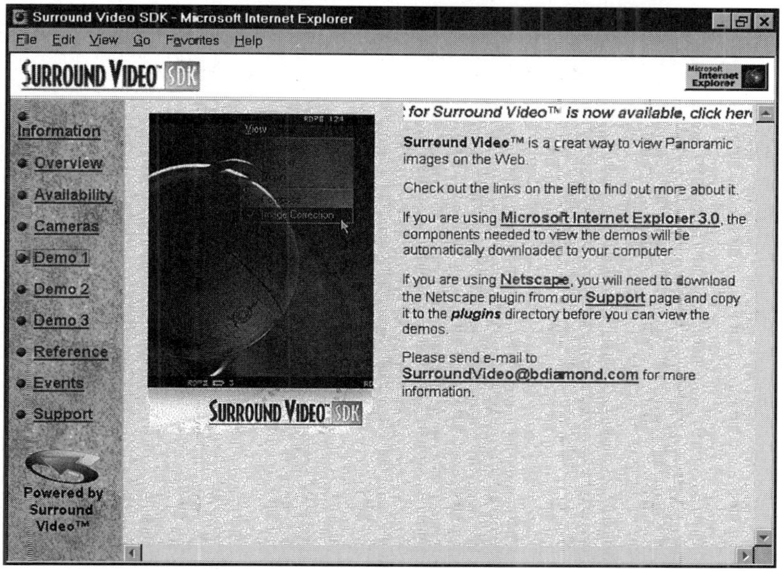

FIGURE 31.1.
Surround Video powered by ActiveX offers a multimedia feast in a full 360 degrees.

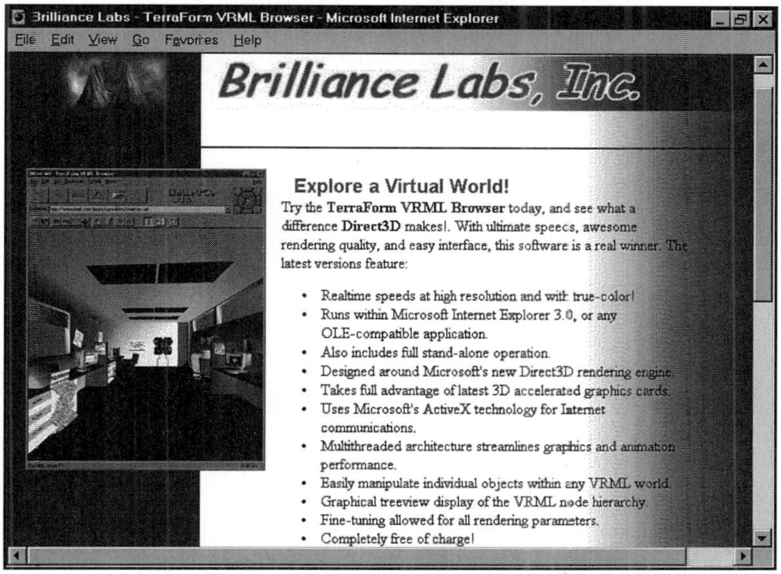

FIGURE 31.2.
Activating VRML with ActiveX and the TerraForm VRML browser.

With ActiveX, you get power and simplicity. One of the latest sensations on the Web is Shockwave from Macromedia. Although Shockwave is a powerful tool for creating interactivity on the Web, its animation and applications carry tremendous overhead. With ActiveX, a company called FutureWave Software delivers interactive full-screen animation with one-tenth of the file size of normal animation. (See Figure 31.3.) You can learn all about FutureWave products here:

```
http://www.futurewave.com
```

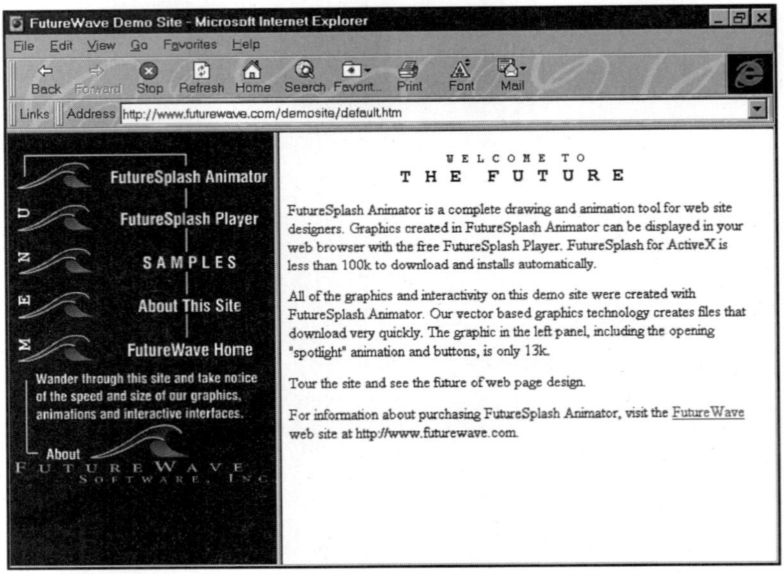

FIGURE 31.3.
Creating powerful animation with minimal bandwidth requirements.

ActiveX Background

ActiveX is a sure winner with powerhouse Microsoft at the helm. To help spread the word about ActiveX to the farthest reaches of cyberspace, Microsoft maintains a comprehensive home page for ActiveX. (See Figure 31.4.) You can find the ActiveX home page at this site:

```
http://www.microsoft.com/activex/
```

Microsoft based ActiveX on the Component Object Model (COM), which allows objects to communicate with each other by using links. Object linking is central to OLE, used widely in Windows applications. COM also forms the basis of both OLE and ActiveX, but OLE and ActiveX serve different functions. OLE is designed for use on desktop computers and carries way too much overhead to use it on the Internet. ActiveX, on the other hand, trims down COM to make object linking practical for Internet use.

When the developers at Microsoft redesigned object linking for the Internet, they streamlined COM considerably, so much so that ActiveX components are 50–75 percent smaller than their OLE counterparts. ActiveX also introduces incremental rendering of components and asynchronous connections. Incremental rendering is used so that users can see almost instantaneous results during downloading, and asynchronous connections speed up downloading considerably.

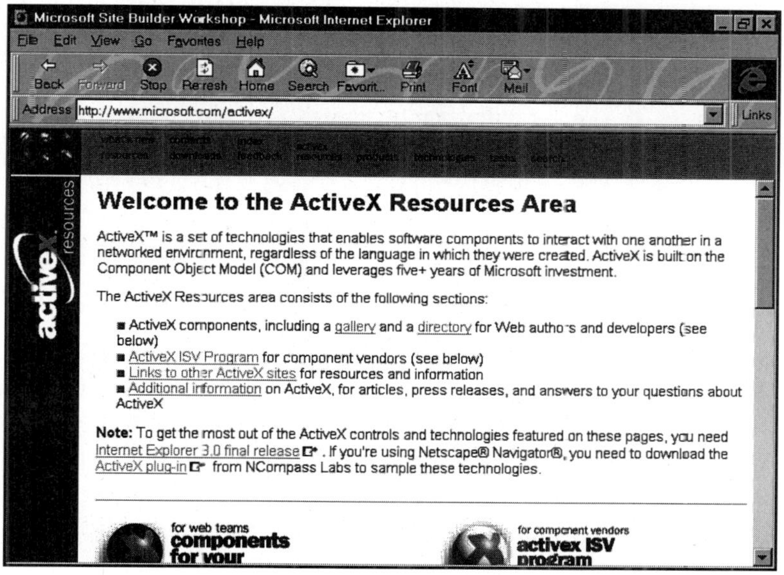

FIGURE 31.4.
The ActiveX home page at Microsoft.

ActiveX Core Technologies

ActiveX is the key to integrated technologies for both clients and servers; its core technologies include the following:

- ActiveX controls
- ActiveX scripting
- ActiveX documents
- The ActiveX server framework

The ActiveX server framework is designed specifically for servers, but ActiveX scripting, ActiveX documents, and ActiveX controls are designed for clients, such as browsers. As Figure 31.5 shows, these core technologies work together to give you live content on the Web.

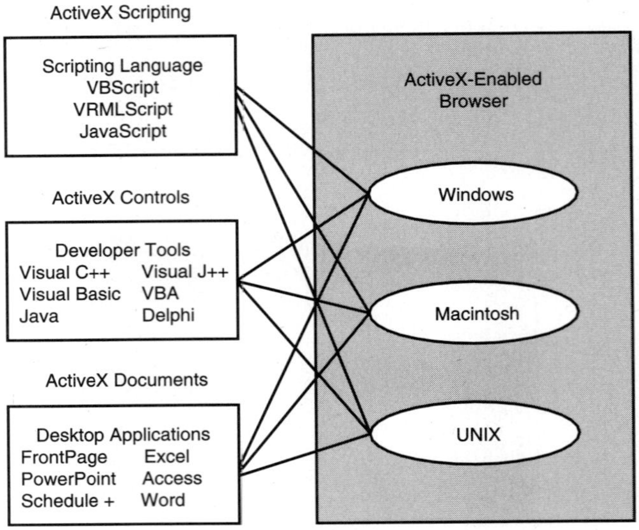

FIGURE 31.5.
ActiveX technologies work together.

ActiveX controls are the key to adding live and interactive multimedia to your Web documents. With ActiveX controls, you can embed and execute software applications in a Web page that let users view and interact with movies, animation, and audio. You can create ActiveX controls with any developer tool that supports OLE, such as Visual C++, Visual J++, and Visual Basic.

ActiveX controls are similar to Netscape plug-ins. Both ActiveX controls and Netscape plug-ins allow you to embed applications in your documents. Just as Netscape lets third-party developers create plug-ins for Navigator, Microsoft is allowing third-party developers to create new ActiveX controls. Already hundreds of cool ActiveX controls are available from Microsoft and from third-party developers. Tracking the vast array of controls would be almost impossible. Fortunately, Microsoft maintains a full directory of available controls (See Figure 31.6.) at this site:

```
http://www.microsoft.com/activexisv/direct.htm
```

Recently, client-side scripting languages have gained popularity. Two of the most popular scripting languages are JavaScript and VBScript. With ActiveX scripting, you can use any client-side scripting language in your documents. You can also link your client-side scripts to Java applets, embedded applications, and ActiveX controls. In Chapter 33, "Integrating ActiveX and VBScript," you will learn how to use ActiveX and VBScript together to create more powerful Web pages.

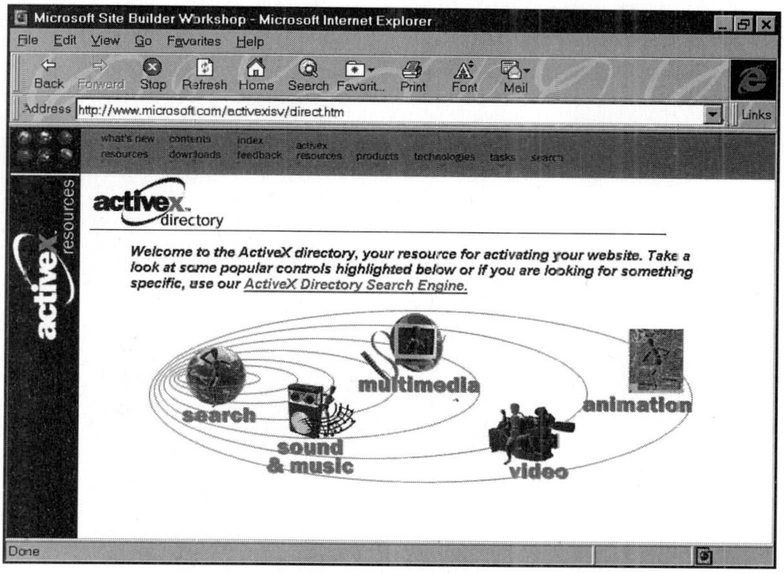

FIGURE 31.6.
A directory to ActiveX controls.

With ActiveX documents, you can import documents formatted for Word, Excel, Powerpoint, Schedule, Access, and many other applications into your Web pages. These documents are imported by using a special viewer inserted into the browser's viewing window. This viewer has its own toolbars, menus, and interface.

The key to ActiveX documents is that the application the document is formatted for must be OLE-compliant. As long as an application is OLE-compliant, you can use ActiveX document technology.

Using ActiveX and ActiveX Controls

Although ActiveX was initially developed for Windows systems, it's designed as a cross-platform solution. Microsoft and several development partners are hard at work bringing ActiveX to Macintosh and UNIX systems.

The showcase browser to support ActiveX is Internet Explorer 3.0. When you use Internet Explorer, you don't have to get any special software to enable ActiveX. However, you might need to check your browser's security options for active content. As shown in Figure 31.7, you should enable the following:

- Downloading of active content
- ActiveX controls and plug-ins
- ActiveX scripts

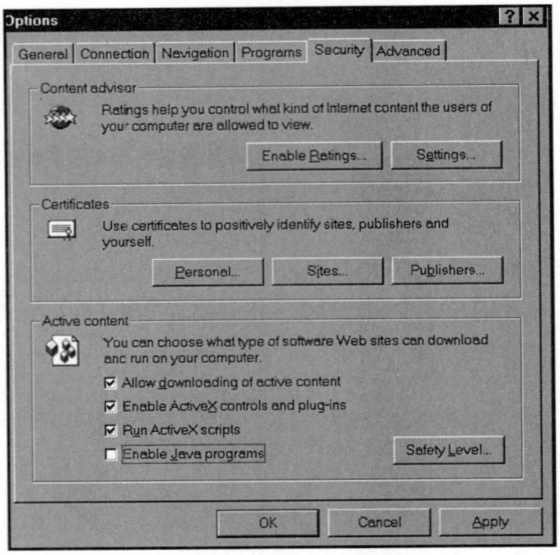

FIGURE 31.7.
Using ActiveX with Internet Explorer.

Internet Explorer isn't the only browser to support ActiveX. Netscape Navigator users can download a plug-in called NCompass. With Ncompass installed, you can use ActiveX controls and ActiveX documents just as you would in any other browser. To get the current version of NCompass, visit NCompass Labs (`www.ncompasslabs.com`).

Although hundreds of cool ActiveX controls are available, you don't have to worry about wading through a myriad of controls spread across hundreds of Web sites. As you have seen, Microsoft maintains a complete directory of controls; it also publishes a gallery of controls created at Microsoft and digitally signed controls available from third-party vendors (`www.microsoft.com/activex/gallery/`). Because the controls in the gallery are authenticated, they're relatively safe to use on your system.

If you visit the ActiveX gallery, you can quickly get your first taste of how easy it is to get and install a new control. Unlike plug-ins, ActiveX controls are readily and immediately available when you visit a page that uses a control. This is because the ActiveX specification requires that all controls support self-registration. To demonstrate this, see how the Popup Window control is installed in a browser.

The first step is to get to the Popup Window control demo page by following the link given in the ActiveX gallery. As you can see from the status bar at the bottom of Figure 31.8, when you reach a page containing a control, your browser immediately gets and starts to install the control. You will know this because the status bar states that the browser is installing components.

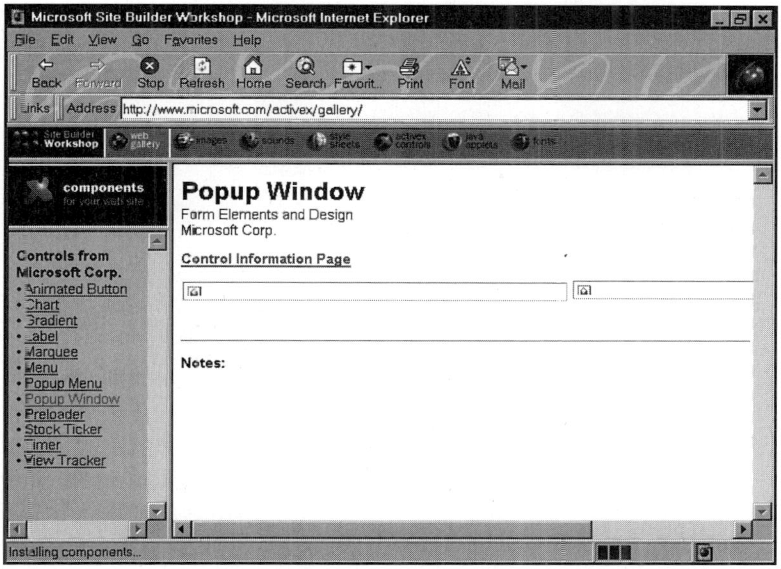

FIGURE 31.8.
Internet Explorer installs components automatically.

When the browser has completely downloaded the control, you'll see the authentication window shown in Figure 31.9. By following links in the authentication window, you can make sure the control you're installing is both secure and safe for your system. If you choose to continue with the installation, the control is instantly added and available for use; if you choose not to, the control is discarded.

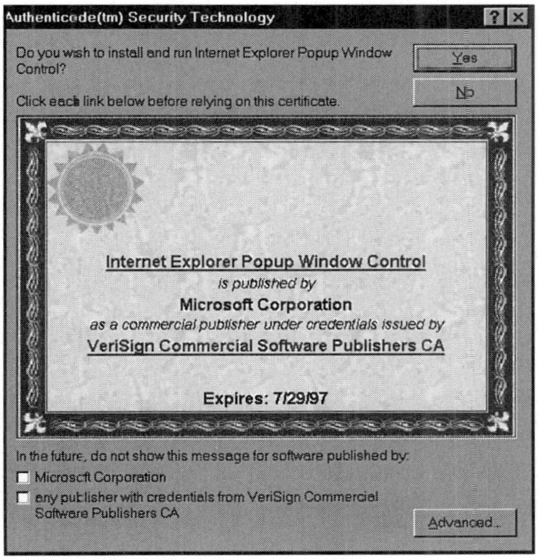

FIGURE 31.9.
An authentication mechanism for ActiveX is built in.

Most controls download and install very quickly, especially at 28.8 Kbps. If you log onto the Internet with a slower modem, you'll be glad to know that you need to download a control only once. After that, the control is always available for use on your system. On my system, the Popup Window control installed completely and ran the demo in less than 10 seconds. The demo page with a popup window is shown in Figure 31.10.

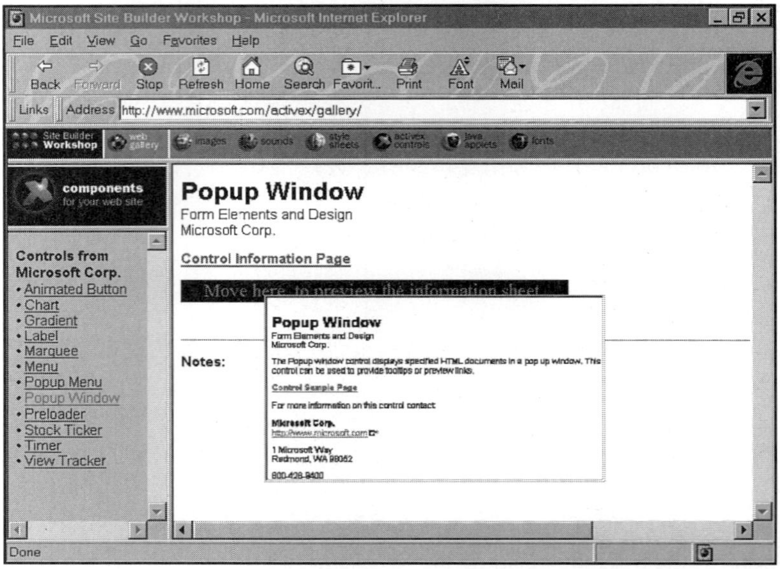

FIGURE 31.10.
Running an installed ActiveX component.

Placing ActiveX Controls on a Web Page

Objects are the key to using ActiveX. When you add an ActiveX control to a Web page, you're placing a special type of object on the page. Objects are defined in a separate specification that will eventually be merged into the upcoming version of HTML, tentatively known as Cougar.

The <OBJECT> tag

To embed an ActiveX control in a Web page, use the `<OBJECT>` tag. This tag tells your browser to insert an object of a specified type into a page. As with most HTML tags, there is a begin and an end `<OBJECT>` tag.

NOTE

The <OBJECT> tag is the proposed replacement for the <APPLET> tag used with Java applets and the <EMBED> tag used with Netscape plug-ins. Although you can add many types of objects to your pages with the <OBJECT> tag, this section focuses on ActiveX objects.

Between the begin and end <OBJECT> tag, you can place the following:

- Markup to be used by browsers that don't support objects
- Object parameters to be used by a browser that supports objects and defined within <PARAM> tags

This means the basic syntax for adding an object is as follows:

```
<OBJECT>
   Additional markup or object parameters
</OBJECT>
```

To identify a specific object type, you must define attributes for your objects. The useful <OBJECT> tag attributes for ActiveX objects are shown in Table 31.1.

Table 31.1 Useful <OBJECT> tag attributes for ActiveX objects.

Attribute Name	*Description*
ALIGN	The alignment of the object
BORDER	The border width to use if the object is a hyperlink
CLASSID	Identifies the object's class
DATA	URL for the object's data
HEIGHT	Sets the object's height
HSPACE	Sets the horizontal spacing around the object
ID	An identifier for the specific instance of the object
NAME	A name to identify an object submitted in a form
TYPE	The MIME type for the object's data
STANDBY	Text to display while the object and data are loaded
SERVER	URL where the control can be installed from
VSPACE	Sets the vertical spacing around the object
WIDTH	Sets the object's width

Most of the attributes shown in the table aren't new to HTML. You have seen the ALIGN, BORDER, HEIGHT, HSPACE, VSPACE, and WIDTH attributes used many times before, especially with the <IMG> tag. These attributes are used exactly as discussed in previous chapters.

NOTE

Because the <OBJECT> tag is part of an advanced specification, it supports the advanced alignments and spacing techniques introduced by HTML 3.2, Netscape Navigator, and Internet Explorer. (Refer to the section "Image Extensions" in Chapter 5, "Designing With HTML 3.2," for more information.)

The CLASSID Attribute

When your browser downloads a control and you choose to install it, the control is registered in the Windows registry, a registry for applications on your system. To make sure operating systems can uniquely identify applications, such as your ActiveX controls, each application has a globally unique identifier (GUID).

Because the identifier is globally unique, an ActiveX control installed on your system has the same GUID as a control installed on any other system. Table 31.2 lists some sample applications and their GUIDs.

Table 31.2. Globally unique identifiers.

Application Name	*GUID*
Internet Explorer	{0002DF01-0000-0000-C000-000000000046}
Macromedia Shockwave	{166B1BCA-3F9C-11CF-8075-444553540000}
LiveScript	{f414c260-6ac0-11cf-b6d1-00aa00bbbb58}
ActiveX Label Control	{99B42120-6EC7-11CF-A6C7-00AA00A47DD2}
ActiveX Popup Control	{4EA34162-CC47-11CF-A5D4-00AA00A47DD2}
ActiveX Popup Window Control	{A23D7C20-CABA-11CF-A5D4-00AA00A47DD2}
ActiveX Popup Menu Control	{7823A620-9DD9-11CF-A662-00AA00C066D2}
ActiveX Preloader Control	{16E349E0-702C-11CF-A3A9-00A0C9034920}
ActiveX Timer Control	{59CCB4A0-727D-11CF-AC36-00AA00A47DD2}

NOTE

In Chapter 33, you will learn how to put the controls identified in Table 31.2 to work. You will also learn about a useful application called the ActiveX Control Pad; with it, you can easily add ActiveX controls to your pages.

In examining the sample GUIDs, notice that the identifier for each application is, indeed, unique and includes alphabetic and numeric characters separated with dashes. The value `{99B42120-6EC7-11CF-A6C7-00AA00A47DD2}` is the GUID for the ActiveX Label Control. This value is also referred to as the CLSID or class ID for the Label Control.

Based on the CLSID value, your system starts the appropriate control. Without a proper CLSID, your system doesn't know which control to use, so the control isn't started. When you use controls in Web pages, you need a way to tell your system about a control; you do this with the `CLASSID` attribute of the `<OBJECT>` tag.

With the `CLASSID` attribute, you refer to controls by their CLSID value, such as this one:

```
<OBJECT CLASSID="clsid:99B42120-6EC7-11CF-A6C7-00AA00A47DD2">
 . . .
</OBJECT>
```

NOTE

In the preceding example, the curly braces are removed from the CLSID. You must remove them from all CLSIDs before referring to them as well.

Right now, you're probably wondering how to get the monstrous CLSID value. The easiest way is through the Registry Editor, which you can run by starting the `regedit.exe` application.

NOTE

Usually, the Registry Editor is in your Windows directory:

```
C:\Windows\Regedit.exe
```

As shown in Figure 31.11, the Registry Editor files entries by category into directories. For OLE and ActiveX objects, the directory you want to examine is the `HKEY_CLASSES_ROOT` directory. Although the Registry Editor features a Find function under the Edit menu, it's useful only if you know the exact name of the object you're searching for, especially if your system is cluttered with applications. Therefore, you should browse for the control you're looking for; to do this, double-click the `HKEY_CLASSES_ROOT` folder.

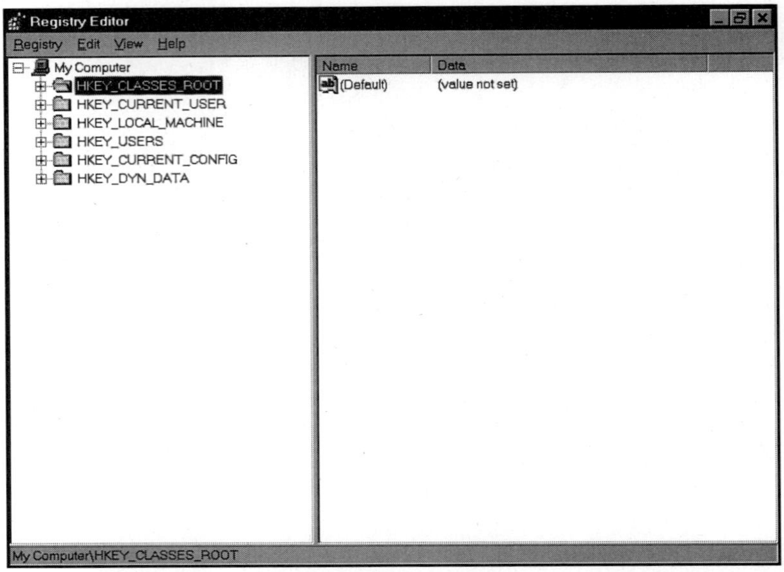

FIGURE 31.11.
The Registry Editor at startup.

With the `HKEY_CLASSES_ROOT` folder open, you can see folders for each registered item. Entries are listed by file extension, name, and GUID. The named entries are what you're looking for. Many ActiveX controls are filed beginning with the keyword *Internet.*

When you find the entry, double-click its folder to see subfolders associated with the entry. (See Figure 31.12.) The CLSID subfolder is the one you want to examine, so double-click it. Now, in the right pane of the Registry Editor, you should see the CLSID associated with the entry.

If you double-click the word `Default` shown in the `Name` field, the Edit String dialog box is displayed. With the CLSID highlighted, you can press Ctrl+C to copy the CLSID to the Clipboard; then when you're ready to use the CLSID, simply paste the value from the Clipboard with Ctrl+V.

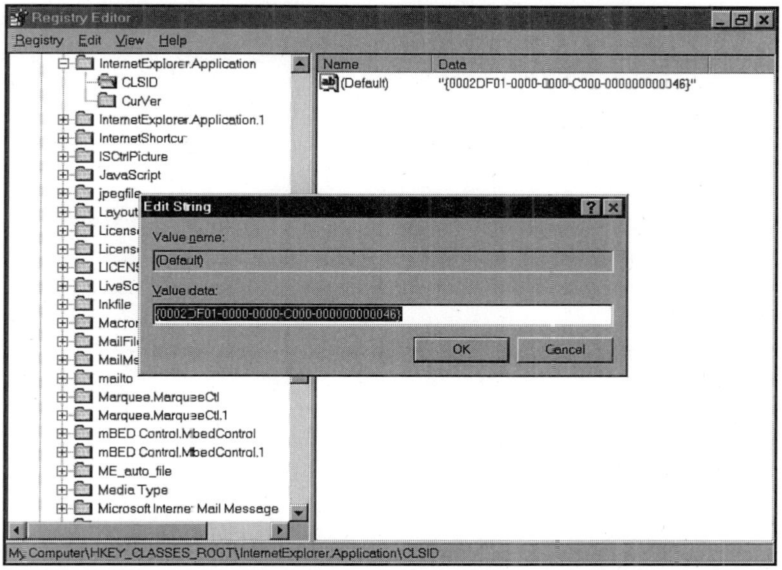

FIGURE 31.12.
Finding the CLSID value for an entry.

Here's how a Label control could be added to a Web page:

```
<HTML>
<HEAD>
<TITLE> The Label Control </TITLE>
</HEAD>
<BODY>
<H2>Using the Label Control </H2>
<OBJECT
     CLASSID="clsid:99B42120-6EC7-11CF-A6C7-00AA00A47DD2"
     WIDTH=350
     HEIGHT=40
     VSPACE=0
     ALIGN=LEFT
>
  . . .
</OBJECT>
</BODY>
</HTML>
```

Creating Object References with ID

Not only do controls added to your page need to be uniquely known by your system, they also need to be uniquely identified on the page so they can be interactive. When you make a control interactive, you identify it with the ID attribute. This ID can then be referred to in a script.

If you're adding a Label control to the page, you could identify the control as follows:

```
<OBJECT
     ID="labelA"
     CLASSID="clsid:99B42120-6EC7-11CF-A6C7-00AA00A47DD2"
>
  . . .
</OBJECT>
```

Then you could refer to the control by name in a script. Uniquely identifying each control you add becomes more important when you add several controls to the same page because scripts interact with individual controls referred to by object. Therefore, if you add two Label controls to a page, each control must be uniquely identified, as shown here:

```
<HTML>
<HEAD>
<TITLE> The Label Control </TITLE>
</HEAD>
<BODY>
<H2>Using the Label Control </H2>
<OBJECT
     ID="labelOne"
     CLASSID="clsid:99B42120-6EC7-11CF-A6C7-00AA00A47DD2"
     WIDTH=350
     HEIGHT=40
     VSPACE=0
     ALIGN=LEFT
>
  . . .
</OBJECT>
<OBJECT
     ID="labelTwo"
     CLASSID="clsid:99B42120-6EC7-11CF-A6C7-00AA00A47DD2"
     WIDTH=350
     HEIGHT=40
     VSPACE=0
     ALIGN=LEFT
>
  . . .
</OBJECT>
</BODY>
</HTML>
```

Using the DATA and TYPE Attributes

The type of object being transferred to a client is identified by a MIME type so that the client knows how to handle and process the object's data. To avoid possible problems with controls, you should identify the MIME type for the control explicitly; you do this with the `TYPE` attribute.

For many ActiveX controls, the MIME type is `application/x-oleobject`, which identifies the control as an application of the experimental OLE object type. You could use this MIME type in an object reference as follows:

```
<OBJECT
      ID="labelOne"
      CLASSID="clsid:99B42120-6EC7-11CF-A6C7-00AA00A47DD2"
      TYPE="application/x-oleobject"
>
  . . .
</OBJECT>
```

Objects you add to the page may need to refer to data files of a specific MIME type. To do this, identify the file by name using the `DATA` attribute, then identify the type of data file with the `TYPE` attribute. To use the data file with a specific ActiveX control, you could define an entry as follows:

```
<OBJECT
      ID="VideoA"
      CLASSID="clsid:00022601-0000-0000-C000-000000000046"
      DATA="SurfsUp.mpeg"
      TYPE="video/mpeg"
>
  . . .
</OBJECT>
```

Self-registering Controls with CODEBASE

Earlier, you learned that all ActiveX controls must be self-registering, which ensures that users can get controls without any problems. To enable self-registering, you must tell the client where to get the source code for a control that isn't registered on the user's system—this is where the `CODEBASE` attribute comes in. You use it to specify the absolute URL path to the control's source code.

Here's the URL path for the Label control:

```
http://activex.microsoft.com/controls/iexplorer/ielabel.ocx
```

Follow the URL path with the version and build of the control you're using, as shown here:

```
http://activex.microsoft.com/controls/iexplorer/ielabel.ocx#version=4,70,0,1161
```

Then assign the URL path and the version information to the `CODEBASE` attribute:

```
<OBJECT
      ID="labelA"
      CLASSID="clsid:99B42120-6EC7-11CF-A6C7-00AA00A47DD2"
      CODEBASE="http://activex.microsoft.com/controls/iexplorer/
➥ielabel.ocx#version=4,70,0,1161"
      TYPE="application/x-oleobject"
      WIDTH=350
      HEIGHT=40
      VSPACE=0
      ALIGN=LEFT
>
  . . .
</OBJECT>
```

TIP

Finding the URL path for the control's source code and version information isn't always easy. The best way to make sure your pages refer to a control's most current version is to visit the control developer's Web site and examine the markup source code for samples that use the control.

Using the STANDBY Attribute

Users new to the Web might not understand what's happening when their browser gets and self-installs a control. You can use the `STANDBY` attribute to keep users informed about what's happening on their system. Any text you assign to the `STANDBY` attribute is displayed while the control is being installed.

You could use the `STANDBY` attribute as follows:

```
<OBJECT
     ID="labelA"
     CLASSID="clsid:99B42120-6EC7-11CF-A6C7-00AA00A47DD2"
     CODEBASE="http://activex.microsoft.com/controls/iexplorer/ielabel.ocx
     ➥#version=4,70,0,1161"
     TYPE="application/x-oleobject"
     WIDTH=350
     HEIGHT=40
     VSPACE=0
     ALIGN=LEFT
     STANDBY="Please wait while the system installs the Label Control . . ."
>
  . . .
</OBJECT>
```

Setting Parameters with the <PARAM> Tag

When you place ActiveX controls on a page, you should set initial properties for the control, such as the label to display with the Label control. You do this with the `<PARAM>` tag, one of the few HTML tags that isn't used in a pair. The `<PARAM>` tag is always placed between the begin and end `<OBJECT>` tags.

Each property you set with a `<PARAM>` tag is passed as a parameter to the control when it's initialized. You identify parameters with the `NAME` attribute and set their values with the `VALUE` attribute, as shown in this example:

```
<OBJECT>
   <PARAM NAME="Caption" VALUE="This is the caption for the label.">
</OBJECT>
```

In the example, the parameter called `Caption` is set to the initial value:

```
This is the caption for the label.
```

Every parameter you pass to a control must be specified in its own <PARAM> tag. Therefore, if you want to set three control properties, you must have three <PARAM> tags:

```
<OBJECT>
   <PARAM NAME="Caption" VALUE="See the Popup Window Control in Action.">
   <PARAM NAME="FontName" VALUE="Times New Roman">
   <PARAM NAME="FontSize" VALUE="12">
</OBJECT>
```

Listing 31.1 shows how you could set parameters for the Label control in a Web page. The sample page is shown in Figure 31.13.

Listing 31.1. Using the Label control.

```
<HTML>
<HEAD>
<TITLE> The Label Control </TITLE>
</HEAD>
<BODY BGCOLOR="#FFFFFF">
<OBJECT
     ID="label0"
     CLASSID="clsid:99B42120-6EC7-11CF-A6C7-00AA00A47DD2"
     CODEBASE="http://activex.microsoft.com/controls/iexplorer/
     ➥ielabel.ocx#version=4,70,0,1161"
     TYPE="application/x-oleobject"
     WIDTH=480
     HEIGHT=500
     VSPACE=20
     HSPACE=10
     ALIGN=LEFT
>

<PARAM NAME="Angle" VALUE="45">
<PARAM NAME="Alignment" VALUE="4" >
<PARAM NAME="BackStyle" VALUE="1" >
<PARAM NAME="Caption" VALUE="Fancy labels are cool!">
<PARAM NAME="FontName" VALUE="Times New Roman">
<PARAM NAME="FontSize" VALUE="30">
<PARAM NAME="ForeColor" VALUE="#f000f0" >

</OBJECT>
<H2 ALIGN=RIGHT> </H2>
<H2 ALIGN=RIGHT>Using the Label Control </H2>
<P> </P>
<P>When your browser downloads a control and you choose to install it, the
 control is registered in the Windows registry, which is a registry for
 applications on your system. To ensure operating systems can uniquely
 identify applications, such as your ActiveX controls, each application
 has a unique identifier.</P>
<P>When you place ActiveX controls on a page, you will usually want to set
initial properties for the control, such as the label to display using
 the Label Control.</P>

</BODY>
</HTML>
```

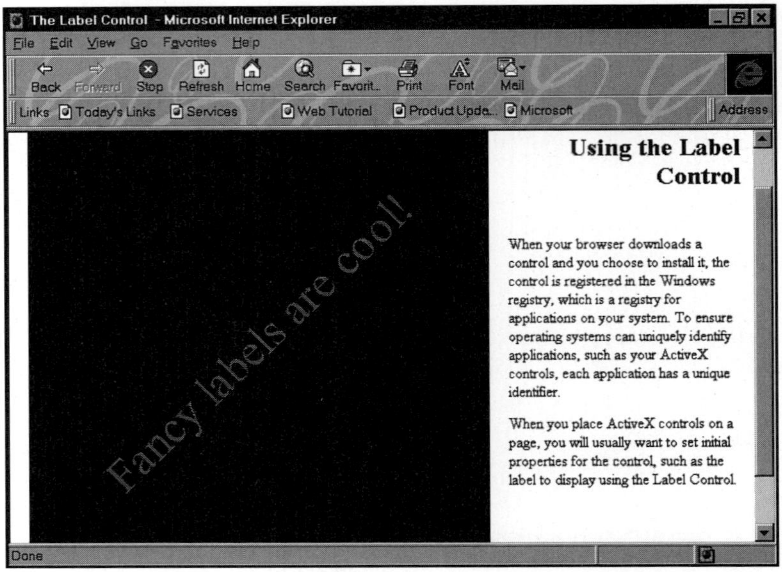

FIGURE 31.13.
Using controls in a Web page.

Summary

ActiveX is the key to activating your Web pages—with it, you can create live documents that have features never before seen on the Web. You can easily put ActiveX client-side technologies to work in your Web pages. With ActiveX scripting, you can add scripts that interact with objects on the page; with ActiveX documents, you can add documents formatted with OLE-compliant applications, such as Word and Excel; and with ActiveX controls, you can embed live objects in the page. These objects can enable everything from 360-degree control over video to networked games.

Adding ActiveX objects to your pages is easy, if you follow the steps outlined in this chapter. To identify the object, use the `<OBJECT>` tag, and to set initial properties for the object, use the `<PARAM>` tag. Together, the `<OBJECT>` and `<PARAM>` tags give you the foundation for fully interactive objects that can come to life before your eyes.

CHAPTER 32

Using VBScript to Enhance Your Web Pages

by William Robert Stanek

IN THIS CHAPTER

Now that you know VBScript basics and have learned about procedures, it's time to move on to the really fun stuff—putting VBScript to work in your Web pages. This chapter covers HTML controls, input boxes, and dynamic writing to pages with VBScript.

With HTML controls, you can create interactive buttons, text areas, checkboxes, and much more. Because VBScript takes advantage of existing HTML controls, you can easily perform complex tasks, such as validating form input. You can even submit your input to a server for processing after validation. Beyond HTML controls are dialog boxes that accept input and scripts that can make dynamic updates to your pages.

Learning About HTML Controls

By combining form elements with a script, you can easily create highly interactive Web pages. For example, to add a button to your page, just use the following line of code:

```
<INPUT TYPE=BUTTON NAME=cmdButton VALUE="Click Me">
```

When you use the `<INPUT>` tag to execute scripts in your page, you're using *intrinsic* HTML controls. These controls are intrinsic because they're built into standard HTML. Controls you can use with VBScript include buttons, text fields, text areas, radio buttons, and checkboxes. Other form element tags you can use with VBScript include `<SELECT>` and `<TEXTAREA>`.

Although you can use the same attributes for these tags you learned about earlier in Chapter 27, "Form Creation and Design," VBScript uses the attributes in unique ways and adds some new attributes, too. Table 32.1 shows a summary of the common attributes.

Table 32.1. Common attributes for HTML controls.

Attribute	*Description*	*Example*
`CHECKED`	The control, such as a radio button or checkbox, is checked when first displayed	`CHECKED`
`DEFAULTVALUE`	The default value for a text or text area control	`DEFAULTVALUE="The beginning "`
`ENABLED`	This attribute is used during testing to enable or disable a control. The default value is `ENABLED=TRUE`.	`ENABLED=FALSE`

Attribute	Description	Example
FORM	The name of the form to which the control relates	FORM="subForm"
LANGUAGE	The scripting language used	LANGUAGE="VBScript"
NAME	The name of the control you're adding to the screen; often used to invoke events	NAME=cmdButton
TYPE	The type of control you're adding to the page	TYPE=BUTTON
VALUE	The label for the control	VALUE="Click Me!"

Using Button Controls

Buttons are one of the coolest controls to add to your page. You can add them anywhere in your page by using the <INPUT> tag and an element type of TYPE=BUTTON.

With button controls, you can boost the fun level of your pages. Figure 32.1 shows a page with three button controls. By passing a parameter from the button to a subroutine call, the same routine can be used to handle input from multiple buttons. Listing 32.1 shows the complete markup for the sample page.

Listing 32.1. Using button controls.

```
<HTML>
<HEAD>
<TITLE>Adding Buttons Controls to Your Pages</TITLE>
<STYLE>
H2  {font: 40pt Times; color: blue}
P  {font: 12pt Times; color: gray; text-indent: .5in; margin-right: 1in}
</STYLE>
</HEAD>

<BODY BGCOLOR="#FFFFFF">
<H2>Using Button Controls</H2>
<P></P>
<CENTER>
<P><INPUT TYPE="BUTTON" NAME="Button1" VALUE="Button One"
```

continues

Listing 32.1. continued

```
LANGUAGE="VBScript" ONCLICK="DisplayDialog 1">
<P><INPUT TYPE="BUTTON" NAME="Button2" VALUE="Button Two"
LANGUAGE="VBScript" ONCLICK="DisplayDialog 2">
<P><INPUT TYPE="BUTTON" NAME="Button3" VALUE="Button Three"
LANGUAGE="VBScript" ONCLICK="DisplayDialog 3">
<P><INPUT TYPE="BUTTON" NAME="Button4" VALUE="Button Four"
LANGUAGE="VBScript" ONCLICK="DisplayDialog 4">
</CENTER>

<HR SIZE=10 NOSHADE>

<SCRIPT LANGUAGE="VBScript">
<!--

Sub DisplayDialog(buttonValue)
     Msgbox "When you clicked on button # " & buttonValue & _
                    " a parameter was passed to the DisplayDialog subroutine."
End Sub

-->
</SCRIPT>
</BODY>
</HTML>
```

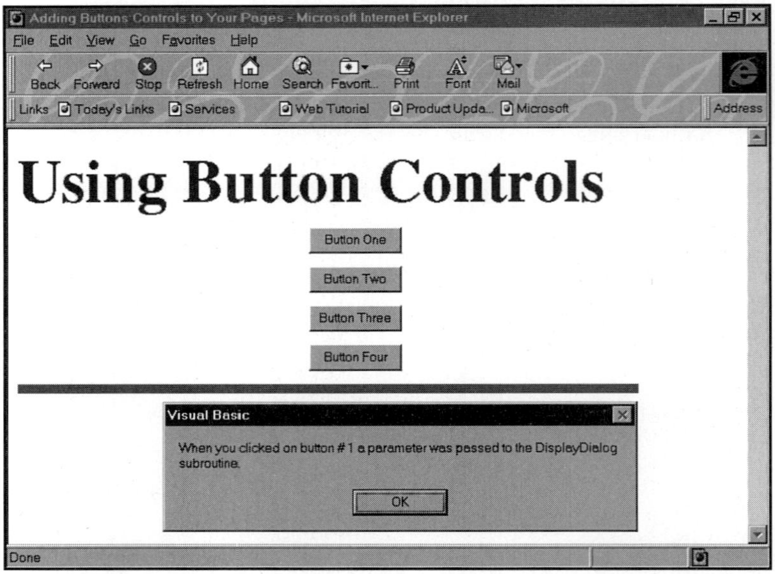

FIGURE 32.1.
Adding button controls to your pages.

By examining the code shown in Listing 32.1, you can learn many things about how buttons are used in Web pages. The following line sets a button on the page with an initial value and a name:

```
<INPUT TYPE=BUTTON VALUE="Click Me" NAME="funButton">
```

For finer control over the button, assign a procedure to execute when the button is clicked by using the `ONCLICK` attribute. You can follow the procedure name with parameters in a comma-separated list. When this button is clicked, one parameter is passed to a procedure called `DisplayDialog`:

```
<INPUT TYPE="BUTTON" NAME="Button1" VALUE="Button One"
LANGUAGE="VBScript" ONCLICK="DisplayDialog 1">
```

The main body of the script in the page is a subroutine called `displayDialog`:

```
Sub DisplayDialog(buttonValue)
     Msgbox "When you clicked on button # " & buttonValue & _
                    " a parameter was passed to the DisplayDialog subroutine."
End Sub
```

The routine accepts a parameter so that it can be used to display messages about any of the buttons being clicked. Although parameter passing is right for some input handling, many times you want each button on the page to drive related and unique events. Following this scenario, the `displayDialog` subroutine would be rewritten as four event-driven subroutines:

```
Sub Button1_OnClick
     Insert code to handle click on Button1
End Sub
Sub Button2_OnClick
     Insert code to handle click on Button2
End Sub
Sub Button3_OnClick
     Insert code to handle click on Button3
End Sub
Sub Button4_OnClick
     Insert code to handle click on Button4
End Sub
```

Other events, methods, and attributes you can use with buttons are shown in Table 32.2.

Table 32.2. Button attributes, events, and methods.

Attributes	*Events*	*Methods*
`Enabled`	`OnClick`	`Click`
`Form`	`OnFocus`	`Focus`
`Name`		
`Value`		

Using Text Controls

With text controls, you can boost interactivity. A text control allows users to input one line of data. You can add a text control anywhere in your page by using the `<INPUT>` tag and an element type of `TYPE=TEXT`. Because `TYPE=TEXT` is the default for the `<INPUT>` tag, you might see this tag used without a `TYPE` attribute. The markup `<INPUT NAME=txtEntry>` is the same as `<INPUT TYPE=TEXT NAME=txtEntry>`.

At the click of a button, your script can display an immediate response to a user's text entry. (See Figure 32.2.) The source code for the sample page is shown in Listing 32.2.

Listing 32.2. Using text controls.

```
<HTML>
<HEAD>
<TITLE>All About Text Controls</TITLE>
<STYLE>
H2  {font: 40pt Times; color: blue}
P  {font: 12pt Times; color: gray; text-indent: .5in; margin-right: 1in}
</STYLE>
</HEAD>

<BODY BGCOLOR="#FFFFFF">
<H2>Using Text Controls</H2>
<P>With text controls, you can boost interactivity to the max. A text control
 allow users to input one line of data. As soon as the user presses the enter
 key or a submission button, your script can display a response.</P>
<CENTER>
<INPUT TYPE=TEXT NAME="funText" SIZE=25 MAXLENGTH=25>
<INPUT TYPE=BUTTON VALUE="Display Entry" NAME="displayButton">
</CENTER>

<HR SIZE=10>

<SCRIPT LANGUAGE="VBScript">
<!--  Option Explicit

Sub displayButton_OnClick
     Msgbox "You entered: " & funText.Value
End Sub

-->
</SCRIPT>
</BODY>
</HTML>
```

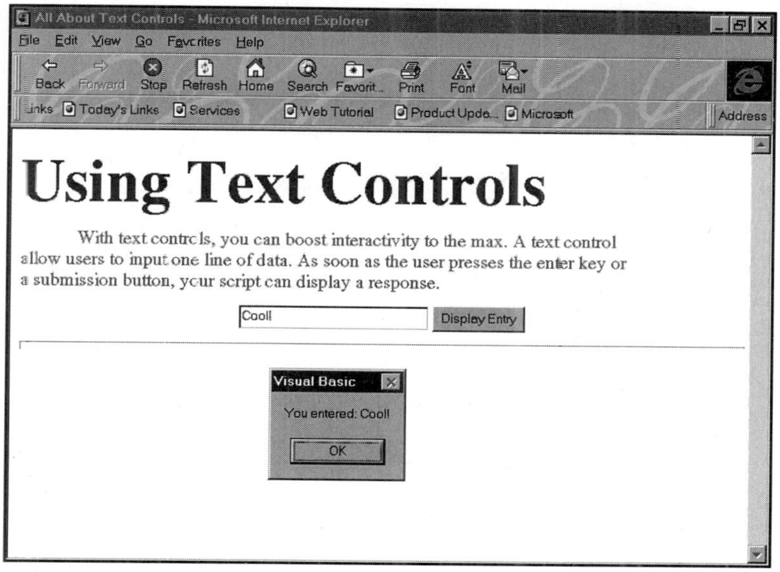

FIGURE 32.2.
Adding text controls to your pages.

If you examine the code shown in Listing 32.2, you can see how text controls are used in Web pages. Because text controls are normally used with buttons, two lines of markup are needed:

```
<INPUT TYPE=TEXT NAME="funText" SIZE=25 MAXLENGTH=25>
<INPUT TYPE=BUTTON VALUE="Display Entry" NAME="displayButton">
```

The first line of markup places the text control on the page. As you can see, you can use any of the valid attributes for text input fields with text controls. The `SIZE` attribute determines the width of the input field, and the `MAXLENGTH` attribute sets the maximum number of characters the user can enter. The script embedded in the page includes a single event-driven subroutine called `displayButton_OnClick`, which automatically displays a message box when the button is clicked.

To have some real fun with text controls, you need to use events directly related to what's happening with the text control itself, such as `OnFocus` and `OnBlur`. These events are driven by the user selecting different text controls on the page. (See Figure 32.3.) To direct output to the text controls, you must insert them in a named form, which allows you to target the form by using a method call. Here's an example of a named form:

```
<FORM NAME=coolForm>
 . . .
</FORM>
```

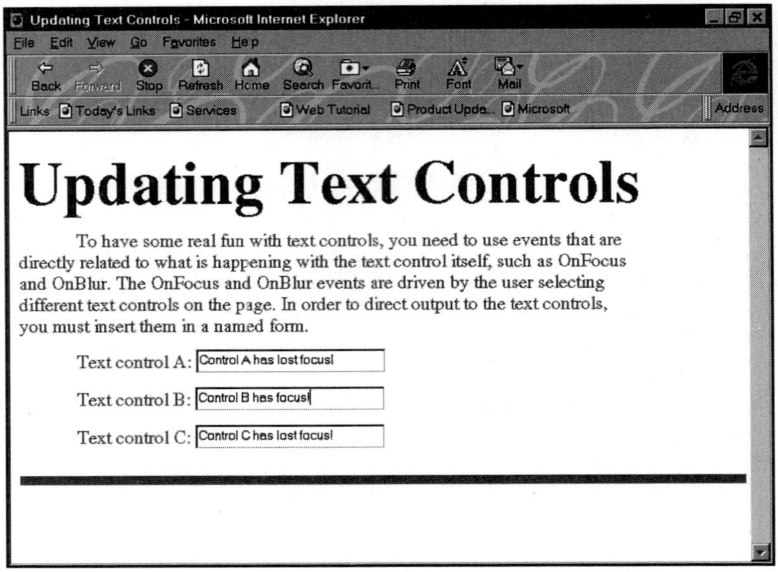

FIGURE 32.3.
Updating text controls on the page.

A named form is used in Listing 32.3 so that the text controls on the page can be updated when they're either selected or deselected.

Listing 32.3. Updating text controls.

```
<HTML>
<HEAD>
<TITLE>Updating Text Controls</TITLE>
<STYLE>
H2  {font: 40pt Times; color: blue}
P  {font: 12pt Times; color: gray; text-indent: .5in; margin-right: 1in}
</STYLE>
</HEAD>

<BODY BGCOLOR="#FFFFFF">
<H2>Updating Text Controls</H2>
<P>To have some real fun with text controls, you need to use
 events that are directly related to what is happening with the text control
 itself, such as OnFocus and OnBlur. The OnFocus and OnBlur events are driven
 by the user selecting different text controls on the page. In order to direct
 output to the text controls, you must insert them in a named form.</P>

<FORM NAME="coolForm">
<P>Text control A: <INPUT TYPE=TEXT NAME="funTextA" SIZE=25 MAXLENGTH=25></P>
<P>Text control B: <INPUT TYPE=TEXT NAME="funTextB" SIZE=25 MAXLENGTH=25></P>
<P>Text control C: <INPUT TYPE=TEXT NAME="funTextC" SIZE=25 MAXLENGTH=25></P>
</FORM>
<HR SIZE=10 NOSHADE>
```

```
<SCRIPT LANGUAGE="VBScript">
<!--  Option Explicit

Sub funTextA_OnFocus()

Dim form
Set form = document.coolForm
form.funTextA.Value = "Control A has focus!"

End Sub

Sub funTextA_OnBlur()

     Dim form
     Set form = document.coolForm
     form.funTextA.Value = "Control A has lost focus!"

End Sub

Sub funTextB_OnFocus()

     Dim form
     Set form = document.coolForm
     form.funTextB.Value = "Control B has focus!"

End Sub

Sub funTextB_OnBlur()

     Dim form
     Set form = document.coolForm
     form.funTextB.Value = "Control B has lost focus!"

End Sub

Sub funTextC_OnFocus()

     Dim form
     Set form = document.coolForm
     form.funTextC.Value = "Control C has focus!"

End Sub

Sub funTextC_OnBlur()

     Dim form
     Set form = document.coolForm
     form.funTextC.Value = "Control C has lost focus!"

End Sub

-->
</SCRIPT>
</BODY>
</HTML>
```

Events, methods, and attributes you can use with text controls are shown in Table 32.3.

Table 32.3. Text control attributes, events, and methods.

Attributes	*Events*	*Methods*
`DefaultValue`	`OnBlur`	`Blur`
`Enabled`	`OnFocus`	`Focus`
`Form`		`Select`
`Maxlength`		
`Name`		
`Size`		
`Value`		

Using Radio Button and Checkbox Controls

Radio button and checkbox controls are used just as you would use their corresponding form elements. You should use radio button controls when you want users to make only one selection and checkbox controls when you want them to make several selections.

One use for radio button and checkbox controls in your Web pages is to create interactive surveys like the one shown in Figure 32.4. Take a look at Listing 32.4 to see how the survey was created.

Listing 32.4. Radio button and checkbox controls.

```
<HTML>
<HEAD>
<TITLE>Using Radio Button Controls</TITLE>
</HEAD>
<STYLE>
H1  {font: 30pt Times; color: blue}
H2  {font: 20pt Times; color: blue}
P  {font: 12pt Times; color: gray; text-indent: .5in; margin-right: 1in}
OL LI  {font: 10pt Arial; color: red}
</STYLE>
<BODY BGCOLOR="#FFFFFF">
<H1>Creating a Survey with Radio Button Controls</H1>

<P>Radio button and check box controls are used just liked you would use their
 corresponding form elements. You should use radio button controls when you
 want users to make only one selection and check box controls when you want
 users to make multiple selections.</P>

<H2>Instant Web Survey</H2>
<OL>
```

```
<LI>Select your age group.<BR>

<INPUT TYPE="RADIO" NAME="userAge" OnClick="setAge('under 18' )"
➥LANGUAGE="VBScript"> Under 18<BR>
<INPUT TYPE="RADIO" NAME="userAge" OnClick="setAge('18-21' )" LANGUAGE="VBScript">
➥18-21<BR>
<INPUT TYPE="RADIO" NAME="userAge" OnClick="setAge('21-25' )" LANGUAGE="VBScript">
➥21-25<BR>
<INPUT TYPE="RADIO" NAME="userAge" OnClick="setAge('26-35' )" LANGUAGE="VBScript">
➥26-35<BR>
<INPUT TYPE="RADIO" NAME="userAge" OnClick="setAge('over 35' )"
➥LANGUAGE="VBScript"> Over 35<BR>

<LI>What do you use the Web for? (Select all that apply).<BR>

<INPUT TYPE="CHECKBOX" NAME="webFun" OnClick="setWeb" LANGUAGE="VBScript"> Fun<BR>
<INPUT TYPE="CHECKBOX" NAME="webBus" OnClick="setWeb" LANGUAGE="VBScript">
➥Business<BR>
<INPUT TYPE="CHECKBOX" NAME="webRes" OnClick="setWeb" LANGUAGE="VBScript">
➥Research<BR>
</OL>

<P><INPUT NAME="theResult" SIZE="65" VALUE="">

<HR SIZE=10 NOSHADE>

<SCRIPT LANGUAGE="VBScript">
<!--
Dim tempAge
Dim tempWeb

Sub setAge(inputAge)
     tempAge = inputAge
     Call displayStatus
End Sub

Sub setWeb()
     Dim Result
     tempWeb = Result
     If webFun.Checked Then
        Result = Result & "fun "
     End If

     If webBus.Checked Then
        Result = Result & "business "
     End If

     If webRes.Checked Then
        Result = Result & "research "
     End If

tempWeb = Result
Call displayStatus

End Sub
```

continues

Listing 32.4. continued

```
Sub displayStatus()
     theResult.Value = "You are " & tempAge & " and use the Web for: " & tempWeb
End Sub

-->
</SCRIPT>
</BODY>
</HTML>
```

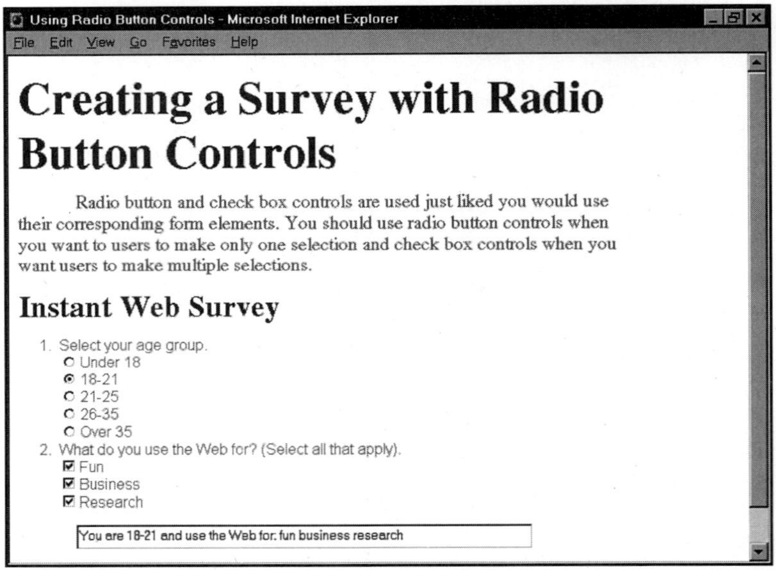

FIGURE 32.4.
Radio button and checkbox controls.

If you examine the code shown in Listing 32.4, you can see that adding radio button and checkbox controls to your page is more complex than adding other controls used previously. However, once you understand the basics of these controls, you can use them like a real pro.

When you add radio button controls, use a single name for all radio buttons in a particular group. In the example, the group `userAge` is used. Next, set up an event with a specific value, using `OnClick`. In the example, the `setAge` subroutine is passed these parameter values: `under 18`, `18-21`, `21-25`, `26-35`, or `over 35`.

When you add checkbox controls, each checkbox is given a unique name. Next, you set up an event to call. In the example, the `setWeb` subroutine is called when a checkbox is selected. Within the subroutine, a series of `If Then` statements assign values to a result variable based on the checkbox's name.

The events, methods, and attributes you can use with radio button and checkbox controls are shown in Table 32.4.

Table 32.4. Radio button and checkbox attributes, events, and methods.

Attributes	*Events*	*Methods*
`Checked`	`OnClick`	`Click`
`Enabled`	`OnFocus`	`Focus`
`Form`		
`Maxlength`		
`Name`		
`Size`		
`Value`		

Using Text Window Controls

Text window controls are almost identical to text controls. The key differences are that with a text window control, users can enter more than one line of text and there's no maximum value for the input's size.

You can use text window controls to let users input large amounts of data. When you create a text window control, you define the size of the window in rows and columns. The number of rows defines the height of the window in lines, and the number of columns defines the width of the window in characters.

The tag used to add a text window control to the page is the <TEXTAREA> tag. Any text between the begin and end <TEXTAREA> tag is used as default text. You can add default text as follows:

```
<TEXTAREA NAME="coolWindow" ROWS=5 COLUMNS=65>
   Insert default text here.
</TEXTAREA>
```

As shown in Figure 32.5, you can use a text window control to gather information from a user, then respond instantly. Examine Listing 32.5 to see how the control was added to the page.

Listing 32.5. Using text window controls.

```
<HTML>
<HEAD>
<TITLE>Using Text Window Controls</TITLE>
</HEAD>
<STYLE>
H1  {font: 40pt Times; color: blue}
P  {font: 12pt Times; color: gray; text-indent: .5in; margin-right: 1in}
</STYLE>
<BODY BGCOLOR="#FFFFFF">
<H1>A Text Window Control Can Gather Comments</H1>
```

continues

Listing 32.5. continued

```
<P>You can use text window controls to allow users to input large amounts of
 data. When you create a text window control, you define the size of the
 window in rows and columns. The number of rows defines the height of the
 window in lines. The number of columns defines the width of the window
 in characters.</P>

<P><TEXTAREA NAME="coolWindow" ROWS=5 COLUMNS=65>
</TEXTAREA></P>
<P><INPUT TYPE=BUTTON VALUE="enterComments" NAME="cmdButton"></P>


<SCRIPT LANGUAGE="VBScript">
<!--
Dim tempAge
Dim tempWeb

Sub coolWindow_OnFocus()
     Alert "We welcome your comments."
End Sub

Sub cmdButton_OnClick()
     Msgbox "Thankyou!"
End Sub

-->
</SCRIPT>
</BODY>
</HTML>
```

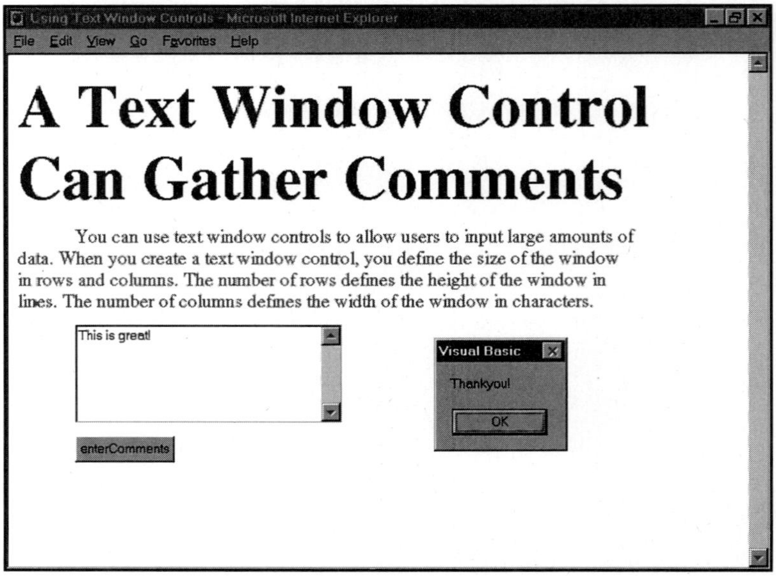

FIGURE 32.5.
Creating text window controls.

Events, methods, and attributes you can use with text controls are shown in Table 32.5.

Table 32.5. Text window control attributes, events, and methods.

Attributes	*Events*	*Methods*
DefaultValue	OnBlur	Blur
Enabled	OnFocus	Focus
Form		Select
Name		
Rows		
Columns		

Using Password Controls

Password controls allow users to enter password information. All text entered in a password control is displayed as asterisks. You can add a password control to your page by using the `<INPUT>` tag and an element type of `TYPE=PASSWORD`. Because a password control is really a disguised text control, the options for a password control are identical to a text control's options.

Figure 32.6 shows how you can use password controls in your Web pages; Listing 32.6 shows how the control was added.

Listing 32.6. Using password controls.

```
<HTML>
<HEAD>
<TITLE>Learning About Password Controls</TITLE>
</HEAD>
<STYLE>
H1  {font: 35pt Times; color: blue}
H2  {font: 25pt Times; color: red}
P  {font: 12pt Times; color: gray; text-indent: .5in; margin-right: 1in}
</STYLE>
<BODY BGCOLOR="#FFFFFF">
<H1>Using Password Controls</H1>
<P>Password controls allow users to enter password information. All text
 entered in a password control is seen as asterisks.</P>

<H2>Enter Your User Name and Password</H2>
<INPUT TYPE=TEXT NAME="userName" SIZE=8 MAXLENGTH=8>
<INPUT TYPE=PASSWORD NAME="userPassword" SIZE=8 MAXLENGTH=8>
<INPUT TYPE=BUTTON VALUE="Validate" NAME="inputButton">

<SCRIPT LANGUAGE="VBScript">
```

continues

Listing 32.6. continued

```
<!--
Sub inputButton_OnClick()

Dim Password
Password = userPassword.Value

If Len(Password) < 8 Then
     Alert "Your password must be at least eight characters in length."
     userPassword.Value = ""
End If

End Sub
-->
</SCRIPT>
</BODY>
</HTML>
```

FIGURE 32.6.
Adding password controls to the page.

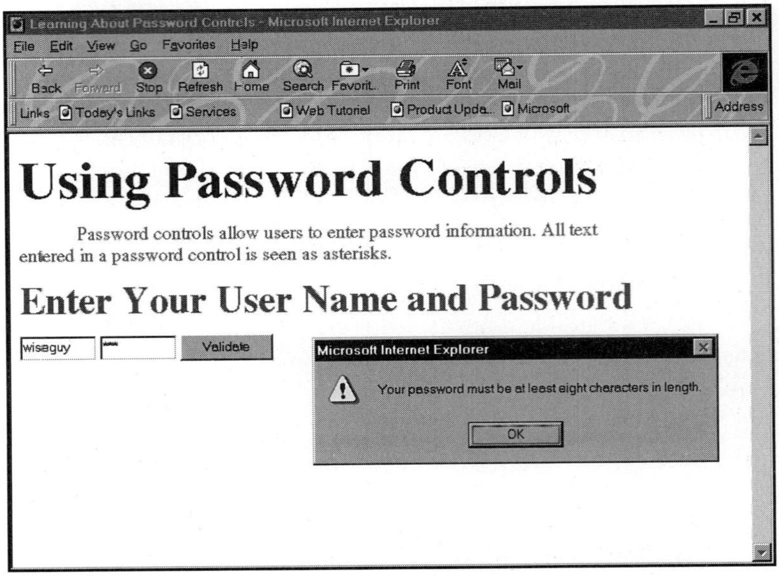

Events, methods, and attributes you can use with text controls are shown in Table 32.6.

Table 32.6. Password control attributes, events, and methods.

Attributes	*Events*	*Methods*
DefaultValue	OnBlur	Blur
Enabled	OnFocus	Focus
Form		Select
Maxlength		
Name		
Size		
Value		

Submitting Input to a Server

VBScript is a powerful tool for adding interactivity to your pages. Still, there are times when you want to submit data to a server. Ideally, you would use VBScript to verify the data before submitting it, which eliminates the back-and-forth traffic between the client and server.

Submitting the contents of a VBScript-enhanced form to a server isn't much different than submitting a normal form. When you want to submit data to a server, you should insert your HTML controls in a `FORM` element:

```
<FORM NAME="myForm" ACTION="http://www.yourserver.com/feedback.pl"
➥METHOD="GET" LANGUAGE="VBScript" OnSubmit="SubmitFeedback">

 Insert HTML controls here.

</FORM>
```

Just as with normal forms, the `FORM` element has an `ACTION` and a `METHOD`. To this, you add three attributes: `Name`, `Language`, and `OnSubmit`. The `Name` attribute gives the form a name so you can refer to it with a method in your script. The optional `Language` attribute identifies the scripting language, and the `OnSubmit` attribute specifies a subroutine to execute after the form is submitted. This subroutine is generally not the one that submits the form's contents to the server; rather, it's the subroutine executed after the contents are submitted to the server.

To submit the form to a server, add a button control to the form. Within a subroutine executed when the button is clicked, add a method reference to submit the form's contents, as shown in this example:

```
Sub custFeedback_OnClick

   document.frmFeedback.Submit

End Sub
```

Figure 32.7 shows a VBScript-enhanced form; the code for that page is given in Listing 32.7.

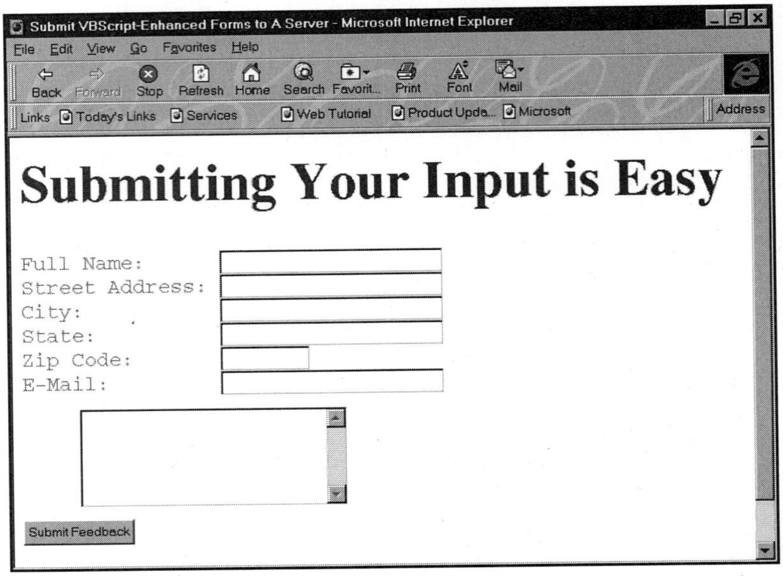

FIGURE 32.7.
VBScript-enhanced feedback form.

Listing 32.7. Submitting input to a server.

```
<HTML>
<HEAD>
<TITLE>Submit VBScript-Enhanced Forms to A Server</TITLE>
<STYLE>
H1  {font: 35pt Times; color: blue}
P  {font: 12pt Times; color: gray; text-indent: .5in; margin-right: 1in}
PRE {font: 14pt Courier; color: red;}
</STYLE>
</HEAD>
<BODY BGCOLOR="#FFFFFF">
<H1>Submitting Your Input is Easy</H1>

<FORM NAME="frmFeedback" ACTION="http://www.yourserver.com/feedback.pl"
METHOD="GET" LANGUAGE="VBScript" OnSubmit="SubmitFeedback">

<PRE>

Full Name:      <INPUT NAME="customerName" SIZE=30>
Street Address: <INPUT NAME="customerAddress" SIZE=30>
City:           <INPUT NAME="customerCity"SIZE=30>
State:          <INPUT NAME="customerState"SIZE=30>
Zip Code:       <INPUT NAME="customerZip"SIZE=10>
E-Mail:         <INPUT NAME="customerEmail"SIZE=30>
</PRE>
<P><TEXTAREA NAME="feedbackWindow" ROWS=5 COLUMNS=65>
</TEXTAREA></P>
<INPUT TYPE="BUTTON" NAME="custFeedback" VALUE="Submit Feedback">
</FORM>
```

```
<HR SIZE=20 NOSHADE>

<SCRIPT LANGUAGE="VBScript">
<!--

dim addCrLf : addCrLf = Chr(13) & Chr(10) & Chr(13) & Chr(10)

Sub custFeedback_OnClick

If Len(document.frmFeedback.customerEmail.value) = 0 then
     Alert "At a minimum, you must enter your e-mail address." & _
           "This allows us to respond to your comments."
Else
     Msgbox "Your feedback will be submitted with an action of " & _
          document.frmFeedback.Action & addCrLf & _
          "Click the OK button to confirm."
     document.frmFeedback.Submit
End If

End Sub

Sub SubmitFeedback
MsgBox "Form was submitted."
MsgBox "The ACTION used is " & document.frmFeedback.Action & addCrLf & _
          "The METHOD used is " & document.frmFeedback.Method & addCrLf & _
          "The ENCODING used is " & document.frmFeedback.Encoding & addCrLf & _
          "The TARGET for results from server is " & document.frmFeedback.Target

End Sub

-->
</SCRIPT>
</BODY>
</HTML>
```

NOTE

This listing contains the VBScript code continuation character. When you see the underscore at the end of a line, it means the line actually continues to the next line, but the programmer decided to break it up so it's easier to read.

If you try to submit the form without filling in the required data, you'll see an alert box. (See Figure 32.8.) Although the current script looks only for the e-mail address, you can easily make other data entries mandatory, too.

When you click the Submit Feedback button, you see the message box shown in Figure 32.9. Although this message box isn't essential to the script's working, it's an example of how you could let users verify that they wanted to submit the form.

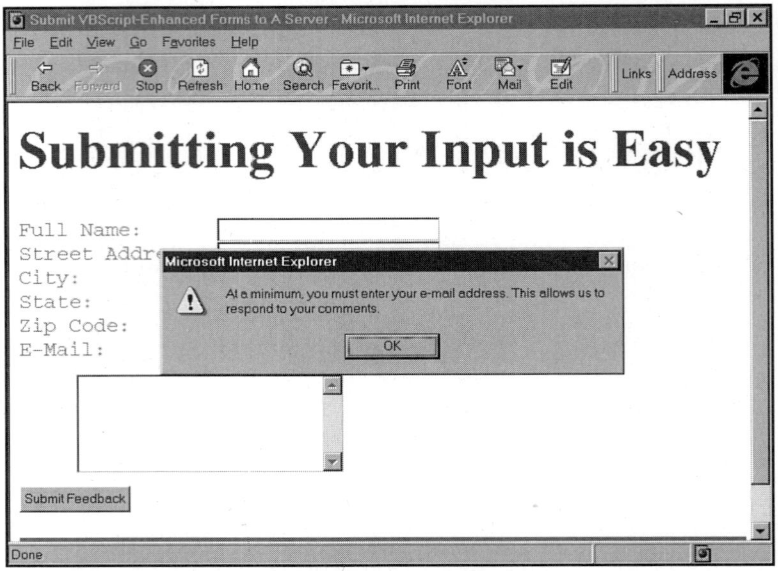

FIGURE 32.8.
If you don't fill out the required fields, an alert box is displayed.

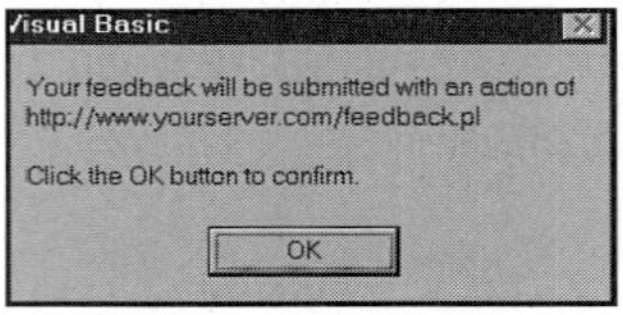

FIGURE 32.9.
If you click the `Submit Feedback` *button, a confirmation dialog box is shown.*

Using Input Boxes

An *input box* is another type of dialog box. (See Figure 32.10.) You can use input boxes to accept input from users and pass the information to your scripts. By default, all input boxes have an input area. To display an input box, use the `InputBox` function as follows:

```
InputBox "Please enter a message to display."
```

Because you expect input from the user, you should always assign the return value to a variable:

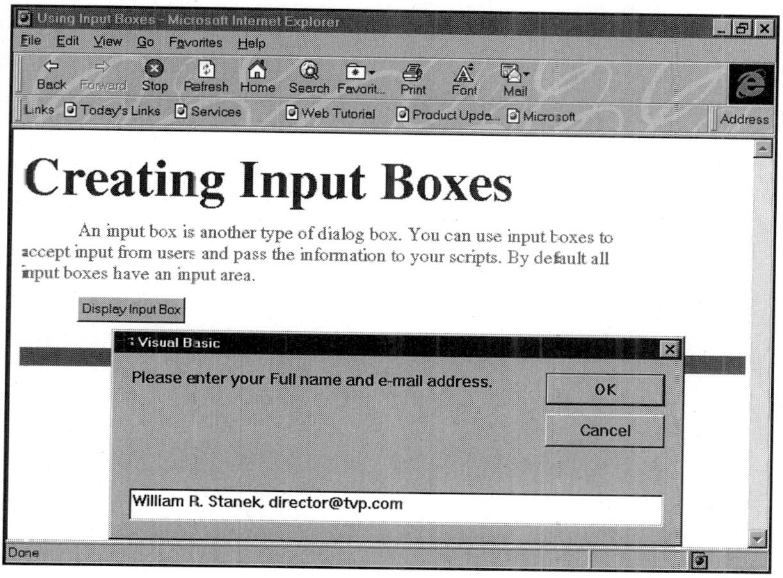

FIGURE 32.10.
Input boxes can be used to gather information from visitors to your Web site.

```
userInput = InputBox ("Please enter a message to display.")
```

You can then evaluate the variable by using an `If Then` or `Select Case` structure, such as the following:

```
Select Case userInput
    Case "A"
      'Insert routine to handle this case
    Case "B"
      'Insert routine to handle this case
    Case "C"
      'Insert routine to handle this case
    Case Else
      'Insert routine to handle unknown or other category
End Select
```

Examine Listing 32.8 to see how input boxes can be used in scripts. By analyzing the script, you can see that an input box is continually displayed until the user enters a valid response. This is handled with a `Do Until` loop.

Listing 32.8. Getting input from the reader with an input box.

```
<HTML>
<HEAD>
<TITLE>Using Input Boxes</TITLE>
<STYLE>
H1  {font: 35pt Times; color: blue}
P  {font: 12pt Times; color: gray; text-indent: .5in; margin-right: 1in}
</STYLE>
</HEAD>
<BODY BGCOLOR="#FFFFFF">

<H1>Creating Input Boxes</H1>
<P>An input box is another type of dialog box. You can use input boxes
 to accept input from users and pass the information to your scripts. By
 default all input boxes have an input area.</P>
<P><INPUT TYPE="BUTTON" NAME="myinputBox" VALUE="Display Input Box"></P>

<HR SIZE=20 NOSHADE>

<SCRIPT LANGUAGE="VBScript">
<!--

dim addCrLf : addCrLf = Chr(13) & Chr(10) & Chr(13) & Chr(10)

Sub myinputBox_OnClick

fullName = InputBox ("Please enter your Full name and e-mail address.")

' Ensures the user enters valid information
Do Until fullName <> ""
   fullName = InputBox ("You did not fill in the InputBox." & addCrLf & _
                        "Please enter your Full name and e-mail address.")
Loop

'Add call to routine that processes input here.

End Sub

-->
</SCRIPT>
</BODY>
</HTML>
```

Input boxes are very versatile and are similar to message boxes in that you can pass parameters to set different display aspects. The basic syntax for an input box is as follows:

```
userInput = InputBox ("The message to display", "Title for input box", "Default
➥reponse",
                      x_position, y_position, helpFile, helpFileContext)
```

The first parameter you've seen many times before; you use it to specify the message to display.

The second parameter lets you specify a title for the input box, such as this:

```
userInput = InputBox ("Please verify with your user name.", "User Validation")
```

With the third parameter, you can specify a default response for the input box. Because users might want to erase the default text, it's always displayed in the input window. You can add a default response to an input box as follows:

```
userInput = InputBox ("Please verify with your user name.",
 "User Validation", "Name: ")
```

By default, input boxes appear in a central position onscreen. The next two parameters allow you to specify the exact positioning of the input box when it's displayed. The `x_position` is the position on the horizontal axis, and the `y_position` is the one on the vertical axis.

The x/y coordinates are determined a little differently from what you may be used to. The upper-left corner of the user's screen is at coordinate `(0,0)`. As you move out to the right in a straight line, the x coordinates grow larger, and as you move down in a straight line, the y coordinates grow larger. Here's an example of selecting the initial display position for the input box:

```
userInput = InputBox ("Please verify with your user name.",
"User Validation",, 0, 100)
```


NOTE

In the previous example, no default response is used. Because it uses parameters that follow the default response parameter, the parameter must still be accounted for, which is why you see two commas following the title information.

The final parameters for the input box are used with help files. Just as you can specify a help file for message boxes, you can also specify one for input boxes.

Figure 32.11 shows how you could use an input box to validate a user's name. In this example, the validated user's name is echoed to a text control on the page. To see how this was done, examine Listing 32.9.

Listing 32.9. Validating input.

```
<HTML>
<HEAD>
<TITLE>Using Input Boxes</TITLE>
<STYLE>
H1  {font: 35pt Times; color: blue}
P  {font: 12pt Times; color: gray; text-indent: .5in; margin-right: 1in}
</STYLE>
</HEAD>
<BODY BGCOLOR="#FFFFFF">

<H1>Input Boxes</H1>
<P ALIGN=CENTER><INPUT TYPE="BUTTON" NAME="myInput"
VALUE="Please validate your user name."></P>
<FORM NAME="myForm">
<P>Returned Validation: <INPUT TYPE=TEXT NAME="textName" SIZE=50 MAXLENGTH=50>
</P>
```

continues

Listing 32.9. continued

```
</FORM>
<HR SIZE=20 NOSHADE>

<SCRIPT LANGUAGE="VBScript">
<!--

Dim addCrLf : addCrLf = Chr(13) & Chr(10) & Chr(13) & Chr(10)
Dim form
Set form = document.myForm

Sub myInput_OnClick

userInput = InputBox ("Please verify with your user name.", "User Validation")

' Ensures the user enters valid information

Do Until userInput <> ""

     userInput = InputBox ("You did not fill in a response!" & addCrLf & _
                "Please verify with your user name.", "User Validation")

Loop

    form.textName.Value = "Your user name — " & userInput & _
     " — has been verified."

End Sub

-->
</SCRIPT>
</BODY>
</HTML>
```

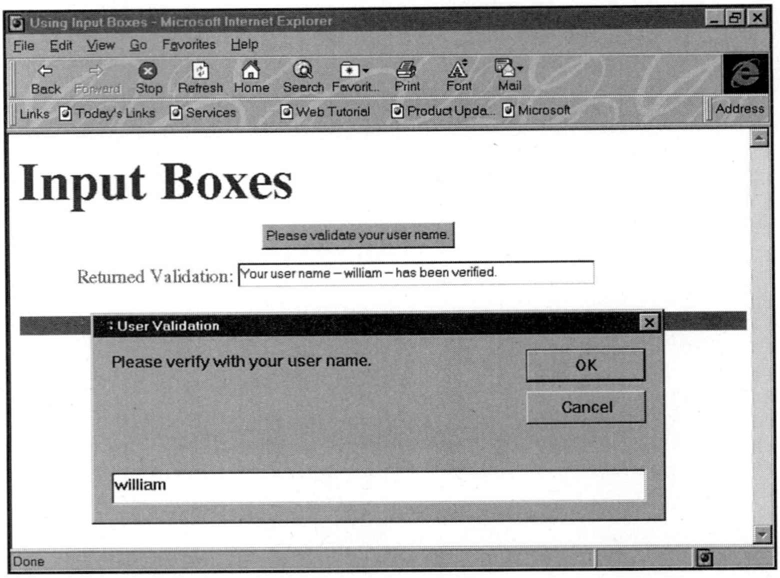

FIGURE 32.11.
Validating user input.

Writing to the Page with VBScript

With VBScript, you can dynamically update the page when it's accessed. You do this by referring to a method of the `document` object. This object has been used in several previous examples when a script needed to refer to a form on the page, such as this:

```
Dim form
Set form = document.myForm
```

In the sample code, a form called `myForm` is referred to by a method call to the `document` object:

```
<FORM NAME="myForm">
<P>Returned Validation: <INPUT TYPE=TEXT NAME="textName" SIZE=50 MAXLENGTH=50>
</P>
</FORM>
```

You can refer to objects of the form by name:

```
form.textName.Value = "Your user name — " & userInput & _
```

Although you can certainly refer to controls placed in forms, you can also write directly to the page. You do this by using the `document.write` method. If you write to a document, you should add HTML markup, as appropriate, in the method call. When the page shown in Listing 32.10 is loaded, the script is automatically executed and the dynamic write updates the page instantly.

Listing 32.10. Using `document.write`.

```
<HTML>
<HEAD>
<TITLE>Writing to Your Pages with VBScript</TITLE>
</HEAD>
<BODY>
<H1>Hello</H1>
<SCRIPT LANGUAGE="VBScript">
<!--

document.write "<H2>And welcome to my VBScript enhanced page!</H2>"

-->
</SCRIPT>
</BODY>
</HTML>
```

To see writing to a page in action, take a look at Figure 32.12. This example uses several dynamic writes and also uses the `Now` function to display the current date and time. To see how this was done, examine Listing 32.11.

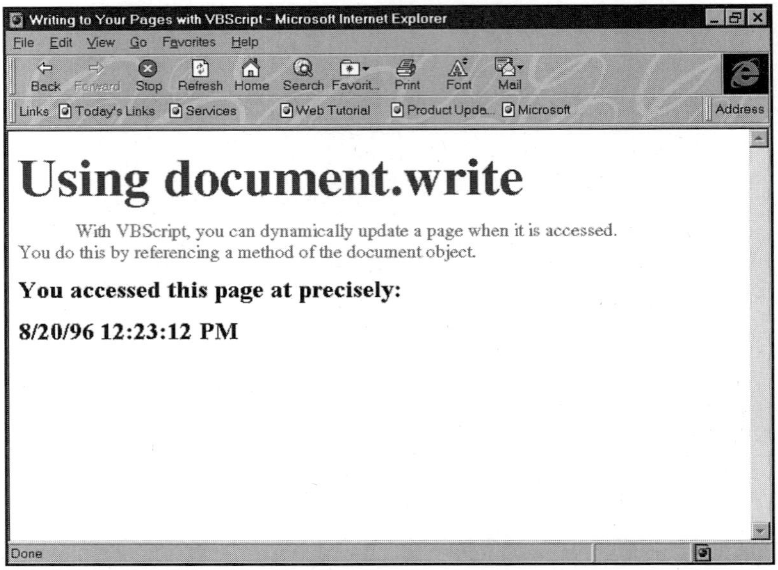

FIGURE 32.12.
Writing to documents dynamically.

Listing 32.11. Dynamic writing to Web pages.

```
<HTML>
<HEAD>
<TITLE>Writing to Your Pages with VBScript</TITLE>
<STYLE>
H1  {font: 35pt Times; color: blue}
P  {font: 12pt Times; color: gray; text-indent: .5in; margin-right: 1in}
</STYLE>
</HEAD>
<BODY BGCOLOR="#FFFFFF">

<SCRIPT LANGUAGE="VBScript">
<!--

document.write "<H1>Using document.write</H1>"
document.write "<P>With VBScript, you can dynamically update a page when it is" _
 & "accessed. You do this by referencing a method of the document object.</P>"
document.write "<H2>You accessed this page at precisely: <BR><BR>" & Now & "</H2>"

-->
</SCRIPT>
</BODY>
</HTML>
```

Using the VBScript concepts you have learned, you can use dynamic writing to customize pages for users. One way to do this is shown in Figure 32.13. In this example, buttons on the page can be used to get customized information on a vacation package.

FIGURE 32.13.
Click a button to get customized information.

Clicking a button updates the page. When you click the first button, the page is updated as shown in Figure 32.14. Examine Listing 32.12 to see how `document.write` was used to update the page dynamically.

FIGURE 32.14.
Sample promotional information.

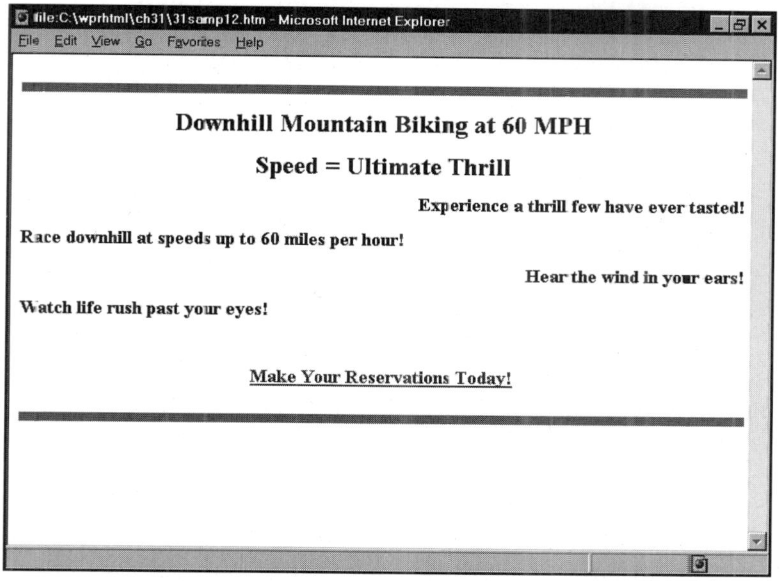

NOTE

When you update a page after it's downloaded, the new material replaces existing material. To compensate for this, you should include all the markup necessary to display the page as you want it to be displayed. In the example, you will see that the subroutines use a <BODY> tag that sets the background color to white.

Listing 32.12. Customized information on demand.

```
<HTML>
<HEAD>
<TITLE>Using VBScript to Dynamically Update Pages</TITLE>
<STYLE>
.classB  {font: 20pt Times;
                color: black;
                background: red;
                margin: .1in}
.classA  {font: 15pt Times;
                font-weight: bold;
                color: red;
                background: black;
                margin: .15in}
H2 { font: 30 pt Times; color: white}

</STYLE>
</HEAD>
<BODY BGCOLOR="Blue">
<IMG SRC="hawaii2.jpg" ALIGN="LEFT" BORDER="0">
<TABLE>
<TR><TH CLASS=classB>Extreme Sports Hawaii Getaways</TH>
<TR><TH  CLASS=classA> </TH>
<TR><TH  CLASS=classA>Vacation to the Max</TH>
<TR><TH  CLASS=classA>Luxury and Style</TH>
<TR><TH  CLASS=classA>On The Edge of Life</TH>
<TR><TH  CLASS=classA>Gear up to Overdrive</TH>
<TR><TH  CLASS=classA>You'll Never Forget</TH>
<TR><TH  CLASS=classA> </TH>
</TABLE>
<BR CLEAR=ALL>
<DIV ALIGN=CENTER>
<H2 ALIGN=CENTER>More Information For Your Extreme Vacation Now!</H2>
<P><INPUT TYPE=BUTTON VALUE="Downhill Mountain Biking at 60 MPH"
➥NAME="m1Vacation"></P>
<P><INPUT TYPE=BUTTON VALUE="Surf Boarding From a 20,000 Ft Sky Dive"
➥NAME="s1Vacation"></P>
<P><INPUT TYPE=BUTTON VALUE="Surf's Up Combo: Wind Surfing,
➥Surf Boarding and Paragliding" NAME="s2Vacation"></P>
</DIV>
<SCRIPT LANGUAGE="VBScript">
<!-- Option Explicit

Sub m1Vacation_OnClick()
```

```
document.write "<BODY BGCOLOR=White>"
document.write "<HR SIZE=10 NOSHADE>"
document.write "<H2 ALIGN=CENTER>Downhill Mountain Biking at 60 MPH</H2>"
document.write "<H2 ALIGN=CENTER>Speed = Ultimate Thrill</H2>"
document.write "<H3 ALIGN=Right>Experience a thrill few have ever tasted!</H3>"
document.write "<H3 ALIGN=Left> Race downhill at speeds up to 60
➥miles per hour!</H3>"
document.write "<H3 ALIGN=Right>Hear the wind in your ears!</H3>"
document.write "<H3 ALIGN=Left>Watch life rush past your eyes!</H3>"
document.write "<P> </P>"
document.write "<H3 ALIGN=CENTER><A HREF=31samp13.htm>Make Your
➥Reservations Today!</A></H3>"
document.write "<HR SIZE=10 NOSHADE>"

End Sub

Sub s1Vacation_OnClick()

document.write "<BODY BGCOLOR=White>"
document.write "<HR SIZE=10 NOSHADE>"
document.write "<H2 ALIGN=CENTER>Surf Boarding From a 20,000 Ft Sky Dive</H2>"
document.write "<H2 ALIGN=CENTER>Altitude = Maximum Challenge</H2>"
document.write "<H3 ALIGN=Right>Experience a thrill few have ever tasted!</H3>"
document.write "<H3 ALIGN=Left> Sky surf while racing toward Earth!</H3>"
document.write "<H3 ALIGN=Right>Spin a 360!</H3>"
document.write "<H3 ALIGN=Left>Hear the wind in your ears!</H3>"
document.write "<P> </P>"
document.write "<H3 ALIGN=CENTER><A HREF=31samp13.htm>Make Your
➥Reservations Today!</A></H3>"
document.write "<HR SIZE=10 NOSHADE>"

End Sub

Sub s2Vacation_OnClick()

document.write "<BODY BGCOLOR=White>"
document.write "<HR SIZE=10 NOSHADE>"
document.write "<H2 ALIGN=CENTER>Surf's Up Combo: Wind Surfing, Surf
➥Boarding and Paragliding</H2>"
document.write "<H2 ALIGN=CENTER>Combo = Thrills X 3</H2>"
document.write "<H3 ALIGN=Right>Wind surf Maui's Best Shores!</H3>"
document.write "<H3 ALIGN=Left> Surf the Pipeline on the North
➥Shore of Oahu!</H3>"
document.write "<H3 ALIGN=Right>Paraglide in Honolulu!</H3>"
document.write "<P> </P>"
document.write "<H3 ALIGN=CENTER><A HREF=31samp13.htm>Make Your
➥Reservations Today!</A></H3>"
document.write "<HR SIZE=10 NOSHADE>"

End Sub

-->
</SCRIPT>

</BODY>
</HTML>
```

Summary

Enhancing your Web pages with VBScript is easy. With HTML controls, you can create interactive buttons, text areas, checkboxes, and much more. Because VBScript takes advantage of existing HTML controls, you can easily perform complex tasks, such as validating form input. You can even submit your input to a server for processing after validation.

Another way to collect information from users is with input boxes, which let you prompt users for information that can be passed back to your script. VBScript also allows you to dynamically update pages based on user input so you can customize pages instantly.

CHAPTER 33

Integrating ActiveX and VBScript

by William Robert Stanek

IN THIS CHAPTER

Strap on your seat belt—it's time to leave the world of static Web pages behind and graduate to the next level of Web publishing. With ActiveX, you can activate your Web site with controls, and by using VBScript, you can add advanced logic and client-side interaction. By integrating ActiveX and VBScript, you can create interactive controls that bring the Web to life.

Using ActiveX with VBScript

Just as you can't create applications without a development language, such as C++ or Visual Basic, and controls, like menus, buttons, and toolbars, you can't create fully interactive Web pages without a scripting language and controls, which is where ActiveX and VBScript enter the picture. ActiveX and VBScript are the perfect partners.

ActiveX supplies the foreground functions, like the menus, buttons, and other controls users see, hear, and experience; VBScript provides the background functions, gluing the controls together and allowing them to call script methods and respond to events.

Changing Object Properties with Method Calls

With VBScript, you can easily change the properties of an ActiveX control. All you need to do is access the control by using the name identifier you assigned to it. This unique identifier is the value assigned to the `ID` attribute of the `<OBJECT>` tag associated with the control and is used to create a reference to the object you're adding to the page.

Using the unique ID of the control, you can change any of its properties by referring to one specifically in a method call to the control. For example, if a control called `LabelA` has a property called `FontName`, you can set the `FontName` property in your script this way:

```
<SCRIPT LANGUAGE="VBScript">
<!--

Sub setFontName
     LabelA.FontName = "Arial"
End Sub

-->
</SCRIPT>
```

NOTE

Determining the acceptable properties for a control you downloaded over the Internet isn't an easy task unless you have documentation. If you got a control you want to use in your Web pages, you should visit the control developer's Web site to get detailed documentation for the control.

To explore this concept further, take another look at the `<OBJECT>` and `<PARAM>` tags. Remember, in the previous chapter, you placed a control on the page with the `<OBJECT>` tag and set its properties by using the `<PARAM>` tag. The Calendar control is a fairly simple one that allows you to insert a calendar into a Web page. You can define the `<OBJECT>` tag for the Calendar control as follows:

```
<OBJECT ID="Calendar1"
    WIDTH=450
    HEIGHT=350
    CLASSID="CLSID:8E27C92B-1264-101C-8A2F-040224009C02"
>
```

In the example, the unique identifier for the Calendar control is `Calendar1`. The control is sized with the `WIDTH` and `HEIGHT` attributes of the `<OBJECT>` tag and is identified to your system with the `CLASSID` attribute.

The Calendar control has many properties you can set, such a default day, month, and year. You can set those properties to initial values with the `<PARAM>` tag:

```
<OBJECT ID="Calendar1"
    WIDTH=450
    HEIGHT=350
    CLASSID="CLSID:8E27C92B-1264-101C-8A2F-040224009C02"
>
    <PARAM NAME="Year" VALUE="1996">
    <PARAM NAME="Month" VALUE="12">
    <PARAM NAME="Day" VALUE="31">
</OBJECT>
```

Those same properties can be accessed in your script by using method calls. As shown here, there would be one method call for each property you want to set:

```
<SCRIPT LANGUAGE="VBScript">
<!--
' Add main body of script here

Sub setCalendar
     Calendar1.Year = 1997
     Calendar1.Month = 1
     Calendar1.Day = 1
End Sub

'Add more subroutines here

-->
</SCRIPT>
```

Examine Listing 33.1 to see how the Calendar control was added to the page. As you can see, the control's initial values are set in a script. Figure 33.1 shows the page with the Calendar control.

Listing 33.1. Setting object properties

```
<HTML>
<HEAD>
<TITLE> The Calendar Control </TITLE>
</HEAD>
<BODY BGCOLOR="#FFFFFF">

<OBJECT ID="Calendar1"
    WIDTH=450
    HEIGHT=350
    CLASSID="CLSID:8E27C92B-1264-101C-8A2F-040224009C02"
>
</OBJECT>

<SCRIPT LANGUAGE="VBScript">
<!--

     Calendar1.Year = 1997
     Calendar1.Month = 1
     Calendar1.Day = 1

-->
</SCRIPT>

</BODY>
</HTML>
```

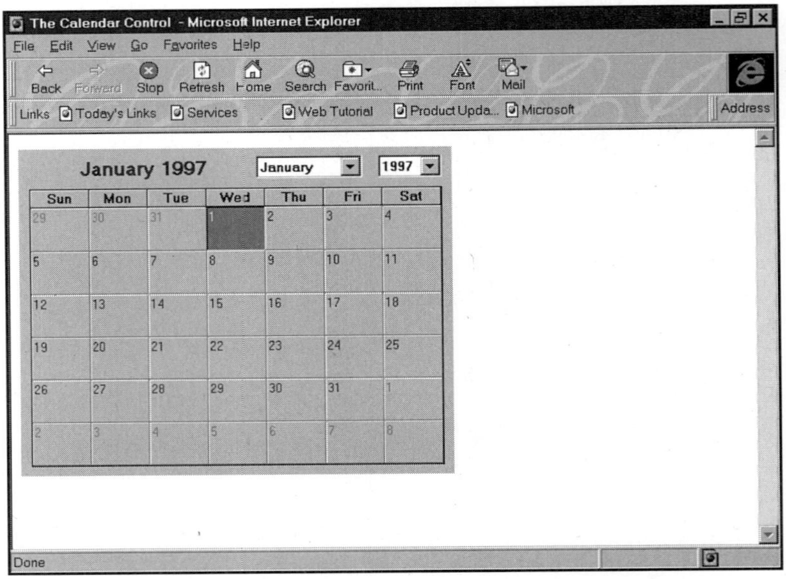

FIGURE 33.1.
Setting a control's properties in a script.

Accessing a Control's Methods

Many controls have methods you can access. Methods differ from properties because they're generally used to perform or simulate an action. For example, the Calendar control has methods for moving around the calendar. Using these methods, you can advance or go back to the next day, month, or year.

Documentation for a control should discuss any methods it uses. To access a control's method, use the same technique you use to change a control's property. The only difference is that instead of using a property name, you use a method name, such as the following:

```
<SCRIPT LANGUAGE="VBScript">
<!--

Sub prevDay
     Calendar1.PreviousDay
End Sub

-->
</SCRIPT>
```

Some methods accept parameters, so you can pass parameters to a method by placing them in parentheses. Each parameter in parentheses is separated by a comma:

```
<SCRIPT LANGUAGE="VBScript">
<!--

Sub paramPassing
     paramControlA.setupBox("What are you trying to do?", "Ensure you use proper
➥values")
End Sub

-->
</SCRIPT>
```

Other methods may return values to your script. Procedures that return values are called *functions*, and generally, functions return a result you want to evaluate or store, such as this one:

```
<SCRIPT LANGUAGE="VBScript">
<!--

Sub storeResult
     result = paramCortrolA.setup
End Sub

-->
</SCRIPT>
```

Using intrinsic HTML controls, you can add more functions to the Calendar control. As you see in Figure 33.2, button controls that allow users to easily manipulate the calendar have been added to the page. If you examine Listing 33.2, you will find that methods of the Calendar control are used to update the calendar when any of the buttons on the page are clicked.

Listing 33.2. Using methods of a control.

```
<HTML>
<HEAD>
<TITLE> The Calendar Control </TITLE>
</HEAD>
<BODY BGCOLOR="#FFFFFF">

<P><OBJECT ID="Calendar1"
    WIDTH=600
    HEIGHT=380
    CLASSID="CLSID:8E27C92B-1264-101C-8A2F-040224009C02"
    ALIGN=LEFT
    HSPACE=1
>
</OBJECT>
<INPUT TYPE="BUTTON" NAME="PreviousDay" VALUE="< Day">
<BR>
<INPUT TYPE="BUTTON" NAME="PreviousMonth" VALUE="<< Month">
<BR>
<INPUT TYPE="BUTTON" NAME="PreviousYear" VALUE="<<¦ Year">
<BR>
<INPUT TYPE="BUTTON" NAME="NextYear" VALUE="Year ¦>>"</P>
<BR>
<INPUT TYPE="BUTTON" NAME="NextMonth" VALUE="Month >>">
<BR>
<INPUT TYPE="BUTTON" NAME="NextDay" VALUE="Day >">
</P>

<SCRIPT LANGUAGE="VBScript">
<!--

     Calendar1.Year = 1997
     Calendar1.Month = 1
     Calendar1.Day = 1

Sub PreviousDay_OnClick
     Calendar1.PreviousDay
End Sub

Sub NextDay_OnClick
     Calendar1.NextDay
End Sub

Sub PreviousMonth_OnClick
     Calendar1.PreviousMonth
End Sub

Sub NextMonth_OnClick
     Calendar1.NextMonth
End Sub

Sub PreviousYear_OnClick
     Calendar1.PreviousYear
End Sub
```

```
Sub NextYear_OnClick
     Calendar1.NextYear
End Sub

-->
</SCRIPT>

</BODY>
</HTML>
```

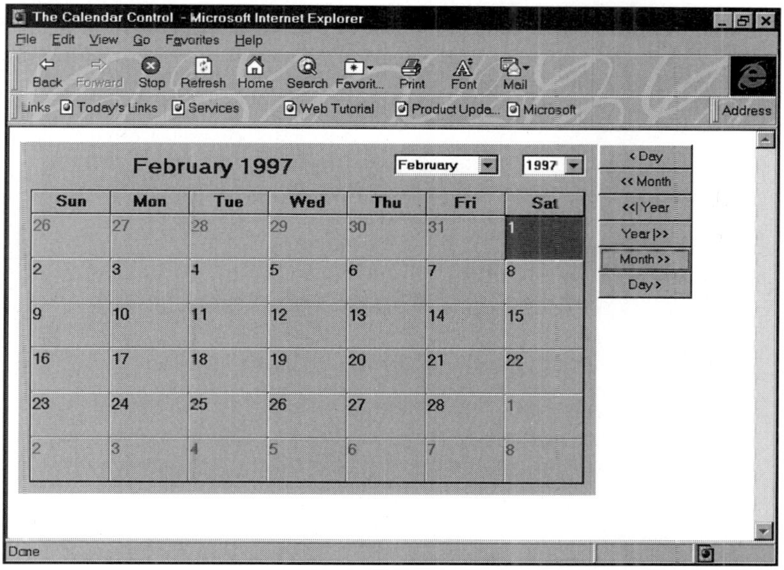

FIGURE 33.2.
Accessing a control's methods in a script.

Using Events of a Control

Just as your scripts can react to user events such as button clicks, your scripts can also react to a control's events. Most controls have events driven by interaction with users. By using events of the Label control, you can react to mouse movements or clicks of mouse buttons.

The way you handle an event, such as a mouse click, is up to you. When a user clicks a mouse button over a Label control, you could rotate the label, display a message box, change the caption for the label, or even dynamically update the document.

To handle an event, you must create a subroutine in your script that executes when the event is triggered. The name of the subroutine must include the identifier of the control to which the event relates, followed by an underscore character, then the name of the event, such as the following:

```
<SCRIPT LANGUAGE="VBScript">
<!--

Sub labelA_Click

labelA.caption = "Mouse click detected"

End Sub

-->
</SCRIPT>
```

In the example, the name of the control whose event you want to handle is `labelA`. The event related to the control is `Click`. Therefore, when the control is clicked, the subroutine `labelA_Click` is automatically executed; it sets the value of the control's caption to `Mouse click detected`.

With events, you can create highly interactive pages. A mouse click on one control can drive other events or updates in other controls. For example, you could add two label controls to a page. When you click one label, the label updates itself and the other label as well. In the following example, clicking on `labelA` changes the angle and caption for itself and another label on the page called `labelB`:

```
<SCRIPT LANGUAGE="VBScript">
<!--

Sub labelA_Click

labelA.angle = labelA.angle + 5
labelB.angle = labelB.angle - 5
labelA.caption = "Mouse click detected"
labelB.caption = "Why not click on me?"

End Sub

-->
</SCRIPT>
```

As shown in Listing 33.3, you can take interaction between Label controls a step further. In this example, two Label controls are added to a Web page. When you click on either control, the caption of the active control is set to `Click` and the angle of the captions for both controls is changed, which makes the labels rotate in different directions. When you double-click either control, the caption of the active control is set to `Double click` and the angles for the controls are interchanged and updated. Figure 33.3 shows the sample page in a browser.

Listing 33.3. Handling a control's events.

```
<HTML>
<HEAD>
<TITLE> An interactive Label Control </TITLE>
</HEAD>
<BODY BGCOLOR="#FFFFFF">
```

```
<OBJECT
      ID="labelA"
      CLASSID="clsid:99B42120-6EC7-11CF-A6C7-00AA00A47DD2"
      CODEBASE="http://activex.microsoft.com/controls/iexplorer/ielabel.ocx
      ➥#version=4,70,0,1161"
      TYPE="application/x-oleobject"
      WIDTH=300
      HEIGHT=300
      VSPACE=10
      HSPACE=10
      ALIGN=LEFT
>

<PARAM NAME="Angle" VALUE="0">
<PARAM NAME="Alignment" VALUE="4" >
<PARAM NAME="BackStyle" VALUE="1" >
<PARAM NAME="Caption" VALUE="Interactive Labels are the best!">
<PARAM NAME="FontName" VALUE="Arial">
<PARAM NAME="FontSize" VALUE="10">
<PARAM NAME="ForeColor" VALUE="#FFFFFF" >

</OBJECT>

<OBJECT
      ID="labelB"
      CLASSID="clsid:99B42120-6EC7-11CF-A6C7-00AA00A47DD2"
      CODEBASE="http://activex.microsoft.com/controls/iexplorer/ielabel.ocx
      ➥#version=4,70,0,1161"
      TYPE="application/x-oleobject"
      WIDTH=300
      HEIGHT=300
      VSPACE=10
      HSPACE=10
      ALIGN=LEFT
>

<PARAM NAME="Angle" VALUE="180">
<PARAM NAME="Alignment" VALUE="4" >
<PARAM NAME="BackStyle" VALUE="1" >
<PARAM NAME="Caption" VALUE="Labels can react to user-driven events">
<PARAM NAME="FontName" VALUE="Arial">
<PARAM NAME="FontSize" VALUE="10">
<PARAM NAME="ForeColor" VALUE="#FFFFFF" >

</OBJECT>

<SCRIPT LANGUAGE="VBScript">
<!--

Sub labelA_Click

labelA.angle = labelA.angle + 5
labelB.angle = labelB.angle - 5
labelA.caption = "Click"

End Sub
```

continues

Listing 33.3. continued

```
Sub labelB_Click

labelA.angle = labelA.angle - 5
labelB.angle = labelB.angle + 5
labelB.caption = "Click"

End Sub

Sub labelA_DblClick

labelA.angle = labelB.angle + 20
labelB.angle = labelA.angle - 20
labelA.caption = "Double Click"

End Sub

Sub labelB_DblClick

labelA.angle = labelB.angle - 20
labelB.angle = labelA.angle + 20
labelB.caption = "Double Click"

End Sub


-->
</SCRIPT>

</BODY>
</HTML>
```

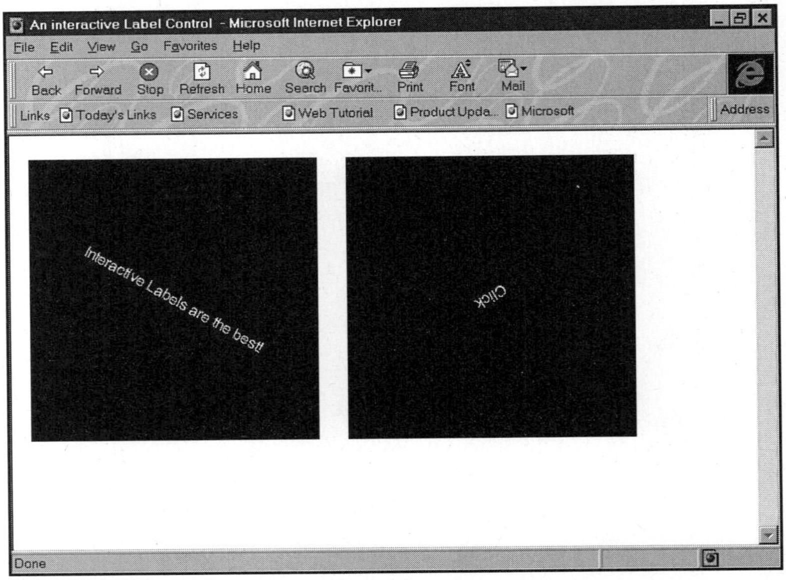

FIGURE 33.3.
Handling a control's events in a script.

Introducing the ActiveX Control Pad

Adding controls to your page isn't always easy, especially if you don't know the acceptable properties, events, and methods for the control you want to use. This is where the ActiveX Control Pad comes in—it's an authoring tool with enhancements for ActiveX. As you know from previous chapters, authoring tools let you easily create HTML pages without having to enter markup manually.

With the ActiveX Control Pad, adding controls to your Web pages is as easy as clicking a button, selecting a control to insert, and entering property values for the control. Once you do that, the Control Pad takes over and inserts the control into the page for you.

The ActiveX Control Pad even features a scripting wizard to automatically generate scripts for your ActiveX controls. It's this feature of the Control Pad that makes it a wonderful tool for integrating ActiveX and VBScript. In the section "Instant Scripts with the Script Wizard," you'll find tips on how the Control Pad can create scripts that interact with controls.

NOTE

Currently, the ActiveX Control Pad is available as a free download from Microsoft at this site:

```
http://www.microsoft.com/workshop/author/cpad
```


Microsoft includes over a dozen ActiveX controls with the ActiveX Control Pad. Yet if you have ever used other ActiveX-compliant products, you probably have several dozen controls available on your system. For example, when you install Internet Explorer 3.0, about a dozen new controls are made available on your system. Further, some controls you install depend on other controls. This means when you install one control, several controls are actually installed on your system.

Table 33.1 shows a combined list of controls that are typically installed when both ActiveX Control Pad and Internet Explorer 3.0 are available on your system. You are not limited to the controls installed with the Control Pad. Any ActiveX control registered on your system can be used in your Web pages.

Table 33.1. Common controls.

Control name	*Description*
ActiveMovie	Plays video files.
ActiveX Image	Displays images in multiple formats, including JPG, GIF, BMP, metafile, and wavelet.
Animated Button	Creates an animated button that uses frame sequences of an AVI video file.
Calendar	Adds a calendar that can be interacted with.
Chart	Creates charts and graphs from data.
Gradient	Creates horizontal lines with gradient coloring.
Label object	Creates text labels that can be rotated.
Marquee	Creates a window for scrolling marquees.
Macromedia Active Shockwave	Allows you to use Shockwave files.
ActiveX Hot Spot	Creates clickable regions on a page.
Menu	Creates a menu that can be easily accessed.
Popup Window	Creates a popup window for tips, notes, and warnings.
Popup Menu	Creates a popup menu for easy site navigation.
Preloader	Loads documents, images, and other media files in the background so they are instantly available when needed.
Stockticker	Displays data that changes continuously.
Timer	Allows you to create timed events that are used to add or remove elements from the page.
ViewTracker	Generates events that can be used to tell when controls are in the viewable part of the browser's window.
Web Browser	Control for displaying any ActiveX document within a page. These documents can include Word documents, Excel spreadsheets, and Access tables.

Many of the controls available from Microsoft deal with Form elements. These controls provide alternatives to using intrinsic HTML controls that depend solely on VBScript and are in a group of controls called Microsoft Forms 2.0. Table 33.2 shows a listing of these controls.

You use form controls as you would intrinsic HTML controls. For example, you can use the Checkbox control to add a checkbox that uses ActiveX to respond to the user's selections. However, you may find that using intrinsic HTML controls with VBScript is much easier than using ActiveX form controls. For this reason, I recommend using only the form controls with unique features, which include the MultiPage control, the Spin Button control, and the TabStrip control.

Table 33.2. Microsoft Forms 2.0 controls.

Control name	*Description*
Checkbox	Adds a checkbox to the page.
Combobox	Adds a drop-down list to the page.
Command Button	Adds a pushbutton to the page.
Frame	Creates a scrollable picture frame for manipulating images.
Image	Adds an image within a form.
Label	Adds a text label to the page.
Listbox	Adds a scrollable list of options to the page.
MultiPage	Allows you to use multiple pages that can be accessed with buttons or tabs; similar to the TabStrip control.
Option Button	Adds a radio button to the page.
Scrollbar	Adds scrollbars to the page.
Spin Button	Adds a button to the page that can be rotated.
TabStrip	Lets user reach several pages with tabs that can be clicked on.
Textbox	Adds a text entry field or text window to the page.
Toggle Button	Adds a button with a toggle state, such as on and off, to the page.

Control Pad Editor Basics

The ActiveX Control Pad is much like any other editor or HTML authoring tool you may have used. You create and edit Web pages by using a basic editor that allows you to enter HTML markup directly into an editor window. The control pad has all the features you would expect in an authoring tool. You can manipulate files, edit files, create new files, save files, and get help by using a menu or a toolbar.

To start the ActiveX Control Pad, use the Start menu on the Windows taskbar. Click `Start | Programs | Microsoft ActiveX Control Pad | Microsoft ActiveX Control Pad`. The second reference to the Control Pad is the actual executable file.

When you start the ActiveX Control Pad, you see the minimal HTML page shown in Figure 33.4. Each file you have open in the Control Pad editor is displayed in a separate window, so you can have several files open at one time.

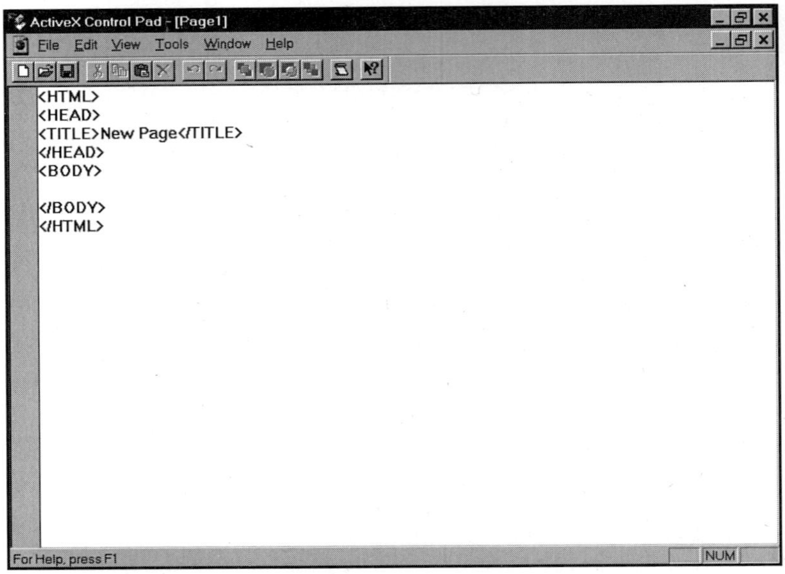

FIGURE 33.4.
Using the ActiveX Control Pad.

There are two types of files you can create with the ActiveX Control Pad:

- HTML
- HTML layout

You can open a new HTML page by choosing `File | New HTML`. When you define a Web page by using the HTML style of the Control Pad, you enter markup directly into the editor window. HTML pages with markup and references to controls are saved with the `.htm` or `.html` extension.

You can use options in the Edit menu to insert ActiveX controls and HTML layout files directly into the page you're currently working on. Because you're using the ActiveX Control Pad, you don't have to worry about creating the markup for controls or layout files; the editor creates this markup for you.

As you can see in Figure 33.5, each new HTML page you open is automatically cascaded. Using options on the Window menu, you can reorganize the windows into a tile or cascade style. When you tile your windows, a single window fills the editor's viewing area. Other pages you have open can then be reached with the Window menu.

FIGURE 33.5.
Creating HTML pages.

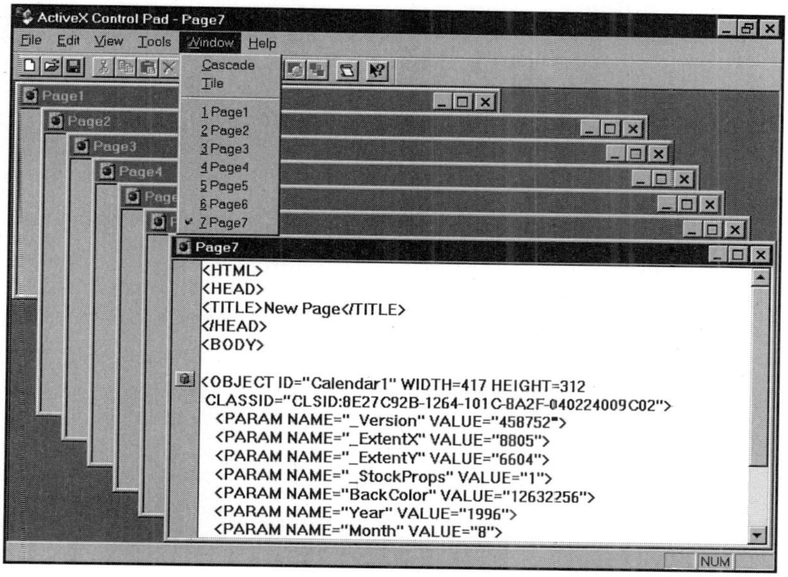

To open a new HTML Layout page, choose `File | New HTML Layout`. HTML Layout pages use a WYSIWYG authoring style, so you can decide where you want to add objects, such as controls, and the editor creates the markup that places the control on the page for you.

The main difference between the HTML editor and the HTML Layout Editor is that the HTML Layout Editor allows you to add controls by using a graphical interface to size, group, and align controls. HTML Layout pages have object references and are saved with the .alx extension. The .alx extension is used for ActiveX Layout Controls.

Although layout pages can be viewed directly in ActiveX-enabled browsers like Internet Explorer, you should insert the layout page into an HTML document so you can add descriptive text and other essentials to finish off the page.

When you open a layout page, you can tell immediately that you're not using the standard editor. As you can see in Figure 33.6, the standard editor window is replaced with a drawing board and a toolbox. From the toolbox, you can select any available controls to place on the drawing board by clicking the appropriate icon. Then you can place the control on the drawing board wherever you want it to be displayed. Any control on the drawing board can be moved, sized, and edited directly.

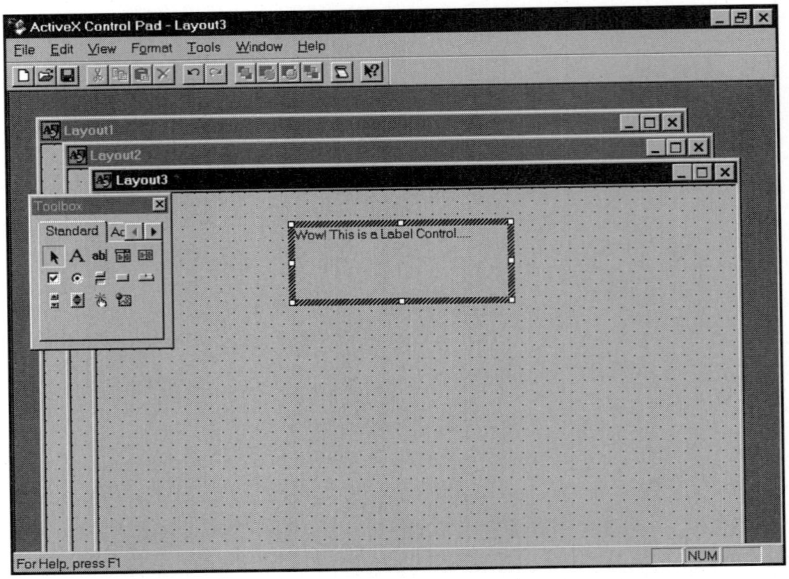

FIGURE 33.6.
Creating HTML Layout pages.

Adding Controls to Your Pages with the Control Pad

Using the Control Pad's built-in editor, you can add ActiveX controls and HTML Layout files to a Web page. Start by opening an existing Web page or creating a new one, then move the cursor to where you want the control or layout file to be inserted. Finally, select the appropriate option from the Edit menu.

Selecting Insert ActiveX Control from the Edit menu opens the dialog box shown in Figure 33.7. This dialog box shows a list of all controls registered on your system. Using the cursor keys or the mouse, you can choose a control to add to the page.

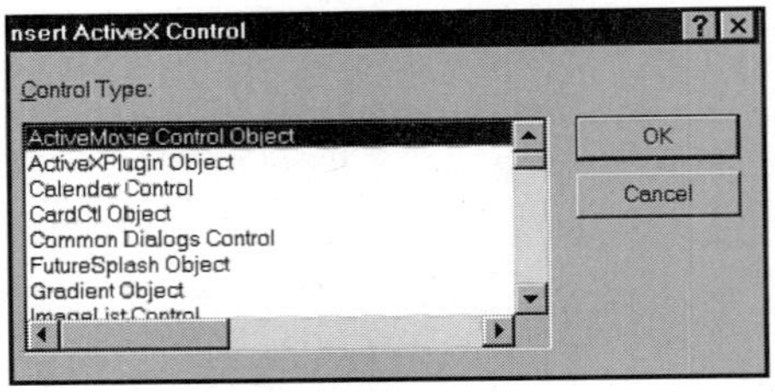

FIGURE 33.7.
Selecting a control to insert.

After selecting a control to insert, the dialog boxes shown in Figure 33.8 open. The Edit ActiveX Control dialog box is a drawing board that allows you to size, move, and edit the control; the Properties dialog box has two columns of entries for each property of the control that you can set. The first column shows the name of a property, and the second column shows the property's default value. Not all properties have default values, though.

FIGURE 33.8.
Control properties and placement.

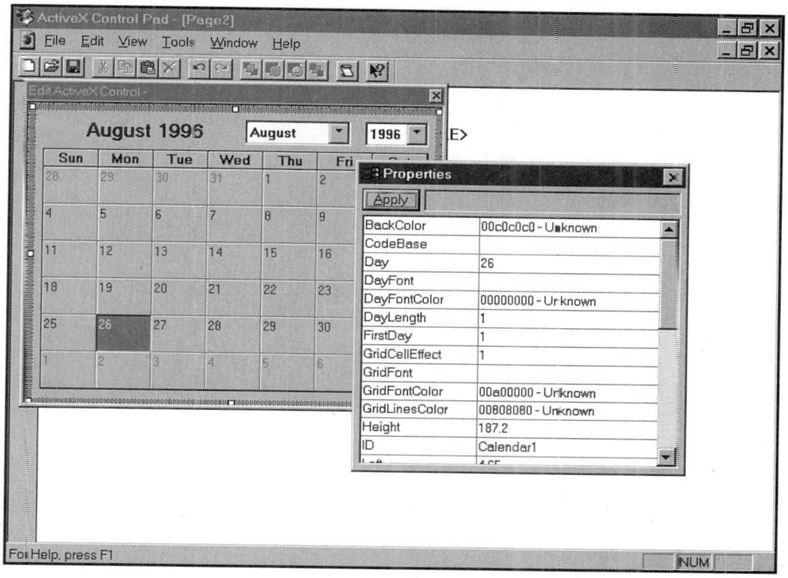

Clicking on an entry in the Properties dialog box lets you edit a text value associated with the property you're setting. You enter this text in the text entry field at the top of the dialog box. If another window is associated with the property you've selected, a button is displayed to the right of the text entry field. Clicking this button opens a dialog box for the property, but you can also double-click the property entry to display this dialog box. When you click on a property that accepts only specific values, such as `On` or `Off`, values are entered for you automatically. Each click of the mouse moves you through the value selections.

Once you set the control's properties, you can add the control to the page simply by closing the Edit ActiveX Control dialog box. When you do this, both the Edit ActiveX Control dialog box and the Properties dialog box for the control should be visible. If the Properties dialog box is closed, the control won't be added to the page. You can reopen a closed Properties dialog box by choosing `Edit | Properties`.

When you close the Edit ActiveX Control dialog box, markup for the control is inserted into the current page. As shown in Figure 33.9, this markup includes definitions for `<OBJECT>` and `<PARAM>` tags. After you insert a control, you can edit its properties at anytime by clicking the cube icon displayed to the left of the control definition; this opens both the Edit ActiveX Control dialog box and the Properties dialog box.

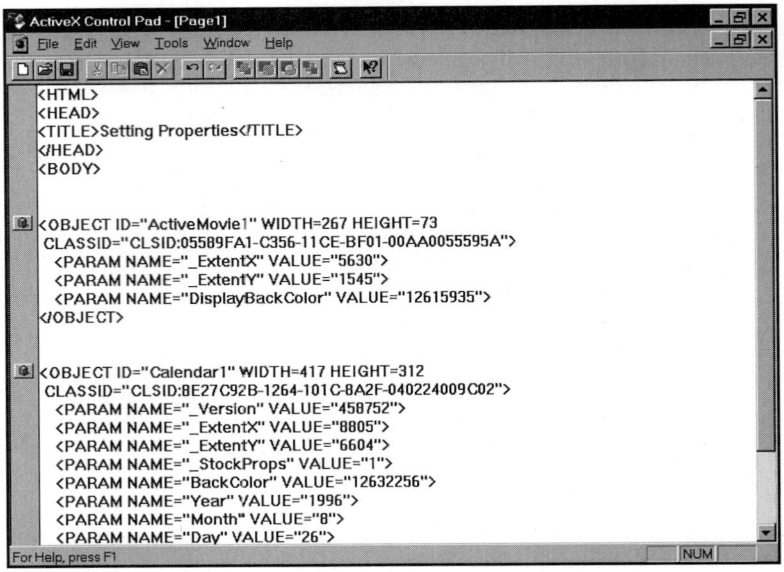

FIGURE 33.9.
A page with controls.

Just about any control you use has properties that set default colors for text, backgrounds, and highlights, so take a look at how you can define color-related properties. Most properties that set colors have a related dialog box called Color where you can select colors by using a graphical interface. If you've played the color-guessing game with your HTML pages before, you know how cool it is to see a color palette and select a color from it at the click of a button.

When the Color dialog box shown in Figure 33.10 is open, you can choose a color simply by clicking on it. After you make a color selection, close the Color dialog box by clicking the OK button. Now the active property is set to the color you selected.

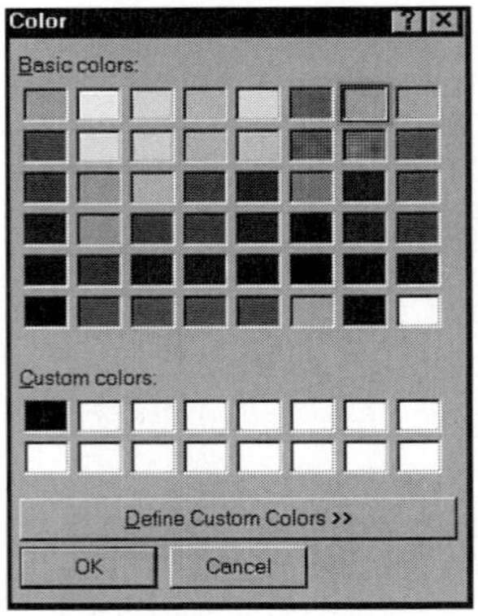

FIGURE 33.10.
Setting a property to a specific color.

If the 48 colors in the basic palette aren't enough, you can create custom colors. The ActiveX Control Pad also lets you store values for up to 16 custom colors to use for other controls or control properties. To create a custom color, click the Define Custom Colors button. As you can see from Figure 33.11, this adds a new area to the Color window.

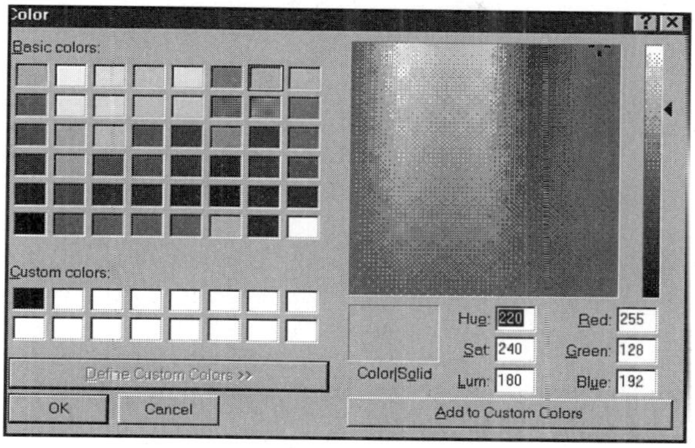

FIGURE 33.11.
Customizing your colors.

You define custom in colors by using one of the following methods:

- Specify the red, green, and blue values for the custom color by filling in the `Red`, `Green`, and `Blue` edit fields. Valid values are between `0` and `255`.
- Specify the hue, saturation, and luminosity values in the `Hue`, `Saturation`, and `Luminosity` edit fields. Valid values are between `0` and `255`.
- To set hue and saturation values by using the color cube, click and drag the mouse across the color spectrum field. To set the luminosity value, move the triangle pointer up or down in the vertical color bar to the right of the color spectrum field.

The `Color/Solid` field displays the dithered and solid colors that correspond to your current color selection. Your system dithers (uses a close approximation of) the true color to correct for the current color settings. When the custom color is set to your liking, click the `OK` button to use the value for the current property.

TIP

If you want to save the custom color, select a rectangle in the Custom Colors grid, create your custom color, and then click the `Add to Custom Colors` button.

Using the Layout Editor

Using the Control Pad's built-in layout editor, you can precisely position controls in a layout file. Although you can open layout files directly in a browser, layout files are usually inserted into other documents.

The only browser that currently supports layout files directly is Internet Explorer, which means layout files pose a potential compatibility problem with most browsers. However, if you use the Control Pad to insert the layout file into your documents, your layout file will be added as an object that any browser capable of using ActiveX should be able to handle.

To create a layout file, choose `New HTML Layout` from the `File` menu. This opens a layout file and the toolbox. The layout area is a drawing board where you can place, size, and edit controls. Unlike the Insert Control dialog box used with standard HTML files, the toolbox has a limited set of controls. The only controls you can use with the toolbox are those installed with the ActiveX Control Pad.

Tabs at the top of the toolbox let you find standard controls and additional controls. On the Standard Controls tab, you'll find the object selector, which you can use to select objects placed on the drawing board. You can select a control to work with just by clicking the control's icon in the toolbox.

Once you select a control, you can add it to the drawing board. Figure 33.12 shows a drawing board with three controls. A Tabstrip control is placed at the top of the layout area; beneath it are two Label controls.

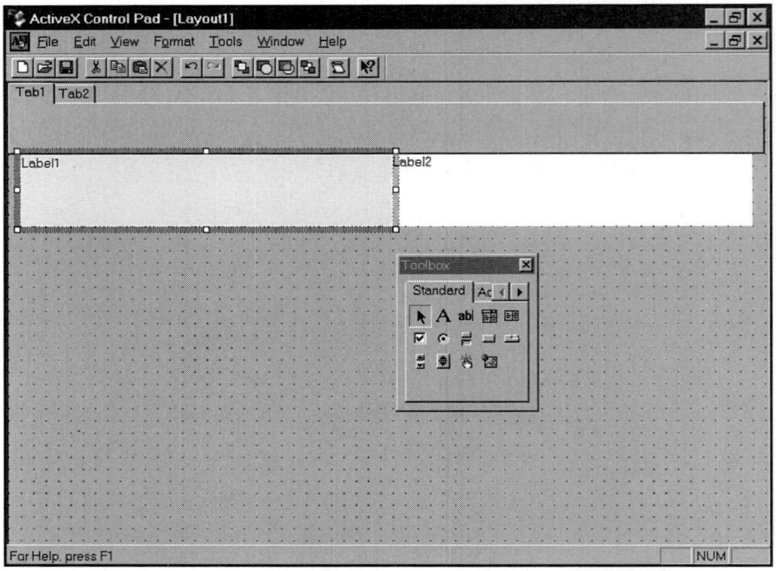

FIGURE 33.12.
Placing controls on the HTML layout editor's drawing board.

After you place controls on the drawing board, you can change their default properties by clicking the control to select it, then either choosing `Properties` from the `Edit` menu or right-clicking the mouse and selecting `Properties` from the pop-up menu. Another way to open the Properties dialog box is to double-click the control.

Some controls can be edited directly on the drawing board. For example, you can change the label for a Label control by clicking the control, backspacing over the current entry, and typing in a new entry.

When you're done creating the layout, save the file. You can then insert the layout in an open HTML page by choosing `Insert HTML Layout` from the `Edit` menu. As you can see in Figure 33.13, the HTML editor identifies layout differently from controls. The cube icon for controls is replaced with a layout icon that shows a capital *A*, a circle, and a square.

The object reference for layout files has some changes worth noting. A parameter called `ALXPATH` is used to refer the file path to the layout you're inserting. As you can see from the figure, this path is set to an absolute location on your file system. Therefore, before you publish a document with a layout file, you must update the file path.

FIGURE 33.13.
Adding layout files to a HTML page.

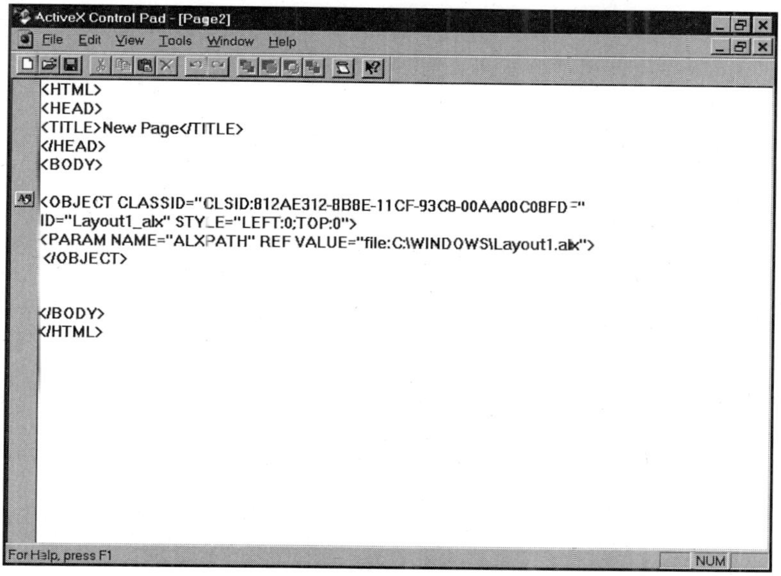

Instant Scripts with the Script Wizard

After you add controls to the page with either the standard editor or the layout editor, you can link the controls to a script. The ActiveX Control Pad supports scripting with VBScript and JavaScript, but by default, it's set to use VBScript. You can check and change the current script settings at any time by choosing `Tools | Options`.

Getting Started with the Script Wizard

To create a script for a control, click the Script Wizard icon on the toolbar or choose `Script Wizard` from the `Tools` menu to open the dialog box shown in Figure 33.14.

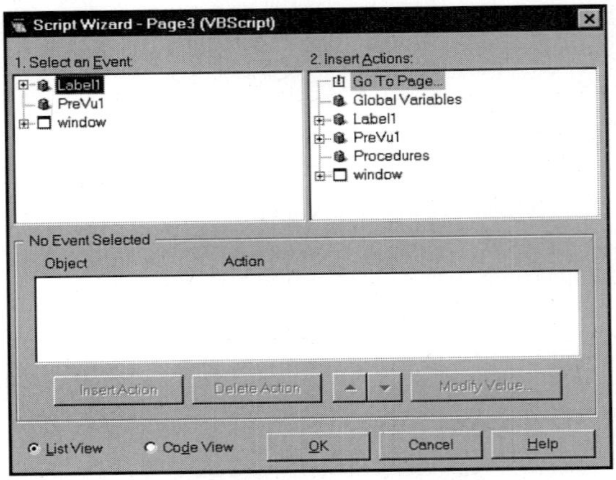

FIGURE 33.14.
Introducing the Script Wizard.

The Script Wizard dialog box is divided into three primary regions. The upper-left part, called the `Select Event` field, is used to select events, and the upper-right part—the `Insert Action` field—is used to select actions to insert. The lower part of the dialog box, the `Edit Script` field, is used to view a summary of currently inserted actions, to delete actions, and to modify actions.

Each control added to the current page is identified in the Script Wizard dialog box. When you first open the dialog box, the controls are shown in the `Select Events` field, along with a special control called *Window* that can be used to set actions for the current page. In this example, the page contains two controls: `Label1` and `PreVu1`. `Label1` identifies a Label control, and `PreVu1` identifies a Popup Window control.

Clicking on a control's entry in the `Select Events` field displays a listing of all events the control can respond to. In Figure 33.15, you see some of the events for the Label control. Some controls, like the Popup Window, have no related events, so clicking on the control's identifier has no effect. To select an event, simply click on it. You can now define actions for it.

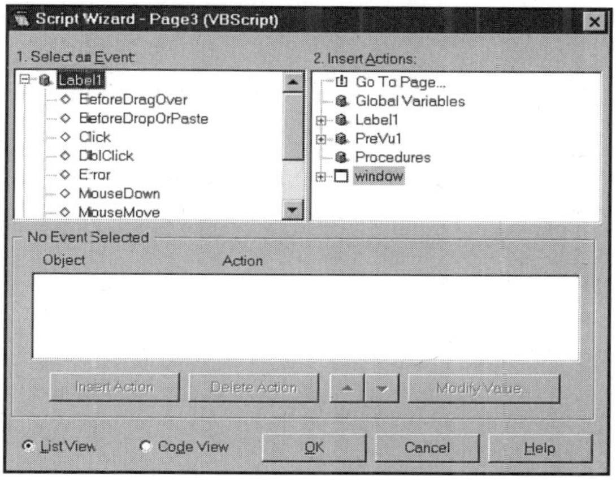

FIGURE 33.15.
A control's events can be selected from a list.

After selecting an event, you can relate it to an action by using the `Insert Action` field. When you open the Script Wizard dialog box, the `Insert Action` field has icons for the controls in the current page, the current page's window, global variables, procedures, and a special event called Go To Page. Under the control names in the `Insert Action` field is a complete list of properties and methods used by the controls.

You can view code instructions in one of two views: list view or code view. In the lower portion of the `Edit Script` field, you can use option buttons to switch views. In list view, script instructions are summarized by action; in code view, the actual script instructions are displayed.

Setting Global Variables

Global variables are those variables you would normally create at the beginning of a script with the `Dim` keyword, such as in these two examples:

```
Dim form
Dim vbYesNoCancel: vbYesNoCancel=3
```

To insert a new global variable, select any event in the `Select an Event` field, move the cursor to the `Insert Action` field, right-click, then select `New Global Variable` from the pop-up menu. This opens the New Global Variable dialog box shown in Figure 33.16, where you enter the name of your global variable, such as `messageText`.

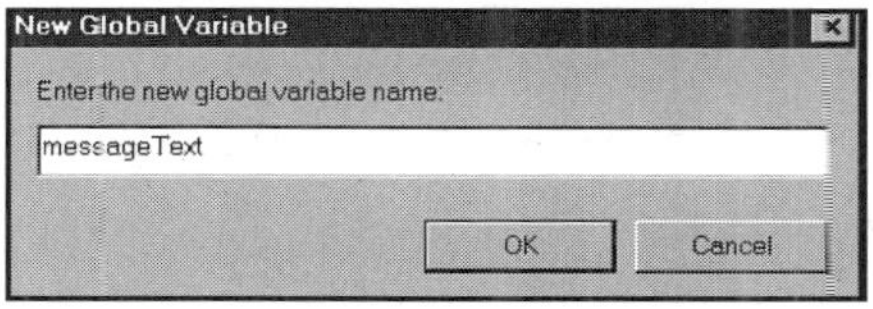

FIGURE 33.16.
Creating a global variable in the Script Wizard.

Once you create global variables, you can click on the `Global Variable` entry in the `Insert Action` field to see a listing of them. To define a value for the variable, double-click on its entry, then enter a value in the dialog box that's displayed. This value can be an actual numeric or text string or a reference to another variable.

Figure 33.17 shows how the `messageText` variable created earlier could be set to a specific value. Be sure to enclose text strings in quotations. When you are done defining the variable, click the `OK` button to close the dialog box.

FIGURE 33.17.
Setting a global variable to a specific value in the Script Wizard.

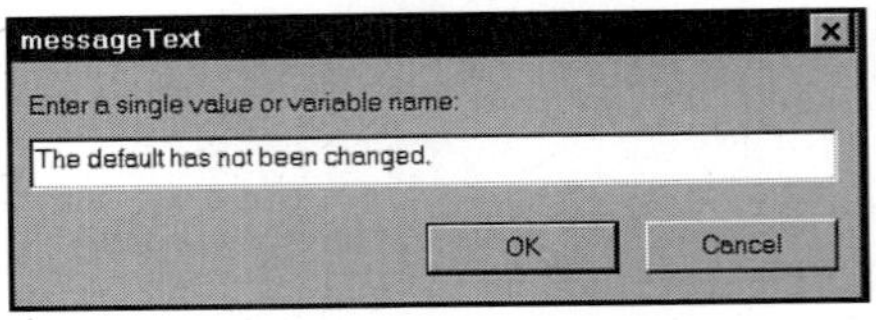

Creating Procedures and Generating Scripts

Script Wizard defines procedures related to events for you, but you can also create your own procedures. Once you create event-driven procedures, they're available for editing. If you're in code view, you can click the `Procedures` icon in the `Select Action` field to see a listing of currently defined procedures.

To insert a new procedure, move the cursor to the `Insert Action` field, right-click, then select `New Procedure` from the pop-up menu. In the `Edit Script` field, you can now define actions for the procedure. The Script Wizard names procedures sequentially. The first procedure you create is `Procedure1`, the second is `Procedure2`, and so on.

If you're in code view, you can define actions for the active procedure. To do this, enter the code directly into the `Edit Script` field, as shown in Figure 33.18.

FIGURE 33.18.
Editing procedures in the Script Wizard.

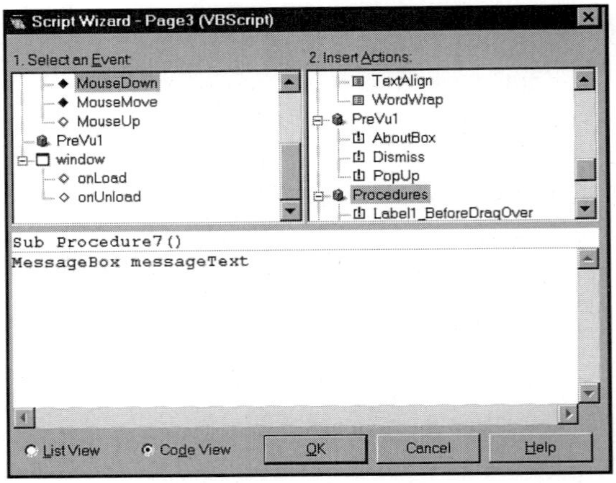

To create an event-driven procedure, select an event for a specific control in the `Select Event` field. Next, choose actions to associate with the event. Actions include setting a control's properties and methods.

In list view, separate dialog boxes are displayed when you double-click on a property or method name in the `Select Event` field. Some dialog boxes allow you to select from lists of acceptable values; others let you enter text strings or set a color-related property with the Color dialog box.

To create an event that changes a label's background style when the mouse moves over the control, first make sure you're in list view, then select the `MouseMovement` event of the Label control by clicking on it in the `Select Event` field. Next, in the `Insert Action` field, double-click on the `BackStyle` property of the Label control. This opens the dialog box shown in Figure 33.19. You can now select the new background style for the label.

FIGURE 33.19.

Generating event-driven procedures in the Script Wizard.

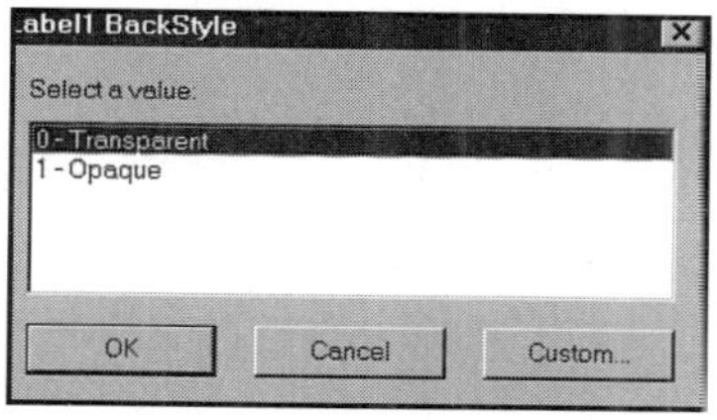

In code view, dialog boxes aren't displayed when you click on a property or method name in the `Select Event` field. Instead, clicking on a property or method name inserts a reference in your code. You must then set the method or property yourself.

If you want to create an event that changes a label's caption when the mouse moves over the control, make sure you're in code view, then select the `MouseMovement` event of the Label control by clicking on it in the `Select Event` field. Next, in the `Insert Action` field, double-click on the `Caption` property of the Label control. As shown in Figure 33.20, this inserts a reference to the `Caption` property into the procedure shown in the `Script Edit` field. Now you can assign a value to the property.

In the Script Wizard, the final step is to generate your script. You do this simply by clicking the `OK` button in the Script Wizard dialog box. The Script Wizard then inserts your script into the current page, as you can see in Figure 33.21. You can edit your script at any time by clicking the Script Wizard icon displayed to the left of the script.

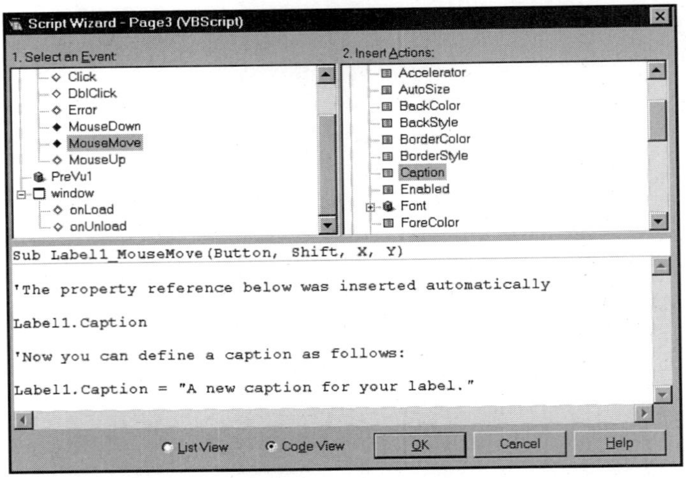

FIGURE 33.20.
Creating event-driven procedures in code view.

Although the sample script is fairly basic, you can use the Script Wizard to generate some enormous scripts. Because the Script Wizard has a point-and-click interface, you can easily generate a 50-line script in five minutes.

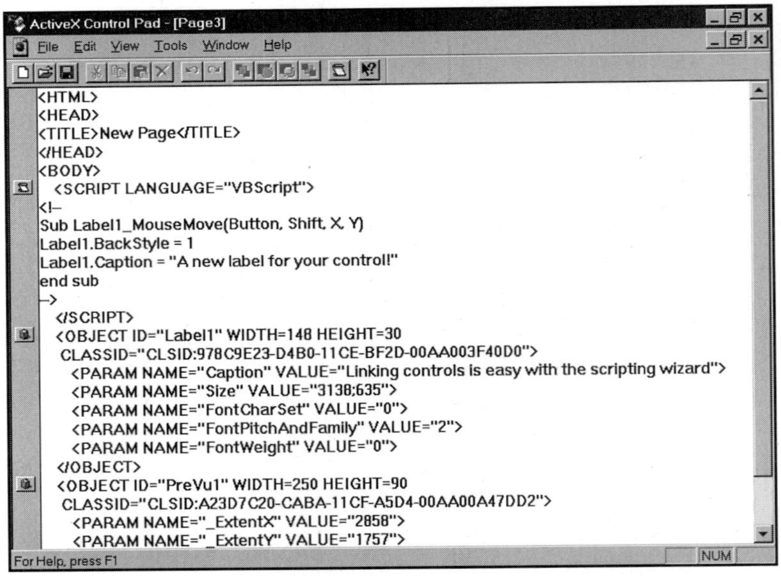

FIGURE 33.21.
A script generated by the Script Wizard.

Summary

ActiveX and VBScript are a powerful combination for activating the Internet. With ActiveX, you can add controls, such as menus, labels, popup windows, and much more, to your pages. With VBScript, you can make the controls interactive. You can even use VBScript to glue controls together, which allows one control to make dynamic updates to others.

Tracking properties, methods, and events for controls is no picnic. Fortunately, Microsoft has created a terrific authoring tool called the ActiveX Control Pad. Not only does it help you integrate ActiveX and VBScript, the Control Pad also gives you instant access to the properties, methods, and events used by controls.

VIII

Part

IN THIS PART

JavaScript and Java

CHAPTER 34

Using JavaScript in Your Web Pages

by Rick Darnell

IN THIS CHAPTER

JavaScript, a scripting extension to HTML, extends your ability to respond to user events without the need for client-server communication or CGI scripting.

In the past, a form typically was submitted to the server for all processing, whether it meant checking a ZIP code or putting information in a database. Each time information was passed back and forth between client and server, it slowed down the process, due to inherently slow communication lines. JavaScript eliminates much of the client-server communication by shifting responses to user events to the client side. Because network transmission is not required, the process goes much faster.

Getting to Know JavaScript

JavaScript is more closely related to a programming language than to HTML tags. JavaScript cannot exist, however, outside of HTML. To function, it must be included as part of a page.

JavaScript was developed by Netscape in conjunction with Sun's Java. You may also know it as LiveScript—the first name it had before the collaboration with Sun.

JAVASCRIPT ISN'T JAVA

Java is an object-oriented programming language used to create standalone applications and applets, special "mini" applications for Web pages. Writing Java programs is easiest when you have some background in programming, such as with C or C++.

Java is compiled into machine-independent bytecodes, which are in turn interpreted by the Java Virtual Machine on the host computer. The bytecodes are generic instructions, such as "print this line," or "create this variable," which are then given nitty-gritty detail by the interpreter on the host machine.

JavaScript shares some of the same syntax and structure as Java, but it provides a much smaller and simpler language for people with HTML or CGI experience. It gets interpreted along with the rest of the page at load time. JavaScript resides only within an HTML document and provides for greater levels of interactivity than basic HTML commands.

For example, JavaScript enables the HTML author to respond to user-initiated events, such as mouse clicks and form activity, without the need for client-server interaction. The result provides quicker operation for the end user and less load on the server.

Although similarities exist between Java and JavaScript, the languages are different and are intended for different uses. A simple form-handling routine that would require a significant amount of coding in Java represents a basic task for JavaScript, but creating a browser such as HotJava in JavaScript is impossible.

Java applets occupy a defined space on the screen, much as an image or other embedded item. Although an applet can communicate with another applet on the same page, communicating with a page's HTML elements requires a substantial amount of code.

JavaScript does not represent a watered-down version of Java for programming beginners. Although related to Java, it provides a solution for client-side scripting in an era when users with high-powered machines get bogged down by client-server communication.

Although many ways exist to control the browser from within a Java applet, simple tasks such as computing a form or controlling frame content become complicated affairs. JavaScript bridges the gap by enabling HTML authors to implement basic HTML functionality and interactivity without hours and hours of codewriting.

The other side of the coin for JavaScript means you have a much smaller set of objects, methods and properties to work with, and they all are focused towards dealing with HTML content. For example, JavaScript does not have the capability to control network connections or download files.

Why Is JavaScript So Hot?

Although based on programming, JavaScript is simple enough to be within easy reach of anyone who feels comfortable with HTML coding. It greatly expands the capabilities of typical HTML pages, without a great deal of hassle.

Look at the following snippet, for example:

```
<SCRIPT LANGUAGE="javascript">
document.writeln("This page last changed on "+document.lastModified());
</SCRIPT>
```

When the page loads, some basic information about itself also is included, such as the time and date the page was saved. Without any further communication with the server, JavaScript accesses the date and displays it for the user. You don't need to remember to update a line of HTML or include a link to a CGI script—when the JavaScript line appears, the process is automatic.

JavaScript also includes the capability to effectively manage multiple frames. Although a page cannot be redrawn, you can control the content in other frames by loading them with new URLs or managing form input.

FRAMES IN REVIEW

Frames enable multiple document windows simultaneously within one browser. Each frame can scroll, hyperlink, reload, and do all of the other things possible with a single browser window. Frames enable creation of useful document groups, such as combining menu and navigation bars with content. They are created with the `<FRAMESET>` tag, with each individual frame defined using `FRAME SRC=URL NAME="name"`.

```
<HTML>
<FRAMESET ROWS="20%,80%">
```

continues

continued

```
        <FRAME SRC="MenuBar.htm" NAME="menu" noresize>
        <FRAMESET COLS="20%,80%">
            <FRAME SRC="NavBar.htm" NAME="nav" noresize>
            <FRAME SRC="Home.htm" NAME="body">
        </FRAMESET>
    </FRAMESET>
    </HTML>
```

Note the nested framesets for creating frames within frames. Be careful when using this feature. Although you can break down the browser screen into individual units, doing so can slow down displays and turn the screen into an unintelligible jigsaw puzzle—especially for a user screen with less than 800×600 resolution.

Assigning names can make referencing frames easier, although referring to individual frames is also possible in JavaScript using the frames array.

When you create a frame, JavaScript adds an entry to its frames array. In the preceding example, JavaScript creates three entries:

```
document.frames[0].namne //"menu"
document.frames[1].name //"nav"
document.frames[2].name //"body"
```

As a general rule, JavaScript always begins numbering with 0, even in arrays. For more information on creating and working with frames, see Chapter 7, "Creating and Enhancing Web Pages with Frames."

One major JavaScript capability is revealed in its capability to handle forms and their elements. Using JavaScript, the information on a form can be validated and checked before it is sent to the server, saving valuable processing and communication time on the server. Client-side form processing also localizes the process, making it much harder for end users to send incompatible data that could cause damage to the server.

Additional characteristics now represent a part of form elements in the shape of events and event handlers. For `INPUT TYPE=` tags such as `BUTTON` and `TEXT`, the page author can check for mouse clicks, changed text, focus, and even change the content of form elements. In addition, submission of forms and other information is controlled by substituting custom actions for the standard submit button formats.

How to Use JavaScript Now

Most HTML editors that handle nonstandard HTML tags enable creation and editing of JavaScript sections to your pages. Several resources available for learning the syntax and idiosyncrasies of JavaScript appear at the end of this chapter.

TIP

One of the most useful sites is the JavaScript online documentation at

`http://home.netscape.com/eng/mozilla/3.0/handbook/javascript/index.html.`

For users to take advantage of your JavaScript-empowered pages, they need to use a compatible browser. This is a short list at present, but more browsers are expected to add this capability, following the example of the two leaders, Netscape and Microsoft.

WARNING

The JavaScript API is not entirely stabilized yet. As Netscape continues its own development and collaboration with Sun, the implementation and workability of some features may change. You should always try your script on more than one browser and platform combination to ensure that your solutions function as planned.

The current browser choices include Netscape Navigator (2.0 and later) and Microsoft Internet Explorer (3.0 and later). Sun HotJava is also scheduled for JavaScript compatibility, although it hasn't been included in any of the beta implementations. NCSA Mosaic also includes support for Java and JavaScript on its wish list, although no date has been set for implementation.

TIP

Like many sites that provide a host of compatibilities, some of which are mutually exclusive, it shows good manners to offer your page in a generic version if crucial content is not usable with a non-JavaScript browser. You can also offer a link to sites where a compatible browser is available for downloading.

The <Script> Tag

As seen in the previous examples in this chapter, JavaScript requires its own special tag to mark its beginning and end. The basic form of the tag appears in the following code:

```
<SCRIPT [LANGUAGE="JavaScript"]>
...statments...
</SCRIPT>
```

A problem can develop when a noncompatible browser is used to view a page embedded with JavaScript statements. Note the following two figures (Figures 34.1 and 34.2). Both show the same HTML document, which includes JavaScript statements (see Listing 34.1); however, Figure 34.1 uses Netscape Navigator 3.0, and Figure 34.2 is viewed with NCSA Mosaic.

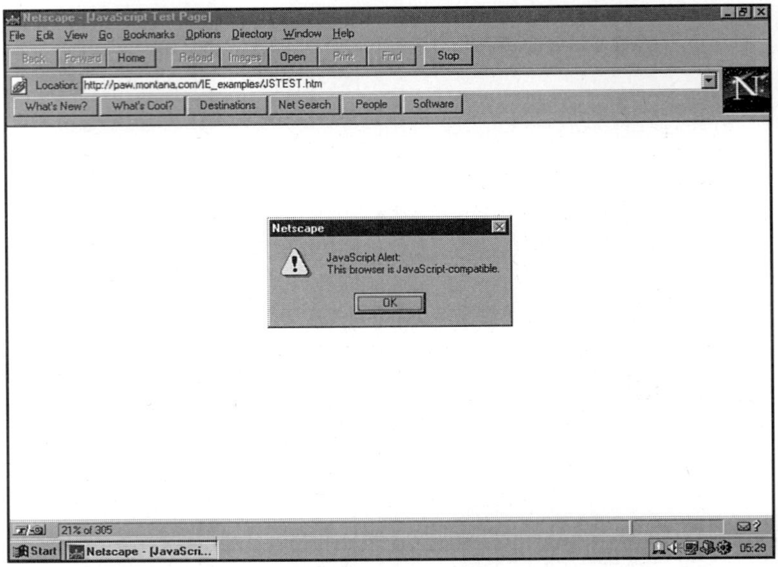

FIGURE 34.1.
JavaScript-compatible Netscape Navigator 3.0 displays this HTML document and processes the JavaScript commands contained in it.

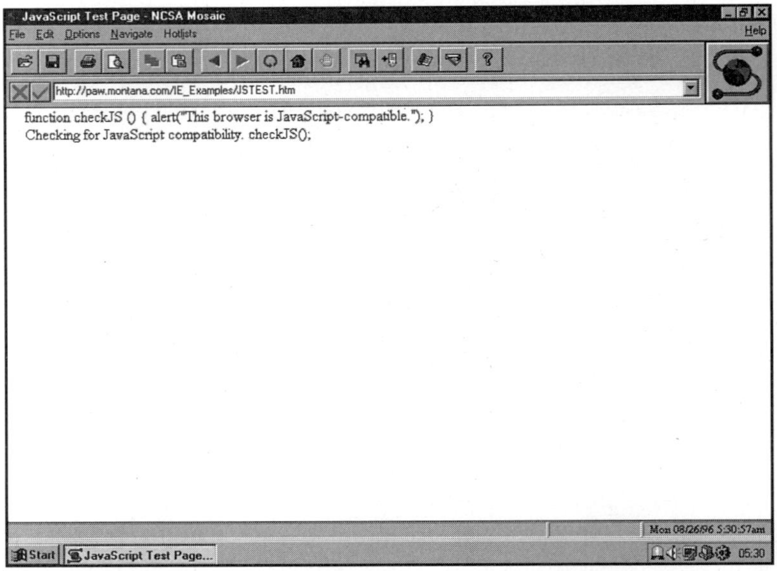

FIGURE 34.2.
The NCSA Mosaic browser is not yet JavaScript-compatible. The `<SCRIPT>` *tags are ignored and the commands are processed as any other text.*

Listing 34.1. The contents of the HTML document used in Figures 34.1 and 34.2.

```
<HTML>
<HEAD>
<TITLE>JavaScript Test Page</TITLE>
<SCRIPT>
function checkJS () {
    alert("This browser is JavaScript-compatible.");
```

```
}
</SCRIPT>
</HEAD>
<BODY>
Checking for JavaScript compatibility.
<SCRIPT>
checkJS();
</SCRIPT>
</BODY>
</HTML>
```

A noncompatible browser ignores the <SCRIPT> tags and displays the JavaScript commands as any other text. For a document including any length of JavaScript, the result produces a screen full of commands and characters otherwise unintelligible to the user.

Hiding Scripts from Incompatible Browsers

Preventing an older or noncompatible browser from incorrectly processing your JavaScript code means correctly using HTML comment tags.

To hide your JavaScript, you must nest a set of HTML comment tags inside the <SCRIPT> tags. A JavaScript comment tag (two forward-slashes) must appear just before the closing comment tag to prevent it from being processed as another line of JavaScript and causing a syntax error (see Figure 34.3).

```
<SCRIPT LANGUAGE="JavaScript">
<!--  Note: An opening HTML comment tag.
...statements...
// --> Note: A JavaScript comment tag (two forward-slashes), followed by a closing
HTML comment tag.
➥</SCRIPT>
```

With proper placement and usage, JavaScript can add vital functionality to your HTML pages without interfering with the capability of noncompatible browsers to interpret the document. Remember, however, that if your page depends on JavaScript for including crucial information or operability, it shows common courtesy to warn users and, if possible, supply a generic version of the document.

Placing Scripts on the Page

The <SCRIPT> tag can appear in either the HEAD or BODY section, although its placement will determine when and how the script gets used.

If placed in the HEAD portion of the document, the script gets interpreted before the page is completely downloaded (see Figure 34.4). This order works especially well for documents that depend on functions. The script is loaded and ready before the user has a chance to interact with any event that actually invokes the function (see Figure 34.5).

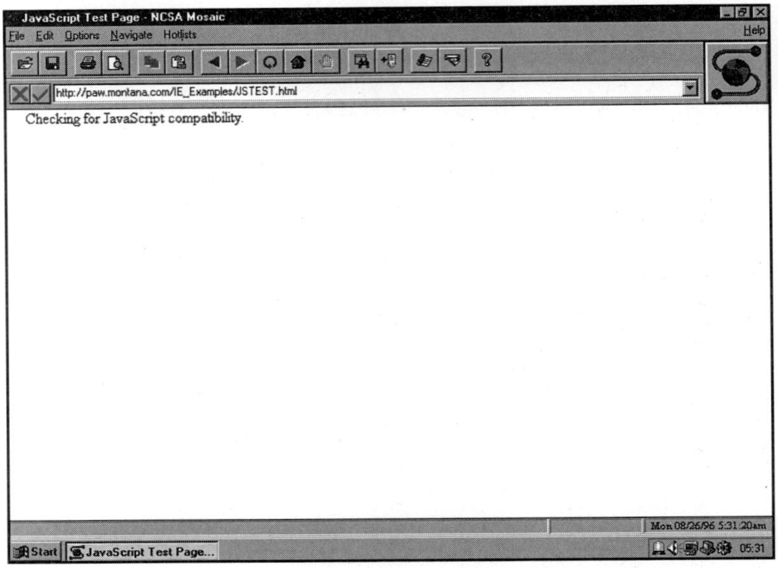

FIGURE 34.3.
NCSA Mosaic with the additional HTML comment tags displays the non-JavaScript content and passes over the part it can't interpret.

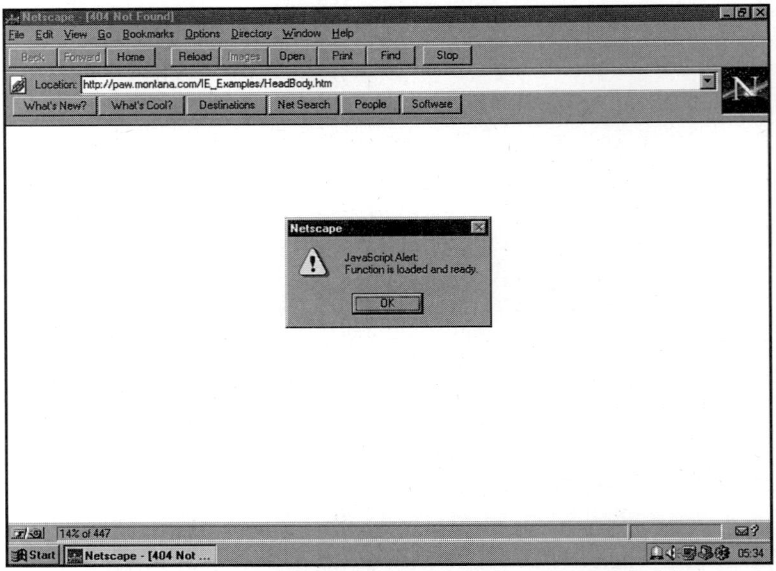

FIGURE 34.4.
The initial screen displayed by Listing 34.2. Note that the first line of JavaScript text and the alert box have appeared, but the text contained in the BODY *portion of the document has not.*

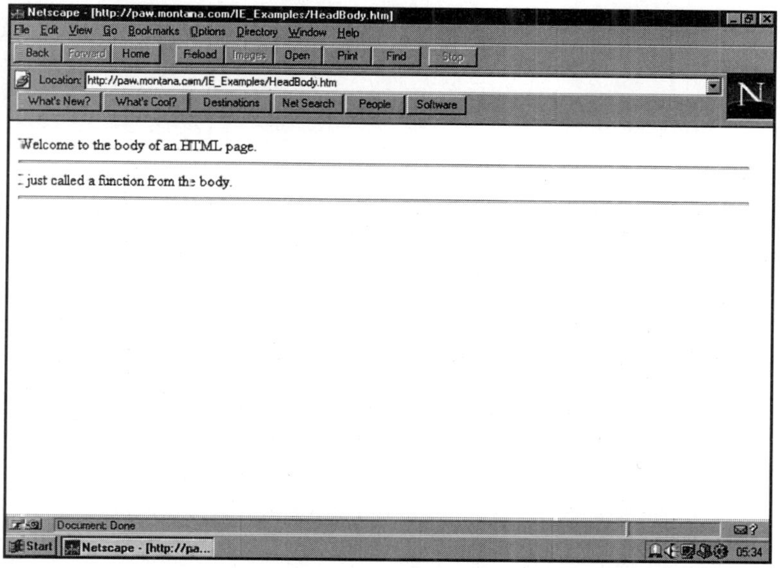

FIGURE 34.5.
The rest of the display generated by Listing 34.2 shows the HTML text in the body of the page and executes the function that was defined in the head.

Listing 34.2. Placing functions in the HEAD portion of the document ensures that they are interpreted before the rest of the document.

```
<HTML>
<HEAD>
<SCRIPT LANGUAGE="javascript">
function printMessage(msgStr) {
    document.writeln("<HR>");
    document.writeln(msgStr);
    document.writeln("<HR>");
}
alert("Function is loaded and ready.");
</SCRIPT>
</HEAD>
<BODY>
Welcome to the body of an HTML page.
<SCRIPT LANGUAGE="javascript">
printMessage("I just called a function from the body.")
</SCRIPT>
</BODY>
</HTML>
```

Using JavaScript in Your Web Page

Many uses exist for JavaScript, and more continue to appear all the time as developers experiment with the possibilities opened with interactive HTML. This section shows a few areas and examples to get you started.

NOTE

A JavaScript ticker, which scrolls a message across the status bar, is absent from this list of applications. With Internet Explorer's <MARQUEE> tag and the availability of multifeatured Java ticker applets, the JavaScript ticker no longer provides an efficient use of browser capability.

Computing Values Without CGI

One application for JavaScript that has gained a degree of popularity is a *form*, which returns values without being processed through a CGI script. One of the easiest ways to implement a form is by assigning a JavaScript function to a submit button rather than a URL. The function then examines the form's values, performs its various operations, and returns a value or values to the page (see Figure 34.6).

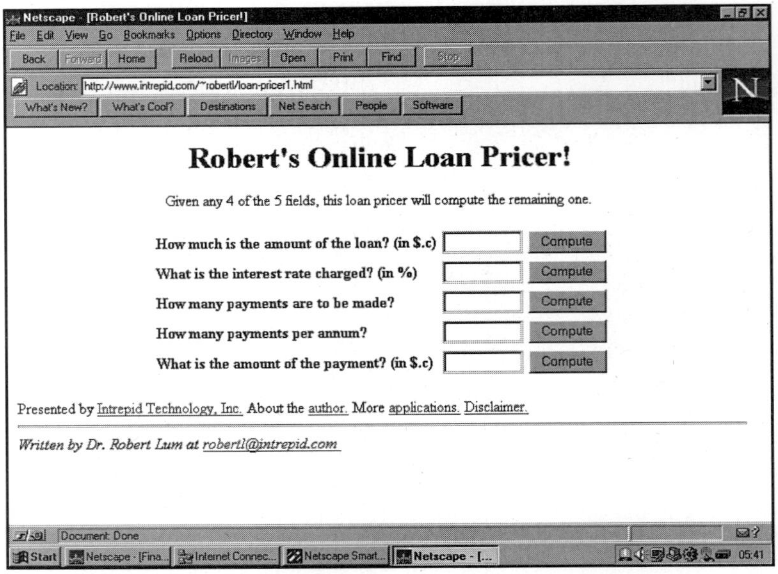

FIGURE 34.6.
This loan calculator accepts a variety of information about the term, payment schedule, and other items, and calculates the value next to the Compute button. The button calls a function that computes the affected value.

The syntax of the new button is `<INPUT TYPE=BUTTON VALUE=Name onClick=JavaScriptFunction()>`. When the button is clicked by the user, the function named after the `onClick` parameter (*JavaScriptFunction()*) is invoked. Other events are also supported by JavaScript, including changing a value or clicking on a field, using the same form of syntax. This enables you to recompute forms as the user enters or changes information (see Figure 34.7).

As the user makes entries throughout the form, the fields that rely on those values are automatically updated and used, in turn, for the next computed value until the tax bill or refund is generated at the bottom.

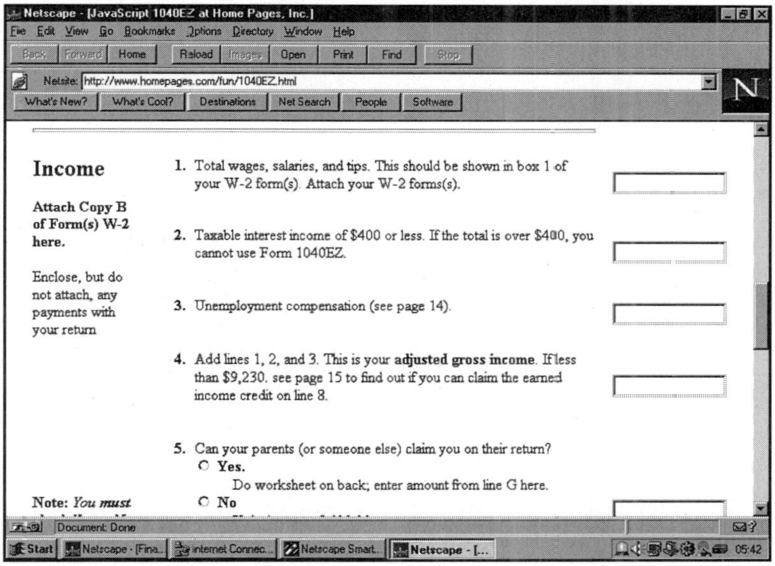

FIGURE 34.7.
One application that received many different treatments in JavaScript is the IRS Form 1040EZ. After a user enters earnings and withholding information, pressing the button computes the tax bill.

Random Numbers

JavaScript includes a method of the `Math` object that generates random numbers, but in its current form it works only on UNIX machines. Another way of generating somewhat-random numbers exists using a user-defined function instead of the built-in method. It is referred to as a *calculated random number*, and can reveal its biases and true nonrandom nature if used repeatedly over a short period of time.

To ensure compatibility for a script across platforms, any script depending on random numbers shouldn't depend exclusively on the `random` method, but instead should rely on a generated number created by a function similar to the following example:

```
function UnixMachine() {
    if (navigator.appVersion.lastIndexOf('Unix') != -1)
        return true
    else
        return false
}

function randomNumber() {
    if UnixMachine()
        num = Math.random()
    else
        num = Math.abs(Math.sin(Date.getTime()));
    return num;
}
```

If the client machine has a UNIX base, `randomNumber` will use the built-in function. Otherwise, it generates a number between 0 and 1 by generating a sine based on the time value.

> **JAVASCRIPT TIME**
>
> Time in JavaScript is measured as the number of milliseconds elapsed since midnight on January 1, 1970, and is accessed by using the `Date` object or an instance of it. The `Date` object is dynamic, ever changing with the time. An instance of the object returns a static value, depending on the current value of `Date` or the date parameter passed to it.
>
> The time is based on the client machine, not the server. One idiosyncrasy occurs in JavaScript's representation of time elements. The `getMonth` and `setMonth` methods both return a value from 0 (January) to 11 (December). When using these two methods, make sure to convert to the 1-12 system the rest of the world recognizes.
>
> ```
> var birthday1 = new Date(96,1,11);
> document.writeln(birthday1.getMonth()); //Returns a 1 (February)
> var birthday2 = new Date("January 11, 1996 06:00:00");
> document.writeln(birthday2.getMonth()); //Returns a 0 (January)
> ```

If you need a constant stream of random numbers, a sine-wave pattern will become evident. In this case, it becomes necessary to show some variation in the process by adding more variation into the calculation. You can do this by substituting a different computation (`cos`, `log`) at various intervals of time.

Status Bar Messages

With event handlers and the `window.status` property, JavaScript enables your browser to display custom messages in the status bar that respond to user actions. One of the most popular implementations is a descriptive line for hyperlinks (see Figure 34.8).

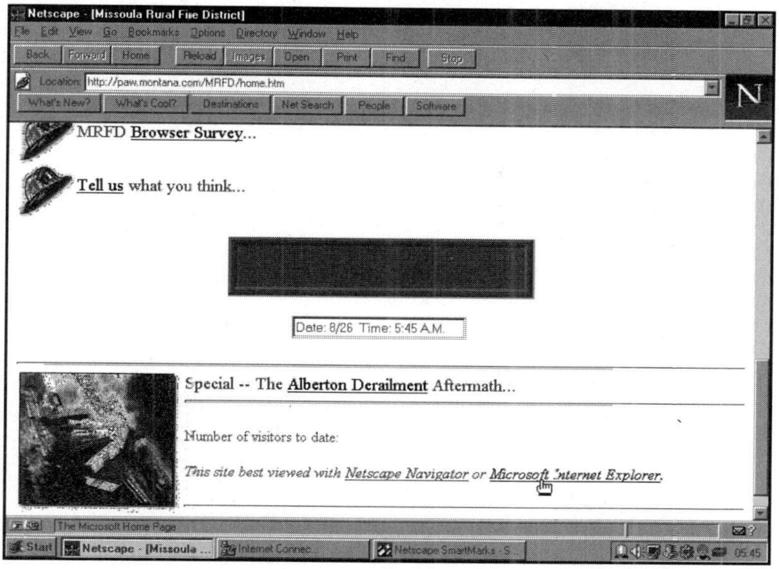

FIGURE 34.8.
A simple addition to the `<A HREF>` tag enables page authors to include useful status-bar messages to respond to actions such as placing the mouse over a hyperlink.

```
Best viewed with
<A HREF="http://www.microsoft.com" onMouseOver="window.status='The Microsoft Home
➥Page';return true">
Microsoft Internet Explorer</A>.
```

One problem with the `status` property is that it becomes the default message until either a browser-generated message overrides it or `status` is set to a different value. In the preceding example, `The Microsoft Home Page` remains in the status bar until another message preempts it.

To work around this problem requires the use of a timer. After passing the mouse over the hyperlink, the message displays, but only for a short time, after which the status bar is reset to a blank display. This setup requires two functions—one to write the message and set the timer, and one to erase the message:

```
timerLength = 1.5;
function writeStatus(str) {
    timeoutVal = timerLength * 1000;
    setTimeout("clearStatus()",timeoutVal);
    window.status = str;

}
function clearStatus() {
    window.status = "";
}
```

This method of generating status bar messages requires more lines of code, but it results in a cleaner operation for custom hyperlink messages. The message appears for the number of seconds assigned to `timerLength`, after which the `clearStatus` function is called to write a null string to the display. To invoke the new method, use the following example:

```
<a href="http://www.microsoft.com/" onMouseOver="writeStatus('Microsoft Home
➥Page'); return true;">
Microsoft</A>
```

Another possibility for this method of generating status-bar displays includes making a copy of the old value of `window.status` and restoring it when the timer expires.

Displaying the Current Date and Time

There are a growing number of ways to display the time on your Web page. Most of them involve server-side includes or objects dependent on helper applications. JavaScript offers live access to the system date, and used in conjunction with a timer feature, allows you to display the current time through a form field.

The first step is to build a simple form to hold the time field:

```
<FORM NAME="Clock">
<INPUT TYPE="Text" NAME="ClockFace">
</FORM>
```

Then, you'll need to fill the field with the date. JavaScript includes its own built-in date object, which can access the system date and store it in a variable. A simple way to do this is with a function:

```
<SCRIPT LANGUAGE="JavaScript">
function getTodayDate()
{
        var today = new Date();
        document.forms[0].todaydate.value = today;
}
</SCRIPT>
```

With these two in place, all that's needed is a way to call the function after the form is loaded:

```
<FORM NAME="Clock">
...
</FORM>
<SCRIPT>
getTodayDate();
</SCRIPT>
```

The date is now displayed on the user's screen (see Figure 34.9) in a static display.

TIP

If the user clicks on the field, he or she can obliterate the date by typing. This is one of the big drawbacks to a static JavaScript date and time display. A live clock, on the other hand, is constantly updated and prevents any permanent change to the field.

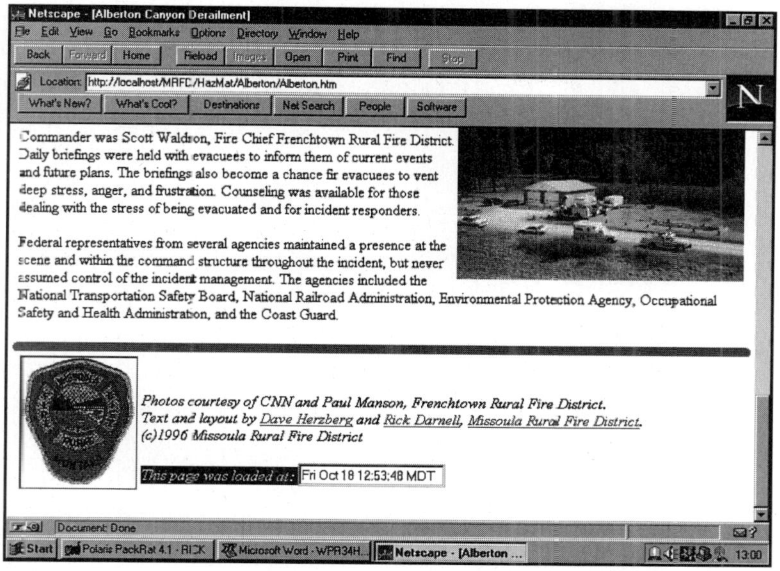

FIGURE 34.9.
When the HTML page is loaded, the value for the clock is calculated and displayed using the JavaScript function. It is a static display—once it's posted, it won't change value with the passing of time.

Displaying a live clock is a better use of JavaScript's capability, and it's not much harder to do. Instead of the `getTodayDate` function, substitute Listing 34.3.

Listing 34.3. A live clock function using JavaScript.

```
<SCRIPT LANGUAGE="JavaScript">
var timerID = null
var timerRunning = false
function stopClock(){
    if(timerRunning)
        clearTimeout(timerID)
    timerRunning = false
}
function startClock(){
    stopClock()
    displayTime()
}
function displayTime(){
    var Today = new Date();
    var mm = Today.getMonth()+1;
    var dd = Today.getDate();
    var hrs = Today.getHours();
    var min = Today.getMinutes();
    var theTime = "Date: " + mm + "/" + dd;
    theTime  += "  Time: " + ((hours > 12) ? hours - 12 : hours);
    theTime  += ((minutes < 10) ? ":0" : ":") + minutes;
    theTimeValue  += (hours >= 12) ? " P.M." : " A.M.";
    document.Clock.clockFace.value = timeValue;
    timerID = setTimeout("displayTime()",60000);
    timerRunning = true;
}
</SCRIPT>
```

To initialize the clock, substitute <BODY onLoad="startclock()"> for your usual <BODY> tag. This initializes the clock and starts it running when the page is loaded by the browser (see Figure 34.10). The time-out setting near the end of the script is used to update the clock every minute. Setting the value to 1000 and adding a variable for the seconds makes the clock seem even more "current."

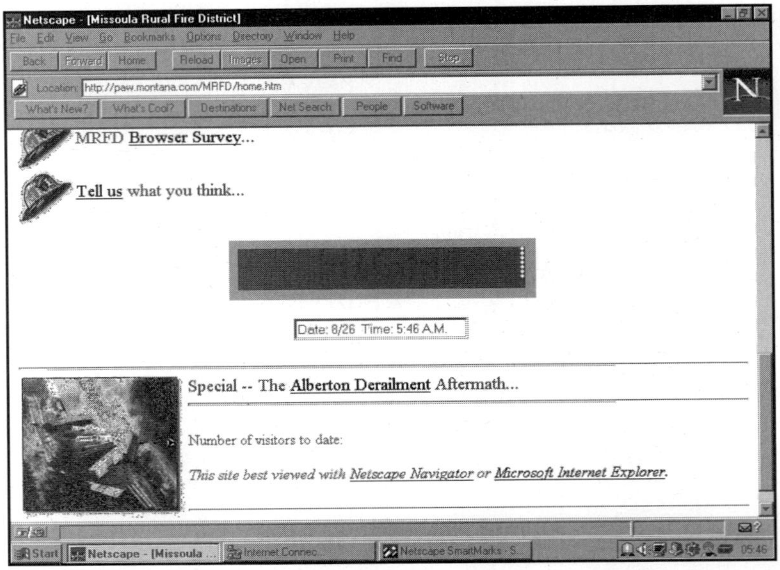

FIGURE 34.10.
The oncreen clock is now in a friendlier format and features constantly updated date and time.

Controlling Browser Behavior

One of the important and powerful capabilities of JavaScript is controlling various aspects of browser behavior and appearance. This feature comes in handy for implementing demonstrations and tours by adding the capability to spawn new browser windows with controllable levels of functionality.

The command syntax to create a new browser window is `windowVar = window.open("URL", "windowName" [, "windowFeatures"])` where:

- `windowVar` represents the name of a variable that holds the information about the new window.
- `URL` refers to an address for the contents of the new window, and can be blank.
- `windowName` represents how the window will be referred to in frame and window references.

- `windowFeatures` provides a list of the individual features of the browser that should be included or excluded. If blank, all features are enabled. If only some features appear, any unmentioned features are disabled.

To include a feature, use the syntax *windowFeature*=yes or *windowFeature*=1. Conversely, to disable a feature use *windowFeature*=no or *windowFeature*=0.

The features include:

- `toolbar` for the row of buttons at the top of the screen
- `status` for the message bar at the bottom of the browser
- `scrollbars` for the buttons and slides to control the part of the document viewed when it exceeds the window boundaries
- `resizable` for user control over the size of the browser
- `width` and `height` in pixels for the initial size of the window

For example, use this code to open a plain window with hotlink-only navigation:

```
//Note: Setting one feature automatically sets all non-mentioned features to false.
window.open("URL", "windowName", "toolbar=no")
```

JavaScript Resources on the Internet

JavaScript gets used and talked about on the Internet frequently, making the Internet one of the first stops for information. You can find up-to-the-minute information on current implementations, bugs, workarounds, and new and creative uses.

Check out the JavaScript-enabled applications found through these resources for ideas and code snippets to include on your pages. If you see something you want to use, be sure to write the author of the page and ask permission first. It's not only good manners, it's the law; JavaScript and HTML documents are covered under copyright. However, in the usually friendly realm of the World Wide Web, most folks are more than happy to share the fruits of their labors.

Netscape

One of the first stops you make should be the home of the people who developed and implemented JavaScript. The Netscape site provides a place to look for new developments and documentation about JavaScript features. The complete JavaScript online documentation (see Figure 34.11) also appears here.

You can access Netscape at `http://home.netscape.com/`. The JavaScript manual is located at `http://home.netscape.com/eng/mozilla/3.0/handbook/javascript/index.html`.

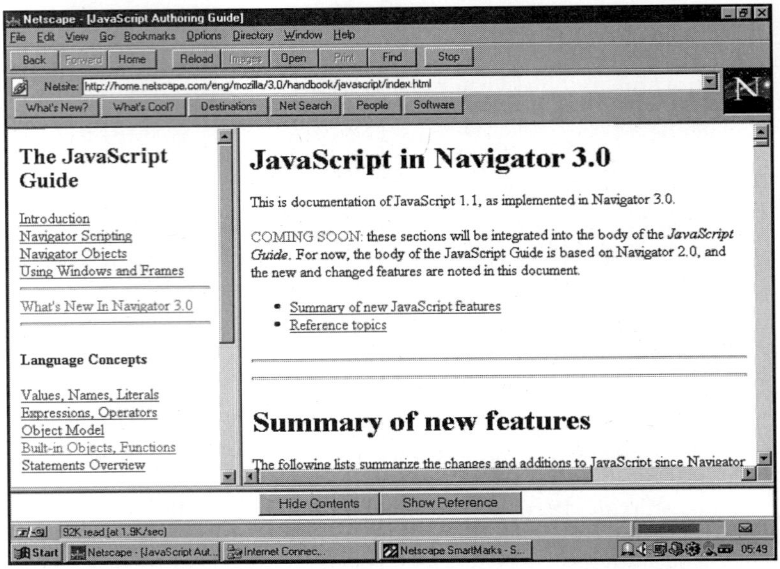

FIGURE 34.11.
The Netscape site has an online manual on JavaScript, including objects, methods, and event handlers. It is also available for download in ZIP format.

Gamelan

This site provides one of the best places for examples of what other people are doing with JavaScript on the Web. Although Gamelan is geared more toward Java, it also includes one of the largest listings of JavaScript sites found anywhere on the Web. By perusing the examples here (see Figure 34.12), you can gain insight from others who have gone before you.

You can access Gamelan at `http://www.gamelan.com/pages/Gamelan.javascript.html`.

JavaScript Index

The JavaScript Index (see Figure 34.13) has a collection of real-life JavaScript examples and experiments, including a growing list of Web pages that illustrate some of JavaScript's features and capabilities. One of the pages included on the Index is a JavaScript Library, an expanding collection of source code from around the Web community.

You can access the JavaScript Index at `http://www.c2.org/~andreww/javascript/`.

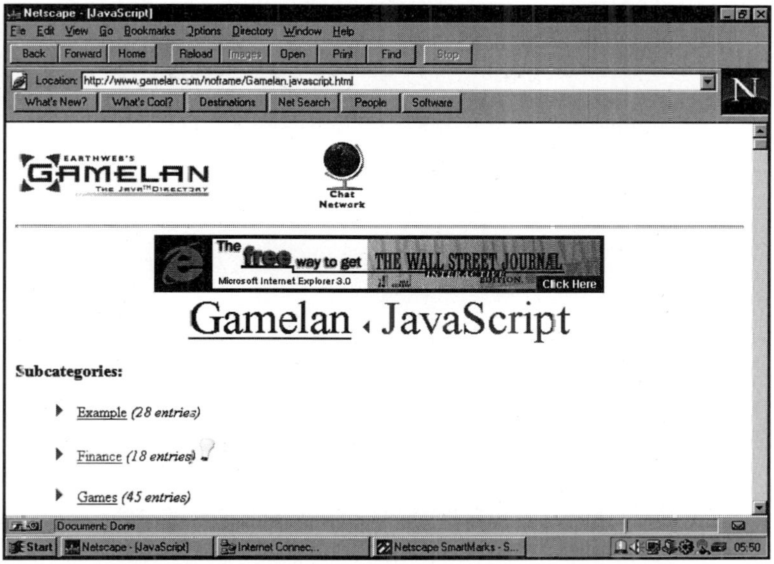

FIGURE 34.12.
The Gamelan site offers one of the premier sites for JavaScript resources on the World Wide Web.

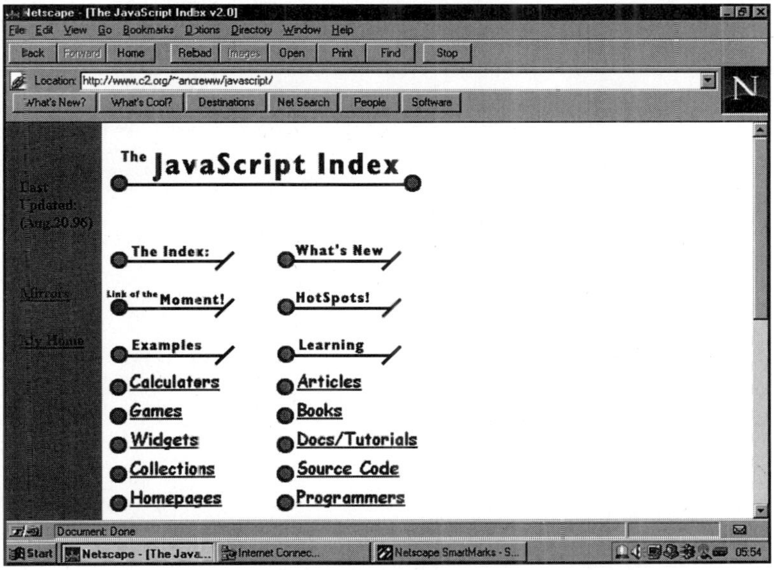

FIGURE 34.13.
The JavaScript Index has a solid source of examples and successful experiments from developers who are making JavaScript one of the fastest growing languages on the Internet.

The Unofficial JavaScript Resource Center

A well-designed site with a great deal of potential, the Unofficial JavaScript Resource (see Figure 34.14) remains shy on content in comparison with similar sites. It includes links to a variety of sites and several tutorials.

You can reach the site at `http://www.ce.net/users/ryan/java/`.

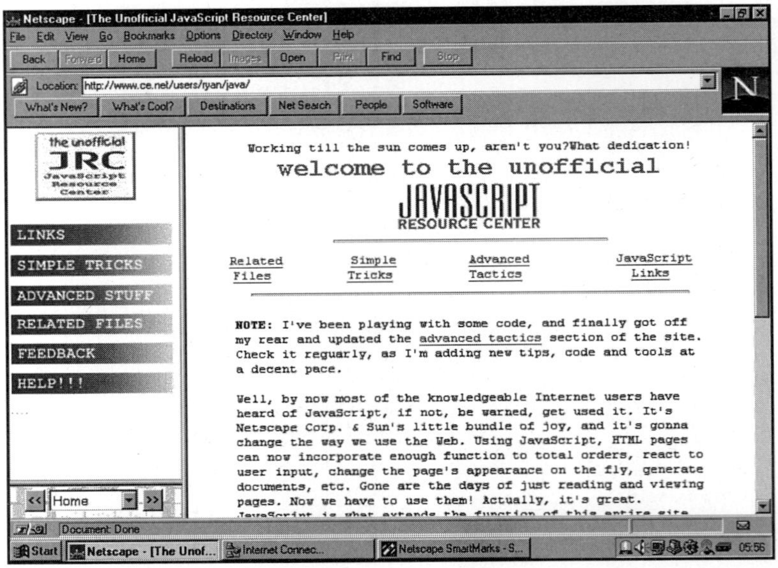

FIGURE 34.14.
The Unofficial JavaScript Resource Center, a growing resource, offers examples and tutorials for getting the most out of scripting on your Web pages.

Summary

JavaScript adds new functionality and interactivity to HTML pages that in the past you could only attain through learning CGI scripting languages such as Perl. By switching the bulk of interactive behavior to the client side, it has also improved the perceived speed of World Wide Web sites as seen by the user.

Although it does have its nuances and idiosyncrasies, taking the time to learn JavaScript will pay off in supporting Web pages with dramatically improved features and functions that users will want to revisit again and again. More information on customizing and creating your own JavaScript-enabled pages is included in the next chapter, "Writing JavaScript Applications."

CHAPTER 35

Writing JavaScript Applications

by Rick Darnell

IN THIS CHAPTER

JavaScript is a scripting language included in HTML pages to increase their interactivity. This runs the gamut from alert boxes and status-bar messages to complex menu systems and form validation.

It's based on Java, so if you're familiar with the way Java works, you'll be up and running with JavaScript in short order. However, because JavaScript is much smaller than Java and is geared specifically towards working with HTML pages, it is easy enough for page authors with no programming experience to use, too.

Creating Scripts

Creating scripts is really quite simple, although you must use proper syntax to ensure success. A knowledge of object-oriented programming will prove useful to anyone creating functions with JavaScript, but it is not a necessity.

New Language, New Terminology

Objects, methods, properties, classes—an object-oriented world has taken off, and a whole new batch of terminology has cropped up to go with it. This section provides a quick primer on the basic terms that get used in conjunction with an object-oriented language such as JavaScript.

> **TIP**
>
> JavaScript is case-sensitive. For example, if your variable is called Bob, you can also have a BOB, bob, and BoB, and each one will be unique.

Object

Objects are at the heart of any object-oriented programming language, and JavaScript is no different. An object is a software model, typically used to represent a real-world object along with a set of behaviors or circumstances. In JavaScript, built-in objects can also represent the structure, action, and state of an HTML page. In object-oriented terminology, the actions are called *methods* and the states are called *properties*. Both of these terms get covered later in this section.

To build an object, you need to know something about it. Consider a squirrel as an example. A squirrel has several physical properties, including sex, age, size, and color. It also has properties relating to its activity, such as running, jumping, eating peanuts, or tormenting dogs. Its methods relate to changes in behavior or state, such as run away, stop and look, or twitch tail and chatter.

This example may seem all well and good, but how do you represent this idea as an object in JavaScript? The basic object creation is a two-step process, beginning with defining a function that outlines the object, and then creating an instance of the object. Using some of the properties listed in the preceding example, you can make a JavaScript squirrel as demonstrated in Listing 35.1.

Listing 35.1. A JavaScript object definition for a squirrel.

```
function squirrel(color) {
    this.color = color;
    this.running = false;
    this.tormentingDog = false;
}

var groundSquirrel = new squirrel("brown")
```

The first part of the script with the `function` tag outlines the initial state for any given squirrel. It accepts one parameter, called `color`, which becomes a property, and adds two more properties, called `running` and `tormentingDog` (both set to `false` by default).

By itself, the function does nothing—it has to be invoked and assigned to a variable. This is what happens in the next step, where a variable called `groundSquirrel` is created, and given the color brown. The following code shows how the object and its properties get represented:

```
groundSquirrel.color // "brown"
groundSquirrel.running // false
groundSquirrel.tormentingDog // false
```

Now, to implement the object as part of an HTML page (see Figure 35.1), include the object definition between the `<HEAD>` tags. To see the object in motion, use Listing 35.2.

Listing 35.2. Use the JavaScript definition of a squirrel in an HTML document similar to this one.

```
<HTML>
<HEAD>
<TITLE>The Squirrel Page</TITLE>
<SCRIPT language="javascript">
<!--
function squirrel(color) {
    this.color = color;
    this.running = false;
    this.tormentingDog = false;
}

// -->
</SCRIPT>
</HEAD>
<BODY>
Making a squirrel...
<BR>
<SCRIPT LANGUAGE="javascript">
```

35
WRITING JAVASCRIPT APPLICATIONS

continues

Listing 35.2. continued

```
var brownSquirrel = new squirrel("brown");
document.writeln("brownSquirrel.color = "+brownSquirrel.color);
document.writeln("<BR>brownSquirrel.running = "+brownSquirrel.running);
document.writeln("<BR>brownSquirrel.tormentingDog = "+brownSquirrel.tormentingDog);
</SCRIPT>
</BODY>
</HTML>
```

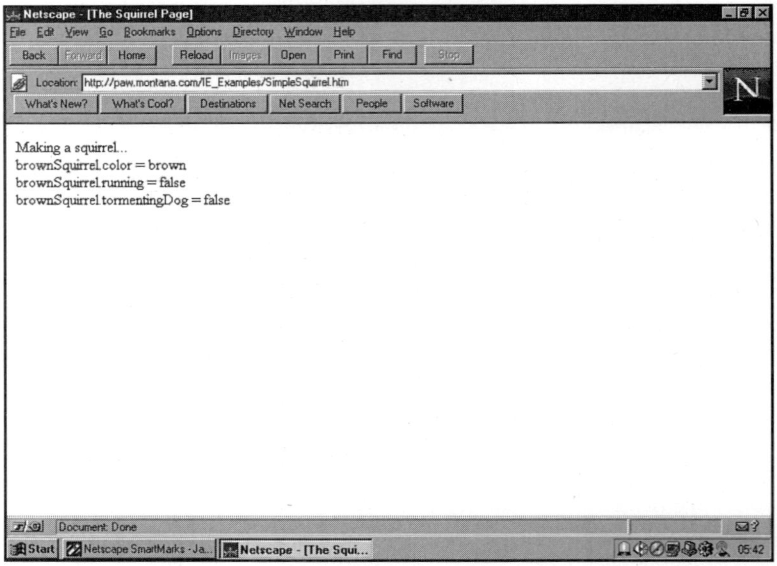

FIGURE 35.1.
The squirrel page creates a simple object and displays its properties.

Class

A class represents the definition for a type of object. Although classes are in Java and not in JavaScript, it is helpful to understand classes because many discussions about either language may refer to them. Simply stated, a class relates to an object as a blueprint relates to a bicycle. A blueprint contains all the information about the bicycle, but you can't ride it. To ride a bicycle, you need to create an instance of it. In object-oriented terminology, this process is called *instantiation.*

Classes can also have *inheritance*, which means they take on the behavior of other classes. A 10-speed bicycle and a tandem bicycle have bicycle characteristics but different specific features and functions. They are considered subclasses of the bicycle class.

Although a JavaScript function has a definition similar to a class, it can operate without instantiation.

Property

Properties are the individual states of an object, typically represented as variables. In the squirrel example, `color`, `running` and `tormentingDog` all represent properties of squirrel. An object's properties can include any of the valid JavaScript variable types.

> **WHICH TYPE IS WHICH?**
>
> A variable's type is the kind of value it holds. Several basic variable types are offered by JavaScript, including string, Boolean, integer, and floating-point decimal.
>
> JavaScript utilizes *loose casting*, which means a variable can assume different types at will. For example:
>
> ```
> squirrel.color = "pink"
> ...statements...
> squirrel.color = 30
> ```
>
> Both color values are valid. In Java, this would cause an error because it incorporates tight casting. After a variable gets assigned a type in Java, it can't be changed.
>
> Loose casting can make life easier when working with JavaScript. When building strings, for example, you can add a string to an integer, and the result will be a string. For example:
>
> ```
> value = 3;
> theResult = value + "is the number." //Results in "3 is the number."
> ```
>
> The downside is that sometimes you can easily forget what a variable thinks it is. It's a good idea to try and keep variables to their original type unless absolutely necessary.

Object properties are accessed using the object's name, followed by a period and the name of the property:

```
squirrel.color
```

Assigning a new value to the property will change it:

```
squirrel.color = "pink"
```

Function

A JavaScript function is a collection of statements that are invoked by using the name of the function and a list of arguments, if used. As a general rule, if you use a set of statements more than once as part of a page, it will probably be easier to include them as a function. Also, any activity used as part of an event handler should get defined as a function for ease of use.

Functions normally appear in the `HEAD` portion of the HTML document to ensure that they are loaded and interpreted before the user has a chance to interact with them.

The syntax to define a function is as follows:

```
function functionName ([arg1] [,arg2] [,...]) {
...statements...
}
```

An example of a function that automatically generates a link to an anchor called `top` at the top of the current page could look like this:

```
function makeTopLink (topLinkText) {
    var topURL = "#top";
    document.writeln(topLinkText.link(topURL));
}
```

This function accepts a text string as its one argument, and it generates a hypertext link similar to using the HTML `<A HREF>` tags:

```
makeTopLink("Return to the top.");
makeTopLink("top");
```

Method

If properties represent the current conditions of the object, methods serve as the knobs and levers that make it perform. Consider the squirrel example again. Defining a squirrel seemed easy enough, but what about making it do something? First, the methods need to be defined as JavaScript functions.

The first method for the squirrel makes him run and quit tormenting the dog:

```
function runAway() {
    this.running = true;
    this.tormentingDog = false;
    document.writeln("The squirrel is running away.");
}
```

The second method makes the squirrel stop moving and tease the dog:

```
function twitchTailChatter () {
    this.tormentingDog = true;
    this.running = false;
    document.writeln("The squirrel is being annoying.");
}
```

A third method levels the playing field between the squirrel and the dog:

```
function dogGetsLucky () {
    this.tormentingDog = false;
    this.running = true;
    document.writeln("The squirrel's tail is a couple of inches shorter.");
}
```

One more method would help you see what happens to the squirrel as his state changes:

```
function showState() {
    document.writeln("<HR><BR>The state of the squirrel is:<UL>")
    document.writeln("<LI>Color: "+this.color+"</LI>");
    document.writeln("<LI>Running: "+this.running+"</LI>");
```

```
    document.writeln("<LI>Tormenting dog: "+this.tormentingDog+"</LI>");
    document.writeln("</UL><HR>");
}
```

TIP

You can include HTML tags in text written to the browser screen using JavaScript's `write` and `writeln` methods. These methods get interpreted like any other HTML text, so formatting can occur for generated content.

Now that you have three methods defined, you need to make them a part of the object. This step amounts to including the method names as part of the object definition:

```
function squirrel(color) {
    this.color = color;
    this.running = false;
    this.tormentingDog = false;
    this.runAway = runAway;
    this.twitchTailChatter = twitchTailChatter;
    this.showState = showState;
}
```

The final step is including the whole package as part of an HTML document, such as Listing 35.3, and seeing whether it works (see Figure 35.2).

Listing 35.3. Using the JavaScript definition of a squirrel and its behavior requires an HTML document similar to this one.

```
<HTML>
<HEAD>
<TITLE>The Squirrel Page</TITLE>
<SCRIPT language="javascript">
<!--
function runAway() {
    this.running = true;
    this.tormentingDog = false;
    document.writeln("The squirrel is running away.");
}

function twitchTailChatter () {
    this.tormentingDog = true;
    this.running = false;
    document.writeln("The squirrel is being annoying.");
}

function showState() {
    document.writeln("The state of "+this.name+" is:<UL>")
    document.writeln("<LI>"+this.name+".color: "+this.color+"</LI>");
    document.writeln("<LI>"+this.name+".running: "+this.running+"</LI>");
    document.writeln("<LI>"+this.name+".tormenting dog: "+this.tormentingDog+"</
```

continues

Listing 35.3. continued

```
LI>");
    document.writeln("</UL><HR>");
}

function squirrel(color,squirrelName) {
    this.name = squirrelName;
    this.color = color;
    this.running = false;
    this.tormentingDog = false;
    this.runAway = runAway;
    this.twitchTailChatter = twitchTailChatter;
    this.showState = showState;
    document.writeln("A squirrel is born...");
}

// -->
</SCRIPT>
</HEAD>
<BODY>
<SCRIPT LANGUAGE="javascript">
var brownSquirrel = new squirrel("brown","brownSquirrel");
brownSquirrel.showState();
brownSquirrel.twitchTailChatter();
brownSquirrel.showState();
brownSquirrel.runAway();
brownSquirrel.showState();
</SCRIPT>
</BODY>
</HTML>
```

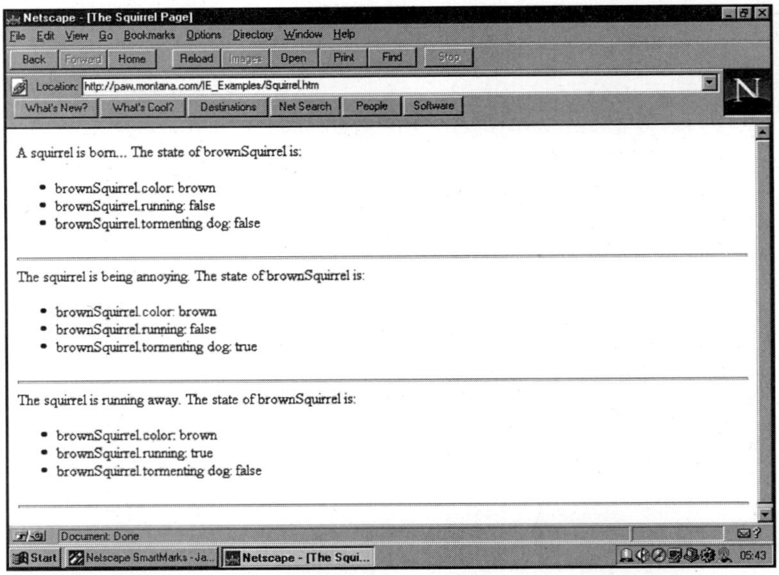

FIGURE 35.2.
The browser screen displays the activity of the JavaScript object as each method is executed.

Event Handlers

One of the features that makes JavaScript so powerful is its ability to respond to events on the Web page. This includes form elements, links and buttons. Unlike the other JavaScript items, event handlers are not included within `<SCRIPT>` tags—they are added as an additional parameter to the item they're monitoring:

```
<INPUT TYPE="text" NAME="state" WIDTH="20" VALUE="MT"
➥onChange="checkState(this.value)">
```

This tag creates a text field, loads it with a default value of `MONTANA`, and adds an event handler to call the function `checkState` when the value of the field changes (see Figure 35.3).

```
function checkState(stateName) {
    if (stateName.toUpperCase() == "MT") {
        window.alert("Glad you're in Montana"); }
    else {
        window.alert("Ride with me Mariah, in Montana."); }
}
```

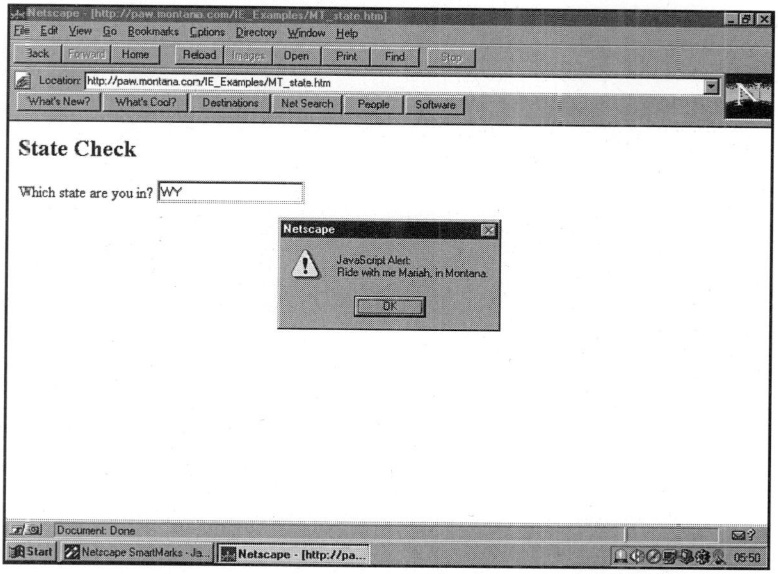

FIGURE 35.3.
An alert box with the appropriate message is generated when JavaScript detects a change in the form field.

This function looks at the value of the field. If it matches the default, it greets the user. Otherwise, it extends an invitation. This function is invoked only if the field changes from its current value. So, if the user changes the field to `Alaska`, then to `Nebraska`, then to `Wyoming`, the function is called three times.

Another useful event handler is the `onClick` event, which can be used for buttons, radio buttons, and lists. One popular use is to call a validation routine before submitting the form contents back to the server. This simplifies your CGI script on the server side by ensuring it receives only good data, and speeds the operation on the user's side.

```
<INPUT TYPE="button" NAME="submit" VALUE="Submit" onClick="validate(this)">
```

Note the difference in the two tags. One includes `this.value` and the other just `this`. When used within the confines of a form, `this` refers to the entire form, while `this.value` refers to the specific form element it's used in. More on validating forms is covered later in this chapter.

JAVASCRIPT AND DOCUMENT ARRAYS

JavaScript represents the various items on an HTML page using arrays. For example, a form is an array of the various elements within it. Consider the following form definition:

```
<FORM NAME="GUEST_INFO">
<INPUT TYPE="TEXT" NAME="Guest_Name">
<INPUT TYPE="TEXT" NAME="Guest_Email">
<SELECT NAME="Background" MULTIPLE>
    <OPTION VALUE="hardcore">Seasoned Web Surfer
    <OPTION VALUE="liar">Business Only
    <OPTION VALUE="newbie">Not For Sure How I Got Here
</SELECT>
```

There are several arrays created when a form is included in a document. The first is an array of forms in the document (`document.forms[`*`index`*`]`). The second is an array of the elements within the form (`document.forms[`*`index`*`].elements[`*`index`*`]`). The last is for list elements (`document.forms[`*`index`*`].elements[`*`index`*`].options[`*`index`*`]`).

The preceding form example results in an array called `document.Guest_Info`, which is also referenced by its position in the document. If it's the first form on the document, it is also called `document.forms[0]` or `document.forms["Guest_Info"]`.

Each of the form elements is an item within another array in the form. So, the second form element is called `document.Guest_Info.Guest_Email`, or another option, `document.Guest_Info.elements[1]`.

The last array represented by this form is for the select elements. The naming of the specific element follows the preceding example, `document.Guest_Info.Background`, followed by one more object, `options[`*`index`*`]`. So, the second item in the select list is the preamble plus `options[1]` or `options["liar"]`.

Although it seems like a terrible amount of typing, this ordering of your documents removes the ambiguity from identifying any item.

TIP

Keep in mind that entire books have been written about JavaScript—don't expect to learn all of the intricacies in one chapter in this book.

Validating Forms

Using CGI scripts to validate forms wastes precious user time and server time to conduct a process that, using JavaScript, is easier and faster on the client's computer. The time required for client-server communication gets reduced, along with the lengthy development cycle necessary for CGI scripts.

With its capability to interact with form elements, JavaScript seems ideally suited to validate information directly on the HTML page. This setup localizes the process and takes advantage of the underutilized client machine. Checking information on the client side also makes it much harder for users to send incompatible or damaging data to the server.

TIP

Generally it's easier to check for valid values than invalid values. If you make a practice of checking for only valid information and rejecting the rest, you should be able to avoid most problems.

Several methods exist to implement form validation, and most include adding a JavaScript function as the action of a submit button. The HTML definition of the submit button could look like this:

```
<INPUT TYPE="BUTTON" NAME="SUBMIT" VALUE="SUBMIT"
➥onClick="checkInformation(this.form)">
```

`checkInformation` is a function that provides verification for the form to ensure that the information meets CGI script expectations. If not, it should return to the document without submitting the form contents to the server. It can also return focus to the offending items. If everything passes inspection, then the function can also use the `submit` method.

```
function checkInformation(thisForm) {
    ...validation statements ...;
    if (validationPassed) {
        thisForm.submit(); }
    return;
}
```

TIP

The `submit()` method sends the contents of the referenced form contents back to the server by the `get` or `post` operation.

You can review or change the submission method through the `method` property of the form, `this.method`. If you want to make sure the contents are sent using `get`, then use a JavaScript command such as `thisForm.method = "get"`.

As mentioned earlier, each form element becomes part of a `form` object with JavaScript. By using the name of the form as the name of the object, you can access each of the elements. If a name is not used, you can also use the `forms` array. The first form on the page is `forms[0]`, the next is `forms[1]`, and so on.

For an example, look at the following form definition:

```
<FORM NAME="validation">
Enter your user name and identification in the boxes.<BR>
Your name: <INPUT TYPE="text" NAME="userName" VALUE=""><BR>
User ID: <INPUT TYPE="text" NAME="userID" WIDTH="9" VALUE=""><BR>
<INPUT TYPE="button" NAME="button" VALUE="Submit" onClick="checkID(this.form)">
</FORM>
```

Each element in this form is represented in JavaScript as

```
document.validation.userName
document.validation.userID
document.validation.button
```

The last element, a button, includes an event handler that calls the function `checkID` with the current form as the argument. Note that you don't need the name of the form in the call because the contents are passed as an argument in `this.form`. In the function (see Listing 35.6), the form is referred to as the name of the argument, `formID`.

Listing 35.6. A function that checks to make sure the lengths of two form elements are correct before submitting the form.

```
function checkID(formID) {
    var validUser = true;
    var validID = true;
    if (formID.userName.length != 10) {
        validUser = false;
        formID.userName.value = "Invalid Entry"; }
    if (formID.userID.length != 9) w
        validID = false;
        formID.userName.value = "Error"; }
    if (validUser && validID) {
        formID.submit(); }
    else {
        alert("Please try again."); }
}
```

To understand the function, work through it section by section. First, two Boolean variables are initialized. These flags indicate whether the validation has been passed when it comes time to check at the end of the function.

Next, the length of a form element named `userName` gets checked. If the value doesn't equal (represented in JavaScript by `!=`) 10, then the valid flag is set to `false`, and the form element receives a new value, which is reflected immediately on the page.

The same process gets repeated for the next form element, `userID`. At the end, if both flags are true (logical and is represented by `&&`), the form is submitted using the `submit` method. If either or both of the flags are `false`, then an alert screen appears.

CAUTION

JavaScript is not a secure way to validate private information, such as passwords and credit-card numbers. Any value you wanted to compare the user's entries to would need to be represented within the script, making it available to prying eyes simply by viewing the document source code.

A Little Math

JavaScript offers a whole host of mathematic operators and functions to help perform whatever computations you need within your scripts.

Operators

The first place to start is with the basic operators used by JavaScript. Like other features of Java and JavaScript, operators borrow their usage and syntax from the C and C+ programming languages.

Basic mathematical operators are called *binary operators*—they need two operands in order to function (see Table 35.1).

Table 35.1. JavaScript binary operators, in order of precedence.

Operator	*Function*
* / %	Multiplication, division, modulus
+ -	Addition, subtraction
<< >> >>>	Bitwise shift left, shift right, shift right/zero fill

There are a few on this list that might not be familiar to you. Modulus is a simple division process that returns only the remainder of the operation.

```
6 % 2 //Returns 0 (2 goes into 6 three times with no remainder)
6 % 4 //Returns 2 (4 goes into 6 once with two leftover)
```

The last set, bitwise operators, shift the bits representing a number left or right. The numbers on both sides are converted to 32-bit integers, and then the bits on the left are moved the number of positions indicated by the number on the right. Bits at the end are discarded.

NOTE

Remember bits and bytes from the early days of computers? They haven't gone away. JavaScript convert numbers in bitwise operations into 32-bit integers. For example, the number 156 is represented as 16 zeros plus 0000000010011100.

Each bit represents a power of two, beginning on the far right with 2^0 and ending with 2^31. To decipher the number, add up the value of each position with a 1. In the 156 example, moving from right to left you would add 0+0+4+8+16+0+0+128.

You can combine all of the binary operators with the assignment operator (=) to simplify other types of equations. For example, to increment a variable by 3 typically requires a statement such as

```
counter = counter + 3
```

This gets the job done, but it does require some extra typing. Combining the assignment and addition operator results in

```
counter += 3
```

The result is exactly the same. This processes the variable on the left and the value on the right using the operator, and it assigns the result to the variable.

The next set of operators you'll use most often are *unary*—they work on a single operand (see Table 35.2).

Table 35.2. JavaScript unary operators.

Operator	*Function*
`++ --`	Increment, decrement
`!`	Complement (Boolean)
`-`	Negation

The increment and decrement operators are used to increase or decrease the value of a number by one. The placement of the operator determines when the calculation takes place. If it is placed after the operand, the operation happens after any other calculation involving it is completed. If placed before, the value is updated, and then the rest of the calculation is finished.

```
count = 1
newValue = count++ //newValue = 1, count = 2
newValue = ++count //newValue = 3, count = 3
```

The complement is used to reverse the value of a Boolean. In the following example, if `ready` is `false`, then `!ready` is true. The text representation of the statement is, "If not ready then..." This is an easier representation than `if (ready == false)`.

```
if (!ready) {
    ... }
```

The last operator reverses the sign of a number from positive to negative and vice versa.

Relational operators are used to compare two values and return a true or false. There are several different options, listing in Table 35.3.

Table 35.3. JavaScript relational operators.

Operator	*Function*
`> <`	Less than, greater than
`<= >=`	Less than or equal, greater than or equal
`== !=`	Equals, doesn't equal
`?:`	Conditional

The first three sets are easy enough to understand. The last one is a special use of the relation, and it is often used to assign a value to a variable. The full syntax is

```
condition ? value if true : value if false
```

This is a shorthand for an `if-then-else` statement. The condition portion of the statement is any operation that results in a Boolean true or false.

TIP

As an alternative to true and false, JavaScript also accepts 1 and 0, respectively. As a general rule, however, using a Boolean expression results in greater clarity.

```
status =   (age>=21) ? "Legal Drinking Age" : "Not Old Enough"
```

This statement evaluates the value of `age`. If the value is at least 21, then `status` is assigned the value `Legal Drinking Age`. If `age` is less than 21, then `status` is assigned `Not Old Enough`.

Functions and Constants

JavaScript includes a built-in object called `Math`. This object contains a whole host of useful functions and constants to save you time and typing. Here are a few of the items you'll find in `Math`.

First are the functions. These provide a handy method for easily computing several different types of equations:

- `Math.abs(arg)`—Returns the absolute (unsigned) value of its argument.
- `Math.ceil(arg)`—Returns the smallest integer greater than or equal to the argument. For example, `Math.ceil(9.14)` returns `10`.
- `Math.floor(arg)`—The opposite of `ceil`, this method returns the largest integer less than or equal to its argument. For example, `Math.floor(2.78)` returns `2`.
- `Math.max(arg1,arg2)`—Returns the largest of the two arguments.
- `Math.min(arg1,arg2)`—Like `max`, this method returns the smaller of the two arguments.
- `Math.round(arg)`—Returns the next-highest or -lowest integer based on the decimal portion of a floating-point number. If the decimal portion is .5 or higher, the next highest value is used.
- `Math.pow(base,exp)`—Returns the base raised to an exponent. While many languages use the caret (^) operator to perform this function, JavaScript uses this method. The caret is reserved for a bitwise operation.
- `Math.sqrt(arg)`—Returns the square root of the argument. If the argument is a negative number, the return value is `0`.
- Trigonometric functions—A standard set of functions related to trigonometry are also available through the Math object, including `cos`, `sin`, `tan`, `acos`, `asin`, and `atan`. The first three accept an argument representing the angle in radians (0 to pi), and return a value from `1` to `-1`. The second set accepts an argument from `1` to `-1`, and returns the angle in radians.

In addition to the methods built into the `Math` object, a set of constant values is also supplied. Because these are not methods and do not accept arguments, they do not use parentheses.

These constant values represent values that are commonly used in math formulas. The most common of these is the value of pi—the ratio of the diameter of the circle to the circumference. The value is approximately 3.1415927 and referred to as `Math.PI`.

JavaScript Internet Resources

It never hurts to have a little help in this world, and working with new technologies and languages like JavaScript is no different. In addition to the resources listed at the end of Chapter 34, here are some other sites you should take a look at to help get you up to speed and productive with scripting on your Web pages.

Netscape

It was mentioned in the last chapter, but it never hurts to mention it again. Netscape developed JavaScript. If you want the latest information on what's new with the language, it always helps to look here. The complete JavaScript online documentation, located at `http://home.netscape.com/eng/mozilla/3.0/handbook/javascript/index.html` (see Figure 35.4), is no longer available for an easy download, but you can save the pages for offline use.

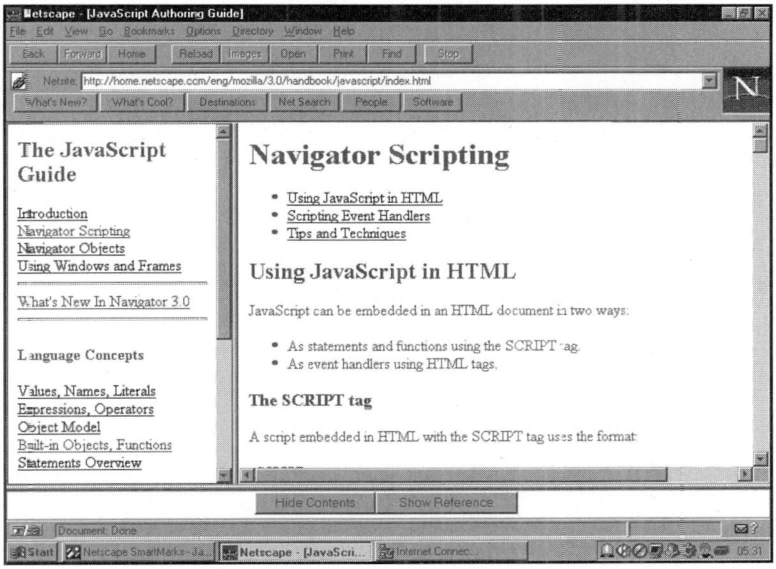

FIGURE 35.4.
The Netscape site has an online manual on JavaScript, including information on integrating Java and JavaScript.

Voodoo JavaScript Tutorial

The Voodoo JavaScript Tutorial (see Figure 35.5) contains a set of lessons covering the various aspects of including JavaScript on your Web pages. This project continues to evolve (with new lessons added periodically), so you may want to check back to see what's new.

You won't find much in the way of advanced material here, but what you find gives you more than enough to get beyond the beginner level.

You can access the site at `http://rummelplatz.uni-mannheim.de/~skoch/js/index.htm`.

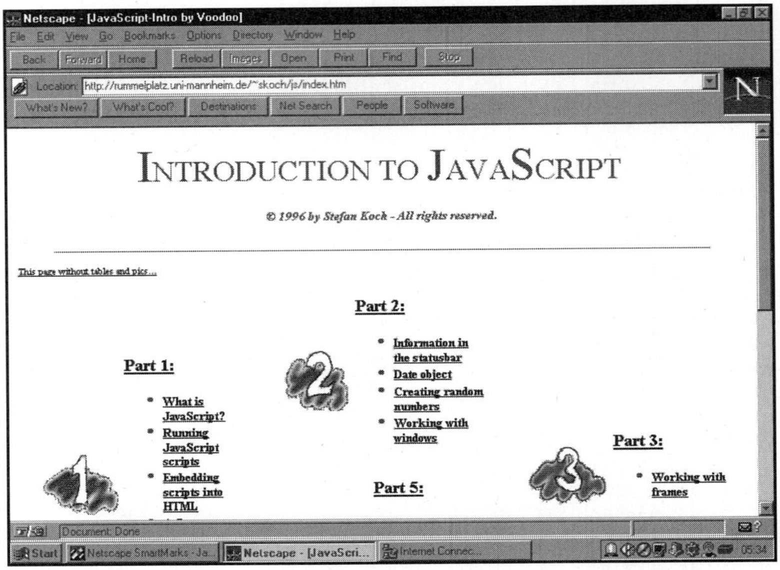

FIGURE 35.5.
The Voodoo JavaScript tutorial provides a good place to pick up the basics of working with JavaScript, in addition to other HTML features such as frames.

JavaScript Newsgroup

This group is frequented by many of the JavaScript gurus, and it provides an excellent source of information, tips, and workarounds. A high level of activity occurs and the threads move quickly, so make sure to check every day if possible.

You can reach the JavaScript Newsgroup at `news://comp.lang.javascript`.

netscape.navigator

It never hurts to have a direct line monitored by the folks who developed JavaScript at Netscape, and netscape.navigator remains the closest thing to that line. JavaScript topics are definitely in the minority in this group, but you can find them if you look.

Note the different news server. The title implies it's secure, but it seems to be readily available for browsing and posting.

To get there, go to: `news://secnews.netscape.com`.

JavaScript Digest

Much like a chain letter, this site serves as a running interactive discussion similar to the newsgroup. Formerly available only in a digest format, it now also comes in a standard form.

To subscribe, send a message to `listproc@inquiry.com` with the message `set javascript mail ack`.

If you have problems receiving the digest, send a message to `listproc@inquiry.com` with the message body `help`. To unsubscribe to the list, send a message to `listproc@inquiry.com` with the message body `unsubscribe JAVASCRIPT`.

Summary

JavaScript is a lot like Java. If you understand Java already, you'll pick up JavaScript that much quicker. If this is your first outing with JavaScript after working with HTML, the learning process may last a little longer, but it is still within easy reach. Once you get used to an object-oriented view of the world, the rest of the process becomes much easier, and you're well on your way to creating interactive and useful Web pages that don't put a huge load on your server.

CHAPTER 36

Including Java Applets in Your Web Pages

by Rick Darnell

IN THIS CHAPTER

Java is one of the hottest topics on the World Wide Web—and for good reason. It offers expanded portability for Web content, including sound and animation, without the use of plug-ins or other helper applications and independent of host hardware. In this sense, Java has helped promote a change in the way page developers think about content on the World Wide Web, similar to the way the World Wide Web changed the way people think about the Internet.

Getting to Know Java

Java is an object-oriented programming language developed by Sun Microsystems, Inc. Although not initially conceived as a way to expand the interactivity and capability of Web pages, it didn't take long for people to see how the platform-independent nature of Java made an ideal fit with the nature of the Internet.

In the past, when an author developed a page with special content beyond the constraints of HTML, an important decision had to be made: either use helper applications or shift the necessary processing to the server. The first solution meant that some content would be inaccessible to some users if they didn't have the helper application or if a helper was unavailable for their system. The second solution meant excluding some content because inherently slow modem lines made animation and sounds unworkable over normal network connections.

Enter Sun's Java. By utilizing a key feature of Java—platform independence—Java applets can implement sound, animation, spreadsheets, e-mail applications, guest books, and virtually anything else you can program, regardless of platform.

Java Safety

Running in a distributed environment, such as an intranet or the World Wide Web, requires safeguards for client computers; a potentially hostile piece of code can do a great deal of damage by erasing files, by formatting disks, and creating other types of damage. Given the way applets are implemented—automatic load and run—you need to ensure the integrity of any piece of code distributed to a broad and uncontrolled audience.

As a Web-page author using Java, you are responsible for ensuring that your applets are clean. The best way is to get them only from trusted sites. Be careful about picking up applets anywhere you find them—the hard drive you save may be your own.

PROGRAMMERS LOVE A CHALLENGE

Java is not bulletproof, however. As quick as it was proclaimed "secure," a dedicated group of programmers went to work to find security holes. And they found them. Through cooperative efforts between Sun, Netscape, Microsoft and others, these are getting corrected, but it's still a dangerous world. There are reports of "black Java" applets which are hostile enough to format system drives and pass secure information across the Internet.

There are a few things you can do to protect yourself and your system:

- Use only the most up-to-date versions of software.
- If your system enables screening applets at the firewall, take advantage of it. If there are applets you'd like to use, make them available internally.
- Don't browse a Java site unless you know it's clean.

As discussed in the introduction, the compiled bytecode is checked extensively for illegal operations and is verified again on the host system before the applet is run. Although these security features limit the scope and capabilities of an applet, they also help ensure against "Trojan horse" viruses and other shenanigans by less-than-scrupulous programmers.

With all of the security features built in, you don't want to implement word processors, spreadsheets, or other interactive applications in Java applets. If you require these programs, consider building a full Java application, which does not contain the security restrictions of an applet.

Although no system can guarantee 100-percent security, Java goes a long way to ensure the protection of client systems from its applets. It uses three security procedures to make the end user safe from malicious attacks:

- Bytecode verification
- Memory layout control
- File access restrictions

Bytecode Verification

After a piece of Java code is loaded into memory, it enters the interpreter, where it gets checked for language compliance before the first statement is executed. This process ensures against corruption or changes to the compiled code between compile time and run time.

Memory Layout

Next, the memory layout is determined for each of the classes, preventing would-be hackers from forging access by deducing anything about the structure of a class or the machine it's running on. Memory allocation is different for each class, depending on its structure and the host machine.

File Access Restrictions

After that, the interpreter security continues to monitor the activity of the applet to make sure it doesn't access the host file system, except as specifically allowed by the client or user. You can extend some implementations of this specific feature to include no file access, period.

Platform Independence

This feature is probably the most important one. One compiled piece of Java code can run on any platform with a Java compiler. Currently, the list of platforms includes Windows 95, Solaris, and Macintosh, but there are people hard at work to expand the possibilities. By its very nature, Java does not contain any implementation-specific syntax. This format means a byte is an 8-bit integer and a float is a 32-bit IEEE 754 floating point number, no matter where the applet runs.

And, with object-oriented code, Java takes advantage of a special programming feature that enables programmers to upgrade capabilities simply by adding a new class. When an applet is upgraded, it is not always necessary to reload the entire applet. A small additional class may be all that's needed.

HotJava

HotJava (see Figure 36.1) represents one of the first applications written entirely in Java. In its initial release, HotJava primarily showed how applets could be included as part of an HTML document. Now, it functions closer to a full-featured browser, supporting all of HTML 1 and 2 specifications. Support for HTML 3.2 is also in the process of integration.

TIP

To download a copy of HotJava, point your browser to `http://java.sun.com/java.sun.com/hotjava.html`. The file size is approximately 3 M.

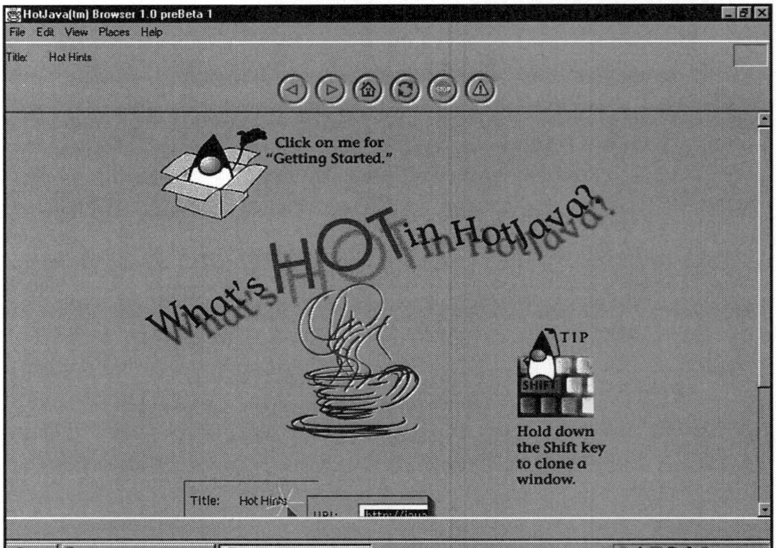

FIGURE 36.1.
The HotJava browser is one of the first stand-alone applications written entirely in the Java language.

HotJava operates differently from most browsers in its basic functioning. Settings, preferences, and other basic maintenance screens get stored in the form of HTML documents and classes.

Stripped down to its most basic level, HotJava knows nothing about anything. Classes are added to the browser so it can understand HTML, e-mail, sound files, and other specialty items. As new content and new formats are developed for Web pages, Java will require only the addition of another class. You won't need a complete upgrade to a new version to take advantage of the latest developments.

The Truth About Java-Powered Pages

When Java was first released in 1995, if you wanted to do something nifty on your Web page with an applet, there were two things you needed:

1. Enough programming language to learn Java.
2. Users with the HotJava browser to view your applet, because it wasn't yet supported by Netscape or Microsoft.

Fortunately, this situation didn't last very long. Enough programmers and Web developers became interested in Java and before long, a whole bunch of applets were available. Second, Netscape adopted Java compatibility for their 2.0 release of Navigator. This was followed closely by Microsoft, who included Java as part of their 3.0 release of Internet Explorer.

NOTE

If you're still interested in writing your own applets, the basics are covered in Chapter 37, "Writing Java Applets." For a detailed programming tutorial, check out *Teach Yourself Java in 21 Days*, available from Sams.net.

HotJava is still available, but it remains a distant choice in the browser market. Although easily customized using Java classes, it's still pretty slow. Sun is not attempting to have it compete with the Big Two, and instead is focusing on intranet and custom markets.

With plenty of applets and Java-compatible browsers, a Java-powered page is as simple as including an applet definition within your HTML document. To wave the Java banner, many page authors also include the Java-Powered icon (see Figure 36.2) as part of the page with the applet or links to other Java pages.

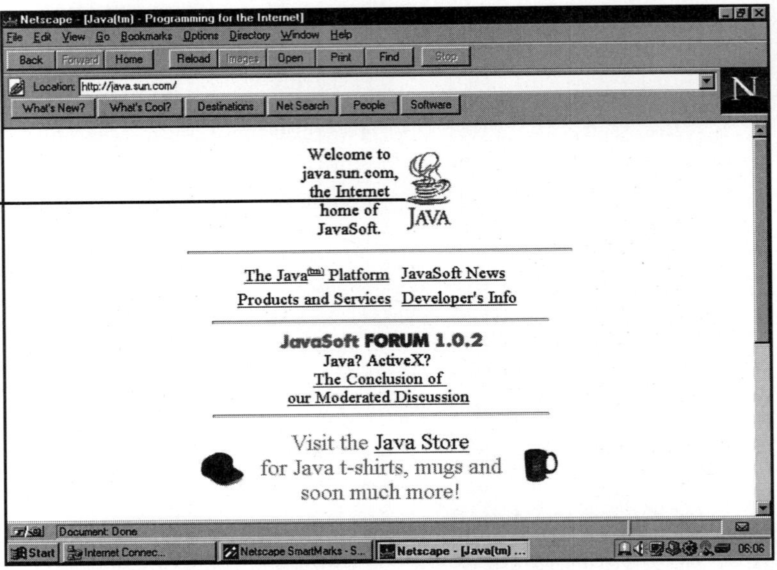

FIGURE 36.2.
The Java-Powered icon is used by many developers to indicate a page with Java applets.

Why Is Everyone So Hyped About Java?

Java holds a great deal of promise for the World Wide Web and computers in general because it provides a solution to the problem of incompatible platforms. Internets and intranets are no longer expected to include similar or directly compatible machines (all UNIX, all Macintosh, or all PC). Because it has a neutral architecture, the same application written in Java can be used by anyone on the network, without concern for which kind of machine the developer used.

For standalone applications, Java's object-oriented structure gives an easy method to upgrade. The class for the upgrade or extension of the application is downloaded into the appropriate class library; then you can run the updated features.

With its modeling capabilities, Java represents a good choice for implementing advanced Web capabilities and content, such as virtual-reality sites or Web crawlers powered by intelligent agents.

How to Use Java Now

The simplest way to implement Java is through embedding applets in your HTML pages. A wide variety of applets are already available for inclusion, including the animation applet included with the Java Development Kit and a plethora of ticker display applets, which scroll a message or graphic in a half million different ways across the applet frame. An example of a ticker applet is included later in this chapter in the section "Applets for Fun and Utility."

NOTE

Although spreading quickly, Java applets do not come with all browsers. Netscape Navigator 2.0 and later, Microsoft Internet Explorer 3.0 and later, and Sun's HotJava support Java applets. NCSA Mosaic has included Java compatibility in its wish list for future upgrades to its product, but no word has been given on when that might happen. If your browser is not Java-compatible, the applet section of the HTML page is ignored.

How Applets and Applications Are Different

Java applications work similarly to standalone programs, such as your browser or word processor. They don't require a third-party intermediary, such as HotJava or the applet viewer. Applets require a Java-compatible browser or the appletviewer for viewing. They operate similarly to other objects embedded in HTML documents, such as Shockwave or RealAudio files, which require assistance to run.

NOTE

The HotJava browser developed by Sun is a Java application that was written and implemented entirely in the Java language.

The fact that applets run on a host system makes them especially suspect and leads to several key security restrictions. Applets have limited capability to interact with their host platform. An applet cannot write files or send files to a printer on the local system. In addition, it cannot read local files or run local applications. Although no system is 100 percent secure, Java goes to great lengths to ensure the integrity of applets generated under its banner.

JAVA APPLETS AND JAVASCRIPT

It has been said a million times, but if you have just started using Java, it bears repeating: Java isn't JavaScript. JavaScript isn't Java.

Java, in applet or application form, is a compiled language with classes and inheritance. HTML pages can include a reference to Java applets, which then get downloaded and run when a compatible browser finds the tag.

JavaScript is an object-based, client-side scripting language developed by Netscape, but it does not include classes or inheritance. JavaScript exists on the HTML page and gets interpreted by a compatible browser along with the rest of the page.

Although they share some common syntax and terminology, the two items work differently and have different uses. Confusing Java and JavaScript only leads to a steeper learning curve.

Using an Applet on a Web Page

Using applets on a Web page requires a two-part process. First, you must make sure your classes and related files, such as images and audio clips, appear in a directory accessible to the HTML page. One common location is in a `classes` subdirectory of the HTML documents. Second, the `<APPLET>` tag that refers to the class is inserted in the Web page, along with any parameters the applet needs to function.

All About the <APPLET> Tag

The `<APPLET>` tag is used to insert the applet on a page, and it takes the following syntax:

```
<APPLET CODE="appletName.class" [CODEBASE="pathToClass"] WIDTH=xxx HEIGHT=xxx
[ALIGN= ][HSPACE= ][VSPACE= ]>
[<PARAMETER name=parameterName value=parameterValue>]
</APPLET>
```

Although it looks like a lot of options, they're actually pretty simple to understand:

- `CODE`—This required line of code identifies the name of the applet. It is case-sensitive and requires the `.class` extension. Don't include the path to the applet with its name. The path is covered in the next option.
- `CODEBASE`—This optional parameter indicates a relative path to the class if it is not stored in the same directory as the HTML file. It can also be a complete URL if the applet resides on a different server.
- `WIDTH/HEIGHT`—Some browsers require these two attributes, some don't. To be safe, use both to specify the size in pixels of the frame that holds the applet.
- `ALIGN`—This option works similarly to the parameter in the `<IMG SRC>` tag by controlling the positioning of HTML text adjacent to the applet's space.
- `HSPACE/VSPACE`—If text from the HTML page is immediately adjacent to the applet, these two parameters allow for some breathing room. The horizontal or vertical space is measured in pixels.

Most applets also require a set of parameters to control their actions. You'll want to check any documentation supplied with the applet to see what's available. There is no limit to the number of parameters you can include within an applet tag. The only rule is that each parameter must appear in a separate `<PARAM>` tag.

Passing Parameters to Applets

Parameters are used to pass information to an applet so the applet knows about the environment it's in and how it should behave. Some applets have one method of running and don't accept any parameters. Most, however, contain some user-definable parameters that can be changed.

The <PARAM> tag enables you to pass information to the applet. The syntax is this:

```
<PARAM NAME=paramName VALUE=paramValue>
```

The parameter name is case-sensitive and must exactly match the parameter name in the applet. If the applet does not provide exceptions for mismatched data types, an incompatible value could cause it not to function. For example, if a parameter calls for an integer and you provide a string, the applet could fail to operate when it attempts to put the string into an integer variable.

There is a small complexity to all of this. You'll notice that some HTML editors that support Java applets include all parameters as strings. The following example passes an integer to the applet as a string:

```
<PARAM NAME="Pause" VALUE="100">
```

What gives? The nuance is that all parameters are sent to the applet as strings, regardless of how you represent them in the parameter tag. The conversion to the appropriate data type happens inside the applet. The moral to this story is to make sure the value you send will convert to the right type. If the "Pause" parameter used in the last example wants an integer, don't send it a string.

The <APPLET> Tag and Non-Java Browsers

There is an additional item you can include within an applet tag that you're probably already familiar with—an <IMG> tag. An image tag within an applet is used with browsers that don't support Java.

When interpreting an HTML document, an incompatible browser ignores any tags it doesn't understand. In this case, that includes the applet and parameter tags. However, it ignores them one at a time instead of finding the closing applet tag and ignoring everything in between. When it reaches the <IMG> tag within your applet definition, it knows what to do and loads the image (see Figure 36.3).

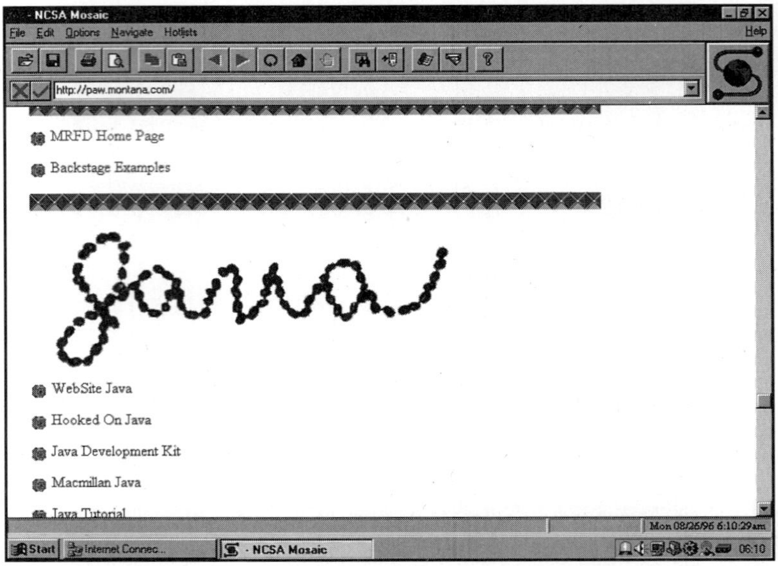

FIGURE 36.3.
Even though NCSA Mosaic is not compatible with Java, it can still display a graphic defined with an `<IMG>` *tag embedded within the* `<APPLET>` *tag.*

Here are some tips to help you use this trick effectively:

- All normal image-tag parameters apply, including source, size and alignment.
- The preferred place to put the `<IMG>` tag is immediately preceding the `</APPLET>` tag. This position is easy to find, and it doesn't clutter the rest of the applet definition.
- If your applet occupied a specific place and size, make sure you include the same settings for the image tag so it fills the same space. For example, if your applet tag was the following:

  ```
  <APPLET CODE="Animator.class" HEIGHT="150" WIDTH="500" ALIGN="LEFT">
  ```

  then your image tag should be something like this:

  ```
  <IMG SRC="/images/explodingBull.gif" HEIGHT="150" WIDTH="500" ALIGN="LEFT">
  ```

TIP

Make sure the actual size of your image matches the dimensions of the applet. If the size defined in the image tag is different from the actual size, it could be distorted on the viewer's screen.

This is an easy way to substitute content for users who don't have Java-compatible browsers. Although all of the benefits of Java are lost, there is at least something for them to view, even if it's a message that they should get a Java browser.

Applets for Fun and Utility

This section provides help on using a selection of applets available on the CD-ROM. These applets are free for you to use on your own Web pages.

Animator

Probably one of the most frequently used, the Java animator applet (see Figure 36.4) comes with the Java Developer's Kit and provides a quick-and-easy way to add animation to your Java-powered page.

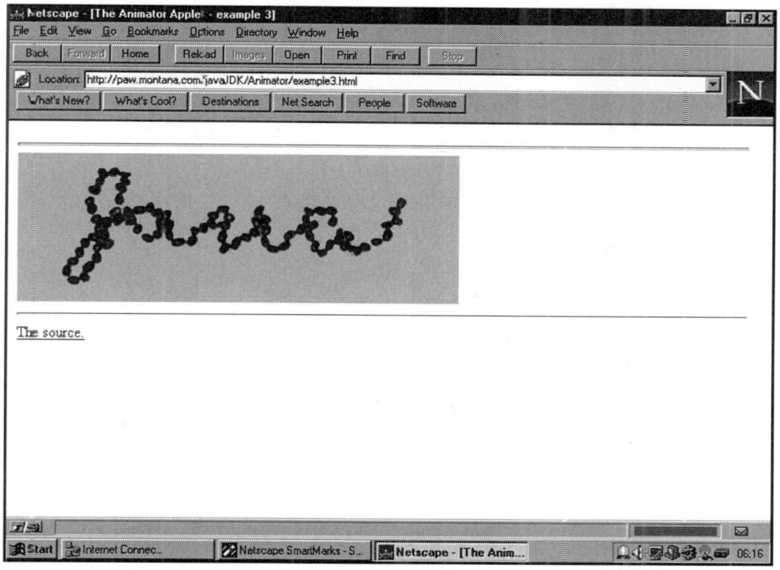

FIGURE 36.4.
The Animator applet is used to display a series of images with an option for frame-specific sounds and soundtracks.

Animator also supports synchronized sound with the animation, but the sound must use the Sun `.au` format. No other sound formats are supported yet. Implementing the applet requires a set of `.gif` or `.jpg` files containing the images that form the animation.

TIP

Try to keep the size of the images as small as possible. Each image has to get downloaded to the client machine, adding significantly to the time required for the applet to load and run.

A wide variety of parameters exist, and they control the operation of Animator. Here's the breakdown and syntax:

<APPLET CODE="Animator.class" WIDTH=*number* HEIGHT=*number*> Width should be at least the width in pixels of the widest frame, whereas height should reflect the size of the tallest frame. Smaller values will result in the image getting clipped.

<PARAM NAME=IMAGESOURCE VALUE="*pathInfo*"> Points to the directory that contains the animation frames. The default directory is the same as the HTML document. By default, the files get named T1.gif, T2.gif, and so on.

<PARAM NAME=STARTUP VALUE="*filename*"> An image that gets displayed while the applet loads and prepares to run.

<PARAM NAME=BACKGROUND VALUE="*filename*"> An image file for use as a background for the animation.

<PARAM NAME=BACKGROUNDCOLOR VALUE="*color,color,color*"> The color for the animation background, represented as an RGB value with a number from 0 to 255 for each of the settings.

<PARAM NAME=STARTIMAGE VALUE=*number*> The first frame in the animation (by default 1).

<PARAM NAME=ENDIMAGE VALUE=*number*> The last frame in the animation.

<PARAM NAME="NAMEPATTERN" VALUE="*dir/prefix*%N.*suffix*"> A pattern to use for generating names based on the STARTIMAGE, ENDIMAGE, and IMAGESOURCE parameters.

<PARAM NAME="PAUSE" VALUE=number> Number of milliseconds to pause between images (default)—can be overridden by PAUSES.

<PARAM NAME="PAUSES" VALUE="number¦number¦..."> Millisecond delay per frame, with each value separated by a vertical bar. Blank uses a default PAUSE value.

<PARAM NAME="REPEAT" VALUE=true> If true, the animation will continue as a loop.

<PARAM NAME="POSITIONS" VALUE="x@y¦x@y..."> Screen positions (x@y) for each frame, represented in pixels and separated by vertical bars. A blank value will use the previous frame's position.

<PARAM NAME="IMAGES" VALUE="number¦number¦..."> Used to define an explicit order for frames, which becomes useful if your frames are out of order or if you want to reverse the sequence (such as "1¦2¦3¦2¦1").

<PARAM NAME="SOUNDSOURCE" VALUE="aDirectory"> Indicates the directory with the audio files. The default is the same directory as the class.

<PARAM NAME="SOUNDTRACK" VALUE="aFile"> An audio file to play throughout the animation as background music.

<PARAM NAME="SOUNDS" VALUE="aFile.au|||||bFile.au"> Plays audio files keyed to individual frames.

<PARAM NAME="HREF" VALUE="aURL"> The URL of the page to visit when user clicks the animation (if not set, a mouse click pauses/resumes the animation).

Clock

This applet displays an analog clock onscreen (see Figure 36.5), complete with a sweeping second hand. Right now, no way exists to control the appearance of the clock. It would, however, be a relatively simple matter to add a parameter to control the size of the clock and whether the second hand appears, and to display of the date and time underneath.

The time gets determined by the host machine. A computer implementation of an analog clock occupies little computer space—just more than 3 K.

```
<applet code="Clock2.class" width=170 height=150>
</applet>
```

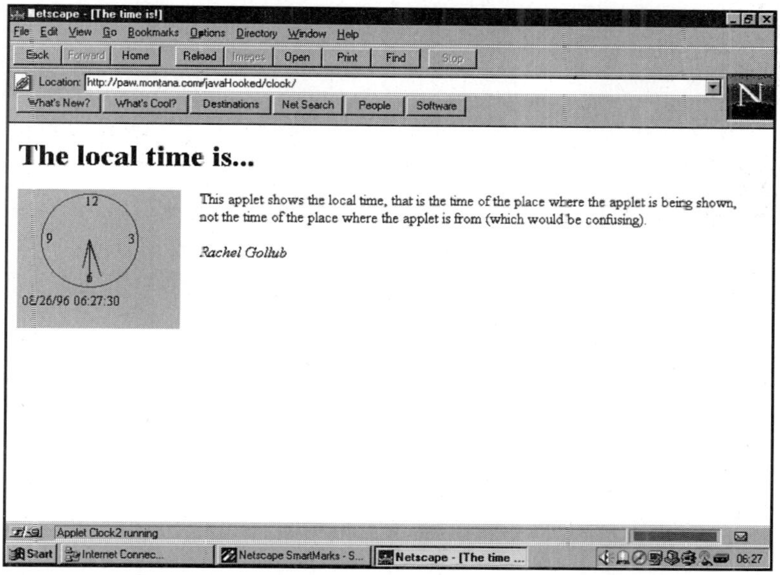

Figure 36.5.
The Clock applet, a small and simple local-time clock to include on a Web page.

Nervous Text

Nervous text (see Figure 36.6) works by combining the basic HTML heading with a dose of really strong coffee and a slab of double chocolate cake. The letters jitter and jump around like Mexican jumping beans on a hot pan.

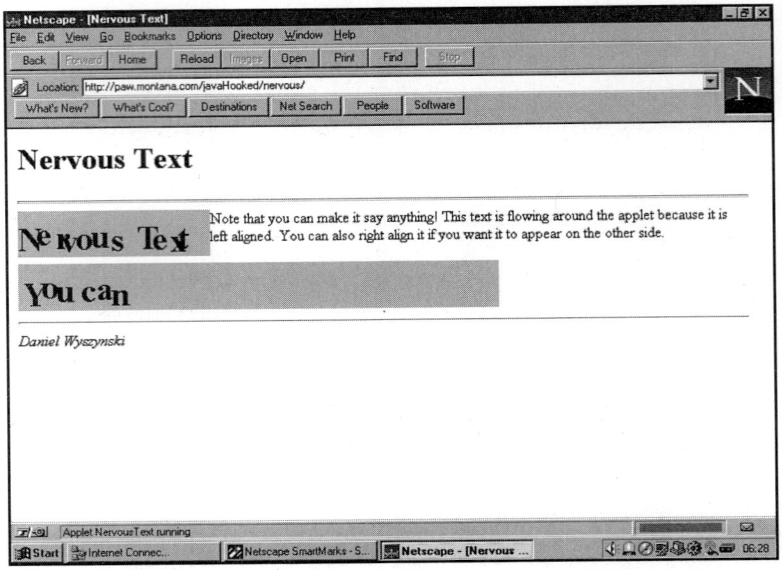

FIGURE 36.6.
The Nervous Text applet moves each letter around in a frantic, haphazard fashion.

Nervous text takes a string of text as its lone parameter. If not included, the default text is `HotJava`. You can also modify the applet's source code to achieve more flexibility, including controlling the size and color of the font.

```
<PARAM NAME=text VALUE="string">
```

Ticker (http://www.uni-kassel.de/fb16/ipm/mt/java/ticker.htm)

This applet (see Figure 36.7) provides one example of the many "ticker tape" applets available. It is one of the improved versions, having made the extra effort to reduce flicker and provide additional control over the text.

It takes a variety of parameters, described here:

`<PARAM NAME=msg VALUE="string">` The message to display.

`<PARAM NAME=speed VALUE=number>` The animation speed, expressed as the number of pixels per 100 milliseconds. The default is 10.

`<PARAM NAME=txtco VALUE="r,g,b">` The color of the message, expressed as an RGB value with numbers from 0 to 255. If omitted, the default is black.

`<PARAM NAME=bgco VALUE="r,g,b">` The color of the background. If omitted, the default appears as light gray.

`<PARAM NAME=shco VALUE="r,g,b">` The color of the message shadow. If omitted, no shadow appears.

`<PARAM NAME=href VALUE="URL">` The ticker can also serve as a hyperlink if the user clicks on the ticker. Either a relative or complete URL is legal.

`<PARAM NAME=hrefco VALUE="r,g,b">` The color of the URL frame. If omitted, the default is blue.

`<PARAM NAME=start VALUE="yy, mm, dd">/<PARAM NAME=exp VALUE="yy, mm, dd">` Dates to start and stop (expire) displaying the applet. If the page gets viewed outside of these dates, as determined by the host machine, the ticker will not display its message. It will still occupy space on the screen, however. You can use either date parameter by itself.

`<PARAM NAME=exfill VALUE="r,g,b">` If the local date falls outside of the start and stop parameters, then the box becomes filled with this color.

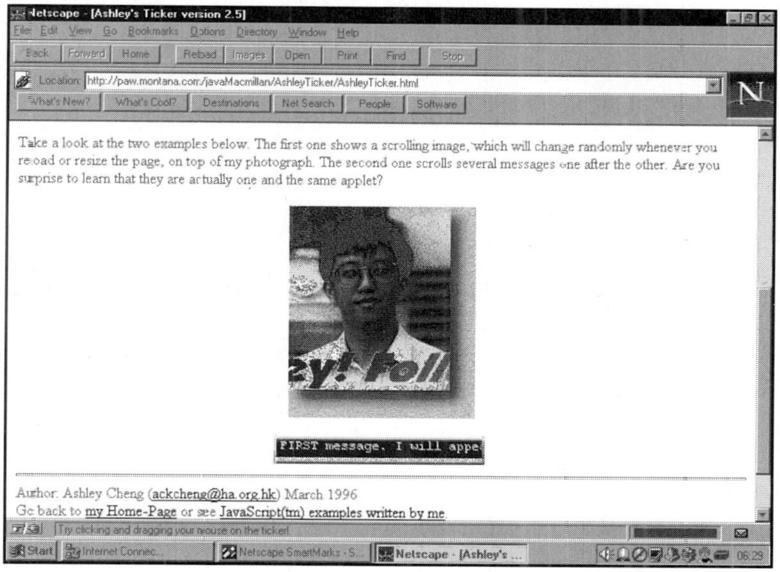

FIGURE 36.7.
The Ticker applet provides a flexible way to display scrolling messages on the browser screen.

Nuclear Power Plant

This little simulation (see Figure 36.8) really doesn't seem useful, unless you plan to run power plants in Russia. It does, however, show a good example of a user interface, object interaction, and animation. After the applet is initialized, you can select one of three powerplant crises—from pump failures to blown turbines. To prevent a meltdown, open and close valves and start pumps as necessary. If you don't work quick enough, the core turns to mush and releases enough radioactivity to ruin everyone's day.

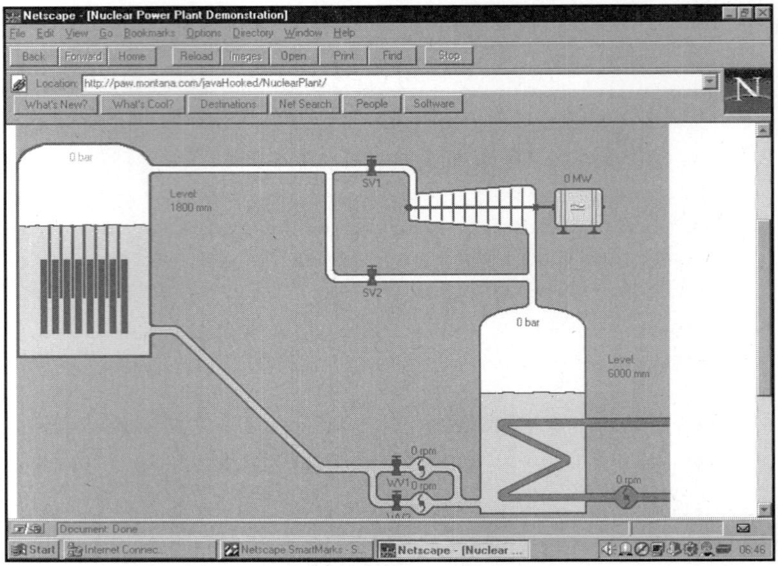

FIGURE 36.8.
The Nuclear Power Plant applet, a creative use of Java as a learning tool and game implementation.

Applet Sources on the Web

Many sources exist for applets on the Web that you can use. Make sure to check the licensing on the applet. Just because an applet appears on a page doesn't mean you can freely use it.

JavaSoft (`http://java.sun.com/`)

JavaSoft, a subsidiary of Sun Microsystems, handles the Java products. Go to their Web site (see Figure 36.9) first when looking for information, documentation, updates, downloads, and other feedback. Originally part of the Sun Web site, JavaSoft received its own space to handle the dramatic increase in attention Java has enjoyed since its release.

JavaWorld (`http://www.javaworld.com/`)

The first online publication devoted entirely to Java, JavaWorld (see Figure 36.10) comes out monthly and includes news and views about Java developments, along with hands-on tips and tricks. Programming contests are a regular feature, and many articles include links to Java-powered sites, source code, and other helpful items.

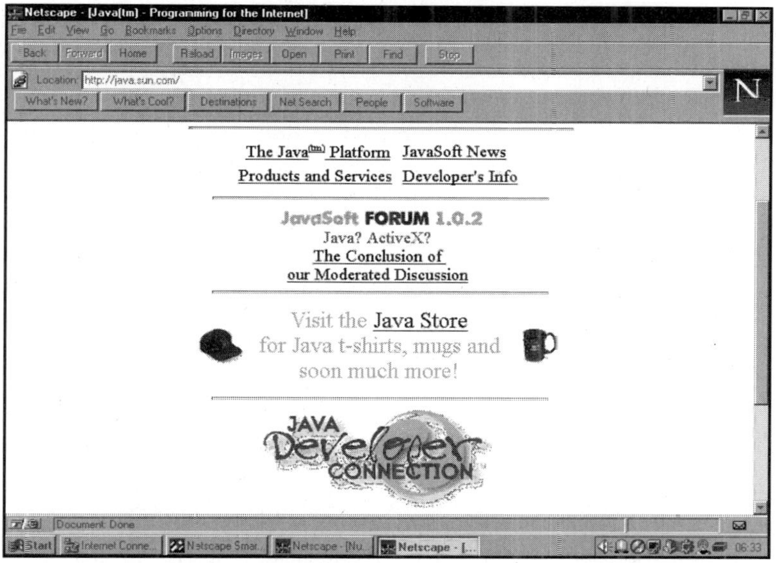

FIGURE 36.9.
The JavaSoft home page includes links to the Java Developer's Kit, HotJava, and other information of use to Java users and developers.

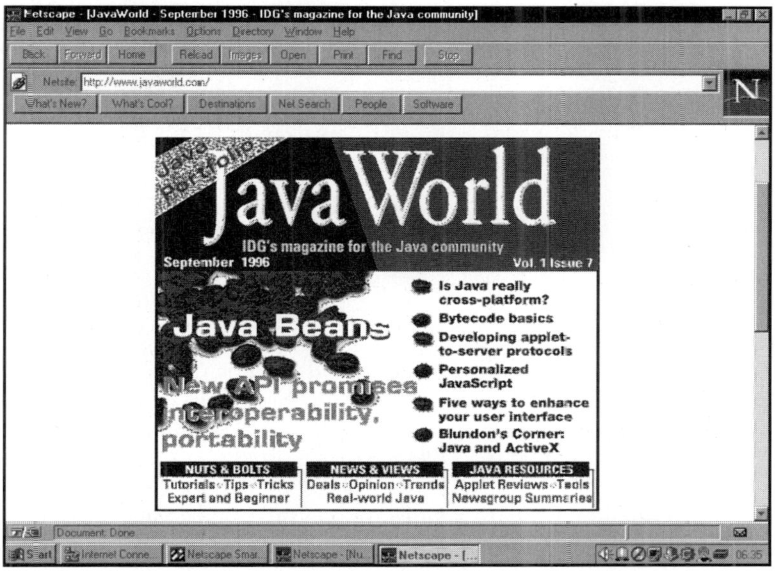

FIGURE 36.10.
JavaWorld includes interviews with the movers and shakers in the Java realm, along with hands-on examples, tutorials, and contests.

Gamelan (`http://www.gamelan.com/`)

This site was developed specifically for the development and advancement of Java. As such, it shows you what the rest of the world is doing with Java. Links appear here to some of the best applets to date for the viewing, and you can download some for use on your pages (see Figure 36.11). It also includes a page devoted to JavaScript for links devoted to pages utilizing Java's cousin. Some of the innovative productions found here include animators, tickers, network utilities, and a Learn to Dance applet.

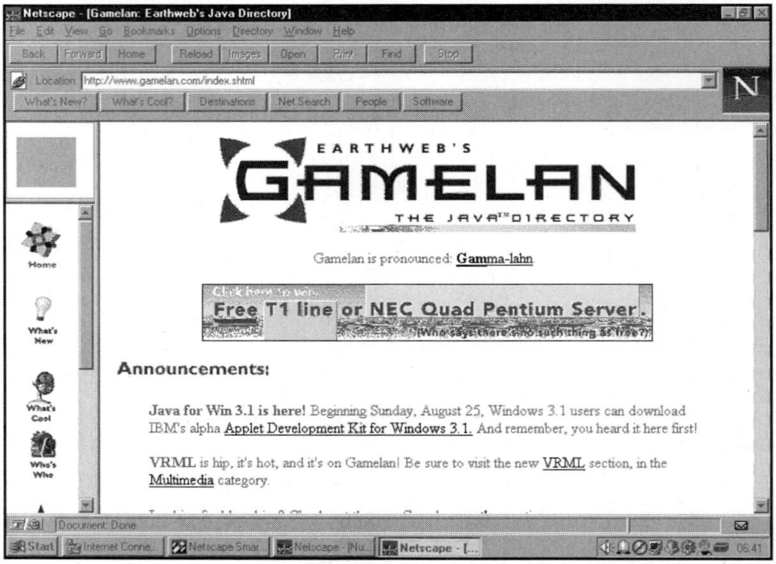

FIGURE 36.11.
Gamelan maintains a comprehensive list of links to applications and applets available on the Web.

Summary

Java use keeps spreading quickly as more and more hardware and software manufacturers pledge support to the language and concepts. Even if you never have the chance to delve deep into the intricacies of building an applet or application from scratch, understanding the basics will help you take full advantage of the powerful capabilities available.

Your introduction to the basics of Java continues in the next chapter. You've looked hard at applets from the outside in this chapter; it's time to see what's on the inside. The next chapter gives an introduction to how an applet is constructed, including defining and creating objects and starting and stopping applet operation.

CHAPTER 37

Writing Java Applets

by Rick Darnell

IN THIS CHAPTER

Sun Microsystems defines Java as, "a simple, robust, secure, object-oriented, platform-independent, dynamic programming environment." At first, all of this Java talk can sound like a lot of voodoo. After you strip away the hype, however, it's easy to see how Java works effectively for implementing simple solutions to potentially complicated challenges in a distributed environment.

What Does the Java Language Offer?

Going back to Sun's description, Java is a language designed to make programming an easier task by hiding the parts which are best handled on a platform-specific basis, and modeling the rest after the way people think. Here's a quick breakdown.

Simple

Java has been designed with C and C++ programmers in mind. C and C++, however, had many hard-to-understand, rarely used features that the Java developers felt caused more pain than benefit. Important functions that come standard to every program, such as memory allocation and pointer arithmetic, automatically get handled by the Java system without needing any acknowledgment from the programmer.

In addition, Java is relatively small. Because of the need to run on a wide variety of platforms, Java applications tend to be smaller than the multi-megabyte applications that dominate the marketplace. The overhead to run a Java program includes 40 K for the basic interpreter and classes, plus an additional 175 K for the standard libraries and threading.

Robust

Java programs must be inherently reliable because any piece of Java byte must be capable of running on any platform. For this reason, a great deal of emphasis gets placed on checking for bugs and problems early in the development process, beginning with basic language implementation.

Use of pointers is a popular example. C++, a close cousin of Java, uses extensive arithmetic to keep track of arrays and other memory variables. This setup enables programmers to take full advantage of a specific platform, but it also creates problems when pointers go awry, overwriting memory and corrupting data. It also prevents a program developed for a Windows environment from working on a UNIX platform.

The Java compiler checks for a wide variety of errors beyond basic syntax, including type casting and method invocations. If you've made a mistake or mistyped, chances are good that your mistake gets flagged by the compiler, which is a far better place than by the interpreter at run time.

Object-Oriented

Object-oriented, probably one of the most overused and confusing terms in computer lingo, really has a simple and easy-to-understand meaning. It facilitates creating clean and portable code by breaking software down into coherent units. Objects become the basic building blocks of the application. Because of their modularity, an object can change without requiring major revision to the other program elements.

Getting The Tools You Need

The first item needed for writing applets is the Java Developer's Kit. This includes a compiler, interpreter, and the classes which are the building blocks of Java applets and applications. You can find the Java Developer's Kit (JDK) on the JavaSoft site at `http://java.sun.com/`.

> **NOTE**
>
> For more information on the differences between Java applications and applets, see Chapter 36, "Including Java Applets in Your Web Pages."

The JDK is a bare-bones resource. It only includes the absolutely essential items to make Java run, plus a handful of applets and the AppletViewer. To create applets, use your favorite text editor or word processor. The only requirement is that it saves your work in a standard text format with a `.java` extension.

In addition to the JDK, there are several other tools available to make developing applets easier.

JavaPad

JavaPad is a simple shareware program for Windows which makes developing Java applets and applications much easier. It includes a text editor for creating the applet source code, and the ability to run your stand-alone application or the AppletViewer.

After you save the `.java` file, JavaPad links to the Java compiler and generates a class file. If there are compiling errors, they're listed in a separate window where you can step through and correct each deficiency (see Figure 37.1).

Although a bare-bones application, JavaPad is a very friendly way to get started with development software. Its home page is `www.modelworks.com/express/`.

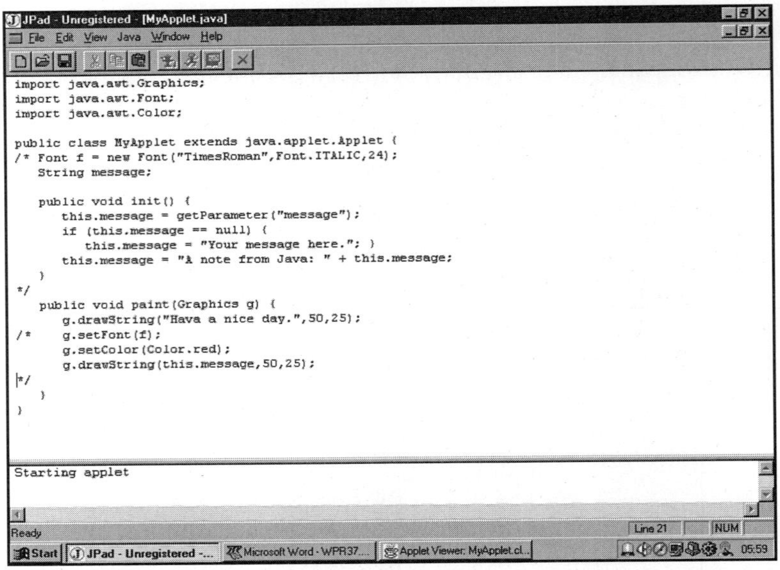

FIGURE 37.1.
JavaPad is a simple and useful program for building Java applications.

Symantec Café

Symantec Café is one of the first integrated development environments produced for Java. It includes all of the features needed by professional programmers, including version control and project management. It also includes an interface editor and graphical debugger. It is available for Windows and Macintosh. More information on ordering or downloading is located at `cafe.symantec.com`.

Sun Java Workshop

Another option is the Java workshop, created by the Java developers. It is every bit the rival of Symantec Café, only available in shareware form. If it has a drawback, it's that it doesn't include a faster compiler than Café, but in every other regard it's a high-quality application and well worth the download time to try. More information on features and availability is located at `www.sun.com/developer-products/java/`.

Creating Java Applets

Creating Java applets is easier if you already have a background in programming. With Java's tight structure, the basic format of an applet is fairly straightforward. You walk through an example here.

TIP

You can access online tutorials and documentation for Java and object-oriented programming from the Sun site, `http://java.sun.com/`.

An Object and Class Primer

Java is object-oriented, meaning that Java programs are built out of sections of code which package data with the instructions that affect it. A *class* is the template from which objects are created.

Think of it as a suburban neighborhood of cookie-cutter tract houses. All of the houses begin as a blueprint, and every house uses the same one. But you can't live in a blueprint, so you have to put the concrete, lumber, pipes, wire, and drywall together to build a house. In Java, this is called instantiation, and an instance of the blueprint is called an object. Many houses (objects) are built from the same blueprint (class).

Applet ABCs

At its simplest, an applet consists of two parts—the class declaration and a paint method. The following snippet contains a breakdown of the common elements for any applet:

```
import java.awt.Graphics;

public class MyApplet extends java.applet.Applet {
    public void paint (Graphics g) {
       your statements here;
    }
}
```

The first line includes a copy of the `Graphics` class from Java's Abstract Windowing Toolkit (AWT), which contains the methods needed for putting graphics, including text, lines, and dots, on the browser screen. This line may also be represented as `import java.awt` if more than the Graphics class is used.

Secondly, the applet is declared. It is `public`, meaning it is available to any other class, and it is a subclass of Java's `Applet` class, which provides the behavior necessary for interaction with the host browser.

The third section defines a method called `paint`, which the Java interpreter looks for to put the information on the screen. It is public to the class, and `void` indicates it does not return a value when it is completed. Its one parameter is an instance of the Graphics class imported on the first line of the program, which is referred to as `g`. This reference can as easily be called `bob` or `hammer`, but `g` is the commonly used convention.

Displaying with the Paint Method

Now that the applet is defined, you need to make it do something. For the `paint` method, include the following line.

```
g.drawString("Hava a nice day.",50,25);
```

After compiling the code and inserting it into an HTML document, you get something that looks like Figure 37.2.

NOTE

For more information on including applets in your Web page, see Chapter 36, "Including Java Applets in Your Web Page."

TIP

To convert your source code into a usable class, type `javac MyApplet.java` at the command prompt to invoke the Sun JDK compiler. If you're using a third-party compiler, follow the instructions provided with it. If any errors are reported, check your spelling and syntax and try again. If the system can't find the Java compiler, make sure its location is included in the system's execution path.

TIP

To test your applet you can use a browser such as Netscape Navigator (2.0 or later) or Microsoft Internet Explorer (3.0 or later). Another alternative is the Java AppletViewer, which is provided with the Java Developer's Kit. For more information, see "Using the Java AppletViewer," later in this chapter.

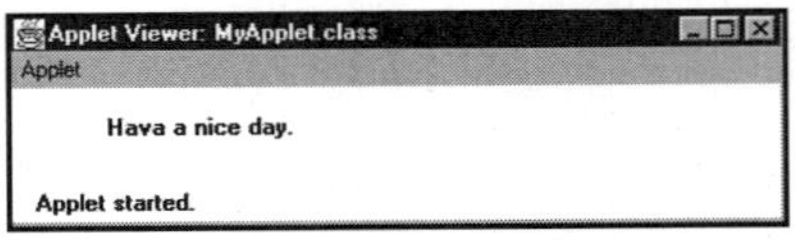

FIGURE 37.2.
MyApplet displays a simple message on the screen.

Of course, applets can do much more. By including some other AWT classes, the text can look better. First, you need the classes that control the font and display color.

```
import java.awt.Font;
import java.awt.Color;
```

Now, after the class declaration, create a variable to hold a new setting for the text.

```
Font f = new Font("TimesRoman",Font.ITALIC,24);
```

After the `paint` method declaration, use the `Graphics.set` methods to set the display before writing to the screen.

```
g.setFont(f);
g.setColor(Color.red);
```

With this extra bit of effort, the applet now looks like Figure 37.3.

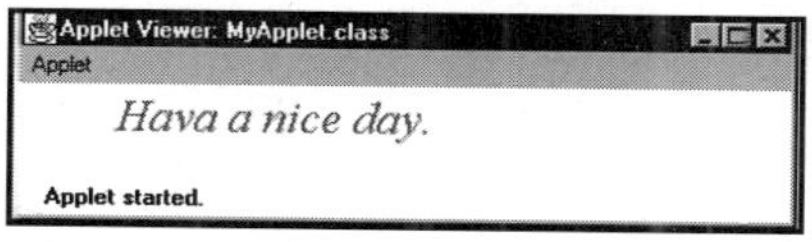

FIGURE 37.3.
MyApplet now displays in a larger font in red after some minor revisions to the code.

Again, this example is limited. The addition of a parameter to control the string makes it more useful to the HTML author. After the class declaration, declare the message as a variable.

```
String message;
```

A new method is also required to initialize the value of `message`.

APPLET ACTIVITIES

In addition to paint, four major activities exist in the life of an applet. If any get omitted, default versions are provided in the `Applet` class. This setup is called inheritance. Providing new methods in the applet is called overriding.

The first activity is initialization, accomplished with the `init` method: `public void init() {...}`. This activity occurs once, immediately after the applet is loaded. Initialization includes creating objects, setting graphics, or defining parameters. It can only happen once in the applet's life.

The second activity is starting, accomplished with the `start` method: `public void start() {...}`. After initialization, activity begins. This activity can also happen if a user activity stopped the applet. Starting can happen many times in the life of an applet. The `paint` method gets invoked somewhere in this method.

The next activity is stopping, accomplished with the `stop` method: `public void stop() {...}`. This activity can be an important method to include because by default the applet continues running and using system resources, even after the user has left the page with the applet. Like `start`, stopping can occur many times in the course of execution.

continues

continued

The last activity is destroying, accomplished with the `destroy` method: `public void destroy() {...}`. Destroying is where an applet throws out its own garbage after completing execution—when the applet is no longer needed or the user exits the browser. Java provides adequate coverage in this department, so you don't need to override this method unless you want to return specific resources to the system.

Initializing the message parameter requires overriding the `init` method for the applet.

```
public void init() {
    this.message = getParameter("message");
    if (this.message == null) {
        this.message = "Your message here."; }
    this.message = "A note from Java: " + this.message;
}
```

This method retrieves the value of the parameter in the HTML document. If a parameter named `message` is not found, then the value is null and `message` is set to the default string, `Your message here.`

NOTE

Java is case-sensitive for all of its variables, even when passed back and forth as parameters. Remember, Bob doesn't bob.

Now you need to update the `paint` method so that it uses the string defined in `init`, rather than the literal string in the `drawString` method.

```
g.drawString(this.message);
```

Using the AppletViewer again now generates the results in Figure 37.4.

To place your own message in the applet, add a `<PARAM>` tag to the HTML source containing the applet. For more information, see "Passing Parameters," later in this chapter. The complete listing for MyApplet appears in Listing 37.1. Note the use of the parameter in the `init` method.

TIP

Listing 37.2 is a sample HTML file which can be used as the basis for inserting or testing applets. Saved in a generic form, it is a very handy and reusable piece of code.

TIP

The file name for the source code must match the name of the applet, including capitalization. Java is case-sensitive in everything it does, including compiling and creating class files.

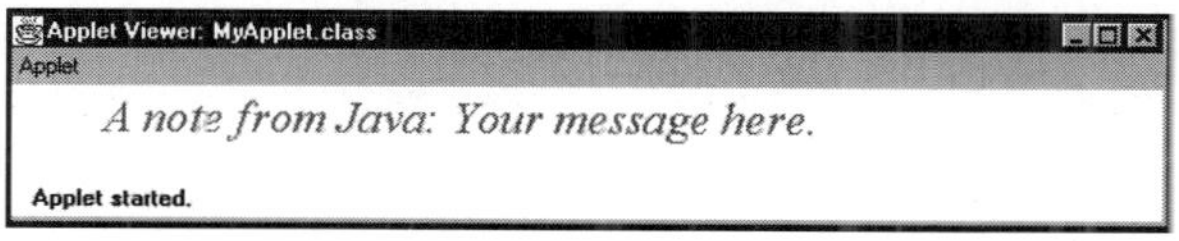

FIGURE 37.4.
The default message generated by MyApplet, after checking for a `message` *parameter and finding none.*

Listing 37.1. A simple applet for displaying text onscreen.

```
import java.awt.Graphics
import java.awt.Font;
import java.awt.Color;

public class MyApplet extends java.applet.Applet {
    Font f = new Font("TimesRoman",Font.ITALIC,24);
    String message;

    public void init() {
        this.message = getParameter("message");
        if (this.message == null) {
            this.message = "Your message here."; }
        this.message = "A note from Java: " + this.message;
    }

    public void paint(Graphics g) {
        g.setFont(f);
        g.setColor(Color.red);
        g.drawString(this.message,50,25);
    }
}
```

Listing 37.2. A sample of an HTML document that can display MyApplet.

```
<HTML>
<HEAD>
<TITLE>The MyApplet</TITLE>
</HEAD>
<BODY>
<HR>
<APPLET CODE="MyApplet.class" WIDTH=400 HEIGHT=50>
<PARAM NAME=message VALUE="Here I am.">
</APPLET>
<HR>
</BODY>
</HTML>
```

Interacting with the User

OK, all the little messages on the screen are neat, but how about actually doing something? The mouse is the preferred weapon on the World Wide Web, so we'll start with reacting to a user doing things with the mouse, beginning with a mouse click.

Looking for a Click

Java divides a mouse click into two parts, `mouseDown` when the button is depressed and `mouseUp` when it's released. This may seem like micro-management, but it's really quite useful.

Think of a drop-down menu. Click and hold to view the menu, and then drag the mouse down to your choice and release the button to select it. In Java, the `mouseDown` indicates the menu is selected and the items are displayed and `mouseUp` indicates a selection is made.

Mouse events are handled by overriding the default method for the particular action. The general syntax follows this example:

```
public boolean mouseDown(Event mdEvent, int x, int y) {
...stuff to do...
}
```

The method returns a Boolean value, true when the button is down, and false when it's up. Its first parameter is the actual event, which is itself an instance of a class. All system events generate a new instance of the Event class, which includes information on the type of event, where it happened, and when it took place. This provides a way to grasp the event and preserve it until your applet processes it. The next two parameters are the screen coordinates of where the event occurs.

A simple way of viewing this activity is to include the following two methods in your applet.

```
public boolean mouseDown(Event mdEvent, int x, int y) {
    System.out.println("Click at " + x + ", " + y);
    return true;
}
public boolean mouseUp(Event muEvent, int x, int y) {
    System.out.println("Release at " + x + ", " + y);
    return true;
}
```

NOTE

The coordinates relate to the space occupied by the applet only. An event object is not created for activities outside of the applet.

Note the last line in both methods, `return true`. This value is used so that other parts of the user interface can work with the event if it needs to. A good rule of thumb is that the event method should return true if it's your method that works with it.

Now, let's use this information for a little target practice. The TargetShoot applet shown in Listing 37.3 looks for a `mouseDown` event, and places a small circle on the screen where it occurs. It gives you the chance to hit the target six times (Figure 37.5).

Listing 37.3. The TargetShoot applet.

```
import java.awt.Graphics;
import java.awt.Color;
import java.awt.Event;

public class TargetShoot extends java.applet.Applet {
    final int shots = 6;
    int xhit[] = new int[shots];
    int yhit[] = new int[shots];
    int shotsTaken = 0;

public void init() {
    setBackground(Color.white);
}

public boolean mouseDown(Event mdEvent, int x, int y) {
    if (shotsTaken < shots)
        bang(x,y);
    else System.out.println("Out of bullets.");
    return true;
}

public void bang(int x, int y) {
    xhit[shotsTaken] = x;
    yhit[shotsTaken] = y;
    shotsTaken++;
    repaint();
}

public void paint(Graphics g) {
    g.setColor(Color.red);
    for (int i = 0; i < shotsTaken; i++) {
        g.fillOval(xhit[i] - 10, yhit[i] - 10, 20, 20);
    }
}

}
```

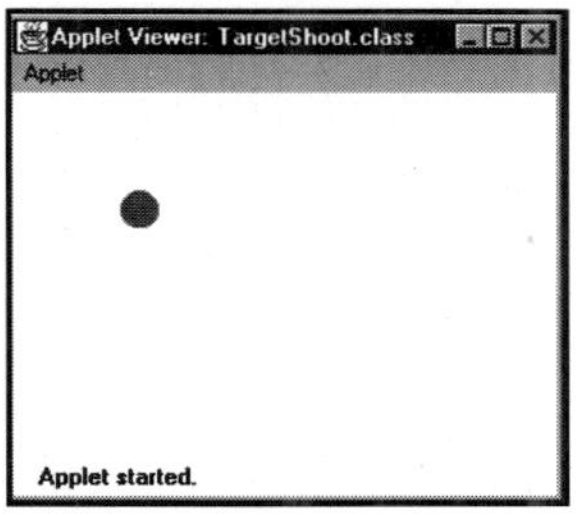

FIGURE 37.5.
The TargetShoot applet places a small red dot on the screen everywhere the user clicks.

Here's what's happening with the applet. The variables which store the maximum number of shots and the current number of shots taken are initialized, along with an array to hold the x and y positions of each one. The `mouseDown` method is used to call the `bang` method when the mouse button is clicked. The `bang` method records the location of the shot and calls the `repaint` method to update the screen. The last method, `paint` sets the color of the hits to blue and paints a circle at each of the locations where a shot has been taken.

Pressing Some Keys

Java can also look for keyboard activity using the `keyDown` method. The syntax of the method is similar to the mouse events.

```
public boolean keyDown(Event kEvt, int key) {
...
}
```

Like the other user input events, `keyDown` needs an event variable as one of its parameters. But instead of x and y coordinates for the location of the event, it accepts an ASCII value representing the key. If you want to turn the value into the actual character, use `char` casting method.

```
theCharacter = (char)key;
```

As part of the `Event` class, a set of key names are provided to make it easier to write code for items like the arrow and directional keys. Table 37.1 lists these key names.

Table 37.1. Key names in the `Event` class.

Event.Property	*Key*
`Event.HOME`	Home Key
`Event.END`	End Key
`Event.PGUP`	Page Up Key
`Event.PGDN`	Page Down Key
`Event.UP`	Up Arrow
`Event.DOWN`	Down Arrow
`Event.LEFT`	Left Arrow
`Event.RIGHT`	Right Arrow

The next task is to display characters on the screen in response to the keyboard. Whatever key the user presses appears on the screen (see Figure 37.6), and pressing the page down key clears the screen. Listing 37.4 provides the code for this task.

Listing 37.4. The KeyPress applet uses the same `Event` class used by the TargetShoot applet.

```
import java.awt.Graphics;
import java.awt.Event;
import java.awt.Font;
import java.awt.Color;

public class KeyPress extends java.applet.Applet {
    char currentKey;
    int valueKey;

public void init() {
    setBackground(Color.white);
    setFont(new Font("TimesRoman",Font.ITALIC,24));
}

public boolean keyDown(Event keyEvent, int key) {
    valueKey = key;
    switch (key) {
    case Event.PGDN:
        setBackground(Color.white);
        currentKey = 0;
        break;
    default:
        currentKey = (char)key;
    }
    repaint();
    return true;
}

public void paint(Graphics g) {
    switch (currentKey) {
    case 74:
        g.drawString("JAVA", 20, 30);
        break;
    case 106:
        g.drawString("java", 20, 30);
        break;
    case 0:
        g.drawString(" ", 20, 30);
        break;
    default:
        g.drawString(String.valueOf(currentKey)+" is ASCII: "+valueKey, 20, 30);
    }
}

}
```

FIGURE 37.6.
The KeyPress applet displays the character pressed and its ASCII value except for upper and lowercase j, when it prints Java.

For the most part, this is a straightforward operation. When a key is pressed, the `keyDown method` checks to see which key is pressed. If it's the page down key, the screen is cleared and nothing is displayed. Otherwise, the value of the key is passed to `currentKey`.

There are a few items included in this applet which are new. First, notice the two uses of the `switch` control. This is in effect a large `if-then` statement. The variable to compare is included in the first line, followed by a series of `case` statements with values. If the variable in the `switch` statement matches the value in the `case` statement, the set of instructions under it are executed. But there's a small hitch.

Normally, once the statements under the specific case are completed, execution passes to the next `case` statement in line. This isn't what we want, and so a `break` command is placed at the end of each `case`. When the program reaches the `break`, control is passed to the end of the entire `switch`. The last line of each `switch` is the optional default. This default is used to guarantee a certain behavior if a match is not found within any of the cases. Because it's the last item, a `break` isn't needed.

Working with Images

Loading and displaying images in Java is an easy task, thanks to the `Image` class located in `java.awt`. The first method to work within `Image` is `getUmage`, which loads the image from the Internet to your applet.

> **NOTE**
>
> Images are not integrated with the applet. Currently, Java only supports GIF and JPEG image files.

To load the image file, `getImage` needs to know where to find it. There are two ways of doing this:

- An URL object with the complete server and path information, such as `http://www.wossomatta.edu/java/images/rocky.gif`.
- An URL object with the base information (`http://www.wossomatta.edu/java/`), and a string with the path or file name of the image file (`images/rocky.gif`).

Although the first method appears to be much simpler, it is not very flexible. If the location of the image changes, you have to change the source code and recompile the applet.

The second form is the preferred method, and includes two options for establishing the base URL:

- `getDocumentBase()`—Returns a URL based on the directory of the HTML document which contains the applet.

- `getCodeBase()`—Returns a string representing the directory of the applet. Its value is dependent on the `CODEBASE` attribute in the `<APPLET>` tag. If the applet is stored in the same directory as the HTML document, this value is empty.

But as it's said, a picture's worth a thousand words, so here are a few examples of how `getImage` works:

- `Image pict = getImage(new URL("http://www.wossomatta.edu/java/images/rocky.gif"));`

  This uses a hard-coded URL to retrieve the image. If the location of the image changes, you need to change the source code and recompile the class in order for the applet to find the file.

- `Image pict = getImage(getDocumentBase(), "images/boris.gif");`

  This applies the path information to the end of the base URL of the HTML document containing the image. If the file is in the document root, then `getDocumentBase` might be `http://www.pottsylvania.gov/`, and the entire URL to the image file is `http://www.pottsylvania.gov/images/boris.gif`.

- `Image pict = getImage(getCodeBase(), "images/boris.gif");`

  Let's assume the HTML document information is the same as the prior example, and now the applet is stored in the directory `javaApplets`. Here's the breakdown on what's where:

  Document—`http://www.pottsylvania.gov/`

  Applet—`http://www.pottsylvania.gov/javaApplets/`

  Image file—`http://www.pottsylvania.gov/javaApplets/images/boris.gif`

It's important to note that at this point the applet has only loaded the image, it hasn't done anything with it. It only exists as an `Image` object called `pict`. Now it's time to display it using a method from the `Graphics` class.

```
public void paint(Graphics g) {
    g.drawImage(pict,10,10,this);
}
```

NOTE

You may have noticed the `this` parameter in the `drawImage` method. Its function is to draw the file contained in the object that calls the method. The `this` parameter always refers to the host object.

That's all there is to it. This form of `drawImage` displays `pict` with the top left corner at the coordinates 10,10. You can also add a second set of numbers to define the width and height of the image when it's painted, enabling you to make it fit anywhere you want.

TIP

Expect image degradation when you expand or contract an image very far beyond its original size. Changing the height to width ratio also distorts the image.

The entire applet to display the image (Figure 37.7) is shown in Listing 37.5. The Animator applet uses these basic operations to display a series of images that gives the appearance of motion.

Listing 37.5. A simple applet to load and display an image.

```
import java.awt.Graphics;
import java.awt.Image;

public class showPict extends java.applet.Applet {

Image pict;

public void init() {
    pict = getImage(getCodeBase(),"images/garden.gif");
}

public void paint(Graphics g) {
    g.drawImage(pict,10,10,this);
}

}
```

FIGURE 37.7.
The showPict applet loads an image from the `images` *subdirectory of the* `javaApplets` *directory.*

Using the Java AppletViewer

During applet development and testing, sometimes it's easier to bypass the unnecessary overhead of a browser. If your browser doesn't support applets, you still need a way to view the applets. At this point, the Java AppletViewer (see Figure 37.8) comes in handy.

FIGURE 37.8.
The Java AppletViewer enables the programmer to view embedded Java applets without the use of a browser. Only the applet is displayed. The rest of the HTML is ignored.

The AppletViewer searches the HTML document for the `<APPLET>` tag, such as the one shown in Listing 37.6. Using the information contained within the tag, it opens a window and runs the applet. Other HTML information on the page is ignored—only the applets appear.

Listing 37.6. A simple HTML document containing an <APPLET> tag.

```
<HTML>
<HEAD>
<TITLE>The animation applet</TITLE>
</HEAD>
<BODY>
<APPLET CODE="Animator.class" WIDTH=460 HEIGHT=160>
<PARAM NAME=imagesource VALUE="images/beans">
<PARAM NAME=endimage VALUE=10>
<PARAM NAME=pause VALUE=200>
</APPLET>
</BODY>
</HTML>
```

The Java AppletViewer is distributed with the Java Developer's Kit and is found in the same directory as the Java compiler and interpreter. To run the AppletViewer, use the following steps:

1. Create a document that references your applet with the appropriate tags and parameters. See Listing 37.6 for an example.
2. From a command line prompt, type **appletviewer *[path/]filename*.html**.

   If the AppletViewer launches from the same directory as the HTML document, you don't need the path name. Otherwise, the path is relative to your current location in the directory structure. The extension `.htm` is also valid for the viewer.
3. Any applets found in the HTML document are loaded and run, with each applet in its own instance of the AppletViewer.
4. Although you cannot change the initial parameters contained within the HTML page from the AppletViewer, you can start the applet from the beginning by choosing `Applet | Restart`. To load it again from memory, select `Applet | Reload`.
5. Leave the applet by choosing `Applet | Quit`.

TIP

The AppletViewer Reload function does not work if the application has been launched from the same directory as the HTML document and classes. For applets, create a subdirectory from your class directory called `HTML`, and place all of your classes and HTML files in it. Call the AppletViewer from the parent directory by using `appletviewer html\filename.html`. This way, you can make changes to the applet, compile it, and use the Reload function to see your changes.

Java Resources on the Web

As a language and as a way of thinking which has found its fame and fortune on the World Wide Web, the Internet remains the primary source of information and tools to learn more about Java. Here are a few of the high spots you may want to look at.

JavaSoft (`http://java.sun.com/`)

JavaSoft, a subsidiary of Sun Microsystems, is the leading figure in the continuing evolution of Java and Java products. Go to their Web site (see Figure 37.9) first when looking for information, documentation, development kit updates, applet downloads, and other feedback. Originally part of the Sun Microsystems Web site, JavaSoft has been created to handle the dramatic increase in attention Java has received since its release.

FIGURE 37.9.
The JavaSoft home page includes links to the Java Developer's Kit, HotJava, and other information of use to Java developers.

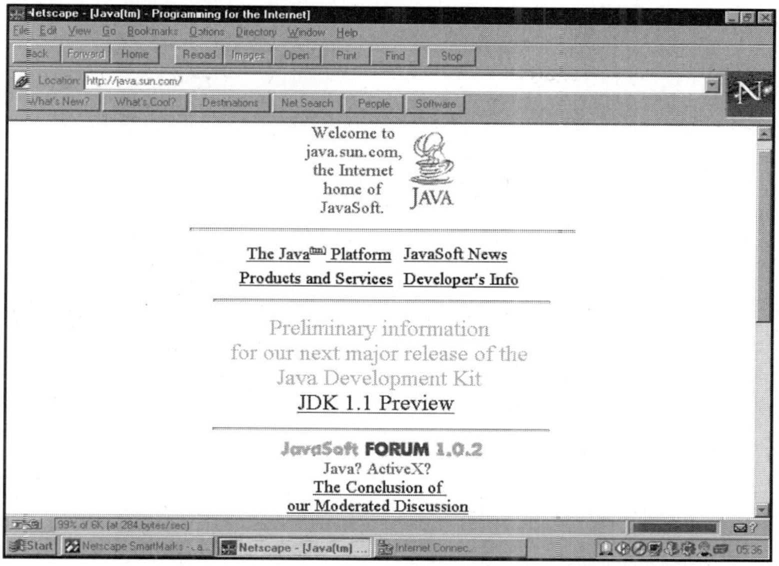

JavaWorld (`http://www.javaworld.com/`)

The first online publication devoted entirely to Java, JavaWorld (see Figure 37.10) is a monthly publication which includes hands-on tips and tricks. A programming contest, "Applet of the Month," is a regular feature. Other articles include links to source code and other helpful items.

FIGURE 37.10.
JavaWorld includes interviews with the movers and shakers in the Java realm, along with hands-on examples, tutorials, and contests.

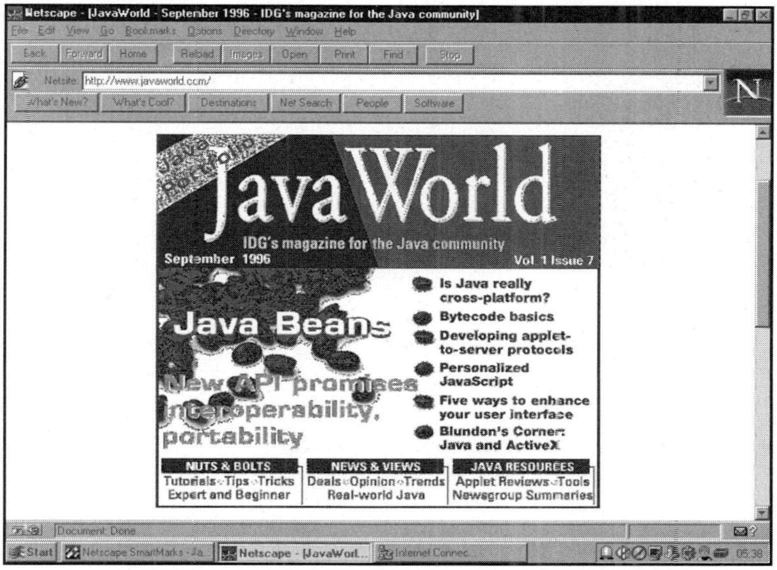

`alt.lang.java`

Although not technically a source for applets, the `alt.lang.java` newsgroup provides a great source of information about Java and its uses. Following the threads can also lead to Java applets and applications, where you can learn from people already making the most of this new language.

Summary

What I've offered on Java in this chapter is a teacup compared to the big coffee machines at Starbuck's. This chapter should have given you an idea of how applets are put together and what tools and methods are used within them to make the applet do something on the Web page.

There's a slew of books available on Java, and more are popping up every day. A good place to get your feet really wet is *Teach Yourself Java in 21 Days* by Laura Lemay and Charles Perkins.

But for now, there's one more ability you can quickly add to your toolkit of Web publishing tools—communication and interaction between JavaScript and Java. The next chapter shows you how to access your applet's methods from JavaScript and how to retrieve information about your Web page from Java using the latest capabilities.

CHAPTER 38

Integrating JavaScript and Java

by Rick Darnell

IN THIS CHAPTER

In Chapters 34 through 37, you learned about how to make Java and JavaScript a part of your Web pages. Standing alone, they are significant developments in their capability to stretch the behavior of your pages far beyond what was ever imagined for the World Wide Web.

They can become even more powerful when harnessed together. As you'll recall from earlier discussions, although Java is powerful enough to add animation, sound and other features within the confines of an applet, it's very cumbersome to directly interact with an HTML page. JavaScript isn't big or powerful enough to match Java's programming power, but it is uniquely suited to work directly with the elements that comprise an HTML document. By combining the best features of both, your applet can interact with your Web page, offering a new level of interactivity for Java and JavaScript.

Setting the Stage

In order for Java and JavaScript to interact on your Web pages, they both have to be active and enabled in the user's browser. To make sure both features are active in Netscape Navigator, follow these simple steps:

1. From the menu bar, choose `Options | Network Preferences`.
2. From the Preferences box, select the `Languages` tab (see Figure 38.1).

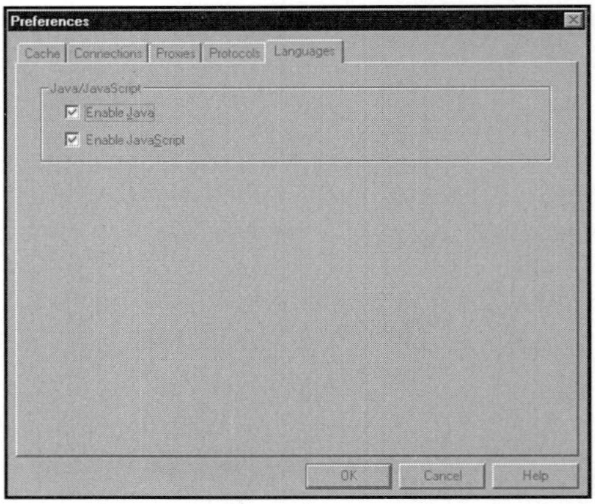

FIGURE 38.1.
The Languages tab from Network Preferences controls whether Java applets and JavaScript commands are processed for HTML documents.

3. Both Java and JavaScript are enabled by default. If this has changed, make sure both boxes are selected.

The process to make sure both languages are active in Microsoft Internet Explorer is similar to the steps for Navigator.

1. From the menu bar, choose `View | Options`.
2. From the Preferences box, select the Security tab (see Figure 38.2).

FIGURE 38.2.
Internet Explorer controls which language features are enabled from the Security tab in the Options dialog box.

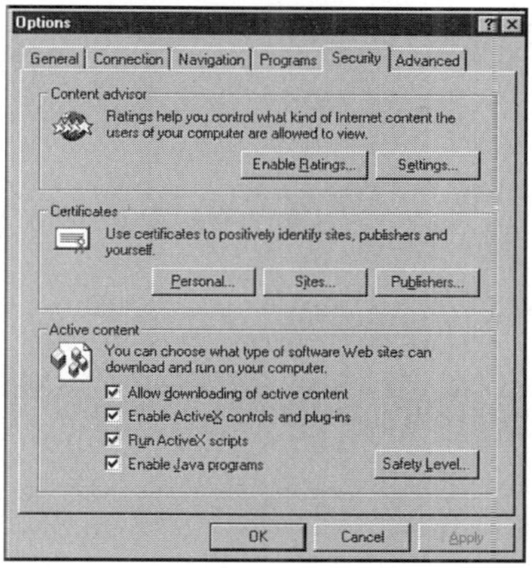

3. Make sure `Enable Java Programs` is selected. The scripting languages available in Internet Explorer, JavaScript, and Visual Basic Script are automatically enabled. There is no way to disable them.

Netscape Navigator also includes a Java Console for displaying applet-generated messages (see Figure 38.3). In addition to system messages such as errors and exceptions, it is where any messages generated by the applet using the `java.lang.System` package, including `System.out.println`, are displayed. To display the console, select `Options | Show Java Console` from the menu bar.

FIGURE 38.3.
The Java Console displays any system messages generated by the applet.

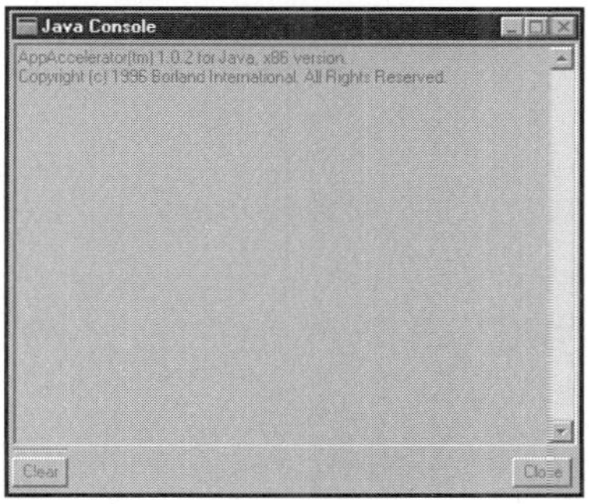

Microsoft Internet Explorer can show the results of system messages also but not in real time like the Navigator Java Console. All messages are saved in `javalog.txt` in `C:\Windows\Java`. To make sure this feature is active, select `View | Options`. In the Advanced tab of the dialog box that appears, make sure that the `Java Logging` box is selected.

Communicating with Java

The first and most commonly used feature of communication is to modify applet behavior from JavaScript. This is really quite easy to do with the right information, and allows your applet to respond to events on the HTML page, including interaction with forms. JavaScript-to-Java syntax is identical to other JavaScript object syntax, so if you're already familiar with this scripting language, adding Java control is an easy step.

Calling Java Methods

Using the new JavaScript `Packages` object, JavaScript can invoke native Java methods directly.

NOTE

Groups of related classes are combined in a construct called a package. Classes from a package are usable by outside classes by using the `import` command.

An example in all applets is the `java` package. One section of the package, `java.awt.Graphics`, is imported into every applet to give the `paint` method the additional methods it needs to add items to the applet screen. Because all applets are outside of the `java` package, its classes or subsets of those classes are imported into the applet for local use.

NOTE

Invoking native Java methods from JavaScript is only possible within Netscape Navigator 3.0 or later. It doesn't work on Microsoft Internet Explorer 3.0.

The syntax to call a Java package directly is

```
[Packages.]packageName.className.methodName
```

The object name is optional for the three default packages—`java`, `sun`, and `netscape`. These three can be referenced by their package name alone:

```
java.className.methodName
sun.className.methodName
netscape.className.methodName
```

Together with the package name, the object and class names can result in some unwieldy and error-prone typing. This is why you can also create new variables using the Package product:

```
var System = Packages.java.lang.System;
System.out.println("Hello from Java in JavaScript.");
```

Controlling Java Applets

Controlling an applet with a script is a fairly easy matter, but it does require a knowledge of the applet you're working with. Any public variable, method, or property within the applet is accessible through JavaScript.

> **TIP**
>
> If you're changing the values of variables within an applet, the safest way is to create a new method within the applet for the purpose. This method can accept the value from JavaScript, perform any error checking, then pass the new value along to the rest of the applet. This helps prevent unexpected behavior or applet crashes.

You need to know which methods, properties and variables are public. Only the public items in an applet are accessible to JavaScript.

> **TIP**
>
> There are two public methods which are common to all applets which you can always use—`start` and `stop`. These provide a handy means to control when the applet is active and running.

> **NOTE**
>
> There are five basic activities common to all applets, as opposed to one basic activity for applications. An applet has more activities to correspond to the major events in its life cycle on the user's browser.
>
> None of the activities have any definitions. You must override the methods with a subclass within your applet.
>
> Initialization—Occurs after the applet is first loaded. This can include creating objects, setting state variables, and loading images.
>
> Starting—After initialization or stopping, an applet is started. The difference between initialization and starting is that initialization only happens once, while starting can occur many times.
>
> Painting—This method is how the applet actually gets information to the screen, from simple lines and text to images and colored backgrounds. Painting can occur a lot of times in the course of an applets life.
>
> *continues*

continued

Stopping–Stopping suspends the applet execution and stops it from using system resources. This can be important since an applet continues to run even after a user leaves the page.

Destroying–This is the extreme form of stop. Destroying an applet begins a clean-up process in which running threads are terminated and objects are released.

With this information in hand, getting started begins with the `<APPLET>` tag. It helps to give a name to your applet to make JavaScript references to it easier to read This isn't absolutely necessary as JavaScript creates an array of applets when the page is loaded. However, it does make for a much more readable page.

```
<APPLET CODE="UnderConstruction" NAME="AppletConstruction" WIDTH=60 HEIGHT=60>
</APPLET>
```

To use a method of the applet from JavaScript, use the following syntax:

```
document.appletName.methodOrProperty
```

TIP

Netscape Navigator 3.0 includes an applets array which is used to reference all of the applets on a page. These are used according to the following syntax.

```
document.applets[index].methodOrProperty
document.applets[appletName].methodOrProperty
```

These two methods also identify the applet you want to control, but the method using the applet's name without the applets array is the easiest to read and requires the least amount of typing.

Like the other arrays, a property of `applets` is `length`, which returns how many applets are in the document.

This array of applets is not currently available in the Microsoft Internet Explorer implementation of JavaScript.

One of the easy methods of controlling applet behavior is starting and stopping its execution. This can be accomplished using the `start` and `stop` methods—common to every applet. Use a form and two buttons to add the functions to your Web page (see Figure 38.4):

```
<FORM>
<INPUT TYPE="button" VALUE="Start" onClick="document.appletName.start()">
<INPUT TYPE="button" VALUE="Stop" onClick="document.appletName.stop()">
</FORM>
```

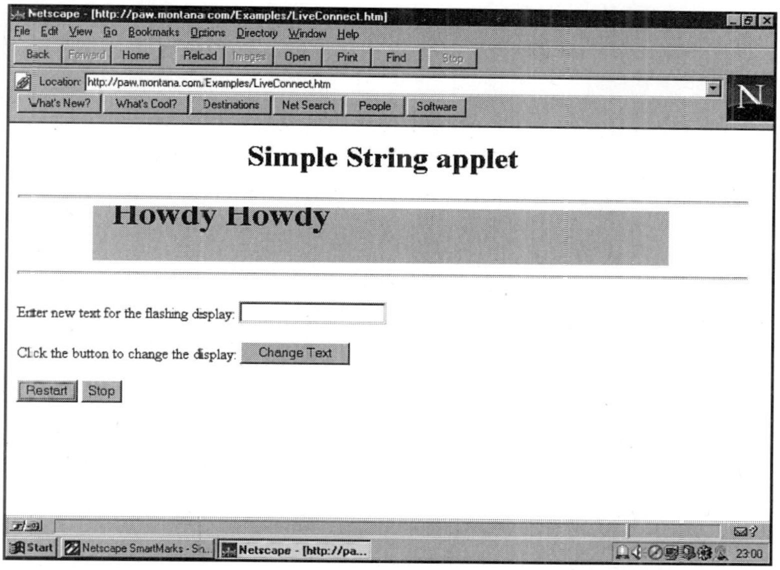

FIGURE 38.4.
One of the simplest methods of controlling an applet is to use buttons to start and stop it.

You can also call other methods, depending on their visibility to the world outside the applet. Any method or variable with a `public` declaration can be called by JavaScript.

TIP

Any variable or method within the applet which doesn't include a specific declaration of scope is `protected` by default. If you don't see the `public` declaration, it's not.

The syntax to call applet methods from JavaScript is simple and can be integrated with browser events such as the preceding button code snippet:

```
document.appletName.methodName(arg1,arg2,arg3)
```

Communicating with JavaScript

With the addition of a new set of classes provided with Netscape Navigator 3.0, Java can take a direct look at your HTML page through JavaScript objects. This requires the use of the `netscape.javascript.JSObject` class when the applet is created.

TIP

`netscape.javascript.JSObject` is included with the other class files under the Netscape directory. In Windows, this is `\Program Files\Netscape\Navigator\Program\java\classes\java_30`. In order for your Java program to compile, create a folder set called `\netscape\javascript` elsewhere on your hard drive, such as under the `\java\lib` folder. Copy the file to the new folder, and make sure your `CLASSPATH` variable includes `C:\java\lib\` in its list. After you restart the computer, the Java compiler should be able to find the new classes. This new package extends the standard Java Object class, so the newly created JSObjects are treated the same as other Java objects are.

TIP

For normal use, the `java` package is all you need to use. The `netscape` package includes methods and properties for Java to reach out to JavaScript and HTML and is covered later in this chapter. The last package, sun, includes platform-specific and system utility classes.

CLASSES IN THE `java` PACKAGE

There are five subsets of classes within the `java` package:

`lang`—These classes and interfaces are the core of the Java language. This subset includes the `Runnable` interface (used for threading) and the basic data types (Boolean, character, class, integer, object, string, etc.). It also includes the `System` class, which provides access to system-level behaviors.

`util`—This group of utility interfaces and classes aren't crucial to running Java, but they provide ways to make programming easier. It includes utilities to generate random numbers, stacks, hash tables, and dates.

`awt`—The Abstract Windowing Toolkit (also known as Another Windows Toolkit) contains the graphical items to help create user interfaces and other graphical items. It includes interfaces for a layout manager and menu container, along with classes for form elements, colors, keyboard and mouse events, fonts, images, menus, and windows.

`io`—Used for passing information in and out of applets and applications, this subset includes classes for sending and receiving input streams and files, not including networking activity (see `net`).

`net`—This subset of classes has the tools and operations for working over a network. This group includes methods and interfaces to handle URLs, URL content, and socket connections.

To include the JSObject class as part of your applet, use the `import` command as you would normally include any other class package.

```
import netscape.javascript.JSObject;
```

An important addition is also necessary in the applet tag—`MAYSCRIPT`. This is a security feature which gives specific permission for the applet to access JavaScript objects.

```
<APPLET CODE="colorPreview.class" WIDTH=50 HEIGHT=50 NAME="Preview" MAYSCRIPT>
```

Without it, any attempt to access JavaScript from the applet results in an exception. If you wish to exclude an applet from accessing the page, simply leave out the MAYSCRIPT parameter.

Java and JavaScript Values

`JSObject` gives Java the ability to look at and change objects defined through JavaScript. This requires certain assumptions, especially when passing or receiving values from Java. Every JavaScript value is assigned some form from `java.lang.Object` to ensure compatibility.

- Objects—Any object sent or received from Java remains in its original object wrapper.
- Java numbers—Since JavaScript doesn't support the variety of numerical types as Java (byte, char, short, int, long, float, and double), they lose their specific type and become a basic JavaScript number.

NOTE

A Java float is a 32-bit floating point number. A version for larger numbers or greater precision behind the decimal point is the double, which is 64 bits long. Bytes, shorts, ints, and longs are all integers of various bit lengths, beginning with 8 bits for the byte and going up to 64 bits for the long. A char is a 16-bit number representing a single Unicode character.

- JavaScript numbers—There's no way to tell what kind of number Java may be receiving from JavaScript. So, all JavaScript numbers are converted to Java floats.
- Booleans and Strings—These are passed essentially unchanged. Java Booleans become JavaScript Booleans and vice versa. The same occurs with strings.

Looking at the JavaScript Window

In order to get a handle on JavaScript objects, including form items and frames, you must create an object to hold the current Navigator window first. `getWindow` provides the means.

First, you'll need to create a new: variable of type `JSObject`:

```
JSObject jsWin;
```

Then, using the JSObject class, assign the window to the variable:

```
jsWin = JSObject.getWindow(this);
```

This type of work is typically accomplished within the applet's `init()` method.

After you have a handle on the window, you can start to break it apart into its various components with `getMember`. This method returns a specific object from the next level of precedence. For example, to get a handle on a form on a Web page with a form called `response`, the following set of statements can be used:

```
jsWin = JSObject.getWindow(this);
JSObject jsDoc = (JSObject) jsWin.getMember("document");
JSObject responseForm = (JSObject) jsDoc.getMember("response");
```

In JavaScript, this form is referred to as `window.document.response`. Note that each JavaScript object is assigned to its own variable in Java and is not a property of a parent object. The form in Java is contained in `responseForm`, not `jsWin.jsDoc.responseForm`.

NOTE

All parts of an HTML document exist in JavaScript in set relationships to each other. This is called instance hierarchy since it works with specific items on the page rather than general classes of items.

At the top of the pyramid is the `window` object. It is the parent of all other objects. Its children include `document`, `location`, `history`, which share a precedence level. `document`'s children include objects specific to the page, such as forms, links, anchors, and applets.

The Java `netscape` package recognizes and uses this hierarchy through its `getWindow` and `getMethod` methods. `getWindow` gets the window object (the highest object), while `getMethod` returns individual members of the next level.

So far, you've only retrieved broad objects, such as windows and forms. Getting a specific value from JavaScript follows the same principles, although now you need a Java variable of the proper type to hold the results instead of an instance of JSObject.

TIP

Don't forget about passing numbers between JavaScript and Java. All JavaScript numbers are converted to a float. You can cast it to another Java type if needed once it's in the applet.

Using the preceding form, let's say there's a text field (`name`), a number (`idNum`), and a checkbox (`member`). Each of these values is retrieved from JavaScript using the following commands:

```
jsWin = JSObject.getWindow(this);
JSObject jsDoc = (JSObject) jsWin.getMember("document");
JSObject responseForm = (JSObject) jsDoc.getMember("response");
JSObject nameField = (JSObject) responseForm.getMember("name");
JSOBject idNumField = (JSObject) responseForm.getMember("idNum");
JSOBject memberField = (JSObject) responseForm.getMember("memberField");
String nameValue = (String) nameField.getMember("value");
Float idNumValue = (Float) idNumField.getMember("value");
Boolean memberValue = (Boolean) memberField.getMember("checked");
```

This chunk of code becomes a bit unwieldy, especially when there are several values needed from JavaScript. If you need to access more than several elements on a page, it helps to create a new method to handle the process.

```
protected JSObject getElement(String formName, String elementName) {
    JSObject jsDoc = (JSObject) JSObject.getWindow().getMember("document");
    JSObject jsForm = (JSObject) jsDoc.getMember(formName);
    JSObject jsElement = (JSObject) jsElement.gerMember(elementName);
    return jsElement;
}
```

This simple method creates the intervening JSObjects needed to get to the form element, making the retrieval as easy as knowing the form and element name.

To change a JavaScript value, use the JSObject `setMember` method in Java. The syntax is `setMember(`*`name`*`, `*`value`*`)`, with the name of the JavaScript object and its new value.

```
JSObject nameField = getElement("response","name");
nameField.setMember("name","Your Name Here");
```

This snippet uses the `getElement` method just defined to get the `name` element from the `response` form, and then uses the JSObject method `setMember` to set its value to `Your Name Here`. This is equivalent to `this.`*`name`*` = `*`newValue`* in JavaScript.

The two methods covered in this section (`getWindow`, `getMember`), are the basic methods used when interfacing with JavaScript. Together, it makes receiving values from an HTML page by way of JavaScript a straightforward task, even if it is a little cumbersome in the number of statements needed to accomplish it.

Getting Values Using Indexes

If your applet is designed to work with a variety of HTML pages which may contain different names for forms and elements, you can use the JavaScript arrays with the JSObject slot methods. If the desired form is always the first to appear on the document and the element is the third, then the form name is `forms[0]` and the element is `elements[2]`.

After retrieving the document object using `getWindow` and `getMember`, use `getSlot(index)` to return a value within it. For example, in an HTML document containing three forms, the second is retrieved into Java using the following commands:

```
JSObject jsWin = JSObject.getWindow(this);
JSObject jsDoc = (JSObject) jsWin.getMember("document");
JSObject jsForms = (JSObject) jsDoc.getMember("forms");
JSObject jsForm1 = (JSObject) jsForms.getSlot(1);
```

Using `setSlot`, the same process is used to load a value into an array. The syntax is

```
JSObject.setSlot(index,value);
```

where the index is an integer and the value is a string, Boolean or float.

TIP

The one rule which must stand firm in this case is the placement of the form and elements within it. When the applet is used with more than one document, the forms and elements must be in the same relative place every time to avoid exceptions and unpredictable results.

Using JavaScript Methods in Java

The `netscape` class package provides two methods to call JavaScript methods from within an applet—`call` and `eval`. The syntax between the two is slightly different, but the outcome is the same. Note that you need a handle for the JavaScript window before you can use these methods.

There are two ways to invoke these methods. The first uses a specific window instance, while the second uses `getWindow` to create a JavaScript window just for the expression.

```
jsWin.callOrEval(arguments)
JSOBject.getWindow().callOrEval(arguments)
```

The `call` method separates the method from its arguments. This is useful for passing Java values to the JavaScript method. The syntax is `call("method", args)`, where the method is the name of the method you want to call and the arguments you want to pass are contained in an array.

`eval`, on the other hand, uses a string which appears identical to the way a method is called within JavaScript. The syntax is `eval("expression")`, where the expression is a complete method name and its arguments, such as `document.writeln("Your name here.'")`. Including it in the `eval` expression results in `eval("document.writeln(\"Your name here.\");")`.

TIP

To pass quotation marks as quotation marks to JavaScript within a Java string, use the backslash character before each occurrence.

Now you have a whole set of tools to get from JavaScript to Java and back again. The marriage of these two Web technologies can open up a whole new world of how to interact with your users. Using simple statements and definitions—already a part of both languages—a previously static Web page can communicate with an applet imbedded in it, and in return react to the output of the applet. It's just one more set of capabilities in your toolbox that you can use to meet your users' needs.

Summary

The last logical step with Java and JavaScript is allowing them to work and communicate with each other. Accessing an applet's methods and public variables from JavaScript and allowing the Java applet to take a look and modify HTML through JavaScript objects extends the capability of both languages, although it still doesn't allow either one to be the complete equal.

As described in Chapter 36, "Including Java Applets in Your Web Pages," Java and JavaScript are tailored to different types of applications. But by being able to coordinate activities between the two, you can extend the interactivity of your Web pages to more powerful and useful levels.

IX
Part

IN THIS PART

Creating VRML Worlds

CHAPTER 39

Introduction to VRML

by Justin Couch

IN THIS CHAPTER

When most people think of the Web they think of the 2D page. Sometimes this is spruced up with some pretty graphics, maybe a bit of sound or video, but seldom do 3D worlds come to mind. With the release of Netscape 3.0, the ability to explore virtual worlds is built into the basic browser with the Live3D plug-in. These virtual worlds are built with the emerging standard called Virtual Reality Modeling Language or VRML.

In this chapter, I present an overview of what VRML is, what you can do with it, how to view it, and some of the basic tools needed to create it. The next chapter presents additional technical issues about how the latest version of the language is written.

What Is VRML?

In its simplest form, VRML allows you to create platform-independent 3D objects. It is a 3D equivalent to HTML, but has more capabilities than just putting a 3D shop on your Web page. VRML and HTML have a number of things in common. Both are written as text files, they can be shown on any type of computer with the appropriate browser, and they are not the first of their kind, but they are the most popular because they are in the right place at the right time.

The first version of VRML was created by taking Silicon Graphics' Open Inventor file format and tweaking it to work with the Internet. This was the result of a meeting at the First International Conference on the World Wide Web. Mark Pesce and Tony Parisi had developed a demo program called Labyrinth that showed the use of a platform-independent graphics format. At this same conference, Tim Berners-Lee and David Ragget (the inventors of HTML and HTTP) held a discussion forum about what was then termed the Virtual Reality Markup Language. Shortly after this, Modeling was substituted for Markup in the name.

VRML's designers wanted to create a platform-independent way to send 3D worlds across the Internet. For this to work, the file format had to describe where objects were placed in 3D space and their attributes such as color. VRML browsers would run on everything from powerful UNIX workstations to humble desktop PCs. Silicon Graphics offered the Open Inventor file format for use which was greatly accepted. A number of changes were made to make it compatible with the Internet and World Wide Web. This was released in May 1995. Following a number of different interpretations, a clarified version called 1.0c was then issued in January 1996.

In December 1995 it was proposed that the next version of VRML incorporate simple behaviors. Like everything else in the development of VRML, new pieces were being done bits at a time. VRML 1.0 described only static scenes. VRML 2.0 included programmable behavior but not the multiuser virtual environments of William Gibson's cyberspace. They could be built on top of VRML 2.0, but multi-user virtual environments are not part of the language specification. The official VRML 2.0 spec was released on August 4, 1996—the opening day of SIGGRAPH, one of the most important conferences for the international graphics community.

VRML 1.0 Versus 2.0

There are now two official versions of VRML. However, unlike HTML versions, there is no backward compatibility. You need to make a choice of the version that you are going to produce. The first version was deliberately limited to creating static scenes. In this way it is not much better than a standard Web page. A user can wander about, click on links to other worlds or pages, and enjoy the scenery, but that is all. The second version of VRML introduces programmable behaviors—meaning that things are really starting to live up to that virtual reality tag.

Along with the addition of behaviors, VRML 2.0 adds many other things. The most important for general world design is the ability to incorporate real 3D sound and video file formats. From a world creator's point of view, however, other changes are even more significant. The major difference between versions is the completely different approach to creating VR worlds. To incorporate behaviors into the version 1.0 file format would have required a lot of messy additions. Worlds which were created in the version 1.0 format can't simply have extra information added to put in the behaviors. A whole new system needed to be drawn up. At the file level everything—even the header—is different.

VRML Product Availability

Judging by the experience with tools for VRML 1.0, you may think that the browsers are available first and then the authoring tools catch up. In fact, it is the other way around. Many of the products that had VRML 1.0 exporters built in were very quickly updated to produce the same output in 2.0 format. However these tools were still only capable of doing the same things—static scenes. This has the immediate advantage that you can get in and start generating output straight away.

Browsers are a lot further from being completed. With the addition of behaviors, VRML 2.0 is much more complex than the original version. At the time of this writing, there were only three browsers available for 2.0 as compared to the 10-15 available for the original version. However Netscape's own VRML browser, Live3D, supports VRML 2.0 from version 2 on. This has the obvious advantage that the capabilities of VRML are available on everyone's desktop sooner rather than later.

Not only are there dedicated VRML browsers and modelers, but almost all of the major 3D modeling packages include support through either plug-in exporters or native capabilities. This has the great advantage that you can use your current skills to create content for a new audience.

For the rest of this chapter, I introduce some of the types of tools that you can use to create VRML files. If you want to know how to write a VRML 2.0 file, take a look at the next chapter for an overview.

Types of Browsers

VRML browsers come in two types: stand-alone and plug-ins for HTML browsers. With the speed at which Netscape is currently moving, your latest version of Navigator includes Live3D, a VRML plug-in, as standard. This is good news, because you can assume that most people have VRML capabilities. However, the Live3D plug-in is only capable of displaying VRML 1.0 files, so you need an alternative to view 2.0 worlds.

If you're going to view only your VRML world, then a stand-alone browser works satisfactorily. However, if you're planning to create mixed HTML and VRML worlds, particularly using Frames, then you need a plug-in browser. Stand-alone browsers offer one advantage—you can run your VRML browser and your HTML browser at the same time. A frames-based approach limits the user's ability to wander —look at full-sized documents—particularly if the user wants the 3D world to be a constant reference point for exploring various documents.

CAUTION

VRML worlds may look different depending on what browser you use, just as HTML pages look different when running on two different browsers. For example, one of the biggest problems with the first-generation browsers was that the colors seemed different between them. Where one browser made the world look very bright, another, even running on the same machine, made it look darker.

Netscape and Live3D

One of the most common VRML browsers on the desktop is Live3D, Netscape's own VRML browser. Live3D is distributed as a standard part of browsers from Navigator version 3 onward. It offers most of the standard features that you find in the other browsers. The browser with Navigator 3 is only capable of viewing VRML 1.0 worlds. To view VRML 2.0 worlds, you need to get one of the browsers mentioned later in the chapter. Netscape will no doubt update their browser to be compliant with 2.0 in the future. The following sections look at how to navigate VRML worlds via the Live3D browser.

Microsoft and ActiveVRML

Before the VRML development community moved to the second version of the VRML specification, a call went out to all interested parties for their proposals. Six submissions were received from Silicon Graphics/Sony, Apple, Microsoft, Sun, IBM, and the German National Research Center for Information Technology (GMD). Of these, the Moving Worlds proposal by SGI and Sony was accepted by popular vote to be the starting point for version 2. As a result, Microsoft took their proposal, which was called ActiveVRML, and started marketing it against VRML 2.0.

Although it does have the potential to read VRML 1.0 files, ActiveVRML is no longer true VRML, as decided by the VRML Architecture Group (VAG)—the controlling body of the VRML standards development group. Microsoft released an alpha version of their ActiveVRML browser in January 1996, but little has been seen of them since then.

Microsoft has stated its support for VRML 2.0 standard by licensing the core technology from DimensionX (`http://www.dimensionx.com/`), which makes Liquid Reality—a Java-based VRML toolkit.

Intervista's WorldView

WorldView is available either as a stand-alone program or as a plug-in to Netscape 1.x and above, as well as for Microsoft's Internet Explorer. WorldView has one advantage over Live3D in that it can run with whatever your favorite browser environment is. The screen shot presented in Figure 39.1 shows the stand-alone version.

One of WorldView's nice features is its ability to nominate your own camera positions while navigating a world and then return back to them. The rendering is very smooth, but it isn't very accurate for handling mesh objects.

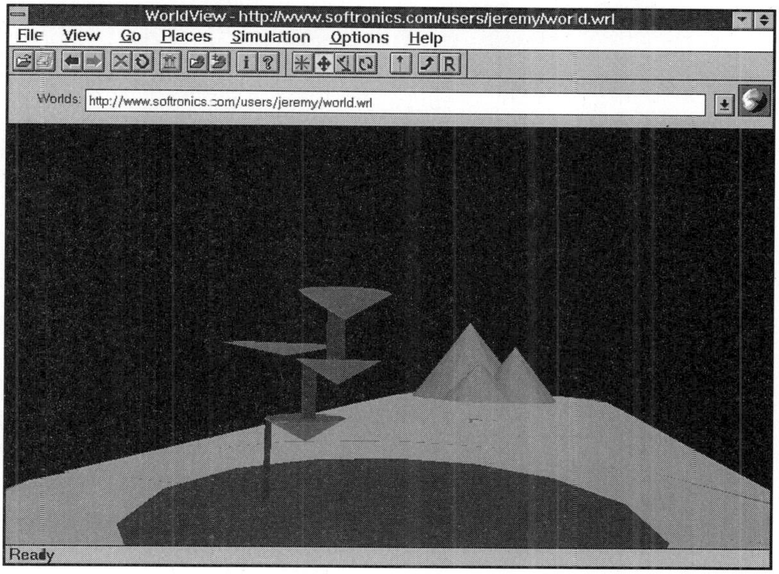

FIGURE 39.1.
InterVista's WorldView Browser.

Chaco Communications VR Scout

VR Scout was the first VRML 1.0 browser released that didn't belong to Silicon Graphics. As a result, it's one of the most developed and stable browsers of the current crop. It is also one of the strictest browsers in terms of compliance with the specification. If your file doesn't load and run in VR Scout, you should definitely go back and fix it up until it does.

The rendering of objects with VR Scout is more accurate than WorldView—particularly large mesh objects (see Figure 39.2). But this means that the performance is not as good even though both programs have the same underlying rendering library. In my general experience, VR Scout performs at about half the speed of WorldView, although it will be different for each person. Accurate measurement is really not possible.

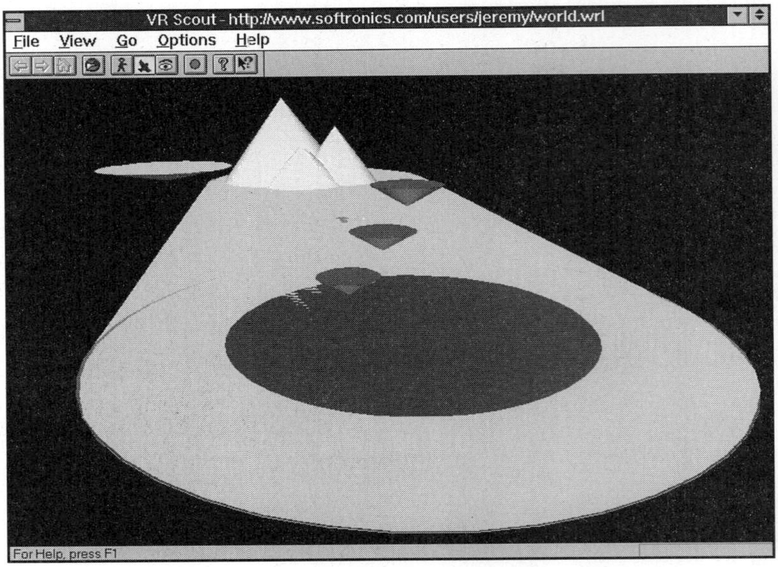

FIGURE 39.2.
Chaco's VR Scout.

SGI's CosmoPlayer

When VRML changed file format so radically from version 1.0, SGI's Open Inventor-based browser, WebSpace, was no longer able to support VRML 2.0. So SGI started from scratch.

CosmoPlayer comes with its own stand-alone converter so that it can be used for VRML 1.0 files. This sometimes causes problems with files that aren't quite compliant with VRML 1.0c because it either won't display them or, even worse, only half displays them. The converter supports Netscape's Spin and SpinGroup extension nodes and turns them into legal VRML 2.0 files using the standard nodes.

Early releases of CosmoPlayer support VRMLScript, which is a derivative of Netscape's JavaScript, for programming simple behaviors. Later versions will also include Java support as well as a Java interface to control the VRML world. Although this does limit some of the potential functionality, all the common behavioral tasks can be constructed. It is available as a Netscape plug-in and Internet Explorer plug-in using the Netscape compatibility option. Figure 39.3 gives you a glimpse of CosmoPlayer.

FIGURE 39.3.
Silicon Graphics' CosmoPlayer. This early beta contains a different dashboard from what you will probably see in the final product.

Sony's CyberPassage

CyberPassage was the first VRML 2.0 browser to be available. (Yes, Sony does produce things other than TVs and stereo systems.) In the second version, it now supports VRML 2.0 and retains the same svelte interface of the first version (see Figure 39.4). CyberPassage only operates as a stand-alone product, which is a bit of a pity, but its very fast rendering puts it ahead of CosmoPlayer on most aspects.

CyberPassage supports Java for scripting, which makes it much more extensible when you need to do that little something extra such as talking to a network or running multithreaded behaviors within a script. It still retains its multi-user capabilities from the first version. These capabilities allow you to participate in virtual worlds with people from around the globe in real-time.

MACINTOSH BROWSERS

The range of browsers for the Macintosh is much more limited. The main one is Live3D, which is included with Netscape Navigator. Live3D is only VRML 1.0-compliant at the time of this writing.

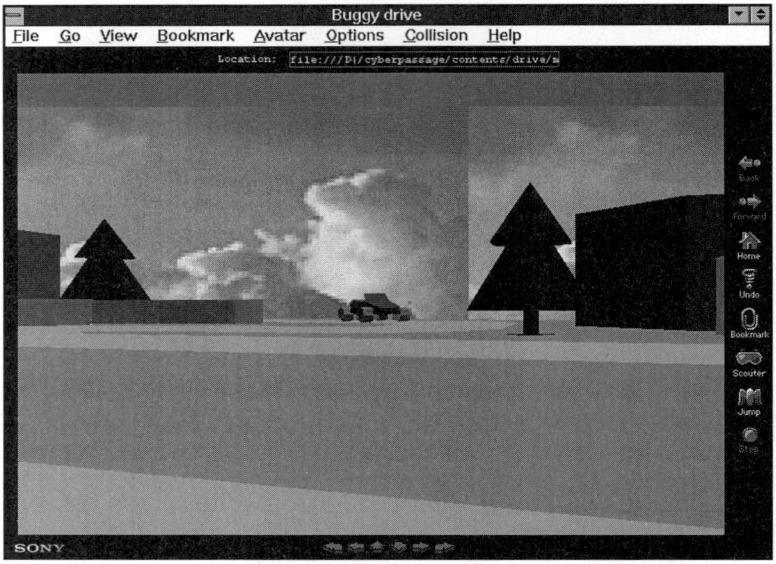

FIGURE 39.4.
The black interface of Sony's CyberPassage makes it fit in with the rest of Sony's electronic products.

VRML Modeling Tools

For most people, the easiest and quickest way to construct a VRML world is to use a modeling package. Modelers can be divided into three categories: those that export to another format and use an external converter, those with internal support through plug-in exporters or native exporters, and those dedicated to VRML tools.

VRML Exports from Traditional Tools

One of the first ways that complex VRML models were constructed was with non-VRML modeling tools like AutoDesk's 3D Studio and Caligari's TrueSpace. These tools export to a standard format like DXF, which then has a third-party converter like `wcvt2pov` change that into VRML. This provides a very quick working base for many VRML worlds because they can leverage existing knowledge to get going.

Today a number of these tools contain plug-in exporters that can automatically produce VRML output files. One of the most widely used is Syndesis Corporation's Interchange, which acts as a plug-in file exporter for most popular modeling tools which supports VRML 2.0 export. However, it only exports static scenes. Another exporter comes from Kinetix which plugs into 3D Studio. This exporter uses the whole capability of the 3DS products. All of your animations and scene details are reproduced in the VRML file.

Dedicated VRML Modelers

One of the more interesting results of VRML is the number of software companies that have released separate, dedicated VRML authoring tools, which are based on their non-VRML modeling tools. The next section looks at several of these.

Like all things, the best way to produce a product is to use a tool designed for the job. There are a wide range of tools available, ranging from those that barely hide VRML from you to those that can create any sort of file format. This section examines three of the most popular tools used in the VRML community today. They are all VRML 1.0 tools, but upgraded versions that export to VRML 2.0 will be released.

The range of tools is quite wide. At one end of the spectrum you have IDS's VRealm Builder. If you really want to learn VRML while you're creating a scene, then VR-Builder is the software for you. It presents a four-view layout on the right side while you see the structure of the VRML file graphically produced on the left (see Figure 39.5).

At the other end of the spectrum is Caligari's Pioneer. Pioneer is a spin-off from Caligari's TrueSpace product, which you may be familiar with already in your other Web graphics work. It contains the same user interface, but has been modified to handle the VRML way of doing things (see Figure 39.6). Pioneer used to be known as Fountain but not much else has changed about it.

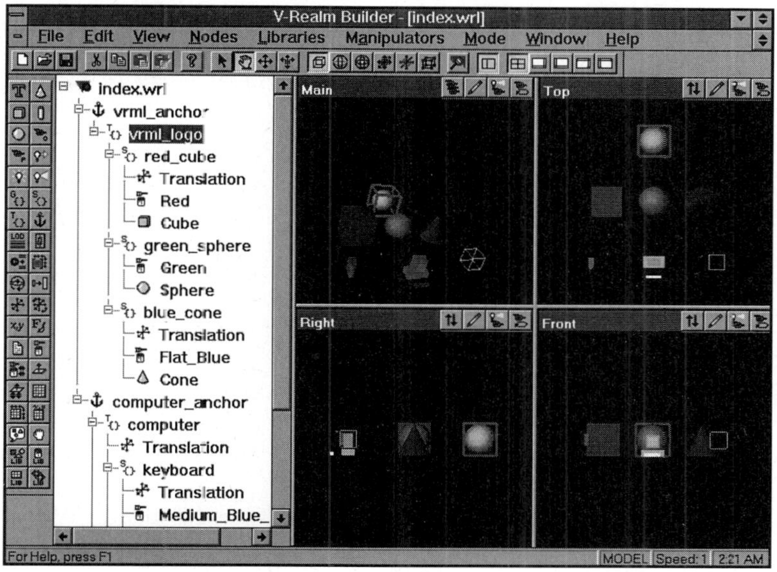

FIGURE 39.5.
VRealm Builder being used to construct the basics of the author's original home world.

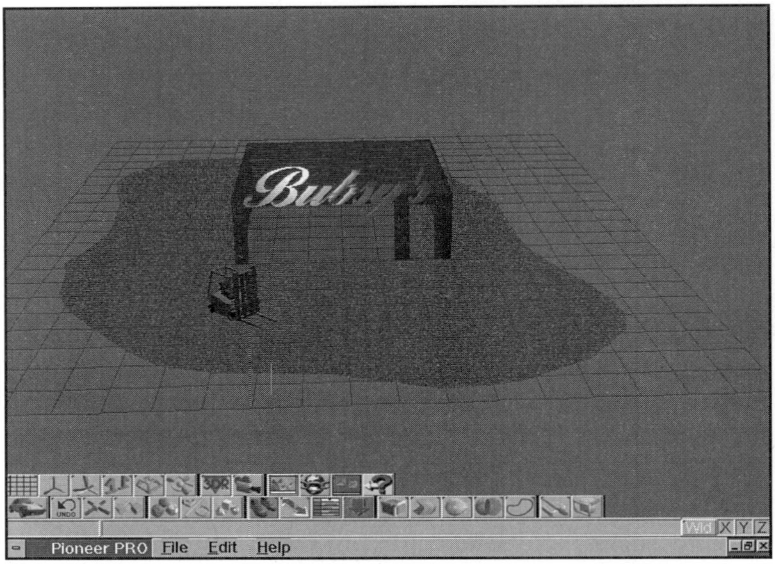

FIGURE 39.6.
Caligari's Pioneer in action.

Naturally there is a whole collection of various modeling tools in between. You can pick the amount of VRML that you want to learn up front and then find a tool for it. With tools like Pioneer, you may never know that you are creating VRML. However at some stage, you will eventually have to learn how to write it in order to tweak the file format and the scene.

Setting up the Web Server

Once you have created your VRML file, you want to be able let the world see it. VRML files end with the extension `.wrl`. Sometimes you may see them end with `.wrl.gz`. These are files that have been compressed to make them smaller. Both kinds are legal, and the Web browsers will handle them properly without you having worry about it.

On the server end, you need to make sure that your Web server is configured for the correct MIME type. Most servers come with the configuration already done, but you need to check that it serves up the type of `x-world/x-vrml` for VRML files. In October 1996, the top-level MIME type of `model` was approved. VRML will belong under this type as the type `model/vrml`.

At the time of writing, no VRML browsers were capable of handling this new type. This capability should be available as new releases of the browsers come out, but it would be best to check before you go ahead and set up this type.

Summary

VRML is now starting to gain critical mass for Web support. With Netscape support in its latest versions of Navigator, you can be sure that any VRML content that you create can be seen by almost everyone visiting your site. There are now a number of modeling tools available to create your content quickly but eventually you need to learn how it works.

In the next chapter, you are shown how to write a VRML 2.0 world by hand. If VRML is of interest to you, then read on because the capabilities are quite wide. VRML will be used for more than just a few personal home pages.

CHAPTER 40

Creating VRML 2.0 Worlds

by Justin Couch

IN THIS CHAPTER

In the preceding chapter, you looked at using various tools to create 3D worlds for the Internet. These tools were based on the original VRML 1.0 standard. In this chapter, I introduce the latest version of the VRML standard: version 2.0

There are quite a few differences between the two versions. To start with, the new version includes the capability to animate the world within the language and add programmable behaviors, using languages such as JavaScript and Java. To accommodate these additions, the whole language has been reconstructed from the ground up.

Why VRML 2.0?

Before introducing the differences between the two versions, there are a couple of choices to be made. The first choice to make is how you want to create your worlds. The original version of VRML is now fairly mature. There are many good tools available to create worlds without even looking at source code. The range of products extend from plug-in modules to traditional 3D modeling tools like 3D Studio to stand-alone applications like Caligari's Pioneer.

VRML 2.0 was released on August 4, 1996, which means that the variety of tools is just not there. Like all new technologies, this means you will be reduced to the most basic of editing tools—the text editor. As usual though, there will be an array of tools hitting the market within months of the release, so if you are not into becoming intimate with Notepad, vi, or emacs, then I suggest you wait a few months before diving into creating 2.0 worlds.

The next choice is what do you want to get from VRML? If all you need to do is create a static object that people can wander around in, then it does not matter what version of VRML you require. The differences between the two versions are such that the new browsers will support VRML 2.0, but not the other way around. Designing for the latest version is probably the best choice because you can always start with the static world and then add the dynamic extras at a later date without a ground up rewrite.

Once you have decided to move to version 2.0, then the final decision is to determine to what extent you want to use it. VRML 2.0 provides more than just 3D scenes. As mentioned in the introduction, VRML now includes the ability to create arbitrary behaviors. It includes native support for 3D sound and video input as well.

Introduction to VRML 2.0

Having decided that VRML 2.0 sounds like a good thing and you wish to learn a bit about it, you need to learn how it works. What makes 2.0 so different from 1.0?

The first thing that you will probably notice is all the field types are different. Like much of the new version, it was discovered that the old types were no longer sufficient to handle behavior and animation so they were scrapped in favor of the new ones. The old MF/SF prefix still applies, but the rest of the types have changed. Most of them are self-explanatory, so they aren't discussed here.

Starting with the File Header

VRML files are characterized by the first line which states the type of file, the version, and the type of character encoding. The standard VRML 1.0 header looks like the following:

```
#VRML V1.0 ascii
```

With the change in specification and the drive towards internationalization of software, version two followed the same path. Now VRML is encoded as UTF8 (a close relative of Unicode used in Windows 95/NT). The new header now looks like the following:

```
#VRML V2.0 utf8
```

In some early files, you may see the words `Draft #n` placed in there as well. This was to indicate to the browser that the file conformed to the draft standard of the specification. This should not worry you because the normal ASCII of your text editor is a subset of UTF8; however, it is good to be warned in case you find any of these floating around.

Organizing the Kids

VRML 1.0, as you may remember, is based on knowing the order in which the nodes are declared to achieve a certain effect. This is no longer the case. Instead, VRML 2.0 uses a tree-type structure in the file. This mimics much of the way the real world works.

Look at your arm and hand, for example. When you decide to move your arm, both the arm and the hand move at the same time. However, you can move the whole hand without moving the arm. The hand represents a child, and the arm is the parent. However, you have two hands, one for each arm, so you only need to declare one hand and include it on both arms.

When you read through a VRML 2.0 file, you will notice that if a node is capable of having children, it includes a field called, naturally enough, `children`. However, the order that you declare the nodes within that `children` field no longer matters. If a node is to effect the properties of another, it must be higher up the hierarchy, rather than just simply placed before it in the file.

Basic Node Concepts

In VRML 1.0, there is no explicit concept of the parent-child relationship. VRML 2.0 is very strict about it. There are a collection of rules about what nodes are legal and where. For instance, a geometry node like `Box` cannot exist by itself. It must be a child of the Shape node.

There are two broad categories of nodes: Group and Leaf nodes. Group nodes are those that can contain other nodes, even more Group nodes, but the Leaf nodes cannot contain others.To confuse the issue a bit, a Leaf node is not strictly the end of the hierarchy. A Shape node is classified as a Leaf node, yet it is the only way that geometry nodes can be made visible. The difference is that the Shape node is only allowed two children, and they are of a specified type; the Group node can contain any number of children of (almost) any type.

If you are still confused, read on. A few examples will illustrate how this works.

Each to His Own

The final difference is how the various parts of the syntax hang together. In VRML 1.0, there is a bit of cross-fertilization of the functionality between nodes. This has been completely removed with the 2.0.

Each node now is designed for a specific purpose. For example, the geometry nodes only contain information about the geometry; what the radius is or how it is for example. They contain no information about where they are located in space or what color they are.

In many ways, you can control the scene much more than before because it is easy to locate the source of a particular problem. A wrong position means that you need to fix the transformation node, not the color node.

A Tree – the First Example

One of the most common items in a VR world based on a real-world theme is the humble tree. This example shows how to use the basics of VRML: color, geometry, transformations, and the node hierarchy.

Starting at the Bottom

The basic tree consists of a brown trunk and a couple of cones to produce the leaves. To start the tree, we need a brown cylindrical trunk. In the previous section, I mentioned that you need a certain relationship between the nodes. Examine the code presented in Listing 40.1.

Listing 40.1. A complete VRML file to produce the trunk of a tree.

```
#VRML V2.0 utf8
Shape {
    appearance Appearance {
        material Material { emissiveColor  0.4 0.4 0.1 }
    }
    geometry Cylinder {
        height 1
        radius 0.25
    }
}
```

In this file, you find there are four nodes used: *Shape*, *Appearance*, *Material*, and *Cylinder*. The Shape node is the overall controlling parent. None of the other nodes are legal unless they have this parent. Next you see that the word `appearance` is written twice. The first one is one of the fields of Shape node, and the second is the declaration of the Appearance node. It seems strange to do this; however, you will notice that this is common right across the VRML nodes. If a node (for example, Shape) is to have a particular node as the child for a field (for example, `Appearance`), then the field is named the same as the node to be used.

It is possible to declare the Shape node without the geometry or Appearance node because defaults have been specified. If you declare it minus the Appearance property, then the cylinder defaults to black in color.

The rest of the description should be fairly straightforward. The Material node defines any color-based properties for the geometry. You will also see shortly that the Appearance node can control other properties as well like texture maps.

Adding the Leaves

Next we need to add the leaves to make it look like a tree. This is done by adding a cone which has been translated to the right position. Anything to do with moving nodes or changing their dimensions is handled by the Transform node, which is illustrated in Listing 40.2.

Listing 40.2. A tree with some leaves.

```
#VRML V2.0 utf8

# The tree trunk
Shape {
    appearance Appearance {
        material Material { emissiveColor  0.41 0.4 0.1 }
    }
    geometry Cylinder {
        height 1
        radius 0.25
    }
}

# A cone for leaves
Transform {
    translation 0 1.5 0
    children [
        Shape {
            appearance Appearance {
                material Material { emissiveColor  0.1 0.6 0.1 }
            }
            geometry Cone {}
        }
    ]
}
```

Any translation properties are handled by the `translation` field and the geometry that is to be translated is placed in the `children` field. The translation does not effect any other nodes except those declared as its children. In VRML 1.0, you need to hide everything inside a huge collection of Separators, and even then leakage of the state causes problems with parts of the scene lower down in the file.

You should also note that the cone is declared with none of the fields set, which is indicated by the empty set of brackets. If you declare a node this way, the node will use the default values. In this case, these values are a cone with a height of 2 and bottom radius of 1.

All of these geometry dimensions are relative to the origin. When you look at a box, the default for the size is written as 2 2 2, which indicates a box which has the extents from +1 to -1 in each of the three directions.

Blowing in the Wind

To make our tree look realistic, you need to make it lean a bit with the breeze. The final tree now has two cones, each of which is tilted a bit to make the tree look like it is leaning with the breeze. This shows the big difference between the two versions of VRML quite dramatically.

Listing 40.3 shows that to produce a compound sway in the top half of the tree you can put in an extra cone and transform it as a child of the original. There is no need to work out relative distances and then how much to rotate each. In this case, you offset this child relative to the parent only.

Listing 40.3. The final tree bending in the breeze.

```
#VRML V2.0 utf8
# The trunk
Shape {
    appearance Appearance {
        material Material { emissiveColor  .41 .40 .1 }
    }
    geometry Cylinder {
        radius .25
        height 1
    }
}
# The leaves. Firstly the bottom cone.
Transform {
    translation 0 1.5 0
    rotation 0 0 1 0.1
    center 0 -0.75 0
    children [
        Shape {
            appearance Appearance {
```

```
                    material Material { emissiveColor .1 .6 .1 }
                }
                # Default cone values look good
                geometry Cone {}
            }

            # Now put in the second cone
            Transform {
                translation 0 .75 0
                rotation 0 0 1 .1
                center 0 -.375 0
                children [
                    Shape {
                        appearance Appearance {
                            material Material { emissiveColor .1 .6 .1 }
                        }
                        geometry Cone {
                            bottomRadius .8
                            height 1.5
                        }
                    }
                ]
            }
        ]
}
```

Besides the `translation` and `rotation` fields, which you can expect to do as their name suggests, there is an extra field: `center`. This locates the center for the rotation to take place about rather than the origin of shape. For these cones, I have set this field to be on the base so that the lean looks more authentic.

Reusing Nodes

If you have to type out (or even cut and paste) the tree every time that you want to use it, you will soon get tired. Luckily, VRML includes a mechanism so that you only need to define an object once and then reuse it.

To define a node to be reused, you use the `DEF` keyword followed by a name and then the node definition. Our tree example then becomes

```
DEF tree Group {
    children [
        # Rest of tree definition...
    ]
}
```

Note that we have to put a Group node around it so that all the parts are collected under one name.

To use that node somewhere else in the file, you use the keyword `USE <name>`. So if we want to create another tree at another location, you put in a transform (to move it to that location) and then `USE` the tree.

```
Transform {
    translation 6 0 5
    children USE tree
}
```

That is all you have to do. There is one thing that you need to watch for. By reusing a node in this way, you only create a pointer to the original. If you change any property in the original, it automatically flows on to all of the copies. For example, if you change the color to red for the leaves, all of the trees appear with red. Depending on what you are trying to achieve, this can be either good or bad.

You are not just limited to defining whole nodes. You can define parts of them but not individual fields. Say you have a nice yellow color that you want to reuse. You can place a `DEF` in front of the Appearance node and then reuse it in another place as the following code shows:

```
Shape {
    appearance DEF gold Appearance {
        material Material { emissiveColor 0.4 0.41 0.1 }
    }
    .....
}
Shape {
    appearance USE gold
    ....
}
```

`DEF` can be used for a variety of other circumstances. It gives a node a name that can be referenced later. As you read through the rest of this chapter, you find that it is used for giving access to view points, scripts, and animation as well as a number of other areas.

Making Worlds More Realistic

You can make a scene a lot more realistic by adding a few extra touches. For example, basic color becomes limiting in anything but a moderate world. VRML 1.0 did not include any object collision detection, so you could walk straight through walls. This section shows you how these effects and more are now created. Again, like the previous section, a lot of the syntax has changed but the basic ideas have stayed the same.

Texture Maps

A texture map is the addition of an image over a piece of geometry. When the tree example was created, the Appearance node was introduced. At this stage all that was demonstrated was the Material node, which allowed you to change the color of the object.

As its name suggests, the Appearance node controls all aspects of how a piece of geometry looks. This can take two forms of color and images. The color is handled by the Material node, which was introduced earlier, and images are handled by a number of nodes. Two fields control images in the Appearance node: `texture` and `textureTransform`.

Texture holds a node that can place an image on the geometry. You might notice that I am being very general with this description. VRML can actually handle three different forms of placing textures. ImageTexture deals with predefined image formats like JPEG or GIFs. PixelTexture contains VRML's own internal uncompressed format (the image is actually stored in the VRML file). The most interesting one is the MovieTexture node, which allows you to place animation on any piece of geometry just by using this node.

A tree is a bit lonely when placed by itself in the middle of scene, so let's build on it a little. To make the world interesting, I have used an IndexedFaceSet node to create an irregularly shaped island. This island is then covered with a grass texture using the ImageTexture node as illustrated by the code in Listing 40.4. Combine this with a few trees and you have a nice little virtual woodlands to play in.

Listing 40.4. The VRML code used to create the island.

```
#VRML V2.0 utf8
Shape {
    appearance Appearance {
        texture ImageTexture { url 'grass.jpg" }
        textureTransform { scale 0.1 0.1 0.1 }
    }
    geometry IndexedFaceSet {
        coord Coordinate {
            point [ 5 0 0, 4.5 0 1, 4 0 2, 3 0 2.5, 2 0 3,
                    4 0 4, 0 0 5, -1 0 4.5, -2 0 4, -2.5 0 3.2,
                   -3 0 2.5, -3.5 0 2.5, -4 0 0.5, -3.5 0 -1, -3.5 0 -2,
                   -3.2 0 -3, -3 0 -4,  -2 0 -4.2, -1 0 -4.6, 0 0 -4.5,
                    1 0 -4, 2 0 -3.5, 3 0 -3, 4 0 -2, -4.5 0 -1
            ]
        }
        coordIndex [ 0, 1, 2, 3, 4, 5, 6, 7, 8, 9, 10, 11, 12, 13, 14,
                     15, 16, 17, 18, 19, 20, 21, 22, 23, 24, 25, 1, -1
        ]
    }
}
```

Note the use of the TextureTransform node. The original grass texture, if unscaled by the file is stretched so that it fits over all of the objects only once. With this new node, I can scale and rotate the texture however I like. In this case, I have reduced the scale by a factor of 10 to get a nice grass effect. The woodlands are shown in Figure 40.1.

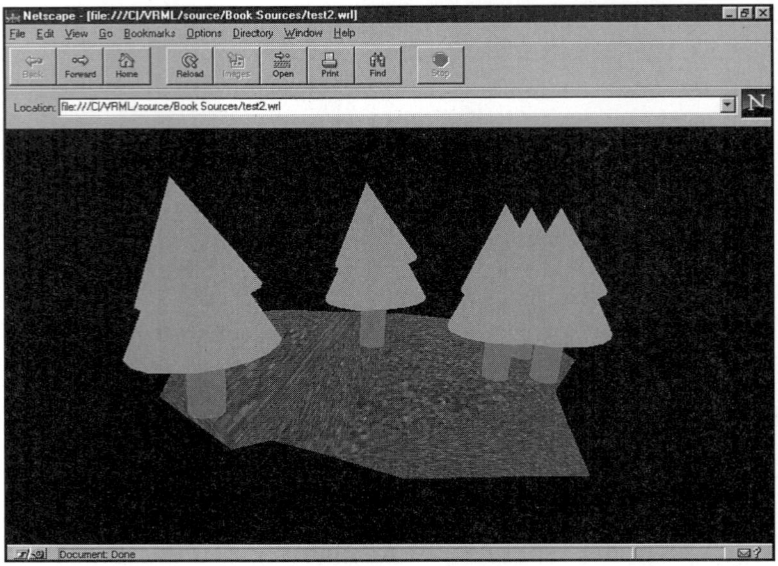

FIGURE 40.1.
The completed woodlands.

Lighting

Next on the list are the light sources. VRML defines 3 sources: PointLight, SpotLight, and DirectionalLight. The names are fairly self-explanatory. A Pointlight is a point in space representing a place where light shines from. The SpotLight focuses a beam of light in a certain direction, but the DirectionalLight puts out parallel rays as thought the light were from an infinite source like the sun.

DirectionalLights are different from the other two sources—they only illuminate objects in the same group as them. So other objects that belong to parent or sibling nodes are not affected by the light source. PointLight and SpotLight do not suffer these restrictions.

One interesting point to note is that VRML does not define shadow behavior. If there is another object between the source and the other object, no shadow is cast. Sometimes this is very frustrating because some types of lighting effects are not possible anymore.

Collisions

One of the problems facing the original VRML specification was that there was no way to prevent a user from walking through objects in the scene. VRML 2.0 defines the Collision node which, while it is not drawn itself, it makes its children collidable. That is, you are no longer able to walk straight through.

There are two fields to use for this behavior. The `children` field is the list of children for which collision detection is turned on. If you want to use some other shape instead, then you can specify a grouping node. These nodes are never drawn, so there is no point associating any color properties with them.

An interesting point to take from this is that if you specify a proxy but no real geometry (for example, the `children` field is empty), then you can have invisible zones that you cannot pass through. This is a very handy trick if you want to constrain a user to a certain volume of space.

Default Views

In both versions of VRML you can specify a list of positions to view the world from. In 2.0, these positions are called viewpoints (1.0 called them cameras). A viewpoint uses the same model as the one used in VRML 1.0. First, you place it somewhere and then you give it an axis to rotate about. The rotation is always relative to the axis pointing in the minus z direction. For example, the following code makes you look 45 degrees to the right of the minus z axis:

```
Viewpoint {
...
orientation 0 1 0 0.782
...
}
```

TIP

Angles are always in radians in VRML. To convert from degrees to radians, divide the angle by 360 and then multiply it by 2π.

The first viewpoint that you declare in a file is the one that is used when you first enter the world. Any after that are then placed in a list that can be dealt with by the browsers. Early beta versions of SGI's CosmoPlayer allowed you to construct a virtual tour by placing the points that you want to visit in order. Each time that you press the page down/page up keys, you move to the next viewpoint.

Included on the CD is the code for a workshop from *Laura Lemay's Web Workshop: 3D Graphics and VRML* written by the same author, which illustrates how a virtual tour can be constructed through a virtual art gallery. Just open the top HTML file and the rest of the world is opened for you. It also illustrates a few more points that I will be raising in later sections of this chapter.

Connecting to the World

One of the great attractions of the Web is that you can place links to any other document anywhere in the world without the user worrying about how to get to it. VRML contains the same capability. Once you have entered the world, you can click on objects to jump to anything that you can place a link to on an HTML page.

Anchors

The Anchor node is the equivalent of the `<anchor>` tag in HTML. It provides the link to another place on the Web. Anything that you can do with a HTML `<A HREF>` tag, you can do within the Anchor node. This link can be a connection to a CGI script, HTML page, VRML world, or anything else.

CGI input is interesting because you can create VRML worlds on the fly just like you can with HTML. A good example of this is Besjon Alavandi's Outland world from Terra Vista (`http://www.webking.com/Outland/`). The introductory page asks you to specify some sizes for the world and then the VRML is generated on the fly. CGI requests are then filled into the anchor fields so that as you travel around the various segments of the world, each bit is dynamically generated.

To use an Anchor node in your world, you simply create your object that you want to put a link on and then put it in the `children` field of the Anchor.

```
Anchor {
    url "http://www.vlc.com.au/"
    children [
        # your children nodes here
    ]
}
```

Inlines

One advantage that VRML has over HTML is the ability to construct a total world from a number of smaller ones. The Inline node allows you to specify the URL to other VRML files and then place them within the world.

A very common use of this node is to create a fast-loading world. This is done by creating a skeleton world that consists of, for example, the basic ground plane, and then the rest of the buildings are inlined. The user gets to see the basic world outline very quickly, and then the details are filled in around them as they wander around.

The syntax of the inline node is very simple:

```
Inline {
    url     "a_building.wrl"
}
```

The inline can then be placed anywhere in the world either by placing it as a child of a `Transform` and then translating it or by setting the `bboxCenter` field (which is the center of the bounding box of the inlined world).

The Parameter Field

One field that has not been demonstrated in the earlier discussion of the Anchor node, is the `parameter` field. This string field allows you to pass parameters along to the target world.

One of the most common uses for the `parameter` field is to use the VRML world to provide links to HTML documents in a multiframed page. The `parameter` field then contains the string

```
"target=name_of_frame"
```

> **TIP**
>
> Netscape introduced some extensions to the original VRML 1.0 specification by providing a `Target` field to the Anchor node that does the same thing but only on multiframed documents.

which then directs the request to that frame. There are also other uses. If the anchor links to a Java applet, it can be used to pass values to it in the same manner as the `<PARAM>` tag does in HTML.

Adding Behaviors

So far, I have compared the differences between VRML 1.0 and 2.0. Now we are heading into the realms that are completely new areas that have been introduced in the latest version.

Animation and its relative, behavior programming, provide true interactive virtual environments. If you feel comfortable with either JavaScript or Java, then you are in luck, because you can use these skills in VRML as well. Because behaviors and animation are a very big and complex topics, I only scratch the surface so that you can then explore it further with other books if you desire.

Events and Animation

The first step along the way to providing interactive behavior is to learn about animation. But there is an even smaller step than this—learning how VRML passes information between nodes to make it all happen.

To pass a bit of information between two nodes, you create an event. To VRML, this is a way of one node informing another that something has changed. An event can be anything from a clock ticking to provide time to the addition of new geometry to the scene.

When you look at the definition of a node in the VRML 2.0 specification, you will notice that some of the fields are specified as `eventIn` or `eventOut`. These are the fields that are used to pass information between nodes (`exposedFields` also does it).

To make two nodes pass events between each other, you must explicitly connect them using the `ROUTE` statement. `ROUTEs` connect an `eventOut` from one node to an `eventIn` on another and both must be of the same field type. For example, you cannot pass an SFInt32 to an MFNode.

```
ROUTE from_node.from_event_out TO to_node.to_event_in
```

`ROUTEs` can be declared anywhere in the file after they have been declared. That is, they are not part of the normal part of the scene structure.

Getting a Sense of Time

When you go to create an animation, you need some sense of time. VRML does not explicitly have time built in to its model. Instead, you use a node that is capable of "sensing" time and passes that as an event to the rest of the world.

TimeSensors are fairly complex so I won't try to describe them all here. For the basic worlds that you will first create, you need to know how to set up a continuous time output. Time in a VRML world runs in seconds and time 0 is midnight GMT on the first of January 1970. (This is the way that time is represented internally on most computer systems.) A TimeSensor has two main fields—`startTime` and `stopTime`. A third field, `loop`, is used to control if you want to make the time loop.

To make a TimeSensor create a continuous time output, you set the `stopTime` to less than the `startTime` and set `loop` to `True`. To make it drive something in the world, you hook the fraction `eventOut` to any node that you desire. The fraction is a value that runs between zero and one inclusive. If you are using a continuous output, you can control the rate at which the fraction output cycle is repeated by setting the appropriate value in the `cycleTime` field. When the TimeSensor gets to `startTime + n * cycleTime`, it outputs a one, and the next value is a zero.

The exact implementation of how the TimeSensor works is up to the browser, and also a close reading of the specification is wise. What has been presented so far should enable you to understand the examples presented in the rest of this chapter.

Making Things Move

There are a couple of ways to make an object move. The first is to create a script that generates the movement for you. To do this, you need a fairly good understanding of the math involved. However, if you want to save yourself work, the second option of using the built-in interpolator nodes is the best way to go.

There are a number of different interpolators for different tasks. The one that you are likely to use most often is the PositionInterpolator. All the interpolators take the same set of parameters. Only the output is different. The input is a fraction between zero and one, and the output is an interpolated value from your defined set of points. The parameters are a set of key points between zero and one and a matching set of values that should be output when the input fraction reaches that key value. If that sounds a bit confusing, consider the following set of values for a position interpolator:

Key	*Value*
0	5 0 0
0.25	0 0 5
0.5	-5 0 0
0.75	0 0 -5
1	5 0 0

This set of values describes a square path that never ends—the last point is the same as the first so that when the TimeSensor returns to zero at the end of a cycle, you are back where you started.

Responding to the User

When you are creating a world with animation in it, you also like to get feedback from the user. The problem with 3D worlds is that there is no place to put a collection of buttons. Instead you make objects in the world respond to user input by placing a sensor on them. VRML contains a reasonably large collection of sensors to achieve many common tasks.

Probably the most common sensor that you will be dealing with is the TouchSensor. This sensor creates an event each time the user touches on the object that you have placed it on. The creators of the VRML standards have been thoughtful enough to define this to work not only with standard mouse input, but also with other 3D devices like datagloves.

The sensor nodes operate a bit differently in syntax to the other nodes. Consider the code in Listing 40.5, which creates a red cube that, when clicked, creates an event.

Listing 40.5. How to use a TouchSensor.

```
#VRML V2.0 utf8
Group {
    children [
        Shape {
            appearance Appearance {
                material Material { emissiveColor 0.8 0 0 }
            }
            geometry Box {}
        },
        TouchSensor {}
    ]
}
```

Instead of the TouchSensor having children to look after, it applies to its siblings. If the children you create also have children in them that contain touch or other sensors, then the lowest one in the tree generates the event.

Apart from the TouchSensors and TimeSensors that you have already learned about, there are a number of sensors that are known as drag sensors. These take the user's input (for example, pressing the first mouse button and then dragging) and then translates that into a motion. For example, SphereSensor makes the cursor follow the path of a sphere. "So where is this useful?" I hear you ask. Consider trying to create the VR equivalent of a slide switch that you might find on your stereo system. These sensors force the mouse (or other input device) to follow a specific path. In the slider case, it is a straight track in 3D space.

Introduction to Scripting

Basic collections of interpolators can do a fair amount of your animation. However, there comes a point in time where you find you need to do more that is not provided by the language. In this case, you need to move on to scripting.

Scripts can be anything from a basic addition of two numbers to generating VRML on the fly. After starting to play with TouchSensors you notice that when you click down on them, a true event is created, but as soon as you release it, a false event is sent. If you are trying to control animation, it only runs while you are holding down the mouse button. What you really need is a toggle behavior.

Enter scripting. A script allows you to create almost any behavior that you want. All it requires is a little bit of programming. No doubt you have already started dabbling with either JavaScript or Java to enhance your Web pages so getting some scripts going doesn't require any more learning.

A Script node is fairly simple. All you need to do is declare a Script node, fill in a couple of required fields, and then add in whatever other fields you like. The most important of the required fields is `url`. This specifies the file that is to be used for the behavior program and is explained for each language. There are two other fields that are not explained here: `mustEvaluate` and `directOutputs`.

Once you have a basic idea of what you require for your script, you can build the node a piece at a time. Let's examine the toggle switch example. Each time that the user presses on the switch, it must change the state of the output. However, we want to make it a little more complex than that. It should only trigger when the button is lifted and over the object.

The last part of the previous section is fairly important to understand. We need to get events for when the TouchSensor is touched but also when the pointer is over the object (it is possible to have clicked on the object and then drag away and release the button when it is not over it). Reading this should then tell you that you need two input events and one output. Also, we need to store the state in between clicks, so an internal field is needed. Listing 40.6 gives you the outline of what is needed on the VRML side of this script. This can then be wired to the code in Listing 40.5 with some routes for the input, and then the output can be used to control something like an animation.

Listing 40.6. Outline of the script declaration to make a toggle button.

```
TOGGLE_BUTTON Script {
    url  ""    # to be filled in later
    field SFBool pointer_over FALSE
    eventIn SFBool isOver
    eventIn SFBool isActive
    eventOut SFBool value_changed
}
```

Using JavaScript

There is not that much difference in using JavaScript in VRML than in a normal Web page. To create a JavaScript behavior, the `url` must either point to a file that ends in `.javascript` or it can embed the code within the VRML file by using the `javascript:url` declaration. With this you can then place all of your code within the one file, but remember—the bigger the file, the longer it takes to download and hence the longer a person must wait before they can start using your world.

So you have decided to place the code inline, what should the code look like? Listing 40.7 shows the code to produce the toggle behavior. Each `eventIn` that has been declared within the VRML definition has a corresponding function. Every time that field gets an event, that function is called.

Listing 40.7. Completing the toggle button behavior with JavaScript.

```
url  "javascript:
    function isOver(value)
    {
        pointer_over = value;
    }
    function isActive(value)
    {
        if((value == FALSE) && (pointer_over == TRUE))
            value_changed = !value_changed;
    }
"
```

Of interest here is that you can read the value of the `eventOut` before assigning a new value to it. In this example, I have only used the first argument. However, it is possible to use two or no arguments for each function. The first argument is the same type as the matching declaration in the VRML code and the second one is the timestamp of when it occurred. If you remember from the TimeSensor description, time is measured in seconds. You can then start an animation five seconds after that event by looking at the timestamp and then adding 5 to it before passing that out as an event to another TimeSensor.

More Complexity with Java

For the more adventurous (or demanding) Web sites, scripts written in Java may be your preferred method. Java is more flexible than VRML script and also runs much faster. One of the prime reasons for using it is the additional capabilities in the libraries such as multithreading and networking.

The process of writing a Java script is different from JavaScript. You need a much closer understanding of how event models work. Java scripting has been designed with the idea that a browser can be written in Java. If you look closely at it, you will notice many similarities to AWT classes.

Due to these restrictions, the Java script lacks some of the nice features like having methods that are directly named after the `eventIns` as in JavaScript. Instead, there are one of two functions that are to be used. The `ProcessEvent()` method is used when you are only dealing with one event at a time and `ProcessEvents()` is used for handling multiple events. The reason for the two separate methods is that browsers may optimize performance by batching a whole heap of events and then send them all to the script at once.

A complete description of the Java API takes more room than is possible so I will show you how to implement the toggle switch example in Java. Listing 40.8 shows the Java source file. Notice that there is much more writing needed to achieve the same effect. In this case, I have used separate methods that are called for each event. However, normally with such a small system, I would write the code all inlined in the event handler.

Listing 40.8. The toggle button code now implemented in Java.

```
// Java source for the toggle button example
import vrml.*;
import vrml.field.*;
import vrml.node.*;

class toggle_button extends Script
{
    private SFBool pointer_over;
    public  SFBool value_changed;

    // initialisation method
    public initialize(void)
    {
        pointer_over = (SFBool)getField("pointer_over");
        value_changed = (SFBool)getEventOut("value_changed");
    }

    private void isOver(ConstSFBool value)
    {
        pointer_over.setValue(value.getValue());
    }

    private void isActive(ConstSFBool value)
    {
        if((value.getValue() == TRUE) &&
           (pointer_over.getValue() == TRUE))
           value_changed.setValue(!value_changed.getValue());
    }

    // the event handler
    public void process_events(Event[] e, int count)
    {
        int i;

        for(i = 0; i < count; I++)
        {
            if(e.getName().eq("isOver"))
                isOver(e.getValue());
            else if (e.getName().eq("isActive"))
                isActive(e.getValue());
        }
    }
}
```

One method that I have not mentioned yet is `initialize()`. It is normally the case in VRML that when the class constructor gets called the VRML values, like field defaults, are not yet valid. To solve this problem, the `initialize` method was added. This method gets called once during the life of that class, just after the VRML world is complete but before the user is allowed to interact with it. In this method, you initialize any Java fields with their VRML equivalent values. This method forms the bridge between the VRML and Java visions of the world.

Building for the Internet

VRML can have many different uses. However, the one that you are most likely to be interested in is to enhance your corporate or personal Web page on the Internet. With this in mind you may want to incorporate some of the following features into you world.

LOD

Not everybody has a high-end workstation on their desk so you need to be careful about performance. Performance is mainly affected by the amount of complexity of your scene. If you load it up with many texture maps and highly complex objects, it will always run slow no matter what sort of machine you are running.

How do you get around this problem? VRML has a node that allows you to control the amount of detail depending on the distance away from an object you are. If you look at an object in the real world, you notice that as you get further away from it you see less and less of the detail. You can simulate this effect with the Level Of Detail (LOD) node.

In this node, you can set a series of distance ranges and what you want to appear within those ranges. Listing 40.9 shows how to use it. The ranges field puts the ranges where you want the transition to be. You need to define one more set of objects than the number of ranges in the range field. This is because they act as the transition point.

It does not really matter what you put for the geometry for each range; they do not even need to look the same. As you see from Listing 40.9, the object for the far distance is a cube and the close object is a sphere.

Listing 40.9. Demonstration of using LOD.

```
#VRML V2.0 utf8
LOD {
    range    5
    levels [
        Shape {
            appearance Appearance {
                material Material { emissiveColor 0.8 0 0 }
            }
            geometry cube {}
        },
        Shape {
            appearance Appearance {
                material Material { emissiveColor 0 0.8 0 }
            }
            geometry sphere {}
        }
    ]
}
```

When you try this out in your browser, you may notice one of two effects. The first is that as you move closer, you go from a cube to a sphere as you would expect. The other possibility is that it only shows the sphere. Why is this so? If you read the specifications closely, it says that the ranges are only a guide to when to change the detail levels. The browser is free to choose what it likes in order to keep the frame rate up. So what ends up happening with a simple model like this is that it always shows the highest detail model (the sphere) because it knows it can do this and still give you nice smooth motion.

Here is one of the other major nasties that you should be aware of. In most of the early VRML browsers, using a world with LOD in it was slower than using it without and running it at the highest detail level. This was due to some poor implementations of the LOD algorithm and also that the browser would load all of the models into memory. If the machine was low on resources, particularly memory, then it would suffer a great performance hit. In the finicky world of the Web user, this is not a good thing.

File Compression

Once you start creating some moderately complex worlds, the file size starts increasing dramatically. Using the complex node types like the `IndexedFaceSet` causes very large file sizes. To minimize the file size, there are a number of approaches.

The first approach that you can take is to remove all of the white space. This is things like the formatting that makes a file readable, extra space at the end of line and between characters. Modeling programs seem to be very good at putting excess white space in—which in itself is not a bad thing because it makes it more readable for you.

Besides removing white space, the next thing to target is too much precision. For just about all worlds, you do not need more than three decimal places. Any more than this and it is, in effect, ignored because it is too small to put on the screen. So to reduce your file size even more then you need, only specify a small amount of precision.

Although reducing white space and precision can save you much in file size, there is one more step for those truly huge files. Compress them. VRML 1.0 allows the use of `gzip` for compressing large files. This is still the same for the latest version. Essentially all the techniques you use for VRML 1.0 can be used in 2.0.

Looking into the future, one of the forthcoming additions to the specification is the binary file format. This file format uses a binary representation of the VRML world rather than the ASCII text format currently being used. This will reduce file size even more than the methods already mentioned in this chapter. However, it is still in the planning stages at the time of writing.

Using Prebuilt VRML

By now you are getting very familiar with the Shape node and how it is used. It is basically the core of a VRML file description. However you soon get tired of typing **appearance Appearance** over and over. Also there are a whole collection of standard objects and scripts that you build into your toolkit. This next section looks at how to extend VRML to handle canned behaviors and new node types.

PROTO

The first thing you may want to do in a file is to create a shortcut to a commonly used function within a world. The Shape node example mentioned in the previous paragraph is a common function. If you want to create a shortcut node only for that file, use the `PROTO` node. Once you have declared a `PROTO` node, you can use it just like any other standard VRML node within that file. To create a node that is used by other files, you need to create another `PROTO` node.

The basic syntax of a `PROTO` node is as follows:

```
PROTO node_name [
    # field and event in declarations
] {
    # VRML code to implement it
}
```

Using this syntax as a base, you can create a simple `PROTO` node for the shape example by providing the geometry and a color. The object is then created. The shape example is declared in Listing 40.10.

Listing 40.10. A simple shape PROTO node.

```
#VRML V2.0 utf8
PROTO SimpleShape [
    field SFNode shapeStyle
    field SFColor shapeColor
]{
    Shape {
        appearance Appearance {
            material Material { emissiveColor IS shapeColor }
        }
        geometry IS shapeStyle
    }
}
```

In this example, you see the appearance of the `IS` keyword. This keyword allows you to associate a field in the declaration with one in the VRML implementation part. You can declare multiple `IS` relationships for the one field in the `PROTO` declaration. The type of group that `PROTO` belongs to is defined by the first node's group typing in the implementation part. In fact, only one top-level node is allowed to be in the implementation.

Now you can use this node however you like in the rest of the VRML file. You need to add this next section of code to the bottom of that listing in 40.10 for it to work.

```
Transform {
    translation 1 0 0
    children [
        SimpleShape {
            shapeType Cube {}
            shapeColor 0 0 0.5
        }
    ]
}
Group {
    children [
        SimpleShape {
            shapeType Sphere { radius 0.5 }
            shapeColor 0.5 0 0.5
        }
    ]
}
```

From this you should see a few nice uses already. Notice that in the second shape that we declared a full sphere with all its fields as well. Anything that you can do with a normal VRML node you can do with PROTOs.

EXTERNPROTO

Although it is useful to declare a shorthand declaration for a node it is more useful to be able to reuse that node across many files. To do this, you need to use the EXTERNPROTO definition. However, you need use the PROTO definition to declare the actual implementation of a node within a file before it can be used by other files.

Once you have the basic file done, you can reuse it by declaring an EXTERNPROTO at the top of the file in which you wish to use it. This is essentially the same as the declaration used for the PROTO with one small difference. Instead of the implementation, there is a list of the URLs and/or URNs to the actual file that defines it. To use the SimpleShape definition from Listing 40.10, declare the code given in Listing 40.11.

Listing 40.11. Using the SimpleShape definition in another file.

```
#VRML V2.0 utf8
EXTERNPROTO ExternShape [
field SFNode shapeStyle
    field SFColor shapeColor
]
"shapelibrary.wrl#SimpleShape"
```

Note the use of #name to get the prototype reference from the file. If you want to create a collection of commonly used prototypes, you can place them all in the one file and reference the individual protos in this way. The name that you use after the # character is the name used in the PROTO definition. This example also demonstrates that you can name an external prototype with a different name than the original definition, which is handy to avoid name clashes if you are using a number of different libraries.

Combining VRML with Other Web Technologies

You are in the Web publishing game and want to know how to combine VRML with all those other technologies that you have spent time learning. As you have seen with scripting, effort to learn Java or JavaScript is beginning to pay off. The next step is integrating VRML with your current Web site.

Apart from using anchors and inlines to provide links to other documents, it is useful to incorporate other technologies. The current incarnation of VRML does not allow you to use 2D text within the environment unless you make it up as a bitmap and then use it as a texture. However, the opposite approach is available; including 3D graphics in your Web page.

There are two approaches available: embedding VRML into a page or creating a multiframe document that has one frame devoted to VRML. To embed a VRML world into a HTML page, use the standard <EMBED> tag that you use to incorporate other technologies.

The more interesting—and probably more widely used technique—is the multiframed document approach. When we looked at the parameter field a little earlier, it showed how a VRML world can control the contents of other frames. Well, the reverse is also true. However, you do not want to replace the VRML world every 30 seconds because they take too long to load. VRML does include one nice feature.

If you have declared your viewpoints with DEF names, you can refer to these from an external document using the # syntax. This time the name used is the DEF name. In the example shown in Figure 40.2, the upper right frame is used to take you to different viewpoints in the VRML world.

Another area that you may wish to keep track of in the near future is an external interface to the VRML world. The VRML development list is working towards getting a standardized external interface so you can do more than just move between camera points. It is likely that the interface will include Java and/or JavaScript variations.

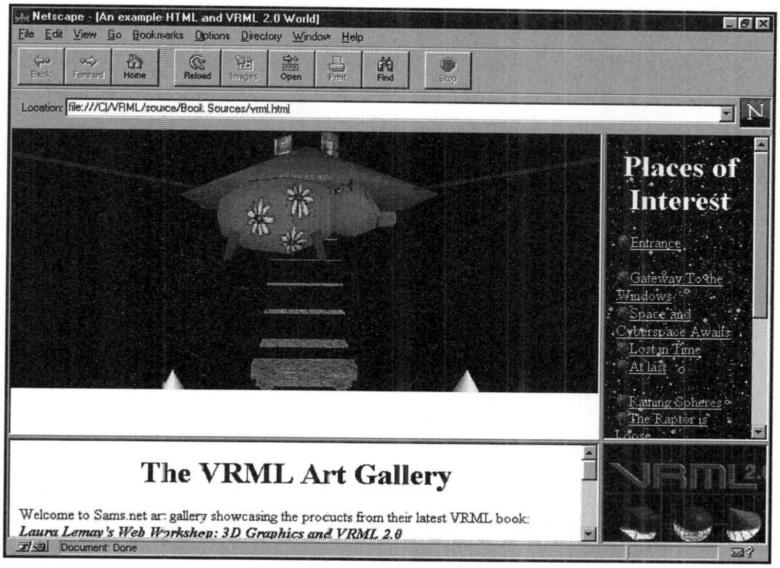

FIGURE 40.2.
A complete multiframed document combining VRML and HTML.

VRML in the Future

So where does this leave VRML for future development? Already I have mentioned that external interfaces and binary file formats are in the works. One area that needs attention is the scripting languages. At the moment, there isn't a required script language so browser writers are free to support either Java or JavaScript—or any others that they want.

However, one of the biggest areas now missing is the inherent support for multiuser virtual environments. When you enter a standard world there will be you and only you in it. There are a number of products like BlackSun's CyberHub Client (`http://www.blacksun.com/`) that add extensions to your existing VRML worlds and your favorite browser (only Live3D and Cosmo are supported in early releases but more are in the works). You can even use Java scripts within the VRML world and use socket interfaces to connect to another server. It all depends on how adventurous you are.

Summary

VRML 2.0 presents a whole new experience for your Web site. Gone are the static worlds and now the interactive 3D environment is ready for your clients. In this chapter, I have only scratched the surface of what you can do with VRML. I suggest that a book fully devoted to VRML 2.0 is a wise investment if you plan to pursue it seriously.

CHAPTER 41

Adding Behaviors with VRMLScript and Java

by John J. Kottler

IN THIS CHAPTER

Like the world itself, the World Wide Web is not flat. However, most of the content on the Web today consists of simple, two-dimensional pages that contain two-dimensional graphics. Only recently, a change has begun to sweep over the Internet and the computer industry. More emphasis is being placed on the three-dimensional world. This is obvious by the immense popularity of three-dimensional games that have saturated the market.

The idea of using three-dimensional objects that can be manually manipulated is becoming more a commonality than a futuristic idea. Businesses and scientists can clearly benefit from the use of three-dimensional drawings to analyze mechanical equipment, chemical compounds, or DNA strands. Simulators are developed using three-dimensional technologies to emulate the real world, and the possibility of three-dimensional operating systems for computers is not far away.

But what about the Internet? Anyone who has browsed the Web can easily be inundated with information. In order to organize some of that information, three dimensions may be clearer than two. In the future, you may find more three-dimensional worlds being created to more easily handle large volumes of data. And as Web technologies continue to evolve, three-dimensional games will become a reality, as will chat rooms where you interact with other three-dimensional people.

The technology that has advanced the prospect of 3D on the Web is VRML, the Virtual Reality Modeling Language. As you have learned from other chapters in this book, this simple language instructs a three-dimensional browser how to paint three-dimensional worlds. The language is fairly straightforward, and numerous development tools available today assist in creating three-dimensional objects for VRML. Unfortunately many VRML sites today suffer from the same afflictions as Web sites in the recent past: the lack of interaction. Users can see a VRML world, walk through it, or rotate it, but they can't actually *do* anything in it.

As the World Turns

Users who are viewing worlds created with VRML 1.0 are very limited in what they can do. Fortunately, just as everything else evolves quickly on the Internet, so has the world of VRML. The newest iteration of VRML 2.0, also referred to as Moving Worlds, is a dynamic virtual reality language. Current information regarding Moving Worlds can be found at the Silicon Graphics Web site: `http://vrml.sgi.com/moving-worlds`.

In addition to new effects and three-dimensional capabilities, with VRML 2.0 it is possible to create worlds where objects spin or move in space. But more importantly, these objects can be *smart* as they move about. Moving Worlds allows three-dimensional objects to interact with computer scripting languages to define the unique characteristics or *behaviors* for those objects. These objects can also interact with each other or with the user to truly make an interactive experience.

In this chapter, you have the opportunity to learn how to make three-dimensional worlds that are dynamic and respond to the actions of the user. You learn about Moving Worlds' newest additions to VRML such as sensors, the script node, and wiring a world with VRMLScript or a Java applet.

Viewing the New World

Moving Worlds still requires the use of a three-dimensional browser. A 3D browser is capable of translating VRML, constructing a three-dimensional scene, and allowing the user to control how the scene is viewed. Most VRML browsers today can be launched by a Web browser such as Netscape's Navigator or Microsoft's Internet Explorer to view a scene related to a Web page. These VRML browsers may either create separate windows for displaying the scene or occupy the same space as the Web page.

In any case, it is important to remember that to see a three-dimensional world created using VRML 2.0, you must use a browser that is compliant with VRML 2.0. A few capable browsers are the following:

- CosmoPlayer by Silicon Graphics (`http://vrml.sgi.com/`)
- CyberPassage by Sony Corporate (`http://vs.sony.co.jp/VS-E/vstop.html`)
- Liquid Reality by DimensionX (`http://www.dimensionx.com/products/lr/`)

These browsers allow you to view VRML 2.0-animated worlds and interact with objects within those worlds. Each of these browsers include sample files that demonstrate the capabilities of VRML 2.0, particularly when used in conjunction with the browser. You will see differences in the way each handles VRML worlds, but they all can display a Moving Worlds three-dimensional world. Figure 41.1 demonstrates a sample of the Sony CyberPassage VRML browser. This browser makes particularly good use of Java applets with the VRML worlds. Several sample files are included with this browser including Drive, a race-track world with an animated car that winds through the curves of the track. In addition, the user can control whether the car moves or is stopped by clicking directly on the car.

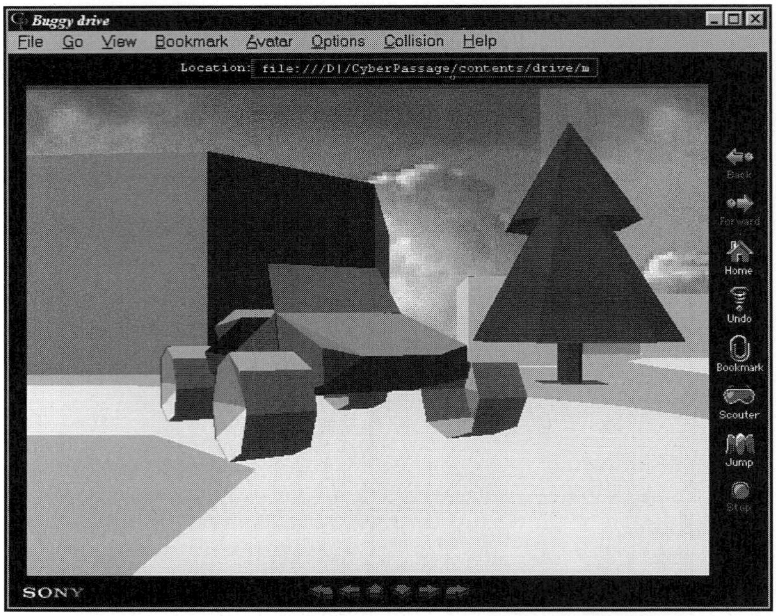

FIGURE 41.1.
Sony's CyberPassage displays Moving Worlds, VRML 2.0 files that feature animation and interaction.

Sensors

In order to accomplish the results shown in Figure 41.1, numerous new interactive capabilities were added to VRML 2.0. For instance, new capabilities that handled the user clicking on the object or touching it were required before the user could click on the car to start it racing around the track. Most of these new interactive capabilities were added to the VRML 2.0 standard in the form of *sensors.*

You can think of these sensors as everyday sensors in the real world. For instance, a common touch sensor is found in the touch-sensitive computer screens in mall kiosks or on some automated teller machines. When you touch the screen, something happens. Likewise, motion sensors may be attached to the outside of a house or business building. When someone or something comes within a predefined distance of the sensor, exterior lights may be lit.

These same sensors are available in VRML 2.0. You find the touch and proximity sensors as well as many others listed in Table 41.1. These sensors all do different tasks but work on the same principle. They monitor activity within the VRML world and send notifications appropriately to programming scripts or other objects when particular events occur.

Table 41.1. Sensors can be set in a VRML 2.0 world to monitor activity.

Sensor Name	*Sensor Action*
`CylinderSensor`	This sensor allows the developer to specify objects of 3D space that are to be rotated around their Y axis, independent of the rest of the scene. This sensor monitors when a user drags the mouse in this region with the button down.
`PlaneSensor`	A developer can specify which objects may be moved along their X and Y axis' independent of the scene. This sensor outputs events when the user drags the mouse with the button down within this region.
`ProximitySensor`	As a user moves closer to a region in 3D space using the VRML browser, specific events are triggered. The developer can use this sensor to make objects run away from the user when the user gets too close.
`SphereSensor`	Similar to `CylinderSensor` and `PlaneSensor`, `SphereSensor` allows the developer to choose which objects in 3D space may be rotated around any axis, independently of the rest of the scene.
`TimeSensor`	Some events occur regularly at a scheduled interval or once at a specific time. The `TimeSensor` monitors an internal clock and triggers events either regularly on a given interval or once when a specific time has occurred. To create objects that update every second, a developer sets the interval for a `TimeSensor`.
`TouchSensor`	Truly interactive worlds allow the user to control them. One method of implementing this control is to note when a user clicks on or "touches" an object. A developer can use the `TouchSensor` to create a switch for turning animation on or off, for example.
`VisibilitySensor`	This sensor determines whether a particular region of the three-dimensional world can be seen by the viewer. If a user can see a particular region monitored by the sensor, an event is triggered. Developers can use this sensor to determine when users can see parts of their world.

Most of the sensors listed in Table 41.1 are associated with particular objects in a VRML scene. For instance, the `TouchSensor` affects all objects within its parent group. Therefore, if a `TouchSensor` is created within a cone transform, as shown in Listing 41.1, you are able to click on the cone and not any other object in the scene. Of course, each object in the scene may have its own sensors with unique functionality.

Listing 41.1. Sensors can be applied to individual objects in VRML 2.0.

```
Transform {
  children [
    DEF TOUCH_SENSOR TouchSensor {}
    Shape {
      appearance Appearance {
        material Material {
          diffuseColor    0 0 1
        }
      }

    geometry Cone{}
    }
  ]
}
```

These sensors open the possibility to create interactive worlds by noting when particular events occur. However sensors alone do not make the world interactive, they need to be connected to other objects or programming logic. In the next section, you learn how to add intelligent behaviors to objects using the `Script` node.

The `Script` Node

As mentioned numerous times already, objects themselves are static but can behave differently when coupled with programming scripts. These scripts can add simple or complex natures to objects in a scene. Anything from simply moving or rotating objects to creating interactive games is possible with scripts.

The `Script` node allows you to add these complex routines and behaviors to your VRML scene. Currently, the `Script` node supports numerous scripting languages such as VRMLScript, JavaScript, and more robust languages such as Java. Each of these languages, as we will see shortly, allows you to give more control over the flow of a world.

TIP

Each scripting language that can be used in Moving Worlds can perform the same basic functions. The difference between these languages becomes more apparent when constructing complex worlds. More complex scenes require faster and more robust languages like Java.

The following outlines the basic scripting node for VRML 2.0:

```
DEF toggle Script {
    field       fieldType   fieldName defaultValue
    eventIn     eventType   eventName
```

```
    eventOut     eventType   eventName
    url          "Script/Applet URL or embedded Script"
    scriptType   "ScriptLanguage"
}
```

field—There may be any number of fields within a `Script` node. These fields are similar to variables in other computer programming languages. Like variables in most languages, the type of data each field holds must be specified in VRML by way of an appropriate field type. Valid VRML field types can be found on the Web at `http://vrml.sgi.com/moving-worlds/spec/part1/fieldsRef.html`. A sample type is `SFBool` to indicate Boolean values.

eventIn—VRML works with objects in three-dimensional space. Therefore, it is not surprising that it is also somewhat object-oriented in nature. `eventIn` specifies the names of functions within the `Script` node that may be invoked by objects outside of the `Script` node. For instance, if there is an object named **MY_CONE** and a function named `MoveCone` within a `Script` node of a VRML scene, that `MoveCone` function needs to be made available to other objects like the cone using `eventIn`. `eventIn` is comparable to methods in object-oriented technology, and there can be as many `eventIn`'s as needed within a `Script` node.

eventOut—Just as a script can expect information to be sent into its functions, a `Script` node may export data to other objects. The data to be made available to other objects is specified using the `eventOut` parameters. `eventOut`'s are equivalent to variables that are defined within a `Script` node that are made available to other objects as well. `eventOut` is similar to properties in object-oriented technology, and there may be numerous `eventOut`'s in a `Script` node.

url—After the functions for receiving input and the variables for sending output are defined in the `Script` node, the actual functions and programming logic must be specified. The `url` parameter of the `Script` node identifies the functions to be associated with that node. The information within the `url` parameter may indicate another location to retrieve scripting commands from or may be used to embed the language directly into the node. It may also be used with an optional `scriptType` parameter to indicate executable languages such as Java.

scriptType—When choosing other languages, such as Java, to handle the script's events, the `scriptType` parameter is essential for specifying what that language is. It is also useful when the `url` parameter points to a file that contains the script, not the actual script itself. In the case of using Java applets, the `scriptType` parameter must be set to `javabc`, for Java byte-codes, when the `url` contains the name of the Java class to use.

TIP

The position for `Script` nodes within a VRML file is irrelevant. Scripts are only invoked as instructed by `ROUTE` statements and therefore can exist at any location in a VRML file. It is recommended that you keep all of the scripts near each other to improve readability of the source VRML file. Typically, scripts are placed near the end, after the scene is described.

The Best Route

`Script` nodes, like most other nodes in VRML, can be placed at any location in a VRML source file. This is because the VRML browser typically reads the entire VRML source file before attempting to display the scene. However, if this is the case, how can a script be instructed to execute when particular events occur? The answer to controlling the flow of events in a VRML world is the `ROUTE` command.

`ROUTE` is a command in VRML that specifies the actions that objects in a world should follow. It specifies what actions in one object can occur to affect other objects. It is not a node, and it can be written on a single line of code. Its sole purpose is to map `eventOut`'s from objects to `eventIn`'s of other objects. This mapping creates a link between objects so that they can communicate with each other and update each other accordingly.

The `ROUTE` command is a fairly straightforward command to understand:

```
ROUTE eventOut_of_Object TO eventIn_of_Object
```

NOTE

A `ROUTE` command must exist for *every* mapping between two objects. If you wish to map three `eventOut`'s of one object to three `eventIn`'s of a second object, you must include three distinct `ROUTE` statements in your VRML source code for each connection.

For example, it's possible to route the output of a sensor to a function in a custom script. The `TouchSensor`, for instance, contains an `isActive` property (`eventOut`). This property can then be routed into a function (`eventIn`) in your own custom script. That way, whenever a user clicks on an object and triggers the `TouchSensor`, a custom function defined in a `Script` node can be executed. With this route, it is possible to monitor when a user clicks on objects in the VRML scene and act appropriately.

Each node in VRML contains its own set of `eventIn`'s and `eventOut`'s. Covering each node with its respective events would require much more than a single chapter. To find out more about specific events for each node, visit the VRML specification site: `http://vrml.sgi.com/moving-worlds/spec/part1/nodesRef.html`.

TIP

Like the `Script` node, `ROUTE` statements may be placed anywhere within the VRML file. However, it is recommended that you either group all routing commands at the end of the file or at least have related commands near their respective `Script` or object nodes.

Introduction to VRMLScript

Now that you have learned about the `Script` node and the `ROUTE` statement in VRML 2.0, you need to begin creating scripts that determine the behavior of objects in a three-dimensional world. VRMLScript is a language that is supported by VRML 2.0 and therefore browsers that are compliant with Moving Worlds. This language, which is a derivative of JavaScript, is exceedingly similar to Java or C programming languages. If you have experience with these languages already, then VRMLScript appears very easy.

VRMLScript is actually a subset of JavaScript. Therefore, it supports much of the same language semantics of JavaScript. The primary difference between VRMLScript and JavaScript is that VRMLScript disregards many of the document and browser class methods and properties necessary for Web pages. VRMLScript does contain a math library and common functions found in JavaScript.

This chapter presents a quick overview of VRMLScript. For more information on the JavaScript scripting language, which is again identical to VRMLScript in many ways, consult Chapters 34–38 of this book or *Teach Yourself JavaScript in 21 Days* or *Netscape 3 Unleashed* by Sams Publishing.

Functions in VRMLScript

As mentioned earlier, functions are essential in scripts. A function is simply a collection of VRMLScript commands that are executed. The important thing to note about functions is that the same group of VRMLScript commands can be executed repeatedly simply by calling that function's name.

The `Script` node maps particular `eventIn` parameters to functions within a `Script` node. In addition, values from other objects can be passed into a function. The function can use those values to determine what other events are happening in the three-dimensional scene you create.

Functions typically take the following format:

```
function functionName(eventIn_Value) {
   VRMLScript Code
}
```

NOTE

More than one function may be inserted within a `Script` node. However, each function must be declared by the `eventIn` parameters of a `Script` node in order for those functions to be publicly available to other objects in the scene.

Assigning Values in VRMLScript

The code between curly braces ({}) in a script's function may be any combination of VRMLScript commands or functions. Often calculations are performed and stored in variables within VRMLScript code. These variables can be assigned using a single = character. Likewise, property values for particular objects may be assigned using the = character. For example, assigning the `on` property of a `DirectionalLight` node named `MY_LIGHT` may be performed with the following statement:

```
MY_LIGHT.on = 1
```

Traditional mathematical functions are accepted within VRMLScript as well, such as multiplication (*), division (/), addition (+), and subtraction (-). Many other mathematical functions are defined within VRML/JavaScript's `math` object. For instance, using `Math.PI` in a line of VRMLScript code returns the value for pi.

TIP

There are numerous shortcuts in C, Java, JavaScript, and VRMLScript for updating variables. By using a variable name followed by two mathematical symbols, it is possible to update the value of that variable. For instance, to update the value of the variable var, the following statements can be used:

```
var++;    // Updates the variable by adding "1" to it, same as "var=var+1"
var-=5;   // Updates the variable by subtracting "5" from it, same as "var=var-5"
```

Conditional Logic

Another common action to perform in programming languages is conditional logic. Conditional logic is an elegant name for simply testing for certain values. Conditional logic typically consists of an `if/then/else` set. The VRMLScript application checks to see *if* some variable is equivalent to a particular value. If it is, *then* the VRMLScript can perform a particular task. If it is not equivalent, then the VRMLScript may have an option to do something *else*.

Conditional statements typically appear as follows:

```
if (variable == value) {
    do some VRMLScript if result is true
}
else {
    do some VRMLScript if result is false
}
```

Conditional statements may be as complex as necessary and can even be nested within each other. In some cases, you may need to test multiple criteria in order to establish a result.

VRMLScript uses typical C/Java/JavaScript notation for testing equivalence (==), non-equivalence (!=), greater than (>), less than (<), greater than or equal to (>=), less than or equal to (<=), logically "ANDing" values together (&&), logically "ORing" values (||), or inverting TRUE/FALSE Boolean values (!).

For example, to test whether an object is a sphere *and* is either red *or* blue, the following condition can be used:

```
if (shape == "sphere" && (color == "Red" || color == "Blue")) {
    ... the object is a red or blue sphere.
}
```

NOTE

Curly braces ({}) are used to surround a group of lines in VRMLScript source code. These braces indicate which lines of code are to be executed together as a group. For example, if an `if` statement is used, it is essential to indicate in the VRMLScript source code exactly which lines are to be executed when the result is true versus those lines that are executed when the result is false.

Looping

Some regions of a VRMLScript application may need to be executed more than once. To make a portion of code repeat numerous times, loops may be used in VRMLScript. There are typically two types of loops available in VRMLScript: the `for` loop and the `while` loop.

For Loop

The `for` loop indicates that a section of source code should execute *for* a particular number of iterations. This loop requires the following syntax:

```
for (loopIndex = startingValue; loopIndex_Condition; loopIndex_Update) {
    VRMLScript code
}
```

The `loopIndex` is a variable that keeps track of how many times the loop has executed. It may be set to a starting value. The `loopIndex_Condition` is similar to an `if` statement that instructs what a loop should look for in order to terminate. If the `loopIndex_Condition` is true, then the code within the loop is executed. When it is false, the loop terminates. Typically, it tests the `loopIndex`'s value to determine whether it has reached the end of the loop's range. Commonly, the `loopIndex` is incremented by one step at a time. However, it is possible to specify that this index update its value differently using the `loopIndex_Update` parameter.

The following are two examples of `for` loops that execute VRMLScript code for a total of 10 iterations:

```
for (n=1; n<=10; n++) {
    some VRMLScript code
}
```

or

```
for (n=20; n>0;n-=2){
    some VRMLScript code
}
```

while Loop

In some cases, you may want to execute a section of code several times without necessarily knowing in advance the exact number of times that loop should occur. The `while` loop allows you to execute a section of VRMLScript as long as the condition within the `while` loop is true. `while` loops use the following syntax:

```
while (condition) {
    do some VRMLScript
}
```

In this case, the `condition` parameter of the `while` loop acts like an `if` statement. When the result of the conditional test is true, the VRMLScript code is executed. Once the result is false, the loop is terminated.

VRML Browser Commands

You will remember that VRMLScript is very similar to JavaScript with the exception of the typical properties and methods found in JavaScript for documents and Web page control. However, VRMLScript also adds several specific commands that can be used with VRML browsers. Table 41.2 lists these specific commands and their functionality within the VRML browser.

Table 41.2. VRMLScript can access numerous methods for the `Browser` object.

Browser Method	*Action Performed*
`getName()`	Returns the name of the VRML browser being used to view a scene as a string.
`getVersion()`	Returns the version number of the VRML browser being used as a string.
`getCurrentSpeed()`	Returns the current speed at which a user is traveling through the VRML world. The value returned is a floating-point number.

Browser Method	*Action Performed*
`getCurrentFrameRate()`	Returns the speed at which scenes can be generated, in frames per second, as a floating-point number returns a VRML scene can be updated as quickly as a browser on a particular computer platform allows. Constraints may include the speed of the hardware, software, or graphics controller.
`getWorldURL()`	Returns a string value containing the current URL used to access the VRML scene displayed in the browser window.
`loadWorld(`*`url`*`)`	Instructs the browser to load another VRML world into the browser window. The `url` parameter specifies the file and location of the VRML file to load.
`replaceWorld(nodes)`	At times it may become necessary to update or replace particular nodes in a world currently viewed in the browser without actually loading a brand new world. The `nodes` parameter allows you to specify a list of nodes to use when replacing the currently viewed scene.
`createVRMLFromURL (url, node, event)`	It is possible to create a 3D scene using another URL for the VRML source. However, retrieving other URLs from the Internet may be a time consuming process. Therefore this method allows you to specify an `eventIn` that is notified when the new node list is successfully read.
`createVRMLFormString(string)`	Three-dimensional scenes may be created on the fly by passing strings that contain VRML commands to the browser. This method sends a string to the browser to be rendered and returns a list of root nodes when completed.
`addRoute(fromNode, fromEventOut, toNode, toEventIn)`	Because objects can be created by way of browser methods at any time, there must be a provision to add routing between new nodes. The `addRoute` method instructs the VRML browser to connect the `eventOut` from one node to the `eventIn` of another node, provided that the events and nodes are named.

continues

Table 41.2. continued

Browser Method	*Action Performed*
`deleteRoute(fromNode, fromEventOut, toNode, toEventIn)`	Just as it is possible to add routes spontaneously to newly created nodes, it is possible to remove them. This method disconnects an `eventOut` from one node and the `eventIn` of a second node.

Seeing the Light

Now that you have had a quick overview of VRMLScript and a familiarity with it, we can examine how it is used in a VRML scene to create an interactive world. A simple example in VRMLScript is to create a world where there is a single white cone in the middle of the world.

Ordinarily this cone appears very dark, therefore a default directional light can be added to give the cone an additional glow of light. Figure 41.2 demonstrates this simple three-dimensional object with the light source applied. In this figure, the Silicon Graphics CosmoPlayer was used to display the VRML world.

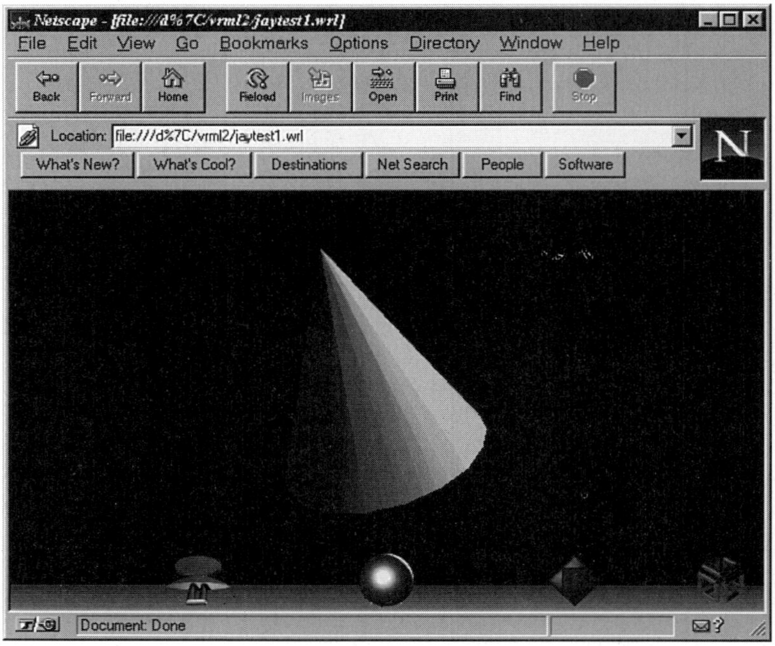

FIGURE 41.2.
A directional light adds a glow to the right half of this 3D cone. The light can be turned on or off by clicking on the cone.

When the light is on and you click on the cone, the light is turned off, and the cone is scarcely visible against the black background. Likewise, if you click on the cone while the light is off, it is turned back on again to reveal the cone.

This simple task of turning a directional light on or off is accomplished using a simple VRML script embedded within a `Script` node and a `TouchSensor`. There are also additional `ROUTE` statements used to direct `eventOut`'s of some nodes into `eventIn`'s of others. To understand how this simple world is constructed, examine its source code in Listing 41.2.

Listing 41.2. The light is controlled using a `TouchSensor` and a simple VRMLScript with routing statements.

```
#VRML V2.0 utf8

DEF MY_LIGHT DirectionalLight {
    on TRUE
}

Transform {
  children [
    DEF TOUCH_SENSOR TouchSensor {}
    Shape {
      appearance Appearance {
        material Material {
          diffuseColor    1 1 1
        }
      }

      geometry Cone{}
    }
  ]
}

DEF toggle Script {
    field    SFBool lightOn FALSE
    eventIn  SFBool isConeClicked
    eventOut SFBool toggle_changed
    url  "vrmlscript:
          function isConeClicked(button_state) {
            if (button_state == 0) {
              if (lightOn == 0)
                lightOn = 1;
              else
                lightOn = 0;
              toggle_changed = lightOn;
            }
          }
         "
}

ROUTE TOUCH_SENSOR.isActive TO toggle.isConeClicked
ROUTE toggle.toggle_changed TO MY_LIGHT.on
```

As you look at the code in Listing 41.2, you will not find much out of the ordinary for creating a simple cone shape in a VRML world. The following sections review what code elements make this simple world interactive.

Touch-Sensitive Cone

The first thing you may notice as you scan down from the top of the source code in Listing 41.2 is the presence of a `TouchSensor`. This `TouchSensor` is named `TOUCH_SENSOR` for reference later on in the source code.

You'll recall that a `TouchSensor` gives an object in VRML 2.0 the ability to have a user click on it in order to perform some action. The `TouchSensor` node can contain numerous events and fields, but the only thing we are concerned with is setting up the `TouchSensor` and triggering a VRMLScript when someone clicks on the cone.

`TouchSensors` are applied to all geometry that falls within the parent node containing the TouchSensor node. In our example, the `TouchSensor` is related to its parent node `Transform`, which was not given a proper name. Therefore, any geometry that appears within this `Transform` is treated as "hot-spots" for the `TouchSensor`. That is, if you can click on any objects within that `transform` and a `TouchSensor` is connected to that `transform`, an action occurs. In our example in Listing 41.2, the only geometric object within the `transform` is a cone, therefore you are only able to click on that cone to initiate an action.

The sensor simply monitors mouse input while the world is viewed. Whenever the mouse passes over objects that contain the `TouchSensor` and the mouse button is clicked, an `eventOut` is triggered from the `TouchSensor`. In this case, the `isActive eventOut` is sent, indicating that a user is actively clicking on the object.

So now that the sensor has been created and an appropriate event is being triggered, what's next? The action of clicking on the cone must be recognized by a script and handled appropriately. This requires the use of a routing statement that connects the `isActive eventOut` from the `TouchSensor` to an appropriate function within a `Script` node. We will review all of the routes that are defined in this scene shortly.

Reading the Script

The next obvious difference in the source code is the addition of a `Script` node. This node allows the VRML browser to control other objects and actions within the three-dimensional world using instructions presented in the node.

The first three lines of the `Script` node declare a variable to be used within the script (`lightOn`), the function `isConeClicked` (which is the node's `eventIn`), and a property named `toggle_changed`, which is an `eventOut`. As you will recall, a `Script` node's `eventIn` declarations match the functions that are available to other objects as methods. Similarly the script node's `eventOut` declarations match variables used in the script that can be read by other objects afterward.

This simple script reads the output of the `TOUCH_SENSOR` output event as input to its own `isConeClicked` function. The `isActive` event from the touch sensor is `TRUE` or 1 when the mouse button is held down and `FALSE` or 0 otherwise. This event is passed to the `isConeClicked` function as the variable `button_state`. When the button is pressed, the `isActive` event of the `TouchSensor` changes from a 0 to a 1, and that result is assigned to the variable `button_state` in the `isConeClicked` function.

Within that function, the script determines whether the light is currently on or off using a variable that toggles its state simultaneously with the directional light `MY_LIGHT`. After the script establishes that the light is either on or off, it changes the state of the light to be the opposite. This is accomplished by first setting the variable within the `Script` node that represents the light to the appropriate value (`1` = on, `0` = off). Another routing statement later takes this variable's result and routes it to the actual light source to complete the action.

NOTE

When writing scripts that respond to `TouchSensors`, it is important to notice that the `TouchSensor` triggers the events and actions continuously. For example, when you hold the mouse button down for a long period of time over the object with the sensor, the sensor sends the `isActive` event to a respective object as long as the mouse button is held down. Therefore, you may consider checking the status of the mouse button (which is indicated by the `isActive` event from the `TouchSensor`). You may wish to only execute the script commands when the mouse button has been released, indicating a complete button click. Listing 41.2 does just this using the condition:

```
if (button_state == 0).
```

TIP

Although it does not matter to the VRML browser that the events and fields appear before the URL, it is a good practice to place them before the actual embedded script code. This makes the code more legible since common programming practices have developers declare variables before the script. Also when reading the script from top to bottom, you will read the variables first and remember them when they are referenced in the code.

Wiring the Light

Now that the script has been designed to check the status of the light and set the new state appropriately, it is time to see how the `TouchSensor`, script, and light are all connected together.

You learned earlier about the `ROUTE` statement in VRML 2.0. This command allows you to control the flow of control for a three-dimensional environment created with Moving Worlds. Routing commands basically inform the browser of the sequence of actions that are to be taken when particular events arise.

In the example shown in Listing 41.2, the `TouchSensor` triggers a script, which in turn triggers a light source in the scene. Therefore, two routing statements are required: one to connect the `TOUCH_SENSOR` sensor to the `toggle` script, and a second to connect the `toggle` script to the light `MY_LIGHT`.

More specifically, the output event's value of the sensor is passed to the input event and ultimately a function of the script. The resulting property value of the script is then sent onto the input event for the light that determines whether the light is on or off. The two lines that accomplish this are:

```
ROUTE TOUCH_SENSOR.isActive TO toggle.isConeClicked
ROUTE toggle.toggle_changed TO MY_LIGHT.on
```

Using Java for More Kick

You can create some fairly complex VRML worlds using the VRMLScript capabilities that have been introduced so far. However, for very complex worlds that require a more robust, object-oriented language, you may consider using something like Java. With Java, truly interactive applications that deal with user's input, network information, and a host of other capabilities are possible.

Fortunately, it is quite simple to tap the capabilities of Java and integrate them with your VRML 2.0 worlds. In the previous section, you learned many of the fundamentals of integrating programmable scripts with Moving Worlds objects. These same techniques will be applied to integrating Java applets with your three-dimensional worlds.

To illustrate connectivity between Java and VRML, consider another example. In this example, we will make a simple cone (we love cones) rotate towards the viewer and appear closer. It will then take several steps to rotate that cone away from the viewer at a further distance away. The animation will continue to swing back and forth as long as the scene is viewed in the VRML browser. In this case, Sony's CyberPassage makes viewing Java-controlled VRML files easy. Sony CyberPassage also includes Java classes that can be incorporated into your Java applets to create these complex VRML worlds. These classes follow standards documented at the Moving Worlds site at Silicon Graphics (`http://vrml.sgi.com/moving-worlds`).

This is a fairly simple animation applet that does not require complicated coding algorithms. However, it is ample for demonstrating the connectivity between VRML and Java. Figures 41.3 through 41.5 show three of the stages of the cone's rotation in order for you to gain a feel for how it will look animated.

Now that you can picture how this animation appears, consider the source code for this animation. Listing 41.3 demonstrates the VRML file that renders the cone. Listing 41.4 displays the Java source code that controls the animation of the VRML cone. The VRML file also connects a `TimeSensor` to a `Script` node that invokes the Java applet described in Listing 41.4.

Listing 41.3. The VRML file for the animated cone consists of the cone, a `TimeSensor`, and a simple script to connect the Java applet.

```
#VRML V2.0 utf8

DEF MY_LIGHT DirectionalLight {
    on TRUE
}

DEF MYCONE_TRANSFORM Transform {
  children [
    Shape {
      appearance Appearance {
        material Material {
          diffuseColor    0 0 1
        }
      }

    geometry Cone{}
    }
  ]
}

DEF TIME_SENSOR TimeSensor{
    loop TRUE
    cycleInterval .250
}

DEF SCRIPT Script{
    url         "MyCone.class"
    scriptType "javabc"

    eventOut   SFRotation MyConeRt
    eventOut   SFVec3f    MyConeTr

    eventIn    SFTime     moveMyCone
}


ROUTE TIME_SENSOR.cycleTime TO SCRIPT.moveMyCone

ROUTE SCRIPT.MyConeTr TO MYCONE_TRANSFORM.set_translation
ROUTE SCRIPT.MyConeRt TO MYCONE_TRANSFORM.set_rotation
```

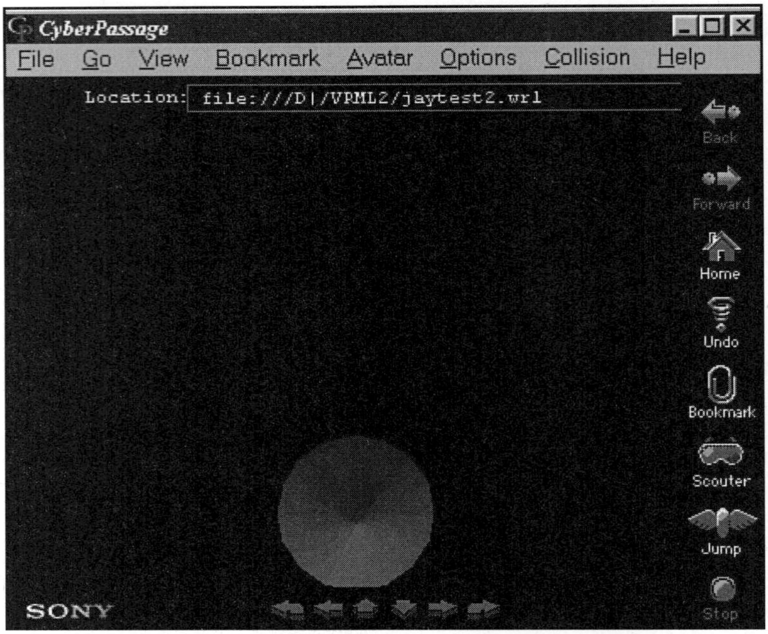

FIGURE 41.3.
In the Java-controlled VRML animation, the cone begins by pointing directly at the user.

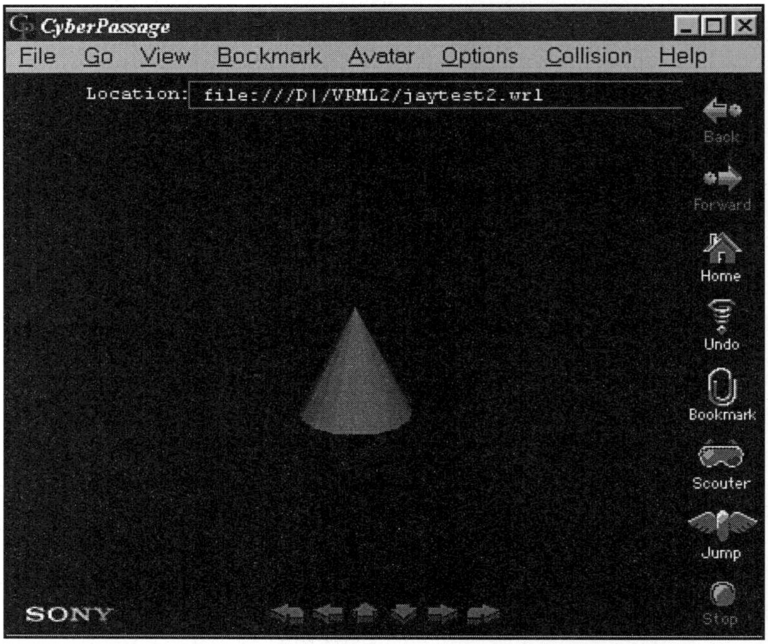

FIGURE 41.4.
In the middle of the same Java-controlled VRML animation, the cone points straight up.

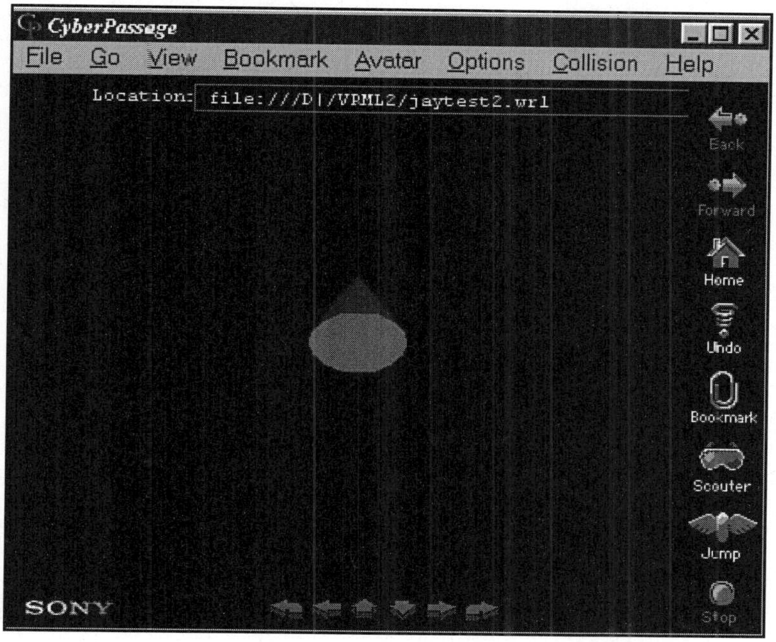

FIGURE 41.5.
The Java-controlled VRML animation ends by pointing the cone away from the user.

Listing 41.4. This Java applet controls the animation of the cone displayed in Figures 41.3–41.5.

```
import vs.*;
import vrml.*;

public class MyCone extends Script{
    // aRad is defined to make degrees to radian conversion easier
    float aRad = (float) (Math.PI/180.0) ;

    // Get the eventOuts from the VRML file
    // These are the properties that get sent to the cone
    // to update its rotation and position
    SFRotation MyConeRt = (SFRotation)getEventOut("MyConeRt");
    SFVec3f MyConeTr = (SFVec3f)getEventOut("MyConeTr");

    // We're going to setup an array of coordinates, so we'll
    // need an index for the array
    int count;
    // Since the animation will bounce back and forth, we'll
    // need to increment or decrement "count" accordingly
    int countDirection = 1;

    float[] positionX;
    float[] positionY;
    float[] positionZ;
    float[] angle;
    float[] translation;
    float[] rotation;
```

continues

Listing 41.4. continued

```
// Constructor my "MyCone" class.  Initialization happens here.
public MyCone()
{

    positionX = new float[9];
    positionY = new float[9];
    positionZ = new float[9];
    angle = new float[9];

    // Translations of objects requires a 3D vector
    // "translation" will hold the X, Y, and Z
    translation = new float[3];

    // Rotations require four parameters:
    // Which axis to rotate around: X, Y, or Z, and the
    // amount of radians to rotate
    rotation = new float[4];

    // Setup all of the animation points
    positionX[0] = 0f;
    positionY[0] = 0f;
    positionZ[0] = 4f;
    angle[0] = 60f;
    positionX[1] = 0f;
    positionY[1] = 0f;
    positionZ[1] = 3f;
    angle[1] = 45f;
    positionX[2] = 0f;
    positionY[2] = 0f;
    positionZ[2] = 2f;
    angle[2] = 30f;
    positionX[3] = 0f;
    positionY[3] = 0f;
    positionZ[3] = 1f;
    angle[3] = 15f;
    positionX[4] = 0f;
    positionY[4] = 0f;
    positionZ[4] = 0f;
    angle[4] = 0f;
    positionX[5] = 0f;
    positionY[5] = 0f;
    positionZ[5] = -1f;
    angle[5] = -15f;
    positionX[6] = 0f;
    positionY[6] = 0f;
    positionZ[6] = -2f;
    angle[6] = -30f;
```

```
        positionX[7] = 0f;
        positionY[7] = 0f;
        positionZ[7] = -3f;
        angle[7] = -40f;
        positionX[8] = 0f;
        positionY[8] = 0f;
        positionZ[8] = -4f;
        angle[8] = -60f;



        // Initialize the count index
        count = 0;
}

    // moveMyCone is invoked every 250ms as defined in
    // the host VRML file.  This method is invoked each
    // time the TimeSensor cycleTime event occurs.
    public void moveMyCone(ConstSFTime time, ConstSFTime ts)
    {
        // Move cone to new X, Y, Z position
        translation[0] = positionX[count];
        translation[1] = positionY[count];
        translation[2] = positionZ[count];
        MyConeTr.setValue(translation);

        // Rotate the cone around its X access
        rotation[0] = 1.0f;
        rotation[1] = 0.0f;
        rotation[2] = 0.0f;
        rotation[3] = angle[count] * aRad;
        MyConeRt.setValue(rotation);

        // Increment/Decrement array index through animation
        count = count + (1*countDirection);

        // When we hit one end of animation, change direction
        if(count >= 9){
            countDirection = -1;
        count = 7;
        }
        if(count < 0){
            countDirection = 1;
            count = 1;
        }
    }
}
```

It's About Time

To make sense of all of this code, first look at the VRML file shown in Listing 41.3. It should be fairly straightforward by now what this VRML file is doing. It renders a scene with a cone, lit by a directional light source.

It also defines a `TimeSensor`. A `TimeSensor` in Moving Worlds is similar to other sensors, including the `TouchSensor` we have reviewed already. It contains `eventOut`'s that can be used to trigger actions to occur in other objects and `eventIn`'s for specifying the sensor's own characteristics. The `TimeSensor` node allows a VRML browser to create an object that checks an internal clock and sends notifications when a particular time has transpired. This `TimeSensor` can be used as an alarm for events that should occur only after a specific amount of time has past. It may also be used as a metronome, sending events on a regular basis. In our example, the `TimeSensor` triggers actions in the script object on a regular interval (every 250ms).

Time to Read the Script

Every 250ms, the `TimeSensor` sends a `cycleTime eventOut` to a `Script` node as specified by a `ROUTE` command near the end of the VRML code listing. This `Script` node is similar to the one we examined earlier with our lighted cone example. The sole purpose of the `Script` node is to determine which methods within the program `Script` are to be used by other objects and what values the program script can post for other objects to use.

In our previous example in this chapter, the `Script` node also embedded the actual scripting commands within the node. In this case, the Java applet that controls the animation cannot be embedded since it is compiled into Java bytecodes. Therefore, the `URL` parameter of this node points to the actual Java class file. Since the `URL` parameter does not contain the actual script language, the VRML browser must know what type of program code it can expect at the location specified. The `scriptType` parameter in Listing 41.3 indicates that the program pointed to by the `URL` is a byte code-compiled Java applet (`javabc` implies *Java Bytecode*).

Route It Out

The final routing statements should come as little surprise. Once the Java applet has determined what the next rotational and translation points should be for the cone during its course of animation, it must update the cone accordingly. The last `ROUTE` commands map the respective properties of the Java applet that contain this information to the appropriate `eventIn` methods for the `Transform` node that contains the cone.

Imported Java

Once you have an understanding of the VRML file for this simple animation, you can begin to examine its accompanying Java applet's source code. As mentioned earlier, Sony CyberPassage provides VRML classes that can be imported into your Java applet. These classes provide numerous functions, but most importantly in this example, they provide the linkage between the `Script` node in the VRML file and the respective methods and properties in the Java applet.

TIP

To make compilation of Java/VRML applets easier, copy the `VRML` and `VS` subdirectories into the Java Developer's Kit (JDK) directory. The best place to move them to make your life easier is within the `classes` subdirectory within your JDK directory. Your JDK directory should then contain a `classes` folder that contains at least four directories: `java`, `sun`, `vrml`, and `vs`.

The first two lines found in Listing 41.4 import the necessary classes for creating Moving Worlds Java applets. One of these classes defines the `Script` class that the applet inherits from, as shown by the first line of code past the `import` statements. The `Script` class contains all of the Application Programming Interface (API) commands necessary to connect your Java applet to the `Script` node in your VRML file. These classes also contain the different field types found in VRML and map them as appropriate variable declarations in Java.

A few lines further into the Java application, you will find the following two lines:

```
SFRotation MyConeRt = (SFRotation)getEventOut("MyConeRt");
SFVec3f MyConeTr = (SFVec3f)getEventOut("MyConeTr");
```

These two lines fetch the `eventOut` information from the `Script` node in the VRML file and map the information to Java variables respectively. The `getEventOut` function finds a particular `eventOut` in a VRML `Script` node to which the Java applet is related. As you can see from these two lines, the rotational values and translation positions are declared using appropriate vectors for VRML.

Initializing the Applet

When the applet is constructed for the first time, its constructor method is invoked. The `MyCone` method is the constructor for this applet, which initializes default values and fills the rotational/translation arrays used for the animation with numbers. The number of four basic arrays that are used: `positionX`, `positionY`, `positionZ`, and `angle`. These arrays are as large as the number of steps in the animation. This particular animation uses nine steps, where each step stores a different rotational and translation value in each of the arrays.

Therefore the first step of the animation, denoted by an index of `0` for the arrays, contains the following settings for the cone's location in 3D space as well as how far it should be rotated:

```
positionX[0] = 0f;
positionY[0] = 0f;
positionZ[0] = 4f;
angle[0] = 60f;
```

The Main Task

The `Script` node found in Listing 41.3 specifically states that the primary method (`eventIn`) for the Java applet is the `moveMyCone` method. Therefore, whenever the script is invoked in the `Script` node, this method is invoked in the Java applet. In this example, this happens when the actual animation is performed.

The method simply finds the position and rotation information for the current step in the animation and assigns the appropriate position vector and rotational properties for export out of the Java applet. The `ROUTE` statements in the VRML file found in Listing 41.3 take the data exported from the Java applet and update the correct object nodes appropriately.

NOTE

Notice that the exported properties (`myConeTr` and `myConeRt`) for the Java applet in Listing 41.4 are set using the `setValue` method. This is essential since the rotational and translation values are treated as arrays of floating-point numbers in the Java applet, but must be converted to appropriate vectors for VRML.

The `moveMyCone` method also updates the pointer to the current frame in the animation and verifies that it has not gone past the beginning or the end of the animation. If it has crossed the bounds at either end, the direction of the animation is reversed by changing the steps in the sequence to increment or decrement. The end result is an animation that appears to swing back and forth.

NOTE

Because a number of steps are played for a consecutive number of times to create the animation, it is tempting to think that a loop would be appropriate to use in the `moveMyCone` method. Although loops can be used, this particular animation is supposed to constantly run in the background. The `TimeSensor` found in the VRML source for this example indicates that an action should be taken every 250 milliseconds. Therefore, every 250 ms the cone's position and rotation can be updated. The `TimeSensor` keeps the VRML world in sync, particularly if other VRML objects are animated with the cone.

In addition, some machines may execute Java code faster than others. If the animation were accomplished completely with a loop, the speed of the animation would vary depending on the machine. Not to mention that a continuous loop may occupy all of the applet's running time and not allow other actions to occur.

Summary

This chapter introduced you to the fundamentals of VRMLScript and the techniques required to attach VRML objects to programmable scripts. You learned the basics of controlling a VRML world with a Java applet and can hopefully expand upon that knowledge to create some truly unique, entertaining, and interactive worlds of your own.

X PART

IN THIS PART

Web Publishing Administration

CHAPTER 42

Managing Large-Scale Projects

by William Robert Stanek

IN THIS CHAPTER

Blockbusters are not written; they are produced. Look at today's hit movies and TV shows. Behind the big scenes, you will find a producer and often a collaborative team. Electronic media are no exception. Behind the big titles, you will find a team—producers, editors, writers, programmers, musicians, and artists. All these people help to organize ideas into a finely polished work. They do this by collaborating—organizing their ideas into a common structure through planning, revision, polishing, and evaluation.

Even when creative works are the result of a single person's efforts, the finished product is still a result of planning, revision, polishing, and fretting over the organization of the work. This is true even for creative people who claim never to use outlines. The simple fact is, finely polished works do not spring to the writer's pen, the painter's canvas, or the musician's note sheets. The best works are the result of effective strategies for thinking, planning, and composing. Helping you manage the development of large-scale projects through effective strategies for thinking, planning, and composing is precisely what this chapter is all about.

In this chapter, you will learn the following:

- Why organization is important
- The building blocks for creating effective Web publications
- Improving ideas—techniques to better organize the Web publication
- Effective strategies for planning and project organization
- Techniques to get the project started
- Techniques to organize the project for the audience
- The use of storyboards to help you organize and link the pages of the publication

Why Organization Is So Important

Web publishing is a new medium for your creativity. Spending a few hours thinking about something that you may spend years, or certainly months, working on makes sense. Getting organized is extremely important, more so when you are working in a new medium. Not only will it save you time, it will help you create a better project. This is true regardless of whether you plan to adapt existing projects or create entirely new projects for your Web-publishing ventures.

Too often, the tendency in Web publishing is to produce an electronic version of the paper-based product. The result is a publication that does not work well and does not appeal to Web users. This is a major problem in Web publishing today. The Web is the ultimate form for Web publications. It is an open-ended multimedia system that will let you seamlessly integrate sound, video, pictures, and text. Most of the publications on the Web are organized like a book—complete with an index. The index is often the starting point for readers of the publication. Yet an electronic extension of a traditional book is not what consumers want.

On the Web, you have only a few minutes to convince readers to stay. If you do not, they are going to go somewhere else for their information as quickly and effortlessly as you can remotely change the channel on your television. Yet, the key to success in Web publishing is not to attract one-time visitors, but to attract repeat visitors to the publication. Publishers on the Web are discovering this the hard way.

The current trend in design on the Web is to create Web publications primarily for repeat visitors while providing a means for the first-time visitor to learn about the publication. Publishers who have adapted this strategy have seen dramatic results, and all because a few innovative thinkers took the time to organize their thoughts before they created publications in the traditional manner.

These innovative thinkers applied some of the processes you will learn in this chapter and came up with better ways to present information. You can apply these processes to any type of Web-publishing project. Creating Web publications can be either a continuous struggle or a logically flowing process. Take the time to organize your thoughts. Not only will the payoff be a better product, it will also mean time and resource savings.

Building Blocks for Creating Effective Publications

Think of the creative process as a building process. Try to build the roof of the house before you lay the foundation and you are going to have serious problems. Pour the concrete for the foundation of the house before you put in the necessary plumbing for water and sewer access and you are going to spend more money than you bargained for.

You build a house one step at a time. You ensure the house has a strong foundation. Buildings with strong foundations tend to weather the seasons and time. When you are almost done with the frame of the house, you build a roof. Although the roof of the house is the top of the structure, you do not stop there. It takes more than a covered frame to make a house. You hire an electrician to do the wiring and bring back the plumber to finish the plumbing. Afterward, you hang plasterboard, add insulation, finish the exterior, add fixtures, and before you know it, you have a house that you can call home.

You build Web publications in the same way—one step at a time, following the activities covered in the previous section. Your start on the project is about as glamorous as the water and sewer pipes waiting for the foundation to be poured around them; just when you are ready to roll back your sleeves and dive into the project with both feet, you may discover you need to conduct research and planning or consider the requirements of the project.

When you finally flesh out the foundation of the project, you start to build the framework. The basic components of any Web publication are the pages that you link together. These pages help you create chapters, articles, and columns that can contain graphics, sound, and even full-motion video. Eventually, you finish composing the project but find you still have to develop its software aspects. Even when you have completed the composing and developing processes, the project still is not finished. You check the structure of the work for flaws. You make sure you have used the right mechanics and format. You examine the fixtures. After all this is done, you finally have a project worthy of publishing.

Try to build the house all at once and you will be overwhelmed. The same is true for any creative process. The way you organize your thoughts can make the difference between a successful project and a failed project. When you are building your Web publication, you need to manage many things—on both a level of general organization and a more specific level of Web-publishing aspects:

- Expectations
- Perceptions
- Strategies
- Goals
- Rules
- Behavior

Managing Expectations

If you mismanage expectations, your project may not turn out as you planned. Your expectations and the expectations of your superiors may be totally different. Before you begin any project, make sure your expectations and the expectations of your supervisors mesh. A good way to do this is to ensure that the communications channels are open and used.

To ensure your project is a smashing success, you should discuss expectations from the beginning of the project. If you develop a rapid prototype of the project, your superiors should be the ones to verify that it meets their expectations. If the prototype does not meet their expectations, maybe the prototype was an example of what not to do for this project, or maybe the expectations were unrealistic. If your prototype meets or exceeds the expectations of your superiors, you have a green light and your project is well on its way to a successful implementation.

You should also manage your personal expectations for the project. Your expectations play a major role in the success of the project. The following is a list of do's and don'ts to help you manage expectations:

- Don't expect the creation and development of the project to flow effortlessly.
- Don't expect first efforts to be perfect.
- Don't expect the completed project to be perfect.
- Do expect to make multiple drafts of the project.
- Do expect to revise, edit, and proof parts of the project.

- Do expect to say the project is "good enough" and that further time spent trying to perfect the project will not be cost-effective.
- Do expect the creation and development process to be challenging and fun.
- Do expect to learn a lot.

Managing Perceptions

Realistic expectations ensure the success of your project. If you perceive the project as an impossibly large undertaking, you may cripple yourself mentally. If you perceive the project as a trivial undertaking, you will not produce your best work.

It is best to find a balance in your perceptions about the project. If you are working on an extremely large project, work on the project in manageable pieces. Do not try to combine the composition and development processes. Take them one at a time. Develop the textual part of the project a chapter, page, or word at a time—whatever it takes to pull you through the project.

As you begin to organize your project, keep in mind that Web publishing is very often a team effort. Few Web publishers will be able to handle all aspects of the publishing process on their own. For this reason, you should have an accurate perception of your abilities and know when it is in the best interest of the project to delegate tasks. For example, if the project requires extensive Java programming and you are not a Java programmer, you will want to consider adding a programmer to the team. Not only will delegating tasks to other team members help ensure the success of the project, it will also take responsibilities off your shoulders and help you avoid feeling overwhelmed.

Managing Strategies

Can you imagine writing 200,000 words and developing hundreds of examples to fill more than 600 pages in a little over three months? The thought of having to do this would overwhelm the best of writers. Yet this is exactly what I had to do to complete my share of the first edition of *Web Publishing Unleashed*. I managed the project by thinking of the work in terms that motivated me. It was not 199,000 words I had to write, it was 1,000 words completed. It was not 550 pages to go, it was 50 pages down. It was not 16 chapters left to write, it was one chapter completed.

Creating a new project is exciting and challenging. You'll be breaking new ground, trying new things, and experimenting with new material. How you think about the project will materially affect the outcome. Manage the project in whatever way will motivate you. If one way of thinking about the project is not motivating you, change tactics. Break up difficult sections of the project. Tackle them one piece at a time. Rotate from section to section, working on each piece a little at a time. Whatever it takes to get the job done.

As a Web publisher, you will often wear many hats. You may have the roles of the writer, graphic designer, composer, editor, and publisher. You may want to develop a strategy with these roles in mind. For example, if you are in the role of the writer and have been staring at a blank page for hours, you may want to change roles for a time. Why not create the preliminary artwork for a particular area of the publication? This will give you a chance to work on another area of the project, and you can return to writing at a later time with a fresh perspective.

Similarly, if you are working on a mundane but necessary part of the project (such as proofreading), think of a way to make the work more interesting or challenging. Bet yourself that you can proof portions of the project in a certain amount of time. And when you succeed, allow yourself a few moments of quiet celebration before you attack the project again.

Do not limit yourself to a few strategies or stick with one strategy when it is obviously not working. Make a list of strategies. If one strategy is not working, switch to a new one. If you do not have a new one, create a new one.

Managing Goals

When you start working on a project, one of the first things you should do is develop goals. Goals are usually developed in the requirements phase. Your goals should take into consideration the complexities and nuances of the project. Goals should be clear and relevant to the problem at hand. You should set major goals relevant to the purpose, scope, and audience of the project. You should also set minor goals or milestones for the stages of the project.

Goals and milestones help you define the project as a series of steps, processes, or achievements. One major goal could be to complete the planning phase of the project. Another major goal could be to complete the design of the project. The series of steps or processes necessary to complete the major goals are the minor goals or milestones. Your first milestone will be to start work on the project. Another milestone may be to select and purchase an authoring tool, such as Microsoft FrontPage.

Managing Rules

As publisher and project manager, you will probably create or be provided rules that pertain specifically to the project—all programming aspects of the project will be written in the C++ programming language, for example, or the Web publication will be written entirely in HTML 2.0. As you start the project, these rules may seem perfectly acceptable. However, as you conduct planning for the project, you may find that C++ isn't the best choice or that HTML 2.0 is too restrictive for your needs. If these early rules cannot be modified to fit the project, you will have problems. You may encounter delays due to loss of efficiency, or the final product may not be what was expected.

No rule should ever be considered absolute. Even the best of rules should be interpreted as guidelines that can vary depending on the situation. Rules for a project should be flexible and make sense. A rule that conflicts with something you are trying to do in the project should be reexamined. The rule may be inappropriate for the situation you are trying to apply it to.

Managing Behavior

A project will never get finished if you avoid working on it. Putting off work until something is due is a poor practice. Quitting when things do not go your way or when you seem to have a block is another poor practice. Even if you thrive on deadlines, plan to work on a project regularly—every day if necessary and possible. You should also plan to work on the project during those times when your thoughts are not flowing. Everyone has bad days and good days. Some days you take more breaks. Some days you work straight through the day and into the night.

You may tend toward other destructive behavior besides avoiding or putting off work. Sometimes publishers go to the opposite extreme. They tear things apart impulsively before letting the work cool off so they can look at it objectively. Never edit, revise, or proof material immediately after it is drafted or put in near-final form.

For example, you have just completed the implementation phase of the project. You have been working on the project 16 hours a day for three weeks. You tell yourself if you do some minor tweaking now the project will be finished. You start correcting minor problems and before you know it, you are changing the master storyboard because things do not seem to fit right, or you are cutting Chapter 18. At this point, an alarm should go off in your mind. Take a break for a day or two before going back to the project. You will be thankful you did.

NOTE

When working on a project, you should back it up regularly. I keep a master copy and at least one backup copy of all projects on floppy disk and on my hard drive. I also have my word processor set to make automatic saves of my work every five minutes. You will be thankful for backups if you delete material in the heat of the moment and later regret it. Disk space is cheap compared to your time and ideas.

Improving Ideas: Techniques to Better Organize

To improve your ideas, you must think in new ways. You must examine the ordinary through different eyes. You must look at the mundane in a new light. You must examine your ideas in fresh ways.

Tapping into your creativity is not a simple process. People have been trying to figure out how to tap into creativity throughout history. One of the great thinkers on the subject of creativity was Abraham Maslow, who discussed creativity in terms of primary and secondary creativity. Secondary creativity is a restrictive creativity—the creativity of adults that is based on the creativity of others. Primary creativity is an innocent or original creativity—the creativity of children, which is blocked off by most adults and a part of our subconscious thoughts. Maslow further said that creativity is not necessarily the trait of those who are geniuses or talented, meaning that the fact that someone is a genius or has certain talents does not mean he is also creative.

Maslow's theories on creativity are very important to help people improve ideas. They suggest that you probably could tap into your creative processes by reaching into your subconscious mind. They suggest you should try to think freely without the inhibitions placed upon you by society or age. They suggest you should look at your ideas through innocent or unjudging eyes. Many modern techniques for aiding the creative process come out of this school of thinking, such as the following:

- Brainstorming
- Freethinking
- Storyboarding

NOTE

Although techniques to improve ideas are most often used at the beginning of projects, they can and should be used any time you want to try to improve your ideas. You may find these techniques especially useful at key stages in project development. For example, if you are considering which type of graphics or sound to include in the project, why not try brainstorming, freethinking, or storyboarding as a way of ensuring you make the best choices?

Brainstorming

One of the most used techniques for boosting creativity is brainstorming. Brainstorming was originally developed as a group problem-solving technique and is designed so that everyone in the group becomes involved in the problem-solving process. Participation, a necessary ingredient for problem-solving, is the key to the success of brainstorming.

To promote the creative process, members of a brainstorming group are given a strict set of rules governing their behavior. These rules are designed to break down the barriers to communication and ensure that all ideas—no matter how far-fetched—are examined. The rules also protect the egos of the group members and promote the need to be a productive member of the group.

The basic rules of brainstorming include the following:

- No evaluation of any idea put forth is permitted.
- Realize that the ideas put forth are simply ideas and not solutions.
- Free your mind by first thinking of the wildest answers to the problem.

- Throw out as many ideas as you can—every idea that comes into your mind.
- Build on the ideas of other group members.
- When the ideas get more difficult to think of, do not stop; the best ideas are just ahead.

One way to get a group brainstorming session going is to start with one person and work around the table or room to the other members. Each person should provide at least one answer or idea to the problem posed. Additionally, someone within the group should be recording the ideas. This allows you to build on ideas in the later stages of the brainstorming session. Following this technique, everyone in the group becomes involved in the problem-solving process.

Similar concepts can be applied to single-person efforts. Brainstorming can boost your creativity tremendously. If you brainstorm, you will tend to be less critical of your work. Eventually, you also will tend to naturally think of more than one approach to solving a problem.

For one-person brainstorming efforts, the following are good techniques to follow:

- Identify the problem, purpose, audience, or subject you want to brainstorm.
- Write this down in the middle of a large piece of paper and circle it.
- Write down all the ideas that come to your mind concerning the topic and circle them.
- Do not stop until you have filled the page.
- Look for patterns or repeated ideas.
- Use these ideas to develop further ideas or to develop solutions.

Freethinking

Freethinking is another effective technique to boost your creativity. When you freethink, you begin by telling yourself, "I will think something!" You think about a topic for a set period, recording your thoughts. Another term for freethinking is freewriting. The latter term tends to be more restrictive than necessary, because the form of your freethinking efforts does not have to be written.

When you freethink, you should record your thoughts in the way that makes you most comfortable—on paper, a tape recorder, or a computer. You should also select a period for freethinking you are comfortable with. Ten minutes may be right for some people. Others may prefer longer or shorter periods. After a freethinking session, you review what you recorded and note the ideas you liked.

Often, several freethinking sessions are necessary to get the best ideas. For most people, two or three successive freethinking sessions may be enough to help generate their best material. Others may wish to try a series of freethinking sessions over a period of several days. The key is to find the freethinking method that works best for you and use it.

Storyboarding

Storyboards are a high-power approach to creative thinking. They are particularly useful for Web publications because of the way they help you structure ideas visually. When you storyboard, you represent each page of the presentation in miniature form on a planning sheet and create a mockup of the project.

The storyboard serves not only as an outline for the presentation, it also lets you visualize the project in a way you otherwise would not be able to. At a glance, you can see the publication from start to finish. This is extremely important in the way you conceptualize the project. The project is no longer a mysterious tangle of documents you have to string together. It has a logical order from beginning to end. Often, being able to see to the end of a complex project is 75 percent of the battle. Techniques used in storyboarding will be discussed in depth in later sections of this chapter.

Effective Strategies for Planning and Project Organization

Creating large Web publications or entire Web sites is ideally a team effort, with each member of the team working in an area of the publication in which they specialize. In the real world, things do not always turn out ideally. Very often, Web publishers must wear many hats. They must be the writer, artist, musician, graphic designer, programmer, editor, and publisher.

The tasks involved in each of these roles can be broken down into three broad categories:

- Composition processes
- Development processes
- Publishing processes

Composition Processes

The processes involved in creating original material can be broadly defined as *composition processes.* In the role of the writer, artist, or musician, the Web publisher creates new material or adapts existing material. This role for the publisher can be limited or extensive, depending on the needs of the publication. The publisher will generally create new material only as necessary. Even if the publisher works directly with writers, artists, or musicians or purchases existing material, at some point the publisher should evaluate the work within the scope of the composition processes.

Contrary to popular opinion, the creative process is not some mythical beast that you must hunt down. You may discover many ways to compose a work and many ways to get to the final product. This is true no matter the form of the creation, but generally, composition processes include seven activities:

- Planning
- Researching
- Composing
- Evaluating
- Revising
- Editing
- Proofing

Before discussing these activities, let's dispel some myths about the creative process. Just because there are seven activities does not mean you have to perform them all. You will use more of these activities when you are working in new mediums. When you are writing about a new subject area, you will tend to use more of the activities than if you were writing about a subject with which you were very familiar. If you are writing for an audience for whom you have never written, you may want to follow the seven steps of the composing process carefully. The same holds true when you are creating a new type of work, such as switching from fiction to nonfiction titles.

You can perform the activities in any order you choose, and you do not have to finish one activity before you start another. Sometimes you create an outline for the work. Sometimes you create the work first, pause to think about the structure, and then plan how to make the work better. Sometimes you tackle the work a section at a time, planning in spurts. Sometimes you are so familiar with your subject or the medium you are working in that planning is a natural part of your thought process.

Although planning is an important stage of the creative process, it is not the most important stage. This is contrary to the traditional school of thought that stressed planning and specifically advised writers to create an outline for everything they wrote. Whether you create an outline or do not create an outline is not going to materially influence the quality of your work. Research into the creative process has shown that what matters most is how you organize your thoughts and the work.

Planning

When you plan, choose the way in which you are going to organize the work. You do this by drawing on experiences or thinking of new ways to create and organize material. Planning also means thinking about the strategies you are going to use to create the work. It involves analyzing the purpose, scope, and audience for the work.

The purpose of the work is the reason you are creating the work or adding to the publication. Are you adding artwork to accent or clarify the story line? Are you adding music to heighten the mood?

The scope of the work defines what the work encompasses or the extent of the work. Scope can sometimes be defined in terms of focus and size. Is the work broadly or narrowly focused? Is the work large or small?

The audience is who you want the work to reach. Is the publication for children or adults? Have you identified a target audience, such as males 16-24, or is the work designed for a general audience?

You have probably seen Broderbund's *Living Books* line on CD-ROM. Popular in this line are the wonderful books by Mercer Mayer such as *Just Grandma and Me, Just Me and My Dad,* and *Just For You.* Although children are the audience for the books, Broderbund did not forget that adults would be the ones purchasing the CD-ROMs. For this reason, the purpose of the books is to provide educational entertainment to children. Given this purpose, the CD-ROM editions of the print books are much larger in scope and were programmed with features to entertain and educate children. A key part of this was to allow children to either interact with the publication or simply let the story be read to them.

Broderbund did not forget the potential for an international audience. Most Living Books enable you to select a language for the book to be read in, such as English, Japanese, or Spanish. This gives the CD-ROMs international appeal and provides another educational outlet. Children in Japan could listen to the English version of the CD-ROM to help them learn English. Children in the U.S. could listen to the Spanish version to help them learn Spanish.

Researching

Researching involves gathering all the information you need to complete the work. This may mean gathering information about eighteenth-century Europe from as many sources as you can to ensure your work has elements authentic from the period. Or it may mean driving to the ocean to photograph or videotape the seagulls and the spray of the waves, so you can later capture the moment in your work.

Composing

Composing is the act of putting your thoughts into a more permanent form. This means putting work on paper or using computer equipment to put work into an appropriate electronic form. The Web publisher will most likely put words into a word processor, transcribe musical notes into a music program, and record brush strokes using a paint program.

The work, as first put down on paper or recorded on a computer, does not have to be the finished product. More than likely, it will simply be a start on a larger work. For the writer, a start on a project could be a few words, a list of thoughts, a paragraph, or pages of writing.

Evaluating

Evaluating involves looking at the work objectively to see if it meets your goals. Ask yourself if the work is right for the purpose and audience for which you are creating it. Often, the best way to be objective about a work you have created is to look at the work as if someone else had created it.

If you find that you cannot be objective about your own work or aren't as objective as you would like, perhaps you need to distance yourself from the work. Take a day off or put on one of your other hats and work on a different part of the project for a few days. This will help you return to the evaluation fresh and ready to think objectively.

Revising

When you revise, you change the structure of the work by adding, deleting, or rearranging. Often you will revise after you have evaluated the work. Revisions can be cosmetic changes involving only a few minor areas of the work, but more often than not revision means major reworking to keep the work focused on the purpose, scope, and audience for which it is intended.

Editing

Whereas revision looks at the structure of the work, editing looks at the style, mechanics, and format of the work. For writing, this means making sure you have used proper spelling, grammar, and punctuation. You would check word choice and format. Great tools to help you through editing are spelling and grammar checkers. These tools might catch 75 percent of your mistakes, but the other 25 percent you will have to catch through careful reading.

During the editing stage, don't forget the nonwritten aspects of your Web publication. You should also edit these aspects as necessary. Do the opening graphics match the tone and style of the graphics you selected in later sections of the publication? Do the sound clips have sections where nothing is audible for a few seconds? Is the video sequence for the home page too long?

Proofing

When you proof something, you are checking the final copy to ensure it is error-free. In traditional publishing, proofing has been a critical area of the composing process. Typos are costly mistakes to correct when material has already gone to press. In Web publishing, this may or may not be the case. Electronic mediums tend to be more liquid than traditional mediums. You can make changes very easily to Web publications.

You may be saying to yourself, "Wait a minute, I have seen typos in publications before". Although most publications have typos, they tend to make you look dumb. For this reason, you will want to correct as many typos as you can, given the time constraints of the project.

Development Processes

The processes involved in developing the software aspects of the Web publication can be broadly defined as *development processes.* In the role of the graphic designer and programmer, the publisher designs and develops the computer-software aspects of the Web publication. As you will see from examples throughout this book, the Web publisher should never have to resort to actual programming. There are many wonderful tools to aid the process of creating the computer-software aspects of the Web publication. You learned about Web publishing tools in Part III, "Web Publishing Environments and Editors."

The programming role of the publisher is more closely related to that of a software developer. The publisher is responsible for the look and interworkings of the publication. The publisher is responsible for selecting the appropriate Web publishing software and tools for her level of expertise and a software process model under which the project will be developed. Fortunately for Web publishers, the software process model of choice will normally be a rapid-prototype model or a modified rapid-prototype model. This is because toolsets exist to aid in the rapid creation of advanced Web-publishing projects and because these tools are of sufficient quality to warrant their use. This section explains what these prototype models involve.

A major strength of the rapid-prototype model is that you can develop the project in linear fashion. You proceed from the working model to the finished product. You can test the prototype in real-world situations or under the scrutiny of the boss. In doing so, you can ensure that what you are creating is what is actually needed. Applying this model to Web publishing projects will also save you time.

This model also works well when you are familiar with traditional approaches to project development and are concerned about using new technologies, such as ActiveX. By developing a rapid prototype, you give yourself the chance to test the new technologies. Before making any further investments, you try out the tools to find out if they meet your needs. This will help you manage the risk of introducing a new technology, while enabling you to assess new techniques.

Although a true rapid-prototype model would include slightly different stages, a modified rapid-prototype model for Web publishing could include six stages:

- Requirements phase
- Rapid-prototype phase
- Specification phase
- Planning phase
- Design phase
- Implementation phase

As you read about each of these phases, it is important to remember that the duration of each phase should be relevant to the size and complexity of the publishing project. The initial project you create using this or any other model will require more time. For a small project or for subsequent projects, you probably could perform all the phases through the design phase in a single eight-hour day.

The implementation phase for electronic projects tends to be the longest phase. Learning about the Web publishing tools you have chosen will probably take up most of your time in your initial project, so the implementation phase may seem excessively long. It is important to remember that each subsequent time you use the tools should be easier than the last. The good news is that Web publishing tools tend to be very user-friendly.

The wonderful thing about Web publishing is that if you take the time to design a good product, you can reuse some of the same specifications and designs in subsequent projects. This will give your company's Web sites and publications a uniform look, and as an added bonus, the payoff in time savings will be substantial.

Finally, remember the rapid-prototype model as a linear part of your project's development life cycle. Unlike the composing processes, each phase of the development process should be conducted in order.

Requirements Phase

In the requirements phase, you try to figure out what your needs are. You do this by first examining the purpose, scope, and audience of the project. Afterward, you examine your reasonable expectations for the project. You translate these needs, goals, and purposes into requirements for the project. Whereas the section on techniques to finish the project provides a sample schedule that lists goals and milestones, the basic needs for any Web publication include the tools the publisher will need to complete the project:

- An authoring tool to aid the creative process, such as FrontPage or SiteMill
- A drawing tool to create graphics, such as CorelDraw! or PaintShop Pro
- A sound tool to create or edit sound, such as SoundApp for the Mac, WHAM for Windows, or SOX for UNIX
- A video tool to play or test video segments, such as an Apple QuickTime player, Video for Windows player, or MPEG player

You will want to think beyond your basic tool needs. You should also consider time, budget, and personnel constraints. If you have only 10 weeks to complete the project, you may need to hire additional team members to get the project finished on time. In this case, hiring a specific number of additional team members would be one of your requirements. If you have a $2,500 budget, you will have to scrutinize every aspect of the budget to keep costs down. In this case, you will probably be extremely selective about the tools you purchase. You will also hire outside help only as necessary. And if the budget constraints are so severe that they would materially affect the success of the project, you will want to ensure your superiors are aware of the situation and possibly make a case for getting a larger budget.

Rapid-Prototype Phase

In the rapid-prototype stage, you roll back your sleeves and dive right into the project. Using the requirements for the project, you create a working model of the publication as quickly as possible. The prototype is far from a completed project. Its structure is rather skeletal, in that not all the pieces work together, but limited interaction with the model is possible. You use this model to figure out your real needs and to find out whether you have selected the right tools to carry you through to the completion of the job.

The traditional school of thought on the rapid-prototype model is that when you are done with this phase, you should discard the rapid prototype. If you do not discard the prototype, you may find yourself wasting time trying to continually build and fix the prototype. The purpose of creating the rapid prototype is to help you figure out real needs and save you time. Clinging to the prototype generally defeats the purpose of creating the prototype in the first place.

Your superiors must understand what this phase is all about. All too often, the prototype is mistaken for a start on the final product when, in fact, it is not. You should manage expectations by ensuring that your superiors understand this phase from day one and recommunicating information about the purpose of the prototype periodically throughout the project.

This said, in certain Web publishing cases you may want to keep parts of the prototype. You may want to reuse or refine for the finished product any creative work (such as graphic icons, art, or sounds) you developed for the rapid prototype. You also may want to keep portions of the interface you created with publishing tools.

Specification Phase

After you develop and verify the prototype, you go on to specify the complete interworkings of the publication. You could do this in a traditional manner, through specification diagrams such as data flow diagrams, state transition diagrams, or petri nets. But these types of diagrams are not really necessary unless you are writing actual programming code for the project. A good way to show how your publication will be linked is by developing a storyboard that graphically shows what the pieces of the project are and how they are linked together. Storyboards are discussed in depth later in this chapter.

Planning Phase

After you verify the specification documents, you should plan the project. Using all the materials you have developed so far for the project, you determine how long the project is going to take and the steps necessary to carry you through the project. For this reason, the planning phase can also be a reality check for project constraints or requirements.

Suppose that after you plan each step of the project you discover that it will take a minimum of six months to complete the project, yet the deadline for project completion given to you by management is three months away. Here, something would have to give, and you would have to work hard to manage perceptions and expectations concerning the project. You may have to renegotiate the deadline, hire additional team members, or eliminate certain time-intensive parts of the project.

The more complex the project, the more involved your planning will be. The plans for a small project could be very basic—a list of steps with deadlines for completion of each step written down on a single piece of paper. The plans for a large project could be rendered in detail on a project-management tool such as Microsoft Project.

Most projects have windows for project steps, such as eight days for planning or three weeks for preliminary design. There could be hundreds of project steps, with multiple steps being performed simultaneously, or a handful of steps, with each step being performed one after the other. Some steps would be dependent on other steps, meaning they could not be started until certain other aspects of the project were completed. Other steps would not be dependent on any other steps and could be performed at any time during the project's development.

Design Phase

After verifying your planning, you go on to the design phase. The design phase is one of the most critical phases of a Web publishing project. During this phase you take the specification documents to another level of detail. You develop the look of the project. You design the layout for the publication and individual pages. By developing a master storyboard for the component parts of the publication, you can make the design phase easier and less time-consuming.

The master storyboard concept is a highly effective way to design. Instead of creating hundreds of individual storyboards, you create templates for the major divisions of the publishing project. These templates form the basis for the individual storyboards. In this way, you have to make only minor adjustments to the individual storyboards and you get a uniform look throughout major sections of the publication.

Implementation Phase

After you verify the designs you have created for the publication, you go on to the implementation phase. This tends to be the longest phase in Web publishing projects, because you actually create the Web publication using the specification and designs you have created. You also integrate the creative materials from the composing processes in this stage.

Publishing Processes

The processes involved in producing the finished product can be broadly defined as *publishing processes.* In the role of the editor and publisher, the Web publisher fine-tunes the publication to give it mass appeal. The publisher must take a hard look at the project with the eyes of an editor, and then take the project through the final five activities:

- Revision
- Editing
- Proofing

- Testing
- Publishing

These activities are similar to the associated activities performed in the composition process, the primary difference being the publisher's role. The publisher is no longer the creator of the work or a collaborator of the work. He or she should review the publishing project with as much objectivity as possible.

Revision

During the revision phase, the publisher is looking for major flaws in the project. The focus of revision is on structure. The publisher will reanalyze the individual parts of the project to ensure the work is focused and consistent throughout. To do this, the publisher might also have to reevaluate the purpose, scope, and audience for the project. Did the project turn out as intended? Is the project larger or more commercially viable than the original concept? Is the project still targeted toward the same audience?

When you revise the publication, you should scrutinize all its parts from start to finish. The soundness of a Web page's structure is extremely important. You should test all links in the storyboard structure to ensure they work as you expect them to.

The depth of the revision often depends on your familiarity with the subject and type of publication. If this is your first project or you are publishing a new type of document, you will want to use a very thorough revision process. A good technique to follow when doing a very thorough revision is the *rule of three.* Under the rule of three, you follow all aspects of the publication from start to finish three times. Each time you revise, you are looking for different structure problems.

The first time through the process, you check for clarity and content. Is everything in the publication clear and placed onscreen in a clear manner? Does the content of each individual part fit in with the publication as a whole? The first revision is the closest inspection of the publication during the revision process.

The second time, you look at the organization and layout of the publication. Is the publication organized in the best way possible? Is the layout of the document the best possible? Is there too much information? Does the screen look cluttered? Is the linking of the pages right? Are the navigation mechanisms easy to use?

The third time, you analyze the publication to see if the overall message meets the proposed purpose and audience. Look at the big picture and ask yourself if the publication is right for the purpose for which it is intended. Is the reading level and style of the publication appropriate for the audience for which it is intended?

Editing

Editing should logically follow revision. There is no point in looking for mechanics and format problems in parts of the publication that might not be in the revised publication. Keeping this rule in mind when you start the publishing process will ultimately save you time.

Back in the editing mode, the publisher looks at the mechanics and format of the work. This is the point when the publisher should refer to a style manual to ensure punctuation, capitalization, and compounding of words are correct. Other good tools for the publisher at this point include grammar reference aids, bad-speller dictionaries, and other types of dictionaries or reference materials to confirm facts.

In a publication such as a Web-published novel, the tendency is to look at chapter text and not the text of titles and headings. Look at all text, no matter where it appears in the publication. If graphics or video contains text, you should scrutinize this text as well. There should be smooth transitions between sections and topics. The capitalization in headings should be consistent throughout the publication.

For the textual portions of the publication, you should look at

- Capitalization
- Grammar
- Punctuation
- Sentence structure
- Spelling
- Word choice and usage

Proofing

At this stage, the publisher proofs the entire project, down to the most minor detail. The most common type of error you will be looking for is the typographical error. Typos may not be as costly in Web publishing, but they will cost you more time and money to fix after a project has been published.

The proofing stage differs from the revision stage and the editing stage in its scope. In revision, you are looking for major problems in structure. In editing, you are looking for problems in mechanics and format. In proofing, you are looking through a magnifying glass for minor problems. Although these three processes can be performed in any order, they work best when done in the preceding order. In this way, you are first looking at the big picture, then you gradually zoom in. Otherwise, you will spend too much time worrying needlessly about minor details before you look at the major problems.

When proofing, you are checking the final copy to ensure it is as error-free as possible. You should recognize that, given your time and budget constraints, you may have to compromise accuracy for timeliness. You should also recognize that there is a definite point of diminishing returns and finding 100 percent of the errors is costly and often not practical. For this reason, most publications contain typos and other types of minor errors. Therefore, the key to proofing is to reduce these errors and not to try to eliminate them.

Testing

When the project is in its final form, the publisher may want to publish the publication or site for users within the office to examine. Testing is not an absolute necessity. Whether you test the project will really depend on your publishing operation. If this is your first large-scale project, you may want to conduct extensive testing. You might also want to conduct extensive testing if you are publishing a new type of site, such as a VRML site that uses ActiveX and VRMLScript, for the first time.

Publishing

Now that you have finally finished your showcase site or publication, you are ready to publish it on the company's intranet or on the World Wide Web. Move your pages, programs, sound, and video to the appropriate directories on the intranet or Web server. Congratulations!

Combining It All

Ideally, during the publication process you would follow the composing processes for the project first. When you finished, you would start the development phases. Finally, you would start the publishing processes. Although this is the ideal situation, life is never ideal. Often, you will want to combine elements from each of the three categories and work on them simultaneously. This is fine.

You can conduct the composition process while you are developing the software aspects of the publication. This will work especially well when you are adapting existing material. It will also work well when you, as the publisher, are collaborating with writers, musicians, or artists to create a project.

The publishing processes are more difficult to integrate into the ongoing creation and development of the project. However, you could create or develop pieces of the project, and then examine those pieces from the viewpoint of the objective publisher. Exercise caution when trying to perform all three processes at once. The tendency is to gloss over the actual publishing process and not scrutinize the project as closely or objectively as you otherwise would have.

Techniques to Get the Project Started

Before you can organize a project, you must start it. Getting the project started is often the hardest thing to do. If you get the project started, the odds are you will probably finish it. The key to starting and finishing the project is to develop good habits for working on the project immediately. Creative people often find themselves at a loss for one of two reasons. They either prefer to avoid work until a deadline is hanging over their head, or they think of reasons why they cannot work.

Human tendency is to put off work until it absolutely has to be done or to think of excuses why the project cannot be started. Procrastination is a mindset that you can overcome through positive thinking and good habits. If you find that you work on the publishing project only when absolutely necessary to meet a deadline, or if you keep promising to start the project but do not, try the ideas in this section.

Give yourself a publishing schedule. The schedule should contain milestones, goals, and an allocation of time. Use the schedule as a flexible and realistic guideline to help you through to project completion. The purpose of the schedule is to help you start thinking about the project and to formalize the steps it will take you to complete the project. You should also use the schedule to help you set regular times to work on the project.

Milestones are generally smaller in scope than goals. A single week could contain many milestones:

Week 1

- Select and purchase reference materials
- Select and purchase authoring tools
- Brainstorm
- Develop weekly schedule overview

Week 2

- Read introduction to authoring-tool manual
- Browse the reference materials to gather ideas
- Freewrite
- Develop weekly schedule
- Start project and complete at least one page

Goals are larger in scope than milestones. Goals for a typical project could be to complete activities or phases in the composition, development, or publishing process. Goals are generally of long duration. You would probably only have one goal per week during the project, such as the following:

- Week 1: Preliminary work on project
- Week 2: Planning
- Week 3: Research
- Week 4: Start project composition

More realistically, the duration of milestones and goals will depend on the time you allocate to the project. The milestones and goals from the previous examples could be rewritten to include the time you dedicate to the project each week and the duration of a task. Although it would be ideal to be able to work full-time on a single project, even full-time publishers often don't have that luxury. Usually they are juggling several projects and can dedicate only a few hours a week to any specific project. If you are working part-time on the project, one of your first goals may be broken down as follows:

Goal: Preliminary work on project. Duration: 2 weeks.

Week 1: 10 hours

- Select and purchase reference materials. Duration: 2 hours.
- Select and purchase authoring tools. Duration: 2 hours.
- Brainstorm. Duration: 2 hours.
- Develop weekly schedule overview. Duration: 3 hours.
- Slack time: 1 hour.

Week 2: 20 hours

- Read introduction to authoring tool manual. Duration: 1 hour.
- Browse the reference materials to gather ideas. Duration: 5 hours.
- Freewrite. Duration: 1 hour.
- Develop weekly schedule. Duration: 8 hours.
- Start project, complete at least one page. Duration: 3 hours.
- Slack time: 2 hours.

There is no harm in building extra time into the schedule to ensure you meet goals. The preceding schedule contains one hour of slack time in the first week and two hours of slack time in the second week. By building slack time into the schedule, you help ensure the project can stay on track, even if there are unexpected delays. Experienced project managers try to build in slack time whenever possible and practical. When you meet a goal, why not celebrate? Take a few hours off, go see the movie you have been wanting to see.

Techniques to Organize for the Audience

The way in which you organize a publication depends largely on who will be using the publication. The success of your publication relies on determining the audience for the publication and adapting the message to the audience. You will certainly organize the publication one way for adults and a different way for children. However, the audience for your publication is usually not in such simple terms. The problem of determining the audience is further complicated because most publications have more than one audience. Nevertheless, correctly determining the target audience can have huge payoffs.

The target audience could be specific (for example, males 16-24) or general (young adults). More often, a publication will have primary audiences and secondary audiences. The primary audience is the group of people for whom the publication is created. The focus and thrust of the publication should be directed toward the primary audience.

The secondary audience is the group of people who will read the publication incidental to its purpose. The secondary audience could include reviewers (people whose job it is to review Web publications), consumer-interest groups (people whose job it is to promote the interests of consumers), or anyone else who might read the publication to determine its quality or to review its content. The secondary audience could also include parents if the publication is directed toward children. Parents may be the ones assessing the moral content of the Web publication before allowing their children to access it.

Often, the primary audience for a publication seems straightforward but is not. Comic books are a good example of this. The reading level of the average comic book is at a sixth-grade level. The look of comic books—with their graphically depicted pows, bangs, and booms—seems to be directed entirely toward children. You may be surprised to learn that, for many comic books, the largest percentage of readers is adults. Look at the price tag on comic books today and the phenomenal popularity of comic books with adult themes. What would have happened to comic books if the companies producing them had not realized that a large portion of their readers is adult?

You can figure out the audience for your publication by the following means:

- Using common sense
- Gathering statistics
- Evaluating trends

Using Common Sense

One of the best tools to analyze the audience for a product is common sense. Realize that the audience probably will not have the same wants, needs, and desires as you. A Web publication may or may not have the same audience as its traditional print counterpart. Try to put yourself in the position of consumers who will view your publication or Web site. Use what you know about people and what you know about the subject of your publication to predict likely responses to questions such as the following:

- What will the reader's initial reaction be?
- What will the reader's expectations be?
- What does the reader consider interesting?
- What features will the reader be looking for?
- What are the selling points for this type of product?
- How will the reader use your product?

- Which reading level should you target?
- Which level of violence or profanity is acceptable to this audience?
- Which level of complexity in the linking and navigation mechanisms is acceptable?

Each of these questions should be answered with the publication's audience in mind. For example, the last question pertains to the complexity of the publication. Publications for adults tend to be more complex and serious. Publications for children tend to be less complex and include more entertainment features.

Gathering Statistics

One of the best ways to determine your audience is to use statistics. Sometimes you can simply ask consumers which type of Web site stops them dead in their tracks. You could do this through a carefully designed survey. Other times, you might want to use existing statistics, such as demographic information, to determine the audience.

Surveys are often an inexpensive way to learn public opinion. Surveys could be provided with product samples passed out at the local shopping mall or given to your associates. Surveys are useful because they can be filled out by many people at the same time. A properly designed survey will be easy to answer and not time-consuming. This way, more people will fill it out.

Demographic information can also provide useful statistics. Demographic information includes age, sex, race, education level, income, and more. This data was probably gathered through surveys and made publicly available. Not all the demographic information available will be relevant to your needs, but some of the data will be extremely important. For instance, if the demographic information reveals that most of the consumers interested in your type of product are females age 40-45 or males over the age of 55, you would certainly adapt the message of your audience differently than if the information reveals the ages are 20–25 for females or 16–22 for males.

Evaluating Trends

Evaluating trends could also help you determine an audience for your product. To do this, you will have to know something about the market for your product. You could begin by looking at similar products from other companies and asking yourself the following:

- What messages do the products carry?
- Toward which target audience are these companies directing their products?
- Are the products being targeted toward secondary audiences as well?

In a new marketplace, trends often shift as companies try to figure out the audience for their products. You may want to look at what other companies are doing when you begin work on the project and again during the project. This way you can judge if the trend is more stable than fluid or more fluid than stable.

Organizing the Publication Through Storyboarding

Developing storyboards for your publication is a critical part of the design process. Storyboards help ensure that the publication is well-designed and that all the pieces of the project fit together. A storyboard can help you reduce complexity by structuring ideas in a less complicated manner.

When you storyboard, you represent each page of the presentation in miniature form on a planning sheet. This enables you to visualize the publication from start to finish. Being able to see the component parts of the entire project makes the project more manageable and less mysterious. You do not have to wonder what is beyond the next page because, when you use the storyboards, you will know what is beyond the next page.

You can represent a single project storyboard as a rectangle. The shape of an individual storyboard makes the storyboard look like little pieces of paper. The storyboard could represent a single page of the publication or a group of pages, like a chapter. Without information in the storyboards, the mockup of the project you create would have little meaning. Although later examples in this chapter will detail how you add information to storyboards, such as chapter headings or titles, the basic idea is to create a template or outline for pages or sections of the publication.

You can extend the idea of storyboards by using lines and arrows to show how the publication is linked. An arrow can show the flow of the publication from one page to the next. Arrows depict how the component parts of the publication link together. By examining the links, you can see the logical structure of the publication and the level of interaction readers will have with the publication. A sample storyboard is shown in Figure 42.1.

FIGURE 42.1.
Creating a storyboard.

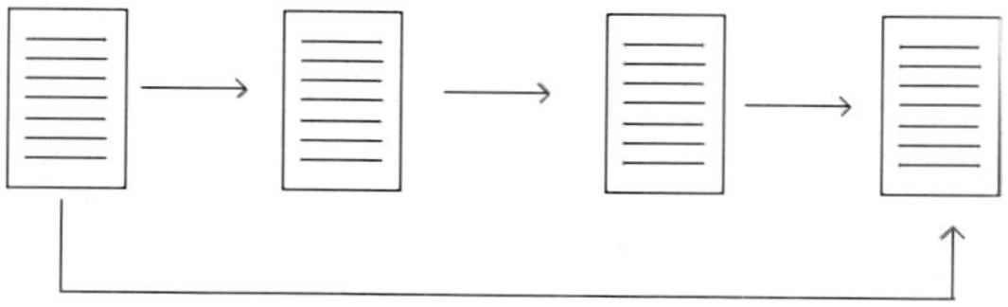

After you have developed the storyboard for your publication, you can immediately find flaws in the design. Finding flaws early in the development of the project will save you time and resources. Having to rebuild the links on a complex project midway through the project could mean disaster. Often, you start a snowball effect. You change one link, and then discover you have to change an associated link. You change the associated link to make sure it leads to the correct page, and then find other links you have to change. Before you know it, you are reworking all the links in the project. At this point, the process may be so involved you will elect to start over rather than try to rework the links.

There are three phases in the storyboard-design process:

- Developing the structure
- Developing the content
- Evaluating the logic

Each phase is progressively more detailed. When you are developing the structure of the project, you are looking at the project-overview level. While keeping in mind that a single storyboard could represent any number of similar pages, you identify the number of storyboards for the project and the logical flow between them. When you are developing the content, you look very closely at the individual parts of the project. You develop the outline for individual storyboards or storyboard templates. When you examine the logic of the project, you scrutinize every detail. You closely examine each storyboard and all links to ensure the project design and flow are correct.

Whether you perform each of the three phases will depend on the size and complexity of the project and your familiarity with the type of project you are publishing. However, each phase that you do perform should be performed in sequence. Even a small project of, say, five to ten storyboards can benefit from the structural development phase. This way, you can easily see

- The structure of the project
- The links of the project
- The project as a whole

Although these phases should be performed in order, the important thing to remember is that the duration of each phase should be relevant to the size and complexity of the project. The initial project you create using this or any other model will require more time than subsequent projects. For a small project or for subsequent projects, you probably could create the entire storyboard process in two hours or less.

If you take the time to design a good storyboard, you may be able to reuse some of the same design concepts in subsequent projects. This way, your publications will have a uniform structure. An added bonus to using reliable design techniques is substantial time savings and a reduction in the amount of resources you will need to complete the project.

Developing Project Structure Using Storyboards

Developing the structure of the project is the first phase in storyboarding. You can organize storyboards in many ways. The structure that is best for your publication depends on the complexity of the project. As complexity increases, you manage it by adopting a more advanced structuring method. Specific design models include

- Linear
- Linear with alternative paths

- Hierarchical
- Combinations of linear and hierarchical
- Integrated web

For a small project or a project with limited complexity, a simple structure is often best. Simple structures include linear and linear with alternative paths. The simplest way to structure a publication is in a *linear* fashion. Using a pure linear structure, you can create a publication with a structure resembling a traditional print publication. Readers move forward and backward in sequence through the pages of the publication.

An *alternative path* structure gives readers more options or paths through the document. By providing alternative paths, you make the structure of the publication more flexible. Instead of being able to move only forward and backward through the publication, readers can follow a branch from the main path. In a linear structure, the branches will rejoin the main path at some point.

The *hierarchical* structure is the most logical structure for a project of moderate complexity. In this structure, you organize the publication into a directory tree. Readers can move from one level of the publication to the next, more detailed, level. They can also go up the tree from the detailed level to a higher level and possibly jump to the top level.

The directory tree closely resembles the way you store files on your hard drive, in a main directory with subdirectories leading to files. You could also think of the hierarchy as a representation of an actual tree. If you invert the tree, the trunk of the tree would be the top level of the publication. The trunk could be the overview of the publication. The large boughs leading from the trunk would be the next level of the document structure. The boughs could be the chapter-overview pages. Branches leading from the boughs would be the next level. They could be pages within chapters.

The *combined linear and hierarchical* structure is one of the most-used forms for Web publications. This is because it is an extremely flexible, but still highly structured, method. Readers can move forward and backward through individual pages. They can navigate through the various levels of the publication by moving up a level or descending to the next level. They can also follow parallel paths through the document.

The most complex structuring method is the *integrated web*. This method lets the reader follow multiple paths from many options. This is a good method to use when you want the reader to be able to browse or wander many times through the publication you have created. Each time through the publication, readers will probably discover something new.

TIP

Something you should keep in mind, no matter the organizational style of the publication, is to include a link to the home page of the publication. This feature is included in most Web publications because it provides a way for readers to get back to beginning at any time. Another key page to provide a link to is the table of contents page.

TIP

Just as the storyboard method can help you visualize the project, it could also help the reader. For a very complex site, you may want to provide a graphical depiction of how the document is organized on a help page. This help page would be a site map that clarifies the layout and navigation mechanisms you have used for the site.

Developing Project Content Using Storyboards

Now that you have developed the structure of the storyboards, you will want to look closer at the individual parts of the project. Developing the content of the storyboards will help you do this. The depth of the content development really depends on the size and complexity of the project.

A traditional way to develop a small project is to develop all content aspects of the storyboard, from the placement of graphics and menu buttons to the placement of text. Similarly, the traditional development method for a large storyboard is to outline each individual storyboard and then progressively work toward more detail as necessary. A better method is to use storyboard templates or master storyboards whenever possible and develop individual storyboards only as necessary.

Developing Master Storyboards

Master storyboards are a highly effective way to design. They make the design process considerably less complex and will save you countless hours of work. Instead of creating hundreds of individual storyboards, you create templates for the major divisions of the publishing project. These templates form the basis for the individual storyboards. In this way, you have to make only minor adjustments to the individual storyboards, and you ensure the look of the publication is consistent throughout.

The main idea behind master storyboards is that you identify repetitious or non-unique features of the publication and let a single master storyboard represent pages with similar features. You do this by looking at the publication in progressive levels of detail. Most publications will have the following:

- Overview pages
- A table of contents
- Topic-overview pages
- Pages within topics
- An index

Start by thinking about the publication as a whole. Are there component parts of the publication that will or should be uniform throughout? The answer is usually yes; the top of the page may contain a header, consistent throughout the publication, and the bottom of the page may contain a similarly consistent footer.

Next, examine the sections of the publication. Multiple sections of the publication will usually have common parts. In a Web-published novel, for example, all chapter pages will probably have the same menu options, such as

- Previous chapter
- Next chapter
- Previous page
- Next page
- Go to chapter index
- Go to help index
- Go to home page
- Search text

The last step is to examine individual sections of the publication for common material. Pages of an index will contain different features or organization from pages of a chapter, but all pages within a chapter or within an index should have similar elements.

After you have examined all aspects of the publication for common parts, you develop the master storyboards. You may have multiple levels of master storyboards, including the following:

- An overall master storyboard
- A master storyboard that can be used in multiple sections
- A master storyboard for individual sections

You may have only one or many master storyboards. The number of master storyboards you have really depends on the size and complexity of your project.

Developing Individual Storyboards

In the design stage, you will rarely develop individual storyboards. This is especially true if you take the time to develop master storyboards. Whether you develop individual storyboards depends on the needs of the project. For a small project, you may want to develop all the storyboards, so you get a precise overview of the publication. For a large project, you may make only simple additions to the individual storyboards, such as adding the titles or headings for associated text.

Sometimes it is essential to develop the content for unique storyboards within the publication to see how they will fit in with the publication as a whole. You develop these storyboards because through them, you can get a better understanding of the publication. The following are examples of unique storyboards:

- Home page
- Table of contents page
- Index page
- Credits page
- Menu pages

Evaluating the Logic of the Storyboard

In the last phase of storyboarding, you evaluate the logic of the storyboard. This process is similar to the editing, revision, and proofing activities of the publishing process. You examine the links between storyboards. You ensure the publication has a logically flowing structure and that all storyboards are properly linked together. Then you examine the outlines the storyboards contain. Here, you are primarily making sure the key elements are placed on the storyboard in the most logical manner.

The storyboarding process is meant to save time, resources, and frustration. Do not spend too much time worrying needlessly about minor details. In this phase, look only for major problems in logic.

Summary

The best Web publications are the result of effective strategies for thinking, planning, and composing. Helping you create the best Web publications using effective strategies is what this chapter was all about. Those strategies include the following:

- You set yourself on the path to success by managing expectations, perceptions, strategies, goals, rules, and behavior.
- You improve your initial ideas through brainstorming, freethinking, and storyboarding.

- You convince yourself to stop procrastinating by setting a flexible and realistic schedule containing milestones, goals, and an allocation of time to help you through to project completion.
- You figure out who the audience for the publication is by using common sense, gathering statistics, and evaluating trends.
- You tackle the project and progress through the composition, development, and publishing processes.
- You reduce complexity in project design by visualizing the publication from start to finish using storyboards. Being able to see the component parts of the entire project makes the project more manageable and less mysterious.

CHAPTER 43

Moving Legacy Publications to the Web

by William R. Stanek

IN THIS CHAPTER

At times it seems the whole world has joined the information revolution. Computers are a part of our everyday lives. Globally, most businesses and hundreds of millions of people own or have access to a computer. Most businesses with more than ten employees have several computers. Often, the computers are connected together in a local area network. Networks can boost productivity, make it easier to communicate without having to leave the desk, and improve the way companies do business.

A growing number of companies have large corporate networks. The company's Wide Area Network may connect hundreds or thousands of computers. A recent trend is to integrate the capabilities of the Internet and the World Wide Web into the corporate information infrastructure.

Thousands of savvy business owners and technical people have recognized the potential for tremendous cost and time savings and have set out to merge years, months, or weeks of existing company publications into the distributed structure of the Internet. The goal of moving legacy publications to the company intranet or Web server is to save time and money, which improves the bottom line. After all, in the end, the bottom line is the only thing that matters.

Putting Legacy Publications to Work for You

Every time there is a product release, product update, or press release, documents are created and distributed to company personnel and customers. This mountain of paper and electronic documents grows with the company.

Over time, the value of the company's legacy documents becomes increasingly apparent, especially when it is necessary to distribute historical or promotional information to large groups of employees or customers. The question soon becomes "How do we tap into all the valuable resources employees have created over the years?" The answer is to integrate key documents into the company's information structure, but before you can move these important documents to your intranet or Web server, you must find them.

Imagine a file cabinet in your office stuffed with cryptically labeled or unlabeled documents, video tapes, music cassettes, and photos, and you have an accurate picture of how the majority of users and organizations store their data in computer systems. Many important documents are in personal directories on hard drives that no one can access, and secretaries spend a lot of time passing floppy disks about the office. Some key documents that could benefit everyone are stored in a location that only one person knows about.

The key to sorting through this mess of documents is getting organized. A clear structure for your directories and files becomes increasingly important as the company grows. Hundreds of files in a single directory are difficult to track and maintain. Therefore, you should carefully consider how to organize both files and directories.

Part of your plan should include procedures for labeling documents. After all, organized information is only useful if you know what the documents contain and what the documents are used for. You should also ask personnel to identify documents that should be made available online. Ideally, these documents would be identified using a priority system based on the usefulness of the documents to particular departments, employees, the company as a whole, and your customers.

After you decide how information should be stored and labeled, turn your ideas into policies that everyone in the company can understand and follow. Then distribute these data storage policies throughout the organization and ensure that everyone knows this is part of your effort to make the company's legacy publications available online, which will in the end save everyone time and money.

Once your data storage policies are in place, organize your documents so they are easy to find and use. The benefit of this is three-fold. Finally, you can get started with the real work of making the documents available online, and when you are finished, you don't have to worry about tracking hundreds or thousands of new files through a maze of file cabinets, desk drawers, and hard drives. Further, you can now easily identify the different file formats that you have to deal with in your conversion effort.

Converting Document Formats

After you identify the file formats you need to convert, you can look for conversion solutions. In an increasingly Internet-aware world, many commercial word processors and publishing environments can save documents in a format that you can use directly on the Web. This means that sometimes your conversion effort is as simple as opening the document you want to move to the Web in the application in which the document was created and saving the document as an HTML-formatted file.

In Chapter 10, "Publishing with Microsoft Internet Assistants", you learned that you can convert Word, Excel, PowerPoint, and Schedule+ documents directly to HTML. Similar solutions exist for other applications, as well. For example, if you use Corel's WordPerfect, you will find that you can convert your documents directly to HTML using Internet Publisher. Internet Publisher is fairly similar to Internet Assistant. Versions of Internet Publisher will soon be available for most applications in Corel's Office Suite.

Though being able to convert your word processor's document format directly into a Web-usable format saves time and money, direct conversion is not always possible. Sometimes you have to convert documents to an intermediate format such as PostScript. Once the legacy file is in the PostScript format, you can integrate it with an Adobe product to create a document in Adobe's Portable Document Format. A growing number of Web-published documents are in PDF.

As discussed earlier in this book, HTML is based on a specific SGML Document Type Definition (DTD). Other DTDs are also available, or waiting to be written, to meet your needs. There are many mature SGML products from which to choose. New and improved products for the Web are announced every month. Common Ground is one example of a recently developed environment that provides a balanced suite of tools to create Web documents from legacy publications.

As detailed in Chapter 9, "An HTML Toolkit: Browsers, Converters, and Editors," tools for converting your documents to Web publications abound. Converters basically enable you to convert your legacy data to another format. Various implementations of converter technology have been applied effectively to create Web documents using software products not originally intended for this purpose.

This is not a new concept. When you send a document to a printer, the document is converted into a format the printer understands. For example, when you write a document using Microsoft Word, Word's file format stores not only content but also formatting commands. When you print the document, a print driver (or Word itself) converts the document's content and formatting commands into a format your printer understands, such as PostScript (PS) or Encapsulated PostScript.

Most word processing programs can also create a print file and store it to disk. The programs and filters associated with this process are similar to the filters used to create Web-formatted documents. Figure 43.1 shows the conversion process.

FIGURE 43.1.
Document conversion from native format to Web format.

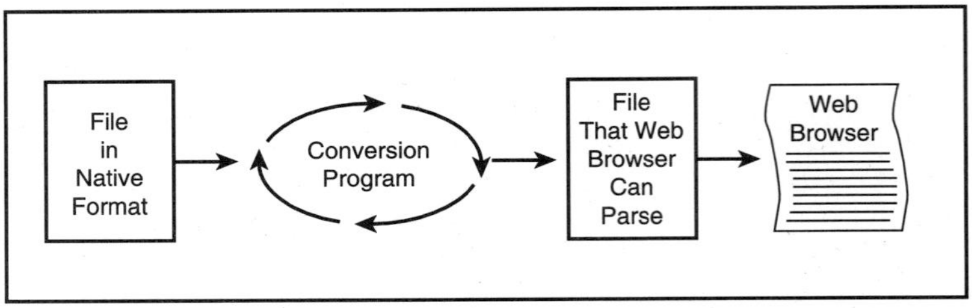

You can apply filter methods to your Web publishing solution in many ways. Theoretically, you can generate a Web document from any formatted document. You can write programs to search for key characteristics and to replace them with a Web formatting tag. You even can parse a flat text file in this way by searching for things like line breaks, headings denoted by Roman numerals, single lines of text, and so on.

The mapping between native document formatting and the target Web format (HTML, SGML, and so on) must be consistent, however. The feasibility of using a custom program diminishes when the original documents have different internal structures.

TIP

Although developing custom software can be an expensive option, this is not always the case. A myriad of inexpensive options for processing documents exists. Developing a program to convert a consistently formatted set of files to a format like HTML is relatively straightforward. In some cases, scripting languages like sed and awk may fulfill your needs. Other options include using the macro capabilities of most commercially available word processors to insert Web tags into your documents.

Microsoft Word's use of document templates (DOT files) lends itself well to filter and conversion routines. By following a well-defined template when creating a Word document, thus maintaining a consistent structure, you can easily convert the Word formatting codes to Web format codes. Methods of converting a Word document to Web format include using macros to replace and insert Web formatted tags before saving a document or running a conversion program on the Word file after saving it.

In either case, this type of conversion involves post-processing, meaning that you must check the document for accuracy after using the converter. Standard Web-formatting errors are detected only after you edit your document. Having to recheck and possibly reprocess your documents after using a converter is characteristic of all filter-based document technologies.

One way to recheck documents is simply to display them in your Web browser and ensure that everything is displayed as it should be. You can also use a program to check the documents for accuracy, such as Quarterdeck's WebAuthor. Figure 43.2 shows the first window that appears in WebAuthor when you launch it from Word. As you can see, WebAuthor has a specific setting for opening HTML documents created in Microsoft Word.

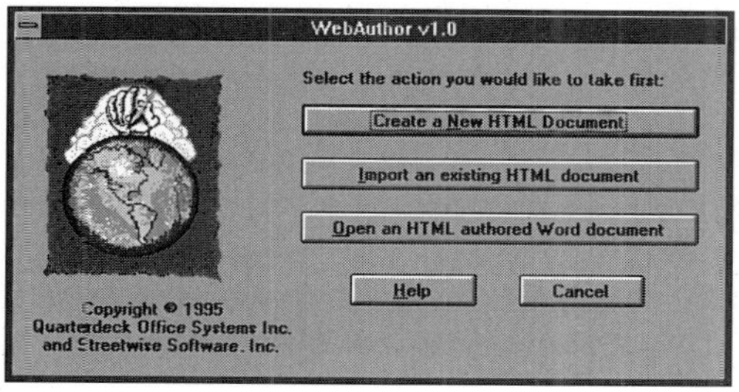

FIGURE 43.2.
Quarterdeck WebAuthor initial window.

If you select `Open an HTML authored Word document`, and then select the filename of your document, WebAuthor opens the file. As it opens the file, it checks the consistency of the document to ensure it is properly formatted HTML. While WebAuthor will not catch all errors, it will catch most of the conversion errors. Figure 43.3 depicts the type of errors WebAuthor reports if it finds poorly formatted HTML code.

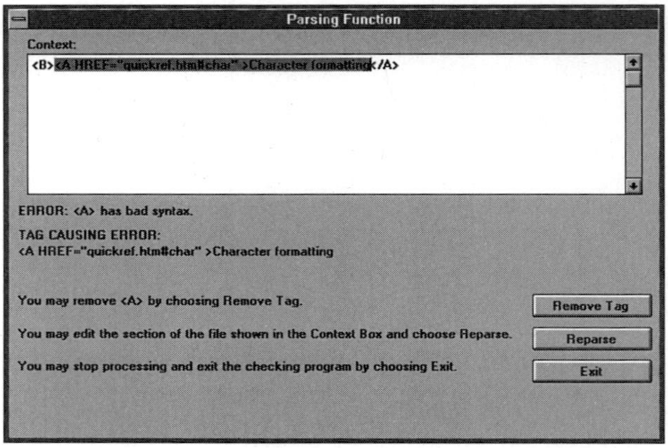

FIGURE 43.3.
QuarterDeck WebAuthor parse error window.

What WebAuthor has actually flagged as "bad syntax" is the `#char` notation. Is WebAuthor wrong? Well, the error as reported is somewhat misleading but is still useful if you take into consideration that the error was found while parsing for HTML tags. WebAuthor interpreted the special character # within `<A HREF...</A>` as non-compliant. What you need to do is move forward with your work by selecting one of the three options Quarterdeck provides for you: remove the tag, edit it and reparse, or exit. Ignoring the "error" is not an option in this case because of the validation criteria built into WebAuthor.

The validation of Web documents after conversion is an essential post-processing activity. This fact can significantly affect costs in converting a large number of documents, even when small discrepancies are found after a document has been converted.

Beyond WebAuthor, you will find dozens of converters that will handle the output of almost every word processing environment. Products like InterLeaf, FrameMaker, and other top-end publishing environments offer either HTML filter and conversion programs or access to third-party providers of such programs.

Two notable applications that make conversion from word processor formats to Web-usable formats easier are the Adobe Acrobat and Common Ground product suites.

The Adobe Acrobat suite of products includes a number of programs for creating and displaying portable documents in Adobe's PDF. Two key programs in this product suite are Adobe Exchange and Adobe Distiller. Adobe Exchange and Adobe Distiller were originally developed to convert PostScript files to electronic hypertext documents; they are now being integrated into Web publishing environments with hypertext PDF files as the target end product. Their ability to more closely approximate a magazine format than HTML or SGML is a strong point that has attracted many mainstream publishers. An example of the Adobe Acrobat Reader format appears in Figure 43.4.

FIGURE 43.4.
Adobe PDF file displayed in Acrobat Reader.

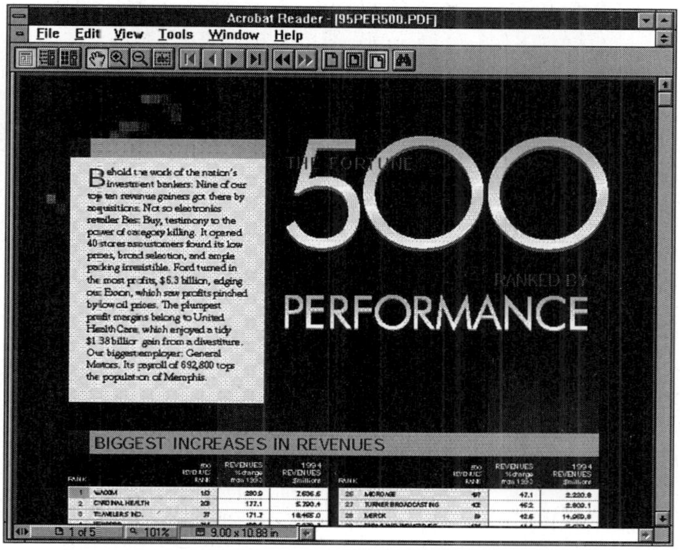

Common Ground is similar in concept to Adobe Acrobat. Common Ground converts your documents to a Digital Paper (DP) format that you can view with their browser, called MiniViewer, on any platform. You can use any publishing suite you want and keep all the composition capabilities you are used to. The online Common Ground document shown in Figure 43.5 looks exactly as it would if you printed it, but you can also include hypertext links in it. The Common Ground MiniViewer is freely distributed, as is the Adobe Acrobat reader, and is catching on quickly on the Web.

With both Adobe Acrobat and Common Ground product suites, you can use your favorite word processor to create documents and then convert them to their portable document format. For example, if you purchased Adobe Acrobat Pro or Adobe Exchange, you can use the Adobe PDFWriter print utility to convert your word processor documents to PDF documents simply by printing them using PDFWriter. In Microsoft Word, the conversion process is as easy as selecting PDFWriter for your printer when you print a document.

FIGURE 43.5.
Digital Paper file displayed in Common Ground.

More on Adobe Acrobat

Adobe Acrobat presents magazine-quality documents to users across multiple platforms by using the Portable Document Format. PDF is basically an extension of Encapsulated Postscript format with the ability to use hypertext linking. All you need to view PDF files is the Adobe Acrobat reader, which is currently available for

DOS

Macintosh

SGI

Sun SPARC and HP UNIX platforms

Windows

Adobe Acrobat is a family of products. While Adobe Acrobat Pro offers the most comprehensive publishing solution, the best value is Adobe Acrobat Exchange. With a retail price of $150, Adobe Acrobat Exchange represents a substantial cost savings over Acrobat Pro, which retails for nearly $600. Most Web publishers will find that Adobe Acrobat Exchange enables them to do everything they would like to do with Adobe's PDF documents. For that reason, this section focuses on Adobe Acrobat Exchange and an extension of Adobe Acrobat Exchange called Adobe Amber.

Adobe Acrobat Exchange

Adobe Acrobat Exchange enables you to create documents in Adobe's PDF. Using Exchange, you can view, print, annotate, build navigational links into, and add security controls to PDF files. Adobe Acrobat Exchange includes an extremely useful print utility called Adobe PDFWriter. In your word processor, you can use PDFWriter as your printer of choice, which will create a PDF document. Another reason to purchase Adobe Acrobat Exchange is that you can increase the functionality of applications using free plug-ins available at Adobe's Web site:

`http://www.adobe.com/acrobat/plugins.html`

Here's a list of some of the free plug-ins:

Movie enables Acrobat Exchange users to add QuickTime and AVI video files to PDF documents.

WebLink enables Acrobat Exchange users to add World Wide Web (URL) links to PDF documents and follow those links to PDF or HTML files anywhere on the Internet.

SuperCrop adds to the toolbar a new crop tool that looks and works like the Adobe Photoshop crop tool.

SuperPrefs adds new preferences to Acrobat Exchange, such as

- `File Open Behavior`. Enables you to specify the maximum number of open documents and automatically closes the least-recently used document if you try to open more documents than the current limit.
- `Acrobat Always On Top`. Makes the Acrobat Exchange window the topmost window at all times.
- `AutoSave Currently Open Docs`. Automatically saves open documents when you quit; the next time you start Acrobat Exchange, the documents will automatically reopen to the same page and position onscreen.

AutoIndex enables users to set up auto index features.

OLE Server enables Acrobat Exchange to act as an OLE server to view PDF documents embedded in other OLE-capable applications.

Monitor Setup gives users better control over color.

Adobe Amber

Adobe Amber is intended to be an update for owners of Adobe Acrobat Exchange and the free Adobe Acrobat reader. In reality, Amber is an Internet-friendly extension of the reader capabilities of Adobe Acrobat products. Although Amber uses some of the Adobe Exchange plug-ins just described, it also has unique features that make it very Internet-friendly. If you have ever become impatient trying to download a large PDF document and wished there were some way you could preview the document as it was downloading, Amber is what you have been looking for.

By combining the built-in features of Amber with an Amber-friendly Web server, Web users finally can view PDF documents one page at a time as the document is downloaded. The capability that makes Web servers "Amber-friendly" is byteserving, the capability to serve a document in byte-sized chunks. The byteserving capability has already been integrated into the Netscape and Open Market server products. Other servers can become Amber-friendly using a CGI script, which Adobe plans to freely distribute.

More good news about Amber is its capability to use URLs within PDF documents. Amber can also be used as a plug-in for the Netscape Navigator 2.0. Currently, Amber is available for free and you can obtain it from

```
http://www.adobe.com/Amber/
```

More on Common Ground

Common Ground is a family of products for creating portable documents. Common Ground presents magazine-quality documents to users across multiple platforms using the Digital Paper format. All you need to view DP files is the Common Ground ProViewer or the MiniViewer. The free MiniViewer is currently available for Windows and Macintosh systems. Viewers are also being developed for UNIX platforms.

You can print Common Ground documents in hard copy form from any system, and they will look exactly as the author intended. This feature represents a significant advantage over many HTML-based browsers that are still working on printing strategies. Common Ground documents can be distributed as executable (EXE) files on diskettes, CDs, networks, and file servers, or by modems or electronic mail. This capability means that many publishers can publish both hard copy and soft copy documents in essentially the same step. It also means that Common Ground documents can be distributed to electronic audiences who are not Web-enabled.

Common Ground works by taking a document created with any Windows or Macintosh application and converting it into a Digital Paper file. This is done using the application's print capability with Common Ground Maker serving as the printer driver. A Common Ground utility called Maker prints your document to a specified disk drive, directory, and file name. The result is a Common Ground document that can be viewed and printed by the Common Ground ProViewer or MiniViewer.

If needed, Maker can combine the document and a MiniViewer into a single executable file that users can view and print even if they do not have Common Ground. The catch is that if you create an executable file on a Windows system, only Windows users will be able to use the file. Similarly, if you create an executable file on a Macintosh system, only Macintosh users will be able to use the file.

Invoke Maker from an application by selecting the Maker printer driver and executing the Print command. Figure 43.6 shows Maker's pop-up Print window.

FIGURE 43.6.
Common Ground Maker window that appears after you select Print.

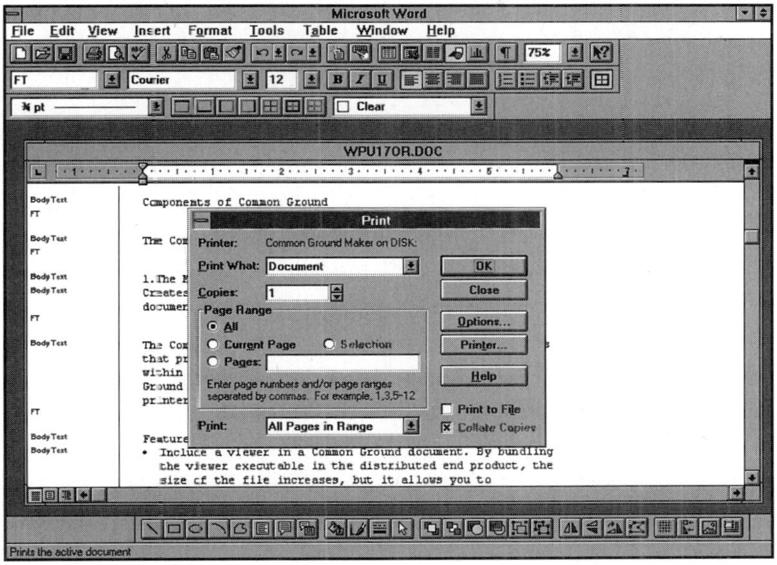

Maker has the following features:

- You can include a viewer in a Common Ground document. By bundling the viewer executable in the distributed end product, the size of the file increases, but you can distribute the document to readers who may not have Common Ground. When embedding a viewer, you can choose either the ProViewer, for which you pay a royalty to Common Ground, or the smaller MiniViewer, which can be distributed freely.
- You can select the page size and the page layout and identify specific pages from your document to include in the Common Ground document. Both text and graphics can be included in your Common Ground file.
- You can apply JPEG compression to color bitmaps in your document, selecting the quality level you desire (and thus affecting the size of the file).
- If you specify that you wish to view the Common Ground document after creating it, the ProViewer is invoked automatically.

Converting FrameMaker Documents

FrameMaker is a huge success as the document system of choice of thousands of corporations, educational institutions, and scientific organizations, especially in UNIX environments. This is largely because FrameMaker is one of the most advanced document systems available. It is also one of the most expensive document system options; FrameMaker has a retail price of between $900 and $1,600, depending on the type of system you are using and the number of licenses purchased. The expense of using FrameMaker as your publishing solution for a distributed networked environment seems astronomical compared to alternatives, primarily because with FrameMaker there is no equivalent reader program, and if there were one, you can be almost certain it would not be free.

Without a reader program, FrameMaker is not a portable document solution. If you want to convert your FrameMaker-formatted documents to a Web-usable format, however, solutions are available. Several FrameMaker-to-HTML conversion products have come on and off the market. Many of the products were freeware or shareware products that have since faded from the Internet or are in limited use.

An exception is a commercial-grade conversion suite, originally developed by CERN and subsequently supported by Harlequin, named WebMaker 2.2. Harlequin's WebMaker 2.2 is an inexpensive Web publishing solution for creating full-featured Web pages from existing FrameMaker documents. It is available for Windows 3.*x*, UNIX, and Macintosh.

CERN developed WebMaker to convert scientific publications written in FrameMaker into HTML format. After WebMaker became available to the public in mid-1994, market demand prompted CERN to select Harlequin to continue developing, supplying, and supporting WebMaker.

With WebMaker, you map FrameMaker tags to HTML tags through a graphical user interface. Error checking alerts you to unmapped tags. WebMaker offers very precise control over FrameMaker-to-HTML mapping. In the reviewed version of WebMaker, there are 169 rules pertaining to the formatting of paragraphs. Rules for paragraphs encompass all primary text elements in your documents, including headings, footnotes, and tables.

A sample of a FrameMaker-to-HTML mapping sequence using WebMaker appears in Figures 43.7 and 43.8. Figure 43.7 shows how WebMaker flags undefined rules. Figure 43.8 shows the dialog box you would use to map rules.

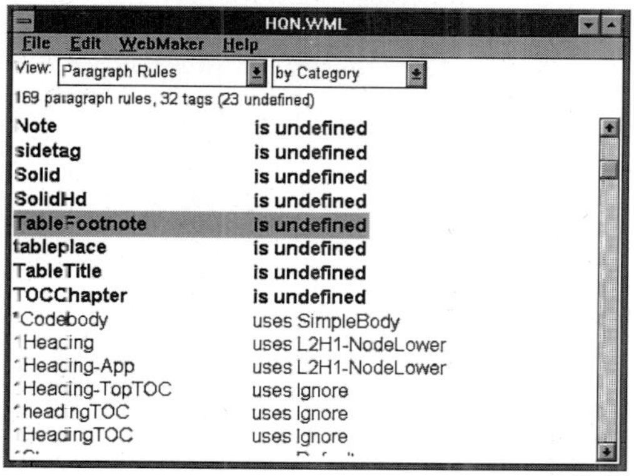

FIGURE 43.7.
WebMaker flags undefined rules as errors.

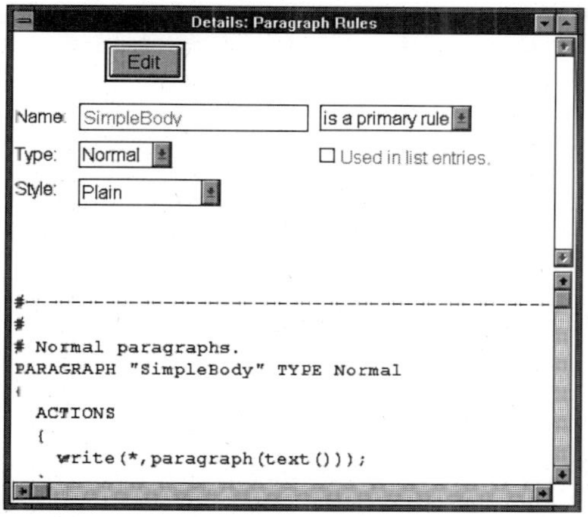

FIGURE 43.8.
Defining a mapping rule.

Download WebMaker 2.2 for evaluation or purchase from the WebMaker pages at Harlequin's Web site:

`http://www.harlequin.com/webmaker/`

Using WebMaker, you can do the following:

- Convert FrameMaker text to HTML
- Convert FrameMaker tables to HTML 3 tables
- Convert all FrameMaker-supported graphic formats to inline GIF format
- Write equations in GIF or HTML 3 format
- Customize the conversion process

Converting TeX Documents

TeX is another document system that enjoys widespread use in corporations, educational institutions, and scientific organizations. TeX's most highly regarded feature is its support of advanced mathematical equations. TeX has a highly structured language syntax, which forms the basis of many popular TeX derivatives such as LaTex. Publishers with TeX conversion requirements should review both TeX-to-LaTeX conversion issues and LaTeX-to-HTML conversion issues before committing to a solution.

LaTeX2HTML is a conversion tool that makes it possible for you to convert documents written in LaTeX (or converted from TeX to LaTeX) into HTML. LaTeX2HTML recreates the basic structure of a paper document as a set of interconnected hypertext nodes that can be explored using automatically generated navigation panels. Any defined annotations, such as cross-references, citations, or footnotes, are converted into hypertext links. Special formatting information, such as special font character mappings for mathematical equations, is converted into GIF images that are placed automatically in the hypertext document.

NOTE

You must use embedded GIF images for converted mathematical equations to present accurately the author's intended notations to users. Remember that HTML only parses data, not formatting information.

LaTeX2HTML is being widely used for preparing electronic books, documentation, scientific papers, lecture notes, training and coursework material, literate programming tools, bibliographic references, and much more. LaTeX2HTML will run on most UNIX systems, but it requires at least Perl version 4. If you've upgraded to Perl 5, there is a version of LaTeX2HTML compatible with Perl version 5.

You can get LaTeX2HTML via FTP from

```
ftp://ftp.tex.ac.uk/pub/archive/support/
```

Moving Databases to the Web

Databases are at the heart of most information systems, and your Web-based information system should be no different. Databases come in many forms.

Often databases are in the form of flat files that are updated by hand. A list of addresses or business contacts in a text document is an example of a flat file. If you maintain flat databases, chances are good that your system administrator has created a program that can extract information from the flat file, such as a person's home address or phone number. Although such databases are simple, they are useful and practical, especially in UNIX environments.

Because flat-file databases are usually formatted as standard ASCII text, using them on your Web or Intranet server is easy. All you have to do is make the file available by moving it to an appropriate directory on the server. Then, using a standard Web browser, anyone can display the file as a text document.

If you have seen text files displayed in a browser, you know that the formatting is not especially appealing. Therefore, you may want to convert the text file to HTML using a converter such as ASCII2HTML or RTF2HTML.

To maintain the usability of the flat file database, you may also want to create a search form users can submit to search the database for entries. You will want to parse the output of the form using a CGI script, and then pass the result to a script that searches the database. Fortunately, you probably have existing search scripts that you can use for this purpose immediately, especially if you use UNIX.

More complex company databases are probably maintained on commercial database systems. The problem with commercial database systems is that they use proprietary formats and interfaces, which makes it extremely difficult to convert your data. The good news is that major database vendors, like Oracle and Sybase, have pulled out all the stops to ensure that their database systems can take advantage of Internet technologies.

Oracle developed a product called WebSystem that consists of Web server and client products that easily integrate with your existing Oracle databases. The key component of WebSystem is Oracle WebServer. The Oracle WebServer provides a complete Web publishing and database solution that combines the power and reliability of Oracle7 Enterprise or Universal Server with the capabilities of the Web.

Sybase offers several solutions for moving your databases to the Web. Their showcase solution integrates Sybase with Silicon Graphics servers to create a powerful Web-ready database solution called WebFORCE CHALLENGE. WebFORCE CHALLENGE features specific modules for conducting online inventory management, transaction management, customer tracking, and marketing using Sybase.

Once you obtain an Internet solution from your database vendor, you will be able to directly access your database on your intranet or Web server. Direct access to your database ensures that the data remains usable and functional on the Web.

Moving Spreadsheets to the Web

Spreadsheets are another valuable type of legacy publication that you may want to make accessible online. Before you move a spreadsheet to the Web, you should ask whether users will want to view or edit the data in a particular spreadsheet. The answer to this question is extremely important.

Creating viewable files out of existing spreadsheet data is easy. One solution is to open the spreadsheet in the application in which it was created, such as Excel or Lotus 1-2-3, and save the spreadsheet as a standard text file with the `.txt` extension. To do this, select `Save As` from the application's `File` menu. Next, as shown in Figure 43.9, select the file type. Keep in mind that any formulas embedded in the spreadsheet are generally not saved in the text file. After you move the file to a directory on the server, anyone will be able to view the spreadsheet data as standard text in a Web browser.

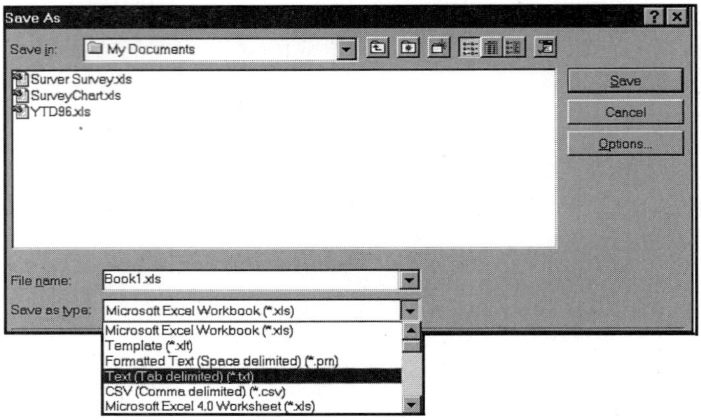

FIGURE 43.9.
Saving a spreadsheet as text in Microsoft Excel.

If you think about it, the columns and rows of a spreadsheet are really the same as the columns and rows of a table, which makes converting a spreadsheet to HTML a snap. Your spreadsheet displayed as an HTML table will be much more appealing than a standard text file. Using the text file you just created, you could add the appropriate HTML markup to create a file containing an HTML table.

Although you could add markup to a basic spreadsheet in a matter of minutes, you probably do not want to convert lengthy spreadsheets by hand. Fortunately, an increasing number of spreadsheet applications have add-ons that support direct conversion of the spreadsheet to HTML: Microsoft has Internet Assistant for Excel, Corel has Internet Publisher for Quattro Pro. Using these conversion tools, you can convert dozens of existing spreadsheets to a Web-viewable format in minutes.

Like database files, spreadsheet data usually needs to be presented on the Web in a more dynamic format than a static page. After all, what good is a spreadsheet if you cannot manipulate it when you need to?

Displaying a spreadsheet in an editable format requires a little more work than converting the spreadsheet to a viewable format, and a lot more ingenuity. To display the spreadsheet in an editable format, you will use the spreadsheet application itself to display the spreadsheet.

The first step is to create HTML pages that reference your spreadsheets. This requires that you reference the spreadsheet by name, such as in the following code:

```
<H2>Spreadsheets</H2>

<P><A HREF="1q96_earnings.xls">First Quarter '96 Earnings</A></P>
<P><A HREF="2q96_earnings.xls">Second Quarter '96 Earnings</A></P>
<P><A HREF="3q96_earnings.xls">Third Quarter '96 Earnings</A></P>
<P><A HREF="4q96_earnings.xls">Fourth Quarter '96 Earnings</A></P>
<P><A HREF="ytd97_earnings.xls">Year-To-Date '97 Earnings</A></P>
```

Launching the spreadsheet application when the user clicks a hypertext link to a spreadsheet data file requires updates to configuration files on your server and client browsers. These updates ensure that your server and browser correctly identify spreadsheet data files and launch the appropriate application to display the files.

Because spreadsheet data files should end in unique extensions, you need to configure your server to send files with these extensions as new MIME types. On most servers, MIME types are stored in a specific configuration file called `mime.types` or `mime.typ`. You need to edit this file and add entries for each spreadsheet application used on your network.

If you use Microsoft Excel, you will add this MIME type entry to the end of the `mime.types` files:

```
application/msexcel     xls     xcl
```

If you use Lotus 1-2-3, you will add this MIME type entry to the end of the `mime.types` files:

```
application/lotus     wks     wk4
```

NOTE

The exact number of spaces between the MIME type and the extension designator does not matter. MIME types are broken down into basic categories, such as application. The application type identifies binary data that can be executed or used with another application. Each data type category has a subtype associated with it. MIME subtypes are defined as primary data types, additionally defined data types, and extended data types. The primary subtype is the primary type of data adopted for use as MIME content types. Additionally defined data types are additional subtypes that have been officially adopted as MIME content types. Extended data types are experimental subtypes that have not been officially adopted as MIME content types.

After you save the MIME configuration file, you should restart your server. You are now ready to configure your browser to launch the spreadsheet application as a helper application. Do this by setting preferences from an options menu within the browser. In Netscape Navigator, when you select `General Preferences` under the `Option` menu, you can use the dialog box shown in Figure 43.10 to configure helper applications.

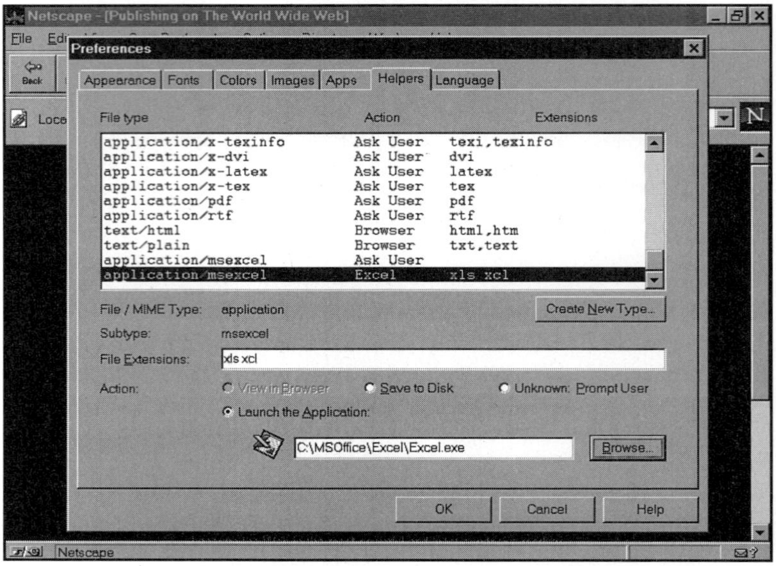

FIGURE 43.10.
Setting preferences in Netscape to launch the spreadsheet application as a helper application.

To set a helper application in Netscape Navigator 3, click the `Create New Type` button. This action opens the Configure New MIME Type dialog box in which you can enter the MIME type and subtype. In the `MIME Type` field, enter the keyword `application`. In the `MIME SubType` field, enter the MIME subtype, such as `msexcel` or `lotus`. Once you enter this information, click the `OK` button to close the Configure New MIME Type dialog box.

In the `File Extension` field of the dialog box shown in Figure 43.10, enter the file extension for the spreadsheet application in a space-separated list, such as `wks wk4`. In the `Action` field, select the radio button labeled `Launch the Application`. Next, click the `Action` field's `Browse` button to open the Select an Appropriate Viewer dialog box. Using this dialog box, search through your file system until you identify the file path to the binary executable for the spreadsheet application. When you are finished, click the `OK` button. After you double-check the accuracy of your helper application entry, click the `OK` button of the Preferences dialog box.

That's it! Now your server and browser are properly configured to launch the spreadsheet application when you need it. Keep in mind that if multiple copies of browsers are separately installed on the network, you will need to configure those browsers as well.

Summary

Making legacy publications available on your intranet or Web server gives employees and customers instant access to the information they need to make decisions. Before you start moving files, you should develop a clear plan that begins with getting the company's data organized.

After your plan is developed and distributed to company personnel, you can start moving legacy publications to the Web. Usually you will want to move files on a prioritized basis that ensures that the most useful legacy data is moved first.

In general, your legacy data will be in one of three formats: document, database, or spreadsheet. Although many document formats are easily converted to HTML, converting database and spreadsheet files often requires some forethought. Thankfully, in an increasingly Internet-aware world, most software vendors are developing tools that make it easier to move legacy publications to the Web. If a specific tool is not available to display the document in a usable format, you can—as you saw with spreadsheets—launch applications directly by configuring your server and browser to recognize and properly handle additional MIME types.

CHAPTER 44

Should You Upgrade to SGML?

by Steven J. DeRose

IN THIS CHAPTER

The World Wide Web has brought more attention to SGML than anything else. Most WWW documents (other than bitmapped graphics) are SGML documents that use the HTML DTD. If you're using HTML, you're using SGML, although there's much more to SGML. On the other hand, most Web browsers don't support any other DTDs besides HTML. This means that all the other SGML data in the world can't be browsed easily on the Web. (But take heart! Several solutions are presented in this chapter.)

This chapter begins by telling you how SGML relates to HTML and what's happening with SGML on the Web already. Then you learn about the practical issues: how to decide whether to go with HTML or SGML for your Web data, and how you can take advantage of each one's strengths and avoid their weaknesses.

How HTML and SGML Relate

People often say that HTML is a subset of SGML. This is nearly right, but it's a bit more complicated. Technically, HTML is an *application* of SGML. This means that it's really a DTD, a set of tags and rules for where the tags can go. SGML is a language for composing DTDs that fit various kinds of documents. There are many applications, and therefore many DTDs. (HTML, the DTD for the World Wide Web, is probably the best-known one.)

You already know that a DTD is always designed for some particular type of document: business letters, aircraft manuals, poetry, and so on. An important question to ask when deciding whether to put some data in HTML or another SGML DTD is, "What kind of documents is the HTML DTD meant for?"

Here is a sample of the kinds of tags that exist in HTML. First, HTML has a lot of tags for marking up common kinds of structures. Here's a partial list:

- Headings: `<H1>`, `<H2>`...
- Divisions (the actual big containers like chapters and sections, that *contain* headings and other data): `<DIV>`
- Basic document blocks (paragraphs, block quotations, footnotes, various kinds of lists): `<P>`, `<BQ>`, `<FN>`, `<OL>`, `<UL>`, `<DL>`
- Tables and equations (only in newer browsers): involve many different element types
- Text emphasis: `<EMPH>`, `<STRONG>`
- Hypermedia links: `<A>`, `<IMG>`
- Interactive forms: `<INPUT>`, `<TEXTAREA>`

HTML also includes several element types that express formatting rather than structure. These pose some portability problems, but they can be useful in cases where you simply *must* have a certain layout:

- Font changing, such as for getting bold and italic type: `<B>`, `<I>`
- Various extensions that work only with certain browsers: `<BLINK>`, `<FONT>`, and so on
- Forced line breaks (most used in code samples, "preformatted text," and similar examples): `<BR>`, `<PRE>`
- Drawing rules, boxes, and so on: `<HR>`

From the selection of element types, you can easily see the kinds of documents HTML is best for: fairly simple documents with sections, paragraphs, lists, and the like. In fact, most of the HTML element types are pretty generic; nearly every DTD has paragraphs and lists in it. One place where HTML excels, however, is in linking. Although it only has a couple of element types for links, those element types can use URLs to point to any data anywhere in the world. For more details on HTML, you may want to read *Special Edition: Using HTML,* from Que Publishing.

So, why use other SGML DTDs? The main reason is that not all documents consist of only these basic kinds of elements. Whenever you run across some other kind of element, you have to "cheat" to express it in HTML. A very common example is the Level 6 heading element in HTML (`H6`). Because the first browsers formatted `H6` headings in small caps and there was no text emphasis tag that would give the same effect, people got in the habit of using `H6` to mean "small caps." Of course, some people also use `H6` as a heading, and many people use it both ways.

This works fine—until something changes. Suppose that a browser comes along that enables users to adjust the text styles for different tags, for example. Someone changes `H6` to look like something besides small caps, and everyone who was counting on small caps is surprised. Sometimes this won't matter, but it might; what if the user wants all the headings big and all the text emphasis small? Or what if the user is blind? When his browser runs across an `H6` element, it wouldn't do any good for his browser to put it in large type, so instead maybe its computer-generated voice says "section" and reads the heading loudly; in the same way, maybe such a browser is not supposed to do anything special for small caps.

The most important problem, though, is that you might want to use the tags for something completely different than formatting later. What if a browser is really friendly and makes automatic outlines by grabbing all the headings? Or what if you want to do a search, but only for text in headings? (You might want to do that because if a word occurs in a heading, it's probably more important than if it just occurs in the main text.)

Using a tag because it gets the right formatting effect is always a problem, usually a delayed one; it works fine when you do it, but the "gotcha" comes later. People working with the distant ancestors of SGML made up a name for this: "tag abuse syndrome."

The only thing to do about tag abuse syndrome is to make sure you have the right types of tags available. Few people would use `<H6>` for small caps if there were a more appropriate emphasis element available. That is exactly why SGML is important for the Web; a lot of documents contain elements that don't fit into the HTML set. Here are some kinds of elements for which tags aren't available in HTML:

- Poetry and drama: STANZA, VERSE, SPEECH, ROLES.
- Computer manual-speak: COMMAND, RESPONSE, MENUNAME.
- Bibliographies, card catalogs, and the like: AUTHOR, TITLE, PUBLISHER, EDITION, SUBJECT-CODE, DATE.
- Back-of-book indexes: ENTRY, SUBENTRY, PAGEREF.
- Dictionaries: ENTRY (of many levels), PRONUNCIATION, ETYMOLOGY, DEFINITION, SAMPLE-QUOTATION.

This problem will continue to exist even though later versions of HTML will add many useful new tags—no one can predict all the kinds of documents that people will invent. SGML provides the solution, because when you need a new kind of element, you can create it. You can avoid problems by trying not to force every kind of document into a single mold (just as you don't try to make a single vehicle do the work of a bicycle, car, and Mack truck).

From time to time, as you tag a document, you might feel as if the right tag just isn't available. How often this happens is a good way to tell how well the DTD you're using fits the document you're working with. If the fit is too poor, the time may come to extend the DTD or switch to an entirely different one—though this shouldn't happen very often. It's better to use the right DTD for each job than to force-fit; to be able to do this, users must have software that handles SGML generically rather than forcing data into any one mold.

TIP

Moving data from one DTD to another can sometimes be easy. It helps to have at least a little skill with some programming tool like Perl, as well as SGML. Even so, the job is not always easy. If the two DTDs use similar structures and differ primarily in tag names, it may be as easy as running some global changes to rename tags. If you aren't using much SGML minimization, non-SGML tools like Perl or even a word processor's Search and Replace command may be enough, because all the tags are right there: you can search for a string like <P> and change it to <PARA>—but remember to allow for tags with attributes! On the other hand, if you're using a log of omitted tags or changing to a very different DTD where you have to add or subtract containers, re-order things, and so on, it can be a lot more work.

There are also special tools available to help transform SGML documents in this way. Among them are OmniMark from Software Exoterica, the SGML Hammer from SoftQuad, and Balise from AIS.

What Data Is Already in SGML?

A lot of data is already available in SGML, and a lot of that has already gone onto the Web. Because SGML was adopted first by large organizations (after all, they had the biggest document problems to solve), those organizations have been able to make a lot of data available.

From Commercial Publishers

Many publishers are moving to SGML for all their documents. Some want to preserve their investment so they can reproduce books even after the latest wiz-bang word processor is history. Some want to simplify the data-conversion they do when authors send in their drafts. Some want to support new forms of multimedia delivery, information retrieval, and so on.

One of the earliest success stories for SGML in publishing is the many-volume Oxford English Dictionary (OED). For many decades, the entire OED used rooms full of 3×5 cards. But in the early 1980s, the publishers decided to go electronic. They worked with Waterloo University and developed sophisticated conversion programs to get the whole dictionary into SGML. One of the hardest tasks was teasing apart 25 or so different uses for italics in the scanned text: book titles, foreign words, emphasis, word origins, and so on. This is just a severe case of tag-abuse syndrome (one they couldn't avoid, since they had to work from scanned text, and scanners can't tell you much about distinctions other than font choice). Success in this conversion made it much easier to keep the dictionary up-to-date; it's also resulted in a great electronic edition that can be searched in very sophisticated ways. Because of the up-front tagging work, if you ask for all the words with Latin origins, you don't also get all the places where "Latin" happens to show up as an emphatic word or in a book title.

Another major SGML publishing project is the Chadwyck-Healey *English Poetry Database*. This project is collecting all English poetry from the earliest stages of English up to 1900 and publishing it on a series of CD-ROMs with sophisticated search software. Some of it everyone has read, some of it only an English professor could love—but it's all going to be there, in SGML.

Journal publishers have recently started using SGML to speed up the review and publishing cycle (see Figure 44.1). Platform and format independence make it easier to ship files to the many people involved. The fact that all kinds of software—from authoring to online and paper delivery systems—can now deal with SGML also makes it a good common format for them.

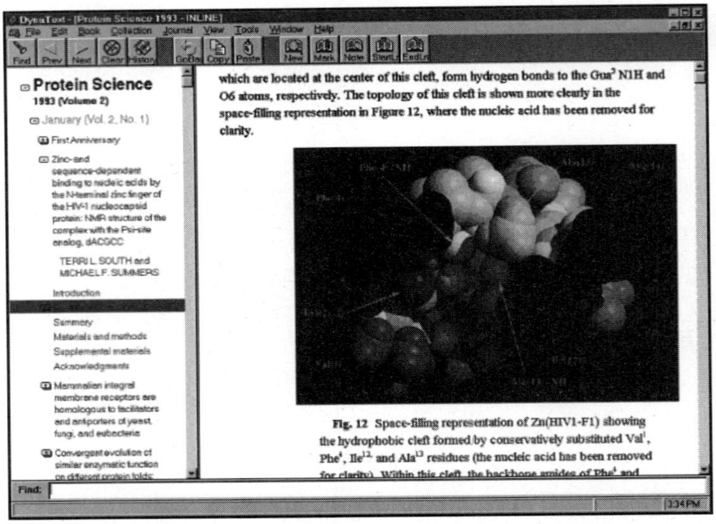

FIGURE. 44.1.
SGML is being used for a variety of sophisticated documents, including technical and scientific journals. Screen shot courtesy of Lightbinders, San Francisco (`http://lbin.com`*).*

From Computer Vendors

When computer companies started using SGML, SGML won the battle. Now that the publications and documentation departments right inside computer companies are demanding good SGML tools, the need is obvious to those companies. When software companies notice a problem, there's a nice side benefit: They not only notice, but can do something about it, and so new tools are beginning to appear.

Silicon Graphics, Inc. was one of the first companies to move its documentation to SGML, calling its system "IRIS InSight" (see Figure 44.2). SGI makes the high-end graphics workstations that bring us a lot of special effects. Novell moved too, and reportedly saves millions of dollars (and trees) per year by shipping NetWare documentation on CD-ROM rather than paper. Novell used SGML to its advantage in moving to the Web; in only a few days, a single person set up over 110,000 pages of NetWare documentation for Web delivery, using a Web server that can convert SGML portions to HTML on demand. The data is still stored and maintained in generic SGML using its original DTDs, and so is always up-to-date without a complicated conversion and update process.

Sun Microsystems, AutoDesk, Phoenix (of BIOS fame), and many others also use SGML heavily, and there are reports that Microsoft does the same in-house. As one SGML Web publisher put it, a lot of the information you *have to* have is going onto the Web in SGML. IBM started using a predecessor of SGML, called GML, long ago, and may have more data in SGML-like forms than anyone.

FIGURE 44.2.
SGI customers access documentation using the IRIS InSight system.

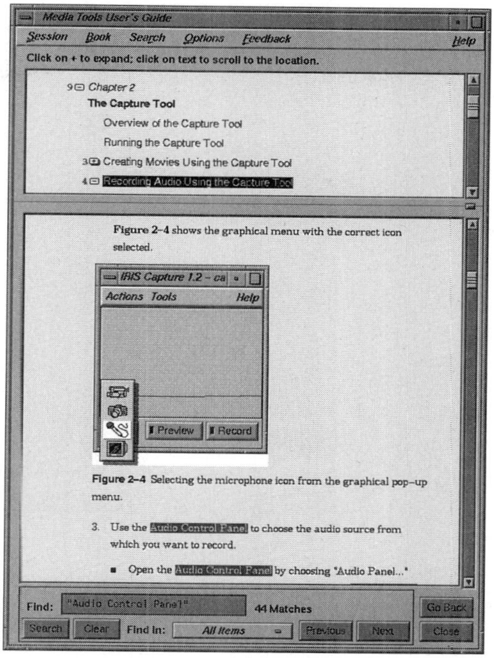

From Libraries and Universities

SGML is being used for *finding aids*, which are the equivalent of catalogs for unique items like special collections of archives, personal papers, and manuscripts. The University of California at Berkeley's library is spearheading this work, quietly converting huge numbers of finding aids into SGML and working with many other libraries to refine a DTD (see Figure 44.3). They can (and do) deliver this information easily on any medium, from CD-ROMs to the Web.

Scholars and teachers also have put a lot of information into SGML and are starting to move it to the Web. The Brown University Women Writers' Project is collecting and coding as many English documents as possible from female authors prior to 1950. Several theological tools, such as CDWord, provide access to sacred texts, commentaries, and the like. And the complete works of philosophers as varied as Nietzsche, Wittgenstein, Pierce, and Augustine are in various stages of conversion to SGML.

The Oxford Text Archive and the Rutgers/Princeton Center for Electronic Texts in the Humanities are developing large literary collections in SGML; some parts are already available on the Web. Many individuals also encode and contribute their favorite literature, as part of research or teaching.

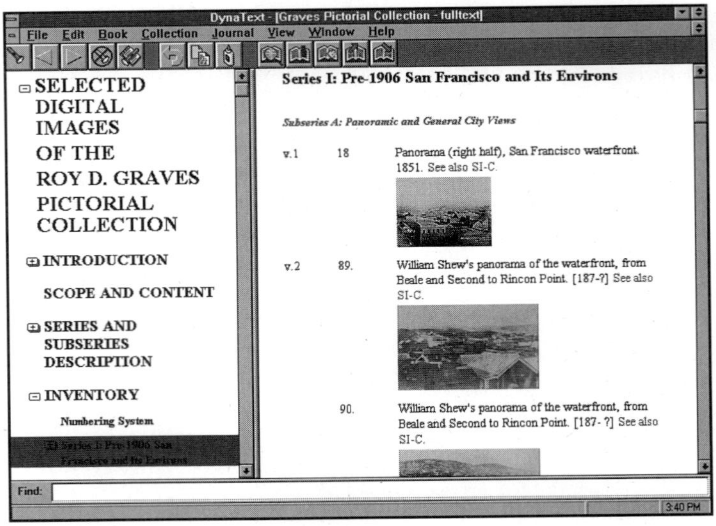

FIGURE 44.3.
Berkeley and many other libraries have cooperated to develop the "Encoded Archival Description" DTD to help give easy access to a wide variety of manuscripts and other collections.

From Industry

High-tech industries moved to SGML very early because of its power for managing large documents. Aircraft and similar industries use many subcontractors; assembling complete manuals using parts from a variety of sources is hard unless you set up some standards. So the aircraft manufacturers and the airlines got together and set up a DTD. The companies that make central-office telephone equipment have done the same.

Not long after these industries went to SGML, the automobile and truck industries did also; companies like Ryder and FreightLiner have improved their speed of repairs and overall reliability using SGML. Other success stories abound in power companies, copier and other office machine companies, and many others.

From Government and the International Community

They say the U.S. Government is the world's biggest publisher, and it's probably true. The Patent Office puts out about 109 megabytes of new patent text per week (not counting figures); the Congressional Record adds a lot, too. Both of these are moving to SGML, though it's a challenge because they must be very careful not to disrupt current practices or delay delivery during the transition.

Internationally, there is much interest in SGML in Europe, and increasing interest in Asia. The International Organization for Standardization (ISO, despite the English word-order), which put SGML together in the first place, uses it for publishing some of its standards.

Why Is This Data in SGML, Not HTML?

Because of all these users, there is a lot of SGML data out there. Why did all these companies choose SGML instead of HTML? Mostly because it's a generic solution; it lets them use tags appropriate to the kinds of documents each one cares about. This means describing the document parts themselves rather than how they should appear on today's output device. This generic approach is why SGML data outlasts the programs that process it, and that can mean huge long-term savings. HTML can do this for a limited number of cases, but not in general. There are other reasons for using SGML:

- *Scalability.* SGML has features, such as entity management, that make it easier to work with large documents. A printed airplane manual often outweighs the plane itself, and the documentation system better not choke.
- *Validation.* SGML's ability to check whether documents really conform to the publisher's rules is important in industry, especially in the current world of liability lawsuits. However, validating a document doesn't ensure it makes sense, any more than spelling correctly ensures it makes sense.
- *Information retrieval.* Big documents are hard to work with, and SGML tagging puts in the "hooks" you need to make search and retrieval software work much better. True containers for big organizing units are especially helpful here, like `CHAPTER` and `SECTION` instead of just `H1` and `H2`.
- *Version management.* High-tech manuals and ancient literature share a common problem because they come in many versions; it can make a big difference which one you get. Although not a true version-management system by itself, SGML has features that form a good foundation for one (such as marked sections, attributes, modularity, boilerplating, and so on).
- *Customizable presentations.* This relates to version management, too. Because SGML doesn't predefine formatting and layout, delivery tools can customize the display for each user as needed—show extra hints for novices, hide secret information, and so on. This is what Ted Nelson (he invented the term *hypertext*) calls *stretchtext*: The document should smoothly expand and contract to match the user's interests.
- *Access for print disabled.* Again because SGML gets away from formatting details, it is easy to convert SGML documents for delivery in Braille, via text-to-speech converters, and so on. Several books have been converted this way in record time.

All these advantages apply to paper production, online delivery, and information retrieval. But once you lay out pages for print, most of these advantages disappear; once all the lines and page breaks are set, the page representation takes over, and getting back to the structure is very difficult.

Five Questions to Ask About Your Data

Given all the advantages of generic SGML for big projects, yet all the simplicity of HTML for simple ones, how do you decide which way to go? There are five questions you can ask that will help you choose.

What Functionality Do I Need?

If your documents fit the HTML model and consist mostly of the kinds of elements HTML provides, HTML is probably a good choice. This is especially true if the documents are also small (tens of pages, not thousands). But if you have big documents or documents with special structures or elements, SGML will take you a lot farther.

If you need to do information retrieval, SGML is also better. You can search HTML, but you can't easily pin down just *where* hits are. This is because the HTML tags don't divide data up as finely as you can with full SGML, and HTML doesn't typically tag large units such as sections. (The tags have only been added in the latest revision, and they're still optional.)

Finally, if you need to deliver in more forms than just the Web, you should consider SGML. Tools are available to turn SGML not only into Web pages, but into paper pages, most kinds of word processor files, CD-ROM publications, Braille, and many other forms. This can all be done with HTML in theory, but it's harder in practice.

Do I Need Flexible Data Interchange?

SGML eases data interchange in several ways. Because it helps you avoid using tags for things they don't quite fit, your data is easier to move to other systems, especially if the tags can take advantage of finer distinctions. For example, if you tag book titles, emphasized words, and foreign words as `<I>` in HTML, you have a problem when you a move to something that can distinguish book titles and emphasis, such as a program to extract and index bibliographies. If you make the finer distinctions, you have a choice later whether to treat the items the same or differently.

Computers are pretty bad at sorting things into meaningful categories when they look the same. You almost need artificial intelligence to decide which italic text is a book title and which is something else. The good news is that computers are really good at the opposite task; if you've already marked up book titles and emphasized words as different things (say, `<TI>` and `<EMPH>`), it's no problem at all for a computer to show them both as italic.

Because of this, interchange is much easier down the road if you break things up early and make as many distinctions as practical. On the other hand, each distinction may be a little extra work, so you need to balance long-term flexibility versus how much time and effort you can put in up front. To figure out this balance, be sure to consider just how long you think your data will last (you're safest to at least double your first guess) and how important your data is.

Importance and lifespan don't always go together. Stock quotes are pretty important when they're current, but after a year only a few specialists ever look at them. At the other extreme, some literature that started out on stone tablets thousands of years ago is still important. Where does your data fit?

How Complex Are Your References and Links?

HTML has great strength as a linking system. This is mostly because URLs can point to any data in any format, and browsers provide a very convenient way to get any of that data. URLs (the most commonly available way of identifying information on the Net, though more advanced ways are coming) can get data via all these protocols (Web-speak for "methods") and others.

Protocol	*Description*
ftp	The data is copied down to your local machine.
http	The data is formatted and shown in the browser itself (or by a helper application for graphics, sound, video, and so on).
e-mail	Communication works like electronic mail.
news	Postings from network newsgroups are retrieved and presented.

HTML does all of this with only a few tags, mainly `<A>` and `<IMG>`. This means that the linking *itself* is not very complex or sophisticated, even though the data that the links point to is. For example, both `<A>` and `<IMG>` are *one-way links*; they live somewhere in document A and point to document B, as shown in Figure 44.4. But if you're in document B, you don't know that document A exists or that it points to you.

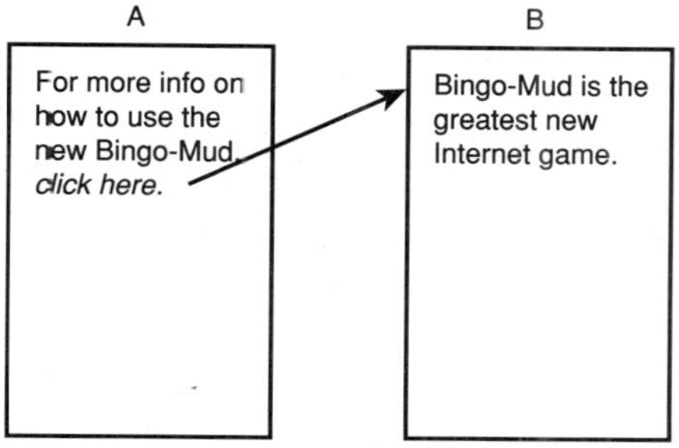

FIGURE 44.4.
The HTML `<A>` *tag makes one-way links.*

If you click a link and travel from document A to document B, most browsers will remember where you were and provide you with a Back button to return to the same document (though perhaps not to the same *place* in that document). That's an important feature, but not at all the same as also being able to get from document B to document A in the first place—with true *two-way links* you know while in document B that there's a link from document A.

NOTE

It's also hard with HTML links to go from document A to a specific place inside document B because URLs normally point to whole files. HTML does give rudimentary support for getting a whole file *and then* scrolling it to some element with a given "name" (like an SGML ID). This is useful, but doesn't help much with larger SGML documents. With large documents, the problem of having to wait for the whole thing to download (even though you only need a small portion of it) becomes very important.

Link precision will probably improve in the future with conventions for a URL to give not only a file, but an ID or other location within a file, and to use this information to optimize downloading, not just scrolling. In fact, some servers already let you add a suffix to a URL to pick out a certain portion. For example, a server could let you put an SGML ID on as if it were a query, and then just serve up the element with that ID (including all its subelements, of course):

```
<a href="http://xyz.org/docs/book.sgm?id=chap4">
```

Though you can simulate a *bi-directional* (or two-way) link in HTML, you have to do it by creating two links (one in document A and one in document B). This poses a couple of problems; the most important one is that you have to actually go in and change both document A and document B, so you can't just do this between any two documents you choose. Even if you can get at both documents to insert the links in the first place, it's easy to forget to update one "half" of the link when you update the other. Such links gradually tend to break.

What do other hypermedia systems do about this? The best ones, SGML-based or not, provide a way to create links that live completely outside of documents, in a special area called a *web*. (That name may change now that it's popular as a shorthand for the World Wide Web.) In that case, the picture looks more like Figure 44.5. Many systems provide both methods, not just one or the other.

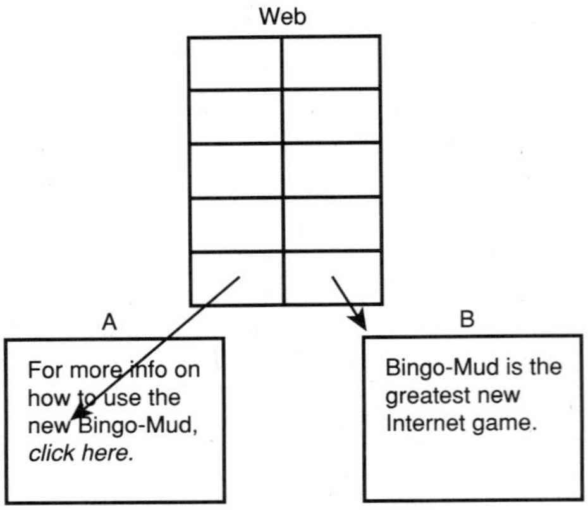

FIGURE 44.5.
An external web lets you create two-way links.

This is a much more powerful system, and you can do it with a number of SGML linking methods, such as HyTime and the TEI guidelines, and some recent systems like Hyper-G. It seems to have originated with the Brown University InterMedia system. Doing links this way has these benefits:

- Because links live outside the documents, anyone can create them without needing permission to change the documents themselves. You can even link in and out of documents on CD-ROM or other unchangeable media. This is especially important for big data like video, because it's still much more effective to keep local copies on CD-ROM or similar media than to download huge files every time they need to be viewed.
- Because documents aren't touched every time a link is attached, they can't be accidentally trashed. Most HTML links have this advantage at one end since the destination document needn't be touched. But the only way for HTML to point to a particular place *inside* a destination document is via an ID; so to do that you may have to add one, and in that case HTML loses even this one-ended advantage.
- Because a set of links is a separate thing, you can collect links into useful groups and ship them, turn them off or on, and so on. Siskel's and Ebert's links to movie-makers' home pages can be in two separate webs, so you can choose to see either or both.

If you don't need this more sophisticated linking, HTML's links may be just fine. Otherwise, you need to go beyond HTML and beyond what current HTML browsers can do. The good news is that such a web can still use URLs and related methods to do the actual references, so you can keep the power HTML gets from them. You can add URL support (or even the `<A>` and `<IMG>` tags themselves) to another DTD that packages them up to provide greater capabilities.

NOTE

TEI and HyTime links provide a very good way to express this kind of linking.

What Kind of Maintenance Is Needed?

There are two areas where HTML files run into maintenance problems that SGML can help with:

- Links tend to break over time.
- HTML itself changes through improvements such as new tags.

While the URLs and other identifiers that HTML uses for links are very powerful, the most common kind right now, the URL itself, is also fragile. A URL names a specific machine on the Internet, and a specific directory and filename on that machine (technically, this doesn't have to be true, but in practice it almost always is). This method has an obvious maintenance problem: What if the file moves? A URL-based link can break in all these ways:

- The owner moves or renames the file, or any of its containing directories (say, to install a bigger disk with a different name).
- The owner creates a new version of the file in the same place and moves the old one elsewhere. (There's an interesting question about which version old links *should* take you to, but you needn't get into that here.)
- The owner's machine gets a new domain name on the Internet (for example, if someone else trademarks the name the owner had).
- The owner moves to a new company or school and takes all of his data with him.

The Internet Engineering Task Force (IETF) is working hard on *Uniform Resource Names* or *URNs*, which let links specify names instead of specific locations. This is like specifying a paper book by author and title, as opposed to "the fifth book on the third shelf in the living room at 153 Main Street." URNs will make links a lot safer against simple changes like the ones just mentioned.

SGML provides a similar solution for part of the problem already, through names called *Formal Public Identifiers* or *FPIs* for entire documents or other data objects. SGML IDs for particular places *within* documents can be used both in general SGML and in HTML. By using FPIs or URNs to identify documents, you can ignore where documents live. When a document is really needed (such as when the reader clicks a link to it), the name is sent off to a "name server" that looks it up and tells where the nearest copy is. This works a lot like library catalogs and like the Internet routing system used for e-mail and other communications.

NOTE

You can make HTML links a little safer against change by using the BASE feature. Very often, a document will have many links that go to nearly the same place as the document itself, such as to several different files living in the same directory on the same network server, or in neighboring directories. When this happens, the beginning of the URLs on those links are all the same, such as

```
http://www.abc.com/u/xyz/docs/aug95/review.htm
http://www.abc.com/u/xyz/docs/aug95/recipe.htm
```

Instead of putting the full URL on every link, you can "factor out" the common part and put it on the BASE element in the header. The links all get much shorter, but the bigger plus is that you can update them all in one step if the server or a directory moves.

```
<BASE ID=b1 HREF="http://www.abc.com/u/xyz/docs/aug95/">
..
<A BASE=b1 HREF="review.htm">
...
<A BASE=b1 HREF="recipe.htm">
```

HTML is constantly being improved. While this is a good thing, it also poses compatibility problems. In HTML 1.0, <P> was not so much the start of an SGML element as a substitute for the Return key. It was an EMPTY element, so the content of the paragraph was never actually part of the P element, and there was normally no <P> tag before the first paragraph in any section. This has been fixed in HTML 2.0, but funny things can happen if you view an old document in a new browser or vice-versa; for example, you might not get a new line for the first paragraph after a heading.

A newer issue is tables. HTML 2.1 adds a way to mark up tables and get good formatting for them; they can even adjust automatically when the reader changes the window-width. But what about tables in earlier documents? Authors often deleted their tables entirely, but when they couldn't, they had to type tables up e-mail style, using HTML's preformatted-text tag (<PRE>) and putting in lots of spaces:

```
<PRE>
....China....1400.million
....India.....800.million
....USA.......250.million
....France.....50.million
....Canada.....25.million
</PRE>
```

These will still work in a new browser (because the <PRE> tag is still around), but they don't get the advantages or capabilities that the new tables support. They won't rewrap to different window widths, you can't wrap text within a single cell, and so on. So you can end up with awful effects like this:

```
    China     1400
million
    India      800
million
    USA        250
million
    France      50
million
    Canada      25
million
```

To get the new capabilities, you have to go in and actually change the documents. This is one reason it's considered bad form in SGML to use spaces for formatting. SGML helps you avoid this painful updating because you can represent your documents in whatever form makes sense for the documents themselves. That form is much less likely to change than the way you have to express it in one fixed DTD or system.

With SGML, if you need to accommodate software that doesn't handle your markup structures, you can use a "down-translation"—that is, a process that throws away anything that a certain HTML version can't handle. For tables, you can mark them up in any table DTD you want (CALS is the most popular) and use a program as needed to translate them to a simpler form— even the HTML 1.0-formatted kind. Then when table support is common in browsers, you just throw the down-translation program away and deliver the same data without conversion.

This works where "up-translation" won't, because computers are so much better at throwing information away than creating it. Tables are a lot like the earlier example with italics. If your DTD distinguishes book titles and a few (or a thousand!) other kinds of italics, it's easy to write a program to turn all of them into just <I> for HTML-only browsers. The reverse is much harder.

Can I Make Do with HTML?

Given all these trade-offs, here are the main things to think about when making the HTML versus full SGML decision for Web delivery:

The form the data is already in. If your data is already in SGML (or in something conceptually similar, like LaTeX), it's much easier to stick with full SGML and have tags that fit your data naturally. This way you don't have to design a complicated set of correspondences, and whatever data conversion you do will be simpler.

The document size and number of authors. If your documents are small, don't have a lot of internal structure, and don't need to be shared among multiple authors or editors, HTML may be all you need. But a little Web-browsing easily shows the bad things that can happen when people try to break big documents into little pieces—the forest can be lost by dividing it into separate trees.

The structures needed for searching. If you need to do searches that target specific data in your documents, you'll probably need SGML to label that data. Doing without it is like doing a personnel database without having names for the fields; if you searched for people with salaries less than $30,000, you'd get not only that, but all the people who are less than 30,000 years old!

The frequency of changes. If your data is going to change frequently, you're better off in SGML, where you can modularize your documents using marked sections, entities, and other features.

All these things relate to each other, so you often can't answer one question without thinking about the others. One example is that frequent changes to a document matter a lot less if the document is really small and you have complete unshared control over it. But if a document is big and several authors have to cooperate to maintain it, frequency of changes matters a lot.

How to Use HTML Safely

If you choose to put your data in HTML rather than another SGML DTD, there are several things you can do to make a later transition easier. These things are also helpful in the short term because they make your HTML more consistent, portable, and reliable.

Make sure your HTML is really valid. Run it through an SGML parser—such as sgmls, yasp, or sp—or use one of the HTML "lint" programs. (They're called that because they go looking around for unwanted dirt that accumulates in dark pockets of HTML documents.) Weblint is one such program; you can find it at

`http://www.unipress.com/weblint.`

Be very careful about quoting attributes. Any attribute value that contains any characters other than letters, digits, periods, and hyphens needs to be quoted (either single or double quotes are fine, but not distinct open/close curly quotes).

TIP

There are a couple of very common HTML errors that you can get away with in some browsers, but that will break others, and will prevent you from using generic SGML tools. The biggest one is failing to quote attributes, as just described. Probably the next biggest is getting comments wrong. These are right:

```
<!-- some text of a comment -->
<!-- another comment, with two text parts -
  -- of which this is the second -->
```

But these are wrong (that is, they're not comments):

```
<!-- this comment never ends --!>
<! This is an SGML syntax error !>
<-- This is just data to SGML -->
<!-- This one -- really -- is not a comment -->
```

Avoid any part of HTML that is labeled "deprecated" in the HTML DTD or its documentation. Deprecated is a polite term standards use to say, "Don't use this; it's dangerous, not recommended for the future, and not even universally supported at present."

Be sure to use the HTML "DIV" containers, not just free-standing headings—especially in larger documents. This makes the structure of your document easier for programs to find and process, and it can also help you find tagging errors.

Avoid colliding with SGML constructs, even if some HTML parsers ignore them. For example, don't depend on an HTML parser failing to know that the string `<![` starts a marked section, that `<?` starts a processing instruction, or that `<!--` starts a comment; always escape such strings, for example, by changing the `<` to `<`.

Challenges of Upgrading

If you decide to put your data in an SGML DTD other than HTML, there are a few "gotchas" to watch out for. None are fatal, but you'll want to start out knowing the rules of the game. The issues are briefly summarized here.

Fewer Browsers to Choose From

At this time, only a few networked information browsers can receive and format SGML regardless of the DTD. Most Web browsers have the HTML tag names built right into the program and require a new release to add new ones. This is true even if the new ones don't require any new formatting capabilities; adding a `BOOK-TITLE` element type won't work, even though you may only want it to mean "show in italics."

The main exception that is already released is a viewer called Panorama, developed by Synex and marketed by SoftQuad. Panorama is an add-on "helper" to existing browsers, like various graphics viewers. This means it does not talk to the network by itself; instead, when a Web browser follows a link and notices that the data coming back claims to be "SGML," it can forward the data to Panorama for display.

If there are Internet-based links in the SGML, Panorama calls the browser back to retrieve them. If the destination is HTML or GIF, it shows up directly in the Web browser. If it's SGML, the browser calls Panorama again.

Another SGML-capable Web browser is a new version of the DynaText SGML delivery system that can view SGML or HTML off a hard disk or CD-ROM, across the Net, out of a database, or from a compiled/indexed form used for big documents. It provides a unified environment for viewing all these data types, as well as graphic and multimedia formats.

Although there aren't many SGML-capable Web browsers, these two are very flexible and give you a lot of control over formatting, style, and other capabilities. Hopefully, more browsers will start to support generic SGML over time.

In the meantime, there are several server-end options available, too. You can always create and maintain documents using full SGML, and then run a conversion program to create HTML from it and put that on the Web. This is especially useful if you have an SGML-based authoring system in use for general publishing or other applications.

There are also Web servers available that can store SGML directly and then translate it to HTML on demand (for example, DynaWeb from Electronic Book Technologies—you can try it out at `http://www.ebt.com`). This method has the advantage that you can adjust the translation rules any time without rerunning a big conversion process over all your data. It also means the translation can be customized as needed, for example, to adjust to whichever browser is calling in, or even to modify the document by inserting real-time information during translation.

A DTD to Choose or Design

Even if you have all the software you need, with full SGML you'll need to answer a question that never arises with HTML: What DTD should I use? Very good DTDs are already available for a wide range of document types, and you can probably put off DTD-building for as long as you want by using them. This makes the task a lot easier. But even so, you have to think about your documents and then learn at least enough about a few DTDs to make a choice. You may also want to tweak an existing DTD—this is easier than starting from scratch, but still takes skills beyond those needed for tagging.

More Syntax to Learn

If you want to make up your own DTDs, you need to deal with all kinds of declarations, parameter entities, content models, and so on; there's a lot of syntax to learn (tools like Near & Far help a lot). If you use an existing DTD, there is less syntax to worry about, but there's still a little more than with HTML.

SGML provides many ways of saving keystrokes in markup, and many special-purpose constructs you never see used in HTML. Using these constructs in an HTML document will result in errors of one kind or another. For example, if you try to "comment out" a block of HTML with a marked section, its content is still there because typical HTML parsers don't recognize marked sections. In fact, for those parsers, the characters `<![ IGNORE [` and `]]>` all count as text content!

```
<P>
<![ IGNORE [ This text is not part of the document, really.
   In fact, it's <EMPH>really </EMPH> not there. ]]>
   And the paragraph goes on right here.
</P>
```

In an HTML application that isn't quite following the rules, this might be taken as just a paragraph that starts with some funny punctuation marks (a really bad HTML implementation might instead complain that you used a tag named `![`). If you got used to this, you might be surprised when you go to a more generic SGML system and discover that the `<![` in your document causes some very different effects—this is something you just have to memorize and know. In this case, the first two lines within the paragraph are not part of the content at all, and a browser shouldn't show them to you.

Using a WYSIWYG SGML editor helps a lot, for the same reasons that using MS Word is a lot easier than typing Microsoft's RTF interchange format directly. But even with the best tools, you can be surprised if you're not aware of such restrictions—for example, you might get a "beep" whenever you try to type `<![` in a paragraph, and not know why.

Benefits of Upgrading

If there's less delivery software to choose from and more to learn, why bother? The reasons are mostly the same ones that influenced big publishers to go with SGML, although which reasons are most important varies from project to project.

Platform Independence

Other SGML DTDs are even better at abstracting formatting than HTML. SGML can be retargeted to anything from a top-line photocomposition system down to text-only browsers like Lynx, Braille composers, and anything in between. SGML itself greatly benefits flexibility. HTML accomplishes this to some extent, but less so because a small and fixed tag set can force authors to think more about display effects and less about describing structure.

Browser Independence

Because generic SGML software (by definition) handles many DTDs, using a new or modified DTD won't faze it. If it works for CALS and TEI, it'll almost certainly work for whatever DTD you choose.

SGML vendors spend a lot of time testing interoperability. A standard demo at trade shows used to be to pass a tape or disk of SGML files from booth to booth throughout the show. Each product had to read the data, do whatever it did with the data (like let you edit or format it), and then write it out to pass on—without trashing it.

The "SGML Open" vendor group gets together regularly online, at shows, and at special meetings to work out agreements on details and make sure SGML documents can move around easily. For example, a popular DTD for tables has a "rotate" attribute to let you lay out tables in either portrait or landscape mode, but doesn't say whether rotation is clockwise or counter-clockwise. The vendors sat down and decided, so now they all do it the same way. Simple agreements like this can save a lot of pain for end users.

NOTE

The central point for finding out about SGML Open activites is `http://www.sgmlopen.org`. Most companies that support SGML are involved in SGML Open, and you can find links to their home pages from the SGML Open Web site, along with links to other useful SGML information.

If you use an SGML-aware server, you can benefit from greater browser independence—even on the Web. Each Web browser has its own strengths and weaknesses. If you can ship slightly different HTML to each one, you can capitalize on the strengths and avoid the weaknesses. This is easier if your data uses a more precise DTD; clients tell servers who they are, so a server that has enough information can down-translate appropriately for each one.

HTML Revision Independence

Keeping your data in SGML also lets you avoid recoding it each time a new HTML feature arrives. You learned earlier about tables—how you'd have to completely rework them if you started by assuming the browser can't support table markup, and then had to change your data when browsers caught up. The same problem came up when Netscape introduced its FRAME element and a lot of reauthoring had to happen. The same problems can happen with any kind of markup. By keeping your documents in DTDs designed to fit, you can leave them untouched and merely adjust a conversion filter.

Appropriate Tag Usage

The biggest fundamental benefit of going to SGML is that your markup can tell the truth about what components are in your document, even if the document doesn't fit into any pre-existing scheme. If the tags you need are there (or, at worst, you can add them yourself), you avoid having to "pun" and use a single tag for a bunch of purposes it may not have been meant for.

NOTE

The question of having the right tag available for the job is very important, so here are a few examples. We've already talked about how sixth-level HTML headings (<H6>) get used to mean small caps, and how italics (<I>) get used to mark many things like emphasis, foreign words, book titles, and so on.

Sometimes preformatted text (<PRE>) gets used for quick-and-dirty tables. Line-break (<BR>) gets used heavily for forcing particular browsers to lay things out a certain way (and usually that way only works well for certain browsers, certain window widths, and so on).

Another big example is equations; since there are not yet HTML elements for doing math, journal publishers and others are stuck turning equations into graphics for Web delivery. This sort of works, but the fine print tends to disappear, and zooming in doesn't help. This is a case where there's dire need for more a more adequate set of tags. And there are already some very good equation DTDs in wide use outside the Web.

Large Document Management

SGML helps you manage the conflict between big documents and slow modems. You can't very well ship a whole manual or a lengthy paper of any kind every time a user wants to see the nth paragraph (even if browsers could handle documents that big, which many can't)—no user would wait for the download to finish. Novell certainly couldn't ship tens of thousand of pages of NetWare manuals every time a user wanted a summary of some installation detail.

The only viable option with documents bigger than several tens to hundreds of pages is to break them up; you can make many smaller documents, say one for each subsection, and a bunch of overview documents that give you access similar to the table of contents in a paper book. This is usually done manually for HTML because HTML documents don't usually contain explicit markup for their larger components. (Some do now that HTML has added the DIV element.) This method works except for these problems:

- If you are also publishing a paper document, you have to maintain two quite different forms.
- The document ends up in many pieces that aren't visibly related; only a person can tell whether some link between HTML files A and B means they're part of the same document, or two somehow-related documents. This makes it hard to maintain consistency between all the parts of your original document.
- If users want to download the whole document for some reason, it's very hard to do. First, they have to find all the pieces, distinguishing "is-part-of" links from "is-related-to" links; then they have to assemble all the parts in the right order and put the larger containing structures in. It's not enough to just pack them end-to-end because some of the connections between lower sections appear only in "header" or "table of contents" documents.
- Users can't scroll smoothly through the complete document; at best, you can carefully provide Next Portion and Previous Portion buttons on every piece.

Internationalization

A final benefit of other SGML DTDs over HTML is that they have more provisions for international and multilingual documents. HTML prescribes the "Latin 1" character set. Latin 1 includes the characters for most Western European languages, but not Eastern European, Asian, or many other languages. Future revisions will probably support "Unicode," a new standard that includes characters for nearly all modern languages. SGML itself lets each document specify a character set and doesn't particularly care whether characters are one, two, or more bytes wide.

Many DTDs also provide a way to mark that individual elements are in different languages. This can have a big effect on display and searching. For example, it helps a lot if you're searching for the English word "die," to not get the German word "die," which means roughly "the," and is very common.

DTDs that specifically mark language are also very helpful when you want to create multilingual documents or documents that can customize to the reader's language. You can create documents where every paragraph has a subelement for each language, and then set up your software to show only the type the user wants; this automatically customizes the document for the reader's own language:

```
<P>
   <ENGLISH>...</>
   <FRENCH>...</>
   <ITALIAN>...</>
   <GERMAN>...</>
   <SPANISH>...</>
   ...
</P>
```

Summary

SGML is especially strong for large or structured documents, documents for which several authors share writing and editing, and documents that have components HTML doesn't provide. A single DTD such as HTML may not provide the types of elements your documents need, in which case you end up using some other type because it gets the desired appearance in the authoring software. This leads to problems down the line. HTML also has only limited support for expressing larger units such as sections, and that makes document management a bit harder.

CHAPTER 45

Setting Up and Administering a Web Server

by John Jung

IN THIS CHAPTER

Eventually, you'll probably want to put all the information in this book to use. To do so, you must have one very important item: a Web server. A Web server is a program that hands out Web pages to whoever asks for them. But Web server software is a special type of software. You can't simply create a Web site by getting the software and running it. There's much more involved in setting up and administering a Web server, as this chapter will explain.

NOTE

This chapter focuses on installing and configuring NCSA and CERN Web servers on a UNIX platform. This was done because most Web servers use either CERN or NCSA. If they aren't, they are typically derivative versions of the two. Additionally, the majority of Web servers are still on UNIX machines.

Jobs of a Web Server

Although you may have been surfing the Web for a while, you might not necessarily know what Web servers do. There is, of course, the obvious job of giving Web pages to users who request them. However, Web servers also have other duties that they must perform. Some of these tasks are done at the request of the Webmaster; others are done at the request of individuals.

User Authentication

One of the most important jobs a Web server must be able to do is to perform user authentication. There are a number of times when you, the Webmaster, don't want everybody to have access to a part of your site. In this case, you use the Web servers to check whether specific users have access to a Web page.

Perhaps your Web site is a commercial venture, and you're selling access to parts of your site. Obviously, you wouldn't want nonpaying users to access those particular parts. If that happened, your company would quickly go out of business. Maybe your company has multiple levels of access to your particular site. The nonpaying customers have a lot of restrictions, the low-paying customers have some, and the high-paying customers have none.

Another possible reason that you would want to restrict user access is to protect information. This protection applies not only to Internet access, but intranet access as well. Large companies often are broken up into smaller groups, each with a different focus. Most of the time, each of these groups wants to keep some of its information private. Perhaps the research and development department has information about upcoming software releases that it doesn't want anybody to know, not even sales and marketing. Perhaps an important customer and a certain group have a constant flow of information between them. Certainly that frequent information exchange should be kept private between the group and the customer.

Scripts

Another task that a Web server should be able to perform is to run scripts. One of the most important parts of a Web site is the CGI script (see Chapter 26, "Writing CGI Scripts"). These scripts can do a number of special functions.

One of the most common functions for a CGI script is to be used in an image map. If you recall from Chapter 20, "Backgrounds, Image Maps, and Creative Layouts," an image map is basically a picture with some defined regions. Each region points to a different part of the Web site, which can make navigating around your site easier. One of the principal components in a traditional image map is the CGI script. This script takes the mouse coordinates of where the user clicks and looks up the position. It finds the URL that corresponds to that position and returns the correct location to the Web browser.

Another use for scripts is to perform a simple form of animation on Web pages. Using the server push method, the Web server is instructed to send out a set of images. These images, all identical in dimension and at the same location, are sent out by a script. This script tells the server the order of the stream of images and regulates when the stream stops.

Servers as Proxies

Another use of Web servers is to act as a proxy server to some other source of information, such as a database or FTP site. In particular, suppose you have a system that contained some sensitive information. To access the information, a person would have to first log in. You could then maintain tight control of the information on a per-user basis. Although this use is workable for small organizations, it may not be a viable option for large companies. In such situations, the people who can have access to the information may not all be in the same office. And the costs for networking all the remote locations together can be expensive.

Consequently, you may want to put the information behind a password-protected Web server. Anybody who doesn't have a Web account can't access the data behind the Web. This method makes it far easier for everybody who should have access to the information to get to it. Additionally, the user and password information for the Web server is centralized, so it is easier to add, delete, and modify the user accounts.

Types of Web Servers

With the tremendous explosion of the Internet, Web sites are popping up all over the place. This fact could lead you to believe that there are a lot of different types of Web servers. In fact, most Web servers use one of two basic types of Web server software, both of which are free. One is the CERN server, which was created by the originators of the Web. The other is the NCSA server, which was created by the authors of Mosaic. Certainly, commercial Web server software exists, but these two are still the most popular. Also, many other available servers often have their roots in one of these two.

CERN

CERN, Conseil Europeen pour la Recherche Nucleaire, was originally founded as a European research center for particle physics. It has since diversified and, along with physics, also does research in electronics and computing. It is here that the World Wide Web was born. Since that time, the World Wide Web Consortium (W3C) has taken over the development of World Wide Web standards.

The CERN, or W3C, server has most of the tools and features that you'd expect from a Web server. The most notable feature lacking with the CERN server, which is in the NCSA server, is the support of SSI (server-side includes). SSIs are basically special markers in Web pages that are modified by the server. This allows Web pages to show you the current time, date, and weather condition, for example. The last major version of the W3C server is 3.0a (subsequent updates have been released to fix security issues). All future Web server development by W3C will be implemented in the Jigsaw Web server, a Java-based Web server that is fully object-oriented and completely modular.

NCSA

The other popular Web server software is the NCSA Web server. NCSA (National Center for Supercomputing Applications) was where one of the first graphic Web browsers, Mosaic, was developed. The NCSA Web server has many of the same features as those found in the CERN server. However, in many respects, the NCSA Web server is noticeably faster than the CERN server.

Though similar to CERN, the NCSA Web server is by far more popular. The basic NCSA Web server has been modified a great deal by other companies. The Apache Web server, for example, has its roots firmly planted in the NCSA program. Also, Netscape Communications' NetSite Communications Server is a derivative from the NCSA program. Additionally, Microsoft's FrontPage Personal Web Server is also a modification of the NCSA server.

Differences Between CERN and NCSA

With two general Web servers, the inevitable question is, "What are the differences between them?" One of the most notable differences is the format of the image map definition file. Although minor, this information is always necessary for Webmasters and Web authors alike.

CERN and NCSA also differ in the features they support. For example, NCSA supports server-side includes. This feature allows the Web server to enhance Web pages that it's sending out. This enhancement typically takes the form of dynamically adding in some sort of information into a Web page. The information added is usually the local time, the local weather condition, or similar data. The CERN server doesn't support this feature.

To be fair, though, CERN has a notable feature not present in the NCSA Web server. That feature is a much finer control of what files are accessible to general users. NCSA, like CERN, allows the Webmaster to easily password-protect directory structures. However, CERN also lets the Webmaster password-protect individual files.

Getting and Installing Web Servers

The two basic types of Web servers are fairly easy to obtain. Because the CERN server was developed by W3C, you can easily download it from its Web page. Similarly, the NCSA Web server is available through NCSA's home page.

Getting and Installing CERN

You can get a copy of the CERN Web server by pointing your Web browser to `ftp://ftp.w3.org/pub/httpd/old/`. There, you'll see a list of all of the available precompiled CERN Web server binaries (see Figure 45.1). Find the system configuration that most closely matches your desired machine, and click it. Depending on the platform you selected, the binaries can take anywhere from about 400 K to 1.5 M.

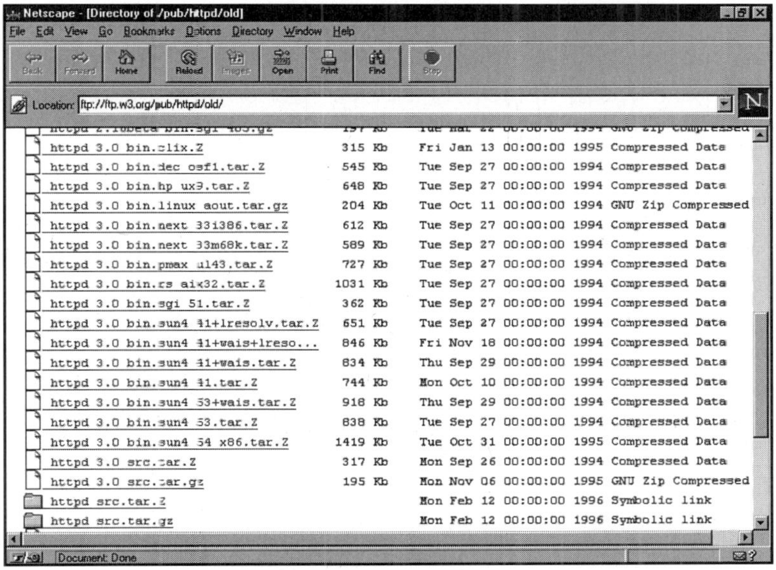

FIGURE 45.1.
The quickest and easiest way to get the CERN binaries is to pick the one you want.

NOTE

There are only precompiled binaries for CERN 3.0, not 3.0a. Because development has stopped on CERN, the only files available for 3.0a are the source code.

CAUTION

The precompiled binaries may not be what you want. They are compiled with a conservative set of build options. If you want to fully customize the CERN Web server, download the source code. You may need to modify the `makefile` and then build the server with the `make` command.

After you download the binary distribution, you must extract the files. Depending on the distribution you selected, you either have to uncompress and untar the file or gunzip and untar the file. Regardless, after you unpack the distribution, you'll have a fully functional copy of the CERN Web server software.

You can install the CERN Web server software anywhere on your file system, and any user can run it. It doesn't have to be run as root or with any special privileges. Next, configure the Web server to suit your needs. You can then run the Web server by going to the `bin` directory and running the `httpd` program.

NOTE

When executing CGI scripts, the CERN Web server takes on the privileges of its owner. Consequently, some files may not be accessible to the scripts.

Getting and Installing NCSA

The NCSA Web server software is very easy to get and install. For the most part, you can simply follow NCSA's OneStep Downloader. This is basically a Web page that behaves similarly to a Microsoft wizard. You're asked a series of questions about your desired configuration, and the custom file is created for you. To enter the OneStep Downloader, point your Web browser to `http://hoohoo.ncsa.uiuc.edu/docs/setup/OneStep.html`. You're asked for your operating system, followed by seven questions, called *directives* (see Figure 45.2). The directives are important questions that directly affect the Web server software itself.

FIGURE 45.2.
The NCSA OneStep Downloader is a great way for first-timers to get the NCSA Web server.

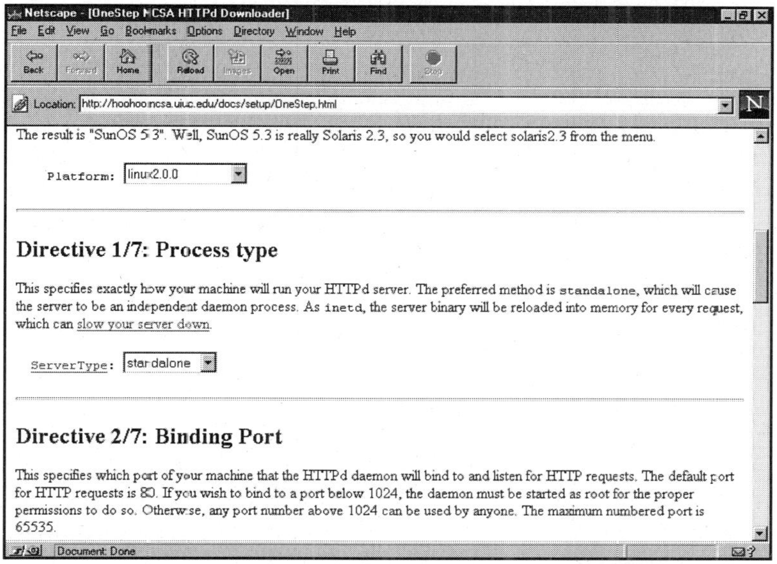

After you've filled in all the questions, click the `Submit Customization` button. Next, you are given a constant update on the status of the custom NCSA distribution. After the updates are done, you are given a hypertext link to click in order to get the custom distribution (see Figure 45.3). Along with the binary built to your specifications, you're given some installation instructions. All you have to do is uncompress and untar the specially created distribution.

FIGURE 45.3.
NCSA's OneStep creates custom archives for easy installation.

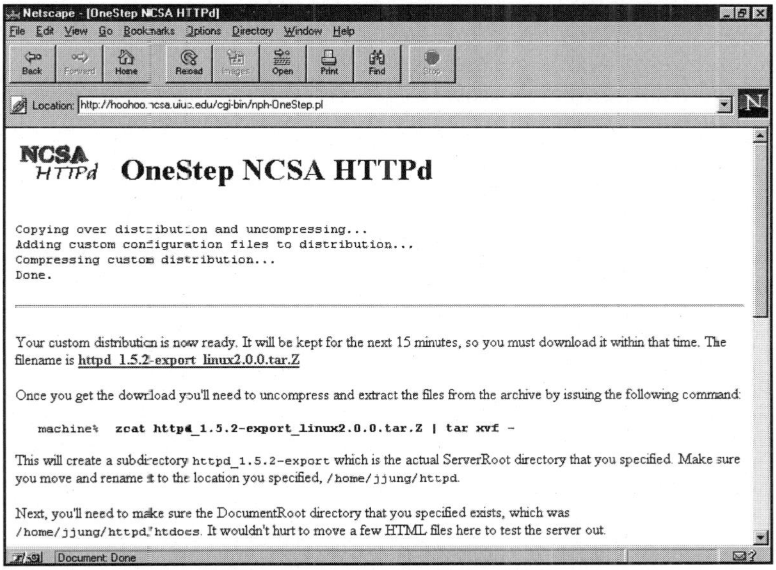

Configuring the CERN Server

Because of the level of content control that the CERN server gives you, there's a fair amount of configuration. Part of the problem with configuring the CERN server is that there are so many different approaches to it. You can store the various parts of the server configuration information in any number of files. Fortunately, though, most people store the server configuration information in one file.

Sample Configuration Files

By default, the CERN Web server comes with a number of sample server configuration files. These files are stored in the `httpd/config` directory, and they all have the extension `.conf`. The CERN configuration file does not have to have a particular file name, however. To use a particular configuration file, run the Web server and use the `-r` command-line option, and then specify the path to the configuration file name. Suppose you downloaded the Web server software and installed it in the `/foo` directory. Also suppose that you wanted to use the `httpd.conf` sample configuration file that came with the server. To do so, you would type in the following:

```
/foo/httpd/bin/httpd -r /foo/httpd/config/httpd.conf
```

Understanding CERN Configuration Files

Probably the most confusing aspect of configuring the CERN Web server is the configuration files. The basic configuration files are straightforward and easy to understand. The problem is that when you want to create more sophisticated configuration files, the syntax starts getting tricky. Most of the general configuration options take just the attributes that they need. Some of the more advanced options require multiple attributes. One needs an entire classification of objects to be defined. Another needs a directory path and some classification to be applied to it. Still another option needs two directory paths so that the Web server can translate URL references.

Some important configuration options should be set regardless of the level of configuration files you want to create:

- The `ServerRoot` option specifies where the top-level Web pages are stored. It needs a single parameter, which is the full path to the location of the Web pages on your machine.
- The `Port` option is used to specify which port CERN will listen to for Web connections. By default, all Web browsers and servers do all their work on port 80.
- The `UserId` option requires a single parameter—the user name or user number.

- The GroupId option also requires a single parameter—the group name or group number.
- The Exec and Pass options each perform similar functions, just for different Web files. Both require two parameters: the URL directory path and the physical directory path. Both options are used for translating URL path names into correct physical path names.

A basic CERN configuration file would look something like the following:

```
ServerRoot   /home/myself/httpd
Port   80
UserId   myself
GroupId   mygroup
Exec   /cgi-bin/*   /home/myself/httpd/cgi-bin/*
Pass   /*   /home/myself/httpd/itip/*
```

Password-Protecting a Directory

One of the most commonly used capabilities of Web servers is the capability to regulate Web page access. As was previously mentioned in the "User Authentication" section, sometimes you don't want everyone to have access to a particular page. For CERN, this form of restriction is accomplished, as with almost everything else, in the configuration file. Unfortunately, to implement such a feature with the W3C server can be somewhat confusing, especially for people who've never used the CERN server before. Password-protecting a particular directory on the Web server involves two elements. The first defines who has access, and the second one defines the directory to be protected.

The first element needed in protecting a directory is to define a classification of users. The Web server uses this classification to determine which users can have access. To define this classification, you must use the Protection option. This option needs two parameters: the name for the classification and its corresponding information. The information for a classification consists of several subelements, UserId, GroupId, ServerId, AuthType, PasswdFile, GroupFile, and GETMask. The UserId and GroupId functions take the same parameters as they do in the main configuration file. The ServerId option has one option, the name of the classification, that is passed to the Web browser. The AuthType option specifies what sort of authentication scheme is used and typically should be set to Basic. The PasswdFile and GroupFile options specify an absolute path and file name for the location of the password and group files. The GETMask option defines which users or groups can submit form information to the protected directory. The following example shows what a typical Protection option should look like:

```
Protection  ITIPWeb  {
   UserId   jjung
   GroupId   users0
   ServerId   ITIPWeb
   AuthType   Basic
   PasswdFile   /home/jjung/httpd/itippasswd
   GroupFile   /home/jjung/httpd/itipgroup
   GETMask   all
}
```

CAUTION

Do not use standard UNIX password or group files for the `PasswdFile` or `GroupFile` options. Though similar in nature, Web password and group information is different from what's used by UNIX.

NOTE

You can create passwords to use with the `PasswdFile` option with the `htadm` utility. This utility is included with the standard distribution of the W3C server.

The second element needed in protecting a directory is the `Protect` option, which takes two parameters. The first parameter is the URL that a user would type in to access a protected directory. The second is the classification rule to be applied to that particular directory. The following is an example of a `Protect` statement:

```
Protect   /private/*     ITIPWeb
```

To better illustrate how these two directives work together, suppose that you're in charge of `http://www.mycom.com/`, which is the organization's main Web page. Further, suppose that there's a `/private` directory off of the main server. You can password-protect the `/private` directory by putting the two preceding examples in your CERN configuration file. When users try to accesss `http://www.mycom.com/private/`, they'll be prompted for a user name and password. The information they enter must match the information contained in the `PasswdFile` directive.

Password-Protecting a File

Other Web servers have no facility to password-protect a single file. A common workaround is to put the file to be protected into a directory. Next, apply a password-protection scheme on that particular directory. Although workable, this solution is inelegant and imperfect because you need a directory for every file you want to password-protect.

In the CERN Web server, you can implement this level of protection by using a file named `.www_acl`. This file consists of a series of lines, each with three options that are separated by colons (:). The first option specifies the file or files that need protecting. The second option controls the privileges that can be performed on those files. This option can be `GET`, `POST`, or `GET,POST`. The final option specifies which individuals or groups have the granted privileges. The following is a sample `.www_acl` file:

```
marketing*.html : GET,POST : sales_marketing
tech*.html: GET,POST : research_development
*.html : GET : me, myself, i
```

NOTE

The .www_acl file is only used when a Protect statement has been applied for that particular directory. So, if you wanted to protect some files in /foo, a Protect statement must exist in the configuration file for /foo. Once the Protect statement is in the configuration file, the server will use the /foo/.www_acl file.

Configuring the NCSA Server

Where the CERN server has one configuration file, maybe two for file protection, the NCSA server has three. Consequently, configuring an NCSA server may be a bit more difficult than configuring a CERN server for first-time Webmasters. That's not to say that NCSA is worse than CERN, just that the learning curve is a little steeper in the beginning. NCSA server configuration is controlled by the httpd.conf, srm.conf, and access.conf files. Each has its own functions and uses for the NCSA server, which are detailed in the following sections.

NOTE

The mime.types file is another configuration file. This file simply lists a MIME type followed by its extension. You need to modify this file if you add more file types to your server.

Along with supporting the usual suite of Web server functions, the NCSA server has a particularly useful feature; it can be configured to work in a multihoming environment. Multihoming is the capability of a Web server to pretend to be more than one Web server. To enable this feature, you need to configure your system and your Web server.

httpd.conf

The httpd.conf file is the main NCSA configuration file and is probably the easiest to understand. There are a number of options that you can specify in this file, each with a particular default. If you got your NCSA distribution with the OneStep Downloader, you pretty much don't have to modify this file. If, however, you've personally built the NCSA server to your specifications, this file will need some tweaking.

There are a number of very important configuration options that you should set in the httpd.conf file:

- The User option takes a single parameter, either the user name or the user number.
- The Group option takes a single parameter as well, either the group name or group number.

- Use the `ServerAdmin` option to specify the e-mail address for the Webmaster.
- By default, the `Port` option is set to 80, which indicates which port the Web server will listen to for Web connections.
- Set the `ServerRoot` option to the absolute path name where the NCSA distribution is stored.

The following is an example of a `httpd.conf` file:

```
User   myself
Group   mygroup
ServerAdmin   myself@mycom.com
ServerRoot   /home/myself/ncsa_httpd
```

srm.conf

The `srm.conf` file, short for Server Resource Map, is the configuration file that specifies a lot of NCSA's behavior. This file is used to control where users' home pages will be, where the default Web pages are, and similar information. As with the `httpd.conf` file, if you received your distribution from the OneStep Downloader, you won't need to change anything. However, there are some important configuration options that you may need to change if you built the NCSA server yourself:

- Probably the most important option in the `srm.conf` file is the `DocumentRoot` option. This option needs a single parameter that specifies the physical directory path for top-level Web pages.
- The `Alias` and `ScriptAlias` options behave similarly to each other. They translate URL-specified path names to physical directory path names. Both take two options; the first is the URL path name, and the second is the physical path name.
- When a user accesses a Web page and doesn't specify a particular HTML file, the NCSA server needs to load a default Web page. You can assign this default with the `DirectoryIndex` option, which lists default Web pages.

The following is an example of a `srm.conf` file:

```
DocumentRoot   /home/myself/ncsa_httpd/htdocs
Alias   /old/   /home/myself/old_pages/
ScriptAlias   /cgi-bin/   /home/myself/ncsa_httpd/cgi-bin/
DirectoryIndex   index.html
```

access.conf

The final important configuration file for the NCSA Web server is the `access.conf` file. This file controls the behavior and protection for directories within a Web site. The syntax for the `access.conf` file is a bit different than for the other two configuration files. Rather than specifying what options are enabled or disabled for the whole system, you do it on a per-directory basis.

The general layout of this file is similar to the way HTML is written. There are starting and ending tags, which affect everything enclosed within. For the `access.conf` file, the starting tag is the `<Directory>` string. This string has one required attribute, the full physical path name for the directory. The ending tag is the `</Directory>` string. Most of the time, you can pretty much leave this file alone. However, there are directory directives that you can apply between the starting and ending tags, if you want:

- Probably the most important directive that can go inside the starting and ending tags is the `Options` directive. This directive enables or disables a series of features within the Web server for the specified directory.
- The `ExecCGI` directive enables CGI scripts to be run from the directory.
- The `Indexes` directive enables the default index files to be used.
- The `Includes` directive allows server-side includes from this directory.
- The `AllowOverride` directive lets you control the options from the global configuration file that can be overridden in this directory.

The following is an example of an `access.conf` file:

```
<Directory /home/myself/other_pages/>
Options Indexes
</Directory>
<Directory /home/myself/ncsa_httpd/htdocs>
Options Indexes ExecCGI
AllowOverride All
</Directory>
```

Multihoming

Multihoming is the capability of a Web server to act as two separate Web servers. Typically, computers on the Internet have only one IP address and a host name. It's very easy for a particular computer to have multiple host names for a particular IP address. However, most UNIX systems have the capability to have two different IP addresses, in addition to having multiple host names. Typically, you can have one IP address per network interface, although some systems allow multiple IP addresses on a single interface.

The NCSA Web server is able to take advantage of a single computer with multiple IPs and make it act as separate systems. This feature is most commonly used by Internet Service Providers (ISPs) and Web Service Providers (WSPs). Often, they'll have many corporate customers, each wanting a different Web site. Consequently, the capability to perform multihoming is important for the business environment.

You can easily configure the NCSA Web server for multihoming by modifying the `httpd.conf` file. To do multihoming, you must use the `<VirtualHost>` option, which follows an HTML-like syntax. Specify two attributes: the IP address of the system you want to multihome and either the string `Required` or `Optional`. Most of the time, you should use `Optional`, which allows the server to start up even if the multihome configuration is bad. After specifying the starting element, you can put in as many configuration options as you want. These options are the same as those used for the nonmultihomed configuration. After specifying the options for the multihomed system, you have to close out the multihoming configuration with the `</VirtualHost>` string.

The following is a sample entry in the `httpd.conf` file for a multihomed system:

```
<VirtualHost 127.0.0.1 Optional>
DocumentRoot    /home/myself/ncsa_httpd/customer_htdocs
ServerName   www.mycom2.com
ServerAdmin   myself2@mycom2.com
ResourceConfig   conf/customer_srm.conf
</VirtualHost>
```

CAUTION

In configuring a multihome system, pay particular attention to the options being used. Some options use the `ServerRoot` as a top-level directory. Other options use absolute path names.

Summary

A number of Web servers are available for your use. Two in particular, CERN and NCSA, are among the more popular, and they're both free. It's up to you as the Webmaster to decide which one is right for you. Take a look at the strengths and weaknesses of each one and determine which is best suited to your needs. Most of the time, you can simply download the precompiled binaries, and they'll work for your system.

The only tricky part about setting up your Web server is the configuration. The CERN server mostly uses just one configuration file, which has a number of configuration options. The NCSA server has three main configuration files, each with a different use and syntax.

CHAPTER 46

Optimizing Your Web Site or Intranet

by Chris Adams and Mark L. Chambers

IN THIS CHAPTER

Once you've designed the content and structure of your Web site or company Intranet, it's tempting to jump directly into the hands-on work: creating HTML, writing Java or CGI code, adding graphics, testing your site, and so on. After all, the design phase is finished, isn't it?

Once your site is up and running, you may be satisfied that it works as planned, but have you really done everything necessary to ensure that your users can retrieve information from it as efficiently as possible? Are you using the right hardware, software, and design techniques to handle a large number of hits without your site slowing to a crawl? In this chapter, we'll discuss how you can optimize your site design for the fastest speeds and highest capacity, even before you go online!

Planning Optimization

The idea behind optimization is simple in theory; you need to streamline each component of your site for fastest access time and lowest system load by intelligently using the resources you have. Any user on the Internet knows just how important efficiency is; transfer speeds have plummeted as the Internet has grown to a size its designers would have thought impossible. If your site is slow as molasses, your users will find the information they're looking for elsewhere or even give up the search entirely. Even if your site is currently working well under full load, optimization is still important. Even a 10 percent gain in efficiency will improve service to every one of your users!

Target the Audience

As a first step in optimizing your site design, you must determine who your target audience is. Unfortunately, those who will access your site are not created equal. The resources available to Internet users vary widely:

- **Hardware.** You will have some users connected using low-end hardware and slower modem speeds. Others surf to the same sites on high-end workstations connected to high-speed T1 or ISDN lines.
- **Multimedia capabilities.** For many of the PC users, video is just barely an option, and there's no guarantee of a sound card either.
- **Browser software.** There's an ever-increasing variety of browsers available, including several different versions of Netscape Navigator and Microsoft Internet Explorer. The older versions will not support many of the features you'd like to incorporate into your site design.

When you design your site, you must consider which section of the market is most important. One approach is simply to appeal to the lowest common denominator and use a minimum of extras on your site: no animated `.gif` images, forms, or frames, and no MIDI music. Don't force multimedia or advanced HTML on your users by default!

However, your target audience may determine whether your site must use the most advanced features; for example, a company that develops multimedia games may decide the company site needs the impact of animated graphics; a record company will probably want sound clips from its latest offerings available on its Web pages.

TIP

You can limit the impact of multimedia on your users that don't have PCs powerful enough to display them or those users that don't want to wait the extra time. Offer multimedia extras on an alternate menu system and let the user pick text or graphical mode on your site's welcome page. If you'd rather keep a single menu system, keep graphics small and offer hotspots that play sound bytes or video clips.

The Delicate Balance

Your design and optimization process will inevitably lead to trade-offs. You can add features, but you will run the risk of locking out many potential users. After you have determined which users you are targeting and decided what resources are available on your end, you can assign a relative priority to the following considerations:

- **Bandwidth and processor time.** Can your site meet the demands placed upon it? Will users get data in what they consider a reasonable amount of time?
- **Client requirements.** Will your target user's computer be able to handle the data it's receiving? Will multimedia extensions be pushing the capabilities of his system?
- **Quality of content.** Will your average user be satisfied with what he's getting? Will it serve his needs? Will it meet your goals?

It's important to look at your projected site as your users will. Follow the same usability procedures that software developers follow; test your site using a computer similar to the average machine available to your target user. Try your site with several browsers. Have friends or co-workers use the site. What may seem intuitive to a computer programmer may be confusing to others. Watch the reactions of your test users and ask why they paused at certain menus or seemed uncertain about what to do.

An Example

Suppose that you are planning a corporate Web site to provide marketing material and technical support for a company that creates commercial animation. Based on reviews of competitors' sites, your site design has enthusiastic support from high-level management. The advertising department has just created a very good promotional video, and one of the VPs has asked you to consider putting an excerpt on the Web site. What would you do?

Establish the priorities:

- Your company's product is highly visual and uses cutting-edge technology. Solid content is a must, but the nature of the product demands that the Web site should also be visually appealing.
- Most of your potential customers will be other companies, and it's safe to assume that they will probably have a direct Internet connection. No need to avoid graphics!
- Fortunately, you can assume your customers will have multimedia PCs.

Based on the above, you should recommend to management a T1 or faster connection hooked up to a fast server. The material online should be more than just raw technical data; you should have enough variety to convince a potential customer that you are delivering a complete solution to their needs. Demonstrating high-quality support is also vital.

As for the video, there's no reason why you shouldn't include it on the site; your target audience has the equipment to view it. However, make sure that you identify its length in megabytes and video format (`.avi` or `.mov`) so that users can decide for themselves whether they want to spend the time to download it. As we mentioned earlier, *never* force multimedia as an automatic default! Illustrate the video link with a few high-quality captured images as well so that potential customers get a preview of what the video contains.

After prioritizing, your Web site has already taken on a certain character. It will have some high-quality images to better demonstrate a graphics product and will provide solid information and support. Those users with more powerful PCs and faster connections can see the best your company has to offer. Clarifying the focus of the site early simplifies the rest of the design phase.

General Optimization Techniques

No matter what you end up putting on your site, a few techniques can offer dramatic improvements. These generic techniques also demonstrate the mindset necessary to successful optimization.

Rethinking Design Goals

When you design your site, you have many goals and considerations in mind. Every decision carries an expense with it. This expense may be in the form of increased bandwidth, higher end-user requirements, server slow-downs, or increased storage space requirements. When optimizing your Web site, you must consider the relative expenses of each decision. Does the added functionality outweigh the performance hit?

In a typical environment, everyone connected to the organization will have features they feel must be present. The trouble with these dream sites is that many of the most requested features tend to be the most expensive in terms of efficiency. After the first version of the site has been created, consider it from an outside perspective. Are the features still worth it? The easiest way to improve a site involves trimming the features lowest on value and highest on expense.

Suppose that you decided it would be worthwhile to include a real-time Real Audio feed on your radio station's home page. Now your server is limping on its knees under the strain of handling the site. Time to consider whether that audio is still worth the trouble!

Other choices might not be so easy. To help you make these choices, ask users for their input. Having a prominently located `mailto:` link to a comments e-mail address is one idea. Better yet would be a form allowing users to rate their favorite features on a scale of one to ten. Such a list could be implemented as shown in Figure 46.1. The code for this form is in Listing 46.1.

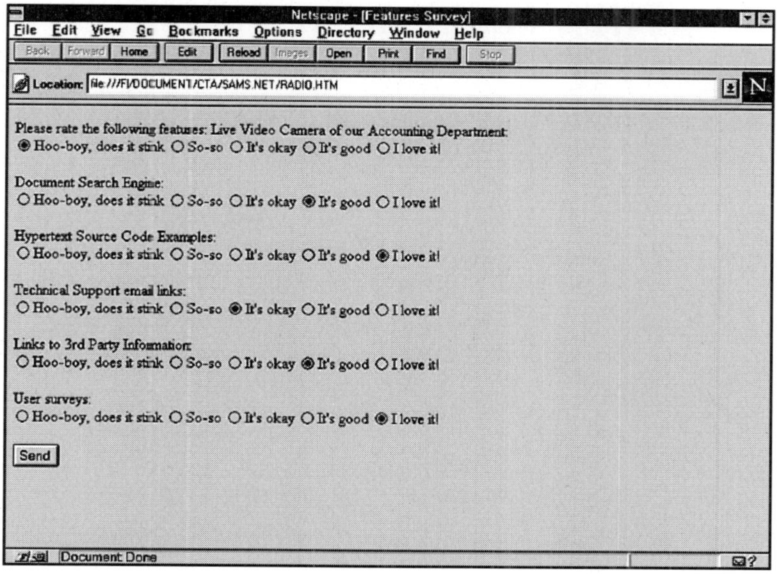

FIGURE 46.1.
This form was created with the HTML code in Listing 46.1.

Listing 46.1. The HTML source code for a user survey designed to rate favorite features of a Web site.

```
<!DOCTYPE HTML PUBLIC "-//W3C//DTD HTML 3.2//EN">
<HTML>
<HEAD>
   <TITLE>Features Survey</TITLE>
   <META NAME="GENERATOR" CONTENT="Mozilla/3.0b6Gold (Win16; I) [Netscape]">
</HEAD>
<BODY>

<P><FORM METHOD="POST" ACTION="http://www.megafoobar.com/cgi-bin/post-query"></P>
Please rate the following features:
Live Video Camera of our Accounting Department:<BR>
<INPUT TYPE="radio" NAME="video" VALUE="bad" CHECKED>Hoo-boy, does it stink
<INPUT TYPE="radio" NAME="video" VALUE="soso">So-so
<INPUT TYPE="radio" NAME="video" VALUE="okay">It's okay
<INPUT TYPE="radio" NAME="video" VALUE="good">It's good
<INPUT TYPE="radio" NAME="video" VALUE="great">I love it!
<P>
Document Search Engine:<BR>
<INPUT TYPE="radio" NAME="searchengine" VALUE="bad">Hoo-boy, does it stink
<INPUT TYPE="radio" NAME="searchengine" VALUE="soso">So-so
<INPUT TYPE="radio" NAME="searchengine" VALUE="okay">It's okay
<INPUT TYPE="radio" NAME="searchengine" VALUE="good" CHECKED>It's good
<INPUT TYPE="radio" NAME="searchengine" VALUE="great">I love it!
<P>
Hypertext Source Code Examples:<BR>
<INPUT TYPE="radio" NAME="sourcecode" VALUE="bad">Hoo-boy, does it stink
<INPUT TYPE="radio" NAME="sourcecode" VALUE="soso">So-so
<INPUT TYPE="radio" NAME="sourcecode" VALUE="okay">It's okay
<INPUT TYPE="radio" NAME="sourcecode" VALUE="good">It's good
<INPUT TYPE="radio" NAME="sourcecode" VALUE="great" CHECKED>I love it!
<P>
Technical Support email links:<BR>
<INPUT TYPE="radio" NAME="supportemail" VALUE="bad">Hoo-boy, does it stink
<INPUT TYPE="radio" NAME="supportemail" VALUE="soso">So-so
<INPUT TYPE="radio" NAME="supportemail" VALUE="okay"CHECKED>It's okay
<INPUT TYPE="radio" NAME="supportemail" VALUE="good">It's good
<INPUT TYPE="radio" NAME="supportemail" VALUE="great">I love it!
<P>
Links to 3rd Party Information:<BR>
<INPUT TYPE="radio" NAME="thirdparty" VALUE="bad">Hoo-boy, does it stink
<INPUT TYPE="radio" NAME="thirdparty" VALUE="soso">So-so
<INPUT TYPE="radio" NAME="thirdparty" VALUE="okay">It's okay
<INPUT TYPE="radio" NAME="thirdparty" VALUE="good" CHECKED>It's good
<INPUT TYPE="radio" NAME="thirdparty" VALUE="great">I love it!
<P>
User surveys:<BR>
<INPUT TYPE="radio" NAME="surveys" VALUE="bad">Hoo-boy, does it stink
<INPUT TYPE="radio" NAME="surveys" VALUE="soso">So-so
<INPUT TYPE="radio" NAME="surveys" VALUE="okay">It's okay
<INPUT TYPE="radio" NAME="surveys" VALUE="good">It's good
<INPUT TYPE="radio" NAME="surveys" VALUE="great" CHECKED>I love it!
<P>
<INPUT TYPE="button" NAME="Send" VALUE="Send">
</FORM>
</BODY>
</HTML>
```

Avoid putting complex graphics on a feedback page. Although it may be attractive, the excessive load time could scare off potential users. Getting an accurate sample is vital! With the information you receive, deciding what to trim should be easy. Don't be afraid to completely redo the site, however, if it turns out that the your users will be significantly better served. On the Web, potential users can pick what suits them best; if you don't provide what they're looking for, someone else will.

Profiling

One of the most powerful tools in any programmer's kit is a profiler. A profiler tracks the time it takes a certain section of code to execute. Examining a profiler log can show where the bottlenecks are within a program. If used wisely, profiling can be one of the most important tools for a Webmaster as well. With a Web site, a profiler can tell you what to optimize. With a large site, merely knowing where to start is a great help.

To profile your Web site, check to see whether your Web server includes usage log capabilities; most servers do. Examine the logs over a statistically useful period of time—perhaps a week or two so you can avoid minor abnormalities. It's also helpful to see whether your server can be set to log the total number of bytes sent over that time period as well; this lets you track load as a percentage of total.

When you have your processed server logs, examine them carefully and identify the slowest resources. There are utilities that can help you sort through a log file; capabilities like sorting by transfer type, location, or speed are invaluable. Generally, if you have any one resource consuming a significant amount of time or space, you should reconsider whether it's worth the expense.

Load Reduction

Load reduction involves looking for a more efficient substitute for existing resources. For instance, it may look good if you use Real Audio data streams. Certainly, it's an improvement over using a `.wav` file. Or is it? A `.wav` file can be cached. As soon as it is transferred (at the full bandwidth of the connection), the server's job is done. Playback characteristics are entirely dependent on the local computer, not the remote server or a network link. Any compression or processing is done once, eliminating a potential performance hit. Plus, a `.wav` file is usually much higher fidelity than a Real Audio feed!

If your existing server is too slow, you may be able to off-load most of the processing to the client side, as shown in this example. In this day of Pentium-level client machines, this solution is certainly feasible. The following sections deal with some potential trouble spots you may want to examine. It would be a good idea to use profiling techniques to see which of these items, if any, are important concerns on your Web site.

Images

You can reduce a lot of overhead by converting images to different file formats. Picking the right file format is very important. By altering the bit-depth (the number of bits stored to record the color value of each pixel), you may reduce file size considerably. By default, most scanners use a 24-bit format. This means that three bytes are stored for each pixel. A single 640 by 480 image uses 921,600 bytes. In many cases, this same image can be reduced to 16- or 8-bit modes, potentially cutting file size by one third. Further reduction may be possible by using the right dithering algorithm. Dithering displays images using clusters of a few different colors instead of a single pixel in any color. It reduces the sharpness of an image, but it also reduces the number of colors needed.

Compression is also very important. `.gif` files use a form of compression that is well-suited for work with computer-generated images (which contain large areas of a single color). `.jpg` files, which use the JPEG compression scheme, are best for working with scanned images; in Figures 46.2 and 46.3, you can see the effects of compression. JPEG compression discards the least noticeable information for dramatic savings. For instance, the image in Figure 46.3 is only five percent of the size of the bitmap file shown in Figure 46.2! JPEG has a quality factor ranging from 1 to 100; at level 100, almost no compression is performed, and the maximum amount of detail is preserved. At level 1, compression is high, but there is noticeable degradation.

FIGURE 46.2.
This picture is a scanned image in bitmap format. Because `.bmp` *images do not allow compression, none was used. This file was stored in a 24-bit color mode.*

As you can see from the examples shown in Figures 46.2 and 46.3, picking the right image format can save considerable space and time. Converting image formats and reducing the size of images with a program such as Paint Shop Pro or Adobe Photoshop can result in further time savings for those using your site.

FIGURE 46.3.
This figure is an optimized JPEG file that is 5 percent of the original size. The JPEG file was reduced to 256 colors (8-bit) and is compressed at a 75 percent quality level.

Common Gateway Interface

CGI scripts allow you to do almost anything, but this functionality comes with a cost. Figure 46.4 is a diagram of a CGI process. Notice that all but the first and last two steps are performed on the server. With a CGI program, any optimization is a big improvement. For proof, just multiply a one-percent increase in speed by a million users.

The following are some general rules concerning CGI optimization:

- Consider changing what language your CGI program is written in. If you pick a more efficient compiler or interpreter, it can lead to big savings in time and memory.
- Optimize your CGI for speed; make sure that all unneeded steps are removed. Depending on your machine, even something as simple as removing most screen output can be important. Cache any results you use more than once.
- If possible, configure your CGI processes to run on a separate machine. If the Web server isn't bogged down running CGI scripts, it will immediately be more responsive.
- Depending on what your CGI script does, you may be able to replace it with a Java applet or even some JavaScript or VBScript. Off-loading processing to the client will save the server machine considerable work.

Frequently Used Files

On any site, there are some files that get used more frequently than others, such as backgrounds or pictures on the first page. If you supply a custom plug-in or ActiveX control to view some of your content, this file will be downloaded quite frequently.

FIGURE 46.4.
A typical CGI setup.

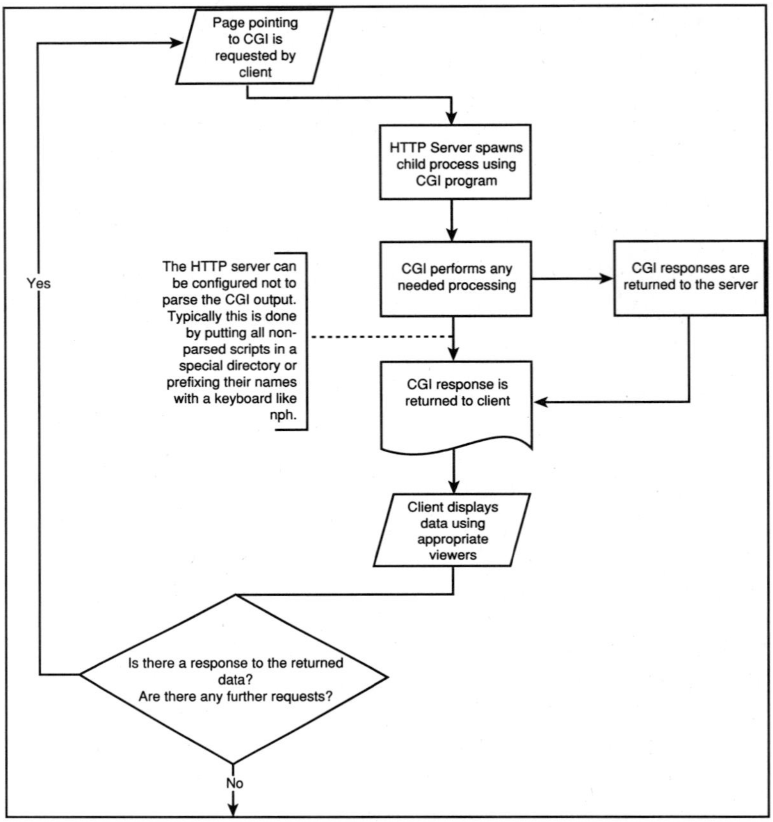

With such high-demand files, even the best attempts at optimization may not take enough load off of the server. Consider adding a separate machine that is devoted to serving these high-traffic items. Because of the nature of the Web, you can easily change your pages to reflect a new location. You may also want to consider establishing a *mirror site*, which is a site that contains identical contents but is located on another machine. Depending on the scale of your site, it may be best to have a server for certain geographic locations, particularly since the slowest links are often those that connect different continents or widely separated locations.

Server Optimization

After you've tried all the various techniques mentioned in the last section, you may still need to upgrade the server machine. Before changing anything, however, find out where the greatest performance hit is coming from! In this section, we discuss physical changes you can make to the server itself to increase performance.

What Kind of Machine Do You Need?

Not all computers are created equal (advertisement claims to the contrary)! There are well-documented examples showing that a better quality system can be significantly faster than a seemingly identical machine. As an example, this chapter was composed on a 100 MHz Pentium with a fast hard drive and a PCI video card. Several benchmarks have rated its performance as being more on par with some 133 MHz Pentiums.

On a server, the most important feature is high bandwidth. On many servers, the capability to pass large amounts of data to and from the disk subsystem is as important as the speed of the network connection. One factor in disk speed is the drive interface. In the desktop world, there are two main types of drives: EIDE/IDE and SCSI. SCSI is usually the best choice for a server. SCSI can handle multiple requests; if you have more than one (E)IDE device on a chain, you will only be able to access one drive at a time. Also, advanced SCSI drives even support multiple transactions. All of this increases speed while serving multiple users. Finally, SCSI drives tend to be focused at the high-performance market; some capabilities simply aren't available in EIDE.

A RAID (Redundant Array of Inexpensive Drives) controller will physically connect several drives but only show a single logical device to an operating system. RAID features can be selected to increase speed (RAID level 0) and provide advanced error correction (RAID levels 1-5), which is very important for mission-critical machines. In general, the maximum throughput for a logical device in a RAID 0 array is equal to the number of drives times the speed of the slowest drive. If you have a two-disk RAID 0 array using 2.5 M/s drives, you can expect around 5 M/s throughput. Couple this with the large disk sizes possible with a RAID array and a six or more drive array can be a compelling option. If you have configured your drives to use something other than RAID 0 (which does no extra error checking) and your controller supports it, you can even replace a failed drive without powering down the server. This feature can be important if your server must be up 24 hours a day, 7 days a week.

Caching will dramatically improve performance on a typical Web site, where certain resources are used far more than others. Many advanced disk controllers come with on-board cache memory. You should upgrade this memory to the largest size supported. Secondly, your server machine should have as much RAM as possible, so be generous when configuring the operating system disk cache.

More RAM will give you the largest available performance increase. Your server should contain as much RAM as the motherboard supports. More RAM generally provides a higher performance increase than even a next-generation processor upgrade. Also, some types of RAM are faster than others. Extended Data-Out (EDO) is currently the best choice, but technologies like Synchronous DRAM (SDRAM) are potentially *much* faster.

Symmetric Multiprocessing (SMP) machines contain several CPUs that share a common memory space. Generally, adding a second processor to an SMP machine provides a performance boost of at least 75 percent, which is cheap compared to the cost of equipping an auxiliary server. To use this capability, your operating system needs to support SMP; current SMP-capable operating systems include Windows NT, OS/2, Novell Netware, Macintosh, and many UNIX variants. Remember that all operating systems are not created equal. In a recent *PC Week* benchmark test, a beta version of IBM's OS/2 Warp Server SMP was up to 4.5 times faster than Windows NT and 30 times faster than Novell Netware on identical hardware.

If you have more than one machine available for use as a server and your network is sufficiently fast enough, you may also be able to link multiple servers across your network. This setup spreads the demand for file access and program execution across more than one machine. The end result is similar to the dedicated CGI machine mentioned earlier: a faster site with a more balanced workload on each server.

Net Connections

Network connections come in many different flavors, and each link in the network connection presents its own set of potential bottlenecks. Again, profiling techniques pay off, so it's time to examine those logs again. In many cases, a connection to the Internet will be the slowest point. Investing in a T1 (1.5 M/s) or T3 (45 M/s) connection can pay off through improved speed. Remember, if you are running a commercial site, it's wise to use a high-quality, high-speed connection.

The gateway is next on the list of bottlenecks. A gateway machine or router must be capable of handling *every* byte transferred beyond the LAN. This is not the place to skimp! Also, the security provided by a sophisticated firewall requires a hefty machine to run, but if a firewall's requirements seem excessive, you may want to evaluate other firewall packages.

Finally, the LAN can be a problem. If your LAN has not only the server but also a significant number of users, peak usage may exceed the capacity of your underlying link. This problem will not only slow site access but may also reduce local productivity. Isolating the server by connecting it directly to the gateway/firewall may be necessary. In any case, a fast fiber-optic network will certainly be welcome.

What if you find that you need a faster connection than you can afford? For most sites, there will be a certain time (or times) of the day where usage is the highest. During the rest of the day, usage is considerably lower. If the normal usage is well within the capabilities of your connection, but the peak load is well beyond them, try one of the following solutions:

- **Division.** Split parts of the site up between different hosts with multiple connections. Also, consider farming out less-used portions of the site to a slower server to free up the main connection.
- **Partners.** What if you can't afford a T3 but have exceeded the capacity of your existing T1? You may be able to share the capacity of a faster link with several other sites with similar usage patterns. If such cooperation is planned carefully, every site will have a faster connection, but the total bandwidth will still be in the T3 range.

This strategy works particularly well if the other sites tend to have different peak times. For example, a popular game site may peak during the evening, but the company it shares a connection with peaks during the business day.

- **Time share.** Depending on your hookup and conditions in your area, you may be able to buy extra bandwidth at peak times. This way, you can maintain reasonable access speeds without the expense of maintaining a faster link all of the time.

Software Optimization

The range of features offered in server software varies widely, and each software publisher is continuously expanding this range. Unfortunately, this variety means that performance will also vary just as widely. Before setting up a Web site, you should evaluate as many different servers (or server suites) as possible.

Picking Servers

What should you compare when evaluating server software? Regardless of what service it provides (HTTP, FTP, Gopher, and so on), you need to consider each of the following issues:

- **Speed.** There are two concerns here: the speed at which requested items are sent and the load placed on the machine to send the items. A CPU-hog may be acceptable if you are either using a very fast machine or you will not be running any other important programs on your server.
- **Response time.** How quickly will a request be handled? The importance of this varies depending on how large the most-used files on your site are. If you are transferring a 1 M image, an extra second isn't going to make a difference, but it may make a difference if you are planning on transferring 40 small clip-art images.
- **Configurability.** How well can you customize the server for your tasks? Can you disable the slowest features? If you have an on-staff programmer, anything that comes with source code can be changed to best serve your site.
- **Price.** How much will the entire package cost? Remember that if you need a feature from the advanced version, the price may go up by an order of magnitude. Also, include your management costs; the time spent configuring and maintaining an inadequate program usually isn't free.
- **Support.** How much help are you going to need from the supplier? If you are willing to do almost all the support yourself, there are many high-quality packages available free on the Internet. Alternately, if you don't want to have a full-time Webmaster/programmer, the extra money spent buying a service contract will be well spent.

- **Quality of all included programs.** It's rare that a single software suite will provide the best solution in every category. Often one good program will be bundled with several mediocre companions. Although the overall price and simplicity may seem appealing, base your decision on the existing capabilities of the entire suite; a promised upgrade or improvement may never ship.

Object Caching

Anyone using the Internet has noticed how slow some areas have become. The Web has been the heaviest load on the Internet for a quite some time, and there is no indication that this will change in the future. This situation is a direct result of the way the Web developed; because it rapidly grew in popularity, in most cases the protocols evolved quickly with more concern for functionality and development speed than efficiency. Now things have cooled down somewhat and more thought is being spent on these neglected issues. One of the most promising technologies involves the addition of caching as an intrinsic part of the protocol.

Consider a popular site such as Yahoo!, Excite, or Netscape; these sites can be almost impossible to use at times because of the number of simultaneous users. However, the vast majority of these users are accessing only a few specific pages. How many people use more than the query form at AltaVista? Figure 46.5 shows what a typical network map of a subsection of the Internet might look like. Every network link is a different speed; in some cases, a long series of faster links might be worse than a shorter slow link.

FIGURE 46.5.
This figure shows the Network relationships between several geographically far points on the Internet.

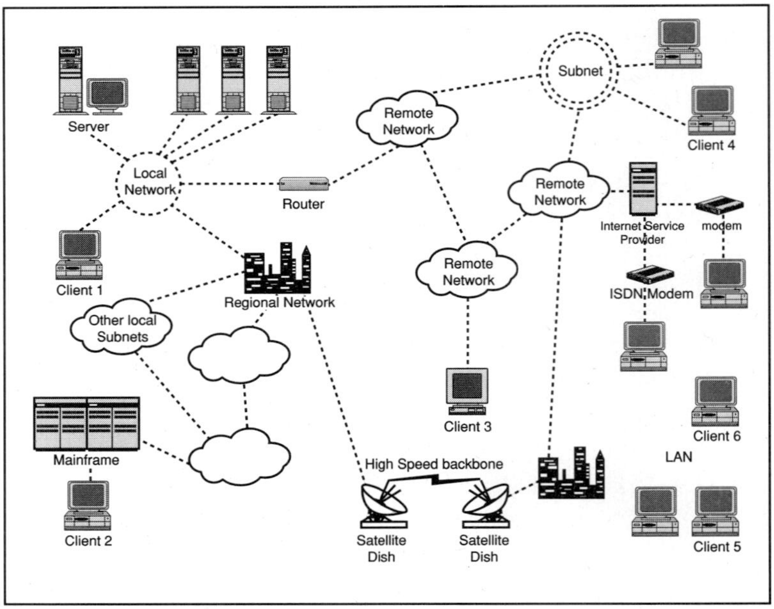

Without caching, when any of the six clients requests a file off of the server, the same process is completed:

1. The client uses Domain Name Server (DNS) entries to get the server's IP address. DNS is a hierarchical protocol; all requests eventually go to the lowest level name server on the same site as the server.
2. The client initiates a socket connection, where a network connection is established to the server using the IP address from step 1.
3. The client sends a request to the server.
4. The server does any needed work, such as running a CGI script or using Reverse DNS to verify the client.
5. The server sends data to the client.
6. The socket is closed by the client, which ends the transaction.

Every step, with the possible exception of step 4, involves a network transmission across the entire link between the client and the server. There are a few spots, such as routers or bridges, where connections will bottleneck. The end result is that a connection between Client 2 and the server slows down every connection with the other clients, even Client 1!

Next, imagine that several network administrators have implemented a cache system. The regional network, the Internet service provider (ISP), and Client 4's subnet have all added cache servers. When Client 5 asks for the main page of the Web site on the server, it is routed through the high-speed connection to the regional network. The cache servers at the ISP and regional network add the IP address and the page to their cache records.

A few minutes later, Client 2 asks for the same page. The requested page is loaded directly off of the regional network's cache server, avoiding the traffic caused by Client 1 and the other machines on the local network. Later, Client 6 initiates the same request. Because the ISP is part of the cache hierarchy, the request is met locally. However, by the time Client 4 asks for the page, the ISP machine has already purged the local copy, so it is reloaded from the next level, the regional network.

Finally, Client 3 requests the same page from this popular site. Normally, this request would go through the two remote networks and the router directly to the server. However, the second network has been suffering from a partial overload and the routing software sends the request the other way instead. Normally, the ISP's cache would have quickly returned the page. Unfortunately, by now the page has been loaded for one hour, and the cache software has expired it. This time the page must be reloaded from the server and so the entire request chain is followed. With the caching software installed, the server handled the local load and only two long-distance requests. Caching allowed faster access for all but the first and last users.

You might have noticed the hierarchical nature of the cache system. Because of the way the cache is designed, a failed local request (at the ISP) went only to the next level (the regional network) instead of going all the way to the server. Coupling this with advanced routing software can yield substantially faster access patterns.

This example was not idle speculation, either. According to the results of "A Case for Caching File Objects Inside Internetworks" (Peter Danzig, Michael Schwartz, and Richard Hall, ACM SIGCOMM '93, Sept. 1993), hierarchical caching could reduce FTP traffic by 50 percent. Similar results are projected for the Web.

The Harvest Object cache is a hierarchical system that has been in operation for over two years at around 100 sites. Tests conducted by its authors show that the Harvest cache system can be up to an order of magnitude faster than the standard CERN cache. The Harvest Cache represents the work of Anawat Chankhunthod, Chuck Neerdaels, and Peter Danzig of the University of Southern California and Michael Schwartz and Duane Wessels of the University of Colorado at Boulder. For more information about this cache, point your Web browser to `http://excalibur.usc.edu/` at the University of Southern California.

Summary

In this chapter, you've learned the basic rules of optimization:

- Profile! If you don't have infinite time and resources, you need to fix the worst problems first.
- Optimize intelligently; try to tune the existing setup before you trim functionality.
- Don't be afraid to rethink your basic design criteria or implementation.
- Above all, optimize for a specific target; you can't provide everything to everyone!

CHAPTER 47

Managing Server Security

by John Jung

IN THIS CHAPTER

Because Web sites are usually very high-profile, they tend to attract a lot of attention. For many organizations, this attention is exactly what they want. The downside to all that exposure is the possibility of people using the Web site to break in to the company. Typically, the more high-profile the company sponsoring the Web site is, the more attempted break-ins there are. Consequently, Webmasters now have to address issues that were typically the domain of network administrators. Obviously, the Webmaster isn't going to replace the network administrator; however, they do share some tasks. This chapter explains what issues are involved in maintaining Web server security.

Internet Security Issues

Probably the most obvious security issue that a Webmaster has to deal with is traffic from the Internet. Because the Internet is likely to generate more network traffic for the site than internal users do, how to handle traffic from the Internet is a very big concern. One of the most important aspects of Web server security is controlling who has direct access to the Web server. Another security issue is making sure that the content of the Web site is inoffensive and follows the company line. Another security issue concerns CGI scripts, which are used in some Web pages.

Remote Access

Traditionally, Web servers are run off of UNIX computers. UNIX, in addition to being extremely powerful, is a true multiuser and multitasking operating system. Also, by nature UNIX is generally a network-dependent environment. Consequently, UNIX servers are one of the most popular targets for unauthorized remote logins. UNIX-based Webmasters have their work cut out for them. Among the more obvious tasks that they should do with the Web server is to ensure that users have secure passwords. One way to ensure the security of passwords is to force users to periodically change them.

Before making your Web site publicly accessible, make sure you've changed a number of system passwords. Aside from the obvious `root` account, there are some other predefined accounts that you should fix. Among them are `bin`, `nobody`, `guest`, `daemon`, and `sys`. Depending on the flavor of UNIX you're using, there might be more, or fewer, predefined accounts. Because these accounts are predefined, they also come with predefined passwords. Not only does your operating system vendor know these passwords, but so do hackers. As a good safety measure, change all the passwords on all predefined accounts.

As a final measure, look at your system from a hacker's point of view. A number of publicly available packages help you to hack into your system. Obviously, you're not trying to do anything malicious, but these packages attempt to find holes in your security. Get some, or all, of these packages and try them out on your system. If a package finds any holes, fix them yourself, or get your system or network administrator to fix them. Additionally, check to see whether your OS vendor has released any operating system patches. If it has, download them and apply them.

Tiger, by Texas A&M University, is one collection of programs. It has no official home page, but you can get a copy of it by pointing your Web browser to `ftp://net.tamu.edu/pub/security/TAMU/tiger-2.2.3.tar.gz`. An older hacking package known as COPS, by Dan Farmer, has an unofficial home page at `http://misbss20.larc.nasa.gov/security/4.0/cops.html`. However, you can't download it directly from that site, as it's intended only for NASA personnel. You can, however, get COPS from `ftp://info.cert.org/pub/cops/1.04/cops_104.tar.Z`. Finally, there's the highly regarded SATAN (Security Administrator's Tool for Analyzing Networks). You can find out more about it by using the URL `http://www.fish.com/satan/`. You can get a copy of its source code from `ftp://ftp.win.tue.nl/pub/security/satan-1.1.1.tar.Z`.

CAUTION

UNIX hacking programs are intended for use by system and network administrators. They will slow down the system they are running on and can take up to several hours in generating a report. They are not intended for general end-user use.

Non-UNIX operating systems are, most of the time, far more secure than UNIX. This difference isn't because the software for UNIX is inferior; it's just that the personal computers aren't designed the same as UNIX is. Specifically, Windows 95 and the Macintosh aren't designed to be as multiuser as UNIX is. Consequently, where most UNIX boxes come enabled with a number of Internet services, the personal operating systems don't. In fact, personal operating systems often require you to install server software.

There is, of course, a middle-ground operating system, Windows NT. This environment is as multiuser and multitasking as UNIX, but is more approachable. This quality is primarily due to Windows NT's built-in user interface. However, it, like the personal operating systems, doesn't have built-in services. It too needs server software to be installed before remote access security issues can become an issue. Additionally, the majority of Windows NT programs require the graphical user interface. This requirement makes it so that only the command line-based programs are accessible to a hacker.

Content Control

Another Internet security issue that concerns Webmasters is the content of the Web site. You, the Webmaster, have to make sure that all the Web pages on your site meet company standards. For example, sensitive company information should not be made available on the public Web server.

You should also watch out for sources of possible lawsuits on your Web page. Make sure there aren't any copyrighted images on your Web site. All images from comic strips, movies, or magazines must be authorized. Also, get rid of any content that may be offensive to users of the site, such as nude pictures or offensive language. Aside from possible lawsuits, such elements may turn off people from your Web site.

Some may feel that talking about Web content has little to do with security. Unfortunately, there are real-life events where hackers have modified content. One such incident happened in August of 1996, when hackers broke into a computer at the Department of Justice. They heavily modified the main Web page, adding profanity, swastikas, and other completely unrelated content. A similar incident happened about a month later to the CIA's Web page, except the modifications were less severe. Although these incidents might have been politically motivated, they could still happen to companies. In fact, high-profile, well-known companies are often the target of unsucessful hacking attempts.

A final aspect of Internet security is to make sure that certain pages are password-protected, if necessary. Especially in large organizations, sometimes it's not a good idea to reveal all information. Suppose you work at a large service-oriented business with different groups for different customers. Further, suppose an information area is created for a particular customer and maintained by a particular group. The area allows the specialized group and its customer to interact with each other in privacy. Obviously, this information area should be protected so that only certain users can access it.

CGI Scripts

CGI scripts are another security concern for most Webmasters. Typically, the Web server software is running as a privileged user. This kind of user often has certain privileges that are beyond the scope of normal users. CGI scripts run with the user and group permissions of the Web server, which means that CGI scripts should be heavily regulated. After all, a malicious CGI script could be written to exploit the Web server's special privileges. In some cases, it would be possible for such a script to delete all or some of the files on your Web server. Either each CGI script should be analyzed and dissected, or each one should go through rigorous testing. Some Web sites completely disable save access to areas where other CGI scripts are stored.

Intranet Security Issues

In addition to dealing with Internet-related security, a Webmaster has to deal with intranet-related security. Just because the intranet is not available to everybody doesn't mean that security should be relaxed. All of the Internet-related problems also exist on an intranet. Most of the solutions just have to be applied in a different fashion. For example, you still have to look out for the content of the Web site by watching out for possible lawsuit issues, such as copyrighted images, but you also have to focus on keeping groups divided. For example, you may not want the sales department to be able to access everything in the development Web pages.

Also, you should watch out for possibly malicious CGI scripts. Although such scripts might not be malicious by design, badly written scripts can cause plenty of problems. As a result, you don't want to give carte blanche to intranet-based scripts. In addition to minimizing the problem of poorly written CGI programs, restricting access to the `cgi-bin` directory can prevent other problems. Suppose a disgruntled employee wrote a malicious script just for vengeance that wreaked havoc on your intranet. Far better to not allow this to happen than to deal with the consequences if it does happen.

Controlling Access

Probably one of the easiest security issues for traditional Webmasters is how to control access. As Webmaster, you want to be able to ensure that Web authors can modify their own Web pages. You wouldn't want somebody to be able to modify someone else's pages. On personal computer operating systems, this type of segregation can be very difficult.

Fortunately, most traditional Web servers are run off of UNIX systems. Consequently, you can use UNIX's built-in user and group permissions. Basically, you can keep users away from each other's files by planning ahead and creating as many groups as possible. Be sure to restrict each user you add by giving him group access only to the files that he needs. Similarly, you should also make sure that all Web pages have appropriate permissions. In particular, avoid giving everybody write access to all Web pages.

Firewalls

So far, I've focused on controlling access permissions of files on the Web server. I've assumed that the people who log on to the system are there because they're supposed to be. But Web server security has another level beyond file protection. The entire system also needs to be protected from unauthorized access. There are a number of approaches that network administrators and Webmasters can take to protect their systems. One common way is to put up something known as a firewall.

What Is a Firewall?

Simply put, a *firewall* separates an internal network from the Internet. It screens and filters all connections coming from the Internet to the internal network and vice versa. This filtering is done through a single, concentrated security checkpoint. All network activity between the Internet and the internal network must go through the firewall. A firewall acts as an electronic gate, allowing in only authorized users. You can manage a number of aspects of this gate as well as keep logs and statistics of activity. Some firewalls even require you to log onto the firewall itself before passing through the gate.

TIP

Using FTP, you can get information on firewalls from mailing list archives at the following URL:

`ftp://ftp.greatcircle.com/ub/firewalls`

A firewall toolkit and papers are available at the following URL:

`ftp://ftp.tis.com/ub/firewalls`

Protection

Believe it or not, there are some inherently insecure services and systems on your internal network. As mentioned in the "Remote Access" section of this chapter, new UNIX machines have a number of predefined passwords. Although it might make sense to change all these passwords for a single machine, this concept becomes unworkable with a large network. It would be a tremendous undertaking for a company with over 2,000 UNIX systems to change all its predefined passwords.

A firewall protects such machines and services that might not be secure. As a result, your internal network is exposed to far fewer risks and dangers. Because the firewall filters out unwanted protocols, there are fewer holes in your network security. This brings peace of mind not only to your network administrators, but also to each individual system administrator.

For example, a firewall could prohibit certain vulnerable services, such as NFS, from entering or leaving your internal network, so you prevent the services by being exploited by outsiders. A firewall also allows your personnel to use the services with less risk of exploitation. Services such as NIS and NFS, which are particularly useful for an internal network, can be used without exposing the network to outside threats. These two services in particular make systems management easier for all administrators.

The problem with firewalls, though, is that they limit access to and from the Internet. In some configurations, you may decide to use a proxy server (see the "Proxy Service" section of this chapter) to filter inbound and outbound access. Although not necessary, proxies can be very useful.

Access Control

A firewall can provide a fine level of access control to internal network machines. For instance, some servers can be made reachable from outside networks. Similarly, other systems can be effectively sealed off from unwanted access. Depending on the level of risk you are willing to accept for your Web site, watch out for outside access to internal network servers. Only under special situations, such as mail servers or RAS services, should you not be too overly concerned. When setting up access control systems, keep the following rule in mind: never provide access to servers or services unless it is required. A good rule of thumb in access control is to keep the available servers and services to a minimum. Following this rule will limit the number of possible break-in points on your system.

Security

A firewall can be less expensive for an organization than security measures on individual machines. Because the firewall is a central filtering point, you can put security software on the firewall system itself. This solution is preferable to distributing such packages to each and every machine on your internal network. In particular, one-time-password systems and other add-on authentication software can be located at the firewall rather than on each system that needs to be accessed from the Internet. As a result, instead of configuring the 2,000 machines on your internal network, you only configure one: the firewall.

Other solutions to your Web site security could involve modifications at each server system. In some cases, such solutions might be preferable to using a firewall. However, firewalls tend to be far simpler to implement because only the firewall machine needs to run specialized software. However, if you have a package-filtering firewall or require your users to log onto the firewall, you'll need more hardware. In all likelihood, you'll need either a router that filters the packages or a dedicated machine.

CAUTION

Don't neglect internal security just because you have a firewall. If a hacker breaks in, your network will be exposed unless you have some internal security policies in place.

Privacy

Privacy should be of great concern for every Web site because all information might be useful to a hacker. Regardless of whether the information appears dangerous, there might be subtle clues that a hacker can pick up on. By using a firewall, Web sites can block access from services such as finger and Domain Name Service (DNS). Typically, people use finger to get information about individual users, such as whether they've read mail and their last login time. However, finger can also be used to retrieve information about the entire system. It can be used to tell how often a system is used and whether users are currently logged on. This information, though by itself harmless, allows hackers to decide whether that system can be attacked. And getting the information in this way doesn't attract the attention of system and network administrators and monitoring software.

Another approach to keeping your internal network private is to maintain separate DNS servers. You could have an internal DNS server that contains all the host names and IP addresses of your internal network. Another external DNS server could be set up to contain only the host names and IP addresses of certain machines. Only those machines that are important to other Internet servers would be on the external DNS. Some Web administrators feel that this setup hides material that otherwise would be useful to hackers.

Logging and Statistics

Firewalls can be configured to log accesses to and from the Internet. This log provides important information about network usage and where possible weak points are in your network. You should have a log of your Web site usage statistics and evidence of probing for a number of reasons. The first reason is to know whether the firewall is withstanding probes and attacks. This information allows you to determine whether the controls on the firewall are adequate. Another reason to track Web server usage statistics is to provide input to network requirements studies and risk-analysis activities.

TIP

A firewall with appropriate alarms that sound when suspicious activity occurs can also provide details on whether the firewall and network are being probed or attacked.

Proxies

Although a firewall might seem like an adequate form of protection, it isn't the only one. Another form of protection for your network, as well as your Web site, is a proxy server. Unlike a firewall, proxies enable you to work with services that might jeopardize your network, but it keeps them from being a threat.

What Are Proxies, Exactly?

A proxy is a program that takes the data of another program and interprets and filters it. A proxy filters information based on the application and service supported by the proxy. This is different from a firewall, which merely filters out data based on what port number it's coming from. Proxy services allow through only those services for which there is a proxy. If an application gateway only contains proxies for FTP and telnet, only FTP and telnet are allowed into the internal network. All other services are completely blocked, even if they pass through the firewall. This degree of security is important. A proxy makes sure that only trustworthy services are allowed through the firewall and prevents untrustworthy services from being implemented on the firewall without your knowledge.

NOTE

If you have used TIA (The Internet Adapter), slirp, or TERM, you probably are familiar with the concept of redirecting a connection. Using these programs, you can redirect a port. Proxy servers work in a similar way by opening a socket on the server and allowing the connection to pass through.

Proxy Service

In terms of Web servers, a *proxy* is a special HTTP server that typically is run on the machine running the firewall. A proxy basically does the following:

- Receives a request from a client inside the firewall
- Sends this request to the remote Web server outside of the firewall
- Reads the response
- Sends the response back to the client

Usually, all of the clients in an internal network use the same proxy. This setup enables the proxy to efficiently cache documents that are requested by several clients.

NOTE

The fact that a proxy service is not transparent to the user means that either the user or the client will have to be made aware of the proxy. Either the user is instructed on how to manage the client in order to access certain services, or the client, such as a Web client, is made proxy-aware.

How Proxies Work with Web Servers

Because proxies are created on an application-by-application basis, they know about the data being sent. Whereas firewalls blindly accept or deny data based on a particular port, proxies can interpret the data. This provides for much more detailed logging information, such as IP addresses, date and time, and other useful information. Another characteristic of proxying is its capability to filter client transactions at the application protocol level. It can control access to services for individual methods, servers, domains, and so on.

Technically speaking, proxy servers act as two separate programs, a client and a server. When a client requests data through the proxy, the proxy intercepts the request. So in this regard, the proxy is the client's server for any such application activity. The proxy then makes the request for information from the specified host. In this regard, the proxy is acting as a client. Finally, the proxy sends the data it received from the server back to the original client. Once again, the proxy is acting as a server to the user client.

NOTE

A complete Web proxy server must speak all of the Web protocols, especially HTTP, FTP, Gopher, and NNTP.

Encryption

With most data that's transferred from a Web client, everything is transmitted in the open. If the Web browser is sending data, it merely sends the exact piece of data, so that if the Web client were told to send the word *test*, the word *test* would be sent. This sort of approach is fine for everyday use and almost all situations with the Web. Unfortunately, it's not perfect, nor preferred, for a number of situations. In particular, if you're sending confidential information, such as a credit card number, this situation is unacceptable. Even though the chances that your credit card number will be seen are remote, the possibility does exist.

To allow data transmissions in which no information is blatantly obvious, the data must be hidden in some form. Although there are many proposed methods of hiding information, the most popular one is to encrypt the transmitted information. What this means is that when a Web browser sends the word *test*, the word doesn't look like *test* while it's on the Internet. Only the destination Web server knows how to decode the encrypted data. After the information is decoded, the Web server can process the information accordingly.

The most popular form of Web data encryption is known as the Secure Sockets Layer (SSL). Although not yet fully accepted, its widespread support makes it likely that it will be fully accepted soon. What SSL does is take the information that's going to be sent over the Internet and encrypts it by using some sophisticated forms of public key cryptography. As a general rule, SSL is very secure. Although it's not completely inpenetrable, it's extremely hard to break.

NOTE

You can find out more about Web security by pointing your browser to

`http://www.genome.wi.mit.edu/WWW/faqs/www-security-faq.html`

NOTE

As a point of reference, Pretty Good Privacy (PGP) uses a technology similar to SSL. It took a concerted effort of many users and workstations over eight months to break a PGP-encoded message.

Most Web sites can work fine without having to encrypt their data. Companies that sell goods over the Internet, however, should look into using some form of encryption. Currently, the only Web servers that can use SSL are those by Netscape and Microsoft. Be aware that implementing SSL, as per Netscape's proposal, is a rather daunting task. As of this writing, there are no available public SSL-capable Web servers.

Accessing Your Server

After all the content for your Web site is created, you'll want to be able to access it. Regardless of whether you're behind a firewall, server access raises several issues. One fact to consider is whether your Web server is an Internet server or an intranet server. Intranet servers are far easier to implement because there is little threat of an unauthorized break-in. Although such a threat still exists, you have better control over it. You probably don't need to worry about firewalls and proxies with an intranet Web server. The only security concerns you deal with relate to user and group permissions.

Internet Web servers are a different matter. For many small-to-medium sized companies, the Webmaster is probably also the systems administrator. Consequently, when you start up a Web site, you have to look at all security concerns. If your site already has a firewall or proxy server, you will have to make sure that the Web server can talk through them. If your organization doesn't have any form of protection, you should look into implementing at least some form of protection.

In large companies, being a Webmaster is a bit easier because you don't have total responsibility for the entire system. Chances are good that some sort of security mechanism is already in place. All you, the Webmaster, have to do is get your Web server to work with it. If your company has a firewall, you'll need to talk to your network administrator. He may need to get justification for opening up a hole in the firewall. If a proxy server is in place, the network and systems administrators may have more work to do. They may need to set up a Web server proxy service for your Web site. Whatever the case, though, you, the Webmaster, won't have that much to do. All you have to do is make sure that the Web server software is made aware of proxies.

Summary

Web server security is a very important part of being a Webmaster. It includes security for the Web server itself as well as its content. To maintain content security, you can use UNIX's built-in set of tools. In keeping with the theme of maintaining content security, you can restrict access to other Web pages by carefully planning out user and group permissions. User accounts enable you to create a corporate-wide Web page, as well as let individual users create their own home pages.

Another aspect of Web server security is to prevent unauthorized people from accessing your system. Two methods of doing this are firewalls and proxy servers. Most Web servers will have no problems talking through a firewall. However, some configuration will be needed to make them proxy-aware.

Part XI

IN THIS PART

Putting It All Together

CHAPTER 48

Designing and Publishing a Perfect Web Page

by Dick Oliver

IN THIS CHAPTER

If you've read the previous 47 chapters—or even skimmed the table of contents—your mind is probably reeling from all the choices and possibilities for your own Web pages. This chapter gives you some complete, hands-on examples of how to make those choices and combine those possibilities intelligently in real-world situations.

The three sample sites presented here all feature real people and businesses. You'll get the inside story on how and why both the multimedia and more conventional elements were used to meet their needs and goals. There is a personal site, a promotional page for an "offline" business, and an online business site. Between all of these, almost all of the technologies and techniques discussed in this book are put into action.

All these sites are included in their entirety on the CD-ROM with this book so you can borrow all the techniques and even some of the content for your own projects. (Obviously, you can't use the logos, names, personal pictures, and copyrighted text or music. But you do have permission to use backgrounds, icons, and general design elements. When in doubt, contact me at `dicko@netletter.com` or contact the people whose names and e-mail addresses are on the pages to ask for specific permission.)

Making a Personal Page More Personal

Sound and action are not just for high-budget, high-bandwidth sites run by giant media moguls. In fact, one of the most popular uses of multimedia on the Web today is for personal home pages. The function of a personal home page is mostly to enable people you meet online to get some idea of who you are and to have some fun making a "page of your own." If you're job-hunting or you happen to be a public figure, your home page may take a more serious bent. But the sound of a human voice and some animation makes anyone's page convey more of a sense of who they are—or who they would like to be!

An Overdue Makeover

I run some popular Web sites, frequent a number of mailing lists and the occasional online chat room, and write books about the Internet. But until recently, my home page was of the old-fashioned snapshot-and-a-few-lines-of-text variety. So I decided to see if I could spice it up using only free or ultra-cheap tools and without taking much time out of my busy schedule. Figure 48.1 and Listing 48.1 show the result, after a couple hours of messing about with it. I'll explain the decisions I made, and why.

FIGURE 48.1.
My home page (`/dicko/dicko.htm` *on the CD-ROM or* `http:/netletter.com/dicko/` *online) flips through four pictures of me, so nobody has to tolerate any one view too long.*

Listing 48.1. /dicko/dicko.htm.

```
<HTML>
<HEAD><TITLE>Dick Oliver's Home Page</TITLE></HEAD>
<BODY BACKGROUND="strip.gif" TEXT="white" LINK="red" VLINK="red" ALINK="white">
<IMG SRC="dickani.gif"> . . . <IMG SRC="dickog.gif"><BR>
 .<P>
So what can you do when you're too dumb to become a physicist or mathematician,
and not quite crazy enough to qualify for free food at the asylum?
Write books, I figure. And software. And what the heck maybe some newsletters
and Web pages, too. But enough about me already.
On to these far more interesting topics:<BR>
<CENTER>
<TABLE>
<TR>
<TD><IMG SRC="see.gif"></TD>
<TD>
<FONT COLOR="cyan"><I>See...</I></FONT><BR>
<A HREF="work.htm"><FONT COLOR="cyan">My work</FONT></A><BR>
<A HREF="family.htm"><FONT COLOR="cyan">My family</FONT></A><BR>
<A HREF="house.htm"><FONT COLOR="cyan">My house</FONT></A><BR>
<A HREF="hotlist.htm"><FONT COLOR="cyan">My hotlist</FONT></A>
</TD>
<TD>
<IMG SRC="hear.gif"></TD>
<TD>
<FONT COLOR="yellow"><I>Hear...</I></FONT><BR>
<A HREF="voice.RA"><FONT COLOR="yellow">My voice</FONT></A><BR>
<A HREF="brillig.RA"><FONT COLOR="yellow">My favorite poem</FONT></A><BR>
```

continues

Listing 48.1. continued

```
<A HREF="ecooro.RA"><FONT COLOR="yellow">My daughters</FONT></A><BR>
<A HREF="dog.RA"><FONT COLOR="yellow">My dog</FONT></A>
</TD>
<TD>
<IMG SRC="get.gif"></TD>
<TD>
<FONT COLOR="red"><I>Get...</I></FONT><BR>
<A HREF="news.htm">My newsletter</A><BR>
<A HREF="books.htm">My books</A><BR>
<A HREF="software.htm">My software</A><BR>
<A HREF="fools.htm">My foolishness</A>
</TD>
</TR>
</TABLE><BR>
Happy? Disgusted? Lonely? Enlightened? Just plain stupid?<BR>
Why not send some e-mail to
<A HREF="mailto:DICKO@netletter.com">
<FONT COLOR="green">DickO@netletter.com</FONT></A>
to tell me about it?<P>
NOTE: To hear the voices, you'll need the
<A HREF="http://www.realaudio.com/">RealAudio player</A>.<P>
</CENTER>
</BODY>
</HTML>
```

Putting a Good Face on It

The first thing I thought about was the background and layout. I wanted something that looked big and bold (like me <grin>) but that was very fast to make and very fast to load and display. So I decided to just make a black-and-white background strip with solid white at the top and solid black down as far as my pages were likely to scroll. The strip is called `/dicko/strip.gif` on the CD-ROM, and because it's mostly solid colors, the big 20×2000 pixel image compresses to less than 1 K. A ragged edge adds a little zest without increasing the file size significantly.

Next, I considered the graphics. The obligatory snapshot of my face seemed too static, so I made an animated sequence of snapshots instead and doctored them up in Paint Shop Pro to prove what an artsy kinda guy I am. Then I used GIF Construction Set to make a multi-image GIF that flips to a new goofy picture of me every 0.6 seconds (see Figure 48.2). A title graphic scanned from my handwriting and some scans of my and my daughter's body parts complete the "DickO look."

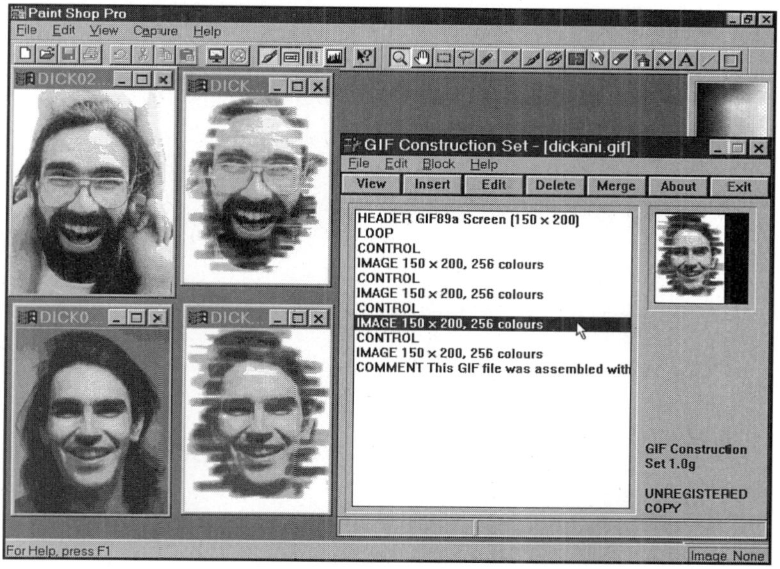

FIGURE 48.2.
A cheap hand scanner and two inexpensive shareware programs (Paint Shop Pro and GIF Construction Set) were all I needed to put together a stylistic animation for my home page.

TIP

I really wanted to make the file sizes small on my page because it will live on my high-volume commercial site where I have to pay for every byte that somebody downloads. So I did something very sneaky with all the pictures. I decreased the color depth to 16 grayscales (using "nearest color" remapping, not "diffusion" dithering). This cut the files to a fraction of their original size. Then I used Paint Shop Pro to colorize them to the 16 colors of my choice and then increased the color depth to 256 colors again.

Both Netscape and Microsoft Explorer do a much better job displaying most 256-color images than 16-color images, so the visual quality most people see is quite a bit better at the higher color depth. Because still only 16 unique color values are being used, however, the compressed file still comes out much smaller than before I brought the images down to 16 colors and back up again.

This trick allowed me to squeeze four relatively large (150X200-pixel) photos into a 28 K GIF file. Before doctoring them, each of the 256-color, 150X200 GIF files was more than 28 K!

The Webmaster's Voice

Most of the links on my home page lead to graphics, text, and other sites I've produced. But the links next to my two-year-old daughter's ear are the parts that probably give the most personal experience of meeting me and my family. The sound of someone's voice—even if it's compressed and distorted a bit—seems to reach a place in the soul that no amount of graphics can touch.

Recording voices is easy enough. In fact, for a personal home page, it would be overkill to use more than a simple recording utility, such as the Windows Sound Recorder and the chintzy microphone that came with my sound card.

The resulting WAV files could be posted as-is or converted with a shareware sound editing program, such as CoolEdit, to the AU format so Netscape Navigator 2.0 could play them without requiring any plug-ins. But I wanted to include fairly lengthy sound samples, such as "my favorite poem" and keep the number of bytes to transfer to an absolute minimum. So, I chose to use the RealAudio encoder (see Figure 48.3) to compress the sound for real-time playback. A 327 K, 8-bit WAV file compresses to about 15 K worth of RealAudio audio and starts playing immediately when the user clicks the links (see Figure 48.4).

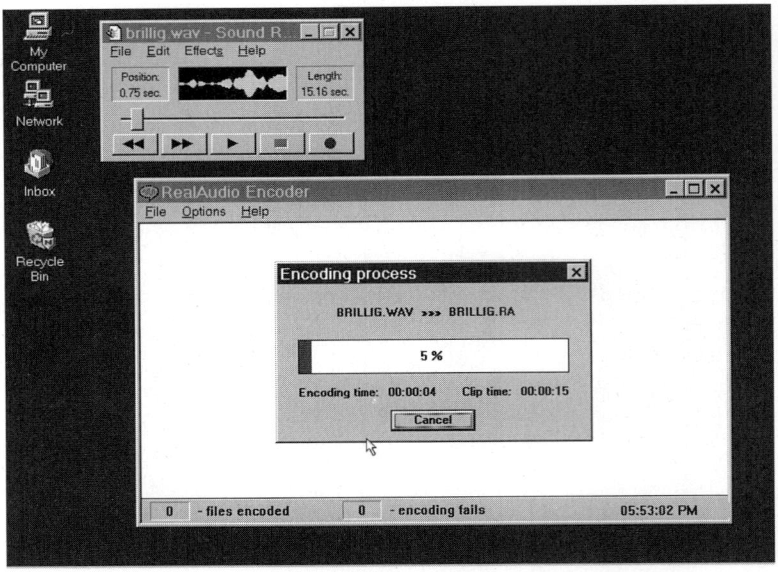

FIGURE 48.3.
It doesn't take a state-of-the-art recording studio to put your voice on the Web. These free programs (the Windows 95 Sound Recorder and RealAudio Encoder) will do just fine.

FIGURE 48.4.
The RealAudio helper application works with any browser and plays back without long download delays. (A RealAudio plug-in is also available for embedded playback.)

The disadvantage of using RealAudio is that not everybody has a plug-in or helper application to play back the `.RA` files. But hey, it's my home page and it's no big deal if somebody can't hear my voice. They can go to `http://www.realaudio.com/` to download the plug-in if they're really intent on hearing me, and I tell them so on the bottom of the page. But of course a used car site pumping out plaid-voiced sales talk might prefer the more universal AU format.

The other obvious choice would have been ToolVox, a similar plug-in that generally achieves better compression and higher quality than RealAudio. But right now, more people have RealAudio—especially the helper application, and I've gotten kind of used to it. By the time you read this, ToolVox will probably be taking the lead in a number of users, so you should seriously consider it as an option for your lengthy sound files. There are other up-and-coming formats, too, but most haven't gained much widespread support yet, and sound quality is still pretty shaky over modem lines. (You'd think a modem hooked to a telephone line could carry telephone-quality voice pretty easily, but there's more to it than that. See Chapter 23, "Creating Online Audio," for all the technical details.)

Notice that I refrained from putting an AVI home video up on my personal Web site. As everybody's bandwidth increases and digital video editing software keeps dropping in price, that might become a viable option. But for now, it would just be too many pixels to push through a poor suffering server just for my personal home page.

An Attention-Grabbing Business Page

Now let's look at a simple business site. Though the goals and concerns of a business are obviously a bit different than those you might have for your personal pages, many of the same decisions need to be made. How can you get big, attention-grabbing graphics while sucking up as little space and time on the server as possible? How can you convey a unique and memorable image without distracting too much from the more prosaic information content?

Festive Java

For the Hawaiian Hard Drive home page in Figure 48.5 and Listing 48.2, we chose a flashy but fun look, mostly conveyed by a large masthead graphic. But the most memorable part of the page is the freeware Java applet under the masthead that creates moving waves of text with rainbow colors flowing through them. Anyone willing to put a link to Integris on their page can freely use this applet, created by Integris Network Services (and included on the CD-ROM in this book).

Having seen and played with lots of nifty little special-purpose Java applets like this one, it is always a delight to actually have a reasonable excuse to use one on a real page. This one seemed like the perfect way to set a festive "Hawaiian mood" without resorting to touristy clichés like palm trees and pineapples, which might turn off many of the Hawaiians for whom this page is intended. (Hawaiian Hard Drive is a free computer newspaper distributed on the islands, and this site offers its readers and advertisers an online version.)

FIGURE 48.5.
This page (`/hhd/hhd.htm` on the CD-ROM or `http://netletter.com/hhd/online`) uses a Java applet (`RnbText.class`) to display "surfing" text.

NOTE

In-word spaces in the following code are intentional. They're necessary due to the width of some characters.

Listing 48.2. /hhd/hhd.htm.

```
<HTML>
<HEAD><TITLE>Hawaiian Hard Drive</TITLE></HEAD>
<BODY BACKGROUND="HHD.JPG">
<CENTER>
<IMG SRC="HHD2.GIF" ALT="Hawaiian Hard Drive"><BR>
<APPLET code="RnbText.class" width=710 height=50>
<param name=text value="H aw aii's C om puter &  Inform ation R esource">
</APPLET> <P>
</CENTER>
<EMBED SRC="aloha.wav" WIDTH=2 HEIGHT=2>
<NOEMBED><BGSOUND SRC="aloha.wav"></NOEMBED><BR>
<FONT SIZE=4>The mission of the Hawaiian Hard Drive newspaper and Web site
is to inform a broad range of computer users and the general general public
of the latest trends in the computer market. Through our writers and
advertisers, you'll find out about software, hardware, applications
and other areas of interest. We are not critics of any hardware or
software platform, and you'll find information that will be useful for DOS,
Mac, and Windows, and other computer users as well. After all, it's not the
machine that counts the most—it's who's using it!<P>
<CENTER>
<HR SIZE=10 NOSHADE>
<APPLET code="RnbText.class" width=120 height=50>
  <param name=text value="Features">
</APPLET><P>
<B><A HREF="webpage.htm">Making Your Own Web Page</A><BR>
<A HREF="virus.htm">A Computer Virus Primer</A><BR>
<A HREF="protect.htm">Software Copyright Protection</A><BR>
<A HREF="dtp.htm">Explore the World of Desktop Publishing</A></B>
<P>
</FONT>
<HR SIZE=10 NOSHADE>
<ADDRESS>
<FONT SIZE=3>
Hawaiian Hard Drive<BR>
94-547 Ukee Street #308<BR>
Waipahu, HI 96797<P>
(808) 677-2464<P>
<A HREF="mailto:PDeptula@aol.com">PDeptula@aol.com</A>
</ADDRESS><P>
All stories are copyright, 1995-1996 by their authors.<BR>
The Java Applet on this page was designed by
<A HREF="http://www.crl.com/~integris">Integris Network Services</A>.<P>
</FONT>
</CENTER>
</BODY>
</HTML>
```

If you scroll down the page (see Figure 48.6), you'll notice that another occurrence of the same `RnbText.class` Java applet is used again for the heading "Features." Once you include a Java applet on a page, no extra download time is incurred if you include another copy elsewhere. Note that visitors to your site will need more computer power to keep both applets working at once, however. With small applets like this one, that isn't much of a concern—but you should avoid including more than one big, graphics-intensive applet on any page.

Generally speaking, you need to be more careful about overburdening the user's computer with too much to do than being careful about the speed with which applets download. This applet, for example, is only 3 K but takes quite a bit of resources to constantly update long strings of text.

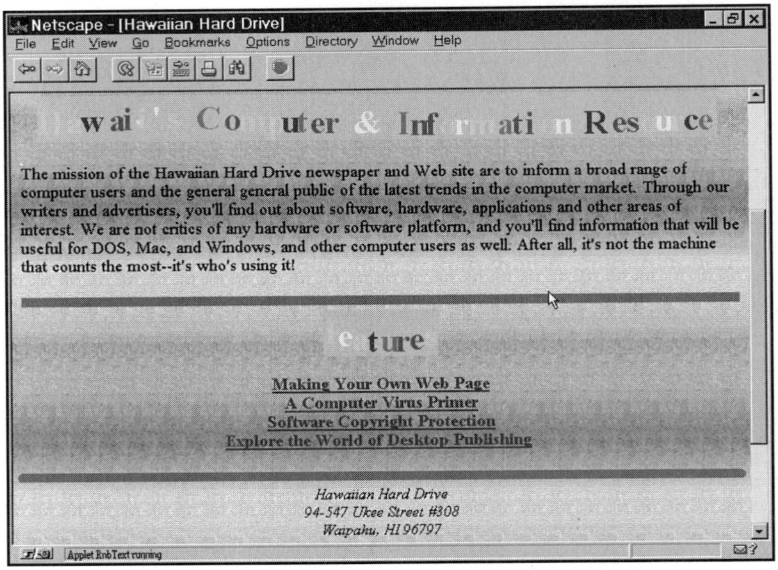

FIGURE 48.6.
If you include more than one copy of an applet on the same page, it still only needs to be downloaded once.

TIP

Even though the latest versions of Netscape Navigator and Microsoft Explorer both support Java applets, many older and more feeble browsers still don't. So you should always make sure that any text displayed by a Java applet (or OLE component) is not strictly necessary for your page to make sense.

The Hawaiian Hard Drive page, for example, still looks fine when the words *Hawaii's Computer & Information Resource* and *Feature* don't appear (see Figure 48.7).

Whenever you use modern enhancements such as Java applets or embedded media, it becomes especially important for you to test how your pages look in other common browsers besides Netscape Navigator. Figure 48.7 shows the page as it looks to Microsoft Internet Explorer 2.0 at 1024×768 resolution. (The previous figures are all at 800×600 resolution, which is by far the most common today.)

FIGURE 48.7.
In Microsoft Internet Explorer 2.0 (shown here at 1024×768 resolution), Java applets don't appear.

Most graphics that look good at 800×600 will look fine (though perhaps a bit small) at 1024×768, but often don't fare so well at the 640×480 resolution, as shown in Figure 48.8. As a rule of thumb, you should always make sure that all graphics, applets, and embedded media at least show enough information at 640×480 to be easily understood. Testing your pages at all three of these common window sizes is very important.

Most commercial online services have switched to Microsoft Explorer and Netscape Navigator instead of their old clunky browsers, too. So you can be assured of looking good to more than 90 percent of the people on the Web if you test your pages with those two browsers. I'd highly recommend testing both with the current version (currently Explorer 3.0 and Navigator 2.0) and with the version before the current one (Explorer 2.0 and Navigator 1.2), however, because a lot of people are quite slow to upgrade once they get used to using something.

FIGURE 48.8.
The page doesn't look quite as perfect at 640×480 resolution, but the important information still shows.

TIP

If you add an old text-based copy of Lynx for DOS to your list of test browsers, you can be sure to please virtually everybody—even the many vision-impaired people who use speech or Braille-reader enabled copies of Lynx to surf the Web.

Even if you don't test with Lynx, you can greatly enhance the readability of your pages for text-based browsers or users with slow modems by always including `ALT=` attributes in your `IMG` tags (for example, `<IMG SRC="hhd.gif" ALT="Hawaiian Hard Drive">`). This is an especially good idea if you use graphics for the title of your page and even more so if the graphics are larger than 5 K or so.

A 13 K image such as the Hawaiian Hard Drive title may seem compact by modern multimedia file standards, but it will take about 13 seconds to load over a 14.4 Kbps modem. Using `ALT=` can make the heading appear that much sooner for users of those modems.

Aloha!

If you have Microsoft Internet Explorer or Netscape Navigator and a WAV-compatible plug-in, the Hawaiian Hard Drive page says "Aloha!" when you load it. Adding a little spoken message like this is pretty much a no-brainer: just record the sound with Windows Recorder or whatever software you like, and put a `<BGSOUND>` tag (for Explorer) and an `<EMBED>` tag (for Navigator) in your page like the following code:

```
<EMBED SRC="aloha.wav" HEIGHT=2 WIDTH=2>
<NOEMBED><BGSOUND SRC="aloha.wav"></NOEMBED>
```

The `WIDTH` and `HEIGHT` values make any display that your plug-in tries to put up so tiny that nobody will pay any attention to it. (Did you notice the tiny little white square just before the text starts on the `/hhd/hhd.htm` page in Figure 48.5? I didn't think so.)

The `<NOEMBED>` tags aren't actually necessary yet, but including them is a good idea because you never know when a browser is going to start supporting both the Netscape and Microsoft extensions. The `<NOEMBED>` tags will ensure that any browser capable of playing the sound with the `<EMBED>` tag will definitely ignore the `<BGSOUND>` tag and not try to play it twice or become otherwise confused.

TIP

If you prefer, you could insert a MIDI music file instead of a WAV sound file. The advantage of MIDI is that it is much more compact, so you can embed a lengthy song. The disadvantage is that the song must be instrumental (with no human voices), and the quality of the playback depends greatly on the quality of each listener's sound card. What sounds sensational on your $300 wavetable card and home stereo speakers may sound rather sickly on most people's el-cheapo multimedia kits.

I test MIDI files for the Web on the noisiest bargain-basement sound card and tinniest headset I have: If the music sounds good with that setup, I know it'll sound good on *any* setup.

For more details on using the `BGSOUND` and `EMBED` tags, refer to Chapter 22, "Adding Multimedia to Your Web Site."

A Flashy and Flexible Online Business Page

One reason we kept the Hawaiian Hard Drive site relatively simple is that its primary purpose is to enhance and publicize an existing "offline" business. As a secondary endeavor to the printed newspaper, cost and time savings were at least as important as a strong presence on the Web.

Now we'll look at a business site where a bit more perfectionism might be in order: The Background Underground is a small Web site that serves as the sole worldwide sales outlet for a small selection of Web-related CD-ROM products. This site isn't there to "support" a business—the site *is* the business.

Small Is Beautiful

As with the other pages discussed in this chapter, a major priority in designing The Background Underground was keeping the size of the files to a minimum.

> **TIP**
>
> For a business site, a little figuring goes a long way toward making intelligent design decisions. For example, before the redesign and name change from "Over the Rainbow," this site was getting around 5,000 hits per week. At current rates, that translates into a cost of about a dollar per month for every kilobyte on the page. So when I designed the page, I could equate some real financial numbers with previous sales figures to know how much bandwidth to budget.
>
> Your mileage will vary and other costs are usually involved for maintaining a good site. But if you design pages for any size commercial site, you should at least figure out the cost-per-kilobyte at projected levels of traffic so you have some idea how much your design choices actually cost *before* you make them.

As important as small file sizes are, it is even more important for an online business to successfully communicate what it offers. And more important than that is to offer something (preferably free) that will attract people to the site. The Background Underground manages this by giving away the best of its wares (background textures for Web pages and other uses) for free, and selling CD-ROMs packed with more backgrounds for those who just can't get enough of the stuff.

So what does this page need to say to its visitors? First, it needs to say, "Here's where you can get background textures free." Second, it needs to show them that the textures are attractive and unique. These two message need to appear very quickly; the ability to click away at a moment's whim makes the Web the ultimate "short attention span theater."

To get the point across in a dramatic way, the page in Figures 48.9 and 48.10 uses a 26-image GIF animation. A new tiled image appears once per second, surrounding a prominent masthead. (In older browsers that don't support GIF animation, just the first image appears.) As Listing 48.3 reveals, the large graphic is made up of many small copies of the same multi-image GIF.

FIGURE 48.9.
The colorful border around this masthead is composed of 24 copies of a single 60×60-pixel image (see `/bgu/bgu.htm` *on the CD-ROM).*

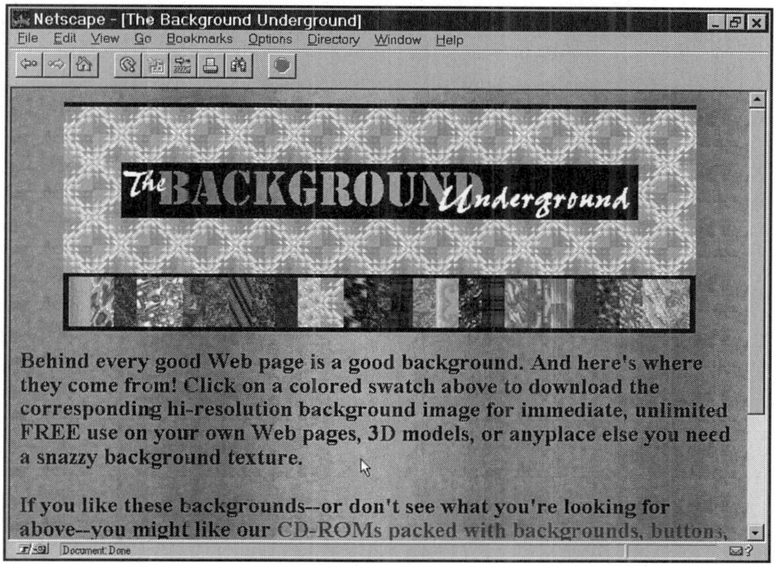

FIGURE 48.10.
The little tile is actually a GIF animation, so the masthead border changes every second.

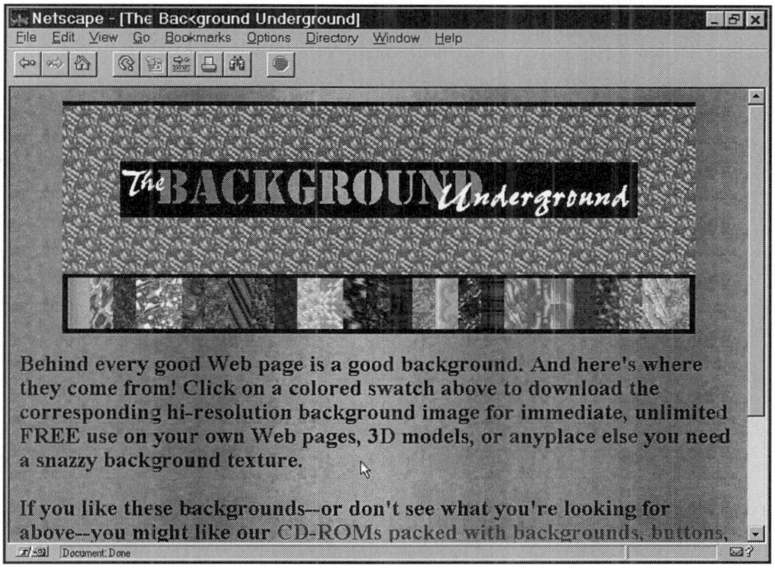

Listing 48.3. /bgu/bgu.htm.

```
<HTML>
<HEAD><TITLE>The Background Underground</TITLE></HEAD>
<BODY BACKGROUND="rainbow.jpg">
<CENTER>
<IMG SRC="topline.gif"><BR>
<IMG SRC="bgani.gif"><IMG SRC="bgani.gif"><IMG SRC="bgani.gif"><IMG
SRC="bgani.gif"><IMG SRC="bgani.gif"><IMG SRC="bgani.gif"><IMG
SRC="bgani.gif"><IMG SRC="bgani.gif"><IMG SRC="bgani.gif"><IMG
SRC="bgani.gif"><IMG SRC="bgani.gif"><BR>
<IMG SRC="bgani.gif"><IMG SRC="bgu.gif"
ALT="The Background Underground"><IMG SRC="bgani.gif"><BR>
<IMG SRC="bgani.gif"><IMG SRC="bgani.gif"><IMG SRC="bgani.gif"><IMG
SRC="bgani.gif"><IMG SRC="bgani.gif"><IMG SRC="bgani.gif"><IMG
SRC="bgani.gif"><IMG SRC="bgani.gif"><IMG SRC="bgani.gif"><IMG
SRC="bgani.gif"><IMG SRC="bgani.gif"><BR>
<IMG SRC="select.gif" USEMAP="select.map"><P>
</CENTER>
<FONT SIZE=5><B>Behind every good Web page is a good background. And
here's where they come from! Click on a colored swatch above to download
the corresponding hi-resolution background image for immediate, unlimited
FREE use on your own Web pages, 3D models, or anyplace else you need
a snazzy background texture.<P>
If you like these backgrounds—or don't see what you're looking for
above—you might like our <A HREF="bguorder.htm">CD-ROMs packed with
backgrounds, buttons, and beautiful Web page accents</A>.<P>
Then be sure to check out Gini Schmitz'
<A HREF="http://netletter.com/cameo/hotlist/hotlist.html">
Texture and Background Wonderland</A>, a hot hotlist of the best background
and Web page graphics sites on the Internet.<P>
</FONT>
</BODY></HTML>
```

TIP

Notice that there is not an embedded MIDI music file with this page nor with the any GIF animation page on the CD-ROM. There's a good reason for this: Have you ever tried listening to music while looking at something rhythmically blink, totally out of sync with the music? To paraphrase Charlie Brown, "Aaaaagh!"

If you want music and motion on the same page, please make a video clip or Shockwave movie where you can synchronize everything well enough to save your viewer's sanity! See Chapter 25, "Adding Interactivity with Shockwave for Director," for help.

As usual, we employed some tricks to get a big, brilliantly colorful image without using big graphics files. The GIF animation is actually tiny—just 60×60 pixels. Also, each of the images in the animation is just 16 colors. So the entire animation of 26 images turns out to be only 53 K. Because GIF animations start displaying when the first image is done downloading, the animation begins almost instantly and continues changing regularly at one-second intervals from then on.

Because each little 60X60 image is a reduced-size background tile, arranging 24 of them next to one another around the masthead makes them look like a giant 660X180-pixel animation with hundreds of unique colors! That this pops up in less than three seconds over a 28.8 Kbps modem seems (to those of us who are used to waiting for huge graphics files) nothing short of miraculous.

By the time visitors look away from the first paragraph of text and the colorful animation, the interlaced 23 K image map underneath the masthead has completed loading—and they probably didn't even notice that it took more than 10 seconds to do so.

Small Is Flexible

Another magical result of using tiles as decorative elements is that you can use the same tiles on a related page in a different arrangement. For example, the order form in Figure 48.11 omits the bottom row of tiles below the masthead to save space. But it will still load with almost no wait at all because all the components that make up the assembled image will be in the browser's memory or cache from the previous page.

FIGURE 48.11.
Because the tile animation and masthead are already in the browser's cache from the main page, the graphics on this order form appear instantly.

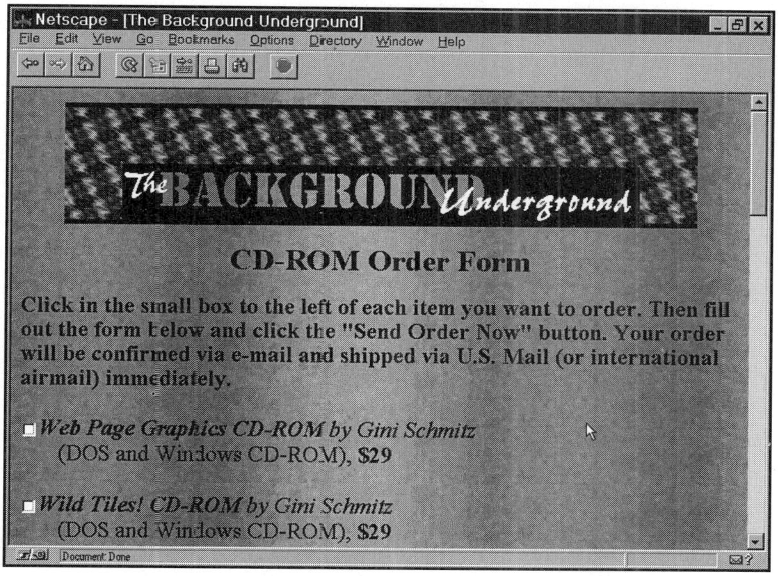

This not only saves time for visitors to the site, it saves money for the site owners because no additional graphics files will be downloaded from the server. So we get two thematic mastheads for the price of one! To sweeten the bargain just a little more, we even used a lone copy of the animated tile as a navigation button at the bottom of the order form (see Figure 48.12).

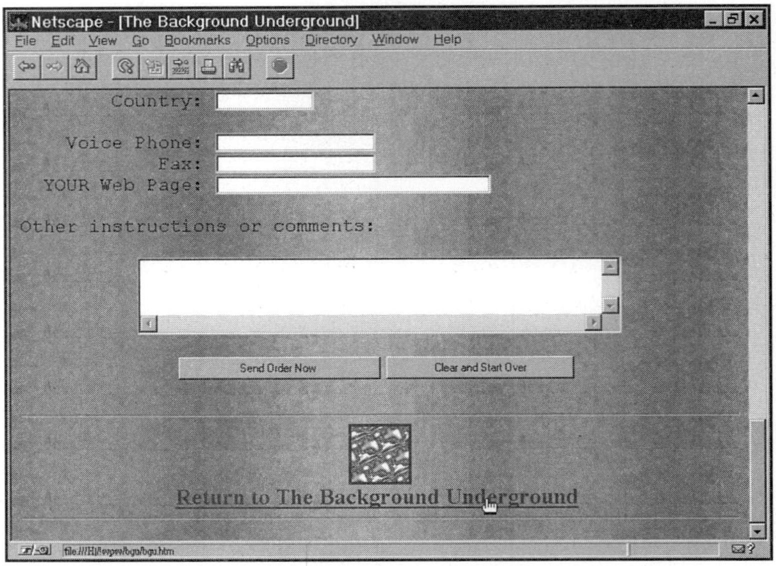

FIGURE 48.12.
A single copy of the animated tile from the masthead border makes a nice icon for the bottom of the page, too.

Breaking Up

All these snap-together graphics look great as long as the user has a big enough window to hold the entire assemblage. Things tend to get a bit strange with smaller windows, however, as demonstrated in Figure 48.13. In this case, the "accident" is kind of neat looking in and of itself and doesn't do anything bad enough to worry about. But if you design with tiles, be sure to test what happens in small windows to make sure that your page is still legible.

Even if you don't sell or give away background tiles, you may find a lot of potential uses for repeating tiles in Web page designs. There aren't many easier or more effective ways to get huge graphics or animations that download as fast as tiny ones do.

And by the way, just in case you need some background tiles to play with, we've included a selection of free tiles on the CD-ROM with this book, accessible from (where else) the Background Underground home page at `/bgu/bgu.htm`. If you want even more backgrounds, check out The Background Underground online at:

```
http://netletter.com/bgu/
```

I promise to add some more bells and whistles to the site by the time this book goes to print, so you'll discover more graphics and animation tricks there, too.

FIGURE 48.13.
When squeezed, designs made from small tiles can fall apart. But at least they usually fall apart in interesting and attractive ways!

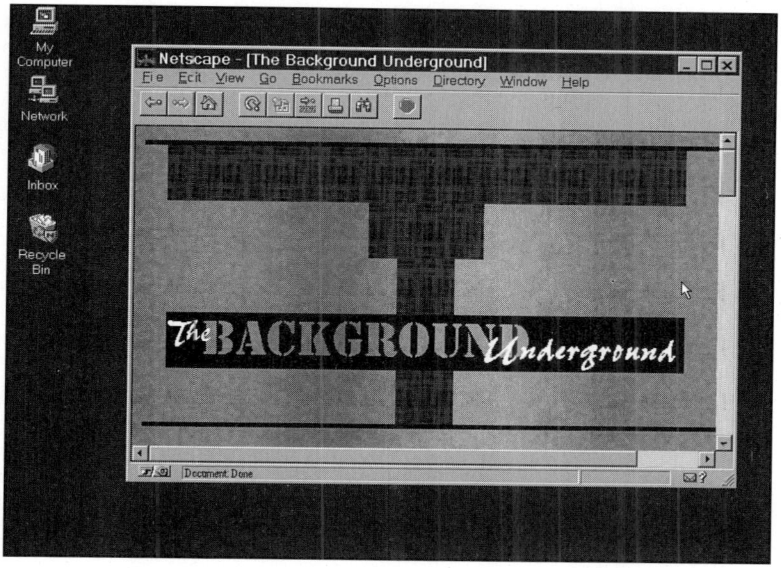

To Shock or Not to Shock?

Many of the effects on the pages presented in this chapter could be achieved quite easily—perhaps *more* easily—using Macromedia Director and Shockwave. Theoretically, "shocked" sites could wipe animated GIFs, embedded sounds, and image maps all into obsolescence with one fell swoop.

But in the real world, you need to invest a lot of money and time to get Director and either learn to use it or hire a seasoned "Director director." And in the real world, the percentage of Web surfers who have the Shockwave plug-in installed is still fairly low (albeit climbing fast). There is also a certain amount of time overhead involved in initiating the plug-in and downloading enough of the Shockwave movie to start playing, even with the new streaming animation feature. The bottom line is that developing Director animations for the vast majority of Web pages would be like taking a helicopter to the grocery store.

This doesn't mean that I don't think Shockwave is a major contribution to the welfare of all humankind. Of course it is. For example, I'm developing a site for a high-end jewelry company where we need flying logos and interactive zooming and the whole nine yards. For stuff like that, Director has no real competition (see Figure 48.14).

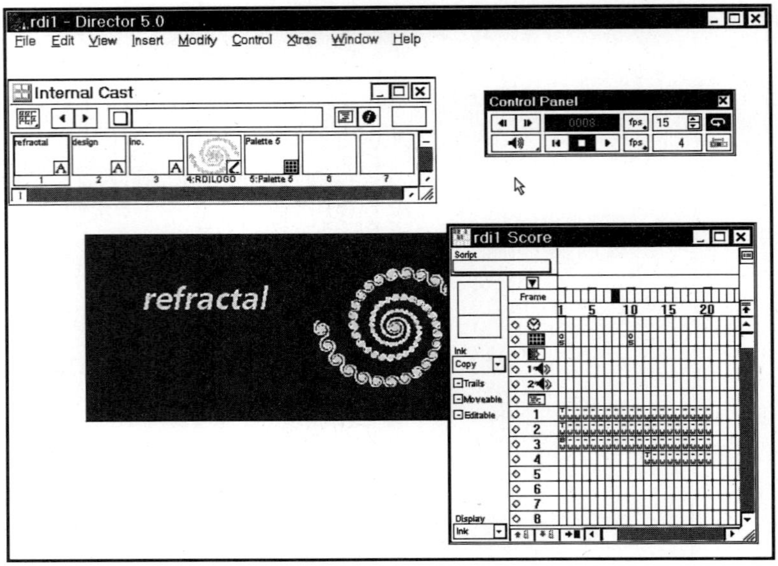

FIGURE 48.14.
Don't underestimate the learning curve, but once you get the hang of it, Director gives you nearly unlimited power for producing animated Web sites.

If you're looking to invest some serious development effort into one or more major sites or you just spent hundreds of dollars for Director and feel like you ought to use the darn thing for heaven's sake, better turn to Chapter 25, "Adding Interactivity with Shockwave for Director," now. For your first few small-business or personal home pages, though?… Get real.

Summary

In this chapter, you've seen several personal and business Web pages. Chapter 49, "Designing and Publishing a Killer Web Site," looks at the bigger picture of producing a cohesive site with many pages.

CHAPTER 49

Designing and Publishing a Killer Web Site

by William Robert Stanek

IN THIS CHAPTER

Publishing on the World Wide Web may be your ticket to success. Success can be measured in many ways. Your success may be increased sales, attracting new clients, or simply gaining widespread visibility for your ideas. Every success story has a beginning, and in Web publishing, the beginning is to create a Web site to tell the world who you are and what you represent.

The difference between a successful site and an unsuccessful site is attention to detail, good content, and good organization. This chapter follows a hands-on approach for creating a Web site. Through practical, step-by-step examples, you learn how to create, organize, and publish your own Web site. The chapter goes on to tell you how you can publicize your site, which is a critical yet all-too-often neglected part of Web publishing. If you don't tell people your site exists, no one will know and no one will visit.

The key to establishing a Web presence and building a name for yourself in cyberspace is to create a killer Web site that will stop Web surfers in their tracks. To do this, you must learn the basics of organizing, creating, and publishing a Web site where you can feature a collection of dozens or hundreds of pages. Following the steps outlined in this chapter, you can become one of the thousands of individuals successfully publishing in cyberspace.

Here are the eight steps for creating, publishing, and publicizing your Web site:

1. Define the Web site.
2. Learn Web-site design concepts.
3. Create the Web site's content.
4. Learn about advanced linking of pages and publications.
5. Add rooms to your Web home.
6. Proof and test your Web site.
7. Publish your Web site.
8. Publicize your Web site.

Defining Your Web Site

You build a Web site one step at a time, and the first step is simply defining what you want to publish on the Web. The basic components of a Web site are the pages you link together. These pages can contain text, graphics, and multimedia. The type of information you can publish on the Web is limited only by your imagination.

You can create a site that has many features, such as community services, product samples, and product information. Your Web site can be a commercial venture or simply an adventure. There are no strict rules that say you must publish either for fun or for profit. Your site can be for profit and still provide the Internet community with a useful resource containing information about you, your company, your products, and your services. Your site can be strictly informational with no sales information whatsoever, providing the Internet community with a fabulous free resource. Your intentions could be to show the world you are the definitive expert in a particular subject area, which may ultimately sell yourself, your ideas, or your company to consumers.

You should carefully consider what you want to publish on the Web. You can start by making a list of your creative projects, the plans for your business, your favorite hobbies, and your areas of interest or expertise. You can use this list to help you decide areas you may want to Web publish in.

Web Site Design Concepts

Competing in a global marketplace requires planning from day one. Before you start building your Web site, you must establish objectives and define what you hope to gain from your Web presence. Establishing an identity for yourself and your company in cyberspace does not come easily. You must use your skills and ideas to sell yourself and your company to the world.

Developing a Strategy

To establish a presence on tomorrow's Web, you must adopt a vision for success focused on global outreach. The Web is the ultimate forum for your ideas. By adding sound, graphics, and video, you can create visually stunning, highly interactive, dynamic documents that will entice readers to visit your site time after time. However, you have only a few minutes to convince readers to read your Web publication. If you do not, they are going to go somewhere else for their information needs as quickly and as effortlessly as you can change the channel on your television by remote control. Therefore, you should carefully organize your ideas and develop a specific strategy before creating a Web site.

Creating Web sites can be either a continuous struggle or a logically flowing process. Take the time to organize your ideas. Not only will the payoff be a better product, it will also mean time and resource savings. Your strategy should focus on four areas:

- The purpose of the site
- The scope of the site
- The audience for the site
- The structure of the site

Defining the Purpose of the Site

The purpose of the site is the reason you are creating the site. Are you creating a Web site to tell the world about your latest book? Are you creating a Web site to tell the world about a service you offer? Are you creating a Web site simply because you want to share your ideas or expertise?

If the purpose of a site is to sell a service or a product to Web users, do not hide that purpose—come right out and say it. This ensures readers are informed about what they are reading. Value the readers' time, and they will probably return if they need the product or service later.

If the purpose of the site is to provide an Internet community service, make sure the readers know that, too. You can build tremendous goodwill by simply providing information free. Why not share a bit of your area expertise with the world?

Defining the Scope of the Site

Another key concept to keep in mind is scope. Scope is sometimes defined in terms of the focus and size of the project. As you organize your thoughts, determine the subject matter you will discuss and how broadly or narrowly you will cover the subject. Will your site be broadly focused and cover many topics related to computer games? Or will it be narrowly focused and cover very specific topics related to Multiuser Dimensions (MUDs)?

After you determine the focus, you should determine the level of detail for the site's subject matter. You could briefly discuss many topics or discuss a few topics at length. If you decide you want to cover a few specific topics at length, you may want to cover the topics on a single Web page. However, if you want to cover many topics at length, you may want to present your ideas on a series of pages with increasing levels of detail. For example, the initial page is an overview page discussing the popularity of Multiuser Dimensions. From this page readers can access other pages that discuss the features of specific MUDs in detail. From the detailed page, readers can access other pages that cover newsgroups, mailing lists, and Web sites related to a specific MUD, and so on. Pages set up in progressive levels of detail is the basic format for a Web site.

Defining the Audience for the Site

Developing a strategy with your audience in mind is also essential to your success, yet determining the group you want the work to reach is not always easy. On the Web, you can reach an extremely diverse global audience, and words written in your native language may be read by people from dozens of countries. A site that specifically focuses on resources for U.S. writers may exclude or alienate writers from dozens of other countries. A site written in Spanish may be read by native speakers from the many Spanish-speaking countries in the world or by the millions of people who speak Spanish as a second language.

TIP

Although English is the dominant language used on the Web, it is not the only language in use on the Web. Many European Web publishers create sites in several languages, and because of this, millions of people who otherwise couldn't enjoy the site can. If you are proficient in a second language, you may want to consider publishing your ideas in both your native and secondary language. You have nothing to lose and everything to gain by ensuring your publication can reach the largest audience possible.

As you consider the potential audience for your ideas, products, or services, focus on specifics of who, what, why, and how:

- Who are you trying to reach?
- What will this group of people be interested in?
- Why would they want to buy your product or service?
- How will you reach them?

Tell yourself you are creating a site for anyone interested in extreme sports who is between the ages of 16 and 35. Readers will be interested in your service because you are the only such service featuring excursions in the Australian outback and the mountains of New Zealand. You will reach readers by featuring a virtual tour and offering a two-for-one discount that is available only to Web surfers. Got the idea?

Defining the Site Structure

Before you start creating the actual markup for pages at your site, you should carefully consider how you will organize the site. Getting organized is extremely important. Not only will it save you time, it will help you create a better site. The quality of your site is what will convince Web users your site is worth visiting.

You can write out the initial structure for your site as an outline or simply as notes you scratch out during a brainstorming session. While you write down your ideas, focus on the purpose, scope, and audience you defined earlier. Key areas of the site you should concentrate on are

The site's home page—This page introduces the site to the world and should provide readers with a brief overview of what is ahead.

The main features of the site—Showcase the content of your site.

The hook—Give readers a reason to come back to your site.

After you develop the basic concept for your Web site, you may want to try to improve your ideas through freethinking, brainstorming, or storyboarding. These and other techniques for unleashing your creativity and better organizing your publications are explored in depth in Chapter 42, "Managing Large-Scale Projects."

Success in Good Organization

You must create a friendly Web site that continues to grow and change. Yet it won't be the size of your site that sells your ideas and products; it will be your vision and ability to find your place in the world community. Two major design concepts you will want to consider immediately are

- The general organization of your information
- The organization of your site's directories and files

Getting Organized

Whether you are thinking on a grand scale or a small scale, the organization of your information is the most important design issue in setting up a Web site. Carefully consider how you will organize your site. The power of Web publishing is that you can seamlessly integrate complex presentations. Behind those complex presentations are dozens, possibly hundreds, of individual pages that can contain text, images, and multimedia. The result can be either an unfriendly place to visit and a nightmare to maintain or, if organized properly, a friendly place to visit and a joy to maintain.

As the Web publisher, you are breathing life into an information infrastructure that may be seen by thousands, possibly millions, of users around the world. When this information infrastructure is in place, you should not haphazardly delete, rename, or rearrange this structure. If you delete, rename, or rearrange your site, not only will you frustrate users, but all links that were leading visitors to your site may become invalid.

NOTE

Your address URLs are the only thing leading visitors to your site. Readers save lists of their favorite places in their browser using a bookmark or hotlist feature. Some users may have published your link as a favorite site on their home page. Many readers also find new places to visit through the lists published by Web databases, and if your pages are in new locations, the reader may not be able to find your site.

Organizing Your Site's Directories and Files

Your site's directory and file structure can play a key role in helping you organize your ideas. Carefully consider how the outside world will regard the structure of your site. You can organize different types of information into directories. You can organize your site into directories that pertain to the projects or publications featured at the site. You can also organize the files within your directories into a logically named structure.

Directory Organization

The base directory of the site should pertain to the overall site or to the organization sponsoring the site. The best way to set up the base directory is to use an index or default page that pertains to the site as a whole. This default page will serve as your home page and will most likely be the first page visitors to your site see. The address URL for your base directory is usually something like this:

```
http://www.your_company.com/
```

or

```
http://www.your_service_provider.com/~you
```

In both cases, a browser accessing the URL would display the default page for your site. As the default page is usually named `index.html`, this means you will want to install a page called `index.html` in the appropriate directory on the Web server. If you are using an ISP's Web server with a virtual domain or an account with Web-publishing privileges, this directory is normally called `public_html` and is located under your user directory.

NOTE

If the `public_html` directory was not created by your service provider, you can easily create it. On a UNIX or DOS-based system, type the command:

```
mkdir public_html
```

The command shown above will make a directory called `public_html` for you. Before you type the command, you should ensure you are in your user directory. One way to do this on a UNIX system is to type the command `cd` on a line by itself as follows:

```
cd
```

Subdirectory Organization

A clear structure for your directories and files becomes increasingly important as your site grows. Hundreds of files in a single directory are difficult to track and maintain. Therefore, you should consider a subdirectory structure at an early stage in your Web site creation. Subdirectories at the site should be logically organized and could pertain to projects, publications, or departments within a company. For example, you could create a directory for each of your projects by category and develop the following structure:

BASE directory	Contains pages that pertain to your company. BASE refers to the default path to your pages, such as `/usr/httpd/docs`.
BOOK directory	Contains pages that pertain to your book-length projects.
BUS directory	Contains pages that pertain to business services you plan to provide.

Each subdirectory would be located under your base directory and could have its own default page associated with it. To access the default page within the BOOK directory, a user could use one of these URLs:

```
http://www.your_company.com/BOOK/
```

```
http://www.your_service_provider.com/~you/BOOK/
```

To access a page called `projects.html` within the BOOK directory, a user could use one of these URLs:

```
http://www.your_company.com/BOOK/projects.html
```

```
http://www.your_service_provider.com/~you/BOOK/projects.html
```

File Organization

Just as it is important to logically name directories, you should also logically name your files. Each file that pertains to a particular presentation could use an element of the project's name to relate it to the project. This is true even if you plan to put individual projects in their own directories and especially important when you plan to publish multiple projects that are closely related. A book publisher that planned to publish extracts of her books on the Web would not want to name the parts of the first book

```
page1.html
page2.html
page3.html
```

or

```
chapter1.html
chapter2.html
chapter3.html
```

A better naming scheme is to relate the parts of the project to the project itself, which will avoid confusion when publishing additional projects and make the site easier to maintain. Imagine a site with a dozen books that has identical names for the pages of the publications. What happens when the new employee you've hired moves pages 12 through 27 for your third book into the directory reserved for your first book?

To relate the parts of the project to the whole, you could prepend an abbreviation for the project or part of the project's title to the file names. For example, the title *Web Publishing Unleashed* could be abbreviated as WPU. You could then prepend the abbreviation to the component parts of the project as follows:

```
wpuch1index.html
wpuch1pg1.html
wpuch1pg2.html
wpuch1pg3.html
wpuch1title.gif
```

Creating the Web Site's Content

A Web site is much more than pages linked together. It is your home on the Web and, as such, it should contain doorways that reduce communications barriers and help spread your ideas to a global audience. Through step-by-step examples, the remainder of this chapter builds a killer Web site. You can use similar pages to form the basis of your Web site and save hours of work.

NOTE

Extreme Sports Hawaii is a fictitious business that I created for use in examples throughout *Web Publishing Unleashed, Professional Reference Edition*. Still, I thought it would be fun to publish this demo site so readers could see it live on the Web. You will find the site at:

```
http://www.tvp.com/writing/
```

Creating the Site's Home Page

The first doorway you will want to establish on the Web is the front door to your Web site, your home page. As the first thing most visitors to your site will see, your home page should be friendly and inviting.

Creating a friendly and inviting home page involves much more than hanging up a virtual welcome mat. It involves creating a well-organized page that reflects who you are and what you plan to do on the Web. The page should follow a sound design that provides an overview of what is available at the site. You can present an overview of content in many ways, but the best way to organize the overview is to make it a sneak preview of what visitors to the site can expect to find.

Your sneak preview can tell the world that you are dull and unimaginative, such as a home page organized like the table of contents you would find in a print publication. A home page organized in such a pure linear fashion may seem a logical way to go, but generally this design has only first-time visitors in mind. While you want to attract new visitors, you also want to attract repeat visitors. If McDonald's attracted only one-time customers, they never would have sold billions of hamburgers. The key in business, even if that business is not-for-profit, is to build a customer base, and you cannot build a customer base if your customers visit your site only once. Therefore, your sneak preview should tell the world this is a place to add to their hot list.

Your home page should grab the reader's attention immediately. The first thing visitors to the home page for Extreme Sports Hawaii (see Figure 49.1) see is an enticing image. The image serves a dual role. It creates a dramatic effect and is a clickable image linked to a contact page.

The remainder of the page provides a teaser to visitors and closes with a text link to the same contact page. This teaser information is given a unique style using a style element.

Ideally, a home page designed to grab the reader's attention will be updated often. You could also rotate a series of cool home pages on a daily basis. This ensures the home page is fresh and new every time the user visits. Listing 49.1 shows the HTML markup for the home page.

Listing 49.1. Home page for Extreme Sports Hawaii.

```
<HTML>
<HEAD>

<TITLE>Welcome to Extreme Sports Hawaii!</TITLE>

<STYLE>
H1  {font: 35pt Times;}
H2  {font: 14pt cursive;
     text-indent: .5in;
     margin-right: 1in;
     margin-left: .5in}
</STYLE>

</HEAD>

<BODY BGCOLOR="#000000" TEXT="#FF0000" LINK="#FF0000"
VLINK="#FF0000" ALINK="#000000">

<P ALIGN="CENTER">
<A HREF="contact.htm"><IMG SRC="lightn.jpg" BORDER="0" ALT=""></A>
</P>

<H2>&quot;In a world without the extreme days slip by one after
 another in boring endless succession. If you long to end the
 monotony, experience the extreme edge and change your life
forever.&quot; </H2>

<H1 ALIGN=CENTER>
<A HREF="contact.htm">More ...</A>
</H1>

</BODY>
</HTML>
```

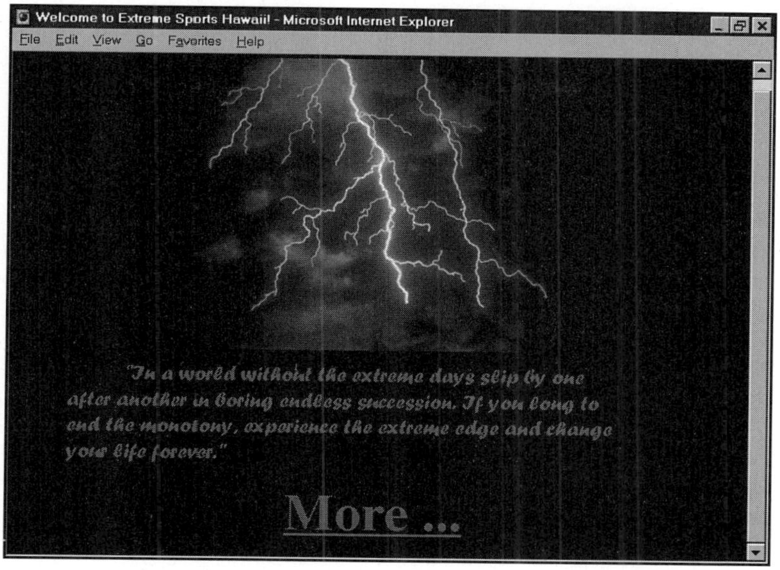

FIGURE 49.1.
Grab the reader's attention immediately with a powerful home page.

Adding a Room to Your Web Home

Your home on the Web should have many rooms. Filling those rooms with wonderful content is not always easy, especially when you have to choose which room to fill first. A new site should build its rooms a little at a time. You should start by building a solid framework for the site that tells the world who you are and what you plan to do. Show visitors you are dedicated to the development of a wonderful resource, and they will return to see how your site is progressing, even if it is in the early stages of development.

Designing a site with content for first-time and repeat visitors is extremely important in creating an inviting place to visit. Yet you also want your house on the Web to be a friendly place to visit. The friendliest sites on the Web are considerate of your time and present information in the right level of detail based on your location within the site.

When you click on the picture of lightning or follow the text link on the Extreme Sports Hawaii home page, you see the page shown in Figure 49.2. This page provides contact information for the business, which includes the address, phone number, and e-mail address. Linking the e-mail address to a `mailto` reference enables visitors to start a mail message in one step. All they need to do is click on the reference.

A background image is used to give the contact page style. Although the background image seems to float in the left margin, the actual image is 800 pixels wide and includes a wide white band that ensures the image will not be repeated both horizontally and vertically.

Although the colors of the image create a stunning contrast, you would not be able to read dark-colored text on the dark section of the background. Similarly, you would not be able to read light-colored text on the light section of the background. This posed a design problem that was solved by centering the elements on the page. As you can see from the figure, centering the text and graphics places them on the light section of the background. Examine Listing 49.2 to see how this was done.

Listing 49.2. Another room for the Web site.

```
<HTML>
<HEAD>

<TITLE>Extreme Sports</TITLE>

</HEAD>

<BODY BACKGROUND="BACK/contactbk.gif" LINK="#FF0000">

<DIV ALIGN=CENTER>

<H1>Extreme Sports Hawaii</H1>
<H3>5300 Kalekaua Honolulu, HI</H3>
<H3>(808) 555-1212</H3>
<H3>
<A HREF="mailto:sports@tvp.com">sports@maxedge.com</A>
</H3>

<P><I>&quot;Extreme to the max.&quot;</I></P>

<P>
<A HREF="vacation.htm" >
<IMG SRC="Surfbord.gif" BORDER=0>
<IMG SRC="Sail.gif" BORDER=0>
<IMG SRC="Surfing.gif" BORDER=0>
</A>
</P>

<H3 ALIGN="CENTER">
<A HREF="vacation.htm">Extreme Getaways You Can't Live Without!</A>
</H3>

</DIV>
</BODY>
</HTML>
```

FIGURE 49.2.
Providing contact information in style.

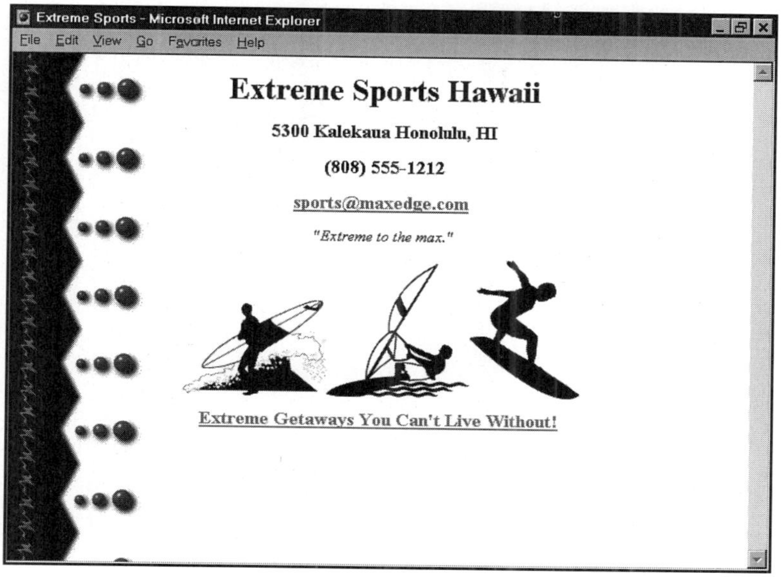

Ongoing Design Is Essential

The design of your site does not stop at your home page. The best sites on the Web have many special areas or mini-sites within the site. These mini-sites can be the star attractions with features that constantly change and grow.

The star attraction of the Extreme Sports Hawaii Web site is the page shown in Figure 49.3. The purpose of this page is to promote the vacation packages available. A fairly advanced style sheet is used to add pizzazz to the table shown at the top of the page. This style sheet uses two classes, which are attached to tags in the table. Sizing the table just right and combining it with a powerful graphic creates a promotional banner at the top of the page.

Visitors to the page can get customized information about a vacation package by clicking on an appropriate button control. This is handled by using VBScript to perform dynamic writes to the page. If visitors want information on downhill mountain biking, they click on the mountain-biking button and the page is updated as shown in Figure 49.4. If visitors want information on sky boarding, they click on the sky-boarding button and the page is updated as shown in Figure 49.5. If visitors want information on a surfing package, they click on the surfing combo button and the page is updated as shown in Figure 49.6. To see how the information page was created, examine Listing 49.3.

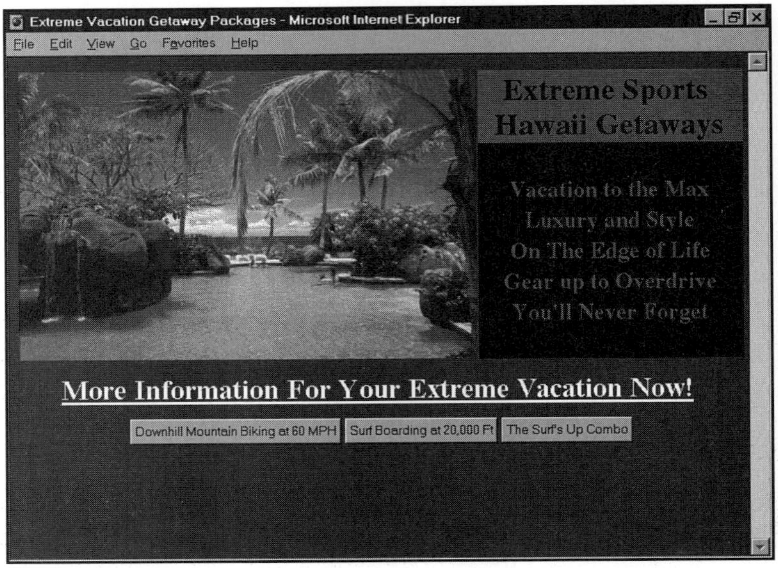

FIGURE 49.3.
Enhancing product pages with style sheets and VBScript.

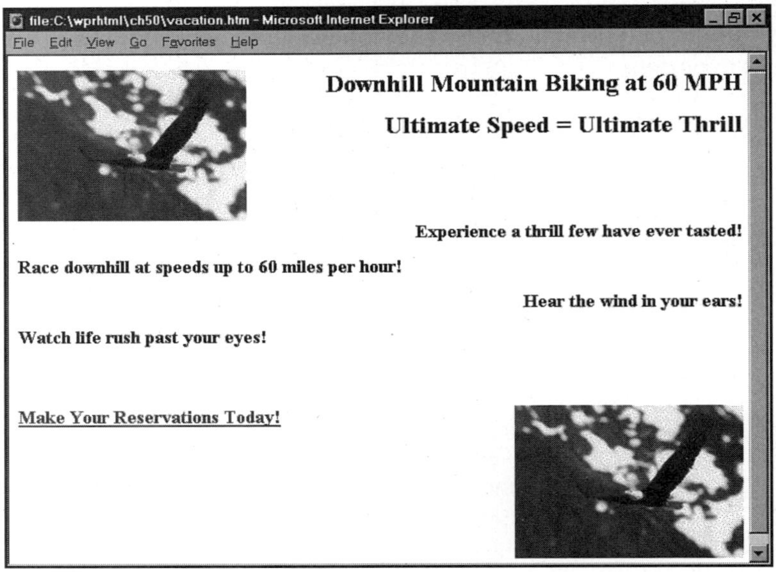

FIGURE 49.4.
Getting information on mountain biking.

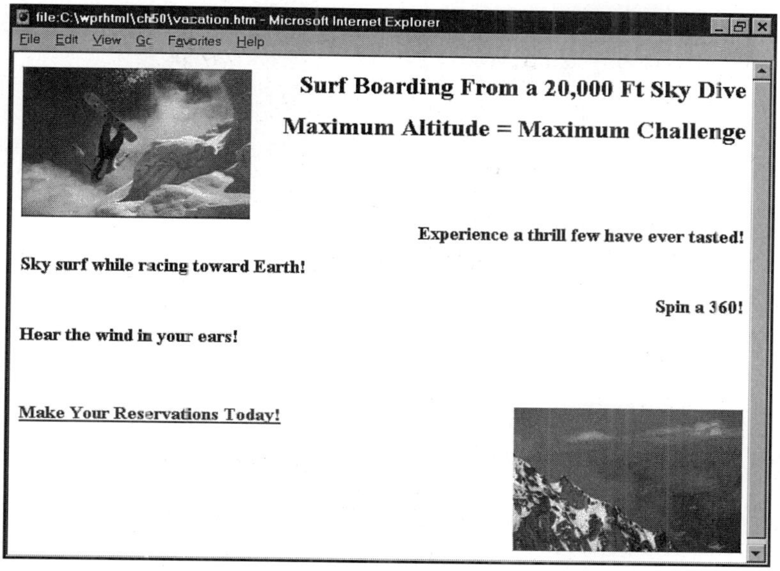

FIGURE 49.5.
Getting information on sky boarding.

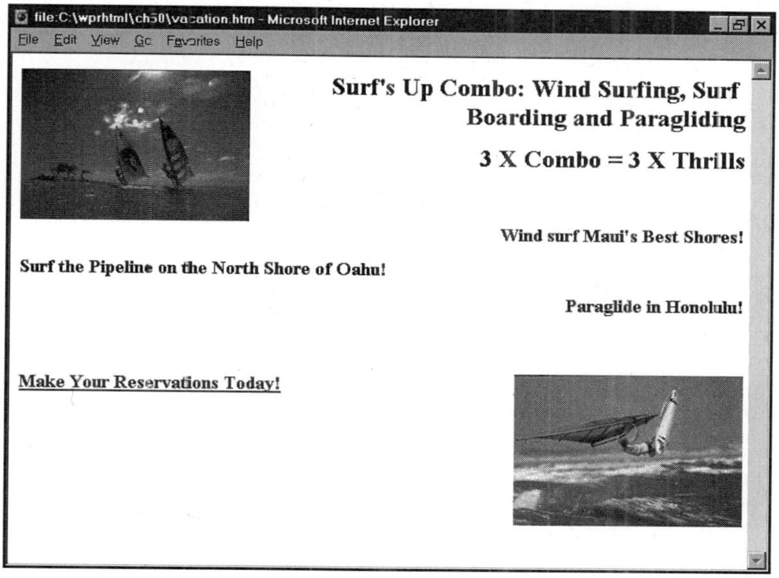

FIGURE 49.6.
Getting information on a surf, sail, and sun combo.

Listing 49.3. Providing vacation information.

```
<HTML>
<HEAD>
<TITLE>Extreme Vacation Getaway Packages</TITLE>

<STYLE>
.classB  {font: 20pt Times;
               color: black;
               background: red;
               margin: .1in}
.classA  {font: 15pt Times;
               font-weight: bold;
               color: red;
               background: black;
               margin: .15in}
H2 { font: 30 pt Times; color: white}

</STYLE>

</HEAD>

<BODY BGCOLOR="Blue" LINK="#FFFFFF">

<IMG SRC="hawaii2.jpg" ALIGN="LEFT" BORDER="0">

<TABLE>
<TR><TH CLASS=classB>Extreme Sports Hawaii Getaways</TH>
<TR><TH  CLASS=classA> </TH>
<TR><TH  CLASS=classA>Vacation to the Max</TH>
<TR><TH  CLASS=classA>Luxury and Style</TH>
<TR><TH  CLASS=classA>On The Edge of Life</TH>
<TR><TH  CLASS=classA>Gear up to Overdrive</TH>
<TR><TH  CLASS=classA>You'll Never Forget</TH>
<TR><TH  CLASS=classA> </TH>
</TABLE>

<BR CLEAR=ALL>

<DIV ALIGN=CENTER>

<H2 ALIGN=CENTER>
<A HREF="info.htm">More Information For Your Extreme Vacation Now!</A>
</H2>

<P>
<INPUT TYPE=BUTTON VALUE="Downhill Mountain Biking at 60 MPH"
➥NAME="m1Vacation">
<INPUT TYPE=BUTTON VALUE="Surf Boarding at 20,000 Ft" NAME="s1Vacation">
<INPUT TYPE=BUTTON VALUE="The Surf's Up Combo" NAME="s2Vacation">
</P>

</DIV>

<SCRIPT LANGUAGE="VBScript">
<!-- Option Explicit

Sub m1Vacation_OnClick()

document.write "<BODY BGCOLOR=White>"
document.write "<IMG SRC=eagle.jpg ALIGN=LEFT BORDER=0>"
```

```
document.write "<H2 ALIGN=RIGHT>Downhill Mourtain Biking at 60 MPH</H2>"
document.write "<H2 ALIGN=RIGHT>Ultimate Speed = Ultimate Thrill</H2>"
document.write "<BR CLEAR=ALL>"
document.write "<H3 ALIGN=Right>Experience a thrill few have ever tasted!</H3>"
document.write "<H3 ALIGN=Left> Race downhill at speeds up to
➥60 miles per hour!</H3>"
document.write "<H3 ALIGN=Right>Hear the wind in your ears!</H3>"
document.write "<H3 ALIGN=Left>Watch life rush past your eyes!</H3>"
document.write "<P> </P>"
document.write "<BR CLEAR=ALL>"
document.write "<IMG SRC=eagle.jpg ALIGN=RIGHT BORDER=0>"
document.write "<H3 ALIGN=LEFT><A HREF=order.htm>Make Your Reservations
➥Today!</A></H3>"

End Sub

Sub s1Vacation_OnClick()

document.write "<BODY BGCOLOR=White>"
document.write "<IMG SRC=airborne.jpg ALIGN=LEFT BORDER=0>"
document.write "<H2 ALIGN=RIGHT>Surf Boarding From a 20,000 Ft Sky Dive</H2>"
document.write "<H2 ALIGN=RIGHT>Maximum Altitude = Maximum Challenge</H2>"
document.write "<BR CLEAR=ALL>"
document.write "<H3 ALIGN=Right>Experience a thrill few have ever tasted!</H3>"
document.write "<H3 ALIGN=Left> Sky surf while racing toward Earth!</H3>"
document.write "<H3 ALIGN=Right>Spin a 360!</H3>"
document.write "<H3 ALIGN=Left>Hear the wind in your ears!</H3>"
document.write "<P> </P>"
document.write "<BR CLEAR=ALL>"
document.write "<IMG SRC=chute.jpg ALIGN=RIGHT BORDER=0>"
document.write "<H3 ALIGN=LEFT><A HREF=order.htm>Make Your Reservations
➥Today!</A></H3>"

End Sub

Sub s2Vacation_OnClick()

document.write "<BODY BGCOLOR=White>"
document.write "<IMG SRC=sail.jpg ALIGN=LEFT BORDER=0>"
document.write "<H2 ALIGN=RIGHT>Surf's Up Combo: Wind Surfing, Surf Boarding
➥and Paragliding</H2>"
document.write "<H2 ALIGN=RIGHT>3 X Combo = 3 X Thrills</H2>"
document.write "<BR CLEAR=ALL>"
document.write "<H3 ALIGN=Right>Wind surf Maui's Best Shores!</H3>"
document.write "<H3 ALIGN=Left> Surf the Pipeline on the North
➥Shore of Oahu!</H3>"
document.write "<H3 ALIGN=Right>Paraglide in Honolulu!</H3>"
document.write "<P> </P>"
document.write "<BR CLEAR=ALL>"
document.write "<IMG SRC=power.jpg ALIGN=RIGHT BORDER=0>"
document.write "<H3 ALIGN=LEFT><A HREF=order.htm>Make Your
➥Reservations Today!</A></H3>"

End Sub

-->
</SCRIPT>

</BODY>
</HTML>
```

Advanced Linking of Your Pages

The linking of pages at your Web site is extremely important. The more navigation mechanisms you provide within the site, the easier it will be for visitors to find their way around.

Your site should follow a flowing design, with multiple routes through the information infrastructure you have created. Readers should be able to advance from overview pages to more detailed pages within your site. They should also be able to go back to your home page and start a new search from any level within the site.

Realize from the start that the structure of the Web is such that readers can enter your site at any level, and you will have a head start on many Web publishers. I don't know how many times I have come across a Web page that gives me no indication of where the page is within the information infrastructure at the site. The worst of these pages become dead-end streets, with no way to return to the site's home page and no way to access any other information at the site. Finding a dead-end street on the Web is frustrating, to say the least, but the reason the dead-end street exists is that its creators lacked foresight. They either thought that all visitors would access the site starting from the front door, or they just never stopped to think about the consequences of creating such a page.

As the Web gets increasingly advanced, good linking becomes increasingly important. To understand why, take another look at the promotional page for vacation packages offered by Extreme Sports Hawaii. Instead of looking at the page in a browser that supports the advanced features used, look at the page in a browser that does not support these features (shown in Figure 49.7).

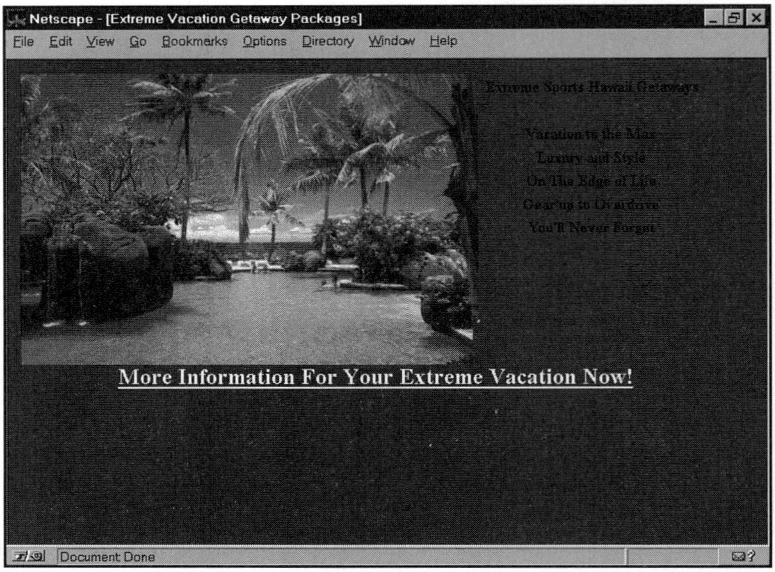

FIGURE 49.7.
The vacation page viewed in a different browser.

The difference between what you see in Figure 49.7 and what you saw in Figure 49.3 is so dramatic that it seems you are seeing two different pages. The customized table with style enhancements is displayed as an ordinary table, and the button controls are gone—vanished because they aren't supported by this browser. If I hadn't designed the page knowing this might happen, the result could have been a dead-end page. Instead, to ensure the table remained readable and distinct beside the image, I used data header tags, which ensures the table data is centered and displayed in bold. I also included a text link that readers could follow for more information. Without this link, the vacation page would lead nowhere. Instead, the vacation page leads to the page shown in Figure 49.8. Listing 49.4 shows the markup for the page.

Listing 49.4. A vacation information page for browsers that don't support VBScript.

```
<HTML>
<HEAD>

<TITLE>Thrill-A-Minute Vacation Extremes</TITLE>

</HEAD>
<BODY BGCOLOR=#FFFFFF LINK="#FF0000">

<DIV ALIGN=CENTER>

<H2>Learn About Our Vacations Today!</H2>
<H3>
<A HREF="#one">Downhill Mountain Biking at 60 MPH</A> ¦¦
<A HREF="#two">Sky Boarding at 20,000 Ft</A> ¦¦
<A HREF="#three">Surfs Up Combo</A>
</H3>
<HR NOSHADE SIZE=10 WIDTH=80%>

</DIV>

<IMG SRC=eagle.jpg ALIGN=LEFT BORDER=0>
<H2 ALIGN=RIGHT><A NAME="one">Downhill Mountain Biking at 60 MPH</A></H2>
<H2 ALIGN=RIGHT>Ultimate Speed = Ultimate Thrill</H2>

<BR CLEAR=ALL>

<H3 ALIGN=Right>Experience a thrill few have ever tasted!</H3>
<H3 ALIGN=Right> Race downhill at speeds up to 60 miles per hour!</H3>
<H3 ALIGN=Right>Hear the wind in your ears!</H3>
<H3 ALIGN=Right>Watch life rush past your eyes!</H3>
<P> </P>

<BR CLEAR=ALL>

<IMG SRC=eagle.jpg ALIGN=RIGHT BORDER=0>
<H3 ALIGN=LEFT><A HREF=order2.htm>Make Your Reservations Today!</A></H3>

<BR CLEAR=ALL>
<HR NOSHADE SIZE=10>
```


continues

Listing 49.4. continued

```
<IMG SRC=airborne.jpg ALIGN=LEFT BORDER=0>

<H2 ALIGN=RIGHT><A NAME="two">Surf Boarding From a 20,000 Ft Sky Dive</A></H2>
<H2 ALIGN=RIGHT>Maximum Altitude = Maximum Challenge</H2>

<BR CLEAR=ALL>

<H3 ALIGN=Right>Experience a thrill few have ever tasted!</H3>
<H3 ALIGN=Right> Sky surf while racing toward Earth!</H3>
<H3 ALIGN=Right>Spin a 360!</H3>
<H3 ALIGN=Right>Hear the wind in your ears!</H3>
<P> </P>

<BR CLEAR=ALL>

<IMG SRC=chute.jpg ALIGN=RIGHT BORDER=0>

<H3 ALIGN=Left><A HREF=order2.htm>Make Your Reservations Today!</A></H3>

<BR CLEAR=ALL>
<HR NOSHADE SIZE=10>

<IMG SRC=sail.jpg ALIGN=LEFT BORDER=0>

<H2 ALIGN=RIGHT><A NAME="three">Surf's Up Combo: Wind Surfing,
Surf Boarding and Paragliding</A></H2>
<H2 ALIGN=RIGHT>3 X Combo = 3 X Thrills</H2>

<BR CLEAR=ALL>

<H3 ALIGN=Right>Wind surf Maui's Best Shores!</H3>
<H3 ALIGN=Right> Surf the Pipeline on the North Shore of Oahu!</H3>
<H3 ALIGN=Right>Paraglide in Honolulu!</H3>
<P> </P>

<BR CLEAR=ALL>

<IMG SRC=power.jpg ALIGN=RIGHT BORDER=0>

<H3 ALIGN=LEFT><A HREF=order2.htm>Make Your Reservations Today!</A></H3>

<BR CLEAR=ALL>
<HR NOSHADE SIZE=10>

</BODY>
</HTML>
```

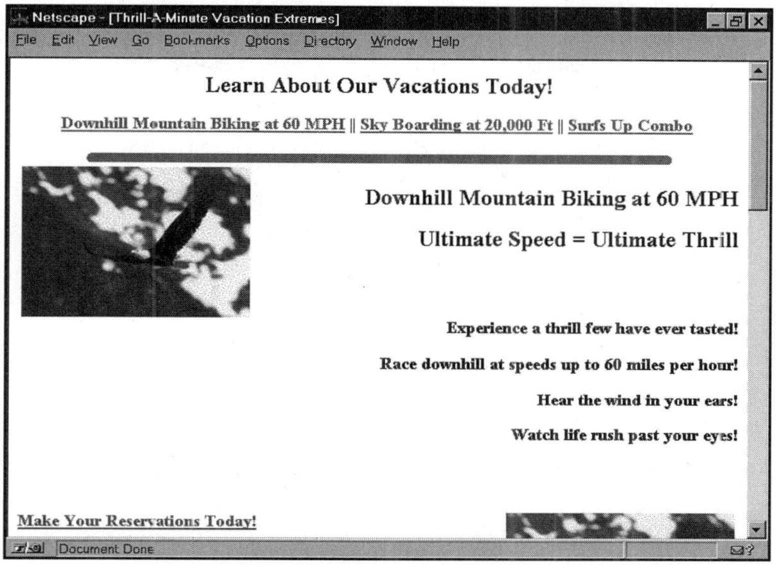

FIGURE 49.8.
A product information page for those who can't use VBScript.

Providing Alternative Paths Through the Site

Now that you know visitors to your site may use different browsers, you can take advantage of this by providing alternative paths through your site for users with different browsers. The traditional way to do this is to place links on the home page that lead to pages designed for different browsers. On some sites, you will find that the home page has links to text-only pages, graphics pages, pages designed for Netscape Navigator, and even separate pages designed for Internet Explorer. These sites create up to five different sets of pages, which means you have to redesign every page as many as five times.

Not only is redesigning a page five different times a tremendous waste of effort, it is not necessary if you understand how HTML and browsers work together. Because users can, and do, turn off the graphics-loading capability of their browsers if they don't want to see graphics, there is no need for separate text-only and graphics pages. All right, maybe the publisher is creating pages for users with a text-only browser such as Lynx. Well, if you've used Lynx, you know the browser inserts the alternative text you provide where the image should be. So instead of creating text-only pages, add alternative text to your image tags when it makes sense to do so. Or better yet, you can get rid of the possibly annoying [Image] reference by defining your image tag as follows:

```
<IMG SOURCE="myImage.gif" ALT="">
```

Creating separate pages for users with advanced browsers isn't necessary either. One way to clearly and easily ensure users with advanced browsers see advanced pages is with frames. Even if you don't want to create multiple windows for a document, you can use frames to provide distinct pages for users with advanced browsers like Internet Explorer and standard browsers like Mosaic. Here is how you can do this:

```
<FRAMESET ROWS="100%%">
<FRAMESET  COLS="100%">
<FRAME SRC="myAdvancedPage.htm">
</FRAMESET>
<NOFRAME>
   Insert markup for standard browsers here.
</NOFRAME>
```

Another way to create pages for both standard and advanced browsers is to follow sound design techniques that ensure your pages are always usable. You do this by designing your pages for all types of browsers—like I did for the vacation page—and providing alternative paths only when necessary.

Because I knew users with advanced browsers would see the dynamic updates to the vacation page, I included a link in the updates that leads to the VBScript-enhanced order page you see in Figure 49.9 and Figure 49.10. This page contains intrinsic HTML controls that will not work in a standard browser. Yet because there is text on the page related to these controls, it is best to ensure that readers with a standard browser do not access this page.

The script on the order page lets visitors see how much a vacation package is going to cost based on the number of people in the party and the length of vacation. Visitors can then submit an order form with their name, address, and phone number. Examine Listing 49.5 to see how this was done.

Listing 49.5. Getting orders online using VBScript.

```
<HTML>
<HEAD>
<TITLE>Make Reservations Today!</TITLE>

<STYLE>
H1  {font: 35pt Times;
     color: blue}
P  {font: 12pt Times;
    color: red;
    text-indent: .5in;
    margin-right: 1in}
</STYLE>

</HEAD>

<BODY BGCOLOR="#FFFFFF">

<H1>
<IMG SRC="power.jpg" ALIGN=LEFT>
Extreme Sports Hawaii Getaways
<IMG SRC="power.jpg" ALIGN=RIGHT>
```

```
</H1>

<BR CLEAR=LEFT>

<H2>Going to the Extreme on a Budget</H2>

<P>To determine the cost of your getaway, enter the order number
 of days you want to stay followed by the number of people in your
 party. Residents of Hawaii must pay an additional sales tax of 7%.</P>

<CENTER>
<HR SIZE=5 NOSHADE WIDTH=80%>
</CENTER>

<PRE>
      Number of days: <INPUT NAME="tripDays" SIZE=3>
    Number of people: <INPUT NAME="tripSize" SIZE=3>
  State of residence: <INPUT NAME="resState" SIZE=2>
</PRE>

<P><INPUT TYPE=BUTTON VALUE="How much to get away from it all
and go to the extreme?" NAME="cmdCost"></P>

<PRE>
    Sub Total                $<INPUT NAME="tripCost" SIZE=10>
    Sales Tax (7% HI only)   $<INPUT NAME="tripTax" SIZE=10>

    Total                    $<INPUT NAME="tripTotal" SIZE=10>
</PRE>

<CENTER>
<HR SIZE=5 NOSHADE WIDTH=80%>
</CENTER>

<FORM NAME="frmOrder" ACTION="http://www.yourserver.com/order.pl"
METHOD="GET" LANGUAGE="VBScript" OnSubmit="SubmitOrder">

<P>Full Name: <INPUT NAME="custName" SIZE=30></P>
<P>Phone Number: <INPUT NAME="custPhone" SIZE=15></P>
<P>Address: <TEXTAREA NAME="custAddress" ROWS=3 COLUMNS=30></TEXTAREA></P>

<P><INPUT TYPE="BUTTON" NAME="custOrder" VALUE="Make Your Reservations!"></P>
</FORM>

<HR SIZE=5>
<P ALIGN=CENTER>
<A HREF="index.htm">Extreme Home Page</A> ¦¦
<A HREF="contact.htm">Contact Information</A> ¦¦
<A HREF="vacation.htm">Vacation Packages</A>
</P>

<SCRIPT LANGUAGE="VBScript">
<!-- Option Explicit

dim addCrLf : addCrLf = Chr(13) & Chr(10) & Chr(13) & Chr(10)

   Sub cmdCost_OnClick()

Dim State
```

continues

Listing 49.5. continued

```
Dim tripLength
Dim tripParty
Dim Cost
Dim Tax
Dim Total

tripLength = tripDays.Value
tripParty = tripSize.Value
State = resState.Value

If Len(tripLength) = 0 Then
    MsgBox "Please enter the length of your getaway."
    Exit Sub
End If

If Len(tripParty) = 0 Then
    MsgBox "Please enter the number of people in your party."
    Exit Sub
End If

Cost = 75.00 * tripLength * tripParty

If State = "HI" Then
     Tax = Cost * 0.07
Else
     Tax = 0
End If

Total = Cost + Tax

tripCost.Value = Cost
tripTax.Value = Tax
tripTotal.Value = Total

End Sub

Sub custOrder_OnClick

If Len(document.frmOrder.custName.value) = 0 then

     Alert "Please enter your full name in the area provided."
     Exit Sub

End If

If Len(document.frmOrder.custAddress.value) = 0 then

     Alert "Please enter your address in the area provided."
     Exit Sub

End If

     Msgbox "Click the OK button to confirm."
     document.frmOrder.Submit
```

```
End Sub

-->
</SCRIPT>

</BODY>
</HTML>
```

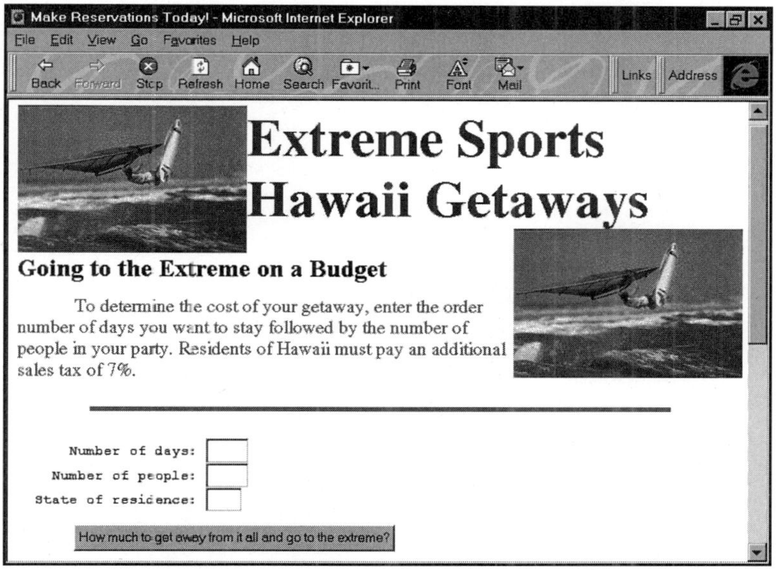

FIGURE 49.9.
Enabling visitors to estimate the cost of their vacations.

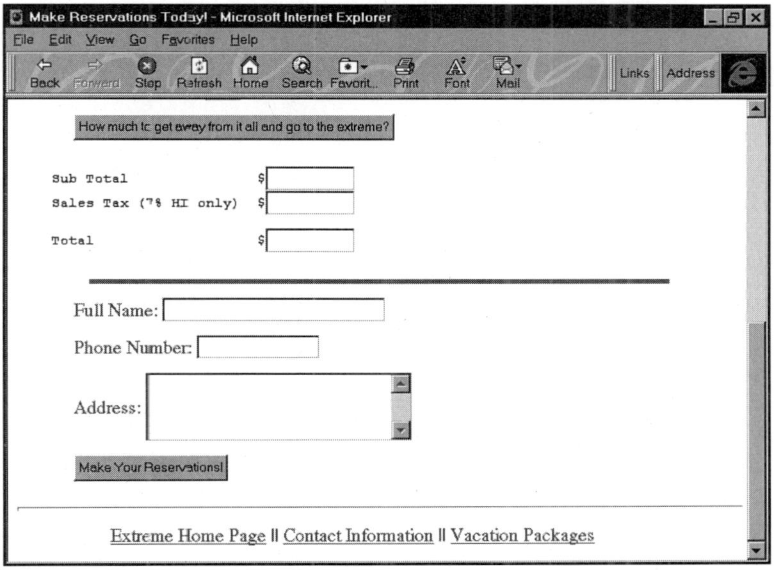

FIGURE 49.10.
Verifying orders with VBScript before submitting them to a server.

As you know, visitors to the Extreme Sports Hawaii Web site who cannot access VBScript enhancements can follow a link to the information page shown in Figure 49.8. This page provides information about vacation packages. Because these visitors should not access the VBScript-enhanced order form, links on the information page lead to the more traditional order form seen in Figure 49.11. Listing 49.6 shows the markup for this page.

Listing 49.6. An order page for browsers that don't support VBScript.

```
<HTML>
<HEAD>
<TITLE>Make Your Reservations Today!</TITLE>
</HEAD>
<BODY BGCOLOR="#FFFFFF">

<H1>
<IMG SRC="power.jpg" ALIGN=LEFT>
Extreme Sports Hawaii Getaways
<IMG SRC="power.jpg" ALIGN=RIGHT>
</H1>

<BR CLEAR=LEFT><H2>Going to the Extreme on a Budget</H2>

<P>Submit the order form and we'll send you detailed information on
vacation packages ideally suited to your needs.</P>

<FORM METHOD="POST" ACTION="http://www.yourserver.com/order.pl">
<PRE>
      Number of days: <INPUT TYPE=TEXT NAME="tripDays" SIZE=3>
    Number of people: <INPUT TYPE=TEXT NAME="tripSize" SIZE=3>
  State of residence: <INPUT TYPE=TEXT NAME="resState" SIZE=2>
           Full Name: <INPUT TYPE=TEXT NAME="custName" SIZE=30>
        Phone Number: <INPUT TYPE=TEXT NAME="custPhone" SIZE=15>
             Address: <TEXTAREA NAME="custAddress" ROWS=2 COLUMNS=30>
</TEXTAREA>
</PRE>

<P><INPUT TYPE=BUTTON VALUE=RESET><INPUT TYPE=BUTTON VALUE=SUBMIT></P>
</FORM>

<HR SIZE=5>
<P ALIGN=CENTER>
<A HREF="index.htm">Extreme Home Page</A> ¦¦
<A HREF="contact.htm">Contact Information</A> ¦¦
<A HREF="vacation.htm">Vacation Packages</A>
</P>

</BODY>
</HTML>
```

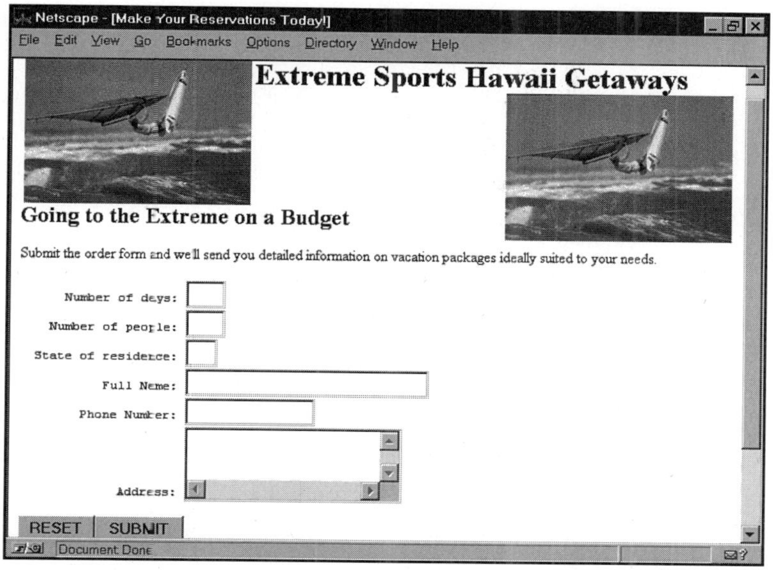

FIGURE 49.11.
An order page for browsers that can't use VBScript.

Proofing Your Web Pages

Proofing is the most neglected aspect of Web publishing. Time and time again I see Web pages with multiple typos and formatting inconsistencies—even at major sites. Pages with glaring typos and inconsistencies reflect poorly on you and your Web-publishing practices.

Proofing is neglected in Web publishing primarily because of the ease with which ideas and words can be published electronically. You can create a page in your word processor or editor and publish it on the Web within minutes after you've finished—even seconds, if you are quick enough. You do not have to spend hours checking spelling and grammar and generally pouring over every punctuation mark on the page, worrying if you have missed something glaringly obvious that is going to cost you a fortune to reprint 10,000 copies. If you make a mistake, you just open the file, correct the mistake, and republish your masterpiece on the Web for the world to see. Right?

Wrong. The quality of your work is a direct reflection on you. Thousands, and possibly millions, of people around the world are going to see your published page. Isn't it worth a few hours of your time to ensure days, weeks, or months of hard work gets the credibility it deserves?

Here are a few tips to help you better proof your Web pages:

- Use spelling and grammar checkers to find the tedious errors, the typos or grammar mistakes you made because you were hurrying to meet a deadline, worn out from long hours at the keyboard, or otherwise.
- Never rely solely on spelling and grammar checkers to find the critical errors; load the page in your browser and read it several times, noting typos or inconsistencies you need to correct.
- For long documents or lengthy projects, reading the document three times, looking for specific problems each time, is often helpful. The first time you proofread, focus on the look of the document, and if you find formatting inconsistencies, missing or misplaced items, correct them. The second time you proofread, check the logic and flow of ideas and words. The third time you proof, scrutinize all the text on the document and check syntax, spelling, capitalization, and punctuation.
- Always check images, figures, and charts on your page. Not only do you want to ensure they are consistent with your textual references, but you also want to check any text that may be included in the graphics. You should even check images you believe do not contain text. You might be surprised to find text and greatly relieved when you find and fix a typo you otherwise would have missed.

Some typos and inconsistencies slip by—the dragon wins every once in a while. But if you find an error after you have already published your page, correct it.

Testing Your Web Pages

Testing all aspects of your Web page before you publish is crucial. At this stage in your Web-publishing operation, you will want to focus on the accuracy of your links and HTML markup. However, as you add features like images and multimedia, you should test these features as well.

Testing Your Links

The easiest way to test links is to load the page in your browser and click on the links one at a time. You will want to ensure that all internal page links access the appropriate section that corresponds to the keyword you have designated. Watch out for multiple sections of the page labeled with the same keyword; this can produce strange results. If you know that a section of your publication is labeled with a certain keyword and the browser jumps to a different section of the page, check the keyword label in the section the browser displays. You probably mislabeled the keyword.

You will also want to ensure all links to other documents are valid and access the appropriate page. If you cannot access a page that you are sure should be available, check the syntax of your links. Did you specify the protocol correctly? Did you use the correct file name extension? Did you forget the tilde (~) symbol?

NOTE

In UNIX, the tilde symbol is used to specify the home directory of a user whose system name follows the tilde. Using the tilde symbol in a URL, you can refer to the Web pages in the user's home directory as follows:

```
http://www.aloha.com/~william/vphp.html
```

The Web server servicing this request would know to look in my home directory for the file called `vphp.html`. Although Web pages are typically in a directory called `public_html` under the user's directory, Web servers know that when you use a tilde in a URL, you are referring to the directory containing the user's Web pages. The process of inferring a directory using the tilde is called *mapping*.

Troubleshooting Problems in Your Web Pages

You've created a wonderful page, but for some reason it just doesn't look right. Troubleshooting problems in your page can be difficult, especially because you created the code and have a mental picture of what you meant to type in your mind's eye. This section contains tips to help you solve common problems. Most problems with your page can be directly attributed to errors in the structure of the page's markup code. Syntax is critically important in HTML. The four most common syntax problems involve the following:

- The tag enclosure set < >
- Pairing of HTML tags
- The double-quotation marks " "
- Nesting of tags

Troubleshooting: This Tag Format Goes On and On

Wait a minute, you say, how come half the text of the page looks like a heading? A tag format that goes on longer than it should is usually caused by one of the following:

- An improperly formed end tag, meaning one of your tags is missing the < or > character
- A missing end tag
- A mismatched pair of HTML tags

A closing tag that is missing the < or > symbol will not be properly interpreted by your browser. As a result, the format will not end until the browser finds a matching end tag. This can cause a section of the text to be displayed in the wrong format. If this element is a header, all text between the associated header opening tag and a matching closing tag will be displayed as a heading. If this element is anchor text, all text between the start of the anchor text and a matching closing tag will be displayed as underlined anchor text.

A missing end tag and a mismatched pair of tags will cause a problem similar to the one already described. Sometimes these problems are difficult to trace because you check the page where the problem ends and find nothing wrong. Don't look where the problem ends; look where it begins. After loading the HTML code for the page in your editor or word processor, go through the code to the section of the page where the begin tag associated with the problem is located and trace the problem forward from there. Tracing the problem forward instead of backward is especially useful when the page contains multiple format problems.

Troubleshooting: There's Text Missing from the Page

Wait a minute, you say, how come half the page is missing? Missing text or objects can usually be traced to those pesky double quotation marks and to misclosed tags that contain URLs. If your page has a " inside a tag, the closing " must be present to avoid potential problems. A tag with a missing double quotation mark may not be properly interpreted by older browsers, and this can produce strange results. If the tag missing the double quotation mark is an anchor tag, all text from the first double quotation mark to the next double quotation mark—no matter where it is located in the text—could be interpreted by your browser as part of an address URL. Address URLs are not displayed on the screen unless you move your mouse pointer to the associated anchor text.

Another problem that may cause missing text is a misclosed tag containing an URL. If a tag containing an URL is not closed properly, your browser could interpret any text following the tag up to the next properly closed tag as part of the URL. This problem is especially difficult to track because, whereas the text following the image will not be displayed, the image with the misclosed tag will often be displayed.

Missing text is also difficult to trace because the problem may seem sporadic. Some browsers, primarily older browsers, display the page with missing text. Others browsers, primarily newer browsers, display the page with no problems. This can make tracking down the source of the problem difficult. Again, don't look where the problem ends—look where the problem begins. After loading the HTML code in your editor or word processor, look at tags that occur before the missing section of text. This should be either the first tag you find with a double quotation mark or URL as you work your way down from the top of the page, or a tag with a double quotation mark that displayed correctly on the page and occurs immediately before the missing section.

NOTE

Any quotation marks you use must be standard ASCII double quotation marks. Some word processors have so-called smart quotes, where the opening quotes look different from closing quotes. If your word processor has this feature, disable it. Smart quotes are not standard ASCII and will not work in your HTML pages.

Troubleshooting: The Format I Want Just Won't Display

Wait a minute, you say, everything looks okay, I've fixed all the bugs, but my browser still won't display the third sentence in bold face. This problem can usually be traced to your browser or to the code. You may want to check your browser's compatibility with character styles. Your browser must be capable of displaying the physical style you have selected. Additionally, when displaying logical styles, the browser ultimately makes the decision about what style to display your text in. A quick way to check to see if you have a compatibility or code problem is to display your page using a different browser. This browser should preferably be one that you know supports the specific style you are trying to use. If the compatible browser won't display the text the way you want, check the code.

The problem in the code could be related to invalid nesting of tags. After loading the HTML code in your editor or word processor, check the section of the page associated with the formatting and ensure all tags are used in parallel fashion. Although you can place the beginning and ending tags for an element fully inside another pair of tags, the tags may not overlap. The emphasis tags overlap with the strong emphasis tags and will cause problems:

```
<EM>Thank you for visiting<STRONG>The Virtual Press</EM></STRONG>
```

The right way to use these tags is to use them in parallel fashion, as follows:

```
<EM>Thank you for visiting<STRONG>The Virtual Press</STRONG></EM>
```

Publishing Your Web Site

The moment of truth has arrived, and you are finally ready to publish the Web site. To publish your Web site, all you need to do is to move your pages to the appropriate directory, either on the Web server or within the public HTML directory of your account. Always contact the server administrator if you are not sure where to put your files.

To publish your Web page, you need access to a Web server. After you have access to a Web server (either through an Internet service provider or your own Web server), you are ready to publish your finished page.

Publishing your Web site is as easy as:

- Checking the names of your files
- Moving your files to appropriate directories
- Checking the mode of the files
- Troubleshooting if necessary

Checking the Names of Your Files

When moving files between different types of platforms, you will want to check the file name to ensure it is appropriate for the system you are moving the file to. Some systems restrict the length of file names. Other systems are case-sensitive, meaning a file with a name in uppercase letters becomes a different file if saved in lowercase letters.

When moving from a DOS/Windows system to a UNIX or Macintosh system, watch out for these potential problems:

- Although DOS file names must be only eight characters long with a three-character extension, some systems do not recognize files with an `.htm` extension as an HTML document. Therefore, after moving your file to the UNIX or Mac system, change the `.htm` extension to `.html`. For example, change `home.htm` to `home.html`. This will ensure the UNIX or Mac Web server will recognize your file as an HTML document.
- Although your file name may have appeared in all uppercase letters on the DOS system, the file name on the UNIX system will likely be in lowercase letters. UNIX systems are case-sensitive and you must reference file names in the appropriate case in your links.

When moving from a Macintosh or UNIX system to a DOS/Windows system, be aware of these differences:

- Before moving your file to a DOS/Windows machine, the file must be renamed to conform to DOS naming conventions. DOS file names must be only eight characters long with a three-character extension. If, for example, your file was called `my_home_document.html`, you could change the name to `homedoc.htm`.
- Watch out for wildcard characters in file names. Whereas on a Macintosh or UNIX system you can use wildcard characters when naming files, you cannot use wildcard characters on a DOS machine.

Moving Your Files

The first step in publishing your page is to move your file to a directory designated for Web pages. Although this directory may reside on the Web server, typically it is mapped to a subdirectory in your home directory called `public_html`. If you are using a Web server someone else has installed, contact the server administrator to find out where to put your pages.

TIP

A mapped directory contains pointers to directories where the actual files reside. Web servers usually map directories to a subdirectory in a user's home directory that you can point to using the tilde followed by the user's system name. Setting up a Web server to map requests is easy. On most servers, your service provider or system administrator can enable this feature by setting a variable called `UserDir` to the subdirectory that will be mapped to users' home directories, such as:

```
UserDir      public_html
```

If this variable is set as shown, requests to `http://www.your_provider.com/~you` would be mapped to the subdirectory called `public_html` in your account, and a Web page called `home.html` could be accessed with the following URL:

```
http://www.your_provider.com/~you/home.html
```

Moving your files to the Web server, or to an Internet account from your home or office system, is easy. The two most common methods to transfer the files are File Transfer Protocol (FTP) and modem transfer.

Using FTP

FTP is a quick and easy way to transfer files, especially if you are transferring files between UNIX systems. The best way to transfer files using FTP is to initiate a binary file transfer. In this way, you do not have to worry about which files are binary and which files aren't.

To start a binary transfer, you could type the following at the shell command prompt:

```
ftp hostname
bin
```

You can transfer multiple files between systems using the `mget` and `mput` commands. You use `mget` to retrieve multiple files from the host you are connected to using FTP, and `mput` to send multiple files to the host you are connected to using FTP. When you are transferring multiple files between systems, another useful FTP command to know is `prompt`. Without toggling the prompt to the off position, your system will prompt you before sending or retrieving each file. Here's how you could toggle the prompt to the off position (if it was on), retrieve all files that start with music, and then quit:

```
ftp aloha.com
bin
prompt
cd /users/music/fun_stuff
mget music*
quit
```

Modem Transfer

Many modem-transfer protocols can be used to transfer files. Some popular transfer protocols are

ASCII

Kermit

Super-Kermit

Xmodem

Xmodem CRC

Xmodem 1K

Ymodem

Ymodem batch or Ymodem-G

Zmodem

Although these transfer protocols are popular, the most popular transfer protocol is the Zmodem transfer protocol. The reason for Zmodem's popularity is its ease of use and reliability. You can initiate a Zmodem transfer within your communications program while connected to the Internet, and there are only two commands you'll ever have to learn:

```
rz     Receive via Zmodem transfer protocol.
sz     Send via Zmodem transfer protocol.
```

From your Internet account, you can type `sz` or `rz` at the shell prompt. If you type `sz` or `rz` and then press Enter, you will get a brief summary of how to use the commands. The most basic format is as follows, where `filename` is the name of the file to transfer:

```
rz filename
```

NOTE

If you own a Macintosh and are transferring files to a different computer platform, you should transfer your files as regular binary files. Other computer platforms cannot read Macintosh binary files, and your files will be unreadable in this format.

Checking the Mode of the File

On some systems, files have strictly defined permissions that can be granted or denied to users. These permissions include the ability to read, write, and execute the file. Permissions are generally set by changing the mode attributed to the file. Make sure that files have the appropriately restricted mode for Web access. On a UNIX system, the mode `705` means that the file is readable, writeable, and executable by you, but only readable and executable by others.

NOTE

The command to change the mode of a file on a UNIX system is `chmod`. The `chmod` command can be used to set permissions for you, your associated group, and others. You can grant or deny permission to read, write, and execute the file. Permissions are generally set using a 3-digit number that equates to the permissions you are setting.

The first digit sets the permissions for you, the owner of the file. The second digit sets the permissions for the group of users you are associated with on the UNIX system. The third digit sets the permissions for anyone else who might use the file. Read permissions are set by adding one to the digit count. Write permissions are set by adding four to the digit count. Execute permissions are set by adding two to the digit count.

A file with the mode of `000` has no permissions. If you changed the mode to `754`, the file would be readable, writeable, and executable by you; readable and executable by anyone in your group; and readable by anyone else.

Troubleshooting Problems with Your Web Site

While publishing your new site, you may encounter problems. Sometimes you just can't access your pages. The first thing you should do is to make sure all files are where they should be. Most of the time, HTML pages and associated files must be in very specific directories in order for the files to be accessed, such as the `public_html` directory. If your files are in the proper directory and you still can't access them, check the following:

- File and directory permissions
- File extensions
- Index files

File and Directory Permissions

All operating systems flag files and directories with permissions. The permissions on files and directories are very important. This is especially true on UNIX systems, where the default file permissions are set according to an involved permission set. If you are having problems accessing the file, check permissions on both the file and the directory the file is in.

NOTE

On a UNIX system, a directory must be executable by the user to be readable. Typically you will want permissions on your public UNIX directories and files set so users can access your files but cannot write to the directory. The command you would use to put your files and directories in this mode is

```
chmod 705 filename
chmod 705 directory_name
or
chmod 755 filename
chmod 755 directory_name
```

NOTE

On a DOS or Windows system, valid modes for files and directories include

```
System
Hidden
Read-only
Executable
```

If you are having problems accessing files and directories, make sure the files are at least readable by the user. Your files and directories should not be hidden.

File Extensions

The file extension you use should match the file type and format. Web servers may use the extension to determine which type of file you are trying to access. Web browsers may use the extension to determine which type of file you are retrieving and the action to take on the file. If you use a UNIX, Macintosh, or Amiga server, your HTML pages should have the extension `.html`.

Although your UNIX, Macintosh, or Amiga server may be configured to recognize the extension of `.htm` as a valid HTML page, it is often easiest to avoid a potential hassle and use the extension `.html`. If you use a Windows-based server, your HTML pages should have the extension `.htm`.

Index Files

Most Web server software wants directories with HTML pages to have an index file. Servers will generally display the index when a user specifies a directory name instead of a file name. If the index file doesn't exist, you may experience problems.

The index file is sometimes called `index.html`, but not always. On a Macintosh server running MacHTTP or WebStar, each folder should have an index file called `default.html`.

Publicizing Your Web Site

You've published your Web site. You have a wonderful Web site or at least a start on what will become a wonderful Web site. Now you have to tell the world about it. In fact, you *must* tell the world about it. On the Internet there are no road maps; unless you tell people you've created a new site, no one is going to find out. Thankfully, dozens of Web sites specialize in spreading the word about Web resources. These sites maintain databases that Web users can search or meander through using links to specific categories.

The good news is that you can register your site with most of these sites for free. All you have to do is tell the site where they can find you and what to expect.

In the past year, more than a dozen new databases have appeared on the Web—and soon, dozens more will be available. Tracking down all these databases individually to ensure maximum exposure to the millions of Web users is difficult and time-consuming, to say the least. Instead of spending an entire day registering your site, one solution would be to register your site only at the major databases—but then the question becomes, which major databases. Here is a list of the major databases and the URLs to their submission pages:

Apollo: `http://apollo.co.uk/`

EINet Galaxy: `http://galaxy.einet.net/cgi-bin/annotate`

GNN: `http://www.gnn.com/gnn/wn/whats-new-form.html`

Harvest: `http://harvest.cs.colorado.edu/Harvest/brokers/register-with-CU-`
`➥gatherers.html"`

HomeCom Global Village: `http://www.homecom.com/global/gc_entry.html`

InfoSeek: `http://www.infoseek.com/doc/FAQ/`

Jump Station: `http://js.stir.ac.uk/jsbin/submit`

Lycos: `http://lycos.cs.cmu.edu/lycos-register.html`

New Rider's WWW Yellow Pages: `http://www.mcp.com/newriders/wwwyp/submit.html`

Nikos: `http://www.rns.com/www_index/new_site.html`

Open Text: `http://opentext.uunet.ca:8080/omw-submit.html`

Starting Point: `http://www.stpt.com/util/submit.html`

Web Crawler: `http://webcrawler.com/WebCrawler/SubmitURLS.html`

What's New Too: `http://newtoo.manifest.com/WhatsNewToo/submit.html`

Whole Internet Catalog: `http://gnn.com/gnn/forms/comments.html"`

World Wide Web Worm: `http://www.cs.colorado.edu/home/mcbryan/WWWWadd.html`

World Wide Web Yellow Pages: `http://www.yellow.com/`

Yahoo: `http://www.yahoo.com/bin/add`

Another solution for registering your site with a database is to use a site that acts as a pointer to the databases. Pointer sites provide a way of automating the registration process; using the fill-out form provided at the site, you can submit your information to multiple databases at the touch of a button. Currently, there are two primary pointer sites: Scott Banister's Submit-It page and HomeCom's Pointers to Pointers page.

The Submit-It page is shown in Figure 49.12. A great thing about the Submit-It page is that all the database sites you see listed at the top of Figure 49.13 are automatically selected to receive your submission. You can tell the site is selected by the X in the box associated with the database. If you don't want to register with a certain site, you click on the box to unselect the site and the X disappears.

After you complete the online form partially depicted in Figure 49.13, you can automatically register your site with more than a dozen Web databases. The key information you enter into this form includes your name, business address, e-mail address, site URL, site title, and a brief description of your site.

FIGURE 49.12.
Use Submit-It to register your site with more than a dozen databases.

The Pointers to Pointers page is shown in Figure 49.14. The organization of this page is very different from the organization of the Submit-It page. Dozens of large, small, and specialized databases are listed in a comprehensive list. Some databases are presented with a checkbox that you must select individually to place an automated submission. Other databases, particularly the specialized databases, are provided only as links that you must visit individually to submit your information.

FIGURE 49.13.
A fill-out form at Submit-It makes submission easy.

HomeCom's page features a fill-out form for automatic submission to databases you have selected. This form is partially depicted in Figure 49.15. The key information you enter into this form includes your name, business address, e-mail address, phone number, fax number, site URL, site title, and a brief description of your site.

FIGURE 49.14.
Use Pointers to Pointers to register your site with large, small, and specialized databases.

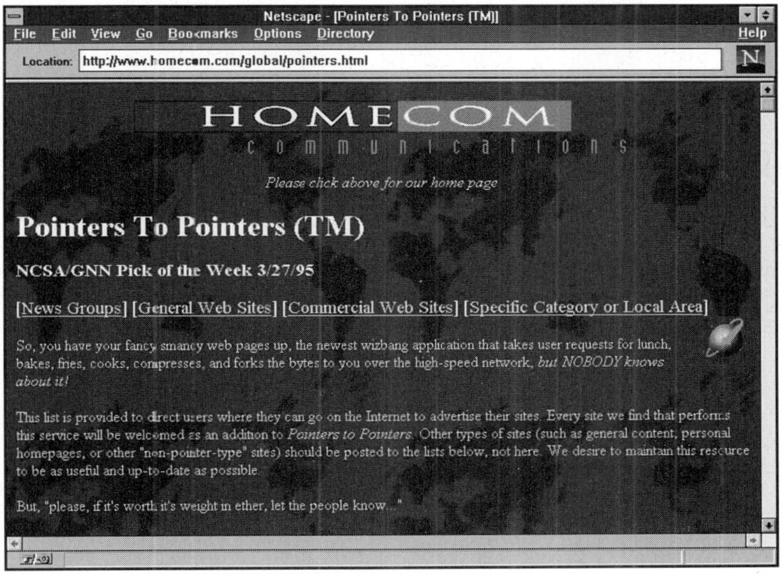

FIGURE 49.15.
The Pointers to Pointers submission form.

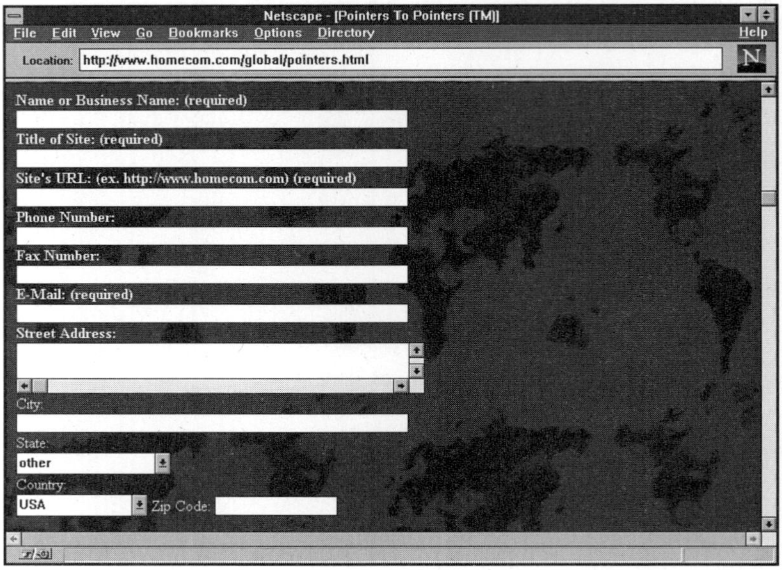

Summary

Creating, publishing, and publicizing your first Web site is easy if you follow the steps outlined in this chapter. If you follow the advice the examples present, your first Web site could have as many as four pages. These include your home page, business background page, personal background page, and a community-service page. Creating a Web site involves much more than creating pages; it involves developing a strategy and focusing on sound design concepts.

To attract visitors, your pages must be friendly and inviting. One way to ensure your pages are friendly is to design them with both first-time and repeat visitors in mind. You should also ensure there are no dead-ends at your site. Dead-ends are frustrating and can easily be avoided by following a sound page design that includes adequate linking. You can use links to create image and text menus, to keep visitors informed, and to provide a feedback mechanism for readers. You can also use links to ensure that all your pages lead somewhere, even if it is only back to your home page.

CHAPTER 50

Creating an Advanced Multimedia Site

by Dick Oliver

IN THIS CHAPTER

The mantra of successful multimedia CD-ROM developers and marketers has been, "It's the content, stupid." In other words, the beauty and utility of the content matter a lot more than how much content there is, how fast it displays, or how many technical bells and whistles you add to it. The same mantra rings true for the Web.

After you have the content, there are essentially three other factors to consider: bandwidth, bandwidth, and bandwidth. The number of bytes per second that fly from your site to most of your visitors is by far the most significant factor in determining what you put on your pages today.

In this chapter, you'll see a site that isn't very practical for the Internet at large, given the current bandwidth of the modem-toting masses. However, literally hundreds of companies are rushing to provide high-bandwidth connections via TV cables, ASDL (Asychronous Digital Subscriber Lines), "copper optics" technologies, satellite services, and pumped-up cellular connections. If even a few of them succeed, the kind of site you see here will become commonplace.

In the meantime, multimedia sites are already becoming commonplace on corporate intranets, where high-bandwidth connections are more economical to maintain. And, of course, you have the luxury of a CD-ROM drive at hand so you can enjoy the music and video as if you had your own T1 line straight to the site and were its only bandwidth-hogging visitor.

Raw Materials

If you're going to make a multimedia site, you need to start with some multimedia. For the examples in this chapter, I started with an AVI music video, a WAV sound file, and a simple logo in a WMF graphics file. All this content was produced by The Sponge Awareness Foundation, or SAF—a couple of mildly deranged young men with too much recording equipment on their hands. Their songs have gotten some national play on the *Dr. Demento* radio show, and the video was used as a sample file on some digital video software CD-ROMs. Continuing in the spirit of that proud heritage, a cutting-edge Web site on the *Web Publishing Unleashed, Professional Reference Edition* CD-ROM seemed in order. (In case you're wondering, no, I'm not one of the two SAF members—despite the coincidence of also being a mildly deranged young man with too much equipment on my hands.)

Capturing Graphics

Notably lacking from this formidable arsenal of content were any thematic icons or background textures, but then again, videos contain a lot of pictures, right? So, I just used the `Capture | Area` command in Paint Shop Pro to steal some frames from the AVI video, and then painted out the backgrounds to make transparent GIF icons, as shown in Figure 50.1. (Paint Shop Pro is a shareware graphics program included on the CD-ROM with this book and discussed in Part IV, "Enhancing Web Pages with Graphics.")

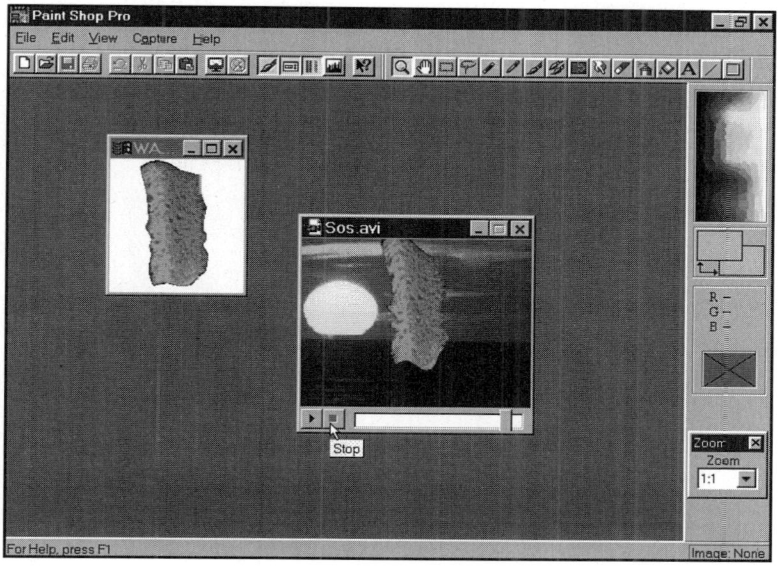

FIGURE 50.1.
Paint Shop Pro can capture anything you can display on your screen for use as a Web page graphic, including the frames in this AVI video.

TIP

Without too much work, you could use Paint Shop Pro to carefully paint the background out from around icons like the dancing sponge in Figure 50.1. But this is the ultimate modern site, so I allowed myself to indulge in the power of Adobe Photoshop's color range selection feature, which made the job much easier and faster.

It's up to you to decide if you're going to be doing this sort of thing often enough to justify the big bucks for Photoshop or another pricey commercial graphics program. Most Webmasters will find it easier and faster to use Paint Shop Pro than to take the time to learn (and pay for) Photoshop.

Instant Backgrounds

A seriously rocking band like SAF clearly requires a seriously rocking background for its Web page. I snagged a thematic design from the climactic ending scene in the music video, in which the Land Where Sponges Never Die morphs and warps into oblivion. I could have used the paint-and-paste technique described in Chapter 20, "Backgrounds, Image Maps, and Creative Backgrounds" for making tilable backgrounds, but there's an even quicker way to tile abstract designs such as this one. Figure 50.2 and the numbered steps that follow it describe how.

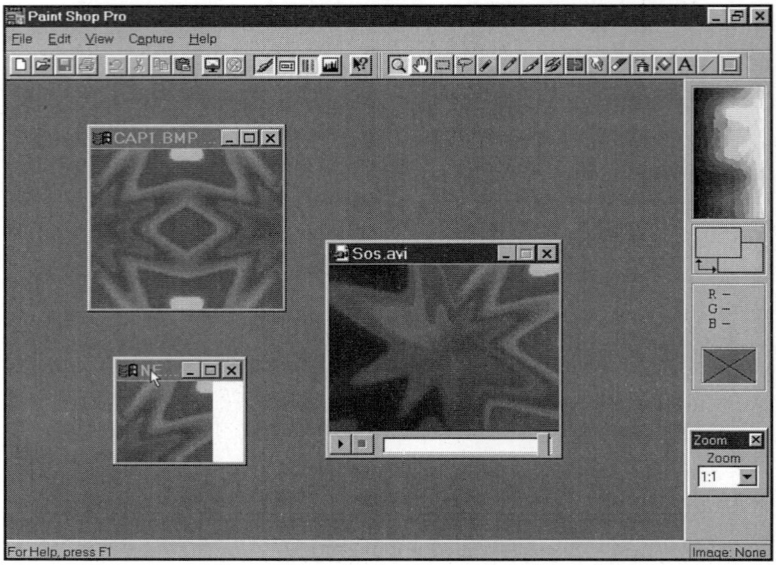

FIGURE 50.2.
The Mirror and Flip commands were used to turn part of this video frame into a background graphic.

1. Open any graphic in Paint Shop Pro, and do any cropping or image manipulation you want. Make sure it is a 256-color or 16-color image, and not a true-color image. (The Mirror and Flip commands in step 4 work slightly differently for true-color images for some strange reason.)
2. Select `Image | Enlarge Canvas` and enlarge the image to twice as wide and twice as tall as it is now. (Remember, the dimensions of the image are always displayed in the lower left corner of the Paint Shop Pro window.) Make sure that `Center Image` is *not* selected, and click `OK`.
3. Use the rectangular selection tool to carefully select the original image area, and select `Edit | Copy`.
4. Select the following commands, in this order:

   `Image | Mirror`

   `Edit | Paste | Into Selection`

   `Image | Flip`

   `Edit | Paste | Into Selection`

   `Image | Mirror`

   `Edit | Paste | Into Selection`

5. You should now have an abstract design that will tile seamlessly as a background! Before saving it, you may want to change its size, select `Colors | Adjust` to lighten or darken it, and perhaps select `Image | Normal Filters | Blur More` to make the edges less severe.

The final tile is `/saf/theland.jpg` on the CD-ROM and is pictured in all the rest of the figures in this chapter. I used the same technique to turn part of the sky of the Land Where Sponges Never Die into another background tile, `/saf/theland2.jpg`. This background is used behind the spinning 3D virtual reality logo in `/saf/saf3d.htm`.

A 3D Virtual Reality Logo

By the way, did I mention yet that there's a spinning 3D virtual reality logo in `/saf/saf3d.htm`? Sure, I could have just put the SAF logo graphic at the top of a home page and called it good, but how about one of those much-too-cool interactive virtual reality thingamabobs instead? Now we're talking.

Way Cool, but Way Easy

The sophisticated way to pull something like this off would be to go into a VRML modeling program (or hack together some VRML by hand) to model each line and shape in the logo with shiny 3D shapes and surfaces. But doing a fairly complex logo that way would probably involve paying a 3D modeling guru (like me) more money than SAF made on their entire 1992 Crumbling City tour of upstate New York. So, yeah, let's think "way cool." But let's think "way easy" (and "way cheap") while we're thinking "way cool," okay?

Time for the old transparent-bitmap-on-a-spinning-box trick! Check out the absurdly simple VRML file in Listing 50.1. Could a single cube at the default size possibly be cool enough to honor the SAF? You bet. As Figure 50.3 demonstrates, this basic VRML cube makes brain-boggling rotating transparent logos in front of a dramatic moving backdrop.

Listing 50.1. `/saf/safcube.wrl`

```
#VRML V1.0 ascii
DEF BackgroundImage Info{ string "THELAND2.jpg" }
SpinGroup {
    rotation 0 1 1 -.1
    Separator {
    Texture2 { filename "saf.gif" }
    Material { diffuseColor    0 0 1 }
    Cube {}
    }
}
```

FIGURE 50.3.
The simple cube described in Listing 50.1 becomes an interactive, animated rendering when embedded in a Web page (`/saf/saf3d.htm`).

Embedding VRML in a Web Page

To see the cube in action, open the `/saf/saf3d.htm` document. If you have a VRML-enabled browser, you'll see the spinning logo in Figure 50.3, and you will be able to control its motion by grabbing it with your mouse. (With Live3D, the left button zooms and pans while the right button rotates.) If you don't have a VRML-enabled browser, you'll see the 3D-looking image in Figure 50.4, but mouse clicking and dragging will have no effect on it.

FIGURE 50.4.
This image, as seen in Internet Explorer 2.0, is only a simulated snapshot of a 3D object. It doesn't move no matter what you do.

Microsoft Internet Explorer 3.0 and Netscape 2.0 plug-ins, such as Live3D, use two different HTML commands to embed VRML worlds into a Web page. Here's how to add the `safecube.wrl` to a page so that both of these browsers will treat it the same:

```
<EMBED SRC="safcube.wrl" WIDTH=500 HEIGHT=240>
<NOEMBED>
<IMG SRC="safsub.gif" DYNASRC="safecube.wrl" WIDTH=500 HEIGHT=240>
</NOEMBED>
```

If you're using Netscape with any VRML plug-in, the `<EMBED>` tag will work. The `<IMG>` tag will try the Microsoft-style `DYNASRC` attribute to insert a 3D world. If both of these tags fail (meaning you don't have a VRML-enabled browser), the `<IMG>` tag will just display the `safsub.gif` image in Figure 50.5.

TIP

To make the `safsub.gif` image, I used Paint Shop Pro's `Capture | Area` command to take a screen shot of Netscape Live3D while it was displaying the VRML cube. This is a handy way to at least give non-VRML users a peek at what they're missing!

The only problem that might come up is for users who have both Internet Explorer 3.0 and Netscape Navigator 3.0 installed at once. In that case, Explorer may interpret the `<EMBED>` command as an instruction to embed a copy of Netscape Navigator with Live3D in the Web page, in which case it will ignore the `DYNASRC` tag. Unfortunately, when Navigator and Live3D 3.0 are embedded in this way, the texture mapping may not work correctly, and users may see a plain blue cube with no logo on it. Although this is a bummer, it's not the end of the world.

FIGURE 50.5.
Some Internet Explorer 3.0 users may not see the texture maps shown in Figure 50.3.

NOTE

Both Netscape and Microsoft are in the process of revamping their approaches to VRML support to accomodate VRML 2.0 and other new technologies, so the appropriate HTML code for inserting VRML is likely to change soon. Keep your eye on `www.microsoft.com` and `home.netscape.com` for the latest VRML browser news.

Links Ahoy!

After whetting visitors' appetites with this virtual reality treat, I gave them some links to the multimedia parts of this multimedia site (see Figure 50.6). As you look over the code for this whole page in Listing 50.2, you may note that I staggered the icons through a creative use of the `IMG ALIGN="left"` attribute. The only other formatting tricks used on this page are some font size and color changes to make the text readable over such a loud background.

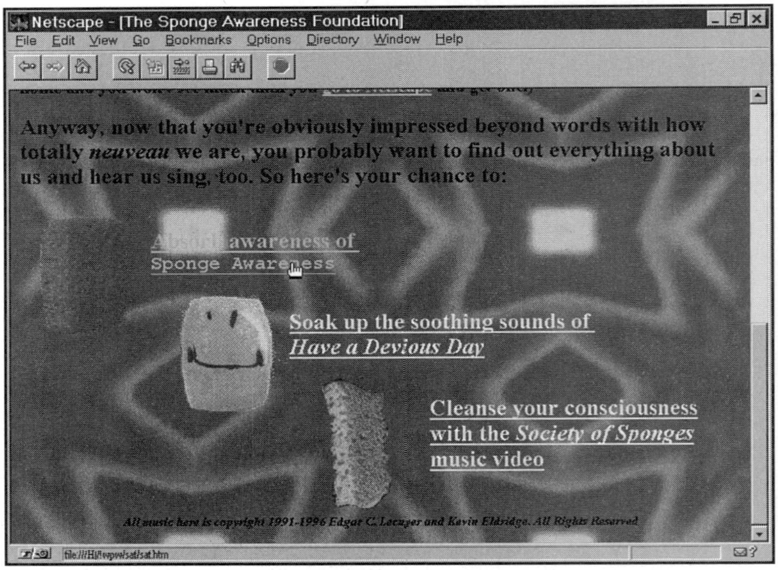

FIGURE 50.6. *Staggered icons, made with* `IMG ALIGN="left"`*, add a little more variety to this otherwise ordinary list of links* (`/saf/saf3d.htm`).

Listing 50.2. /saf/saf3d.htm.

```
<HTML>
<HEAD><TITLE>The Sponge Awareness Foundation</TITLE></HEAD>
<BODY BACKGROUND="theland.jpg"
  TEXT="black" VLINK="silver" LINK="yellow" BGCOLOR="red">
<CENTER>
<TT><FONT SIZE=7><B>The Sponge Awareness Foundation</B></FONT></TT><BR>
<FONT SIZE=5>
```

```
<I><B>"We're not a rock band, but we play one on TV."</B></I></FONT><P>
<EMBED SRC="safcube.wrl" WIDTH=500 HEIGHT=240>
<NOEMBED><IMG SRC="safsub.gif" DYNASRC="safecube.wrl"
WIDTH=500 HEIGHT=240></NOEMBED><P>
</CENTER>

<FONT SIZE=5><B>Welcome to our much-too-cool, cutting-edge, high-bandwidth
Web-site-on-a-CD-ROM. The innocent looking logo at the top of this page is
really one of those unbelievably nifty 3D virtual reality thingamabobs.
Try flying around it by clicking and dragging with the right mouse button.
Bet you think we're slick now, hey?

<FONT SIZE=4>(You do if you have Live3D or another VRML texture-mapping plug-in
installed,that is. Otherwise, you can click till the cows come home and you won't
see much until you <A HREF="http://home.netscape.com/">go to Netscape</A> and
get one. Or if you're using an old-fashioned VRML helper app, you can
<A HREF="safcube.wrl" click here to view the 3D logo</A>.)<P></FONT>

Anyway, now that you're obviously impressed beyond words with how totally
<I>neuveau</I> we are, you probably want to find out everything about us
and hear us sing, too. So here's your chance to:</B><P></FONT>

<A HREF="saf.htm"><IMG SRC="engorged.gif" ALIGN="left" BORDER=0><BR>
<H2>Absorb awareness of <BR><TT>Sponge Awareness</TT></A></H2>
<A HREF="devious.htm"><IMG SRC="devious.gif" ALIGN="left" BORDER=0><BR>
<H2>Soak up the soothing sounds of <BR><I>Have a Devious Day</I></A></H2>
<A HREF="sos.htm"><IMG SRC="warped.gif" ALIGN="left" BORDER=0><BR>
<H2><B>Cleanse your consciousness with the <I>Society of Sponges</I>
music video</A></H2>
<BR CLEAR="all"><P>
<CENTER><FONT SIZE=2>
<I>All music here is copyright 1991-1996 Edgar C. Lecuyer and Kevin Eldridge.
All Rights Reserved</I></FONT></CENTER>
</BODY>
</HTML>
```

Yet Another GIF Animation

If you've read my Chapter 19, "Animating Graphical Images" and Chapter 48, "Designing and Publishing a Perfect Web Page," you've probably figured out that I like GIF animations. It probably won't be a big surprise, then, when you load `/saf/saf.htm` or click the `Absorb awareness of Sponge Awareness` link in the `saf3d.htm` document.

Sure enough, I couldn't resist. Figures 50.7 and 50.8 confirm that the image at the top of `/saf/saf.htm` is just what you expected: flashing colors, winking eye, that kind of thing. I won't list the HTML for this page because it's nothing too special. Chapter 19 gives you the skinny on how to make GIF animations like this if you haven't become addicted to them already.

FIGURE 50.7.
An ordinary boring logo on a party site like this one? No way (`/saf/saf.htm`).

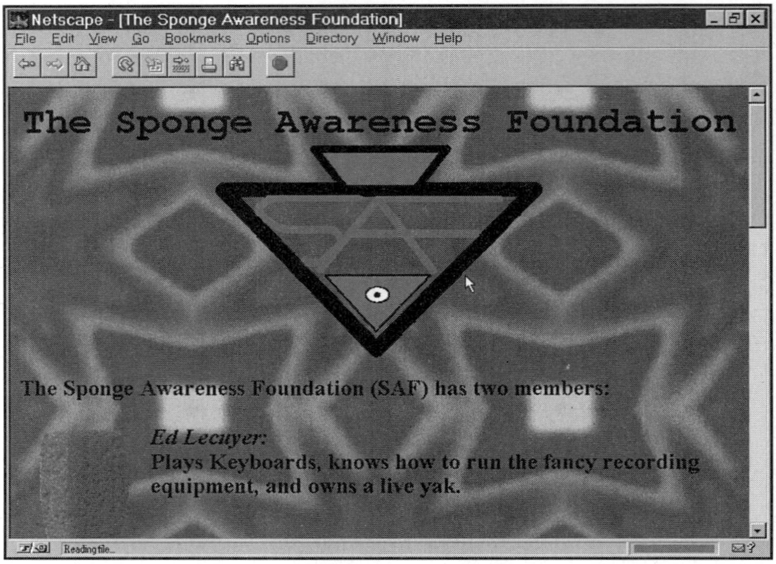

FIGURE 50.8.
Even a tiny touch of color animation can add a lot of spice to a bland page of text (`/saf/saf.htm`).

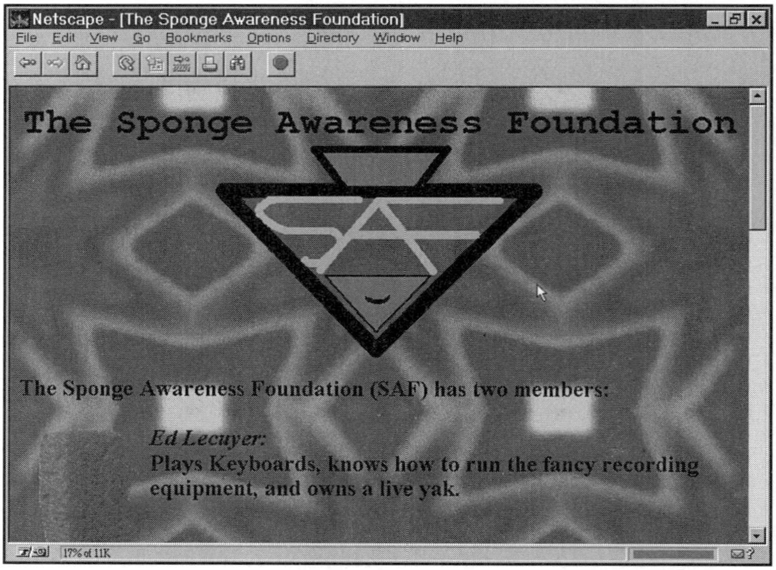

Sound Check

Making a full-length song play when a page loads is no different than playing a quick sound bite like the "Aloha!" discussed in Chapter 48. The simplicity of Listing 50.3 is proof that it isn't rocket science to blast rock-and-roll through a Web page. Notice that both the Netscape

<EMBED> tag and the Microsoft <BGSOUND> tag are included and that a link is also provided for people who only have a helper app such as Windows Media Player.

The only other thing to notice about this document is that the 400-pixel width of the background combined with a centered graphic make a lovely symmetrical design when viewed at 800×600 resolution (Figure 50.9). This doesn't look as nice at other window sizes, but so many people use 800×600 resolution that effects like this are well worth cultivating.

FIGURE 50.9.
People who view this page at 800×600 resolution get an extra nice visual layout to complement the music they hear.

Listing 50.3. /saf/devious.htm.

```
<HTML>
<HEAD><TITLE>Have a Devious Day</TITLE></HEAD>
<BODY BACKGROUND="theland.jpg"
  BGCOLOR="red" TEXT="black" LINK="yellow" VLINK="silver">
<CENTER>
<FONT SIZE=6><TT><B>The Sponge Awareness Foundation</B></TT></FONT><BR>
<B>Presents</B><P>
<FONT SIZE=7>Have a Devious Day</FONT><BR>
<IMG SRC="devious.gif"><BR>
<EMBED SRC="devious.wav" WIDTH=145 HEIGHT=60>
<NOEMBED><BGSOUND="devious.wav"></NOEMBED>
</TABLE>
</TD></TR></TABLE>
</CENTER>
<FONT SIZE=5><B>
If you have a WAV-compatible Web browser or plug-in, you can click on the
play button above to enjoy the music. If you only have a WAV helper app that
doesn't support embedding (which means there isn't a play button above to
click on), you can just
```

continues

Listing 50.3. continued

```
<A HREF="devious.wav">click here to play the song.</A><P>
If you don't have a sound card and speakers, I'm afraid there's not much we
can do for you here. Try yodeling in the shower instead.
(No, it's fun--really!)<P>
Oh, did we mention that this song, recorded in 1992, has never before been
publicly released? So you're pretty lucky to have this opportunity to hear
it, don't you think? We thought so.<P>
<CENTER>
<A HREF="saf3d.htm"><BR>
<IMG SRC="saf3d.gif" BORDER=0><BR>Click your heels three times, Dorothy...</A>
</CENTER>
</B></FONT>
</BODY>
</HTML>
```

The TV Table

Embedding video that is compatible with both the Netscape and Microsoft extensions to HTML is as simple as embedding sound or VRML files. On the `/saf/sos.htm` page pictured in Figure 50.10, I added nested table borders around the video window, so viewers could get that cozy and comfortable boob-tube feeling even before the video begins.

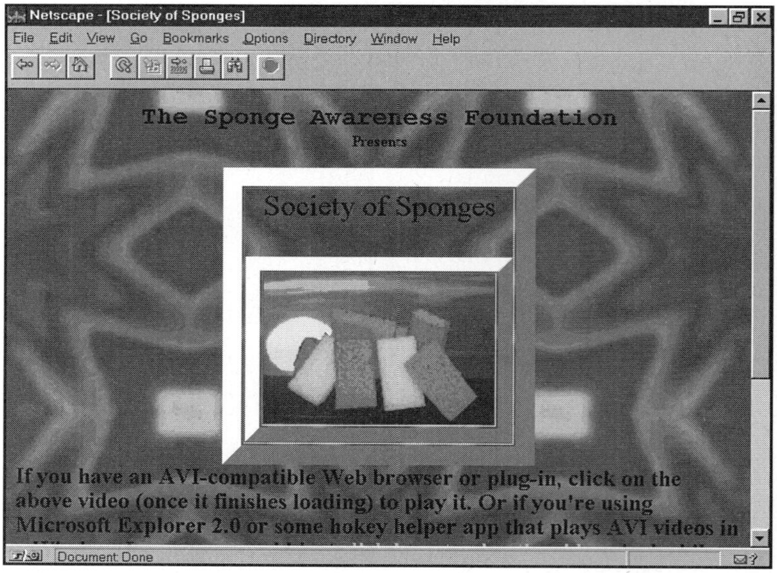

FIGURE 50.10.
Make it look like a TV, and Americans will watch anything.

As discussed in Chapter 22, "Adding Multimedia to Your Web Site," it may be impossible to specify `WIDTH` and `HEIGHT` attributes for the `<EMBED>` tag that work well with both Netscape plug-ins (see Figure 50.10) and embedded helper applications that display playback controls (see Figure 50.11). Though the video may get squashed a bit, it will at least be viewable in both situations.

FIGURE 50.11.
Internet Explorer 3.0 will try to fit an embedded helper app, including any controls, in the same space that the Netscape LiveVideo plug-in (refer to Figure 50.10) just puts the video.

Writing the HTML to implement the embedded video was just slightly easier than programming the clock on my VCR. (OK, it was a lot easier. The real reason you can't buy books about VCR programming is that they can't find any authors who have figured it out.) As with the embedded VRML world, the `<EMBED>`, `<NOEMBED>`, `<IMG DYNSRC>`, and `<IMG SRC>` tags are all used together:

```
<EMBED SRC="sos.avi" WIDTH=320 HEIGHT=200>
<NOEMBED>
<IMG DYNASRC="sos.avi" WIDTH=320 HEIGHT=200 SRC="sponges.jpg">
</NOEMBED>
```

If you're using Netscape Navigator 2.0 (or higher) and an AVI plug-in is installed, it will play `sos.avi` using the `<EMBED>` tag (refer to Figure 50.10). If no AVI plug-in is installed, or if a non-Netscape browser is being used, the `<IMG>` tag will come into play. If Microsoft Internet Explorer 3.0 is being used, it will either use Object Linking and Embedding (OLE) to embed an AVI player with the `EMBED` tag, or it will see the `DYNASRC` attribute and embed the `sos.avi` video. Any other browser will just see the `<IMG>` attribute and display `sponges.jpg` instead (see Figure 50.12). Isn't standardization wonderful?

And the plot thickens: If a user of an aging browser sees those sponges just sitting there, but still wants to see the video, she or he can click the link provided a little further down the page to display the video in a separate window (see Figure 50.13). If this page were online instead of on a CD-ROM, those users would have to wait for the whole video to download before they could start viewing it.

FIGURE 50.12.
Browsers that don't support embedded video (such as Explorer 2.0) will politely display a still image instead.

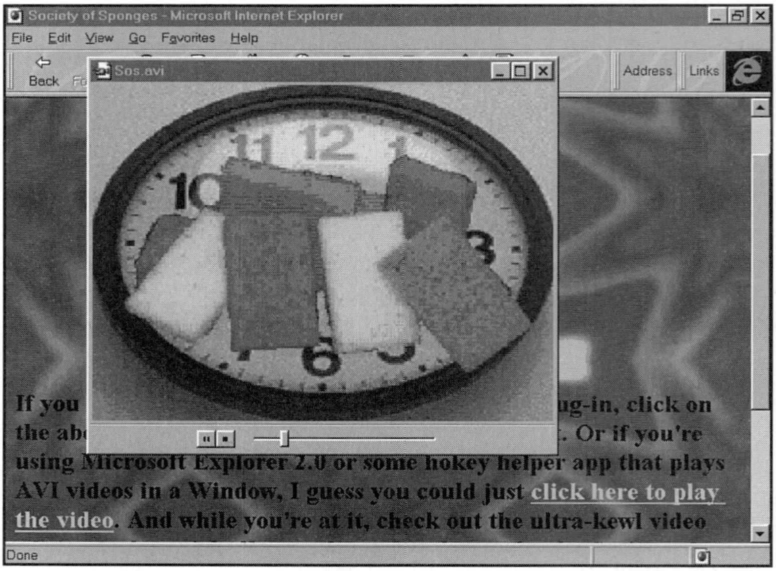

FIGURE 50.13.
Almost everybody has some sort of helper app to display video clips, so you should always provide a clickable link to your media even if you also embed it.

Listing 50.4 reveals the whole sos.htm document, just to prove there's nothing else fishy up my sleeve this time.

Listing 50.4. /saf/sos.htm.

```
<HTML>
<HEAD><TITLE>Society of Sponges</TITLE></HEAD>
<BODY BACKGROUND="theland.jpg"
  BGCOLOR="red" TEXT="black" LINK="yellow" VLINK="silver">
<CENTER>
<FONT SIZE=6><TT><B>The Sponge Awareness Foundation</B></TT></FONT><BR>
<B>Presents</B><P>
<TABLE BORDER=20>
<TR><TD><CENTER>
<FONT SIZE=6>Society of Sponges</FONT></CENTER><BR>
<TABLE BORDER=15>
<TR><TD><EMBED SRC="sos.avi"
WIDTH=240 HEIGHT=160><NOEMBED><IMG DYNASRC="sos.avi"
WIDTH=320 HEIGHT=200 SRC="sponges.jpg"></NOEMBED></TD></TR>
</TABLE>
</TD></TR></TABLE>
</CENTER>
<FONT SIZE=5><B>
If you have an AVI-compatible Web browser or plug-in, click on the above video
(once it finishes loading) to play it. Or if you're using Microsoft
Explorer 2.0 or some hokey helper app that plays AVI videos in a Window,
I guess you could just <A HREF="sos.avi">click here to play the video</A>.
And while you're at it, check out the ultra-kewl video editing and special
effects software used to make the Society of Sponges video, at
<A HREF=" http://www.andatech.com/">the Andover Advanced Technologies
web site</A>.<P>
<CENTER>
<A HREF="saf3d.htm"><BR>
<IMG SRC="saf3d.gif" BORDER=0><BR>Enough of this. Take me home now.</A>
</CENTER>
</B></FONT>
</BODY>
</HTML>
```

NOTE

If this were really and truly the high-bandwidth site of the far distant future, we could make a bigger table full of multiple copies of the video for that totally-hip "TV store" look. Such things are easy enough to code in HTML. Now if somebody would just run fiber optics to every home and business in the world already....

Onward and Upward!

The sample pages in this chapter obviously haven't even begun to exhaust the possibilities for enhancing this modern site. Here are some of the ways to add even more cutting-edge features to this site:

- Add an interactive Shockwave animation like the ones discussed in Chapter 25, "Adding Interactivity with Shockwave for Director."
- Use ActiveX controls or OCX-compatible plug-ins to link Windows programs directly into the Web page, as discussed in Chapter 31, "Exploring ActiveX and ActiveX Controls."
- Insert Java applets as demonstrated in Chapter 36, "Including Java Applets in Your Web Pages."
- Use JavaScript or Visual Basic to link parts of the page together, as suggested in Chapter 34, "Using JavaScript in Your Web Pages," and Chapter 32, "Using VBScript to Enhance Your Web Pages."

Of course the possibilities explode if you are (or are willing to hire) a programmer. You can then produce your own custom OC components, Java applets, or CGI scripts.

A no less ambitious way to add sophistication to a high-bandwidth site is to improve the production quality of the audio-visual media files you post there. Alas, this book would need many thousands more pages if it were to include a complete course on cinematography and interactive multimedia production!

Summary

This chapter has followed the development of a multimedia Web site from designing the background and layout to embedding VRML, sound, and video in the Web pages. This book gives you the chance to fully participate in the world of online, interactive media today. And those who are involved today will undoubtedly be a step ahead tomorrow, when professional-quality audio-visual productions can be successfully served over the Internet—or the speedier parts of it, at least.

IN THIS PART

XII
PART

Appendixes

APPENDIX A

Sources for Additional Information

IN THIS APPENDIX

In this appendix, you'll find the URLs for all kinds of information about the World Wide Web, HTML, developing Web presentations, and locations of tools to help you write HTML documents. With this list, you should be able to find just about anything you need on the Web.

NOTE

Some of the URLs in this section refer to FTP sites. Some of these sites may be very busy during business hours, and you may not be able to immediately access the files. Try again during non-prime hours.

Also, some of these sites, for mysterious reasons, may be accessible through an FTP program, but not through Web browsers. If you are consistently getting refused from these sites using a browser, and you have access to an FTP program, try that program instead.

Collections of HTML and WWW Development Information

Yahoo!'s WWW Section

Linkname: Computers: World Wide Web

`http://www.yahoo.com/Computers/World_Wide_Web/`

The Virtual Library

Linkname: The Web Developer's Virtual Library

`http://WWW.Stars.com/`

The Ten Commandments of HTML FAQ

`http://www.visdesigns.com/design/commandments.html`

World Wide Web FAQ

`http://www.boutell.com/faq/`

NCSA: A Beginner's Guide to HTML Home Page

`http://www.ncsa.uiuc.edu/General/Internet/WWW/HTMLPrimer.html`

The Developer's JumpStation

Linkname: OneWorld/SingNet WWW & HTML Developer's JumpStation

`http://oneworld.wa.com/htmldev/devpage/dev-page.html`

The Repository

Linkname: Subjective Electronic Information Repository

`http://cbl.leeds.ac.uk/nikos/doc/repository.html`

The Home of the WWW Consortium

Linkname: The World Wide Web Consortium (W3C)

`http://www.w3.org/`

Netscape's HTML Assistance Pages

Linkname: Creating Net Sites

`http://home.netscape.com/assist/net_sites/index.html`

The Spider's Web Pages on the Web

Linkname: (BOBAWORLD) World Wide Web

`http://miso.wwa.com/~boba/`

The HTML Writer's Guild

Linkname: The HTML Writer's Guide Website

`http://www.hwg.org`

Web Directories

ALIWEB, a great Web index

Linkname: Welcome to ALIWEB

`http://web.nexor.co.uk/public/aliweb/aliweb.html`

An Index of Indexes

Linkname: WebCrawler Searching

`http://www.webcrawler.com/`

Galaxy

Linkname: TradeWave Galaxy

`http://www.einet.net/galaxy.html`

Point

Linkname: POINTReview: The Written Word on Web Culture

`http://www.pointcom.com/`

W3 Virtual Library

Linkname: The World-Wide Web Virtual Library: Subject Catalogue

`http://www.w3.org/hypertext/DataSources/bySubject/Overview.html`

Yahoo!

Linkname: Yahoo!

`http://www.yahoo.com/`

Web Search Tools

CUSI

Linkname: CUSI Services

`http://Web.nexor.co.uk/susi/cusi.html`

excite

Linkname: Excite Home

`http://www.excite.com/`

InfoSeek

Linkname: InfoSeek

`http://www.infoseek.com`

Lycos

Linkname: Welcome to Lycos

`http://www.lycos.com/`

Browsers

A general list

Linkname: WWW Client Software products

`http://www.w3.org/hypertext/WWW/Clients.html`

Netscape (Windows, Windows 95, Mac, X)

Linkname: Download Netscape Software

`http://home.netscape.com/comprod/mirror/index.html`

Microsoft Internet Explorer 2.0 (Windows 95)

Linkname: Download Microsoft Internet Explorer 2.0

`http://www.microsoft.com/ie/ie.htm`

NCSA Mosaic (X, Windows, Mac)

Linkname: NCSA Mosaic Home Page

`http://www.ncsa.uiuc.edu/SDG/Software/Mosaic/NCSAMosaicHome.html`

Lynx (UNIX and DOS)

Linkname: About Lynx

`http://www.cc.ukans.edu/about_lynx/`

WinWeb (Windows)

Linkname: WinWeb and MacWeb

`http://galaxy.tradewave.com/EINet/WinWeb/WinWebHome.htmlNew`

MacWeb (Macintosh)

Linkname: WinWeb and MacWeb

`http://galaxy.tradewave.com/EINet/WinWeb/WinWebHome.htmlNew`

Arena (X)

Linkname: Welcome to Arena

`http://www.w3.org/pub/WWW/Arena/`

Emacs-W3 (for Emacs)

Linkname: The Emacs World Wide Web Browser

`http://www.cs.indiana.edu/elisp/w3/docs.html`

Netscape Navigator for OS/2 Warp

Linkname: OS/2 Warp/Netscape Navigator for OS/2 Warp

`http://www.internet.ibm.com/browsers/netscape/warp/`

Specifications for HTML, HTTP, and URLs

The HTML Level 2 specification

Linkname: HTML 2.0 Proposed Standard Materials

`http://www.w3.org/hypertext/WWW/MarkUp/html-spec/index.html`

The HTML 3.2 specification

Linkname: Introducing HTML 3.2

`http://www.w3.org/pub/WWW/MarkUp/Wilbur`

The HTTP specification

Linkname: Overview of HTTP

`http://www.w3.org/pub/WWW/Protocols/`

Netscape's Extensions to HTML 2.0

Linkname: Extensions to HTML

`http://home.netscape.com/assist/net_sites/html_extensions.html`

Netscape's Extensions to HTML 3.0

Linkname: Extensions to HTML

`http://home.netscape.com/assist/net_sites/html_extensions_3.html`

Mosaic Tables

Linkname: HTML Tables in NCSA Mosaic

`http://www.ncsa.uiuc.edu/SDG/Software/XMosaic/table-spec.html`

Pointers to URL, URN, and URI information and specifications

Linkname: UR* and The Names and Addresses of WWW objects

`http://www.w3.org/hypertext/WWW/Addressing/Addressing.html`

Microsoft Internet Explorer

Linkname: HTML Enhancements

`http://www.microsoft.com/ie/ie3/htmlext.htm`

Java and JavaScript

The Sun Microsystems Java home page

Linkname: Java: Programming for the Internet

`http://java.sun.com/`

A Java Applet and JavaScript Directory

Linkname: Gamelan

`http://www.gamelan.com/`

Yahoo! Java Directory

Linkname: Yahoo - Computers and Internet:Languages:Java

`http://www.yahoo.com/Computers_and_Internet/Programming_Languages/Java/`

Netscape Navigator Family Page

`http://home.netscape.com/comprod/products/navigator/`

JavaWorld magazine

`http://www.javaworld.com/`

A JavaScript Index

Linkname: The JavaScript Index

`http://www.c2.org/~andreww/javascript/`

JavaScript Programming

Linkname: Learn Advanced JavaScript Programming

`http://www.geocities.com/SiliconValley/9000/`

JavaScript Tips

Linkname: JavaScript Tip of the Week - webreference.com

`http://webreference.com/javascript/`

Other JavaScript Information

Linkname: JavaScript 411 Home Page

`http://www.freqgrafx.com/411/`

Linkname: Club Java is sponsored by Virtual Rendezvous®

`http://rendezvous.com/java/`

Linkname: The Java Developer

`http://www.digitalfocus.com/digitalfocus/faq/`

Linkname: THE JAVA URN

`http://www.nebulex.com/URN/`

Tools for Images

Some good information about transparent GIFs

Linkname: Transparent Background Images

`http://members.aol.com/htmlguru/transparent_images.html`

giftrans

Linkname: source for giftrans

`ftp://ftp.rz.uni-karlsruhe.de/pub/net/www/tools/`

LView Pro for Windows (at the OAK Simtel Mirror)

`ftp://oak.oakland.edu/pub/simtelnet/win3/graphics/`

LView Pro for Windows 95 (at the OAK Simtel Mirror)

`ftp://oak.oakland.edu/simtelnet/win95/graphics/`

Graphic Converter for Macintosh (at the HyperArchive sumex-aim Mirror)

`http://hyperarchive.lcs.mit.edu/HyperArchive/Archive/`
`➥gst/grf/`

GIF Converter for Macintosh (at the HyperArchive sumex-aim Mirror)

`http://hyperarchive.lcs.mit.edu/HyperArchive/Archive/gst/grf/`

Transparency (Macintosh)

`http://hyperarchive.lcs.mit.edu/HyperArchive/Archive/gst/grf/`

GIFTool (Unix)

http://www.homepages.com/tools/

Sound and Video

SOX (UNIX and DOS sound Converter)

http://www.spies.com/Sox/

WAVany (Windows sound converter)

ftp://ftp.radio-msu.net/mirror/Coast/win3/sound/

WHAM (Windows sound converter)

ftp://gatekeeper.dec.com/pub/micro/msdos/win3/sounds/wham133.zip

SoundAPP (Macintosh sound converter)

http://hyperarchive.lcs.mit.edu/HyperArchive/Archive/_Graphic_&_Sound_Tool/
➥_Sound/

FastPlayer (Macintosh Quicktime player and "flattener")

ftp://ftp.ncsa.uiuc.edu/Mosaic/Mac/Helpers/fast-player-110.hqx

QFlat (Windows QuickTime "flattener")

ftp://venice.tcp.com/pub/anime-manga/software/viewers/qtflat.zip

Sparkle (MPEG player and converter for Macintosh)

http://hyperarchive.lcs.mit.edu/HyperArchive/Archive/_Graphic_%26_Sound_Tool/
➥_Movie

XingCD (AVI to MPEG converter)

http://www.xingtech.com/

AVI-Quick (Macintosh converter for AVI to Quicktime)

http://hyperarchive.lcs.mit.edu/HyperArchive/Archive/_Graphic_%26_Sound_Tool/
➥_Movie

SmartVid Conversion Utility

ftp://ftp.intel.com/pub/IAL/Indeo_video/indeo/utilities/smartv.exe

The MPEG FAQ

Linkname: MPEG Moving Picture Expert Group FAQ

http://www.vol.it/MPEG/

Information on making MPEG movies

Linkname: How to make MPEG movies

`http://www.arc.umn.edu/GVL/Software/mpeg.html`

Servers

CERN HTTPD

Linkname: W3C httpd Administration

`http://www.w3.org/pub/WWW/Daemon/User/Admin.html`

NCSA HTTPD

Linkname: NCSA httpd Overview

`http://hoohoo.ncsa.uiuc.edu/docs/Overview.html`

NCSA HTTPD for Windows

Linkname: Windows httpd

`http://www.city.net/win-httpd/`

MacHTTP

Linkname: MacHTTP Info

`http://www.starnine.com/machttp/machttpsoft.html`

Web Providers

An index from HyperNews

Linkname: Leasing a Server

`http://union.ncsa.uiuc.edu/HyperNews/get/www/leasing.html`

Gateway Scripts and the Common Gateway Interface (CGI)

Yahoo!'s CGI List

Linkname: Yahoo - Computers and Internet:Internet:World Wide Web:CGI - Common Gateway Interface

`http://www.yahoo.com/Computers_and_Internet/Internet/World_Wide_Web/`

CGI___Common_Gateway_Interface

Linkname: The Common Gateway Interface

`http://hoohoo.ncsa.uiuc.edu/cgi/`

The spec for CGI

Linkname: The Common Gateway Interface Specification

`http://hoohoo.ncsa.uiuc.edu/cgi/interface.html`

Information about CGI in CERN HTTPD

Linkname: CGI/1.1 script support of the CERN Server

`http://www.w3.org/hypertext/WWW/Daemon/User/CGI/Overview.html`

A library of C programs to help with CGI deveopment

Linkname: EIT's CGI Library

`http://wsk.eit.com/wsk/dist/doc/libcgi/libcgi.html`

An index to HTML-related programs written in Perl

Linkname: Index of Perl/HTML archives

`http://www.seas.upenn.edu/~mengwong/perlhtml.html`

An archive of CGI Programs at NCSA

Linkname: CGI sample scripts

`ftp://ftp.ncsa.uiuc.edu/Web/httpd/Unix/ncsa_httpd/cgi`

Un-CGI, a program to decode form input

Linkname: Un-CGI

`http://www.hyperion.com/~koreth/uncgi.html`

Forms and Image Maps

The original NCSA forms documentation

Linkname: The Common Gateway Interface: FORMS

`http://hoohoo.ncsa.uiuc.edu/cgi/forms.html`

Mosaic form support documentation

Linkname: Mosaic for X Version 2.0 Fill-Out Form Support

`http://www.ncsa.uiuc.edu/SDG/Software/Mosaic/Docs/fill-out-forms/overview.html`

Image maps in CERN HTTPD

Linkname: Clickable image support in W3C httpd

`http://www.w3.org/hypertext/WWW/Daemon/User/CGI/HTImageDoc.html`

Image maps in NCSA

Linkname: NSCA Tutorial: Imagemap

`http://hoohoo.ncsa.uiuc.edu/docs/tutorials/imagemapping.html`

Some Perl scripts to manage forms

Linkname: The cgi-lib.pl Home Page

http://www.bio.cam.ac.uk/web/form.html

Mapedit: A tool for Windows and X11 for creating image map files

Linkname: Mapedit

http://www.boutell.com/mapedit/

WebMap (Macintosh map creator)

http://hyperarchive.lcs.mit.edu/HyperArchive/Archive/_Text_Processing/_HTML

HTML Editors and Converters

A list of converters and editors, updated regularly

Linkname: Tools for WWW Providers

http://www.w3.org/hypertext/WWW/Tools/

A better list of converters

Linkname: Computers:World Wide Web:HTML Converters

http://www.yahoo.com/Computers_and_Internet/Internet/World_Wide_Web/HTML_Converters/

A great list of editors

Linkname: Computers:World Wide Web:HTML Editors

http://www.yahoo.com/Computers_and_Internet/Internet/World_Wide_Web/HTML_Editors/

NCSA Converters to and from HTML

Linkname: HTML Converters

http://union.ncsa.uiuc.edu/HyperNews/get/www/html/converters.html

Other

Tim Berners-Lee's style guide

Linkname: Style Guide for Online Hypertext

http://www.w3.org/hypertext/WWW/Provider/Style/Overview.html

The Yale HyperText Style Guide

Linkname: Yale C/AIM WWW Style Manual

http://info.med.yale.edu/caim/StyleManual_Top.HTML

APPENDIX B

HTML Reference

by Stephen Le Hunte

IN THIS APPENDIX

Table B.1. How to quickly find information about a particular tag in this appendix.

The vast range of HTML markup currently supported by available HTML user agents (Web browsers, such as Netscape, Mosaic, and so on) can be broadly divided into the following sections. Some elements described may not be supported by all browsers. Where an element is known to be supported by specific browsers, the element description will be labelled as such.

This appendix is divided into the following sections:

Document Structure Elements

Anchor Element

Block Formatting Elements

Character Data

Dynamic HTML Documents

Form Elements

Frames

Image Element

Information Type and Character Formatting Elements

List Elements

Table Elements

Table B.1 on the previous pages provides a list of these sections as well as all the tags described in each section. Page numbers are provided so you can find what you need quickly.

NOTE

Stephen Le Hunte (cmlehunt@swan.ac.uk), the author of this appendix, is an independent software developer and freelance technical author specializing in HTML and WinHelp. He is currently studying for his Ph.D. at the University of Wales Swansea.

Document Structure Elements

These elements are required within an HTML document. Apart from the prologue document identifier, they represent the only HTML elements that are explicitly required for a document to conform to the standard.

The essential document structure elements are

```
<HTML>...</HTML>

<HEAD>...</HEAD>

<BODY>...</BODY>
```

Prologue Identifiers

In order to identify a document as HTML, each HTML document should start with the prologue:

```
<!DOCTYPE HTML PUBLIC "-//IETF//DTD HTML 2.0//EN">
```

However, it is worth noting that if the document does not contain this type declaration, a browser should infer it. The above document identifier identifies the document as conforming to the HTML 2.0 DTD.

<HTML>...</HTML>

The `<HTML>` element identifies the document as containing HTML elements. It should immediately follow the prologue document identifier, and it serves to surround all of the remaining text, including all other elements. Browsers use the presence of this element at the start of an HTML document to ensure that the document is actually HTML, according to the `text/html` MIME type. The document should be constructed as follows:

```
<!DOCTYPE HTML PUBLIC "-//IETF//DTD HTML 2.0//EN">
<HTML>
  The rest of the document should be placed here.
</HTML>
```

The HTML element is not visible upon browser rendering and can contain only the `<HEAD>` and `<BODY>` elements.

<HEAD>...</HEAD>

The `<HEAD>` element of an HTML document is used to provide information about the document. It requires the `<TITLE>` element between `<HEAD>` and `</HEAD>` tags:

```
<HEAD>
  <TITLE>Introduction to HTML</TITLE>
</HEAD>
```

The `<HEAD>` and `</HEAD>` tags do not directly affect the look of the document when rendered.

The following elements are related to the `<HEAD>` element. Although they don't directly affect the look of the document when rendered, you can use them to provide important information to the browser. To do so, you employ the following elements, all of which should be included within the `<HTML>...</HTML>` tags.

`<BASE>`	Allows the base address of HTML document to be specified
`<ISINDEX>`	Allows keyword searching of the document
`<LINK>`	Indicates relationships between documents

<META>	Specifies document information usable by server/clients
<NEXTID>	Creates unique document identifiers
<STYLE>	Specifies styles within the document when used by browsers that support use of style sheets
<TITLE>	Specifies the title of the document

NOTE

The <TITLE> element is the only element described here that is required as part of the <HEAD> of an HTML document for conformance to any HTML standard.

<BODY>...</BODY>

The body of an HTML document, as its name suggests, contains all the text and images that make up the page, together with all the HTML elements that provide the control and formatting of the page. The format is

```
<BODY>
  The rest of the document included here
</BODY>
```

The <BODY>...</BODY> tags should be directly enclosed by the <HTML>...</HTML> tags.

The <BODY> and </BODY> tags themselves do not directly affect the look of the document when rendered, but they are required in order for the document to conform to the specification standard. Various attributes of the opening <BODY> tag can be used to set up various page-formatting settings.

The ability to specify background images and colors for HTML documents was first implemented by Netscape and has since been implemented by most other browsers. It should be noted that the following elements may not be supported by every browser.

BACKGROUND

Recent versions of the proposed HTML 3.2 specification have added a BACKGROUND attribute to the <BODY> element. The purpose of this attribute is to specify a URL pointing to an image that is to be used as a background for the document. In most browsers, this background image is used to tile the full background of the document-viewing area. Consider the following code:

```
<BODY BACKGROUND="imagename.gif">
  Rest of the document goes here
</BODY>
```

It would cause whatever text, images, and so on that appeared in the body of the document to be placed on a background consisting of the imagename.gif graphics file, being tiled to cover the viewing area (like bitmaps are used for Windows wallpaper). Most browsers that support this attribute allow the use of .GIF and .JPG images for document backgrounds, whereas Internet Explorer supports those, plus Windows .BMP files.

BGCOLOR

The BGCOLOR attribute to BODY is not currently in the proposed HTML 3.2 specification, but is supported by Netscape, the Internet Explorer, NCSA Mosaic, and many other browsers, and is being considered for inclusion in HTML 3.2. It allows the setting of the color of the background without having to specify a separate image that requires another network access to load. The format is

```
<BODY BGCOLOR="#rrggbb">
  Rest of document goes here
</BODY>
```

where #rrggbb is a hexadecimal (base 16) red-green-blue triplet used to specify the background color.

Recently, browsers have begun allowing the use of special names to define certain colors. Appendix D, "Color Table," presents a list of all the color names recognized by popular browsers and also includes their corresponding hexadecimal triplet values.

Note that using color names is browser specific, so you have greater control over the displayed colors if you use the #rrggbb values instead.

If you change the background colors or patterns within a presentation, remember to verify that the foreground still looks good on the new background.

NOTE

Color Considerations

Most graphical browsers allow the downloading of embedded images to be turned off to allow for faster downloading and display of the HTML document. If you turn off downloading for embedded images, background images will not be loaded or displayed. If this happens and no BGCOLOR attribute was specified, all of the foreground text and link-color attributes (TEXT, LINK, VLINK, and ALINK) will be ignored. This is so that documents are not rendered illegibly if the text color scheme authored for use over the set image clashes with the default browser background.

BGPROPERTIES

In Internet Explorer, you can watermark HTML documents by fixing a background image so that it doesn't scroll as a normal background image does. To give a page with a background image a watermarked background, add BGPROPERTIES=FIXED to the <BODY> element as follows:

```
<BODY BACKGROUND="filename.gif" BGPROPERTIES=FIXED>
```

LEFTMARGIN

This Internet Explorer attribute allows you to set the left margin of the document. For example

```
<BODY LEFTMARGIN="40">This document is indented 40 pixels from the left-hand
edge of the browser window</BODY>
```

If you set `LEFTMARGIN` to `0`, the page will start at the very left-hand side of the page.

LINK, VLINK, and ALINK

These link attributes allow you to control the color of link text. `VLINK` stands for visited link, and `ALINK` stands for active link (this sets the color that the link text will be for the time that it is clicked on). Generally, the default colors of these attributes are `LINK=blue (#0000FF)`, `VLINK=purple (#800080)`, and `ALINK=red (#FF0000)`. The format for these attributes is the same as that for `BGCOLOR` and `TEXT`:

```
<BODY LINK="#rrggbb" VLINK="#rrggbb" ALINK="#rrggbb">
  Rest of document goes here
</BODY>
```

You can also use color names rather than hexadecimal values for these attributes. See Appendix D for a complete list of color names and their hexadecimal values.

TEXT

The `TEXT` attribute can be used to control the color of all the normal text in the document. This basically consists of all text that is not specially colored to indicate a link. The format of `TEXT` is the same as that of `BGCOLOR`:

```
<BODY TEXT="#rrggbb">
  Rest of document goes here
</BODY>
```

You can also use color names rather than hexadecimal values for these attributes. See Appendix D for a complete list of color names and their hexadecimal values.

TOPMARGIN

This Internet Explorer-specific attribute allows the top margin of the document to be set. For example,

```
<BODY TOPMARGIN="40">This document is indented 40 pixels from the top hand
edge of the browser window</BODY>
```

If you set `TOPMARGIN` to `0`, the page will start at the very top of the page.

<BASE...>

The <BASE...> element allows you to set the URL of the document itself, to help browsers in situations where the document might be read out of context. It is especially useful in allowing browsers to determine any partial URLs or relative paths that might be specified (for example, in <A HREF> elements or in paths used to specify <IMG SRC=> (images)). The <BASE> element should appear within the bounds of the <HEAD> element only.

Where the base address is not specified, the browser uses the URL it used to access the document to resolve any relative URLs.

HREF

The <BASE> element has one standard attribute, HREF, that identifies the URL. The URL should be fully qualified as in this example:

```
<BASE HREF="http://www.myhost.com/">
```

This code specifies www.myhost.com to be the base from which all relative URLs should be determined.

TARGET

Netscape (from version 2.0) and Internet Explorer (from version 3.0) add one other attribute to the <BASE> element. With the introduction of targeted windows, you can use the TARGET attribute as you use it in anchors (<A>). This allows you to pick a default-named target window for every link in a document that does not have an explicit TARGET attribute. Its format is

```
<BASE TARGET="default_target">
```

<ISINDEX...>

The <ISINDEX> element tells the browser that the document is an index document. As well as reading it, the reader can use a keyword search.

Readers can query the document with a keyword search by adding a question mark to the end of the document address, followed by a list of keywords separated by plus signs.

NOTE

The <ISINDEX> element is usually generated automatically by a server. If added manually to an HTML document, the browser assumes that the server can handle a search on the document. To use the <ISINDEX> element, the server must have a search engine that supports this element.

ACTION

Netscape provides the ACTION attribute for the <ISINDEX> element. When used in the <ISINDEX> element, it explicitly specifies the CGI script or program to which the text string in the input box should be passed. For example:

```
<ISINDEX ACTION="Websearch">
```

This code passes the text entered into the input box on the page to the CGI script Websearch.

> **NOTE**
>
> Websearch in the preceding example is a hypothetical CGI script. The ACTION attribute must point to a properly configured script on the host machine.

PROMPT

Netscape provides the PROMPT attribute for the <ISINDEX> element. PROMPT allows you to specify text that should be placed before the text-input field of the index. The syntax is

```
<ISINDEX PROMPT="Any_text_string: ">
```

where Any_text_string is the text you want to be displayed before the input box.

<LINK...>

The <LINK> element indicates a relationship between the document and some other object. A document may have any number of <LINK> elements.

The <LINK> element is empty (does not have a closing element), but takes the same attributes as the Anchor element. (For example REL, REV, METHODS, TITLE, HREF and so on.)

The <LINK> element would typically be used to provide pointers to related indexes, or glossaries. Links can also be used to indicate a static tree structure in which the document was authored by pointing to a parent, next, and previous document, for example.

Servers may also allow links to be added by those who do not have the right to alter the body of a document.

The <LINK> element represents one of the primary style sheet inclusion mechanism elements. It can be used to specify the location of the style sheet that is to be used for the document. For example:

```
<HTML>
<HEAD>
<TITLE>This HTML document uses a style sheet</TITLE>
<LINK REL="stylesheet" TYPE="text/css" HREF="http://www.stylesheets.com/sheets/
formal.css" TITLE="formal">
```

```
</HEAD>
<BODY>
  Rest of the document goes here
</BODY>
</HTML>
```

In the preceding HTML fragment, the `<LINK>` element points to the file "formal.css" at the given URL. It tells the browser that:

- the file addressed is a style sheet, by explicitly giving the "text/css" MIME type;
- the file's RELationship to the HTML document is that it is a "stylesheet";
- the stylesheet's `TITLE` is "formal."

NOTE

The above HTML fragment represents part of a *"work in progress"* specification of the W3C (World Wide Web Consortium).

For more information about these specific attributes, see the `<A>` section, and for more general information about style sheets, see the style sheets section.

<NEXTID...>

The `<NEXTID>` element, included in old HTML specifications, is not widely supported and its use is not recommended. Previously, it could be used to provide information about the name of new `<A>` elements when a document is being edited.

<TITLE>...</TITLE>

Every HTML document must have a `<TITLE>` element. As its name suggests, it is used to specify the title of the document in question. Unlike headings, titles are not typically rendered in the text of a document itself. Normally, browsers will render the text contained within the `<TITLE>...</TITLE>` elements in the title bar of the browser window.

The `<TITLE>` element must occur within the head of the document and may not contain anchors, paragraph elements, or highlighting. Only one title is allowed in a document.

NOTE

Although the length of the text specified in the `<TITLE>...</TITLE>` elements is unlimited, for display reasons, most browsers will truncate it. For this reason, title text should be kept short but should be enough to uniquely identify the document. For instance, a short title such as *Introduction* may be meaningless out of context, but if the title were *An Introduction to HTML Elements,* then it would be obvious what the document is about.

This is the only element that is required within the <Head> element.

```
<HEAD>
  <TITLE>Welcome to the HTML Reference</TITLE>
</HEAD>
```

<META...>

The <META> element is used within the <Head> element to embed document meta-information not defined by other HTML elements. Such information can be extracted by servers/clients for use in identifying, indexing, and cataloguing specialized document meta-information.

Although it is generally preferable to use named elements that have well-defined semantics for each type of meta-information, such as title, this element is provided for situations where strict SGML parsing is necessary and the local DTD is not extensible.

In addition, HTTP servers can read the content of the document head to generate response headers corresponding to any elements defining a value for the attribute HTTP-EQUIV. This provides document authors a mechanism (not necessarily the preferred one) for identifying information that should be included in the response headers for an HTTP request.

Attributes of the <META> element are listed in the following sections.

CONTENT

The meta-information content to be associated with the given name and/or HTTP response header.

If the document contains

```
<META HTTP-EQUIV="Expires" CONTENT="Sat, 06 Jan 1990 00:00:01 GMT">
<META HTTP-EQUIV="From" CONTENT="nick@htmlib.com">
<META HTTP-EQUIV="Reply-to" CONTENT="stephen@htmlib.com"
```

then the HTTP response header would be

```
Expires: Sat, 06 Jan 1990 00:00:01 GMT
From: nick@htmlib.com
Reply-to: stephen@htmlib.com
```

Commonly, HTML documents can be seen to contain a listing of repeated terms. Some Web search/indexing engines use the "Keywords" information generated either from the server, or from those specified in <META HTTP-EQUIV="Keywords" CONTENT="..."> markup to determine the content of the specified document and to calculate their "relevance rating" (how relevant the document is to the specific search string) for the search results.

When the HTTP-EQUIV attribute is not present, the server should not generate an HTTP response header for this meta-information. For example,

```
<META NAME="IndexType" CONTENT="Service">
```

Do *not* use the `<META>` element to define information that should be associated with an existing HTML element.

The following is an inappropriate use of the `<META>` element

```
<META NAME="Title" CONTENT="Welcome to the HTML Reference">
```

Do *not* name an `HTTP-EQUIV` equal to a responsive header that should typically only be generated by the HTTP server. Some inappropriate names are "Server," "Date," and "Last-modified." Whether a name is inappropriate depends on the particular server implementation. It is recommended that servers ignore any `<META>` elements that specify HTTP-equivalents equal (case-insensitively) to their own reserved response headers.

The `<META>` element is particularly useful for constructing Dynamic documents via the Client Pull mechanism. This uses the following syntax:

```
<META HTTP-EQUIV="Refresh" CONTENT="x">
```

which causes the browser to believe that the HTTP response when the document was retrieved from the server included the following header:

```
Refresh: x
```

and causes the document to be re-loaded in *x* seconds.

> **NOTE**
>
> In the preceding example, where the document refreshes, loading itself, the browser will infinitely reload the same document over and over. The only way out of this situation would be for the user to either activate some hyperlink on the page, loading a different document, or to press the "Back" button to reload a previous document.

This can be useful to provide automatic redirection of browsers. For instance, if the element was

```
<META HTTP-EQUIV="Refresh" CONTENT="2; URL=http://some.site.com/otherfile.html">
```

then the `Refresh` directive would cause the file at `http://some.site.com/otherfile.html` to be loaded after 2 seconds. Although this generally works if the URL specified is partial, you should use a fully qualified URL to ensure its proper functioning.

HTTP-EQUIV

This attribute binds the element to an HTTP response header. If the semantics of the HTTP response header named by this attribute is known, then the contents can be processed based on a well-defined syntactic mapping whether or not the DTD includes anything about it. HTTP header names are not case-sensitive. If not present, the `NAME` attribute should be used to identify this meta-information, and it should not be used within an HTTP response header.

NAME

Meta-information name. If the name attribute is not present, then name can be assumed equal to the value HTTP-EQUIV.

Anchor Element

The Anchor text is probably the single most useful HTML element. It is the element that is used to denote hyperlinks—the entire essence of HTML as a hypertext application.

<A...>...</A>

Anchor elements are defined by the <A> element. The <A> element accepts several attributes, but either the NAME or HREF attribute is required.

Attributes of the <A> element are decribed in the following sections.

HREF

If the HREF (Abbreviated from Hypertext REFerence) attribute is present, the text between the opening and closing anchor elements becomes a hypertext link. If this hypertext is selected by readers, they are moved to another document, or to a different location in the current document, whose network address is defined by the value of the HREF attribute. Typically, hyperlinks specified using this element would be rendered in underlined blue text, unless the LINK attribute of the <BODY> element has been specified.

```
See <A HREF="http://www.htmlib.com/">HTMLib</A> for more information about the
HTML Reference.
```

In this example, selecting the text "HTMLib" takes the reader to a document located at http://www.htmlib.com.

With the HREF attribute, the form HREF="#identifier" can refer to another anchor in the same document, or to a fragment of another document, that has been specified using the NAME attribute (see below).

```
The <A HREF="document.html#pre">&lt;PRE&gt;</A> provides details about the
preformatted text element.
```

In this example, selecting "<PRE>" (< and > are character data elements and render as < and >, respectively. In this case they are used so that <PRE> is actually rendered on the screen, (so that the browser doesn't think that the following text is preformatted text). Selecting the link takes the reader to another anchor (that is, <A NAME="pre"><PRE></A>) in a different document (document.html). The NAME attribute is described below. If the anchor is in another document, the HREF attribute may be relative to the document's address or the specified base address, or can be a fully qualified URL.

Table B.2. Several other forms of the HREF attribute permitted by browsers.

<A HREF="http://...">	Makes a link to another document located on a World Wide Web server.
<A HREF="ftp://...">	Makes a link to an FTP site. Within an HTML document, normally a connection to an anonymous FTP site would be made. Some browsers, however, allow connections to private FTP sites. In this case, the anchor should take the form ftp://lehunte@htmlib.com and the browser would then prompt the user for a password for entry to the site.
<A HREF="gopher://... >	Makes a link to a Gopher server.
<A HREF="mailto:...">	Activating such a link would bring up the browsers mailing dialogue box (providing it has mailing capabilities; otherwise, whatever default e-mail software is installed on the system should be activated) allowing the user to send mail messages to the author of the document, or whoever's address is specified in the mailto attribute. NCSA Mosaic supports use of the TITLE attribute for the anchor element when used with mailto: links. It allows the author to specify the subject of the mail message that will be sent. Netscape allows specification of the subject line by using the following syntax: <A HREF="mailto:lehunte@htmlib.com?subject=The HTML Reference is fantastic"> link text</A>
<A HREF="news:...">	Makes a link to a Usenet newsgroup. Care should be taken in using such links because the author cannot know what newsgroups are carried by the local news server of the user.
<A HREF="newsrc:...">	Makes a link to a specific newsrc file. The newsrc file is used by Usenet news reading software to determine what groups, carried by the news server, the reader subscribes to.
<A HREF="nntp://...">	Can be used to specify a different news server to that which the user may normally use.
<A HREF="telnet://...">	Activating such a link would initiate a Telnet session (using an external application) to the machine specified after the telnet:// label.
<A HREF="wais://...">	Makes a link that connects to a specified WAIS index server.

METHODS

The METHODS attributes of anchors and links provide information about the functions that the user may perform on an object. These are more accurately given by the HTTP protocol when it is used, but it may, for similar reasons as for the TITLE attribute, be useful to include the information in advance in the link. For example, the browser may choose a different rendering as a function of the methods allowed; for example, something that is searchable may get a different icon or link text display method.

The value of the METHODS attribute is a comma-separated list of HTTP methods supported by the object for public use.

NAME

If present, the NAME attribute allows the anchor to be the target of a link. The value of the NAME attribute is an identifier for the anchor, which may be any arbitrary string but must be unique within the HTML document.

```
<A NAME="pre">&lt;PRE&gt;</A> gives information about...
```

Another document can then make a reference explicitly to this anchor by putting the identifier after the address, separated by a hash sign as follows:

```
<A HREF="document.html#pre">
```

REL

The REL attribute gives the relationship(s) described by the hypertext link from the anchor to the target. The value is a comma-separated list of relationship values, which will have been registered by the HTML registration authority. The REL attribute is only used when the HREF attribute is present.

REV

The REV attribute is the same as the REL attribute, but the semantics of the link type are in the reverse direction. A link from A to B with REL="X" expresses the same relationship as a link from B to A with REV="X". An anchor may have both REL and REV attributes.

TARGET

With the advent of Frame page formatting, browser windows can now have names associated with them. Links in any window can refer to another window by name. When you click on the link, the document you asked for will appear in that named window. If the window is not already open, Netscape will open and name a new window for you.

The syntax for the targeted windows is

```
<A HREF="download.html" TARGET="reference">Download information</A>
```

This would load the document download.html in the frame that has been designated as having the name reference. If no frame has this name, then Netscape will open a new browser window to display the document in.

NOTE

The use of targeted browser windows is supported by those browsers that currently support the use of <FRAME> page layout (Netscape and Internet Explorer). If the targetted document is part of a frameset, there are various reserved names that can be used to allow smooth window transition. For more information, see <FRAMES>.

TITLE

The TITLE attribute is informational only. If present, the TITLE attribute should provide the title of the document whose address is given by the HREF attribute.

This may be useful as it allows the browser to display the title of the document being loaded as retrieval starts—providing information before the new document can be viewed. It is up to individual browsers to specify how they display the title information, but usually, it is displayed in the title bar at the top of the browser window. Some documents (such as gopher or ftp directory listings) do not themselves contain title information within the document. The TITLE attribute can be used to provide a title to such documents. As mentioned earlier, Mosaic supports use of the TITLE attribute to specify the subject of a mail message sent when the user activates a <A HREF="mailto:..."> link.

URN

If present, the URN attribute specifies a uniform resource name (URN) for a target document. The precise specification for URNs has not yet been defined and so its use is not recommended.

Block-Formatting Elements

Block formatting elements are used for the formatting of whole blocks of text within an HTML document, rather than single characters. They should all (if present) be within the body of the document (that is, within the <BODY>...</BODY> elements).

The essential block formatting elements are

<ADDRESS>...</ADDRESS>	Format an address section
<BASEFONT SIZE=...>	Specifying the default font size for the document
<BLOCKQUOTE>...</BLOCKQUOTE>	To quote text from another source

 	Force a line break
<CENTER>...</CENTER>	Centering text on the page
<COMMENT>...</COMMENT>	To enclose text as a comment
<DFN>...</DFN>	Defining Instance
<DIV>...</DIV>	Allow centering, or left/right justification of text
<FONT ...>...</FONT>	Setting/changing the font size, color, and type
<HR>	Renders a sizeable hard line on the page
<Hx>...</Hx>	Format six levels of heading
<LISTING>...</LISTING>	Text formatting
<MARQUEE>	Highlighted scrolling text
<NOBR>	Specifying that words aren't to be broken
<P>...</P>	Specify what text constitutes a paragraph and its alignment
<PLAINTEXT>	For text formatting
<PRE>...</PRE>	Use text already formatted
<WBR>	Specifying that a word is to be broken if necessary
<XMP>...</XMP>	Text formatting

<ADDRESS>...</ADDRESS>

As its name suggests, the <ADDRESS>...</ADDRESS> element can be used to denote information such as addresses, authorship credits, and so on.

Typically, an address is rendered in an italic typeface and may be indented, though the actual implementation is at the discretion of the browser. The <ADDRESS> element implies a paragraph break before and after, as shown in the following:

```
<ADDRESS>
Mr. Cosmic Kumquat<BR>
SSL Trusters Inc.<BR>
1234 Squeamish Ossifrage Road<BR>
Anywhere<BR>
NY 12345<BR>
U.S.A.
</ADDRESS>
```

<BASEFONT ...>

This changes the size of the <BASEFONT> that all relative <FONT SIZE=+...> changes are based on. It defaults to 3, and has a valid range of 1–7.

```
<BASEFONT SIZE=5>
```

FACE

This attribute allows changing of the face of the HTML document `<BASEFONT>` exactly as it works for `<FONT FACE= ...>`.

> **NOTE**
>
> This attribute is Internet Explorer specific.

COLOR

This allows the `<BASEFONT>` color for the HTML document to be set (as such it is similar to the `TEXT` attribute of the `<BODY>` element). Colors can either be set by using one of the reserved color names or as a hex `rrggbb` triplet value.

> **NOTE**
>
> The `<BASEFONT SIZE=...>` element is supported only by Netscape and the Internet Explorer, with the `...FACE` and `...COLOR` attributes being Internet Explorer specific. This kind of presentation markup can also be specified within a style sheet.

<BLOCKQUOTE>...</BLOCKQUOTE>

The `<BLOCKQUOTE>` element can be used to contain text quoted from another source.

Typically, `<BLOCKQUOTE>` rendering would be a slight extra left and right indent, and possibly rendered in an italic font. The `<BLOCKQUOTE>` element causes a paragraph break, and provides space above and below the quote.

```
In "Hard Drive", a former Microsoft project manager has said,
<BLOCKQUOTE>
"Imagine an extremely smart, billionaire genius who is 14 years old and subject to
temper tantrums"
</BLOCKQUOTE>
```


The line break element specifies that a new line must be started at the given point. The amount of line space used is dependent on the particular browser, but is generally the same as it would use when wrapping a paragraph of text over multiple lines.

B HTML Reference

NOTE

Some browsers may collapse repeated <BR> elements, to render as if only one had been inserted.

```
<P>
Mary had a little lamb<BR>
Its fleece was white as snow<BR>
Everywhere that Mary went<BR>
She was followed by a little lamb.
```

With the addition of floating images (that is, the ability to align an embedded image to the left or right of the browser display window, allowing text flow around the image) it became necessary to expand the <BR> element. Normal <BR> still just inserts a line break. A `CLEAR` attribute was added to <BR>, so:

- `CLEAR=left` will break the line, and move vertically down until you have a clear left margin (that is, where there are no floating images).
- `CLEAR=right` does the same for the right margin.
- `CLEAR=all` moves down until both margins are clear of images.

The `CLEAR` attribute (as well as floating images) are currently only supported by Netscape and the Internet Explorer.

<CENTER>

All lines of text between the begin and end of the <CENTER> element are centered between the current left and right margins. This element was introduced by the Netscape authors because it was claimed that using <P ALIGN= CENTER > "broke" existing browsers when the <P> element was used as a container (that is, with a closing </P> element).

The element is used as shown below and any block of text (including any other HTML elements) can be enclosed between the centering elements.

```
<CENTER>All this text would be centered in the page</CENTER>
```

NOTE

Most browsers will internally work around this element to produce the desired format, but it is an element introduced by Netscape authors.

<COMMENT>...</COMMENT>

The `<COMMENT>` element can be used to "comment" out text. As such, it is similar to the `<!-- ... -->` element.

Any text placed between the `<COMMENT>` and `</COMMENT>` elements will not render on the screen, allowing comments to be placed in HTML documents. For example,

```
<COMMENT>This text won't render. I can say what I like here, it won't appear
</COMMENT>
```

would not render on the screen.

NOTE

This element is only supported by Internet Explorer and Mosaic.

<DFN>...</DFN>

Use of the `<DFN>` element is currently only supported by Internet Explorer.

The `<DFN>` element can be used to mark the Defining Instance of a term. For example, the first time some text is mentioned in a paragraph.

Typically, it will render italicized; for example,

```
<DFN>Internet Explorer</DFN> is Microsoft's Web browser.
```

would render as

Internet Explorer is Microsoft's Web browser.

<DIV>...</DIV>

NOTE

Use of the `<DIV>` element is currently only supported by Netscape (after version 2.0).

The `<DIV>` element, as described in the HTML 3.2 specification, should be used with a `CLASS` attribute, to name a section of text as being of a certain style as specified in a style sheet. Netscape has implemented the `DIV` element to work as the `<P ALIGN= ...>` element. Essentially, text surrounded by the <DIV>...</DIV> elements will be formatted according to the description attached to the ALIGN attribute within the <DIV> elements. For example:

```
<DIV ALIGN="left">This text will be displayed left aligned in the browser
window.</DIV>

<DIV ALIGN="center">This text will be centered.</DIV>

<DIV ALIGN="right">This text will be displayed aligned to the right of the
browser window.</DIV>
```

<FONT ...>

Netscape 1.0 (and above) and Microsoft's Internet Explorer support different sized fonts within HTML documents. This should be distinguished from Headings.

The element is <FONT SIZE=value>. Valid values range from 1–7. The default FONT size is 3. The value given to size can optionally have a + or – character in front of it to specify that it is relative to the document <BASEFONT>. The default <BASEFONT SIZE= ...> is 3, and is specified with the <BASEFONT SIZE ...> element.

```
<FONT SIZE=4>changes the font size to 4</FONT>

<FONT SIZE=+2>changes the font size to BASEFONT SIZE ... + 2</FONT>
```

NOTE

The <FONT SIZE=...> element is currently only supported by Netscape and Internet Explorer.

Microsoft's Internet Explorer supports the ability to change the font color as well as face type. It adds COLOR and FACE attributes to the <FONT> element. Netscape will support the use of the COLOR attribute only.

COLOR = *#rrggbb* or COLOR = *color*

The color attribute sets the color for the text that will appear on the screen. #rrggbb is a hexadecimal color denoting an RGB color value. Alternately, the color can be set to one of the available predefined colors (see Table B.1). These color names can be used for the BGCOLOR, TEXT, LINK, ALINK, and VLINK attributes of the <BODY> tag as well.

```
<FONT COLOR="#ff0000">This text is red.</FONT>
```

or

```
<FONT COLOR="Red">This text is also red.</FONT>
```

NOTE

The use of names for coloring text is currently only supported by the Microsoft Internet Explorer and Netscape. Also, it should be noted that HTML attributes of this kind (that format the presentation of the content) can also be controlled via the use of style sheets.

FACE=*name* [,*name*] [,*name*]

The FACE attribute sets the typeface that will be used to display the text on the screen. The typeface displayed must already be installed on the user's computer. Substitute typefaces can be specified in case the chosen type face is not installed on the user's computer. If no exact font match can be found, the text will be displayed in the default type that the browser uses for displaying normal text.

```
<FONT FACE="Courier New, Comic Sans MS"> This text will be displayed in either
Courier New, or Comic Sans MS, depending on which fonts are installed on the
browsers system. It will use the default 'normal' font if neither are installed.
</FONT>
```

NOTE

When using this element, care should be taken to try to use font types that will be installed on the user's computer if you want the text to appear as desired. Changing the font face is Internet Explorer specific and can also be set within a style sheet.

<HR>

A Horizontal Rule element is a divider between sections of text such as a full-width horizontal rule or equivalent graphic.

```
<HR>
<ADDRESS>April 12, 1996, Swansea</ADDRESS>
</BODY>
```

The <HR> element specifies that a horizontal rule of some sort (the default being a shaded engraved line) be drawn across the page. It is possible to control the format of the horizontal rule.

<HR ALIGN=left¦right¦center>

Because horizontal rules do not have to be the width of the page, it is necessary to allow the alignment of the rule to be specified. Using the above values, rules can be set to display centered, left-aligned, or right-aligned.

<HR COLOR=*name*¦*#rrggbb*>

Internet Explorer allows the specifying of the hard rule color. Accepted values are any of the Internet Explorer supported color names, or any acceptable `rrggbb` hex triplet.

<HR NOSHADE>

For those times when a solid bar is required, the `NOSHADE` attribute lets the author specify that the horizontal rule should not be shaded at all.

<HR SIZE=*number*>

The `SIZE` attribute lets the author give an indication of how thick they wish the horizontal rule to be. The number value specifies how thick the rule will be, in pixels.

<HR WIDTH=number¦percent>

The default horizontal rule is always as wide as the page. With the `WIDTH` attribute, the author can specify an exact width in pixels, or a relative width measured in percent of the browser display window.

<H*x*>...</H*x*>

HTML defines six levels of heading. A Heading element implies all the font changes, paragraph breaks before and after, and white space necessary to render the heading.

The highest level of headings is `<H1>`, followed by `<H2>...<H6>`.

Example of use:

```
<H1>This is a first level heading heading</H1>
Here is some normal paragraph text
<H2>This is a second level heading</H2>
Here is some more normal paragraph text.
```

The rendering of headings is determined by the browser, but typical renderings (as defined in the HTML 2.0 specification) are

`<H1>...</H1>`	Bold, very large font, centered. One or two blank lines above and below.
`<H2>...</H2>`	Bold, large font, flush-left. One or two blank lines above and below.
`<H3>...</H3>`	Italic, large font, slightly indented from the left margin. One or two blank lines above and below.
`<H4>...</H4>`	Bold, normal font, indented more than `H3`. One blank line above and below.

<H5>...</H5>	Italic, normal font, indented as H4. One blank line above.
<H6>...</H6>	Bold, indented same as normal text, more than H5. One blank line above.

NOTE

Heading alignments described above can be overriden by the use of <CENTER> elements, or by ALIGNing the heading (see below).

Although heading levels can be skipped (for example, from H1 to H3), this practice is not recommended as skipping heading levels may produce unpredictable results when generating other representations from HTML. For example, much talked about automatic contents/index generation scripts could use heading settings to generate contents "trees" where <H2> would be considered to label the start of a section that is a sub-section of a section denoted by a <H1> element and so on.

Included in the HTML 3.2 specification is the ability to align Headings.

ALIGN=*left*¦*center*¦*right* can be added to the <H1> through to <H6> elements. For example,

```
<H1 ALIGN=center>This is a centered heading</H1>
```

would align a heading of style 1 in the center of the page.

NOTE

This element is currently only supported by Mosaic and Netscape. The Internet Explorer supports only the center value, centering the heading.

<LISTING>...</LISTING>

The <LISTING> element can be used to presents blocks of text in fixed-width font, and so is suitable for text that has been formatted on screen. As such, it is similar to the <PRE> and <XMP> elements, but has a different syntax.

Typically, it will render as fixed width font with white space separating it from other text. It should be rendered such that 132 characters fit on the line.

NOTE

Only Netscape actually complies with this.

The following

```
Some might say<LISTING>that two heads</LISTING>are better than one
```

would render as

```
Some might say

that two heads

are better than one.
```

NOTE

The Internet Explorer and Netscape will translate any special characters included within `<LISTING>` elements. That is, if characters such as `<`, `>`, are used, they will be translated to < and >. Mosaic treats the text contained within the elements literally.

<MARQUEE>...</MARQUEE>

NOTE

This element is currently only supported by Microsoft Internet Explorer.

The `<MARQUEE>` element allows the author to create a region of text that can be made to scroll across the screen (much like the Windows Marquee screen saver):

```
<MARQUEE>This text will scroll from left to right slowly</MARQUEE>
```

ALIGN

This attribute can be set to `TOP`, `MIDDLE`, or `BOTTOM` and specifies that the text around the marquee should align with the top, middle, or bottom of the marquee.

```
<MARQUEE ALIGN=TOP>Hello in browser land.</MARQUEE>Welcome to this page
```

The text "Welcome to this page'" would be aligned with the top of the Marquee (which scrolls the text "Hello in browser land" across the screen).

NOTE

Until the Marquee width is limited by setting the `WIDTH` attribute, the Marquee will occupy the whole width of the browser window and any following text will be rendered below the Marquee.

BEHAVIOR

This can be set to SCROLL, SLIDE, or ALTERNATE. It specifies how the text displayed in the Marquee should behave. SCROLL (the default) makes the Marquee test start completely off one side of the browser window, scroll all the way across and completely off the opposite side, then start again. SLIDE causes the text to scroll in from one side of the browser window, then stick at the end of its scroll cycle. ALTERNATE means bounce back and forth within the marquee.

```
<MARQUEE BEHAVIOR=ALTERNATE>This marquee will "bounce" across the screen</
MARQUEE>
```

BGCOLOR

This specifies a background color for the marquee, either as an rrggbb hex triplet or as one of the reserved color names. (See <BODY BGCOLOR> for more information.)

DIRECTION

This specifies in which direction the <MARQUEE> text should scroll. The default is LEFT, which means that the text will scroll to the left from the right-hand side of the <MARQUEE>. This attribute can also be set to RIGHT, which would cause the marquee to scroll from the left to the right.

HEIGHT

This specifies the height of the marquee, either in pixels (HEIGHT=*n*) or as a percentage of the screen height (HEIGHT=n%).

HSPACE

This attribute is the same as that for <IMG> (images). It is used to specify the number of pixels of free space at the left- and right-hand sides of the <MARQUEE> so that the text that flows around it doesn't push up against the sides.

LOOP

LOOP=n specifies how many times a marquee will loop when activated. If n=-1, or LOOP=INFINITE is specified, the marquee action will loop indefinitely.

NOTE

If text is enclosed in a <MARQUEE>...</MARQUEE> element set, then it defaults to an infinite loop action.

SCROLLAMOUNT

Specifies the number of pixels between each successive draw of the marquee text. That is, the amount for the text to move between each draw.

SCROLLDELAY

SCROLLDELAY specifies the number of milliseconds between each successive draw of the marquee text. That is, it controls the speed at which text draw takes place.

```
<MARQUEE SCROLLDELAY=1 SCROLLAMOUNT=75>Hello.</MARQUEE>
```

This marquee would be extremely fast.

VSPACE

This attribute is the same as that for <IMG> (images). It is used to specify the number of pixels of free space at the top and bottom edges of the <MARQUEE> so that the text that flows around it doesn't push up against the sides.

NOTE

If you wish to set the <FONT> to be displayed in the <MARQUEE>, then the <MARQUEE> definition should be enclosed inside the <MARQUEE>.

```
<FONT FACE="Comic Sans MS"><MARQUEE>Hello!</MARQUEE></FONT>
```

WIDTH

This specifies the width of the marquee, either in pixels (WIDTH=n) or as a percentage of the screen height (WIDTH=n%).

<NOBR>...</NOBR>

The <NOBR> element stands for NO BReak. This means all the text between the start and end of the <NOBR> elements cannot have line breaks inserted. Although <NOBR> may be essential for those character sequences that don't want to be broken, it should be used carefully; long text strings inside of <NOBR> elements can look rather odd, especially if during viewing, the user adjusts the page size by altering the window size.

NOTE

The <NOBR> element is supported only by Netscape and Internet Explorer.

<P>...</P>

The paragraph element indicates a paragraph of text. No specification has ever attempted to define exactly the indentation of paragraph blocks and this may be a function of other elements, style sheets, and so on.

Typically, paragraphs should be surrounded by a vertical space of between one and one and a half lines. With some browsers, the first line in a paragraph may be indented.

```
<H1>The Paragraph element</H1>
<P>The paragraph element is used to denote paragraph blocks</P>.
<P>This would be the second paragraph.</P>
```

Included in the HTML 3.2 specification is the ability to align paragraphs.

Basically, the `ALIGN=left¦center¦right` attribute and values have been added to the `<P>` element.

```
<P ALIGN=LEFT> ... </P>
```

All text with in the paragraph will be aligned to the left side of the page layout. This setting is equal to the default `<P>` element.

```
<P ALIGN=CENTER> ... </P>
```

All text within the paragraph will be aligned to the center of the page. (See also `<CENTER>...</CENTER>`.)

```
<P ALIGN=RIGHT> ... </P>
```

All text will be aligned to the right side of the page.

NOTE

Internet Explorer supports only the use of the left and center values, while Mosaic and Netscape support the use of all three values.

<PLAINTEXT>

The `<PLAINTEXT>` element can be used to represent formatted text. As such, it is similar to the `<XMP>` and `<LISTING>` element. However, the `<PLAINTEXT>` element should be an open element, with no closing element. Only Netscape supports this element according to any HTML specification. Internet Explorer and Mosaic will both allow the use of a `</PLAINTEXT>` closing element. Netscape will treat the closing element literally and display it.

Typically, it will render as fixed width font with white space separating it from other text.

```
I live<PLAINTEXT>in the rainiest part of the world.
```

would render as

```
I live

in the rainiest part of the world.
```

As said above, anything following the opening <PLAINTEXT> element should be treated as text. Only Netscape behaves like this. Internet Explorer and Mosaic will allow the use of a closing </PLAINTEXT> element, allowing discrete blocks of <PLAINTEXT> formatted text to be displayed.

<PRE>...</PRE>

The Preformatted Text element presents blocks of text in fixed-width font, and so is suitable for text that has been formatted on screen, or formatted for a mono-spaced font.

The <PRE> element may be used with the optional WIDTH attribute, which is an HTML Level 1 feature. The WIDTH attribute specifies the maximum number of characters for a line and allows the browser to determine which of its available fonts to use and how to indent the text (if at all). If the WIDTH attribute is not present, a width of 80 characters is assumed. Where the WIDTH attribute is supported, widths of 40, 80 and 132 characters should be presented optimally, with other widths being rounded up.

Within preformatted text, any line breaks within the text are rendered as a move to the beginning of the next line. The <P> element should not be used, but if it is found, it should be rendered as a move to the beginning of the next line. It is possible to use Anchor elements and character highlighting elements are allowed. Elements that define paragraph formatting (headings, address, and so on) must not be used. The horizontal tab character (encoded in US-ASCII and ISO-8859-1 as decimal 9) represents a special formatting case. It should be interpreted as the smallest positive nonzero number of spaces which will leave the number of characters so far on the line as a multiple of 8. (However, despite being allowed, its use is not recommended.)

NOTE

It is at the discretion of individual browsers how to render preformatted text, and where "beginning of a new line" is to be implied, the browser can render that new line indented if it sees fit.

Example of use:

```
<PRE WIDTH="80">
This is an example of preformatted text.
</PRE>
```

NOTE

Within a preformatted text element, the constraint that the rendering must be on a fixed horizontal character pitch may limit or prevent the ability of the browser to render highlighting elements specially.

<WBR>

The <WBR> element stands for Word BReak. This is for the very rare case when a <NOBR> section requires an exact break. Also, it can be used any time the browser can be helped by telling it where a word is allowed to be broken. The <WBR> element does not force a line break (
 does that); it simply lets the browser know where a line break is allowed to be inserted if needed.

NOTE

<WBR> is supported only by Netscape and the Internet Explorer.

<XMP>...</XMP>

The <XMP> element can be used to presents blocks of text in fixed-width font, and so is suitable for text that has been formatted on screen. As such, it is similar to the <PRE> and <LISTING> elements, but has a different syntax.

Typically, it will render as fixed-width font with white space separating it from other text. It should be rendered such that 80 characters fit on the line. For example,

```
The <XMP>Netscape Navigator</XMP>supports colored tables.
```

would render as:

```
The
Netscape Navigator
doesn't support colored tables.
```

NOTE

The Internet Explorer will translate any special characters included within <XMP> elements. That is, if characters such as `<`, `>` and so on are used, they will be translated to < and >. Netscape and Mosaic treat the text contained within the elements literally.

Character Data

Within an HTML document, any characters between the HTML elements represent text. An HTML document (including elements and text) is encoded by means of a special character set described by the `charset` parameter as specified in the `text/html` MIME type. Essentially, this is restricted to a character set known as `US-ASCII` (or ISO-8859-1), which encodes the set of characters known as Latin Alphabet No. 1 (commonly abbreviated to Latin-1). This covers the characters from most Western European Languages. It also covers 25 control characters, a soft hyphen indicator, 93 graphical characters and 8 unassigned characters.

It should be noted that non-breaking space and soft hyphen indicator characters are not recognized and interpreted by all browsers, and due to this, their use is discouraged.

There are 58 character positions occupied by control characters. See Control Characters for details on the interpretation of control characters.

Because certain special characters are subject to interpretation and special processing, information providers and browser implementors should follow the guidelines in the Special Characters section.

In addition, HTML provides character entity references and numerical character references to facilitate the entry and interpretation of characters by name and by numerical position.

Because certain characters will be interpreted as markup, they must be represented by entity references as described in character and/or numerical references.

Character Entity References

Many of the Latin-1 set of printing characters may be represented within the text of an HTML document by a character entity.

The reasons why it may be beneficial to use character entity references instead of directly typing the required characters are as described in the numerical entity references. That is, character entity references compensate for keyboards that don't contain the required characters (such as characters common in many European languages) and where the characters may be recognised as SGML coding.

A character entity is represented in an HTML document as an SGML entity whose name is defined in the HTML DTD. The HTML DTD includes a character entity for each of the SGML markup characters and for each of the printing characters in the upper half of Latin-1, so that one may reference them by name if it is inconvenient to enter them directly:

> the ampersand (`&`), double quotes (`"`), lesser (`<`) and greater (`>`) characters

```
Kurt G&ouml;del was a famous logician and mathematician.
```

NOTE

To ensure that a string of characters is not interpreted as markup, represent all occurrences of <, >, and & by character or entity references.

Table B.3 contains the possible numeric and character entities for the ISO-Latin-1 (ISO8859-1) character set. Where possible, the character is shown.

NOTE

Not all browsers can display all characters, and some browsers may even display characters different from those that appear in the table. Newer browsers seem to have a better track record for handling character entities, but be sure to test your HTML files extensively with multiple browsers if you intend to use these entities.

Table B.3. ISO-Latin-1 character set.

Character	*Numeric Entity*	*Hex Value*	*Character Entity (if any)*	*Description*
	&#00;–&#08;	00–08		Unused
		09		Horizontal tab
0A		Line feed
	&#11;–&#31;	0B–1F		Unused
		20		Space
!	!	21		Exclamation mark
“	"	22	"	Quotation mark
#	#	23		Number sign
$	$	24		Dollar sign
%	%	25		Percent sign
&	&	26	&	Ampersand
‘	'	27		Apostrophe
(	(	28		Left parenthesis
)	)	29		Right parenthesis
*	*	2A		Asterisk
+	+	2B		Plus sign

continues

Table B.3. continued

Character	*Numeric Entity*	*Hex Value*	*Character Entity (if any)*	*Description*
,	,	2C		Comma
-	-	2D		Hyphen
.	.	2E		Period (fullstop)
/	/	2F		Solidus (slash)
0–9	0–9	30-39		Digits 0–9
:	:	3A		Colon
;	;	3B		Semicolon
<	<	3C	<	Less than
=	=	3D		Equals sign
>	>	3E	>	Greater than
?	?	3F		Question mark
@	@	40		Commercial at
A–Z	A–Z	41-5A		Letters A–Z
[	[	5B		Left square bracket
\	\	5C		Reverse solidus (backslash)
]	]	5D		Right square bracket
^	^	5E		Caret
—	_	5F		Horizontal bar
`	`	60		Grave accent
a–z	a–z	61-7A		Letters a–z
{	{	7B		Left curly brace
|			7C		Vertical bar
}	}	7D		Right curly brace
~	~	7E		Tilde
	&#127;–	;7F-A0		Unused
¡	¡	A1		Inverted exclamation point

Character	*Numeric Entity*	*Hex Value*	*Character Entity (if any)*	*Description*
¢	¢	A2		Cent sign
£	£	A3		Pound sterling
¤	¤	A4		General currency sign
¥	¥	A5		Yen sign
¦	¦	A6		Broken vertical bar
§	§	A7		Section sign
¨	¨	A8		Umlaut (dieresis)
©	©	A9	© (NHTML)	Copyright
ª	ª	AA		Feminine ordinal
«	«	AB		Left angle quote, guillemot left
¬	¬	AC		Not sign
-		AD		Soft hyphen
®	®	AE	® (HHTM)	Registered trademark
¯	¯	AF		Macron accent
°	°	B0		Degree sign
±	±	B1		Plus or minus
²	²	B2		Superscript two
³	³	B3		Superscript three
´	´	B4		Acute accent
µ	µ	B5		Micro sign
¶	¶	B6		Paragraph sign
·	·	B7		Middle dot
¸	¸	B8		Cedilla
¹	¹	B9		Superscript one
º	º	BA		Masculine ordinal
»	»	BB		Right angle quote, guillemot right

continues

Table B.3. continued

Character	Numeric Entity	Hex Value	Character Entity (if any)	Description
1/4	¼	BC		Fraction one-fourth
1/2	½	BD		Fraction one-half
3/4	¾	BE		Fraction three-fourths
¿	¿	BF		Inverted question mark
À	À	C0	À	Capital A, grave accent
Á	Á	C1	Á	Capital A, acute accent
Â	Â	C2	Â	Capital A, circumflex accent
Ã	Ã	C3	Ã	Capital A, tilde
Ä	Ä	C4	Ä	Capital A, dieresis or umlaut mark
Å	Å	C5	Å	Capital A, ring
Æ	Æ	C6	Æ	Capital AE dipthong (ligature)
Ç	Ç	C7	Ç	Capital C, cedilla
È	È	C8	È	Capital E, grave accent
É	É	C9	É	Capital E, acute accent
Ê	Ê	CA	Ê	Capital E, circumflex accent
Ë	Ë	CB	Ë	Capital E, dieresis or umlaut mark
Ì	Ì	CC	Ì	Capital I, grave accent
Í	Í	CD	Í	Capital I, acute accent

Character	Numeric Entity	Hex Value	Character Entity (if any)	Description
Î	Î	CE	Î	Capital I, circumflex accent
Ï	Ï	CF	Ï	Capital I, dieresis or umlaut mark
Ð	Ð	D0	Ð	Capital Eth, Icelandic
Ñ	Ñ	D1	Ñ	Capital N, tilde
Ò	Ò	D2	Ò	Capital O, grave accent
Ó	Ó	D3	Ó	Capital O, acute accent
Ô	Ô	D4	Ô	Capital O, circumflex accent
Õ	Õ	D5	Õ	Capital O, tilde
Ö	Ö	D6	Ö	Capital O, dieresis or umlaut mark
×	×	D7		Multiply sign
Ø	Ø	D8	Ø	Capital O, slash
Ù	Ù	D9	Ù	Capital U, grave accent
Ú	Ú	DA	Ú	Capital U, acute accent
Û	Û	DB	Û	Capital U, circumflex accent
Ü	Ü	DC	Ü	Capital U, dieresis or umlaut mark
Ý	Ý	DD	Ý	Capital Y, acute accent
	Þ	DE	Þ	Capital THORN, Icelandic
	ß	DF	ß	Small sharp s, German (sz ligature)

continues

Table B.3. continued

Character	Numeric Entity	Hex Value	Character Entity (if any)	Description
à	à	E0	à	Small a, grave accent
á	á	E1	á	Small a, acute accent
â	â	E2	â	Small a, circumflex accent
ã	ã	E3	ã	Small a, tilde
ä	ä	E4	&aauml;	Small a, dieresis or umlaut mark
å	å	E5	å	Small a, ring
æ	æ	E6	æ	Small ae dipthong (ligature)
ç	ç	E7	ç	Small c, cedilla
è	è	E8	è	Small e, grave accent
é	é	E9	é	Small e, acute accent
ê	ê	EA	ê	Small e, circumflex accent
ë	ë	EB	ë	Small e, dieresis or umlaut mark
ì	ì	EC	ì	Small i, grave accent
í	í	ED	í	Small i, acute accent
î	î	EE	î	Small i, circumflex accent
ï	ï	EF	ï	Small i, dieresis or umlaut mark
ð	ð	F0	ð	Small eth, Icelandic
ñ	ñ	F1	ñ	Small n, tilde

Character	Numeric Entity	Hex Value	Character Entity (if any)	Description
ò	ò	F2	ò	Small o, grave accent
ó	ó	F3	ó	Small o, acute accent
ô	ô	F4	ô	Small o, circumflex accent
õ	õ	F5	õ	Small o, tilde
ö	ö	F6	ö	Small o, dieresis or umlaut mark
÷	÷	F7		Division sign
ø	ø	F8	ø	Small o, slash
ù	ù	F9	ù	Small u, grave accent
ú	ú	FA	ú	Small u, acute accent
û	û	FB	û	Small u, circumflex accent
ü	ü	FC	ü	Small u, dieresis or umlaut mark
ý	ý	FD	ý	Small y, acute accent
	þ	FE	þ	Small thorn, Icelandic
ÿ	ÿ	FF	ÿ	Small y, dieresis or umlaut mark

Control Characters

Control characters are non-printable characters that are typically used for communication and device control, as format effectors, and as information separators.

In SGML applications, the use of control characters is limited in order to maximise the chance of successful interchange over heterogenous networks and operating systems. In HTML, only three control characters are used: Horizontal Tab (HT, encoded as 9 decimal in US-ASCII and ISO-8859-1), Carriage Return, and Line Feed.

Horizontal Tab is interpreted as a word space in all contexts except preformatted text. Within preformatted text, the tab should be interpreted to shift the horizontal column position to the next position which is a multiple of 8 on the same line; that is, `col := ((col+8) div8) * 8` (where `div` is integer division).

Carriage Return and Line Feed are conventionally used to represent end of line. For Internet Media Types defined as `text/*`, the sequence CR/LF is used to represent an end of line. In practice, `text/html` documents are frequently represented and transmitted using an end of line convention that depends on the conventions of the source of the document; frequently, that representation consists of CR only, LF only, or CR/LF combination. In HTML, end of line in any of its variations is interpreted as a word space in all contexts except preformatted text. Within preformatted text, HTML interpreting agents should expect to treat any of the three common representations of end-of-line as starting a new line.

Numeric Character References

In addition to any mechanism by which characters may be represented by the encoding of the HTML document, it is possible to explicitly reference the printing characters of the Latin-1 character encoding using a numeric character reference.

There are two principle cases for using a numeric character reference. Firstly, some keyboards may not provide the necessary characters (such as those that use accents, cedilla's, dieresis marks and so on,) commonly used in European languages. Secondly, some characters would be interpreted as SGML coding (for example, the ampersand &, double quotes " and lesser < and greater than > characters) and so should be referred to by numerical references.

Numeric character references are represented in an HTML document as SGML entities whose name is number sign (#) followed by a numeral from 32-126 and 161-255. The HTML DTD includes a numeric character for each of the printing characters of the Latin-1 encoding, so that one may reference them by number if it is inconvenient to enter them directly: the ampersand (`&`), double quotes (`"`), lesser (`<`), and greater (`>`) characters.

The following entity names are used in HTML, always prefixed by an ampersand (&) and followed by a semicolon. See Table B.2.

Special Characters

Certain characters have special meaning in HTML documents. There are two printing characters which may be interpreted by an HTML application to have an effect on the format of the text.

Space

This is interpreted as a single word space (the section of a paragraph of text where the text can be broken if necessary—for example, where lines can be broken for text wrapping) except where it is used within `<PRE>...</PRE>` elements. Within preformatted text elements, a space is interpreted as a nonbreaking space.

Hyphen

This is interpreted as a hyphen glyph in all contexts.

The following entity names are used in HTML, always prefixed by an ampersand (&) and followed by a semicolon. They represent particular graphic characters which have special meanings in places in the markup, or may not be part of the character set available to the writer.

Glyph	*Name*	*Syntax*	*Description*
<	lt	<	Less than sign
>	gt	>	Greater than sign
&	amp	&	Ampersand
"	quot	"	Double quote sign

Document Sound

> **NOTE**
>
> Two different elements now exist for employing in-line sound directly in an HTML document. The first is BGSOUND; this element is currently only supported by Microsoft Internet Explorer. The other is SOUND, which is currently only supported by NCSA Mosaic. Mosaic does also support a limited version of Microsoft's BGSOUND element. Netscape can support in-line sound via the plug-in mechanism. See <EMBED> for more details.

The BGSOUND element allows authors to create pages that will play sound clips, or background soundtracks while the page is being viewed. Sounds can either be samples (.WAV or .AU format) or MIDI (.MID format).

<BGSOUND>

The HTML used to insert a background sound into a page is

```
<BGSOUND SRC="start.wav">
```

The BGSOUND element accepts the following attributes.

SRC

This attribute specifies the address of a sound to be played.

LOOP=*n*

This attribute specifies how many times a sound will loop when activated. If n=-1 or LOOP=INFINITE is specified, the sound will loop indefinitely.

Mosaic supports use of the SOUND element for playing inline sound. This element allows the playing of *.WAV files in pages.

NOTE

The SOUND element is only supported by Mosaic.

The syntax is

```
<SOUND SRC="filename.wav">
```

The <SOUND> element supports the following attributes:

LOOP=infinite and DELAY=sec.

LOOP=infinite will play the sound sample continuously while the page is being viewed.

DELAY=sec will delay playing of the sound file for the specified number of seconds after the page and sound file have finished loading.

NOTE

Although Mosaic will support the use of the BGSOUND element (for .WAV file), it will not play in-line *.MID MIDI files without launching an external application as defined in the Helper Application set up.

Dynamic Documents

Recent advances in browser technology have been pushing the idea of active content. To this end, there are a number of methods that HTML authors should be aware of:

- **Server-push**. This mechanism has generally been used for providing animation within Web pages, whereby the Web server serves the page that the browser has requested, and keeps the client (browser) to server connection open and keeps repeatedly sending down chunks of data as long as the connection is kept open. To be able to take advantage of such a mechanism requires an in-depth knowledge of MIME types, the for non-HTTP transport protocol, and CGI scripting or programming. As such, it is not really recommended other than programmers.
- **Client-pull**. As seen in the discussion of the `<META>` element, this method provides a useful automatic redirection mechanism for serving Web pages. The server serves the browser the requested page (which contains `META` information) which makes the browser believe it has received certain HTTP response headers, which typically would be used to make the browser retrieve a different document. For more details, see the `<META>` element.

Server-Push

Server-push allows for dynamic document updating via a server to client connection that is kept open. This method (as opposed to client-pull) is totally controlled by the server, but the perpetual open connection occupies valuable server resources. Its main advantage over client-pull is that using server-push, it is possible to replace a single inline image in a page repeatedly. All that is needed is that the `SRC` attribute of the image to be updated points to a URL that continually pushes image data through the open HTTP connection.

The exact server-push mechanism is technically complex and is outside the scope of this reference. What is presented below is a brief outline of the method. Those that are interested in utilizing server-push in CGI scripts or Web server-based executable applications should visit the Netscape Web site (`http://home.netscape.com/`) for more information. Note that only Netscape supports the use of server-push.

When a Web server receives a request for an HTML document, it typically sends a single set of data (the actual HTML document). Many pieces of data can be sent encapsulated in a single message by using the MIME type `multipart/mixed`. The message is split into separate data sections, each provided with its own MIME type (given in the content header) so that the browser can distinguish between the different data in the different sections of the message. Server-push utilizes a variation on this MIME type, called `multipart/x-mixed-replace` (the `x-` represents the fact that the MIME type is experimental and has not achieved standardized use). It is by virtue of the "replace" section that certain sections of the message can be replaced. Essentially, the server does not push down the entire message at once. It will send down sections (data-chunks) of the message when it sees fit (or as controlled by the server-push script or application). When the browser sees a separator (sent down in the `multipart/x-mixed-replace` message), it just sits and waits for the next data object to be sent, which it then uses to replace the data previously sent by the server.

Forms

Perhaps the biggest advance that the HTML 2.0 specification made over its predecessors was the inclusion of elements that allowed for users to input information. These elements are the <FORM> elements. They provide for the inclusion of objects like text boxes, choice lists, and so on and have proved invaluable for recent HTML applications, particularly search engines, database query entries, and the like.

It should be noted that while these HTML elements can be used to easily define the presentation of the form to the user, the real value behind any form is in what it does with the information that is entered. For a form to do anything more than send a straight text dump of the form data (including control characters) to an e-mail address, the form data will need to be passed to some kind of CGI script, or server-based executable for processing. (CGI scripting is outside of the scope of this reference; ample reference material is available elsewhere for those interested.)

The following elements are used to create forms:

<FORM>...</FORM>	A form within a document
<INPUT ...>...</INPUT>	One input field
<OPTION>	One option within a Select element
<SELECT>...<SELECT>	A selection from a finite set of options
<TEXTAREA ...>...</TEXTAREA>	A multi-line input field

Each variable field is defined by an INPUT, TEXTAREA, or OPTION element and must have a NAME attribute to identify its value in the data returned when the form is submitted.

A very simple form for eliciting user response would be:

```
<H1 ALIGN="center">Comment Form</H1>
<FORM METHOD="POST" ACTION="http://www.htmlib.com/formscript.cgi">
<CENTER>
Your name: <INPUT NAME="name" size="20">
Your e-mail address: <INPUT NAME="email" size="20">
<P>I think the HTML Reference is:
  <SELECT NAME="Choice">
    <OPTION>Outstanding
    <OPTION>Very good
    <OPTION>Good
    <OPTION>Average
    <OPTION>Below Average
    <OPTION>Awful
    <OPTION SELECTED>My response would be "indecent" under the CDA Act.
  </SELECT>
<P>If you have any further comments, please enter them here:<BR>
  <TEXTAREA NAME="Comments" ROWS="10" COLS="40" WRAP="Virtual">
  </TEXTAREA>
<P><INPUT TYPE=SUBMIT> <INPUT TYPE=RESET>
</CENTER>
</FORM>
```

Different platforms will have different native systems for navigating within the input fields of a form. (For example, Windows users can use the Tab key to move from one field to the next through the order that the fields appear within the form.) Different browsers may also display different text on any buttons included in the form. For example, Netscape defaults to displaying "“Submit Query" for a button specified by `<INPUT TYPE=SUBMIT>`, while Internet Explorer and Mosaic display just "Submit" on such a button. Figure B.1 shows the form resulting from the preceding HTML fragment.

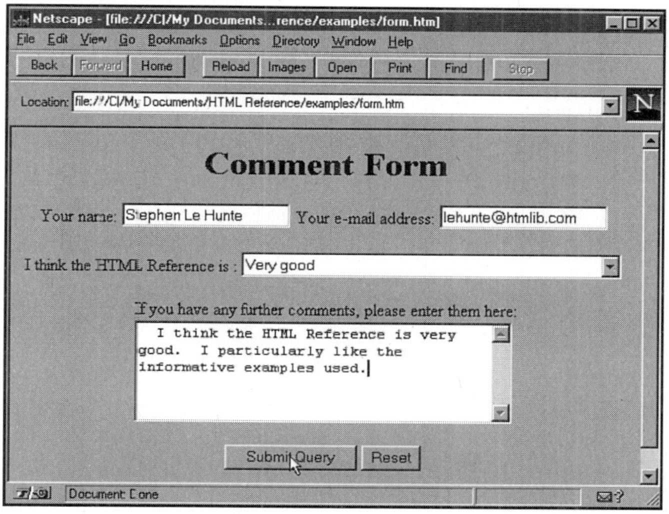

FIGURE B.1.
The Windows 95 version of Atlas Preview 1 (3.0 beta 2) showing Netscape's support for use of the `<TEXTAREA WRAP="virtual">` *element.*

HTTP File Upload

It is possible to write forms that ask for files as input, rather than data input by input boxes and other simple elements such as checkboxes and radio buttons.

An example of such a form would be:

```
<FORM ENCTYPE="multipart/form-data" ACTION="_URL_" METHOD=POST>
Send this file: <INPUT NAME="userfile" TYPE="file">
<INPUT TYPE="submit" VALUE="Send File">
</FORM>
```

NOTE

This method of file upload is Netscape specific and is essentially adoption of another IETF Internet Draft by the Netscape authors. The Internet Draft in question, "Form based file upload in HTML," details adding the `FILE` option to the `TYPE` attribute of the `INPUT` element,

continues

allowing an ACCEPT attribute for the INPUT element (which would be a list of MIME types—essentially detailing what files are allowed to be uploaded as the contents of the form) and allowing the ENCTYPE of a form to be multipart/form-data. This MIME type essentially wraps the form data (including that presented in any other input fields) as a data stream, with discrete boundaries between the information sections. For a more detailed description, readers should check the HTTP file upload specification.

The display method is largely at the discretion of the browsers that support this method. Netscape (Windows versions) display a "Browse..." button beside the input box, which brings up the standard open/save dialog box, allowing the choice of any local file for upload.

<FORM>...</FORM>

The <FORM> element is used to delimit a data input form. There can be several forms in a single document, but the <FORM> element can not be nested. (That is, a form can't contain another form.)

```
<FORM ACTION='_URL_" METHOD="GET¦POST" ENCTYPE="MIME type">
```

The ACTION attribute is a URL specifying the location to which the contents of the form data fields are submitted to elicit a response. As mentioned before, this could be simply a direction to an e-mail address, but generally, would be used to point towards some kind of server-based CGI script/application that handles the forwarding of form data. If the ACTION attribute is missing, the URL of the document itself is assumed. The way data is submitted varies with the access protocol of the URL to which the form data is sent and with the values of the METHOD and ENCTYPE attributes.

Generally, the METHOD attribute specifies a method of accessing the URL specified in the ACTION attribute. Generally, the method will be either GET or POST. The GET method is ideal for form submission where the use of the form data does not require external processing. For example, with database searches, there is no lasting effect caused by the query of the form (that is, the query runs its search through the database and reports the results). However, when the form is used to provide information, for example, that updates a database, then the POST method should be used, with the ACTION attribute pointing to a CGI script that executes the form data processing.

The ENCTYPE specifies the media type used to encode the form data. The default ENCTYPE is the MIME type application/x-www-form-urlencoded.

<INPUT>

The <INPUT> element represents a field whose contents may be edited or activated by the user. Attributes of the <INPUT> element are listed in the following sections.

ALIGN

To be used with the TYPE=IMAGE setting, this attribute specifies the alignment of the image. It takes the same values as the ALIGN in the <IMG> element.

CHECKED

To be used with a TYPE=CHECKBOX or TYPE=RADIO setting, this indicates that the checkbox or radio button is selected.

MAXLENGTH

To be used with TYPE=TEXT setting, this indicates the maximum number of characters that can be entered into a text field. This can be greater than specified by the SIZE attribute, in which case the field will scroll appropriately. The default number of characters is unlimited.

NAME

This attribute represents the name that will be used for the data when transferring the form's contents. The NAME attribute is required for most input types and is normally used to provide a unique identifier for a field, or for a logically related group of fields.

SIZE

Specifies the size or precision of the field according to its type. For example, to specify a field with a visible width of 24 characters:

```
INPUT TYPE=text SIZE="24"
```

SRC

To be used with the TYPE=IMAGE, this attribute represents a URL specifying the desired image.

TYPE

Defines the type of data the field accepts. Defaults to free text. Several types of fields can be defined with the type attribute:

BUTTON

This can be used to embed buttons directly into HTML documents, that add functionality when used in conjunction with Visual Basic Script. The NAME attribute is used to give the button a unique name, which can be used to set its function in the script. The VALUE attribute specifies the text that is displayed on the button in the document.

CHECKBOX

Used for simple Boolean attributes (where a field will be chosen, or not) or for attributes that can take multiple values at the same time. The latter is represented by a number of checkbox fields, each of which has the same name. Each selected checkbox generates a separate name/value pair in the submitted data, even if this results in duplicate names. The default value for checkboxes is "on." This field type requires the `NAME` and `VALUE` attributes; `CHECKED` is an optional attribute.

FILE

Netscape now supports a `FILE` option to the `TYPE` attribute of the `INPUT` element, allowing an `ACCEPT` attribute for the `INPUT` element (which is a list of media types or type patterns allowed for the input) and allowing the `ENCTYPE` of a form to be `multipart/form-data`. This allows the inclusion of files with form information, which could prove invaluable, for example, for companies providing technical support, or service providers, requesting data files.

HIDDEN

With this input type, no field is presented to the user, but the content of the field is sent with the submitted form. This value may be used to transmit state information about client/server interaction.

IMAGE

An image field upon which you can click with a pointing device, causing the form to be immediately submitted. The coordinates of the selected point are measured in pixel units from the upper-left corner of the image, and are returned (along with the other contents of the form) in two name/value pairs. The x-coordinate is submitted under the name of the field with `.x` appended, and the y-coordinate is submitted under the name of the field with `.y` appended. The `NAME` attribute is required. The image itself is specified by the `SRC` attribute, exactly as for the Image element.

> **NOTE**
>
> In a future version of the HTML specification, the `IMAGE` functionality may be folded into an enhanced `SUBMIT` field.

PASSWORD

`PASSWORD` is the same as the `TEXT` attribute, except that text is not displayed as it is entered.

RADIO

RADIO is used for attributes that accept a single value from a set of alternatives. Each radio button field in the group should be given the same name. Only the selected radio button in the group generates a name/value pair in the submitted data. Radio buttons require an explicit VALUE and NAME attribute. CHECKED is an optional attribute and can be used to specify which options are selected for initial form display.

RESET

RESET is a button that, when pressed, resets the form's fields to their specified initial values. The label to be displayed on the button may be specified just as for the SUBMIT button.

SUBMIT

SUBMIT is a button that, when pressed, submits the form. You can use the VALUE attribute to provide a non-editable label to be displayed on the button. The default label is browser-specific. If a SUBMIT button is pressed in order to submit the form, and that button has a NAME attribute specified, then that button contributes a name/value pair to the submitted data. Otherwise, a SUBMIT button makes no contribution to the submitted data.

TEXT

TEXT is used for single-line text-entry fields. It should be used in conjunction with the SIZE and MAXLENGTH attributes to set the maximum amount of text that can be entered. For textual input that requires multiple lines, use the <TEXTAREA> element for text fields which can accept multiple lines. Explicit VALUE and NAME attributes are also required.

TEXTAREA

TEXTAREA is used for multiple-line text-entry fields. Use in conjunction with the SIZE and MAXLENGTH attributes.

VALUE

When used with TYPE= ... attributes, this attribute sets the initial displayed value of the field if it displays a textual or numerical value. If the TYPE= ... attribute is one which only allows Boolean values (that is, chosen or not chosen) then this specifies the value to be returned when the field is selected.

<OPTION>

The <OPTION> element can only occur within a <SELECT> element. It represents one choice, and can take these attributes:

SELECTED

Indicates that this option is initially selected.

VALUE

When present indicates the value to be returned if this option is chosen. The returned value defaults to the contents of the `<OPTION>` element.

The contents of the `<OPTION>` element is presented to the user to represent the option. It is used as a returned value if the `VALUE` attribute is not present.

<SELECT ...>...</SELECT>

The `<SELECT>` element allows the user to chose one of a set of alternatives described by textual labels. Every alternative is represented by the `<OPTION>` element.

Attributes used with the `<SELECT>` are listed in the following sections.

MULTIPLE

The `MULTIPLE` attribute is needed when users are allowed to make several selections, for example, `<SELECT MULTIPLE>`.

NAME

Specifies the name that will submitted as part of a name/value pair.

SIZE

Specifies the number of visible items. If this is greater than one, then the resulting form control will be a list.

The `SELECT` element is typically rendered as a pull down or pop-up list. For example:

```
<SELECT NAME="Choice">
  <OPTION>Outstanding
  <OPTION>Very good
  <OPTION>Good
  <OPTION>Average
  <OPTION>Below Average
  <OPTION>Awful
  <OPTION SELECTED>My response would be "indecent" under the CDA Act.
</SELECT>
```

<TEXTAREA>...</TEXTAREA>

The `TEXTAREA` element lets users enter more than one line of text.

Any text included up to the end element (</TEXTAREA>) is used to initialize the field's value. This end element is always required even if the field is initially blank. When submitting a form, lines in a TEXTAREA should be terminated using CR/LF.

In a typical rendering, the ROWS and COLS attributes determine the visible dimension of the field in characters. The field is rendered in a fixed-width font. Browsers should allow text to extend beyond these limits by scrolling as needed.

Recent versions of Netscape (from version 2.0) have introduced the WRAP attribute in the TEXTAREA element: Now it is possible to specify how to handle word-wrapping display in text input areas in forms.

<TEXTAREA WRAP=OFF>	The default setting. Wrapping doesn't happen. Lines are sent exactly as typed.
<TEXTAREA WRAP=VIRTUAL>	The display word-wraps, but long lines are sent as one line without new-lines.
<TEXTAREA WRAP=PHYSICAL>	The display word-wraps, and the text is transmitted at all wrap points.

NOTE

Word wrapping in a TEXTAREA text box is supported by Netscape only.

Advanced Page Formatting

NOTE

The use of Frames is currently only supported by recent versions of Netscape (from version 2.0) and Internet Explorer (3.0 and above).

Frames allow the browser display window to be subdivided into separate sections. Each section can be updated or have new documents loaded into it separately from the remaining frame sections. As such, a frame-based layout can be especially useful for HTML applications where some information is required across a whole range of pages (such as a table of contents or title graphics)

Frames are generated by three elements: <FRAMESET>, <FRAME> elements, and <FRAME>.

Frame Document

A frame document has a basic structure very much like a normal HTML document, except the BODY container is replaced by a FRAMESET container which describes the sub-HTML documents, or Frames, that will make up the page.

```
<HTML>
<HEAD>
</HEAD>
<FRAMESET>

</FRAMESET>
</HTML>
```

No HTML that would normally be included within the <BODY> section of an HTML document should be included within the <FRAMESET> ... </FRAMESET> elements.

Frame Syntax

<FRAMESET>

This is the main container for a frame. It has two attributes ROWS and COLS. The <FRAMESET> element has a matching end element, and within the FRAMESET you can only have other nested <FRAMESET>, <FRAME>, or <NOFRAMES> elements.

ROWS="row_height_value_list"

This takes a list of values, separated by comma marks. They can represent either absolute pixel, percentage, or relative scaling values. The total set by the values given in the ROWS attribute should not exceed 100% (as the total rows are extended across the whole available browser display window).

If any of the values are single numerical values, then these are considered to be absolute pixel values. It is not recommended to fix a frameset by using a complete set of pixel values, because browsers use a variety of different screen resolutions when viewing documents, and the layout may become distorted. Percentage values can be given for this attribute. If the total percentage values given exceed 100% then all values will be scaled down by the browser so that the total is 100%. The remaining value option is to use a * character. This tells the browser that the frame is a relative size frame and should be displayed accordingly. Numerical values can be used with the * character, to scale the relative frame sections within the browser window.

To specify a three-part, vertical framed layout where the first section uses 20 percent of the display window, the second uses 100 pixels, and the third section uses the remaining screen, use:

```
<FRAMESET ROWS="20%, 100, *>
```

To split the layout into two vertical frames, the first using a quarter of the display window, the second using three-quarters of the window, use:

```
<FRAMESET ROWS="25%, 75%>
```

This would be exactly the same as using `<FRAMESET ROWS="*, 3*">`.

COLS="*column_width_list*"

The `COLS` attribute takes as its value a comma separated list of values that is of the exact same syntax as the list described above for the `ROWS` attribute.

The `<FRAMESET>` element can be nested. In this way, frame sections can be set up where the display window can be split into either horizontal or vertical sections, with any of these being further sub-divided by nested `<FRAMESET>` elements.

<FRAME>

This element defines a single frame in a frameset. It has eight possible attributes: `SRC`, `NAME`, `MARGINWIDTH`, `MARGINHEIGHT`, `SCROLLING`, `NORESIZE`, `FRAMEBORDER` and `FRAMESPACING`. The `<FRAME>` element is not a container, so it has no matching end tag.

SRC="*url*"

This attribute is used to specify the HTML document that will be used as the display in the particular frame section of the frameset.

NAME="*frame_name*"

The NAME attribute is used to assign a name to a frame so it can be targeted by links in other documents, by using `<A HREF="_URL_" TARGET="frame_name">`. (These would usually be from other documents in the same frameset.) The `NAME` attribute is optional; by default all windows are unnamed.

Names must begin with an alphanumeric character. Several reserved names have been defined, which start with an underscore.

These are currently:

`_blank`	Always load this link into a new, unnamed window.
`_self`	Always load this link over the document that originated the link.
`_parent`	Always load this link over the parent frame. (becomes self if the frame has no parent, or is the parent frame).
`_top`	Always load this link at the top level (becomes self if the frame is the top frame).

NOTE

Although these are reserved names for the NAME attribute of the <FRAME> element, they should only be referred to using an anchor target. That is, used to target specific windows, allowing smoother transition between framed documents and between framed and non-framed documents (for example, when providing a link to documents on a foreign server that may not be framed documents). Although Internet Explorer supports the naming of frames for document navigation and hyperlinking, it doesn't support the use of the `_blank` reserved name for opening a document in a new browser window. Also, unlike Netscape, Internet Explorer will not open a new window for a link whose TARGET value has not been defined by a NAME attribute.

MARGINWIDTH="*value*"

This accepts an absolute pixel value and forces indentation from the left- and right-hand side of the frame pane according to the number of pixels. It cannot be set to a value less than 1 as this would cause the contents of the frame to be displayed right up against the left-hand margin. By default, the browser will choose its own `MARGINWIDTH` when trying to produce the best possible display.

MARGINHEIGHT="*value*"

This is analogous to the `MARGINWIDTH` attribute, but it controls the top and bottom margins.

SCROLLING="yes¦no¦auto"

This attribute can be used to control the appearance of any scrollbars that may appear as a result of the frame contents being too much to display in the set pane. Using "no" may be dangerous, because the HTML author cannot know the resolution/display window size of the client browser and so information may not be displayable.

NORESIZE

By default, all frames specified in a framed document can be resized by the client. Setting this flag (it requires no value) prevents the frame from being resized.

FRAMEBORDER="yes¦no"

This is an Internet Explorer–specific attribute, which allows control of the frame border display. With this attribute set to "no," the borders for the specific frame are not drawn.

FRAMESPACING="*value*"

This attribute is also Internet Explorer–specific and allows the setting of extra space around frames, to give the appearance of floating frames. The "value" should be the distance required around the frame in pixels.

```
<FRAME FRAMESPACING="40" ...>
```

would present the frame with an invisible "border" of 55 pixels.

<NOFRAMES>

This element is provided for HTML authors who want to create alternative content for browsers that cannot display frames. This is especially useful if the author is making the very first document of the site a framed document. It should be noted that this element is not actually recognized by non-frame capable browsers. As with any HTML, if the browser does not recognize the element, it ignores it. Browsers that cannot display frames would ignore all the `<FRAMESET>` and `<FRAME>` elements, but will display whatever is enclosed in the `<NOFRAMES> ... </NOFRAMES>` elements, which can be any HTML at all, because that is what it recognizes. On the other hand, frame-capable browsers will preferentially display what is set up by the frame elements, unless they provide any mechanism where the display of frames can be turned off, in which case they may display this alternative content.

The Main Frame Setup Document

The main document that sets up the example frame is as follows:

```
<HTML>
<!--HTMLIB.HTM-->
<HEAD>
<TITLE>The HTML Reference Library</TITLE>
</HEAD>
<BASEFONT SIZE=3>

<FRAMESET ROWS="85,*,65">
<FRAME SCROLLING="no" NAME="title" NORESIZE SRC="title.htm">
<FRAMESET COLS="40%,60%">
<FRAME SCROLLING="yes" NAME="toc" SRC="toc.htm">
<FRAME SCROLLING="yes" NAME="main page" SRC="main.htm">
</FRAMESET>
<FRAME SCROLLING="no" NAME="HLP buttons" NORESIZE SRC="buttons.htm">

<NOFRAME>

</NOFRAME>
</FRAMESET>
</HTML>
```

A Line-by-Line Breakdown

```
<FRAMESET ROWS="85,*,65">
```

This line divides the page into three regions, the top region being 85 pixels in height, the bottom region being 65 pixels in height, the middle region occupying the rest of the browser window.

```
<FRAME SCROLLING="no" NAME="title" NORESIZE SRC="title.htm">
```

This line sets the top region of the window (the region that is 85 pixels high) to be a non-scrolling, non-resizable region. Its name is title (so, any other link that specifies "title" with its `TARGET` attribute would be displayed in this region).

```
<FRAMESET COLS="40%,60%">
```

This is a nested `<FRAMESET>` element and splits the middle region of the browser window into two sections horizontally. The left-hand section being 40 percent of the frame width, the right-hand section being the remaining 60 percent of the frame width. (This could also have been achieved using `<FRAMESET COLS="2*, 3*>`.)

```
<FRAME SCROLLING="yes" NAME="toc" SRC="toc.htm">
<FRAME SCROLLING="yes" NAME="main page" SRC="main.htm">
```

These two lines (as the other `<FRAME>` line above) set the attributes for the two middle sections of the page. That is, they name the regions `toc` and `main page`, respectively, and link the regions to the two pages to be displayed in the regions.

```
</FRAMESET>
```

This line closes the subframes that were opened in the middle section of the main framed regions.

```
<FRAME SCROLLING="no" NAME="buttons" NORESIZE SRC="buttons.htm">
```

This line defines the properties of the remaining main region of the window, the bottom region that is 65 pixels high. It defines it as a non-scrolling, non-resizable region (ideal for navigation tools).

The Title Document

NOTE

This document contains no mark up relevant to the use of the frames, but has been included for reasons of completeness.

This document is the Title for the paged document. It resides in the top frame, which is a non-scrolling, non-resizeable frame. Hence the title will always be displayed in the same place. Note that for frame subdocuments, titles are not required. The title of the site will always be taken from the main frame page.

```
<HTML>
<!--TITLE.HTM-->
<BODY>
<BASEFONT SIZE=3>
<CENTER>
<H2 ALIGN=center>Hello and Welcome to the HTML Reference Library</H2>
<BR>
</CENTER>
</BODY>
</HTML>
```

The Contents Document

This is the Table of Contents page. It appears on the left scrolling frame region. This section has been used (in this example) for a stationary table of contents.

```
<HTML>
<!--TOC.HTM-->
<BODY>
<BASEFONT SIZE=2>
<CENTER>
Please Select a Volume<BR><BR>
<A HREF="lang.htm" TARGET="main page"><B>1) The HTML Language</B></A><BR>
<A HREF="qr.htm" TARGET="main page"><B>2) Quick Reference Guide</B></A><BR>
<A HREF="author.htm" TARGET="main page"><B>3) Contacting the Author</B></A><BR>
<A HREF="new.htm" TARGET="main page"><B>4) New in this version</B></A><BR>
</CENTER>
</BODY>
</HTML>
```

The use of the `TARGET` attribute in the anchor means that when each link is activated, the document accessed will be displayed in the frame region named `main page`. Thus, any documents accessed from the table of contents will appear in the framed region to the right of the table of contents.

The Main Text Document

NOTE

This document contains no mark up relevant to the use of the frames, but has been included for reasons of completeness.

This document is the document that appears in the right hand framed region of the page the first time the page is accessed.

```
<HTML>
<!--MAIN.HTM-->
<BODY>
This reference, using the Internet Draft as an information base is an on-line
reference library of currently supported HTML elements - their syntax, and
use.<BR>
It assumes that the user has knowledge of the World Wide Web and the various
browsers available. Information on specific browsers, or the broader topic
of 'The World Wide Web' can be obtained by reading the World Wide Web FAQ.<BR>
</BODY>
</HTML>
```

The Navigation Buttons Document

NOTE

This document contains no mark up relevant to the use of the frames, but has been included for reasons of completeness.

This document resides at the bottom of the framed document. This region is a non-scrollable, non-resizable region. As such, it is ideal for a set of navigation buttons or other tools, as these could be. For the purposes of this example, the buttons are just a graphic image.

```
<HTML>
<!--BUTTONS.HTM-->
<BODY>
<CENTER>
<IMG SRC="buttons.gif"><BR>
<FONT SIZE=1>&copy; Stephen Le Hunte 1995</FONT>
</CENTER>
</BODY>
</HTML>
```

The HTML Language Document

NOTE

This document contains no mark up relevant to the use of the frames, but has been included for reasons of completeness.

This document is accessed by choosing the first option from the table of contents. When accessed, it would be displayed in the right-hand section of the middle regions.

```
<HTML>
<!--LANG.HTM-->
<BODY>
<CENTER><B>The HTML Language</B></CENTER>
<BR>
```

```
The vast range of HTML MarkUp currently supported by available browsers
(Web browsers, such as Netscape, Mosaic etc.) can be divided into the
following sections. Some elements featured here may not be supported by
all browsers. Where an element is known to be supported by specific
browsers, the element description will be labeled as such.<BR>
</BODY>
</HTML>
```

Inline Images

Recently, the <IMG> element has undergone the largest enhancements of all HTML 2.0 elements, on the way to newer HTML standardization. This is due to the <IMG> element being probably the second most important markup element (behind the Anchor element) as it handles all embedded graphical content in HTML documents.

The attributes commonly supported by the <IMG> element have had some recent additions to allow client-side image maps, embedded inline video clips, and embedded inline VRML worlds.

NOTE

Formats

Netscape and Mosaic (and most other browsers) will only support use of .GIF and JPG images within HTML documents. This can be extended with Netscape, by embedding image formats within pages, providing the format is one that the user will have software to handle installed on their system, or they have a plug-in module specifically to handle that type of image (see <EMBED>). Also, Netscape natively supports (that is, the browser can display) progressive JPEG images.

Internet Explorer will allow the use of GIF, JPEG, progressive JPEG images, PNG (portable network graphics) images and also BMP files, giving the author a wider variety of image formats from which to choose.

Netscape now fully supports the GIF89a format, which means that multi-image GIF files can be used to create animation sequences. Users are encouraged to seek out the GIF Construction Kit for more details and tools for the preparation of multi-image GIF files.

<IMG...>

The Image element is used to incorporate inline graphics (typically icons or small graphics) into an HTML document. This element cannot be used for embedding other HTML text. Browsers that cannot render inline images ignore the Image element unless it contains the ALT attribute.

The Image element, which is empty (no closing element), has these attributes:

ALIGN

The `ALIGN` attribute accepts the values `left`, `right`, `top`, `texttop`, `middle`, `absmiddle`, `baseline`, `bottom`, and `absbottom`, which specifies the alignment of the image and that of the following line of text.

> **NOTE**
>
> Not all browsers support the left and right alignment of images and will render embedded images on their own paragraph space in the browser window.

These attribute values to the `ALIGN` option require some explanation. First, the values `"left"` and `"right"`. Images with those alignments are a *floating* image type.

`ALIGN=left` will align the image on the left-hand edge of the browser display window and subsequent text will wrap around the right-hand side of that image.

`ALIGN=right` will align the image on the right-hand edge of the browser display window and subsequent text will wrap around the left-hand side of that image.

The use of floating images and wrap around text can cause some formatting problems. Using `<BR CLEAR=left¦right¦all>` is recommended to achieve the desired page formatting effect.

`ALIGN=top` allows any text following the image to align itself with the top of the tallest item in the line. (That is, the top of the image.)

`ALIGN=texttop` allows any text following the image to align itself with the top of the tallest text in the line (this is usually but not always the same as `ALIGN=top`).

`ALIGN=middle` aligns the baseline of the current line with the middle of the image.

`ALIGN=absmiddle` aligns the middle of the current line with the middle of the image.

`ALIGN=baseline` aligns the bottom of the image with the baseline of the current line.

`ALIGN=bottom` aligns the bottom of the image with the baseline of the current line.

`ALIGN=absbottom` aligns the bottom of the image with the bottom of the current line.

ALT

This attribute allows the setting of text as an alternative to the graphic for rendering in non-graphical environments, or when the user has de-activated the auto-loading of images. Alternate text should be provided by the browser whenever the graphic is not rendered.

```
<IMG SRC="triangle.gif" ALT="Warning:"> Be sure to read these instructions.
```

Internet Explorer uses any ALT text that is set as a "Tool Tip" that is displayed whenever the mouse pauses over an image for which the ALT text has been specified.

BORDER=*value*

This lets the document author control the thickness of the border around an image displayed.

It is useful is the image is to be a hyperlink, in that the BORDER can be set to 0 to avoid the display of the standard blue hypertext link border.

ISMAP

The ISMAP (is map) attribute identifies an image as an image map. Image maps are graphics in which certain regions are mapped to other documents. By clicking on different regions, different resources can be accessed from the same graphic. Example of use:

```
<A HREF="http://machine/htbin/imagemap/sample">
<IMG SRC="sample.gif" ISMAP></A>
```

NOTE

To be able to employ this type of image map in HTML documents, the HTTP server which will be controlling document access must have the correct cgi-bin software installed to control image map behavior. That is, the document must have access to an image map handling script and the map file defining the graphic hot-spots.

Recent browsers allow a simpler form of image map, known as client-side image maps. Although this is currently a proposed extension to HTML, it is widely supported by browsers. For details, see Client Side Image Maps.

LOWSRC

Using the LOWSRC attribute, it is possible to use two images in the same space. The syntax is

```
<IMG SRC="hiquality.gif" LOWSRC="lowquality.gif">
```

Browsers that do not recognize the LOWSRC attribute cleanly ignore it and simply load the image specified by the SRC attribute.

Browsers that support this attribute, however, will load the image called lowquality.gif on their first layout pass through the document. When the rest of the document has been completely loaded and formatted on the page, the browser will then redraw the page and load the image specified by the standard SRC attribute. This allows the author to specify a low-resolution (or smaller file size version of the main image—perhaps a grayscale version) image to be displayed initially while the document is loading, which is later replaced by the higher quality version.

Any graphic file format that the browser supports can be used interchangeably within the LOWSRC and SRC attributes. You can also specify width and height values in the IMG element, and both the high-resolution and low-resolution versions of the image will be appropriately scaled to match. However, if no width and height values have been set, the values used for the LOWSRC image (that is, the dimensions of that image) will be used to re-scale the SRC image. This is to minimize page format disruption that would be caused by the browser trying to load two different sized images into the same page space.

```
<IMG ALIGN="left" SRC="mosaic.gif" HSPACE="20" ALT="Mosaic logo">Mosaic,
from the <B>N</B>ational <B>C</B>entre for <B>S</B>upercomputing
<B>A</B>pplications represents the original graphical browser which
Netscape development was based on.
<BR CLEAR="all">
<HR>
<IMG ALIGN="right" SRC="netscape.gif" HSPACE="20" ALT="Netscape logo">Netscape,
from <B>Netscape Communications</B>, after initial development from Mosaic,
stormed away and became more or less the <I>de facto</I> Web browser.
<BR CLEAR="all">
<HR>
<IMG ALIGN="left" SRC="iexplore.gif" HSPACE="20" ALT="Internet Explorer logo">
Internet Explorer, from <B>Microsoft</B>, exhibits Microsoft's serious
intentions to enter the Web browser market and compete head-to-head with
Netscape.
<BR CLEAR="all">
<HR>
```

SRC

The value of the SRC attribute is the URL of the image to be displayed. Its syntax is the same as that of the HREF attribute of the <A> element. SRC is the only mandatory attribute of the <IMG> element. Image elements are allowed within anchors.

```
<IMG SRC ="warning.gif">Be sure to read these instructions.
```

The SRC attribute can accept fully qualified, or partial, relative URL's, or even just image names (providing the image is located in the same directory as the HTML document).

VSPACE=*value* HSPACE=*value*

For the *floating* images (that is, those displayed with an ALIGN=left¦right attribute) it is likely that the author does not the text wrapped around the image to be pressed up against the image. VSPACE controls the vertical space above and below the image, while HSPACE controls the horizontal space to the left and right of the image. Value should be a pixel value.

WIDTH=*value* HEIGHT=*value*

The WIDTH and HEIGHT attributes allow the browser to determine the text layout surrounding images before the entire image has been downloaded, which can significantly speed up display of the document text. If the author specifies these, the viewer of the document will not have to wait for the image to be loaded over the network and its size to be calculated. Internet Explorer uses image placement mechanisms, so that if the display of in-line images has been turned off, the space that the images would occupy in the page is marked as if the image were there (with any ALT text being displayed in the place holder). This allows authors to be sure that the text layout on the page will be as desired, even if the user is not displaying the images.

Client-Side Image Maps

Before this image map method was implemented by browsers, using image maps required communication with the Web server on which the HTML documents were located in order to determine the action to be taken when an area of the image had been clicked on. This produced unnecessary server-side overheads. The client-side image map specification (designed by Spyglass) allows for all of the processing of the image map action to be done by the browser. It allows the use of image maps within HTML documents that are not being distributed by conventional means (that is, from a Web server). For example, using client-side image maps allows image map functionality for HTML documents on CD-ROMs and so on.

Basically, adding the USEMAP attribute to an <IMG> element indicates that the image is a client-side image map. The USEMAP attribute can be used with the ISMAP attribute to indicate that the image can be processed as either a client-side or server-side image map (useful to ensure browser independence of HTML documents). The value used in the USEMAP attribute specifies the location of the map definition to use with the image, in a format similar to the HREF attribute on anchors. If the argument to USEMAP starts with a #, the map description is assumed to be in the same document as the IMG tag.

```
<IMG SRC="../images/image.gif" USEMAP="maps.html#map1">
```

This would use the map described as "map1" in maps.html as the overlay for the image file image.gif. The map definition (see below) can be included either within the HTML document itself where the image is embedded, or in a completely separate file.

The different active regions of the image are described using MAP and AREA elements.

<MAP>

The map describes each region in the image and indicates the location of the document to be retrieved when the defined area is activated. The basic format for the MAP element is as follows:

```
<MAP NAME="name">
<AREA [SHAPE="shape"] COORDS="x,y,..." [HREF="reference"] [NOHREF]>
</MAP>
```

The name specifies the name of the map so that it can be referenced by an <IMG USEMAP=> element. The shape gives the shape of the specific area. Currently the only shape defined is "RECT", but the syntax is defined in such a way to allow other region types to be added. If the SHAPE attribute is omitted, SHAPE="RECT" is assumed. The COORDS attribute gives the coordinates of the shape, using image pixels as the units. For a rectangle, the coordinates are given as "left,top,right,bottom". The rectangular region defined includes the lower-right corner specified, that is, to specify the entire area of a 100x100 image, the coordinates would be "0,0,99,99".

The NOHREF attribute indicates that clicks in this region should perform no action. An HREF attribute specifies where a click in that area should lead. Note that a relative anchor specification will be expanded using the URL of the map description as a base, rather than using the URL of the document from which the map description is referenced. If a BASE tag is present in the document containing the map description, that URL will be used as the base to resolve partial URLs.

<AREA>

An arbitrary number of AREA elements may be specified. If two areas intersect, the one which appears first in the map definition takes precedence in the overlapping region. For example, a button bar in a document might use a 200 pixel by 80 pixel image and appear like this:

```
<MAP NAME="buttonbar">
<AREA SHAPE="RECT" COORDS="10,10,40,70" HREF="../index.html">
<AREA SHAPE="RECT" COORDS="60,10,90,70" HREF="../download.html">
<AREA SHAPE="RECT" COORDS="110,10,140,70" HREF="../email.html">
<AREA SHAPE="RECT" COORDS="160,10,190,70" HREF="../reference.html">
</MAP>
<IMG SRC="../images/tech/bar.gif" USEMAP="#buttonbar">
```

NOTE

The TARGET attribute can be used within the <AREA> element, allowing the use of client-side image maps within framed dcouments. For more information about the use of TARGET attributes, see the <FRAME> section.

Inline Video

Microsoft's Internet Explorer allows the user to embed .AVI (Audio Video Interleave) video clips in HTML documents. This is done by adding several new attributes, notably DYNSRC (Dynamic Source) to the <IMG> element. Using the <IMG> element for this purpose makes it possible to add video clips to pages, but also have browsers not enabled for video display still images in their place.

NOTE

In future versions of Internet Explorer, proprietary additions by Microsoft are to be deprecated (that is, their support will be removed) in favor of open standard mechanisms for the embedding of objects, such as video and executable content. Netscape can support the embedding of video clips through its plug-in mechanism using the <EMBED> element. See <EMBED> for more details.

CONTROLS

This attribute has no values. It is a flag that if set, displays the standard Windows AVI control panel to allow the user to control the display of the video clip.

DYNSRC

This attribute specifies the address of a video clip to be displayed in the window. It stands for Dynamic Source.

```
<IMG SRC="filmclip.gif" DYNSRC="filmclip.avi">
```

Internet Explorer will display the movie `filmclip.avi`; other browsers will display the image `filmclip.gif`.

The attributes used to control the playing of the video clip are as follows.

LOOP

Specifies how many times a video clip will loop when activated. If `n=-1`, or if `LOOP=INFINITE` is specified, the video will loop indefinitely.

LOOPDELAY

Specifies, in milliseconds, how long a video clip will wait between play loops.

NOTE

As seen in the first example on this page, because the `DYNSRC` is an attribute of the `IMG` element, other attributes of the `IMG` element, such as `HEIGHT`, `WIDTH`, `HSPACE`, `VSPACE`, `BORDER`, and so on, are also acceptable and, if specified, will format the display window for the video clip.

START

This attribute specifies when the video clip should start playing. It accepts values of `FILEOPEN` or `MOUSEOVER`. `FILEOPEN` means that the video will start playing as soon as it has finished downloading from the Web server, or distribution source. This is the default value. MOUSEOVER means start playing when the user moves the mouse cursor over the animation. It is possible to specify both of these values together.

Inline VRML Worlds

NOTE

As with other <IMG> related object embedding mechanisms (that is, inline video), future versions of the Internet Explorer will support open standard object embedding mechanisms, instead of relying on proprietary extensions as detailed here.

Microsoft's Internet Explorer (from version 2) has added the ability to include inline embedded VRML viewable by installing the Virtual Explorer plug-in module, available from the Microsoft Windows 95 Web site (http://www.microsoft.com/windows). It does this by adding the VRML attribute to the <IMG> element.

As the attribute is used in the <IMG> element, it supports many of the other attributes of the <IMG> element, such as HEIGHT, WIDTH, VSPACE, HSPACE, and so on.

For example;

```
<IMG SRC="picture.gif" VRML="world.wrl" HEIGHT=250 WIDTH=300>
```

The preceding example would embed the VRML world, world.wrl, into the HTML document, with the navigation controls below the embedding pane. The pane is displayed according to the dimensions specified. For browsers other than Virtual Explorer (Internet Explorer with the VRML add-on), the picture picture.gif would be displayed.

NOTE

Embedding of VRML worlds is also supported by Netscape, using the Netscape Live3D plug-in module and the <EMBED> element. See <EMBED> for more details.

Information Type and Character Formatting Elements

The following information type and character formatting elements are supported by most browsers.

NOTE

Different information type elements may be rendered in the same way. The following are what are sometimes called logical formatting elements. They suggest to the browser that the enclosed text should be rendered in a way set by the browser, rather than physically fixing the display type. Elements that do this are character formatting elements (see below, also known as physical elements) that produce strict rendering of the text.

Information type elements:

`<CITE>...</CITE>`	Citation
`<CODE>...</CODE>`	An example of code
`<EM>...</EM>`	Emphasis
`<KBD>...</KBD>`	User-typed text
`<SAMP>...</SAMP>`	A sequence of literal characters
`<STRONG>...</STRONG>`	Strong typographic emphasis
`<VAR>...</VAR>`	Indicates a variable name
`<!-- ... -->`	Defining comments

Character formatting elements:

`<B>...</B>`	Boldface type
`<BIG>...</BIG>`	Big text
`<BLINK>...</BLINK>`	Blinking text
`<I>...</I>`	Italics
`<SMALL>...</SMALL>`	Small text
`<STRIKE>...</STRIKE>` (or `<S>...</S>`)	Text that has been struck through
`<SUB>...</SUB>`	Subscript
`<SUP>...</SUP>`	Superscript
`<TT>...</TT>`	TypeType (or Teletype)
`<U>...</U>`	Underlined text

Although character formatting elements (physical elements) may be nested within the content of other character formatting elements, browsers are not required to render nested character-level elements distinctly from non-nested elements:

```
plain <B>bold <I>italic</I></B>
```

may be rendered the same as

```
plain <B>bold </B><I>italic</I>
```

<!-- Comments -->

To include comments in an HTML document that will be ignored by the browser, surround them with <!-- and -->. After the comment delimiter, all text up to the next occurrence of --> is ignored. Hence comments cannot be nested. White space is allowed between the closing -- and >, but not between the opening <! and --. Comments can be used anywhere within an HTML document and are generally used as markers to improve the readability of complex HTML documents.

For example:

```
<HEAD>
<TITLE>The HTML Reference</TITLE>
<!-- Created by Stephen Le Hunte, April 1996 -->
</HEAD>
```

> **NOTE**
>
> Some browsers incorrectly consider a > sign to terminate a comment.

<B>...</B>

The Bold element specifies that the text should be rendered in boldface, where available. Otherwise, alternative mapping is allowed.

```
The instructions <B>must be read</B> before continuing.
```

would be rendered as:

The instructions **must be read** before continuing.

<BIG>...</BIG>

The <BIG> element specifies that the enclosed text should be displayed, if practical, using a big font (compared with the current font). This is an HTML 3.0 element and may not be widely supported.

```
This is normal text, with <BIG>this bit</BIG> being big text.
```

would be rendered as:

This is normal text, with this bit being big text.

NOTE

Use of this element is currently supported by Netscape and the Internet Explorer only. They also allow the <BIG>...</BIG> element to be used surrounding the _{...} and ^{...} elements to force rendering of the sub/superscript text as normal size text as opposed to the default slightly smaller text normally used.

The exact appearance of the big text will change depending on any `<FONT SIZE=...>` and `<BASEFONT SIZE=...>` settings, if specified.

<BLINK>

Surrounding any text with this element will cause the selected text to *blink* on the viewing page. This can serve to add extra emphasis to selected text.

```
<BLINK>This text would blink on the page</BLINK>.
```

NOTE

The <BLINK>...</BLINK> element is currently only supported by Netscape.

<CITE>...</CITE>

The Citation element specifies a citation and is typically rendered in an italic font. For example, the following

```
This sentence contains a <CITE>citation reference</CITE>.
```

would look like:

This sentence contains a *citation reference.*

<CODE>...</CODE>

The Code element should be used to indicate an example of code and is typically rendered in a monospaced font. This should not be confused with the Preformatted Text (<PRE>) element.

```
The formula is: <CODE>x=(-b+/-(b^2-4ac)^1/2)/2a</CODE>.
```

It would look like:

The formula is: `x=(-b+/-(b^2-4ac)^1/2)/2a.`

<EM>...</EM>

The Emphasis element indicates typographic emphasis and is typically rendered in an italic font.

```
The <EM>Emphasis</EM> element typically renders as Italics.
```

would render:

> The *Emphasis* element typically renders as Italics.

<I>...</I>

The Italic element specifies that the text should be rendered in italic font, where available. Otherwise, alternative mapping is allowed.

```
Anything between the <I>I elements</I> should be italics.
```

would render as:

> Anything between the *I elements* should be italics.

<KBD>...</KBD>

The Keyboard element can be used to indicate text to be typed by a user and is typically rendered in a monospaced font. It might commonly be used in an instruction manual.

```
To login to the system, enter <KBD>"GUEST"</KBD> at the command prompt.
```

would render as:

> To login to the system, enter `"GUEST"` at the command prompt.

<SAMP>...</SAMP>

The Sample element can be used to indicate a sequence of literal characters and is typically rendered in a monospaced font.

```
A sequence of <SAMP>literal characters</SAMP> commonly renders in a monospaced
font.
```

would render as:

> A sequence of `literal characters` commonly renders in a monospaced font.

<SMALL>...</SMALL>

The `<SMALL>` element specifies that the enclosed text should be displayed, if practical, using a small font (compared with the current font). This is an HTML 3.2 element and may not be widely supported.

```
This is normal text, with <SMALL>this bit</SMALL> being small text.
```

would be rendered as:

This is normal text, with this bit being small text.

NOTE

Use of this element is currently supported by Netscape and the Internet Explorer only. They also allow the <SMALL>...</SMALL> element to be used surrounding the _{...} and ^{...} elements to force rendering of the sub/superscript text as text even smaller than the default slightly smaller (compared to the normal) text normally used.

The exact appearance of the small text will change depending on any <FONT SIZE=...> and <BASEFONT SIZE=...> settings, if specified.

<STRIKE>...</STRIKE>

The <STRIKE>...</STRIKE> element states that the enclosed text should be displayed with a horizontal line striking through the text. Alternative mappings are allowed if this is not practical. This is an HTML 3.2 element and may not be widely supported.

```
This text would be <STRIKE>struck through</STRIKE>.
```

would be rendered as:

This text would be ~~struck through~~.

NOTE

Although use of the <STRIKE> element is currently supported by Netscape and Mosaic, the element contained in current versions of the HTML 3.2 specification, is <S>...</S>, which is supported by Mosaic, but not Netscape. The Microsoft Internet Explorer supports either version of the element.

<STRONG>...</STRONG>

The Strong element can be used to indicate strong typographic emphasis and is typically rendered in a bold font.

```
The instructions <STRONG>must be read</STRONG> before continuing.
```

would be rendered as:

The instructions **must be read** before continuing.

_{...}

The <SUB> element specifies that the enclosed text should be displayed as a subscript, and, if practical, using a smaller font (compared with normal text). This is an HTML 3.2 element and may not be widely supported.

```
This is the main text, with <SUB>this bit</SUB> being subscript.
```

This is the main text, with $_{\text{this bit}}$ being subscript.

NOTE

The selected text will be made a superscript to the main text, formatting the selected text slightly smaller than the normal text. Netscape and the Internet Explorer can be forced to make subscripts even smaller by compounding the _{...} element with the <SMALL>...</SMALL> element, or be forced to render the subscript the same size as the normal text, by compounding the _{...} element with the <BIG>...</BIG> element.

The exact appearance of the subscript text will change depending on any <FONT SIZE=...> and <BASEFONT SIZE=...> settings, if specified.

^{...}

The <SUP> element specifies that the enclosed text should be displayed as a superscript, and, if practical, using a smaller font (compared with normal text). This is an HTML 3.2 element and may not be widely supported.

```
This is the main text, with <SUP>this bit</SUP> being superscript.
```

This is the main text, with $^{\text{this bit}}$ being superscript.

NOTE

The selected text will be made a superscript to the main text, formatting the selected text slightly smaller than the normal text. Netscape and the Internet Explorer can be forced to make superscripts even smaller by compounding the ^{...} element with the <SMALL>...</SMALL> element, or be forced to render the superscript the same size as the normal text, by compounding the ^{...} element with the <BIG>...</BIG> element.

The exact appearance of the superscript text will change depending on any <FONT SIZE=...> and <BASEFONT SIZE=...> settings, if specified.

<TT>...</TT>

The Teletype element specifies that the text should be rendered in fixed-width typewriter font where available. Otherwise, alternative mapping is allowed.

```
Text between the <TT> typetype elements</TT> should be rendered in fixed-width
typewriter font.
```

would render as:

> Text between the `typetype elements` should be rendered in fixed-width typewriter font.

<U>...</U>

The `<U>...</U>` elements state that the enclosed text should be rendered, if practical, underlined. This is an HTML 3.2 element and may not be widely supported.

```
The <U>main point</U> of the exercise...
```

would be rendered as:

> The main point of the exercise...

NOTE

As yet, Netscape doesn't support use of the `<U>` element.

<VAR>...</VAR>

The Variable element can be used to indicate a variable name and is typically rendered in an italic font.

```
When coding, <VAR>LeftIndent()</VAR> must be a variable.
```

would render as:

> When coding, *LeftIndent()* must be a variable.

List Elements

HTML supports several types of lists, all of which may be nested. If used they should be present in the `<BODY>` of an HTML document.

`<DL>...</DL>`	Definition list
`<DIR>...</DIR>`	Directory list

`<MENU>...</MENU>`	Menu list
`<OL>...</OL>`	Ordered list
`<UL>...</UL>`	Unordered list

<DIR>...</DIR>

A Directory List element can be used to present a list of items, which may be arranged in columns, typically 24 characters wide. Some browsers will attempt to optimize the column width as a function of the widths of individual elements.

A directory list must begin with the `<DIR>` element which is immediately followed by a `<LI>` (list item) element:

```
<DIR>
<LI>A-H
<LI>I-M
<LI>M-R
<LI>S-Z
</DIR>
```

<DL>...</DL>

Definition lists are typically rendered by browsers, with the definition term `<DT>` flush left in the display window with the definition data `<DD>` rendered in a separate paragraph, indented after the definition term. Individual browsers may also render the definition data on a new line, below the definition term.

Example of use:

```
<DL>
<DT>&lt;PRE&gt;<DD>Allows for the presentation of preformatted text.
<DT>&lt;P&gt;<DD>This is used to define paragraph blocks.
</DL>
```

The layout of the definition list is at the discretion of individual browsers. However, generally, the `<DT>` column is allowed one-third of the display area. If the term contained in the `<DT>` definition exceeds this in length, it may be extended across the page with the `<DD>` section moved to the next line, or it may be wrapped onto successive lines of the left-hand column.

Single occurrences of a `<DT>` element without a subsequent `<DD>` element are allowed and have the same significance as if the `<DD>` element had been present with no text.

The opening list element must be `<DL>` and must be immediately followed by the first term (`<DT>`).

The definition list type can take the `COMPACT` attribute, which suggests that a compact rendering be used, so as to minimize inefficient display window space. Generally, this will be displayed as a table, with the definition terms and data being rendered on the same line.

```
<DL COMPACT>
<DT>&lt;PRE&gt;<DD>Allows for the presentation of preformatted text.
<DT>&lt;P&gt;<DD>This is used to define paragraph blocks.
</DL>
```

<MENU>...</MENU>

Menu lists are typically rendered as discrete items on a single line. This arrangement is more compact than the rendering of an unordered list. Typically, a menu list will be rendered as a bulleted list, but this is at the discretion of the browser.

A menu list must begin with a `<MENU>` element which is immediately followed by a `<LI>` (list item) element:

```
<MENU>
<LI>First item in the list.
<LI>Second item in the list.
<LI>Third item in the list.
</MENU>
```

<OL>...</OL>

The Ordered List element is used to present a numbered list of items, sorted by sequence or order of importance and is typically rendered as a numbered list, but this is at the discretion of individual browsers.

> **NOTE**
>
> The list elements are not sorted by the browser when displaying the list. (This sorting should be done manually when adding the HTML elements to the desired list text.) Ordered lists can be nested.

An ordered list must begin with the `<OL>` element which is immediately followed by a `<LI>` (list item) element:

```
<OL>
<LI>Click on the desired file to download.
<LI>In the presented dialog box, enter a name to save the file with.
<LI>Click 'OK' to download the file to your local drive.
</OL>
```

The Ordered List element can take the `COMPACT` attribute, which suggests that a compact rendering be used.

As mentioned above, the average ordered list counts 1, 2, 3, ... and so on. The `TYPE` attribute allows authors to specify whether the list items should be marked with:

`(TYPE=A)`	Capital letters. For example, A, B, C ...

(TYPE=a)	Small letters. For example, a, b, c ...
(TYPE=I)	Large Roman numerals. For example, I, II, III ...
(TYPE=i)	Small Roman numerals. For example, i, ii, iii ...
(TYPE=1)	The default numbers. For example, 1, 2, 3 ...

For lists that wish to start at values other than 1, the new attribute START is available.

START is always specified in the default numbers and will be converted based on TYPE before display. Thus START=5 would display either an *E*, *e*, *V*, *v*, or *5* based on the TYPE attribute. For examples, changing the preceding example to:

```
<OL TYPE=a START=3>
<LI>Click on the desired file to download.
<LI>In the presented dialog box, enter a name to save the file with.
<LI>Click 'OK' to download the file to your local drive.
</OL>
```

would present the list as using lower-case letters, starting at *c*.

To give even more flexibility to lists, the TYPE attribute can be used with the <LI> element. It takes the same values as <OL> and it changes the list type for that item and all subsequent items. For ordered lists, the VALUE attribute is also allowed, which can be used to set the count for that list item and all subsequent items.

NOTE

The TYPE attribute used in the <OL> element and the <LI> element and the START attribute in the <OL> element are supported only by Netscape and Internet Explorer.

<UL>...</UL>

The Unordered List element is used to present a list of items which is typically separated by white space and/or marked by bullets, but this is at the discretion of individual browsers.

An unordered list must begin with the <UL> element, which is immediately followed by a <LI> (list item) element: Unordered lists can be nested.

```
<UL>
<LI>First list item
<LI>Second list item
<LI>Third list item
</UL>
```

The Unordered List element can take the COMPACT attribute, which suggests that a compact rendering be used.

The basic bulleted list has a default progression of bullet types that changes—from a solid disc, to a circle, to a square—as you move through indented levels. The TYPE attribute can be used in the <UL> element so that no matter what the indent level the bullet type can be specified thus:

```
TYPE=disc

TYPE=circle

TYPE=square
```

To give even more flexibility to lists, the TYPE attribute to the <LI> element is also allowed. It takes the same values as <UL> and it changes the list type for that item and all subsequent items.

NOTE

The TYPE attribute when used in the <UL> and <LI> elements is supported by Netscape only.

Tables

At present, the table HTML elements are

`<TABLE>...</TABLE>`	The table delimiter
`<TR ...>...</TR>`	Used to specify number of rows in a table
`<TD ...>...</TD>`	Specifies table data cells
`<TH ...>...</TH>`	Table header cell
`<CAPTION ...>...</CAPTION>`	Specifies the table caption

Internet Explorer has introduced support for various HTML 3.0 table elements. Those introduced are

`<THEAD>...</THEAD>`	Specifies the Table head
`<TBODY>...</TBODY>`	Specifies the Table body
`<TFOOT>...</TFOOT>`	Specifies the Table footer
`<COLGROUP>...</COLGROUP>`	Used to group column alignments
`<COL>...</COL>`	Used to specify individual column alignments

Also, some new attributes have been introduced. These are

`<TABLE BACKGROUND="...">`	Specifies a background image for the table
`<TH BACKGROUND="...">`	Specifies a background image for the table header
`<TD BACKGROUND="...">`	Specifies a background image for table data cell

`<TABLE FRAME="...">`	Specifies the appearance of the Table frame
`<TABLE RULES="...">`	Specifies the appearance of the Table dividing lines

<TABLE>...</TABLE>

This is the main wrapper for all the other table elements, and other table elements will be ignored if they aren't wrapped inside of a `<TABLE>...</TABLE>` element. By default, if tables have no borders, borders will be added if the `BORDER` attribute is specified.

The `<TABLE>` element has the following attributes.

ALIGN="left¦right"

Some browsers (Internet Explorer and Netscape) support the `ALIGN` attribute to the `<TABLE>` element. Like that used for *floating images*, it allows a table to be aligned to the left or right of the page, allowing text to flow around the table. Also, as with floating images, it is necessary to have knowledge of the `<BR CLEAR=...>` element to be able to organize the text display so as to minimize poor formatting.

BACKGROUND

Internet Explorer supports the placing of images in the `<TABLE>` element. (Also in the `<TD>` and `<TH>` elements) If used in the `<TABLE>` element, the image in question will be tiled behind all of the table cells. Any of the supported graphic file formats can be used as a graphic behind a table.

BGCOLOR="*#rrggbb*¦*color name*"

Internet Explorer and Netscape support use of this attribute (also supported in the `<BODY>` element). It allows the background color of the table to be specified, using either the specified *color names* or a `rrggbb` hex triplet.

BORDER

This attribute can be used to both control and set the borders to be displayed for the table. If present, then a border will be drawn around all data cells. The exact thickness and display of this default border is at the discretion of individual browsers. If the attribute isn't present, then the border is not displayed, but the table is rendered in the same position as if there were a border (that is, allowing room for the border). It can also be given a value, that is, `BORDER=<value>`, which specifies the thickness of the table border. The border value can be set to 0, which regains all the space that the browser has set aside for any borders (as in the case where no border has been set).

BORDERCOLOR="*#rrggbb*¦*color name*"

Internet Explorer includes support for this attribute which sets the border color of the table. Any of the predefined color names can be used, as well as any color defined by a rrggbb hex triplet. It is necessary for the BORDER attribute to be present in the main <TABLE> element for border coloring to work.

BORDERCOLORDARK="*#rrggbb*¦*color name*"

Internet Explorer allows the use of the BORDERCOLORDARK attribute to independently set the darker color to be displayed on a 3D <TABLE> border. It is the opposite of BORDERCOLORLIGHT. Any of the predefined color names can be used, as well as any color defined by a rrggbb hex triplet. It is necessary for the BORDER attribute to be present in the main <TABLE> element for border coloring to work.

NOTE

The BGCOLOR, BORDERCOLOR, BORDERCOLORLIGHT and BORDERCOLORDARK attributes can also be used in <TH>, <TR>, and <TD> elements, with the color defined in the last element overriding those defined before. For example, if a <TD> element contains a BORDERCOLOR attribute setting, the setting specified will be used instead of any color settings that may have been specified in the <TR> element, which in turn overrides any color settings in the <TABLE> element.

BORDERCOLORLIGHT="*#rrggbb*¦*color name*"

Internet Explorer allows use of the BORDERCOLORLIGHT attribute to independently set the lighter color to be displayed on a 3D <TABLE> border. It is the opposite of BORDERCOLORDARK. Any of the pre-defined *color names* can be used, as well as any color defined by a rrggbb hex triplet. It is necessary for the BORDER attribute to be present in the main <TABLE> element for border coloring to work.

CELLPADDING=*value*

The CELLPADDING is the amount of white space between the borders of the table cell and the actual cell data (whatever is to be displayed in the cell). It defaults to an effective value of 1. This example gives the most compact table possible:

```
<TABLE BORDER=0 CELLSPACING=0 CELLPADDING=0>
```

CELLSPACING=*value*

The CELLSPACING is the amount of space inserted between individual table data cells. It defaults to an effective value of 2.

FRAME

Only Internet Explorer supports the use of this attribute. It requires the BORDER attribute to be set and affects the display of the table borders. It can accept any of the following values:

void	This removes all the external borders.
above	This displays external borders at the top of the table only.
below	This displays external borders at the bottom of the table only.
hsides	This displays external borders at the horizontal sides of the table. That is, at the top and bottom of the table.
lhs	This displays external borders at the left-hand edges of the table only.
rhs	This displays external borders at the right-hand edges of the table only.
vsides	This displays external borders at both left- and right-hand edges of the table.
box	This displays a box around the table (that is, top, bottom, left- and right-hand sides).

HEIGHT=*value_or_percent*

If used, this attribute can specify either the exact height of the table in pixels, or the height of the table as a percentage of the browser display window.

RULES

Internet Explorer supports this new attribute. It requires the BORDER value to be set and may only be used in tables where the <THEAD>, <TBODY>, and <TFOOT> sections have been set. It affects the display of the internal table borders ("rules"). It can accept the following values:

none	This removes all the internal rules.
basic	This displays horizontal borders between the <THEAD>, <TBODY> and <TFOOT> sections.
rows	This displays horizontal borders between all rows.
cols	This displays horizontal borders between all columns.
all	This displays all the internal rules.

VALIGN="top¦bottom"

The Internet Explorer supports this attribute that specifies the vertical alignment of the text displayed in the table cells. The default (which is also used if the attribute is not set) is centeraligned.

WIDTH=*value_or_percent*

If used, this attribute can specify either the exact width of the table in pixels, or the width of the table as a percentage of the browser display window.

<CAPTION ...>...</CAPTION>

This represents the caption for a table. `<CAPTION>` elements should appear inside the `<TABLE>` but not inside table rows or cells. The caption accepts an alignment attribute that defaults to `ALIGN=top` but can be explicitly set to `ALIGN=bottom`. Like table cells, any document body HTML can appear in a caption. Captions are, by default, horizontally centered with respect to the table, and they may have their lines broken to fit within the width of the table.

The `<CAPTION>` element can accept the following attributes.

ALIGN="top¦bottom¦left¦center¦right"

The `ALIGN` attribute controls whether the caption appears above or below the table, using the top and bottom values, defaulting to top. The Internet Explorer allows the `<CAPTION>` element to be left, right or center aligned. For the Internet Explorer to set the `<CAPTION>` at the top or bottom of the table, it is necessary to use the `VALIGN` attribute.

VALIGN="top¦bottom"

The Internet Explorer allows use of the `VALIGN` attribute inside the `<CAPTION>` element. It specifies whether the caption text should be displayed at the top or bottom of the table.

<COL>...</COL>

This element, which is Internet Explorer–specific, can be used to specify the text alignment for table columns. It accepts the following attributes.

ALIGN="center¦justify¦left¦right"

This sets the text alignment within the column group. The default value is `"center"`.

SPAN=*value*

This can be used to set the number of columns upon which the `ALIGN` attribute is to act.

<COLGROUP>...</COLGROUP>

This element, which is Internet Explorer–specific, can be used to group columns together to set their alignment properties. It accepts the following attributes:

B HTML REFERENCE

ALIGN="center¦justify¦left¦right"

This sets the text alignment within the column group. The default value is "center".

SPAN=*value*

This can be used to set the number of columns upon which the ALIGN and VALIGN attributes are to act.

VALIGN="baseline¦bottom¦middle¦top"

This sets the vertical text alignment within the column group.

<TBODY>...</TBODY>

This element, which is Internet Explorer–specific, is used to specify the body section of the table. It is somewhat analogous to the <BODY> element. It does directly affect the rendering of the table on the screen, but is required if you want RULES to be set in the <TABLE> .

<TD ...>...</TD>

This stands for table data, and specifies a standard table data cell. Table data cells must only appear within table rows. Each row need not have the same number of cells specified, as short rows will be padded with blank cells on the right. A cell can contain any of the HTML elements normally present in the body of an HTML document.

Internet Explorer will allows the use of <TD></TD> to specify a blank cell, that will be rendered with a border (providing a border has been set). Other browsers will require some character within a data cell for it to be rendered with a border.

<TD ...>...</TD> can accept the following attributes.

ALIGN="left¦center¦right"

This attribute controls whether text inside the table cell(s) is aligned to the left, right or center.

BACKGROUND

Internet Explorer supports the placing of images inside the <TD> element. (Also in the <TABLE>, <TD>, and <TH> elements.) If used in the <TD> element, the image in question will be tiled behind the particular data cell. Any of the supported graphic file formats can be used as a graphic behind a table.

BGCOLOR="*#rrggbb¦color name*"

Internet Explorer and Netscape support use of this attribute (also supported in the <BODY> element). It allows the background color of the data cell to be specified, using either the specified color names or a rrggbb hex triplet.

BORDERCOLOR="*#rrggbb¦color name*"

Internet Explorer includes support for this attribute which sets the border color of the data cell. Any of the pre-defined *color names* can be used, as well as any color defined by a rrggbb hex triplet. It is necessary for the BORDER attribute to be present in the main <TABLE> element for border coloring to work.

BORDERCOLORDARK="*#rrggbb¦color name*"

Internet Explorer allows use of the BORDERCOLORDARK attribute to independently set the darker color to be displayed on a 3D <TD> border. It is the opposite of BORDERCOLORLIGHT. Any of the predefined color names can be used, as well as any color defined by a rrggbb hex triplet. It is necessary for the BORDER attribute to be present in the main <TABLE> element for border coloring to work.

NOTE

The BGCOLOR, BORDERCOLOR, BORDERCOLORDARK and BORDERCOLORLIGHT attributes can also be used in <TABLE>, <TH>, and <TR> elements, with the color defined in the last element overriding those defined before. For example, if a <TD> element contains a BORDERCOLOR attribute setting, the setting specified will be used instead of any color settings that may have been specified in the <TR> element, which in turn overrides any color settings in the <TABLE> element.

BORDERCOLORLIGHT="*#rrggbb¦color name*"

Internet Explorer allows use of the BORDERCOLORLIGHT attribute to independently set the lighter color to be displayed on a 3D <TD> border. It is the opposite of BORDERCOLORDARK. Any of the predefined color names can be used, as well as any color defined by a rrggbb hex triplet. It is necessary for the BORDER attribute to be present in the main <TABLE> element for border coloring to work.

COLSPAN="*value*"

This attribute can appear in any table cell (<TH> or <TD>) and it specifies how many columns of the table this cell should span. The default COLSPAN for any cell is 1.

HEIGHT=*value_or_percent*

If used, this attribute can specify either the exact height of the data cell in pixels, or the height of the data cell as a percentage of the browser display window. Only one data cell can set the height for an entire row, typically being the last data cell to be rendered.

NOWRAP

If this attribute appears in any table cell (<TH> or <TD>) it means the lines within this cell cannot be broken to fit the width of the cell. Be cautious in use of this attribute as it can result in excessively wide cells.

ROWSPAN="*value*"

This attribute can appear in any table cell (<TH> or <TD>) and it specifies how many rows of the table this cell should span. The default ROWSPAN for any cell is 1. A span that extends into rows that were never specified with a <TR> will be truncated.

VALIGN="top¦middle¦bottom¦baseline"

The VALIGN attribute controls whether text inside the table cell(s) is aligned to the top, to the bottom, or vertically centered within the cell. It can also specify that all the cells in the row should be vertically aligned to the same baseline.

WIDTH=*value_or_percent*

If used, this attribute can specify either the exact width of the data cell in pixels, or the width of the data cell as a percentage of the table being displayed. Only one data cell can set the width for an entire column, typically being the last data cell to be rendered.

<TFOOT>...</TFOOT>

This element, which is Internet Explorer–specific, is used to specify the footer section of the table. It does directly affect the rendering of the table on the screen, but is required if you want RULES to be set in the <TABLE> .

<TH ...>...</TH>

This stands for table header. Header cells are identical to data cells in all respects, with the exception that header cells are in a bold font, and have a default ALIGN=center.

<TH ...>...</TH> can contain the following attributes:

ALIGN="left¦center¦right"

This attribute controls whether text inside the table cell(s) is aligned to the left, right or center of the cell.

BACKGROUND

Internet Explorer supports the placing of images inside the <TH> element. (Also in the <TABLE>, <TD> and <TH> elements) If used in the <TH> element, the image in question will be tiled behind the particular data cell. Any of the supported graphic file formats can be used as a graphic behind a table.

BGCOLOR="*#rrggbb¦color name*"

Internet Explorer and Netscape support use of this attribute (also supported in the <BODY> element). It allows the background color of the header cell to be specified, using either the specified color names or a rrggbb hex triplet.

BORDERCOLOR="*#rrggbb¦color name*"

Internet Explorer includes support for this attribute which sets the border color of the header cell. Any of the pre-defined *color names* can be used, as well as any color defined by a rrggbb hex triplet. It is necessary for the BORDER attribute to be present in the main <TABLE> element for border coloring to work.

BORDERCOLORDARK="*#rrggbb¦color name*"

Internet Explorer allows use of the BORDERCOLORDARK attribute to independently set the darker color to be displayed on a 3D <TH> border. It is the opposite of BORDERCOLORLIGHT. Any of the predefined color names can be used, as well as any color defined by a rrggbb hex triplet. It is necessary for the BORDER attribute to be present in the main <TABLE> element for border coloring to work.

NOTE

The BGCOLOR, BORDERCOLOR, BORDERCOLORDARK and BORDERCOLORLIGHT attributes can also be used in <TABLE>, <TD>, and <TR> elements, with the color defined in the last element overriding those defined before. For example, if a <TD> element contains a BORDERCOLOR attribute setting, the setting specified will be used instead of any color settings that may have been specified in the <TR> element, which in turn overrides any color settings in the <TABLE> element.

BORDERCOLORLIGHT="#rrggbb¦color name"

Internet Explorer allows use of the BORDERCOLORLIGHT attribute to independently set the lighter color to be displayed on a 3D <TH> border. It is the opposite of BORDERCOLORDARK. Any of the predefined color names can be used, as well as any color defined by a rrggbb hex triplet. It is necessary for the BORDER attribute to be present in the main <TABLE> element for border coloring to work.

COLSPAN="value"

This attribute can appear in any table cell (<TH> or <TD>) and it specifies how many columns of the table this cell should span. The default COLSPAN for any cell is 1.

HEIGHT=value_or_percent

If used, this attribute can specify either the exact height of the data cell in pixels, or the height of the data cell as a percentage of the browser display window. Only one data cell can set the height for an entire row, typically being the last data cell to be rendered.

NOWRAP

This attribute specifies that the lines within this cell cannot be broken to fit the width of the cell. Be cautious in use of this attribute as it can result in excessively wide cells.

ROWSPAN="value"

This attribute can appear in any table cell (<TH> or <TD>) and it specifies how many rows of the table this cell should span. The default ROWSPAN for any cell is 1. A span that extends into rows that were never specified with a <TR> will be truncated.

VALIGN="top¦middle¦bottom¦baseline"

The VALIGN attribute controls whether text inside the table cell(s) is aligned to the top or bottom or vertically centered within the cell. It can also specify that all the cells in the row should be vertically aligned to the same baseline.

WIDTH=value_or_percent

If used, this attribute can specify either the exact width of the data cell in pixels, or the width of the data cell as a percentage of the table being displayed. Only one data cell can set the width for an entire column, typically being the last data cell to be rendered.

<THEAD>...</THEAD>

This element, which is Internet Explorer–specific, is used to specify the head section of the table. It is somewhat analogous to the <HEAD> element. It does directly affect the rendering of the table on the screen, but is required if you want RULES to be set in the <TABLE> .

<TR ...>...</TR>

This stands for table row. The number of rows in a table is exactly specified by how many <TR> elements are contained within it, regardless of cells that may attempt to use the ROWSPAN attribute to span into non-specified rows.

The <TR> element can have the following attributes.

ALIGN="left¦center¦right"

This controls whether text inside the table cell(s) is aligned to the left, right or center of the cell.

BGCOLOR="*#rrggbb¦color name*"

Internet Explorer and Netscape support use of this attribute (also supported in the <BODY> element). It allows the background color of the table to be specified, using either the specified color names or a rrggbb hex triplet.

BORDERCOLOR="*#rrggbb¦color name*"

Internet Explorer includes support for this attribute which sets the border color of the row. Any of the predefined color names can be used, as well as any color defined by a rrggbb hex triplet. It is necessary for the BORDER attribute to be present in the main <TABLE> element for border coloring to work.

BORDERCOLORDARK="*#rrggbb¦color name*"

Internet Explorer allows use of the BORDERCOLORDARK attribute to independently set the darker color to be displayed on a 3D <TR> border. It is the opposite of BORDERCOLORLIGHT. Any of the predefined color names can be used, as well as any color defined by a rrggbb hex triplet. It is necessary for the BORDER attribute to be present in the main <TABLE> element for border coloring to work.

NOTE

The BGCOLOR, BORDERCOLOR, BORDERCOLORLIGHT and BORDERCOLORDARK attributes can also be used in <TABLE>, <TH>, and <TD> elements, with the color defined in the last element overriding those defined before. For example, if a <TD> element contains a BORDERCOLOR attribute setting, the setting specified will be used instead of any color settings that may have been specified in the <TR> element, which in turn overrides any color settings in the <TABLE> element.

BORDERCOLORLIGHT="#rrggbb¦color name"

Internet Explorer allows use of the BORDERCOLORLIGHT attribute to independently set the lighter color to be displayed on a 3D <TR> border. It is the opposite of BORDERCOLORDARK. Any of the predefined color names can be used, as well as any color defined by a rrggbb hex triplet. It is necessary for the BORDER attribute to be present in the main <TABLE> element for border coloring to work.

VALIGN="top¦middle¦bottom¦baseline"

This attribute controls whether text inside the table cell(s) is aligned to the top, to the bottom, or vertically centered within the cell. It can also specify that all the cells in the row should be vertically aligned to the same baseline.

Table Examples

Here are some sample HTML <TABLE> fragments with accompanying screenshots.

A Simple Table

```
<TABLE BORDER>
<TR>
<TD>Data cell 1</TD><TD>Data cell 2</TD>
</TR>
<TR>
<TD>Data cell 3</TD><TD>Data cell 4</TD>
</TR>
</TABLE>
```

FIGURE B.2.
A simple four-cell table.

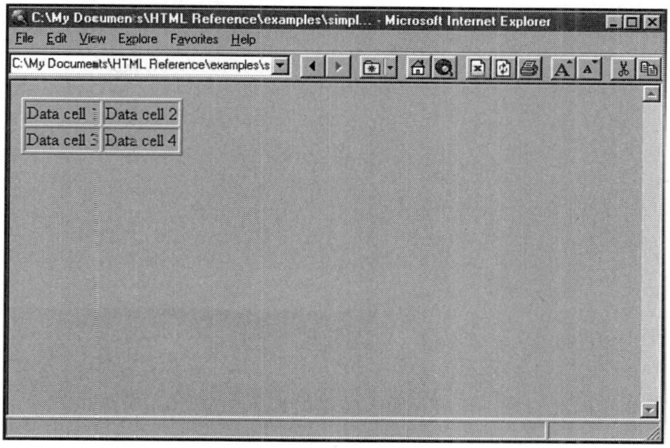

A Table Using ROWSPAN

```
<TABLE BORDER>
<TR>
<TD ROWSPAN=2>This cell spans two rows</TD>
<TD>These cells</TD><TD>would</TD>
</TR>
<TR>
<TD>contain</TD><TD>other data</TD>
</TR>
</TABLE>
```

FIGURE B.3.
A table with spanning rows.

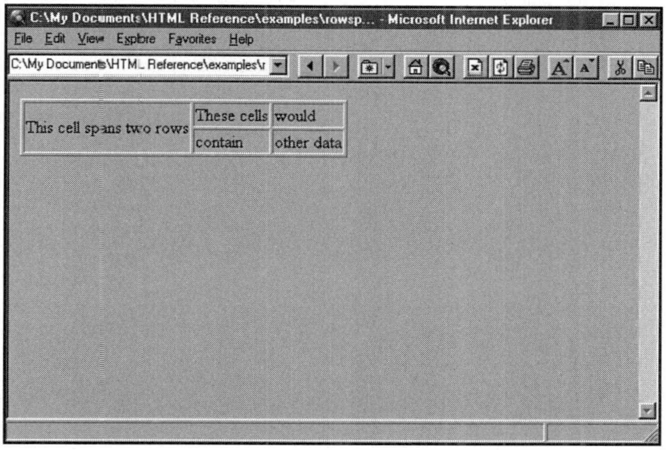

A Table Using COLSPAN

```
<TABLE BORDER>
<TR>
<TD>Data cell 1</TD>
<TD COLSPAN=2>This cell spans 2 columns</TD>
</TR>
<TR>
<TD>Data cell 2</TD><TD>Data cell 3</TD><TD>Data cell 4</TD>
</TR>
</TABLE>
```

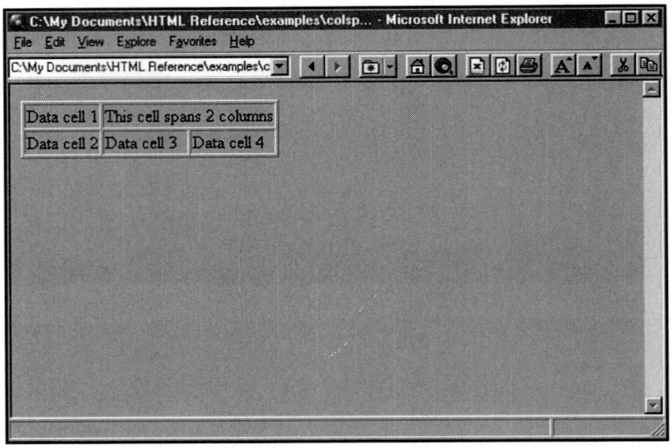

FIGURE B.4.
A table with spanning columns.

A Table Using Headers

```
<TABLE BORDER>
<TR>
<TH>Netscape</TH><TH>Internet Explorer</TH><TH>Mosaic</TH>
</TR>
<TR>
<TD>X</TD><TD>X</TD><TD>-</TD>
</TR>
<TR>
<TD>X</TD><TD>-</TD><TD>X</TD>
</TR>
</TABLE>
```

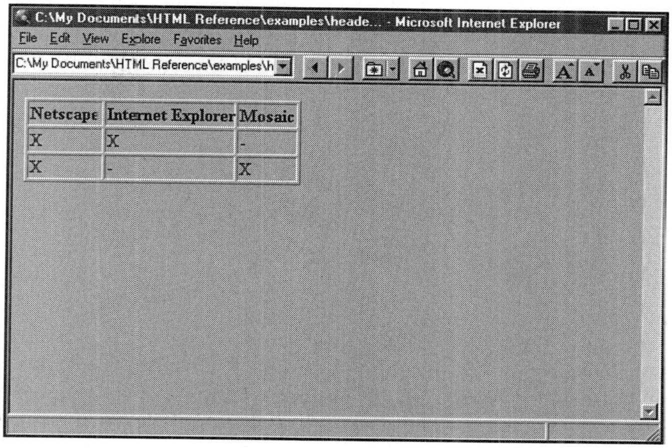

FIGURE B.5.
Table headers.

A Table Using All of the Above

```
<TABLE BORDER>
<TR>
<TD><TH ROWSPAN=2></TH>
<TH COLSPAN=3>Browser</TH></TD>
</TR>
<TR>
<TD><TH>Netscape</TH><TH>Internet Explorer</TH><TH>Mosaic</TH></TD>
</TR>
<TR>
<TH ROWSPAN=2>Element</TH>
<TH>&lt;DFN&gt;</TH><TD>-</TD><TD>X</TD><TD>-</TD>
</TR>
<TR>
<TH>&lt;DIR&gt;</TH><TD>X</TD><TD>X</TD><TD>X</TD>
</TR>
</TABLE>
```

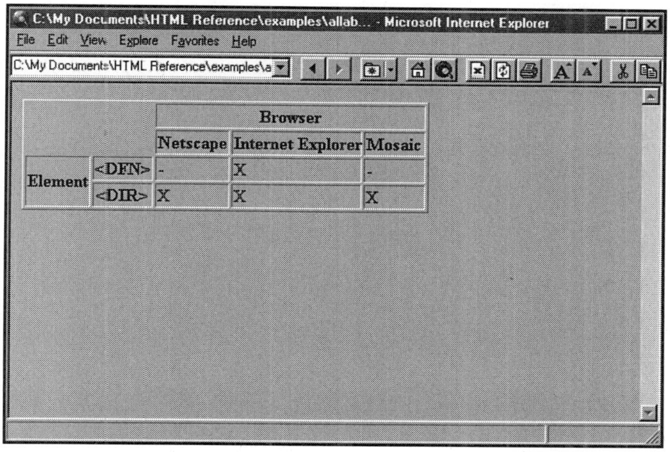

FIGURE B.6.
A complex table.

A Table Using ALIGN/VALIGN

This table adds `ALIGN` and `VALIGN` attributes to the preceding example to improve the layout of the table.

```
<TABLE BORDER>
<TR>
<TD><TH ROWSPAN=2></TH>
<TH COLSPAN=3>Browser</TH></TD>
</TR>
<TR>
<TD><TH>Netscape</TH><TH>Internet Explorer</TH><TH>Mosaic</TH></TD>
</TR>
<TR>
<TH ROWSPAN=2 VALIGN=top>Element</TH>
<TH>&lt;DFN&gt;</TH>
<TD ALIGN=center>-</TD>
<TD ALIGN=center>X</TD>
<TD ALIGN=center>-</TD>
</TR>
<TR>
<TH>&lt;DIR&gt;</TH>
<TD ALIGN=center>X</TD>
<TD ALIGN=center>X</TD>
<TD ALIGN=center>X</TD>
</TR>
</TABLE>
```

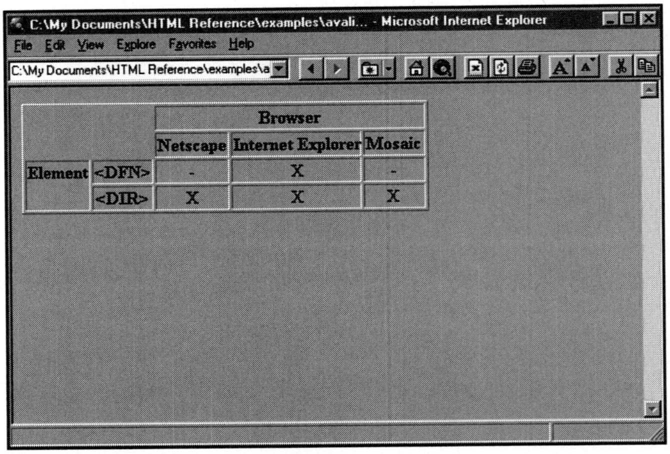

FIGURE B.7.
Improving the layout of a table.

Nested Tables

To show that tables can be nested within each other. This table uses the ROWSPAN table, including the "simple" table inside one of the data cells.

```
<TABLE BORDER>
<TR>
<TD ROWSPAN=2>This cell spans two rows
<TABLE BORDER>
<TR>
<TD>Data cell 1</TD><TD>Data cell 2</TD>
</TR>
<TR>
<TD>Data cell 3</TD><TD>Data cell 4</TD>
</TR>
</TABLE>
</TD>
<TD>These cells</TD><TD>would</TD>
</TR>
<TR>
<TD>contain</TD><TD>other data</TD>
</TR>
</TABLE>
```

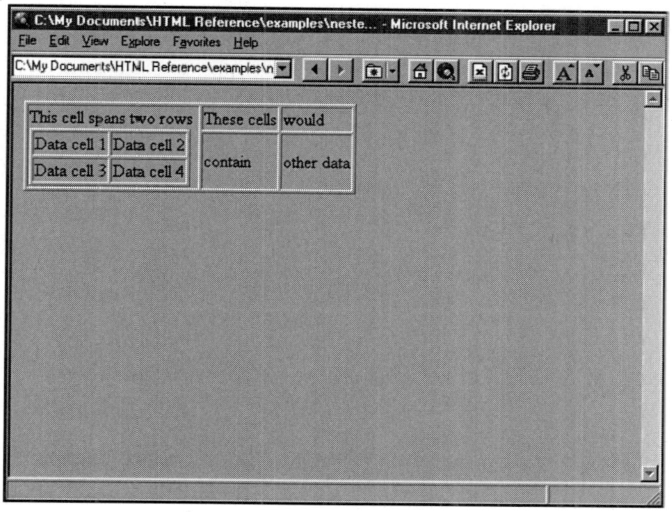

FIGURE B.8.
Nesting one table inside another.

Floating Tables

```
<TABLE ALIGN=left BORDER WIDTH=50%>
<TR>
<TD>This is a two row table</TD>
</TR>
<TR>
<TD>It is aligned to the left of the page</TD>
</TR>
</TABLE>
This text will be to the right of the table, and will fall neatly beside the table
<BR CLEAR=all>
<HR>
<TABLE ALIGN=right BORDER WIDTH=50%>
<TR>
<TD>This is a two row table</TD>
</TR>
<TR>
<TD>It is aligned to the right of the page</TD>
</TR>
</TABLE>
This text will be to the left of the table, and will fall neatly beside the table
<BR CLEAR=all>
<HR>
```

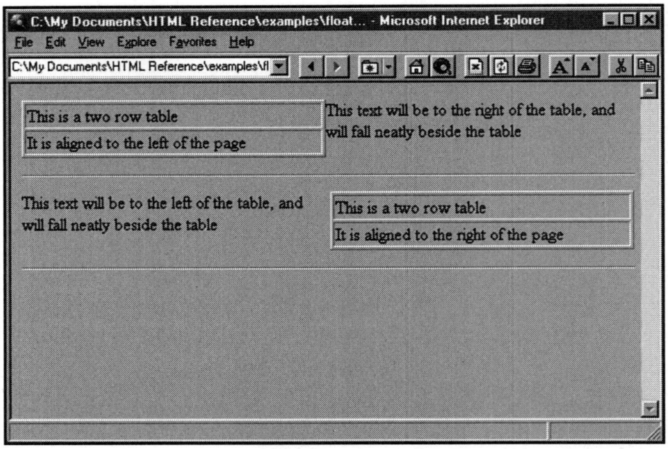

FIGURE B.9.
Tables that can float in the document.

A Colored Table

```
<TABLE BORDER BGCOLOR=Silver BORDERCOLOR=Black WIDTH=50%>
<TR>
<TD>This is the first cell</TD>
<TD>This is the second cell</TD>
</TR>
<TR BORDERCOLOR=Red BGCOLOR=Green>
<TD>This is the third cell</TD>
<TD>This is the fourth cell</TD>
</TR>
<TR BORDERCOLOR=Red BGCOLOR=Green>
<TD BORDERCOLOR=Yellow>This is the fifth cell</TD>
<TD BGCOLOR=White>This is the sixth cell</TD>
</TR>
</TABLE>
```

FIGURE B.10.
Color can be added to cells.

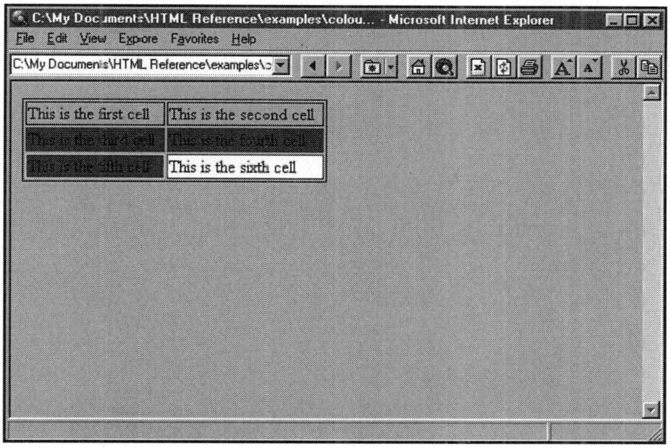

An HTML 3.2 Table

> **NOTE**
>
> The following HTML table is at present only supported by Internet Explorer.

```
<TABLE BORDER FRAME=hsides RULES=cols>
<COL ALIGN=left>
<COLGROUP SPAN=3 ALIGN=center VALIGN=middle>
<THEAD>
<CAPTION ALIGN=center><FONT SIZE=+1><B>A section of the Comparison Table</B>
</FONT>
</CAPTION>
<TR>
<TD>Element</TD><TD><B>Internet Explorer</B></TD><TD><B>Netscape</B>
</TD><TD><B>Mosaic</B></TD>
```

```
</TR>
</THEAD>
<TBODY>
<TR>
<TD>&lt;B&gt;</TD><TD>X</TD><TD>X</TD><TD>X</TD>
</TR>
<TR>
<TD>&lt;BASE ...&gt;</TD><TD>X</TD><TD>X</TD><TD>X</TD>
</TR>
<TR>
<TD>  ...HREF</TD><TD>X</TD><TD>X</TD><TD>X</TD>
</TR>
<TR>
<TD>  ...TARGET</TD><TD>X</TD><TD>X</TD><TD></TD>
</TR>
<TR>
<TD>&lt;BASEFONT ...&gt;</TD><TD>X</TD><TD>X</TD><TD></TD>
</TR>
<TR>
<TD VALIGN=top>  ...SIZE</TD><TD>X<BR><FONT SIZE=-1>(only visible<BR>when
FONT<BR>SIZE= used<BR>as well)</FONT></TD><TD VALIGN=top>X</TD><TD></TD>
</TR>
<TR>
<TD>  ...FACE</TD><TD>X</TD><TD></TD><TD></TD>
</TR>
<TR>
<TD VALIGN=top>&lt;BGSOUND ...&gt;</TD><TD VALIGN=top>X</TD><TD>
</TD><TD>X<BR><FONT SIZE=-1>(will spawn<BR>player for<BR>.mid files)
</FONT></TD>
</TR>
</TBODY>
<TFOOT></TFOOT>
</TABLE>
```

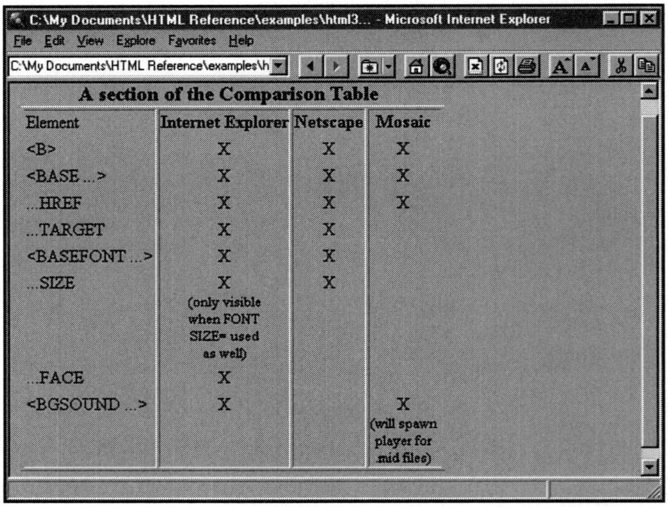

FIGURE B.11.
A complex table created for Internet Explorer.

APPENDIX C

Browser Comparison Chart

by Stephen Le Hunte

Table C.1 lists all the HTML 3.2 elements and attributes and indicates which browsers support them.

Table C.1. Comparison of HTML across three popular browsers.

Element	*Attribute*	*Internet Explorer*	*Netscape Navigator*	*NCSA Mosaic*
`<!-- ...>`		✓	✓	✓
`<!DOCTYPE ...>`		✓	✓	✓
`<A ...>`		✓	✓	✓
	`...HREF`	✓	✓	✓
	`Mailto : ...TITLE`			✓
	`...NAME`	✓	✓	✓
	`...TITLE`	✓	✓	✓
	`...REL`	✓	✓	✓
	`...REV`	✓	✓	✓
	`...URN`	✓	✓	✓
	`...METHODS`	✓	✓	✓
	`...TARGET`		✓	
`<ADDRESS>`		✓	✓	✓
`<APPLET ...>`			✓	
	`...CODEBASE`		✓	
	`...CODE`		✓	
	`...ALT`		✓	
	`...NAME`		✓	
	`...WIDTH/HEIGHT`		✓	
	`...ALIGN`		✓	
	`...VSPACE/HSPACE`		✓	
	`...PARAM NAME/VALUE`		✓	
`<B>`		✓	✓	✓
`<BASE ...>`		✓	✓	✓
	`...HREF`	✓	✓	✓
	`...TARGET`		✓	
`<BASEFONT ...>`		✓	✓	

Element	*Attribute*	*Internet Explorer*	*Netscape Navigator*	*NCSA Mosaic*
	...SIZE	✓ (only visible when FONT SIZE=used too)	✓	
	...FACE	✓		
<BGSOUND ...>		✓		✓ (will spawn player for .mid files)
	...LOOP	✓		✓
	...DELAY			✓
<BIG>		✓	✓	
<BLINK>			✓	
<BLOCKQUOTE>		✓	✓	✓
<BODY ...>		✓	✓	✓
	...BACKGROUND	✓	✓	✓
	...TEXT	✓	✓	✓ (using color names is reliable)
	...LINK	✓	✓	✓
	...VLINK	✓	✓	✓
	...ALINK		✓	
	...BGCOLOR	✓	✓	✓
	...BGPROPERTIES	✓		
	...LEFTMARGIN	✓		
	...TOPMARGIN	✓		
 		✓	✓	✓
	...CLEAR	✓	✓	
<CAPTION>		✓	✓	✓
	...ALIGN	✓ (top, bottom, left, right, center)	✓ (top, bottom)	✓ (top, bottom)

continues

Table C.1. continued

Element	*Attribute*	*Internet Explorer*	*Netscape Navigator*	*NCSA Mosaic*
	...VALIGN	✓ (top, bottom)		
<CENTER>		✓	✓	✓
<CITE>		✓	✓	✓
<CODE>		✓	✓	✓
<COL>		✓		
	...SPAN	✓		
	...ALIGN	✓		
<COLGROUP>		✓		
	...SPAN	✓		
	...ALIGN	✓		
	...VALIGN	✓		
<COMMENT>		✓		✓
<DFN>		✓		
<DIR>		✓ (no bullet)	✓	✓
<DIV>			✓	
	...ALIGN		✓ (left, right, center)	
<DL>		✓	✓	✓
<DT>		✓	✓	✓
<DD>		✓	✓	✓
	...COMPACT		✓	
<DT>		✓	✓	✓
<EM>		✓	✓	✓
<EMBED ...>			✓	
<FONT ...>		✓	✓	
	...SIZE	✓	✓	
	...COLOR	✓	✓	
	...FACE	✓		

Element	*Attribute*	*Internet Explorer*	*Netscape Navigator*	*NCSA Mosaic*
<FORM>		✓	✓	✓
<FRAME ...>			✓	
	...SRC		✓	
	...NAME		✓	
	...MARGINWIDTH		✓	
	...MARGINHEIGHT		✓	
	...SCROLLING		✓	
	...NORESIZE		✓	
	...FRAMEBORDER	✓		
	...FRAMESPACING	✓		
<FRAMESET ...>		✓	✓	
	...ROWS	✓	✓	
	...COLS	✓	✓	
<H ALIGN= ...>		✓ (center only)	✓ (right, left, center)	✓ (right, left, center)
<H1>		✓	✓	✓
<H2>		✓	✓	✓
<H3>		✓	✓	✓
<H4>		✓	✓	✓
<H5>		✓	✓	✓
<H6>		✓	✓	✓
<HEAD>		✓	✓	✓
<HR ...>		✓	✓	✓
	...SIZE	✓	✓	✓
	...WIDTH	✓	✓	✓
	...ALIGN	✓	✓	✓
	...NOSHADE	✓	✓	✓
	...COLOR	✓		
<HTML>		✓	✓	✓
<I>		✓	✓	✓

continues

C BROWSER COMPARISON CHART

Table C.1. continued

Element	*Attribute*	*Internet Explorer*	*Netscape Navigator*	*NCSA Mosaic*
`<IMG ...>`		✓	✓	✓
	`...ALIGN`	✓	✓	✓ (top, middle, bottom only)
	`...ALT`	✓	✓	✓
	`...ISMAP`	✓	✓	✓
	`...SRC`	✓	✓	✓
	`...WIDTH`	✓	✓	✓
	`...HEIGHT`	✓	✓	✓ (image can't be distorted)
	`...BORDER`	✓ (only when image is a link)	✓	
	`...VSPACE`	✓	✓	
	`...HSPACE`	✓	✓	
	`...LOWSRC`		✓	
	`...USEMAP`	✓	✓	✓
	`...VRML`	✓		
`<INPUT ...>`		✓	✓	✓
	`...ALIGN`	✓	✓	✓
	`...CHECKED`	✓	✓	✓
	`...MAXLENGTH`	✓	✓	✓
	`...NAME`	✓	✓	✓
	`...SIZE`	✓	✓	✓
	`...SRC`	✓	✓	✓
	`...TYPE`	✓	✓	✓
	`...VALUE`	✓	✓	✓
`<ISINDEX ...>`		✓	✓	✓
	`...PROMPT`	✓	✓	
`<KBD>`		✓	✓	✓
`<LI>`		✓	✓	✓

Element	*Attribute*	*Internet Explorer*	*Netscape Navigator*	*NCSA Mosaic*
<LINK ...>		✓	✓	✓
<LISTING>		✓ (will translate special characters)	✓ (renders characters to the line and translates special characters)	✓
<MAP ...>		✓	✓	✓
	...SHAPE	✓	✓	✓
	...COORDS	✓	✓	✓
	...AREA	✓	✓	✓
<MARQUEE ...>		✓		
	...ALIGN	✓		
	...BEHAVIOR	✓		
	...BGCOLOR	✓		
	...DIRECTION	✓		
	...HEIGHT	✓		
	...WIDTH	✓		
	...HSPACE	✓		
	...LOOP	✓		
	...SCROLLAMOUNT	✓		
	...SCROLLDELAY	✓		
	...VSPACE	✓		
<MENU>		✓ (no bullet)	✓	✓
<META ...>		✓	✓	✓
	...HTTP-EQUIV	✓	✓	✓
	...NAME	✓	✓	✓
	...CONTENT	✓	✓	✓
<NEXTID ...>		✓	✓	✓
<NOBR>		✓	✓	

continues

Table C.1. continued

Element	*Attribute*	*Internet Explorer*	*Netscape Navigator*	*NCSA Mosaic*
<NOFRAMES>		✓	✓	
<OBJECT>		✓		
<PARAM>		✓		
<OL ...>		✓	✓	✓
	...TYPE	✓	✓	
	...START	✓	✓	
	...VALUE	✓	✓	
<OPTION>		✓	✓	✓
<P>		✓	✓	✓
	...ALIGN	✓ (center only)	✓ (left, right, center)	✓ (left, right, center)
<PLAINTEXT>		✓ (allows closing element)	✓	✓ (allows closing element)
<PRE>		✓	✓	✓
<S>		✓		✓
<SAMP>		✓	✓	✓
<SCRIPT ...>		✓	✓	
	...LANGUAGE	✓	✓	
	...SRC	✓	✓	
<SELECT>		✓	✓	✓
<SMALL>		✓	✓	
<SOUND ...>				✓ (.wav only)
	...SRC			✓
	...DELAY			✓
<STRIKE>		✓	✓	✓
<STRONG>		✓	✓	✓
<SUB>		✓	✓	✓
<SUP>		✓	✓	✓

Element	Attribute	Internet Explorer	Netscape Navigator	NCSA Mosaic
<TABLE ...>		✓	✓	✓
	...BORDER	✓	✓	✓
	...CELLSPACING	✓	✓	✓
	...CELLPADDING	✓	✓	✓
	...WIDTH	✓	✓	✓
	...HEIGHT	✓	✓	✓
	...ALIGN	✓	✓	
	...VALIGN	✓		
	...BGCOLOR	✓		
	...BORDERCOLOR	✓		
	...BORDERCOLORLIGHT	✓		
	...BORDERCOLORDARK	✓		
	...BACKGROUND	✓		
	...FRAME	✓		
	...RULES	✓		
<TBODY>		✓		
<TD ...>		✓	✓	✓
	...ROWSPAN	✓	✓	✓
	...COLSPAN	✓	✓	✓
	...ALIGN	✓	✓	
	...VALIGN	✓	✓	✓
	...WIDTH	✓	✓	
	...HEIGHT	✓		
	...NOWRAP	✓	✓	
	...BGCOLOR	✓		
	...BORDERCOLOR	✓		
	...BORDERCOLORLIGHT	✓		
	...BORDERCOLORDARK	✓		
	...BACKGROUND	✓		

continues

Table C.1. continued

Element	*Attribute*	*Internet Explorer*	*Netscape Navigator*	*NCSA Mosaic*
`<TEXTAREA ...>`		✓	✓	✓
	`...NAME`	✓	✓	✓
	`...ROWS`	✓	✓	✓
	`...COLS`	✓	✓	✓
	`...WRAP`		✓	
`<TFOOT>`		✓		
`<TH ...>`		✓	✓	✓
	`...ROWSPAN`	✓	✓	✓
	`...COLSPAN`	✓	✓	✓
	`...ALIGN`	✓	✓	✓
	`...VALIGN`	✓	✓	✓
	`...WIDTH`	✓	✓	
	`...HEIGHT`	✓		
	`...NOWRAP`	✓	✓	
	`...BGCOLOR`	✓		
	`...BORDERCOLOR`	✓		
	`...BORDERCOLORLIGHT`	✓		
	`...BORDERCOLORDARK`	✓		
	`...BACKGROUND`	✓		
`<THEAD>`		✓		
`<TITLE>`		✓	✓	✓
`<TR ...>`		✓	✓	✓
	`...ALIGN`	✓	✓	✓
	`...VALIGN`	✓	✓	✓
	`...BGCOLOR`	✓		
	`...BORDERCOLOR`	✓		
	`...BORDERCOLORLIGHT`	✓		
	`...BORDERCOLORDARK`	✓		

Element	*Attribute*	*Internet Explorer*	*Netscape Navigator*	*NCSA Mosaic*
<TT>		✓	✓	✓
<U>		✓		✓
<UL>		✓	✓	✓
<VAR>		✓	✓	✓
<WBR>		✓	✓	
<XMP>		✓ (will translate special characters)	✓	✓

APPENDIX D

Color Table

by Wes Tatters

Table D.1 contains a list of all the color names recognized by Navigator 2.0 and also includes their corresponding hexadecimal Triplet values. To see all these colors correctly, you must have a 256-color or better video card and the appropriate video drivers installed. Also, depending on the operating system and computer platform you are running, some colors may not appear exactly as you expect them to.

Table D.1. Color values and HEX triplet equivalents.

Color Name	*HEX Triplet*	*Color Name*	*HEX Triplet*
ALICEBLUE	#A0CE00	DARKGREEN	#006400
ANTIQUEWHITE	#FAEBD7	DARKKHAKI	#BDB76B
AQUA	#00FFFF	DARKMAGENTA	#8B008B
AQUAMARINE	#7FFFD4	DARKOLIVEGREEN	#556B2F
AZURE	#F0FFFF	DARKORANGE	#FF8C00
BEIGE	#F5F5DC	DARKORCHID	#9932CC
BISQUE	#FFE4C4	DARKRED	#8B0000
BLACK	#000000	DARKSALMON	#E9967A
BLANCHEDALMOND	#FFEBCD	DARKSEAGREEN	#8FBC8F
BLUE	#0000FF	DARKSLATEBLUE	#483D8B
BLUEVIOLET	#8A2BE2	DARKSLATEGRAY	#2F4F4F
BROWN	#A52A2A	DARKTURQUOISE	#00CED1
BURLYWOOD	#DEB887	DARKVIOLET	#9400D3
CADETBLUE	#5F9EA0	DEEPPINK	#FF1493
CHARTREUSE	#7FFF00	DEEPSKYBLUE	#00BFFF
CHOCOLATE	#D2691E	DIMGRAY	#696969
CORAL	#FF7F50	DODGERBLUE	#1E90FF
CORNFLOWERBLUE	#6495ED	FIREBRICK	#B22222
CORNSILK	#FFF8DC	FLORALWHITE	#FFFAF0
CRIMSON	#DC143C	FORESTGREEN	#228B22
CYAN	#00FFFF	FUCHSIA	#FF00FF
DARKBLUE	#00008B	GAINSBORO	#DCDCDC
DARKCYAN	#008B8B	GHOSTWHITE	#F8F8FF
DARKGOLDENROD	#B8860B	GOLD	#FFD700
DARKGRAY	#A9A9A9	GOLDENROD	#DAA520

Color Name	HEX Triplet	Color Name	HEX Triplet
GRAY	#808080	MEDIUMBLUE	#0000CD
GREEN	#008000	MEDIUMORCHID	#BA55D3
GREENYELLOW	#ADFF2F	MEDIUMPURPLE	#9370DB
HONEYDEW	#F0FFF0	MEDIUMSEAGREEN	#3CB371
HOTPINK	#FF69B4	MEDIUMSLATEBLUE	#7B68EE
INDIANRED	#CD5C5C	MEDIUMSPRINGGREEN	#00FA9A
INDIGO	#4B0082	MEDIUMTURQUOISE	#48D1CC
IVORY	#FFFFF0	MEDIUMVIOLETRED	#C71585
KHAKI	#F0E68C	MIDNIGHTBLUE	#191970
LAVENDER	#E6E6FA	MINTCREAM	#F5FFFA
LAVENDERBLUSH	#FFF0F5	MISTYROSE	#FFE4E1
LEMONCHIFFON	#FFFACD	NAVAJOWHITE	#FFDEAD
LIGHTBLUE	#ADD8E6	NAVY	#000080
LIGHTCORAL	#F08080	OLDLACE	#FDF5E6
LIGHTCYAN	#E0FFFF	OLIVE	#808000
LIGHTGOLDENRODYELLOW	#FAFAD2	OLIVEDRAB	#6B8E23
LIGHTGREEN	#90EE90	ORANGE	#FFA500
LIGHTGREY	#D3D3D3	ORANGERED	#FF4500
LIGHTPINK	#FFB6C1	ORCHID	#DA70D6
LIGHTSALMON	#FFA07A	PALEGOLDENROD	#EEE8AA
LIGHTSEAGREEN	#20B2AA	PALEGREEN	#98FB98
LIGHTSKYBLUE	#87CEFA	PALETURQUOISE	#AFEEEE
LIGHTSLATEGRAY	#778899	PALEVIOLETRED	#DB7093
LIGHTSTEELBLUE	#B0C4DE	PAPAYAWHIP	#FFEFD5
LIGHTYELLOW	#FFFFE0	PEACHPUFF	#FFDAB9
LIME	#00FF00	PERU	#CD853F
LIMEGREEN	#32CD32	PINK	#FFC0CB
LINEN	#FAF0E6	PLUM	#DDA0DD
MAGENTA	#FF00FF	POWDERBLUE	#B0E0E6
MAROON	#800000	PURPLE	#800080
MEDIUMAQUAMARINE	#66CDAA	RED	#FF0000

continues

Table D.1. continued

Color Name	*HEX Triplet*
ROSYBROWN	#BC8F8F
ROYALBLUE	#4169E1
SADDLEBROWN	#8B4513
SALMON	#FA8072
SANDYBROWN	#F4A460
SEAGREEN	#2E8B57
SEASHELL	#FFF5EE
SIENNA	#A0522D
SILVER	#C0C0C0
SKYBLUE	#87CEEB
SLATEBLUE	#6A5ACD
SLATEGRAY	#708090
SNOW	#FFFAFA
SPRINGGREEN	#00FF7F
STEELBLUE	#4682B4
TAN	#D2B48C
TEAL	#008080
THISTLE	#D8BFD8
TOMATO	#FF6347
TURQUOISE	#40E0D0
VIOLET	#EE82EE
WHEAT	#F5DEB3
WHITE	#FFFFFF
WHITESMOKE	#F5F5F5
YELLOW	#FFFF00
YELLOWGREEN	#9ACD32

APPENDIX E

MIME Types and File Extensions

by Laura Lemay

Table E.1 lists the file extensions and MIME content-types supported by many popular Web servers. If your server does not list an extension for a particular content-type or if the type you want to use is not listed at all, you will have to add support for that type to your server configuration.

Table E.1. MIME types and HTTPD support.

MIME Type	*What It Is (If Noted)*	*File Extensions*
`application/acad`	AutoCAD Drawing files	`dwg, DWG`
`application/arj`		`arj`
`application/clariscad`	ClarisCAD files	`CCAD`
`application/drafting`	MATRA Prelude drafting	`DRW`
`application/dxf`	DXF (AutoCAD)	`dxf, DXF`
`application/excel`	Microsoft Excel	`xl`
`application/i-deas`	SDRC I-DEAS files	`unv, UNV`
`application/iges`	IGES graphics format	`igs, iges, IGS, IGES`
`application/mac-binhex40`	Macintosh BinHex format	`hqx`
`application/msword`	Microsoft Word	`word, w6w, doc`
`application/mswrite`	Microsoft Write	`wri`
`application/octet-stream`	Uninterpreted binary	`bin`
`application/oda`		`oda`
`application/pdf`	PDF (Adobe Acrobat)	`pdf`
`application/postscript`	PostScript	`ai, PS, ps, eps`
`application/pro_eng`	PTC Pro/ENGINEER	`prt, PRT, part`
`application/rtf`	Rich Text Format	`rtf`
`application/set`	SET (French CAD standard)	`set, SET`
`application/sla`	Stereolithography	`stl, STL`
`application/solids`	MATRA Prelude Solids	`SOL`
`application/STEP`	ISO-10303 STEP data files	`stp, STP, step, STEP`
`application/vda`	VDA-FS Surface data	`vda, VDA`
`application/x-director`	Macromedia Director	`dir, dcr, dxr`
`application/x-mif`	FrameMaker MIF Format	`mif`

MIME Type	*What It Is (If Noted)*	*File Extensions*
application/x-csh	C-shell script	csh
application/x-dvi	TeX DVI	dvi
application/x-gzip	GNU Zip	gz, gzip
application/x-hdf	NCSA HDF Data File	hdf
application/x-latex	LaTeX source	latex
application/x-netcdf	Unidata netCDF	nc,cdf
application/x-sh	Bourne shell script	sh
application/x-stuffit	Stiffut Archive	sit
application/x-tcl	TCL script	tcl
application/x-tex	TeX source	tex
application/x-texinfo	Texinfo (Emacs)	texinfo,texi
application/x-troff	Troff	t, tr, roff
application/x-troff-man	Troff with MAN macros	man
application/x-troff-me	Troff with ME macros	me
application/x-troff-ms	Troff with MS macros	ms
application/x-wais-source	WAIS source	src
application/x-bcpio	Old binary CPIO	bcpio
application/x-cpio	POSIX CPIO	cpio
application/x-gtar	GNU tar	gtar
application/x-shar	Shell archive	shar
application/x-sv4cpio	SVR4 CPIO	sv4cpio
application/x-sv4crc	SVR4 CPIO with CRC	sv4crc
application/x-tar	4.3BSD tar format	tar
application/x-ustar	POSIX tar format	ustar
application/x-winhelp	Windows Help	hlp
application/zip	ZIP archive	zip
audio/basic	Basic audio (usually µ-law)	au, snd
audio/x-aiff	AIFF audio	aif, aiff, aifc
audio/x-pn-realaudio	RealAudio	ra, ram
audio/x-pn-realaudio-plugin	RealAudio (plug-in)	rpm
audio/x-wav	Windows WAVE audio	wav

continues

Table E.1. continued

MIME Type	*What It Is (If Noted)*	*File Extensions*
`image/gif`	GIF image	`gif`
`image/ief`	Image Exchange Format	`ief`
`image/jpeg`	JPEG image	`jpg, JPG, JPE, jpe, JPEG, jpeg`
`image/pict`	Macintosh PICT	`pict`
`image/tiff`	TIFF image	`tiff, tif`
`image/x-cmu-raster`	CMU raster	`ras`
`image/x-portable-anymap`	PBM Anymap format	`pnm`
`image/x-portable-bitmap`	PBM Bitmap format	`pbm`
`image/x-portable-graymap`	PBM Graymap format	`pgm`
`image/x-portable-pixmap`	PBM Pixmap format	`ppm`
`image/x-rgb`	RGB Image	`rgb`
`image/x-xbitmap`	X Bitmap	`xbm`
`image/x-xpixmap`	X Pixmap	`xpm`
`image/x-xwindowdump`	X Windows dump (xwd) format	`xwd`
`multipart/x-zip`	PKZIP Archive	`zip`
`multipart/x-gzip`	GNU ZIP Archive	`gzip`
`text/html`	HTML	`html, htm`
`text/plain`	Plain text	`txt, g, h, C, cc, hh, m, f90`
`text/richtext`	MIME Richtext	`rtx`
`text/tab-separated-values`	Text with tab-separated values	`tsv`
`text/x-setext`	Struct enhanced text	`etx`
`video/mpeg`	MPEG video	`mpeg, mpg, MPG, MPE, mpe, MPEG, mpeg`
`video/quicktime`	QuickTime Video	`qt, mov`
`video/msvideo`	Microsoft Windows Video	`avi`
`video/x-sgi-movie`	SGI Movieplayer format	`movie`
`x-world/x-vrml`	VRML Worlds	`wrl`

APPENDIX F

JavaScript Reference

by Arman Danesh and Stephen LeHunte

IN THIS APPENDIX

While Sun was developing the much-lauded Java programming language, Netscape was busy developing a lightweight scripting language called LiveScript. This was then re-defined and renamed JavaScript. With JavaScript, you can provide almost limitless interactivity in your Web pages. The scripting language allows the you to access events such as startups, document loads, exits, and user mouse clicks. You can also use JavaScript to directly control objects, such as the browser status bar, frames, and even the browser display window. JavaScript also provides interactivity between plug-in modules and Java applets.

After providing a brief overview of creating dynamic documents with JavaScript, this appendix provides a reference section organized by object with properties and methods listed by the objects they apply to. A final reference section covers independent functions in JavaScript not connected with a particular object, as well as operators in JavaScript.

NOTE

JavaScript is currently only fully supported by the Netscape Navigator (version 2 and above). Certain scripts may be supported by the Internet Explorer. For more information on JavaScript (including the entire script language documentation), visit the Netscape Web site (`http://home.netscape.com/`). The information provided here only details how to include JavaScript scripts within HTML documents, not how to author actual scripts. Such information is well beyond the scope of this appendix.

Dynamic Documents with JavaScript

As mentioned earlier, JavaScript represents a heavily stripped-down and redefined version of the Java programming language. It can be used to control almost any part of the browser (as defined in the JavaScript object model) and to respond to various user actions such as form input and page navigation. It is particularly valuable because all processing duties are written in the script (embedded into the HTML document), so the entire process defined by the script is carried out on the client side, without the need to refer back to a server.

For example, you can write a JavaScript script to verify that numeric information has been entered into a form requesting a telephone number or zip code. Without any network transmission, an HTML script with embedded JavaScript can interpret the entered text and alert the user with an appropriate message dialog.

A script is embedded in HTML within a `<SCRIPT>` element:

```
<SCRIPT>...</SCRIPT>
```

The text of a script is inserted between `<SCRIPT>` and its end element. Attributes within the `<SCRIPT>` element are specified as follows:

```
<SCRIPT LANGUAGE="JavaScript">
  Script functions go here
</SCRIPT>
```

The `LANGUAGE` attribute is required unless the `SRC` attribute is present and specifies the scripting language.

The optional `SRC` attribute can be used to specify a URL that loads the text of a script.

```
<SCRIPT LANGUAGE="language" SRC=url>
```

When a JavaScript-enabled HTML document is retrieved by a browser that supports JavaScript, the script functions are evaluated and stored. The functions defined within the script are executed only upon certain events within the page (for example, when the user moves the mouse over an object, or enters text in a text box, and so on).

So that non-JavaScript capable browsers do not display the text of the script (browsers will display anything they don't recognize as HTML as text on the page), the script should be enclosed within comment elements:

```
<SCRIPT LANGUAGE="JavaScript">
<!-- Begin to hide script contents from old browsers.
  Script contents go here.
  End the hiding here.-->
</SCRIPT>
```

JavaScript Objects and Their Properties

This section describes JavaScript objects and their properties. Objects are presented in alphabetical order for easy reference.

The anchor Object

See the `anchors` property of the `document` object.

The button Object

The `button` object reflects a push button from an HTML form in JavaScript.

Properties

`name`	A string value containing the name of the button element.
`value`	A string value containing the value of the button element.

Methods

`click()`	Emulates the action of clicking on the button.

Event Handlers

`onClick`	Specifies JavaScript code to execute when the button is clicked.

The `checkbox` Object

The `checkbox` object makes a check box from an HTML form available in JavaScript.

Properties

`checked`	A Boolean value indicating if the check box element is checked.
`defaultChecked`	A Boolean value indicating if the check box element was checked by default (that is, reflects the `CHECKED` attribute).
`name`	A string value containing the name of the check box element.
`value`	A string value containing the value of the check box element.

Methods

`click()`	Emulates the action of clicking on the check box.

Event Handlers

`onClick`	Specifies JavaScript code to execute when the check box is clicked.

The `Date` Object

The `Date` object provides mechanisms for working with dates and times in JavaScript. Instances of the object can be created with the following syntax:

```
newObjectName = new Date(dateInfo)
```

In this example, *`dateInfo`* is an optional specification of a particular date and can be one of the following, where the latter two options represent integer values:

```
"month day, year hours:minutes:seconds"
year, month, day
year, month, day, hours, minutes, seconds
```

If no *`dateInfo`* is specified, the new object will represent the current date and time.

Methods

`getDate()`	Returns the day of the month for the current `Date` object as an integer from 1 to 31.
`getDay()`	Returns the day of the week for the current `Date` object as an integer from 0 to 6 (where 0 is Sunday, 1 is Monday, and so on).
`getHours()`	Returns the hour from the time in the current `Date` object as an integer from 0 to 23.
`getMinutes()`	Returns the minutes from the time in the current `Date` object as an integer from 0 to 59.
`getMonth()`	Returns the month for the current `Date` object as an integer from 0 to 11 (where 0 is January, 1 is February, and so on).
`getSeconds()`	Returns the seconds from the time in the current `Date` object as an integer from 0 to 59.
`getTime()`	Returns the time of the current `Date` object as an integer representing the number of milliseconds since January 1, 1970 at 00:00:00.
`getTimezoneOffset()`	Returns the difference between the local time and GMT as an integer representing the number of minutes.
`getYear()`	Returns the year of the week for the current `Date` object as a two-digit integer representing the year less 1900.

`parse(`*`dateString`*`)`	Returns the number of milliseconds between January 1, 1970 at 00:00:00 and the date specified in *`dateString`*. *`dateString`* should take the format
	`Day, DD Mon YYYY HH:MM:SS TZN`
	`Mon DD, YYYY`

`setDate(`*`dateValue`*`)`	Sets the day of the month for the current `Date` object. *`dateValue`* is an integer from 1 to 31.
`setHours(`*`hoursValue`*`)`	Sets the hours for the time for the current `Date` object. *`hoursValue`* is an integer from 0 to 23.
`setMinutes(`*`minutesValue`*`)`	Sets the minutes for the time for the current `Date` object. *`minutesValue`* is an integer from 0 to 59.
`setMonth(`*`monthValue`*`)`	Sets the month for the current `Date` object. *`monthValue`* is an integer from 0 to 11 (where 0 is January, 1 is February, and so on).

`setSeconds(secondsValue)`	Sets the seconds for the time for the current `Date` object. *`secondsValue`* is an integer from 0 to 59.
`setTime(timeValue)`	Sets the value for the current `Date` object. *`timeValue`* is an integer representing the number of milliseconds since January 1, 1970 at 00:00:00.
`setYear(yearValue)`	Sets the year for the current `Date` object. *`yearValue`* is an integer greater than 1900.
`toGMTString()`	Returns the value of the current `Date` object in GMT as a string using Internet conventions in the following form: `Day, DD Mon YYYY HH:MM:SS GMT`
`toLocaleString()`	Returns the value of the current `Date` object in the local time using local conventions.
`UTC(yearValue, monthValue, dateValue, hoursValue, minutesValue, secondsValue)`	Returns the number of milliseconds since January 1, 1970 at 00:00:00 GMT. *`yearValue`* is an integer greater than 1900. *`monthValue`* is an integer from 0 to 11. *`dateValue`* is an integer from 1 to 31. *`hoursValue`* is an integer from 0 to 23. *`minutesValue`* and `secondsValue` are integers from 0 to 59. *`hoursValue`*, *`minutesValue`*, and *`secondsValue`* are optional.

The document Object

The `document` object reflects attributes of an HTML document in JavaScript.

Properties

`alinkColor`	The color of active links as a string or a hexadecimal triplet.
`anchors`	Array of anchor objects in the order they appear in the HTML document. Use `anchors.length` to get the number of anchors in a document.
`bgColor`	The color of the document's background.
`cookie`	A string value containing cookie values for the current document.
`fgColor`	The color of the document's foreground.
`forms`	Array of form objects in the order the forms appear in the HTML file. Use `forms.length` to get the number of forms in a document.
`lastModified`	String value containing the last date of modification of the document.

`linkColor`	The color of links as a string or a hexadecimal triplet.
`links`	Array of link objects in the order the hypertext links appear in the HTML document. Use `links.length` to get the number of links in a document.
`location`	A string containing the URL of the current document.
`referrer`	A string value containing the URL of the calling document when the user follows a link.
`title`	A string containing the title of the current document.
`vlinkColor`	The color of followed links as a string or a hexadecimal triplet.

Methods

`clear()`	Clears the document window.
`close()`	Closes the current output stream.
`open(`*`mimeType`*`)`	Opens a stream which allows `write()` and `writeln()` methods to write to the document window. *`mimeType`* is an optional string which specifies a document type supported by Navigator or a plug-in (for example, `text/html`, `image/gif`, and so on).
`write()`	Writes text and HTML to the specified document.
`writeln()`	Writes text and HTML to the specified document followed by a newline character.

The `form` Object

The `form` object reflects an HTML form in JavaScript. Each HTML form in a document is reflected by a distinct instance of the `form` object.

Properties

`action`	A string value specifying the URL which the form data is submitted to.
`elements`	Array of objects for each form element in the order in which they appear in the form.
`encoding`	String containing the MIME encoding of the form as specified in the `ENCTYPE` attribute.
`method`	A string value containing the method of submission of form data to the server.
`target`	A string value containing the name of the window to which responses to form submissions are directed.

Methods

`submit()`	Submits the form.

Event Handlers

`onSubmit`	Specifies JavaScript code to execute when the form is submitted. The code should return a true value to allow the form to be submitted. A false value prevents the form from being submitted.

The `frame` Object

The `frame` object reflects a frame window in JavaScript.

Properties

`frames`	An array of objects for each frame in a window. Frames appear in the array in the order in which they appear in the HTML source code.
`parent`	A string indicating the name of window containing the frameset.
`self`	An alternative for the name of the current window.
`top`	An alternative for the name of the top-most window.
`window`	An alternative for the name of the current window.

Methods

`alert(`*`message`*`)`	Displays *`message`* in a dialog box.
`close()`	Closes the window.
`confirm(`*`message`*`)`	Displays *`message`* in a dialog box with OK and Cancel buttons. Returns true or false based on the button clicked by the user.
`open(`*`url`*`,`*`name`*`,`*`features`*`)`	Opens *`url`* in a window named *`name`*. If *`name`* doesn't exist, a new window is created with that name. *`features`* is an optional string argument containing a list of features for the new window. The feature list contains any of the following name/value pairs separated by commas and without additional spaces:

`toolbar=[yes,no,1,0]`	Indicates if the window should have a toolbar.
`location=[yes,no,1,0]`	Indicates if the window should have a location field.
`directories=[yes,no,1,0]`	Indicates if the window should have directory buttons.
`status=[yes,no,1,0]`	Indicates if the window should have a status bar.
`menubar=[yes,no,1,0]`	Indicates if the window should have menus.
`scrollbars=[yes,no,1,0]`	Indicates if the window should have scroll bars.
`resizable=[yes,no,1,0]`	Indicates if the window should be resizable.
`width=`*`pixels`*	Indicates the width of the window in pixels.
`height=`*`pixels`*	Indicates the height of the window in pixels.

`prompt(`*`message`*`,`*`response`*`)`	Displays *`message`* in a dialog box with a text entry field with the default value of *`response`*. The user's response in the text entry field is returned as a string.
`setTimeout(`*`expression`*`,`*`time`*`)`	Evaluates *`expression`* after *`time`* where *`time`* is a value in milliseconds. The time out can be named with the structure: `name = setTimeOut(expression,time)`
`clearTimeout(`*`name`*`)`	Cancels the time out with the name `name`.

The `hidden` Object

The `hidden` object reflects a hidden field from an HTML form in JavaScript.

Properties

name	A string value containing the name of the hidden element.
value	A string value containing the value of the hidden text element.

The `history` Object

The `history` object allows a script to work with the Navigator browser's history list in JavaScript. For security and privacy reasons, the actual content of the list is not reflected into JavaScript.

Properties

`length`	An integer representing the number of items on the history list.

Methods

`back()`	Goes back to the previous document in the history list.
`forward()`	Goes forward to the next document in the history list.
`go(`*`location`*`)`	Goes to the document in the history list specified by *`location`*. *`location`* can be a string or integer value. If it is a string it represents all or part of a URL in the history list. If it is an integer, *`location`* represents the relative position of the document on the history list. As an integer, *`location`* can be positive or negative.

The `link` Object

The `link` object reflects a hypertext link in the body of a document.

Properties

`target`	A string value containing the name of the window or frame specified in the `TARGET` attribute.

Event Handlers

`onClick`	Specifies JavaScript code to execute when the link is clicked.
`onMouseOver`	Specifies JavaScript code to execute when the mouse is over the hypertext link.

The `location` Object

The `location` object reflects information about the current URL.

Properties

`hash`	A string value containing the anchor name in the URL.
`host`	A string value containing the hostname and port number from the URL.
`hostname`	A string value containing the domain name (or numerical IP address) from the URL.
`href`	A string value containing the entire URL.
`pathname`	A string value specifying the path portion of the URL.
`port`	A string value containing the port number from the URL.
`protocol`	A string value containing the protocol from the URL (including the colon, but not the slashes).
`search`	A string value containing any information passed to a `GET` CGI-BIN call (that is, an information after the question mark).

The `Math` Object

The `Math` object provides properties and methods for advanced mathematical calculations.

Properties

`E`	The value of Euler's constant (roughly 2.718) used as the base for natural logarithms.
`LN10`	The value of the natural logarithm of 10 (roughly 2.302).
`LN2`	The value of the natural logarithm of 2 (roughly 0.693).
`PI`	The value of PI—used in calculating the circumference and area of circles (roughly 3.1415).
`SQRT1_2`	The value of the square root of one-half (roughly 0.707).
`SQRT2`	The value of the square root of two (roughly 1.414).

Methods

`abs(`*`number`*`)`	Returns the absolute value of *`number`*. The absolute value is the value of a number with it's sign ignored so `abs(4)` and `abs(-4)` both return 4.

`acos(number)`	Returns the arc cosine of *number* in radians.
`asin(number)`	Returns the arc sine of *number* in radians.
`atan(number)`	Returns the arc tangent of *number* in radians.
`ceil(number)`	Returns the next integer greater than *number*—in other words, rounds up to the next integer.
`cos(number)`	Returns the cosine of *number* where *number* represents an angle in radians.
`exp(number)`	Returns the value of `E` to the power of *number*.
`floor(number)`	Returns the next integer less than *number*—in other words, rounds down to the nearest integer.
`log(number)`	Returns the natural logarithm of *number*.
`max(number1,number2)`	Returns the greater of *number1* and *number2*.
`min(number1,number2)`	Returns the smaller of *number1* and *number2*.
`pow(number1,number2)`	Returns the value of *number1* to the power of *number2*.
`random()`	Returns a random number between zero and one.
`round(number)`	Returns the closest integer to *number*—in other words rounds to the closest integer.
`sin(number)`	Returns the sine of *number* where *number* represents an angle in radians.
`sqrt(number)`	Returns the square root of number.
`tan(number)`	Returns the tangent of *number* where *number* represents an angle in radians.

The `navigator` Object

The `navigator` object reflects information about the version of Navigator being used.

Properties

`appCodeName`	A string value containing the code name of the client (for example, "Mozilla" for Netscape Navigator).
`appName`	A string value containing the name of the client (for example, "Netscape" for Netscape Navigator).

`appVersion`	A string value containing the version information for the client in the form `versionNumber (platform; country)`
`userAgent`	A string containing the complete value of the user-agent header sent in the HTTP request. This contains all the information in `appCodeName` and `appVersion`: `Mozilla/2.0b6 (Win32; I)`

The `password` Object

The `password` object reflects a password text field from an HTML form in JavaScript.

Properties

`defaultValue`	A string value containing the default value of the password element (that is, the value of the `VALUE` attribute).
`name`	A string value containing the name of the password element.
`value`	A string value containing the value of the password element.

Methods

`focus()`	Emulates the action of focusing in the password field.
`blur()`	Emulates the action of removing focus from the password field.
`select()`	Emulates the action of selecting the text in the password field.

The `radio` Object

The `radio` object reflects a set of radio buttons from an HTML form in JavaScript. To access individual radio buttons, use numeric indexes starting at zero. For instance, individual buttons in a set of radio buttons named `testRadio` could be referenced by `testRadio[0]`, `testRadio[1]`, and so on.

Properties

`checked`	A Boolean value indicating if a specific button is checked. Can be used to select or deselect a button.

`defaultChecked`	A Boolean value indicating if a specific button was checked by default (that is, reflects the `CHECKED` attribute).
`length`	An integer value indicating the number of radio buttons in the set.
`name`	A string value containing the name of the set of radio buttons.
`value`	A string value containing the value of a specific radio button in a set (that is, reflects the `VALUE` attribute).

Methods

`click()`	Emulates the action of clicking on a radio button.

Event Handlers

`onClick`	Specifies JavaScript code to execute when a radio button is clicked.

The `reset` Object

The `reset` object reflects a reset button from an HTML form in JavaScript.

Properties

`name`	A string value containing the name of the reset element.
`value`	A string value containing the value of the reset element.

Methods

`click()`	Emulates the action of clicking on the reset button.

Event Handlers

`onClick`	Specifies JavaScript code to execute when the reset button is clicked.

The `select` Object

The `select` object reflects a selection list from an HTML form in JavaScript.

Properties

`length`	An integer value containing the number of options in the selection list.

`name`	A string value containing the name of the selection list.
`options`	An array reflecting each of the options in the selection list in the order they appear. The options property has its own properties:
`defaultSelected`	A Boolean value indicating if an option was selected by default (that is, reflects the `SELECTED` attribute).
`index`	An integer value reflecting the index of an option.
`length`	An integer value reflecting the number of options in the selection list.
`name`	A string value containing the name of the selection list.
`options`	A string value containing the full HTML code for the selection list.
`selected`	A Boolean value indicating if the option is selected. Can be used to select or deselect an option.
`selectedIndex`	An integer value containing the index of the currently selected option.
`text`	A string value containing the text displayed in the selection list for a particular option. `value` A string value indicating the value for the specified option (that is, reflects the `VALUE` attribute).
`selectedIndex`	Reflects the index of the currently selected option in the selection list.

Event Handlers

`onBlur`	Specifies JavaScript code to execute when the selection list loses focus.
`onFocus`	Specifies JavaScript code to execute when focus is given to the selection list.
`onChange`	Specifies JavaScript code to execute when the selected option in the list changes.

The `string` Object

The `string` object provides properties and methods for working with string literals and variables.

Properties

`length`	An integer value containing the length of the string expressed as the number of characters in the string.

Methods

`anchor(`*`name`*`)`	Returns a string containing the value of the string object surrounded by an `A` container tag with the `NAME` attribute set to *`name`*.
`big()`	Returns a string containing the value of the string object surrounded by a `BIG` container tag.
`blink()`	Returns a string containing the value of the string object surrounded by a `BLINK` container tag.
`bold()`	Returns a string containing the value of the string object surrounded by a `B` container tag.
`charAt(`*`index`*`)`	Returns the character at the location specified by *`index`*.
`fixed()`	Returns a string containing the value of the string object surrounded by a `FIXED` container tag.
`fontColor(`*`color`*`)`	Returns a string containing the value of the string object surrounded by a `FONT` container tag with the `COLOR` attribute set to *`color`* where *`color`* is a color name or an RGB triplet.
`fontSize(`*`size`*`)`	Returns a string containing the value of the string object surrounded by a `FONTSIZE` container tag with the size set to *`size`*.
`indexOf (`*`findString`*`, `*`startingIndex`*`)`	Returns the index of the first occurrence of *`findString`*, starting the search at *`startingIndex`* where *`startingIndex`* is optional—if it is not provided, the search starts at the start of the string.
`italics()`	Returns a string containing the value of the string object surrounded by an `I` container tag.
`lastIndexOf (`*`findString`*`, `*`startingIndex`*`)`	Returns the index of the last occurrence of *`findString`*. This is done by searching backwards from *`startingIndex`*, which is optional and assumed to be the last character in the string if no value is provided.
`link(`*`href`*`)`	Returns a string containing the value of the string object surrounded by an `A` container tag with the `HREF` attribute set to *`href`*.
`small()`	Returns a string containing the value of the string object surrounded by a `SMALL` container tag.
`strike()`	Returns a string containing the value of the string object surrounded by a `STRIKE` container tag.
`sub()`	Returns a string containing the value of the string object surrounded by a `SUB` container tag.

`substring (firstIndex, lastIndex)`	Returns a string equivalent to the substring starting at *`firstIndex`* and ending at the character before *`lastIndex`*. If *`firstIndex`* is greater than *`lastIndex`*, the string starts at *`lastIndex`* and ends at the character before *`firstIndex`*.
`sup()`	Returns a string containing the value of the string object surrounded by a `SUP` container tag.
`toLowerCase()`	Returns a string containing the value of the string object with all characters converted to lowercase.
`toUpperCase()`	Returns a string containing the value of the string object with all characters converted to uppercase.

The `submit` Object

The `submit` object reflects a submit button from an HTML form in JavaScript.

Properties

`name`	A string value containing the name of the submit button element.
`value`	A string value containing the value of the submit button element.

Methods

`click()`	Emulates the action of clicking on the submit button.

Event Handlers

`onClick`	Specifies JavaScript code to execute when the submit button is clicked.

The `text` Object

The `text` object reflects a text field from an HTML form in JavaScript.

Properties

`defaultValue`	A string value containing the default value of the text element (that is, the value of the `VALUE` attribute).
`name`	A string value containing the name of the text element.
`value`	A string value containing the value of the text element.

Methods

`focus()`	Emulates the action of focusing in the text field.
`blur()`	Emulates the action of removing focus from the text field.
`select()`	Emulates the action of selecting the text in the text field.

Event Handlers

`onBlur`	Specifies JavaScript code to execute when focus is removed from the field.
`onChange`	Specifies JavaScript code to execute when the content of the field is changed.
`onFocus`	Specifies JavaScript code to execute when focus is given to the field.
`onSelect`	Specifies JavaScript code to execute when the user selects some or all of the text in the field.

The `textarea` Object

The `textarea` object reflects a multi-line text field from an HTML form in JavaScript.

Properties

`defaultValue`	A string value containing the default value of the `textarea` element (that is, the value of the `VALUE` attribute).
`name`	A string value containing the name of the `textarea` element.
`value`	A string value containing the value of the `textarea` element.

Methods

`focus()`	Emulates the action of focusing in the `textarea` field.
`blur()`	Emulates the action of removing focus from the `textarea` field.
`select()`	Emulates the action of selecting the text in the `textarea` field.

Event Handlers

`onBlur`	Specifies JavaScript code to execute when focus is removed from the field.
`onChange`	Specifies JavaScript code to execute when the content of the field is changed.

`onFocus`	Specifies JavaScript code to execute when focus is given to the field.
`onSelect`	Specifies JavaScript code to execute when the user selects some or all of the text in the field.

The `window` Object

The `window` object is the top-level object for each window or frame and is the parent object for the document, location, and history objects.

Properties

`defaultStatus`	A string value containing the default value displayed in the status bar.
`frames`	An array of objects for each frame in a window. Frames appear in the array in the order in which they appear in the HTML source code.
`length`	An integer value indicating the number of frames in a parent window.
`name`	A string value containing the name of the window or frame.
`parent`	A string indicating the name of the window containing the frameset.
`self`	An alternative for the name of the current window.
`status`	Used to display a message in the status bar—this is done by assigning values to this property.
`top`	An alternative for the name of the top-most window.
`window`	An alternative for the name of the current window.

Methods

`alert(`*`message`*`)`	Displays *`message`* in a dialog box.
`close()`	Closes the window.
`confirm(`*`message`*`)`	Displays *`message`* in a dialog box with OK and Cancel buttons. Returns true or false based on the button clicked by the user.

`open(url,name,features)`	Opens *`url`* in a window named *`name`*. If *`name`* doesn't exist, a new window is created with that name. `features` is an optional string argument containing a list of features for the new window. The feature list contains any of the following name/value pairs separated by commas and without additional spaces:

`toolbar=[yes,no,1,0]`	Indicates if the window should have a toolbar
`location=[yes,no,1,0]`	Indicates if the window should have a location field
`directories=[yes,no,1,0]`	Indicates if the window should have directory buttons
`status=[yes,no,1,0]`	Indicates if the window should have a status bar
`menubar=[yes,no,1,0]`	Indicates if the window should have menus
`scrollbars=[yes,no,1,0]`	Indicates if the window should have scroll bars
`resizable=[yes,no,1,0]`	Indicates if the window should be resizable
`width=`*`pixels`*	Indicates the width of the window in pixels
`height=`*`pixels`*	Indicates the height of the window in pixels

`prompt(message,response)`	Displays *`message`* in a dialog box with a text entry field with the default value of *`response`*. The user's response in the text entry field is returned as a string.

`setTimeout(expression,time)`	Evaluates `expression` after `time` where `time` is a value in milliseconds. The time out can be named with the structure. `name = setTimeOut(expression,time)`
`clearTimeout(name)`	Cancels the time out with the name `name`.

Event Handlers

`onLoad`	Specifies JavaScript code to execute when the window or frame finishes loading.
`onUnload`	Specifies JavaScript code to execute when the document in the window or frame is exited.

Independent Functions, Operators, Variables, and Literals

This section describes JavaScript's independent functions, operators, variables, and literals.

Independent Functions

`escape(character)`	Returns a string containing the ASCII encoding of `character` in the form `%xx` where `xx` is the numeric encoding of the character.
`eval(expression)`	Returns the result of evaluating `expression` where `expression` is an arithmetic expression.
`isNaN(value)`	Evaluates value to see if it is `NaN`. Returns a Boolean value. This function is only available on UNIX platforms where certain functions return `NaN` if their argument is not a number.
`parseFloat(string)`	Converts `string` to a floating-point number and returns the value. It continues to convert until it hits a non-numeric character and then returns the result. If the first character cannot be converted to a number, the function returns `"NaN"` (zero on Windows platforms).

`parseInt(string,base)`	Converts *`string`* to an integer of base *`base`* and returns the value. It continues to convert until it hits a non-numeric character and then returns the result. If the first character cannot be converted to a number, the function returns `"NaN"` (zero on Windows platforms).
`unescape(string)`	Returns a character based on the ASCII encoding contained in *`string`*. The ASCII encoding should take the form `"%integer"` or `"hexadecimalValue"`.

Operators

JavaScript provides the following categories of operators:

- Assignment operators
- Arithmetic operators
- Bitwise operators
- Logical operators
- Logical comparison operators
- Conditional operators
- String operators

After each type of operator is discussed, operator precedence in JavaScript is presented.

Assignment Operators

`=`	Assigns value of right operand to the left operand
`+=`	Adds the left and right operands and assigns the result to the left operand
`-=`	Subtracts the right operand from the left operand and assigns the result to the left operand
`*=`	Multiplies the two operands and assigns the result to the left operand
`/=`	Divides the left operand by the right operand and assigns the value to the left operand
`%=`	Divides the left operand by the right operand and assigns the remainder to the left operand

Arithmetic Operators

`+`	Adds the left and right operands
`-`	Subtracts the right operand from the left operand

`*`	Multiplies the two operands
`/`	Divides the left operand by the right operand
`%`	Divides the left operand by the right operand and evaluates to the remainder
`++`	Increments the operand by one (can be used before or after the operand)
`--`	Decreases the operand by one (can be used before or after the operand)
`-`	Changes the sign of the operand

Bitwise Operators

Bitwise operators deal with their operands as binary numbers but return JavaScript numerical value.

AND (or `&`)	Converts operands to integers with 32 bits, pairs the corresponding bits, and returns one for each pair of ones. Returns zero for any other combination.
OR (or `¦`)	Converts operands to integers with 32 bits, pairs the corresponding bits, and returns one for each pair where one of the two bits is one. Returns zero if both bits are zero.
XOR (or `^`)	Converts operands to integers with 32 bits, pairs the corresponding bits, and returns one for each pair where only one bit is one. Returns zero for any other combination.
`<<`	Converts the left operand to an integer with 32 bits and shifts bits to the left the number of bits indicated by the right operand—bits shifted off to the left are discarded and zeros are shifted in from the right.
`>>>`	Converts the left operand to an integer with 32 bits and shifts bits to the right the number of bits indicated by the right operand—bits shifted off to the right are discarded and zeros are shifted in from the left.
`>>`	Converts the left operand to an integer with 32 bits and shifts bits to the right the number of bits indicated by the right operand—bits shifted off to the right are discarded and copies of the leftmost bit are shifted in from the left.

Logical Operators

`&&`	Logical "and"—returns true when both operands are true; otherwise it returns false.
`¦¦`	Logical "or"—returns true if either operand is true. It only returns false when both operands are false.
`!`	Logical "not"—returns true if the operand is false and false if the operand is true. This is a unary operator and precedes the operand.

Comparison Operators

- `==` Returns true if the operands are equal
- `!=` Returns true if the operands are not equal
- `>` Returns true if the left operand is greater than the right operand
- `<` Returns true if the left operand is less than the right operand
- `>=` Returns true if the left operand is greater than or equal to the right operand
- `<=` Returns true if the left operand is less than or equal to the right operand

Conditional Operators

Conditional expressions take one form:

```
(condition) ? val1 : val2
```

If *`condition`* is true, the expression evaluates to *`val1`*; otherwise it evaluates to *`val2`*.

String Operators

JavaScript provides two string-concatenation operators:

- `+` This operator evaluates to a string combining the left and right operands.
- `+=` This operator is a shortcut for combining two strings.

Operator Precendence

JavaScript applies the rules of operator precedence as follows (from lowest to highest precedence):

- Comma `,`
- Assignment operators `= += -= *= /= %=`
- Conditional `? :`
- Logical or `||`
- Logical and `&&`
- Bitwise or `|`
- Bitwise xor `^`
- Bitwise and `&`
- Equality `== !=`
- Relational `< <= > >=`
- Shift `<< >> >>>`
- Addition/subtraction `+ -`

Multiply/divide/modulus	`* / %`
Negation/increment	`! - ++ —`
Call, member	`() []`

APPENDIX G

ActiveX and VBScript Reference

by Stephen LeHunte

IN THIS APPENDIX

Recent advances in browser technology have been pushing the idea of active content. To this end, here are a couple of products that HTML authors should be aware of:

- ActiveX
- Visual Basic Script

The recent technology from Microsoft is based around ActiveX controls (previously known as OLE controls). A new control requirement specification has meant that OLE controls previously burdened with code inappropriate for use on the Internet can now be much more streamlined, making it possible to embed them as `<OBJECT>`s into Web pages. This (like Java) allows almost limitless activity and interactivity within Web pages. To produce ActiveX controls though, you must have a good deal of programming skill. Casual HTML authors, however, will be able to rely on taking advantage of many freely available controls, as they can with JavaScript scripts and Java applets at the moment. (This mechanism is Internet Explorer-specific.)

Visual Basic Script is a lightweight yet fully compatible version of Visual Basic. Designed for use on the Internet, Visual Basic Script allows full automation, customization, and scripting within Web pages. Coming into its own when used to control ActiveX controls, Visual Basic is the easiest to learn of the available methods for creating dynamic content. (This mechanism is Internet Explorer-specific.)

Microsoft ActiveX Technology

Microsoft's ActiveX technology, recently announced and supported by Internet Explorer 3.0 only (although Microsoft is co-developing a plug-in module for Netscape that will allow Netscape to employ ActiveX controls), represents a huge advance in the capabilities of Internet Explorer. ActiveX has relaxed the OLE control requirements to practically nothing. Although previous OLE controls (such as the `.OCX` files shipped with Visual Basic) contained a lot of baggage inappropriate to use on the Internet, new ActiveX controls (conforming to the redesigned control requirements specification) can be a lot more streamlined, facilitating the easier production of high-quality dynamic content for HTML documents. (It's easier to create ActiveX controls than previous OLE controls, but it still requires a great degree of programming knowledge. Casual HTML authors, though, will no doubt be able to take advantage of a multitude of freely available ActiveX controls in time.)

Internet Explorer 3.0 allows for the use of ActiveX controls, active scripts (such as Visual Basic Script), and active documents. ActiveX can be used to encapsulate practically any application or applet for use within HTML documents.

NOTE

The embedding mechanism, using the `<OBJECT>` element, has been designed in coalition with the W3C, a technical report of which can be found at `http://www.w3.org/pub/www/TR/WD-object.html`.

The specific method of construction of ActiveX controls is outside the scope of this reference, but some (very) simple examples of the use of a couple of ActiveX controls are presented later in this appendix.

Microsoft recently made available a number of ActiveX controls as a brief demonstration of the possibilities of the technology. For details on how to use these, see the ActiveX control pack section and the Microsoft ActiveX gallery at the Internet Explorer 3.0 Web site. Also see the ActiveVRML and ActiveMovie Web sites at `http://www.microsoft.com/intdev/avr/` and `http://www.microsoft.com/advtech/ActiveMovie/Amstream.htm`, respectively.

Using ActiveX Controls

This HTML fragment uses the `label` and `new` button ActiveX controls, using the `new` button's built-in graphic image. The screen capture in Figure H.1 was created using Internet Explorer 3.0 Alpha, which is the only browser at present that supports the use of ActiveX controls. For more details on ActiveX controls, see the section "ActiveX Control Pack" later in this appendix.

```
<HTML>
<HEAD>
<TITLE>Label Control</TITLE>
</HEAD>
<BODY>
<OBJECT classid="clsid:{99B42120-6EC7-11CF-A6C7-00AA00A47DD2}"
  id=lbl1
  width=100
  height=220
  align=left>
  <param name="angle" value="80" >
  <param name="alignment" value="2' >
  <param name="BackStyle" value="0' >
  <param name="caption" value="The HTML Reference">
  <param name="FontName" value="Arial">
  <param name="FontSize" value="24'>
  <param name="FontBold" value="1">
```

```
  <param name="frcolor" value="8421376">
</OBJECT>
<BR><BR>
Welcome to the new Reference pages
<OBJECT
  classid="{642B65C0-7374-11CF-A3A9-00A0C9034920}"
  id=newb
  width=31
  height=19>
  <PARAM NAME="date" value="6/1/1997">
</OBJECT>
</BODY>
</HTML>
```

FIGURE G.1.
Example of ActiveX controls.

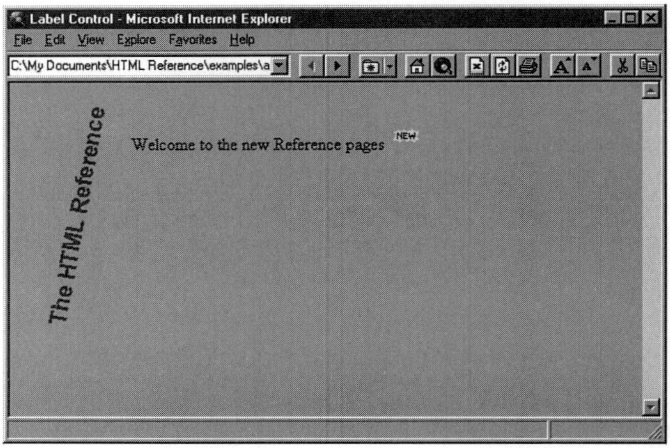

ActiveX/Visual Basic Script Examples

The following examples use both the Timer and the Label ActiveX controls (both available in the ActiveX control pack from the Microsoft Web site). They are exceedingly simple but serve to show how easy it is.

NOTE

They will require Internet Explorer 3.0 and the ActiveX controls to be installed.

The first example uses the Timer control to alter the text color and alignment angle of the text displayed by the Label controls at regular intervals. The Label ActiveX control supports the `Click` event, and so actions that are carried out when the control is clicked can be attributed to this Label. In this case, it simply displays an Alert dialogue, with the text "Hello" on it.

```
<HTML>
<HEAD>
<OBJECT classid="{59CCB4A0-727D-11CF-AC36-00AA00A47DD2}"
        id=timer
        align=left
        width=1
        height=1>
  <param name="TimeOut" value="100">
  <param name="enable" value="1">
</OBJECT>
<TITLE>Label Control</TITLE>
<SCRIPT LANGUAGE="VBS">
<!--
Sub timer_time
  lbl1.forecolor= rnd() * 166777216
  lbl2.forecolor= rnd() * 166777216
  lbl3.forecolor= rnd() * 166777216
  lbl1.Angle=(lbl1.Angle+5) mod 360
  lbl3.Angle=(lbl3.Angle-10) mod 360
End Sub
Sub lbl1_Click
  Alert "Hello"
End Sub
-->
</SCRIPT>
</HEAD>
<BODY BGCOLOR=#c0c0c0>
<CENTER>
<TABLE
  WIDTH=50%
  BORDER=5
  BORDERCOLORLIGHT=green
  BORDERCOLORDARK=navy
  RULES=none
  FRAME=box>
<COLGROUP SPAN=4 ALIGN=center VALIGN=top>
<THEAD></THEAD>
<TBODY>
<TR>
<TD>
<OBJECT  classid="clsid:{99B42120-6EC7-11CF-A6C7-00AA00A47DD2}"
  id=lbl1
  width=90
  height=90>
  <param name="angle" value="30" >
  <param name="alignment" value="2" >
  <param name="BackStyle" value="0" >
  <param name="caption" value="The HTML">
  <param name="FontName" value="Arial">
  <param name="FontSize" value="20">
  <param name="FontBold" value="1">
  <param name="frcolor" value="8421376'>
</OBJECT>
</TD>
<TD>
```

```
<OBJECT classid="clsid:{99B42120-6EC7-11CF-A6C7-00AA00A47DD2}"
  id=lbl2
  width=200
  height=20
  align=center>
  <param name="angle" value="0" >
  <param name="alignment" value="3" >
  <param name="BackStyle" value="0" >
  <param name="caption" value="Reference Library is">
  <param name="FontName" value="Arial">
  <param name="FontSize" value="22">
  <param name="FontBold" value="1">
  <param name="frcolor" value="8421376">
</OBJECT>
</TD>
<TD>
<OBJECT classid="clsid:{99B42120-6EC7-11CF-A6C7-00AA00A47DD2}"
  id=lbl3
  width=90
  height=90>
  <param name="angle" value="-30" >
  <param name="alignment" value="2" >
  <param name="BackStyle" value="0" >
  <param name="caption" value="Great!">
  <param name="FontName" value="Arial">
  <param name="FontSize" value="24">
  <param name="FontBold" value="1">
  <param name="frcolor" value="8421376">
</OBJECT>
</TD>
</TR>
</TBODY>
<TFOOT></TFOOT>
</TABLE>
<FONT SIZE=+1>
</CENTER>
</BODY>
</HTML>
```

The second example is in a similar vein and is a mock version of the infamous Nervous Text Java applet. Again, it uses the `Timer` control to control the random setting of the Label alignments and to rotate them.

```
<HTML>
<HEAD>
<OBJECT classid="{59CCB4A0-727D-11CF-AC36-00AA00A47DD2}"
        id=timer1
        align=left
        width=1
        height=1>
<param name="TimeOut" value="100">
<param name="enable" value="1">
</OBJECT>
<TITLE>Label Testing</TITLE>
<SCRIPT LANGUAGE="VBS">
<!--
```

```
Sub timer1_time
  label1.Alignment= rnd() * 4
  label2.Alignment= rnd() * 4
  label3.Alignment= rnd() * 4
  label4.Alignment= rnd() * 4
  label5.Alignment= rnd() * 4
  label6.Alignment= rnd() * 4
  label7.Alignment= rnd() * 4
  label8.Alignment= rnd() * 4
  label9.Alignment= rnd() * 4
  label10.Alignment= rnd() * 4
  label1.Angle= rnd() * 90
  label2.Angle= rnd() * 90
  label3.Angle= rnd() * 90
  label4.Angle= rnd() * 90
  label5.Angle= rnd() * 90
  label6.Angle= rnd() * 90
  label7.Angle= rnd() * 90
  label8.Angle= rnd() * 90
  label9.Angle= rnd() * 90
  label10.Angle= rnd() * 90
End Sub
-->
</SCRIPT>
</HEAD>
<BODY BGCOLOR=#c0c0c0>
<CENTER>
<TABLE
  BORDER=5
  BORDERCOLORLIGHT=green
  BORDERCOLORDARK=navy
  RULES=none
  FRAME=box>
<THEAD></THEAD>
<TBODY>
<TR>
<TD>
<OBJECT classid="clsid:{99B42120-6EC7-11CF-A6C7-00AA00A47DD2}"
  id=label1
  width=30
  height=30>
  <param name="angle" value="0" >
  <param name="alignment" value="2" >
  <param name="BackStyle" value="0" >
  <param name="caption" value="I">
  <param name="FontName" value="Arial">
  <param name="FontSize" value="20">
  <param name="FontBold" value="1">
  <param name="frcolor" value="8421376">
</OBJECT>
</TD>
<TD>
<OBJECT classid="clsid:{99B42120-6EC7-11CF-A6C7-00AA00A47DD2}"
```

```
  id=label2
  width=30
  height=30
  align=center>
  <param name="angle" value="0" >
  <param name="alignment" value="3" >
  <param name="BackStyle" value="0" >
  <param name="caption" value="'">
  <param name="FontName" value="Arial">
  <param name="FontSize" value="20">
  <param name="FontBold" value="1">
  <param name="frcolor" value="8421376">
</OBJECT>
</TD>
<TD>
<OBJECT classid="clsid:{99B42120-6EC7-11CF-A6C7-00AA00A47DD2}"
  id=label3
  width=30
  height=30>
  <param name="angle" value="0" >
  <param name="alignment" value="2" >
  <param name="BackStyle" value="0" >
  <param name="caption" value="m">
  <param name="FontName" value="Arial">
  <param name="FontSize" value="20">
  <param name="FontBold" value="1">
  <param name="frcolor" value="8421376">
</OBJECT>
</TD>
<TD>
<OBJECT classid="clsid:{99B42120-6EC7-11CF-A6C7-00AA00A47DD2}"
  id=label4
  width=30
  height=30>
  <param name="angle" value="0" >
  <param name="alignment" value="2" >
  <param name="BackStyle" value="0" >
  <param name="caption" value=" ">
  <param name="FontName" value="Arial">
  <param name="FontSize" value="20">
  <param name="FontBold" value="1">
  <param name="frcolor" value="8421376">
</OBJECT>
</TD>
<TD>
<OBJECT classid="clsid:{99B42120-6EC7-11CF-A6C7-00AA00A47DD2}"
  id=label5
  width=30
  height=30>
  <param name="angle" value="0" >
  <param name="alignment" value="2" >
  <param name="BackStyle" value="0" >
  <param name="caption" value="S">
  <param name="FontName" value="Arial">
```

```
    <param name="FontSize" value="20">
    <param name="FontBold" value="1">
    <param name="frcolor" value="8421376">
  </OBJECT>
  </TD>
  <TD>
  <OBJECT classid="clsid:{99B42120-6EC7-11CF-A6C7-00AA00A47DD2}"
    id=label6
    width=30
    height=30>
    <param name="angle" value="0" >
    <param name="alignment" value="2" >
    <param name="BackStyle" value="0" >
    <param name="caption" value="c">
    <param name="FontName" value="Arial">
    <param name="FontSize" value="20">
    <param name="FontBold" value="1">
    <param name="frcolor" value="8421376">
  </OBJECT>
  </TD>
  <TD>
  <OBJECT classid="clsid:{99B42120-6EC7-11CF-A6C7-00AA00A47DD2}"
    id=label7
    width=30
    height=30>
    <param name="angle" value="0" >
    <param name="alignment" value="2" >
    <param name="BackStyle" value="0" >
    <param name="caption" value="a">
    <param name="FontName" value="Arial">
    <param name="FontSize" value="20">
    <param name="FontBold" value="1">
    <param name="frcolor" value="8421376">
  </OBJECT>
  </TD>
  <TD>
  <OBJECT classid="clsid:{99B42120-6EC7-11CF-A6C7-00AA00A47DD2}"
    id=label8
    width=30
    height=30>
    <param name="angle" value="0" >
    <param name="alignment" value="2" >
    <param name="BackStyle" value="0" >
    <param name="caption" value="r">
    <param name="FontName" value="Arial">
    <param name="FontSize" value="20">
    <param name="FontBold" value="1">
    <param name="frcolor" value="8421376">
  </OBJECT>
  </TD>
  <TD>
  <OBJECT classid="clsid:{99B42120-6EC7-11CF-A6C7-00AA00A47DD2}"
```

```
  id=label9
  width=30
  height=30>
  <param name="angle" value="0" >
  <param name="alignment" value="2" >
  <param name="BackStyle" value="0" >
  <param name="caption" value="e">
  <param name="FontName" value="Arial">
  <param name="FontSize" value="20">
  <param name="FontBold" value="1">
  <param name="frcolor" value="8421376">
</OBJECT>
</TD>
<TD>
<OBJECT classid="clsid:{99B42120-6EC7-11CF-A6C7-00AA00A47DD2}"
  id=label10
  width=30
  height=30>
  <param name="angle" value="0" >
  <param name="alignment" value="2" >
  <param name="BackStyle" value="0" >
  <param name="caption" value="d">
  <param name="FontName" value="Arial">
  <param name="FontSize" value="20">
  <param name="FontBold" value="1">
  <param name="frcolor" value="8421376">
</OBJECT>
</TD>
</TR>
</TBODY>
<TFOOT></TFOOT>
</TABLE>
</BODY>
</HTML>
```

For a list of the `CLASSID` attributes of the controls in the ActiveX control pack available from Microsoft, see the next section.

ActiveX Control Pack

The ActiveX control pack, available from the Microsoft Web site, contains the following controls:

- Label
- Timer
- Animated button
- Chart

- New button
- Pre-loader
- Intrinsic controls

Also, separately available are the ActiveMovie and ActiveVRML controls. Presented here are the unique `CLASSID` identification numbers, together with a list of properties. For the latest information about their properties or for later releases of the controls, you should check the Microsoft Web site.

Almost any ActiveX control (such as those shipped with Visual Basic) can be embedded within HTML documents.

Each of the ActiveX controls is described in more detail in the following subsections.

<OBJECT> ... </OBJECT>

The `<OBJECT>` element provides a way for the ActiveX controls and other media to be embedded directly into HTML documents. It assumes the role of the `<IMG>` element, providing an insertion mechanism for media other than static images. As far as the Internet Explorer is concerned, the `<OBJECT>` element can be used for the inclusion of ActiveX OLE controls and Java applets.

NOTE

The `<OBJECT>` element is currently supported only by Internet Explorer. The object insertion mechanism is the subject of a W3C working draft available at `http://www.w3.org/pub/WWW/TR/WD-object.html`. For this and other W3C working drafts, you should visit the W3C site at `http://www.w3.org/pub/World Wide Web/TR/`.

An example of the syntax is as follows. This example inserts a Label ActiveX control into the page:

```
<OBJECT CLASSID="clsid:{99B42120-6EC7-11CF-A6C7-00AA00A47DD2}"
  ID=lbl1
  WIDTH=90
  HEIGHT=90>
  <PARAM NAME="angle" VALUE="30" >
  <PARAM NAME="alignment" VALUE="2" >
  <PARAM NAME="BackStyle" VALUE="0" >
  <PARAM NAME="caption" VALUE="Hello there">
  <PARAM NAME="FontName" VALUE="Arial">
  <PARAM NAME="FontSize" VALUE="20">
  <PARAM NAME="FontBold" VALUE="1">
  <PARAM NAME="frcolor" VALUE="8421376">
</OBJECT>
```

The object being inserted into the HTML document in this case is referred to by its `CLASSID`. This is a unique identifier for the `label` control, according to the Component Object Model `CLASSID` URL scheme. (`CLASSID`s can be found by searching in the Registry under `HKEY_CLASSES_ROOT` under the file type name (in this case, `SprLbl.SprLblCtl`) or by searching through the `CLSID` section of `HKEY_CLASSES_ROOT`. Searching for the file type is easier. The `ID` attribute identifies the specific label with a unique name, allowing interaction with and dynamic updating of the object's properties via active OLE scripting (for example, Visual Basic Script). Some objects will require certain code to implement them. This should be referenced by using the `CODE` attribute. Also, the `DATA` attribute can be used to point to a persistent data stream to initialize the object's state. The use of the above attributes is control-dependent, so exhaustive examples cannot be given.

In keeping with the role of the `<OBJECT>` element as a media insertion element (using `<IMG>`), various standard formatting attributes, such as `HEIGHT`, `WIDTH`, `ALIGN`, `BORDER`, `HSPACE`, `VSPACE`, and so on, can also be used to define the positioning of the object on the page.

The `PARAM` element allows a list of named property values (used to initialize an OLE control, plug-in module, or Java applet) to be represented as a sequence of `PARAM` elements. Note that `PARAM` is an empty element and should appear without an end tag. The `NAME` attribute defines the property to be defined, and the `VALUE` attribute defines the property value. For instance, in the preceding example, the line:

```
<PARAM NAME="caption" VALUE="Hello there">
```

sets the value of the property `caption` to be `"Hello there"`. (In this case, this property represents the text that will be displayed for the label.) Object properties are entirely control-dependent, so you should read the reference documentation for any control to find out what properties can be set using the `PARAM` element.

The Label Control—IELABEL.OCX

The Label ActiveX control allows the setting of labels within HTML documents. Labels are text strings that can be aligned at any angle, in any color, and in any font. The Label control has the following properties:

`Caption`	Specifies text to be displayed.
`Angle`	Specifies in degrees, counter-clockwise, how far the text is to be rotated.
`Alignment`	Specifies how to align text in the control. Possible values are

	`0`	Align to left.
	`1`	Align to right.
	`2`	Centered.
	`3`	Align to top.
	`4`	Align to bottom.
`BackStyle`	Control background. Possible values are	
	`0`	Transparent.
	`1`	Opaque.
`FontName`	Name of TrueType font for the label text.	
`FontSize`	Size of the font for the label text.	
`FontItalic`	Flag for italic text.	
`FontBold`	Flag for bold text.	
`FontUnderline`	Flag for underline text.	
`FontStrikeout`	Flag for strikeout text.	
`frcolor`	Specifies the color of the text to be used. This accepts a single value that can be calculated by working out the RRGGBB triplet for the color you desire and then converting the whole triplet to a decimal value. (Instead of treating it as a triplet of two figures for each color component, treat it as a six-figure hexadecimal number.)	

For all flag values, anything that isn't `0` is treated as a `1`. Using a value of `1` specifies the flag to be true.

The Label control accepts the `Click` event (for the purposes of scripting added functionality to the control).

The `CLASSID` of the Label control is as follows:

```
classid="{99B42120-6EC7-11CF-A6C7-00AA00A47DD2}"
```

Something like the following could typically be used in HTML for the Label control:

```
<OBJECT
  classid="{99B42120-6EC7-11CF-A6C7-00AA00A47DD2}"
```

```
  id=label
  width=150
  height=500
  vspace=0
  align=left>
  <PARAM NAME="angle" VALUE="45">
  <PARAM NAME="alignment" VALUE="2">
  <PARAM NAME="BackStyle" VALUE="0">
  <PARAM NAME="caption" VALUE="Stephen">
  <PARAM NAME="FontName" VALUE="Times New Roman">
  <PARAM NAME="FontSize" VALUE="20">
</OBJECT>
```

The Timer Control—`IETIMER.OCX`

The Timer control can be used to trigger events periodically. It does not appear rendered on the screen. It accepts the following properties:

`Enable` To enable/disable the Timer. Possible values are

- `1` Enabled state.
- `0` Disabled state.

`TimeOut` Interval (in milliseconds) at which `Time` event be triggered. When set to a negative or `0` value, Timer will behave as in disabled state.

The Timer supports just one event:

`Time` When the timer is enabled and has a positive `TimeOut` value, this event is invoked at every interval (that is, when the timer reaches its `TimeOut` value).

The `CLASSID` of the Timer control is as follows:

```
classid="{59CCB4A0-727D-11CF-AC36-00AA00A47DD2}"
```

Something like the following would typically be used in HTML for the Timer control:

```
<OBJECT
  classid="{59CCB4A0-727D-11CF-AC36-00AA00A47DD2}"
  id=timer
  align=middle>
  <PARAM NAME="TimeOut" VALUE="100">
  <PARAM NAME="enable" VALUE="1">
</OBJECT>
```

This would cause whatever events are scripted in the sub `timer_time` event routine to occur every 0.1 seconds.

The Animated Button—IEANBTN.OCX

The Animated button control displays various frame sequences of an AVI movie depending on the button state, which can be in any of four states:

`Default`	When the mouse cursor and focus are both not on the control
`Down`	When the control receives `LButton` click
`Focus`	When the control gets focus
`Mouseover`	When mouse moves over the control

The Animated button accepts the following properties:

`DefaultFrEnd`	The End Frame for `Default` state
`DefaultFrStart`	The Start Frame for `Default` state
`DownFrEnd`	The End Frame for `Down` state
`DownFrStart`	The Start Frame for `Down` state
`FocusFrEnd`	The End Frame for `Focus` state
`FocusFrStart`	The Start Frame for `Focus` state
`MouseoverFrEnd`	The End Frame for `Mouseover` state
`MouseoverFrStart`	The Start Frame for `Mouseover` state
`URL`	The URL location of the AVI file to be used

The Animated button, by nature of its very use, supports the following events:

```
ButtonEvent_Click
ButtonEvent_DblClick
ButtonEvent_Focus
```

The `CLASSID` of the Animated button control is as follows:

```
classid="{0482B100-739C-11CF-A3A9-00A0C9034920}"
```

Something like the following would typically be used in HTML for the Animated button control:

```
<OBJECT
  classid="{0482B100-739C-11CF-A3A9-00A0C9034920}"
  id=anbtn
  width=320
  height=240
  align=center
  hspace=0
  vspace=0>
```

```
  <PARAM NAME="defaultfrstart" VALUE="0">
  <PARAM NAME="defaultfrend" VALUE="7">
  <PARAM NAME="mouseoverfrstart" VALUE="8">
  <PARAM NAME="mouseoverfrend" VALUE="15">
  <PARAM NAME="focusfrstart" VALUE="16">
  <PARAM NAME="focusfrend" VALUE="23">
  <PARAM NAME="downfrstart" VALUE="24">
  <PARAM NAME="downfrend" VALUE="34">
  <PARAM NAME="URL" VALUE="welcome3.avi">
</OBJECT>
```

The Chart Control—IECHART.OCX

The Chart control allows the embedding of graphical charts in an HTML document. It supports the following chart types:

Area Chart
Bar Chart
Column Chart
Line Chart
Pie Chart
Point Chart
Stocks Chart

Each chart type has three different styles that can be employed:

Chart Type	*Styles*
Area Chart	Simple Chart.
	Stacked Chart.
	100%.
Bar Chart	Simple Chart.
	Stacked Chart.
	100%.
Column Chart	Simple Chart.
	Stacked Chart.
	100%.
Line Chart	Simple Chart.
	Stacked Chart.
	100%.

Pie Chart	Simple Chart.
	One wedge of the chart is offset by some distance from the center.
Point Chart	Simple Chart.
	Stacked Chart.
	100%.
Stocks Chart	With `Open`, `High`, `Low`, and `Close` values.
	Simple Chart.
	Connected Chart.

The `IECHART` control supports the following properties:

`Rows`	Specifies number of rows in the data series.
`Columns`	Specifies number of columns in the data series.
`HorizontalGrid`	Specifies horizontal grids.
`VerticalGrid`	Specifies vertical grids.
`ChartType`	Specifies the type of chart you want. This property can take the following values:

Pie Chart	`0`
Point Chart	`1`
Line Chart	`2`
Area Chart	`3`
Column Chart	`4`
Bar Chart	`5`

Stocks Chart	`6` (for `High`, `Low`, `Close` values).
Stocks Chart	`7` (for `Open`, `High`, `Low`, `Close` values).
`ChartStyle`	This property can assume one of the following values:

Simple	`0`
Stacked	`1`
100%	`2`

`RowIndex`	Specifies the row index, used along with the `DataItem` property.
`ColumnIndex`	Specifies the column index, used along with the `DataItem` property.

DataItem	Specifies a data value—entry is identified by RowIndex and ColumnIndex properties. For example, to specify a data value of 3 for row 2, column 4, you would set the RowIndex property to 2, ColumnIndex property to 4, and then set the DataItem property value to 3.
ColorScheme	Specifies which pre-defined set of colors you would like to use. These colors will be used to fill regions. The possible values this property can take: 0, 1, or 2.

The CLASSID of the Chart control is as follows:

```
classid="{FC25B780-75BE-11CF-8B01-444553540000}"
```

Something like the following would typically be used in HTML for the Chart control:

```
<OBJECT
  classid="{FC25B780-75BE-11CF-8B01-444553540000}"
  id=chart1
  width=300
  height=150
  align=center
  hspace=0
  vspace=0>
  <PARAM NAME="ChartStyle" VALUE="1">
  <PARAM NAME="ChartType" VALUE="0">
  <PARAM NAME="hgridStyle" VALUE="0">
  <PARAM NAME="vgridStyle" VALUE="0">
  <PARAM NAME="colorscheme" VALUE="0">
  <PARAM NAME="backstyle" VALUE="2">
  <PARAM NAME="rows" VALUE="4">
  <PARAM NAME="columns" VALUE="4">
  <PARAM NAME="data[0][0]" VALUE="40">
  <PARAM NAME="data[0][1]" VALUE="50">
  <PARAM NAME="data[0][2]" VALUE="30">
  <PARAM NAME="data[0][3]" VALUE="60">
</OBJECT>
```

This particular example will render a pie chart with one slice pulled out from the center, using the color scheme of red, green, blue, and yellow.

The New Button Control—IENEWB.OCX

The New Button control can be used to display a New button alongside some text. It has a fairly typical new graphic built in.

It has just two properties:

Date	The date until which this image needs to be displayed
Image	The URL specifying the image (if the default image is unsatisfactory)

The CLASSID for the New button is as follows:

```
classid="{642B65C0-7374-11CF-A3A9-00A0C9034920}"
```

The HTML to include the default New button graphic, until the author's next birthday, would be as follows:

```
<OBJECT
  classid="{642B65C0-7374-11CF-A3A9-00A0C9034920}"
  id=ienewb
  width=31
  height=19>
  <PARAM NAME="date" VALUE="6/1/1997">
</OBJECT>
```

NOTE

Care should be taken when specifying the date. Readers' systems may use a different date format. The above uses a format of day/month/year, that is, a standard British format.

The Pre-loader Control—IEPRELD.OCX

The Pre-loader control downloads a single URL and then fires an event. It can be used to pre-load large data files (such as images) so that by the time the user actually gets to a page, much of the data is already in the cache. It is not displayed on the reader's screen.

The Pre-loader accepts two properties:

`URL`	The URL to be downloaded
`enable`	Enable (1) the pre-loader or disable (0) it

It allows for the following scriptable events:

`Complete`	Downloading is completed.
`Error`	Error was encountered.

The CLASSID of the Pre-loader is as follows:

```
classid="{16E349E0-702C-11CF-A3A9-00A0C9034920}"
```

If the following HTML were in a page, the next page of which contained the movie `welcome3.avi`, then while the user was reading the initial page, the video clip would be in the process of loading. A message would also pop up when the video had finished pre-loading.

```
<OBJECT
  id=movie
  classid="{16E349E0-702C-11CF-A3A9-00A0C9034920}"
  width=1
  height=1>
  <PARAM NAME="_extentX" VALUE="1">
  <PARAM NAME="_extentY" VALUE="1">
  <PARAM NAME="URL" VALUE="welcome3.avi">
  <PARAM NAME="enable" VALUE="1">
</OBJECT>
<script language="VBS">
sub movie_complete
  MsgBox "Movie ready, proceed when ready"
end sub
</script>
```

The Intrinsic Controls—HTMLCTL.OCX (Registered During Internet Explorer 3.0 Setup)

The following control names can be used on any form within an HTML document. They accept the properties typical of the normal form element's attributes.

Control	*Element*
`ButtonCtl` Object	`INPUT TYPE=BUTTON`
`CheckboxCtl` Object	`INPUT TYPE=CHECKBOX`
`ComboCtl` Object	`SELECT MULTIPLE`
`ListCtl` Object	`SELECT`
`PasswordCtl` Object	`INPUT TYPE=PASSWORD`
`RadioCtl` Object	`INPUT TYPE=RADIO`
`TextAreaCtl` Object	`TEXTAREA`
`TextCtl` Object	`INPUT NAME`

The Active Movie Control—AMOVIE.OCX

Together with ActiveVRML, this represents the most advanced ActiveX control. Active Movies use the Active Movie Streaming format, which essentially is a single data stream that contains time-stamped media. That is, the ASF format is an architectural wrapper, defining a file format that contains the various media elements (which can include video, sound, and URLs), all being time-stamped so that they display synchronized as authored. The major advantage of this format is that it is a streaming format; that is, the data contained in the `.ASF` file is transmitted and played across networks in real time, instead of the Web browser having to download the entire file before playing can begin.

As would be expected, the ActiveMovie control supports a vast array of properties, 37 in total (only considering those unique to itself), three methods, and four events. It's recommended that you obtain the ActiveMovie SDK/add-on example files from Microsoft if you wish to pursue use of this data format. See `http://www.microsoft.com/advtech/ActiveMovie/Amstream.htm` for more information.

The `CLASSID` of the ActiveMovie control is as follows:

```
CLASSID="{05589FA1-C356-11CE-BF01-00AA0055595A}"
```

As an example, the following would include a file called `STEVE.ASF` within an HTML document. The ActiveMovie data stream will start automatically and return to the start of the file when playing has finished. The playing controls are also shown within the page.

```
<OBJECT CLASSID="{05589FA1-C356-11CE-BF01-00AA0055595A}"
  HEIGHT=400
  WIDTH=340
  ID=ActiveMovie
  align=left>
  <PARAM NAME="FileName" VALUE="steve.asf">
  <PARAM NAME="AutoStart" VALUE="1">
  <PARAM NAME="ShowControls" VALUE="1">
  <PARAM NAME="ShowDisplay" VALUE="1">
  <PARAM NAME="AutoRewind" VALUE="1">
</OBJECT>
```

If the user has the ActiveMovie player installed, ActiveMovie stream format files can also be forced to play by using standard client-pull techniques.

The ActiveVRML Control—AVVIEW.DLL

The ActiveVRML control allows the embedding of Active VRML animation scripts within HTML documents. ActiveVRML is Microsoft's attempt to further the VRML specification, by adding even scripting capabilities to VRML. It allows for animated VRML objects. For more information, visit the ActiveVRML Web site in the following Note.

NOTE

The ActiveVRML control requires Internet Explorer 3.0 and the DirectX support files to be installed. A "lite" version of the DirectX SDK is available from the ActiveVRML Web site

`http://www.microsoft.com/intdev/avr/`

The ActiveVRML control accepts the following properties:

`DataPath`	This points to the `.AVR` ActiveVRML animation script.
`Expression`	An expression written into the ActiveVRML which provides control information.
`Border`	This can be `true` or `false`, and it determines the appearance, or non-appearance, of a border around the scene.

The `CLASSID` for the ActiveVRML control is as follows:

```
classid="{389C2960-3640-11CF-9294-00AA00B8A733}"
```

The HTML including an ActiveVRML scene, entitled `steve.avr`, would be as follows:

```
<OBJECT
  CLASSID="{389C2960-3640-11CF-9294-00AA00B8A733}"
  ID="AVView"
  WIDTH=300
  HEIGHT=250>
  <PARAM NAME="DataPath" VALUE="steve.avr">
  <PARAM NAME="Expression" VALUE="model">
  <PARAM NAME="Border" VALUE=FALSE>
</OBJECT>
```

Visual Basic Script

Visual Basic Script represents a further step toward active Web pages. Like JavaScript, Visual Basic Script provides scripting, automation, and customization capabilities for Web browsers. It is a subset of the Visual Basic programming language that is fully compatible with Visual Basic and Visual Basic for Applications.

To use Visual Basic Script within an HTML document, the code needs to be wrapped in `<SCRIPT> ... </SCRIPT>` elements, just like in JavaScript. As with JavaScript, the `LANGUAGE` attribute is required, in this case needing the value `"VBS"`. Visual Basic Script comes into its own when used in conjunction with ActiveX OLE controls, which allow for full automation with any OLE-compliant application and can be used for almost any purpose on a page, allowing for truly interactive Web sites to be created relatively easily.

The following code assumes that a button named `btnHello` has been created somewhere on the HTML document:

```
<SCRIPT LANGUAGE="VBS">
<!-- These comment delimiters ensure the code is hidden from those browsers
that do not support Visual Basic Script
Sub btnHello_OnClick
   MsgBox "Hello, it's a fine day"
End Sub
-->
</SCRIPT>
```

The `btnHello` button responds to being clicked by displaying a message box with the text `Hello, it's a fine day`. For information on how to embed ActiveX controls, see the `<OBJECT>` element. (The button in the above example can be embedded into an HTML document using a standard `<INPUT TYPE=BUTTON>` element. For more details, see Appendix B, "HTML Reference," in the section "Forms.")

As with JavaScript, a complete description of Visual Basic Script is well outside the scope of this reference, and you are encouraged to visit `http://www.microsoft.com/vbscript/` for more information and a complete copy of the language documentation.

APPENDIX H

What's on the CD?

IN THIS APPENDIX

On the *Web Publishing Unleashed, Professional Reference Edition* CD-ROM, you will find all the sample files that have been presented in this book along with a wealth of other applications and utilities.

> **NOTE**
>
> Please refer to the `readme.wri` file on the CD-ROM (Windows) or the `Guide to the CD-ROM` (Macintosh) for the latest listing of software.

Windows Software

ActiveX

- Microsoft ActiveX Control Pad and HTML Layout Control
- Sample controls

CGI

- CGI*StarDuo and CGI*StarDuo95
- CGI PerForm command language interpreter for Common Gateway Interface (CGI) application design
- Several sample CGI scripts and libraries

GNU

- GNU Licenses

GZIP

- Gzip compression utility

HTML Tools

- Microsoft Internet Assistants for Access, Excel, PowerPoint, Schedule+, and Word
- W3e HTML Editor
- CSE 3310 HTML Validator
- Hot Dog 32-bit HTML editor
- HoTMetaL HTML editor
- HTMLed HTML editor

- HTML Assistant for Windows
- WebEdit Pro HTML editor
- Web Weaver HTML editor
- ImageGen
- Sample Icons and Backgrounds

Java

- Sun's Java Developer's Kit for Windows 95/NT, version 1.0.2
- Sample Java applets
- Sample JavaScripts
- Trial version of Jamba for Windows 95/NT
- Jpad IDE
- JPad Pro Java IDE demo
- Kawa IDE
- Studio J++ demo
- Javelin IDE demo
- JDesigner Pro database wizard for Java

Graphics, Video and Sound Applications

- Goldwave sound editor, player, and recorder
- MapThis image map utility
- MPEGPLAY MPEG viewer
- Paint Shop Pro 3.12 graphics editor and graphic file format converter for Windows
- SnagIt screen capture utility
- ThumbsPlus image viewer and browser

Perl

- Perl 4
- Perl 5.002
- Perl 5 build 109 for Windows NT

Explorer

- Microsoft Internet Explorer v3.01 for Windows 95 and NT

Utilities

- Microsoft viewers for Excel, PowerPoint, and Word
- Adobe Acrobat viewer
- Microsoft PowerPoint Animation Player and Publisher
- WinZip for Windows NT/95
- WinZip Self-Extractor

Macintosh Software

HTML Tools

- BBEdit 3.5.1
- BBEdit 4 demo
- HTML Web Weaver v2.5.2
- WebMap v1.01f imagemap creator
- HTML.edit v1.7
- HTML Editor for the Macintosh v1.0
- Images and backgrounds

Graphics, Video, and Sound Applications

- Graphic Converter v2.1.4
- GIFConverter v2.3.7
- Fast Player v1.1
- Sparkle 2.4.5
- SoundApp v1.5.1

Utilities

- ZipIt for Macintosh
- ScrapIt Pro
- Adobe Acrobat

About Shareware

Shareware is not free. Please read all documentation associated with a third-party product (usually contained in files named `readme.txt` or `license.txt`) and follow all guidelines.

I

INDEX

Symbols

A

C

D

E

F

H

I

J

K

L

P

Q

R

S

W

X-Y-Z

Teach Yourself Web Publishing with HTML 3.2 in 14 Days, Professional Reference Edition

Laura Lemay

This book is the updated edition of Lemay's previous bestseller, *Teach Yourself Web Publishing with HTML in 14 Days, Premier Edition.* In it, readers will find advanced topics such as adding audio, video, and animation to Web pages.

This book also explores the use of CGI scripts, tables, HTML 3.0, the Netscape and Internet Explorer extensions, Java applets and JavaScript, and VRML.

$59.99 USA, $81.95 CDN *ISBN: 1-57521-096-7, 1,104 pp.*

Laura Lemay's Web Workshop: Microsoft FrontPage

Laura Lemay and Denise Tyler

This is a clear hands-on guide to maintaining Web pages with Microsoft's FrontPage. Written in the conversational style of Laura Lemay, it is packed with many interesting, colorful examples that demonstrate specific tasks of interest to the reader.

The included CD-ROM has all the templates, backgrounds, and materials you need.

$39.99 USA, $56.95 CDN *ISBN: 1-57521-149-1, 400 pp.*

Microsoft FrontPage 97 Unleashed, Second Edition

William Stanek

FrontPage 97 works directly with the Microsoft Office 97 suite of products. Its built-in WYSIWYG (What You See Is What You Get) editor is the best and most popular Web authoring tool on the market. New and experienced FrontPage users need this book to show them how to use the new version's power to add multimedia, sound, animation, and Office 97 documents to a Web site.

The included CD-ROM contains all the examples, built-in templates, Web publishing resources, and more.

$49.99 USA, $70.95 CDN *ISBN: 1-57521-226-9, 1,000 pp.*

Laura Lemay's Web Workshop: ActiveX and VBScript

Paul Lomax and Rogers Cadenhead

ActiveX is an umbrella term for a series of Microsoft products and technologies that add activity to Web pages. VBScript is an essential element of the ActiveX family. With it, you can add animation, multimedia, sound, graphics, and interactivity to a Web site. This book is a compilation of individual workshops that show you how to use VBScript and other ActiveX technologies within your Web site.

The included CD-ROM contains the entire book in HTML format, a hand-picked selection of the best ActiveX development tools, scripts, templates, backgrounds, borders, and graphics.

$39.99 USA, $56.95 CDN *ISBN: 1-57521-207-2, 450 pp.*

Laura Lemay's Web Workshop: 3D Graphics and VRML 2.0

Laura Lemay, Justin Couch, and Kelly Murdock

This book is the easiest way for readers to learn how to add three-dimensional virtual worlds to Web pages. It describes the new VRML 2.0 specification, explores the wide arrray of existing VRML sites on the Web, and steps readers through the process of creating their own 3D Web environments.

The included CD-ROM contains the book in HTML format, a hand-picked selection of the best VRML and 3D graphics tools, and a collection of ready-to-use virtual worlds.

$39.99 USA, $56.95 CDN *ISBN: 0-672-143-2, 400 pp.*

Laura Lemay's Web Workshop: Graphics and Web Page Design

Laura Lemay and James Rudnick

With the number of Web pages increasing daily, only the well-designed pages will stand out and grab the attention of people browsing the Web. This book illustrates, in classic Laura Lemay style, how to design attractive Web pages that will be visited over and over again.

The included CD-ROM contains HTML editors, graphics software, and royalty-free graphics and sound files.

$55.00 USA, $77.95 CDN *ISBN: 1-57521-125-4, 500 pp.*

Laura Lemay's Web Workshop: JavaScript

Laura Lemay

In this book, readers will explore various aspects of Web publishing, everything from JavaScript and interactivity to graphics design to Netscape Navigator Gold, in greater depth than the *Teach Yourself* books.

The included CD-ROM includes the complete book in HTML format, publishing tools, templates, graphics, backgrounds, and more.

$39.99 USA, $56.95 CDN *ISBN: 1-57521-141-6, 400 pp.*

Web Programming Unleashed

Breedlove, et al.

This comprehensive tome explores all aspects of the latest technology craze, Internet programming. This book gives timely, expert advice on ways to exploit the full potential of the Internet.

The included CD-ROM includes complete source code for all applications in the book, additional programs with accompanying source code, and several Internet application resource tools.

$49.99 USA, $70.95 CDN *ISBN: 1-57521-117-3, 1,200 pp.*

Book ISBN 1-57521-198-x

Installing the CD-ROM

The companion CD-ROM contains all the source code and project files developed by the authors, plus an assortment of evaluation versions of third-party products. To install the CD-ROM, please follow the steps in the sections below.

Windows 95 / NT 4 Installation Instructions

1. Insert the CD-ROM into your CD-ROM drive.
2. From the Windows 95 desktop, double-click the My Computer icon.
3. Double-click the icon representing your CD-ROM drive.
4. Double-click the icon titled `setup.exe` to run the CD-ROM installation program.

Windows NT 3.5x1 Installation Instructions

1. Insert the CD-ROM into your CD-ROM drive.
2. From File Manager or Program Manager, choose `File | Run`.
3. Type **<*drive*>:\setup** and press Enter, where **<*drive*>** corresponds to the drive letter of your CD-ROM. For example, if your CD-ROM is drive D, type **D:\SETUP** and press Enter.
4. Follow the on-screen instructions.

NOTE

Windows NT 3.5x1 users will be unable to access the `\WIN95NT4` directory because it was left in its original long file name state with a combination of uppercase and lowercase letters. This was done to allow Windows 95 and Windows NT 4 users direct access to those files on the CD. All other directories were translated in compliance with the Windows NT 3.5x1 operating system and may be accessed without trouble. (Note: Attempting to access the `\WIN95NT4` directory will cause no harm, you just won't be able to read its contents.)

Macintosh Installation Instructions

1. Insert the CD-ROM into your CD-ROM drive.
2. When an icon for the CD appears on your desktop, open the disc by double-clicking its icon.
3. Double-click the icon named `Guide to the CD-ROM` and follow the directions that appear.